THE
OXFORD BOOK OF
HUMOROUS
PROSE

THE
OXFORD BOOK
OF
HUMOROUS
PROSE

From William Caxton to P. G. Wodehouse

A CONDUCTED TOUR

by

FRANK MUIR

Oxford New York
OXFORD UNIVERSITY PRESS
1990

Oxford University Press, Walton Street, Oxford OX2 6DP
Oxford New York Toronto
Delhi Bombay Calcutta Madras Karachi
Petaling Jaya Singapore Hong Kong Tokyo
Nairobi Dar es Salaam Cape Town
Melbourne Auckland
and associated companies in
Berlin Ibadan

Oxford is a trade mark of Oxford University Press

British Library Cataloguing in Publication Data
The Oxford book of humorous prose: William Caxton to
P. G. Wodehouse: a conducted tour.
1. Humorous prose in English. Anthologies
I. Muir, Frank, 1920–
828'.08
ISBN 0–19–214106–6

Library of Congress Cataloging in Publication Data
The Oxford book of humorous prose: William Caxton to
P. G. Wodehouse: a conducted tour   chosen
and edited by Frank Muir.
1. English prose literature. 2. American prose literature.
3. English wit and humor. 4. American wit and humor.
I. Muir, Frank.
828'.08—dc20   PR1285.O94   1990
ISBN 0–19–214106–6

Text processing by the Oxford Text System
Printed in the United States of America

This book is—as most things have been—
for Polly
and for Jamie *and* Sally

Contents

Introduction

THIS book is intended to be not only an anthology *raisonnée* but also a gesture of gratitude and a commemoration.

Gratitude for the vast stock of harmless pleasure which five centuries of humorous writing have left us, and a commemoration of its authors. Upon many of these authors the spirit of humour must have alighted quite unbidden, like a mustard seed upon a damp flannel, and driven the unfortunate recipients willy-nilly to ignore criticism, toothache, poverty, fatigue, boredom, rejection by their loved ones, and the onset of baldness in pursuit of the elusive stuff.

Theorizing about humour is kept to a minimum because for one thing the reader knows more about comedy than I do. That is to say, every reader knows precisely what he, or she, finds funny, which is more than any author can know about the reader.

Another reason for touching theory lightly is that this is not a book about humour but a presentation of it, and the writers who wrote it, and I think that most of us who are involved in humour professionally tend to be wary of philosophers' claims to have discovered how comedy and laughter work. We suspect that there is a bit of unfathomable mystery in humour somewhere along the line, and our fear is that our ability to create it was a God-given gift which was arbitrarily bestowed upon us and if we start mucking about with it it might just as arbitrarily be taken away again, leaving us to soldier on with no comic invention left, only experience and professionalism. And experience and professionalism in humour, like punctuality and personal hygiene in life, are always welcome, of course, but not really the point of it.

Nor are theories of what makes people laugh of practical help to the writer. For a humorist to study a theory of laughter before starting work would be like a Victorian bridegroom thumbing through steel-engravings in a medical textbook on Married Love before putting the light out; informative perhaps but not conducive to stimulation of the creative urge.

The only theory I am prepared to offer is my own personal theory about comedy, which is that *all* theories about comedy are right but none of them is completely right. They all seem to have a piece missing. For instance, George Meredith's theory that comedy and laughter belong to the intellect and not to the emotions has a lot going for it but there is not much intellectual involvement in a baby's gurgling laugh when somebody bends over its cot wearing a funny hat.

One of the difficulties when discussing things which make us laugh is that almost everybody uses the words 'comedy', 'wit', 'buffoonery', 'humour', and so on more or less indiscriminately. This does not matter much in conversation because it is usually clear what the speaker means, but it does matter in a book like this in which the words are technical terms.

So we must have naming of parts.

For the purposes of this book, the following words are taken to mean the following things:

🖝 COMEDY. The word was invented by the Greeks in 486 BC to describe a new kind of theatrical presentation which complemented their productions of tragedy. It was derived from the Greek word *komos*, 'a revel', and comedy was, in essence, everything that tragedy was not. Tragedy dealt in a bracing manner with the fall from power and eventual death of heroic figures and the (usually rather bloody) inevitability of fate.

Comedy was light-hearted and filthy and dealt with the goings-on of everyday folk like corrupt religious leaders, golden-hearted prostitutes, venal slaves, and bent magistrates. Aristotle summed it up as 'an imitation of men who are inferior but not altogether vicious'. Tragedy was about heroes, gods, and unhappy endings. Comedy was about ordinary citizens and happy endings.

Philosophers, including Cicero, anxious to make this widely popular but often breathtakingly obscene branch of theatre purposeful and therefore respectable, pronounced that comedy was in fact much more meaningful than it seemed; that it had an equally important function to perform as the purifying catharsis of a good dose of tragedy. Ever since the plays of Aristophanes, they explained, the classical role of comedy had been 'to correct the irrational and immoral conduct of the foolish' by pointing at them the finger of mockery. The laughter this produced was supposed to ring hideously in the ears of the foolish who would cower back, whimpering, and mend their ways. The curious myth that comedy had curative powers (has any rotter in history ever been known to have turned saintly on being laughed at?) was believed until well into the eighteenth century.

A weapon in the armoury of this kind of comedy was satire, much used by the Greeks and Romans. Satire was a violent attack on somebody or something judged to be wicked or foolish using invective, parody, mockery, or anything else which might wound. In its pure form satire was not comic at all but brilliantly horrific (Swift's *Modest Proposal* to reduce the Irish population by cooking and eating the babies, George Orwell's appalling new world of *Nineteen Eighty-Four*). But mixed in with the fun and games it gave much of classical comedy its cutting edge. It is in this classical interpretation of the word that such works as Dante's *The Divine Comedy* and Robert Burton's *Anatomy of Melancholy* are classified as comedies.

After Caxton introduced printing to England, comedy of all kinds was widely disseminated in prose and the word comedy was no longer used only in connection with plays and poems. Its usage broadened until it is now an imprecise, hold-all term for any literary or dramatic piece which aims to amuse.

In this book, comedy is taken to consist largely of three elements, wit, buffoonery, and humour.

➥ WIT is the aristocratic aspect of comedy.

The original meaning of wit was sharp intelligence, wisdom, a vestige of which lingers in sentences like 'he had the wit to realize he wasn't wanted'.

Wit was essentially aristocratic because it was an intellectual sport played between gentlemen using ideas as shuttlecocks. The language of wit was rich in poetic references and paradoxes and puns which only expensively educated minds could bandy. It was also so much in use in upper social circles as an offensive weapon that Aristotle defined wit as 'educated insult'.

During the seventeenth century the word began to be used to describe not only a brilliant and concise thought, as in Pope's definition of true wit as 'nature to advantage dressed, / What oft was thought but ne'er so well expressed', but a brilliant thought which was also amusing. From then on a shaft of wit was expected to be entertaining as well as intellectually adroit. An example of this kind of wit was the Revd Sydney Smith's summing up of an *Edinburgh Review* piece full of declamation and invective by Henry Brougham: 'long yet vigorous like the penis of a jackass.'

But wit was not there to be laughed at. It was to be admired with a lift of an eyebrow or a half-smile or a nod of appreciation but not much more than that. Because of this it was the only aspect of comedy which a gentleman in the eighteenth century could practise in public; polite society would not tolerate the sight of gentlemen roaring with laughter.

To this modern age, which perhaps overpraises the tonic effect of collapsing into honks of uncontrollable mirth, it might seem incredible that an eighteenth-century gentleman was permitted by polite society to be seen kissing a male friend in the street, weeping piteously, spitting, relieving himself on the lawn of Lambeth Palace, but not laughing. Dean Swift admitted to having laughed only twice in his life. Pope claimed that he had never laughed at all. Lord Chesterfield wrote instructively to his thick son: 'Since I have had the full use of my reason, nobody has ever heard me laugh.' Even the clubbable Oliver Goldsmith wrote in *The Deserted Village* of 'The loud laugh that speaks the vacant mind.'

Samuel Johnson's laughter-inducing frolics were much cherished by his friends (Hannah More: 'The old genius was extremely jocular . . . you would have imagined we had been at some comedy had you heard our peals of laughter'; Arthur Murphy, the actor and writer: 'With great powers of mind, wit and humour were his shining talents'; Fanny Burney: 'Dr Johnson has more fun, and comical humour, and love of nonsense about him than almost anybody I ever saw') but these qualities were hardly mentioned by Boswell in the *Life*. Boswell was not going to diminish his hero by showing him to possess what was to eighteenth-century society evidence of a flawed and second-rate character, so he played down this most amiable side of Johnson's nature.

➧ BUFFOONERY, overt comicality, popular fun, is the opposite end of the scale to wit in just about every respect. Cheap and cheerful, it is that section of comedy whose sole purpose is to induce laughter. Laughter as loud and long and public as possible. It makes use, sometimes figuratively, of things such as funny hats and red noses to help induce a comical mood and it can be a social weapon of attack. But if it fails to arouse laughter it is nothing at all.

Buffoonery was a large element in Greek comedy and proved to have staying power; it was the wandering comic troupes who kept a strand of theatre going during the Dark Ages when legitimate drama had been suppressed.

Telling jokes is the most widespread form of buffoonery, probably because a joke is self-contained and the easiest device with which to trigger off laughter. And a bout of helpless laughter is highly prized in the modern world. It is today's equivalent of a swig of opium, not curing pain and worry but obscuring the symptoms for a few brief moments: the nearest thing in life to complete escapism next to the climax of love-making.

The jokes of most social and professional comedians ventilate our sexual anxieties and confirm our racial and other prejudices (Hazlitt wrote, 'for every joke there is a sufferer'). Laughing at our worries reduces their threat to us. And laughing at silly people who are not as bright or rich as we are makes us feel warm and secure. So the effect of buffoonery is opposite to that of classical comedy. In classical comedy, the aim of laughter is to benefit the person laughed at. With jokes, the laugh reassures the laugher.

➧ HUMOUR. In between wit and buffoonery lies the third, and as far is this book is concerned the most interesting subdivision of comedy—humour. If wit belongs mainly to the well-educated classes and buffoonery to the lower-classes, humour is middle-class.

In medieval times a 'humour' was any of the four cardinal fluids—blood, phlegm, choler, and melancholy, or black bile—which coursed round the body and according to their relative strengths determined a person's mental and physical state. When one of the fluids predominated then a person's character was dominated by that particular 'humour'. He would become either over-passionate (too much blood), dull and droopy (overdose of phlegm), quick-tempered and irascible (choler flowing too strongly), or gloomy and dejected (a touch too much of the melancholy, or black bile). Such a man was said to be in a 'humour'. Or, if he carried on behaving peculiarly, to be a 'humorist'.

This rather simplistic view of eccentricity lasted well, its peak perhaps being the end of the sixteenth century with the production of Ben Jonson's plays, *Every Man In His Humour* in 1598 (with Shakespeare in the cast), and *Every Man Out of His Humour* in 1599. But by the beginning of the eighteenth century the word 'humorist' had moved across to describe not the eccentric person but the writer who described the eccentricities.

Helped by the efforts of Joseph Addison and Sir Richard Steele, 'humour', in its new meaning, took root and became favoured light reading amongst

Augustan Age literate citizens, who were mostly from the rapidly expanding middle-classes.

Humour, long before it had a name, was not the invention of Greek playwrights or patrician Roman poets but of ordinary people and is the oldest of the three divisions of comedy, probably dating back to when Og first stood upright in the cave and knocked himself senseless, and Ug laughed and told Ig all about it. For humour is observational. Unlike wit and buffoonery, humour, like life and art, is quite useless and has no function to perform apart from being itself. And it is a contribution to culture which England has given the world; not Britain, not Scotland, Ireland, or Wales—but England.

The claim that the English originated humour was made by Sir William Temple (an Englishman). Sir William, diplomat, essayist, married to Dorothy Osborne, made his point about humour in an essay entitled 'Of Poetry' in his *Miscellanea*, Part II, published in 1690.

Nobody has yet disproved Sir William's claim.

His view was that England's humour was the product of richness of the soil, the inequality of our climate, and liberty. Liberty, because much humour came from the perception of odd and incongruous ways in which some people behaved, and despotic government as practised over much of Europe resulted in 'uniformity of character and all cut from only two patterns, the gentry and the common people'. Humorous behaviour, Sir William argued, needed a free society in which to flourish, and the Anglo-Saxons in England's temperate climate developed a kind of stubborn individuality which was peculiarly suited to humour. 'We have more humour because every man follows his own, and takes a pleasure, perhaps a pride, in showing it.'

A telling point which Sir William made about the Englishness of humour was that no other nation had the word humour in its language. The French had their equivalents of 'comedy' and 'wit' and 'buffoonery' but their word *humeur* meant 'disposition' or 'mood'. The Germans, the Italians, the French, all enjoyed upper-class wit and proletariat clowning but only the English, it seems, took pleasure in the middle area, in the recording of 'small but significant human traits'. Wit was concerned with ideas and buffoonery with deeds, humour with people.

The other nations of Europe not only failed to develop an equivalent to the English sense of humour but could not understand it. Visitors were dismayed by the strange, alien flippancy which they encountered in English conversation and literature, by the English nation's affection for the oddities of human behaviour, by the way that the English used irony to a degree unknown across the Channel, not only literary irony employed in satirical humour, for example, Jonathan Swift in his *Advice to Servants* ('never wear socks when you wait at meals . . . most ladies like the smell of young men's toes') but also in ordinary conversation when wrong words were used but the sense came through clearly (the novelist E. Arnot Robertson heard a woman say to a friend: 'Did you read about that silly woman committing suicide? I've got varicose veins but people with varicose veins don't commit suicide—they've got more sense'). European visitors found these deviations from their own pursuit of man as a high-minded, rational being not only baffling but rather distasteful.

As late as 1861 the French philosopher and historian, Hippolyte Taine, the theorist of the French *naturalisme* movement and a major influence on Emile Zola, visited England and wrote a book about his findings, *Notes sur l'Angleterre* (1872). In this he came to the conclusion that the English idea of humour was untranslatable into French because in France they not only did not have the word humour but 'they have not the idea'.

Cockney humour seemed to Taine to consist of 'grim savagery and gloom' (heaven knows what piece of Cockney impudence the philosopher so wildly misinterpreted; rhyming slang? The teasing of a foreigner? Elsewhere in the book M. Taine explained to his French readers that Englishwomen had big teeth because they ate a lot of meat and huge feet because they frequently walked across meadows, so his observations on England can be taken as being *naturalistique* but not very *réalistique*).

The English sense of humour seeped over the borders into Scotland, Wales, and across to Ireland, making its mark on their own jocular literature, and emigrants took English humour across the seas with them to America, Canada, Australia, and finally New Zealand.

At the beginning of the last century, American and Canadian humorous prose consisted of English humour written by Englishmen, or imitations of it written by North Americans, Australian funny prose did not exist at all and New Zealand had forty more years to wait before being colonized. But once they had all got their nations going the migrants began to mould the English humour they had brought with them to their new requirements.

Canada was too close geographically to America, and New Zealand to Australia for the smaller nations not to be deeply influenced by their massive neighbours and their humour was inevitably much the same, but the native humour of the North Americans developed along different routes to that of Australians and New Zealanders.

Whilst English humour was in the middle of a century and a half of being polite and warmly sentimental—its best period according to J. B. Priestley—with Charles Dickens as its epitome and the 'scribbling barristers' protecting the values of the new middle-classes in *Punch*, the pioneer writers of frontier humour in *ante bellum* America, mostly solid citizens in thick suits, waist-coats, and watch-chains, were developing a different approach, a strain of irreverent, snook-cocking humour which was political, irascible, and frequently had as its hero a small-time crook or con-man (ironically, the precursor of this strain was Judge Haliburton, a Canadian lawyer who eventually became an English Member of Parliament).

Like all frontier humour, including that of medieval Middle Europe, early American and Australian went in for bragging and tall stories such as the

Davy Crockett yarns in America and 'the Speewah' tales in Australia, but as the two nations progressed, their humour parted company.

The pieces in this book indicate that there was, more frequently than with other nations, a streak of cruelty present in American humour. Not sadistic but callous, most remarkably expressed in the difficult-to-read but important stories featuring Sut Lovingood. The petty con-man, or cruel, or actively political stories lasted until the great hinge of American writing, Mark Twain, swung humour into the modern world. Then, with the centre of humour moving from the pioneer areas of Down East and the Deep South and the West Coast into Chicago and New York, American humour became urban and smart and the swift wisecrack was born and the *New Yorker* and other magazines gave America the lead in intelligent, mildly sophisticated comicality.

Australian pioneer life presented different problems to those living it and its humour in these pages takes different directions. It was kinder than North American humour, kinder to women and unashamed in its appreciation of the value of 'mateship'. 'Mateship' was an enormously important factor of early Australian life and with its built-in dislike of superfluous chatter it gave Australian (and New Zealand) humour prose a leathery, laconic style which is unmistakable and unique.

Early Australian humour was not political like American humour of the same period because, quite simply, all ordinary Australians were so implacably against authority in the shape of Australia's politicians and police that there was hardly any mileage left in writing about it.

The constant exchange of humorous literature between America and Britain (a great deal of it pirated), from Dickens and *Punch* in one direction to Mark Twain and the *New Yorker* in the other, meant that the comic writing of the two nations grew closer together. And the growth during this century of radio and movies and television with worldwide distribution has meant that the differences in the ways in which nations once expressed their humour are unfortunately giving way to a bland, internationally acceptable kit of humorous values.

However, it seems that the word 'humour', or rather 'humor', is still suspect in the USA. When I was on an author tour there in 1976, my American publisher begged me not to mention the word 'humor' in describing my book to the book-trade. 'Say it's comedy,' he pleaded, 'say it's wit, but don't for God's sake call it "humor". In this country "humor" means books about batty old ladies being silly in English villages which Brentanos put their only copy of on the bottom shelf next to the U-Fix-It photo frames.'

Fifteen years ago, Oxford University Press asked me whether I would take a long, deep look at humorous prose written in the English language and trace its development, in America, Canada, Australia, and New Zealand as well as in Britain, since William Caxton.

As far as both parties were aware, this was the first time that this sort of survey had been attempted on such a scale, which is not surprising as humour only became socially acceptable, and therefore deemed worthy of consideration, about a hundred years ago. In the late nineteenth century, after a period beginning in the early 1700s of nothing but boot-faced rhetoric and grave demeanours on all important occasions, a sense of humour became a social asset. And then virtually a necessity.

Nowadays most Englishmen who follow soccer and like a drink with the lads on a Friday night would not mind much being labelled a drunk or a sex maniac because beneath these lurks an oblique suggestion of the macho. But very few of them, or their wives, would willingly admit to having no sense of humour. It is peculiarly gratifying to read in Harold Nicolson's essay, 'The English Sense of Humour', that 'in all the rich and varied literature of English invective the first public figure to be accused of possessing no sense of humour was Mr Gladstone'.

Having been immersed in humorous prose of all kinds for so many years whilst working on this book, I am now fairly certain that I can recognize humour when I see it without it having to leap up and bite me in the thigh, but I would not claim to know much more about it than that, except for the following brief points.

I would give as a working definition of English humour: an odd, embarrassing or funny incident experienced or observed, and described later in a plain manner, which might or might not call for laughter.

The English sense of humour is an agreeable mixture of a sense of fun and a sense of proportion, which is not at all the same thing as a taste for buffoonery. Perhaps a small axiom could be proposed: beware of people who only laugh at jokes.

A joke has a measurable potential of laughter; there are snigger-sized jokes, guffaw-sized jokes, and hearty laughter-sized jokes. Humour has no such limitations. A piece might only give the reader quiet pleasure. On the other hand if it catches the reader off-guard and in the right mood (in my case the first time I read Patrick Campbell's account of his visit to Dublin Public Library to research numismatics, and every time I have reread it since) its effect can be violent and prolonged, inducing, in my case, uncontrollable surges of laughter, hiccups, and a curious snoring noise in trying to regain breath.

Humour does not put a value on itself by announcing that it is going to make you laugh. To tell somebody that they are going to find a piece hilarious (even the Paddy Campbell piece which I happened to find so funny) is to dictate to them what their sense of humour should be, and a sense of humour is a most personal possession, not to be tampered with. Any attempt to manipulate it results in its owner wanting very much to find the piece recommended less than hilarious and rather disappointing.

It took some twelve years to assemble a representative selection of five hundred years of humorous prose. It would have taken far longer had dramatic works not been reluctantly excluded on the grounds that these extra excerpts would have made the book dangerously heavy. Frail readers under eight stone reading in bed and reaching out to put the book back on to the bedside table might well have been levered out of bed and flung to the floor by its weight.

The long period of research meant reading notoriously solemn authors to make sure thay they really were humourless, as well as selecting the most typical extracts from amusing authors whose every line was worth quoting—the trick is to choose a piece in which the author writes most like himself—but friends helped by making out reading lists and by ploughing through volumes on my behalf to find out whether there was anything in them of potential interest. I am particularly grateful to Susan Matthews (now Dr Susan Matthews) who over several years read deeply and thoughtfully, was strong on the early centuries and dug up several authors whom I would otherwise have missed entirely, and Josh Cunningham who read indefatigably and wrote witty précis.

What emerged from the vast amount of material collected was that pure English humour, besides being itself, also functioned over the centuries like good stock in cookery, enriching other kinds of comedy and giving them added flavour. Wit with humour proved to be more appreciated than wit being clever all by itself, satire expressed through humour was found to be more widely effective, jokes built on humorous observation had a deeper appeal. So although this book quotes much pure humour it also quotes a great deal of humour in its modified forms, witty humour, satirical humour, comical humour, and so on.

Comedy does not work in a vacuum. Its audience has to be in the right mood of expectancy and confidence, a mood which a comedian must create with his opening remarks. In literature, a humorous writer has to set the receptive mood he wants his reader to be in with his opening paragraphs. In order to cover so much ground it has been necessary in this book to lay violent hands on humorous pieces, to truncate them, edit them, modernize them, and in the case of major humorists to put together a mini-anthology of their range and styles. To print those detached fragments cold and alone would be doing the authors a grave disservice and make the book the literary equivalent of a bag of broken biscuits.

So the quoted humorous pieces are set within a commentary which introduces them by describing how the extracts came to be written, or why, with perhaps facts or anecdotes or gossip about the author, or what was going on at the time, the aim being to bring the reader up to the beginning of each piece in a good frame of mind to appreciate it.

A piece was chosen to be included if it was (1) a classic example of the genre, or a good representation of the humorous prose of a particular country, (2) a shock coming from the pen of an author not normally regarded as being humorous at all, (3) regarded as hilarious many years ago but now monumentally unfunny, (4) a step forward in humorous prose technique or subject-matter, (5) wonderfully written, (6) I just liked it.

Also included are samples of the work of much-admired authors of the past who are now forgotten, and of the good second-rate humorists who provided such a large proportion of professional magazine humour. There are also occasional selections of jokes to indicate where the public sense of humour had got to in various centuries, and samplings of the contemporary state of the pun (skippable).

The success of humour depends strongly upon the accuracy of its observation. It is possible that, by its nature, a collection of real humour could provide a subtler picture of how ordinary life was lived than could solemn sources.

Sir William concluded his essay 'Of Poetry' with a paragraph which was much admired in his day and much quoted (and plagiarized) later. It seems to sum up, in its beautiful prose, the modest but worthwhile role of humour in the great scheme of things:

When all is done, human life is, at the greatest and the best, but like a froward child, that must be played with and humoured a little to keep it quiet till it falls asleep, and then the care is over.

F.M.

Thorpe,
September 1989

THE
OXFORD BOOK OF
HUMOROUS
PROSE

THE starting-point is William Caxton.
     One reason for this is that there is a logic in beginning with England's first printer of books, but a better reason is perhaps that in his own writings Caxton reveals a sense of humour which though five hundred years old is recognizably in the English tradition; a mixture of a sense of fun and a sense of proportion.

Caxton was a rich wool-merchant trading in Bruges but his real interest was translating continental literature into plain, clear English. To facilitate this he bought one of the new, secret German machines which printed from movable type, returned to England, and set up a printing shop in the precincts of Westminster Abbey.

The first book he printed in England—England's first printed book—was Dictes or Sayengis of the Philosophres (1477), a translation from the French made by one of Caxton's patrons, the great Earl Rivers. The noble Earl asked Caxton to go through the manuscript and correct any errors and Caxton found one. Earl Rivers had left out some adverse comments which Socrates had made on women.

However affable Earl Rivers may have been with Caxton when they were, say, discussing their mutual interest in good prose, the fact remains that Caxton was a tradesman and Earl Rivers was brother-in-law of the King, Edward IV (Shakespeare gave Earl Rivers a walk-on part in Richard III in which he trails along behind his sister the Queen speaking lines like 'She may, my lord, for—'). In real life Rivers was highly religious, a famous womanizer, dubbed 'the handsomest man living' and important enough to be murdered by Richard of York.

In those savage and unstable times it would have been prudent and forgivable for Caxton either not to have mentioned in his epilogue that the powerful Earl had left out a chunk of text or to have bent over backwards to be tactful about it.

Caxton chose instead to have a bit of fun:

I have done what I can to oversee this his said book and examined as near as I could how it accords with the original, being in French. And I find nothing discordant therein, save only in the dictes and sayings of Socrates, wherein I find that my said lord hath left out certain and divers conclusions touching women. Wherefore I wonder why my said lord hath not written them, or what has moved him so to do, or what cause he had at that time. But I suppose that some fair lady hath desired him to leave it out of his book, or else he was amorous on some noble lady, for whose love he would not put it in his book . . . Socrates was a Greek born in a far country from here, which country is very different from this one and men and women of different natures than they be here in this country, and I well know that whatever women are like in Greece, the women of this country be right good, wise, pleasant, humble, discreet, sober, chaste, obedient to their husbands, true, trustworthy, steadfast, ever busy and never idle, temperate in speech, and virtuous in all their works—or at least should be so. For these reasons my said lord, as I suppose, thought it was not necessary to put in his book the sayings of the author Socrates concerning women . . .

But as I had commandment by my said lord to correct and amend where I should find fault, and other find I none save that he hath left out those dictes and sayings about the women of Greece; therefore in obeying his commandments, as I am not certain whether the passage was in my lord's copy or not, or else peradventure the wind had blown the leaf over at the time of translation, I propose to write the sayings of the Greek Socrates which apply to the women of Greece and not to them of this realm, whom I suppose he never knew.

> William Caxton (1422?–91), Epilogue: *Dictes or Sayengis of the Philosophres* (1477). Text modernized.

Caxton did not print any jest books, although they were hugely popular at the time. The nearest he got—and it was a near-miss—was his printing of his own translation of Aesop. His source was a German rag-bag of old medieval 'jests'.

Caxton translated all these and then he found he was still a page or two short for his sheets so he added three 'tales' of his own. They were, in fact, three jokes. These jokes have not been traced in earlier continental compilations so they are almost certainly current stories which were going the rounds of London at the time and which Caxton liked and put into his own words for his book.

Here is one of them (not at all a bad joke in the mildly salacious range). It is almost certainly the first printed joke in the English language:

There was in a certain town a widower who wooed a widow to have and wed her as his wife, and at last they were agreed and betrothed. And when a young woman, being servant with the widow, heard thereof she came to her mistress and said to her:

'Alas, mistress, what have you done?'

'Why?' said she.

'I have heard say,' said the maid, 'that ye be betrothed and shall wed so-and-so.'

'And what then?' said the widow.

'Alas,' said the maid, 'I am distressed for you because I have heard say that he is a dangerous man, for he lay so often and knew so much carnally his other wife that she died thereof. I am afraid in case the like thing should befall you.'

The widow thought. She smiled quietly. She said:

'Forsooth, I would not mind being dead. Is there not but sorrow and care in this world?'

> *The Fables of Aesop* (1484). Text modernized.

S TUDYING *old jest books is a punishing experience for a modern reader. Within minutes a drowsy numbness pains the senses. The jests are mainly directed against priests, nuns, townsmen, magistrates, simpletons, and so on, and most of them now seem deeply unfunny. There is also a depressingly large number of simple scatological jokes, a typical example being 'what is the most cleanliest leaf among all other leaves? It is holly leaves, for nobody will not wipe his arse with them.'*

But jest books qualify as 'humorous prose', and they are interesting because they were popular not only when printing began but also for centuries beforehand and, indeed, ever since. And not all the jokes are awful. Here are some which have stood the test. Having been reprinted endlessly they are the jokes which centuries of readers have found funny:

There came unto Rome a certain gentleman very like Augustus. The emperor noticed him and demanded of him if his mother had sometimes been to Rome.

'No,' said the gentleman. 'But my father hath often been.'

The Schoolemaster or Teacher of Table Philosophie (1583).

> ➥ *This joke, like Caxton's, was surprisingly sophisticated and a fairly complicated thought process was required before its point became apparent. But unlike Caxton's it was one of the many jests which were of great age. It has been traced back to the early fifth century when Macrobius's version ran 'Dic mihi, adulescens, fuit aliquando mater tua Romae?' Negavit ille nec contentus adjecit: 'Sed pater meus saepe.'*

A Judge upon the bench did ask an old man how old he was: 'My Lord,' said he, 'I am eight and fourscore': 'And why not fourscore and eight?' said the Judge; the other replied, 'because I was eight before I was fourscore'.

John Taylor, the Water-Poet (1580–1653), *Wit and Mirth* (1630).

A nobleman (as he was riding) met with a yeoman of the country, to whom he said, 'My friend, I should know thee. I do remember I have often seen thee.'

'My good lord,' said the countryman, 'I am one of your honour's poor tenants, and my name is T. I.' 'I remember thee better now' (saith my lord) 'There were two brothers but one is dead. I pray, which of you doth remain alive?'

Ibid.

> ➥ This story is still in circulation. Nowadays it is usually told about twin undergraduates and some notably vague Oxford don like Dr Spooner.

A wench accused a fellow for a rape. The judge asked her whether he offered her any violence, as to bind her hands, or otherwise.

'Yes,' saith she, 'he bound my hands, and he would have bound my legs too, but he could not bring them together. I thank God I kept them far enough asunder.'

A Banquet of Jeasts (1630). Text modernized.

One was praising a wench's chastity, whom a stander-by knew to be a whore, wherefore he said to him, 'Is she chaste? Pray, had she never a child?'

The first answered him, 'Indeed she had a child, but it was a very little one.'

Gratiae Ludentes (1638).

> Frederick Marryat appropriated this joke for the first chapter of *Mr Midshipman Easy*, where a nursemaid was being interviewed:
> ' "Not a married woman and she has a child?"
> "If you please, ma'am, it was a very little one." '

A melting Sermon being preached in a Country Church, all fell a weeping, except a Country man, who being ask'd why he did not weep with the rest?

'Because' (says he) 'I am not of this Parish.'

Delight and Pastime (1697).

A waterman, being very drunk, sat down in frosty weather on the shore near the Tower wharf at a low water, on a moonshine night, and fell fast asleep, and slept so long that the tide came in and flowed by degrees even up to his mouth, the moon shining in his face. Whereupon, suddenly awaking, he said, 'No more drink, I thank you heartily. But a few more bedclothes, if you please, and then put out the candle.'

A Banquet of Jeasts (1630). Text modernized.

EVEN more popular than jest books were books of sermons, and the two were slightly connected. It had been a practice for centuries for priests to keep their largely illiterate congregations awake during the sermon by making use of exempla, which were jokes or folk-tales from jest books with a little moral tagged on the end.

King Edward VI's court preacher, Hugh Latimer, later to be burnt at the stake for heresy, was well known for using jests in his sermons. As he usually split his sermon into two parts and each was enormously long, the young King, who was sickly, must have been grateful for anything approaching light relief:

And here by the way I will tell you a merry toy. Master More was once sent in commission into Kent to help to try [find] out, if it might be, what was the cause of Goodwin sands, and the shelf that stopped up Sandwich haven. Thither cometh Master More, and calleth the country afore him, such as were thought to be men of experience, and men that could of likelihood best certify him of that matter concerning the stopping of Sandwich haven. Among others came in before him an old man, with a white head, and one that was thought to be little less than an hundred years old. When Master More saw this aged man, he thought it expedient to hear him say his mind in this matter; for, being so old a man, it was likely that he knew most of any man in that presence and company. So Master More called this old aged man unto him, and said: 'Father,' said he, 'tell me, if ye can, what is the cause of this great arising of the sands and shelves here about this haven, the which stop it up that no ships can arrive here? Ye are the eldest man that I can espy in all this company, so that if any man can tell any cause of it, ye of likelihood can say most in it; or at leastwise more than any other man here assembled.'

'Yea forsooth, good master,' quoth this old man, 'for I am well nigh an hundred years old, and no man here in this company any thing near unto mine age.'

'Well then,' said Master More, 'how say you in this matter? What think ye to be the cause of these shelves and flats that stop up Sandwich haven?'

'Forsooth sir,' quoth he, 'I am an old man; I think that Tenterton steeple is the cause of Goodwin sands. For I am an old man, sir,' quoth he, 'and I may [can] remember the building of Tenterton steeple; and I may remember when there was no steeple at all there. And before that Tenterton steeple was in building, there was no manner of speaking of any flats or sands that stopped the haven; and therefore I think that Tenterton steeple is the cause of the destroying and decay of Sandwich haven.'

And even so, to my purpose, is preaching of God's word the cause of rebellion, as Tenterton steeple was cause Sandwich haven is decayed.

> Hugh Latimer DD (1485?–1555), Last sermon preached before King Edward VI (16 Mar. 1550).
>
> ➴ But the old man with the white head was probably right. Legend has it that the Goodwin Sands was once a farm owned by the saxon Earl Godwine who left it to the church. The bishops failed to maintain its sea-wall and it became a sandy waste. The sand drifted ashore and began to block up Sandwich harbour. Money was raised to clear the harbour but the bishops used the money instead to build Tenterden steeple.

━━━━━━

Books which helped readers to improve themselves were as popular in the early years of printing as they are now. Roger Ascham, a teacher and classics scholar—he became Latin Secretary to King Edward VI and managed to remain so under Queen Mary and then Queen Elizabeth, a triumph of self-preservation—wrote Toxophilus to help the nation improve its archery. He also wanted to set a higher style of literary composition and so encourage other learned men to write their books in English rather than the customary Latin or Greek. The book was dedicated to Henry VIII. Ascham was successful on all three counts; archery improved, his literary style was much admired and helped the growth of vernacular writing, and Henry VIII awarded him a pension.

His descriptions of the various neurotic postures adopted by archers when loosing *their arrows could just as well describe how modern darts players throw. Or Wimbledon finalists serve for match point:*

Some shooteth, his head forward, as though he would bite the mark; another stareth with his eyes, as though they should fly out; another winketh with one eye, and looketh with the other; some make a face with writhing their mouth and countenance so, as though they were doing you wot what; another bleareth out his tongue; another biteth his lips; another holdeth his neck awry. In drawing some set such a compass, as though they would turn about and bless all the field; others heave their hands now up now down, that a man cannot discern whereat they would shoot; another waggeth the upper end of his bow one way, the nether end another way. Another will stand pointing his shaft at the mark a good while, and, by and by, he will give him a whip, and away before a man wit. Another maketh such a wrestling with his gear, as though he were able to shoot no more as long as he lived. Another draweth softly to the middle, and, by and by, it is gone you cannot know how. Another draweth his shaft low at the breast, as though he would shoot at a roving mark, and by and by, he lifteth his arm up prick height. Another maketh a wrenching with his back, as though a man pinched him behind. Another cowereth down, and layeth out his buttocks, as though he would shoot at crows. Another setteth forward his left leg, and draweth back with head and shoulders, as though he pulled at a rope, or else were afraid of the mark. Another draweth his shaft well, until within two fingers of the head, and then he stayeth a little, to look at his mark, and, that done, pulleth it up to his head and looseth it . . . Another I saw which, at every shot, after the loose, lifted up his right leg so far that he was ever in jeopardy of falling. Some stamp forward, and some leap backward . . .

Some will give two or three strides forward, dancing and hopping after his shaft, as long as it flieth, as though he were a mad man. Some, which fear to be too far gone, run backwards, as it were to pull his shaft back. Another runneth forward, when he feareth to be short, heaving after his arms, as though he would help his shaft to fly.

Roger Ascham (1515–68), Toxophilus (1545), Book II.

━━━━━━━━

O NE *of the perils of Tudor and Elizabethan life was the increasing number of vagrants. Farm-workers out of a job at the dissolution of the vast monastery estates and disbanded soldiers and sailors joined the already huge mass of beggars, petty thieves, and gypsies trailing round the countryside. The gypsies were well organized with their own cant dialect and secret signs and these became common to most rogues and vagabonds.*

Thomas Harman called himself a 'poore gentleman' but he was well-

*off enough to live comfortably at Crayford, in Kent. Because of ill health he stayed
at home most of the time and began to take an interest in the many beggars who
came to his door. He asked them questions and took notes. In 1566 he published
the results of his researches in a book which he called A* Caveat *for* Common
Cursitors, *Commonly called* Vagabonds. *The book was hugely successful and
made Harman the father of English 'rogue' literature. He told the stories of each of
the twenty-four classes of thief and tramp, and provided a glossary of 'thieves cant'
which became the foundation of all English cant dictionaries.*

From this one book rose a literary genre which includes The Beggar's Opera,
much of Dickens, Mayhew's London Labour and the London Poor, *and a
thousand Hollywood gangster movies.*

*Chapter XIX tells the story of a 'walking mort'. The glossary reveals that a
'walking mort' was a female beggar who went round cottages pretending that she
had been recently bereaved and asking for money. It also tells us that a 'mort' was
a harlot, so we now know what sort of girl she was and the two sources of her
income.*

*Harman was clearly rather taken with the girl. He gives her a little pious rebuke
at the beginning but soon drops into a gently teasing attitude. The mood if anything
is one of sympathy. The writing has touches of reality which not only heighten the
humour but lift the piece way above any similar contemporary prose, such as the
confession by the neighbour's wife of an earlier grope, the husband's attempts at
domestic chit-chat with his wife before rushing out to the barn, his frustrated
embarrassment when rescued by his farmhand, the girl's evident pleasure at telling
her tale.*

*For the purposes of the plot it should be remembered that in those days the word
'hose' did not mean stockings but close-fitting breeches:*

A WALKING MORT

The last summer, *Anno Domini* 1566, being in familiar talk with a walking
mort that came to my gate, I learned by her what I could and I thought I
had gathered as much for my purpose as I desired. I began to rebuke her for
her lewd life and beastly behaviour, declaring to her what punishment was
prepared and heaped up for her in the world to come for her filthy living and
wretched conversation [immorality].

'God help!' quoth she, 'how should I live? None will take me into service.
But I labour in harvest-time honestly.'

'I think but a while with honesty,' quoth I.

'Shall I tell you?' quoth she. 'The best of us all may be amended. But yet, I
thank God, I did one good deed within this twelve months.'

'Wherein?' quoth I.

Saith she, 'I would not have it spoken of again.'

'If it be meet and necessary,' quoth I, 'it shall lie under my feet.'

'What mean you by that?' quoth she.

'I mean,' quoth I, 'to hide the same and never to discover it to any.'

'Well,' quoth she, and began to laugh as much as she could, and swear by the Mass that if I disclosed the same to any, she would never more tell me anything.

'The last summer,' quoth she, 'I was great with child, and I travelled into East Kent by the sea-coast, for I lusted marvellously after oysters and mussels, and gathered many, and in the place where I found them, I opened them and ate them still. At last, in seeking more, I reached after one, and stepped into a hole and fell in into [up to] the waist, and there did stick, and I would have drowned if the tide had come, and espying a man a good way off, I cried as much as I could for help. I was alone. He heard me, and repaired to me as fast as he might, and finding me there fast sticking, I required for God's sake his help. And whether it was with striving and forcing myself out, or for joy I had of his coming to me, I had a great colour in my face, and looked red and well-coloured. And, to be plain with you, he liked me so well as he said that I should there lie still, an [unless] I would not grant him that he might lie with me. And, by my troth, I wist not what to answer, I was in such a perplexity. For I knew the man well. He had a very honest woman to his wife, and was of some wealth; and, on the other side, if I were not holp [helped] out, I should there have perished, and I granted him that I would obey to his will.

'Then he plucked me out. And because there was no convenient place near hand, I requested that I might go wash myself, and make myself somewhat cleanly, and I would come to his house and lodge all night in his barn, whither he might repair to me, and accomplish his desire.

' "But let it not be," quoth he, "before nine of the clock at night for then there will be small stirring."

' "And I may repair to the town," quoth I, "to warm and dry myself"; for this was about two of the clock in the afternoon.

' "Do so," quoth he; "for I must be busy myself to look out my cattle hereby before I can come home."

'So I went away from him, and glad was I.'

'And why so?' quoth I.

'Because,' quoth she, 'his wife, my good dame, is my very friend, and I am much beholden to her. And she hath done me so much good ere this, that I were loath now to harm her any way.'. . .

'Why,' quoth I, 'what an it had been any other man, and not your good dame's husband?'

'The matter had been the less,' quoth she.

'Tell me, I pray thee,' quoth I, 'who was the father of your child?'

She studied a while, and said that it had a father.

'But what was he?' quoth I.

'Now, by my troth, I know not,' quoth she. 'You bring me out of my matter [story], so you do.'

'Well, say on,' quoth I.

'Then I departed straight to the town and came to my dame's house and showed [told] her of my misfortune, also of her husband's usage in all points, and that I showed her the same for good will, and bid her take better heed to her husband, and to herself. So she gave me great thanks, and made me good cheer, and bid me in any case that I should be ready at the barn at that time and hour we had appointed.

' "For I know well," quoth this good wife, "my husband will not break with thee. And one thing I warn [ask] thee, that thou give me a watchword aloud when he goeth about to have his pleasure of thee, and that shall be 'Fie, for shame, fie,' and I shall be hard by you with help. But I charge thee, keep this secret until all be finished. And hold," saith this goodwife; "here is one of my petticoats I give thee."

' "I thank you, good dame," quoth I, "and I warrant you I will be true and trusty unto you."

'So my dame left me sitting by a good fire with meat and drink; and with the oysters I brought with me, I had great cheer. She went straight and repaired to her gossips [cronies] dwelling thereby, and, as I did after understand, she made her moan to them, what a naughty [wicked], lewd, lecherous husband she had, and that she could not have his company for harlots, and that she was in fear to take some filthy disease of him, he was so common a man, having little respect whom he had to do withal.

' "And," quoth she, "now here is one at my house, a poor woman that goeth about the country, that he would have had to do withal [wanted to lie with]. Wherefore, good neighbours and loving gossips, as you love me, and as you would have help at my hand another time, devise some remedy to make my husband a good man, that I may live in some surety without disease, and that he may save his soul that God so dearly bought."

'After she had told her tale, they cast their piercing eyes all upon her. But one stout [determined] dame amongst the rest had these words: "As your patient bearing of troubles, your honest behaviour among us your neighbours, your tender and pitiful heart to the poor of the parish, doth move us to lament your case, so the unsatiable carnality of your faithless husband doth instigate and stir us to devise and invent some speedy redress for your case and the amendment of his life. Wherefore, this is my counsel, an [if] you will be advertised [advised] by me, for I say to you all, unless it be this goodwife, who is chiefly touched in this matter, I have the next cause: he was in hand with me not long ago an company had not been present, which was by a marvellous chance, he had, I think, forced me. For often he hath been tampering with me, and yet have I sharply said him nay. Therefore, let us assemble secretly into the place where he has appointed to meet this gillot [wanton] that is at your house, and lurk privily in some corner till he begin to go about his business. And then methought I heard you say even now that you had a watchword, at which word we will all step forth, being five of us besides you, for you shall be none [of our number] because it is your husband, but get you to bed at your accustomed hour. We will carry each of us a good birchen rod in our laps, and we will be muffled for knowing [to be unrecognized]. And see that you go home and acquaint that walking mort with the matter; for we must have her help to hold, for always four must hold and two lay on."

' "Alas!" saith this goodwife, "he is too strong for you all. I would be loath for my sake you should receive harm at his hand."

' "Fear you not," quoth these stout women. "Let her not give the watch-word until his hosen be about his legs. And I trow we will all be with him to bring [be upon] him before he shall have leisure to pluck them up again."

'They all with one voice agreed to the matter, that the way she had devised was the best. So this goodwife repaired home. But before she departed from her gossips she showed them at what hour they should privily come in on the back-side, and where to tarry their good hour. So by the time she came in, it was almost night, and [she] found the walking mort still sitting by the fire, and declared to her all this new device [plan] above said, which [she] promised faithfully to fulfil to her small power as much as they had devised.

'Within a quarter of an hour after, in cometh the goodman [rogue], who said that he was about [attending to] his cattle.

' "Why, what have we here, wife, sitting by the fire? And if she have eat and drunk, send her into the barn to her lodging for this night, for she troubleth the house."

' "Even as you will, husband," saith his wife. "You know she cometh once in two years to these quarters. Away," saith this goodwife, "to your lodging!"

' "Yes, good dame," saith she, "as fast as I can."

'Thus, by looking one on the other, each knew other's mind, and so departed to her comely couch.

'The goodman of the house shrugged him for joy, thinking to himself, "I will make some pastime with you anon"; and, calling to his wife for his supper, set him down, and was very pleasant, and drank to his wife, and fell to his mammerings [eating], and munched apace, nothing understanding [knowing] of the banquet that was a-preparing for him after supper, and, according to the proverb, that sweet meat will have sour sauce. Thus, when he was well refreshed, his spirits being revived [he] entered into familiar talk with his wife of many matters, how well he had spent that day to both their profits, saying some of his cattle were like to have been drowned in the ditches, driving others of his neighbours' cattle out that were in his pastures, and mending his fences that were broken down. Thus profitably he had consumed the day, nothing talking of his helping out of the walking mort out of the mire, neither of his request nor yet of her promise. Thus feeding her with friendly fantasies [he] consumed two hours and more.

'Then feigning how he would see in what case his horse were in and how they were dressed, [he] repaired covertly into the barn, whereas his friendly foes lurked privily, unless it were this mannerly [respectable] mort, that comely couched on a bottle [bundle] of hay.

' "What, are you come?" quoth she. "By the mass, I would not for a hundred pound that my dame should know that you were here, either [nor] any else of your house."

' "No, I warrant thee,' said this goodman, "they be all safe and fast enough at their work, and I will be at mine anon"; and lay down by her, and straight would have had to do with her.

' "Nay, fie" saith she, "I like not this order. If ye lie with me, you shall surely untruss you and put down your hosen, for that way is most easiest and best."

' "Sayest thou so?" quoth he, "Now, by my troth, agreed."

'And when he had untrussed himself and put down, he began to assault the unsatiable fort.

' "Why," quoth she, that was without shame, saving for her promise, "and are you not ashamed?"

' "Never a whit," saith he. "Lie down quickly."

' "Now fie, for shame, fie," saith she aloud, which was the watchword.

'At the which word, these five furious, sturdy, muffled gossips flings [leap] out, and takes sure hold of this betrayed person, some plucking his hosen down lower, and binding the same fast about his feet; then binding his hands, and knitting a handkercher about his eyes, that he should not see. And when they had made him sure and fast, then they laid him on until they were windless.

' "Be good," saith this mort, "unto my master, for the passion of God!" and laid on as fast as the rest and still ceased not to cry upon them to be merciful unto him and yet laid on apace.

'And when they had well beaten him, that the blood brast [burst] plentifully out in most places, they let him lie, still bound—with this exhortation, that he should from that time forth know his wife from other men's, and that this punishment was but a flea-biting in respect of that which should follow if he amended not his manners. Thus leaving him blustering, blowing, and foaming for pain and melancholy that he neither might or could be revenged of them, they vanished away, and had this mort with them, and safely conveyed her out of the town.

'Soon after cometh into the barn one of the goodman's boys, to fet [set out] some hay for his horse; and finding his master fast bound and grievously beaten with rods, was suddenly abashed and would have run out again to have called for help. But his master bade him come unto him and unbind him; "and make no words," quoth he, "of this. I will be revenged well enough." Yet notwithstanding, after better advice [further consideration], the matter being unhonest he thought it meeter [better] to let the same pass, and not, as the proverb saith, to awake the sleeping dog.

'And, by my troth,' quoth this walking mort, 'I come now from that place,

and was never there sithence [since] this part was played, which is somewhat
more than a year. And I hear a very good report of him now, that he loveth
his wife well, and useth [behaves] himself very honestly. And was not this a
good act, now? How say you?'

'It was prettily handled,' quoth I. 'And is here all?'

'Yea,' quoth she, 'here is the end.'

> Thomas Harman (fl.1567), *A Caveat for Common Cursitors, Vulgarly called
> Vagabonds* (1566).

———

*IN Elizabeth's time the Common Man was fiercely patriotic and regarded
foreigners across the Channel as inferior beings with unfortunate habits. Merchants, adventurers, and courtiers tended to take a different view. They came
increasingly to regard the Continent as a useful area in which they could extend
their business interests and also improve their position in society by contact with
older cultures and more sophisticated social behaviour.*

*Thomas Nashe, a coarse, aggressive and passionate controversialist whose sense
of humour kept breaking through, spoke up sturdily for the Common Englishman:*

What is there in France to be learned more than in England, but falsehood
in fellowship, perfect slovenry, to love no man but for my pleasure, to swear
Ah par la mon Dieu when a man's hams are scabbed? For the idle traveller, I
mean not for the soldier, I have known some that have continued there by
the space of half-a-dozen years, and when they come home they have hid a
little wearish [wizened] lean face under a broad French hat, kept a terrible
coil [disturbance] with the dust in the street in their long cloaks of grey paper,
and spoke English strangely. Nought else have they profited by their travel,
save learnt to distinguish of the true Bordeaux grape, and know a cup of
neat Gascoigne wine from wine of Orleance. Yea, and peradventure this also,
to esteem of the pox as a pimple, to wear a velvet patch on their face, and
walk melancholy with their arms folded.

From Spain what bringeth our traveller? A skull-crowned hat of the fashion
of an old deep porringer, a diminutive alderman's ruff with short strings like
the droppings of a man's nose, a close-bellied doublet coming down like a
peak behind as far as the crupper, and cut off before by the breast-bone like
a partlet or neckercher, a wide pair of gaskins which ungathered would make
a couple of women's riding kirtles, huge hangers [straps on the sword-belt]
that have half a cow-hide in them, a rapier that is lineally descended from
half-a-dozen dukes at the least. Let his cloak be as long or as short as you
will; if long, it is faced with Turkey grogeran [coarse silk] ravelled; if short,
it hath a cape like a calf's tongue and is not so deep in his whole length, nor
hath so much cloth in it, I will justify as only the standing cape of a Dutch-

man's cloak. I have not yet touched all, for he hath in either shoe as much taffatie for his tyings as would serve for an ancient; which serveth him (if you will have the mystery of it) of the own accord for a shoe-rag. A soldier and a braggart he is (that's concluded). He jetteth strouting [strutting], dancing on his toes with his hands under his sides. If you talk with him, he makes a dishcloth of his own country in comparison of Spain, but if you urge him more particularly wherein it exceeds, he can give no instance but 'in Spain they have better bread than any we have'; when, poor hungry slaves, they may crumble it into water well enough and make misers [slops] with it, for they have not a good morsel of meat except it be salt piltchers to eat with it all the year long, and, which is more, they are poor beggars and lie in foul straw every night.

Italy, the paradise of the earth and the epicure's heaven, how doth it form our young master? It makes him to kiss his hand like an ape, cringe his neck like a starveling, and play at heypass, repass come aloft [gesture like a conjuror], when he salutes a man. From thence he brings the art of atheism, the art of epicurizing, the art of whoring, the art of poisoning, the art of sodomitry. The only probable good thing they have to keep us from utterly condemning it is that it maketh a man an excellent courtier, a curious carpet knight; which is, by interpretation, a fine close lecher, a glorious hypocrite. It is now a privy note amongst the better sort of men, when they would set a singular mark or brand on a notorious villain, to say he hath been in Italy.

Thomas Nashe (1567–1601), *The Unfortunate Traveller* (1594).

———

THOMAS DELONEY *was a silk weaver by trade but his pleasure was writing; first comical ballads, then rather more weighty ballads on topical excitements such as the Spanish Armada, the Duchess of Suffolk's calamity, and popular murders. He also wrote three books which helped to pioneer the writing of stories about ordinary, good people rather than great men or rogues.*

The Gentle Craft *was written in praise of shoemakers. In the following extract two young maidservants meet in the street and their thoughts turn instantly to men. Margaret, who fancies a handsome shoemaker, describes to her friend how blissful she imagines married life must be:*

It chanced that Margaret, having occasion to go into London, it was her good fortune to meet with Gillian of the *George*, whom her mistress had sent thither to buy comfits and carraways, with divers other sweet-meats, for that they had a banquet bespoken by divers gallant which that night appointed to come thither. But so soon as Margaret spied her, she smiled, saying: 'Gillian now in good sadness, well met (if thou be met a maid [virgin]).'

'And ill met' (quoth she) 'not meeting so good a maid as myself.'

'Tush' (said Margaret) 'It is good for us to think well of ourselves, for there is enough that think ill of us.'

'Marry, I defy them' (quoth Gillian) 'that thinks ill of me, and I respect as little their speech, as they do my profit. For a woman with a good life fears no man with an evil tongue.'

'If you be so hot [furious]' (quoth Margaret) 'where the wind blows so cold, what will you be like by that time supper is ready, where the fire will be as fierce as your choler [anger] is great? And mistake me not, good Gillian, though I said men think ill of us, I mean not thereby that any go about to blemish our good names. But I suppose they think not so well of us as they might do that do not love us so well as to marry us.'

'Nay' (said Gillian) 'if that be all, I am at a good point; for though my maidenhead be somewhat burdensome to bear, yet I had rather keep it than bestow it on a bad husband: but though I say it, though I be but a poor wench, I have choice of husbands enough, and such as I am assured in my conscience would both love me well and keep me gallantly.'

'Wherefore then do you not marry?' (quoth Margaret) 'In my opinion it is the pleasingest life that may be, when a woman shall have her husband come home and speak in this sort [manner] to her: "How now wife? How dost thou my sweetheart? What wilt thou have? Or what dost thou lack?" And therewithall kindly embracing her, gives her a gentle kiss, saying: "Speak, my pretty mouse. Wilt thou have a cup of claret-wine, white-wine, or sack to supper?" And then perhaps he carves unto her the leg of capon, or the wing of a chicken, and if there be one bit better than other, she hath the choice of it. And if she chance to long for anything, by and by it is sent for with all possible speed, and nothing is thought too dear to do her good. At last, having well refreshed themselves, she sets her silver whistle to her mouth and calls her maid to clear the board: then going to the fire, he sets her on his knee, and wantonly stroking her cheek, amorously he chucks her under the chin, fetching many stealing touches at her ruby lips, and so soon, as he hears the bell ring eight a clock, he calls her to go to bed with him. O how sweet do these words sound in a woman's ears? But when they are once close between a pair of sheets, O Gillian, then, then . . .'

'Why, what of that?' (quoth she).

'Nay, nothing' (saith Margaret) 'but they sleep soundly all night.'

Thomas Deloney (1543?–1600?), *The Gentle Craft* (1597).

———————

THE *playwright Thomas Dekker was a prolific contributor to this 'common-man literature' and his works are a rich and amusing source of detail about middle-class life in Elizabethan and Jacobean London. The Guls Hornebooke, which appeared in 1609, was an ironic version of the popular 'courtesy' books which set*

out to teach the socially-ambitious how to better themselves. The Guls Hornebooke *purported to teach a decent young country lad how to turn himself into an
oafish town gallant; a good idea which Dekker lifted from a Dutch book, Dedekind's*
Grobianus.

*The most famous piece in the book is the passage in which Dekker gives in-
structions to the would-be gallant on how to behave at the playhouse. It was the
practice, until Garrick put a stop to it in the eighteenth century, for nobility, fops,
and young bloods generally to pay sixpence and sit on the stage itself during
performances. The piece suggests that Dekker had suffered much from loutish
interference during his plays: it seems to come from the heart:*

Present not yourself on the stage (especially at a new play), until the quaking
Prologue hath (by rubbing) got colour into his cheeks, and is ready to give
the trumpets their cue that he is upon point to enter. For then it is time, as
though you were one of the properties, or that you dropped out of the
hangings, to creep from behind the arras with your *tripos* or three-footed
stool in one hand and a teston [silver sixpence] mounted between a forefinger
and a thumb in the other . . .

Before the play begins, fall to cards. You may win or lose (as fencers do in
a prize [bout]) and beat one another by confederacy, yet share the money
when you meet at supper. Notwithstanding, to gull the ragamuffins that
stand aloof gaping at you, throw the cards (having first torn four or five of
them) round about the stage just upon the third sound [of the trumpet: to
signal the play's commencement], as though you had lost . . .

Now, sir, if the writer be a fellow that hath either epigrammed you, or
hath had a flirt at your mistress, or hath brought [ridiculed] either your
feather, or your red beard, or your little legs, etc., on the stage, you shall
disgrace him worse than by tossing him in a blanket, or giving him the
bastinado in a tavern, if, in the middle of his play (be it pastoral or comedy,
moral or tragedy) you rise with a screwed and discontented face from your
stool to be gone. No matter whether the scenes be good or no; the better
they are, the worse do you distaste them. And, being on your feet, sneak not
away like a coward, but salute all your gentle acquaintance that are spread
either on the rushes or on stools about you, and draw what troop you can
from the stage after you. The mimics [actors] are beholden to you for allowing
them elbow-room. Their poet cries, perhaps 'A pox go with you!' but care
not for that—there's no music without frets.

Marry, if either the company or indisposition of the weather bind [compel]
you to sit it out, my council is that you turn plain ape, take up a rush,
and tickle the earnest ears of your fellow gallants, to make other fools fall
a-laughing; mew at passionate speeches, blare at merry, find fault with the
music, whew at the children's action, whistle at the songs . . .

Thomas Dekker (1570?–1641?), The Guls Hornebooke (1609)

O F the many straightforward manuals teaching social survival perhaps Henry
Peacham's is the most beguiling. His approach is not ironic. The book is a
serious attempt to prevent innocent visitors to big cities from being instantly parted
from their money. But his touch is light:

Take a private chamber wherein you may pass your spare time in doing
something or other, and what you call for, pay for, without going upon the
score, especially in city alehouses, where in many places you shall be torn
out of your skin, if it were possible, even for a debt of twopence . . .

Keep out of throngs and public places where multitudes of people are—for
saving your purse. The fingers of a number go beyond your sense of feeling.
A tradesman's wife of the Exchange one day, when her husband was following some business in the city, desired him he would give her leave to go
see a play, which she had not done in seven years. He bade her take his
apprentice along with her and go, but especially to have a care of her purse,
which she warranted him she would. Sitting in a box among some gallants
and gallant wenches and returning when the play was done, she returned
to her husband and told him she had lost her purse.

'Wife,' quoth he, 'did I not give you warning of it? How much money was
there in it?'

Quoth she, 'Truly, four pieces, six shillings, and a silver toothpicker.'

Quoth her husband, 'Where did you put it?'

'Under my petticoat, between that and my smock.'

'What,' quoth he, 'did you feel nobody's hand there?'

'Yes,' quoth she, 'I felt one's hand there, but I did not think he had come
for that.'

So much for the guard of the purse.

Henry Peacham (1576–1643?), *The Art of Living in London* (1642)

S IR JOHN HARINGTON, *godson of Queen Elizabeth, poet, wit, miscellaneous
writer, inventor of the valve-flushing water-closet, and commander of horse
under Essex in Ireland, much enjoyed the gossip and scandal of court life under
King James I.*

*In 1606 the king's brother-in-law, Christian IV of Denmark, paid a state visit
and was expensively entertained by King James. Happily Sir John was present and
described the goings-on with relish in a letter to a friend:*

I came here a day or two before the Danish King came, and from the day he
did come until this hour, I have been well nigh overwhelmed with carousal
and sports of all kinds. The sports began each day in such manner and such
sort, as well nigh persuaded me of Mahomet's paradise. We had women, and

indeed wine too, of such plenty, as would have astonished each sober beholder. Our feasts were magnificent, and the two royal guests did most lovingly embrace each other at table. I think the Dane hath strangely wrought on our good English nobles; for those, whom I could never get to taste good liquor, now follow the fashion and wallow in beastly delights. The ladies abandon their sobriety, and are seen to roll about in intoxication. In good sooth the parliament did kindly to provide his Majesty so seasonably with money, for there hath been no lack of good living; shows, sights, and banquetings, from morn to eve.

One day, a great feast was held, and, after dinner, the performance of Solomon his Temple and the coming of the Queen of Sheba was made, or (as I may better say) was meant to have been made, before their Majesties, by device of the Earl of Salisbury and others . . . The Lady who did play the Queen's part did carry most precious gifts to both their Majesties; but, forgetting the steps arising to the canopy, overset her caskets into his Danish Majesty's lap, and fell at his feet, though I rather think it was in his face. Much was the hurry and confusion; cloths and napkins were at hand, to make all clean.

His Majesty then got up and would dance with the Queen of Sheba; but he fell down and humbled himself before her, and was carried to an inner chamber and laid on a bed of state; which was not a little defiled with the presents of the Queen which had been bestowed on his garments; such as wine, cream, jelly, beverage, cakes, spices, and other good matters.

The entertainment and show went forward, and most of the presenters [actors] went backward, or fell down, wine did so occupy their upper chambers.

Now did appear, in rich dress, Hope, Faith, and Charity: Hope did assay to speak, but wine rendered her endeavours so feeble that she withdrew, and hoped the King would excuse her brevity.

Faith was then all alone, for I am certain she was not joined with good works, and left the court in a staggering condition.

Charity came to the King's feet, and seemed to cover the multitude of sins her sisters had committed; in some sort she made obeisance and brought gifts, but said she would return home again, as there was no gift which heaven had not already given his Majesty. She then returned to Hope and Faith, who were both sick and spewing in the lower hall.

Next came Victory, in bright armour, and presented a rich sword to the King, who did not accept it but put it by with his hand; and, by a strange medley of versification, did endeavour to make suit to the King. But Victory did not triumph long; for after much lamentable utterance, she was led away like a silly captive, and laid to sleep in the outer steps of the antechamber.

Now did Peace make entry, and strive to get in front of the King; but I grieve to tell how great wrath she did discover [show] unto those of her attendants; and, much contrary to her semblance, most rudely made war with her olive branch, and laid on the pates of those who did oppose her coming.

Sir John Harington (1561–1612), Letter to Mr Secretary Barlow (1606). *Nugae Antiquae*.

════════

R OBERT BURTON *wrote* The Anatomy of Melancholy *under the pseudonym 'Democritus Junior'. Democritus, a Greek philosopher of the fifth century* BC, *was known as 'the laughing philosopher' because it was believed that his reaction to the follies of mankind was to poke fun at them.*

In his preface to The Anatomy of Melancholy, *Burton explained that he wrote the book to rid himself of his own melancholia. This it failed to do; Bishop Kennet wrote that Burton's only relief from despondency was to lean over the foot-bridge at Oxford and listen to the bargemen swearing at each other.*

But the book amused a great number of readers, including Samuel Johnson, and was a direct influence on later writers such as Laurence Sterne and Charles Lamb.

Its medieval, Rabelaisian technique of amassing great lists of adjectives and descriptive phrases with a generous sprinkling of Latin tags and quotations from the classics is now unfunny and somewhat heavy going but it was then much enjoyed. Here is a typical (but untypically brief) passage telling of the blindness of love:

Every lover admires his mistress, though she be very deformed of herself, ill-favoured, wrinkled, pimpled, pale, red, yellow, tanned, tallow-faced, have a swollen juggler's platter face, or a thin, lean, chitty face, have clouds in her face, be crooked, dry, bald, goggle-eyed, blear-eyed, or with staring eyes, she looks like a squis'd cat, holds her head still awry, heavy, dull, hollow-eyed, black or yellow about the eyes, or squint-eyed, sparrow-mouthed, Persian hook-nosed, have a sharp fox nose, a red nose, China flat, great nose *nare simo patuloque* [snub and flat nose], a nose like a promontory, gubber-tushed, rotten teeth, black, uneven, brown teeth, beetle-browed, a witch's beard, her breath stink all over the room, her nose drop winter and summer, with a Bavarian poke under her chin, a sharp chin, lave-eared, with a long crane's neck, which stands awry too, *pendulis mammis* 'her dugs like two double jugs,' or else no dugs, in that other extreme, bloody fallen fingers, she have filthy, long unpared nails, scabbed hands or wrists, a tanned skin, a rotten carcass, crooked back, she stoops, is lame, splea-footed, 'as slender in the middle as a cow in the waist', gouty legs, her ankles hang over her shoes, her feet stink, she breed lice, a mere changeling, a very monster, an oaf imperfect, her whole complexion savours, an harsh voice, incondite gesture, vile gait, a vast virago, or an ugly tit, a slug, a fat fustilugs, a truss, a long lean rawbone, a skeleton, a sneaker (*si latent meliora puta* [think that what is not seen is better]), and to thy judgement looks like a mard in a lantern, whom thou couldst not fancy for the world, but hatest, loathest, and wouldst have spit in her face, or blow thy nose in her bosom, *remedium amorus* [a cure for love] to another man, a dowdy, a slut, a scold, a nasty, rank, rammy, filthy, beastly quean, dishonest peradventure, obscene, base, beggarly, rude, foolish, untaught, peevish, Irus' daughter, Thersites' sister, Grobian's scholar; if he love her once, he admires her for all this, he takes no notice of any such errors, or imperfections of body and mind, *Ipsa haec delectant, veluti Balbinum polypus Agnæ* [These very things charm him, as Agna's polypus did Balbinus]; he had rather have her than any woman in the world. Robert Burton (1577–1640), *The Anatomy of Melancholy* (1621).

─────────

D URING *the first part of the seventeenth century a literary form called 'characters' became popular. This dated back to the* Characters of Theo-phrastus *of Lesbos (371–287* BC), *a book in which the philosopher described thirty different types of people.*

This kind of short, descriptive essay fitted the seventeenth-century taste for brevity and for exploration of individual behaviour. The medieval theory, still believed, was that a person's temperament was determined by the mixture of his or her bodily fluids, or humours, and when one fluid got the upper hand, vapour wafted up to the brain and that person became noticeably melancholic, or sanguine, or choleric, or phlegmatic in their behaviour. He or she was then said to be 'humorous' (see Ben Jonson's plays, Every Man in His Humour *and* Every Man Out of His Humour).

Thus writers took to devising characters, particularly in plays, whose behaviour depended on one dominant mood or peculiarity. The seventeenth-century writers of 'characters' went further and tried to describe individuals who at the same time exemplified types, which was a tentative move towards the beginning of the English Novel.

The first Englishman to write a book of characters was Sir Thomas Overbury, a poet and courtier. Perhaps a better poet than courtier because he was eventually committed to the Tower for intrigue and poisoned there by Lady Essex.

The following character by Sir Thomas is noteworthy for being our first entry to be smothered in puns:

A WATER-MAN

Is one that hath learnt to speak well of himself; for always he names himself *the first man*. If he had betaken himself to some richer trade, he could not have choosed but done well; for in this (though it be a mean one) he is still plying it and putting himself forward. He is evermore telling strange news, most commonly lies. If he be a sculler, ask him if he be married, he'll equivocate and swear he's a single man. Little trust is to be given to him, for he thinks that day he does best, when he fetches most men over. His daily labour teaches him the art of dissembling: for like a fellow that rides to the pillory, he goes not the way he looks. He keeps such a bawling at *Westminster* that if the lawyers were not acquainted with it, an order would be taken with him. When he is upon the water he is fare-company: when he comes ashore he mutinies, and contrary to all other trades, is most surly to gentlemen when they tender payment: the play-houses only keep him sober; and as it doth many other gallants, make him an afternoons man. London-bridge is the most terrible eye-sore to him that can be. And to conclude, nothing but a *great press* makes him fly from the river; nor anything but a great *frost* can teach him any good manners.

Sir Thomas Overbury (1581–1613), Characters (1614).

———————

T HE *technique of writing characters, the piling-up of detail, the careful placing of a character in the right setting, the listing of the little eccentricities, crept into other forms of prose, notably biography.*

Here is a portrait by Lord Shaftesbury, the most eminent statesman of his time, of a nobly born squire who was of the Old School; a dying breed:

Mr Hastings, by his quality, being the son, brother, and uncle to the Earls of Huntingdon, and his way of living, had the first place amongst us. He was peradventure an original in our age, or rather the copy of our nobility in ancient days in hunting and not warlike times; he was low, very strong and very active, of a reddish flaxen hair, his clothes always green cloth, and never all worth when new five pound.

His house was perfectly of the old fashion . . . the great hall strewed with marrow-bones, full of hawks' perches, hounds, spaniels, and terriers, the upper sides of the hall hung with the fox-skins of this and the last year's killing, here and there a polecat intermixed; guns, keepers' and huntsmen's poles in abundance.

The parlour was a large long room, as properly furnished; on a great hearth paved with brick lay some terriers and the choicest hounds and spaniels; seldom but two of the great chairs had litters of young cats in them, which were not to be disturbed, he always having three or four attending him at dinner, and a little white round stick of fourteen inches long lying by his trencher, that he might defend such meat as he had no mind to part with to them.

The windows, which were very large, served as places to lay his arrows, crossbows, stonebows, and other such-like accoutrements; the corners of the room full of the best choice hunting and hawking poles; an oyster-table at the lower end, which was of constant use twice a day all the year round, for he never failed to eat oysters before dinner and supper through all seasons: the neighbouring town of Poole supplied him with them.

The upper part of this room had two small tables and a desk, on the one side of which was a church Bible, on the other the Book of Martyrs; on the tables were hawks' hoods, bells and such like, two or three old green hats with their crowns thrust in so as to hold ten or a dozen eggs, which were of a pheasant kind of poultry he took much care of and fed himself; tables, dice, cards and boxes were not wanting. In the hole of the desk were store of tobacco-pipes that had been used.

On one side of this end of the room was the door of a closet, wherein stood the strong beer and the wine, which never came thence but in single glasses, that being the rule of the house exactly observed, for he never exceeded in drink nor permitted it.

On the other side was a door into an old chapel not used for devotion; the pulpit, as the safest place, was never wanting of a cold chine of beef, pasty of venison, gammon of bacon, or great apple-pie, with thick crust extremely baked. His table cost him not much, though it was very good to eat at, his sports supplying all but beef and mutton, except Fridays, when he had the best sea-fish as well as other fish he could get, and was the day that his neighbours of best quality most visited him. He never wanted a London pudding, and always sang it in with 'my part lies therein-a'.

He drank a glass or two of wine at meals, very often syrup of gilliflower in his sack, and had always a tun glass without feet stood by him holding a pint of small beer, which he often stirred with a great sprig of rosemary.

He was well natured but soon angry, calling his servants bastard and cuckoldy knaves, in one of which he often spoke truth to his knowledge, and sometimes in both, though of the same man.

He lived to a hundred, never lost his eye-sight, but always wrote and read without spectacles, and got to horse without help. Until past fourscore he rode to the death of a stag as well as any.

Anthony Ashley Cooper, first Earl of Shaftesbury (1621–83), Fragment of Autobiography (c.1680).

━━━━━━━━━━

U NLIKE *a 'character', which tried to give a fairly full description of an individual and a type, an 'anecdote' could be merely a brush-stroke which put a little colour on. It could be something the subject said, or a little incident, or even— sometimes best of all—pure gossip, so long as it gave the reader a whiff of what the person was really like.*

The 'anecdote' or 'secret history' was a form which appealed strongly to those who had humour and a magpie mind. The sprightliest practitioner of this kind of anecdote, if not its founding father, was the antiquarian and unrepentant Gossip of Gossips, John Aubrey:

SIR THOMAS MORE

In his *Utopia* his law is that the young people are to see each other stark-naked before marriage. Sir William Roper, of Eltham in Kent, came one morning, pretty early, to my Lord, with a proposal to marry one of his daughters. My Lord's daughters were then both together abed in a truckle-bed in their father's chamber asleep. He carries Sir William into the chamber and takes the sheet by the corner and suddenly whips it off. They lay on their backs, and their smocks up as high as their arm-pits. This awakened them and immediately they turned on their bellies. Quoth Roper, 'I have seen both sides', and so gave a pat on the buttock, he made choice of, saying 'Thou art mine'. Here was all the trouble of the wooing.

SIR WALTER RALEIGH

He loved a wench well; and one time getting up one of the Maids of Honour up against a tree in a Wood ('twas his first Lady) who seemed at first boarding to be something fearful of her Honour, and modest, she cried, 'Sweet Sir Walter, what do you me ask? Will you undo me? Nay, sweet Sir Walter! Sweet Sir Walter! Sir Walter!' At last, as the danger and the pleasure at the same time grew higher, she cried in the ecstacy, 'Swisser Swatter Swisser Swatter!' She proved with child.

JOHN COLET

John Colet, DD, Dean of St Paul's, London. After the Conflagration [Great Fire] (his Monument being broken) somebody made a little hole towards the upper edge of his coffin, which was closed like the coffin [casing] of a pie and was full of a Liquor which conserved the body. Mr Wyld and Ralph Greatorex tasted it and 'twas of a kind of insipid taste, something of an ironish taste. The coffin was of lead, and laid in the wall about 2 foot $\frac{1}{2}$ above the surface of the floor.

This was a strange rare way of preserving a corpse: perhaps it was a pickle, as of beef, whose saltness in so many years the lead might sweeten and render insipid. The body felt, to the probe of a stick which they thrust into a chink, like boiled brawn.

JOHN SELDEN

He was of Hart-hall in Oxon, and Sir Giles Mompesson told me that he was then of that house, and that he was a long scabby-polled boy, but a good student.

Thence he came to the Inner-Temple. He was quickly taken notice of for his learning, and was Solicitor and Steward to the Earl of Kent, whose Countess, being an ingenious woman and loving men, would let him lie with her, and her husband knew it. After the Earl's death he married her. He did lie with Mistress Williamson (one of my Lady's women) a lusty bouncing woman, who robbed him on his death-bed. I remember in 1646, or 1647, they did talk also of my Lady's she-blackamoor.

I remember my saddler (who wrought [worked] many years to that family) told me that Mr Selden had got more by his prick than he had done by his practice. He was no eminent practicer at the Bar.

He was very tall, I guess about six foot high, sharp oval face, head not very big, long nose inclining to one side, full popping eye (gray). He was a poet.

EDWARD DE VERE: EARL OF OXFORD

This Earl of Oxford, making of his low obeisance to Queen Elizabeth, happened to let a Fart, at which he was so abashed and ashamed that he went to travel, 7 years. On his return the Queen welcomed him home, and said, My Lord, I had forgot the Fart.

John Aubrey (1626–97), Brief Lives (ed. Oliver Lawson Dick, 1949).

———————

*L*ORD MACAULAY *suggested in an essay that the love-story of Dorothy Osborne and William (later Sir William) Temple had the makings of a good five-volume novel.*

They met at an inn on the Isle of Wight where their two parties were putting up for the night. William was aged 20 and spirited and Dorothy was aged 21 and beautiful. They fell in love.

There were huge problems. William's father, Sir John, was a Puritan Member of Parliament while Dorothy's father, Sir Peter, commanded Guernsey for King Charles I. And both parents strongly disapproved of the match for other reasons as well: William's father wanted his son to marry a woman who would bring him more wealth and position. Dorothy's family disliked William intensely and urged her to accept one of the other suitors who wooed her, one of whom was Henry Cromwell, fourth son of the Protector (Henry gave her an Irish greyhound). But they loved each other and held on and after seven years of courtship the opposition died away. As they were preparing for the marriage Dorothy caught smallpox and was badly disfigured. They married and were happy.

During their seven years courtship William was abroad and they kept in touch by writing to each other. His letters to her have been lost but Dorothy's still exist; perceptive, loving, warm with humour:

You would both have pitied and laughed at me, if you could have seen how woodenly I entertained the widow who came hither the day before, and surprised me very much. Not being able to say anything, I got her to cards, and there with a great deal of patience lost my money to her, or rather I gave it as my ransom. In the midst of our play in comes my blessed [carrier's] boy with your letter, and in earnest I was not able to disguise the joy it gave me, though one was by [i.e. her brother] that is not much your friend, and took notice of a blush that for my life I could not keep back. I put up the letter in my pocket, and made what haste I could to lose the money I had left that I might take occasion to go fetch some more, but I did not make such haste back again I can assure you, I took enough time to have coined myself some money if I had had the art on't . . .

My dreams are yours, and I have got such a habit of thinking of you that any other thought intrudes and grows uneasy to me. I drink your health every morning in a drench that would poison a horse I believe, and 'tis the only way I have to persuade myself to take it; 'tis the infusion of steel and makes me so horribly sick that every day at ten a clock I am making my will, and taking leave of all my friends. You will believe that you are not forgot then.

Dorothy Osborne (1627–95), *The Letters of Dorothy Osborne to William Temple* (ed. Moore Smith, 1928), 5 Mar. 1652–3.

What an age do we live in where 'tis a miracle if in ten couples that are married two of them live so as not to publish it to the world that they cannot agree . . . A kinswoman of ours . . . had a husband who was not always himself, and when he was otherwise his humour was to rise in the night, and with two bedstaves tabor [beat] upon the table an hour together. She took care every night to lay a great cushion upon the table for him to strike on that nobody might hear him and so discover his madness. But 'tis a sad thing that all one's happiness is only that the world does not know you are miserable. For my part I think it were very convenient that all such as intend to marry should live together in the same house some years of probation, and if in all that time they never disagreed they should then be permitted to marry if they pleased. But how few would do it then! I do not remember that I ever saw or heard of any couple that were bred up so together (as many you know are, that are designed for one another from children) but they always disliked one another extremely, and parted if it were left in their choice. If people proceeded with this caution the world would end sooner than is expected, I believe . . .

Ibid., Oct. 1653.

Just now I have news brought me of the death of an old, rich knight that has promised me these seven years to marry me whensoever his wife died, and now he's dead before her, and has left her such a widow it makes me mad to think on't; £1200 a year jointure and £20,000 in money and personal estate; and all this I might have had if Mr Death had been pleased to have taken her instead of him: well who can help these things? But since I cannot have him, would you had her! What say you, shall I speak a good word for you? She will marry for certain, and though perhaps my brother may expect

I should serve him in it [speak on his behalf], yet if you give me commission I'll say I was engaged beforehand for a friend and leave him to shift for himself. You would be my neighbour if you had her and I should see you often.

Ibid., 28 May 1653.

A DIFFERENT *dish of tea altogether were the letters (and life) of the dramatist, Sir George Etherege, who was the archetypal Restoration roué.*

He was a playwright whose three witty comedies paved the way for the great wave of Restoration comedies of manners ; he was a bully-boy who beat up watchmen with his crony, Lord Rochester ; it was widely believed that he bought his knighthood in order to persuade a rich widow to marry him ; he lived with England's first prominent actress, Elizabeth Barry, who had a child by him ; he wangled a diplomatic job from Charles II and went off to Ratisbon where he shocked the staid German society by carousing, having musicians in the house playing at all hours, and keeping an actress as his mistress.

In 1686 Sir George's old friend George Villiers, second Duke of Buckingham, according to a contemporary report 'worn to a thread with whoring', decided to leave London and court intrigue and retire to a country life in Yorkshire.

Sir George hears of this and writes him a letter:

To the Duke of Buckingham
November 12,
Ratisbon 1686.

My Lord,

I received the news of your Grace's retiring into Yorkshire, and leading a sedate contemplative life there, with no less astonishment than I should hear of his Christian Majesty's turning Benedictine monk, or the Pope's wearing a long periwig and setting up for a flaming beau in the seventy-fourth year of his age. We have a picture here in our town-hall which I never look upon but it makes me think on your Grace; and I dare swear you'll say there is no dishonour done you, when you hear whose it is: In short, 'tis that of the famous Charles the V, who (amidst all the magnificence that this foolish world affords, amidst all his African laurels and Gallic triumphs) freely divested himself of the empire of Europe, and his hereditary kingdoms, to pass the remainder of his life in solitude and retirement.

Is it possible that your Grace (who has seen ten times more luxury than that Emperor ever knew, conversed with finer women, kept politer company, possessed as much too of the true real greatness of the world as ever he enjoyed) should in age still capable of pleasure, and under a fortune whose very ruins would make up a comfortable Electorate here in Germany, is it possible, I say, that your Grace should leave the play at the beginning of the fourth act, when all the spectators are in pain to know what will become of the hero, and what mighty matters he is reserved for, that set out so advantageously in the first? That a person of your exquisite taste, that has breathed the air of courts ever from your infancy, should be content, in that part of your life which is most difficult to be pleased and most easy to be disgusted, to take up with the conversation of country parsons; a sort of people, whom to my knowledge, your Grace never much admired; and do penance in the nauseous company of lawyers, whom I am certain you abominate.

To raise our astonishment higher, who could ever have prophesied (though he had a double gift of Nostradamus's spirit) that the Duke of Buckingham who never vouchsafed his embraces to any ordinary beauty, would ever condescend to sigh and languish for the heiress apparent of a thatched cottage, in a straw hat, flannel petticoat, stockings of as gross a yarn as the Blue-Coat Boy's caps at the Chelsea Royal Hospital, and a smock (the Lord defend me from the wicked idea of it!) of as coarse a canvas as ever served an apprenticeship to a mackerel boat? Who could have believed, till matter of fact had confirmed the belief of it, (and your Grace knows that matter of fact is not to be disputed) that the most polished refined epicure of his age, that had regaled himself in the most exquisite wines of Italy, Greece, and Spain, would, in the last scene of his life, debauch his constitution in execrable Yorkshire ale? And that he, who all his life time had either seen princes his play-fellows or companions, would submit to the nonsensical chat and barbarous language of farmers and higglers?

This, I confess, so much shocks me that I cannot tell what to make on't . . .

Later in the letter comes the paragraph in which Sir George gives us a Restoration rake's philosophy on drinking:

To unbosom myself frankly and freely to your Grace, I always looked upon drunkenness to be an unpardonable crime in a young fellow, who without any of these foreign helps, has fire enough in his veins to enable him to do justice to Caelia whenever she demands a tribute from him. In a middle-aged man, I consider the bottle only as subservient to the nobler pleasures of love; and he that would suffer himself to be so far infatuated by it as to neglect the pursuit of a more agreeable game I think deserves no quarter from the ladies: In old age, indeed, when tis convenient very often to forget and steal from ourselves, I am of opinion that a little drunkenness, discreetly used, may as well contribute to our health of body as tranquillity of soul.

I am, my Lord, your Grace's most obedient servant

G. Etherege.

Sir George Etherege (1635?–91), *Buckingham's Miscellaneous Works* (1704).

*A*N *author at the other end of the social scale from Sir George was Ned Ward,*
semi-educated hack-writer and keeper of the Bacchus *tavern in Moorfields.*
In a foreword to one of his books he finds similarities between the life of a Grub
Street scribbler like himself and of a member of an equally precarious profession:

The condition of an author is much like that of a strumpet, both exposing
our reputations to supply our necessities, till at last we contract such ill
habits, thro' our practices, that we are equally troubled with an itch to be
always doing: and if the reason be requir'd, why we betake ourselves to so
scandalous a profession, as whoring and pamphleteering, the same executive
answer will serve us both, viz, that the unhappy circumstances of a narrow
fortune, hath forc'd us to do that, for our substance, which we are much
ashamed of.

The only difference between us, in this particular, wherein the jilt has the
advantage: we do our business first, and stand to the courtesies of our
benefactors to reward us after: while the other, for her security, makes her
rider pay for his journey, before he mounts the saddle.

Edward Ward (1667–1731), Foreword to A Trip to Jamaica (1698).

*T*OM BROWN *was a contemporary of Ned Ward; better educated but more*
profligate, prepared reluctantly to provide Grub Street printers with a pamph-
let, a satire, a poem, a scurrilous personal attack, an obituary, or anything which
might earn him a whore, a pint of wine, or sleeping space on a floor—probably in
that order of precedence.

He is best remembered now for supposedly having extemporized a curiously
durable little verse in order to escape some punishment when he was an under-
graduate at Oxford under the formidable Dr Fell:

> I do not love thee, Dr Fell.
> The reason why I cannot tell.
> But this I know and know full well,
> I do not love thee, Dr Fell.

In the following piece Tom Brown writes as a fop aghast at hearing that a fellow
exquisite has decided to turn soldier:

Lord! what will the degeneracy of this age come to? That a gentleman that
understands dressing to perfection, and has spent so many hours at Locket's
and the Blue Posts to cultivate his palate, should ever be such a sot as in
cold blood, and of his own true accord, to visit that hellish country where
the burgomasters and the boors conspire between them to infect the very air
with their belches. Rot my diaphragm, if the nasty word has not polluted my
ink, so that I'm forced to put some orange-water into the standish to correct
the unsavoury smell. Really, Tam, to think of the miseries thou must endure

this summer is as bad as going up the Monument; it has made me giddy, confound me, and my head turns round like a weather-cock. In the first place, to lie in a damned sneaking tent, where you can scarce turn yourself round, with no curtains to your bed: nay, not so much as a looking-glass in its lowest signification. Then no other powder to scent your periwig but the dust of the plains and gunpowder, and to stink worse of the latter than Cheapside did formerly on a Lord Mayor's Day; upon those unrighteous things called marches, no such thing as a sedan-chair to be got. For your comfort, Tam, you must walk through thick and thin with no waiter behind you to clean your shoes, among a herd of shirtless rascals that stink worse than polecats . . .

To come now, Tam, to the field of battle; those ill-bred whoreson things called bullets are no respecters of persons. A pox on them, they observe no distinction between a fine gentleman and a dragooner. Perhaps it would not grieve a man to lose his life upon a good occasion! (I speak this by way of supposition only) but to survive the untimely fate of one's beloved wig, to see one's embroidered coat mangled and hacked, is enough to break the heart of Hercules, if he were alive, and had a true sense of things . . .

Pray retire a moment or two to your closet; lay your hand upon your heart, and ask it cooly and soberly how it would relish that most extraordinary accomplishment, a wooden leg? Think what a decent figure you'll make in a lady's chamber with so fine a qualification . . .

Faith, Tam, I dare trust my thought no longer with such a melancholy theme. So hoping you'll be so kind to your self as to consider more of this matter, I am

Votre très humble Serviteur.

Tom Brown (1663–1704), Amusements Serious and Comical (1700).

A piece more typical of Tom Brown's usual raunchy style was his description of a trip on the river. The boatmen's elaborate swearing, which was traditional and practised with pride as a kind of occupational folk-art, gave Tom Brown an opportunity to exercise his undoubted talent for vulgar and salacious dialogue. How old Robert Burton would have enjoyed being in the boat with them all:

THE THAMES

No sooner had we put off into the middle of the stream, but our Charon and his assistant (being jolly fellows) began to scatter the verbal wild-fire on every side of them, their first attack being on a couple of fine ladies, with a footman in the stern.

'How now, you two confederate brimstones, where are you swimming with your fine top-knots, to invite Irish bully or Scotch Highlander to scour your cloven furbelows for a petticoat pension? I'll warrant your poor cuckolds are hovering about the Exchange to hear what news from Flanders, whilst you, like a couple of hollow-bellied whores, are sailing up to Spring-Gardens to cram one end with roasted fowls, and the other with raw sausages.'

One of the ladies taking courage, plucked up a female spirit of revenge, and facing us with the gallantry of an Amazon, made the following return, 'Get you home, you old cuckold. Look under your wife's bed and see what a lusty gardener has been planting, a son of a whore in your parsley-bed. O how fond the old fool will be of the fruits of another man's labour, when the midwife vouches the bastard to be the true picture of his daddy! Out, you old rogue, gray before you're good, and bald before you're mannerly; hold your bawling, you rusty old churl, whose dogged countenance makes you look as if you were begot by a tanner's mastiff. Talk not to a woman, you surly whelp, for you are fit for nothing but, like the breed you come from, to crawl upon all-fours, and cry bow-wow at a Bear-garden.'

No sooner had we saluted each other with these water-compliments as we passed by . . . but we fell foul (in words I mean) upon a nimble pair of oars, freighted with a couple of scarlet officers, and between them a lady furbelowed with all the colours of a rainbow. No sooner were they come up a broadside of us, but our bold son of Neptune, seconded by his man, began a vigorous attack upon the sons of Mars, who sat hugging their Venus, as the two elders did Susanna.

''Efaith, noble captain, you lay close seige; I dare swear, at the very first assault love's fortress will surrender upon your own terms; 'though I can tell you this for your comfort, as soon as your ammunition is spent and your guns are dismounted you'll be forced to quit the possession. But whatever you do, take care before you enter that the castle is not on fire; for if it should, you had better break up your siege than go any farther.'

'Hold your tongue, you old swabber,' replies one of the heroes, 'and pull off milord mayor's jacket and louse yourself, or else, you rogue, we will have you whipped in Bridewell, for suffering his lordship's livery to be over-run with vermin, to the dishonour of the city.'

'You are mistaken, captain,' cries Bullface, 'a louse is a soldier's companion, and not a waterman's; therefore pray look in your own collar, for a red-coat and a creeper are inseparable companions, as a dog and a flea, virginity and a crab-louse.'

'Out, you nasty fellows,' cries the lady, 'what, an old man and a beast!'

'Why how now, Madam Rainbow,' cries our advocate, 'what so young a wench and so notorious a strumpet, to have two soldiers at a time to relieve your concupiscence, when Venus herself, the damnedst whore in the heavens, was contented with one, though she had fifty times your beauty.'

The next diverting scene that the river afforded us, was a very warm engagement between a Western barge and a boatful of Lambeth gardeners, by whom Billingsgate was much outdone in stupendous obscenity, tonitrous verbosity, and malicious scurrility. So that the reader may have a taste of their modest dialect and incomparable breeding, I have ventured to stain the paper with some of their spiteful eloquence.

'B, a, a, sheep-stealers,' cried the gardeners to the bargemen, 'what kin are you to Tom Collet of Staines, that beat his own father, stood pimp to his mother, lay with his sister, and b——d his brother, all in one night. He was a Western bargeman, you rogues, he was so.'

'Foh, you nasty dogs,' replied the bargemen, 'that get your bread by the drippings of other people's fundaments; well may you pray for the dunghill, for if that should fail you, no turd, no gardener. Who was that, you rogues, that dung'd in his own cap at Stocks-market, and carried home the old gold to enrich his radish-bed? Out upon you, for a pack of snail-picking Adamites! Who was it that took the old woman from weeding, and gave her a flirt under the burgamy pear tree, and when he was caught by his apprentice, gave the boy a holiday, that he should not tell his mistress?'

With this sort of Billingsgate fecundity we were merrily entertained till we had arrived at that port to which we had consigned ourselves, where we quitted our boat.

                                                                        Ibid.

————————

THE *early years of the eighteenth century saw the beginnings of some profound social changes and in reflecting these, humorous prose moved off in a quite new direction.*

In the Bloodless Revolution of 1688 the Protestant landowners and businessmen had, as it were, beaten the court Catholics and the country was now committed to having a Protestant monarchy; and the Protestant ethic was 'work and prosper'. There was a yearning for stability, for less warmongering and political strife, more moderation in everything, and much less of the Tom Brown kind of gutter buffoonery.

The bawdy wit of much Restoration theatre suddenly seemed immoral and rather nasty. Societies for the Suppression of Vice sprang up. 'Correctness', 'order', 'decorum' were the kind of virtues now admired.

Unrestrained behaviour like laughing aloud was suppressed among gentlefolk; Swift claimed that he had only laughed twice in his life. Pope could not remember ever having laughed.

It was in this moral climate that two friends of Swift and Pope, Joseph Addison and Richard Steele, developed a new and hugely successful kind of amusing prose which became known as 'polite' humour.

The rising professional and middle classes could, and did, read, and there was a keen market for newsletters and periodicals in London's coffee-house society. It was a tiny readership by modern standards but large enough then to enable two respectable writer/politicians like Addison and Steele to earn some useful money. Thus journalism and the writing of prose became tolerated as moderately respectable professions for gentlemen.

In 1709 Richard (later Sir Richard) Steele founded The Tatler, *a thrice-weekly sheet of news, verse, comment, and stories. To help him write it he called upon his old school hero Addison and they got on well. Steele was feckless and improvident, given to hanging about town until all hours but he had a boyish charm which shows in his letters to his long-suffering wife, his 'dear Prue', actually a rich and somewhat shrewish lady.*

Steele would scribble her a little note wherever he happened to find himself at night and wing it off to her by messenger:

> Five in the Evening,
> 19 September, 1708

Dear Prue,

I send you seven pennyworth of walnuts at five a penny, which is the greatest proof I can give you at present of my being, with my whole heart, yours.

The little horse comes back with the boy, who returns with him for me on Wednesday evening; in the mean time, I believe, it will be well that he runs in the Park.

I am Mrs Binn's servant.

Since I writ this I came to the place where the boy was order'd with the horses; and, not finding him, sent this bearer, lest you should be in fears, the boy not returning.

P.S. There are but 29 walnuts.

> 30 September. 1710
> From the Pier.
> One in the morning.

Dear Prue,

I am very sleepy and tir'd, but could not think of closing my eyes till I had told you that I am, dearest creature, yr most affectionate and faithful husband.

> 16 February, 1716–1717

Sober or not, I am ever yours.

His quirky, boyish humour popped up constantly in his work. Here is a little 'filler' paragraph from The Tatler, *no. 217. He wrote under the pseudonym 'Isaac Bickerstaff':*

ADVERTISEMENT

The Season now coming on in which the Town will begin to fill, *Mr Bickerstaff* gives Notice, That from the *First of October* next, he will be much wittier than he has hitherto been.

———

J OSEPH ADDISON *had a quite different personality. He was as shy as Steele was gregarious and although an MP, he was for years too bashful to make a speech. His Latin verse was much admired.*

If Steele had a touch of the Restoration rake in his nature, Addison was wholly of the new Augustan Age, and as Steele frittered his money away so Addison grew richer. Steele was the innovator, the born journalist with the original ideas, but it was Addison who improved and refined them. Addison's graceful, cool, balanced prose style was recognized immediately as being of the highest order, and throughout the world his essays were regarded as models of their kind for the next two hundred years.

In 1711 Addison and Steele began The Spectator, *a daily journal aimed at educating middle-class readers in the Augustan virtues. Each number was to be a short essay—the journal was printed on one sheet of paper—and there was to be no political venom, no savage satire, no biting wit, no attacks upon individuals. Humorous essays were not to mock foolish behaviour but to encourage readers to smile amiably at the mild eccentricities of good people.*

This might sound like humour with the nerve taken out, and indeed to modern readers that is what it is, but it was what the early eighteenth century wanted. The Spectator *was hugely successful and 'polite' humour, together with the 'sentimental' stage comedies pioneered by Steele, had an enormous influence, laying a somewhat clammy hand on humour for something like a hundred and fifty years. The vulgar sound of laughter was not sought.*

At the end of the century Robert Southey suggested that the aim of polite humour was to inculcate 'a silent and transient simper'.

Addison loathed the fashion for Italian opera which gripped The Town. In 1711 the Haymarket theatre had a success with the opera Hydaspes, *the high spot of which was a scene in which the hero, played by a castrated Neapolitan singer named Nicolini, had to wrestle with what many reports insisted was a real lion. Addison went along and, in an early example of investigative journalism, wrote of what he discovered:*

There is nothing that of late years has afforded matter of greater amusement to the town than Signior Nicolini's combat with a lion in the Hay-Market, which has been very often exhibited to the general satisfaction of most of the nobility and gentry in the kingdom of Great Britain.

Upon the first rumour of this intended combat, it was confidently affirmed, and is still believed by many in both galleries, that there would be a tame lion sent from the Tower every opera night, in order to be killed by Hydaspes; this report, though altogether groundless, so universally prevailed in the upper regions of the play-house, that some of the most refined politicians in those parts of the audience, gave it out in whisper, that the lion was a cousin-german of the tiger who made his appearance in King William's days, and that the stage would be supplied with lions at the public expense, during the whole session. Many likewise were the conjectures of the treatment which this lion was to meet with from the hands of Signior Nicolini; some supposed that he was to subdue him in *recitatico*, as Orpheus used to serve the wild beasts in his time, and afterwards to knock him on the head; some fancied that the lion would not pretend to lay his paws upon the hero, by reason of the received opinion, that a lion will not hurt a virgin. Several, who pretended to have seen the opera in Italy, had informed their friends, that the lion was to act a part in high Dutch, and roar twice or thrice to a thorough bass, before he fell at the feet of Hydaspes. To clear up a matter that was so variously reported, I have made it my business to examine whether this pretended lion is really the savage he appears to be, or only a counterfeit.

But before I communicate my discoveries, I must acquaint the reader, that upon my walking behind the scenes last winter, as I was thinking on something else, I accidentally justled against a monstrous animal that extremely startled me, and, upon my nearer survey of it, appeared to be a lion-rampant. The lion, seeing me very much surprised, told me, in a gentle voice, that I might come by him if I pleased: *For* (says he) *I do not intend to hurt anybody.* I thanked him very kindly, and passed by him. And in a little time after saw him leap upon the stage, and act his part with very great applause. It has been observed by several, that the lion has changed his manner of acting twice or thrice since his first appearance; which will not seem strange, when I acquaint my reader that the lion has been changed upon the audience three several times. The first lion was a candle-snuffer, who being a fellow of a testy, choleric temper over-did his part, and would not suffer himself to be killed so easily as he ought to have done; besides, it was observ'd of him, that he grew more surly every time he came out of the lion; and having dropped some words in ordinary conversation, as if he had not fought his best, and that he suffered himself to be thrown upon his back in the scuffle, and that he would wrestle with Mr Nicolini for what he pleased, out of his lion's skin, it was thought proper to discard him: and it is verily believed to this day, that had he been brought upon the stage another time, he would certainly have done mischief. Besides, it was objected against the first lion, that he reared himself so high upon his hinder paws, and walked in so erect a posture, that he looked more like an old man than a lion.

The second lion was a tailor by trade, who belonged to the play-house, and had the character of a mild and peaceable man in his profession. If the former was too furious, this was too sheepish, for his part; insomuch that after a short modest walk upon the stage, he would fall at the first touch of Hydaspes, without grappling with him, and giving him an opportunity of showing his variety of Italian trips: It is said, indeed, that he once gave him a rip in his flesh-colour doublet, but this was only to make work for himself, in his private character of a tailor. I must not omit that it was this second lion who treated me with so much humanity behind the scenes.

The acting lion at present is, as I am informed, a country gentleman, who does it for his diversion, but desires his name may be concealed. He says very handsomely in his own excuse, that he does not act for gain, that he indulges an innocent pleasure in it, and that it is better to pass away an evening in this manner, than in gaming and drinking; but at the same time says, with a very agreeable raillery upon himself, that if his name should be known, the ill-natured world might call him, *The Ass in the Lion's skin*. This gentleman's temper is made out of such a happy mixture of the mild and the choleric, that he out-does both his predecessors, and has drawn together greater audiences than have been known in the memory of man.

I must not conclude my narrative, without taking notice of a groundless report that has been raised, to a gentleman's disadvantage, of whom I must declare myself an admirer; namely, that Signior Nicolini and the lion have been seen sitting peaceably by one another, and smoking a pipe together, behind the scenes; by which their common enemies would insinuate, it is but a sham combat which they represent upon the stage: but upon enquiry I find, that if any such correspondence has passed between them, it was not till the combat was over, when the lion was to be looked upon as dead, according to the received rules of the drama. Besides, this is what is practised every day in Westminster-Hall, where nothing is more usual than to see a couple of lawyers, who have been tearing each other to pieces in the court, embracing one another as soon as they are out of it.

The Spectator, no. 13 (15 Mar. 1711).

● Sutherland Edwards, in his *History of the Opera*, records that in *Hydaspes* the hero, played in London by Nicolini whose voice was soprano modulating to contralto, is suddenly inspired with manly courage on spotting his mistress in the crowd, appeals to the lion to surrender in a minor key and then strangles it in the relative major.

———

T HE *height of Addison's polite humour was reached with the papers he wrote about the old, whimsical country squire, Sir Roger de Coverley. The character was, typically, invented by Steele but polished and perfected by Addison. In keeping with* The Spectator's *policy of not fomenting party politics the old Tory squire was not, for once, pictured in the usual Whig way as a drunken, ignorant, fox-hunting lout but as an old-fashioned country gentleman whose little foibles only make him more endearing. Addison's humour in these pieces was refined to the point of being non-existent, but as a substitute for humour he gave us good-humour, the pleasant observations of a writer who was much liked for his own kindness and sunny nature.*

It would probably be true to say that Sir Roger de Coverley was the best-known and most beloved of all the eighteenth-century literary characters invented to amuse.

Here is Sir Roger at Church:

I am always very well pleased with a country Sunday; and think, if keeping holy the seventh day were only a human institution, it would be the best method that could have been thought of for the polishing and civilizing of mankind. It is certain the country-people would soon degenerate into a kind of savages and barbarians, were there not such frequent returns of a stated time, in which the whole village meet together with their best faces, and in their cleanliest habits, to converse with one another upon indifferent subjects, hear their duties explained to them, and join together in adoration of the supreme being. Sunday clears away the rust of the whole week, not only as it refreshes in their minds the notions of religion, but as it puts both the sexes upon appearing in their most agreeable forms, and exerting all such qualities as are apt to give them a figure in the eye of the village. A country-fellow distinguishes himself as much in the *church-yard*, as a citizen does upon the *Change*; the whole parish-politics being generally discussed in that place either after sermon or before the bell rings.

My friend Sir Roger being a good church-man, has beautified the inside of his church with several texts of his own choosing: he has likewise given a handsome pulpit-cloth, and railed-in the communion-table at his own expense. He has often told me, that at his coming to his estate he found his parishioners very irregular; and that in order to make them kneel and join in the responses, he gave every one of them a hassock and a common-prayer book: and at the same time employed an itinerant singing-master, who goes about the country for that purpose, to instruct them rightly in the tunes of the psalms; upon which they now very much value themselves, and indeed out-do most of the country churches that I have ever heard.

As Sir Roger is landlord to the whole congregation, he keeps them in very good order, and will suffer no body to sleep in it besides himself; for if by chance he has been surprised into a short nap at sermon, upon recovering out of it he stands up and looks about him, and if he sees anybody else nodding, either wakes them himself, or sends his servants to them. Several other of the old knight's particularities break out upon these occasions: sometimes he will be lengthening out a verse in the singing-psalms, half a minute after the rest of the congregation have done with it; sometimes, when he is pleased with the matter of his devotion, he pronounces Amen three or four times to the same prayer; and sometimes stands up when everybody else is upon their knees, to count the congregation, or see if any of his tenants are missing.

I was yesterday very much surprised to hear my old friend, in the midst of the service, calling out to one John Matthews to mind what he was about, and not disturb the congregation. This John Matthews it seems is remarkable for being an idle fellow, and at that time was kicking his heels for his diversion. This authority of the knight, though exerted in that odd manner which accompanies him in all circumstances of life, has a very good effect upon the parish, who are not polite enough to see anything ridiculous in his behaviour; besides that, the general good sense and worthiness of his character, make his friends observe these little singularities as foils that rather set off than blemish his good qualities.

As soon as the sermon is finished, nobody presumes to stir till Sir Roger is gone out of the church. The knight walks down from his seat in the chancel between a double row of his tenants, that stand bowing to him on each side; and every now and then enquires how such an one's wife or mother, or son, or father do whom he does not see at church; which is understood as a secret reprimand to the person that is absent.

Ibid., no. 112 (9 July 1711).

LETTER-WRITING *was a favourite form of amusement and self-expression among the leisured and literate classes, particularly among those fashionable ladies whose day was unencumbered by domestic or any other labours. Many embarked on voluminous correspondence with family and friends which they kept up busily until death loosened their grip on the quill.*

One of the most enthusiastic of those early eighteenth-century letter writers was the splendid Lady Mary Wortley Montagu, daughter of the Duke of Kingston. She taught herself Latin as a child, read everything she could lay her hands on, eloped for love with Edward Wortley Montagu only to find him boring, had a daughter who married Lord Bute who became Prime Minister, became friends with and then quarrelled with Alexander Pope, travelled widely abroad, introduced inoculation into England, and expired at the age of 74, allegedly with the words, 'It has all been most interesting'.

Here is Lady Mary, then a girl of 20, writing to an older friend and seeing significance in a dozing bride:

Next to the great ball, what makes the most noise is the marriage of an old maid, who lives in this street, without a portion, to a man of £7,000 *per annum*, and they say £40,000 in ready money. Her equipage and liveries outshine anybody's in town. He has presented her with £3,000 in jewels; and never was man more smitten with these charms that had lain invisible for these forty years; but, with all his glory, never bride had fewer enviers, the dear beast of a man is so filthy, frightful, odious, and detestable. I would turn away such a footman, for fear of spoiling my dinner, while he waited at table. They were married on Friday, and came to church *en parade* on Sunday. I happened to sit in the pew with them, and had the honour of seeing Mrs Bride fall fast asleep in the middle of the sermon, and snore very comfortably; which made several women in the church think the bridegroom not quite so ugly as they did before. Envious people say 'twas all counterfeited to please him, but I believe that to be scandal.

Lady Mary Wortley Montagu (1689–1762), Letter to Mrs Hewet (1709).

ANOTHER *voluminous writer of letters was Lady Mary Wortley Montagu's one-time friend, Alexander Pope. The poet was a master of the small man-œuvre, the complicated little intrigue,—Lady Bolingbroke said that 'he could hardly drink tea without a strategem'—and a great many of his letters were 'political' in that they were written for eventual publication to justify himself or to make some point. But he occasionally wrote letters simply to charm and amuse.*

Here Pope writes to a friend about an old house to which he has been invited to stay:

You must expect nothing regular in my description of a house that seems to be built before rules were in fashion; the whole is so disjointed and the parts so detached from each other and yet so joining again one cannot tell how, that (in a poetical fit) you would imagine it had been a village in Amphion's time, where twenty cottages had taken a dance together, were all out, and stood still in amazement ever since. A stranger would be grievously dis-appointed who should ever think to get into this house the right way; one would expect after entering through the porch to be let into the hall; alas nothing less; you find yourself in a brewhouse. From the parlour you think to step into the drawing-room; but upon opening the iron-nailed door, you are convinced by a flight of birds about your ears, and a cloud of dust in your eyes, that it is the pigeon-house. On each side our porch are two chimneys, that wear their greens on the outside, which would do as well within, for whenever we make a fire, we let the smoke out of the windows. Over the parlour window hangs a sloping balcony, which time has turned to a very convenient pent-house. The top is crowned with a very venerable tower, so like that of the church just by, that the jackdaws build in it as if it were the true steeple.

The great hall is high and spacious, flanked with long tables, images of ancient hospitality; ornamented with monstrous horns, about twenty broken pikes, and a match-lock musket or two, which they say were used in the civil wars . . .

Our best room above is very long and low, of the exact proportion of a bandbox: it has hangings of the finest work in the world, those, I mean, which Arachne spins out of her own bowels; indeed the roof is so decayed, that after a favourable shower of rain, we may (with God's blessing) expect a crop of mushrooms between the chinks of the floors.

All this upper story has for many years had no other inhabitants than certain rats, whose very age renders them worthy of this venerable mansion, for the very rats of this ancient seat are grey. Since these had not quitted it, we hope at least this house may stand during the small remainder of days these poor animals have to live, who are now too infirm to remove to another: they have still a small subsistence left them in the few remaining books of the library.

Alexander Pope (1688–1744), Letter from Stanton Harcourt.

➤ While he was staying with his friend Lord Harcourt at Stanton Harcourt,

two rustic lovers were struck by lightning. Pope wrote an epitaph and sent
it to Lady Mary Wortley Montagu. It read:

> 'Here lye two poor lovers
> who had the mishap,
> Tho' very chaste people,
> to die of a Clap.'

Lady Mary was not amused.

JONATHAN SWIFT, *friend of Pope, could hardly be called a 'humorous writer'.
His satire was deeply felt and bitterly expressed and when Swift was angry his
sense of fun was put aside; but mockery through humour is part of a satirist's
armoury and Swift called for a smile whenever it suited his purpose.*

In Part 3 of Gulliver's Travels, *Gulliver visited the flying island of Laputa and
met some of its inhabitants.*

They were extremely brainy:

Their heads were all reclined to the right, or the left; one of their eyes turned
inward, and the other directly up to the zenith. Their outward garments were
adorned with the figures of suns, moons, and stars, interwoven with those
of fiddles, flutes, harps, trumpets, guitars, harpsichords, and many more
instruments of music, unknown to us in Europe. I observed here and there
many of the habit of servants, with a blown bladder fastened like a flail to
the end of a short stick, which they carried in their hands. In each bladder
was a small quantity of dried pease or little pebbles (as I was afterwards
informed). With these bladders they now and then flapped the mouths and
ears of those who stood near them, of which practice I could not then
conceive the meaning. It seems, the minds of these people are so taken up
with intense speculations, that they neither can speak, or attend to the
discourses of others, without being roused by some external taction upon the
organs of speech and hearing; for which reason, those persons who are able
to afford it always keep a flapper (the original is *climenole*) in their family, as
one of their domestics, nor ever walk abroad or make visits without him.
And the business of this officer is, when two or more persons are in company,
gently to strike with his bladder the mouth of him who is to speak, and the
right ear of him or them to whom the speaker addresseth himself. This *flapper*
is likewise employed diligently to attend his master in his walks, and upon
occasion to give him a soft flap on his eyes; because he is always so wrapped
up in cogitation, that he is in manifest danger of falling down every precipice,
and bouncing his head against every post; and in the streets, of jostling
others or being jostled himself into the kennel.

Jonathan Swift (1667–1745), *Gulliver's Travels* (1726).

Gulliver moved on to make a small tour of the Academy of Projectors at the town of Lagado, where the projects being worked upon were a comment on the many idiotic and hopeless inventions then being promoted in Britain:

The first man I saw was of a meagre aspect, with sooty hands and face, his hair and beard long, ragged and singed in several places. His clothes, shirt, and skin were all of the same colour. He had been eight years upon a project for extracting sunbeams out of cucumbers, which were to be put into vials hermetically sealed, and let out to warm the air in raw inclement summers. He told me, he did not doubt in eight years more, that he should be able to supply the Governor's gardens with sunshine at a reasonable rate; but he complained that his stock was low, and entreated me to give him something as an encouragement to ingenuity, especially since this had been a very dear season for cucumbers. I made him a small present, for my Lord had furnished me with money on purpose, because he knew their practice of begging from all who go to see them . . .

I saw another at work to calcine ice into gunpowder, who likewise showed me a treatise he had written concerning the malleability of fire, which he intended to publish.

There was a most ingenious architect who had contrived a new method for building houses, by beginning at the roof and working downwards to the foundation, which he justified to me by the like practice of those two prudent insects, the bee and the spider . . .

I was complaining of a small fit of the colic, upon which my conductor let me into a room, where a great physician resided, who was famous for curing that disease by contrary operations from the same instrument. He had a large pair of bellows with a long slender muzzle of ivory. This he conveyed eight inches up the anus, and drawing in the wind, he affirmed he would make the guts as lank as a dried bladder. But when the disease was more stubborn and violent, he let in the muzzle while the bellows was full of wind, which he discharged into the body of the patient, then withdrew the instrument to replenish it, clapping his thumb strongly against the orifice of the fundament; and this being repeated three or four times, the adventitious wind would rush out, bringing the noxious along with it (like water put into a pump) and the patient recover . . .

I visited many other apartments, but shall not trouble my reader with all the curiosities I observed, being studious of brevity.   Ibid.

When Swift's purpose was not to savage some aspect of human fatuity or villainy which enraged him but simply to mock some item of social behaviour which peeved him, he could be as amusing as most of his contemporaries.

Perhaps his most sustained exercise in humorous mockery was his Directions to Servants. *This was an ironic piece, in the manner of* Grobianus *and of* Dekker's The Guls Hornebooke, *which purported to be a manual instructing servants how to carry out their duties.*

In the following extract from Chapter III, the skills of being a footman are taught, such as waiting at table:

There is a great controversy about the most convenient and genteel way of holding your plate, when you wait on your Master, and his company, at meals; some butlers stick it between the frame of the back of the chair, which is an excellent expedient, where the make of the chair will allow it: Others, for fear the plate should fall, grasp it so firmly, that their thumb reacheth to the middle of the hollow; which however, if your thumb be dry, is no secure method; and therefore in that case, I advise your wetting the bowl of it with your tongue: As to that absurd practice of letting the back of the plate lie leaning on the hollow of your hand, which some ladies recommend, it is universally exploded, being liable to so many accidents. Others again, are so refined, that they hold their plate directly under the left arm-pit, which is the best situation for keeping it warm; but this may be dangerous in the article of taking away a dish, where your plate may happen to fall upon some of the company's heads. I confess myself to have objected against all these ways, which I have frequently tried; and therefore I recommend a fourth, which is to stick your plate up to the rim inclusive in the left side between your waistcoat and your shirt: This will keep it at least as warm as under your arm-pit, or ockster, (as the Scots call it); this will hide it so, as strangers may take you for a better servant, too good to hold a plate; this will secure it from falling and thus disposed, it lies ready for you to whip it out in a moment, ready warmed, to any guest within your reach, who may want it. And lastly, there is another convenience in this method, that if, any time during your waiting, you find yourselves going to cough or sneeze, you can immediately snatch out your plate, and hold the hollow part close to your nose or mouth, and, thus prevent spurting any moisture from either, upon the dishes or the ladies head-dress: You see gentlemen and ladies observe a like practice on such an occasion, with a hat or a handkerchief: yet a plate is less fouled and sooner cleaned than either of these; for, when your cough or sneeze is over, it is but returning your plate to the same position, and your shirt will clean it in the passage . . .

If you are bringing up a joint of meat in a dish and it falls out of your hands, before you get into the dining room, with the mat on the ground, and the sauce spilled, take up the meat gently, wipe it with the lap of your coat, then put it again into the dish, and serve it up; and when your lady misses the sauce, tell her it is to be sent up in a plate by itself. When you carry up a dish of meat, dip your fingers in the sauce, or lick it with your tongue, to try whether it be good and fit for your master's table . . .

While Grace is saying after meat, do you and your brethren take the chairs from behind the company, so that when they go to sit again, they may fall backwards, which will make them all merry; but be you so discreet as to hold your laughter till you get to the kitchen, and then divert your fellow-servants . . .

Never wear socks when you wait at meals, on the account of your own health, as well as of them who sit at table; because as most ladies like the smell of young mens toes, so it is a sovereign remedy against vapours.

Directions to Servants (1745).

H EARTY *laughter in public might have been frowned upon by polite society but impolite society still hunted the wild guffaw, as no doubt did polite society when consenting adults met in private. Joke-books flourished. Most were the usual rehash of old publications but a small volume of 247 jokes was published in 1739 which proved to be the most famous and durable of them all:* Joe Miller's Jests or, The Wit's Vade Mecum.

Edition followed edition for more than a century, each being enlarged with contemporary jokes until by the mid-nineteenth century an American edition had 1,286 items, and the name 'Joe Miller' had become synonymous with 'a be-whiskered chestnut of a joke'.

Joe Miller was a well-known actor of the time, and it has been said that putting his name to a joke-book was a joke in itself in that he was notoriously lugubrious. The book was actually compiled by a Grub Street playwright and hack writer called John Mottley. Although a few of the jokes are familiar from earlier compilations a great number of them were almost certainly new stories which were circulating among the actors and writers who were Mottley's friends.

Some of the stories give an indication of the way that the range of this kind of broad humour was being extended; for instance jokes about toasted-cheese-eating Welshmen were being joined by jokes about the curious logic of Irishmen:

A gentleman who had been out a shooting brought home a small bird with him, and having an Irish servant, he ask'd him, if he had shot that little bird, yes, he told him; Arrah by my shoul, honey, reply'd the Irish man, it was not worth powder and shot, for this little thing would have died in the fall.

Joe Miller's Jests or, The Wit's Vade Mecum (1739), no. 120.

Regional characteristics were being used in jokes; for example, the pre-eminence of Yorkshiremen:

A gentleman coming to an inn in Smithfield, and seeing the hostler expert and tractable about the horses, asked, how long he had lived there? And what countryman he was? I'se Yerkshire, said the fellow, an ha' lived sixteen years here. I wonder reply'd the gentleman, that in so long a time, so clever a fellow as you seem to be, have not come to be master of the inn yourself. Ay, said the hostler, but maister's Yerkshire too.

Ibid., no. 156.

It is clear from the many gamey jokes in Joe Miller's Jests, *and the book's great success, that a significant proportion of Augustan Age readers enjoyed not only a polite Addisonian essay but also prose that was indecorous, impolite, and thoroughly ungenteel:*

A gentlewoman, who thought her servants always cheated her, when they went to Billingsgate to buy fish, was resolved to go thither one day herself, and asking the price of some fish, which she thought too dear, she bid the fish-wife about half what she asked. Lord, madam, said the woman, I must have stole it to sell it at that price, but you shall have it if you will tell me what you do to make your hands look so white. Nothing, good woman, answered the gentlewoman, but wear dog-skin gloves. D—mn you for a lying bitch, replied the other, my husband has wore dog-skin breeches these ten years, and his a—se is as brown as a nutmeg.

Ibid., no. 115.

Mr H—rr—n, one of the commissioners of the Revenue in Ireland, being one night in the pit, at the Play-house in Dublin, Monoca Gall, the orange girl, famous for her wit and her assurance, striding over his back, he popp'd his hands under her petticoats: Nay, Mr Commissioner, said she, you'll find no goods there but what have been fairly entered.

Ibid., no. 3.

Lady C——g and her two daughters having taken lodgings at a leather-breeches maker's in Piccadilly, the sign of the Cock and Leather-Breeches, was always put to the blush when she was obliged to give any body direction to her lodgings, the sign being so odd a one; upon which my Lady, a very good sort of woman, sending for her landlord, a jolly young fellow, told him, she liked him and his lodgings very well, but she must be obliged to quit them on account of his sign, for she was ashamed to tell any body what it was. O! dear madam, said the young fellow, I would do any thing rather than lose so good lodgers, I can easily alter my sign; so I think, answered my Lady, and I'll tell you how you may satisfy both me and my daughters: Only take down your Breeches and let your Cock stand.

Ibid., no. 25.

NEWSPAPERS *proliferated, both in London and in the provinces. It was a cutthroat game. Printers had to set up the type and print off their copies early in the morning in the hope that their pedlars would be selling them round the coffee houses before their rivals showed up. Provincial papers mostly relied on London papers for their copy and rival messengers were often waylaid on the road to make them late in delivering their vital source material.*

For this and other reasons there was often a shortage of hard news to print and editors had to make use of 'fillers', short, self-contained paragraphs which could be used to complete a column or to pad out a virtually newsless issue. Most of these items described some small local event, such as a wedding or the murder of somebody unimportant, but others were clearly included because of their entertainment value. It was the beginning of humorous reportage:

A certain person having yesterday the curiosity to hold a conversation with a female prisoner through the chequer door, in the postern of Newgate, and attempting a greater intimacy than was strictly decent, before he could recover his hand from the bottom of the door, his new acquaintance robbed his head, which before seemed not overwell-furnish'd, and he went away swearing and cursing, without his hat.

The Daily Post (c.1720).

In 1730–1 a printer, Edward Cave, decided to found a new sort of periodical. Instead of being a series of essays by one hand it would be a compilation of 'the essays and intelligence which appeared in the two hundred half sheets which the London press threw off monthly . . . and probably as many more half sheets printed elsewhere in the three kingdoms'.

As the function of the journal was to act as a storehouse he called it by a synonym of that word, and so the Gentleman's Magazine *became the first publication to descibe itself as a 'magazine'.*

With so many news-sheets to call upon nationwide the magazine had access to an endless supply of humorous fillers:

Monday, 24 (November). A butcher was robbed in a very gallant manner by a woman well mounted on a side saddle, and near Romford in Essex. She presented a pistol to him, and demanded his money; he being amazed at her behaviour told her, he did not know what she meant; when a gentleman coming up, told him he was a brute to deny the lady's request, and if he did not gratify her desire immediately, he would shoot him through the Head; so he gave her his watch and 6 guineas.

Gentleman's Magazine (Nov. 1735).

The story of a man at Birmingham's burying his wife on a Tuesday marrying again on Thursday, having a child born to him on Friday, and hanging himself on Saturday, which has been inserted in most of the news papers in town and country, we are well assured from that town is entirely without foundation.

Ibid. (Sept. 1732).

WHEN a writer has a humorous turn of mind it seems that, like an underground spring, it may stay out of sight for a time but it will eventually surface, often unexpectedly. Jonathan Richardson was an amiable man, a well-known painter of sound but rather dull portraits. He was also an author, often writing in partnership with his son Jonathan whose career as a portraitist was less successful; perhaps because he was so short-sighted that he could barely make out the face which he was trying to paint.

Here, in the opening of a serious book about Milton, father and son describe the poet's person:

He was rather a middle sized than a little man, and well proportioned; Latterly he was—no; not short and thick, but he would have been so, had he been something shorter and thicker than he was.

> Jonathan Richardson, father and son (1665–1745; 1694–1771), *Explanatory Notes and Remarks on 'Paradise Lost'* (1734).

———

B ENJAMIN FRANKLIN, *that most American of Americans, was a voluminous author whose output ranged from writing* Poor Richard's Almanack *to helping draft the* Declaration of Independence. *He was suitably grave when writing about important political and scientific issues but at other times his humour would bubble, spring-like, to the surface. Unlike Alexander Pope and a great many others he had no thought of writing for posterity but for the need of the moment, which sometimes took the form of getting down on paper an idea which amused him.*

Here, in the form of a letter, he is 'Advising a Young Man as to the Selection of a Mistress'. There was no young man, and Franklin did not write the piece for publication but simply for the fun of it:

To * * * *   [Philadelphia,] 25 June, 1745.

My Dear Friend:

I know of no medicine fit to diminish the violent natural inclinations you mention; and if I did, I think I should not communicate it to you. Marriage is the proper remedy. It is the most natural state of man, and therefore the state in which you are most likely to find solid happiness. Your reasons against entering into it at present appear to me not well founded. The circumstantial advantages you have in view by postponing it, are not only uncertain, but they are small in comparison with that of the thing itself, the being married and settled. It is the man and woman united that make the compleat human being. Separate, she wants his force of body and strength of reason; he, her softness, sensibility and acute discernment. Together they are more likely to succeed in the world. A single man has not nearly the value he would have in the state of union. He is an incomplete animal. He resembles the odd half of a pair of scissors. If you get a prudent, healthy wife, your industry in your profession, with her good economy, will be a fortune sufficient.

But if you will not take this counsel and persist in thinking a commerce with the sex inevitable, then I repeat my former advice, that in all your amours you should prefer old women to young ones.

You call this a paradox and demand my reasons. They are these:

1. Because they have more knowledge of the world, and their minds are better stored with observations, their conversation is more improving, and more lastingly agreeable.

2. Because when women cease to be handsome they study to be good. To maintain their influence over men, they supply the diminution of beauty by an augmention of utility. They learn to do a thousand services small and great, and are the most tender and useful of friends when you are sick. Thus they continue amiable. And hence there is hardly such a thing to be found as an old woman who is not a good woman.

3. Because there is no hazard of children, which irregularly produced may be attended with much inconvenience.

4. Because through more experience they are more prudent and discreet in conducting an intrigue to prevent suspicion. The commerce with them is therefore safer with regard to your reputation. And with regard to theirs, if the affair should happen to be known, considerate people might be rather inclined to excuse an old woman, who would kindly take care of a young man, form his manners by her good counsels, and prevent his ruining his health and fortune among mercenary prostitutes.

5. Because in every animal that walks upright, the deficiency of the fluids that fill the muscles appears first in the highest part. The face first grows lank and wrinkled; then the neck; then the breast and arms; the lower parts continuing to the last as plump as ever: so that covering all above with a basket, and regarding only what is below the girdle, it is impossible of two women to know an old one from a young one. And as in the dark all cats are grey, the pleasure of corporal enjoyment with an old woman is at least equal, and frequently superior; every knack being, by practice, capable of improvement.

6. Because the sin is less. The debauching a virgin may be her ruin, and make her for life unhappy.

7. Because the compunction is less. The having made a young girl miserable may give you frequent bitter reflection; none of which can attend the making an old woman happy.

8thy & lastly. They are so grateful!!

Thus much for my paradox. But still I advise you to marry directly; being sincerely

Your affectionate Friend,

BENJAMIN FRANKLIN

Benjamin Franklin (1706–90), Manuscripts of Franklin, State Department, Washington.

CHRISTOPHER SMART *was a short, shy, impoverished, slightly deranged poet and Grub Street hack. His bouts of mild lunacy, which twice caused him to be 'immured in the madhouse', took the form of dropping to his knees and praying incessantly. This was harmless enough, but the world took against him when he tried to make everybody present kneel down and join him. He was a friend of Samuel Johnson, who stoutly defended Smart: 'His infirmities were not noxious to society. He insisted on people praying with him, and I'd as lief pray with Kit Smart as with any one else. Another charge was that he did not love clean linen; and I have no passion for it.'*

In 1751 Smart began a threepenny journal called The Midwife, or the Old Woman's Magazine, *which he wrote under the pseudonym 'Mary Midnight'. In those pieces his odd humour did not so much bubble up as gush forth, fizzing:*

A letter from Mrs Mary Midnight to the Royal Society, containing some new and curious Improvements upon the CAT-ORGAN.

Gentlemen,

I need not inform persons of your infinite experience and erudition, that the Cat-Organ, as it has hitherto been made use of, was no more than what followeth, viz. A plain harpsichord, which instead of having strings and jacks, consists of cats of different sizes, included in boxes, whose voices express every note in the gamut, which is extorted from the imprison'd animals, by placing their tails in grooves, which are properly squeezed by the impression of the organist's fingers on the keys.—This instrument, unimproved as it was, I have often heard with incredible delight; but especially in the Grand and the plaintive—This delight grew upon me every time I was present at its performance. At length I shut myself up for seven years to study some additions and improvements, which I have at length accomplished, agreeable to my warmest wishes, and which I with all due submission now lay before you.

In the first place then it is universally known and acknowledged that these animals, at the time of their amours, are the most musical creatures in nature; I would therefore recommend it to all and singular Cat-Organists, to have a most especial regard to the time of cater-wawling, particularly if they have any thing very august or affecting to exhibit.

Secondly, it is also very well known that the best voices are improved by castration. I therefore never have less than eight geldings in my treble cleft.—And here I cannot help informing you of an experiment I lately made on an Italian boar-cat, and an English one of the same gender; and I solemnly protest that, after the operation, my country animal had every whit as delicate, piercing, and comprehensive a tone as the foreigner.—And I make no sort of doubt but some of our harmonious Englishmen would shine with an equal lustre, if they had the same ADVANTAGES as the Italians.—This may be worth the consideration of the people in power:—For, if this experiment had been tryed with success, how many thousand pounds would it have save this nation?

Thirdly, of the forte and Piano.—I must not omit to tell you, gentlemen, that my Cat-Organ resembles a double harpsichord; for as that has two rows of keys, so mine has two layers of cats.—The upper row on which I play piano, or softly, consists of cats, both of a lesser size, and whose tails are squeezed by a much less degree of pressure; that is, by nothing but the bare extremity of the key.—But the lower row, on which I play forte, or loudly, contains an harmonious society of banging grimalkins; and whose tails are severely pricked by brass-pins, inserted at the end of the key for that purpose.

Fourthly, Of the shake [a trill-like ornament in keyboard playing].—There was one enormous defect in this instrument, before I took it in hand, and that was in the shake; the imperfectness of which gave me great offence.— But as it is now managed, it has the most ravishing effect in the world.— There are between all the keys little wires fixed almost imperceptibly.—These go underneath 'till they reach each puss's throat.—At the extremity of these wires are placed horizontally wrens' quills, about the length of a quarter of an inch.—when the artist therefore has a mind to form his shake, he touches the wires, which soon sends the quills in a tickle, tickle, tickle, up to the cat's throat, and causes the most gurgling, warbling, shaking, quaking, trembling, murmuring sound in the World . . .

I am,

Gentlemen,

Your most obedient humble Servant

M. MIDNIGHT

Christopher Smart (1722–71), *The Midwife, or Old Woman's Magazine* (1751).

The Midwife ran for three years and Smart's flow of comic inventiveness never seemed to falter. Many of his ideas had a modern, Goon Show incongruity, like his scholarly paper which began 'It is an universally acknowledged Truth, founded on Fact, and the common experience of Mankind, THAT IF ANY PERSON, OR PERSONS, CUT THEIR NAILS ON A MONDAY MORNING, WITHOUT THINKING OF A FOX'S TAIL, THEY WILL CERTAINLY COME TO GREAT RICHES.' Or the report of a debate at the Robin-Hood tavern on 'Whether 'tis best to oil a Man's Wig with Honey or Mustard'.

The Midwife was a typical Grub Street journal in that its aim was not to be admired in the small world of polite society but to be a popular success in the much larger community of the more rough and ready middle-classes. Thus Smart was able to venture on to subjects which would have been too vulgar for Addison and Steele. Like this paper, mocking the Society of Antiquarians, on the discovery of a fossilized turd:

A Letter from Mrs Midnight, to the Society of Antiquarians, giving them an account of a very curious petrification found near Penzance, in the County of Cornwall.

Gentlemen,

As my worthy friend Mr Powallis of Penzance, was taking an evening's walk in the fields, he accidentally trod upon something, which having all the appearance of an human excrement, made him immediately congratulate himself upon his good luck. But upon a stricter scrutiny it appeared to be a pebble, which both in shape and colour perfectly resembled what he at first took it for. He carried it home to his lady, who at first sight cried out, my dear, you have brought home a —— mentioning a word, which I am sorry should ever drop from a woman of her decency and discretion. However, upon handling it she was pacified, and diverted herself by now and then depositing it in the parlour, to the confusion of the housemaid, and sometimes dropping it in company, for the entertainment and astonishment of her friends. At length a gentleman who was an excellent antiquarian, and likewise profoundly learned in minerals and fossils, happened to pay Mr Powallis a visit; and upon inspection declared with transport, that it was the greatest curiosity in Europe. 'This (says he) is really an *bona fide* a petrified excrement, and as it was found in the fields, is a valuable monument of ancient simplicity; when our fathers (how unlike the effeminacy of our moderns!) used to do their business in the most pastoral and unaffected manner, and (as the Divine Milton sings)

> Every Shepherd laid his tail
> Under the hawthorne in the vale.'

This gentleman is now in possession of the petrifaction which he obtained from Mr Powallis, who (because he was his very intimate friend) let him have it at the easy expense of fifty pound. I wish, gentlemen of the Society, it was mine to bestow, I declare I should not hesitate a moment about the disposal of it. But, as it is, you will be content with a description of it, which I shall attempt in as brief a manner, as I may: This rarity then, which you may either call an artificial piece of nature, or a natural piece of art, is about seven inches long, and about three-and-a-half diameter; (I mean in the centre) for, towards the end, it's taper, and is (as a certain poet says by a lady's shape): 'Fine by Degrees and beautifully less'.

Your most humble Servant,

M. MIDNIGHT

Ibid.

I N *the 1680s the publication of* Letters *written by a* Turkish Spy, *translated from the French, established a new genre. The letters were supposed to have been written by Mahmut, a Turkish spy living in Paris, whose job it was to report back on the social and political affairs of the European nations, which gave the author an opportunity to satirize contemporary life and manners by describing them through the eye of an alien to whom everything was odd and different.*

This literary device proved so useful that the Turkish Spy *was followed by many imitations in the eighteenth century, notably* Lettres Persanes *by Montesquieu, published in 1721, in which a Persian visitor observed and reflected upon life in France.*

In 1760 Oliver Goldsmith, working as a hack for the publisher Newbery's journal The Public Ledger, *borrowed the device and began* The Chinese Letters, *purporting to be a series of letters written home by a visiting Chinese philosopher, Lien Chi Altanghi (not a wholly successful attempt at a Chinese name, perhaps). The letters had little in the way of hard satire but were infused with Goldsmith's particular gaiety and charm.*

In 1762 Goldsmith collected the letters together and published them as a book, which he called The Citizen of the World. *It was rather more than a bundle of letters because there was also a frail narrative thread and a wisp of plot. And there is one character, Beau Tibbs, who might have come straight out of a Charles Dickens' novel except that Beau Tibbs appeared eighty years before* The Pickwick Papers.

Here the Chinese philosopher is taken to Beau Tibbs's house to meet his lady wife:

My little Beau yesterday overtook me again in one of the public walks, and, slapping me on the shoulder, saluted me with an air of the most perfect familiarity. His dress was the same as usual, except that he had more powder in his hair, wore a dirtier shirt, a pair of temple spectacles, and his hat under his arm.

As I knew him to be a harmless, amusing little thing, I could not return his smiles with any degree of severity; so we walked forward on terms of the utmost intimacy, and in a few minutes discussed all the usual topics preliminary to particular conversation. The oddities that marked his character, however, soon began to appear; he bowed to several well-dressed persons, who, by their manner of returning the compliment, appeared perfect strangers. At intervals he drew out a pocket-book, seeming to take memorandums before all the company, with much importance and assiduity. In this manner he led me through the length of the whole walk, fretting at his absurdities, and fancying myself laughed at not less than him by every spectator. When we were got to the end of our procession, 'Blast me,' cries he with an air of vivacity, 'I never saw the Park so thin in my life before! There's no company at all to-day; not a single face to be seen.' 'No company!' interrupted I, peevishly; 'no company where there is such a crowd? why, man, there's too much. What are the thousands that have been laughing at us but company?' 'Lord, my dear,' returned he with the utmost good-humour, 'you seem immensely chagrined; but, blast me, when the world laughs at me, I laugh at the world, and so we are even. My Lord Trip, Bill Squash the Creolian, and I, sometimes make a party at being ridiculous; and so we say and do a thousand things for the joke's sake. But I see you are grave, and if you are for a fine, grave, sentimental companion, you shall dine with me and my wife to-day; I must insist on't. I'll introduce you to Mrs Tibbs, a lady of as elegant qualifications as any in nature: she was bred (but that's between ourselves) under the inspection of the Countess of All Night. A charming body of voice; but no more of that—she will give us a song. You shall see my little girl, too, Carolina Wilhelmina Amelia Tibbs, a sweet, pretty creature! I design her for my Lord Drumstick's eldest son; but that's in friendship—let it go no farther: she's but six years old, and yet she walks a minuet, and plays on the guitar immensely already. I intend she shall be as perfect as possible in every accomplishment. In the first place, I'll make her a scholar; I'll teach her Greek myself, and learn that language purposely to instruct her; but let that be a secret.'

Thus saying, without waiting for a reply, he took me by the arm and hauled me along. We passed through many dark alleys and winding ways; for, from some motives to me unknown, he seemed to have a particular aversion to every frequented street; at last, however, we got to the door of a dismal-looking house in the outlets of the town, where he informed me he chose to reside for the benefit of the air. We entered the lower door, which ever seemed to lie most hospitably open; and I began to ascend an old and creaking staircase, when, as he mounted to show me the way, he demanded whether I delighted in prospects; to which, answering in the affirmative, 'Then,' says he, 'I shall show you one of the most charming in the world out of my window; you shall see the ships sailing and the whole country for twenty miles round, tip top, quite high. My Lord Swamp would give ten thousand guineas for such a one; but, as I sometimes pleasantly tell him, I always love to keep my prospects at home, that my friends may visit me the oftener.'

By this time we were arrived as high as the stairs would permit us to ascend, till we came to what he was facetiously pleased to call the first floor down the chimney; and knocking at the door, a voice from within demanded, 'Who's there?' My conductor answered that it was him. But this not satisfying the querist, the voice again repeated the demand; to which he answered louder than before; and now the door was opened by an old woman with cautious reluctance. When we were got in, he welcomed me to his house with great ceremony, and turning to the old woman, asked where was her lady. 'Good troth,' replied she in a peculiar dialect, 'she's washing your twa shirts at the next door, because they have taken an oath against lending out the tub any longer.' 'My two shirts!' cried he in a tone that faltered with confusion, 'what does the idiot mean?' 'I ken what I mean weel enough,' replied the other; 'she's washing your twa shirts at the next door, because—' 'Fire and fury, no more of thy stupid explanations!' cried he; 'go and inform her we have got company. Were that Scotch hag', continued he, turning to me, 'to be for ever in my family, she would never learn politeness, nor forget that absurd poisonous accent of hers, or testify the smallest specimen of breeding or high life; and yet it is very surprising, too, as I had her from a parliament man, a friend of mine from the Highlands, one of the politest men in the world; but that's a secret.'

We waited some time for Mrs Tibbs' arrival, during which interval I had a full opportunity of surveying the chamber and all its furniture, which consisted of four chairs with old wrought bottoms, that he assured me were his wife's embroidery; a square table that had been once japanned; a cradle in one corner, a lumbering cabinet in the other; a broken shepherdess, and a mandarine without a head, were stuck over the chimney; and round the walls several paltry unframed pictures, which, he observed, were all his own drawing. 'What do you think, sir, of the head in the corner, done in the manner of Grisoni? There's the true keeping in it; it is my own face, and though there happens to be no likeness, a Countess offered me a hundred for its fellow; I refused her, for, hang it, that would be mechanical, you know.'

The wife at last made her appearance, at once a slattern and a coquette; much emaciated, but still carrying the remains of beauty. She made twenty apologies for being seen in such odious *déshabillé*, but hoped to be excused, as she had stayed out all night with the Countess, who was excessively fond of the horns. 'And, indeed, my dear,' added she, turning to her husband, 'his lordship drank your health in a bumper.' 'Poor Jack!' cries he, 'a dear, good natured fellow; I know he loves me. But I hope, my dear, you have given orders for dinner; you need make no great preparations neither, there are but three of us; something elegant, and little, will do—turbot, an ortolan, a—' 'Or what do you think, my dear,' interrupts the wife, 'of a nice pretty bit of ox-cheek, piping hot, and dressed with a little of my own sauce?' 'The very thing!' replies he; 'it will eat best with some smart bottled beer; but be sure to let us have the sauce his Grace was so fond of. I hate your immense loads of meat; that is country all over; extremely disgusting to those who are in the least acquainted with high life.' By this time my curiosity began to abate and my appetite to increase: the company of fools may at first make us smile, but at last never fails of rendering us melancholy; I therefore pretended to recollect a prior engagement, and after having shown my respect to the house, according to the fashion of the English, by giving the old servant a piece of money at the door, I took my leave; Mrs Tibbs assuring me that dinner, if I stayed, would be ready at least in less than two hours.

Oliver Goldsmith (1730?–74), The Citizen of the World (1762).

L ITERATE *society in the middle of the eighteenth century was strongly conscious of class distinctions, but the journals themselves were strangely classless as far as their contributors were concerned. At one end of the scale there were poor writers like Goldsmith who had failed to make a living as an unqualified physician and had turned literary hack, and his friend Samuel Johnson who could be described as a failed provincial schoolmaster. In the middle there were numerous gentlemen of wit and scholarship such as Bonnell Thornton and George Colman who co-owned and wrote* The Connoisseur. *At the top end there were the nobly born* dilettanti: *one publication,* The World, *had amongst its contributors Horace Walpole, the Earl of Cork, and Lord Chesterfield.*

Most of the unruly elements which Addison and Steele had tried to expunge from the essay form, like personal attacks, satire intended to draw blood, and political wrangling, had crept back again, but one figure remained staunchly Augustan in his writings, Philip Dormer Stanhope, fourth Earl of Chesterfield. He admired wit but disapproved of hilarity, and wrote to his son 'Frequent laughter is the characteristic of folly and ill-manners'. His witty essays were designed to be received with a nod of approval or at most a wry smile.

Here is a wry-smile-seeking piece by Lord Chesterfield on the subject of ladies' maquillage:

I have taken great pains to inform myself of the growth and extent of this heinous crime of self-painting . . . and I am sorry to say that I have found it to be extremely epidemical. The present state of it, in its several degrees, appears to be this.

The inferior class of women, who always ape their betters, make use of a sort of rough coat, little superior to the common lath and plaster, which comes very cheap, and can be afforded out of the casual profits of the evening . . .

The generality of women of fashion make use of a superior stucco . . . which does not require a daily renewal, and will, with some slight occasional repairs, last as long as their curls, and stand a pretty strong collision.

As for the transcendent and divine powder, with an exquisite varnish superinduced to fix it, it is by no means common, but is reserved for the ladies not only of the first rank, but of the most considerable fortunes, it being so very costly, that few pin-monies can keep a face in it, as a face of condition ought to be kept . . .

Talking upon this subject lately with a friend, he said that in his opinion a woman who painted white gave the public a pledge of her chastity, by fortifying it with a wall which she must be sure that no man would desire either to batter or scale.

Philip Dormer Stanhope, fourth Earl of Chesterfield (1694–1773).

THE *eighteenth century produced some oddities in humorous prose. The name of William Blake, poet, engraver, and mystic, does not immediately conjure up thoughts of either vulgar laughter or wry smiles yet he wrote what he intended to be a funny story,* An Island in the Moon. *It seems that in the 1780s his friends, including the painter John Flaxman, introduced Blake into polite society. Blake recoiled from it and wrote the satire to mock the pretensions and insincerities which he met. It is a curious piece without much form and constantly breaking into verse but at least Blake was able to rescue three of the poems and include them in* Songs of Innocence.

A short extract is enough to give the flavour:

Then Scopprell and Miss Gittipin coming in, Scopprell took up a book & read the following passage:—

'An Easy of Huming Understanding, by John Lookye Gent.'

'John Locke,' said Obtuse Angle.

'O, ay—Lock,' said Scropprell.

'Now here,' said Miss Gittipin,—'I never saw such company in my life. You are always talking of your books. I like to be where we talk. You had better take a walk, that we may have some pleasure. I am sure I never see any pleasure. There's Double Elephant's Girls, they have their own way & there's Miss Filligreework, she goes out in her coaches, & her footman & her mains, & Stormonts & Balloon hats, & a pair of gloves every day, & the Sorrows of Werter, & Robinsons, & the Queen of France's Puss colour, & my Cousin Gibble Gabble says that I am like nobody else. I might as well be in a nunnery. There they go in Postchaises and Stages to Vauxhall and Ranelagh. And I hardly know what a coach is, except when I go to Mr Jacko's. He knows what riding is, & his wife is the most agreeable woman. You hardly know she has a tongue in her head, & he is the funniest fellow, & I do believe he'll go in partnership with his master, & they have black servants lodge at their house. I never saw such a place in my life. He says he has six & twenty rooms in his house, and I believe it, & he is not such a liar as Quid thinks he is.'

'Poo! Poo! Hold your tongue. Hold your tongue,' said the Lawgiver.

This quite provok'd Miss Gittipin, to interrupt her in her favourite topic, & she proceeded to use every Provoking speech that ever she could, & he bore it more like a Saint than a Lawgiver, and with great solemnity he address'd the company in these words:—

'They call women the weakest vessel, but I think they are the strongest. A girl has always more tongue than a boy. I have seen a little brat no higher than a nettle, & she had as much tongue as a city clark; but a boy would be such a fool, not have any thing to say, &, if any body ask'd him a question he would put his head into a hole and hide it. I am sure I take but little pleasure. You have as much pleasure as I have. There I stand &

bear every fool's insult. If I had only myself to care for, I'd wring off their noses.'

> William Blake (1757–1827), *An Island in the Moon* (c.1785). *Collected Writings* (ed. G. Keynes).

━━━━━━━━

ARTHUR COLLIER *was a clergyman and a writer on metaphysical subjects. He had two daughters, Sarah and Jane, who became friendly with literary figures such as the novelists Samuel Richardson and Henry Fielding. In 1753 one of these quiet, gentle, unmarried ladies published a remarkable book,* An Essay on the Art of ingeniously Tormenting; with proper rules for the Exercise of that Pleasant Art.

Jane Collier's humour was pungent and original. Here is her advice to parents with too many offspring:

Suppose your stock of children too large; and that, by your care for their support, you should be abridged of some of your own luxuries and pleasures. To make away with the troublesome and expensive brats, I allow, would be the desirable thing: but the question is, how to effect this without subjecting yourself to that punishment which the law has thought proper to affix to such sort of jokes. Whipping and starving, with some caution, might do the business: but, since a late execution for a fact of that kind may have given a precedent for the magistrates to examine into such affairs, you may, by these means, find your way to the gallows, if you are low enough for such a scrutiny into your conduct: and, if you are too high to have your actions punished, you may possibly be a little ill spoken of amongst your acquaintance. I think, therefore, it is best not to venture, either your neck, or your reputation, by such a proceeding; especially as you may effect the thing, full as well, by following the directions I have given, of holding no restraint over them.

Suffer them to climb, without contradiction, to heights from whence they may break their necks: let them eat every thing they like, and at all times; not refusing them the richest meats, and highest sauces, with as great a variety as possible; because even excess in one dish of plain meat cannot, as I have been told by physicians, do much harm. Suffer them to sit up as late as they please at night, and make hearty meat-suppers; and even in the middle of the night, if they call for it, don't refuse the poor things some victuals. By this means, nobody can say you starve your children: and if they should chance to die of a surfeit, or of an ill habit of body, contracted from such diet, so far will you be from censure, that your name will be recorded for a kind and indulgent parent. If any impertinent person should hint to you, that this manner of feeding your children was the high road to destruction, you may answer, 'That the poor people suffer their children to eat and drink what they please, not feeding them upon bread-pudden, milk and water, and such stuff, as the physicians advise; and (you may say) where do you see anything more healthful, than the children of the poor?'

Jane Collier (*fl.* mid-eighteenth century), *The Art of Tormenting* (1753).

———

ANOTHER *oddity of eighteenth-century humour, in an entirely different vein, was a book called* Biographical Memoirs of Extraordinary Painters, *written in 1776 by William Beckford.*

Beckford was as odd as his book. He was born with what might be termed a golden spoon in his mouth as he was the son of an immensely rich merchant who had twice been Lord Mayor of London. He was privately educated—his music teacher was Mozart—and his fortune allowed him to indulge his epicurean fancy for collecting vast quantities of objets d'art *and books. He bought Edward Gibbon's library in Lausanne then locked the door and sat down to read it. He wrote an Oriental romance,* Vathek, *in French. It was translated into English by an obscure clergyman and was so successful that it began a fashion for steamy, colourful tales of the mysterious East. He rebuilt the family mansion at Fonthill in an extravagant Gothic manner with an enormous entrance hall and a tower three hundred feet high. The tower fell down. He replaced it with another which also fell down. For twenty years he lived at Fonthill, a recluse, attended by a steward, a doctor, a French abbé and a dwarf. Eventually he ran short of money and retired to Bath where the grounds of his house are now the cemetery.*

The DNB *comments, 'Beckford's was, on the whole, a wasted life'.*

When he was 16 he read a book of biographies of the great Flemish painters, Vie des Peintres Flamand. *The style of the book, indeed of that kind of adulatory biography, so incensed the sensitive and precocious lad that he sat down and wrote a parody of it.*

Here are some extracts, beginning with a mocking of the Flemish painters' preoccupation with anatomy and the study of corpses.

His subject in this biography is keen young Rouzinski, whose father is leader of a robber band:

His father's band frequently bringing bodies to their caves, he amused himself with dissecting and imitating the several parts, till he attained such a perfection in muscular expression as is rarely seen in the works of the greatest masters. His application was surprising; for his curiosity to examine the human structure being inflamed, he pursued the study with such eagerness as those who are not amateurs cannot easily imagine. Every day discovered some new artery, or tendon to his view . . .

In the Spring he used early in the morning to quit his cave, and frequently trussing a body over his shoulders, repaired to a wood, and delighted himself with exploring it. Instead of carrying with him in his walks a nice pocket edition of some Elzevir classic, he never was without a leg or an arm, which he went slicing along, and generally accompanied his operations with a melodious whistling; for he was of a cheerful disposition.

Religion in the Low countries at that time was austere and the Flemish painters painted a society in which a high moral tone was not only admired but required. Beckford touches on this in describing the painter Watersouch's admiration of the lady artist Merian:

He adored the extreme nicety of her touch, and not a little admired that strict sense of propriety which had induced her to marriage; for it seems she had chosen Jean Graff of Nuremburg for her husband, merely to study the *Nude* in a modest way.

> William Beckford (1759–1844), *Biographical Memoirs of Extraordinary Painters* (1780).

———————

Another *odd piece is not odd in itself but in the fact that the writer was one of the last representatives of a breed which flourished in the publishing boom of the eighteenth century: the gifted amateur author. The word 'amateur', like its synonym 'dilettante', did not in those days carry the sense of being inferior to a professional, of toying with something rather than working at it. Both words simply meant doing something for the love of it and not for the money.*

Henry William Bunbury had a gift for caricature, a buoyant sense of humour, and plenty of money, so he is down in the dictionaries of biography as 'amateur artist, caricaturist, and writer'. In fact he was much admired as an artist by his friends Horace Walpole, Goldsmith, and Sir Joshua Reynolds, and his humorous book on riding went into several editions and eventually a sequel.

Here he gives basic advice to beginners:

The height of a horse is perfectly immaterial, provided he is higher behind than before. Nothing is more pleasing to a traveller than the sensation of continually getting forward: whereas the riding of a horse of contrary make is like swarming the banisters of a stair-case, when, though perhaps you really advance, you feel as if you were going backwards . . . The less he lifts his fore legs, the easier he will move for his rider, and he will likewise brush all the stones out of his way, which might otherwise throw him down. If he turns out his toes as well as he should do, he will then disperse them to the right and the left, and not have the trouble of kicking the same stone of a second time . . .

If, then, you bend your body well forward, your rump sticking properly out behind, with your legs projected, I shall have hopes of you; you cannot, I think, fail of soon equalling my most sanguine expectations; and, after having attained this excellence (an excellence, let me tell you, arrived at by but few, and those men of the first knowledge and science, such as the fellows of Colleges, the Liverymen of London, or, perhaps, the crew of a man of war) I would advise you, without delay, to attempt another step towards equestrian perfection; that is, on riding either eastward or westward, to make your toes point due north and south, or vice versa.

'Geoffrey Gambado' (H. W. Bunbury) (1750–1811), *An Academy for Grown Horsemen* (1787).

THE *agreeable practice of letter-writing continued to keep families in contact and friendships in repair as the eighteenth century progressed.*

Sir John Dalrymple was a Scottish judge and the author of many legal works with such titles as Essay towards a General History of Feudal Property in Great Britain under various Heads *and* Considerations on the Policy of Entails in Great Britain. *Samuel Johnson and Boswell visited him at his estate on their Highland journey but arrived late and the visit was not a happy one, perhaps not helped by the fact that although Sir John shared Johnson's interest in making chemical experiments Sir John was more successful at it: he had discovered how to turn herrings into soap.*

Humour based on the problems and disasters of country life has been the theme of a great many writers since the eighteenth century but the subject has probably never been treated so thoroughly and laconically as by the Scottish lawyer in a letter to his uncle:

My Dear Sir,—Your shirts are safe. I have made many attempts upon them; but Bess, who has in honesty what she wants in temper, keeps them in safety for you.

You ask me what I have been doing? To the best of my memory, what has passed since I came home is as follows.

Finding the roof bad, I sent slaters, at the peril of their necks, to repair it. They mended three holes, and made thirty themselves.

I pulled down as many walls round the house as would have fortified a town. This was in summer: but now that winter is come, I would give all the money to put them up again, that it cost me to take them down.

I thought it would give a magnificent air to the old hall, to throw the passage into it. After it was done, I went out of town to see how it looked. It was night when I went into it; the wind blew out the candle from the over-size of the room; upon which, I ordered the partition to be built up again, that I might not die of cold in the midst of summer.

I ordered the old timber to be thinned; to which, perhaps, the love of lucre a little contributed. The workmen, for every tree they cut, destroyed three, by letting them fall on each other. I received a momentary satisfaction from hearing that the carpenter I employed had cut off his thumb in felling a tree. But this pleasure was soon allayed, when, upon examining his measure, I found that he had measured false, and cheated me of 20 *per cent.*

Instead of addle-horses I bought mares, and had them covered with an Arabian. When I went, some months after, to mount them, the groom told me, I should kill the foals; and now I walk on foot, with the stable full of horses, unless when, with much humility, I ask to be admitted into the chaise, which is generally refused me.

Remembering, with a pleasing complacency, the Watcombe pigs, I paid thirty shillings for a sow with pig. My wife starved them. They ran over to a madman, called Lord Adam Gordon, who distrained them for damage; and the mother, with ten helpless infants, died of bad usage.

Loving butter much, and cream more, I bought two Dutch cows, and had plenty of both. I made my wife a present of two more: she learned the way to market for their produce; and I have never got a bowl of cream since.

I made a fine hay-stack; but quarrelled with my wife as to the manner of drying the hay, and building the stack. The hay-stack took fire; by which I had the double mortification of losing my hay, and finding my wife had more sense than myself.

I kept no plough; for which I thank my Maker; because then I must have wrote this letter from a gaol.

I paid twenty pounds for a dunghill, because I was told it was a good thing; and, now, I would give anybody twenty shillings to tell me what to do with it.

I built, and stocked a pigeon-house; but the cats watched below, the hawks hovered above; and pigeon-soup, roasted pigeon, or cold pigeon-pie, have I never seen since.

I fell to drain a piece of low ground behind the house; but I hit upon the tail of the rock, and drained the well of the house; by which I can get no water for my victuals.

I entered into a great project for selling lime, upon a promise from one of my own farmers to give me land off his farm. But when I went to take off the ground, he laughed, said he had choused [swindled] the Lawyer, and exposed me to a dozen law-suits for breach of bargains, which I could not perform.

I fattened black cattle and sheep; but could not agree with the butchers about the price. From mere economy, we ate them ourselves, and almost killed all the family with surfeits.

I bought two score of six-year-old wethers for my own table; but a butcher, who rented one of the fields, put my mark upon his own carrion sheep; by which I have been living upon carrion all the summer.

I brewed much beer; but the small turned sour, and the servants drank all the strong.

I found a ghost in the house, whose name was M'Alister, a pedlar, that had been killed in one of the rooms at the top of the house two centuries ago. No servant would go on an errand after the sun was set, for fear of M'Alister, which obliged me to send off one set of my servants. Soon after the housekeeper, your old friend Mrs Brown, died, aged 90; and then the belief ran, that another ghost was in the house, upon which many of the new set of servants begged leave to quit the house, and got it.

In one thing only I have succeeded. I have quarrelled with all my neighbours; so that, with a dozen gentlemen's seats in my view, I stalk alone like a lion in a desert.

I thought I should have been happy with my tenants, because I could be insolent to them without their being insolent to me. But they paid me no rent; and in a few days I shall have above one half of the very few friends I have in the country in a prison.

Such being the pleasures of a country life, I intend to quit them all in about a month, to submit to the mortification of spending the spring in London, where, I am happy to hear, we are to meet. But I am infinitely happier to hear that Mrs Dalrymple is doing so well. May God preserve her long to you! for she is a fine creature.

Just when I was going to you last spring, I received a Letter from Bess, that she was dying. I put off my journey to Watcombe, and almost killed myself with posting to Scotland, where I found Madam in perfect good health—Yours always, my dear Jack,

John Dalrymple

Sir John Dalrymple (1726–1810), Letter to Admiral Dalrymple, Cranstoun (1 Jan. 1772).

———

ARGUABLY *the most delightful letter-writer in the eighteenth century, or perhaps any century, was Horace Walpole, who devoted most of his literary energy to this form of expression and during the whole of his enormous correspondence hardly wrote one dull paragraph let alone a dull page. Byron called the letters 'incomparable'.*

Horace Walpole was the fourth son of the Prime Minister, Sir Robert Walpole, who appointed his son to enough sinecure posts to enable him to live the comfortable life of a dilettante, connoisseur and collector of objets d'art and vertu. He never married.

Walpole had a town house in Arlington Street, but in 1747 he bought the lease of a cottage in Twickenham from a Mrs Chenevix, the owner of a famous toyshop in Suffolk Street.

Walpole's taste was for the Gothic and he tricked out his cottage as a tiny Gothic castle complete with fake battlements, renamed it Strawberry Hill—the house still stands—and filled it with items to his taste.

He was severe on tastes which differed from his own. His eye missed little when he paid a visit to the beautiful but illiterate and wildly immoral Lady Chudleigh:

I breakfasted the day before yesterday at Ælia Laelia Chudleigh's. There was a concert for Prince Edward's birthday, and at three, a vast cold collation, and all the town. The house is not fine, nor in good taste, but loaded with finery. Execrable varnished pictures, chests, cabinets, commodes, tables, stands, boxes, riding on one another's backs, and loaded with terrenes, filligree, figures, and everything upon earth. Every favour she has bestowed is registered by a bit of Dresden china. There is a glass-case full of enamels, eggs, ambers, lapis lazuli, cameos, toothpick-cases, and all kinds of trinkets, things that she told me were her playthings; another cupboard, full of the finest japan, and candlesticks and vases of rock crystal, ready to be thrown down, in every corner. But of all curiosities, are the conveniences in every bedchamber: great mahogany projections, with brass handles, cocks, etc. I could not help saying, it was the loosest family I ever saw. Adieu!

Horace Walpole (1717–97), Letter to George Montagu (27 Mar. 1760).

🍂 A very early reference to water-closets. These were virtually unknown in town houses, which had no drains. The devices probably emptied into a distant pit in the servants' quarters.

Like most entertaining letter-writers Walpole had an excellent ear for gossip:

You will be diverted with what happened to Mr Meynell lately. He was engaged to dine at a formal old lady's, but stayed so late hunting that he had not time to dress, but went as he was, with forty apologies. The matron very affected, and meaning to say something very civil, cried, 'Oh! Sir, I assure you I can see the gentleman through a pair of buckskin breeches as well as if he was in silk or satin.'

   I am sure I can't tell you anything better, so good night!

Letter to George Montagu, Esq. (23 June 1759)

Walpole, being the Prime Minister's son and later fourth Earl of Orford, had a privileged position from which to observe great events. Nothing awed him. Even the funeral of George II was described to his friends with his usual mixture of perception, playfulness, and wit:

Do you know, I had the curiosity to go to the burying t'other night; I had never seen a royal funeral; nay, I walked as a rag of quality, which I found would be, and so it was, the easiest way of seeing it. It is absolutely a noble sight. The Prince's Chamber, hung with purple, and a quantity of silver lamps, the coffin under a canopy of purple velvet, and six vast chandeliers of silver on high stands, had a very good effect. When we came to the chapel of Henry the Seventh, all solemnity and decorum ceased—no order was observed, people sat or stood where they could or would, the yeomen of the guard were crying out for help, oppressed by the immense weight of the coffin, the Bishop read sadly, and blundered in the prayers, the fine chapter,

Man that is born of a woman, was chanted, not read, and the anthem, besides being unmeasurably tedious, would have served as well for a nuptial. The real serious part was the figure of the Duke of Cumberland, heightened by a thousand melancholy circumstances.

He had a dark brown adonis [a kind of wig], and a cloak of black cloth, with a train of five yards. Attending the funeral of a father, however little reason he had so to love him, could not be pleasant. His leg extremely bad, yet forced to stand upon it near two hours, his face bloated and distorted with his late paralytic stroke, which has affected, too, one of his eyes, and placed over the mouth of the vault, into which, in all probability, he must himself so soon descend—think how unpleasant a situation! He bore it all with a firm and unaffected countenance.

This grave scene was fully contrasted by the burlesque Duke of Newcastle. He fell into a fit of crying the moment he came into the chapel, and flung himself back in a stall, the Archbishop hovering over him with a smelling bottle—but in two minutes his curiosity got the better of his hypocrisy, and he ran about the chapel with his glass to spy who was or was not there, spying with one hand, and mopping his eyes with t'other. Then returned the fear of catching cold, and the Duke of Cumberland, who was sinking with heat, felt himself weighed down, and turning round, found it was the Duke of Newcastle standing upon his train to avoid the chill of the marble.

Letter to George Montague (13 Nov. 1760).

S AMUEL JOHNSON, *essayist, poet, political pamphleteer, compiler of the first great English dictionary, was the son of a respected but poor bookseller in Lichfield. He went to London to earn his living by his pen and nearly starved. Gradually he got under way; doing hack work for Edward Cave's* Gentleman's Magazine; *getting his poems published; having his play* Irene *staged by Garrick; writing his own periodical essays as* The Rambler. *Publishers, politicians and the reading public came to realize that Johnson was an author of formidable intellect: not, perhaps, a great original thinker but the possessor of a mind of extraordinary power and clarity. He finished up with two honorary doctorates, a state pension, and the distinction of being the dominant figure in the eighteenth-century world of letters. He was dubbed by Tobias Smollett, 'the Grand Cham of Literature'.*

The modern image of Johnson, mostly derived from an essay by Lord Macaulay, is of a vast, ungainly figure dressed in shabby clothes, his head lolling sideways, solemn from a fear of God, insensitive, prejudiced, brutal in controversy. But the way his friends wrote about him gives a different picture. The authoress Hannah More took tea with Johnson and wrote afterwards to her sister: 'The old genius was extremely jocular . . . You would have imagined we had been at some comedy had you heard our peals of laughter.' Arthur Murphy the actor and writer, wrote: 'He was surprized to be told, but it is certainly true, that, with great powers of mind, wit and humour were his shining talents.' Fanny Burney confided to her diary: 'Dr Johnson has more fun, and comical humour, and love of nonsense about him than almost anyone I ever saw.'

The 'old genius' managed to suppress his love of fun and nonsense in most of his writings because much of what he wrote had a sterner purpose than to provide amusement. But when it was proper to be trivial, as in some of his periodical essays, his touch was appropriately light.

Here is an essay on the growth of advertising in newspapers:

The practice of appending to the narratives of public transactions more minute and domestic intelligence, and filling the newspapers with advertisements, has grown up by slow degrees to its present state.

Genius is shewn only by invention. The man who first took advantage of the general curiosity that was excited by a siege or battle, to betray the readers of news into the knowledge of the shop where the best puffs and powder were to be sold, was undoubtedly a man of great sagacity, and profound skill in the nature of man. But when he had once shewn the way, it was easy to follow him; and every man now knows a ready method of informing the public of all that he desires to buy or sell, whether his wares be material or intellectual; whether he makes clothes, or teaches the mathematics; whether he be a tutor that wants a pupil, or a pupil that wants a tutor.

Whatever is common is despised. Advertisements are now so numerous that they are very negligently perused, and it is therefore become necessary to gain attention by magnificence of promises, and by eloquence sometimes sublime and sometimes pathetic.

Promise, large promise, is the soul of an advertisement. I remember a 'wash-ball' that had a quality truly wonderful, it gave 'an exquisite edge to the razor'. And there are now to be sold 'for ready money only', some 'duvets for bed-coverings, of down, beyond comparison superior to what is called otter down', and indeed such, that its 'many excellencies cannot be here set forth'. With one excellence we are made acquainted, 'it is warmer than four or five blankets, and lighter than one'.

There are some, however, that know the prejudice of mankind in favour of modest sincerity. The vender of the 'Beautifying Fluid' sells a lotion that repels pimples, washes away freckles, smooths the skin, and plumps the flesh; and yet, with generous abhorrence of ostentation, confesses, that it will not 'restore the bloom of fifteen to a lady of fifty'.

The true pathos of advertisements must have sunk deep into the heart of every man that remembers the zeal shewn by the seller of the anodyne necklace, for the ease and safety 'of poor toothing infants', and the affection with which he warned every mother, that 'she would never forgive herself' if her infant should perish without a necklace.

Samuel Johnson (1709–84), *The Idler*, no. 40 (20 Jan. 1759).

One of the stock subjects for periodical essay writers was mildly eccentric social behaviour.

Here Johnson draws a sketch of a lady afflicted with an obsession which is not unknown today:

I am the unfortunate husband of a 'buyer of bargains'. My wife has somewhere heard, that a good housewife 'never' has any thing to 'purchase when it is wanted'. This maxim is often in her mouth, and always in her head. She is not one of those philosophical talkers that speculate without practice, and learn sentences of wisdom only to repeat them; she is always making additions to her stores; she never looks into a broker's shop, but she spies something that may be wanted some time; and it is impossible to make her pass the door of a house where she hears 'Goods selling by auction'.

Whatever she thinks cheap, she holds it the duty of an oeconomist to buy; in consequence of this maxim, we are incumbered on every side with useless lumber. The servants can scarcely creep to their beds through the chests and boxes that surround them. The carpenter is employed once a week in building closets, fixing cupboards, and fastening shelves, and my house has the appearance of a ship stored for a voyage to the colonies.

I had often observed that advertisements set her on fire, and therefore, pretending to emulate her laudable frugality, I forbad the newspaper to be taken any longer; but my precaution is vain; I know not by what fatality, or by what confederacy, every catalogue of 'genuine furniture' comes to her hand, every advertisement of a warehouse newly opened is in her pocket-book, and she knows before any of her neighbours, when the stock of any man 'leaving off trade' is to be 'sold cheap for ready money'.

Such intelligence, is to my dear one the Siren's song. No engagement, no duty, no interest can withhold her from a sale, from which she always returns congratulating herself upon her dexterity at a bargain; the porter lays down his burden in the hall, she displays her new acquisitions, and spends the rest of the day in contriving where they shall be put.

As she cannot bear to have any thing uncomplete, one purchase necessitates another; she has twenty feather-beds more than she can use, and a late sale has supplied her with a proportionable number of Witney blankets, a large roll of linen for sheets, and five quilts for every bed, which she bought because the seller told her, that if she would clear his hands he would let her have a bargain.

Thus by hourly encroachments my habitation is made narrower and narrower; the dining-room is so crowded with tables that dinner scarcely can be served; the parlour is decorated with so many piles of china, that I dare not step within the door; at every turn of the stairs I have a clock, and half the windows of the upper floors are darkened that shelves may be set before them.

This, however, might be borne, if she would gratify her own inclinations without opposing mine. But I who am idle am luxurious, and she condemns me to live upon salt provision. She knows the loss of buying in small quantities, we have therefore whole hogs and quarters of oxen. Part of our meat is tainted before it is eaten, and part is thrown away because it is spoiled; but she persists in her system, and will never buy any thing by single pennyworths.

The common vice of those who are still grasping at more, is to neglect that which they already possess; but from this failing my charmer is free. It is the great care of her life that the pieces of beef should be boiled in the order in which they are bought; that the second bag of pease shall not be opened till the first are eaten; that every feather-bed shall be lain on in its turn; that the carpets should be taken out of the chests once a month and brushed, and the rolls of linen opened now and then before the fire. She is daily enquiring after the best traps for mice; and keeps the rooms always scented by fumigations to destroy the moths. She employs workmen, from time to time, to adjust six clocks that never go, and clean five jacks that rust in the garret; and a woman in the next alley lives by scouring the brass and pewter, which, are only laid up to tarnish again.

She is always imagining some distant time in which she shall use whatever she accumulates; she has four looking-glasses which she cannot hang up in her house, but which will be handsome in more lofty rooms; and pays rent for the place of a vast copper in some warehouse, because when we live in the country we shall brew our own beer.

Of this life I have long been weary, but know not how to change it; all the married men whom I consult advise me to have patience; but some old bachelors are of opinion, that since she loves sales so well, she should have a sale of her own, and I have, I think, resolved to open her hoards, and advertise an auction.

I am, Sir,

Your very humble servant,

PETER PLENTY

Ibid., no. 35 (16 Dec. 1758).

Johnson's best-known work was his massive dictionary, which took him eight years to complete. Perhaps the best proof of Johnson's independent spirit and real humour lies within those two folio volumes. What other eighteenth-century English writer, let alone Frenchman, German or Italian, would have put jokes into a dictionary?:

BOOT OF A COACH. The space between the coachman and the coach.

DULL. 8. Not exhilarating; as, to make dictionaries is dull work.

EAME. Uncle: a word still used in the wilder parts of Staffordshire.

> ✎ A small local joke. Johnson's home town, Lichfield, was reckoned by its inhabitants to be highly civilized, 'the Athens of Staffordshire'.

EXCISE. A hateful tax levied upon commodities, and adjudged not by the common judges of property, but wretches hired by those to whom excise is paid.

GRUBSTREET. Originally the name of a town in Moorfields in London, much inhabited by writers of small histories, dictionaries, and temporary poems; whence any mean production is called *grubstreet*.

> Johnson had great sympathy for those forced, as he once was, to write 'mean productions' for starvation wages. He followed the entry with a quotation from the *Greek Anthology* which translates:
>
> > 'Hail, Ithica!
> > After toil and bitter woe I am
> > glad to reach your soil.'

LEXICOGRAPHER. A Writer of dictionaries; a harmless drudge.

MONSIEUR. A term of reproach for a Frenchman.

MUSHROOM. 2. An upstart; a wretch risen from the dunghill; a director of a company.

NETWORK. Any thing reticulated, or recussated, at equal distances, with interstices between the intersections.

NOVEL. A small tale, generally of love.

OATS. A grain, which in England is generally given to horses, but in Scotland supports the people.

> This famous definition might well not have been a joke at all. The dictionary is remarkably free from Johnson's usual ribbing of the Scots and during his lifetime the above statement was literally true. On the other hand . . .

PATRON. One who countenances, supports or protects. Commonly a wretch who supports with insolence, and is paid with flattery.

PENSION. An allowance made to any one without an equivalent. In England it is generally understood to mean pay given to a state hireling for treason to his country.

> Johnson eventually received a state pension of £300, enough to live on in modest comfort, but he would not modify this definition in later editions of the dictionary.

SHEEP. The animal that bears wool: remarkable for its usefulness and innocence.

STAMMEL. Of this word I know not the meaning.

VERMICELLI. A paste rolled and broken in the form of worms.

WHIST. A game at cards, requiring close attention and silence.

TO WORM. 2. To deprive a dog of something, nobody knows what, under the tongue, which is said to prevent him, nobody knows why, from running mad.

A Dictionary of the English Language (1755).

━━━━━━━━

H UMOROUS *prose, until now mainly found in essays, letters, and other forms of non-fiction, took on lusty new life with the birth and development of what is usually called the English novel.*

Daniel Defoe is sometimes credited with being the father of the English novel, although many of his books were fiction based upon fact. The case rests upon him being our first major author to write fiction in which the characters had ordinary names and behaved believably, and in which there was a realistic sense of time. But his books lacked some of the other ingredients of the English novel like subtlety of form and the development and interplay of character. His stories tended to run on and on and the aim in life of his heroes and heroines was social and financial security. One does not look to Defoe for humour.

The other author named as father of the novel is Samuel Richardson, who was the first novelist to base whole books on the close-up, almost claustrophobic personal dilemmas of his characters, which he developed along psychological lines in minute detail.

If Defoe could be said to have invented what is now called 'faction', that is to say fiction inextricably mixed up with facts about real people and events, then Richardson could be said to have invented the 'best-seller'.

Within months of the publication of the first volumes of Pamela *the book was a spectacular success. It swept across Europe, was translated into four languages, and imitated in many more. So great a hit was it that it was said at the time that those who had not read it found themselves out of every conversation, and when the serving-girl heroine finally succeeded in marrying her would-be seducer they rang the church bells in Slough, Buckinghamshire.*

It is hardly surprising that Pamela *was such a success, particularly with the vast army of lady's-maids and other female house-servants who were avid readers of romances. It was really a version of the Cinderella story and told of the plight of a maidservant lusted after by her employer, Squire B. He was aided in his evil machinations by his wicked housekeeper, Mrs Jervis, but Pamela's virtue was so impregnable that all his attempts at seduction and finally rape were staunchly rebuffed and he eventually married her.*

The morality of Pamela *was warmly applauded from the pulpit but Richardson had a prurient streak and lingered somewhat gloatingly over details of the sexual struggling, so the book also had its dirty bits. Lady Mary Wortley Montagu dismissed* Pamela *as 'the joy of chambermaids of all nations'.*

Richardson's work, like Defoe's, was virtually humourless, but Pamela *did great service to humour by so infuriating the playwright and magistrate Henry Fielding that he burst into prose with a rollicking parody of it.*

It was the moral hypocrisy in Pamela *which dismayed Fielding.* Pamela *had fought to retain her virginity seemingly so that she could eventually get the best price for it—marriage to a brute who had tried repeatedly to deflower her but who represented a step up for her socially and financially.*

In Fielding's parody Shamela *('In which, the many notorious Falsehoods and Misrepresentations of a Book called* PAMELA *are exposed and refuted'), the virtuous Pamela became a slut who had already had a child by the local clergyman, Parson Williams, and was scheming to marry her salacious but stupid employer, Squire Booby. The housekeeper, Mrs Jewkes, was egging her on, hoping thereby to make enough money to open a brothel.*

This saintly group is described in action by Pamela in a letter home to her dear mother, an ex-whore:

Shamela Andrews *to Mrs* Henrietta Maria Honora Andrews *at her lodgings at the* Fan *and* Pepper-Box *in* Drury-Lane.

Dear Mamma,

As soon as I had breakfasted, a Coach and Six came to the Door, and who should be in it but my Master.

I immediately run up into my Room, and stript, and washed, and drest my self as well as I could, and put on my prettiest round-ear'd cap, and pulled down my stays, to shew as much as I could of my bosom, (for Parson Williams says, that is the most beautiful part of a woman) and then I practised over all my airs before the glass, and then I sat down and read a chapter in the Whole Duty of Man.

Then Mrs Jewkes came to me and told me, my master wanted me below, and says she, Don't behave like a fool; No, thinks I to my self, I believe I shall find wit enough for my master and you too.

So down goes I into the parlour to him. Pamela, says he, the moment I came in, you see I cannot stay long from you, which I think is a sufficient proof of the violence of my passion. Yes, Sir, say I, I see your honour intends to ruin me, that nothing but the destruction of my vartue will content you.

O what a charming Word that is, rest his Soul who first invented it.

How can you say I would ruin you, answered the Squire, when you shall not ask any thing which I will not grant you. If that be true, says I, good your honour let me go home to my poor but honest parents; that is all I have to ask, and do not ruin a poor maiden, who is resolved to carry her vartue to the grave with her.

Hussy, says he, don't provoke me, don't provoke me, I say. You are absolutely in my power, and if you won't let me lie with you by fair means, I will by force. O la, Sir, says I, I don't understand your paw [obscene] words.— Very pretty treatment indeed, says he, to say I use paw words; Hussy, Gipsie,

Hypocrite, Saucebox, Boldface, get out of my sight, or I will lend you such a kick in the —— I don't care to repeat the word, but he meant my hinder part. I was offering to go away, for I was half afraid, when he called me back, and took me round the neck and kissed me, and then bid me go about my business.

I went directly into my room, where Mrs Jewkes came to me soon afterwards. So madam, says she, you have left my master below in a fine pet, he hath threshed two or three of his men already; it is might pretty that all his servants are to be punished for your impertinence.

Harkee, madam, says I, don't you affront me, for if you do, d—n me (I am sure I have repented for using such a word) if I am not revenged.

How sweet is revenge: sure the sermon book is in the right, in calling it the sweetest morsel the Devil ever dropped into the mouth of a sinner.

Mrs Jewkes remembered the smart of my nails too well to go farther, and so we sat down and talked about my vartue till dinner-time, and then I was sent for to wait on my master. I took care to be often caught looking at him, and then I always turned away my eyes and pretended to be ashamed. As soon as the cloth was removed, he put a bumper of champagne into my hand, and bid me drink—O la I can't name the health. Parson Williams may well say he is a wicked Man.

Mrs Jewkes took a glass and drank the dear monysyllable; I don't understand that word but I believe it is baudy. I then drank towards his honour's good pleasure. Ay, hussy, said he, you can give me pleasure if you will; Sir, says I, I shall be always glad to do what is in my power, and so I pretended not to know what he meant. Then he took me into his lap.—O Mamma, I could tell you something if I would—and he kissed me and I said I won't be slobbered about so, so I won't and he bid me get out of the room for a saucy baggage, and said he had a good mind to spit in my face.

Sure no man ever took such a method to gain a woman's heart.

I had not been long in my chamber before Mrs Jewkes came to me and told me, my master would not see me any more that evening, that is, if he can help it; for, added she, I easily perceive the great ascendant you have over him; and to confess the truth, I don't doubt but you will shortly be my mistress.

What says I, dear Mrs Jewkes, what do you say? Don't flatter a poor girl, it is impossible his honour can have any honourable design upon me. And so we talked of honourable designs till supper-time. And Mrs Jewkes and I supped together upon a hot buttered Apple-Pie; and about ten o'clock we went to bed.

We had not been a bed half an hour, when my master came to the room in his shirt as before. I pretended not to hear him, and Mrs Jewkes laid hold of one arm, and he pulled down the bed-cloaths and came into bed on the other Side, and took my other arm and laid it under him, and fell a kissing one of my Breasts as if he would have devoured it; I was then forced to

awake, and began to struggle with him, Mrs Jewkes crying why don't you do it? I have one arm secure, if you can't deal with the rest I am sorry for you. He was as rude as possible to me; but I remembered, Mamma, the instructions you gave me to avoid being ravished, and followed them, which soon brought him to terms, and he promised me on quitting my hold, that he would leave the bed.

O Parson Williams, how little are all the men in the world compared to thee.

Your dutiful daughter
Shamela.

Henry Fielding (1707–54) *An Apology for the Life of Mrs Shamela Andrews* (1741).

It seems that writing the bawdy romp, Shamela, *which was only the length of a longish short story, did not satisfy Fielding's deep need to say what he thought about the kind of lip-service morality which Richardson had sold so successfully, so he immediately began another parody of* Pamela, *this time a full-length novel which he called* The Adventures of Joseph Andrews. *Later he wrote* Tom Jones, *one of the great novels of the language, but Joseph Andrews was his comic masterpiece.*

Fielding changed the heroine's sex and recounted the adventures of Pamela's brother Joseph, a footman as pious and virtuous as his sister. Joseph was in the employ of Squire B's aunt, the lecherous Lady Booby, who was bent on seducing the handsome lad.

The same ambition was nursed by her ladyship's equally amorous housekeeper, the unlovely Mrs Slipslop, who was described thus:

She was a maiden gentlewoman of about forty-five years of age, who having made a small slip in her youth had continued a good maid ever since. She was not at this time remarkably handsome; being very short, and rather too corpulent in body, and somewhat red, with the addition of pimples in the face. Her nose was likewise rather too large, and her eyes too little; nor did she resemble a cow so much in her breath, as in two brown globes which she carried before her; one of her legs was also a little shorter than the other, which occasioned her to limp as she walked. This fair creature had long cast the eyes of affection on Joseph, in which she had not met with quite so good success as she probably wished, though besides the Allurements of her native charms, she had given him tea, sweetmeats, wine, and many other delicacies, of which by keeping the keys, she had the absolute command. Joseph however, had not returned the least gratitude to all these favours, not even so much as a kiss; though I would not insinuate she was so easily to be satisfied: for surely then he would have been highly blameable. The truth is, she was arrived at an Age when she thought she might indulge herself in any liberties with a man, without the danger of bringing a third person into the world to betray them. She imagined, that by so long a self-denial, she had not only made amends for the small slip of her Youth above hinted at:

but had likewise laid up a quantity of merit to excuse any future failings. In a word, she resolved to give a loose to her amorous inclinations, and pay off the debt of pleasure which she found she owed herself, as fast as possible.

The Adventures of Joseph Andrews (1742).

Joseph wandered into the room so Mrs Slipslop poured him a full glass of ratafia, sat him down and turned on him the full force of her eloquence.

The comical misuse of words in speech was an old device, well known to Shakespeare, but Fielding's use of it in Mrs Slipslop's speeches proved so popular that until Sheridan arrived on the scene thirty years later and did it much better with Mrs Malaprop and her 'malapropisms,' the practice was given Mrs Slipslop's name (see Grose's Classical Dictionary of the Vulgar Tongue *(1785): 'SLIP-SLOPPING. Misnaming and misapplying any hard word: from the character of Mrs Slipslop, in Fielding's "Joseph Andrews" '):*

'Sure nothing can be a more simple *Contract* in a woman, than to place her affections on a boy. If I had ever thought it would have been my fate, I should have wished to die a thousand deaths rather than live to see that day. If we like a man, the lightest hint sophisticates. Whereas a boy *proposes* upon us to break through all the *Regulations* of modesty, before we can make any *Oppresion* upon him.'

Joseph, who did not understand a word she said, answered, '*Yes Madam*'; 'Yes Madam!' replied *Mrs Slipslop* with some warmth, 'Do you intend to *result* my passion? Is it not enough, ungrateful as you are, to make no return to all the favours I have done you: but you must treat me with *Ironing?* Barbarous monster! how have I deserved that my passion should be *resulted* and treated with *Ironing?*' 'Madam,' answered *Joseph*, 'I don't understand your hard words: but I am certain, you have no occasion to call me ungrateful: for so far from intending you any wrong, I have always loved you well as if you had been my own mother.' 'How, Sirrah!' says Mrs *Slipslop* in a rage: 'Your own mother! Do you *assinuate* that I am old enough to be your mother? I don't know what a stripling may think: but I believe a man would *refer* me to any Green-Sickness silly girl *whatsomeever*: but I ought to despise you rather than be angry with you, for *referring* the conversation of girls to that of a woman of sense.' 'Madam,' says Joseph, 'I am sure I have always valued the honour you did me by your conversation; for I know you are a woman of learning.' 'Yes but, *Joseph*,' said she a little softened by the compliment to her learning, 'If you had a Value for me, you certainly would have found some method of showing it me; for I am *convicted* you must see the value I have for you. Yes, *Joseph*, my eyes whether I would or no, must have declared a passion I could not conquer.—Oh! *Joseph*!—'

Ibid.

Fielding based the structure of the story on Don Quixote. *The Quixote-like journey which Joseph and his friend Parson Adams made back to their home village enabled Fielding to involve the pair in a variety of predicaments and bring in a number of*

memorable minor characters, like the untrustworthy, hen-pecked Mr Tow-wouse,
keeper of the inn where Joseph recovered after being attacked and left for dead, the
inn-keeper's nagging wife, and the cause of the nagging, Betty, the compliant
chambermaid:

Betty . . . had some good qualities. She had good-nature, generosity and
compassion, but unfortunately her constitution was composed of those warm
ingredients, which, though the purity of courts or nunneries might have
happily controlled them, were by no means able to endure the ticklish situation of a chambermaid at an inn, who is daily liable to the solicitations of
lovers of all complexions, to the dangerous addresses of fine gentlemen of the
army, who sometimes are obliged to reside with them a whole year together,
and above all are exposed to the caresses of footmen, stage-coachmen, and
drawers; all of whom employ the whole artillery of kissing, flattering, bribing,
and every other weapon which is to be found in the whole armory of love,
against them.

Betty, who was but one and twenty, had now lived three years in this
dangerous situation, during which she had escaped pretty well. An ensign
of foot was the first person who made any impression on her heart;
he did indeed raise a flame in her, which required the care of a surgeon to
cool.

While she burnt for him, several others burnt for her. Officers of the army,
young gentlemen travelling the Western Circuit, inoffensive squires, and
some of graver character were set afire by her charms!

At length, having perfectly recovered the effects of her first unhappy
passion, she seemed to have vowed a state of perpetual chastity. She was
long deaf to all the sufferings of her lovers, till one day at a neighbouring
fair, the rhetoric of John, the Hostler, with new straw hat, and a pint of wine,
made a second conquest over her.

She did not however feel any of those flames on this occasion, which had
been the consequence of her former amour; nor indeed those other ill effects,
which prudent young women very justly apprehend from too absolute an
indulgence to the pressing endearments of their lovers. This latter, perhaps,
was a little owing to her not being entirely constant to John, with whom she
permitted Tom Whipwell the state-coachman, and now and then a handsome
young traveller, to share her favours.

Mr Tow-wouse had for some time cast the languishing eyes of affection on
this young maiden. He had laid hold on every opportunity of saying tender
things to her, squeezing her by the hand, and sometimes of kissing her lips:
for as the violence of his passion had considerably abated to Mrs Tow-wouse;
so like water, which is stopped from its usual current in one place, it naturally
sought a vent in another. Mrs Tow-wouse is thought to have perceived this
abatement, and probably it added very little to the natural sweetness of her
temper: for though she was as true to her husband, as the dial to the sun,

she was rather more desirous of being shone on, as being more capable of feeling his warmth.

Ever since Joseph's arrival, Betty had conceived an extraordinary liking to him, which discovered itself more and more, as he grew better and better; till that fatal evening, when, as she was warming his bed, her passion grew to such a height, and so perfectly mastered both her modesty and her reason, that after many fruitless hints, and sly insinuations, she at last threw down the warming-pan, and embracing him with great eagerness, swore he was the handsomest creature she had ever seen.

Joseph in great confusion leapt from her, and told her, he was sorry to see a young woman cast off all regard to modesty: but she had gone too far to recede, and grew so very indecent, that Joseph was obliged, contrary to his inclination, to use some violence to her, and taking her in his arms, he shut her out of the room, and locked the door.

How ought Man to rejoice, that his chastity is always in his own power, that if he hath sufficient strength of mind, he hath always a competent strength of body to defend himself: and cannot, like a poor weak woman, be ravished against his will.

Betty was in the most violent agitation at this disappointment. Rage and lust pulled her heart, as with two strings, two different ways; one moment she thought of stabbing Joseph, the next, of taking him in her arms, and devouring him with kisses; but the latter passion was far more prevalent. Then she thought of revenging his refusal on herself: but whilst she was engaged in this meditation, happily death presented himself to her in so many shapes of drowning, hanging, poisoning, etc. that her distracted mind could resolve on none.

In this perturbation of spirit, it accidentally occurred to her memory, that her master's bed was not made. She therefore went directly to his room; where he happened at that time to be engaged at his bureau. As soon as she saw him, she attempted to retire: but he called her back, and taking her by the hand, squeezed her so tenderly, at the same time whispering so many soft things into her ears, and, then pressed her so closely with his kisses, that the vanquished fair-one, whose passions were already raised, and which were not so whimsically capricious that one man only could lay them, though perhaps, she would rather preferred that one: The vanquished fair-one quietly submitted, I say, to her master's will, who had just attained the accomplishment of his bliss, when Mrs Tow-wouse unexpectedly entered the room, and caused all that confusion which we have before seen, and which it is not necessary at present to take any farther notice of: since without the assistance of a single hint from us, every reader of any speculation, or experience, though not married himself, may easily conjecture, that it concluded with the discharge of Betty, the submission of Mr Tow-wouse, with some things to be performed on his side by way of gratitude for his wife's goodness in being reconciled to him, with many hearty promises never to offend any more in the like manner: and lastly, his quietly and contentedly bearing to be reminded of his transgressions, as a kind of penance, once or twice a day, during the Residue of his Life.

Ibid.

Once Joseph was joined at the inn by Parson Adams the parody element disappeared almost completely from the book, as though Fielding had suddenly found that he enjoyed writing about his new character more than he did further lampooning Samuel Richardson.

Abraham Adams was the 'Quixote' of the story; a physically strong, slightly vain, desperately poor parson who was truly holy but unworldy, absent-minded, and guileless.

Towards the end of the book Parson Adams and Joseph stay the night at Lady Booby's country house. Also present are Joseph's chaste sweetheart Fanny, Mrs Slipslop, and a lecherous rake, Beau Didapper, who has designs on Fanny. The plot of the mix-ups that occur that night are echoed in Smollett's Humphrey Clinker *and again in Dickens's* Pickwick Papers. *It might well be the archetype of all 'wrong bedroom' chapters:*

Containing several curious Night-Adventures, in which Mr Adams fell into many Hair-breadth 'Scapes, partly owing to his Goodness, and partly to his Inadvertency.

About an hour after they had all separated (it being now past three in the morning), Beau Didapper, whose passion for Fanny permitted him not to close his eyes, but had employed his imagination in contrivances how to satisfy his desires, at last hit on a method by which he hoped to effect it. He had ordered his servant to bring him word where Fanny lay, and had received his information; he therefore arose, put on his breeches and nightgown, and stole softly along the gallery which led to her apartment; and, being come to the door, as he imagined it, he opened it with the least noise possible and entered the chamber.

A savour now invaded his nostrils which he did not expect in the room of so sweet a young creature, and which might have probably had no good effect on a cooler lover. However, he groped out the bed with difficulty, for there was not a glimpse of light, and, opening the curtains, he whispered in Joseph's voice (for he was an excellent mimic), 'Fanny, my angel! I am come to inform thee that I have discovered the falsehood of the story we last night heard. I am no longer thy brother, but thy lover; nor will I be delayed the enjoyment of thee one moment longer. You have sufficient assurances of my constancy not to doubt my marrying you, and it would be want of love to deny me the possession of thy charms.'—So saying, he disencumbered himself from the little clothes he had on, and, leaping into bed, embraced his angel, as he conceived her, with great rapture.

If he was surprised at receiving no answer, he was no less pleased to find his hug returned with equal ardour. He remained not long in this sweet confusion; for both he and his paramour presently discovered their error. Indeed it was no other than the accomplished Slipslop whom he had engaged; but, though she immediately knew the person whom she had mistaken for Joseph, he was at a loss to guess at the representative of Fanny. He had so little seen or taken notice of this gentlewoman, that light itself would have afforded him no assistance in his conjecture.

Beau Didapper no sooner had perceived his mistake than he attempted to escape from the bed with much greater haste than he had made to it; but the watchful Slipslop prevented him. For that prudent woman, being disappointed of those delicious offerings which her fancy had promised her pleasure, resolved to make an immediate sacrifice to her virtue. Indeed she wanted an opportunity to heal some wounds, which her late conduct had, she feared, given her reputation; and, as she had a wonderful presence of mind, she conceived the person of the unfortunate beau to be luckily thrown in her way to restore her lady's opinion of her impregnable chastity. At that instant, therefore, when he offered to leap from the bed, she caught fast hold of his shirt, at the same time roaring out, 'O thou villain! who hast attacked my chastity, and, I believe, ruined me in my sleep; I will swear a rape against thee, I will prosecute thee with the utmost vengeance.'

The beau attempted to get loose, but she held him fast, and when he struggled she cried out 'Murder! murder! rape! robbery! ruin!'

At which words, parson Adams, who lay in the next chamber, wakeful, and meditating on the pedlar's discovery, jumped out of bed, and, without staying to put a rag of clothes on, hastened into the apartment whence the cries proceeded. He made directly to the bed in the dark, where, laying hold of the beau's skin (for Slipslop had torn his shirt almost off), and finding his skin extremely soft, and hearing him in a low voice begging Slipslop to let him go, he no longer doubted but this was the young woman in danger of ravishing, and immediately falling on the bed, and laying hold on Slipslop's chin, where he found a rough beard, his belief was confirmed; he therefore rescued the beau, who presently made his escape, and then, turning towards Slipslop, received such a cuff on his chops, that, his wrath kindling instantly, he offered to return the favour so stoutly, that had poor Slipslop received the fist, which in the dark passed by her and fell on the pillow, she would most probably have given up the ghost.

Adams, missing his blow, fell directly on Slipslop, who cuffed and scratched as well as she could; nor was he behindhand with her in his endeavours, but happily the darkness of the night befriended her. She then cried she was a woman; but Adams answered, she was rather the devil, and if she was he would grapple with him; and, being again irritated by another stroke on his chops, he gave her such a remembrance in the guts, that she began to roar loud enough to be heard all over the house. Adams then, seizing her by the hair (for her double clout had fallen off in the scuffle), pinned her head down to the bolster, and then both called for lights together.

The Lady Booby, who was as wakeful as any of her guests, had been alarmed from the beginning; and, being a woman of a bold spirit, she slipt on a nightgown, petticoat, and slippers, and taking a candle, which always burnt in her chamber, in her hand, she walked undauntedly to Slipslop's room; where she entered just at the instant as Adams had discovered, by the two mountains which Slipslop carried before her, that he was concerned with a female. He then concluded her to be a witch, and said he fancied those breasts gave suck to a legion of devils.

Slipslop, seeing Lady Booby enter the room, cried 'Help! or I am ravished,' with a most audible voice: and Adams, perceiving the light, turned hastily, and saw the lady (as she did him) just as she came to the feet of the bed; nor did her modesty, when she found the naked condition of Adams, suffer her to approach farther. She then began to revile the parson as the wickedest of all men, and particularly railed at his impudence in choosing her house for the scene of his debaucheries, and her own woman for the object of his bestiality.

Poor Adams had before discovered the countenance of his bedfellow, and, now first recollecting he was naked, he was no less confounded than Lady Booby herself, and immediately whipt under the bedclothes, whence the chaste Slipslop endeavoured in vain to shut him out. Then putting forth his head, on which, by way of ornament, he wore a flannel nightcap, he protested his innocence, and asked ten thousand pardons of Mrs Slipslop for the blows he had struck her, vowing he had mistaken her for a witch.

Lady Booby then casting her eyes on the ground, observed something sparkle with great lustre, which, when she had taken it up, appeared to be a very fine pair of diamond buttons for the sleeves. A little farther she saw lie the sleeve itself of a shirt with laced ruffles. 'Heyday!' says she, 'what is the meaning of this?' 'O, madam,' says Slipslop, 'I don't know what hath happened, I have been so terrified. Here may have been a dozen men in the room.' 'To whom belongs this laced shirt and jewels?' says the lady. 'Undoubtedly,' cries the parson, 'to the young gentleman whom I mistook for a woman on coming into the room, whence proceeded all the subsequent mistakes; for if I had suspected him for a man, I would have seized him, had he been another Hercules, though, indeed, he seems rather to resemble Hylas.'

He then gave an account of the reason of his rising from bed and the rest, till the lady came into the room; at which, and the figures of Slipslop and her gallant, whose head only were visible at the opposite corners of the bed, she could not refrain from laughter; nor did Slipslop persist in accusing the parson of any motions towards a rape. The lady therefore desired him to return to his bed as soon as she was departed, and then ordering Slipslop to rise and attend her in her own room, she returned herself thither.

When she was gone, Adams renewed his petitions for pardon to Mrs Slipslop, who, with a most Christian temper, not only forgave, but began to move with much courtesy towards him, which he taking as a hint to begin, immediately quitted the bed, and made the best of his way towards his own; but unluckily, instead of turning to the right, he turned to the left, and went to the apartment where Fanny lay, who (as the reader may remember) had not slept a wink the preceding night, and who was so hagged out with what had happened to her in the day, that, notwithstanding all thoughts of her Joseph, she was fallen into so profound a sleep, that all the noise in the adjoining room had not been able to disturb her.

Adams groped out the bed, and, turning the clothes down softly, a custom Mrs Adams had long accustomed him to, crept in, and deposited his carcase on the bed-post, a place which that good woman had always assigned him.

As the cat or lap-dog of some lovely nymph, for whom ten thousand lovers languish, lies quietly by the side of the charming maid, and, ignorant of the scene of delight on which they repose, meditates the future capture of a mouse, or surprisal of a plate of bread and butter: so Adams lay by the side of Fanny, ignorant of the paradise to which he was so near; nor could the emanation of sweets which flowed from her breath overpower the fumes of tobacco which played in the parsons's nostrils.

And now sleep had not overtaken the good man, when Joseph, who had secretly appointed Fanny to come to her at the break of day [to make an early start on their journey], rapped softly at the chamber-door, which when he had repeated twice, Adams cried, 'Come in, whoever you are.' Joseph thought he had mistaken the door, though she had given him the most exact directions; however, knowing his friend's voice, he opened it, and saw some female vestments lying on a chair.

Fanny waking at the same instant, and stretching out her hand on Adams's beard, she cried out,—'O heavens! where am I?' 'Bless me! where am I?' said the parson. Then Fanny screamed, Adams leapt out of bed, and Joseph stood, as the tragedians call it, like the statue of Surprise.

'How came she into my room?' cried Adams. 'How came you into hers?' cried Joseph, in an astonishment.

'I know nothing of the matter' answered Adams, 'but that she is a vestal for me. As I am a Christian, I know not whether she is a man or woman. He is an infidel who doth not believe in witchcraft. They as surely exist now as in the days of Saul. My clothes are bewitched away too, and Fanny's brought into their place.' For he still insisted he was in his own apartment: but Fanny denied it vehemently, and said his attempting to persuade Joseph of such a falsehood convinced her of his wicked designs.

'How!' said Joseph in a rage, 'hath he offered any rudeness to you?' She answered—She could not accuse him of any more than villanously stealing to bed to her, which she thought rudeness sufficient, and what no man would do without a wicked intention.

Joseph's great opinion of Adams was not easily to be staggered, and when he heard from Fanny that no harm had happened he grew a little cooler; yet still he was confounded, and, as he knew the house, and that the women's apartments were on this side Mrs Slipslop's room, and the men's on the other, he was convinced that he was in Fanny's chamber. Assuring Adams therefore of this truth, he begged him to give some account how he came there. Adams then, standing in his shirt, which did not offend Fanny, as the curtains of the bed were drawn, related all that had happened; and when he had ended Joseph told him,—It was plain he had mistaken by turning to the right instead of the left. 'Odso!' cries Adams, 'that's true: as sure as sixpence, you have hit on the very thing.'

He then traversed the room, rubbing his hands, and begged Fanny's pardon, assuring her he did not know whether she was man or woman. That innocent creature firmly believing all he said, told him she was no longer angry, and begged Joseph to conduct him into his own apartment, where he should stay himself till she had put her clothes on.

Joseph and Adams accordingly departed, and the latter soon was convinced of the mistake he had committed; however, whilst he was dressing himself, he often asserted he believed in the power of witchcraft notwithstanding, and did not see how a Christian could deny it.

Ibid.

——

THE splendidly named Tobias Smollett was a Scot who went to sea as a surgeon's mate, became an unsuccessful physician ashore and then devoted himself to making a living in literature. He translated Don Quixote *and Le Sage's* Gil Blas, *and was much influenced, as were Fielding and Laurence Sterne, by the picaresque novel (from the Spanish* picaro, *a rogue) which took the form of describing the survival of a non-hero through a series of loosely-knit adventures, some dangerous, some comical.*

Smollett was noted for his aggression and bad temper—Laurence Sterne came up against him when travelling through Italy and dubbed him 'Smelfungus'—and much of his writing was coarse-grained and morbidly concerned with cruelty and nastiness, but it had great vitality and a powerful narrative flow.

The continental travelling resulted in Sterne writing the gentle and sensitive Sentimental Journey *and Smollett producing* Travels Through France and Italy; *cantankerous and violently critical of foreign ways but full of accurate observation recorded in lean, strong prose.*

Here Smollett comes across a filthy French habit at the dining table:

There is nothing so vile or repugnant to nature; but you may plead prescription for it, in the customs of some nation or other. A Parisian likes mortified flesh: a native of Legiboli will not taste his fish till it is quite putrefied: the civilized inhabitants of Kamschatka get drunk with the urine

of their guests, whom they have already intoxicated: the Nova Zemblans
make merry on train-oil: the Greenlanders eat in the same dish with their
dogs: the Caffres, at the Cape of Good Hope, piss upon those whom they
delight to honour, and feast upon a sheep's intestines with their contents, as
the greatest dainty that can be presented. A true-bred Frenchman dips his
fingers, imbrowned with snuff, into his plate filled with ragout: between
every three mouthfuls, he produces his snuff-box, and takes a fresh pinch,
with the most graceful gesticulations; then he displays his handkerchief,
which may be termed the flag of abomination, and, in the use of both, scatters
his favours among those who have the happiness to sit near him.

Tobias Smollett (1721–71), *Travels in France and Italy* (1766).

*The ladies of France did little to mollify Smollett's exasperation with the nasty
ways of foreigners.*

Will custom exempt from the imputation of gross indecency a French lady,
who shifts her frowsy smock in presence of a male visitant, and talks to him
of her *lavement*, her *medicine*, and her *bidet*! An Italian *signora* makes no
scruple of telling you, she is such a day to begin a course of physic for the
pox. The celebrated reformer of the Italian comedy introduces a child be-
fouling itself on the stage, OE, NO TI SENTI? BISOGNA DESFASSARLO, (*fa cenno che
sentesi mal odore*). I have known a lady handed to the house of office by her
admirer, who stood at the door, and entertained her with *bon mots* all the
time she was within. But I should be glad to know, whether it is possible for
a fine lady to speak and act in this manner, without exciting ideas to her
own disadvantage in the mind of every man who has any imagination left,
and enjoys the entire use of his senses, howsoever she may be authorised by
the customs of her country?

Ibid.

*In his novels Smollett seemed more interested in the bad aspects of his characters
than in their good qualities and he devised much unpleasantness for them to endure,
but this was coupled with a facility for endless comic invention. He was the first
novelist to write about life in the navy, and one of his creations, the ex-sailor
Commodore Hawser Trunnion, is generally accepted as being the first major fully-
realized comical character in the English novel.*

*The Commodore, an irascible one-eyed sea-dog, lived in retirement with Lieu-
tenant Hatchway—who had one leg—as his companion. His house was protected
against surprise attack from the enemy with battlements and a moat, and inside it
was run like a ship-of-the-line with everybody sleeping in hammocks and taking
their turn on watch. The Commodore spoke entirely in naval jargon, which was a
comical innovation at that time.*

*The Commodore is to be married to Grizzle Pickle, aunt of the novel's 'hero',
Peregrine. He decides to ride to the church on horseback, navigating his steed by*

compass. In keeping with the best traditions of the Royal Navy, the Commodore is
hopeless on a horse:

The fame of this extraordinary conjunction spread all over the county; and
on the day appointed for their spousals, the church was surrounded by an
inconceivable multitude. The commodore, to give a specimen of his gallantry,
by the advice of his friend Hatchway, resolved to appear on horseback on
the grand occasion, at the head of all his male attendants, whom he had
rigged with the white shirts and black caps formerly belonging to his barge's
crew; and he bought a couple of hunters for the accommodation of himself
and his lieutenant. With this equipage then he set out from the garrison for
the church, after having dispatched a messenger to apprise the bride that he
and his company were mounted.

She got immediately into the coach, accompanied by her brother and his
wife, and drove directly to the place of assignation, where several pews were
demolished and divers persons almost pressed to death, by the eagerness of
the crowd that broke in to see the ceremony performed. Thus arrived at the
altar, and the priest in attendance, they waited a whole half hour for the
commodore, at whose slowness they began to be under some apprehension,
and accordingly dismissed a servant to quicken his pace.

The valet having rode something more than a mile, espied the whole troop
disposed in a long field, crossing the road obliquely, and headed by the
bridegroom and his friend Hatchway, who, finding himself hindered by a
hedge from proceeding farther in the same direction, fired a pistol, and stood
over to the other side, making an obtuse angle with the line of his former
course; and the rest of the squadron followed his example, keeping always
in the rear of each other like a flight of wild geese.

Surprised at this strange method of journeying, the messenger came up,
and told the commodore that his lady and her company expected him in the
church, where they had tarried a considerable time, and were beginning to
be very uneasy at his delay; and therefore desired he would proceed with
more expedition. To this message Mr Trunnion replied,—'Hark ye, brother,
don't you see we make all possible speed? go back, and tell those who sent
you, that the wind has shifted since we weighed anchor, and that we are
obliged to make very short trips in tacking, by reason of the narrowness of
the channel: and that as we lie within six points of the wind, they must
make some allowance for variation and leeway.' 'Lord, sir!' said the valet,
'what occasion have you to go zig-zag in that manner? do but clap spurs to
your horses, and ride straight forward, and I'll engage you shall be at the
church-porch in less than a quarter of an hour.' 'What! right in the wind's
eye?' answered the commander, 'ahey! brother, where did you learn your
navigation? Hawser Trunnion is not to be taught at this time of day how to
lie his course, or keep his own reckoning. And as for you, brother, you best
know the trim of your own frigate.'...

The commodore and his crew had, by dint of turning, almost weathered the parson's house that stood to windward of the church, when the notes of a pack of hounds unluckily reached the ears of the two hunters which Trunnion and the lieutenant bestrode. These fleet animals no sooner heard the enlivening sound, than, eager for the chase, they sprung away all of a sudden, and straining every nerve to partake of the sport, flew across the fields with incredible speed, overleaped hedges and ditches, and everything in their way, without the least regard to their unfortunate riders.

The lieutenant, whose steed had got the heels of the other, finding it would be great folly and presumption in him to pretend to keep the saddle with his wooden leg, very wisely took the opportunity of throwing himself off in his passage through a field of rich clover, among which he lay at his ease; and seeing his captain advancing at full gallop, hailed him with the salutation of 'what cheer, ho!' The commodore, who was in infinite distress, eyeing him askance, as he passed, replied with a faltering voice,—'O damn you! you are safe at anchor; I wish to God I were as fast moored.' Nevertheless, conscious of his disabled heel, he would not venture to try the experiment which had succeeded so well with Hatchway, but resolved to stick as close as possible to his horse's back, until Providence should interpose on his behalf. With this view he dropped his whip, and with his right hand laid fast hold on the pummel, contracting every muscle in his body to secure himself in the seat, and grinning most formidably, in consequence of this exertion.

In this attitude he was hurried on a considerable way, when all of a sudden his view was comforted by a five-bar gate that appeared before him, as he never doubted that there the career of his hunter must necessarily end. But, alas! he reckoned without his host: Far from halting at this obstruction, the horse sprung over it with amazing agility, to the utter confusion and disorder of his owner, who lost his hat and periwig in the leap, and now began to think in earnest that he was actually mounted on the back of the devil. He recommended himself to God, his reflection forsook him, his eyesight and all his other senses failed, he quitted the reins, and, fastening by instinct on the mane, was in this condition conveyed into the midst of the sportsmen, who were astonished at the sight of such an apparition . . .

Our bridegroom finding himself at last brought up, or in other words, at the end of his career, took the opportunity of this first pause, to desire the huntsmen would lend him a hand in dismounting; and was by their condescension safely placed on the grass, where he sat staring at the company as they came in, with such wildness of astonishment in his looks, as if he had been a creature of another species, dropt among them from the clouds . . .

Trunnion was set upon the squire's own horse, and led by his servant in the midst of this cavalcade, which proceeded to a neighbouring village, where they had bespoke dinner, and where our bridegroom found means to provide himself with another hat and wig. With regard to his marriage, he bore his disappointment with the temper of a philosopher; and the exercise he had undergone having quickened his appetite, sat down at table in the midst of his new acquaintances, making a very hearty meal, and moistening every morsel with a draught of the ale, which he found very much to his satisfaction.   *The Adventures of Peregrine Pickle* (1751).

Smollett's last and most agreeable novel was The Expedition of Humphry Clinker, *which was published in 1771, the year of his death at the age of 50. It was a much mellower and kindlier piece of work than anything he had published before, and it had more humour.*

As usual it was a picaresque story, telling in a series of letters the travels through England and Scotland of Matthew Bramble, an old bachelor, and his party. Among those present were Bramble's spinster sister Tabitha, a husband-hungry virago; his nephew Jerry, a cheerful lad; his niece, the sweet and pretty Lydia; and his maid, Winifred Jenkins.

Lieutenant Obadiah Lismahago, a poor and argumentative Scot, joined them later. Humphry Clinker himself, a ragged ostler, appeared a third of the way through and was taken on by Bramble as a servant.

Five of the group wrote letters telling their friends how the expedition was progressing. The maid, like Fielding's Mrs Slipslop, and Sheridan's Mrs Malaprop in The Rivals *four years later, used any words which sounded vaguely like the ones she had in mind.*

The following letter, nevertheless, is an interesting and accurate account of some aspects of life in Edinburgh in the late eighteenth century—including the sanitary arrangements necessary in a city built on solid rock:

To Mrs Mary Jones, at Brambleton-hall.

Dear Mary,
The 'squire has been so kind as to rap my bit of nonsense under the kiver of his own sheet—O, Mary Jones! Mary Jones! I have had trials and trembulation. God help me! I have been a vixen and a griffin these days—Sattin has had power to temp me in the shape of van Ditton, the young 'squire's wally de shamble; but by God's grease he did not purvail—I thoft as how, there was no arm in going to a play at Newcastle, with my hair dressed in the Parish fashion; and as for the trifle of paint, he said as how my complexion wanted rouch, and so I let him put it on with a little Spanish owl; but a mischievous mob of colliers, and such promiscous ribbel rabble, that could bare no smut but their own, attacked us in the street, and called me *hoar* and painted *Issabel*, and splashed my close, and spoiled me a complete set of blond lace triple ruffles, not a pin the worse for the ware—They cost me seven good sillings, to lady Griskin's woman at London . . .

And now, dear Mary, we have got to Haddingborrough, among the Scots, who are civil enuff for our money, thof I don't speak their lingo—But they should not go for to impose upon foreigners; for the bills in their houses say, they have different *easements* to let; and behold there is nurro geaks in the whole kingdom, nor any thing for poor sarvants, but a barrel with a pair of tongs thrown across; and all the chairs in the family are emptied into this here barrel once a-day; and at ten o'clock at night the whole cargo is flung out of a back windore that looks into some street or lane, and the maid calls *gardy loo* to the passengers, which signifies Lord have mercy upon you! and this is done every night in every house in Haddingborrough; so you may guess, Mary Jones, what a sweet savour comes from such a number of profuming pans; but they say it is wholsome, and, truly, I believe it is; for being in the vapours, and thinking of Issabel and Mr Clinker, I was going into a fit of astericks, when this fiff, saving your preference, took me by the nose so powerfully that I sneezed three times, and found myself wonderfully refreshed; and this to be sure is the raisin why there are no fits in Haddingborrough . . .

Remember me kindly to Saul and the kitten—I hope they got the horn-buck, and will put it to a good yuse, which is the constant prayer of,

Dear Molly,
your loving friend,

Addingborough, July 18.   Win. Jenkins.

The Expedition of Humphry Clinker (1771).

Smollett had five colourfully different characters writing the letters so he was able to make ironic humour from descriptions of the same event as seen from opposing points of view.

Here the delights of a visit to the famous pleasure gardens of Ranelagh and Vauxhall are described by the charming Lydia in a letter to her friend Laetitia:

To Miss Laetitia Willis, at Gloucester.

My dear Letty,

Ranelagh looks like the inchanted palace of a genie, adorned with the most exquisite performances of painting, carving and gilding, enlightened with a thousand golden lamps, that emulate the noon-day sun; crowded with the great, the rich, the gay, the happy, and the fair; glittering with cloth of gold and silver, lace, embroidery, and precious stones. While these exulting sons and daughters of felicity tread this round of pleasure, or regale in different parties, and separate lodges, with fine imperial tea and other delicious refreshments, their ears are entertained with the most ravishing delights of musick, both instrumental and vocal. There I heard the famous Tenducci, a thing from Italy—It looks for all the world like a man, though they say it is not. The voice, to be sure, is neither man's nor woman's; but it is more melodious than either; and it warbled so divinely, that, while I listened, I really thought myself in paradise.

At nine o'clock, in a charming moonlight evening, we embarked at Ranelagh for Vauxhall, in a wherry, so light and slender, that we looked like so many fairies sailing in a nut-shell . . .

Image to yourself, my dear Letty, a spacious garden, part laid out in delightful walks, bounded with high hedges and trees, and paved with gravel; part exhibiting a wonderful assemblage of the most picturesque and striking objects, pavilions, lodges, groves, grottoes, lawns, temples, and calcades; porticoes, colonades, and rotundos; adorned with pillars, statues, and painting: the whole illuminated with an infinite number of lamps, disposed in different figures of suns, stars and constellations; the place crowded with the gayest company, ranging through those blissful shades, of supping in different lodges on cold collations, enlivened with mirth, freedom, and good-humour, and animated by an excellent band of musick. Among the vocal performers I had the happiness to hear the celebrated Mrs ——, whose voice was so loud and so shrill, that it made my head ake through excess of pleasure . . .

I wish my weak head may not grow giddy in the midst of all this gallantry and dissipation; though, as yet, I can safely declare I could safely give up all these tumultuous pleasures, for country solitude, and a happy retreat with those we love; among whom my dear Willis will always possess the first place in the breast of her

ever affectionate
Lydia Melford.

London, May 31.

Ibid.

The elderly, grumpy, hypochondriacal Matthew Bramble also visited Ranelagh.

In a letter to his physician friend he describes what he thinks of the pleasure gardens:

To Dr Lewis.

Dear Doctor,

What are the amusements at Ranelagh? One half of the company are following one another's tails, in an eternal circle; like so many blind asses in an olive-mill, where they can neither discourse, distinguish, nor be distinguished; while the other half are drinking hot water, under the denomination of tea, till nine or ten o'clock at night, to keep them awake for the rest of the evening. As for the orchestra, the vocal music especially, it is well for the performers that they cannot be heard distinctly. Vauxhall is a composition of baubles, overcharged with paltry ornaments, ill conceived, and poorly executed; without any unity of design, or propriety of disposition. It is an unnatural assembly of objects, fantastically illuminated in broken masses; seemingly contrived to dazzle the eyes and divert the imagination of the vulgar—Here a wooden lion, there a stone statue; in one place, a range of things like coffee-house boxes, covered atop; in another, a parcel of ale-house benches; in a third, a puppet-show representation of a tin cascade; in a fourth, a gloomy cave of a circular form, like a sepulchral vault half lighted; in a fifth, a scanty slip of grass-plat, that would not afford pasture sufficient for an ass's colt. The walks, which nature seems to have intended for solitude, shade, and silence, are filled with crowds of noisy people, sucking up the nocturnal rheums of an aguish climate; and through these gay scenes, a few lamps glimmer like so many farthing candles.

When I see a number of well-dressed people, of both sexes, sitting on the covered benches, exposed to the eyes of the mob; and, which is worse, to the cold, raw, night-air, devouring sliced beef, and swilling port, and punch, and cider, I can't help compassionating their temerity, while I despise their want of taste and decorum; but, when they course along those damp and gloomy walks, or crowd together upon the wet gravel, without any other cover than the cope of Heaven, listening to a song, which one half of them cannot possibly hear, how can I help supposing they are actually possessed by a spirit, more absurd and pernicious than any thing we meet with in the precincts of Bedlam? In all probability, the proprietors of this, and other public gardens of inferior note, in the skirts of the metropolis, are, in some shape, connected with the faculty of physic, and the company of undertakers; for, considering that eagerness in the pursuit of what is called pleasure, which now predominates through every rank and denomination of life, I am persuaded, that more gouts, rheumatisms, catarrhs, and consumptions are caught in these nocturnal pastimes, *sub dio*, than from all the risques and accidents to which a life of toil and danger is exposed.

yours always,

London, May 29th.   Matt. Bramble.

Ibid.

---

*L*AURENCE STERNE'S *contribution to the development of the comic English novel was to turn the form upside down, or perhaps inside out, and send it galloping off in all directions.* The Life and Opinions of Tristram Shandy, Gent. *was so eccentric in style that families were divided and friendships put to the test—and still are—in arguments over whether it was a work of comic genius or a boring muddle.*

Famous men took sides. The novelists Samuel Richardson and Tobias Smollett were vehemently critical. Samuel Johnson, offended by the book's many indecencies (and even more offended by being at a party where Sterne handed round a filthy picture) said, at a time when sales were drooping a little, 'Nothing odd will do long. Tristram Shandy *did not last.' Horace Walpole found the book 'insipid and tedious'. Oliver Goldsmith called Sterne 'a bawdy blockhead'. On the other hand, Bishop Warburton recommended the book to 'the best company in town', and Garrick loved it. Lord Ossory commissioned Reynolds to paint Sterne's portrait. Noblemen such as Lord Rockingham and Earl Bathurst took him up and his social life was so busy that it was said that every minute of his time was booked for a month ahead.*

Sterne was an Irishman, a not-very-holy parson with a parish in Yorkshire. He took to writing in his early forties and found that he enjoyed it. Unlike Richardson and Fielding he was no moralist; he wrote to be famous. In 1760 the first two volumes of Tristram Shandy *were published in York, but Dodsley the London bookseller took a few. The book's success with London society was so spectacular that Dodsley commissioned Sterne to write a further volume a year for the rest of his life. Sterne lived long enough to write nine.*

It was certainly an odd book. Among its physical eccentricities were its strange punctuation, with lavish use of dashes and rows of asterisks; a black page to commemorate the death of parson Yorick; a blank page for readers to write down their own mental picture of the desirable Widow Wadnam; a marbled page; the Roman Catholic form for excommunication, with a Latin version on the left-hand page; the words and music of 'Lillabullero'; and chapters which varied greatly in length.

Here is one chapter in its entirety:

CHAPTER FIVE

Is this a fit time, said my father to himself, to talk of *pensions* and *grenadiers?*

> Laurence Sterne (1713–1768), *The Life and Opinions of Tristram Shandy, Gent.,* vol. iv (1761).

What upset those readers who could not get on with the book was its lack of any apparent shape. The title itself made no sense as the book described the life of Uncle Toby, if anybody, and the opinions of Walter Shandy, Tristram's father. Tristram himself was conceived on page one but was not born until volume IV and vanished from the story altogether in volume VI.

Sterne based the circumstances of Tristram's absent-minded conception on the philosopher John Locke's theory of the association of ideas. Mr Shandy had formed the habit of performing two marital duties on the first Sunday night of every month: winding the clock and obliging Mrs Shandy with her conjugal rights. These two events became so associated in Mrs Shandy's mind, 'that my poor mother could never hear the said clock wound up,—but the thoughts of some other things popped into her head—& vice versa':

CHAPTER ONE

I wish either my father or my mother, or indeed both of them, as they were in duty both equally bound to it, had minded what they were about when they begot me; had they duly considered how much depended upon what they were then doing;—that not only the production of a rational Being was concerned in it, but that possibly the happy formation and temperature of his body, perhaps his genius and the very cast of his mind;—and, for aught they knew to the contrary, even the fortunes of his whole house might take their turn from the humours and dispositions which were then uppermost:— Had they duly weighed and considered all this, and proceeded accordingly,— I am verily persuaded I should have made a quite different figure in the world, from that in which the reader is likely to see me.—Believe me, good folks, this is not so inconsiderable a thing as many of you may think it;—you have all, I dare say, heard of the animal spirits, as how they are transfused from father to son &c. &c.—and a great deal to that purpose:—Well, you may take my word, that nine parts in ten of a man's sense or his nonsense, his successes and miscarriages in this world depend upon their motions and activity, and the different tracts and trains you put them into, so that when they are once set a-going, whether right or wrong, 'tis not a halfpenny matter,—away they go cluttering like hey-go-mad; and by treading the same steps over and over again, they presently make a road of it, as plain and as smooth as a garden-walk, which, when they are once used to, the Devil himself sometimes shall not be able to drive them off it.

Pray, my dear, quoth my mother, *have you not forgot to wind up the clock?—Good G—!* cried my father, making an exclamation, but taking care to moderate his voice at the same time,—*Did ever woman, since the creation of the world, interrupt a man with such a silly question?*

Ibid., vol i.

The long pseudo-scholastic digressions in the manner of Rabelais and Robert Burton, and the little unresolved plots which circled each other and interlocked like a conjuror's magic rings, were not haphazard. Sterne had it all under control and the book, however eccentric, was a work of art.

For the first time dialogue was written with the fits and starts and repetitions of vernacular speech. It was the first major novel to involve itself in unromantic domestic affairs. It, and Sentimental Journey, *were the first works to develop the 'sentimental' approach, the subjective writing which is more concerned with the effect of an event on the senses of the beholder than with the event itself. It was the first tentative step towards the 'stream of consciousness' writings which were to be developed much later by Virginia Woolf and James Joyce.*

What made Tristram Shandy *last, and prove Johnson wrong, was the quality and originality of the humour. At the heart of the book were four memorable and lovable characters: 'my father', Walter Shandy, was a retired merchant with a compulsion to turn every issue into a philosophical disputation. Unhappily nobody would dispute with him. His brother, Uncle Toby, had been wounded in the groin at the siege of Namur and happily spent his retirement restaging sieges in miniature on his bowling-green. He was helped by his servant Corporal Trim—wounded in the knee—who was loyal and voluble. Walter was unable to argue with Uncle Toby because Uncle Toby, kind and willing though he was, was incapable of understanding anything which could not be expressed in siege terminology so usually said nothing and whistled 'Lillabullero'.*

Walter tried hard to dispute with his wife but the good Mrs Shandy was no philosopher and, to his frustration, placidly agreed with everything he said:

It was a consuming vexation to my father, that my mother never asked the meaning of a thing she did not understand.

—That she is not a woman of science, my father would say—is her misfortune—but she might ask a question.

My mother never did.—In short, she went out of the world at last without knowing whether it turned *round* or stood *still*.—My father had officiously told her above a thousand times which way it was,—but she always forgot.

Ibid., vol. vi, chap. 39

In those days one of the really important milestones in a small boy's life, a kind of gentile bar-mitzvah, *was when he was big enough to be taken out of the tunics which all children wore and put into his first pair of real, grown-ups' breeches.*

The decision to do this with Tristram occupied a whole chapter:

CHAPTER FIFTEEN

—I'll put him, however, into breeches, said my father,—let the world say what it will.

Ibid., vol. vi.

The details of the breeching had to be properly discussed with Mrs Shandy so 'my father' resolved on holding what he called two beds of justice. *These were discussions held in bed over two nights, one night being the first Sunday of the month—the significance of which we are fully aware—and the other on the previous night. 'My father' reasoned that the mood of each night would be different so truth would lie in a compromise between the two discussions.*

We join them on the Sunday:

We should begin, said my father, turning himself half-round in bed, and shifting his pillow a little towards my mother's, as he opened the debate—We should begin to think, Mrs Shandy, of putting this boy into breeches.—

We should so,—said my mother.—We defer it, my dear, quoth my father, shamefully.—

I think we do, Mr Shandy,—said my mother,

—Not but the child looks extremely well, said my father, in his vest and tunics.—

He does look very well in them,—replied my mother.—

—And for that reason it would be almost a sin, added my father, to take him out of 'em.—

—It would so,—said my mother:—But indeed he is growing a very tall lad,—rejoined my father.

—He is very tall for his age, indeed,—said my mother.—

—I can not (making two syllables of it) imagine, quoth my father, who the deuce he takes after.—

I cannot conceive, for my life,—said my mother.

Humph!—said my father.

(The dialogue ceased for a moment.)

—I am very short myself,—continued my father, gravely.

You are very short, Mr Shandy,—said my mother . . .

I am resolved, however, quoth my father, breaking silence the fourth time, he shall have no pockets in them.—

—There is no occasion for any, said my mother.—

I mean in his coat and waistcoat,—cried my father.

—I mean so too,—replied my mother.

—Though if he gets a gig or a top—Poor souls! it is a crown and scepter to them,—they should have where to secure it.—

—Order it as you please, Mr Shandy, replied my mother.—

—But don't you think it right? added my father, pressing the point home to her.

Perfectly, said my mother, if it pleases you, Mr Shandy.—

—There's for you! cried my father, losing temper—Pleases me! You never will distinguish, Mrs Shandy, nor shall I ever teach you to do it, betwixt a point of pleasure and a point of convenience.—This was on the Sunday night;—and further this chapter sayeth not.

Ibid., vol.vi, chap. 18.

One of the most extraordinary and original features of Sterne's style was his way of occasionally describing an incident, a gesture, a posture, in minute detail.

The effect was as if the book was illustrated, but with word-pictures rather than drawings:

I cannot conceive how it is possible, quoth my uncle Toby, for such a thing as a sermon to have got into my Stevinus.

I think 'tis a sermon, replied Trim;—but if it please your Honours, as it is a fair hand, I will read you a page;—for Trim, you must know, loved to hear himself read, almost as well as talk . . .

Begin, Trim,—and read distinctly, quoth my father.—I will, an' please your honour, replied the corporal, making a bow, and bespeaking attention with a slight movement of his right hand . . .

—But before the corporal begins, I must first give you a description of his attitude;—otherwise he will naturally stand represented, by your imagination, in an uneasy posture,—stiff,—perpendicular,—dividing the weight of his body equally upon both legs;—his eye fixed, as if on duty,—his look determined,—clinching the sermon in his left hand, like his firelock:—In a word, you would be apt to paint Trim, as if he was standing in his platoon ready for action:—His attitude was as unlike all this as you can conceive.

He stood before them with his body swayed and bent forward, just so far, as to make an angle of 85 degrees and a half upon the plane of the horizon;—which sound orators, to whom I address this, know very well to be the true persuasive angle of incidence:—in any other angle you may talk and preach—'tis certain;—and it is done every day;—but with what effect,—I leave the world to judge!

The necessity of this precise angle of 85 degrees and a half, to a mathematical exactness,—does it not show us, by the way,—how the arts and sciences mutually befriend each other?

How the deuce Corporal Trim, who knew not so much as an acute angle from an obtuse one, came to hit it so exactly;—or whether it was chance, or nature, or good sense or imitation, &c. shall be commented upon in that part of this cyclopædia of arts and sciences, where the instrumental parts of the eloquence of the senate, the pulpit, the bar, the coffee-house, the bed-chamber, and fire-side, fall under consideration.

He stood,—For I repeat it, to take the picture of him in at one view, with his body swayed, and somewhat bent forwards,—his right leg firm under him, sustaining seven-eighths of his whole weight,—the foot of his left leg, the defect of which was no disadvantage to his attitude, advanced a little,—not laterally, nor forwards, but in a line betwixt them;—his knee bent, but that not violently,—but so as to fall within the limits of the line of beauty;—and I add, of the line of science too;—for consider, it had one-eighth of his body to bear up;—so that, in this case, the position of the leg is determined,—because the foot could be no further advanced, or the knee more bent, than what would allow him mechanically, to receive an eighth part of his whole weight under it,—and to carry it too.

☞ This I recommend to painters:—need I add,—to orators?—I think not; for, unless they practise it,—they must fall upon their noses.

So much for Corporal Trim's body and legs.—He held the sermon loosely,—not carelessly, in his left hand, raised something above his stomach, and detached a little from his breast;—his right arm falling negligently by his side, as nature and the laws of gravity ordered it,—but with the palm of it open and turned towards his audience, ready to aid the sentiment, in case it stood in need.

Corporal Trim's eyes and the muscles of his face, were in full harmony with the other parts of him;—he looked frank,—unconstrained,—something assured,—but not bordering upon assurance.

Let not the critic ask how Corporal Trim could come by all this;—I've told him it shall be explained;—but so he stood before my father, my uncle Toby, and Dr Slop,—so swayed his body, so contrasted his limbs, and with such an oratorical sweep throughout the whole figure,—a statuary might have modelled from it;—nay, I doubt whether the oldest Fellow of a College,—or the Hebrew Professor himself, could have much mended it.

Trim made a bow, and read as follows: Ibid., vol. ii, chap. 15 ff.

Our boy hero proved to be accident-prone. Apart from being conceived at a moment when his parents' concentration had wavered, Dr Slop applied the forceps wrongly in delivery and broke his nose. Then his father wanted him to be christened Trismegistus but the maid forgot the name on her way to the font and he was named Tristram instead.

Perhaps worst of all, Uncle Toby cut the sash-weights out of a window-frame to melt down into miniature cannon and the little boy had a most unfortunate accident:

—'Twas nothing,—I did not lose two drops of blood by it—'twas not worth calling in a surgeon, had he lived next door to us—thousands suffer by choice, what I did by accident.—Dr Slop made ten times more of it than there was occasion:—some men rise, by the art of hanging great weights upon small wires,—and I am this day (August the 10th, 1761) paying part of the price of this man's reputation.—O 'twould provoke a stone, to see how things are carried on in this world!—The chamber-maid had left no ******* *** under the bed: —Cannot you contrive, master, quoth Susannah, lifting up the sash with one hand, as she spoke, and helping me up into the window-seat with the other,—cannot you manage, my dear, for a single time, to **** *** ** *** ******?

I was five years old.—Susannah did not consider that nothing was well hung in our family,—so slap came the sash down like lightning upon us;— Nothing is left,—cried Susannah,—nothing is left—for me, but to run my country.—

My uncle Toby's house was a much kinder sanctuary; and so Susannah fled to it.

Ibid., vol. v, chap. 17.

The sub-plot, such as it was, disappeared and reappeared throughout the nine volumes, sometimes with several chapters interrupting a speech. It concerned the delectable Widow Wadman's pursuit of Uncle Toby.

Widow Wadman lives next door and her bower adjoins Uncle Toby's bowling-green battleground, which gives her opportunities to corner the good man and try to stir his romantic inclinations, if any, into action:

—I am half distracted, Captain Shandy, said Mrs Wadman, holding up her cambric handkerchief to her left eye, as she approached the door of my uncle Toby's sentry-box—a mote—or sand—or something—I know not what, has got into this eye of mine—do look into it—it is not in the white.—

In saying which, Mrs Wadman edged herself close in beside my uncle Toby, and squeezing herself down upon the corner of his bench, she gave him an opportunity of doing it without rising up—Do look into it—said she.

Honest soul! thou didst look into it with as much innocency of heart, as ever child looked into a raree-shew-box; and 'twere as much a sin to have hurt thee.

—If a man will be peeping of his own accord into things of that nature— I've nothing to say to it.—

My uncle Toby never did: and I will answer for him, that he would have sat quietly upon a sopha from June to January, (which, you know, takes in both the hot and cold months) with an eye as fine as the Thracian Rhodope's besides him, without being able to tell, whether it was a black or a blue one.

The difficulty was to get my uncle Toby, to look at one, at all.

'Tis surmounted. And

I see him yonder, with his pipe pendulous in his hand, and the ashes falling out of it—looking—and looking—then rubbing his eyes—and looking again, with twice the good-nature that ever Galileo looked for a spot in the sun.

—In vain! for by all the powers which animate the organ—widow Wadman's left eye shines this moment as lucid as her right—there is neither mote, or sand, or dust, or chaff, or speck, or particle of opake matter floating in it—There is nothing, my dear paternal uncle! but one lambent delicious fire, furtively shooting out from every part of it, in all directions, into thine.—

—If thou lookest, uncle Toby, in search of this mote one moment longer—thou are undone . . .

An eye is for all the world exactly like a cannon, in this respect; That it is not so much the eye or the cannon, in themselves, as it is the carriage of the eye—and the carriage of the cannon, by which both the one and the other are able to do so much execution. I don't think the comparison a bad one: However, as 'tis made and placed at the head of the chapters as much for use as ornament, all I desire in return, is, that whenever I speak of Mrs Wadnam's eyes (except once in the next period) that you keep it in your fancy.

I protest, Madam, said my uncle Toby, I can see nothing whatever in your eye.

It is not in the white; said Mrs Wadman: my uncle Toby looked with might and main into the pupil—

Now of all the eyes, which ever were created—from your own, Madam, up to those of Venus herself, which certainly were as venereal a pair of eyes as ever stood in a head—there never was an eye of them all, so fitted to rob my uncle Toby of his repose, as the very eye, at which he was looking—it was not, Madam, a rolling eye,—a romping or a wanton one—nor was it an eye sparkling—petulant or imperious—of high claims and terrifying exactions, which would have curdled at once that milk of human nature, of which my uncle Toby was made up—but 'twas an eye full of gentle salutations—and soft responses—speaking—not like the trumpet stop of some ill-made organ, in which many an eye I talk to holds coarse converse—but whispering soft—like the last low accents of an expiring saint—'How can you live comfortless, Captain Shandy, and alone, without a bosom to lean your head on—or trust your cares to?'

It was an eye—

But I shall be in love with it myself, if I say another word about it.

—It did my uncle Toby's business.   *Ibid., vol. viii, chap. 24.*

There is, however, a tiny black cloud threatening Mrs Wadman's dreams of re-married bliss: Uncle Toby's war wound. That it is in his groin is common knowledge but vital details have not been revealed. Precisely how much damage has been done, and to precisely what, become matters of great concern to the prospective bride.

Corporal Trim and Uncle Toby often discussed their respective wounds. One day on the bowling-green they compare notes on the pain they had each suffered at the time:

There is no part of the body, an' please your honour, where a wound occasions more intolerable anguish than upon the knee.—

Except the groin; said my uncle Toby. An' please your honour, replied the corporal, the knee, in my opinion, must certainly be the most acute, there being so many tendons and what-d'ye-call-'ems all about it.

It is for that reason, quoth my uncle Toby, that the groin is infinitely more sensible;—there being not only as many tendons and what-d'ye-call-'ems (for I know their names as little as thou dost)—about it,—but moreover,—
* * *
Mrs Wadman, who had been all the time in her arbour,—instantly stopp'd her breath—unpinn'd her mob at the chin, and stood upon one leg—

Ibid., vol. viii, chap. 19.

Widow Wadman and her maid Bridget, who has taken a strong physical fancy to Corporal Trim, decide on a two-pronged attack to get to the truth of the matter. They invite the two men to call.

Ten days later the ex-warriors, in their most splendid clothes, present themselves at the cottage. Uncle Toby sits on the sofa near Mrs Wadman, who pretends to darn an apron as she works the conversation round to the vital question:

—And whereabouts, dear Sir, quoth Mrs Wadman, a little categorically, did you receive this sad blow?—In asking this question, Mrs Wadman gave a slight glance towards the waistband of my uncle Toby's red plush breeches, expecting naturally, as the shortest reply to it, that my uncle Toby would lay his fore-finger upon the place—It fell out otherwise—for my uncle Toby having got his wound before the gate of St Nicholas, in one of the traverses of the trench, opposite to the salient angle of the demi-bastion of St Roch; he could at any time stick a pin upon the identical spot of ground where he was standing when the stone struck him: this struck instantly upon my uncle Toby's sensorium—and with it, struck his large map of the town and citadel of Namur and its environs, which he had purchased and pasted down upon a board, by the corporal's aid, during his long illness—it had lain, with other military lumber in the garret ever since, and accordingly the corporal was detached into the garret to fetch it.

My uncle Toby measured off thirty toises, with Mrs Wadman's scissars, from the returning angle before the gate of St Nicholas; and with such a virgin modesty laid her finger upon the place, that the goddess of Decency, if then in being—if not, 'twas her shade—shook her head, and with a finger wavering across her eyes—forbid her to explain the mistake.

Unhappy Mrs Wadman!

Ibid., vol. ix, chap. 26.

Corporal Trim carries the map down to the kitchen. It is now Bridget's turn to close with the enemy. The encounter provides Bridget little in the way of vital intelligence but leads to a warm haze of asterisks:

And here is the Maes—and this is the Sambre; said the corporal, pointing with his right hand extended a little towards the map and his left upon Mrs Bridget's shoulder—but not the shoulder next him—and this, said he, is the town of Namur—and this the citadel—and there lay the French—and here lay his honour and myself—and in this cursed trench, Mrs Bridget, quoth the corporal, taking her by the hand, did he receive the wound which crushed him so miserably *here*.—In pronouncing which, he slightly pressed the back of her hand towards the part he felt for—and let it fall.

We thought, Mr Trim, it had been more in the middle,—said Mrs Bridget.

That would have undone us for ever—said the Corporal.

—And left my poor mistress undone too—said Bridget.

The corporal made no reply to the repartee, but by giving Mrs Bridget a kiss.

Come—come—said Bridget, holding the palm of her left hand parallel to the plane of the horizon, and sliding the fingers of the other over it, in a way which could not have been done, had there been the least wart or protruberance—'Tis every syllable of it false, cried the corporal, before she had half finished the sentence.

—I know it to be fact, said Bridget, from credible witnesses.

—Upon my honour, said the corporal, laying his hand upon his heart, and blushing as he spoke, with honest resentment—'tis a story, Mrs Bridget, as false as hell—Not, said Bridget, interrupting him, that either I or my mistress care a halfpenny about it, whether 'tis so or no—only that when one is married, one would choose to have such a thing by one at least—

It was somewhat unfortunate for Mrs Bridget, that she had begun the attack with her manual exercise; for the corporal instantly * * * * * *
* *
* *
* * * *.   Ibid., vol. ix, chap. 28.

The Widow Wadman finally succeeds in winning the Captain's heart and hand. Walter Shandy's immediate reaction to the news is probably as perspicacious a comment on marriage as any to be found in literature:

I have an article of news to tell you, Mr Shandy, quoth my mother, which will surprise you greatly.—

Now my father was then holding one of his second beds of justice, and was musing within himself about the hardships of matrimony, as my mother broke silence.—

'—My brother Toby, quoth she, is going to be married to Mrs Wadman.'

—Then he will never, quoth my father, be able to lie *diagonally* in his bed again, as long as he lives.

Ibid., vol. vi, chap. 39.

Sterne's other great work was his travel book, A Sentimental Journey through France and Italy, *which was another huge success. Although* Tristram Shandy *had run into considerable criticism from the literary world and the Church for its indecencies, it is interesting to find that among the list of subscribers printed in the first edition of* Sentimental Journey *are 6 Dukes, 3 Marquesses, 4 Earls, 1 Viscount, 28 Lords, 2 Bishops, 10 Reverends, and the Archbishop of York.*

Sentimental Journey *was almost as idiosyncratic and innovative as* Tristram Shandy. *The very title put into the language a new, vogue word 'sentimental,' quite possibly coined by Sterne, which he used to describe a state of mind in which 'sentiment,' that is, emotional response, predominated over reason. Sterne himself was deeply sentimental. He sobbed quite a lot in his letters and wept frequently in his travels when faced with such affecting sights as a donkey eating a thistle.* Tristram Shandy *and* Sentimental Journey *made such sentimental behaviour fashionable, and Sterne's sentimentalism had a strong influence on continental literature as well as on British writers such as Burns, Bulwer Lytton, Dickens, and Robert Louis Stevenson.*

Sterne began his seven months' continental journey in 1785, hoping to improve his health as the consumption which showed itself when he was at university was tightening its grip. England and France happened to be at war at the time but in those days war was less than total and influential gentlemen could always arrange a passport for such an international celebrity as the great writer Sterne.

The book of his travels was published, uncompleted, in 1768. His lungs had finally collapsed and he died in his Bond Street lodgings.

Sentimental Journey *was not about mountains and cataracts or politics and princes ; it was an emotional record of the tiny, commonplace adventures which he met with on the road, and the feelings which they aroused in him at the time. There was none of the coarseness found in* Tristram Shandy. *Yet, perhaps because of his consumption, which must have frequently given him a running temperature, a delicate vein of eroticism pulsed just below the surface of the humour.*

At the end of the book, on the road to Lyon, he found himself held up by a fall of rock and having to put up for the night at 'a little decent kind of an inn by the roadside'. He took possession of his bedroom, got the fire going, ordered supper and was thanking heaven it was no worse when a voiture rolled to a stop at the inn door.

Inside were a lady and her maid-servant :

As there was no other bed-chamber in the house, the hostess, without much nicety, led them into mine, telling them, as she ushered them in, that there was nobody in it but an English gentleman—that there were two good beds in it, and a closet within the room which held another—the accent in which she spoke of this third bed did not say much for it—however, she said there were three beds, and but three people—and she durst say, the gentleman would do any thing to accommodate matters.—I left not the lady a moment to make a conjecture about it—so instantly made a declaration I would do any thing in my power.

As this did not amount to an absolute surrender of my bed-chamber, I still felt myself so much the proprietor, as to have a right to do the honours of it—so I desired the lady to sit down—pressed her into the warmest seat— called for more wood—desired the hostess to enlarge the plan of the supper, and to favour us with the very best wine.

The lady had scarce warmed herself five minutes at the fire, before she began to turn her head back, and give a look at the beds; and the oftener she cast her eyes that way, the more they returned perplexed—I felt for her— and for myself; for in a few minutes, what by her looks, and the case itself, I found myself as much embarrassed as it was possible the lady could be herself.

That the beds we were to lay in were in one and the same room, was enough simply by itself to have excited all this—but the position of them, for they stood parallel, and so very close to each other as only to allow space for a small wicker chair betwixt them, rendered the affair still more oppressive to us—they were fixed up moreover near the fire, and the projection of the chimney on one side, and a large beam which crossed the room on the other, formed a kind of recess for them that was no way favourable to the nicety of our sensations—if any thing could have added to it, it was, that the two beds were both of 'em so very small, as to cut off every idea of the lady and the maid lying together; which in either of them, could it have been feasible, my lying besides them, though a thing not to be wished, yet there was nothing in it so terrible which the imagination might not have pass'd over without torment.

As for the little room within, it offered little or no consolation to us; 'twas a damp cold closet, with a half-dismantled window-shutter, and with a window which had neither glass or oil-paper in it to keep out the tempest of the night. I did not endeavour to stifle my cough when the lady gave a peep into it; so it reduced the case in course to this alternative—that the lady should sacrifice her health to her feelings, and take up with the closet herself, and abandon the bed next mine to her maid—or that the girl should take the closet, &c. &c.

The lady was a Piedmontese of about thirty, with a glow of health in her cheeks.—The maid was Lyonoise of twenty, and as brisk and lively a French girl as ever moved.—There were difficulties every way—and the obstacle of the stone in the road, which brought us into the distress, great as it appeared whilst the peasants were removing it, was but a pebble to what lay in our way now—I have only to add, that it did not lessen the weight which hung upon our spirits, that we were both too delicate to communicate what we felt to each other upon the occasion.

We sat down to supper; and had we not had more generous wine to it than a little inn in Savoy could have furnished, our tongues had been tied up till necessity herself had set them at liberty—but the lady having a few bottles of Burgundy in her voiture, sent down her Fille de Chambre for a couple of them; so that by the time supper was over, and we were left alone, we felt ourselves inspired with a strength of mind sufficient to talk, at least, without reserve upon our situation. We turned it every way, and debated and considered it in all lights in the course of a two hours negociation; at the end of which the articles were settled finally betwixt us, and stipulated for in form and manner of a treaty of peace—and I believe with as much religion and good faith on both sides, as in any treaty which had yet had the honour of being handed down to posterity.

They were as follows:

First. As the right of the bed-chamber is in Monsieur—and he thinking the bed next to the fire to be the warmest, he insists upon the concession on the lady's side of taking up with it.

Granted, on the part of Madame; with a proviso, That as the curtains of that bed are of a flimsy transparent cotton, and appear likewise too scanty to draw close, that the Fille de Chambre, shall fasten up the opening, either by corking pins or needle and thread, in such manner as shall be deemed a sufficient barrier on the side of Monsieur.

2dly. It is required on the part of Madame, that Monsieur shall lay the whole night through in his robe de chambre.

Rejected: inasmuch as Monsieur is not worth a robe de chambre; he having nothing in his portmanteau but six shirts and a black silk pair of breeches.

The mentioning the silk pair of breeches made an entire change of the article—for the breeches were accepted as an equivalent for the robe de chambre; and so it was stipulated and agreed upon that I should lay in my black silk breeches all night.

3dly. It was insisted upon, and stipulated for by the lady, that after Monsieur was got to bed, and the candle and fire extinguished, that Monsieur should not speak one single word the whole night.

Granted; provided Monsieur's saying his prayers might not be deemed an infraction of the treaty.

There was but one point forgot in this treaty, and that was the manner in which the lady and myself should be obliged to undress and get to bed—there was but one way of doing it, and that I leave to the reader to devise; protesting as I do it, that if it is not the most delicate in nature, 'tis the fault of his own imagination—against which this is not my first complaint.

Now when we were got to bed, whether it was the novelty of the situation, or what it was, I know not; but so it was, I could not shut my eyes; I tried this side and that, and turned and turned again, till a full hour after midnight; when nature and patience both wearing out—O my God! said I—

—You have broke the treaty, Monsieur, said the lady, who had no more slept than myself.—I begged a thousand pardons—but insisted it was no more than an ejaculation—she maintained 'twas an entire infraction of the treaty—I maintained it was provided for in the clause of the third article.

The lady would by no means give up her point, though she weakened her barrier by it; for in the warmth of the dispute, I could hear two or three corking pins fall out of the curtain to the ground.

Upon my word and honour, Madam, said I—stretching out my arm out of bed by way of asseveration—

—(I was going to have added, that I would not have trespassed against the remotest idea of decorum for the world)—

—But the Fille de Chambre hearing there were words between us, and fearing that hostilities would ensue in course, had crept silently out of her closet, and it being totally dark, had stolen so close to our beds, that she had got herself into the narrow passage which separated them, and had advanced so far up as to be in a line betwixt her mistress and me—

So that when I stretched out my hand, I caught hold of the Fille de Chambre's

A Sentimental Journey through France and Italy (1768).

———

STERNE'S *influence on the development of the novel was profound. He showed that the conventional pattern of the novel did not have to be followed; that the author could give rein to his imagination in the manner in which he told his story as well as in the story's content. He also demonstrated that humour could be used for its own sake. Many writers down to the present day have acknowledged their debt to Sterne's peculiar, inventive genius, which broke the mould before it had even set.*

His books were widely imitated by his contemporaries all over Europe but most of them ignored his humour and concentrated on the sentimentalism, which resulted in a decade or so of tear-stained, solemn novels about saintly men of feeling (for example, Henry Brooke's The Fool of Quality *(1766–70): five volumes of sensitive weeping).*

One of the exceptions was the minor novelist, Robert Bage. Bage was a paper-manufacturer who branched off into making iron, lost a lot of money with the financial collapse of his foundry, and at the age of 53 set about becoming less poor by writing novels. Bage was not at all a sentimentalist. He was a cheerful materialist, some said 'without morals or religion', and his six successful novels were full of lively humour.

In the preface to his first novel, Mount Henneth, *Bage explains to the critics why he has taken up writing and then obligingly reviews his work on their behalf:*

PREFACE

A Novel, according to the present usages, may be sent into the world with a preface, or without. I chose the former, not with any intention to pre-instruct the reader in the nature of the work, for novels have all one nature; but to soften the severity of this criticism, by information of the reasons, which drew me in to write.

It is very easy to say I wrote it for my own amusement, and published it to satisfy the importunity of some very judicious friends, who could not bear that so many beauties should lie concealed in the drawer of a cabinet. But as I intend to be upon honour with my reader, in point of veracity, I must candidly confess, I have been determined by far different motives. In short, my three daughters assure me, that I write in a very tasty manner; and that it is two years, bating two months, since I made each of them a present of a new silk gown.

Now you must know, my dear Readers, that I live a great way from London, and have a pretty mechanical way of doing certain things, which has procured me some reputation; and, till lately, as much wealth as any man who thinks of the snug and quiet comforts of life, only, would desire.

But I don't know how it is, people are oftener dunning me for money than usual; and to be sure, I do not pay the ready for raw materials, as I was wont. The proximate cause of this, I am unable to discover; but the predisposing and occasional causes, I once presumed to think, lay hid in the heads or tails of the female part of my family, which, within a few years, have suffered an amazing expansion.

This, my daughters assure me, is an error of the first concoction. It is true, they say, ladies, in their stile of life, must conform to the fashion, and people who don't understand things, are apt to imagine that this must be attended with a great deal of expence; but people who know life, like my daughters, know how to make a little go a great way. In short, I am now convinced I have injured the dear creatures by my suspicions, and to make them amends, have laid the whole burden to the account of the American war.

But my daughters must have new silk gowns.

Now Messieurs, the Reviewers, will kindly inform the world, that in their opinion, I might have been better, and quite as profitably employed in getting up a few more of my mechanical matters. But, with submission to their better judgments, a man cannot be always making ———.

These gentlemen I believe are generally, and may they be always, better employed, than in reading such books as mine. I have been indebted to their salutary admonitions for many a crown, which fair title pages would otherwise have drawn out of my pocket.

Willingly would I, in gratitude, do them any kindness that lies within the compass of my small abilities. Willingly will I review these books myself, and save their heads the many necessary aches which must otherwise ensue.

Henneth Castle, Etc. Etc. Etc.

'If readers expect to find, in these volumes, any thing like wit, humour, plot, character, or keeping, they will be much disappointed. The work puts us in mind of Doctor Johnson's sarcasm of Macklin's conversation, a perpetual renovation of hope, with perpetual disappointment. To say the least we can of it, it is bad in the beginning, worse and worse in its progress, but the end is heaven.'

Into what egregious folly does gratitude sometimes betray simple minded people!

Books of this class are printed, published, bought, read, and deposited in the lumber garret, three months before the Reviewers say a syllable of the matter.

What a dunderhead!

If, after all, the WORLD will deny me its confidence, will buy, read, judge by itself: do not, dear gentlemen, for gallantry's, for pity's sake, do not *go out of your way* for the sake of establishing my veracity.

'But if your book be as bad as you say, it is incumbent on us to give the earliest notice, in order to save the WORLD its money, as we have heretofore done yours.'

Oh! that you had seen my daughters!

Robert Bage (1728–1801), Mount Henneth (1781).

D URING *the last quarter of the eighteenth century a literary phenomen occured: the rise and rapid predominance of women novelists.*

There had always been women who wrote ; there was Mrs Aphra Behn, daughter of a barber and spy for King Charles II, the world's first professional authoress who wrote rather gamey plays, poetry, and romances, died in 1689, and was appropriately entombed in the cloisters of Westminster Abbey. There were the eighteenth-century 'blue-stocking' essayists like Mrs Chapone and Mrs Montagu, lady diarists like Lady Mary Wortley Montagu, poetesses like Anna Seward, 'The Swan of Lichfield', and female playwrights like Mrs Centlivre, but the novel had been a masculine domain, much concerned with adventure, low-life, bawdiness (if only to point a moral), villainy, and similar un-ladylike pursuits. A young lady of quality had very little which she could, with propriety, write a novel about.

But the social life of the gentry was changing, particularly in what was expected of a marriage. Arranged marriages, really business mergers in terms of land, still happened, but usually only between eldest sons and heiresses. There was now more leisure, and husbands and wives were together more of the time, so younger sons, and girls with small marriage settlements, looked for affection and companionship in their partners. Best of all was to fall in love and be loved in return. But for a girl the path of romance was fraught with real perils. She was, to modern standards, incredibly vulnerable. Her reputation was vital to her if she was to make any kind of decent match, and she could lose her reputation in a moment, not only by some small indiscretion but by sheer accident. Then she was lost.

Here at last there was *something to write about; and who better to write about the excitements and alarums of courtship than a woman?*

At the age of 17 Fanny Burney, daughter of the distinguished historian of music Dr Charles Burney, noted in her diary 'I am now going to charm *myself for the third time with poor Sterne's* Sentimental Journey.'

Little Miss Burney, self-educated, genteel, shy but full of fun, had always scribbled stories and verses, and she decided that she would write a novel for her own amusement. Her father, like most fathers, thought that novels were a frivolous waste of time—he had only one novel in his library—so Fanny wrote in secret. When it was finished she persuaded her brother to try it out on the trade. The bookseller Lowndes bought it for £30 plus ten bound copies and in 1778, when Fanny was 26, Evelina, or a Young Lady's Entrance into the World was published anonymously.

It was an immense success. Her father's friends loved it: the great Samuel Johnson thought that some of the passages were worthy of Samuel Richardson and he almost knew the book by heart; Sir Joshua Reynolds would not put it down at the dinner table and was fed whilst still reading it, and he and Edmund Burke stayed up half the night to finish it. It was a moment of keen pleasure when those friends discovered that the anonymous author was the charming young lady whose company they so enjoyed. Fanny noted in her diary that when she heard of the book's success she ran out into the garden and danced round a mulberry tree.

Fanny went on to write another success, Cecilia; to please her father she became second keeper of the robes to the Queen at Windsor Castle, an exhausting and deeply tedious appointment; carried on writing her diary, a most readable journal; married a French émigré, General d'Arblay; and somewhere along the way lost her girlish laughter, developed middle-age word-spread and wrote Camilla *and* The Wanderer *which are now virtually unreadable.*

Fanny Burney's talent was perhaps limited, but the contribution which she made to the development of the lightly humorous novel was considerable. The ecstatic reception which Samuel Johnson and his friends gave to Evelina *might puzzle the modern reader to whom the book would seem to be just another example of what librarians call 'Light Love'. But* Evelina *was the original. It was the first novel of social life on a small scale; the first novel of manners, the first realistic depiction of a girl in love, and of class discrimination among the middle classes, and Fanny Burney's writings greatly affected the work of later women novelists, particularly Jane Austen.*

In the last chapter of Cecilia *occurred a passage in which Fanny Burney suddenly burst into capital letters and gave Jane Austen the eventual title, and perhaps the theme, of her best-known novel. The heroine Cecilia's old friend was reflecting on all that had happened: '"The whole of this unfortunate business," said Dr Lyster, "has been the result of PRIDE and PREJUDICE . . . Yet this, however, remember; if to PRIDE and PREJUDICE you owe your miseries, so wonderfully is good and evil balanced, that to PRIDE and PREJUDICE you will also owe their termination."'*

Not surprisingly the list of subscribers to Fanny Burney's next novel, Camilla, *included 'Miss J. Austen, Steventon'.*

Evelina *tells of a 17-year-old, gauche, genteel, country-bred young lady's entry into the fashionable world, of the difficulties she has with some rather vulgar members of her family, and her finally successful love for a handsome and utterly decent young milord.*

Although Evelina is befriended by the kindly Lady Howard and is clearly going to turn out at the end of the book to be at the very least the long-lost daughter of a baronet, her grandmother was a barmaid who had married a Frenchman, Duval, and inherited a fortune.

The form of the book is epistolary, mostly letters written by Evelina to the kind old clergyman who brought her up.

During Evelina's 'coming-out' season in London she has to divide her time between two quite different social worlds, Lady Howard's genteel, aristocratic circle which includes the handsome Lord Orville with whom she has secretly fallen in love, and life with her relations, the Branghtons, who are tradesmen with a silversmith's shop in Snow-Hill. They take in lodgers.

The two worlds constantly overlap. One night she might be taken to the play at Drury-Lane and enjoy the delicious excitement of being in a side-box with Lord Orville. The next night she might be taken to the Opera by the embarrassing Branghtons:

In a short time . . . we arrived at one of the door-keeper's *bars.* Mr Branghton demanded for what part of the house they took money? They answered the pit, and regarded us all with great earnestness. The son then advancing, said, 'Sir, if you please, I beg that I may treat Miss.'

'We'll settle that another time,' answered Mr Branghton, and put down a guinea.

Two tickets of admission were given to him.

Mr Branghton, in his turn, now stared at the door-keeper, and demanded what he meant by giving him only two tickets for a guinea?

'Only two, Sir!' said the man, 'why don't you know that the tickets are half a guinea each?'

'Half a guinea each!' repeated Mr Branghton, 'why I never heard of such a thing in my life! And pray, Sir, how many will they admit?'

'Just as usual, Sir, one person each.'

'But one person for half a guinea!—why I only want to sit in the pit, friend.'

'Had not the Ladies better sit in the gallery, Sir; for they'll hardly chuse to go into the pit with their hats on?'

'O, as to that,' cried Miss Branghton, 'if our hats are too high, we'll take them off when we get in. I shan't mind it, for I did my hair on purpose.'

Another party then approaching, the door-keeper could no longer attend to Mr Branghton, who, taking up the guinea, told him it should be long enough before he'd see it again, and walked away.

The young ladies, in some confusion, expressed their surprise, that their *papa* should not know the Opera prices, which, for their parts, they had read in the papers a thousand times.

'The price of stocks', said he, 'is enough for me to see after; and I took it for granted it was the same thing here as at the play-house.'

'I knew well enough what the price was,' said the son, 'but I would not speak, because I thought perhaps they'd take less, as we're such a large party.'

The sisters both laughed very contemptuously at this idea, and asked him if he ever heard of *people's abating* any thing at a public place?

'I don't know whether I have or no,' answered he, 'but I'm sure if they would, you'd like it so much the worse.'

'Very true, Tom,' cried Mr Branghton; 'tell a woman that any thing is reasonable, and she'll be sure to hate it.'

'Well,' said Miss Polly, 'I hope that Aunt and Miss will be on our side, for Papa always takes part with Tom.'

'Come, come,' cried Madame Duval, 'if you stand talking here, we shan't get no place at all.'

Mr Branghton then enquired the way to the gallery, and, when we came to the door-keeper, demanded what was to pay.

'The usual price, Sir,' said the man.

'Then give me change,' cried Mr Branghton, again putting down his guinea.

'For how many, Sir?'

'Why—let's see,—for six.'

'For six, Sir? why you've given me but a guinea.'

'*But* a guinea! why how much would you have? I suppose it i'n't half a guinea apiece here too?'

'No, Sir, only five shillings.'

Mr Branghton again took up his unfortunate guinea, and protested he would submit to no such imposition. I then proposed that we should return home, but Madame Duval would not consent, and we were conducted, by a woman who sells books of the Opera, to another gallery-door, where, after some disputing, Mr Branghton at last paid, and we all went upstairs.

Madame Duval complained very much of the trouble of going so high, but Mr Branghton desired her not to hold the place too cheap, 'for, whatever you may think,' cried he, 'I assure you I paid pit price; so don't suppose I come here to save my money.'

'Well, to be sure,' said Miss Branghton, 'there's no judging of a place by the outside, else, I must needs say, there's nothing very extraordinary in the staircase.'

But, when we entered the gallery, their amazement and disappointment became general. For a few instants, they looked at one another without speaking, and then they all broke silence at once.

'Lord, Papa,' exclaimed Miss Polly, 'why you have brought us to the one shilling gallery!'

'I'll be glad to give you two shillings, though,' answered he 'to pay. I was never so fooled out of my money before, since the hour of my birth. Either the door-keeper's a knave, or this is the greatest imposition that ever was put upon the public.'

'*Ma foi*,' cried Madame Duval, 'I never sat in such a mean place in all my life;—why it's as high!—we shan't see nothing.'

'I thought at the time', said Mr Branghton, 'that three shillings was an exorbitant price for a place in the gallery, but as we'd been asked so much more at the other doors, why I paid it without many words; but then, to be sure, thinks I, it can never be like any other gallery,—we shall see some *crinkum-crankum* or other for our money;—but I find it's as arrant a take-in as ever I met with.'

'Why it's as like the twelvepenny gallery at Drury-lane', cried the son, 'as two peas are one to another. I never knew father so bit before.'

'Lord,' said Miss Branghton, 'I thought it would have been quite a fine place,—all over I don't know what,—and done quite in taste.'

In this manner they continued to express their dissatisfaction till the curtain drew up; after which, their observations were very curious. They made no allowance for the customs, or even for the language of another country, but formed all their remarks upon comparisons with the English theatre.

Notwithstanding my vexation at having been forced into a party so very disagreeable, and that, too, from one so much—so very much the contrary—yet, would they have suffered me to listen, I should have forgotten every thing unpleasant, and felt nothing but delight in hearing the sweet voice of Signor Millico, the first singer; but they tormented me with continual talking.

'What a jabbering they make!' cried Mr Branghton; 'there's no knowing a word they say. Pray what's the reason they can't as well sing in English?—but I suppose the fine folks would not like it, if they could understand it.'

'How unnatural their action is!' said the son; 'why now who ever saw an Englishman put himself in such out-of-the-way postures?'

'For my part,' said Miss Polly, 'I think it's very pretty, only I don't know what it means.'

'Lord, what does that signify?' cried her sister; 'mayn't one like a thing without being so very particular?—You may see that Miss likes it, and I don't suppose she knows more of the matter than we do.'

A gentleman, soon after, was so obliging as to make room in the front row for Miss Branghton and me. We had not sooner seated ourselves, than Miss Branghton exclaimed, 'Good gracious! only see!—why, Polly, all the people in the pit are without hats, dressed like any thing!'

'Lord, so they are,' cried Miss Polly, 'well, I never saw the like!—it's worth coming to the Opera if one saw nothing else.' . . .

I was then able to distinguish the happy party I had left; and I saw that

Lord Orville had seated himself next to Mrs Mirvan. Sir Clement had his eyes perpetually cast towards the five-shilling gallery, where I suppose he concluded that we were seated; however, before the Opera was over, I have reason to believe that he had discovered me, high and distant as I was from him. Probably he distinguished me by my head-dress.

At the end of the first act, as the green curtain dropped, to prepare for the dance, they imagined that the Opera was done, and Mr Branghton expressed great indignation that he had been *tricked* out of his money with so little trouble. 'Now if any Englishman was to do such an impudent thing as this,' said he, 'why he'd be pelted;—but here, one of these outlandish gentry may do just what he pleases, and come on, and squeak out a song or two, and then pocket your money without further ceremony.'

However, so determined he was to be dissatisfied, that, before the conclusion of the third act, he found still more fault with the Opera for being too long, and wondered whether they thought their singing good enough to serve us for supper.

During the symphony of a song of Signor Millico's, in the second act, young Mr Branghton said, 'It's my belief that that fellow's going to sing another song!—why there's nothing but singing!—I wonder when they'll speak.'

This song, which was slow and pathetic, caught all my attention, and I leaned my head forward to avoid hearing their observations, that I might listen without interruption; but, upon turning round, when the song was over, I found that I was the object of general diversion to the whole party; for the Miss Branghtons were tittering, and the two gentlemen making signs and faces at me, implying their contempt of my affectation.

This discovery determined me to appear as inattentive as themselves; but I was very much provoked at being thus prevented enjoying the only pleasure, which, in such a party, was within my power.

'So, Miss,' said Mr Branghton, 'you're quite in the fashion, I see;—so you like Operas? well, I'm not so polite; I can't like nonsense, let it be never so much the taste.'

'But pray, Miss,' said the son, 'what makes that fellow look so doleful while he's singing?'

'Probably because the character he performs is in distress.'

'Why then I think he might as well let alone singing till he's in better cue: it's out of all nature for a man to be piping when he's in distress. For my part, I never sing but when I'm merry; yet I love a song as well as most people.'

When the curtain dropped, they all rejoiced.

How do *you* like it?—and how do *you* like it? passed from one to another with looks of the utmost contempt. 'As for me,' said Mr Branghton, 'they've caught me once, but if ever they do again, I'll give 'em leave to sing me to Bedlam for my pains: for such a heap of stuff never did I hear; there isn't one ounce of sense in the whole Opera, nothing but one continued squeaking and squalling from beginning to end.'

'If I had been in the pit,' said Madame Duval, 'I should have liked it vastly, for music is my passion; but sitting in such a place as this, is quite unbearable.'

Miss Branghton, looking at me, declared, that she was not genteel enough to admire it.

Miss Polly confessed, that, if they would but sing English she should like it very well.

The brother wished he could raise a riot in the house, because then he might get his money again.

And, finally, they all agreed, that it was *monstrous dear*.

Fanny Burney (1752–1840), *Evelina* (1778).

Evelina is shuttled between the haut monde *and the* bourgeoisie, *not having much fun in either camp because Lord Orville seems to have too little regard for her and the Branghton's lodger a great deal too much.*

Young Mr Smith, who rents the Branghton's first-floor room above the shop, is nouveau semi-riche *and not tortured by self-doubts. Evelina attends two delightful balls with Lady Howard's group and then finds herself invited to a public ball with Mr Smith and the Branghtons. There she has an infuriating experience which might well have suggested to Jane Austen the famous proposal scene in* Pride and Prejudice *between Mr Collins the clergyman and Elizabeth Bennet:*

The ball was at *the long room* at Hampstead.

This room seems very well named, for I believe it would be difficult to find any other epithet which might, with propriety, distinguish it, as it is without ornament, elegance, or any sort of singularity, and merely to be marked by its length.

I was saved from the importunities of Mr Smith, the beginning of the evening, by Madame Duval's declaring her intention to dance the first two dances with him herself. Mr Smith's chagrin was very evident, but as she paid no regard to it, he was necessitated to lead her out . . .

For a few moments I very much rejoiced at being relieved from this troublesome man; but scarce had I time to congratulate myself, before I was accosted by another, who begged *the favour of hopping a dance* with me.

I told him that I should not dance at all; but he thought proper to importune me, very freely, not to be so cruel; and I was obliged to assume no little haughtiness before I could satisfy him I was serious . . .

I knew not whether to be glad or sorry, when Madame Duval and Mr Smith returned. The latter instantly resumed his tiresome entreaties, and Madame Duval said she would go to the card-table: and as soon as she was accommodated, she desired us to join the dancers.

I will not trouble you with the arguments which followed . . . In truth, I had no power to attend to him, for all my thoughts were occupied in re-tracing the transactions at the two former balls at which I had been present. The party—the conversation—the company—O how great the contrast!

In a short time, however, he contrived to draw my attention to himself, by his extreme impertinence; for he chose to express what he called his *admiration* of me, in terms so open and familiar, that he forced me to express my displeasure with equal plainness.

But how was I surprised, when I found he had the temerity—what else can I call it?—to impute my resentment to doubts of his honour; for he said, 'My dear Ma'am, you must be a little patient; I assure you I have no bad designs, I have not upon my word; but, really, there is no resolving on such a thing as matrimony all at once; what with the loss of one's liberty, and what with the ridicule of all one's acquaintance,—I assure you, Ma'am, you are the first lady who ever made me even demur on this subject; for, after all, my dear Ma'am, marriage is the devil!'

'Your opinion, Sir,' answered I, 'of either the married or the single life, can be of no manner of consequence to me, and therefore I would by no means trouble you to discuss their different merits.'

'Why, really, Ma'am, as to your being a little out of sorts, I must own I can't wonder at it, for, to be sure, marriage is all in all with the ladies; but with us gentlemen it's quite another thing! Now only put yourself in my place,—suppose you had such a large acquaintance of gentlemen as I have,— and that you had already been used to appear a little—a little smart among them,—why now, how should you like to let yourself down all at once into a married man?'

I could not tell what to answer; so much conceit, and so much ignorance, both astonished and silenced me.

'I can assure you, Ma'am,' added he, 'there is not only Miss Biddy,— though I should have scorned to mention her, if her brother had not blabbed, for I'm quite particular in keeping ladies' secrets,—but there are a great many other ladies that have been proposed to me,—but I never thought twice of any of them,—that is, not in a *serious* way,—so you may very well be proud,' offering to take my hand, 'for I assure you, there is nobody so likely to catch me at last as yourself.'

'Sir,' cried I, drawing myself back as haughtily as I could, 'you are totally mistaken, if you imagine you have given me any pride I felt not before, by this conversation; on the contrary, you must allow me to tell you, I find it too humiliating to bear with it any longer.'...

Indeed, the extreme vanity of this man makes me exert a spirit which I did not, till now, know that I possessed: but I cannot endure that he should think me at his disposal.

The rest of the evening passed very quietly, as Mr Smith did not again attempt speaking to me; except, indeed, after we had left the room, and while Madame Duval was seating herself in the coach, he said, in a voice of *pique*,

'Next time I take the trouble to get any tickets for a young lady, I'll make a bargain beforehand that she sha'n't turn me over to her grandmother.'

Ibid.

———————

Maria Edgeworth *was born in England but spent a great deal of her life in Edgeworthstown in Ireland looking after her father's estate. And writing.*

She was so tiny as a child that efforts were made to lengthen her by hanging her up by the neck. She remained short. She also had bad eyesight which doses of the then popular tar-water did nothing to improve. In spite of these trusted eighteenth-century remedies she survived and became a pioneer writer for and about children. More importantly, she began writing stories about Ireland's past, and these inspired Sir Walter Scott to try writing about the past of his own native heath.

Maria Edgeworth was also the first major regional novelist; the first author to point out the essential Irishness of the Irish.

Her work was highly regarded; Jane Austen sent her a copy of Emma, *and the success of the Irish regional novels inspired Sir Walter Scott once again, this time to try to do the same sort of thing for the Scottishness of the Scots.*

In her novel Ennui, *which tells of the effects of unrestrained Irishness on a non-Irish traveller, a rather haughty English milord, stricken with the eighteenth-century English malady of boredom, attempts to relieve his condition by making a visit to his remote estates in Ireland:*

I travelled in a light barouche, and with my own horses. My own man (an Englishman), and my cook (a Frenchman), followed in a hackney chaise; I cared not how, so that they kept up with me; the rest was their affair. At night, my gentleman complained bitterly of the Irish post carriages, and besought me to let him follow at an easier rate the next day; but to this I could no means consent; for how could I exist without my own man and my French cook?

In the morning, just as I was ready to set off, and had thrown myself back in my carriage, my Englishman and Frenchman came to the door, both in so great a rage, that the one was inarticulate and the other unintelligible. At length the object of their indignation spoke for itself. From the inn yard came a hackney chaise, in a most deplorable crazy state; the body mounted up to a prodigious height, on unbending springs, nodding forwards, one door swinging open, three blinds up, because they could not be let down, the perch tied in two places, the iron of the wheels half off, half loose, wooden pegs for linch-pins, and ropes for harness. The horses were worthy of the harness; wretched little dog-tired creatures, that looked as if they had been driven to the last gasp, and as if they had never been rubbed down in their lives; their bones starting through their skin; one lame, the other blind; one with a raw back, the other with a galled breast; one with his neck poking down over his collar, and the other with his head dragged forward by a bit of a broken bridle, held at arm's length by a man dressed like a mad beggar, in half a hat and half a wig, both awry in opposite directions; a long tattered great-coat, tied round his waist by a hay-rope; the jagged rents in the skirts of his coat showing his bare legs marbled of many colours; while something like stockings hung loose about his ankles. The noises he made by way of threatening or encouraging his steeds, I pretend not to describe.

In an indignant voice I called to the landlord, 'I hope these are not the horses—I hope this is not the chaise, intended for my servants.'

The innkeeper, and the pauper who was preparing to officiate as postilion, both in the same instant exclaimed, '*Sorrow* better chaise in the county!'

'Sorrow!' said I; 'what do you mean by sorrow?'

'That there's no better, plase your honour, can be seen. We have two more, to be sure; but one has no top, and the other no bottom. Any way there's no better can be seen than this same.'

'And these horses!' cried I; 'why, this horse is so lame he can hardly stand.'

'Oh, plase your honour, tho' he can't stand, he'll go fast enough. He has a great deal of the rogue in him, plase your honour. He's always that way at first setting out.'

'And that wretched animal with the galled breast!'

'He's all the better for it, when once he warms; it's he that will go with the speed of light, plase your honour. Sure, is not he Knockecroghery? and didn't I give fifteen guineas for him, barring the luck penny, at the fair of Knockecroghery, and he rising four years old at the same time?'

I could not avoid smiling at this speech: but my gentleman, maintaining his angry gravity, declared, in a sullen tone, that he would be cursed if he went with such horses; and the Frenchman, with abundance of gesticulation, made a prodigious chattering, which no mortal understood.

'Then I'll tell you what you'll do,' said Paddy; 'you'll take four, as becomes gentlemen of your quality, and you'll see how we'll powder along.'

And straight he put the knuckle of his fore-finger in his mouth, and whistled shrill and strong; and, in a moment, a whistle somewhere out in the fields answered him.

I protested against these proceedings, but in vain; before the first pair of horses were fastened to the chaise, up came a little boy with the others fresh from the plough. They were quick enough in putting these to; yet how they managed it with their tackle, I know not. 'Now we're fixed handsomely', said Paddy.

'But this chaise will break down the first mile.'

'Is it this chaise, plase your honour? I'll engage it will go the world's end. The universe wouldn't break it down now; sure it was mended but last night.'

Then seizing his whip and reins in one hand, he clawed up his stockings with the other: so with one easy step he got into his place, and seated himself, coachman-like, upon a well-worn bar of wood, that served as a coach-box. 'Throw me the loan of a trusty Bartly, for a cushion,' said he. A frieze coat was thrown up over the horses' heads—Paddy caught it. 'Where are you, Hosey?' cried he. 'Sure I'm only rowling a wisp of straw on my leg', replied Hosey. 'Throw me up,' added this paragon of postilions, turning to one of the crowd of idle bystanders. 'Arrah, push me up, can't ye?'

A man took hold of his knee, and threw him upon the horse; he was in his seat in a trice; then clinging by the mane of his horse, he scrambled for the bridle, which was under the other horse's feet—reached it, and, well satisfied with himself, looked round at Paddy, who looked back to the chaise-door at my angry servants, 'secure in the last event of things'. In vain the Englishman in monotonous anger, and the Frenchman in every note of the gamut, abused Paddy: necessity and wit were on Paddy's side; he parried all that was said against his chaise, his horses, himself, and his country, with invincible comic dexterity, till at last, both his adversaries, dumb-founded, clambered into the vehicle, where they were instantly shut up in straw and darkness. Paddy, in a triumphant tone, called to *my* postilions, bidding them 'get on, and not be stopping the way any longer'.

Without uttering a syllable, they drove on; but they could not nor could I, refrain from looking back to see how those fellows would manage. We saw the fore-horses make towards the right, then to the left, and every way but straight forwards; whilst Paddy bawled to Hosey—'Keep the middle of the road, can't ye? I don't want ye to draw a pound at-all-at-all.'

At last, by dint of whipping, the four horses were compelled to set off in a lame gallop; but they stopped short at a hill near the end of the town, whilst a shouting troop of ragged boys followed, and pushed them fairly to the top. Half an hour afterwards, as we were putting on our drag-chain to go down another steep hill,—to my utter astonishment, Paddy, with his horses in full gallop, came rattling and *chehupping* past us. My people called to warn him that he had no *drag*: but still he cried 'Never fear!' and shaking the long reins, and stamping with his foot, on he went thundering down the hill. My Englishmen were aghast.

'The turn yonder below, at the bottom of the hill, is as sharp and ugly as ever I see', said my postilion, after a moment's stupefied silence. 'He will break their necks, as sure as my name is John.'

Quite the contrary: when we had dragged and undragged, and came up to Paddy, we found him safe on his legs, mending some of his tackle very quietly.

'If that had broken as you were going down the steep hill,' said I, 'it would have been all over with you, Paddy.'

'That's true, plase your honour: but it never happened me going down hill—nor never will, by the blessing of God, if I've any luck.'

With this mixed confidence in a special providence, and in his own good luck, Paddy went on, much to my amusement. It was his glory to keep before us; and he rattled on till he came to a narrow part of the road, where they were rebuilding a bridge. Here there was a dead stop. Paddy lashed his horses, and called them all manner of names; but the wheel horse, Knockecroghery, was restive, and at last began to kick most furiously. It seemed inevitable that the first kick which should reach the splinter-bar, at which it was aimed, must demolish it instantly. My English gentleman and my Frenchman both put their heads out of the only window which was pervious and called most manfully to be let out. 'Never fear,' said Paddy. To open the door for themselves was beyond their force or skill. One of the hind wheels, which had belonged to another carriage, was too high to suffer the door to be opened, and the blind at the other side prevented their attempts, so they were close prisoners. The men who had been at work on the broken bridge came forward, and rested on their spades to see the battle. As my carriage could not pass, I was also compelled to be a spectator of this contest between man and horse.

'Never fear,' reiterated Paddy; 'I'll engage I'll be up wid him. Now for it, Knockecroghery! Oh, the rogue, he thinks he has me at a *nonplush*, but I'll show him the *differ*.'

After this brag of war, Paddy whipped, Knockecroghery kicked; and Paddy, seemingly unconscious of danger, sat within reach of the kicking horse, twitching up first one of his legs, then the other, and shifting as the animal aimed his hoofs, escaping every time as it were by miracle. With a mixture of temerity and presence of mind, which made us alternately look upon him as a madman and a hero, he gloried in the danger, secure of success, and of the sympathy of the spectators.

'Ah! didn't I *compass* him cleverly then? Oh, the villain, to be browbating me! I'm too cute for him yet. See there, now, he's come to; and I'll be his bail he'll go *asy* enough wid me. Ogh! he has a fine spirit of his own, but it's I that can match him: 'twould be a poor case if a man like me cou'dn't match a horse any way, let alone a mare, which this is, or it never would be so vicious.'

After this hard-fought battle, and suitable rejoicing for the victory, Paddy walked his subdued adversary on a few yards to allow us to pass him; but, to the dismay of my postilions, a hay-rope was at this instant thrown across the road, before our horses, by the road-makers, who, to explain this proceeding, cried out, 'Plase your honour, the road is so dry, we'd expect a trifle to wet it.'

'What do these fellows mean?' said I.

'It's only a tester or a hog they want, your honour, to give 'em to drink your honour's health,' said Paddy.

'A hog to drink my health?'

'Ay, that is a thirteen, plase your honour; all as one as an English shilling.'

I threw them a shilling: the hay-rope was withdrawn, and at last we went on. We heard no more of Paddy till evening. He came in two hours after us, and expected to be doubly paid *for driving my honour's gentlemen* so well.

I must say that on this journey, though I met with many delays and disasters; though one of my horses was lamed in shoeing by a smith, who came home drunk from a funeral; and though the back panel of my carriage was broken by the pole of a chaise; and though one day I went without my dinner at a large desolate inn, where nothing was to be had but whiskey; and though one night I lay in a little smoky den, in which the meanest of my servants in England would have thought it impossible to sleep; and though I complained bitterly, and swore it was impracticable for a gentleman to travel in Ireland; yet I never remember to have experienced, on any journey, less ennui.

Maria Edgeworth (1767–1849), *Ennui* (1809).

MISS ELIZABETH HAMILTON—*known to her readers as Eliza Hamilton although she preferred to be called Mrs Hamilton—was, like Maria Edgeworth, another of those impecunious and sickly Georgian ladies, in her case a prey to gout and bad eyesight, who somehow managed to get through enough work in a day to cripple a shire horse.*

Mrs Hamilton was what is called, rather bleakly, a 'miscellaneous writer'. She was a Scot of ancient family whose philanthropic work and sympathetic stories on behalf of the Scottish agricultural poor, not forgetting her much-beloved ballad 'My ain Fireside' which, emotionally rendered, has moistened many a cheek at Burns Night Suppers ever since, made her a famous and important figure of her time. When she died, Maria Edgeworth wrote a moving obituary.

But not all Mrs Hamilton's books were serious in intent. She cut loose with Memoirs of Modern Philosophers *which was an ironic tilt at those amateur philosophers, like Tristram Shandy's father, who argued on principles which they believed in but did not wholly understand.*

Mrs Hamilton herself believed in good old Scottish common sense but in the book her anti-heroine, Bridgetina Botherim, is a New Thinker who uses fashionable vogue-words like 'energized', believes in both reason and sensibility and has no sense at all.

In the story Bridgetina has set her cap at an agreeable young man called Henry, but to her surprise and dismay her peculiar behaviour has put him off. She makes a rational decision (in accordance with her sensibilities) on how to heal the breach:

The three following days were employed by Bridgetina in the composition of a letter, which she determined should be a master-piece of fine writing. It was, indeed, the very essence of philosophy, and flower of eloquence. The style was sublime and energetic, adorned in every sentence by strings of double and treble epithets, and all the new-coined noun-verbs and verb-nouns that have of late so much enriched the English language. As to the arguments, the reader must have formed a very inadequate idea of Bridgetina's powers, if he does not believe them to be unanswerable. After having carefully taken a copy, which she resolved should on some future day be generously presented to the public, she consigned the letter to the care of Jenny, with instructions to give it into Henry's own hand, and diligently to observe the expression of his countenance while he perused it.

The twenty minutes of Jenny's absence appeared an age to Bridgetina. She took her station at the window, and at length had the happiness of seeing her messenger of love appear, loaded to her wish, with a packet still larger than her own. 'He has written! He has written!' cried she, in an ecstasy. 'He has at length deigned to enter into a discussion on the important truths it has been my glory to promulgate. My powers shall be again called forth in an answer. Our correspondence shall be printed. It shall be published. It shall be called *The Sweet Sensations of Sensibility*, or the Force of Argument. But here she comes. Give me the letter. But before I open it, let me know how he received mine. I see by this it must have arrived in a moment of impression. Did he not kiss the seal? Did he not in trembling ecstasy press it to his throbbing bosom? Tell me, tell me all, I conjure you.'

'He did not kiss a bit of it, that I saw, Ma'am,' returned Jenny. 'He only took it out of my hand, and said Pshaw.'

'Pshaw! What does Pshaw signify? What is its etymology? From whence its derivation? I must look to the dictionary. But did you mark his looks, as he perused the important pages? Did you observe where he changed colour, where he appeared struck with admiration, and where thrilled with delight?'

'I could see nothing of all which you says, Ma'am: for though I told him as how that you desired me to see him pruse it, he only said Phoh! and walked into his closet.'

'Charming delicacy! But here, here it is that I shall view the portrait of his soul. Here the high-wrought frenzied emotions of his bosom are doubtless portrayed. Here—'

'Bless me, Ma'am, how pale you look! Aye, that is the very letter I carried to the gentleman, sure enough. The seal not so much as broken! I'll be bound he never read a word on't. Well now, I vow I never saw a more ungenteeler thing done in all my life; and if I was you, Ma'am, (thof to be sure, you must know best) but I should ha' my fingers burnt before I should write another sullebul to such a grumpish sort of a gentleman.'

'My epistle of fourteen pages, my precious essay on philosophy and love, returned without a perusal—returned in a blank cover! O hideous perversion of intellect! O prejudices, obstinate and invincible! Has he no sense of justice, no sense of the duty he owes society, that he thus deprives of her usefulness one of its most valuable members? O Jenny, Jenny, I can energize no longer.'

Eliza Hamilton (1758–1816), *Memoirs of Modern Philosophers* (1800).

➧ It seems that Bridgetina was based upon a real person, the celebrated New Thinker and feminist Mary Hays, author of a biography of illustrious women which ran to six volumes. Charles Lamb wrote of her:

'G— forbid
I should
pass my days
with Miss H—s.'

═════════

*T*HE *rise of the woman novelist and the novel of manners reached its peak with Jane Austen.*

Virginia Woolf wrote that Jane Austen, of all the great novelists, was the most difficult to catch in the act of greatness. It could also be said that of the great humorists Jane Austen is as difficult as any to catch in the act of being overtly humorous. Her humour suffused almost everything she wrote but, with one or two exceptions, like Mr Collins in Pride and Prejudice, *not through comical characters; nor through the sort of near-farcical predicaments which Fielding, Smollett, Sterne, and Fanny Burney contrived. Jane Austen's humour was largely in her tone of voice, her choice of words, the manner in which she described people and places; above all, in her cool, detached irony.*

Jane Austen's ironic touch might well have owed something to the example set by Henry Fielding, the master of irony. In Fielding's Joseph Andrews, *when the innkeeper's termagant wife discovers her husband seducing the chamber-maid, the erring husband gets away with it except for 'quietly and contentedly bearing to be reminded of his Transgressions, as a kind of Penance, once or twice a day, during the Residue of his life'.*

Jane Austen has a similar scene of a husband, Lord Middleton, being reprimanded for behaving disgracefully, but being a Jane Austen novel the husband's crime is merely to invite two girl cousins to his home without first consulting his good wife.

The punishment meted out by Lady Middleton is the same as that administered by the innkeeper's wife but scaled down a little so as to be perfectly in character:

As it was impossible, however, now to prevent their coming, Lady Middleton resigned herself to the idea of it with all the philosophy of a well-bred woman, contenting herself with merely giving her husband a gentle reprimand on the subject five or six times every day.

Jane Austen (1775–1817), *Sense and Sensibility* (1811).

The ladies and the gentlemen who people the novels do not, as it were, wander on but are properly introduced in a descriptive paragraph; a sketch which, with small,

*precise brush-strokes, tells us not all, because Miss Austen writes implicitly, but
all we need to know at this point:*

Vanity was the beginning and end of Sir Walter Elliot's character; vanity of
purpose and of situation. He had been remarkably handsome in his youth;
and, at fifty-four, was still a very fine man. Few women could think more of
their personal appearance than he did; nor could the valet of any new-made
lord be more delighted with the place he held in society. He considered the
blessing of beauty as inferior only to the blessing of a baronetcy; and the Sir
Walter Elliot, who united these gifts, was the constant object of his warmest
respect and devotion.

Persuasion (1818).

Mrs Ferrars was a little, thin woman, upright, even to formality, in her figure,
and serious, even to sourness, in her aspect. Her complexion was sallow;
and her features small, without beauty, and naturally without expression;
but a lucky contraction of the brow had rescued her countenance from the
disgrace of insipidity by giving it the strong characters of pride and ill nature.

Sense and Sensibility (1811).

All that could be done was to sit down at the end of the counter which
seemed to promise the quickest succession; one gentleman only was standing
there, and it is probable that Elinor was not without hope of exciting his
politeness to a quicker dispatch. But the correctness of his eye and the delicacy
of his taste proved to be beyond his politeness. He was giving orders for
a toothpick-case for himself, and till its size, shape, and ornaments were
determined, all of which, after examining and debating for a quarter of an
hour over every toothpick-case in the shop, were finally arranged by his own
inventive fancy, he had no leisure to bestow any other attention on the two
ladies than what was comprised in three or four very broad stares; a kind of
notice which served to imprint on Elinor the remembrance of a person and
face of strong, natural, sterling insignificance.

Ibid.

*Jane Austen's eye for the telling detail and her gift for the swift, destructive phrase
were not assumed for the purposes of her novel-writing but were part of her nature,
as extracts from letters to her sister Cassandra and others show:*

He seems a very harmless sort of young Man—nothing to like or dislike in
him;—goes out shooting and hunting with the two others all the morning—
and plays at whist & making queer faces in the evening.

Only think of Mrs Holder's being dead!—Poor woman, she has done the only
thing in the World she could possibly do, to make one cease to abuse her.

We had a Miss North and a Mr Gould of our party; the latter walked home
with me after tea. He is a very young man, just entered Oxford, wears
spectacles, and has heard that 'Evelina' was written by Dr Johnson.

Dr Gardiner was married yesterday to Mrs Percy and her three daughters.

You express so little anxiety about my being murdered under Ash Park Copse by Mrs Hulbert's servant, that I have a great mind not to tell you whether I was or not.

Mrs Blount was the only one much admired. She appeared exactly as she did in September, with the same broad face, diamond bandeau, white shoes, pink husband, and fat neck.

Mrs Hall of Sherborne, was brought to bed yesterday of a dead child, some weeks before she expected, owing to a fright. I suppose she happened unawares to look at her husband.

Letters.

Miss Austen's clear, and sometimes glittering, eye was devoid of sentimentality. Even towards babies:

A fond mother, though in pursuit of praise for her children the most rapacious of human beings, is likewise the most credulous; her demands are exorbitant; but she will swallow anything; and the excessive affection of the Miss Steeles towards her offspring were viewed therefore by Lady Middleton without the smallest surprise or distrust. She saw with maternal complacency all the impertinent incroachments and mischievous tricks to which her cousins submitted. She saw their sashes untied, their hair pulled about their ears, their work-bags searched, and their knives and scissors stolen away, and felt no doubt of it being a reciprocal enjoyment. It suggested no other surprise than that Elinor and Marianne should sit so composedly by, without claiming a share in what was passing.

'John is in such spirits today!' said she, on his taking Miss Steele's pocket handkerchief and throwing it out of window. 'He is full of monkey tricks.'

And soon afterwards, on the second boy's violently pinching one of the same lady's fingers, she fondly observed, 'How playful William is!'

'And here is my sweet little Annamaria,' she added, tenderly caressing a little girl of three years old, who had not made a noise for the last two minutes; 'And she is always so gentle and quiet. Never was there such a quiet little thing!'

But unfortunately in bestowing these embraces, a pin in her ladyship's head-dress, slightly scratching the child's neck, produced from this pattern of gentleness such violent screams as could hardly be outdone by any creature professedly noisy. The mother's consternation was excessive; but it could not surpass the alarm of the Miss Steeles, and everything was done by all three, in so critical an emergency, which affection could suggest as likely to assuage the agonies of the little sufferer. She was seated in her mother's lap, covered with kisses, her wound bathed with lavender-water, by one of the Miss Steeles, who was on her knees to attend her, and her mouth stuffed with sugar-plums by the other. With such a reward for her tears, the child was too wise to cease crying.

Sense and Sensibility.

In Emma, *Emma and her party are invited to a strawberry-gathering picnic. One of the party is the garrulous Mrs Elton, and the conversation at the strawberry-beds, with enthusiasm for strawberries gradually wilting in the hot sunshine, must be been one of the earliest examples of the stream-of-consciousness writing which Sterne had experimented with in* Tristram Shandy.

Mrs Elton, in all her apparatus of happiness, her large bonnet and her basket, was very ready to lead the way in gathering, accepting, or talking—strawberries, and only strawberries, could now be thought or spoken of. 'The best fruit in England—every body's favourite—always wholesome. These the finest beds and finest sorts.—Delightful to gather for one's self—the only way of really enjoying them.—Morning decidedly the best time—never tired—every sort good—hautboy infinitely superior—no comparison—the others hardly eatable—hautboys very scarce—Chili preferred—white wood finest flavour of all—price of strawberries in London—abundance around Bristol—Maple Grove—cultivation—beds when to be renewed—gardeners thinking exactly different—no general rule—gardeners never to be put out of their way—delicious fruit—only too rich to be eaten much of—inferior to cherries—currants more refreshing—only objection to gathering strawberries the stooping—glaring sun—tired to death—could bear it no longer—must go and sit in the shade.'

Emma (1816).

England was at war with France and the political situation at home was troubled but neither subject intruded into the novels, no doubt for the very good reason that neither war nor politics intruded much into the lives of the rural gentry of the early 1800s; war was fought by small, professional armies and politics was mainly the concern of the great landowners and London place-seekers.

Sexual passion had little place, either. More probably because it, too, was not a subject for discussion in that small area of society rather than because of prudery on Jane Austen's part. In fact she did deal with the sexual impulse, humorously and not at all timidly, in a fragment from an unfinished novel.

Sir Edward Denham, inspired by reading in Samuel Richardson's novel Clarissa Harlowe *of Robert Lovelace's brutal seduction and ruination of Clarissa, is convinced that he is destined to conduct his own wooing along similar lines:*

Sir Edward's great object in life was to be seductive.—With such personal advantages as he knew himself to possess, and such talents as he did also give himself credit for, he regarded it as his duty.—He felt that he was formed to be a dangerous man—quite in the line of the Lovelaces.—The very name of Sir Edward he thought, carried some degree of fascination with it.—To be generally gallant and assiduous about the fair, to make fine speeches to every pretty girl, was but the inferior part he had to play.—Miss Heywood, or any other young woman with any pretensions to beauty, he was entitled (according to his own views of society) to approach with high compliment and rhapsody on the slightest acquaintance; but it was Clara alone on whom he had serious designs; it was Clara whom he meant to seduce.

Her seduction was quite determined on. Her situation in every way called for it. She was his rival in Lady Denham's favour, she was young, lovely and dependent.—He had very early seen the necessity of the case, and had now been long trying with cautious assiduity to make an impression on her heart, and to undermine her principles.—Clara saw through him, and had not the least intention of being seduced—but she bore with him patiently enough to confirm the sort of attachment which her personal charms had raised.—A greater degree of discouragement indeed would not have affected Sir Edward. He was armed against the highest pitch of disdain or aversion.—If she could not be won by affection, he must carry her off. He knew his business.— Already had he had many musings on the subject. If he *were* constrained so to act, he must naturally wish to strike out something new, to exceed those who had gone before him—and he felt a strong curiosity whether the neighbourhood of Timbuctoo might not afford some solitary house adapted for Clara's reception;—but the expense alas! of measures in that masterly style was ill-suited to his purse, and prudence obliged him to prefer the quietest sort of ruin and disgrace for the object of his affections.

Sanditon (ed. R. W. Chapman; 1926).

When Fanny Burney wrote Evelina, *novels were still widely regarded as rubbish, trivial romances to beguile the servant classes. But Richardson, Fielding, Smollett, and Sterne had demonstrated that novels could also be intelligent, morally instructive (except Sterne), and amusing (except Richardson) and during the last half of the century novels became increasingly popular among all classes. Most towns had circulating libraries which also sold trinkets, lottery tickets, and toys, and the local circulating library became the female equivalent of the male coffee-house where genteel ladies could meet each other to exchange books, gossip, and scandal. The novel had achieved some kind of social respectability.*

The majority of the new novel-readers were women and perhaps it was because Jane Austen knew that most of her readers would understand from their own experience what she was getting at that she was able to write about feminine behaviour and emotions with such unprecedented subtlety:

A family of ten children will always be called a fine family, where there are heads, and arms, and legs enough for the number; but the Morlands had little other right to the word, for they were in general very plain, and Catherine, for many years of her life, as plain as any. She had a thin awkward figure, a sallow skin without colour, dark lank hair, and strong features . . .

Such was Catherine Morland at ten. At fifteen appearances were mending . . . her love of dirt gave way to an inclination for finery, and she grew clean as she grew smart; she had now the pleasure of sometimes hearing her father and mother remark on her personal improvement. 'Catherine grows quite a good-looking girl; she is almost pretty to-day,' were the words which caught her ears now and then; and how welcome were the sounds! To look *almost* pretty is an acquisition of higher delight to a girl who has been looking plain the first fifteen years of her life than a beauty from her cradle can ever receive.

Northanger Abbey (1818).

A year or two later, Catherine is taken to Bath by a kindly neighbour. The modest Catherine and her flighty friend, Isabella Thorpe, are visiting the Pump Room when Isabella notices two young men glancing meaningfully in her direction. Isabella reacts as would any pretty ingenue *of her age:*

'For Heaven's sake, let us move away from this end of the room.' [said Isabella] 'Do you know, there are two odious young men who have been staring at me this half-hour. They really put me quite out of countenance. Let us go and look at the arrivals. They will hardly follow us there.'

Away they walked to the book; and while Isabella examined the names, it was Catherine's employment to watch the proceedings of these alarming young men.

'They are not coming this way, are they? I hope they are not so impertinent as to follow us. Pray let me know if they are coming. I am determined I will not look up.'

In a few moments Catherine, with unaffected pleasure, assured her that she need not be longer uneasy, as the gentlemen had just left the Pump Room.

'And which way are they gone?' said Isabella, turning hastily round. 'One was a very good-looking young man.'

'They went towards the churchyard.'

'Well, I am amazingly glad I have got rid of them! And now, what say you to going to Edgar's Buildings with me, and looking at my new hat? You said you should like to see it.'

Catherine readily agreed. 'Only,' she added, 'perhaps we may overtake the young men.'

'Oh! never mind that. If we make haste we shall pass by them presently, and I am dying to show you my hat.'

'But if we only wait a few minutes, there will be no danger of our seeing them at all.'

'I shall not pay them any such compliment, I assure you. I have no notion of treating men with such respect. *That* is the way to spoil them.'

Catherine had nothing to oppose against such reasoning; and therefore, to show the independence of Miss Thorpe, and her resolution of humbling the sex, they set off immediately as fast as they could walk, in pursuit of the two young men.

Ibid.

The most popular of Jane Austen's six published books proved to be Pride and Prejudice, *perhaps the finest example we have of courtship comedy in the novel of manners.*

The book's opening sentence sets the tone precisely:

It is a truth universally acknowledged, that a single man in possession of a good fortune, must be in want of a wife.
Pride and Prejudice (1813).

Mrs Bennet, whose chief concern in life was to get her daughters married, was in want of five single men of good fortune but for just one to move into nearby Netherfield Park was an encouraging start, particularly as he had an aristocratic friend. The complicated process of match-making began.

Soon another suitor appeared: Mr Bennet's nephew, the egregious young clergyman, Mr Collins. As Mr Bennet had five daughters and no male heirs the estate was entailed and Mr Collins would eventually inherit, so marriage to one of the Bennet girls seemed to Mrs Bennet to be wholly desirable.

Mrs Bennet was a rather silly woman, but her problem of finding suitable husbands for five daughters with no dowries was then a very real one. Young ladies and their mothers reading the book in 1813 would have had the situations in the novel considerably heightened for them by their awareness of the underlying seriousness of the girls' predicament. Marriage was the only comfortable future open to genteel young women, and suitable husbands were in desperately short supply: at that time one girl in four ended her life unmarried. Hence the high incidence of comical maiden aunts in eighteenth- and early nineteenth-century plays and novels.

There was, however, one snag with having Mr Collins as a husband: he was unspeakably awful: a self-regarding, pompous prig whose fawning admiration for his patron, the viciously haughty Lady Catherine de Bourgh, seeped through most of his conversation. His proposal of marriage was accepted in the end, not by one of the Bennet girls but by their friend Charlotte Lucas, who knew exactly what sort of man she was marrying but, accepting that it was probably her last chance, coolly and bravely took it, hoping that she could make some sort of tolerable life for herself even with him.

Almost as brave a decision as marrying Mr Collins was turning him down; he was, after all, respectable and well off. Before turning his attention to Charlotte Lucas, Mr Collins had, in a famous episode, proposed to Elizabeth Bennet, the liveliest and wittiest of the Bennet daughters. Mr Collins's mind at the time was so full of his own point of view that there was no room left in it for him to take any notice of Elizabeth's feelings in the matter.

The result is one of the most delicately insufferable proposals yet endured by a novel's heroine:

On finding Mrs Bennet, Elizabeth, and one of the younger girls together, soon after breakfast, he addressed the mother in these words,

'May I hope, Madam, for your interest with your fair daughter, Elizabeth, when I solicit for the honour of a private audience with her in the course of this morning?'

Before Elizabeth had time for any thing but a blush of surprise, Mrs Bennet instantly answered,

'Oh dear!—Yes—certainly.—I am sure Lizzy will be very happy—I am sure she can have no objection.—Come, Kitty, I want you upstairs.' And gathering her work together, she was hastening away, when Elizabeth called out,

'Dear Ma'am, do not go.—I beg you will not go.—Mr Collins must excuse me.—He can have nothing to say to me that any body need not hear. I am going away myself.'

'No, no, nonsense, Lizzy.—I desire you will stay where you are.'—And upon Elizabeth's seeming really, with vexed and embarrassed looks, about to escape, added, 'Lizzy, I *insist* upon your staying and hearing Mr Collins.'

Elizabeth would not oppose such an injunction—and a moment's consideration making her also sensible that it would be wisest to get it over as soon and as quietly as possible, she sat down again, and tried to conceal by incessant employment the feelings which were divided between distress and diversion. Mrs Bennet and Kitty walked off, and as soon as they were gone Mr Collins began.

'Believe me, my dear Elizabeth, that your modesty, so far from doing you any disservice, rather adds to your other perfections. You would have been less amiable in my eyes had there *not* been this little unwillingness; but allow me to assure you I have your respected mother's permission for this address. You can hardly doubt the purport of my discourse, however your natural delicacy may lead you to dissemble; my attentions have been too marked to be mistaken. Almost as soon as I entered the house I singled you out as the companion of my future life. But before I am run away with by my feelings on this subject, perhaps it will be advisable for me to state my reasons for marrying—and moreover for coming into Hertfordshire with the design of selecting a wife, as I certainly did.'

The idea of Mr Collins, with all his solemn composure, being run away with by his feelings, made Elizabeth so near laughing that she could not use the short pause he allowed in any attempt to stop him farther, and he continued:

'My reasons for marrying are, first, that I think it a right thing for every clergyman in easy circumstances (like myself) to set the example of matrimony in his parish. Secondly, that I am convinced that it will add very greatly to my happiness; and thirdly—which perhaps I ought to have mentioned earlier, that it is the particular advice and recommendation of the very noble lady whom I have the honour of calling patroness. Twice has she condescended to give me her opinion (unasked too!) on this subject; and it was but the very Saturday night before I left Hunsford—between our pools at quadrille, while Mrs Jenkinson was arranging Miss de Bourgh's foot-stool, that she said, "Mr Collins, you must marry. A clergyman like you must marry.—Chuse properly, chuse a gentlewoman for *my* sake; and for your *own*, let her be an active, useful sort of person, not brought up high, but able to make a small income go a good way. This is my advice. Find such a woman as soon as you can, bring her to Hunsford, and I will visit her." Allow me, by the way, to observe, my fair cousin, that I do not reckon the notice and kindness of Lady Catherine de Bourgh as among the least of the advantages in my power to offer. You will find her manners beyond any thing I can describe; and your wit and vivacity I think must be acceptable to her, especially when tempered with the silence and respect which her rank will inevitably excite. Thus much for my general intention in favour of matrimony; it remains to be told why my views were directed to Longbourn instead of my own neighbourhood, where I assure you there are many amiable young women. But the fact is, that being, as I am, to inherit this estate after the death of your honoured father (who, however, may live many years longer), I could not satisfy myself without resolving to chuse a wife from among his daughters, that the loss to them might be as little as possible, when the melancholy event takes place—which, however, as I have already said, may not be for several years. This has been my motive, my fair cousin, and I flatter myself it will not sink me in your esteem. And now nothing remains but for me to assure you in the most animated language of the violence of my affection. To fortune I am perfectly indifferent, and shall make no demand of that nature on your father, since I am well aware that it could not be complied with; and that one thousand pounds in the 4 per cents, which will not be yours till after your mother's decease, is all that you may ever be entitled to. On that head, therefore, I shall be uniformly silent; and you may assure yourself that no ungenerous reproach shall ever pass my lips when we are married.'

It was absolutely necessary to interrupt him now.

'You are too hasty, Sir,' she cried. 'You forget that I have made no answer. Let me do it without farther loss of time. Accept my thanks for the compliment you are paying me. I am very sensible of the honour of your proposals, but it is impossible for me to do otherwise than decline them.'

'I am not now to learn,' replied Mr Collins, with a formal wave of the hand, 'that it is usual with young ladies to reject the addresses of the young man whom they secretly mean to accept, when he first applies for their favour; and that sometimes the refusal is repeated a second or even a third time. I am therefore by no means discouraged by what you have just said, and shall hope to lead you to the altar ere long.'

'Upon my word, Sir,' cried Elizabeth, 'your hope is rather an extraordinary one after my declaration. I do assure you that I am not one of those young ladies (if such young ladies there are) who are so daring as to risk their happiness on the chance of being asked a second time. I am perfectly serious in my refusal.—You could not make *me* happy, and I am convinced that I am the last woman in the world who would make *you* so.—Nay, were your friend Lady Catherine to know me, I am persuaded she would find me in every respect ill qualified for the situation.'

'Were it certain that Lady Catherine would think so,' said Mr Collins very gravely—'but I cannot imagine that her ladyship would at all disapprove of you. And you may be certain that when I have the honour of seeing her again I shall speak in the highest terms of your modesty, economy, and other amiable qualifications.'

'Indeed, Mr Collins, all praise of me will be unnecessary. You must give me leave to judge for myself, and pay me the compliment of believing what I say. I wish you very happy and very rich, and by refusing your hand, do all in my power to prevent your being otherwise. In making me the offer, you must have satisfied the delicacy of your feelings with regard to my family, and may take possession of Longbourn estate whenever it falls, without self-reproach. This matter may be considered, therefore, as finally settled.' And rising as she thus spoke, she would have quitted the room, had not Mr Collins thus addressed her.

'When I do myself the honour of speaking to you next on this subject I shall hope to receive a more favourable answer than you have now given me; though I am far from accusing you of cruelty at present, because I know it to be the established custom of your sex to reject a man on the first application, and perhaps you have even now said as much to encourage my suit as would be consistent with the true delicacy of the female character.'

'Really, Mr Collins,' cried Elizabeth, with some warmth, 'you puzzle me exceedingly. If what I have hitherto said can appear to you in the form of encouragement, I know not how to express my refusal in such a way as may convince you of its being one.'

'You must give me leave to flatter myself, my dear cousin, that your refusal of my addresses is merely words of course. My reasons for believing it are briefly these:—It does not appear to me that my hand is unworthy your acceptance, or that the establishment I can offer would be any other than highly desirable. My situation in life, my connections with the family of De Bourgh, and my relationship to your own, are circumstances highly in my favour; and you should take it into farther consideration that in spite of your manifold attractions, it is by no means certain that another offer of marriage may ever be made to you. Your portion is unhappily so small that it will in all likelihood undo the effects of your loveliness and amiable qualifications. As I must therefore conclude that you are not serious in your rejection of me, I shall chuse to attribute it to wish of increasing my love by suspense, according to the usual practice of elegant females.'

'I do assure you, Sir, that I have no pretension whatever to that kind of elegance which consists in tormenting a respectable man. I would rather be paid the compliment of being believed sincere. I thank you again and again for the honour you have done me in your proposals, but to accept them is absolutely impossible. My feelings in every respect forbid it. Can I speak plainer? Do not consider me now as an elegant female intending to plague you, but as a rational creature speaking the truth from her heart.'

'You are uniformly charming!' cried he, with an air of awkward gallantry; 'and I am persuaded that when sanctioned by the express authority of both your excellent parents, my proposals will not fail of being acceptable.'

To such perseverance in self-deception Elizabeth would make no reply, and immediately and in silence withdrew; determined, if he persisted in considering her repeated refusals as flattering encouragement, to apply to her father, whose negative might be uttered in such a manner as must be decisive, and whose behaviour at least could not be mistaken for the affectation and coquetry of an elegant female.   Ibid.

─────────

*I*F *the eighteenth century began as the Age of Reason it ended as the Age of Sentiment: Sense gave way to Sensibility.*

Neoclassical literature and painting had Daphnis and Chloe lolling about in all-purpose glades; trees, of a suitable shape to fit the composition, were painted 'brown as an old violin'.

Romantics at the end of the century looked at nature more closely and realistically and began to write of daffodils fluttering and dancing in the breeze: painters painted trees the way they looked, green and glistening with moisture.

The Romantic Revival, as this change of approach in the arts is usually called, not only made sentimentality fashionable but considerably widened the scope of novelists in other ways. Once the neoclassical rules were loosened the body of creative thought spilled out in all directions, and not always towards more naturalism. One of Romanticism's more bizarre manifestations was a morbid interest in medievalism, mystery, implicit eroticism, melancholy, orientalism, and violence, exemplified by the origination in England of the Gothic novel. The first successful example and the book which created a fashion for supernatural romances was The Castle of Otranto *by Horace Walpole, published in* 1764.

Many imitations and variations followed, notably The Monk *by Matthew Lewis,* 1795 *(blasphemy and miscellaneous depravity, written in ten days when he was* 19; *it contains the deathless line: 'God Almighty! It was the bleeding nun!'), and* Vathek, An Arabian Tale *by William Beckford,* 1787 *(sex and Oriental cruelty; Beckford claimed that he wrote it at the age of 22 in French in three days and two nights without taking his clothes off).*

Gothic novels became immensely popular with lending library subscribers, and in 1798 Jane Austen began a novel, entitled Susan, *to show 'the pernicious effect of too much novel-reading on an imaginative young girl who believed that Gothic novels were true to life'. The novel was published in 1818 under the title* Northanger Abbey.

Meanwhile the same idea had occurred to an Irish-born poet and political satirist, Eaton Stannard Barrett, who in 1813 published a highly successful comic novel warning young ladies of the effect that over-indulgence in Gothic novels could have on 'a Fair Romance Reader'. It is broad satire; a wild parody of the Gothic style and its overblown romantic prose:

CHAPTER I

'Blow, blow, thou wintry wind.'
—*Shakespeare.*

'Blow, breezes, blow.'
—*Moore.*

It was on a nocturnal night in autumnal October; the wet rain fell in liquid quantities, and the thunder rolled in an awful and Ossianly manner. The lowly but peaceful inhabitants of a small but decent cottage were just sitting down to their homely but wholesome supper, when a loud knocking at the door alarmed them. Bertram armed himself with a ladle. 'Lack-a-daisy!' cried old Margueritone, and little Billy seized the favourable moment to fill his mouth with meat. Innocent fraud! happy childhood!

'The father's lustre and the mother's bloom.'

Bertram then opened the door, when, lo! pale, breathless, dripping and with a look that would have shocked the Royal Humane Society, a beautiful female tottered into the room. 'Lack-a-daisy! ma'am,' said Margueritone, 'are you wet?' 'Wet?' exclaimed the fair unknown, wringing a rivulet of rain from the corner of her robe; 'O ye gods, wet!' Margueritone felt the justice, the gentleness of the reproof, and turned the subject, by recommending a glass of spirits.

'Spirit of my sainted sire.'

The stranger sipped, shook her head, and fainted. Her hair was long and dark, and the bed was ready; so since she seems in distress, we will leave her there awhile, lest we should betray an ignorance of the world in appearing not to know the proper time for deserting people.

On the rocky summit of a beetling precipice, whose base was lashed by the angry Atlantic, stood a moated and turreted structure called Il Castello di Grimgothico. As the northern tower had remained uninhabited since the death of its late lord, Henriques de Violenci, lights and figures were, *par consequence*, observed in it at midnight. Besides, the black eyebrows of the present baron had a habit of meeting for several years, and *quelque fois*, he paced the picture-gallery with a hurried step. These circumstances combined, there could be no doubt of his having committed murder . . .

CHAPTER II

'Oh!'
— *Milton.*

'Ah!'
— *Pope.*

One evening, the Baroness de Violenci, having sprained her left leg in the composition of an ecstatic ode, resolved not to go to Lady Penthesilea Rouge's rout. While she was sitting alone at a plate of prawns, the footman entered with a basket, which had just been left for her. 'Lay it down, John,' said she, touching his forehead with her fork. The gay-hearted young fellow did as he was desired and capered out of the room. Judge of her astonishment when she found, on opening it, a little cherub of a baby sleeping within. An oaken cross, with 'Hysterica' inscribed in chalk, was appended at its neck, and a mark, like a bruised gooseberry, added interest to its elbow. As she and her lord had never had children, she determined, *sur le champ*, on adopting the pretty Hysterica. Fifteen years did this worthy woman dedicate to the progress of her little charge; and in that time taught her every mortal accomplishment. Her sigh, particularly, was esteemed the softest in Europe.

But the stroke of death is inevitable; come it must at last, and neither virtue nor wisdom can avoid it. In a word, the good old Baroness died, and our heroine fell senseless on her body.

'O what a fall was there, my countrymen!'

But, alas! misfortunes are often gregarious, like sheep. For one night, when our heroine had repaired to the chapel, intending to drop her customary tear on the tomb of her sainted benefactress, she heard on a sudden,

'Oh, horrid horrible, and horridest horror!'

the distant organ peal a solemn voluntary. While she was preparing, in much terror and astonishment, to accompany it with her voice, four men in masks rushed from among some tombs and bore her to a carriage, which instantly drove off with the whole party. In vain she sought to soften them by swoons, tears, and a simple little ballad; they sat counting murders and not minding her. As the blinds of the carriage were closed the whole way, we waive a description of the country which they traversed. Besides, the prospect within the carriage will occupy the reader enough; for in one of the villains Hysterica discovered—Count Stilletto! She fainted. On the second day the carriage stopped at an old castle, and she was conveyed into a tapestried apartment— in which rusty daggers, mouldering bones, and ragged palls lay scattered in all the profusion of feudal plenty—where the delicate creature fell ill of an inverted eyelash, caused by continual weeping . . .

CHAPTER III

'Sure such a day as this was never seen!'
—*Thomas Thumb.*

'The day, th' important day!'
—*Addison.*

'O giorno felice!'
—*Italian.*

The morning of the happy day destined to unite our lovers was ushered into the world with a blue sky, and the ringing of bells. Maidens, united in bonds of amity and artificial roses, come dancing to the pipe and tabor; while groups of children and chickens add hilarity to the union of congenial minds. On the left of the village are some plantations of tufted turnips; on the right a dilapidated dog-kennel 'With venerable grandeur marks the scene,' while everywhere the delighted eye catches monstrous mountains and minute daisies. In a word,

'All nature wears one universal grin.'

The procession now set forward to the church. The bride was habited in white drapery. Ten signs of the Zodiac, worked in spangles, sparkled round its edge, but Virgo was omitted at her desire, and the bridegroom proposed to dispense with Capricorn. Sweet delicacy! She held a port of myrtle in her hand, and wore on her head a small lighted torch emblematical of Hymen . . . The marriage ceremony passed off with great spirit, and the fond bridegroom, as he pressed her to his heart, felt how pure, how delicious are the joys of virtue.

Eaton Stannard Barrett (1786–1820), *The Heroine, or Adventures of a Fair Romance Reader* (1813).

———————

Part *of the Romantic movement was a growing awareness of locality, a feeling for regionalism which turned writers' minds to contemplating what was happening in their own back yards rather than in London, Edinburgh, or Dublin.*

Following Maria Edgeworth's success in writing about Ireland came a burst of novels and short stories (always a favourite Irish literary form) trying to pin down the authentic flavour of Irish speech and humour. Usually, unhappily, by means of impenetrable dialect full of knobbly, incomprehensible words.

An early success was achieved by Gerald Griffin, a dramatist, poet, and novelist who was born in Limerick and wrote about Southern Ireland. His best-known novel, The Collegians, *was adapted by Dion Boucicault into the successful stage comedy* The Colleen Bawn.

Here is a Griffin story. Mr Hardress sends for the local barber to trim his hair. The barber turns out to be as talkative as only an Irish barber can be but during the course of the one-way conversation Mr Hardress does at least learn a new recipe.

It is for limestone broth:

He had scarcely taken his seat before the toilet [dressing-table], when a soft tap at the door, and the sound of a small squeaking voice, announced the arrival of the hair-cutter. On looking round him, Hardress beheld a small, thin-faced, red-haired little man, with a tailor's shears dangling from his finger, bowing and smiling with a timid and conciliating air. In an evil hour for his patience, Hardress consented that he should commence operations.

'The piatez [potatoes] were very airly this year, sir,' he modestly began, after he had wrapped a check apron about the neck of Hardress, and made the other necessary arrangements.

'Very early, indeed. You needn't cut so fast.'

'Very airly, sir—the white-eyes especially. Them white-eyes are fine piatez. For the first four months I wouldn't ax a better piatie than a white-eye, with a bit o'bacon, if one had it; but after that the meal goes out of 'em, and they gets wet and bad. The cups arn't so good in the beginnin' o' the saison, but they hould better. Turn your head more to the light, sir, if you plase. The cups, indeed, are a fine substantial, lasting piatie. There's great nutriment in 'em for poor people, that would have nothin' else with them but themselves, or a grain o' salt. There's no piatie that eats better, when you have nothin' but a bit o' the little one (as they say) to eat with a bit o' the big. No piatie that eats so sweet with point.'

'With point?' Hardress repeated, a little amused by this fluent discussion of the poor hair-cutter upon the varieties of a dish which, from his childhood, had formed almost his only article of nutriment, and on which he expatiated with as much cognoscence and satisfaction as a fashionable gourmand might do on the culinary productions of Eustache Ude. 'What is point?'

'Don't you know what that is, sir? I'll tell you in a minute. A joke that them that has nothin' to do, an' plenty to eat, make upon the poor people that has nothin' to eat, and plenty to do. That is, when there's dry piatez on the table, and enough of hungry people about it, and the family would have, maybe, only one bit o' bacon hanging up above their heads, they'd peel a piatie first, and then they'd *point* it up at the bacon, and they'd fancy that it would have the taste o' the mait when they' be aitin' it after. That's what they call point, sir. A cheap sort o' diet it is (Lord help us!) that's plenty enough among the poor people in this country. A great plan for making a small bit o' pork go a long way in a large family.'

'Indeed it is but a slender sort of food. Those scissors you have are dreadful ones.'

'Terrible, sir. I sent my own over to the forge before I left home, to have an eye put in it; only for that, I'd be smarter a deal. Slender food it is, indeed. There's a deal o' poor people here in Ireland, sir, that are run so hard at times, that the wind of a bit o' mait is as good to 'em as the mait itself to them that would be used to it. The piatez are everythin'; the *kitchen* [anything eaten with the potatoes] little or nothin'. But there's a sort o' piatez (I don't know did your honour ever taste 'em) that's getting greatly in vogue now among 'em, an' is killin' half the country,—the white piatez, a piatie that has great produce, an' requires but little manure, and will grow in very poor land; but has no more strength nor nourishment in it than if you had boiled a handful o' saw-dust and made gruel of it, or put a bit of a deal board between your teeth and thought to make a breakfast of it. The black bulls themselves are better; indeed, the black bulls are a deal a better piatie than they're thought. When you'd peel 'em, they look as black as indigo, an' you'd have no mind to 'em at all; but I declare they're very sweet in the mouth, an' very strengthenin'. The English reds are a nate piatie, too; and the apple piatie (I don't know what made 'em be given up), an' the kidney (though delicate o' rearing); but give me the cups for all, that will hould the meal in 'em to the last, and won't require any inthricket tillage. Let a man have a middling-sized pit o'cups again the winter, a small *caish* [pig] to pay his rent, an' a handful o' turf behind the doore, an' he can defy the world.'

'You know as much, I think,' said Hardress, 'of farming as of hair-cutting.'

'Oyeh, if I had nothin' to depend upon but what heads comes across me this way, sir, I'd be in a poor way enough. But I have a little spot o' ground besides.'

'And a good taste for the produce.'

' 'Twas kind father for me to have that same. Did you every hear tell, sir, of what they call limestone broth?'

'Never.'

' 'Twas my father first made it. I'll tell you the story, sir, if you'll turn your head this way a minute.'

Hardress had no choice but to listen.

'My father went once upon a time about the country, in the idle season, seeing would he make a penny at all by cutting hair, or setting razhurs and penknives, or any other job that would fall in his way. Well an' good—he was one day walking alone in the mountains of Kerry, without a hai'p'ny in his pocket (for though he travelled a-foot, it cost him more than he earned), an' knowing there was but little love for a country Limerick man in the place where he was, on being half perished with the hunger, an' evening drawing nigh, he didn't know well what to do with himself till morning. Very good— he went along the wild road; an' if he did, he soon sees a farmhouse at a little distance o' one side—a snug-looking place, with the smoke curling up out of the chimney, an' all tokens of good living inside. Well, some people would live where a fox would starve. What do you think did my father do? He wouldn't beg (a thing one of our people never done yet, thank heaven!)

an' he hadn' the money to buy a thing, so what does he do? He takes up a couple o' the big limestones that were lying on the road in his two hands, an' away with him to the house. "Lord save all here!" says he, walkin' in the doore. "And you kindly," says they. "I'm come to you," says he, this way, looking at the two limestones, "to know would you let me make a little limestone broth over your fire, until I'll make my dinner?" "Limestone broth!" says they to him again; "what's that, aroo?" "Broth made o' lime-stone," says he; "what else?" "We never heard of such a thing," says they. "Why, then, you may hear it now," says he, "an' see it also, if you'll gi' me a pot an' a couple o' quarts o' soft water." "You can have it an' welcome," says they. So they put down the pot an' the water, an' my father went over an' tuk a chair hard by the pleasant fire for himself, an' put down his two limestones to boil, and kep stirrin' them round like stirabout. Very good—well, by-an'-by, when the water began to boil—"'Tis thickening finely," says my father; "now if it had a grain o' salt at all, 'twould be a great improvement to it." "Raich down the salt-box, Nell," says the man o' the house to his wife. So she did. "Oh, that's the very thing, just," says my father, shaking some of it into the pot. So he stirred it again awhile, looking as sober as a minister. By-an'-by, he takes the spoon he had stirring it, an' tastes it. "It is very good now," says he, "although it wan something yet." "What is it?" says they. "Oyeh, wisha nothing," says he; "maybe 'tis only fancy o' me." "If it's anything we can give you," says they, "you're welcome to it." "'Tis very good as it is," says he; "but when I'm at home, I find it gives it a fine flavour just to boil a little knuckle o' bacon, or mutton trotters, or anything that way along with it." "Raich hether that bone o' sheep's head we had at dinner yesterday, Nell," says the man o' the house. "Oyeh, don't mind it," says my father; "let it be as it is." "Sure if it improves it, you may as well," says they. "Baithershin'!" [Be it so] says my father, putting it down. So after boiling it a good piece longer, "'Tis as fine limestone broth," says he, "as ever was tasted; an' if a man had a few piatez," says he, looking at a pot of 'em that was smokin' in the chimney-corner, "he couldn't desire a better dinner." They gave him the piatez, and he made a good dinner of themselves an' the broth, not forgetting the bone, which he polished equal to chaney [china] before he let it go. The people themselves tasted it, an' thought it as good as any mutton broth in the world.'

Gerald Griffin (1803-40).

═══════════

THE *Romantic interest in regional literature quickly spread from Ireland to Scotland. In 1814 Walter Scott published* Waverley, *a novel about the Scottish Jacobite Rebellion of 1745, and Scott freely acknowledged that the inspiration to write a novel about Scotland and the Scots came from Maria Edgeworth's success in writing about Ireland.*

After Waverley, Scott produced a rapid succession of further novels about Auld Scotland and the success of these first initiated and then catered for a new kind of popular literature—the Romantic historical novel. Scott virtually created the modern historical novel, and in doing so also more or less invented Bonnie Scotland.

Although Scott's novels were usually drawn on a huge canvas and were full of action and strong emotion—what he called 'my big bow-wow strain'—some of his minor comic characters were very well drawn. Like Meg Dods, the innkeeper in Scott's St Ronan's Well, a practitioner of the fine old Scottish love of vituperation.

Mrs Dods is an aggressive woman at the best of times and only too ready to launch into spirited abuse of Lady Penelope of the big house and the smart folk she invites down from Edinburgh, as Mr Tyrrel, the book's hero, discovers when he asks Mrs Dods why the mineral waters of the Well are so highly thought of:

'I dinna ken, sir—they used to be thought good for naething, but here and there for a puir body's bairn, that had gotten the cruells [King's Evil], and could not afford a penniworth of salts. But my Leddy Penelope Penfeather had fa'an ill, it's like, as nae other body had ever fell ill, and sae she was to be cured some gate naebody was ever cured, which was naething mair than reasonable—and my leddy, ye ken, has wit at wull, and has a' the wise folk out from Edinburgh at her house at Windywa's younder, which it is her leddyship's will and pleasure to call Air-castle—and they have a' their different turns, and some can clink [beat out] verses, wi' their tale, as weel as Rob Burns or Allan Ramsay—and some rin up hill and down dale, knapping [breaking] the chucky stanes [pebbles] to pieces wi' hammers, like sae mony road-makers run daft—they say it is to see how the warld was made!—and some that play on all manner of ten-stringed instruments—and a wheen [small group of] sketching souls, that ye may see perched like craws on every craig in the country, e'en working at your ain trade, Mister Francie; forby men that had been in foreign parts, or said they had been there, whilk is a' ane, ye ken, and maybe twa or three draggle-tailed misses, that wear my Leddy Penelope's follies when she has dune wi' them, as her queans [sluts] of maids wear her second-hand claithes. So, after her leddy-ship's happy recovery, as they ca'd it, down cam the hail tribe of wild geese, and settled by the Well, to dine thereout on the bare grund, like a wheen tinklers; and they had sangs, and tunes, and healths, nae doubt, in praise of the fountain, as they ca'd the Well, and of Leddy Penelope Penfeather; and, lastly, they behov'd a' to take a solemn bumper of the spring, which, as I am tauld, made unco havoc among them or they wan hame; and this they ca'd Pick-nick, and a plague to them! And sae the jig was begun after her leddyship's pipe, and mony a mad measure has been danced sin' syne; for down cam masons and murgeon-makers [workmen who demolish old buildings], and preachers and player-folk, and Episcopalians and Methodists, and fools and fiddlers, and Papists and pie-bakers, and doctors and drugsters; by the shop-folk, that sell trash and trumpery at three prices—and so up got the bonny new Well, and down fell the honest auld town of St Ronan's, where blythe decent folk had been heartsome eneugh for mony a day before ony o' them were born, or ony sic vapouring fancies kittled in their cracked brains.'

Sir Walter Scott (1771–1832), *St Ronan's Well* (1824).

———

JOHN GALT *was a Scot whose humour was gentle and parochial. He was a Lowlander from Ayrshire who wrote an enormous number of historical novels, poems, travel pieces, and plays, most of which were on exotic themes and are now forgotten. Then he turned to writing about the country life of Ayrshire, which he knew well, and he produced three novels which became minor classics of Scottish regional humour.*

Annals of the Parish purported to be the personal chronicle of the Revd Micah Balwhidder; an account of the events which occurred in the village of Dalmailing in Ayrshire from 1760—the year in which George III became king—to 1810. The Revd Micah Balwhidder did not lead an exciting life and hardly anything happened at all in Dalmailing between 1760 and 1810 but it was all most interesting to him, and much of the pleasure of the book is in the minister's Pooter-like naïvety and unconscious humour.

He begins his annals by observing an uncanny similarity between his own life and that of his Sacred Majesty King George III:

In the same year, and on the same day of the same month, that his Sacred Majesty King George, the third of the name, came to his crown and kingdom, I was placed and settled as the minister of Dalmailing. When about a week thereafter this was known in the parish, it was thought a wonderful thing, and every body spoke of me and the new king as united in our trusts and temporalities, marvelling how the same should come to pass, and thinking the hand of Providence was in it, and that surely we were pre-ordained to fade and flourish in fellowship together; which has really been the case, for in the same season that his Most Excellent Majesty, as he was very properly styled in the proclamations for the general fasts and thanksgivings, was set by as a precious vessel which had received a crack or a flaw, and could only be serviceable in the way of an ornament, I was obliged, by reason of age and the growing infirmities of my recollection, to consent to the earnest entreaties of the Session, and to accept of Mr Amos to be my helper. I was long reluctant to do so, but the great respect that my people had for me, and the love that I bore towards them, over and above the sign that was given to me in the removal of the royal candlestick from its place, worked upon my heart and understanding, and I could not stand out. So, on the last Sabbath of the year 1810, I preached my last sermon, and it was a moving discourse. There were few dry eyes in the kirk that day, for I had been with the aged from the beginning—the young considered me as their natural pastor—and my bidding them all farewell was, as when of old among the heathen, an idol was taken away by the hands of the enemy.

John Galt (1779–1839), *Annals of the Parish* (1821).

The first Mrs Balwhidder had died some years previously. Much later, in 1796, the admirably economic second Mrs Balwhidder was also taken. The Minister feels that he should obtain a third Mrs Balwhidder:

In the month of February my second wife was gathered to the Lord. She had been very ill for some time with an income [pain] in her side, which no medicine could remove. I had the best doctors in the country-side to her, but their skill was of no avail, their opinions being, that her ail was caused by an internal abscess, for which physic has provided no cure. Her death was to me a great sorrow, for she was a most excellent wife, industrious to a degree, and managed everything with so brisk a hand, that nothing went wrong that she put it to. With her I had grown richer than any other minister in the presbytery; but above all, she was the mother of my bairns, which gave her a double claim upon me.

I laid her by the side of my first love, Betty Lanshaw, my own cousin that was, and I inscribed her name upon the same headstone; but time had drained my poetical vein, and I have not yet been able to indite an epitaph on her merits and virtues, for she had an eminent share of both. Her greatest fault—the best have their faults—was an over-earnestness to gather geer [bits and pieces], in the doing of which I thought she sometimes sacrificed the comforts of a pleasant fire-side, for she was never in her element but when she was keeping the servants eydent at their work. But, if by this she substracted something from the quietude that was most consonant to my nature, she has left cause, both in bank and bond, for me and her bairns to bless her great household activity.

She was not long deposited in her place of rest till I had occasion to find her loss. All my things were kept by her in a most perjinct [precise] and excellent order, but they soon fell into an amazing confusion, for, as she often said to me, I had a turn for heedlessness; insomuch, that although my daughter Janet was grown up, and able to keep the house, I saw that it would be necessary, as soon as decency would allow, for me to take another wife. I was moved to this chiefly by foreseeing that my daughter would in time be married, and taken away from me, but more on account of the servant lasses, who grew out of all bounds, verifying the proverb, 'Well kens the mouse when the cat's out of the house'. Besides this, I was now far down in the vale of years, and could not expect to be long without feeling some of the penalties of old age, although I was still a hail and sound man. It therefore behoved me to look in time for a helpmate, to tend me in my approaching infirmities.

Upon this important concern I reflected, as I may say, in the watches of the night, and, considering the circumstances of my situation, I saw it would not do for me to look out for an overly young woman, nor yet would it do for one of my ways to take an elderly maiden, ladies of that sort being liable to possess strong-set particularities. I therefore resolved that my choice should lie among widows of a discreet age; and I had a glimmer in my mind of speaking to Mrs Malcolm, but when I reflected on the saintly steadiness of her character, I was satisfied it would be of no use to think of her. Accordingly, I bent my brows, and looked towards Irville, which is an abundant trone [market-place] for widows and other single women; and I fixed my purpose on Mrs Nugent, the relic of a Professor in the University of Glasgow, both because she was a well-bred woman, without any children to plea about the interest of my own two, and likewise because she was held in great estimation by all who knew her, as a lady of a Christian principle.

It was sometime in the summer, however, before I made up my mind to speak to her on the subject; but one afternoon, in the month of August, I resolved to do so, and, with that intent, walked leisurely over to Irville, and after calling on the Revd Dr Dinwiddie, the minister, I stepped in, as if by chance, to Mrs Nugent's. I could see that she was a little surprised at my visit; however, she treated me with every possible civility, and her servant lass bringing in the tea things, in a most orderly manner, as punctually as the clock was striking, she invited me to sit still, and drink my tea with her; which I did, being none displeased to get such encouragement. However, I said nothing that time, but returned to the Manse, very well content with what I had observed, which made me fain to repeat my visit. So, in the course of the week, taking Janet, my daughter, with me, we walked over in the forenoon, and called at Mrs Nugent's first, before going to any other house; and Janet saying, as we came out to go to the minister's, that she thought Mrs Nugent an agreeable woman, I determined to knock the nail on the head without farther delay.

Accordingly, I invited the minister and his wife to dine with us on the Thursday following; and before leaving the town, I made Janet, while the minister and me were handling a subject, as a sort of thing of common civility, go to Mrs Nugent, and invite her also. Dr Dinwiddie was a gleg [clever] man, of a jocose nature; and he, guessing something of what I was ettling at, was very mirthful with me, but I kept my own counsel till a meet season.

On the Thursday, the company, as invited, came, and nothing extra-ordinary was seen, but in cutting up, and helping a hen, Dr Dinwiddie put one wing on Mrs Nugent's plate, and the other wing on my plate, and said, there have been greater miracles than these two wings flying together, which was a sharp joke, that caused no little merriment, at the expence of Mrs

Nugent and me. I, however, to show that I was none daunted, laid a leg also on her plate, and took another on my own, saying, in the words of the Reverend Doctor, there have been greater miracles than that these two legs should lie in the same nest, which was thought a very clever come off; and at the same time, I gave Mrs Nugent a kindly nip on her sonsy [agreeably plump] arm, which was breaking the ice in as pleasant a way as could be. In short, before any thing passed between ourselves on the subject, we were set down for a tristed pair; and this being the case, we were married as soon as a twelvemonth and a day had passed from the death of the second Mrs Balwhidder; and neither of us have had occasion to rue the bargain. It is, however, but a piece of justice due to my second wife to say, that this was not a little owing to her good management; for she had left such a well plenished house, that her successor said, we had nothing to do but to contribute to one another's happiness.

Ibid.

PERHAPS even more popular with Scottish readers than John Galt's Annals of the Parish _was_ The Life of Mansie Wauch, Tailor in Dalkeith. _This was written, originally as stories for_ Blackwood's _magazine, by Galt's friend David Macbeth Moir, a literary doctor. Their styles were similar in that both books purported to be autobiographies and both described with relish and much detail the life led by simple Scottish folk, but_ Mansie Wauch _was not set in a village but in a small, bustling country town, and its humour was vigorous and not at all ironic._

In Chapter IV the author recalls his plight when, as a small but rapidly elongating lad, love beckoned:

I was sent to school, where I learned to read and spell, making great progress in the Single's and Mother's Carritch. Na, what is more, few could fickle me in the Bible, being mostly able to spell it all over, save the second of Ezra and the seventh of Nehemiah, which the Dominie himself could never read through twice in the same way.

My father, to whom I was born, like Isaac to Abraham, in his old age, was an elder in the Relief Kirk, respected by all for his canny and douce behaviour, and, as I have observed before, a weaver to his trade. The cot and the kail-yard [cottage and back-yard] were his own, and had been auld granfaither's; but still he had to ply the shuttle from Monday to Saturday, to keep all right and tight. The thrums [short lengths of wool left over from weaving] were a perquisite of my own, which I niffered [swapped] with the gundy-wife [seller of sweets] for Gibraltar rock, cut-throat, gib, or bulls-eyes.

Having come into the world before my time, and being of a pale face and delicate make, Nature never could have intended me for the naval or military line, or for any robustious trade or profession whatsoever. No, no, I never liked fighting in my life; peace was aye in my thoughts. When there was any riot in the streets, I fled, and scougged myself [skulked] at the chumley-lug as quickly as I dowed; and, rather than double a nieve [clench a fist] to a school-fellow, I pocketed many shabby epithets, got my paiks [beatings], and took the coucher's [coward's] blow from laddies that could hardly reach up to my waistband.

Just after I was put to my 'prenticeship, having made free choice of the tailoring trade, I had a terrible stound [hard time] of calf-love. Never shall I forget it. I was growing up, long and lank as a willow-wand. Brawns to my legs there were none, as my trowsers of other years too visibly effected to show. The long yellow hair hung down, like a flax-wig, the length of my lantern jaws, which looked, notwithstanding my yapness [readiness] and stiff appetite, as if eating and they had broken up acquaintanceship. My blue jacket seemed in the sleeves to have picked a quarrel with the wrists, and had retreated to a tait [bunch of wool] below the elbows. The haunch-buttons, on the contrary, appeared to have taken a strong liking to the shoulders, a little below which they showed their tarnished brightness. At the middle of the back the tails terminated, leaving the well-worn rear of my corduroys, like a full moon seen through a dark haze. Oh! but I must have been a bonny lad.

My first flame was the minister's lassie [maid], Jess, a buxom and forward quean, two or three years older than myself. I used to sit looking at her in the kirk, and felt a droll confusion when our een [eyes] met. It dirled [gave a twinge of pain] through my heart like a dart, and I looked down at my psalm-book sheepish and blushing. Fain would I have spoken to her, but it would not do; my courage aye failed me at the pinch, though she whiles gave me a smile when she passed me. She used to go to the well every night with her twa stoups, to draw water after the manner of the Israelites at gloaming; so I thought of watching to give her the two apples which I had carried in my pouch for more than a week for that purpose. How she laughed when I stappit them into her hand, and brushed bye without speaking! I stood at the bottom of the close listening, and heard her laughing till she was like to split. My heart flap-flappit in my breast like a pair of fanners [winnowers]. It was a moment of heavenly hope; but I saw Jamie Coom, the blacksmith, who I aye jealoused was my rival, coming down to the well. I saw her give him one of the apples; and hearing him say, with a loud gaffaw, 'Where is the tailor?' I took to my heels, and never stopped till I found myself on the little stool by the fireside, and the hamely sound of my mother's wheel bum-bumming in my lug [ear], like a gentle lullaby.

Every noise I heard flustered me, but I calmed in time, though I went to my bed without my supper. When I was driving out the gaislings to the grass on the next morn, who was it my ill fate to meet but the blacksmith. 'Ou, Mansie,' said Jamie Coom, 'are ye gaun to take me for your best man? I hear you are to be cried [to have the marriage banns read out] in the kirk on Sunday?'

'Me!' answered I, shaking and staring.

'Yes!' said he, 'Jess the minister's maid told me last night, that you had been giving up your name at the manse. Ay, it's ower true—for she showed me the apples ye gied her in a present. This is a bonny story, Mansie, my man, and you only at your 'prenticeship yet.'

Terror and despair had struck me dumb. I stood as still and as stiff as a web of buckram. My tongue was tied, and I could not contradict him. Jamie faulded his arms, and gaed away whistling, turning every now and then his sooty face over his shoulder, and mostly sticking his tune, as he could not keep his mouth screwed for laughing. What would I not have given to have laughed too!

There was no time to be lost; this was the Saturday. The next rising sun would shine on the Sabbath. Ah, what a case I was in! I could mostly have drowned myself, had I not been frighted. What could I do? My love had vanished like lightning; but oh, I was in a terrible gliff! Instead of gundy [sweets], I sold my thrums to Mrs Walnut for a penny, with which I bought at the counter a sheet of paper and a pen; so that in the afternoon I wrote out a letter to the minister, telling him what I had been given to hear, and begging him, for the sake of mercy, not to believe Jess's word, as I was not able to keep a wife.

> David Macbeth Moir (1798–1851), *The Life of Mansie Wauch, Tailor in Dalkeith* (1828).

———

LITTLE *Miss Ferrier of Edinburgh, spinster and author, was neither a blue-stocking nor a prim literary recluse but a warmly individual, free-speaking Scottish lady. When a friend wrote to say that she had an idea for a story, old Miss Ferrier wrote back, 'I begin to suspect that I am with book myself.'*

Susan Ferrier wrote three lively, humorous novels describing different aspects of Scottish life. The books were much admired by her contemporaries including Lord Macaulay and the Revd Sydney Smith, and she was befriended by Sir Walter Scott (the friendliest and most generous of all authors towards other authors).

Her first novel, Marriage, *was designed to warn young ladies against marrying for the wrong reasons, and the writing contained much social satire and high comedy, particularly when the heroine, Juliana Courtland, daughter of an English earl, travels to Scotland with her newly acquired husband, Henry, to avoid his London creditors.*

Elegant, snobbish, and spoilt, Lady Juliana is appalled to find that Henry's family lives in what is to her the squalor of the ancient Highland way of life.

Apart from Henry's father, the old Laird, the family is feminine; three aunts, described as 'long-chinned spinsters', and five massive 'awkward purple girls' named Belle, Becky, Betty, Babby, and Beenie.

The family does its kindly best to keep Lady Juliana entertained, even holding a ball for her in the castle:

The interval, which seemed of endless duration to the hapless Lady Juliana, was passed by the aunts in giving sage counsel as to the course of life to be pursued by married ladies. Worsted stockings and quilted petticoats were insisted upon as indispensable articles of dress; while it was plainly insinuated, that it was utterly impossible any child could be healthy, whose mother had not confined her wishes to barley broth and oatmeal porridge.

'Only look at thae young lambs,' said Miss Grizzy, pointing to the five great girls; 'see what pickters of health they are! I'm sure I hope, my dear niece, your children will be just the same—only boys, for we are sadly in want of boys. It's melancholy to think we have not a boy among us, and that a fine auntient race like ours should be dying away for want of male heirs.' And the tears streamed down the cheeks of the good spinster as she spoke.

The entrance of the gentlemen put a stop to the conversation.

Flying to her husband, Lady Juliana began to whisper, in very audible tones, her enquiries, whether he had yet got any money—when they were to go away, &c. &c.

'Does your Ladyship choose any tea?' asked Miss Nicky, as she disseminated the little cups of coarse black liquid.

'Tea! oh no, I never drink tea—I'll take some coffee though; and Psyche [her dog] doats on a dish of tea.'—And she tendered the beverage, that had been intended for herself, to her favourite.

'Here's no coffee,' said Douglas, surveying the tea-table; 'but I will ring for some,' as he pulled the bell.

Old Donald answered the summons.

'Where's the coffee?' demanded Miss Nicky.

'The coffee!' repeated the Highlander: 'troth, Miss Nicky, an' it's been clean forgot.'

'Well, but you can get it yet?' said Douglas. 'Deed, Maister Harry, the night's owre far gane for't noo; for the fire's a' ta'en up, ye see,' reckoning with his fingers, as he proceeded; 'there's parritch makin' for oor supper; and there's patatees boiling for the beasts; and—'

'I'll see about it myself,' said Miss Nicky, leaving the room, with old Donald at her back, muttering all the way.

The old Laird, all this while, had been enjoying his evening nap; but, that now ended, and the tea equipage being dismissed, starting up, he asked what they were about, that the dancing was not begun.

'Come, my Leddy, we'll set the example,' snapping his fingers, and singing, in a hoarse voice,

'The mouse is a merry beastie,
And the moudiwort wants the een;
But folk sall ne'er get wit,
Sae merry as we twa ha'e been.'

'But whar's the girlies?' cried he; 'Ho! Belle, Becky, Betty, Babby, Beenie— to your posts!'

The young ladies, eager for the delights of music and dancing, now entered, followed by Coil, the piper, dressed in the native garb, with cheeks seemingly ready blown for the occasion. After a little strutting and puffing, the pipes were fairly set agoing in Coil's most spirited manner. But vain would be the attempt to describe Lady Juliana's horror and amazement at the hideous sounds that for the first time assailed her ear. Tearing herself from the grasp of the old gentleman, who was just setting off in the reel, she flew shrieking to her husband, and threw herself trembling into his arms, while he called loudly to the self-delighted Coil to stop.

'What's the matter—what's the matter?' cried the whole family, gathering around.

'Matter!' repeated Douglas furiously, 'you have frightened Lady Juliana to death with your infernal music. What did you mean,' turning fiercely to the astonished piper, 'by blowing that confounded bladder?'

Poor Coil gaped with astonishment; for never before had his performance on the bagpipe been heard but with admiration and applause.

'A bonny bargain, indeed, the canna stand the pipes,' said the old gentleman, as he went puffing up and down the room; 'She's no the wife for a Heelandman. Confoonded blather, indeed! By my faith, ye're no blate!'

'I declare it's the most distressing thing I ever met with,' sighed Miss Grizzy; 'I wonder whether it could be the sight or sound of the bagpipe that frightened our dear niece. I wish to goodness Lady Maclaughlan was here!'

'It's impossible the bagpipe could frighten any body,' said Miss Jacky, in a high voice: 'nobody with common sense could be frightened at a bagpipe.'

Mrs Douglas here mildly interposed, and soothed down the offended pride of the Highlanders, by attributing Lady Juliana's agitation entirely to surprise. The word operated like a charm; all were ready to admit, that it was a surprising thing when heard for the first time. Miss Jacky remarked, that we are all liable to be surprised; and the still more sapient Grizzy said, that indeed it was most surprising the effect that surprise had upon some people. For her own part, she could not deny, but that she was very often frightened when she was surprised.

Douglas, meanwhile, was employed in soothing the terrors, real or affected, of his delicate bride; who declared herself so exhausted with the fatigue she had undergone, and the sufferings she had endured, that she must retire for the night. Henry, eager to escape from the question and remarks of his family, gladly availed himself of the same excuse; and, to the infinite mortification of both aunts and nieces, the ball was broke up.

Susan Ferrier (1782–1854), *Marriage* (1818).

TALES *of simple rural life in Scotland were known as 'kail-yard stories'.*
The pioneer in England of a new form of essentially middle-class rural humour—herbaceous-border stories?—where nature was described naturalistically and the comedy of village manners was accurately and affectionately observed, was Mary Russell Mitford.

Miss Mitford was born in 1787 and was a true eighteenth-century daughter in her unquestioning devotion to her father. Fanny Burney went into royal service at Windsor knowing that it would be bad for her health and harmful to her work as a writer because her father wanted her to and it never occurred to her to question his wishes. Mary Mitford's father was even more inconsiderate. At the age of 10 Mary picked a ticket in a lottery and won £20,000, an enormous sum of money in those days. Within a few years her father had spent the lot and the family had to live frugally in a labourer's cottage near Reading, supported by what Mary could earn by her pen.

She wrote a number of tragic dramas for the stage, some of which were mildly successful both in England and America, but real success came in 1819 when the first of her countryside stories appeared in the Lady's Magazine, *under the title 'Our Village'. The circulation of the magazine rose from 250 to 2000; Mary Russell Mitford became famous; the village, Three Mile Cross on the Basingstoke to Reading road, became a tourist attraction; babies were named after Miss Mitford's villagers and pet greyhounds; her earnings rose dramatically; her father managed to spend the money as it came in, and the family continued to live in near-poverty.*

In 1842 her father died, loved and respected to the last by his daughter.

Compared to the large canvasses worked upon by novelists, Miss Mitford's stories are the literary equivalent of that most English of art forms, the water-colour. They are delicate and charming, observant and feminine.

Here, setting the pattern for stories about small but real personal predicaments, is Miss Mitford's account of an unfortunate shopping expedition:

THE BLACK VELVET BAG

Have any of my readers ever found great convenience in the loss, the real loss, of actual tangible property, and been exceedingly provoked and annoyed when such property was restored to them? If so, they can sympathize with a late unfortunate recovery, which has brought me to great shame and disgrace. There is no way of explaining my calamity but by telling the whole story.

Last Friday fortnight was one of those anomalies in weather with which we English people are visited for our sins; a day of intolerable wind, an insupportable dust; an equinoctial gale out of season; a piece of March unnaturally foisted into the very heart of May; just as, in the almost parallel misarrangement of the English counties, one sees (perhaps out of compliment to this peculiarity of climate, to keep the weather in countenance as it were) a bit of Wiltshire plumped down in the very middle of Berkshire, whilst a great island of the county palatine of Durham figures in the centre of canny Northumberland. Be this as it may, on that remarkable windy day did I set forth to the good town of B——, on the feminine errand called shopping. Every lady who lives far in the country, and seldom visits great towns, will understand the full force of that comprehensive word; and I had not been shopping for a long time. I had a dread of the operation, arising from a consciousness of weakness. I am a true daughter of Eve, a dear lover of bargains and bright colours; and knowing this have generally been wise enough to keep, as much as I can, out of the way of temptation. At last a sort of necessity arose for some slight purchases, in the shape of two new gowns from London, which cried aloud for making. Trimmings, ribands, sewing-silk, and lining—all were called for. The shopping was inevitable, and I undertook the whole concern at once, most heroically resolving to spend just so much and no more; and half comforting myself that I had a full morning's work of indispensable business, and should have no time for extraneous extravagance.

There was, to be sure, a prodigious accumulation of errands and wants. The evening before, they had been set down in great form, on a slip of paper, headed thus—'things wanted.' To how many and various catalogues that title would apply, from the red bench of the peer, to the oaken settle of the cottager—from him who wants a blue riband, to him who wants bread and cheese! My list was astounding. It was written in double columns, in an invisible hand; the long intractable words were brought into the ranks by the Procrustes mode—abbreviations; and as we approached the bottom, two or three were crammed into one lot, clumped as the bean-setters say, and designated by a sort of shorthand, a hieroglyphic of my own invention. In good open printing my list would have cut a respectable figure as a catalogue, and filled a decent number of pages—a priced catalogue too; for, as I had a given sum to carry to market, I amused myself with calculating the proper and probable cost of every article; in which process I most egregiously cheated the shopkeeper and myself, by copying, with the credulity of hope, from the puffs in newspapers, and expecting to buy fine solid wearable goods at advertising prices. In this way I stretched my money a great deal farther than it would go, and swelled my catalogue, so that at last, in spite of compression and shorthand, I had no room for another word, and was obliged to crowd several small, but important articles, such as cotton, laces, pins, needles, shoe-strings, etc., into that very irregular and disorderly storehouse—that place where most things deposited are lost—my memory, by courtesy so called.

The written list was safely consigned, with a well-filled purse, to my usual repository, a black velvet bag; and, the next morning, I and my bag, with its nicely balanced contents of wants and money, were safely conveyed in a little open carriage to the good town of B——. There I dismounted, and began to bargain most vigorously, visiting the cheapest shops, cheapening the cheapest articles, yet wisely buying the strongest and the best; a little astonished at first to find everything so much dearer than I had set it down, yet soon reconciled to this misfortune by the magical influence which shopping possesses over a woman's fancy—all the sooner reconciled, as the monitory list lay unlooked at, and unthought of, in its grave receptacle, the black velvet bag. On I went, with an air of cheerful business, of happy importance, till my money began to wax small. Certain small aberrations had occurred too in my economy. One article that had happened, by rare accident, to be below my calculation, and indeed, below any calculation, calico at ninepence, fine, thick, strong, wide calico, at ninepence (did ever man hear of anything so cheap?), absolutely enchanted me, and I took the whole piece; then after buying for M—— a gown, according to order, I saw one that I liked better, and bought that too. Then I fell in love, was actually captivated, with a sky-blue sash and handkerchief—not the poor, thin, greeny colour which usually passes under that dishonoured name, but the rich full tint of the noonday sky, and a cap-riband, really pink, that might have vied with the inside leaves of a moss-rose. Then, in hunting after cheapness, I got into obscure shops, where, not finding what I asked for, I was fain to take something that they had, purely to make a proper compensation for the trouble of lugging out drawers and answering questions. Lastly, I was fairly coaxed into some articles by the irresistibility of the sellers—by the demure and truth-telling look of a pretty quaker, who could almost have persuaded the head off one's shoulders, and who did persuade me that ell-wide muslin would go as far as yard and a half; and by the fluent impudence of a lying shopman, who under cover of a well-darkened window, affirmed, on his honour, that his brown satin was a perfect match to my green pattern, and forced the said satin down my throat accordingly. With these helps, my money melted all too fast; at half-past five my purse was entirely empty; and, as shopping with an empty purse has by no means the relish and savour of shopping with a full one, I was quite willing and ready to go home to dinner, pleased as a child with my purchases, and wholly unsuspecting the sins of omission, the errands unperformed, which were the natural result of my unconsulted memoranda and my treacherous memory.

Home I returned, a happy and proud woman, wise in my own conceit, a thrifty fashion-monger, laden like a pedlar, with huge packages in stout brown holland, tied up with whipcord, and genteel little parcels, papered and packthreaded in shopmanlike style. At last we were safely stood in the pony-chaise, which had much ado to hold us, my little black bag lying, as usual, in my lap; when, as we ascended the steep hill out of B——, a sudden puff of wind took at once my cottage-bonnet and my large cloak, blew the bonnet off my head, so that it hung behind me, suspended by the riband, and fairly snapped the string of the cloak, which flew away, much in the style of John Gilpin's, renowned in story. My companion, pitying my plight, exerted himself manfully to regain the fly-away garments, shoved the head into the bonnet, or the bonnet over the head (I do not know which phrase best describes the manœuvre), with one hand, and recovered the refractory cloak with the other. This last exploit was certainly the most difficult. It is wonderful what a tug he was forced to give before that obstinate cloak could be brought round: it was swelled with the wind like a bladder, animated, so to say, like a living thing, and threatened to carry pony and chaise and riders and packages backward down the hill, as if it had been a sail and we a ship. At last the contumacious garment was mastered. We righted; and by dint of sitting sideways and turning my back on my kind comrade, I got home without any further damage than the loss of my bag, which, though not missed before the chaise had been unladen, had undoubtedly gone by the board in the gale; and I lamented my old and trusty companion, without in the least foreseeing the use it would probably be of to my reputation.

Immediately after dinner (for in all cases, even when one has bargains to show, dinner must be discussed) I produced my purchases. They were very much admired; and the quantity, when spread out in our little room, being altogether dazzling and the quality satisfactory, the cheapness was never doubted. Everybody thought the bargains were exactly such as I meant to get—for nobody calculated; and the bills being really lost in the lost bag, and the particular prices just as much lost in my memory (the ninepence calico was the only article whose cost occurred to me), I passed, without telling anything like a fib, merely by a discreet silence, for the best and thriftiest bargainer that ever went shopping. After some time spent very pleasantly in admiration on one side and display on the other, we were interrupted by the demand for some of the little articles which I had forgotten. 'The sewing silk, please, ma'am, for my mistress's gown.' 'Sewing silk! I don't know—look about.' Ah, she might look long enough—no sewing-silk was there. 'Very strange!' Presently came other inquiries: 'Where's the tape, Mary?' 'The tape?' 'Yes, my dear; and the needles, pins, cotton, stay-laces, boot-laces!' 'The bobbin, the ferret, shirt-buttons, shoe-strings?' quoth she of the sewing-silk, taking up the cry, and forthwith began a search as bustling, as active, and as vain, as that of our old spaniel Brush after a hare that had stolen away from her form. At last she suddenly desisted from her rummage. 'Without doubt, ma'am, they are in the reticule, and all lost,' said she, in a very pathetic tone. 'Really,' cried I, a little conscience-stricken, 'I don't recollect; perhaps I might forget.' 'Depend on it, my love, that Harriet's right,' interrupted one, whose interruptions are always kind; 'those are just the little articles that people put in reticules, and you never could forget so many things; besides, you wrote them down.' 'I don't know—I am not sure.' But I was not listened to; Harriet's conjecture had been metamorphosed into a certainty; all my sins of omission were stowed in the reticule, and before bedtime the little black bag held forgotten things enough to fill a sack.

Never was reticule so lamented by all but its owner; a boy was immediately dispatched to look for it, and, on his returning empty-handed, there was even a talk of having it cried. My care, on the other hand, was all directed to prevent its being found. I had had the good luck to lose it in a suburb of B—— renowned for filching, and I remembered that the street was, at that moment, full of people; the bag did actually contain more than enough to tempt those who were naturally disposed to steal for stealing's sake, so I went to bed in the comfortable assurance that it was gone for ever. But there is nothing certain in this world—not even a thief's dishonesty. Two old women, who had pounced at once on my valuable property, quarrelled about the plunder, and one of them, in a fit of resentment at being cheated in her share, went to the mayor of B—— and informed against her companion. The mayor, an intelligent and active magistrate, immediately took the disputed bag and all its contents into his own possession, and as he is also a man of great politeness, he restored it as soon as possible to the right owner. The very first thing that saluted my eyes when I awoke on the morning, was a note from Mr Mayor, with a sealed packet. The fatal truth was visible; I had recovered my reticule, and lost my reputation. There it lay, that identical black bag, with its name-tickets, its cambric handkerchief, its empty purse, its unconsulted list, its thirteen bills, and its two letters; one from a good sort of lady-farmer, inquiring the character of a cook, with half a sonnet written on the blank pages; the other from a literary friend, containing a critique on the plot of a play, advising me not to kill the king too soon, with other good counsel, such as might, if our mayor had not been a man of sagacity, have sent a poor authoress, in a Mademoiselle-Scuderi-mistake, to the Tower.

That catastrophe would hardly have been worse than the real one. All my omissions have been found out. My price list has been compared with the bills. I have forfeited my credit for bargaining. I am become a byword for forgetting. Nobody trusts me to purchase a paper of pins, or to remember the cost of a penny riband. I am a lost woman. My bag is come back, but my fame is gone.

Mary Russell Mitford (1787–1855), *Our Village* (1824).

EVEN *in those troubled times at the beginning of the nineteenth century when there was much concern over increasing government restriction on freedom of expression, a growing national debt, problems with the price of bread, weariness with the Georges as kings, etc. etc., or perhaps* because *the times were troubled, senses of humour seemed to have been as sprightly as ever and correspondence between friends as amusing.*

The painter Benjamin Robert Haydon was a friend of Miss Mitford and painted a not very good portrait of her. His ambitions as a painter of huge historical canvases exceeded his talent and he eventually committed suicide, but he wrote extremely well and his letters were delightful:

18 August, 1826.

The other night I paid my butcher; one of the miracles of these times, you will say. Let me tell you I have all my life been seeking for a butcher whose respect for genius predominated over his love of gain. I could not make out, before I dealt with this man, his excessive desire that I should be his customer; his sly hints as I passed his shop that he had 'a bit of South Down, very fine; a sweetbread, perfection; and a calf's foot that was all jelly without bone!'

The other day he called and I had him sent up into the painting-room. I found him in great admiration of *Alexander*. 'Quite alive, sir!' 'I am glad you think so,' said I. 'Yes, sir; but as I have said often to my sister, you could not have painted that picture, sir, if you had not eat my meat, sir!' 'Very true, Mr Sowerby.' 'Ah! sir I have a fancy for *genius*, sir!' 'Have you, Mr Sowerby?' 'Yes, sir; Mrs Siddons, sir, has eat my meat, sir; never was *such a woman for chops*, sir!' and he drew up his beefy, shiny face, clean-shaved, with a clean blue cravat under his chin, a clean jacket, a clean apron, and a pair of hands that would pin an ox to the earth if he was obstreperous—'Ah! sir, she was a wonderful crayture!' 'She was, Mr Sowerby.' 'Ah! sir, when she used to act that there character, you see (but Lord, such a head! as I say to my sister)—that there woman, sir, that murders a king between 'em!' 'Oh, Lady Macbeth.' 'Ah! sir, that's it—Lady Macbeth—I used to get up with the butler behind her carridge when she acted, and, as I used to see her looking quite wild, and all the people quite frightened. Ah, ha! my lady says I, if it wasn't for my meat, though, you wouldn't be able to do *that*!'

'Mr Sowerby, you seem to be a man of feeling; will you take a glass of wine?' After a bow or two, down he sat, and by degrees his heart opened. 'You see, sir, I have fed Mrs Siddons, sir; John Kemble, sir; Charles Kemble, sir; Stephen Kemble, sir; and Madam Catalani, sir; Morland the painter, and, I beg your pardon, sir, and *you*, sir.' 'Mr Sowerby, you do me honour.' 'Madam Catalani, sir, was a wonderful woman for sweetbreads; but the Kemble family, sir, the gentlemen, sir, rump-steaks and kidneys in general was their taste; but Mrs Siddons, sir, she liked chops, sir, as much as you do, sir,' etc., etc. I soon perceived that the man's ambition was to feed genius. I shall recommend you to him; but is he not a capital fellow? . . . Think of Lady Macbeth eating chops!

Is this not a peep behind the curtain?

Benjamin Haydon (1786–1846), Letter to Mary Russell Mitford (1826).

G REAT *ladies were still writing to other great ladies with intent to*
amuse:

Castle Howard
September 1804

... Lord C, has very gloomy fits, *mais au milieu de la tempête on peut entrevoir des beaux jours*, during which he is pleasant and tells some funny stories— amongst others of a man whom nothing could put out of his way, or *dérouter* in the least. To try him one night Lord Somebody and a large party at a house in the country made him dead drunk, rubbed him all over with sirrup, rolled him in a feather bed and then hid themselves in his room to watch his recovery. When he woke he walked slowly up to the glass, and, upon be- holding himself, quietly said—'A bird, by God,' and went and sat down again. I tell you this because I nearly expired when I heard it and though it does not do as well *écrit*, I like to fancy I see you laugh at the same things that I did.

Addio, adored Emma.

> Letter from Harriet Cavendish to her mother, the Duchess of Devonshire (1804).

A NOTHER *letter of the same period was written by Miss Marjorie Fleming to a young relation. Miss Fleming read history and wrote poems and diaries (and was, of course, a friend of Sir Walter Scott).*
She was aged 5:

My dear Isa,
I now sit down to answer all your kind and beloved letters which you was so good as to write to me. This is the first time I ever wrote a letter in my Life. There are a great many Girls in the Square and they cry just like a pig when we are under the painful necessity of putting it to Death. Miss Potune a Lady of my acquaintance praises me dreadfully. I repeated something out of Dean Swift, and she said I was fit for the stage, and you may think I am primmed up with majistick Pride, but upon my word felt myselfe turn a little birsay—birsay is a word which is a word that William composed which is as you may suppose a little enraged. This horrid fat simpleton says that my Aunt is beautiful which is entirely impossible for that is not her nature ...

> Marjorie Fleming (1803–11), Letter to Isabella Keith (1809).

E VERY *so often a work was published which, like an annual in the flower garden, made a brilliant show during its short life and then disappeared without trace. Such a book was* Thinks-I-to-myself, *published in 1811 and written by a gentleman who resolutely hid from fame behind the pseudonym* 'Thinks-I-to-myself, Who?'.

The book was an immediate success, going rapidly through ten editions plus a printing in Amsterdam. The title became a catch-phrase, and Charles Dibdin the younger wrote a popular song, 'Thinks-I-to-myself, Thinks-I', *which was sung by Grimaldi at Covent Garden and Sadler's Wells and subsequently whistled, hummed, and played endlessly on barrel-organs in the streets of London and the fashionable spas.*

It was an amusing and lightly satirical novel, set in Jane Austen country, which made fun of fashionable and pretentious social behaviour and was not nearly as coy a piece of work as its awful title promised. It was in the form of an autobiography, supposedly written by a young man who spoke little but thought a lot. In the text he prefixed his more important thoughts with the phrase Thinks-I-to-myself, *hence the title.*

In this scene the narrator describes an agonizing social occasion, frequent in those days, when a friend's child is persuaded to recite poetry. In this case the artiste is Mrs Fidget's small son who is aged 4 and formidably ungifted:

At last, however, upon my mother's tapping the pretty child under the chin, and taking him *kindly* by the hand, and expressing (Heaven bless her!) the *most ardent wish* and *desire* to be so *indulged,* he did condescend to advance into the middle of the room, and was upon the point of beginning, when Mrs Fidget most considerately interposed, to procure him to put his right foot a little forwarder, with the toe more out, and to direct him about the proper motion, that is, the *up-lifting* and *down-dropping* of his right arm during the performance. One of his sisters, in the mean time, seating herself near to him, for fear of any accidental slip or failure in the young gentleman's miraculous memory.

His first attempt was upon *Pope's Universal Prayer,* but unfortunately, of the fourth line, he managed constantly to make but one word, and that so odd a one, that the sound but ill atoned for the manifest ignorance of the sense.

> 'Father of all, in every age,
>   In every clime ador'd
> By saint, by savage, and by sage,
>   Jovajovalord!'

Jovajovalord! This was the word, and the only word that could be got out of his mouth, and *Thinks-I-to-myself,* it would be well if no greater blunders had ever been committed with regard to that insidious line; however, in consequence of this invincible misnomer, the Universal Prayer was laid by, and other pieces successively proposed, till it was at length unanimously determined, that what he *shone most in,* was King Lear's Address to the Tempest, and this was accordingly fixed upon as his *chef-d'œuvre* in the art of oratory.

Some preliminaries, however, in this instance appeared to be necessary. It was not reasonable to suppose young Master could address a storm without some sort of *symptoms* at least of a *real* storm. It was agreed upon, therefore, that he should not commence his speech till he heard a rumbling noise proceed from the company present, and we were all desired to bear our part in this fictitious thunder; how we all thundered, I cannot pretend to say, but so it was, that in due time, by the aid of such noises as we could severally and jointly contribute, the storm began most nobly, when the young orator stepping forward, his eyes and right hand raised, and his right foot protruded *secundem artem,* he thus began:

'Blow winds and cwack your cheeks!'—

'Crack your cheeks,' my love, says his sister; 'What can you mean by cwack your cheeks? what's that, pray?'

'Aye, what is that,' says Mrs Fidget;—'but I believe, ma'am,' adds she, turning to my mother, 'I must make his excuses for him; you must know, he cannot be brought yet to pronounce an R, do all we can, so that he always leaves it quite out, or he pronounces it exactly like a W.'

Thinks-I-to-myself many do the like.

'We choose speeches for him, therefore,' continues Mrs Fidget; 'in which there are many R's on purpose to conquer the difficulty, if we can; begin again, my dear,' says she, 'and remember not to leave our your RRs'; so he began afresh.

'Blow winds, and cwack your cheeks! *wage*

'*Wage,* my dear,' says Mrs Fidget, 'do pray try to say rage.'

'Wage
You Catawacts and hurwy canoes, spout
Till you have dwenched our steeples, dwown'd the cocks!'

'Bless me,' exclaims Mrs Fidget, 'you might as well not speak at all as speak so; I defy any body to understand what you mean by dwown'd the cocks!' The little gentleman, however, proceeded spite of the RRs.

'You sulphwous and thought executing fires,
Vaunt—couwiers of oak-cleaving thunder-bolts,
Singe my white head—and thou, all-shaking thunder,
Stwike flat the thick wotundity o' th' world;
Cwack nature's mould, all germins spill at once
That make ungwateful man.
Wumble thy belly-full, spit fire, spout wain!'

'O dear, dear, dear,' says Mrs Fidget, 'that will never do; wumble thy belly-full, spit fire, and spout wain! who ever heard of such things? Better, my love, have done with that and try the Bard,' but the Bard beginning

'Wuin seize thee, wuthless king,'

put us too much in mind of 'wumble your belly-full,' to be proceeded with, and therefore little master was at last bidden to descend from such flights, and try his *Fable*; but even his Fable, which chanced to be the first of *Gay*, happening, most unfortunately, to begin with an R, his setting off here was as bad as ever, viz.

'Wemote from cities lived a swain—'

however he got through about ten lines, making, as I observed, a dead pause at the end of every one, and not disposing very discreetly, either of his *accents* or his *stops*; his delivery being as nearly as possible, just as follows: his accents falling on the words printed in italics; and his pauses as noted by the perpendicular and horizontal bars.

'His *head* was | *silver'd* | o'er with *age*—
And *long* ex- | *perience* | made him *sage*—
His *hours* in | *cheerful* | *labour* flew—
Nor Envy *nor* | *Ambition* knew—'

At the beginning of every couplet I also found his right arm regularly went up, and precisely at the end and close of every rhyme came plump down again. Most happily at the end of the eleventh line the young gentleman's miraculous memory was *non-plus'd*, and neither mama, nor any of his sisters, nor either of the Pug-dogs could at all help him out.

'Thinks-I-to-Myself, Who?' (Edward Nares) (1762–1841). *Thinks-I-to-Myself* (1811).

➤ Few readers, of course, will need to be reminded that the fourth line of Pope's *Universal Prayer*, rendered by the little orator as 'Jovajovalord', reads 'Jehovah, Jove, or Lord!'

━━━━━━━

THE *anonymous author of the jauntily humorous novel* Thinks-I-to-myself *turned out to be the Reverend Dr Edward Nares, Regius Professor of Modern History at Oxford, son-in-law of the Duke of Marlborough. He managed to hang on to his anonymity during the time that his book was a popular best-seller but achieved unsought fame soon after for quite a different reason.*

There was a deeply serious side to Dr Nares. He was a scholar and a historian, and in 1832 he began to publish an enormous, exhaustive biography of William Cecil, Lord Burghley. This vast tome was reviewed by Thomas Babington Macaulay in the Edinburgh Review *and the hapless Dr Nares became famous after all, not for his humour but for being the wretched author who was savaged in one of Macaulay's most brutally critical essays:*

BURLEIGH AND HIS TIMES

Memoirs of the Life and Administration of the Right Honourable William Cecil Lord Burghley, Secretary of State in the Reign of King Edward the Sixth, and Lord High Treasurer of England in the Reign of Queen Elizabeth. Containing an Historical View of the Times in which he lived, and of the many eminent and illustrious Persons with whom he was connected; with Extracts from his Private and Official Correspondence and other Papers, now first published from the Originals.

    By the Reverend Edward Nares, DD, Regius Professor of Modern History in the University of Oxford. 3 vols. 4to. London: 1828, 1832.

The work of Dr Nares has filled us with astonishment similar to that which Captain Lemuel Gulliver felt when he first landed in Brobdingnag, and saw corn as high as the oaks in the New Forest, thimbles as large as buckets, and wrens of the bulk of turkeys. The whole book, and every component part of it, is on a gigantic scale. The title is as long as an ordinary preface: the prefatory matter would furnish out an ordinary book; and the book contains as much reading matter as an ordinary library. We cannot sum up the merits of the stupendous mass of paper which lies before us better than by saying that it consists of about two thousand closely printed quarto pages, that it occupies fifteen hundred inches cubic measure, and that it weighs sixty pounds avoirdupois. Such a book might, before the deluge, have been considered as light reading by Hilpa and Shalum [Old Testament characters who lived to a very great age]. But unhappily the life of man is now threescore years and ten; and we cannot but think it somewhat unfair in Dr Nares to demand from us so large a portion of so short an existence.

Compared with the labour of reading through these volumes, all other labour, the labour of thieves on the treadmill, of children in factories, of negroes in sugar plantations, is an agreeable recreation. There was, it is said, a criminal in Italy, who was suffered to make his choice between Guicciardini [a sixteenth-century statesman and historian who wrote an enormously long, detailed, and bleak history of Italy] and the galleys. He chose the history. But the war of Pisa was too much for him. He changed his mind, and went to the oar. Guicciardini, though certainly not the most amusing of writers, is a Herodotus or a Froissart, when compared to Dr Nares. It is not merely in bulk, but in specific gravity also, that these memoirs exceed all other human compositions. On every subject which the Professor discusses, he produces three times as many pages as another man; and one of his books is as tedious as another man's three. His book is swelled to its vast dimensions by endless repetitions, by episodes which have nothing to do with the main action, by quotations from books which are in every circulating library, and by reflections which, when they happen to be just, are so obvious that they must necessarily occur to the mind of every reader. He employs more words in expounding and defending a truism than any other writer would employ in supporting a paradox. Of the rules of historical perspective, he has not the faintest notion. There is neither foreground nor background in his deline-ation. The wars of Charles the Fifth in Germany are detailed at almost as much length as Robertson's Life of that prince. The troubles of Scotland are related as fully as M'Crie's Life of John Knox. It would be most unjust to deny that Dr Nares is a man of great industry and research; but he is so utterly incompetent to arrange the materials which he has collected that he might as well have left them in their original repositories.

Neither the facts which Dr Nares has discovered, nor the arguments which he urges, will, we apprehend, materially alter the opinion generally en-tertained by judicious readers of history concerning his hero. Lord Burleigh can hardly be called a great man.

Thomas Babington Macaulay (1800–59), Edinburgh Review (Apr. 1832).

➧ As was his custom in his *Edinburgh Review* essays, Macaulay then went on to give, in 12,000 words, *his* opinion of Lord Burleigh. Poor Dr Nares tried to rescue his dented reputation as a scholar by publishing 'A few Observations on the "Edinburgh Review" of Dr Nares's *Memoirs of Lord Burghley*', but this made no impact. Trying to better Macaulay with a pamphlet was like trying to stop an army tank by dabbing at it with a feather duster.

―――――――――

*T*HERE *is one figure in literature who is inseparable from any consideration of humour in the nineteenth century or any century, the Revd Sydney Smith.*

Natural, unforced humour welled from him and pervaded his critical reviews, his political tracts, his family life, his work as a churchman and, above all, his conversation. He expressed himself through humour not to make himself the centre of attention or because he was a performer manqué *but because he could not help it. Being humorous was to Sydney Smith as necessary and inevitable as breathing out.*

He was one of the co-founders of the Edinburgh Review *and wrote for it, but almost all his most memorable remarks were made in conversation so it could be argued that they have no place in a book concerned with humorous prose. One answer to that would be to claim that all his sayings were subsequently printed in collections of his letters and in various memoirs and so rate as prose. The real answer is that it would be unthinkable to leave him out.*

In religion he was a Social Christian who believed in tolerance, doing good and keeping cheerful. He was no theologian. When asked his opinion of the Revd Henry Millman's History of Christianity, *he said:*

'No man should write on such subjects unless he is prepared to go the whole lamb.'

He campaigned hard for Catholic emancipation but detested Methodism. Towards the end of his life he began to get very tired and had a short holiday at the seaside to try and recover his strength. When asked how he felt he replied:

'I feel so weak, both in body and mind, that I verily believe, if the knife were put into my hand, I should not have strength or energy enough to stick it into a Dissenter.'

He was quite unawed by the Church establishment and treated the Church of England hierarchy as playfully as he treated everybody else:

Someone asked if the Bishop of —— was going to marry. 'Perhaps he may,' said Sydney Smith; 'Yet how can a Bishop marry? How can he flirt? The most he can say is, "I will see you in the vestry after service."'

'I have, alas, only one illusion left, and that is the Archbishop of Canterbury.'

'The Dean of —— deserves to be preached to death by wild curates.'

'I must believe in the Apostolic Succession, there being no other way of accounting for the descent of the Bishop of Exeter from Judas Iscariot.'

Sydney Smith seemed to blossom in any kind of company, and he had the gift of being able to enhance any conversation with some illuminating analogy or a wholly original flight of fancy:

'When so showy a woman as Mrs —— appears at a place, though there is no garrison within twelve miles, the horizon is immediately clouded with majors.'

'I once dissuaded a youth from entering the army, on which he was bent, at the risk of breaking his mother's heart, by asking him how he would prevent his sword from getting between his legs. It quite staggered him; he never solved the difficulty and took to peace instead of war.'

All his life he was almost excessively fond of good food. When he was very ill and was on a light diet without any meat, he whispered to his friend General Fox:

'Ah, Charles! I wish I were allowed even the wing of a roasted butterfly.'

One of his most famous speeches was made in Taunton in 1832. The Reform Bill had been passed by the Commons but failed to get through the House of Lords. To Sydney Smith and to most people with his humane common sense the passing of the Bill was vital and inevitable. The political effect of his ironically humorous attack on the Lords' hostility to the Reform Bill was considerable:

'I do not mean to be disrespectful, but the attempt of the Lords to stop the progress of reform, reminds me very forcibly of the great storm of Sidmouth and of the conduct of the excellent Mrs Partington on that occasion. In the winter of 1824 there set in a great flood upon that town—the tide rose to an incredible height—the waves rushed in upon the houses, and every thing was threatened with destruction. In the midst of this sublime and terrible storm, Dame Partington, who lived upon the beach, was seen at the door of her house with mop and pattens, trundling her mop, squeezing out the sea-water, and vigorously pushing away the Atlantic Ocean. The Atlantic was roused. Mrs Partington's spirit was up; but I need not tell you that the contest was unequal. The Atlantic Ocean beat Mrs Partington. She was excellent at a slop, or a puddle, but she should not have meddled with a tempest. Gentlemen, be at your ease—be quiet and steady. You will beat Mrs Partington.'

🙟 The speech was published in *The Times*, prints with Wellington as Dame Partington were rushed into the shops and 'Mrs Partington' became a folklore figure. She was later appropriated by a humorist in the USA who turned her into an American version of Mrs Malaprop.

Perhaps the Revd Sydney Smith showed at his best when in 1808 the Residence Bill was passed requiring all clergymen to live in their parishes, instead of living comfortably elsewhere and paying a local curate to perform their duties. Smith's appointed parish was Foston, a small and remote village in Yorkshire. He loved London life, the company of other wits, the intellectual stimulation of politics and literature, and food, and he loathed the countryside. But, without complaint, off he went with his family to build a new life—and a new vicarage:

A diner-out, a wit, and a popular preacher, I was suddenly caught up by the Archbishop of York, and transported to my living in Yorkshire, where there had not been a resident clergyman for a hundred and fifty years. Fresh from London, not knowing a turnip from a carrot, I was compelled to farm three hundred acres, and without capital to build a parsonage-house.

I asked and obtained three years' leave from the Archbishop, in order to effect an exchange, if possible; and fixed myself meantime at a small village two miles from York, in which was a fine old house of the time of Queen Elizabeth, where resided the last of the squires, with his lady, who looked as if she had walked straight out of the ark, or had been the wife of Enoch. He was a perfect specimen of the Trullibers of old; he smoked, hunted, drank beer at his door with his grooms and dogs, and spelt over the county paper on Sundays.

At first, he heard I was a Jacobin and a dangerous fellow, and turned aside as I passed: but at length, when he found the peace of the village undisturbed, harvests much as usual, Juno and Ponto uninjured, he first bowed, then called, and at last reached such a pitch of confidence that he used to bring his papers, that I might explain the difficult words to him; actually discovered that I had made a joke, laughed till I thought he would have died of convulsions, and ended by inviting me to see his dogs.

All my efforts for an exchange having failed, I asked and obtained from my friend the Archbishop another year to build in. And then I set my shoulder to the wheel in good earnest; sent for an architect; he produced plans which would have ruined me. I made him my bow: 'You build for glory, Sir; I, for use.' I returned him his plans, with five-and-twenty pounds, and sat down in my thinking chair, and in a few hours Mrs Sydney and I concocted a plan which has produced what I call the model of parsonage-houses.

I then took to horse to provide bricks and timber; was advised to make my own bricks, of my own clay; of course, when the kiln was opened, all bad; mounted my horse again, and in twenty-four hours had bought thousands of bricks and tons of timber. Was advised by neighbouring gentlemen to employ oxen: Bought four,—Tug and Lug, Hawl and Crawl; but Tug and Lug took to fainting, and required buckets of sal-volatile, and Hawl and Crawl to lie down in the mud. So I did what I ought to have done at first,—took the advice of the farmer instead of the gentleman; sold my oxen, bought a team of horses, and at last, in spite of a frost which delayed me six weeks, in spite of walls running down with wet, in spite of the advice and remonstrances of friends who predicted our death, in spite of an infant of six month, who had never been out of the house, I landed my family in my new house nine months after laying the first stone, on the 20th March; and performed my promise to the letter to the Archbishop, by issuing forth at midnight with a lantern to meet the last cart, with the cook and the cat, which had stuck in the mud, and fairly established them before twelve o'clock at night in the new parsonage-house;—a feat, taking ignorance, inexperience, and poverty into consideration, requiring, I assure you, no small degree of energy.

It made me a very poor man for many years, but I never repented it. I turned schoolmaster, to educate my son, as I could not afford to send him to school. Mrs Sydney turned schoolmistress, to educate my girls, as I could not afford a governess. I turned farmer, as I could not let my land. A manservant was too expensive; so I caught up a little garden-girl, made like a milestone, christened her Bunch, put a napkin in her hand, and made her my butler. The girls taught her to read, Mrs Sydney to wait, and I undertook her morals; Bunch became the best butler in the country.

I had little furniture, so I bought a cart-load of deals, took a carpenter (who came to me for parish relief, called Jack Robinson) with a face like a full-moon, into my service; established him in a barn, and said, 'Jack, furnish my house.' You see the result!

At last it was suggested that a carriage was much wanted in the establishment; after diligent search, I discovered in the back settlements of a York coachmaker an ancient green chariot, supposed to have been the earliest invention of the kind. I brought it home in triumph to my admiring family. Being somewhat dilapidated, the village tailor lined it, the village blacksmith repaired it; nay (but for Mrs Sydney's earnest entreaties), we believe the village painter would have exercised his genius upon the exterior; it escaped this danger however, and the result was wonderful. Each year added to its charms: it grew younger and younger; a new wheel, a new spring; I christened it the *Immortal*; it was known all over the neighbourhood; the village boys cheered it, and the village dogs barked at it; but '*Faber meae fortunae*' was my motto, and we had no false shame . . .

Smith filled his house and farm with all sorts of weird and ingenious labour-saving inventions, some of which worked. He also turned one room of the parsonage into a dispensary so that he could doctor his villagers himself rather than leave them to the care of those he called 'the professional and graduated homicides'. His daughter records:

'Ring the bell for Annie Kay.' Kay appeared. 'Bring me my medicine-book, Annie Kay. Kay is my apothecary's boy, and makes up my medicines.' Kay appears with the book. 'I am a great doctor; would you like to hear some of my medicines?' 'Oh yes, Mr Sydney.' 'There is the Gentle-jog, a pleasure to take it,—the Bull-dog, for more serious cases,—Peter's puke,—Heart's delight, the comfort of all the old women in the village,—Rub-a-Tub, a capital embrocation,—Dead-stop, settles the matter at once,—Up-with-it-then needs no explanation; and so on. Now, Annie Kay, give Mrs Spratt a bottle of Rub-a-dub; and to Mr Coles a dose of Dead-stop and twenty drops of laudanum.'

'This is the house to be ill in' (turning to us) 'indeed everybody who comes is expected to take a little something; I consider it a delicate compliment when my guests have a light illness here. We have contrivances for everything. Have you seen my patent armour? No? Annie Kay, bring my patent armour. Now, look here: if you have a stiff neck or swelled face, here is this sweet case of tin filled with hot water, and covered with flannel, to put round your neck, and you are well directly. Likewise, a patent tin shoulder, in case of rheumatism. There you see a stomach-tin, the greatest comfort in life; and lastly, here is a tin slipper, to be filled with hot water, which you can sit with in the drawing-room, should you come in chilled, without wetting your feet. Come and see my apothecary's shop.'

We all went downstairs, and entered a room filled entirely on one side with medicines, and on the other with every description of groceries and household or agricultural necessaries; in the centre, a large chest, forming a table, and divided into compartments for soap, candles, salt, and sugar.

'Here you see,' said he, 'every human want before you:—

> Man wants but little here below,
> As beef, veal, mutton, pork, lamb, venison show;'

spreading out his arms to exhibit everything, and laughing. 'Life is a difficult thing in the country, I assure you, and it requires a good deal of forethought to steer the ship, when you live twelve miles from a lemon.'

The Church authorities and the government decided that the highest office to which they could safely promote that wise, witty, erudite, and good man was to make him Canon of St Paul's. This was a small promotion and the timidity of the authorities shows that, then as now, although a sense of humour is most welcome in a friend it is deeply distrusted in a public figure.

Sydney Smith summed it up when he said to his brother Bobus, a distinguished lawyer:

'You and I are exceptions to the law of nature. You have risen by your gravity, I have sunk by my levity.'

A Memoir of the Reverend Sydney Smith (1771–1845), by his daughter, Lady Holland, with a Selection from his Letters, edited by Miss Austen (1855).

---

*P*ERIODICALS, *then as now, were happy to wring what humour they could from topical issues. A fruitful source of topical humour was any kind of innovation, however progressive, which tampered with the traditional way of doing things: the public reaction, nourished by the periodicals, was almost always one of furious denunciation followed by mockery.*

Until the beginning of the nineteenth century the students of Oxford and Cambridge were tested for their degree by the medieval method of oral questioning. Lord Eldon, Lord Chancellor, graduated from University College, Oxford, in 1770 and from his own report it is clear that an eighteenth-century oral examination was not exactly an ordeal: 'I was examined in Hebrew and History: "What is the Hebrew for the Place of a Skull?" said the Examiner. "Golgotha," I replied. "Who founded University College?" I answered "King Alfred". "Very well, sir," said the Examiner, "then you are competent for your degree."'

This comfortable, sleepy way of drifting into a degree was transformed at the beginning of the nineteenth century by the introduction of something quite new: written examination papers; carefully considered questions which had to be answered in full, in writing.

Many prominent citizens considered this a dangerous innovation, weakening the power of patronage and the influence of family connections. The Times newspaper found the whole thing worrying and then mockable. In 1816 they published the first in what has turned out to be a useful line for humorists—the spoof exam paper.

Here is The Times's parody of the Cambridge University Examination, stuffed with topical references familiar to all Times readers—then:

UTOPIA UNIVERSITY, UNDECEMBER 9657

1. Give a comparative sketch of the principal English theatres, with the dates of their erection, and the names of the most eminent candle-snuffers at

each. What were the stage-boxes? What were the offices of prompter—
ballet-master—and scene-shifter? In what part of the theatre was the one-
shilling gallery? Distinguish accurately between operas and puppet-shows.

2. Where was Downing-street? Who was prime-minister when Cribb defeated Molineux—and where did the battle take place? Explain the terms
milling—fibbing—cross buttock—neck and crop—bang up—and—prime.

3. Give the dates of all the parliaments from their first institution to the
period of the hard frost on the Thames. In what month of what year was Mr
Abbot elected Speaker? Why was he called *'the little man in the wig?'* When
the Speaker was out of the chair, where was the mace put?

4. Enumerate the principal houses of call in and about London, marking
those of the Taylors, Bricklayers, and Shoe-makers, and stating from what
Brewery each house was supplied with Brown Stout. Who was the tutelary
Saint of the Shoemakers? At what time was his feast celebrated? Who was
Saint Swithin? Do you remember any remarkable English proverb respecting
him?

5. Give a ground plan of Gilead-house. Mention the leading topics of the
Guide to Health, with some account of the Anti-Impetigines—Daffy's Elixir—
Blaine's Distemper Powders—Ching's Worm Lozenges—and Hooper's Female
Pills.

6. Give characters of Wat Tyler, Jack Cade, and Sir Francis Burdett. Did the
latter return from the Tower by water or land? On what occasion did Mr
Lethbridge's 'hair stand on *ind*'? Correct the solecism, and give the reason of
your alteration.

7. Enumerate the roads on which double toll was taken on the Sundays. Did
this custom extend to Christmas-day and Good Friday? Who was toll-taker
at Tyburn, when Mrs Brownrigg was executed?

8. Distinguish accurately between Sculls and Oars—Boat, and Punt—Jackass, and Donkey—Gauger, Exciseman, and Supervisor—Pantaloons, Trowsers, Gaiters, and Over-alls.—At what place of education were any of these
forbidden? Which? and Why?

9. Express the following words in the Lancashire, Derbyshire, London, and
Exmoor dialects—Bacon—Poker—You—I—Doctor—and Turnpike-gate.

10. Mention the principal Coach Inns in London, with a correct list of the
Coaches which set out from the Bolt-in-Tun. Where were the chief stands of
Hackney Coaches?—and what was the No. of that in which the Princess
Charlotte drove to Connaught-house? To what stand do you suppose this
removed after it set her down?

11. Give a succinct account, with dates, of the following persons—Belcher—Mr Waithman—Major Cartwright—Martin Van Butchell—and Edmund Henry Barker.

12. Draw a Map of the Thames with the surrounding country, marking particularly Wapping, Blackwall, Richmond, and the Isle of Dogs. Distinguish between Newcastle-on-Tyne, and Newcastle-under-Line—Gloucester and Double Gloucester—and the two Richmonds. What celebrated teacher flourished at one of them?—and who were his most eminent disciples?

13. What were the various sorts of paper in use amongst the English? To what purpose was *whited-brown* chiefly applied? What was size? Distinguish between this and college Sizings, and state the ordinary expense of papering a room.

14. 'For every one knows little *Matt's* an M.P.' Frag. Com. Inc. ap. Morn. Chron. vol. 59, p. 1624.
    What reasons can you assign for the general knowledge of this fact? Detail at length, the ceremony of chairing a Member. What were the Hustings? Who paid for them? Explain the abbreviations—Matt. M.P—Tom—Dick—F.R.S.—L.L.D.—and A.S.S.

15. What was the distinguishing title of the Mayors of London? Did any other city share the honour? Give a list of the Mayors of London from Sir Richard Whittington to Sir William Curtis, with an account of the Cat of the first, and the Weight of the last. What is meant by Lord Mayor's day? Describe the *Apothecaries'* Barge, and give some account of Marrow-bones and Cleavers.

16. When was Spyring and Marsden's Lemon Acid invented? Distinguish between this and Essential Salt of Lemons. Enumerate the principal Patentees, especially those of Liquid Blacking.

17. Scan the following lines—

> But for shaving and tooth-drawing,
> Bleeding, cabbaging and sawing,
> Dicky Gossip, Dicky Gossip is the man!

What is known of the character and history of Dicky Gossip?

The Times (25 Jan. 1816).

THE *poet Robert Southey was offered the editorship of* The Times *at £2,000 a year but refused the honour although he later accepted the position of Poet Laureate for an annual sum equal to the value of 42 gallons of canary wine. Southey was not only a poet but also a 'bookman' of the old school, a tireless reader and a voluminous writer of dramas, translations, reviews, biographies, and histories.*

The heaviest burden laid upon Poet Laureates was to produce two patriotic odes a year, to celebrate the New Year and the monarch's birthday. These odes inevitably turned out to be pompous and deeply boring and are now possibly the most tedious body of poetry in the language. Robert Southey's birthday odes—though he did try hard to put a stop to the ode-writing tradition—were no exception.

But Southey could write humorously when there was a place for it. Between 1834 and 1838 he published anonymously five volumes of a miscellany which he called The Doctor *(two more volumes were published posthumously). This work was a collection of his own pieces on random subjects together with anecdotes and little stories, loosely held together in close imitation of* Tristram Shandy, *by a Shandy-like Dr Dove and family.*

In the book occurred the first printing of The Story of the Three Bears, *which was probably not by Southey but a traditional story with which parents diverted infant tears. The trick was that the power of the storyteller's voice was supposed to change according to which bear was speaking, 'in the manner that our way of printing it may sufficiently indicate'.*

The Great Bear's terrifying bellow was represented in gigantic type, the Middle Bear's in much smaller type and the Little, Small, Wee Bear's in type which was barely visible. The unwelcome visitor in this original version was not a girl but 'an impudent, bad old woman' who finally jumped out of the bedroom window and legged it for the woods. It seems that the winsome Goldilocks was a Victorian addition.

Southey's own contributions to the book, that is, most of it, ranged in style from dazzling erudition to fugitive humorous essays, some of which seem astonishingly modern.

To Southey the theme of the following piece was no doubt merely an amusing conceit, but a hundred and fifty years later Southey's little joke is now taken seriously by zealous feminists:

In letter-writing, every person knows that male and female letters have a distinct sexual character, they should therefore be generally distinguished thus,

Hepistle and Shepistle.

And as there is the same marked difference in the writing of the two sexes I would propose

Penmanship and Penwomanship.

Erroneous opinions in religion being promulgated in this country by women as well as men, the teachers of such false doctrines may be divided into

Heresiarchs and Sheresiarchs,

so that we should speak of

> the Heresy of the Quakers
> the Sheresy of Joanna Southcote's people.

The troublesome affection of the diaphragm, which every person has experienced, is upon the same principle to be called according to the sex of the patient

> Hecups or Shecups,

which upon the principle of making our language truly British is better than the more classical form of

> Hiccups and Haeccups,

In its objective use the words become

> Hiscups or Hercups,

and in like manner Histerics should be altered into Herterics, the complaint never being masculine.

So also instead of making such words as agreeable, comfortable, &c. adjectives of one termination, I would propose,

> *Masculine:* agreabeau,   *Feminine:* agreabelle
> comfortabeau   comfortabelle
> miserabeau   miserabelle,
> &c. &c.

These things are suggested as hints to Mr Pytches, to be by him perpended in his improvement of our Dictionary.

Robert Southey (1774–1843), *The Doctor* (1834–8, 1847).

———

J OHN KEATS, *like Southey and most major poets of the time, did not write poetry to amuse, but writing letters was another matter. Keats had a gift for friendship and the warmth of his relationship with his friends and with his brothers and sister was expressed in the long letters which he, like Mozart, dashed off at great speed to tell them everything that he was doing and thinking and feeling. The letters sparkled with puns and humorous observation.*

In July 1818, after the publication of Endymion, *he went on a tour of the north of England and Scotland with a friend, scribbling exuberant letters home, even after tramping twenty miles a day. His thoughts poured out too swiftly for him to bother much with such literary niceties as spelling and punctuation.*

Here is his account of first seeing the Highland Fling danced. He concludes it with a little poetic analogy:

July 1st—We are this morning at Carlisle—After Skiddaw, we walked to Ireby the oldest market town in Cumberland where we were greatly amused by a country dancing school, holden at the Sun, it was indeed 'no new cotillon fresh from France'. No they kickit & jumpit with mettle extraordinary, & whiskit, & fleckit, & toe'd it, & go'd it, & twirld it, & wheel'd it, & stampt it, and sweat'd it, tattooing the floor like mad: The differenc [sic] between our country dances & these scotch figures, is about the same as leisurely stirring a cup o' Tea & beating up a batter pudding.

> John Keats (1795–1821), *Letters of John Keats*, ed. Robert Gittings, Letter to his younger brother, Tom Keats (1818).

Keats's other brother had married and had sailed with his bride Georgiana to make his fortune in the southern states of America. Keats wrote to his brother and sister-in-law jointly, saving up the letters until he had a packet large enough to ship. He was as affectionate towards his sister-in-law as he was towards his own blood relations, addressing her as 'sister'.

Knowing the difficulties Georgiana must have been facing in settling in to their new and alien life, and putting aside his own miseries—the death of his brother Tom, his own health, the hostile reception given to Endymion—*he did his best to try to cheer her up:*

I want very very much a little of your wit my dear sister—a Letter or two of yours just to bandy back a pun or two across the Atlantic and send a quibble [old word for a pun] over the Floridas—Now you have by this time crumpled up your large Bonnet, what do you wear—a cap! do you put your hair in papers of a night? do you pay the Miss Birkbeck's a morning visit—have you any tea?—or do you milk and water with them?—What place of Worship do you go to—the Quakers the Moravians, the Unitarians or the Methodists— Are there any flowers in bloom you like—any beautiful heaths—Any streets full of corset makers. What sort of shoes have you to fit those pretty feet of yours? Do you desire Compts. to one another? Do you ride on Horseback? What do you have for breakfast, dinner and supper? without mentioning lunch and bever and wet [drink] and snack—and a bit to stay one's stom- ach—Do you get any spirits?—now you might easily distill some whiskey— and going into the woods set up a whiskey shop for the Monkeys—Do you and the Miss Birkbecks get groggy on any thing—a little so so ish so as to be obliged to be seen home with a Lantern—You may perhaps have a game at puss in the corner—Ladies are warranted to play at this game though they have not whiskers. Have you a fiddle in the Settlement—or at any rate a jew's harp—which will play in spite of one's teeth—When you have nothing else to do for a whole day I tell you how you may employ it—First get up and when you are dress'd, as it would be pretty early, with a high wind in the woods give George a cold Pig [a splash of cold water to wake him up] with my Complements. Then you may saunter into the nearest coffee-house and after taking a dram and a look at the chronicle—go and frighten the wild boars upon the strength—you may as well bring one home for breakfast serving up the hoofs garnished with bristles and a grunt or two to accompany the singing of the kettle—then if George is not up give him a colder Pig always with my Compliments—When you are both set down to breakfast I advise you to eat your full share—but leave off immediately on feeling yourself inclined to anything on the other side of the puffy—avoid that for it does not become young women—After you have eaten your breakfast—keep your eye upon dinner—it is the safest way—You should keep a Hawk's eye over your dinner and keep hovering over it till due time then pounce taking care not to break any plates—While you are hovering with your dinner in prospect you may do a thousand things—put a hedgehog into Georges hat—pour a little water into his rifle—soak his boots in a pail of water—cut his jacket round into shreds like a roman kilt or the back of my grandmother's stays—sew *off* his buttons.

Letter to George and Georgiana Keats (14 Feb.–3 May, 1819).

A NOTHER *unlikely writer of amusing nonsense was the poet and translator of Omar Khayyam, Edward Fitzgerald. He was a minor poet, a shy man, but such was his personal charm that many major poets and authors were close friends, including Alfred Tennyson and his two brothers, George Crabbe, Thackeray, Carlyle, and James Spedding, the editor of Bacon's works.*

Fitzgerald kept up a steady correspondence with his distinguished literary friends and they enjoyed the benefit of many a thoughtful, Fitzgerald observation. As here, on the wig worn by the composer Handel:

Handel's was not a bagwig, which was simply so named from the little stuffed black silk watch-pocket that hung down behind the back of the wearer. Such were Haydn's and Mozart's—much less influential on the character: much less ostentatious in themselves: not towering so high, nor rolling down in following curls so low as to overlay the nature of the brain within. But Handel wore the Sir Godfrey Kneller wig: greatest of wigs: one of which some great General of the day used to take off his head after the fatigue of the battle and hand over to his valet to have the bullets combed out of it. Such a wig was a fugue in itself.

Edward Fitzgerald (1809–83), Letter to Frederic Tennyson (31 Mar. 1842).

Fitzgerald was a semi-recluse, living a quiet life in the country and pottering about in boats. His friend Spedding wrote of him, 'Edward Fitzgerald is the Prince of Quietists . . . His tranquillity is like a pirated copy of the peace of God.' Fitzgerald wrote of Spedding, or rather of Spedding's magnificently domed head:

That portrait of Spedding which Laurence has given me: not swords, nor cannon, nor all the Bulls of Bashan butting at it, could, I feel sure, discompose that venerable forehead. No wonder that no hair can grow at such an altitude: no wonder his view of Bacon's virtue is so rarefied that the common conscience of men cannot endure it. Thackeray and I occasionally amuse ourselves with the idea of Spedding's forehead: we find it somehow or other in all things, just peering out of all things: you see it in a milestone, Thackeray says. He also draws the forehead rising with a sober light over Mont Blanc, and reflected in the lake of Geneva. We have great laughing over this. The forehead is at present in Pembrokeshire, I believe: or Glamorganshire: or Monmouthshire: it is hard to say which. It has gone to spend its Christmas there.

Letter to Frederic Tennyson (16 Jan. 1841).

A FFECTIONATE *mocking of a friend's appearance was one thing but Thomas De Quincey's description of William Wordsworth had more of a bite to it. De Quincey had been friendly with Wordsworth for some time but he fell out with the Great Man over some real or imagined slight.*

Later, in an essay, he achieved a small revenge by drawing a pen picture of his ex-friend on a Nature Ramble:

Wordsworth was, upon the whole, not a well-made man. His legs were pointedly condemned by all the female connoisseurs in legs that ever I heard lecture upon that topic; not that they were bad in any way which would force itself upon your notice—there was no absolute deformity about them; and undoubtedly they had been serviceable legs beyond the average standard of human requisition; for I calculate, upon good data, that with these identical legs Wordsworth must have traversed a distance of 175 to 180,000 English miles—a mode of exertion which, to him, stood in the stead of wine, spirits, and all other stimulants whatsoever to the animal spirits; to which he has been indebted for a life of unclouded happiness, and we for much of what is most excellent in his writings. But, useful as they have proved themselves, the Wordsworthian legs were certainly not ornamental; and it was really a pity, as I agreed with a lady in thinking, that he had not another pair for evening dress parties—when no boots lend their friendly aid to masque our imperfections from the eyes of female rigorists—the *elegantes formarum spectarices*. A sculptor would certainly have disapproved of their contour . . .

But the worst part of Wordsworth's person was the bust: there was a narrowness and a droop about the shoulders which became striking, and had an effect of meanness when brought into close juxtaposition with a figure of a most statuesque order. Once on a summer morning, walking in the vale of Langdale with Wordsworth, his sister, and Mr J—, a native Westmoreland clergyman, I remember that Miss Wordsworth was positively mortified by the peculiar illustration which settled upon this defective conformation. Mr J—, a fine towering figure, six feet high, massy and columnar in his proportions, happened to be walking, a little in advance, with Wordsworth; Miss Wordsworth and myself being in the rear; and from the nature of the conversation which then prevailed in our front rank, something or other about money, devises, buying and selling, we of the rear-guard thought it requisite to preserve this arrangement for a space of three miles or more; during which time, at intervals, Miss W— would exclaim, in a tone of vexation, 'Is it possible?—can that be William? How very mean he looks!' and could not conceal a mortification that seemed really painful, until I, for my part, could not forbear laughing outright at the serious interest which she carried into this trifle. She was, however, right as regarded the mere visual judgment.

Wordsworth's figure, with all its defects, was brought into powerful relief by one which had been cast in a more square and massy mould; and in such a case it impressed a spectator with a sense of absolute meanness, more especially when viewed from behind, and not counteracted by his countenance; and yet Wordsworth was of a good height, just five feet ten, and not a slender man; on the contrary, by the side of Southey his limbs looked thick, almost in a disproportionate degree.

But the total effect of Wordsworth's person was always worst in a state of motion; for, according to the remark I have heard from many country people, 'he walked like a cade'—a cade being some sort of insect which advances by an oblique motion [a 'cade' was, in fact, the country word for a tottering, new-born lamb: perhaps slightly preferable from Wordsworth's point of view to an ant]. This was not always perceptible, and in part depended (I believe) upon the position of his arms; when either of these happened (as was very customary) to be inserted into the unbuttoned waistcoat, his walk had a wry or twisted appearance; and not appearance only—for I have known it, by slow degrees, gradually to edge off his companion from the middle to the side of the highroad.

Thomas De Quincey (1785–1859), Recollections of the Lakes and the Lake Poets (1840).

―――――

THERE *is a story that when Charles Lamb was very young he was taken by his sister for a walk through a cemetery. Even at that age he read everything he could find and he insisted on stopping at every tombstone and reading the inscriptions in praise of the dear departed. On the way out he said to his sister, 'Mary, where are all the naughty people buried?'*

Whether the story is true or not does not really matter because like most good anecdotes it illuminates the subject, and suggests the originality of mind, the element of common sense, and the powers of observation which made Charles Lamb's humorous prose so particular.

Thomas Carlyle once visited Charles Lamb at Lamb's cottage at Enfield. Carlyle was aged 34, a serious-minded young apostle of Man as Hero. Lamb was by then 56, a retired clerk who wrote little essays for periodicals. Perhaps in an effort to entertain his austere Scottish guest, Lamb observed cheerfully: 'There are just two things I regret in England's history: first, that Guy Fawkes's plot did not take effect (there would have been so glorious an explosion); second, that the Royalists did not hang Milton (then we might have laughed at them) . . .'

Carlyle was not at all the right audience for Lamb's humour. He wrote of that meeting, 'Charles Lamb I sincerely believe to be in some considerable degree insane. A more pitiful, ricketty, gasping, staggering, stammering Tom-fool I do not know . . . Besides, he is now a confirmed, shameless drunkard . . . Poor Lamb! Poor England, when such a despicable abortion is named genius!'

Strong stuff, even for a period when criticism was frequently personal and vitriolic, but a certain amount of truth lay beneath the venom. There was insanity in Lamb's family; he himself was confined for a short time in a sanatorium and his sister Mary murdered their mother in a fit of madness, which resulted in him having to take care of her for the rest of her life. He had an ugly stammer, he smoked too much, and drank too much, although it is probable that only a little drink quickly made him very drunk.

But there was another side to the picture. Lamb was poor all his life. In order to provide for his sister as well as himself he tried to supplement his wages as a clerk in the East India Office by authorship, by writing essays, criticisms, children's stories, even puns and epigrams for the Morning Post *at sixpence a joke. Little of his work was appreciated during his lifetime by the reading public, neither did it bring him in much money (when* The Essays of Elia *was reprinted in book form his royalties amounted to £30. He never received it).*

Yet he was loved by a huge circle of friends, some not in the public eye and others very much so, the latter including Southey, Walter Savage Landor, Wordsworth, Coleridge, Hazlitt, Leigh Hunt, and Tom Hood. He was loved not only for his mildly eccentric behaviour but also for his natural charm, loyalty, lack of self-pity, and, of course, for his humour. None of these ever wavered in spite of his appalling domestic difficulties. He confessed to Southey that anything awful made him laugh. He once misbehaved at a funeral, and during Hazlitt's wedding (to a clearly unsuitable bride) he laughed so much that he was almost thrown out three times.

His humour was frequently autobiographical. Here, in a letter to a friend, he describes his feelings in the umpteenth week of a nasty cold in the head:

Dear B.B.

Do you know what it is to succumb under an insurmountable day-mare,— 'a whoreson lethargy,' Falstaff calls it,—an indisposition to do anything, or to be anything,—a total deadness and distaste, a suspension of vitality,—an indifference to locality,—a numb, soporifical, good-for-nothingness,—an ossification all over,—an oysterlike insensibility to the passing events,—a mind-stupor,—a brawny defiance to the needles of a thrusting-in conscience? Did you ever have a very bad cold, with a total irresolution to submit to water-gruel processes? This has been for many weeks my lot and my excuse. My fingers drag heavily over this paper, and to my thinking it is three-and-twenty furlongs from here to the end of this demi-sheet. I have not a thing to say; nothing is of more importance than another; I am flatter than a denial or a pancake; emptier than Judge Park's wig when the head is in it; duller than a country stage when the actors are off it; a cipher, an O! I acknowledge life at all, only by an occasional convulsional cough, and a permanent phlegmatic pain in the chest. I am weary of the world; and the world is weary of me. My day is gone into twilight, and I don't think it worth the expense of candles. My wick hath a thief in it, but I can't muster courage to snuff it. I inhale suffocation; I can't distinguish veal from mutton; nothing interests me. 'Tis twelve o'clock, and Thurtell is just now coming out upon the New Drop, Jack Ketch alertly tucking up his greasy sleeves to do the last office of mortality, yet cannot I elicit a groan or a moral reflection. If you told me the world will be at an end tomorrow, I should just say, 'Will it?' I have not volition enough left to dot my i's, much less to comb my eyebrows; my eyes are set in my head; my brains are gone out to see a poor relation in Moorfields, and they did not say when they'd come back again; my skull is a Grub Street attic, to let—not so much as a joint stool or a cracked jordan [chamber pot] left in it; my hand writes, not I, from habit, as chickens run about a little, when their heads are off. O for a vigorous fit of gout, cholic, toothache,—an earwig in my auditory, a fly in my visual organs! Pain is life—the sharper, the more evidence of life; but this apathy, this death!

Charles Lamb (1775–1834), Letter to Bernard Barton (9 Jan. 1824).

Lamb's stutter made it impossible for him to take part in long conversations and he developed a technique of diverting the flow with a quick pun or a joke (at one party a lady asked him in all seriousness, 'Mr Lamb, how do you like babies?' Lamb replied 'B-b-boiled, ma'am'). He wrote of himself in a mock autobiography 'Stammers abominably and is therefore more apt to discharge his occasional conversation in a quaint aphorism, or a poor quibble, than in set and edifying speeches.'

But writing was another matter. In his essays Lamb was able to express himself smoothly and coherently, he could elaborate, he could develop a flight of fancy, and in his own good time he could find exactly the right words. The result was that in simple, beautiful prose he was the equal of Addison and in fanciful humour he was the master:

A DISSERTATION UPON ROAST PIG

Mankind, says a Chinese manuscript, which my friend M. was obliging enough to read and explain to me, for the first seventy thousand ages ate their meat raw, clawing or biting it from the living animal, just as they do in

Abyssinia to this day. This period is not obscurely hinted at by their great
Confucius in the second chapter of his Mundane Mutations, where he des-
ignates a kind of golden age by the term Cho-fang, literally the Cooks' holiday.
The manuscript goes on to say, that the art of roasting, or rather broiling
(which I take to be the elder brother) was accidentally discovered in the
manner following. The swine-herd, Ho-ti, having gone out into the woods
one morning, as his manner was, to collect mast [nuts and acorns] for his
hogs, left his cottage in the care of his eldest son Bo-bo, a great lubberly boy,
who being fond of playing with fire, as younkers of his age commonly are,
let some sparks escape into a bundle of straw, which kindling quickly, spread
the conflagration over every part of their poor mansion, till it was reduced to
ashes. Together with the cottage (a sorry antediluvian make-shift of a building, you may think it) what was of much more importance, a fine litter of
new-farrowed pigs, no less than nine in number, perished. China pigs have
been esteemed a luxury all over the East, from the remotest periods that we
read of. Bo-bo was in the utmost consternation, as you may think, not so
much for the sake of the tenement, which his father and he could easily build
up again with a few dry branches, and the labour of an hour or two, at any
time, as for the loss of the pigs. While he was thinking what he should say to
his father, and wringing his hands over the smoking remnants of one of
those untimely sufferers, an odour assailed his nostrils, unlike any scent
which he had before experienced. What could it proceed from?—not from
the burnt cottage—he had smelt that smell before—indeed this was by no
means the first accident of the kind which had occurred through the negligence of this unlucky young fire-brand. Much less did it resemble that of
any known herb, weed, or flower. A premonitory moistening at the same
time overflowed his nether lip. He knew not what to think. He next stooped
down to feel the pig, if there were any signs of life in it. He burnt his fingers,
and to cool them he applied them in his booby fashion to his mouth. Some of
the crumbs of the scorched skin had come away with his fingers, and for the
first time in his life (in the world's life indeed, for before him no man had
known it) he tasted—*crackling*! Again he felt and fumbled at the pig. It did
not burn him so much now, still he licked his fingers from a sort of habit.
The truth at length broke into his slow understanding, that it was the pig
that smelt so, and the pig that tasted so delicious; and, surrendering himself
up to the new-born pleasure, he fell to tearing up whole handfuls of the
scorched skin with the flesh next it, and was cramming it down his throat in
his beastly fashion, when his sire entered amid the smoking rafters, armed
with retributory cudgel, and finding how affairs stood, began to rain blows
upon the young rogue's shoulders, as thick as hail-stones, which Bo-bo
heeded not any more than if they had been flies. The tickling pleasure, which
he experienced in his lower regions, had rendered him quite callous to any
inconveniences he might feel in those remote quarters. His father might lay
on, but he could not beat him from his pig, till he had fairly made an end of

it, when, becoming a little more sensible of his situation, something like the following dialogue ensued.

'You graceless whelp, what have you got there devouring? Is it not enough that you have burnt me down three houses with your dog's tricks, and be hanged to you, but you must be eating fire, and I know not what—what have you got there, I say?'

'O father, the pig, the pig, do come and taste how nice the burnt pig eats.'

The ears of Ho-ti tingled with horror. He cursed his son, and he cursed himself that ever he should beget a son that should eat burnt pig.

Bo-bo, whose scent was wonderfully sharpened since morning, soon raked out another pig, and fairly rending it asunder, thrust the lesser half by main force into the fists of Ho-ti, still shouting out 'Eat, eat, eat the burnt pig, father, only taste—O Lord,'—with such-like barbarous ejaculations, cramming all the while as if he would choke.

Ho-ti trembled every joint while he grasped the abominable thing, wavering whether he should not put his son to death for an unnatural young monster, when the crackling scorching his fingers, as it had done his son's, and applying the same remedy to them, he in his turn tasted some of its flavour, which, make what sour mouths he would for a pretence, proved not altogether displeasing to him. In conclusion (for the manuscript here is a little tedious) both father and son fairly sat down to the mess, and never left off till they had despatched all that remained of the litter.

Bo-bo was strictly enjoined not to let the secret escape, for the neighbours would certainly have stoned them for a couple of abominable wretches, who could think of improving upon the good meat which God had sent them. Nevertheless, strange stories got about. It was observed that Ho-ti's cottage was burnt down now more frequently than ever. Nothing but fires from this time forward. Some would break out in broad day, others in the night-time. As often as the sow farrowed, so sure was the house of Ho-ti to be in a blaze; and Ho-ti himself, which was the more remarkable, instead of chastising his son, seemed to grow more indulgent to him than ever. At length they were watched, the terrible mystery discovered, and father and son summoned to take their trial at Pekin, then an inconsiderable assize town. Evidence was given, the obnoxious food itself produced in court, and verdict about to be pronounced, when the foreman of the jury begged that some of the burnt pig, of which the culprits stood accused, might be handed into the box. He handled it, and they all handled it, and burning their fingers, as Bo-bo and his father had done before them, and nature prompting to each of them the same remedy, against the face of all the facts, and the clearest charge which judge had ever given,—to the surprise of the whole court, towns-folk, strangers, reporters, and all present—without leaving the box, or any manner of consultation whatever, they brought in a simultaneous verdict of Not Guilty.

The judge, who was a shrewd fellow, winked at the manifest iniquity of the decision: and, when the court was dismissed, went privily, and bought up all the pigs that could be had for love or money. In a few days his Lordship's town house was observed to be on fire. The thing took wing, and now there was nothing to be seen but fires in every direction. Fuel and pigs grew enormously dear all over the district. The insurance offices one and all shut up shop. People built slighter and slighter every day, until it was feared that the very science of architecture would in no long time be lost to the world. Thus this custom of firing houses continued, till in process of time, says my manuscript, a sage arose, like our Locke, who made a discovery, that the flesh of swine, or indeed of any other animal, might be cooked (*burnt*, as they called it) without the necessity of consuming a whole house to dress it. Then first began the rude form of a gridiron. Roasting by the string, or spit, came in a century or two later, I forget in whose dynasty. By such slow degrees, concludes the manuscript, do the most useful, and seemingly the most obvious arts, make their way among mankind.——

Without placing too implicit faith in the account above given, it must be agreed, that if a worthy pretext for so dangerous an experiment as setting houses on fire (especially in these days) could be assigned in favour of any culinary object, that pretext and excuse might be found in ROAST PIG.

Essays of Elia (1823).

DURING *the later years of Lamb's life some new forms of the novel were attracting readers. The old social stories of Manners had been joined by the Silver Fork novel, which provided the largely middle-class readership with titillating glimpses of amorous intrigue and social manœuvring amongst the upper classes. One of the earliest and most popular of these was Bulwer Lytton's* Pelham, or The Adventures of a Gentleman, *published in 1828. The hero Pelham, like Lytton himself and a later author of Silver Fork novels Benjamin Disraeli, was a politically ambitious dandy. In the book the masculine but foppish Pelham startled London society by forsaking the bright colours then worn by gentlemen in the evening for plain black. This started a fashion in real life and British manhood has ever since appeared on formal evening occasions dressed like undertakers.*

Silver Fork novels, amusing enough though they were in scenes which included amusing people, did not set out primarily to be humorous.

But another kind of story, which began to be popular a year or so after Pelham, *had to make its readers laugh or it had failed. It was a new style of broad humour, usually taking the form of a series of farcical incidents built round a central comical character.*

In the 1830s Robert Smith Surtees, a failed solicitor from an ancient Durham family, began and edited The New Sporting Magazine. *For this he wrote a series*

of comical sketches featuring Mr John Jorrocks, a well-off, self-made, cockney
grocer who was obsessed with riding to hounds. The sketches became extremely
popular and were published in book form in 1838 as Jorrock's Jaunts and Jollities.
More Jorrocks books followed.

Jorrocks, the old-fashioned London merchant with an order-book in the pocket of
his riding jacket so that he could dispose of some of his teas during the chase, cared
more for hunting than anything else in the world, including his dear wife:

'Unting is all that's worth living for—all time is lost wot is not spent in
'unting—it is like the hair we breathe—if we have it not we die—it's the
sport of kings, the image of war without its guilt, and only five-and-twenty
per cent of its danger . . .

'Unting fills my thoughts by day, and many a good run I have in my sleep.
Many a dig in the ribs I give Mrs J. when I think they're running into the
warmint . . . No man is fit to be called a sportsman wot doesn't kick his wife
out of bed of a haverage once in three weeks!

Robert Smith Surtees (1803–64), Handley Cross (1843).

Jorrocks was vulgar but shrewd, good-natured yet not to be put upon. Also,
considering that he was in his sixties and incompetent in the saddle, and that his
horse Arterxerxes was enormous, he was the possessor of a kind of fearful courage:

Twang, twang, twang went Mr Jorrocks's horn, sometimes in full, sometimes
in divided notes and half screeches. The hounds turn and make for the point.
Governor, Adamant, Dexterous, and Judgment came first, then the body of
the pack, followed by Benjamin at full gallop on Xerxes, with his face and
hands all scratched and bleeding from the briars and brushwood, that Xerxes,
bit in teeth, had borne him triumphantly through. Bang—the horse shot past
Mr Jorrocks, Benjamin screaming, yelling, and holding on by the mane,
Xerxes doing with him just what he liked, and the hounds getting together
and settling to the scent. 'My vig, wot a splitter!' cried Mr Jorrocks in astonishment, as Xerxes took a high stone wall out of the cover in his stride,
without disturbing the coping, but bringing Ben right on to his shoulder—
'Hoff, for a fi' pun note! hoff for a guinea 'at to a Gossamer!' exclaimed Mr
Jorrocks, eyeing his whipper-in's efforts to regain the saddle. A friendly chuck
of Xerxes's head assists his endeavours, and Ben scrambles back to his place.
A gate on the left let Mr Jorrocks out of cover, on to a good sound sward,
which he prepared to take advantage of by getting Arterxerxes short by the
head, rising in his stirrups, and hustling him along as fast as he could lay
his legs to the ground. An open gate at the top fed the flame of his eagerness,
and not being afraid of the pace so long as there was no leaping, Jorrocks
sent him spluttering through a swede turnip field as if it was pasture. Now
sitting plum in his saddle, he gathered his great whip together, and proceeded
to rib-roast Arterxerxes in the most summary manner, calling him a great

lurching, rolling, lumbering, beggar, vowing that if he didn't lay himself
out and go as he ought, he'd 'boil him when he got 'ome'. So he jerked and
jagged, and kicked and spurred, and hit and held, making indifferent progress
compared to his exertions. The exciting cry of hounds sounded in front and
now passing on to a very heavy, roughly-ploughed upland, our master saw
the hind-quarters of some half-dozen horses, the riders of which had been in
the secret, disappearing through the high quick fence at the top.

'Dash my vig, 'ere's an unavoidable leap, I do believe,' said he to himself,
as he neared the headland, and saw no way out of the field but over the
fence—a boundary one; 'and a werry hawkward place it is too,' added he,
eyeing it intently, 'a yawnin' blind ditch, a hugly quick fence on the top,
and may be, a plough or 'arrow turned teeth huppermost, on the far side.

'Oh, John Jorrocks, John Jorrocks, my good friend, I wishes you were well
over with all my 'eart—terrible place indeed! Give a guinea 'at to be at the
far side,' so saying, he dismounted, and pulling the snaffle-rein of the bridle
over his horse's head, he knotted the lash of his ponderous whip to it, and
very quietly slid down the ditch and climbed up the fence, 'Who-a-ing' and
crying to his horse to 'stand still,' expecting every minute to have him atop
of him. The taking-on place was wide, and two horses having gone over
before him, had done a little towards clearing the way, so having gained his
equilibrium at the top, Mr Jorrocks began jerking and coaxing Arterxerxes
to induce him to follow, pulling at him much in the style of a school-boy
who catches a log of wood in fishing.

'Come hup! my man,' cried Mr Jorrocks, coaxingly, jerking the rein; but
Arterxerxes only stuck his great resolute fore legs in advance, and pulled the
other way. 'Gently, old fellow!' cried he, 'gently Arterxerxes, my bouy!'
dropping his hand, so as to give him more line, and then trying what effect a
jerk would have, in inducing him to do what he wanted. Still the horse stood
with his great legs before him. He appeared to have no notion of leaping.
Jorrocks began to wax angry. 'Dash my vig, you hugly brute!' he exclaimed,
grinning with rage at the thought of the run he was losing, 'dash my vig, if
you don't mind what you're arter, I'll get on your back and bury my spurs i'
your sides. COME HUP! I say, YOU HUGLY BEAST!' roared he, giving a tremendous
jerk of the rein, upon which the horse flew back, pulling Jorrcoks downwards
in the muddy ditch. Arterxerxes then threw up his heels and ran away, whip
and all . . .

And to crown the day's disasters, when at length our fat friend got his
horse and his hounds and his damaged Benjamin scraped together again,
and re-entered Handley Cross, he was yelled at, and hooted, and rid-coat!
rid-coat!-ed by the children, and made an object of unmerited ridicule by the
fair but rather unfeeling portion of the populace.

'Lauk! here's an old chap been to Spilsby!' shouted Betty Lucas, the
mangle-woman, on getting a view of his great mud-stained back.

'Hoot! he's always tumblin' off, that 'ard chap,' responded Mrs Hardbake, the itinerant lolly-pop seller, who was now waddling along with her tray before her.

'Sich old fellows have no business out a-huntin'!' observed Miss Rampling, the dressmaker, as she stood staring, bonnet-box on arm.

Then a marble-playing group of boys suspended operations to give Jorrocks three cheers; one, more forward than the rest, exclaiming, as he eyed Arterxerxes, 'A! what a shabby tail! A! what a shabby tail!'

Next as he passed the Barley-mow beer-shop, Mrs Gallon, the landlady, who was nursing a child at the door, exclaimed across the street, to Blash, the barber's pretty but rather wordy wife—

'A-a-a! ar say Fanny!—old Fatty's had a fall!'

To which Mrs Blash replied, with a scornful toss of her head, at our now admiring friend—

'*Hut!* he's always on his back, that old feller'.

'Not 'alf as often as you are, old gal!' retorted the now indignant Mr Jorrocks, spurring on out of hearing.   Ibid.

Mr Jorrocks rode hard (on the flat) and, when the hunt was over and Arterxerxes was snugly stabled, he ate enormously and drank deeply—to the point of immobility.

As he gently explained to a Duke who had unthinkingly invited Jorrocks merely to dinner:

'Where I dine I sleep, and where I sleep I breakfast, your Greece.'

Hillingdon Hall (1845).

In one famous scene he finishes the evening in the company of the brandy bottle and James Pigg, his stable manager and huntsman. After they have drunk innumerable toasts, including one to each of the hounds by name, Mr Jorrocks begins to worry that it might rain and spoil his next morning's hunting:

'Look out of the winder, James, and see what'un a night it is,' said he to Pigg, giving the log a stir, to ascertain that the hiss didn't proceed from any dampness in the wood.

James staggered up, and after a momentary grope about the room—for they were sitting without candles—exclaimed, 'Hellish dark, and smells of cheese!'

'Smells o' cheese!' repeated Mr Jorrocks, looking round in astonishment; 'smells o' cheese!—vy, man, you've got your nob i' the cupboard—this be the vinder.'

Handley Cross (1843).

THE *Jorrocks books were not in the first eleven of contemporary literature,
perhaps because their fox-hunting background had its limitations, but Surtees
could be described in cricketing terms as being in his day the vice-captain of
the second eleven. And much more importantly, the popular success of Jorrocks
had, unwittingly, an enormous influence on the development of the English
comic novel.*

*A well-known illustrator and caricaturist, Robert Seymour, had seen how pop-
ular the Jorrocks stories were and suggested to a newish publishing house, Chapman
and Hall, that he should engrave a series of comical sporting prints featuring a
group of cockney sports enthusiasts who would be known as the 'Nimrod Club'.
The work was to be published monthly in 'shilling numbers'. This form of production was cheap and had an enormous potential readership as the parts were not
only sold in bookshops but also hawked round villages and remote areas by pedlars
and higglers.*

*Chapman and Hall were interested. Industrialization was changing the face of
England, cities and towns were growing fast as former farm labourers moved to
where the new factories were being built, railways were steadily taking over from
stage-coaches, and the success of the Jorrocks stories showed that a profitable
market existed in nostalgia for the eighteenth-century open-air life, for the Henry
Fielding world of rolling hills, white roads and bustling inns, particularly if this
was mixed with nineteenth-century standards of better food and drink and cleaner
beds (Jorrocks slept comfortably after his day's adventures).*

*Chapman and Hall looked around for a hack writer to supply the text to link
Seymour's pictures and decided to try a young Parliamentary reporter who was
about to publish a collection of humorous newspaper articles and was already under
contract to them to write a piece for their monthly magazine. He was Charles
Dickens, aged 23.*

*What was extraordinary was that the young Dickens, desperately in need of the
money so that he could get married, would only take the job on his own terms: he
pointed out that he knew very little about sport and insisted that he be allowed to
widen the brief and write about anything that took his fancy. He also wanted the
pictures to illustrate his text rather than the other way round. All was agreed.
Dickens thought up the character of Mr Pickwick and began his chore of delivering
12,000 words every thirty days. Seymour illustrated the first number and then,
weighed down by financial and other problems, committed suicide. Other young
illustrators were considered—including William Makepeace Thackeray—but the
job eventually went to a friend of Thackeray, Hablot Knight Browne, aged 19.
Browne took the pseudonym 'Phiz' to complement Dickens's pen-name 'Boz' (presumably pronounced 'Boaze,' to rhyme with 'hose': Dickens's younger brother was
nicknamed 'Moses' in honour of the Vicar of Wakefield and 'Moses', 'facetiously
pronounced through the nose', became 'Boses' and eventually 'Boz').*

*The whole project had turned about: Dickens, instead of just doing the menial
task of linking the all-important pictures, now had artistic control over both the
story and the illustrations. He extended the text from twenty-four pages to*

thirty-two to give himself more room to develop his scenes and he cut the number of illustrations per issue from four to two.

In April 1836 the first of the twenty monthly parts of The Posthumous Papers of the Pickwick Club *was published. Nothing much happened. About five hundred were sold which was not profitable. Then with the fourth number, which introduced Sam Weller and took the four members of the Pickwick Club back to London, the sales began to increase dramatically. By the time the twelfth number was issued the circulation was forty times larger, exceeding twenty thousand copies a month. Charles Dickens was famous, Chapman and Hall were much richer, and* The Pickwick Papers *had become the most spectacularly successful publication in the history of the novel.*

Dickens was the most theatrical of novelists—he almost became an actor before meeting Chapman and Hall—and he brought on most of his comic characters as though they were actors in a play, first describing the setting and then how the character was dressed and what he or she looked like. When the character spoke he or she almost always had an individual, comical trick of speech.

Here is the scene in the highly important part four where we first meet Sam Weller, boot boy of the White Hart Inn, High Street, Borough:

There are in London several old inns, once the head-quarters of celebrated coaches in the days when coaches performed their journeys in a graver and more solemn manner than they do in these times; but which have now degenerated into the abiding and booking places of country waggons. The reader would look in vain for any of these ancient hostelries, among the Golden Crosses and Bull and Mouths, which rear their stately fronts in the improved streets of London. If he would light upon any of these old places, he must direct his steps to the obscurer quarters of the town; and there in some secluded nooks he will find several, still standing with a kind of gloomy sturdiness, amidst the modern innovations which surround them . . .

It was in the yard of one of these inns—of no less celebrated a one than the White Hart—that a man was busily employed in brushing the dirt off a pair of boots, early on the morning succeeding the events narrated in the last chapter. He was habited in a coarse-striped waistcoat, with black calico sleeves, and blue glass buttons; drab breeches and leggings. A bright red handkerchief was wound in a very loose and unstudied style round his neck, and an old white hat was carelessly thrown on one side of his head. There were two rows of boots before him, one cleaned and the other dirty, and at every addition he made to the clean row, he paused from his work, and contemplated his work with evident satisfaction . . .

A loud ringing of one of the bells, was followed by the appearance of a smart chambermaid in the upper sleeping gallery, who, after tapping at one of the doors, and receiving a request from within, called over the balustrades—

'Sam!'

'Hallo,' replied the man with the white hat.

'Number twenty-two wants his boots.'

'Ask number twenty-two, wether he'll have 'em now, or wait till he gets 'em,' was the reply.

'Come, don't be a fool, Sam,' said the girl coaxingly, 'the gentleman wants his boots directly.'

'Well, you *are* a nice young 'ooman for a musical party, you are,' said the boot-cleaner. 'Look at these here boots—eleven pair o' boots; and one shoe as b'longs to number six, with the wooden leg. The eleven boots is to be called at half-past eight and the shoe at nine. Who's number twenty-two, that's to put all the others out? No, no, reg'lar rotation, as Jack Ketch said, wen he tied the men up. Sorry to keep you a waitin,' sir, but I'll attend to you directly.'

Saying which, the man in the white hat set to work upon a top-boot with increased assiduity.

Charles Dickens (1812–70), The Pickwick Papers (1836).

Sam Weller leaves his job at the White Hart and joins Mr Pickwick. 'When I wos first pitched neck and crop into the world, to play at leap-frog with its troubles,' he explains happily, 'I wos a carrier's boy at startin': then a vagginer's, then a helper, then a boots. Now I'm a gen'l'm'n's servant.' Cocky and respectful at the same time, he takes it upon himself to protect his benevolent, innocent employer. Sam is a London street-arab who survived and he seems to know every inch of London, as Mr Pickwick discovers when, shaken after an unpleasant session with lawyers, he asks Sam where he can get a glass of warm brandy and water:

'Second court on the right hand side—last house but vun on the same side the vay—take the box as stands in the first fire-place, 'cos there an't no leg in the middle o' the table, wich all the others has, and it's wery inconwenient.'

The public house is much used by stage-coachmen. One of them, a very fat, red-faced, elderly pipe-smoker, keeps staring at Sam and Mr Pickwick. Eventually:

The stout man having blown a thick cloud of smoke from his pipe, a hoarse voice, like some strange effort of ventriloquism, emerged from beneath the capacious shawls which muffled his throat and chest, and slowly uttered these sounds—'Wy, Sammy!'

'Who's that, Sam?' inquired Mr Pickwick.

'Why, I wouldn't ha' believed it, sir,' replied Mr Weller with astonished eyes. 'It's the old 'un.'

'Old one,' said Mr Pickwick. 'What old one?'

'My father, sir,' replied Mr Weller. 'How are you, my ancient?' With which beautiful ebullition of filial affection, Mr Weller made room on the seat beside him for the stout man, who advanced pipe in mouth and pot in hand, to greet him.

'Wy, Sammy,' said the father, 'I han't seen you, for two year and better.'

'Nor more you have, old codger,' replied the son. 'How's mother in law?'

Mr Weller senior counsels his son on the misfortunes of the married state while Mr Pickwick gradually realizes that he has now acquired a coachman as well as a servant to accompany him on his jaunts.

Dickens's creative powers were extraordinary even in this his first book. He invented almost a hundred characters for The Pickwick Papers, *most of them comical and almost all of them memorable.*

One of the oddest and most beguiling is Mr Alfred Jingle, itinerant actor and part-time confidence trickster. He joins the Pickwickians in the first number when they are setting out to Rochester by stage-coach and subsequently bobs up from time to time in the story, usually engaged in some small, hopeless swindle.

As usual, Dickens first takes him into the Make-Up and Wardrobe departments and, as it were, kits him out:

He was about the middle height, but the thinness of his body, and the length of his legs, gave him the appearance of being much taller. The green coat had been a smart dress garment in the days of swallow-tails, but had evidently in those times adorned a much shorter man than the stranger, for the soiled and faded sleeves scarcely reached to his wrists. It was buttoned closely up to his chin, at the imminent hazard of splitting the back; and an old stock, without a vestige of shirt collar, ornamented his neck. His scanty black trousers displayed here and there those shiny patches which bespeak long service, and were strapped very tightly over a pair of patched and mended shoes, as if to conceal the dirty white stockings, which were nevertheless distinctly visible. His long black hair escaped in negligent waves from beneath each side of his old pinched-up hat; and glimpses of his bare wrists might be observed between the tops of his gloves, and the cuffs of his coat sleeves. His face was thin and haggard; but an indescribable air of jaunty impudence and perfect self-possession pervaded the whole man.

Mr Jingle has a peculiar way of rattling out his words in quick spurts, like a rifleman's rapid-fire (Mr Weller senior called it 'the gift o' the gab wery gallopin''). The four innocent Pickwickians are tremendously impressed by him and take down his stories in their special tour notebooks:

'Sportsman, sir?' abruptly turning to Mr Winkle.
    'A little, sir,' replied the gentleman.
    'Fine pursuit, sir—fine pursuit.—Dogs, sir?'
    'Not just now,' said Mr Winkle.
    'Ah! you should keep dogs—fine animals—sagacious creatures—dog of my own once—Pointer—surprising instinct—out shooting one day—entering enclosure—whistled—dog stopped—whistled again—Ponto—no go; stock still—called him—Ponto, Ponto—wouldn't move—dog transfixed—staring at a board—looked up, saw an inscription—"Gamekeeper has orders to shoot all dogs found in this enclosure"—wouldn't pass it—wonderful dog—valuable dog that—very.'

'Singular circumstance that,' said Mr Pickwick. 'Will you allow me to make a note of it?'

'Certainly, sir, certainly—hundreds of anecdotes of the same animal—Fine girl, sir' (to Mr Tracy Tupman, who had been bestowing sundry anti-Pickwickian glances on a young lady by the roadside).

'Very!' said Mr Tupman.

'English girls not so fine as Spanish—noble creatures—jet hair—black eyes—lovely forms—sweet creatures—beautiful.'

'You have been in Spain, sir?' said Mr Tracy Tupman.

'Lived there—ages.'

'Many conquests, sir?' inquired Mr Tupman.

'Conquests! Thousands. Don Bolaro Fizzgig—Grandee—only daughter—Donna Christina—splendid creature—loved me to distraction—jealous father—high-souled daughter—handsome Englishman—Donna Christina in despair—prussic acid—stomach pump in my portmanteau—operation performed—old Bolaro in ecstasies—consent to our union—join hands and floods of tears—romantic story—very.'

'Is the lady in England now, sir?' inquired Mr Tupman, on whom the description of her charms had produced a powerful impression.

'Dead, sir—dead,' said the stranger, applying to his right eye the brief remnant of a very old cambric handkerchief. 'Never recovered the stomach pump—undermined constitution—fell a victim.'

'And her father?' inquired the poetic Snodgrass.

'Remorse and misery,' replied the stranger. 'Sudden disappearance—talk of the whole city—search made everywhere—without success—public fountain in the great square suddenly ceased playing—weeks elapsed—still a stoppage—workmen employed to clean it—water drawn off—father-in-law discovered sticking head first in the main pipe, with a full confession in his right boot—took him out, and the fountain played again, as well as ever.'

'Will you allow me to note that little romance down, sir?' said Mr Snodgrass, deeply affected.

Ibid.

Another character out of the run of normal comic invention was Mr Leo Hunter, a grave gentleman who called on Mr Pickwick when the Pickwickians were visiting the market town of Eatanswill (i.e. 'Eat and swill'. Dickens still frequently used the ancient device of labelling characters and places with names which described their chief characteristics.)

The well-off, artistic lady who appoints herself cultural leader of a provincial town is not a particularly original figure of fun, but behind most of these formidable ladies there lurks a figure more neglected by literature, a barely discernible husband. This is certainly true of Eatanswill's literary leader and collector of visiting celebrities, Mrs Leo Hunter (i.e. 'lionizer').

Mr Leo Hunter is so profoundly honoured at being the husband of Mrs Leo

Hunter that he uses her visiting card when he calls rather than presume to have a card of his own:

Mr Pickwick's conscience had been somewhat reproaching him for his recent neglect of his friends at the Peacock; and he was just on the point of walking forth in quest of them, on the third morning after the election had terminated, when his faithful valet put into his hand a card, on which was engraved the following inscription:—

Mrs Leo Hunter

The Den.   Eatanswill.

'Person's a waitin',' said Sam, epigrammatically.

'Does the person want me, Sam?' inquired Mr Pickwick.

'He wants you particklar; and no one else'll do, as the Devil's private secretary said ven he fetched avay Doctor Faustus,' replied Mr Weller.

'*He.* Is it a gentleman?' said Mr Pickwick.

'A wery good imitation o' one, if it an't,' replied Mr Weller.

'But this is a lady's card,' said Mr Pickwick.

'Given me by a gen'lm'n, hows'ever,' replied Sam, 'and he's waitin' in the drawing-room—said he'd rather wait all day, than not see you.'

Mr Pickwick, on hearing this determination, descended to the drawing-room, where sat a grave man, who started up on his entrance, and said, with an air of profound respect:

'Mr Pickwick, I presume?'

'The same.'

'Allow me, sir, the honour of grasping your hand. Permit me, sir, to shake it,' said the grave man.

'Certainly,' said Mr Pickwick.

The stranger shook the extended hand, and then continued.

'We have heard of your fame, sir. The noise of your antiquarian discussion has reached the ears of my wife, sir; *I* am *Mr* Leo Hunter'—the stranger paused, as if he expected that Mr Pickwick would be overcome by the disclosure; but seeing that he remained perfectly calm, proceeded.

'My wife, sir—Mrs Leo Hunter—is proud to number among her acquaintances all those who have rendered themselves celebrated by their works and talents. Permit me, sir, to place in a conspicuous part of the list the name of Mr Pickwick, and his brother members of the club that derives its name from him.'

'I shall be extremely happy to make the acquaintance of such a lady, sir,' replied Mr Pickwick.

'You *shall* make it, sir,' said the grave man. 'To-morrow morning, sir, we give a public breakfast—a *fête champêtre*—to a great number of those who have rendered themselves celebrated by their works and talents. Permit Mrs Leo Hunter, sir, to have the gratification of seeing you at the Den.'

'With great pleasure,' said Mr Pickwick.

'Mrs Leo Hunter has many of these breakfasts, sir' resumed the new acquaintance—'"feasts of reason, sir, and flows of soul", as somebody who wrote a sonnet to Mrs Leo Hunter on her breakfasts, feelingly and originally observed.'

'Was *he* celebrated for his works and talents?'

'He was, sir,' said the grave man, 'all Mrs Leo Hunter's acquaintances are; it is her ambition, sir, to have no other acquaintances.'

'It is a very noble ambition,' said Mr Pickwick.

'When I inform Mrs Leo Hunter, that that remark fell from *your* lips, sir, she will indeed be proud,' said the grave man. 'You have a gentleman in your train, who has produced some beautiful little poems, I think, sir.'

'My friend Mr Snodgrass has a great taste for poetry,' replied Mr Pickwick.

'So has Mrs Leo Hunter, sir. She doats on poetry, sir. She adores it; I may say that her whole soul and mind are wound up, and entwined with it. She has produced some delightful pieces, herself, sir. You may have met with her Ode to an Expiring Frog, sir.'

'I don't think I have,' said Mr Pickwick.

'You astonish me, sir,' said Mr Leo Hunter. 'It created an immense sensation. It was signed with an "L" and eight stars, and appeared originally in a Lady's Magazine. It commenced

> "Can I view thee panting, lying
> On thy stomach, without sighing;
> Can I unmoved see thee dying
> On a log,
> Expiring frog!"'

'Beautiful!' said Mr Pickwick.

'Fine,' said Mr Leo Hunter, 'so simple.'

'Very,' said Mr Pickwick.

'The next verse is still more touching. Shall I repeat it?'

'If you please,' said Mr Pickwick.

'It runs thus,' said the grave man, still more gravely.

> "Say, have fiends in shape of boys,
> With wild halloo, and brutal noise,
> Hunted thee from marshy joys,
> With a dog,
> Expiring frog!"'

'Finely expressed,' said Mr Pickwick.

'All point, sir,' said Mr Leo Hunter, 'but you shall hear Mrs Leo Hunter repeat it. *She* can do justice to it, sir. She will repeat it, in character, sir, to-morrow morning.'

'In character!'

'As Minerva. But I forgot—it's a fancy-dress breakfast.'

Ibid.

Half-way through writing the twenty numbers of The Pickwick Papers *Charles Dickens, now aged 24, married and famous, negotiated with another publisher to begin a new monthly serial. So during the last half of* The Pickwick Papers *he was also writing the first half of* Oliver Twist. *At the conclusion of* The Pickwick Papers *he made a deal with Chapman and Hall to retain a share of copyright and to begin immediately on another long part-work. So while he was still working on* Oliver Twist *he was also writing* Nicholas Nickleby. *Although outstandingly successful as a novelist he continued throughout his career to write for and edit newspapers and magazines (also to take part in amateur dramatics, go for fast walks, play with his ten children, pursue charity projects, keep in touch socially with a huge circle of distinguished friends, and, latterly, give public readings of his works in England and America. He also had a girl friend).*

When he was being an editor, Dickens was always exhorting his contributors to 'Brighten it! Brighten it!', whether the piece was a story or a factual scientific paper. It was his own working maxim. Even his later novels with serious social themes were tragicomic rather than tragic. He managed to inject humour even into a scene between Nicholas Nickleby and the criminally brutal headmaster of Dotheboys Hall, Wackford Squeers:

There ranged themselves in front of the schoolmaster's desk, half-a-dozen scarecrows, out at knees and elbows, one of whom placed a torn and filthy book beneath his learned eye.

'This is the first class in English spelling and philosophy, Nickleby,' said Squeers, beckoning Nicholas to stand beside him. 'We'll get up a Latin one, and hand that over to you. Now, then, where's the first boy?'

'Please, sir, he's cleaning the back parlour window,' said the temporary head of the philosophical class.

'So he is, to be sure,' rejoined Squeers. 'We go upon the practical mode of teaching, Nickleby; the regular education system. C-l-e-a-n, clean, verb active, to make bright, to scour. W-i-n, win, d-e-r, der, winder, a casement. When the boy knows this out of the book, he goes and does it. It's just the same principle as the use of the globes. Where's the second boy?'

'Please, sir, he's weeding the garden,' replied a small voice.

'To be sure,' said Squeers, by no means disconcerted. 'So he is. B-o-t, bot, t-i-n, tin, bottin n-e-y, ney, bottiney, noun substantive, a knowledge of plants. When he has learned that bottinney means a knowledge of plants, he goes and knows 'em. That's our system, Nickleby; what do you think of it?'

'It's a very useful one, at any rate,' answered Nicholas.

'I believe you,' rejoined Squeers, not remarking the emphasis of his usher. 'Third boy, what's a horse?'

'A beast, sir,' replied the boy.

'So it is,' said Squeers. 'Ain't it, Nickleby?'

'I believe there is no doubt of that, sir,' answered Nicholas.

'Of course there isn't,' said Squeers. 'A horse is a quadruped, and quadruped's Latin for beast, as every body that's gone through the grammar, knows,
or else where's the use of having grammars at all?'

The Life and Adventures of Nicholas Nickleby (1838–9).

*Dickens wrote superb introductions to bring on his minor characters. Perhaps no
other author except Jane Austen has written such humorous, economical, vividly
descriptive paragraphs.*

*Although some of the characters might seem too grotesque to have been drawn
from life there is a recognizable grain of truth embedded in most of them and many
of them are clearly portraits of real people.*

*Here are some examples of Dickens's introductions. In the opening lines of
Dombey and Son we meet Mr Dombey the successful business man and his infant
son:*

Dombey was about eight-and-forty years of age. Son about eight and forty
minutes. Dombey was rather bald, rather red, and though a handsome
well-made man, too stern and pompous in appearance to be prepossessing.
Son was very bald, and very red, and though (of course) an undeniably fine
infant, somewhat crushed and spotty in his general effect, as yet.

Dombey and Son (1847–8).

*It is decided that for the good of his health young Paul Dombey must go to Brighton,
to Mrs Pipchin's 'infantine Boarding-House of a very exclusive description', which
is also a preparatory school:*

This celebrated Mrs Pipchin was a marvellous ill-favoured, ill-conditioned
old lady, of a stooping figure, with a mottled face, like bad marble, a hook
nose, and a hard grey eye, that looked as if it might have been hammered at
on an anvil without sustaining any injury. Forty years at least had elapsed
since the Peruvian mines had been the death of Mr Pipchin; but his relict
still wore black bombazeen, of such a lustreless, deep, dead, sombre shade,
that gas itself couldn't light her up after dark, and her presence was a
quencher to any number of candles. She was generally spoken of as 'a great
manager' of children; and the secret of her management was, to give them
everything that they didn't like, and nothing that they did—which was found
to sweeten their dispositions very much. She was such a bitter old lady, that
one was tempted to believe there had been some mistake in the application
of the Peruvian machinery, and that all her waters of gladness and milk of
human kindness, had been pumped out dry, instead of the mines.   Ibid.

*Dombey junior moves on to a young gentleman's boarding-school, an Academy
kept by the splendid Doctor Blimber:*

The Doctor's walk was stately, and calculated to impress the juvenile mind
with solemn feelings. It was a sort of march; but when the Doctor put out

his right foot, he gravely turned upon his axis, with a semi-circular sweep towards the left; and when he put out his left foot, he turned in the same manner towards the right. So that he seemed, at every stride he took, to look about him as though he were saying, 'Can anybody have the goodness to indicate any subject, in any direction, on which I am uninformed? I rather think not.'

Ibid.

In David Copperfield, *the young David's troubles begin in earnest when his mother remarries. He dislikes his stepfather, Mr Murdstone, a petty tyrant whose religion is 'austere and wrathful'. Mr Murdstone's sister arrives to join the household:*

A gloomy-looking lady she was; dark, like her brother, whom she greatly resembled in face and voice; and with very heavy eyebrows, nearly meeting over her large nose, as if, being disabled by the wrongs of her sex from wearing whiskers, she had carried them to that account. She brought with her, two uncompromising hard black boxes, with her initials on the lids in hard brass nails. When she paid the coachman she took her money out of a hard steel purse, and she kept the purse in a very jail of a bag which hung upon her arm by a heavy chain, and shut up like a bite. I had never, at that time, seen such a metallic lady altogether as Miss Murdstone was.

The History of David Copperfield (1849–50).

In Bleak House, *Miss Summerson, who narrates most of the story, is taking dancing lessons at Mr Turveydrop's dancing academy. Mr Turveydrop does not teach at his school, he merely graces it occasionally with his famous presence.*

Mr Turveydrop is celebrated for his Deportment:

Just then, there appeared from a side door, old Mr Turveydrop, in the full lustre of his Deportment.

He was a fat old gentleman with a false complexion, false teeth, false whiskers, and a wig. He had a fur collar, and he had a padded breast to his coat, which only wanted a star or a broad blue ribbon to be complete. He was pinched in, and swelled out, and got up, and strapped down, as much as he could possibly bear. He had such a neckcloth on (puffing his very eyes out of their natural shape), and his chin and even his ears so sunk into it, that it seemed as though he must inevitably double up, if it were cast loose. He had, under his arm, a hat of great size and weight, shelving downward from the crown to the brim; and in his hand a pair of white gloves, with which he flapped it, as he stood poised on one leg, in a high-shouldered, round-elbowed state of elegance not to be surpassed. He had a cane, he had an eye-glass, he had a snuff-box, he had rings, he had wristbands, he had everything but any touch of nature; he was not like youth, he was not like age, he was not like anything in the world but a model of Deportment.

'Father! A visitor. Miss Jellyby's friend, Miss Summerson.'

'Distinguished', said Mr Turveydrop, 'by Miss Summerson's presence.' As he bowed to me in that tight state, I almost believe I saw creases come into the whites of his eyes.

Bleak House (1852–3).

In Hard Times, *the awful Mr Bounderby (another of those significant names) has a housekeeper, Mrs Sparsit—a seemingly genteel widow:*

Mr Bounderby sat looking at her, as, with the points of a stiff, sharp pair of scissors, she picked out holes for some inscrutable ornamental purpose, in a piece of cambric. An operation which, taken in connexion with the bushy eyebrows and the Roman nose, suggested with some liveliness the idea of a hawk engaged upon the eyes of a tough little bird.

Hard Times (1854).

Mr Bounderby himself is a familiar type probably suggested to Dickens by an encounter or two in real-life.
   He is the self-made man of riches and power who boasts of his humble origins:

He was a rich man: banker, merchant, manufacturer, and what not. A big, loud man, with a stare, and a metallic laugh. A man made out of a coarse material, which seemed to have been stretched to make so much of him. A man with a great puffed head and forehead, swelled veins in his temples, and such a strained skin to his face that it seemed to hold his eyes open, and lift his eyebrows up. A man with a pervading appearance on him of being inflated like a balloon, and ready to start. A man who could never sufficiently vaunt himself a self-made man. A man who was always proclaiming, through that brassy speaking-trumpet of a voice of his, his old ignorance and his old poverty. A man who was the Bully of humility.

Ibid.

When a new, strong character like Mr Bounderby was introduced, he or she usually took centre-stage for a page or so and delivered what was virtually a monologue.
   In Mr Bounderby's case this turns out to be a scene in which he overdoes it in trying to impress the feeble Mrs Gradgrind with the rigours of his poverty-stricken upbringing (all lies, as it turns out). This scene has been echoed many times since and has become a kind of hardy perennial of humorous sketches:

In the formal drawing-room of Stone Lodge, standing on the hearthrug, warming himself before the fire, Mr Bounderby delivered some observations to Mrs Gradgrind on the circumstance of its being his birthday. He stood before the fire, partly because it was a cool spring afternoon, though the sun shone; partly because the shade of Stone Lodge was always haunted by the ghost of damp mortar; partly because he thus took up a commanding position, from which to subdue Mrs Gradgrind.

   'I hadn't a shoe to my foot. As to a stocking, I didn't know such a thing by name. I passed the day in a ditch, and the night in a pigsty. That's the way I spent my tenth birthday. Not that a ditch was new to me, for I was born in a ditch.'

   Mrs Gradgrind, a little, thin, white, pink-eyed bundle of shawls, of surpassing feebleness, mental and bodily; who was always taking physic without any effect, and who, whenever she showed a symptom of coming to life, was invariably stunned by some weighty piece of fact tumbling on her; Mrs Gradgrind hoped it was a dry ditch?

'No! As wet as a sop. A foot of water in it,' said Mr Bounderby.

'Enough to give a baby cold,' Mrs Gradgrind considered.

'Cold? I was born with inflammation of the lungs, and of everything else, I believe, that was capable of inflammation,' returned Mr Bounderby. 'For years, ma'am, I was one of the most miserable little wretches ever seen. I was so sickly, that I was always moaning and groaning. I was so ragged and dirty, that you wouldn't have touched me with a pair of tongs.'

Mrs Gradgrind faintly looked at the tongs, as the most appropriate thing her imbecility could think of doing.

'How I fought through it, I don't know,' said Bounderby. 'I was determined, I suppose. I have been a determined character in later life, and I suppose I was then. Here I am, Mrs Gradgrind, anyhow, and nobody to thank for my being here, but myself.'

Mrs Gradgrind meekly and weakly hoped that his mother—

'*My* mother? Bolted, ma'am!' said Bounderby.

Mrs Gradgrind, stunned as usual, collapsed and gave it up.

'My mother left me to my grandmother,' said Bounderby; 'and, according to the best of my remembrance, my grandmother was the wickedest and the worst old woman that ever lived. If I got a little pair of shoes by any chance, she would take 'em off and sell 'em for drink. Why, I have known that grandmother of mine lie in her bed and drink her fourteen glasses of liquor before breakfast!'

Mrs Gradgrind, weakly smiling, and giving no other sign of vitality, looked (as she always did) like an indifferently executed transparency of a small female figure, without enough light behind it.   Ibid.

In Martin Chuzzlewit, *another introduction and subsequent monologue brings on one of Dickens's most splendid grotesques, Mrs Sairey Gamp, a sick-room attendant before the days of professional nursing who also obliged her customers as a midwife and a layer-out of corpses.*

Mrs Gamp, gross, insensitive, illiterate, just managed to keep herself alive in her poor and cruel corner of existence by doing unpleasant work which was always in demand, by using her strongly developed native cunning, and by constantly praising herself to others by quoting the words of her good friend Mrs Harris, who was a figment of Mrs Gamp's imagination.

Mr Pecksniff fetches Mrs Gamp in a cab to lay out the remains of the late Mr Chuzzlewit:

She was a fat old woman, this Mrs Gamp, with a husky voice and a moist eye, which she had a remarkable power of turning up, and only showing the

white of it. Having very little neck, it cost her some trouble to look over
herself, if one may say so, at those to whom she talked. She wore a very
rusty black gown, rather the worse for snuff, and a shawl and bonnet to
correspond. In these dilapidated articles of dress she had, on principle, arrayed
herself, time out of mind, on such occasions as the present; for this at once
expressed a decent amount of veneration for the deceased, and invite the
next of kin to present her with a fresher suit of weeds: an appeal so frequently
successful, that the very fetch and ghost of Mrs Gamp, bonnet and all, might
be seen hanging up, any hour in the day, in at least a dozen of the second-
hand clothes shops about Holborn. The face of Mrs Gamp—the nose in
particular—was somewhat red and swollen, and it was difficult to enjoy her
society without becoming conscious of a smell of spirits. Like most persons
who have attained to great eminence in their profession, she took to hers
very kindly; insomuch that, setting aside her natural predilections as a
woman, she went to a lying-in or a laying-out with equal zest and relish . . .

*The cab journey with Mr Pecksniff gives Mrs Gamp the opportunity to talk a little
about her work as a layer-out of corpses and also, more importantly, to drop a
hint or two to Mr Pecksniff as to her terms and conditions of employment:*

'Ah!' repeated Mrs Gamp; for it was always a safe sentiment in cases of
mourning. 'Ah dear! When Gamp was summoned to his long home, and I
see him a-lying in Guy's Hospital with a penny-piece on each eye, and his
wooden leg under his left arm, I thought I should have fainted away. But I
bore up.' . . .
     'You have become indifferent since then, I suppose?' said Mr Pecksniff.
'Use is second nature, Mrs Gamp.'
     'You may well say second natur, sir,' replied that lady. 'One's first ways is
to find sich things a trial to the feelings, and so is one's lasting custom. If it
wasn't for the nerve a little sip of liquor gives me (I never was able to do
more than taste it), I never could go through with what I sometimes has to
do. "Mrs Harris," I says, at the very last case as ever I acted in, which it was
but a very young person, "Mrs Harris," I says, "leave the bottle on the
chimley-piece, and don't ask me to take none, but let me put my lips to it
when I am so dispoged, and then I will do what I am engaged to do, according
to the best of my ability." "Mrs Gamp," she says, in answer, "if ever there
was a sober creetur to be got at eighteenpence a day for working people,
and three and six for gentlefolk—night watching",' said Mrs Gamp, with
emphasis, '"being a extra charge—you are that inwallable person." "Mrs
Harris," I says to her, "don't name the charge, for if I could afford to lay all
my fellow creeturs out for nothink, I would gladly do it, sich is the love I
bears 'em. But what I always says to them as has the management of matters,
Mrs Harris"': here she kept her eye on Mr Pecksniff; '"be they gents or be
they ladies, is, don't ask me whether I won't take none, or whether I will,

but leave the bottle on the chimley-piece, and let me put my lips to it when I am so dispoged.'''

The Life and Adventures of Martin Chuzzlewit (1843–4).

A little later we are given some glimpses of Mrs Gamp going about her errands of mercy.

We find her taken on as a night-nurse to watch over a very sick young man at an inn. She begins by ordering the supplies she will need to get him through the night:

'I think, young woman,' said Mrs Gamp to the assistant-chambermaid, in a tone expressive of weakness, 'that I could pick a little bit of pickled salmon, with a nice little sprig of fennel, and a sprinkling of white pepper. I takes new bread, my dear, with jest a little pat of fresh butter, and a mossel of cheese. In case there should be such a thing as a cowcumber in the 'ouse, will you be so kind as bring it, for I'm rather partial to 'em, and they does a world of good in a sick room. If they draws the Brighton Old Tipper here, I takes that ale at night, my love; it bein' considered wakeful by the doctors. And whatever you do, young woman, don't bring more than a shillin's-worth of gin-and-water warm when I rings the bell a second time; for that is always my allowance, and I never takes a drop beyond!'

Ibid.

Mrs Gamp then, for the first time, regards the semi-delirious patient in her care:

Mrs Gamp solaced herself with a pinch of snuff, and stood looking at him with her head inclined a little sideways, as a connoisseur might gaze upon a doubtful work of art. By degrees, a horrible remembrance of one branch of her calling took possession of the woman; and stooping down, she pinned his wandering arms against his sides, to see how he would look if laid out as a dead man. Hideous as it may appear, her fingers itched to compose his limbs in that last marble attitude.

'Ah!' said Mrs Gamp, walking away from the bed, 'he'd make a lovely corpse.'

Ibid.

Another of Dickens's memorable grotesques in the same novel is the most unctuous and hypocritical of Dickens's whole gallery of unctuous hypocrites, the architect and land-surveyor, Mr Pecksniff. Pecksniff does not actually design buildings or survey land, he mostly collects rents and instructs pupils. This last means taking in a few young men on payment of a premium, pawning the mathematical instruments they have brought with them and setting them to draw elevations of Salisbury Cathedral for two or three years. This leaves him free to get on with his principal preoccupation which is trying to swindle young Martin Chuzzlewit out of his father's money.

For a change Mr Pecksniff and his two maiden daughters, who are no longer in the first flush of youth, are not described by Dickens before we meet them. Instead, a gust of wind blows the front door shut just as Mr Pecksniff is entering his house and knocks him down the steps. One of the Miss Pecksniffs, fearing an intruder, opens the door and peers out but fails to spot the recumbent figure of her father:

With a sharply delivered warning relative to the cage and the constable, and the stocks and the gallows, Miss Pecksniff was about to close the door again, when Mr Pecksniff (being still at the bottom of the steps) raised himself on one elbow, and sneezed.

'That voice!' cried Miss Pecksniff. 'My parent!'

At this exclamation, another Miss Pecksniff bounced out of the parlour: and the two Miss Pecksniffs, with many incoherent expressions, dragged Mr Pecksniff into an upright posture.

'Pa!' they cried in concert. 'Pa! Speak! Do not look so wild, my dearest Pa!'

But as a gentleman's looks, in such a case of all others, are by no means under his own control, Mr Pecksniff continued to keep his mouth and his eyes very wide open, and to drop his lower jaw, somewhat after the manner of a toy nut-cracker: and as his hat had fallen off, and his face was pale, and his hair erect, and his coat muddy, the spectacle he presented was so very doleful, that neither of the Miss Pecksniffs could suppress an involuntary screech.

'That'll do,' said Mr Pecksniff. 'I'm better.'

'He's come to himself!' cried the youngest Miss Pecksniff.

'He speaks again!' exclaimed the eldest . . .

The door closed, both young ladies applied themselves to tending Mr Pecksniff's wounds in the back parlour . . . These injuries having been comforted externally, with patches of pickled brown paper, and Mr Pecksniff having been comforted internally, with some stiff brandy-and-water, the eldest Miss Pecksniff sat down to make the tea, which was all ready. In the meantime the youngest Miss Pecksniff brought from the kitchen a smoking dish of ham and eggs, and, setting the same before her father, took up her station on a low stool at his feet, thereby bringing her eyes on a level with the teaboard . . .

Then comes Dickens's nicely ironic description of Mr Pecksniff's character and personal appearance:

It has been remarked that Mr Pecksniff was a moral man. So he was. Perhaps there never was a more moral man than Mr Pecksniff: especially in his conversation and correspondence. It was once said of him by a homely admirer, that he had a Fortunatus's purse of good sentiments in his inside. In this particular he was like the girl in the fairy tale, except that if they were not actual diamonds which fell from his lips, they were the very brightest paste, and shone prodigiously. He was a most exemplary man: fuller of virtuous precept than a copy-book. Some people likened him to a direction-board, which is always telling the way to a place, and never goes there: but these were his enemies; the shadows cast by his brightness; that was all. His very throat was moral. You saw a good deal of it. You looked over a very low fence of white cravat (whereof no man had ever beheld the tie, for he fastened it behind), and there it lay, a valley between two jutting heights of collar, serene and whiskerless before you. It seemed to say, on the part of Mr Pecksniff, 'There is no deception, ladies and gentlemen, all is peace, a holy calm pervades me.' So did his hair, just grizzled with an iron-grey, which was all brushed off his forehead, and stood bolt upright, or slightly drooped in kindred action with his heavy eyelids. So did his person, which was sleek though free from corpulency. So did his manner, which was soft and oily. In a word, even his plain black suit, and state of widower, and dangling double eyeglass, all tended to the same purpose, and cried aloud, 'Behold the moral Pecksniff !'

And so into the first of the many little improving moral discourses which Mr Pecksniff bestowed upon his daughters :

'Even the worldly goods of which we have just disposed,' said Mr Pecksniff, glancing round the table which he had finished, 'even cream, sugar, tea, toast, ham,—'

'And eggs,' suggested Charity in a low voice.

'And eggs,' said Mr Pecksniff, 'even they have their moral. See how they come and go! Every pleasure is transitory. We can't even eat, long. If we indulge in harmless fluids, we get the dropsy; if in exciting liquids, we get drunk. What a soothing reflection is that!'

'Don't say *we* get drunk, Pa,' urged the eldest Miss Pecksniff.

'When I say we, my dear,' returned her father, 'I mean mankind in general; the human race, considered as a body, and not as individuals. There is nothing personal in morality, my love. Even such a thing as this,' said Mr Pecksniff, laying the forefinger of his left hand on the brown paper patch on the top of his head, 'slight casual baldness though it be, reminds us that we are but'—he was going to say 'worms,' but recollecting that worms are not remarkable for heads of hair, he substituted 'flesh and blood'.   Ibid.

Perhaps Dickens's greatest and most popular comic small-part player was Mr Micawber who appeared only very briefly but wholly memorably as landlord to the young David Copperfield.

Mr and Mrs Micawber were based on the more likeable aspects of Dickens's parents ; thus Mr Micawber, like Dickens's father, was mercurial in temperament, constantly in financial difficulties yet quite sure in his own mind that something would turn up and save his bacon.

Mrs Micawber, like Mrs Dickens, was unshakeably loyal to her husband and devoted to her children. Like many of Dickens's characters, including the two Wellers and Mr Pecksniff, Mr Micawber was an orator. He constantly embarked on rich, orotund speeches but no sooner had he got into his stride than his rhetoric ran out of steam and he had to conclude lamely with saying 'in short . . .' and then putting his thoughts into a simple colloquial phrase.

Young David Copperfield, aged 10, has been given a job as bottle-washer by the dread Mr Murdstone, who has arranged for the boy to board with one of the firm's part-time (and unsuccessful) salesmen:

The counting-house clock was at half past twelve, and there was general preparation for going to dinner, when Mr Quinion tapped at the counting-house window, and beckoned me to go in. I went in, and found there a stoutish, middle-aged person, in a brown surtout and black tights and shoes, with no more hair upon his head (which was a large one and very shining) than there is upon an egg, and with a very extensive face, which he turned full upon me. His clothes were shabby, but he had an imposing shirt-collar on. He carried a jaunty sort of stick, with a large pair of rusty tassels to it; and a quizzing-glass hung outside his coat,—for ornament, I afterwards found, as he very seldom looked through it, and couldn't see anything if he did.

'This,' said Mr Quinion, in allusion to myself, 'is he.'

'This,' said the stranger, with a certain condescending roll in his voice, and a certain indescribable air of doing something genteel, which impressed me very much, 'is Master Copperfield. I hope I see you well, sir?'

I said I was very well, and hoped he was. I was sufficiently ill at ease, Heaven knows; but it was not in my nature to complain much at that time of my life, so I said I was very well, and hoped he was.

'I am,' said the stranger, 'thank Heaven, quite well. I have received a letter from Mr Murdstone, in which he mentions that he would desire me to receive into an apartment in the rear of my house, which is at present unoccupied—and is, in short, to be let as a—in short,' said the stranger, with a smile and in a burst of confidence, 'as a bedroom—the young beginner whom I now have the pleasure to—' and the stranger waved his hand, and settled his chin in his shirt-collar.

'This is Mr Micawber,' said Mr Quinion to me.

'Ahem!' said the stranger, 'that is my name.'

'Mr Micawber is known to Mr Murdstone. He takes orders for us on commission, when he can get any. He has been written to by Mr Murdstone, on the subject of your lodgings, and he will receive you as a lodger.'

'My address,' said Mr Micawber, 'is Windsor Terrace, City Road. I—in short,' said Mr Micawber, with the same genteel air, and in another burst of confidence—'I live there.'

I made him a bow.

'Under the impression,' said Mr Micawber, 'that your peregrinations in this metropolis have not as yet been extensive, and that you might have some difficulty in penetrating the arcana of the Modern Babylon in the direction of the City Road,—in short,' said Mr Micawber, in another burst of confidence, 'that you might lose yourself—I shall be happy to call this evening, and install you in the knowledge of the nearest way.'

I thanked him with all my heart, for it was friendly in him to offer to take that trouble. *The History of David Copperfield.*

That evening Mr Micawber escorts David Copperfield to his home where Mrs Micawber is introduced:

Arrived at his house in Windsor Terrace (which I noticed was shabby like himself, but also, like himself, made all the show it could), he presented me to Mrs Micawber, a thin and faded lady, not at all young, who was sitting in the parlour (the first floor was altogether unfurnished, and the blinds were kept down to delude the neighbours), with a baby at her breast. This baby was one of the twins; and I may remark here that I hardly ever, in all my experience of the family, saw both the twins detached from Mrs Micawber at the same time. One of them was always taking refreshment. Ibid.

Mr Micawber, abetted by his wife, lives a rich and happy life in the private world of his own romantic imagination. In the real world his creditors are closing in and the household in Windsor Terrace is in real financial trouble. But the Micawbers cannot stay miserable for long before rebounding to the other extreme, perhaps because their optimism is more real to them than are the unpleasant facts.

Even when creditors take to gathering in the street outside and hurling abuse up at the Micawber windows:

At these times, Mr Micawber would be transported with grief and mortification, even to the length (as I was once made aware by a scream from his wife) of making motions at himself with a razor; but within half-an-hour afterwards, he would polish up his shoes with extraordinary pains, and go out, humming a tune with a greater air of gentility than ever. Mrs Micawber was quite as elastic. I have known her to be thrown into fainting fits by the king's taxes at three o'clock, and to eat lamb chops, breaded, and drink warm ale (paid for with two tea-spoons that had gone to the pawnbroker's) at four. On one occasion, when an execution had just been put in, coming home through some chance as early as six o'clock, I saw her lying (of course with a twin) under the grate in a swoon, with her hair all torn about her face; but I never knew her more cheerful that very same night, over a veal cutlet before the kitchen fire, telling me stories about her papa and mama, and the company they used to keep.

Ibid.

Mr Micawber has a spell in the debtor's jail and then Mrs Micawber's family persuade the Micawbers to leave London and live in Plymouth, where the family is situated and where a job for Mr Micawber might be arranged. It is a sad parting for David Copperfield but Mr Micawber rises magnificently to the occasion:

'My dear young friend,' said Mr Micawber, 'I am older than you; a man of experience in life, and—and of some experience, in short, in difficulties, generally speaking. At present, and until something turns up (which I am, I may say, hourly expecting), I have nothing to bestow but advice. Still my advice is so worth taking, that—in short, that I have never taken it myself, and am the'—here Mr Micawber, who had been beaming and smiling, all over his head and face, up to the present moment, checked himself and frowned—'the miserable wretch you behold.'

'My dear Micawber!' urged his wife.

'I say,' returned Mr Micawber, quite forgetting himself, and smiling again, 'the miserable wretch you behold. My advice is, never do tomorrow what you can do today. Procrastination is the thief of time. Collar him!'

'My poor papa's maxim,' Mrs Micawber observed.

'My dear,' said Mr Micawber, 'your papa was very well in his way, and Heaven forbid that I should disparage him. Take him for all in all, we ne'er shall—in short, make the acquaintance, probably, of anyone else possessing, at his time of life, the same legs for gaiters, and able to read the same description of print, without spectacles. But he applied that maxim to our marriage, my dear; and that was so far prematurely entered into, in consequence, that I never recovered the expense.'

Mr Micawber looked aside at Mrs Micawber, and added: 'Not that I am sorry for it. Quite the contrary, my love.' After which he was silent for a minute or so.

'My other advice, Copperfield,' said Mr Micawber, 'you know. Annual income twenty pounds, annual expenditure nineteen nineteen and six, result happiness. Annual income twenty pounds, annual expenditure twenty pounds ought and six, result misery. The blossom is blighted, the leaf is withered, the god of day goes down upon a dreary scene, and—and in short you are for ever floored. As I am!'

To make his example the more impressive, Mr Micawber drank a glass of punch with an air of great enjoyment and satisfaction, and whistled the College Hornpipe.

Ibid.

Earlier, in Nicholas Nickleby, *Dickens had used his mother as the basis for another sympathetic character. In keeping with the novel's melodramatic style (Nicholas actually told the wicked uncle that he would not darken his doorstep again) Nicholas was a dashing hero and his sister Kate a chaste and demure heroine. In order to leaven the Nickleby family scenes with a little humour Dickens made their mother a nice but rather vague little woman who constantly harked back—as did his own mother and Mrs Micawber—to the more genteel life which she had once enjoyed.*

What brings Mrs Nickleby to life as a character is the trick she has, always so charming to strangers and so maddening for the family, of losing her train of thought almost as soon as she has got on it:

'Kate, my dear,' said Mrs Nickleby, 'I don't know how it is, but a fine, warm, sunny day like this, with the birds singing in every direction, always puts me in mind of roast pig, with sage and onion sauce, and made gravy.'

'That's a curious association of ideas, is it not, mamma?'

'Upon my word, my dear, I don't know,' replied Mrs Nickleby. 'Roast pig—let me see. On the day five weeks after you were christened we had a roast—no, that couldn't have been a pig either, because I recollect there were a pair of them to carve, and your poor papa and I could never have thought of sitting down to two pigs; they must have been partridges. Roast pig! I hardly think we ever could have had one, now I come to remember; for your papa could never bear the sight of them in the shops, and used to say that they always put him in mind of very little babies, only the pigs had much fairer complexions; and he had a horror of little babies, too, because he couldn't very well afford any increase to his family, and had a natural dislike to the subject. It's very odd now; what could have put that in my head? I recollect dining once at Mrs Bevan's, in that broad street round the corner by the coachmaker's, where the tipsy man fell through the cellar-flap of an empty house, nearly a week before the quarter-day, and wasn't found till the new tenant went in—and we had roast pig there. It must be that, I think, that reminds me of it, especially as there was a little bird in the room that would keep on singing all the time of dinner—at least, not a little bird, for it was a parrot, and he didn't sing exactly, for he talked and swore dreadfully; but I think it must have been that—indeed I am sure it must. Shouldn't you say so, my dear?'

'I should say there was not a doubt about it, mamma,' returned Kate, with a cheerful smile.   *The Life and Adventures of Nicholas Nickleby.*

Besides the comedy scenes with the great grotesques and the comical supporting characters there are many enjoyable smaller moments of humour in the books; sometimes when a chord of recognition is struck in the reader, like being reminded of what it feels like to get up very early in the morning:

The dead winter-time was in full dreariness when I left my chambers for ever, at five o'clock in the morning. I had shaved by candle-light, of course, and was miserably cold, and experienced that general all-pervading sensation of getting up to be hanged which I have usually found inseparable from untimely rising under such circumstances.   *Christmas Stories* (1860).

Or the revelation of what longings occupy the thoughts of manufacturers' representatives when they live in lodgings:

'There is no such passion in human nature, as the passion for gravy among commercial gentlemen.' [Mrs Todgers].

The Life and Adventures of Martin Chuzzlewit.

Or a comment on those nobly born bully-boys, left-overs from Georgian society, who were still making a nuisance of themselves in the 1830s:

'He has a very nice face and style, really,' said Mrs Kenwigs.

'He certainly has,' added Miss Petowker. 'There's something in his appearance quite—dear, dear, what's that word again?'

'What word?' inquired Mr Lillyvick.

'Why—dear me, how stupid I am,' replied Miss Petowker, hesitating. 'What do you call it, when Lords break off door-knockers and beat policemen, and play at coaches with other people's money, and all that sort of thing?'

'Aristocratic?' suggested the collector.

'Ah! aristocratic,' replied Miss Petowker; 'something very aristocratic about him, isn't there?'

The Life and Adventures of Nicholas Nickleby.

Or the care and concentration expended on penning a letter by somebody who has only just learnt to write.

In this instance Joe Gargery, the blacksmith:

At my own writing-table, pushed into a corner and cumbered with little bottles, Joe sat down to his great work, first choosing a pen from the pen-tray as if it were a chest of large tools, and tucking up his sleeves as if he were going to wield a crowbar or sledge-hammer. It was necessary for Joe to hold on heavily to the table with his left elbow, and to get his right leg well out behind him, before he could begin, and when he did begin, he made every down-stroke so slowly that it might have been six feet long, while at every up-stroke I could hear his pen spluttering extensively. He had a curious idea that the inkstand was on the side of him where it was not, and constantly dipped his pen into space, and seemed quite satisfied with the result. Occasionally, he was tripped up by some orthographical stumbling-block, but on the whole he got on very well indeed, and when he had signed his name, and had removed a finishing blot from the paper to the crown of his head with his two forefingers, he got up and hovered about the table, trying the effect of his performance from various points of view as it lay there, with unbounded satisfaction.

Great Expectations (1860–1).

Or the delights of a christening feast on an achingly cold day in winter:

'Mr John,' said Mr Dombey, 'will you take the bottom of the table, if you please? What have you got there, Mr John?' 'I have got a cold fillet of veal here, Sir. What have *you* got there, Sir,' 'This,' returned Mr Dombey, 'is some cold preparation of calf's head, I think. I see cold fowls—ham—patties—salad—lobster. Miss Tox will do me the honour of taking some wine? Champagne to Miss Tox.' There was a toothache in everything. The wine was so bitterly cold that it forced a little scream from Miss Tox, which she had great difficulty in turning into a 'Hem!'. The veal had come from such an airy pantry that the first taste of it had struck a sensation as of cold lead into Mr Chick's extremities. Mr Dombey alone remained unmoved. He might have been hung up for sale at a Russian fair as a specimen of a frozen gentleman.

Dombey and Son.

Dickens's novels were criticized as being 'literature for semi-illiterates' because the monthly parts were enjoyed by hundreds of thousands of working-class men and women who only read with difficulty and whose horizons of understanding were limited. Indeed many thousands of ordinary people who vastly enjoyed Dickens could not read at all; they met in groups in a room or the village hall and the parts—sometimes rented and sometimes bought between them—were read aloud by the schoolmaster or a literate neighbour.

Giving pleasure through literature to such a huge and new audience would be regarded by most people nowadays as being well worth doing, which is how Dickens looked at it: he wrote to appeal to the masses, but he wanted to be respected as a serious author, and unfortunately for his ambitions, what the public liked was his humour and his broad comical effects; they really wanted him to supply endless variations on The Pickwick Papers.

But the particular, if reluctant, genius of Dickens as a comic novelist is to be found not only in Pickwick Papers. *It is also at its best in the scenes featuring Mr Vincent Crummles and his touring theatrical troupe in* Nicholas Nickleby.

Nicholas Nickleby and Smike, on the run from London, meet Mr Crummles at an inn and go with him to Portsmouth to join his company. The episode shows Dickens's love of everything to do with the theatre; it shows his skill as a reporter in its evocation of the sights and smells behind the scenes of a small provincial theatre; it shows his creative energy as he seemingly effortlessly fills the stage with a new set of odd and colourful characters; and it shows Dickens's compassion.

Mr Vincent Crummles may be a fraud, an untalented old ham, but he does try; he is, in his way, a professional, and Dickens manages to make him both absurd and oddly likeable:

As Mr Crummles had a strange four-legged animal in the inn stables, which he called a pony, and a vehicle of unknown design, on which he bestowed the appellation of a four-wheeled phaeton, Nicholas proceeded on his journey next morning with greater ease than he had expected: the manager and himself occupying the front seat: and the Master Crummleses and Smike being packed together behind, in company with a wicker basket defended from wet by a stout oilskin, in which were the broad-swords, pistols, pigtails, nautical costumes, and other professional necessaries of the aforesaid young gentlemen.

The pony took his time upon the road, and—possibly in consequence of his theatrical education—evinced, every now and then, a strong inclination to lie down. However, Mr Vincent Crummles kept him up pretty well, by jerking the rein, and plying the whip; and when these means failed, and the animal came to a stand, the elder Master Crummles got out and kicked him. By dint of these encouragements, he was persuaded to move from time to time, and they jogged on (as Mr Crummles truly observed) very comfortably for all parties.

'He's a good pony at bottom,' said Mr Crummles, turning to Nicholas.

He might have been at bottom, but he certainly was not at top, seeing that his coat was of the roughest and most ill-favoured kind. So Nicholas merely observed that he shouldn't wonder if he was.

'Many and many is the circuit this pony has gone,' said Mr Crummles, flicking him skilfully on the eyelid for old acquaintance' sake. 'He is quite one of us. His mother was on the stage.'

'Was she?' rejoined Nicholas.

'She ate apple-pie at a circus for upwards of fourteen years,' said the manager; 'fired pistols, and went to bed in a nightcap; and, in short, took the low comedy entirely. His father was a dancer.'

'Was he at all distinguished?'

'Not very,' said the manager. 'He was rather a low sort of pony. The fact is, he had been originally jobbed out by the day, and he never quite got over his old habits. He was clever in melodrama too, but too broad—too broad. When the mother died, he took the port-wine business.'

'The port-wine business!' cried Nicholas.

'Drinking port-wine with the clown,' said the manager; 'but he was greedy, and one night bit off the bowl of the glass, and choked himself, so his vulgarity was the death of him at last.'

The descendant of this ill-starred animal requiring increased attention from Mr Crummles as he progressed in his day's work, that gentleman had very little time for conversation. Nicholas was thus left at leisure to entertain himself with his own thoughts, until they arrived at the drawbridge at Portsmouth, when Mr Crummles pulled up.

'We'll get down here,' said the manager, 'and the boys will take him round to the stable, and call at my lodgings with the luggage. You had better let yours be taken there, for the present.'

Thanking Mr Vincent Crummles for his obliging offer, Nicholas jumped out, and, giving Smike his arm, accompanied the manager up High Street on their way to the theatre; feeling nervous and uncomfortable enough at the prospect of an immediate introduction to a scene so new to him.

They passed a great many bills, pasted against the walls and displayed in windows, wherein the names of Mr Vincent Crummles, Mrs Vincent

Crummles, Master Crummles, Master P. Crummles, and Miss Crummles, were printed in very large letters, and everything else in very small ones; and, turning at length into an entry, in which was a strong smell of orange-peel and lamp-oil, with an under-current of saw-dust, groped their way through a dark passage, and, descending a step or two, threaded a little maze of canvas screens and paint-pots, and emerged upon the stage of the Portsmouth Theatre.

'Here we are,' said Mr Crummles.

It was not very light, but Nicholas found himself close to the first entrance on the prompt side, among bare walls, dusty scenes, mildewed clouds, heavily daubed draperies, and dirty floors. He looked about him; ceiling, pit, boxes, gallery, orchestra, fittings, and decorations of every kind,—all looked coarse, cold, gloomy, and wretched.

'Is this a theatre?' whispered Smike, in amazement. 'I thought it was a blaze of light and finery.'

'Why, so it is,' replied Nicholas, hardly less surprised; 'but not by day, Smike—not by day.'

The manager's voice recalled him from a more careful inspection of the building, to the opposite side of the proscenium, where, at a small mahogany table with rickety legs and of an oblong shape, sat a stout, portly female, apparently between forty and fifty, in a tarnished silk cloak, with her bonnet dangling by the strings in her hand, and her hair (of which she had a great quantity) braided in a large festoon over each temple.

'Mr Johnson,' said the manager (for Nicholas had given the name which Newman Noggs had bestowed upon him in his conversation with Mrs Kenwigs), 'let me introduce Mrs Vincent Crummles.'

'I am glad to see you, sir,' said Mrs Vincent Crummles, in a sepulchral voice. 'I am very glad to see you, and still more happy to hail you as a promising member of our corps.'

The lady shook Nicholas by the hand as she addressed him in these terms; he saw it was a large one, but had not expected quite such an iron grip as that with which she honoured him.

'And this,' said the lady, crossing to Smike, as tragic actresses cross when they obey a stage direction, 'and this is the other. You too, are welcome, sir.'

'He'll do, I think, my dear?' said the manager, taking a pinch of snuff.

'He is admirable,' replied the lady. 'An acquisition, indeed.'

As Mrs Vincent Crummles recrossed back to the table, there bounded on to the stage from some mysterious inlet, a little girl in a dirty white frock with tucks up to the knees, short trousers, sandaled shoes, white spencer, pink gauze bonnet, green veil and curl papers; who turned a pirouette, cut twice in the air, turned another pirouette, then, looking off at the opposite wing, shrieked, bounded forward to within six inches of the footlight, and fell into a beautiful attitude of terror . . .

'Very well, indeed,' said Mr Crummles; 'bravo!'

'Bravo!' cried Nicholas, resolved to make the best of everything, 'Beautiful!'

'This, sir,' said Mr Vincent Crummles, bringing the maiden forward, 'this is the infant phenomenon—Miss Ninetta Crummles.'

'Your daughter?' inquired Nicholas.

'My daughter—my daughter,' replied Mr Vincent Crummles; 'the idol of every place we go into, sir. We have had complimentary letters about this girl, sir, from the nobility and gentry of almost every town in England.'

'I am not surprised at that,' said Nicholas; 'she must be quite a natural genius.'

'Quite a—!' Mr Crummles stopped: language was not powerful enough to describe the infant phenomenon. 'I'll tell you what, sir,' he said; 'the talent of this child is not to be imagined. She must be seen, sir—seen—to be ever so faintly appreciated. There; go to your mother, my dear.'

'May I ask how old she is?' inquired Nicholas.

'You may, sir,' replied Mr Crummles, looking steadily in his questioner's face, as some men do when they have doubts about being implicitly believed in what they are going to say. 'She is ten years of age, sir.'

'Not more?'

'Not a day.'

'Dear me!' said Nicholas, 'it's extraordinary.'

It was; for the infant phenomenon, though of short stature, had a comparatively aged countenance, and had moreover been precisely the same age—not perhaps to the full extent of the memory of the oldest inhabitant, but certainly for five good years. But she had been kept up late every night, and put upon an unlimited allowance of gin-and-water from infancy, to prevent her growing tall, and perhaps this system of training had produced in the infant phenomenon these additional phenomena.

The Life and Adventures of Nicholas Nickleby.

BEFORE *the War of Independence almost all American literature was British colonial in style and subject. Even Benjamin Franklin confessed that he had modelled his prose on the essays of Bacon and Joseph Addison.*

The first novel to attempt a naturalistic description of life in the very un-British backwoods of America was published in five books between 1792 and 1815. The author was Hugh Henry Brackenridge, born in Scotland but taken to the frontier village of Pittsburgh, in Pennsylvania, at the age of 5 and later, in true American fashion, becoming successively a teacher, army chaplain, playwright, lawyer, politician, and eventually Supreme Court Judge.

It is an overlong, rambling, picaresque satire, with whiffs of Don Quixote,

Hudibras, *and* Tom Jones, *telling of the wanderings of Captain Farrago, a likeable and intelligent Democrat, and his half-cunning, half-stupid servant Teague O'Regan. The humour is enjoyable enough, but it was written in the early days of the Union and shows no specifically American characteristics except for the good Captain's practical, non-European attitude towards duelling (echoed later by Mark Twain).*

Captain Farrago has been 'called out' by an Army major. He writes back:

Major Valentine Jacko,
US Army.

Sir,—

I have two objections to this duel matter.

The one is, lest I should hurt you; and the other is, lest you should hurt me.

I do not see any good it would do me to put a bullet through any part of your body. I could make no use of you when dead for any culinary purpose as I would a rabbit or a turkey. I am no cannibal to feed on the flesh of men. Why, then, shoot down a human creature of which I could make no use? A buffalo would be better meat. For though your flesh may be delicate and tender, yet it wants that firmness and consistency which takes and retains salt. At any rate, it would not be fit for long sea voyages. You might make a good barbecue, it is true, being of the nature of a racoon or an opossum, but people are not in the habit of barbecuing anything human now. As to your hide, it is not worth taking off, being little better than that of a year-old colt.

It would seem to me a strange thing to shoot at a man that would stand still to be shot at, inasmuch as I have heretofore been used to shoot at things flying or running or jumping. Were you on a tree now like a squirrel, endeavoring to hide yourself in the branches, or like a racoon that after much eyeing and spying, I observe at length in the crotch of a tall oak with boughs and leaves intervening, so that I could just get a sight of his hinderparts, I should think it pleasurable enough to take a shot at you. But, as it is, there is no skill or judgment requisite to discover or take you down.

As to myself, I do not much like to stand in the way of anything harmful. I am under apprehension that you might hit me. That being the case, I think it most advisable to stay at a distance. If you want to try your pistols, take some object, a tree or a barn door, about my dimensions. If you hit that, send me word and I shall acknowledge that if I had been in the same place, you might also have hit me.

John Farrago
Late Captain, Pennsylvania Militia.

Hugh Henry Brackenridge (1748–1816), *Modern Chivalry, or the Adventures of Captain John Farrago and Teague O'Regan his Servant* (1792–1815).

H UGH HENRY BRACKENRIDGE *is little read nowadays but the works of his contemporary and fellow pioneer of early American humour, Washington Irving, have become minor classics.*

Irving's History of New York, *generally accepted as being 'the first great book of comic literature written by an American', was a topical satire on Thomas Jefferson, literary pedantry, floridly written histories, the ambition of politicians, the perfidy of businessmen, and so on, and it created a tremendous stir in 1809 when it was published.*

To modern readers without a key to who or what is being satirized it reads more like a jolly burlesque.

Here is a brief taste of the most famous episode:

CHAPTER VIII

Containing the Most Horrible Battle Ever Recorded in Poetry or Prose; With the Admirable Exploits of Peter Headstrong.

'Now had the Dutchmen snatched a huge repast,' and finding themselves wonderfully encouraged and animated thereby, prepared to take the field. Expectation, says the writer of the Stuyvesant manuscript—Expectation now stood on stilts. The world forgot to turn round, or rather stood still, that it might witness the affray; like a round-bellied alderman, watching the combat of two chivalrous flies upon his jerkin. The eyes of all mankind, as usual in such cases, were turned upon Fort Christina. The sun, like a little man in a crowd at a puppet-show, scampered about the heavens, popping his head here and there, and endeavoring to get a peep between the unmannerly clouds that obtruded themselves in his way. The historians filled their ink-horns—the poets went without their dinners, either that they might buy paper and goose-quills, or because they could not get anything to eat. Antiquity scowled sulkily out of its grave, to see itself outdone—while even Posterity stood mute, gazing in gaping ecstasy of retrospection on the eventful field . . .

There came on the intrepid Peter—his brows knit, his teeth set, his fists clenched, almost breathing forth volumes of smoke, so fierce was the fire that raged within his bosom. His faithful squire Van Corlear trudged valiantly at his heels, with his trumpet gorgeously bedecked with red and yellow ribbons, the remembrances of his fair mistresses at the Manhattoes. Then came waddling on the sturdy chivalry of the Hudson . . .

For an instant the mighty Peter paused in the midst of his career, and mounting on a stump, addressed his troops in eloquent Low Dutch, exhorting them to fight like *duyvels,* and assuring them that if they conquered, they should get plenty of booty—if they fell, they should be allowed the satisfaction, while dying, of reflecting that it was in the service of their country— and after they were dead, of seeing their names inscribed in the temple of renown, and handed down, in company with all the other great men of the year, for the admiration of posterity.—Finally, he swore to them, on the word of a governor (and they knew him too well to doubt it for a moment), that if he caught any mother's son of them looking pale, or playing craven, he would curry his hide till he made him run out of it like a snake in spring time. Then lugging out his trusty sabre, he brandished it three times over his head, ordered Van Corlear to sound a charge, and shouting the words 'St Nicholas and the Manhattoes!' courageously dashed forwards. His warlike followers, who had employed the interval in lighting their pipes, instantly stuck them into their mouths, gave a furious puff, and charged gallantly under cover of the smoke.

The Swedish garrison, ordered by the cunning Risingh not to fire until they could distinguish the whites of their assailants' eyes, stood in horrid silence on the covert-way, until the eager Dutchmen had ascended the glacis. Then did they pour into them such a tremendous volley, that the very hills quaked around, and were terrified even unto an incontinence of water, insomuch that certain springs burst forth from their sides, which continue to run unto the present day. Not a Dutchman but would have bitten the dust beneath that dreadful fire, had not the protecting Minerva kindly taken care that the Swedes should, one and all, observe their usual custom of shutting their eyes and turning away their heads at the moment of discharge.

> Washington Irving (1783–1859), *A History of New York, From the Beginning of the World to the End of the Dutch Dynasty, by Dietrich Knickerbocker* (1809).

Irving became the first American author to achieve international fame but his books were still European literature written by an American. He, like Benjamin Franklin, tried to write fluent, balanced prose in the manner of Addison and Goldsmith. He became a friend of Sir Walter Scott and Lord Byron, he lived and worked in London, Paris, Germany, and Spain, and he was strongly influenced by mid-European folklore: in his most popular publication, The Sketch Book, *the two most successful stories were based upon old German folktales,* The Legend of Sleepy Hollow, *and* Rip Van Winkle.

Much of Irving's writing, like that of his idol Addison, was more non-solemn than hilarious, yet because of elements in Rip Van Winkle *Irving is considered to be, if not exactly a founding father of American humour at least a founding great-uncle.*

Rip Van Winkle is a very early example of the 'frame' story, a device much used by later American humorists for preventing an unbelievable story emerging as just plain silly. The trick is to give the yarn a narrator, usually a detached and reliably intelligent observer. In Rip Van Winkle *it is the pedantic old Dutch-American, Dietrich Knickerbocker, who introduces the whole thing and makes out a case for it being true.*

But perhaps the reason for the huge and lasting popularity of Rip Van Winkle *might be that it is the first story to articulate the alternative American dream. If the Great American Dream is to work hard, get on, and become very rich and*

*famous, e.g. President, then the Great Alternative American Dream is to avoid
doing any work at all and go fishing instead:*

There lived, many years since, while the country was yet a province of Great
Britain, a simple, good-natured fellow, of the name of Rip Van Winkle.
He was a descendant of the Van Winkles who figured so gallantly in the
chivalrous days of Peter Stuyvesant, and accompanied him to the siege of
Fort Christina. He inherited, however, but little of the martial character of
his ancestors. I have observed that he was a simple, good-natured man; he
was, moreover, a kind neighbor, and an obedient, henpecked husband.
Indeed, to the latter circumstance might be owing that meekness of spirit
which gained him such universal popularity; for those men are most apt to be
obsequious and conciliating abroad, who are under the discipline of shrews
at home. Their tempers, doubtless, are rendered pliant and malleable in the
fiery furnace of domestic tribulation; and a curtain-lecture is worth all the
sermons in the world for teaching the virtues of patience and long-suffering.
A termagant wife may, therefore, in some respects be considered a tolerable
blessing; and if so, Rip Van Winkle was thrice blessed . . .

The great error in Rip's composition was an insuperable aversion to all
kinds of profitable labor. It could not be from the want of assiduity or perseverance; for he would sit on a wet rock, with a rod as long and heavy as a
Tartar's lance, and fish all day without a murmur, even though he should
not be encouraged by a single nibble. He would carry a fowling-piece on his
shoulder for hours together, trudging through woods and swamps, and up
hill and down dale, to shoot a few squirrels or wild pigeons. He would never
refuse to assist a neighbor even in the roughest toil, and was a foremost man
at all country frolics, for husking Indian corn, or building stone fences; the
women of the village, too, used to employ him to run errands, and to
do such little odd jobs as their less obliging husbands would not do for
them. In a word, Rip was ready to attend to anybody's business but his
own; but as to doing family duty, and keeping his farm in order, he found it
impossible . . .

In fact, he declared it was of no use to work on his farm; it was the most
pestilent little piece of ground in the whole country; everything about it went
wrong, and would go wrong, in spite of him . . .

Rip Van Winkle, however, was one of those happy mortals, of foolish,
well-oiled dispositions, who take the world easy, eat white bread or brown,
whichever can be got with least thought or trouble, and would rather starve
on a penny than work for a pound. If left to himself, he would have whistled
life away in perfect contentment; but his wife kept continually dinning in
his ears about his idleness, his carelessness, and the ruin he was bringing on
his family. Morning, noon, and night, her tongue was incessantly going,
and everything he said or did was sure to produce a torrent of household
eloquence.

The only way Rip can escape from 'the labour of the farm and the clamour of his wife' is to shoulder his gun and take to the mountains to shoot squirrels. On one of these expeditions he is sitting under a tree as evening draws in when he hears his name being called and sees a strange figure toiling up the rocks bearing something on his shoulders:

He was a short square-built old fellow, with thick bushy hair, and a grizzly beard. His dress was of the antique Dutch fashion,—a cloth jerkin strapped round his waist—several pair of breeches, the outer one of ample volume, decorated with rows of buttons down the sides, and bunches at the knees. He bore on his shoulder a stout keg, that seemed full of liquor, and made signs for Rip to approach and assist him with the load. Though rather shy and distrustful of this new acquaintance, Rip complied with his usual alacrity; and mutually relieving one another, they clambered up a narrow gully, apparently the dry bed of a mountain torrent. As they ascended, Rip every now and then heard long, rolling peals, like distant thunder, that seemed to issue out of a deep ravine, or rather cleft, between lofty rocks, toward which their rugged path conducted. He paused for an instant, but supposing it to be the muttering of one of those transient thunder-showers which often take place in mountain heights, he proceeded. Passing through the ravine, they came to a hollow, like a small amphitheatre, surrounded by perpendicular precipices . . .

On entering the amphitheatre, new objects of wonder presented themselves. On a level spot in the centre was a company of odd-looking personages playing at ninepins. They were dressed in a quaint, outlandish fashion; some wore short doublets, others jerkins, with long knives in their belts, and most of them had enormous breeches, of similar style with that of the guide's. Their visages, too, were peculiar: one had a large beard, broad face, and small piggish eyes; the face of another seemed to consist entirely of nose, and was surmounted by a white sugar-loaf hat, set off with a little red cock's tail. They all had beards, of various shapes and colors. There was one who seemed to be the commander. He was a stout old gentleman, with a weather-beaten countenance; he wore a laced doublet, broad belt and hanger, high-crowned hat and feather, red stockings, and high-heeled shoes, with roses in them. The whole group reminded Rip of the figures in an old Flemish painting, in the parlor of Diminie Van Shaick, the village parson, and which had been brought over from Holland at the time of the settlement.

What seemed particularly odd to Rip was, that, though these folks were evidently amusing themselves, yet they maintained the gravest faces, the most mysterious silence, and were, withal, the most melancholy party of pleasure he had ever witnessed. Nothing interrupted the stillness of the scene but the noise of the balls, which, whenever they were rolled, echoed along the mountains like rumbling peals of thunder.

As Rip and his companion approached them, they suddenly desisted from their play, and stared at him with such fixed, statuelike gaze, and such strange, uncouth, lack-lustre countenances, that his heart turned within him, and his knees smote together. His companion now emptied the contents of the keg into large flagons, and made signs to him to wait upon the company. He obeyed with fear and trembling; they quaffed the liquor in profound silence, and then returned to their game.

By degrees Rip's awe and apprehension subsided. He even ventured, when no eye was fixed upon him, to taste the beverage, which he found had much of the flavor of excellent Hollands. He was naturally a thirsty soul, and was soon tempted to repeat the draught. One taste provoked another; and he reiterated his visits to the flagon so often that at length his senses were overpowered, his eyes swam in his head, his head gradually declined, and he fell into a deep sleep . . .

Rip's sleep was indeed deep. On waking up:

He looked round for his gun, but in place of the clean, well-oiled fowling-piece, he found an old firelock lying by him, the barrel incrusted with rust, the lock falling off, and the stock worm-eaten. He now suspected that the grave roisterers of the mountain had put a trick upon him, and, having dosed him with liquor, had robbed him of his gun. Wolf, too, had disappeared, but he might have strayed away after a squirrel or partridge. He whistled after him, and shouted his name, but all in vain; the echoes repeated his whistle and shout, but no dog was to be seen. . .

More surprises await Rip as he clambers down to the mountains to his village:

As he rose to walk, he found himself stiff in the joints, and wanting in his usual activity. 'These mountain beds do not agree with me,' thought Rip, 'and if this frolic should lay me up with a fit of the rheumatism, I shall have a blessed time with Dame Van Winkle.' With some difficulty he got down into the glen: he found the gully up which he and his companion had ascended the preceding evening; but to his astonishment a mountain stream was now foaming down it, leaping from rock to rock, and filling the glen with babbling murmurs . . .

As he approached the village he met a number of people, but none whom he knew, which some what surprised him, for he had thought himself acquainted with every one in the country round. Their dress, too, was of a different fashion from that to which he was accustomed. They all stared at him with equal marks of surprise, and whenever they cast their eyes upon him, invariably stroked their chins. The constant recurrence of this gesture induced Rip, involuntarily, to do the same, when, to his astonishment, he found his beard had grown a foot long! . . . The very village was altered; it was large and more populous. There were rows of houses which he had never seen before, and those which had been his familiar haunts had disappeared.

Strange names were over the doors—strange faces at the windows—everything was strange . . .

He locates his house but finds it derelict. The windows are broken and the roof has fallen in:

He now hurried forth, and hastened to his old resort, the village inn—but it too was gone. A large rickety wooden building stood in its place, with great gaping windows, some of them broken and mended with old hats and petticoats, and over the door was painted, The Union Hotel, by Jonathan Doolittle. Instead of the great tree that used to shelter the quiet little Dutch inn of yore, there now was reared a tall naked pole, with something on top that looked like a red nightcap, and from it was fluttering a flag, on which was a singular assemblage of stars and stripes;—all this was strange and incomprehensible. He recognized on the sign, however, the ruby face of King George, under which he had smoked so many a peaceful pipe; but even this was singularly metamorphosed. The red coat was changed for one of blue and buff, a sword was held in the hand instead of a sceptre, the head was decorated with a cocked hat, and underneath was painted in large characters, GENERAL WASHINGTON . . .

It finally emerges that Rip had slept for twenty years, having been caught up in some strange, mystical, once-every-twenty-years visitation by the ghosts of old Hendrick Hudson and his crew, the discoverers of the river. Rip's nagging wife is dead having broken a blood-vessel 'in a fit of passion at a New England peddler'.
And so:

[Rip] had got his neck out of the yoke of matrimony and could go in and out whenever he pleased. Being arrived at that happy age when a man can be idle with impunity, he took his place once more on the bench at the inn-door, and was reverenced as one of the patriarchs of the village.

'Rip Van Winkle', *The Sketch-Book* (1819–20).

━━━━━━━

ANOTHER *early nineteenth-century American writer steeped in European literary tradition was Edgar Allan Poe, who had been to school in England as a lad. Poe was hardly a key figure in the development of humorous prose in the United States but it is interesting that he even attempted a form so different from his usual melancholy romanticism.*

Poe could not fit into society as he saw it and society was in no hurry to fit him in; the first real recognition he received was on publication of his poem The Raven *four years before he died. But for years he was a hard-working editor, journalist and critic, with a prodigious output of miscellaneous articles and stories among which were some humorous pieces.*

Here is one, a magazine short story—a form which he did much to encourage. As one would expect from Edgar Allan Poe, it is an exercise in Gothic humour with scenes of social satire and a message that nothing is quite what it seems.

At a function the writer meets a tremendously impressive-looking Brigadier who had survived a hand-to-hand swamp-fight with Bugaboo and Kickapoo Indians. The writer is intrigued and becomes obsessed with finding out what happened during the fight to make the mysterious Brigadier such a revered local celebrity:

THE MAN THAT WAS USED UP

Pleurez, pleurez, mes yeux, et fondez vous en eau
La moitié de ma vie a mis l'autre au tombeau.
                                        —Corneille

I cannot just now remember when or where I first made the acquaintance of that truly fine-looking fellow, Brevet Brigadier-General John A. B. C. Smith. Someone *did* introduce me to the gentleman, I am sure—at some public meeting, I know very well—held about something of great importance, no doubt—at some place or other, I feel convinced,—whose name I have unaccountably forgotten. The truth is—that the introduction was attended, upon my part, with a degree of anxious embarrassment which operated to prevent any definite impressions of either time or place. I am constitutionally nervous—this, with me, is a family failing, and I can't help it. Especially, the slightest appearance of mystery—of any point I cannot exactly comprehend— puts me at once into a pitiable state of agitation.

There was something, as it were, remarkable—yes, remarkable, although this is but a feeble term to express my full meaning—about the entire individuality of the personage in question. He was, perhaps, six feet in height, and of a presence singularly commanding. There was an *air distingué* pervading the whole man, which spoke of high breeding, and hinted at high birth. Upon this topic—the topic of Smith's personal appearance—I have a kind of melancholy satisfaction in being minute. His head of hair would have done honor to a Brutus; nothing could be more richly flowing, or possess a brighter gloss. It was of a jetty black; which was also the color, or more properly the no color, of his unimaginable whiskers. You perceive I cannot speak of these latter without enthusiasm; it is not too much to say that they were the handsomest pair of whiskers under the sun. At all events, they encircled, and at times partially over-shadowed, a mouth utterly unequalled. Here were the most entirely even, and the most brilliantly white of all conceivable teeth. From between them, upon every proper occasion, issued a voice of surpassing clearness, melody, and strength. In the matter of eyes, also, my acquaintance was pre-eminently endowed. Either one of such a pair was worth a couple of the ordinary ocular organs. They were of a deep hazel exceedingly large and lustrous; and there was perceptible about them, ever and anon, just that amount of interesting obliquity which gives pregnancy to expression.

The bust of the General was unquestionably the finest bust I ever saw. For your life you could not have found a fault with its wonderful proportion. This rare peculiarity set off to great advantage a pair of shoulders which would have called up a blush of conscious inferiority into the countenance of the marble Apollo. I have a passion for fine shoulders, and may say that I never beheld them in perfection before. The arms altogether were admirably modelled. Nor were the lower limbs less superb. These were, indeed, the *plus ultra* of good legs. Every connoisseur in such matters admitted the legs to be good. There was neither too much flesh nor too little,—neither rudeness nor fragility. I could not imagine a more graceful curve than that of the *os femoris*, and there was just that due gentle prominence in the rear of the *fibula* which goes to the confirmation of a properly proportioned calf. I wish to God my young and talented friend Chiponchipino, the sculptor, had but seen the legs of Brevet Brigadier-General John A. B. C. Smith.

But although men so absolutely fine-looking are neither as plenty as raisins or blackberries, still I could not bring myself to believe that the *remarkable* something to which I alluded just now,—that the odd air of *je ne sais quoi* which hung about my new acquaintance,—lay altogether, or indeed at all, in the supreme excellence of his bodily endowments. Perhaps it might be traced to *manner*;—yet here again I could not pretend to be positive. There *was* a primness, not to say stiffness, in his carriage—a degree of measured and, if I may so express it, of rectangular precision attending his every movement, which, observed in a more diminutive figure, would have had the least little savor in the world of affectation, pomposity, or constraint, but which, noticed in a gentleman of his undoubted dimensions, was readily placed to the account of reserve, *hauteur*—of a commendable sense, in short, of what is due to the dignity of colossal proportion.

The kind friend who presented me to General Smith whispered in my ear some few words of comment upon the man. He was a *remarkable* man—a *very* remarkable man—indeed one of the *most* remarkable men of the age. He was an especial favourite, too, with the ladies—chiefly on account of his high reputation for courage.

'In *that* point he is unrivalled—indeed he is a perfect desperado—a downright fire-eater, and no mistake,' said my friend, here dropping his voice excessively low, and thrilling me with the mystery of his tone.

'A downright fire-eater, and *no* mistake. Showed *that*, I should say, to some purpose, in the late tremendous swamp-fight, away down South, with the Bugaboo and Kickapoo Indians.' (Here my friend opened his eyes to some extent.) 'Bless my soul!—blood and thunder, and all that!—*prodigies* of valor!—heard of him of course?—you know he's the man—'

'Man alive, how *do* you do? why, how *are* ye? very glad to see ye, indeed!' here interrupted the General himself, seizing my companion by the hand as he drew near, and bowing stiffly but profoundly, as I was presented. I then thought (and I think so still) that I never heard a clearer nor a stronger voice, nor beheld a finer set of teeth; but I *must* say that I was sorry for the interruption just at that moment, as, owing to the whispers and insinuations aforesaid, my interest had been greatly excited in the hero of the Bugaboo and Kickapoo campaign.

However, the delightfully luminous conversation of Brevet Brigadier-General John A. B. C. Smith soon completely dissipated this chagrin. My friend leaving us immediately, we had quite a long *tête-à-tête*, and I was not only pleased but *really*—instructed. I never heard a more fluent talker, or a man of greater general information. With becoming modesty, he forbore, nevertheless, to touch upon the theme I had just then most at heart—I mean the mysterious circumstances attending the Bugaboo war—and, on my own part, what I conceive to be a proper sense of delicacy forbade me to broach the subject; although, in truth, I was exceedingly tempted to do so. I perceived, too, that the gallant soldier preferred topics of philosophical inter-est, and that he delighted, especially, in commenting upon the rapid march of mechanical invention. Indeed, lead him where I would, this was a point to which he invarably came back.

'There is nothing at all like it,' he would say; 'We are a wonderful people, and live in a wonderful age. Parachutes and railroads—man-traps and spring-guns! Our steam-boats are upon every sea, and the Nassau balloon packet is about to run regular trips (fare either way only twenty pounds sterling) between London and Timbuctoo. And who shall calculate the im-mense influence upon social life—upon arts—upon commerce—upon lit-erature—which will be the immediate result of the great principles of electromagnetics! Nor, is this all, let me assure you! There is really no end to the march of invention. The most wonderful—the most ingenious—and let me add, Mr—Mr—Thompson, I believe, is your name—let me add, I say the most *useful*—the most truly *useful*—mechanical contrivances are daily springing up like mushrooms, if I may so express myself, or, more figuratively, like—ah—grasshoppers—like grasshoppers, Mr Thompson—about us and ah—ah—ah—around us!'

Thompson, to be sure, is not my name; but it is needless to say that I left General Smith with a heightened interest in the man, with an exalted opinion of his conversational powers, and a deep sense of the valuable privileges we enjoy in living in this age of mechanical invention. My curiosity, however, had not been altogether satisfied, and I resolved to prosecute immediate inquiry among my acquaintances touching the Brevet Brigadier-General him-self, and particularly respecting the tremendous events *quorum pars magna fuit* during the Bugaboo and Kickapoo campaign.

The first opportunity which presented itself, and which (*horresco referens*) I did not in the least scruple to seize, occurred at the Church of the Reverend Doctor Drummummupp, where I found myself established, one Sunday, just at sermon time, not only in the pew, but by the side of that worthy and communicative little friend of mine, Miss Tabitha T. Thus seated, I congratulated myself, and with much reason, upon the very flattering state of affairs. If any person knew anything about Brevet Brigadier-General John A. B. C. Smith, that person, it was clear to me, was Miss Tabitha T. We telegraphed a few signals and then commenced, *sotto voce*, a brisk *tête-à-tête*.

'Smith!' said she, in reply to my very earnest inquiry; 'Smith!—why, not General A. B. C.? Bless me, I thought you knew all about him! This is a wonderfully inventive age! Horrid affair that!—a bloody set of wretches, those Kickapoos!—fought like a hero—prodigies of valor—immortal renown. Smith!—Brevet Brigadier-General John A. B. C.!—why, you know he's the man—'

'Man,' here broke in Doctor Drummummupp, at the top of his voice, and with a thump that came near knocking the pulpit about our ears—'man that is born of a woman hath but a short time to live; he cometh up and is cut down like a flower!' I started to the extremity of the pew, and perceived by the animated looks of the divine, that the wrath which had nearly proved fatal to the pulpit had been excited by the whispers of the lady and myself. There was no help for it; so I submitted with a good grace, and listened, in all the martyrdom of dignified silence, to the balance of that very capital discourse.

Next evening found me a somewhat late visitor at the Rantipole Theatre, where I felt sure of satisfying my curiosity at once, by merely stepping into the box of those exquisite specimens of affability and omniscience, the Misses Arabella and Miranda Cognoscenti. That fine tragedian, Climax, was doing Iago to a very crowded house, and I experienced some little difficulty in making my wishes understood; especially as our box was next the slips, and completely overlooked the stage.

'Smith!' said Miss Arabella, as she at length comprehended the purport of my query; 'Smith!—why, not General John A. B. C.?'

'Smith!' inquired Miranda, musingly, 'God bless me, did you ever behold a finer figure?'

'Never, madam, but do tell me—'

'Or so inimitable grace?'

'Never, upon my word! But pray, inform me—'

'Or so just an appreciation of stage effect?'

'Madam!'

'Or a more delicate sense of the true beauties of Shakespeare? Be so good as to look at that leg!'

'The devil!' and I turned again to her sister.

'Smith!' said she, 'why, not General John A. B. C.? Horrid affair that, wasn't it?—great wretches, those Bugaboos—savage and so on—but we live in a wonderfully inventive age!—Smith!—O yes! great man!—perfect desperado!—immortal renown!—prodigies of valor! *Never heard!*' (This was given in a scream.) 'Bless my soul!—why, he's the man—'

> '—mandragora
> Nor all the drowsy syrups of the world
> Shall ever medicine thee to that sweet sleep
> Which thou ow'dst yesterday!'

here roared out Climax just in my ear, and shaking his fist in my face all the time, in a way that I *couldn't* stand, and I *wouldn't*. I left the Misses Cognoscenti immediately, went behind the scenes forthwith, and gave the beggarly scoundrel such a thrashing as I trust he will remember till the day of his death.

At the *soirée* of the lovely widow, Mrs Kathleen O'Trump, I was confident that I should meet with no similar disappointment. Accordingly, I was no sooner seated at the card-table, with my pretty hostess for a *vis-à-vis*, than I propounded those questions the solution of which had become a matter so essential to my peace.

'Smith!' said my partner, 'why, not General John A. B. C.? Horrid affair that, wasn't it?—diamonds did you say?—terrible wretches those Kickapoos!—we are playing *whist*, if you please, Mr Tattle—however, this is the age of invention, most certainly the age, one may say—*the* age *par excellence*—speak French?—oh, quite a hero—perfect desperado!—*no hearts*, Mr Tattle? I don't believe it—immortal renown and all that!—prodigies of valor! *Never heard!*—why, bless me, he's the man—'

'Mann!—*Captain* Mann!' here screamed some little feminine interloper from the farthest corner of the room. 'Are you talking about Captain Mann and the duel?—oh, I *must* hear—do tell—go on, Mrs O'Trump!—do now go on!' And go on Mrs O'Trump did—all about a certain Captain Mann, who was either shot or hung, or should have been both shot and hung. Yes! Mrs. O'Trump, she went on, and I—I went off. There was no chance of hearing anything further that evening in regard to Brevet Brigadier-General John A. B. C. Smith.

Still I consoled myself with the reflection that the tide of ill-luck would not run against me forever, and so determined to make a bold push for information at the rout of that bewitching little angel, the graceful Mrs Pirouette.

'Smith!' said Mrs P., as we twirled about together in a *pas de zéphyr*, 'Smith!—why, not General John A. B. C.? Dreadful business that of the Bugaboos, wasn't it?—dreadful creatures, those Indians!—*do* turn out your toes! I really am ashamed of you—man of great courage, poor fellow!—but this is a wonderful age for invention—O dear me, I'm out of breath—quite a desperado—prodigies of valor—*never heard!*—can't believe it—I shall have to sit down and enlighten you—Smith! why, he's the man—'

'Man-*Fred*, I tell you!' here bawled out Miss Bas-Bleu, as I led Mrs Piourette

to a seat. 'Did ever anybody hear the like? It's Man-*Fred*, I say, and not at all
by any means Man-*Friday*.' Here Miss Bas-Bleu beckoned to me in a very
peremptory manner; and I was obliged, will I nill I, to leave Mrs. P. for the
purpose of deciding a dispute touching the title of a certain poetical drama of
Lord Byron's. Although I pronounced, with great promptness, that the true
title was Man-*Friday*, and not by any means Man-*Fred*, yet when I returned
to seek Mrs Pirouette she was not to be discovered, and I made my retreat
from the house in a very bitter spirit of animosity against the whole race of
the Bas-Bleus.

Matters had now assumed a really serious aspect, and I resolved to call at
once upon my particular friend, Mr Theodore Sinivate; for I knew that here
at least I should get something like definite information.

'Smith!' said he, in his well-known peculiar way of drawling out his
syllables; 'Smith!—why, not General John A. B. C.? Savage affair that with
the Kickapo-o-o-os, wasn't it? Say, don't you think so?—perfect despera-
a-ado—great pity, 'pon my honor!—wonderfully inventive age!—pro-o-
odigies of valor! By the by, did you ever hear about Captain Ma-a-a-a-n?'

'Captain Mann be d——d!' said I; 'please to go on with your story.'

'Hem!—oh well!—quite *la même cho-o-ose*, as we say in France. Smith,
eh? Brigadier-General John A-B-C? I say'—(here Mr S. thought proper to put
his finger to the side of his nose)—'I say, you don't mean to insinuate now,
really and truly, and conscientiously, that you don't know all about that
affair of Smith's as well as I do, eh? Smith? John A-B-C? Why, bless me, he's
the ma-a-an—'

'*Mr* Sinivate,' said I, imploringly, '*is* he the man in the mask?'

'No-o-o!' said he, looking wise, 'nor the man in the mo-o-on.'

This reply I considered a pointed and positive insult, and so left the house
at once in high dudgeon, with a firm resolve to call my friend, Mr Sinivate,
to a speedy account for his ungentlemanly conduct and ill-breeding.

In the meantime, however, I had no notion of being thwarted touching
the information I desired. There was one resource left me yet. I would go to
the fountainhead. I would call forthwith upon the General himself, and
demand, in explicit terms, a solution of this abominable piece of mystery.
Here, at least, there should be no chance for equivocation. I would be plain,
positive, peremptory—as short as pie-crust—as concise as Tacitus or
Montesquieu.

It was early when I called, and the General was dressing, but I pleaded
urgent business, and was shown at once into his bedroom by an old negro
valet, who remained in attendance during my visit. As I entered the chamber,
I looked about, of course, for the occupant, but did not immediately perceive
him. There was a large and exceedingly odd-looking bundle of something
which lay close by my feet on the floor, and, as I was not in the best humor
in the world, I gave it a kick out of the way.

'Hem! ahem! rather civil that, I should say!' said the bundle, in one of the smallest, and altogether the funniest little voices, between a squeak and a whistle, that I ever heard in all the days of my existence.

'Ahem! rather civil that, I should observe.'

I fairly shouted with terror, and made off, at a tangent, into the farthest extremity of the room.

'God bless me, my dear fellow!' here again whistled the bundle, 'what—what—what—why, what *is* the matter? I really believe you don't know me at all.'

What *could* I say to all this—what *could* I? I staggered into an armchair, and, with staring eyes and open mouth, awaited the solution of the wonder.

'Strange you shouldn't know me though, isn't it?' presently resqueaked the nondescript, which I now perceived was performing upon the floor some inexplicable evolution, very analogous to the drawing on of a stocking. There was only a single leg, however, apparent.

'Strange you shouldn't know me though, isn't it? Pompey, bring me that leg!' Here Pompey handed the bundle a very capital cork leg, already dressed, which it screwed on in a trice; and then it stood up before my eyes.

'And a bloody action it *was*,' continued the thing, as if in a soliloquy; 'but then one mustn't fight with the Bugaboos and Kickapoos, and think of coming off with a mere scratch. Pompey, I'll thank you now for that arm. Thomas' (turning to me) 'is decidedly the best hand at a cork leg; but if you should ever want an arm, my dear fellow, you must really let me recommend you to Bishop.' Here Pompey screwed on an arm.

'We had rather hot work of it, that you may say. Now, you dog, slip on my shoulders and bosom. Pettit makes the best shoulders, but for a bosom you will have to go to Ducrow.'

'Bosom!' said I.

'Pompey, will you *never* be ready with that wig? Scalping is a rough process after all; but then you can procure such a capital scratch at De L'Orme's.'

'Scratch!'

'Now, you nigger, my teeth! For a *good* set of these you had better go to Parmly's at once; high prices, but excellent work. I swallowed some very capital articles, though, when the big Bugaboo rammed me down with the butt end of his rifle.'

'Butt end! ram down!! my eye!!'

'O yes, by the by, my eye—here, Pompey, you scamp, screw it in! Those Kickapoos are not so very slow at a gouge; but he's a belied man, that Dr Williams, after all; you can't imagine how well I see with the eyes of his make.'

I now began very clearly to perceive that the object before me was nothing more or less than my new acquaintance, Brevet Brigadier-General John A. B. C. Smith. The manipulations of Pompey had made, I must confess, a very striking difference in the personal appearance of the man. The voice, however, still puzzled me no little; but even this apparent mystery was speedily cleared up.

'Pompey, you black rascal,' squeaked the General, 'I really do believe you would let me go out without my palate.'

Hereupon, the negro, grumbling out an apology, went up to his master, opened his mouth with the knowing air of a horse-jockey, and adjusted therein a somewhat singular-looking machine, in a very dexterous manner, that I could not altogether comprehend. The alteration, however, in the entire expression of the General's countenance was instantaneous and surprising. When he again spoke, his voice had resumed all that rich melody and strength which I had noticed upon our original introduction.

'D—n the vagabonds!' said he, in so clear a tone that I positively started at the change, 'D—n the vagabonds! they not only knocked in the roof of my mouth, but took the trouble to cut off at least seven eights of my tongue. There isn't Bonfanti's equal, however, in America, for really good articles of this description. I can recommend you to him with confidence,' (here the General bowed) 'and assure you that I have the greatest pleasure in so doing.'

I acknowledged his kindness in my best manner, and took leave of him at once, with a perfect understanding of the true state of affairs—with a full comprehension of the mystery which had troubled me so long. It was evident. It was a clear case. Brevet Brigadier-General John A. B. C. Smith was the man—was *the man that was used up.*

Edgar Allan Poe (1809–49), 'The Man That Was Used Up'.

➥ A strangely prophetic little story. Now, a hundred and fifty years or so later, extensive spare-part surgery is a grim reality.

TRULY *American humour, idiosyncratic, local, nourished by the soil, began to emerge in the early 1830s. Ironically perhaps, from New England. And the best market for American humorous prose turned out to be not the literary journal or the book as in Europe but the newspaper column.*

In the 1830s America had many literary magazines and journals but they were usually financially precarious, had small circulations, and paid their contributors very little if anything. On the other hand newspapers were comparatively prosperous, needed copy daily, and had a surprisingly strong literary content. Elementary education available to nearly everybody in 'the little red schoolhouse' meant that most people could read, and they had, and still have, a seemingly insatiable appetite for reading newspapers.

No sooner had a new frontier town been established with a saloon, a store, a bank, and a church than a wagon arrived with some founts of type and a hand printing-machine, and a new newspaper, however poorly written and smudged, was on the streets. For at least the next hundred years American humorous writers, almost without exception, were newspapermen.

In the same year that Charles Dickens was starting his career as a reporter, Seba Smith, born in a log cabin in the state of Maine, was beginning to write a humorous column for the Portland Courier, *the first daily newspaper north of Boston, which he owned and edited. The column took the form of a series of letters from a Yankee ex-peddler, Major Jack Downing, who was supposed to be a confidential adviser to the President, Andrew Jackson. This gave Seba Smith the opportunity for satirical comment on the political world as seen through the eyes of a simple but shrewd rustic.*

The character of Major Jack Downing was an important contribution to modern American humour; the prototype of a long line of whimsical, home-spun philosophers commenting on the current scene, including David Ross Locke's 'Petroleum V. Nasby', Finley Peter Dunne's 'Mr Dooley', Will Rogers, and even modern political humorists like Mort Sahl.

The column was pirated and widely imitated and, as a final accolade, the cartoons depicting Major Jack became the basis for the symbol of the US, Uncle Sam.

In the following letter Major Jack, on an exhausting tour down East with the President, writes home to Downingville warning Uncle Joshua to prepare for an official visit:

To Uncle Joshua Downing, Post Master, up in Downingville, in the State of Maine. This to be sent by my old friend, the Editor of the Portland Courier, with care and speed.

Philadelphia, June 10, 1833.

Dear Uncle Joshua,—We are coming on full chisel. I've been trying, ever since we started, to get a chance to write a little to you; but when we've been on the road I couldn't catch my breath hardly long enough to write my name, we kept flying so fast; and when we made any stop, there was such a jam round us there wasn't elbow room enough for a miskeeter to turn round without knocking his wings off.

I'm most afraid now we shall get to Downingville before this letter does, so that we shall be likely to catch you all in the suds before you think of it. But I understand there is a *fast mail* goes on that way, and I mean to send it by that, so I'm in hopes you'll get it time enough to have the children's faces washed and their heads combed, and the gals get on their clean gowns. And if Sargent Joel *could* have time enough to call out my old Downingville Company and get their uniforms brushed up a little, and come down the road as fur as your new barn to meet us, there's nothing that would please the President better. As for the victuals, most any thing wont come amiss; we are as hungry as bears after travelling a hundred miles a day. A little fried pork and eggs, or a pot of baked beans and an Indian pudding would suit us much better than the soft stuff they give us here in these great cities.

The President wouldn't miss seeing you for any thing in the world, and he will go to Downingville if he has legs and arms enough left when he goes to Portland to carry him there. But for fear any thing should happen that he shouldn't be able to come, you had better meet us in Portland, say about the 22nd, and then you can go up to Downingville with us, you know.

This travelling with the President is capital fun after all, if it wasn't so plaguy tiresome. We come into Baltimore on a Rail Road, and we flew over the ground like a harrycane. There isn't a horse in this country that could keep up with us, if he should go upon the clean clip. When we got to Baltimore, the streets were filled with folks as thick as the spruce trees down in your swamp. There we found Black Hawk, a little, old, dried up Indian king.—And I thought the folks looked at him and the prophet about as much as they did at me and the President. I gave the President a wink that this Indian fellow was taking the shine off of us a little, so we concluded we wouldn't have him in our company any more, and shall go on without him.

I cant stop to tell you in this letter how we got along to Philadelphy, though we had a pretty easy time some of the way in the steam-boats. And I cant stop to tell you of half of the fine things I have seen here. They took us up into a great hall this morning as big as a meeting-house, and then the folks begun to pour in by thousands to shake hands with the President; federalists and all, it made no difference. There was such a stream of 'em coming in that the hall was full in a few minutes, and it was so jammed up round the door that they couldn't get out again if they were to die. So they had to knock out some of the windows and go out t'other way.

The President shook hands with all his might an hour or two, till he got so tired he couldn't hardly stand it. I took hold and shook for him once in awhile to help him along, but at last he got so tired he had to lay down on a soft bench covered with cloth and shake as well as he could, and when he couldn't shake he'd nod to 'em as they come along. And at last he got so beat out, he couldn't only wrinkle his forward and wink. Then I kind of stood behind him and reached my arm round under his, and shook for him about a half an hour as tight as I could spring. Then we concluded it was best to adjourn for to-day.

And I've made out to get away up into the garret in the tavern long enough to write this letter. We shall be off tomorrow or next day for York, and if I can possibly get breathing time enough there, I shall write to you again.

Give my love to all the folks in Downingville, and believe me your loving neffu,

Major Jack Downing.

Seba Smith (1792–1868), *The Life and Writings of Major Jack Downing of Downingville* (1833).

IN 1835, *two years after the first appearance of Major Jack Downing, another humorous Yankee, Sam Slick the Clockmaker, became the talking point of newspaper readers. These sketches by Thomas Chandler Haliburton, really observations on rural Down-East life, were extremely popular not only throughout the United States and Canada but world-wide. According to Josh Billings, Haliburton was the pioneer of a style of humour which inspired his own writings and that of Artemus Ward, Mark Twain, and other expounders of American cracker-barrel regional humour.*

Haliburton, though a major figure in the development of modern American humour, was not American at all but Canadian. He was a judge of the Supreme Court of Nova Scotia and wrote his pieces for The Nova Scotian *with the intention of stirring up the notoriously placid and somnolent farmers of the Eastern seaboard. He was the first Canadian author to win an international reputation; indeed he was probably the first well-known Canadian author. He was unquestionably the first, and only, North American humorist to sit in Britain's House of Commons as the MP for Launceston.*

They are frame stories. In a typical example, Sam Slick the enterprising Yankee demonstrates to his friend the narrator how he uses applied psychology to persuade frugal Nova Scotians to pay out good money for his cheap clocks:

'How is it,' said I to Sam Slick, 'that you manage to sell such an immense number of clocks, which certainly can't be called necessary articles, among people with whom there seems to be so great a scarcity of money?'

Sam looked me in the face and said in a confidential tone, 'Why, I don't care if I do tell you, for the market is glutted and I shall quit this circuit. It's done by a knowledge of soft sawder [flattery] and human nature.'

'Here is Deacon Flint's. I've got but one clock left and I guess I'll sell it to him.'

At the gate of a most comfortable looking farmhouse stood Deacon Flint, a respectable old man who had understood the value of time better than most of his neighbors, to judge by the appearances of his place.

After the usual salutation, an invitation to alight was accepted by Sam. He said that he wished to take leave of Mrs Flint before he left Colchester, Nova Scotia.

We had hardly entered the house before Sam, pointing to the view from the window, said, 'If I was to tell them down in Connecticut that there was such a farm as this away Down East here in Nova Scotia, they wouldn't believe me. Why, there ain't such a location in all New England!' Sam praised the fine bottom land and admiringly said that the 'water privilege' alone must be worth three or four thousand dollars—'twice as good as that Governor Case paid fifteen thousand dollars for. I wonder, Deacon, you don't put up a carding mill on it. The same works would carry a turning lathe, a shingle machine, a circular saw—'.

'Too old,' said the Deacon. 'Too old for all these speculations.'

'Old!' repeated Sam. 'Not you! Why, you're worth half a dozen of the young men we see nowadays. You're young enough to—'. Here he said something in a lower tone of voice which I did not distinctly hear, but whatever it was, the Deacon was pleased. He smiled and said he did not think of such things now.

'But your beasts,' the Deacon said. 'Your beasts must be put in and have a feed.'

As the old gentleman closed the door after him, Sam drew near to me and said in an undertone, 'That's what I call soft sawder.'

He was cut short by the entrance of Mrs Flint.

'Just come to say goodbye, Mrs Flint,' he told her.

'What!' said she. 'Have you sold all your clocks?'

'Yes, and very low, too. Money is scarce and I wished to close the concern. I'm wrong in saying all, for I have just one left. Neighbor Steel's wife asked to have the refusal of it but I guess I won't sell it. I had but two of them, this one and the feller of it that I sold to Governor Lincoln. General Green, the Secretary of State for Maine, said he'd give me fifty dollars for this here one. It has composition wheels and patent axles. It's a beautiful article, a real first chop, and no mistake, genuine superfine. But I guess I'll take it back. And, besides, Squire Hawk might think kind of hard that I didn't give him the offer.'

'Dear me,' said Mrs Flint. 'I should like to see it. Where is it?'

'Oh, it's in a chest of mine over the way at Tom Tape's store. I guess he can ship it on to Eastport.'

'Just let's look at it,' said Mrs Flint. 'That's a good man.'

Sam Slick, willing to oblige, soon produced the clock, a gaudy, highly varnished trumpery affair. He placed it on the chimney piece, where its beauties were pointed out and duly appreciated by Mrs Flint whose admiration was about ending in a proposal to buy when Deacon Flint returned from giving his directions about the care of the horses.

The Deacon praised the clock. He too thought it a handsome one. But the Deacon was a prudent man. He had a watch, he was sorry, but he had no occasion for a clock.

Sam said, 'I guess you're in the wrong furrow this time, Deacon. It ain't for sale. And if it was, I reckon Neighbor Steel's wife would have it, for she gives me no peace about it.'

Mrs Flint said Mr Steel had enough to do, poor man, to pay his interest without buying clocks for his wife.

'It's no concern of mine,' said Sam, 'what he has to do, as long as he pays me. But I guess I don't want to sell it. And, besides, it comes too high. That clock couldn't be made at Rhode Island under forty dollars.'

Suddenly Sam started and said, 'Why, it ain't possible!' He looked at his watch. 'Why, as I'm alive, it's four o'clock, and if I ain't been two hours here! How on earth shall I reach River Philip tonight? I tell you what, Mrs

Flint. I'll leave the clock in your care until I return on my way to the States. I'll set it a-going and put it to the right time.'

As soon as this operation was performed, he delivered the key to the Deacon, telling him to wind it up every Saturday night.

When we were mounted and on our way, Sam said. 'That I call human nature. Now, that clock is sold for forty dollars. It cost me just six dollars and fifty cents. Mrs Flint will never let Mrs Steel have the refusal, nor will the Deacon learn until I call for the clock how hard it is to give up.'

'We can do without any article of luxury we never had, but once we've had it, it's not in human nature to surrender it voluntarily. Of fifteen thousand sold by myself and my partners in this Province, twelve thousand were left in this manner. And only ten clocks were ever returned when we came back around.'

Said Sam Slick, 'You see, we trust to soft sawder to get the clocks in the house and to human nature that they never come out of it.'

Thomas Chandler Haliburton (1796–1865), *The Clockmaker* (1836).

————————————

FRANCES MIRIAM WHITCHER *was a quiet lady who was married to a clergyman in New York and wrote, anonymously, little humorous stories about Yankee village life which were much enjoyed and reprinted later in several volumes. The only details she would reveal to her editors about herself was that she had:*

> Hands and feet
> Of respectable size,
> Mud-coloured hair,
> And dubious eyes.

Her stories were recollections of a widow, Hezekiah Bedott, and were gentle and observant. The interesting point about them is that when they began to appear in the 1840s they were the first ever American stories to be built entirely round a humorous female character.

Here the Widow Bedott recounts, in her own good time, an occasion when her late husband was in a deeply philosphical mood:

He was a wonderful hand to moralize, husband was, specially after he begun to enjoy poor health. He made an observation once, when he was in one of his poor turns, that I shall never forget the longest day I live.

He says to me one winter evenin as we was a-settin by the fire—I was a-knittin. I was always a great knitter—and he was smokin, though the doctor used to tell him he'd be better off to leave tobacco alone. When he was well, he used to take his pipe and smoke a spell after he'd got the chores done up, and when he warn't well, he used to smoke the biggest part of the time.

Well, he took his pipe out of his mouth and turned toward me, and I knowed somethin was comin, for he had a particular way of lookin round when he was a-goin to say anything uncommon. Well, he says to me, 'Silly,'—my name was Prisilly, naturally, but he generally called me 'Silly' because 'twas handier, you know—well, he says to me, 'Silly,' and he looked pretty solemn, I tell you! He had a solemn countenance, and after he got to be deacon 'twas more so, but since he'd lost his health he looked solemner than ever, and certainly you wouldn't wonder at it if you knew how much he underwent. He was troubled with a pain in his chest and mazin weakness in the spine of his back, besides the pleurisy in his side, and bein broke of his rest of nights because he was put to it for breath when he laid down. Why, it's an unaccountable fact that when that man died he hadn't seen a well day in fifteen year, though when he was married and for five or six year after, I shouldn't desire to see a ruggeder man than he was. But the time I'm a-speakin of, he'd been out of health nigh upon ten year, and, oh dear sakes! How he had altered since the first time I ever see him! That was to a quiltin to Squire Smith's a spell before Sally was married. I'd no idea *then* that Sal Smith was a-goin to be married to Sam Pendergrass. She'd been keepin company with Mose Hewlitt for better'n a year, and everybody said that was a settled thing, and lo and behold! All of a sudden she up and took Sam Pendergrass. Well, that was the first time I ever see my husband, and if anybody'd a-told me then that I should ever marry him, I should a-said—

But lawful sakes! I was a-goin to tell you what he said to me that evenin, and when a body begins to tell a thing I believe in finishin on it some time or other. Some folks have a way of talkin round and round and round for evermore. Now there's Miss Jenkins, she that was Poll Bingham before she was married—but what husband said to me was this. He says to me, 'Silly'.

Says I, 'What?' I didn't say, 'What, Hezekiah?' for I didn't like his name. The first time I ever heard it I near killed myself a-laughin. 'Hezekiah Bedott!' says I. 'Well, I would give up if I had such a name!' But then, you know, I had no more idea of marryin the feller than you have this minute of marryin the governor. I suppose you think it's curious we should name our oldest son Hezekiah. Well, we done it to please Father and Mother Bedott. It's his name, and he and Mother Bedott both used to think that names had ought to go down from generation to generation. But we always called him Kiah, you know. That boy is a blessin! I ain't the only one that thinks so, I guess. Now, don't you ever tell anybody that I said so, but between you and me, I rather guess that if Kesiah Winkel thinks she's a-goin to catch Kiah Bedott, she is a little out of her reckonin!

Well, husband he says to me, 'Silly'. And says I, 'What?' though I'd no idea what he was a-goin to say, didn't know but what it was somethin about his sufferins, though he warn't apt to complain, but used to say that he wouldn't wish his worst enemy to suffer one minute as he did all the time, but that can't be called grumblin—think it can? Why, I've seen him when you'd a-thought no mortal could a-helped grumblin, but he didn't. He and me went once in the dead of winter in a one-hoss sleigh out to see a sister of his. You know the snow is deep in this section of the country. Well, the hoss got stuck in one of them snow banks, and there we set, unable to stir, and to cap it all, husband was took with a dreadful crick in his back. Now that is what I call a predicament!

Most men would a-swore, but husband didn't. We might a-been settin there to this day, far as I know, if there hadn't a-happened to come along a mess of men in a double team, and they pulled us out.

But husband says to me—I could see by the light of the fire, for there didn't happen to be any candle burnin, if I don't disremember, though my memory is sometimes rather forgetful, but I know we weren't apt to burn candles exceptin when we had company—I could see by the light of the fire that his mind was uncommon solemnized. Says he to me, 'Silly'.

I says to him, 'What?'

He says to me, says he, 'We're all poor creatures'.

Frances Miriam Whitcher (1814–52), *The Widow Bedott Papers* (1856).

➤ Mrs Whitcher eventually confessed to being the author of the famous Widow Bedott papers. The neighbours rose in fury at being depicted and her husband, the vicar, was aghast at finding he had a literary wife. She left him, and New York, and spent her remaining years in a village on the Mohawk river.

YANKEE *humour, popular and influential though it was, was only one of the many forms which burst into print in the first half of the century.*

Another kind, even more indigenously American, was the humour of the frontier, of the backwoodsman, the Mississippi riverman, the bear hunter. The harsh, physical life of the frontier was hardly conducive to the pursuit of literature but it was fallow ground for the good old-fashioned art of story-telling and the oral frontier humour of the old South, West, and South-West, retold in print, shaped the character of much early American humorous prose.

The frontiersman as represented in the oral tall stories had qualities which are now somewhat unfashionable: he was coarse and violent, racist, confident of the superiority of horse-sense over book-learning, crudely behaved to women, a tremendous eater and drinker, and a mighty braggart.

The frontier tall tales recounting the gargantuan exploits of these heroes were usually supposed to be based upon real frontiersmen and some of the most popular myths were told about Davy Crockett.

Crockett was a real person. He was born in Tennessee in 1786, went to work at the age of 12, ran away from home at 13, fought with Andrew Jackson in the war against the Creek Indians, was elected to the Tennessee legislature, stood for Congress and was elected as a Democrat, turned Whig, and was changed by Whig propagandists from a fine upstanding, plain-speaking backwoods politician into a vote-winning frontier myth. He lost his seat in 1835, said 'You may all go to hell and I will go to Texas', joined the army in Texas and in 1836 was killed at the battle of the Alamo.

Tall stories about Davy Crockett, that is to say oral folk-tales collected by the Whig political journalists and literary hacks and published in newspapers and almanacs, were extremely popular; over fifty Davy Crockett almanacs were published between 1835 and 1856.

Here is one tall tale telling how Davy Crockett wakes one very cold morning and gets his breakfast:

One January morning it was so all-screwen-up cold that the forest trees war so stiff that they couldn't shake, and the very day-break froze fast as it war tryin' to dawn. The tinder-box in my cabin would no more ketch fire than a sunk raft at the bottom o' the sea. Seein' that daylight war so far behind time, I thought creation war in a fair way for freezin' fast.

'So,' thinks I, 'I must strike a leetle fire from my fingers, light my pipe, travel out a few leagues, and see about it.'

Then I brought my knuckles together like two thunder clouds, but the sparks froze up afore I could begin to collect 'em—so out I walked, and endeavored to keep myself unfriz by goin' at a hop, step, and jump gait, and whislin' the tune of 'fire in the mountains!' as I went along in three double quick time. Well, arter I had walked about twenty-five miles up the peak o' Daybreak Hill, I soon discovered what war the matter. The airth had actually friz fast in her axis, and couldn't turn round; the sun had got jammed between two cakes o' ice under the wheels, an' thar he had bin shinin' and workin' to get loose, till he friz fast in his cold sweat.

'C-r-e-a-t-i-o-n!' thought I, 'this are the toughest sort o' suspension, and it mustn't be endured—somethin' must be done, or human creation is done for.'

It war then so antedeluvian and premature cold that my upper and lower teeth an' tongue war all collapsed together as tight as a friz oyster. I took a fresh twenty pound bear off o' my back that I'd picked up on the road, an' beat the animal agin the ice till the hot ile began to walk out on him at all sides. I then took an' held him over the airth's axes, an' squeezed him till I thaw'd 'em loose, poured about a ton on it over the sun's face, give the airth's cog-wheel one kick backward, till I got the sun loose—whistled 'Push along, keep movin'!' an' in about fifteen seconds the airth gin a grunt, and begun movin'—the sun walked up beautiful, salutin' me with sich a wind o' gratitude that it made me sneeze. I lit my pipe by the blaze o' his top-knot, shouldered my bear, an' walked home, introducin' the people to fresh daylight with a piece of sunrise in my pocket, with which I cooked my bear steaks, an' enjoyed one o' the best breakfasts I had tasted for some time.

Anon. (1835).

—————————

THE old South-West, and indeed America as a whole, has always had a soft spot for confidence tricksters. There is a long line of heroes in humorous stories who were petty swindlers by profession, beginning with Sam Slick the Clockmaker, including most of the characters in stories by such writers as O. Henry and Damon Runyon and ending with many of the roles played in movies by star comedians like W. C. Fields and Bob Hope.

This somewhat amoral attitude to tricksters, of enjoying them as entertainers rather than condemning them as petty criminals, was probably due to another national characteristic, particularly strong in frontier and backwoods areas, of trying to be self-sufficient and to rely on 'gut reaction' and personal judgement rather than on wisdom and education. Thus the con-man was admired for his resourcefulness and it was the wretched dupe who was blamed for not having enough nous to realize what was going on.

One of the most popular of the old South-West, pre-Civil War fictitious con-men was Captain Simon Suggs (his motto was 'It is good to be shifty in a new country'). Suggs was created by Johnson J. Hooper in the 1840s for a Whig newspaper which he edited called the East Alabamian. The pieces were reprinted by newspapers throughout the United States and even reached England where Thackeray pronounced Hooper to be the most promising young writer in America.

Besides being a confidence trickster by trade, Simon Suggs was also a gambler (another admired occupation), a backwoodsman, and a military hero (those so-called officers, like Major Jack Downing, were not career army officers but commanders of the local militia, which usually consisted of a handful of farm-lads and assorted layabouts).

In this episode the gallant Captain, down on his luck, braves the wild preaching and the steamy goings-on at a highly suspect Revivalist camp-meeting in order to out-swindle the fundamentalist brethren and hijack some of their takings:

Captain Suggs found himself as poor at the conclusion of the Creek war as he had been at its commencement. Although no 'arbitrary', 'despotic', 'corrupt', and 'unprincipled' judge had fined him a thousand dollars for his proclamation of martial law at Fort Suggs, or the enforcement of its rules in the case of Mrs Haycock; yet somehow—the thing is alike inexplicable to him and to us—the money which he contrived, by various shifts, to obtain, melted away and was gone forever. To a man like the Captain, of intense domestic affections, this state of destitution was most distressing. 'He could stand it himself—didn't care a d—n for it, no way,' he observed, 'but the old woman and the children; that bothered him!'. . .

Having uttered the exclamation we have repeated—and perhaps, hurriedly walked once or twice across the room—Captain Suggs drew on his famous old green-blanket overcoat, and ordered his horse, and within five minutes was on his way to a camp-meeting, then in full blast on Sandy Creek, twenty miles distant, where he hoped to find amusement, at least. When he arrived there, he found the hollow square of the encampment filled with people, listening to the mid-day sermon, and its dozen accompanying 'exhortations'. A half-dozen preachers were dispensing the word; the one in the pulpit, a meek-faced old man, of great simplicity and benevolence. His voice was weak and cracked, notwithstanding which, however, he contrived to make himself heard occasionally, above the din of the exhorting, the singing, and the shouting which were going on around him. The rest were walking to and fro (engaged in the other exercises we have indicated), among the 'mourners'—a host of whom occupied the seat set apart for their especial use—or made personal appeals to the mere spectators. The excitement was intense. Men and women rolled about on the ground, or lay sobbing or shouting in pro-miscuous heaps. More than all, the negros sang and screamed and prayed. Several, under the influence of what is technically called 'the jerks', were plunging and pitching about with convulsive energy. The great object of all seemed to be, to see who could make the greatest noise—

> 'And each—for madness ruled the hour—
> Would try his own expressive power.'

'Bless my poor old soul!' screamed the preacher in the pulpit; 'ef yonder aint a squad in that corner that we aint got one outen yet! It'll never do'—raising his voice—'you must come outen that! Brother Fant, fetch up that youngster in the blue coat! I see the Lord's a-workin' upon him! Fetch him along—glory—yes!—hold to him!'

'Keep the thing warm!' roared a sensual seeming man, of stout mould and florid countenance, who was exhorting among a bevy of young women, upon whom he was lavishing caresses. 'Keep the thing warm, breethring!—come to the Lord, honey!' he added, as he vigorously hugged one of the damsels he sought to save . . .

Near these last stood a delicate woman in that hysterical condition in which the nerves are incontrollable, and which is vulgarly—and most blas-phemously—termed the 'holy laugh'. A hideous grin distorted her mouth, and was accompanied with a maniac's chuckle; while every muscle and nerve of her face twitched and jerked in horrible spasms.

Amid all this confusion and excitement Suggs stood unmoved. He viewed the whole affair as a grand deception—a sort of 'opposition line' running against his own, and looked on with a sort of professional jealousy. Sometimes he would mutter running comments upon what passed before him.

'Well now,' said he, as he observed the full-faced brother who was 'offi-ciating' among the women, 'that ere feller takes *my* eye!—thar he's been this half-hour, a-figurin amongst them galls, and's never said the fust word to nobody else. Wonder what's the reason these here preachers never hugs up the old women? Never seed one do it in my life—the sperrit never moves 'em that easy! It's nater tho'; and the women, *they* never flocks round one o' the old dried-up breethring—bet two to one old splinter-legs thar,'—nodding at one of the ministers—'won't git a chance to say turkey to a good-lookin gall to-day! Well! who blames 'em? Nater will be nater, all the world over; and I judge ef I was a preacher, I should save the purtiest souls fust, myself!'

While the Captain was in the middle of this conversation with himself, he caught the attention of the preacher in the pulpit, who inferring from an indescribable something about his appearance that he was a person of some consequence, immediately determined to add him at once to the church if it could be done; and to that end began a vigorous, direct personal attack.

'Breethring,' he exclaimed, 'I see yonder a man that's a sinner; I *know* he's a sinner! Thar he stands,' pointing at Simon, 'a missubble old crittur, with his head a-blossomin for the grave! A few more short years, and d-o-w-n he'll go to perdition, lessen the Lord have mer-cy on him (Come up here, you old hoary-headed sinner, a-n-d git down upon your knees, a-n-d put up your cry for the Lord to snatch you from the bottomless pit! You're ripe for the devil—you're b-o-u-n-d for hell, and the Lord only knows what'll become on you!'

'D—n it,' thought Suggs, 'ef I only had you down in the krick swamp for a minit or so, *I'd* show you who's old! *I'd* alter your tune *mighty* sudden, you sassy, 'saitful old rascal!' But he judiciously held his tongue and gave no utterance to the thought.

The attention of many having been directed to the Captain by the preach-er's remarks, he was soon surrounded by numerous well-meaning, and doubtless very pious persons, each one of whom seemed bent on the ap-plication of his own particular recipe for the salvation of souls. For a long time the Captain stood silent, or answered the incessant stream of ex-hortations only with a sneer; but at length, his countenance began to give token of inward emotion. First his eye-lids twitched—then his upper lip quivered—next a transparent drop formed on one of his eye-lashes, and a similar one on the tip of his nose—and, at last, a sudden bursting of air from nose and mouth, told that Captain Suggs was overpowered by his emotions. At the moment of the explosion, he made a feint as if to rush from the crowd, but he was in experienced hands, who well knew that the battle was more than half won.

'Hold to him!' said one—'it's a-workin in him as strong as a Dick horse!'

'Pour it into him,' said another, 'it'll all come right directly!'

'That's the way I love to see 'em do,' observed a third; 'when you begin to draw the water from their eyes, taint gwine to be long afore you'll have 'em on their knees!'

And so they clung to the Captain manfully, and half dragged, half led him to the mourners' bench; by which he threw himself down, altogether unmanned, and bathed in tears . . . Great was the rejoicing of the brethren, as they sang, shouted, and prayed around him—for by this time it had come to be generally known that the 'convicted' old man was Captain Simon Suggs, the very 'chief of sinners' in all that region.

The Captain remained grovelling in the dust during the usual time, and gave vent to even more than the requisite number of sobs, and groans, and heart-piercing cries. At length, when the proper time had arrived, he bounced up, and with a face radiant with joy, commenced a series of vaultings and tumblings, which 'laid in the shade' all previous performances of the sort at that camp-meeting. The brethren were in ecstasies at this demonstrative evidence of completion of the work; and whenever Suggs shouted 'Gloree!' at the top of his lungs, every one of them shouted it back, until the woods rang with echoes.

The effervescence having partially subsided, Suggs was put upon his pins to relate his experience, which he did somewhat in this style—first brushing the tear-drops from his eyes, and giving the end of his nose a preparatory wring with his fingers, to free it of the superabundant moisture:

'Friends,' he said, 'it don't take long to curry a short horse, accordin' to the old sayin', and I'll give you the perticklers of the way I was "brought to a knowledge"'—here the Captain wiped his eyes, brushed the tip of his nose and snuffled a little—'in less'n no time.'

'Praise the Lord!' ejaculated a bystander.

'You see I come here full o' romancin' and devilment, and jist to make game of all the purceedins. Well, sure enough, I done so for some time, and was a-thinkin' how I should play some trick—'

'Dear soul alive! *don't* he talk sweet!' cried an old lady in black silk—'whar's John Dobbs? You Sukey!' screaming at a negro woman on the other side of the square—'ef you don't hunt up your mass John in a minute, and have him here to listen to the 'sperience, I'll tuck you up when I git home and give you a hundred and fifty lashes, madam!—see ef I don't!' . . .

'And so from that I felt somethin' a-pullin' me inside—'

'Grace! grace! nothin' but grace!' exclaimed one; meaning that 'grace' had been operating in the Captain's gastric region.

'And then,' continued Suggs, 'I wanted to git off, but they hilt me, and bimeby I felt so missuble, I had to go yonder'—pointing to the mourners' seat—'and when I lay down thar it got wuss and wuss, and 'peared like somethin' was a-mashin' down on my back—'

'That was his load o' sin,' said one of the brethren—'never mind, it'll tumble off presently, see ef it don't!' and he shook his head professionally and knowingly . . . 'And arter awhile,' Suggs went on, ''peared like I fell into a trance, like, and I seed—'

'Now we'll git the good on it!' cried one of the sanctified.

'And I seed the biggest, longest, rip-roarnest, blackest, scaliest—' Captain Suggs paused, wiped his brow, and ejaculated, 'Ah, L-o-r-d!' so as to give full time for curiosity to become impatience to know what he saw.

'Sarpent! warn't it?' asked one of the preachers.

'No, not a sarpent,' replied Suggs, blowing his nose.

'Do tell us what it war, soul alive!—whar is John?' said Mrs Dobbs.

'Alligator!' said the Captain.

'Alligator!' repeated every woman present, and screamed for very life . . .

'Well,' said the Captain in continuation, 'the allegator kept a-comin' and a-comin' to'ards me, with his great long jaws a-gapin' open like a ten-foot pair o' tailor's shears—'

'Oh! oh! oh! Lord! gracious above!' cried the women.

'Satan!' was the laconic ejaculation of the oldest preacher present, who thus informed the congregation that it was the devil which had attacked Suggs in the shape of an alligator.

'And then I concluded the jig was up, 'thout I could block his game some way; for I seed his idee was to snap off my head.'

The women screamed again.

'So I fixed myself jist like I was purfectly willin' for him to take my head, and rather he'd do it as not'—here the women shuddered perceptibly—'and so I hilt my head straight out'—the Captain illustrated by elongating his neck—'and when he come up and was a gwine to *shet down* on it, I jist pitched in a big rock which chocked him to death, and that minit I felt the weight slide off, and I had the best feelins—sorter like you'll have from *good* sperrits—any body ever had!' . . .

Captain Suggs was now the 'lion of the day'. Nobody could pray so well, or exhort so movingly, as 'brother Suggs'. Nor did his natural modesty prevent the proper performance of appropriate exercises. With the reverend Bela Bugg (him to whom, under providence, he ascribed his conversion) he was a most especial favorite. They walked, sang, and prayed together for hours.

'Come, come up; thar's rooms for all!' cried brother Bugg, in his evening exhortation. 'Come to the "seat", and ef you won't pray for yourselves, let me pray for you!'

'Yes!' said Simon, by way of assisting his friend; 'it's a game that all can win at! Ante up! ante up, boys—friends I mean—don't back out!'. . .

And thus the Captain continued, until the services were concluded, to assist in adding to the number at the mourners' seat; and up to the hour of retiring, he exhibited such enthusiasm in the cause, that he was unanimously voted to be the most efficient addition the church had made during that meeting.

The next morning, when the preacher of the day first entered the pulpit, he announced that 'brother Simon Suggs', mourning over his past iniquities, and desirous of going to work in the cause as speedily as possible, would take up a collection to found a church in his own neighbourhood, at which he hoped to make himself useful as soon as he could prepare himself for the ministry, which the preacher didn't doubt, would be in a very few weeks, as 'brother Suggs' was a man of mighty good judgement, and of a great discourse. The funds were to be collected by 'brother Suggs', and held in trust by brother Bela Bugg, who was the financial officer of the circuit, until some arrangement could be made to build a suitable house.

'Yes, breethring,' said the Captain, rising to his feet; 'I want to start a little 'sociation close to me, and I want you all to help. I'm mighty poor myself, as poor as any of you—don't leave, breethring'—observing that several of the well-to-do were about to go off—'don't leave; ef you aint able to afford any thing, jist give your blessin' and it'll be all the same!'

This insinuation did the business, and the sensitive individuals reseated themselves.

'It's mighty little of this world's goods I've got,' resumed Suggs, pulling off his hat and holding it before him; 'but I'll bury *that* in the cause any how,' and he deposited his last five-dollar bill in the hat.

There was a murmur of approbation at the Captain's liberality throughout the assembly.

Suggs now commenced collecting, and very prudently attacked first the gentlemen who had shown a disposition to escape. These, to exculpate themselves from anything like poverty, contributed handsomely.

'Look here, breethring,' said the Captain, displaying the bank-notes thus received, 'brother Snooks has drapt a five wi' me, and brother Snodgrass a ten! In course 'taint expected that you that *aint as well off as them*, will give *as much*; let every one give *accordin'* to ther means.'

This was another chain-shot that raked as it went! 'Who so low' as not to be able to contribute as much as Snooks and Snodgrass?

'Here's all the *small* money I've got about me,' said a burly old fellow, ostentatiously handing to Suggs, over the heads of a half dozen, a ten dollar bill.

'That's what I call maganimus!' exclaimed the Captain; 'that's the way *every* rich man ought to do!'

These examples were followed, more or less closely, by almost all present, for Simon had excited the pride of purse of the congregation, and a very handsome sum was collected in a very short time.

The reverend Mr Bugg, as soon as he observed that our hero had obtained all that was to be had at that time, went to him and inquired what amount had been collected. The Captain replied that it was still uncounted, but that it couldn't be much under a hundred.

'Well, brother Suggs, you'd better count it and turn it over to me now. I'm goin' to leave presently.'

'No!' said Suggs—'can't do it!'

'Why?—what's the matter?' inquired Bugg.

'It's got to be prayed over, fust!' said Simon, a heavenly smile illuminating his whole face.

'Well,' replied Bugg, 'les go one side and do it!'

'No!' said Simon, solemnly.

Mr Bugg gave a look of inquiry.

'You see that krick swamp?' asked Suggs—'I'm gwine down in *thar*, and I'm gwine to lay this money down *so*'—showing how he would place it on the ground—'and I'm gwine to git on these here knees'—slapping the right one—'and I'm *n-e-v-e-r* gwine to quit the grit ontwell I feel it's got the blessin'! And nobody aint got to be thar but me!'

Mr Bugg greatly admired the Captain's fervent piety, and bidding him God-speed, turned off.

Captain Suggs 'struck for' the swamp sure enough, where his horse was already hitched. 'Ef them fellers aint done to a cracklin,' he muttered to himself as he mounted, 'I'll never bet on two pair agin! They're peart at the snap game, theyselves, but they're badly lewed this hitch! Well! Live and let live is a good old motter, and it's my sentiments adzactly!' And giving the spur to his horse, off he cantered.

Johnson J. Hooper (1815–62), *Some Adventures of Captain Simon Suggs, Late of the Tallapoosa Volunteers* (1845).

IN *the early years of this century the English author and statesman Augustine Birrel observed that 'the essence of American humour consists in speaking lightly of dreadful subjects'.*

What certainly emerges from early American humorous prose is a running streak of violence and cruelty. In fact an element of mild sadism has continued to be a characteristic of American comedy, not only in prose but also in oral jokes and in visual comedy like the violence in the Tom and Jerry movie cartoons, the Three Stooges poking fingers into each other's eyes, and even the Marx Brothers' humiliation of large ladies.

Undoubtedly the most crude and cruel character of the early humour was Sut Lovingood, a lanky lad who was a poor white in the mountains of Tennessee. Sut had a hard, brutish life and his sole pleasures were drinking a lot of corn whisky and playing cruel jokes on the people he lived amongst. His creator, George Washington Harris, was quite a character himself, a Tennessee River steamboat captain—a tough trade in those days—and then a wealthy jewellery-maker and engraver, and finally a writer. He was a belligerent man, violently pro-slavery, and he lived uneasily among the liberal, anti-slavery folk of East Tennessee, which may have encouraged him to release his aggressiveness through his stories.

The Sut Lovingood yarns were afire with Rabelaisian extravagances and were something quite new to American humorous writing, highly regarded when news-papers first published them but argued over ever since; Mark Twain liked them and was indebted to them (many believe Huckleberry Finn to be a watered-down version of the awful Sut) and William Faulkner found them admirable, but others did not; Edmund Wilson wrote of Sut, 'he is a peasant squatting in his own filth'. Nevertheless, the vividness and earthiness of the stories were in the true tradition of the oral story-telling of the old frontier South-West, and Sut resembled Europe's Til Eulenspiegel in the sad uselessness of his life, his one gift the ability to invent sadistic pranks.

The story of Sut and the quilting at Mrs Yardley's is a small masterpiece of ante-bellum humour in spite of its extraordinary bouts of gratuitous violence.

The old frontier social custom of holding a 'quilting' is described realistically: we are told about the various types of quilts; how the girls and women sew happily together knowing that later there will be sweet toddy, hugging, dancing, and men in abundance; and the men are lured with the promise of food, fiddles, girls, and whiskey. The words 'kissin' and 'huggin' seem to be euphemisms for what actually went on. As at Simon Suggs's camp-meeting, there is a heady, sensual atmosphere at the quilting and Sut gives us a transparently erotic description of the advantages to be gained from 'huggin' a young widow.

The language, too, is realistic and it is interesting to find Sut using words and phrases which have changed meaning or become obsolete in England but have survived in the Tennessee mountains: 'disappoint' in its old meaning as used by Samuel Johnson of 'thwart' or 'balk'; 'nigh unto' for 'near', 'as lief be' for 'willingly be'.

The trouble with the extreme realism of the language is that it makes it hard going indeed for most modern readers. The nineteenth century was the period when a great many writers, particularly humorists, were obsessed with trying to reproduce regional dialects phonetically with absolute accuracy. The result, at first glance, is a seemingly impenetrable jungle of hanging apostrophes and unfamiliar syllables to be hacked through.

One solution to the problem is to take a run at it and read the story as fast as possible out loud (and alone):

MRS YARDLEY'S QUILTING

'That's one durn'd nasty muddy job, an' I is jis' glad enuf tu take a ho'n ur two, on the straingth ove hit.'

'What have you been doing, Sut?'

'Helpin tu salt ole Missis Yardley down.'

'What do you mean by that?'

'Fixin her fur rotten cumfurtably, kiverin her up wif sile, tu keep the buzzards frum cheatin the wurms.'

'Oh, you have been helping to bury a woman.'

'That's hit, by golly!... George, did yu know ole Missis Yardley?'

'No.'

'Well, she wer a curious 'oman in her way, an' she wore shiney specks. Now jis' listen: Whenever yu see a ole 'oman ahine a par ove *shiney* specks, yu keep yer eye skinn'd; they am dang'rus in the extreme. Thar is jis' no knowin what they can du ...'

'What caused the death of Mrs Yardley, Sut?'

'Nuffin, only her heart stop't beatin 'bout losin a nine dimunt quilt. True, she got a skeer'd hoss tu run over her, but she'd a-got over that ef a quilt hadn't been mix'd up in the catastrophy. Yu see quilts wer wun ove her speshul gifts; she run strong on the bed-kiver question. Irish chain, star ove Texas, sun-flower, nine dimunt, saw teeth, checkerboard, an' shell quilts; blue, an' white, an' yaller, an' black coverlids, an' callickercumfurts reigned triumphan' 'bout her hous'. They wer packed in drawers, layin in shelfs full, wer hung four dubbil on lines in the lof, packed in chists, piled on cheers, an' were everywhar, even ontu the beds, an' wer changed every bed-makin. She told everybody she cud git to listen tu hit that she ment tu give every durn'd one ove em tu Sal when she got married. Oh, Lordy! what es fat a gal es Sal Yardley cud ever do wif half ove em, an' sleepin wif a husbun at that, is more nor I ever cud see through. Jis' think ove her onder twenty layer ove quilts in July, an' yu in thar too. Gewhillikins! George, look how I is sweatin' now, an' this is December. I'd 'bout as lief be shet up in a steam biler wif a three hundred pound bag ove lard, es tu make a bisiness ove sleepin wif that gal—'twould kill a glass-blower.

'Well, tu cum tu the serious part ove this conversashun, that is how the old quilt-mersheen an' coverlid-loom cum tu stop operashuns on this yeath. She hed narrated hit thru the neighborhood that nex Saterday she'd gin a quiltin—three quilts an' one cumfurt to tie. "Goblers, fiddils, gals, an' whisky", wer the words she sent tu the men-folk, an' more tetchin ur wakenin words never drap'd ofen an 'oman's tongue. She sed tu the gals, "Sweet toddy, huggin, dancin, an' huggers in 'bundance". Them words struck the gals rite in the pit ove the stumick, an' spread a ticklin sensashun bof ways, ontil they scratched their heads wif one han, an' thar heels with tuther.

'Everybody, he an' she, what were baptized b'levers in the righteousnes ove quiltins wer thar, an' hit jis' so happen'd that everybody in them parts, frum fifteen summers tu fifty winters, were unannamus b'levers. Strange, warn't hit? Hit wer the bigges' quiltin ever Missis Yardley hilt, an' she hed hilt hundreds; everybody wer thar, 'scept the constabil an' suckit-rider, two dam easily-spared pussons; the numbers ni ontu even too; jis' a few more boys nur girls; that made hit more exhitin, fur hit gin the gals a chance to kick an squeal a littil, wifout eny risk ove not gittin kissed at all, an' hit gin reasonabil grouns fur a few scrimmages among the he's. Now es kissin an' fightin' am the pepper an' salt ove all soshul getherins, so hit were more espishully wiv this ove ours. Es I swung my eyes over the crowd, George, I thought quiltins, managed in a morril an' sensibil way, truly good things— good fur free drinkin, good fur free eatin, good fur free huggin, good fur free dancin, good fur free fightin, an' goodest ove all fur populatin a country fas'.

'The mornin come, still, saft, sunshiney; cocks crowin, hens singin, birds chirpin, tuckeys gobblin—jis' the day tu sun quilts, kick, kiss, squeal, an' make love.

'All the plow-lines an' clothes-lines wer straiched tu every post an' tree. Quilts purvailed. Durn my gizzard ef two acres roun that ar house warn't jis' one solid quilt, all out a-sunnin, an' tu be seed. They dazzled the eyes, skeered the hosses, gin the wimen the heart-burn, an' perdominated.

'To'ards sundown the he's began tu drap in. Yearnis' needil-drivin commenced tu lose groun, threads broke often, thimbils got los,' an' quilts needed another roll. Gigglin, winkin, whisperin, smoofin ove har, an' gals a-ticklin anuther, wer a-gainin every inch ove groun what the needils los'. Did yu ever notis, George, at all soshul getherins, when the he's begin tu gether, that the young she's begin tu tickil one anuther an' the ole maids swell thar tails, roach up thar backs, an' sharpen thar nails ontu the bed-posts and door jams, an' spit an' groan like cats a-courtin . . . ?

'But then, George, gals an' ole maids haint the things tu fool time away on. Hits widders, by golly, what am the rale sensibil, steady-goin, never-skeerin, never-kickin, willin, sperrited, smoof pacers. They cum clost up tu the hoss-block, standin still wif that purty, silky years playin, an' the naik-veins a-throbbin, an' waits fur the word, which of course yu gives, arter yu finds yer feet well in the stirrup, an' away they moves like a cradil on cushioned rockers, or a spring buggy runnin in damp san'. A tetch ove the bridil, an' they knows yu wants em tu turn, an' they dus hit es willin es ef the idea were thar own. I be dod rabbited ef a man can't 'propriate happiness by the skinful ef he is in contack wif sumbody's widder, an' is smart. Gin me a willin widder, the yeath over: what they don't know, haint worth larnin. They hes all been tu Jamakey an' larnt how sugar's made, an' knows how tu sweeten wif hit; an' by golly, they is always ready tu use hit. All yu hes tu du is tu find the spoon, an' then drink comfort till yer blind. Next to good sperrits an' my laigs, I likes a twenty-five year ole widder, wif roun ankils, an' bright eyes, honestly an' squarly lookin intu yurn, an' sayin as plain es a partrige sez "Bob White", "Don't be afraid ove me; I has been thar; yu know hit ef yu hes eny sense, an' thar's no use in eny humbug, ole feller—cum ahead!"

'Ef yu onderstans widders nater, they ken save yu a power ove troubil, onsartinty, an' time, an' ef yo is enterprisin yu gits mons'rous well paid fur hit. The very soun ove thar littil shoe-heels speak full trainin, an' hes a knowin click as they tap the floor; an' the rustle ove thar dress sez, "I dar yo to ax me."

'When yu hes made up yer mind tu court one, jis' go at hit like hit were a

job ove rail-maulin. Ware yer workin close, use yer common, every-day
moshuns an' words, an' abuv all, fling away yer cinnament ile vial an' burn
all yer love songs. No use in tryin tu fool em, fur they sees plum thru yu, a
durn's sight plainer than they dus thru thar veils. No use in a pasted shut;
she's been thar. No use in borrowin a cavortin fat hoss; she's been thar. No
use in har-dye; she's been thar. No use in cloves, tu kill whisky breff; she's
been thar. No use in buyin clost curtains fur yer bed, fur she has been thar.
Widders am a speshul means, George, fur ripenin green men, killin off weak
ones, an' makin 'ternally happy the soun ones.

'Well, as I sed afore, I flew the track an' got ontu the widders. The fellers
begun tu ride up an' walk up, sorter slow, like they warn't in a hurry, the
durn'd 'saitful raskils, hitchin thar critters tu enythin they cud find. One
red-comb'd, long-spurr'd, dominecker feller, frum town, in a red an' white
gridiron jackid an' patent leather gaiters, hitched his hoss, a wild, skeery,
wall-eyed devil, inside the yard palins, tu a cherry tree lim'. Thinks I, that
hoss hes a skeer intu him big enuf tu run intu town, an' perhaps beyant hit,
ef I kin only tetch him off; so I got intu thinkin.

'One aind ove a long clothes-line, wif nine dimunt quilts ontu hit, were
tied tu the same cherry tree that the hoss wer. I tuck my knife and socked it
thru every quilt, 'bout the middil, an' jis' below the rope, an' tied them thar
wif bark, so they cudent slip. Then I went tu the back aind, an' ontied hit
from the pos,' knottin in a hoe-handil, by the middil, tu keep the quilts from
slippin off ef my bark strings failed, an' laid hit on the groun. Then I went tu
the tuther aind: that wer 'bout ten foot tu spar, a-lyin on the groun arter
tyin tu the tree. I tuck it atwix Wall-eye's hine laigs, an' tied hit fas' tu bof
stirrups, an' then cut the cherry tree lim' betwix his bridil an' the tree, almos'
off. Now, mine yu thar wer two ur three uther ropes full ove quilts atween
me an' the hous', so I were purty well hid frum thar. I jis' tore off a palin
frum the fence, an' tuck hit in bof hans, an' harter raisin hit 'way up
yander, I fotch hit down, es hard es I cud, flatsided to'ards the groun, an' hit
acksidentally happen'd to hit Wall-eye, 'bout nine inches ahead ove the root
ove his tail. Hit landed so hard that hit made my hands tingle, an' then
busted intu splinters. The first thing I did wer tu fell ove mysef, on the same
spot what hit hed hit the hoss. I cudent help duin hit to save my life, an' I
swar I felt sum ove Wall-eye's sensashun, jis' es plain. The fust thing he did,
were tu tare down the lim' wif a twenty foot jump, his head to'ards the hous'.
Thinks I, now yu hev dun hit, yu durn'd wall-eyed fool! tarin down that lim'
wer the beginn ove all the troubil, an' the hoss did hit hissef; my conshuns
felt clar es a mountin spring, an' I were in a frame ove mine tu observe
things es they happen'd, an' they soon begun tu happen purty clost arter
one another rite then, an' thar, an' tharabouts, clean ontu town, thru hit,
an' still wer a-happenin, in the woods beyant thar nigh untu eleven mile
frum ole man Yardley's gate, an' four beyant town.

'The fust line ove quilts he tried tu jump, but broke hit down; the nex one he ran onder; the rope cotch ontu the ho'n ove the saddil, broke at bof ainds, an' went along wif the hoss, the cherry tree lim' an' the fust line ove quilts, what I hed proverdensally tied fas' tu the rope. That's what I calls foresight, George. Right furnint the frunt door he cum in contack wif ole Missis Yardley herself, an' anuther ole 'oman; they wer a-holdin a nine dimunt quilt spread out, a-'zaminin hit, an' a-praisin hits perfeckshuns. The durn'd onmannerly, wall-eyed fool run plum over Missis Yardley, frum ahine, stompt one hine foot through the quilt, takin hit along, a-kickin ontil he made hits corners snap like a whip. The gals screamed, the men hollered wo! an' the ole 'oman were toted intu the hous' limber es a wet string, an' every word she sed wer, "Oh, my preshus nine dimunt quilt!"

'Wall-eye busted thru the palins, an' Dominicker sed 'im, made a mortal rush fur his bitts, wer too late fur them, but in good time for the strings ove flyin quilts, got tangled among em, an' the gridiron jackid patren wer los' tu my sight amung star an' Irish chain quilts; he went frum that quiltin at the rate ove thuty miles tu the hour. Nuffin lef on the lot ove the hole consarn, but a nine biler hat, a par ove gloves, an' the jack ove hearts . . .

'Well arter they'd tuck the ole 'oman up stairs an' camfired her tu sleep, things begun tu work agin. The widders broke the ice, an' arter a littil gigilin, goblin, an' gabblin, the kissin begun. *Smack!*—"Thar, now," a widder sed that. *Pop!*—"Oh, don't!" *Pfip!*—"Oh, yu quit!" *Plosh*—"Go *way* yu awkerd critter, yu kissed me in the eye!" another widder sed that. *Bop!*—"Now yu ar satisfied, I recon, big mouf!" *Vip!*—"That hain't fair!" *Spat!*—"Oh, Lordy, May, cum pull Bill away; he's a-tanglin my har." *Thut!*—"I jis' d-a-r-e yu tu du that agin!" a widder sed that, too. Hit sounded all 'roun that room like poppin co'n in a hot skiller, an' wer pow'ful sujestif.

'Hit kep on ontil I be durn'd ef *my* bristles didn't begin tu rise, an' sumthin like a cold buckshot wud run down the marrow in my back-bone 'bout every ten secons, an' then run up agin, tolerabil hot. I kep a swallerin wif nuthin tu swaller, an' my face felt swell'd; an' yet I were fear'd tu make a bulge. Thinks I, I'll ketch one out tu herself torreckly, an' then I guess we'll rastl. Purty soon Sal Yardley started fur the smoke-'ous, so I jis' gin my head a few short shakes, let down one ove my wings a-trailin, an' sirkiled roun her wif a side twis' in my naik, steppin sidewise, an' a-fetchin' up my hinmos foot wif a sorter jerkin slide at every step. Sez I, "Too coo-took a-too". She onderstood hit, an stopt, sorter spreadin her shoulders. An' jis' es I hed pouch'd out my mouf, an' were reachin forrid wif hit, fur the article hitsef, sumthin interfared wif me, hit did. George, wer yu ever ontu yer hans an' knees, an' let a hell-tarin big, mad ram, wif a ten yard run, but yu yearnis'ly, jis' onst, right squar ontu the pint ove yer back-bone?'

'No, you fool; why do you ask?'

'Kaze I wanted tu know ef yu cud hev a realizin' noshun ove my shock. Hits scarcely worth while tu try tu make yu onderstan the case by words only, onless yu hev been tetched in that way. Gr-eat golly! the fust thing I felt, I tuck hit tu be a back-ackshun yeathquake; an' the fust thing I seed wer my chaw'r terbacker a-flyin over Sal's head like a skeer'd bat. My mouf wer pouch'd out, ready fur the article hitsef, yu know, an' hit went outen the roun hole like the wad outen a pop-gun-thug! an' the fust thing I know'd, I wer a-flyin over Sal's head, too, an' a-gainin on the chaw'r terbacker fast. I were straitened out strait, toes hinemos,' middil fingernails foremos', an' the fust thing I hearn wer, "Yu dam Shanghi!" Great Jerus-a-lam! I lit ontu my all fours jis' in time tu but the yard gate ofen hits hinges, an' skeer loose sum more hosses—kep on in a four-footed gallop, clean acrost the lane afore I cud straiten up, an' yere I cotch up wif my chaw'r terbacker, stickin flat agin a fence-rail. I hed got so good a start that I thot hit a pity to spoil hit, so I jis' jump'd the fence an' tuck thru the orchurd. I tell you I dusted these yere close, fur I tho't hit were arter me.

'Arter runnin a spell, I ventered tu feel roun back thar, fur sum signs ove what hed happened tu me. George, arter two pow'ful hard tugs, I pull'd out the vamp an' sole ove one ove ole man Yardley's big brogans, what he hed los' amung my coat-tails. Dre'full dre'full! Arter I got hit away frum thar, my flesh went fas' asleep, from abuv my kidneys tu my knees; about now, fur the fust time, the idear struck me, what hit wer that hed interfar'd wif me, an' los' me the kiss. Hit wer ole Yardley hed kicked me. I walked fur a month like I wer straddlin a thorn hedge. Sich a shock, at sich a time, an' on sich a place—jis' think ove hit! hit am tremenjus, haint hit? The place feels num, right now.'

'Well, Sut, how did the quilting come out?'

'How the hell du yu 'speck me tu know? I warn't thar eny more.'

George Washington Harris (1814–69), *Sut Lovingood. Yarns Spun by a Nat'ral Born Durn'd Fool* (1867).

'T he *last frontier*, *California and the western seaboard, fell to the humorists about the time of the gold and silver rushes of the forties and fifties.*

One of the most interesting of those West Coast pioneer writers of humour was George Horatio Derby. Derby was originally from the East, a graduate of West Point who became an army officer in the Topographical Bureau, was badly wounded—and disillusioned—in action in Mexico, and was assigned to mapping duties on the Pacific coast. He was well read, witty, a practical joker, and a great favourite with the literary saloon society of San Francisco where he spent his leaves. For fun he began to write humorous pieces for local newspapers, comments and reports supposedly written by 'John Phoenix', or 'Squibob', both highly gullible pseudo-pedants. Friends made a collection of these and published them in a book entitled Phoenixiana *which made a great impact, was reprinted in England and was hailed as a fine example of 'the new humour of the West'.*

*John Phoenix's important contribution to the scheme of things was probably
that his humour, though it could be boisterous enough in keeping with life on the
Barbary Coast, was frequently much more urbane and subtle than most frontier
humour—sometimes even whimsical: Artemus Ward recalled in a book that John
Phoenix once put his frail and aged mother aboard the boat to San Francisco with
the caution: 'Dear mother, be virtuous and you will be happy.'*

*In the subjects he chose for his humour and in his calm and disrespectful style
he laid the foundations of modern humorous journalism and has been called 'the
first of the great modern American humorists'.*

*With the discovery of precious minerals and concern with where the new rail-
roads should best be routed there was a nationwide rage for anything to do with
geology, mining, and technology. New inventions proliferated.*

Even, according to 'John Phoenix', in dentistry:

TUSHMAKER'S TOOTHPULLER

Dr Tushmaker was never regularly bred as a physician or surgeon, but he
possessed naturally a strong mechanical genius and a fine appetite; and
finding his teeth of great service in gratifying the latter propensity, he concluded that he could do more good in the world, and create more real
happiness therein, by putting the teeth of its inhabitants in good order, than
in any other way; so Tushmaker became a dentist. He was the man that first
invented the method of placing small cog-wheels in the back teeth for the
more perfect mastication of food, and he claimed to be the original discoverer
of that method of filling cavities with a kind of putty, which, becoming hard
directly, causes the tooth to ache so grievously that it has to be pulled,
thereby giving the dentist two successive fees for the same job. Tushmaker
was one day seated in his office, in the city of Boston, Massachusetts, when
a stout old fellow, named Byles, presented himself to have a back tooth
drawn. The dentist seated his patient in the chair of torture, and, opening
his month, discovered there an enormous tooth, on the right-hand side,
about as large, as he afterwards expressed it, 'as a small Polyglot Bible'. I
shall have trouble with this tooth, thought Tushmaker, but he clapped on
his heaviest forceps, and pulled. It didn't come. Then he tried the turn-screw,
exerting his utmost strength, but the tooth wouldn't stir. 'Go away from
here,' said Tushmaker to Byles, 'and return in a week, and I'll draw that
tooth for you, or know the reason why.' Byles got up, clapped a handkerchief
to his jaw, and put forth. Then the dentist went to work, and in three days
he invented an instrument which he was confident would pull anything. It
was a combination of the lever, pulley, wheel and axle, inclined plane, wedge
and screw. The castings were made, and the machine put up in the office,
over an iron chair, rendered perfectly stationary by iron rods going down
into the foundations of the granite building. In a week old Byles returned;
he was clamped into the iron chair, the forceps connected with the machine
attached firmly to the tooth, and Tushmaker, stationing himself in the rear,

took hold of a lever four feet in length. He turned it slightly. Old Byles gave a groan and lifted his right leg. Another turn; another groan, and up went the leg again. 'What do you raise your leg for?' asked the doctor. 'I can't help it,' said the patient. 'Well,' rejoined Tushmaker, 'that tooth is bound to come out now.'

He turned the lever clear round with a sudden jerk, and snapped old Byles's head clean and clear from his shoulders, leaving a space of four inches between the severed parts! They had a *post-mortem* examination—the roots of the tooth were found extending down the right side, through the right leg, and turning up in two prongs under the sole of the right foot! 'No wonder', said Tushmaker, 'he raised his right leg.' The jury thought so too, but they found the roots much decayed; and five surgeons swearing that mortification would have ensued in a few months, Tushmaker was cleared on a verdict of 'justifiable homicide'. He was a little shy of that instrument for some time afterward; but one day an old lady, feeble and flaccid, came in to have a tooth drawn, and thinking it would come out very easy, Tushmaker concluded, just by way of variety, to try the machine. He did so, and at the first turn drew the old lady's skeleton completely and entirely from her body, leaving her a mass of quivering jelly in her chair! Tushmaker took her home in a pillow-case. She lived seven years after that, and they called her the 'India-rubber Woman'. She had suffered terribly with the rheumatism, but after this occurrence never had a pain in her bones. The dentist kept them in a glass case. After this, the machine was sold to the contractor of the Boston Custom-house, and it was found that a child of three years of age could, by a single turn of the screw, raise a stone weighing twenty-three tons. Smaller ones were made on the same principle, and sold to the keepers of hotels and restaurants. They were used for boning turkeys. There is no moral to this story whatever, and it is possible that the circumstances may have become slightly exaggerated. Of course, there can be no doubt of the truth of the main incidents.

'John Phoenix' (George Horatio Derby) (1823–61), *Phoenixiana; or, Sketches and Burlesques by John Phoenix* (1855).

Although life was still somewhat primitive in California it was not entirely lacking in culture. Music was particularly enjoyed.

In a piece which anticipates by a century some similarly helpful programme notes made by Robert Benchley in the New Yorker, *'John Phoenix' explains to readers of the San Diego* Herald *some of the subtleties of an imaginative new work by a local composer:*

CRITIQUE OF *THE PLAINS*
PAR JABEZ TARBOX

This glorious composition was produced for the first time in this or any other country by a very full orchestra (the performance taking place immediately after supper) and a chorus composed of the entire Sauer Kraut

Verein, the Wie Gehtes Association, and the Pike Harmonic Society, assisted by Messrs. John Smith and Joseph Brown who held the coats, fanned them, and furnished water during the more overpowering passages.

The Plains does not depend for its success upon its plot, its theme, its school, or its master, for it has very little if any of them, but upon its soul-subduing, all-absorbing, highfaluting effect upon the audience.

The symphony opens upon the wide and boundless plains, Longitude 115 W., Latitude 35° 21′ 03″ N., and about sixty miles from the west bank of the Pitt River. These data are beautifully and clearly expressed by a long-drawn note from an E-flat clairionet. The sandy nature of the soil, sparsely dotted with bunches of cactus and artemesia, the extended view, flat and unbroken to the horizon, save by the rising smoke in the extreme verge from a Piute village, are represented by the bass drum. A few notes on the piccolo call the attention to a solitary antelope picking up mescal beans in the foreground. The sun, having an altitude of 36° 27′, blazes down upon the scene in indescribable majesty. Gradually the sounds roll forth in a song of rejoicing to the God of Day:

> 'Of thy intensity
> 'And great immensity
> 'Now then we sing:
> 'Beholding in gratitude
> 'Thee in this latitude,
> 'Curious thing.'

Which swells out into, 'Hey, Jim along, Jim along, Josey!' Then *decrescendo*, dies away, and dries up.

Suddenly we hear approaching a train from Pike County, consisting of seven families with forty-six wagons, each drawn by thirteen oxen. Each family consists of a man in butternut-colored clothing driving the oxen, a wife in butternut-colored clothing riding in the wagon holding a butternut baby, and seventeen butternut children running promiscuously about the establishment. All are barefooted, dusty, and smell unpleasantly.

All these circumstances are expressed by pretty rapid fiddling for some minutes, winding up with a puff from the orpheclide. It is impossible to misunderstand the description.

Now rises o'er the plains in mellifluous accents the grand Pike County Chorus:

> 'Oh, we'll soon be thar
> 'In the land of gold,
> 'Through the forest old,
> 'O'er the mounting cold,
> 'With spirits bold—
> 'Oh, we come, we come,
> 'And we'll soon be thar.
> 'Gee up, Bolly! Whoo up! Whoo haw!'

The train now encamps. The unpacking of the kettles and mess pans, the unyoking of the oxen, the gathering about the various camp fires, the frizzling of the pork, are so clearly expressed by the music that the most untutored savage could comprehend it. Indeed, so vivid and lifelike was the representation, that a lady sitting near us involuntarily exclaimed aloud, '*Thar! That pork's burning!*' And it was truly interesting to watch the gratified expression of her face when, by a few notes of the guitar, the pan was removed from the fire and the blazing pork extinguished.

This is followed by the beautiful *aria:*

> 'Oh, marm! I want a pancake'

Then that touching *recitative:*

> 'Shet up, or I will spank you!'

To which succeeds a grand *crescendo* movement representing the flight of the child with the pancake, the pursuit of the mother, and the final arrest and summary punishment of the former, represented by rapid and successive strokes of the castanet.

The turning in for the night follows, and the deep and stertorious breathing of the encampment is well given by the bassoon, while the sufferings and trials of an unhappy father with an unpleasant infant are touchingly set forth by the cornet.

The NIGHT ATTACK of the Piutes, the fearful cries of the demonic Indians, the shrieks of the females and children, the rapid and effective fire of the rifles, the stampede of the oxen, their recovery and the final repulse—the Piutes being routed after a loss of thirty-six killed and wounded, while the Pikes lose but one scalp, from an old fellow who wore a wig and lost it in the scuffle. All this is faithfully given and excites the most intense interest in the minds of the hearers.

Then follows the grand chorus:

> 'Oh, We give them fits,
> 'The Injun Piutes.
> 'With our six-shooters—
> 'We give 'em particular fits.'

After which we have a charming *recitative* to a frightened infant, which is really one of the most charming gems in the performance:

> 'Now, dern your skin, *can't* you be easy!'

Morning succeeds. The sun rises magnificently (octavo flute)—breakfast is eaten in a rapid movement on three sharps—the oxen are caught and yoked up, with a small drum and triangle—the watches, purses, and other valuables of the conquered Piutes are stored away in a camp kettle, to a small movement on the piccolo.

The train moves on with a grand chorus:

> 'We'll soon be thar.
> 'Gee up, Bolly! Whoo hup! Whoo haw!
> 'Whup! Whoo haw!
> 'Gee!
> 'Whup! Whoo haw!
> 'Gee!'

The immense expense attending the production of this magnificent work, the length of time required to prepare the chorus, the incredible number of instruments destroyed at each rehearsal, have hitherto prevented Mr Tarbox from placing it before the American public. It has remained for San Diego to show herself superior to her sister cities of the Union in musical taste and appreciation and in high-souled liberality by patronizing this immortal prodigy.

We trust every citizen of San Diego and Vallecetos will listen to it ere it is withdrawn. And if there yet lingers in San Francisco one spark of musical fervor or a remnant of taste for pure harmony, we can only say that the *Southerner* sails from that place to San Diego once a fortnight and that the passage money is but forty-five dollars.

Ibid.

UNTIL 1891 there was no international copyright agreement between America and Great Britain and a brisk trade existed in cheap pirated editions of British novels, to the fury of authors like Charles Dickens who found themselves widely read and famous in the USA but no richer for it.

Although 'book-learning' had been notoriously resisted by frontiersmen it seems that in the pioneer days of California, although the state had only recently been prised away from Mexico and there was no rail link with the rest of America—goods and passengers had to get there by sea round the Cape or by a dangerous stage-coach journey across the Rockies—there seems to have been, surprisingly perhaps, a demand not only for classical music but also for good literature.

As early as 1867 Bret Harte, Californian newspaper columnist and writer of hugely popular 'local colour' poems and short stories—'The Heathen Chinee', 'The Luck of Roaring Camp'—published his first book, a collection of pieces originally written for the San Francisco newspapers, Golden Era and The Californian. It is a measure of how familiar with English novels the newspaper-readers of early San Francisco must have been that Harte's book, which was highly successful, was a collection of literary parodies of classic novels including works by Charles Dickens and Charlotte Brontë. Here is an extract from the beginning of Harte's burlesque of Jane Eyre:

CHAPTER I

As a child I was not handsome. When I consulted the triangular bit of looking-glass which I always carried with me, it showed a pale, sandy, and freckled face, shaded by locks like the colour of sea-weed when the sun strikes it in deep water. My eyes were said to be indistinctive; they were a faint ashen-grey; but above them rose—my only beauty—a high, massive, domelike forehead, with polished temples, like door-knobs of the purest porcelain.

Our family was a family of governesses. My mother had been one, and my sisters had the same occupation. Consequently, when, at the age of thirteen, my eldest sister handed me the advertisement of Mr Rawjester, clipped from that day's *Times*, I accepted it as my destiny. Nevertheless, a mysterious presentiment of an indefinite future haunted me in my dreams that night, as I lay upon my little snow-white bed. The next morning, with two band-boxes tied up in silk handkerchiefs, and a hair trunk, I turned my back upon Minerva Cottage for ever.

CHAPTER II

Blunderbore Hall, the seat of James Rawjester, Esq., was encompassed by dark pines and funereal hemlocks on all sides. The wind sang weirdly in the turrets and moaned through the long-drawn avenues of the park. As I approached the house I saw several mysterious figures flit before the windows, and a yell of demoniac laughter answered my summons at the bell. While I strove to repress my gloomy forebodings, the housekeeper, a timid, scared-looking old woman, showed me into the library.

I entered, overcome with conflicting emotions. I was dressed in a narrow gown of dark serge, trimmed with black bugles. A thick green shawl was pinned across my breast. My hands were encased with black half-mittens worked with steel beads; on my feet were large pattens, originally the property of my deceased grandmother. I carried a blue cotton umbrella. As I passed before a mirror, I could not help glancing at it, nor could I disguise from myself the fact that I was not handsome.

Drawing a chair into a recess, I sat down with folded hands, calmly awaiting the arrival of my master. Once or twice a fearful yell rang through the house, or the rattling of chains, and curses uttered in a deep, manly voice broke upon the oppressive stillness. I began to feel my soul rising with the emergency of the moment.

'You look alarmed, miss. You don't hear anything, my dear, do you?' asked the housekeeper nervously.

'Nothing whatever,' I remarked calmly, as a terrible scream, followed by the dragging of chairs and tables in the room above, drowned for a moment my reply. 'It is the silence, on the contrary, which has made me foolishly nervous.'

The housekeeper looked at me approvingly, and instantly made some tea for me.

I drank seven cups; as I was beginning the eighth, I heard a crash, and the next moment a man leaped into the room through the broken window.

CHAPTER III

The crash startled me from my self-control. The housekeeper bent towards me and whispered:

'Don't get excited. It's Mr Rawjester—he prefers to come in sometimes in this way. It's his playfulness, ha! ha! ha!'

'I perceive,' I said calmly. 'It's the unfettered impulse of a lofty soul breaking the tyrannizing bonds of custom,' and I turned towards him.

He had never once looked at me. He stood with his back to the fire, which set off the Herculean breadth of his shoulders. His face was dark and expressive, his under-jaw squarely formed and remarkably heavy. I was struck with his remarkable resemblance to a Gorilla.

As he absently tied the poker into hard knots with his nervous fingers, I watched him with some interest. Suddenly he turned towards me:

'Do you think I'm handsome, young woman?'

'Not classically beautiful,' I returned calmly; 'but you have, if I may so express myself, an abstract manliness—a sincere and wholesome barbarity which, involving as it does the naturalness'—but I stopped, for he yawned at that moment—an action which singularly developed the immense breadth of his lower jaw—and I saw that he had forgotten me. Presently he turned to the housekeeper:

'Leave us.'

The old woman withdrew with a courtesy.

Mr Rawjester deliberately turned his back upon me and remained silent for twenty minutes. I drew my shawl the more closely around my shoulders and closed my eyes.

'You are the governess?' at length he said.

'I am, sir.'

'A creature who teaches geography, arithmetic, and the use of the globes—ha!—a wretched remnant of femininity—a skimp pattern of girlhood with a premature flavour of tea-leaves and morality. Ugh!'

I bowed my head silently.

'Listen to me, girl!' he said sternly; 'this child you have come to teach—my ward—is not legitimate. She is the offspring of my mistress—a common harlot. Ah! Miss Mix, what do you think of me now?'

'I admire', I replied calmly, 'your sincerity. A mawkish regard for delicacy might have kept this disclosure to yourself. I only recognize in your frankness that perfect community of thought and sentiment which should exist between original natures.'

I looked up; he had already forgotten my presence, and was engaged in pulling off his boots and coat. This done, he sank down in an armchair by the fire, and ran the poker wearily through his hair. I could not help pitying him.

The wind howled fearfully without, and the rain beat furiously against the windows. I crept towards him and seated myself on a low stool beside his chair.

Presently he turned, without seeing me, and placed his foot absently in my lap. I affected not to notice it. But he started and looked down.

'You here yet, Carrothead? Ah, I forgot. Do you speak French?'

'*Oui, Monsieur.*'

'*Taisez-vous!*' he said sharply, with singular purity of accent. I complied. The wind moaned fearfully in the chimney, and the light burned dim. I shuddered in spite of myself. 'Ah, you tremble, girl!'

'It is a fearful night.'

'Fearful! Call you this fearful—ha! ha! ha! Look! you wretched little atom, look! and he dashed forward, and, leaping out of the window, stood like a statue in the pelting storm, with folded arms. He did not stay long, but in a few minutes, he returned by way of the hall chimney. I saw from the way that he wiped his feet on my dress that he had again forgotten my presence.

'You are a governess. What can you teach?' he asked, suddenly and fiercely thrusting his face in mine.

'Manners!' I replied calmly.

'Ha! teach *me!*'

'You mistake yourself,' I said, adjusting my mittens. 'Your manners require not the artificial restraint of society. You are radically polite; this impetuosity and ferociousness is simply the sincerity which is the basis of a proper deportment. Your instincts are moral; your better nature, I see is religious. As St Paul justly remarks—see chap. 6, 8, 9, and 10—'

He seized a heavy candlestick, and threw it at me. I dodged it submissively, but firmly.

'Excuse me, Miss Mix—but I can't stand St Paul. Enough—you are engaged.'

Bret Harte (1839–1902), *Condensed Novels and Other Papers* (1867).

━━━━━━━━━

AMERICAN *writers were not the first to guard their privacy by writing under comical pseudonyms; Sir Walter Scott coined many, including 'Chrystal Croftangry', 'Malachi Malagrowther', and 'Jedediah Cleishbotham'; Thackeray wrote under even more, including 'Charles Yellowplush', 'Mulligan of Kil-*

ballymulligan', and 'Ikey Solomons Jnr', but by the middle of the nineteenth century the practice of writing under bizarre names had become widespread among American humorists. Robert H. Newell wrote satirical pieces about the Government's loony bureaucratic practices under the name 'Orpheus C. Kerr' (which is a pun, a little strained perhaps, on 'office-seeker'). Mortimer Thompson wrote inventive sketches for the New York Tribune *as 'Q. K. Philander Doesticks'. The most successful of those early humorists with comical names was David Ross Locke who wrote as 'Petroleum Vesuvius Nasby'.*

David Ross Locke began as an itinerant printer in Ohio and ended as owner and editor of the Toledo Blade. *He was a campaigning editor, writing powerfully in favour of President Lincoln and the abolition of slavery.*

When the Civil War broke out Locke began a satirical column in his paper purporting to be letters from 'Petroleum V. Nasby', a Copperhead (a Northerner who sympathized with the South). Nasby was presented as a red-nosed, venal, dissolute, illiterate country preacher in the Deep South, violently defending slavery and the Confederacy and on the make for a sinecure job as village postmaster under the Democrats. Nasby was such an offensive bigot that he makes his modern television equivalents, Archie Bunker and Alf Garnett, look like woolly liberals.

The Petroleum V. Nasby letters were immensely successful. It is believed that President Lincoln declared Nasby to be worth a division of infantry to the Union cause, and was fifteen minutes late for a meeting with the English Ambassador, or delayed outlining the Emancipation Proclamation to his cabinet (the legends vary a little) in order to read to them the latest Nasby letter.

Here is a late example of Nasby in action. The piece uses the usual humorous writing tricks like bad grammar and comical (i.e. tortuous) spelling, but Nasby is interestingly autobiographical at the beginning and steadily repellent throughout:

POST OFFIS, CONFEDRIT X ROADS

(wich is in the Stait uv Kentucky),

November 25, 1867.

After many more tribulations, like the Wanderin Jew, I wended my weary way to Kentucky, where, at Confedrit X Roads, I hoped to spend the few remaining years uv my life. Here the glad noos come! The Tyrant Linkin had bin laid low—*halleloogy!* Saint Androo Johnson was elevated where he could reward the Democrisy, wich ever hed bin his troo love, Southern man that he wuz. I wuz happy and contented. Under the Administration uv President Johnson, upon whose head blessins! I wuz at last give the enjoyment uv that end of the hopes uv all Democrats—a post offis! The Post Offis at Confedrit X Roads (wich is in the Stait uv Kentucky) has four saloons within a stone's throw, and a distillery ornamentin the landscape only a quarter uv a mile from where I write these lines, with the ruins of a burnt nigger school house in sight uv my winder.

I wanted nothin more. I hoped to be allowed to live here and thus forever, and when Death should come, he would find me at Bascom's Saloon, enjoying the delightful company uv them wich I am proud to call my friends.

But, alars! It wuz not to be so. I am ever vigilant and have to tare myself loose from comforts and friends when the Democrisy is threatened.

There was trouble in one uv the Southren counties uv Ohio. In a reliably Democratic township in that country is a settlement uv niggers, who, in the old time, ran away from Kentucky, and settled there where they could hev what they earned, wich wuz jest so much swindled out uv Kentucky. Of course, comin from Kentucky, these niggers are, many uv em, as near white as they can be. One uv em who carried with him the name uv his master, and, as he says, father, Lett, is as near a white man as may be, and has married a wench who wuz a shade whiter than he. Ther children are jest a touch whiter than both uv em. Uv these he had three daughters, rangin from sixteen to twenty.

Now this Lett is a disturber. He hed a farm uv perhaps 200 akers, and wuz taxed heavy for school purposes, but his children wuzn't, uv course, allowed to attend the school. None uv the nigger children were. But Lett got the idea into his head that there wuzn't no propriety in his payin taxes without enjoyin the benefits arizin from em, and aided and abetted by other niggers, who were wicked enough to complain uv paying taxes to the support uv white schools, he sent his daughters to the school, directin em to present themselves boldly, take their seats quietly, and study perseverinly. They did so. The schoolmarm, who wuz a young huzzy from Noo Hampsheer, where they persecute the saints, gave em seats and put em into classes—think uv that!—with white children.

There wuz trouble in that township. I wuz sent for to-wunst, and gladly I come. I wuz never so gratified in my life. Hed smallpox broken out in that school, there wouldn't hev bin half the eggscitement in the township. It wuz the subjick uv universal talk everywhere, and the Democrisy was a bilin like a pot.

I met the trustees uv the township, and demanded if they intended tamely to submit to this outrage? I askt em if they intended to hev their children set side by side with the children uv Ham, who in the Bible wuz condemned to a position uv inferiority forever? Can you, I askt, so degrade yourselves, and so blast the self-respect uv your children?

And, bilin up with indignashen, they answered, 'Never' and yoon-animously requested me to accompany em to the school house, that they might expel these disgustin beings who hed obtrooded themselves among those uv superior race.

On the way to the school house, wich wuz perhaps a mile distant, I askt the Board if they knowed these girls by sight. No, they replied, they hed never seed em. 'I hev bin told,' said I, 'that they are nearly white.'

'They are,' said one uv em. 'Quite white.'

'It matters not,' said I. 'There is somethin in the nigger at wich the instink of the white man absolootely rebels, and from wich it instinktively recoils. So much experience hev I had with em, that put me in a dark room with one uv em, no matter how little nigger there is in em, and that unerrin instink would betray em to me, wich, by the way, goes to prove that the dislike we hev to em is not the result of prejudis, but is part uv our very nacher, and one uv its highest and holiest attriboots.'

Thus communin, we entered the school house. The schoolmarm wuz there, as bright and as crisp as a Janooary mornin. The scholars wuz ranged on the seats, a studyin as rapidly as possible.

'Miss,' said I, 'we are informed that three nigger wenches, daughters uv one Lett, a nigger, is in this school, a-minglin with our daughters as a ekal. Is it so?'

'The Misses Lett are in this school,' said she, 'and I am happy that they are among my best pupils.'

'Miss,' said I sternly, 'pint em out to us!'

'Wherefore?' says she.

'That we may bundle em out!' said I.

'Bless me!' said she. 'I reely couldn't do that. Why expel em?'

'Because,' said I, 'no nigger shel contaminate the white children uv this districk. No such disgrace shel be put onto em.'

'Well,' said this aggravatin schoolmarm, wich was from Noo Hampsheer, 'you put em out.'

'But show me wich they are,' said I.

'Can't you detect em, sir?' said she. 'Don't their color betray em? If they are so near white that you can't detect em at a glance, it strikes me that it can't hurt very much to let em stay.'

I wuz sorely puzzled. There wuzn't a girl in the room that looked at all niggery. But my reputashen wuz at stake. Noticin three girls setting together who wuz somewhat dark complected and whose black hair waved, I went for em and shoved em out.

Here the tragedy okkerred. At the door I met a man who rode four miles in his zeal to assist us. He had always hed an itchin to pitch into a nigger, and as he could do it now safely, he proposed not to lose the chance. I wuz a-putting the girls out, and hed jest dragged em to the door, when I met him entering in.

'What is this?' he said, with a surprised look.

'We're puttin out these cussed wenches, who is contaminatin your children and mine,' said I. 'Ketch hold uv that disgustin one yonder!' said I.

'Wenches!' said he. 'You damned scoundrel! Them are my girls!'

And without waiting for an explanashen, the infooriated monster sailed into me, the schoolmarm laying over one of the benches explodin in laughter. The three girls assisted their parent, and between em, in about four minutes, I wuz insensible. One uv the trustees, pityin my woes, took me to the nearest railrod station, and somehow, how I know not, I got home.

When the Almighty made niggers, he ought to hev made em so that mixin with the sooperior race would hev bin an impossibility. I write these lines propped up in bed at my boarding house, my face beaten to a jelly, and perfectly kivered with stickin plaster. My nose, always the beauty and glory uv my face, is enlarged to twice its fair proportions. My lips resemble sausages. My left ear is forever no more, and what little hair was a-hangin around my venerable temples is gone—my head is as bald as a billiard ball, and twict its normal size . . .

I hev only to say that when I go on sech a trip again, I shel require as condishen precedent that the Afrikins to be put out shel hev enuff Afrikin into em to prevent sech mistakes. But, good Lord, what haven't I suffered in this cause?

PETROLEUM V. NASBY, P.M.

(wich is Postmaster).

David Ross Locke (1833–88), Column in Toledo *Blade* (1867).

═══════════

ANOTHER *humorist much admired by Abraham Lincoln was Charles Farrar Browne. Beginning like so many others as a wandering printer, he began to be noticed as a writer when, for the* Cleveland Plain Dealer, *he invented the character of 'Artemus Ward', a travelling showman who was illiterate but full of Down East gumption and cheerful contempt for sentimentality and pretension.*

Charles Farrar Browne transformed misspelling and bad grammar from devices to indicate a character's lack of education into a comic art. It was how Artemus Ward expressed himself rather than what happened to him that made him a unique figure in American humour; his prose is lean but alive with colloquial aphorisms, literary and historical references which are not quite right but do their job, and good old backwoods horse sense.

America had then, and still has, a highly organized system of lecture circuits, and the old 'lyceum tours' proved to be a valuable source of income to those writers who were at ease on a stage. Before the Civil War the lyceums were a popular source of self-education and the most sought-after lecturers were writers with something serious to say. Ralph Waldo Emerson, for instance, proclaimed 'the lyceum is my podium' and earned most of his income from lecturing. When his lectures became too familiar on the circuit he passed them on to his printer to be published as essays.

After the Civil War the public taste turned from education to entertainment and the lectures on Science and Morality gave way to Swiss bell-ringers and personal appearances of such popular comical figures as Petroleum V. Nasby and Artemus Ward.

Charles Farrar Browne managed to transfer Artemus Ward from page to podium with brilliant success and his 'moral lectures' drew full houses wherever he went.

No longer able to get laughs from his adroit use of misspelling, he filled the gap by giving Artemus Ward a curiously lugubrious manner and a mock-pompous attitude which was in contrast to his manifest incompetence. In effect the appearances were hilarious send-ups of the 'improving' lectures so familiar to lyceum audiences.

In 1866 he went to England where his comic lectures were if anything even more popular. He contributed regularly to Punch, *and was hailed as 'America's first national humorist'. The following year his lungs collapsed and he died at Southampton, aged 33.*

The lecture which was such a success in England was 'Artemus Ward among the Mormons', the story of a trip he had once made to Utah. The lecture was based upon the following prose account of his visit. When published it had delighted his readers and infuriated the Mormons:

A VISIT TO BRIGHAM YOUNG

It is now goin on 2(too) yeres, as I very well remember, since I crossed the Planes for Kaliforny, the Brite land of Jold. While crossin the Planes all so bold I fell in with sum noble red men of the forest (N.B.—this is rote Sarcasticul. Injins is Pizin, whar ever found), which thay Sed I was their Brother, & wanted for to smoke the Calomel of Peace with me. Thay then stole my jerkt beef, blankits, etsettery, skalpt my origin grinder, & scooted with a Wild Hoop. Durin the Cheaf's techin speech he sed he shood meet me in the Happy Huntin Grounds. If he duz, thare will be a fite. But enuff of this ere. Reven Noose Muttons, as our skoolmaster, who has got Talent into him, cussycally obsarve.

I arrove at Salt Lake in doo time. At Camp Scott there was a lot of U.S. sogers, hosstensibly sent out thare to smash the Mormins, but really to eat Salt vittles & play poker & other beautiful but sumwhat onsartin games. I got acquainted with sum of the officers. Thay lookt putty scrumpshus in their Bloo coats with brass buttings onto um & ware very talented drinkers, but so fur as fitin is consarned I'd willingly put my wax figgers agin the hull party.

My desire was to exhibit my grate show in Salt Lake City, so I called on Brigham Yung, the grate mogull among the Mormins, and axed his permishun to pitch my tent and onfurl my banner to the jentle breezis. He lookt at me in a austeer manner for a few minits, and said:—

'Do you bleeve in Solomon, Saint Paul, the immaculateness of the Mormin Church and the Latter-day Revelashuns?'

Sez I, 'I'm on it!' I make it a pint to get along plesunt, tho I didn't know what under the Son the old feller was drivin at. He sed I mite show.

'You air a marrid man, Mister Yung, I bleeve?' sez I, preparin to rite him some free parsis.

'I hev eighty wives, Mister Ward. I sertinly am marrid.'

'How do you like it as far as you hev got?' sed I.

He sed 'middlin', and axed me wouldn't I like to see his famerly, to which I replide that I wouldn't mind minglin with the fair Seck & Barskin in the winnin smiles of his interestin wives. He accordinly tuk me to his Scareum. The house is powerful big, & in a exceedin large room was his wives & children, which larst was squawkin and hollerin enuff to take the roof rite orf the house. The wimin was of all sizes and ages. Sum was pretty & sum was Plane—sum was helthy and sum was on the Wayne—which is verses, the sich was not my intentions, as I don't 'prove of puttin verses in Proze rittins, tho ef occashun requires I can Jerk a Poim ekal to any of them Atlantic Munthly fellers.

'My wives, Mister Ward,' sed Yung.

'Your sarvant, marms,' sed I, as I sot down in a cheer which a red-heded female brawt me . . .

'Besides these wives you see here, Mister Ward,' said Yung, 'I hav eighty more in varis parts of this consecrated land which air Sealed [bound to a male Mormon as one of his 'spiritual wives'] to me.'

'Which?' sez I, getting up & staring at him.

'Sealed, Sir! sealed.'

'Whare bowts?' sez I.

'I sed, Sir, that they was sealed!' He spoke in a tragerdy voice.

'Will they probly continner on in that stile to any grate extent, Sir?' I axed.

'Sir,' sed he, turning as red as a biled beet, 'don't you know that the rules of our Church is that I, the Profit, may hev as meny wives as I wants?'

'Jes so,' I sed. 'You are old pie, ain't you?'

'Them as is Sealed to me—that is to say, to be mine when I wants um— air at present my sperretooul wives,' sed Mister Yung.

'Long may they wave' sez I, seein I shood git into a scrape ef I didn't look out.

In a privit conversashun with Brigham I learnt the following fax: It takes him six weeks to kiss his wives. He don't do it only onct a yere, & sez it is wuss nor cleanin house. He don't pretend to know his children, thare is so many of um, tho they all know him. He sez about every child he meats call him Par, & he takes it for grantid it is so. His wives air very expensiv. They allers want suthin & ef he don't buy it for um they set the house in a uproar. He sez he don't have a minit's peace. His wives fite among theirselves so much that he has bilt a fiting room for thair speshul benefit, & when too of 'em get into a row he has em turned loose into that place, where the dispoot is settled accordin to the rules of the London prize ring. Sumtimes thay abooz hisself individooally. Thay hev pulled the most of his hair out at the roots & he wares meny a horrible scar upon his body, inflicted with mop-handles, broom-sticks, and sich. Occashunly they git mad & scald him with biling hot water. When he got eny waze cranky thay'd shut him up in a dark closit, previshly whippin him arter the stile of muthers when thare orfspring git onruly. Sumtimes when he went in swimmin thay'd go to the banks of the Lake & steal all his close, thereby compellin him to sneek home by a sir-cootius rowt, drest in the Skanderlus stile of the Greek Slaiv. 'I find that the keers of a marrid life way hevy onto me,' sed the Profit, '& sometimes I wish I'd remaned singel.' I left the Profit and startid for the tavern whare I put up to. On my way I was overtuk by a lurge krowd of Mormins, which they surroundid me & statid they were goin into the Show free.

'Wall,' sez I, 'ef I find a individooal who is going round letting folks into his show free, I'll let you know.'

'We've had a Revelashun biddin us go into A. Ward's Show without paying nothin!' thay showted.

'Yes,' hollered a lot of femaile Mormonesses, ceasin me by the cote tales & swingin me round very rapid, 'we're all going in free! So sez the Revelashun!'

'What's Old Revelashun got to do with my show?' sez I, getting putty rily. 'Tell Mister Revelashun,' sed I, drawin myself up to my full hite and lookin round upon the ornery krowd with a proud & defiant mean, 'tell Mister Revelashun to mind his own bizness, subject only to the Konstitushun of the United States!'

'Oh, now, let us in, that's a sweet man,' said several femailes, puttin thare arms round me in luvin style. 'Become 1 of us. Becum a Preest & hav wives Sealed to you.'

'Not a Seal!' sez I, startin back in horror at the idee.

'Oh stay, Sir, stay,' sed a tall gawnt femaile, ore whoos hed 37 summirs hev parsd, 'stay, & I'll be your Jentle Gazelle.'

'Not ef I know it, you won't,' sez I. 'Awa, you skanderlus femaile, awa! Go and be a Nunnery!' *That's what I sed*, JES SO.

'& I,' sed a fat, chunky femaile, who must hav wade more than too hundred lbs., 'I will be your sweet gidin Star!'

Sez I, 'Ile bet two dollars and a half you won't!' Whare ear I may Rome Ile still be troo 2 thee, Oh Betsy Jane! (N.B.—Betsy Jane is my wife's Sir naime.)

'Wiltist though not tarry here in the promist Land?' sed several of the meserabil critters.

'Ile see you all essenshally cussed be 4 I wiltist!' roared I, as mad as I cood be at thare infernal noncents. I girdid up my Lions & fled the Seen. I packt up my duds & Left Salt Lake, which is a 2nd Soddum & Germorrer, inhabitid by as theavin & onprincipled a set of retchis as ever drew Breth in eny spot on the Globe.

Charles Farrar Browne (1834–67), *Artemus Ward: His Book* (1862).

CHARLES FARRAR BROWNE *wrote his first piece at the age of 17 for the journal which he was helping to print, the Boston humorous weekly* The Carpet-Bag. *Besides launching Browne as an author, the 1 May 1852 edition of* The Carpet-Bag *also contained the first published prose of 'John Phoenix' and the first published story from the pen of a 16-year-old boy, Samuel L. Clemens.*

Although The Carpet-Bag *only managed to keep going for two years it played an important part in providing a link between the old, pre-Civil War frontier humour and the new humour which young writers were contributing. Its printer, editor, and occasional contributor was Benjamin Penhallow Shillaber, the creator of a famous and much-beloved comic character, Mrs Partington.*

The good Mrs Partington, whom Shillaber admitted he named for no particular reason after the Revd Sydney Smith's Mrs Partington who failed to hold the Atlantic Ocean back with a broom, was a kindly Yankee village lady, addicted to cat-nip tea and almanacs, who chattered away on all manner of subjects with happy ignorance.

Three books of Mrs Partington's sayings were published. Here is a random selection of the sort of remarks which made her famous. The point about Mrs Partington, of course, is that she is the American version of Mrs Malaprop:

She remarked to us, quite recently, that there were so many intimations of her now-a-days she hardly knew how to indemnify herself.

She prefers the Venus de Medicine to any other statute she knows of.

That Ike, who has just returned from France, 'speaks French like a Parishioner'.

'Here's Dr. Johnson's Dictionary,' said Mrs Partington, as she handed it to Ike; 'study it contentively, and you will gain a great deal of inflammation.'

'I am not so young as I was once, and I don't believe I shall ever be, if I live to the age of Samson, which, heaven knows as well as I do, I don't want to, for I wouldn't be a centurion or an octagon and survive my factories and become idiomatic by any means. But then there is no knowing how a thing will turn out until it takes place, and we shall come to an end some day, though we may never live to see it.'

Benjamin Penhallow Shillaber (1814–90), *Life and Sayings of Mrs Partington* (1854).

✒ Mrs Partington was the inspiration for Tom's Aunt Polly in Mark Twain's *Tom Sawyer*.

Another development was the rise of the 'paragraphist', the writer who could express his humour in a single paragraph or a brief piece only one or two paragraphs long.

Almanacs, both serious and comic, Christmas annuals, gift books, all sold in vast numbers and needed humorous paragraphs as fillers, and self-contained paragraphs became an increasingly conspicuous feature in newspaper columns and magazines. The art of writing short, pithy humorous paragraphs, which was probably perfected by early Punch *writers, seemed to fall easily to American pens. It is still practised with most wit and finesse in the* New Yorker *but is now a universal technique.*

One of the most popular of the pioneer American paragraphists was Henry Wheeler Shaw. 'With me', he once said, 'everything must be put in two or three lines.'

Shaw had drifted around as a riverboat captain, farmer, and estate agent until at the age of 42 he settled in New York State as an auctioneer and began to write bits for local newspapers. The fame and prosperity of 'Artemus Ward' as a humorist and lecturer impressed him and he decided to follow the same path. He invented a character, 'Josh Billings', a Yankee cracker-box philosopher abrim with home-spun aphorisms and bucolic wit, and set about writing short paragraphs, ostensibly by 'Josh Billings', with the same kind of humorous misspelling that 'Artemus Ward' was using so effectively. It worked. Shaw struck gold. His pieces were collected into several highly successful books, he lectured most profitably, and for eleven years he published his annual Farmer's Allminax.

Some of the Josh Billings pieces are very brief indeed:

FOUND

A Malteese soprano kat, about 12 months old, singing old hundred on a picket fence, late last thursda nite, whichever persons owns sed kat will find him (or her, according to circumstancis) in a vakant lot, just bak ov our hous, still butiful in death.

WOMAN

Woman iz the glass ware ov kreashun. She iz luvly, and brittle, but she hez run up everything we really enjoy in this life from 25 cents to par. Adam, without Eve, would hav been az stupid a game az playing checkures alone. There haz been more butiful things sed in her praze than thare haz ov enny other animate thing, and she iz worthy ov them all. She is not an angell tho, and i hope she wont never go into the angell bizness. Angells on earth dont pay. The only mistake that woman haz ever made iz to think she iz a better man than Adam.

Perhaps the most popular of all the Josh Billings paragraphs were those describing animals:

THE BELLICOSE GOAT

The goat iz a coarse wollen sheep, with a cracked voice and a sanguine digestion. They had rather steal a rotten turnip out ov a garbage barrell than cum honestly bi a peck of oats. They strike from the hed insted ov the shoulder, and are az likely tew hit the mark az a bumblebee iz. They are faithfull kritters in the hour ov adversity, and will stick tew a man az long az he lives in a shanty. They kan klimb evrything but a greased pole, and are alwus poor in the boddy. What they eat seems tew all go tew appetight. A phatt goat would be a literary curiosity.

THE BRINY CODFISH

The codfish iz the fruit ov the oshun, which accounts for their being so salt.
They are good eating for a wet day; they are better than an umbreller to
keep a man dry. They want a good deal ov freshning before they are eaten,
and want freshning a good deal afterwards. If i can have plenty ov codfish
for breakfast, i can generally manage tew make the other two meals out of
cold water.

Henry Wheeler Shaw (1818–85), *Josh Billings, His Sayings* (1865).

A CURIOUS *form of short prose piece which became hugely popular after
the Civil War and lasted well into the present century was the humorous
fable.*

*The fable's appeal to writers was clearly its flexibility of length as a filler for a
newspaper column and its convenience as a form; it accommodated any humorous
writing style from rustic ignorance to mock pedantry, and its formal shape, with
its concluding 'moral', made it a relatively easy vehicle for satirical or amusing
comment.*

*Like the fables of the ancients, most of the post-Civil War American fables were
about animals.*

*One of the earliest of the humorous fable writers was George Thomas Lanigan, a
Canadian journalist who moved across the border and eventually worked for the
New York* World *and Philadelphia* Record. *Lanigan's touch was light and urbane.
Once, on reading in a London newspaper that somebody (or something) called the
Akhoond of Swat had died, he sat down and wrote a famous threnody on the
departed which concluded with the memorable couplet:*

'The Akhoond of Swat
is not!'

Here is a brace of Lanigan's odd, off-beat fables:

THE OSTRICH AND THE HEN

An Ostrich and a Hen chanced to occupy adjacent apartments, and the
former complained loudly that her rest was disturbed by the cackling of her
humble neighbour. 'Why is it,' he finally asked the Hen, 'that you make such
an intolerable noise?' The Hen replied, 'Because I have laid an egg.' 'Oh no,'
said the Ostrich, with a superior smile, 'it is because you are a Hen, and
don't know any better.'

Moral.—The moral of the foregoing is not very clear, but it contains some
reference to the Agitation for Female Suffrage.

THE FOX AND THE CROW

A Crow, having secured a Piece of Cheese, flew with its Prize to a lofty Tree, and was preparing to devour the Luscious Morsel, when a crafty Fox, halting at the foot of the Tree, began to cast about how he might obtain it. 'How tasteful,' he cried, in well-feigned Ecstasy, 'is your Dress! It cannot surely be that your Musical Education has been neglected. Will you not oblige—?' 'I have a horrid Cold,' replied the Crow, 'and never sing without my Music, but since you press me—At the same time, I should add that I have read Aesop, and been there before.' So saying, she deposited the Cheese in a safe Place on the Limb of the Tree, and favoured him with a Song. 'Thank you', exclaimed the Fox, and trotted away, with the Remark that Welsh Rabbits never agreed with him, and were far inferior in Quality to the animate Variety.

Moral.—The foregoing Fable is supported by a whole Gatling Battery of Morals. We are taught (1) that it Pays to take the Papers; (2) that Invitation is not Always the Sincerest Flattery; (3) that a Stalled Rabbit with Contentment is better than No Bread, and (4) that the Aim of Art is to Conceal Disappointment.

George Thomas Lanigan (1845–86), *Fables by G. Washington Aesop* (1878).

A POPULAR *humorist who used the fable form with great success at the turn of the century was George Ade, warmly recommended by S. J. Perelman as 'undoubtedly one of the greatest humorists, if not the most outstanding, America has yet come up with'.*

Ade was from Indiana but wrote for newspapers in Chicago. His particular contribution to humour—apart from continually coming up with lines of the quality of 'the music teacher came twice each week to bridge the awful gap between Dorothy and Chopin', and 'she was a town-and-country soprano of the kind often used to augment grief at a funeral'—was his ability to reproduce slang in print. For the first time readers could read how ordinary Americans actually spoke:

THE PROFESSOR WHO WANTED TO BE ALONE

Now it happens that in America a man who goes up hanging to a Balloon is a Professor.

One day a Professor, preparing to make a Grand Ascension, was sorely pestered by Spectators of the Yellow-Hammer Variety, who fell over the Stay-Ropes or crowded up close to the Balloon to ask Fool Questions. They wanted to know how fur up he Calkilated to go and was he Afeerd and how often had he did it. The Professor answered them in the Surly Manner peculiar to Showmen accustomed to meet a Web-Foot Population. On the Q.T. the

Prof. had Troubles of his own. He was expected to drop in at a Bank on the following Day and take up a Note for 100 Plunks. The ascension meant 50 to him, but how to Corral the other 50? That was the Hard One.

This question was in his Mind as he took hold of the Trapeze Bar and signaled the Farm Hands to let go. As he trailed Skyward beneath the buoyant silken Bag he hung by his Knees and waved a glad Adieu to the Mob of Inquisitive Yeomen. A Sense of Relief came to him as he saw the Crowd sink away in the Distance.

Hanging by one Toe, and with his right Palm pressed to his Eyes, he said: 'Now that I am Alone, let me Think, let me Think.'

There in the Vast Silence He Thought.

Presently he gave a sigh of Relief.

'I will go to my Wife's Brother and make a Quick Touch,' he said. 'If he refuses to Unbelt I will threaten to tell his Wife of the bracelet he bought in Louisville.'

Having reached this Happy Conclusion, he loosened the Parachute and quickly descended to the Earth.

Moral: Avoid Crowds

THE NINNY WHO SWAM AWAY FROM THE LIFE PRESERVER

Once there was a Citizen who put in most of his Time acting as Custodian of a Thirst.

He could inhale through a Straw, bury his Nose in it or leave it flow from the Original Package.

After he had bombarded the Innards with Aqua Fortis for a matter of 20 years, he awoke one Morning suffering from a combination of Pin-Wheels, Moving-Pictures and a General Alarm of Fire.

Doc came in answer to a Hurry-Up and found that he was on the Job about 8 years too late.

The Patient had something like 15 Things the matter with him ranging from Cirrhosis of the Liver to Water on the Brain, although the latter did not sound Reasonable.

He had six Weeks in which to settle up his Affairs before receiving the Wreaths and Pillows.

During that time he chopped on the Fire-Water because he somewhat blamed the Old Stuff for sending him away at 42 when he might have stuck around to be 87.

His Pals came to see him just before he winked out.

They found him very white and drawn and sort of Aghast at the Record he had established.

After the funeral the Pall-Bearers took off many Dark Gloves and flew at the High Balls.

One of them expresses the Opinion that what killed Jim was cutting out the Stimulants. The Shock was too much for him.

All the other Diagnosticians nodded their heads gravely.

And the host went to the Cellar for another Load.

Moral: It is absolutely Harmless unless Discontinued.

George Ade (1866–1944), Fables in Slang (1899).

A DIFFERENT *use of the fable form was made by Ambrose Bierce, a powerful force in Pacific Coast journalism and perhaps the first humorous columnist to get away with insisting that not a word of his copy be altered or deleted.*

Bierce was a brilliant but strange man; he had been severely wounded in the head during the Civil War and might have become slightly unhinged. He was tall and lean and looked less like an American than a French cartoonist's idea of an English milord. Bierce's fables, written for various newspapers under his pseudonym 'Dod Grile', were a useful vehicle for Bierce's peculiar, macabre humour:

OFFICER AND THUG

A Chief of Police who had seen an Officer beating a Thug was very indignant, and said he must not do so any more on pain of dismissal.

'Don't be too hard on me,' said the Officer, smiling; 'I was beating him with a stuffed club.'

'Nevertheless,' persisted the Chief of Police, 'it was a liberty that must have been very disagreeable, though it may not have hurt. Please do not repeat it.'

'But,' said the Officer, still smiling, 'it was a stuffed Thug.'

In attempting to express his gratification the Chief of Police thrust out his right hand with such violence that his skin was ruptured at the arm-pit and a stream of sawdust poured from the wound. He was a stuffed Chief of Police.

CAT AND KING

A Cat was looking at a King, as permitted by the proverb.

'Well,' said the monarch, observing her inspection of the royal person, 'how do you like me?'

'I can imagine a King,' said the Cat, 'whom I should like better.'

'For example?'

'The King of Mice.'

The sovereign was so pleased with the wit of the reply that he gave her permission to scratch his Prime Minister's eyes out.

Ambrose Bierce (1842–1913?).

The date of Ambrose Bierce's death has a query attached to it because in 1913 it seems he became disillusioned with American civilization, walked into the Mexican jungle and did not come out again. His fate is unknown.

Before seeking what he called 'the good kind darkness' he had collected his work into twelve volumes. He had also assembled a book of cynical and sardonic definitions with which he had spiced his columns during his years in California. He called it The Devil's Dictionary. *In this he berated the great many things which he detested. These included the Common Man ('a lout of the stables'), Socialism, railways, religion, the United States ('universal blank of ignorance, crudity, conceit, tobacco-chewing, ill-dressing, unmannerly manners and general barbarity'), and women.*

Bierce was an important humorist in that his degree of bitterness, his élitist contempt for the ordinary, and his cosmopolitan, erudite style of writing were not only unusual in American humour of that period but a foretaste of the direction in which some of it was going to go in the future.

Here is a sampler of definitions from The Devil's Dictionary:

ABSTAINER, *n.* A weak person who yields to the temptation of denying himself a pleasure.

AFFECTIONATE, *adj.* Addicted to being a nuisance. The most affectionate creature in the world is a wet dog.

BANG, *v.t.* The cry of a gun. The arrangement of a woman's hair which suggests the thought of shooting her: hence the name.

BELLADONNA, *n.* In Italian a beautiful lady; in English a deadly poison. A striking example of the essential identity of the two tongues.

BORE, *n.* A person who talks when you wish him to listen.

BRANDY, *n.* A cordial composed of one part thunder-and-lightning, one part remorse, two parts bloody murder, one part death-hell-and-the-grave, two parts clarified Satan and four parts Holy Moses.

CHEMISE, *n.* Don't know what it means.

CHOP, *n.* A piece of leather skilfully attached to a bone and administered to the patients at restaurants.

DEBAUCHEE, *n.* One who has so earnestly pursued pleasure that he has had the misfortune to overtake it.

MACARONI, *n.* An Italian food made in the form of a slender, hollow tube. It consists of two parts—the tubing and the hole, the latter being the part that digests.

RHUBARB, *n.* Vegetable essence of stomach ache.

RED-SKIN, *n.* A North-American Indian, whose skin is not red—at least on the outside.

SAINT, *n*. A dead sinner revised and edited.

> *The Devil's Dictionary* (1911). Originally published as *The Cynic's Word Book* (1906).

A MERICAN *humour was by no means isolated from Europe. There was a constant interchange of both authors and humorous prose.* Punch *was popular and was widely imitated in America, and before a copyright agreement was reached between Britain and America, books by British novelists were systematically pirated in vast numbers. Many American writers, including Washington Irving, Nathaniel Hawthorne, and Thomas Chandler Haliburton ('Sam Slick') had careers which took them to England. Charles Farrar Browne ('Artemus Ward') was a hit in England with his comedy lectures and contributions to* Punch, *and Ambrose Bierce was a successful freelance humorous writer in England, no mean achievement.*

Not only Britain enjoyed American humour. It was widely read in most English-speaking countries and even had a following in Scandinavia; between 1878 and 1879 a three-volume anthology of current American humour was translated into Swedish by three writers, one of whom was—of all people—August Strindberg.

One internationally famous American post-bellum humorist was Edgar Wilson 'Bill' Nye, who was also, for a time, the most popular newspaper humorist in the United States. Nye was a poor boy from Maine. He drifted about doing odd jobs, taught in a school, practised law in Laramie, Wyoming, then becoming Laramie's postmaster. He began writing little dry, rather sardonic sketches of small-town life for local newspapers and suddenly found himself a success, his column reprinted throughout the United States.

Here is the sort of thing which he did better than anybody of his day. It is from his column in the Laramie Boomerang.

His success as a humorous journalist enabled him to give up his job of running the local post-office.

As the position of postmaster is a political appointment, Bill Nye writes a suitably formal and dignified letter of resignation to his ultimate employer:

A RESIGN

Post-office Divan, Laramie City, W.T.,
Oct. 1, 1883.

TO THE PRESIDENT OF THE UNITED STATES:

Sir.—I beg leave at this time to officially tender my resignation as postmaster at this place, and in due form to deliver the great seal and the key to the front door of the office. The safe combination is set on the numbers 33, 66 and 99, though I do not remember at this moment which comes first, or how many times you revolve the knob, or which direction you should turn it at first in order to make it operate.

There is some mining stock in my private drawer in the safe, which I have not yet removed. This stock you may have, if you desire it. It is a luxury, but you may have it. I have decided to keep a horse instead of this mining stock. The horse may not be so pretty, but it will cost less to keep him.

You will find the postal cards that have not been used under the distributing table, and the coal down in the cellar. If the stove draws too hard, close the damper in the pipe and shut the general delivery window.

Looking over my stormy and eventful administration as postmaster here, I find abundant cause for thanksgiving. At the time I entered upon the duties of my office the department was not yet on a paying basis. It was not even self-sustaining. Since that time, with the active co-operation of the chief executive and the heads of the department, I have been able to make our postal system a paying one, and on top of that I am now able to reduce the tariff on average-sized letters from three cents to two.

Through all the vicissitudes of a tempestuous term of office I have safely passed. I am able to turn over the office today in a highly improved condition, and to present a purified and renovated institution to my successor.

Acting under the advice of Gen. Hatton, a year ago, I removed the feather bed with which my predecessor, Deacon Hayford, had bolstered up his administration by stuffing the window, and substituted glass. Finding nothing in the book of instructions to postmasters which made the feather bed a part of my official duties, I filed it away in an obscure place and burned it in effigy, also in the gloaming. This act maddened my predecessor to such a degree, that he then and there became a candidate for justice of the peace on the Democratic ticket. The Democratic party was able, however, with what aid it secured from the Republicans, to plow the old man under to a degree.

It was not long after I had taken my official oath before an era of unexampled prosperity opened for the American people. The price of beef rose to a remarkable altitude, and other vegetables commanded a good figure and a ready market. We then began to make active preparations for the introduction of the strawberry-roan two-cent stamps and the black-and-tan postal note. One reform has crowded on the heels of another, until the country is today upon the foam-crested waves of permanent prosperity.

Mr President, I cannot close this letter without thanking yourself and the heads of departments at Washington for your active, cheery and prompt co-operation in these matters. I need not say that I herewith transmit my resignation with great sorrow and genuine regret. We have toiled on together month after month, asking for no reward except the innate consciousness of rectitude and the salary as fixed by law. Now we are to separate. Here the roads seem to fork, as it were, and you and I, and the cabinet, must leave each other at this point.

You will find the key under the door-mat, and you had better turn the cat out at night when you close the office. If she does not go readily, you can make it clearer to her mind by throwing the cancelling stamp at her.

If Deacon Hayford does not pay up his box-rent, you might as well put his mail in the general delivery, and when Bob Head gets drunk and insists on a letter from one of his wives every day in the week, you can salute him through the box delivery with an old Queen Anne tomahawk, which you will find near the Etruscan water-pail. This will not in any manner surprise either of these parties.

Tears are unavailing. I once more become a private citizen, clothed only with the right to read such postal cards as may be addressed to me personally, and to curse the inefficiency of the post-office department. I believe the voting class to be divided into two parties, viz: Those who are in the postal service, and those who are mad because they cannot receive a registered letter every fifteen minutes of each day, including Sunday.

Mr President, as an official of this Government I now retire. My term of office would not expire until 1886. I must, therefore, beg pardon for my eccentricity in resigning. It will be best, perhaps, to keep the heart-breaking news from the ears of European powers until the dangers of a financial panic are fully past. Then hurl it broadcast with a sickening thud.

'Bill Nye' (Edgar Wilson Nye) (1850–96), *Bill Nye and Boomerang* (1881).

THE post-bellum literary comedians, ranging from Artemus Ward and Josh Billings to Ambrose Bierce and George Ade, tended to be national in identity rather than regional. Their humour, unlike that of the old characters such as Sam Slick, Davy Crockett, Sut Lovingood, no longer sprang from the attitudes and speech of a particular state or frontier but was more like a series of humorous comments on general topics made by a comical figure of no fixed abode.

A move back was made by a group of post-Civil War writers known as 'local colourists'. Their stated intention was to make their readers more aware of being part of a united nation by writing realistic, colourful descriptions of life in one small locality. One of the pioneer local colourists was Bret Harte, the journalist and parodist whose stories and verse about California were the first great success of the movement.

Understandably, the local colourists did not concern themselves much with the confused post-Civil War period in which they lived but harked back to the more romantic pre-Civil War days. Bret Harte's big success, The Luck of Roaring

Camp and other Sketches, was published in 1870 but was about life in the Californian mining camps twenty years earlier.

The somewhat sentimental and nostalgic pictures of pre-Civil War America—the fields of cotton, the mansions and mint-juleps of Old Georgia, the comradely perils of the Old West, and so on—which were so carefully drawn by the local colourists, became established myths. The myths, in their turn, became the source of innumerable and enormously long romantic novels, and any number of Hollywood motion pictures starring Clark Gable or Gary Cooper.

One local colourist, Joel Chandler Harris, thought back into his past in the Old South but came up not with more myth but with a memory of the stories told to him as a boy by Negro slaves. Harris grew up in the 1850s in a small town in Georgia. He was illegitimate and penniless and spent much of his time playing with slave children from a plantation and listening to old African folk tales which told of an exciting, funny, wondrous world in which animals talked to each other and the weaker creature always won in the end.

By the 1870s Harris had become a successful newspaperman, senior writer on the Atlantic Constitution. But this was the new, bustling South, swarming with businessmen busily sinking mines and laying railroads and intent on making education scientific and utilitarian. This was a world which was not at all to the taste of the little newspaperman, who was literary, gentle, and painfully shy (he recoiled with horror at Mark Twain's suggestion that he give comic lectures). In an effort to give children's imagination the sort of stimulation that had awakened his own, he began to write stories, tales supposedly told by an old, Negro house-servant, Uncle Remus.

Uncle Remus was no chuckly, cuddly old stage-negro; in fact 'he did no great amount of work. . . was reasonably vain of his appearance', and with the white grown-ups he was 'dictatorial, overbearing and quarrelsome'. But he loved telling stories to the little boy of the house and the Brer Rabbit stories he told were the old traditional animal legends which Harris remembered slaves telling him in his own childhood.

In 1880 Harris published the first of many collections of Uncle Remus tales. They not only charmed the American nation (and a good deal of the rest of the world) but they accurately represented Negro speech and character for the first time and directly influenced Mark Twain and later writers. It has been said that Harris's works were among the first, and remain the greatest, in the school of Negro folk stories, and are among the most unforgettable books in American literature.

The stories were simple yet proved gripping to generations of nineteenth-century American children who nearly fell out of bed with excitement as they waited to hear whether tonight was the night when Brer Fox would finally manage to eat Brer Rabbit.

Harris made the tales into a continuing saga. The second story, picking up where the first left off, was based upon one of the oldest of traditional Negro folk tales; the one where the fox uses a tar-baby as a lure to catch Brer Rabbit.

Notice the rhythmic repetition of the phrase 'en Brer Fox, he lay low', like a line in a Blues song:

THE WONDERFUL TAR-BABY STORY

'Didn't the fox never catch the rabbit, Uncle Remus?' asked the little boy the next evening.

'He come mighty nigh it, honey, sho's you bawn—Brer Fox did. One day after Brer Rabbit fool him wid dat calamus root, Brer Fox went ter wuk en got 'im some tar, en mix it wid some turkentime, en fix up a contrapshun what he call a Tar-Baby, en he tuck dish yere Tar-Baby en he sot 'er in de big road, en den he lay off in de bushes fer ter see wat de news wuz gwineter be. En he didn't hatter wait long, nudder, kaze bimeby here come Brer Rabbit pacin' down de road—lippity-clippity, clippity-lippity—dez ez sassy ez a jaybird. Brer Fox, he lay low. Brer Rabbit come prancin' 'long twel he spy de Tar-Baby, en den he fotch up on his behime legs like he was 'stonished. De Tar-Baby, she sot dar, she did, en Brer Fox, he lay low.

'"Mawnin'!" sez Brer Rabbit, sezee; "nice wedder dis mornin'," sezee.

'Tar-Baby ain't sayin' nuthin', en Brer Fox, he lay low.

'"How duz zo' sym'tums seem to segashuate?" sez Brer Rabbit, sezee.

'Brer Fox, he wink his eye slow, en de Tar-Baby, she ain't sayin' nuthin'.

'"How you come on, den? Is you deaf?" sez Brer Rabbit, sezee; "kaze if you is, I can holler louder," sezee.

'Tar-Baby stay still, en Brer Fox, he lay low.

'"Youer stuck up, dat's w'at you is," says Brer Rabbit, sezee, "en I'm gwineter kyore you, dat's w'at I'm a gwineter do," sezee.

'Brer Fox, he sorter chuckle in his stummick, he did, but Tar-Baby ain't sayin' nuthin'.

'"I'm gwineter larn you howter talk ter 'specttuble fokes ef hit's de las' ack," says Brer Rabbit, sezee. "Ef you don't take off dat hat en tell me howdy, I'm gwineter bus' you wide open," sezee.

'Tar-Baby stay still, en Brer Fox, he lay low.

'Brer Rabbit kept on axin' 'im, en de Tar-Baby, she keep on sayin' nuthin' twel presently Brer Rabbit draw back wid his fis', he did, en blip he tuck 'er side er de head. Right dar's whar he broke his molasses jug. His fis' stuck, en he can't pull loose. De tar hilt 'im.

'But Tar-Baby, she stay still, en Brer Fox, he lay low.

'"Ef you don't lemme loose, I'll knock you agin," sez Brer Rabbit, sezee, en wid dat he fotch 'er a wipe wid de udder han', en dat stuck. Tar-Baby, she ain't sayin' nuthin', en Brer Fox, he lay low.

'"Tu'n me loose, fo' I kick de natal stuffin' outen you," sez Brer Rabbit, sezee, but de Tar-Baby, she ain't sayin' nuthin'. She des hilt on, en Brer Rabbit lose de use er his feet in de same way.

'Brer Fox, he lay low. Den Brer Rabbit squall out dat ef de Tar-Baby don't tu'n 'im loose he butt 'er cranksided. En den he butted, en his head got stuck.

Den Brer Fox, he santered fort', lookin' des ez innercent ez wunner yo' mammy's mockin'-birds.

'"Howdy, Brer Rabbit," sez Brer Fox, sezee. "You look sorter stuck up dis mawnin," sezee, en den he rolled on de groun', en laft twel he couldn't laff no mo'. "I 'speck you'll take dinner wid me dis time, Brer Rabbit. I done laid in some calamus root, en I ain't gwineter take no skuse," sez Brer Fox, sezee.'

Here Uncle Remus paused, and drew a two-pound yam out of the ashes.

'Did the fox eat the rabbit?' asked the little boy to whom the story had been told.

'Dat's all de fer de tale goes,' replied the old man. 'He mout, en den agin he moutent. Some say Jedge B'ar come along and loosed 'im—some say he didn't. I hear Miss Sally callin'. You better run 'long.'

> Joel Chandler Harris (1848–1908), *Uncle Remus: His Songs and his Sayings* (1881).

---

*M*ANY *humorous sketches and stories before the Civil War may have been about cunning characters and low life but most of them were written by prosperous citizens who were judges, newspaper editors, literary-minded business-men and similar gentlefolk; for example, Washington Irving (businessman and diplomat), Haliburton (judge and politician), 'John Phoenix' (Army officer). They wrote from compulsion rather than for the money. There was little money available to pay authors in those days.*

About the middle of the century it became possible for the first time for an American author to earn a reasonable living from writing humour. And a very good living indeed if the pieces were reprinted in books and the author became famous enough to appear on the lucrative lecture circuits.

Professionals began to take over from the gifted amateurs. The result was an increase in comicality, in going for laughs for their own sake, and the development of technical tricks like the atrocious grammar and eccentric spelling popularized by the new and broader comic writers and performers christened the 'Phunny Phellows'.

But one very good thing came out of humorous writing becoming a profitable career and that was the attraction into its ranks of a young ex-riverboat pilot, ex-printer, ex-miner named Samuel L. Clemens, who as 'Mark Twain' became America's most famous humorous writer.

Samuel Clemens, like Charles Dickens, was a professional author who made his living from his writings. Like Dickens he adopted a more profitable way of dis-tributing his books; in Clemens's case by using book agents to push sales rather than leaving the books to take their chance on the shelves of book stores. Like Dickens he had an improvident, Micawber-like father, a loving mother, and a childhood during which money was scarce. And, like Dickens, he became his

country's most popular writer without entirely winning over the literary critics,
who were happy to acknowledge his genius as an entertainer but found his output
uneven and anyway tended not to rate entertainment all that high in the qualities
they sought for in a book.

Not that all this bothered Samuel Clemens much; he strongly disliked the work
of many highly praised authors including Sir Walter Scott, Jane Austen, and James
Fenimore Cooper, and had little respect for 'literature' as such:

A classic . . . something that everybody wants to have read and nobody
wants to read.

> Samuel L. Clemens ('Mark Twain') (1835–1910), *Mark Twain's Speeches*
> (1910).

Clemens deliberately and unrepentently avoided 'the gentle tradition' and aimed
for a mass-readership:

My books are water: those of the great geniuses are wine. Everybody drinks
water.

> *Mark Twain's Notebook*, ed. Albert Bigelow Paine (1935).

The masses bought enough Mark Twain books to make him two fortunes. Perhaps
his twenty-five books did not rate as literary 'wine' but they were funny, vigorous,
opinionated, full of common sense, enriched here and there with a tincture of
Dickensian sentiment, and immensely readable.

The journalist in him came out in the keenness of his observation, but even
little descriptive passages were lit by his imagination and the originality of his
humour:

Two beautiful deer came sauntering across the grounds and stopped and
looked me over as impudently as if they thought of buying me. Then they
seemed to conclude that they could do better for less money, and sauntered
indolently away.

> *S.L.C. to C.T.*
> Private printing, New York (1925).

There was exactly one mahogany tree on the island [Bermuda]. I know this
to be reliable because I saw a man who said he had counted it many a time
and could not be mistaken. He was a man with a harelip and a pure heart,
and everybody said he was as true as steel. Such men are all too few.

> *Tom Sawyer Abroad* (1894).

It seems to me that in the matter of intellect the ant must be a strangely
overrated bird. During many summers, now, I have watched him, when I
ought to have been in better business, and I have yet to come across a living
ant that seemed to have any more sense than a dead one . . . I am persuaded
that the average ant is a sham. I admit his industry, of course; he is the
hardest working creature in the world—when anybody is looking—but his

leather-headedness is the point I make against him. He goes out foraging, he
makes a capture, then what does he do? Go home? No—he goes anywhere
but home. He doesn't know where home is. His home may be only three feet
away—no matter, he can't find it. He makes his capture, as I have said; it is
generally something which can be of no sort of use to himself or anybody
else; it is usually seven times bigger than it ought to be; he hunts out the
awkwardest place to take hold of it; he lifts it bodily up in the air by main
force, and starts; not toward home, but in the opposite direction; not calmly
and wisely, but with a frantic haste which is wasteful of his strength; he
fetches up against a pebble, and instead of going around it, he climbs over it
backwards dragging his booty after him, tumbles down on the other side,
jumps up in a passion, kicks the dust off his clothes, moistens his hands,
grabs his property viciously, yanks it this way, then that, shoves it ahead of
him a moment, turns tail and lugs it after him another moment, gets madder
and madder, then presently hoists it into the air and goes tearing away in an
entirely new direction; comes to a weed; it never occurs to him to go around
it; no, he must climb it; and he does climb it, dragging his worthless property
to the top—which is as bright a thing to do as it would be for me to carry a
sack of flour from Heidelberg to Paris by way of Strasburg steeple; when he
gets up there he finds it is not the place; takes a cursory glance at the scenery
and either climbs down again or tumbles down, and starts off once more . . .
in as violent a hurry as ever . . . to see if he can't find an old nail, or something
else that is heavy enough to afford entertainment and at the same time
valueless enough to make an ant want it . . .

It is strange, beyond comprehension, that so manifest a humbug as the
ant has been able to fool so many nations and keep it up for so many ages
without being found out.

A Tramp Abroad (1880).

*Samuel Clemens grew up in Hannibal, Missouri, a small town on the banks of the
busy Mississippi river. After some meagre schooling he drifted from one job to
another as most boys tended to do who did not know what they wanted to do except
avoid hard work:*

I had once been a grocery clerk, for one day, but had consumed so much
sugar in that time that I was relieved from further duty by the proprietor;
said he wanted me outside, so that he could have my custom. I had studied
law an entire week, and then given it up because it was so prosy and tiresome.
I had engaged briefly in the study of blacksmithing, but wasted so much time
trying to fix the bellows so that it would blow itself, that the master turned
me adrift in disgrace, and told me that I would come to no good. I had been
a bookseller's clerk for a while, but the customers bothered me so much I
could not read with any comfort, and so the proprietor gave me a furlough
and forgot to put a limit on it. I had clerked in a drug store part of a summer,
but my prescriptions were unlucky, and we appeared to sell more stomach

pumps than soda water. So I had to go. I had made of myself a tolerable printer, under the impression that I would be another Franklin some day.

Roughing It (1872).

In fact he was apprenticed to a printer at the age of 13 and 'stuck type' for three years, printing and contributing to his brother Orion's local newspaper.

Brother Orion turned out to be as financially incapable as their father. After a few more temporary jobs the young Samuel Clemens decided to try his luck in South America but changed his mind in mid-stream aboard a Mississippi riverboat and persuaded the captain, Horace Bixby, to accept him, on tick, as an apprentice steamboat pilot. He won his licence in 1859 and happily plied his trade between St Louis and New Orleans.

Those few good years spent as a riverboat captain on the Mississippi went into his memory as a kind of mine of stories, tall tales, and colourful characters to be dug up later when they were needed. His best work was to be at least partly autobiographical and his experiences of life on the river proved eventually to be a far richer and more profitable lode than any he might have located when he later tried to mine silver:

In that brief, sharp schooling I got personally and familiarly acquainted with all the different types of human nature that are to be found in fiction, biography, or history. When I find a well-drawn character in fiction or biography I generally take a warm personal interest in him, for the reason that I have known him before—met him on the river.

Life on the Mississippi (1883).

The Civil War broke out and traffic on the Mississippi stopped. Clemens, in an impulsive moment, joined a detachment of Confederate volunteers. His military zeal evaporated after two weeks and he deserted. His brother Orion had managed to wangle himself a job as secretary to the governor of Nevada and Samuel decided to go out west with him.

Travelling west by stage-coach in those days was not dull:

During the preceding night an ambushed savage had sent a bullet through the pony-rider's jacket, but he had ridden on just the same, because pony-riders were not allowed to stop and inquire into such things except when killed. As long as they had life enough left in them they had to stick to the horse and ride, even if the Indians had been waiting for them for a week, and were entirely out of patience . . . [our driver] said the place to keep a man 'huffy' was down on the Southern Overland among the Apaches, before the company moved the stage line up on the northern route. He said the Apaches used to annoy him all the time down there, and that he came as near as anything to starving to death in the midst of abundance, because they kept him so leaky with bullet holes that he 'couldn't hold his vittles'. This person's statements were not generally believed. *Roughing It.*

Clemens tried prospecting and silver mining in Nevada without success, failed in a timber speculation, and then tried journalism, writing for the Virginia City Ter-ritorial Enterprise *at twenty-five dollars a week.*

He found that he enjoyed writing; it was not, to him, hard work. His output was the usual Phunny Phellow kind of newspaper column then in fashion, jaunty sketches full of word-play and burlesque.

One of his most successful parodies was of the reminiscences of an elderly, retired riverboat pilot, Isaiah Seller, which appeared in the New Orleans Picayune. *So devastating was Clemens's mockery of the old pilot's dull and pompous literary style that Seller never wrote again.*

Seller's articles had been published under his pseudonym: 'Mark Twain'.

Perhaps to expiate his hatchet job on Seller by keeping the old man's nom-de-plume alive, or more likely because the ambitious young writer Clemens recognized a good pseudonym when he saw one, he appropriated it for himself and ever after was known professionally as Mark Twain. Ultimately, of course, the derivation of 'mark twain!' was the shout of a riverboat's leadsman when he found that his line was wet up to the second knot, indicating that the water was two fathoms deep, the minimum for a laden boat.

Mark Twain (Mark II) moved to San Francisco and worked on the Morning Call, *and as San Francisco correspondent of the Virginia City* Territorial Enterprise. *He was fired by the editor of the* Morning Call *and moved to another San Francisco newspaper, but after two or three months he was in trouble again and had to leave town.*

Exiled from San Francisco, he spent three months at the little pocket-mining camp of Jackass Hill with friends, two old, unsuccessful miners named Jim Gillis and Jim Stoker. It rained heavily and there was little to do but sit around the cabin fire and talk, or go to the tiny hotel at Angel's Camp and talk. The hotel had a French cook who made four kinds of soup which, Twain noted glumly in his notebook, were known to the locals as 'Hellfire, General Debility, Insanity, and Sudden Death'.

Those three months spent listening to Jim Gillis and his friends telling traditional old frontier yarns and 'elaborate impromptu lies', turned out to be as important a period for Twain as his piloting days on the Mississippi. Their kind of story-telling appealed to him enormously and he persuaded himself that this was what he should be trying to do in print instead of wasting his time on ephemeral journalism. He studied Jim Gillis's technique, noting how 'he just builds a story as it goes along, careless of whither it is proceeding, enjoying each fresh fancy as it flashes from the brain and caring not at all whether the story shall ever end brilliantly and satisfactorily'. He practised writing the stories down, speaking them out aloud in various ways until he found the form which best translated the oral effects into writing.

Back in San Francisco he was encouraged to turn author by Bret Harte and other friends. Artemus Ward turned up on a lecture tour and Twain recounted to him an old mining-camp yarn which had taken his fancy. Ward asked Twain to write it out, as his new book, Artemus Ward; His Travels, *was a bit short and his publisher wanted more copy to plump it out a little. Twain wrote the story, called it* Jim Smiley and his Jumping Frog, *and sent it off to New York but the publisher could not use it and passed it on to a newspaper-editor friend. It was printed in the New York* Saturday Press *and immediately caught the public's fancy; so much so that it was swiftly reprinted in numerous newspapers both in America and in England. James Russell Lowell pronounced it to be 'the finest piece of humorous literature yet produced in America'. Mark Twain, with his first published short story, had become a celebrated author.*

The 'Frog' is a frame story with two narrators; the first is a slightly pompous 'Mark Twain' and the second is Simon Wheeler, a story-teller clearly based on Twain's old friend Jim Gillis. Wheeler, in the ambling, discursive manner of Gillis, recounts how Jim Smiley, a compulsive and cunning gambler who bets on everything and usually wins, comes up against a naïve stranger:

THE CELEBRATED JUMPING FROG OF CALAVERAS COUNTY

In compliance with the request of a friend of mine, who wrote me from the East, I called on good-natured, garrulous old Simon Wheeler, and inquired after my friend's friend, Leonidas W. Smiley, as requested to do, and I hereunto append the result. I have a lurking suspicion that *Leonidas W.* Smiley is a myth; and that my friend never knew such a personage; and that he only conjectured that if I asked old Wheeler about him, it would remind him of his infamous *Jim* Smiley, and he would go to work and bore me to death with some exasperating reminiscence of him as long and as tedious as it should be useless to me. If that was the design, it succeeded.

I found Simon Wheeler dozing comfortably by the bar-room stove of the dilapidated tavern in the decayed mining camp of Angel's, and I noticed that he was fat and bald-headed, and had an expression of winning gentleness and simplicity upon his tranquil countenance. He roused up, and gave me good-day. I told him a friend had commissioned me to make some inquiries about a cherished companion of his boyhood named *Leonidas W.* Smiley—Rev. *Leonidas W.* Smiley, a young minister of the Gospel, who he had heard was at one time a resident of Angel's Camp. I added that if Mr Wheeler could tell me anything about this Rev. Leonidas W. Smiley, I would feel under many obligations to him.

Simon Wheeler backed me into a corner and blockaded me there with his chair, and then sat down and reeled off the monotonous narrative which follows this paragraph. He never smiled, he never frowned, he never changed his voice from the gentle-flowing key to which he tuned his initial sentence, he never betrayed the slightest suspicion of enthusiasm; but all through the interminable narrative there ran a vein of impressive earnestness and sincerity, which showed me plainly that, so far from his imagining that there was anything ridiculous or funny about his story, he regarded it as a really important matter, and admired its two heroes as men of transcendent genius in *finesse*. I let him go on in his own way, and never interrupted him once:

Rev. Leonidas W. H'm, Reverend Le—well, there was a feller here once by the name of Jim Smiley, in the winter of '49—or maybe it was the spring of '50—I don't recollect exactly, somehow, though what makes me think it was one or the other is because I remember the big flume warn't finished when he first came to the camp; but any way, he was the curiousest man about always betting on anything that turned up you ever see, if he could get anybody to bet on the other side; and if he couldn't he'd change sides. Any way that suited the other man would suit *him*—any way just so's he got a bet, *he* was satisfied. But still he was lucky, uncommon lucky; he most always come out winner. He was always ready and laying for a chance; there couldn't be no solit'ry thing mentioned but that feller'd offer to bet on it, and take any side you please, as I was just telling you. If there was a horserace, you'd find him flush or you'd find him busted at the end of it; if there was a dog-fight, he'd bet on it; if there was a cat-fight, he'd bet on it; if there was a chicken-fight, he'd bet on it; why, if there was two birds setting on a fence, he would bet you which one would fly first; or if there was a camp-meeting, he would be there reg'lar to bet on Parson Walker, which he judged to be the best exhorter about here, and he was, too, and a good man. If he even see a straddle-bug start to go anywheres, he would bet you how long it would take him to get to—to wherever he was going to, and if you took him up, he would foller that straddle-bug to Mexico but what he would find out where he was bound for and how long he was on the road. Lots of the boys here has seen that Smiley and can tell you about him. Why, it never made no difference to *him*—he'd bet on *any* thing—the dangest feller. Parson Walker's wife laid very sick once, for a good while, and it seemed as if they warn't going to save her; but one morning he come in, and Smiley up and asked him how she was, and he said she was considerable better—thank the Lord for his inf'nit' mercy—and coming on so smart that with the blessing of Prov'dence she'd get well yet; and Smiley, before he thought, says, 'Well, I'll risk two-and-a-half she don't anyway.'

Thish-yer Smiley had a mare—the boys called her the fifteen-minute nag, but that was only in fun, you know, because, of course, she was faster than that—and he used to win money on that horse, for all she was so slow and always had the asthma, or the distemper, or the consumption, or something of that kind. They used to give her two or three hundred yards start, and then pass her under way; but always at the fag-end of the race she'd get excited and desperate-like, and come cavorting and straddling up, and scattering her legs around limber, sometimes in the air, and sometimes out to one side amongst the fences, and kicking up m-o-r-e dust and raising m-o-r-e racket with her coughing and sneezing and blowing her nose—and *always* fetch up at the stand just about a neck ahead, as near as you could cipher it down.

And he had a little small bull-pup, that to look at him you'd think he warn't worth a cent but to set around and look ornery and lay for a chance to steal something. But as soon as money was upon him he was a different dog; his under-jaw'd begin to stick out like the fo'-castle of a steamboat, and his teeth would uncover and shine like the furnaces. And a dog might tackle him and bully-rag him, and bite him, and throw him over his shoulder two or three times, and Andrew Jackson—which was the name of the pup—Andrew Jackson would never let on but what he was satisfied, and hadn't expected nothing else—and the bets being doubled and doubled on the other side all the time, till the money was all up; and then all of a sudden he would grab that other dog jest by the j'int of his hind leg and freeze to it—not chaw, you understand, but only just grip and hang on till they throwed up the sponge, if it was a year. Smiley always come out winner on that pup, till he harnessed a dog once that didn't have no hind legs, because they'd been sawed off in a circular saw, and when the thing had gone along far enough, and the money was all up, and he come to make a snatch for his pet holt, he see in a minute how he'd been imposed on, and how the other dog had him in the door, so to speak, and he 'peared surprised, and then he looked sorter discouraged-like, and didn't try no more to win the fight and so he got shucked out bad. He gave Smiley a look, as much as to say his heart was broke, and it was *his* fault, for putting up a dog that hadn't no hind legs for him to take holt of, which was his main dependence in a fight, and then he limped off a piece and laid down and died. It was a good pup, was that Andrew Jackson, and would have made a name for hisself if he'd lived, for the stuff was in him and he had genius—I know it, because he hadn't no opportunities to speak of, and it don't stand to reason that a dog could make such a fight as he could under them circumstances if he hadn't no talent. It always makes me feel sorry when I think of that last fight of his'n, and the way it turned out.

Well, thish-yer Smiley had rat-tarriers, and chicken cocks, and tom-cats and all of them kind of things, till you couldn't rest, and you couldn't fetch nothing for him to bet on but he'd match you. He ketched a frog one day, and took him home, and said he cal'lated to educate him; and so he never done nothing for three months but set in his back yard and learn that frog to jump. And you bet you he *did* learn him, too. He'd give him a little punch behind, and the next minute you'd see that frog whirling in the air like a doughnut—see him turn one summerset, or maybe a couple, if he got a good start, and come down flat-footed and all right, like a cat. He got him up so in the matter of ketching flies, and kep' him in practice so constant, that he'd nail a fly every time as fur as he could see him. Smiley said all a frog wanted was education, and he could do 'most anything—and I believe him. Why, I've seen him set Dan'l Webster down here on this floor—Dan'l Webster was the name of the frog—and sing out, 'Flies, Dan'l, flies!' and quicker'n you could wink he'd spring straight up and snake a fly off'n the counter there, an flop down on the floor ag'in as solid as a gob of mud, and fall to scratching the side of his head with his hind foot as indifferent as if he hadn't no idea he'd been doin' any more'n any frog might do. You never see a frog so modest and straightfor'ard as he was, for all he was so gifted. And when it come to fair and square jumping on a dead level, he could get over more ground at one straddle than any animal of his breed you ever see. Jumping on a dead level was his strong suit, you understand; and when it come to that, Smiley would ante up money on him as long as he had a red. Smiley was monstrous proud of his frog, and well he might be, for fellers that had travelled and been everywheres, all said he laid over any frog that ever *they* see.

Well, Smiley kep' the beast in a little lattice box, and he used to fetch him downtown sometimes and lay for a bet. One day a feller—a stranger in the camp, he was—come acrost him with his box, and says:

'What might be that you've got in the box?'

And Smiley says, sorter indifferent-like, 'It might be a parrot, or it might be a canary, maybe, but it ain't—it's only just a frog.'

And the feller took it, and looked at it careful, and turned it round this way and that, and says, 'H'm—so 'tis, Well, what's *he* good for?'

'Well,' Smiley says, easy and careless, 'he's good enough for *one* thing, I should judge—he can out jump any frog in Calaveras County.'

The feller took the box again, and took another long, particular look, and give it back to Smiley, and says, very deliberate, 'Well,' he says, 'I don't see no p'ints about that frog that's any better'n any other frog.'

'Maybe you don't,' Smiley says. 'Maybe you understand frogs and maybe you don't understand 'em; maybe you've had experience, and maybe you ain't only a amature, as it were. Anyways, I've got *my* opinion and I'll risk forty dollars that he can outjump any frog in Calaveras County.'

And the feller studied a minute, and then says, kinder sad like, 'Well, I'm only a stranger here, and I ain't got no frog; but if I had a frog, I'd bet you.'

And then Smiley says, 'That's all right—that's all right—if you'll hold my box a minute, I'll go and get you a frog.' And so the feller took the box, and put up his forty dollars along with Smiley's and set down to wait.

So he set there a good while thinking and thinking to hisself, and then he got the frog out and prized his mouth open and took a teaspoon and filled him full of quail shot—filled him pretty near up to his chin—and set him on the floor. Smiley he went to the swamp and slopped around in the mud for a long time, and finally he ketched a frog, and fetched him in, and give him to this feller, and says:

'Now, if you're ready, set him alongside of Dan'l, with his forepaws just even with Dan'l's, and I'll give the word.' Then he says, 'One—two—three— *git!*' and him and the feller touched up the frogs from behind, and the new frog hopped off lively, but Dan'l give a heave, and hysted up his shoulders— so—like a Frenchman, but it warn't no use—he couldn't budge; he was planted as solid as a church, and he couldn't no more stir than if he was anchored out. Smiley was a good deal surprised, and he was disgusted too, but he didn't have no idea what the matter was, of course.

The feller took the money and started away; and when he was going out at the door, he sorter jerked his thumb over his shoulder—so—at Dan'l, and says again, very deliberate, 'Well,' he says, '*I* don't see no p'ints about that frog that's any better'n any other frog.'

Smiley he stood scratching his head and looking down at Dan'l a long time, and at last says, 'I do wonder what in the nation that frog throwed off for—I wonder if there ain't something the matter with im—he 'pears to look mighty baggy, somehow.' And he ketched Dan'l up by the nap of the neck, and hefted him, and says, 'Why blame my cats if he don't weigh five pounds!' and turned him upside down and he belched out a double handful of shot. And then he see how it was, and he was the maddest man—he set the frog down and took out after that feller, but he never ketched him. And—

(Here Simon Wheeler heard his name called from the front yard, and got up to see what was wanted.) And turning to me as he moved away, he said: 'Jest set where you are, stranger, and rest easy—I ain't going to be gone a second.'

But, by your leave, I did not think that a continuation of the history of the enterprising vagabond *Jim* Smiley would be likely to afford me much information concerning the Rev. *Leonidas W.* Smiley, and so I started away.

At the door I met the sociable Wheeler returning, and he buttonholed me and recommenced:

'Well, thish-yer Smiley had a yaller, one-eyed cow that didn't have no tail, only jest a short stump like a bannanner, and—'

However, lacking both time and inclination, I did not wait to hear about the afflicted cow, but took my leave.

The Celebrated Jumping Frog of Calaveras County (1865).

● The *Jumping Frog* enjoyed a long life. Twain recycled it many times with small changes and the title varied between *Jim Smiley and his* . . ., *The Celebrated* . . ., and *The Notorious* . . .

Mark Twain had found his voice. Literally, because he next discovered that he could talk to people as successfully as he could write for them, and in 1866 he became, and remained until his death, an accomplished and increasingly well-paid humorous lecturer and after-dinner speaker.

In 1867 he joined the steamship Quaker City *for a tour through Europe and the Holy Land. The result was a hugely successful travel book,* The Innocents Abroad, *which was just the tonic that American readers wanted after the miseries of the Civil War years. A hundred thousand copies were sold in its first three years and it is still selling.*

The Innocents Abroad *was something new in travel writing; 'little old Europe' as seen through the eyes of a humorous, sceptical, high-spirited, patriotic democrat*

from the West, unimpressed by European scenery when compared with his own
mighty landscapes back home, scornful of European inherited titles and wealth,
and repelled by the un-American standards of hygiene which he met everywhere:

This Civita Vecchia is the finest nest of dirt, vermin, and ignorance we have
found yet, except that African perdition they call Tangier, which is just like
it. The people here live in alleys two yards wide, which have a smell about
them which is peculiar, but not entertaining. It is well the alleys are not
wider, because they hold as much smell now as a person can stand, and, of
course, if they were wider they would hold more, and then the people would
die . . .

They are very uncleanly—these people—in face, in person and in dress.
When they see anybody with a clean shirt on, it arouses their scorn. The
women wash clothes, half the day, at the public tanks in the streets, but they
are probably somebody else's. Or maybe they keep one set to wear and
another to wash; because they never put on any that have ever been washed.

The Innocents Abroad (1869).

In Marseilles they make half the fancy toilet soap we consume in America,
but the Marseillaise only have a vague theoretical idea of its use, which they
have obtained from books of travel, just as they have acquired an uncertain
knowledge of clean shirts, and the peculiarities of the gorilla, and other
curious matters. This reminds me of poor Blucher's note to the land-lord in
Paris:

'*Monsieur le* landlord—Sir: *Pourquoi* don't you *mettez* some *savon* in your
bedchambers? *Est-ce que vous pensez* I will steal it? *La nuit passee* you charged
me *pour deux chandelles* when I only had one; *hier vous avez* charged me *avec*
glace when I had none at all; *tout les jours* you are coming some fresh game
or other on me, *mais vous ne pouvez pas* play this *savon* dodge on me twice.
Savon is a necessary *de la vie* to anybody but a Frenchman, *et je l'aurai hors*
de cet hotel or make trouble. You hear me. *Allons.*

Blucher.'

Ibid.

> ☙ This was an early example of the comic mixing of French and English
> now known as 'Franglais'.

Another reason for the popularity of The Innocents Abroad *was Twain's refusal*
as a no-nonsense American to be awed by the great works of art which he was
shown. He treated European art and antiquity with a cheeky irreverence.
In Rome:

I wish to say one word about Michael Angelo Buonarotti—I used to worship
the mighty genius of Michael Angelo—that man who was great in poetry,
painting, sculpture, architecture—great in everything he undertook. But I
do not want Michael Angelo for breakfast—for luncheon—for tea—for supper—for between meals. I like a change occasionally. In Genoa he designed

everything; he designed the Lake of Como; in Padua, Verona, Venice, Bologna, whom did we ever hear of, from guides, but Michael Angelo? In Florence he painted everything, nearly, and what he did not design he used to sit on a favourite stone and look at, and they showed us the stone. In Pisa he designed everything but the old shot-tower, and they would have attributed that to him if it had not been so awfully out of the perpendicular. He designed the piers of Leghorn and the custom-house regulations of Civita Vecchia. But here—here it is frightful. He designed St Peter's; he designed the Pope; he designed the Pantheon, the uniform of the Pope's soldiers, the Tiber, the Vatican, the Coliseum, the Capitol, the Tarpeian Rock, the Berberini Palace, St John Lateran, the Campagna, the Appian Way, the Seven Hills, the Baths of Caracalla, the Claudian Aqueduct, the Cloaca Maxima— the eternal bore designed the Eternal City, and, unless all men and books do lie, he painted everything in it! Dan said the other day to the guide, 'Enough, enough, enough! Say no more! Lump the whole thing! Say that the Creator made Italy from designs by Michael Angelo!'

I never felt so fervently thankful, so soothed, so tranquil, so filled with a blessed sense of peace, as I did yesterday when I learnt that Michael Angelo was dead.   Ibid.

The Innocents Abroad *was a cunning mixture of styles which changed rapidly ; a humorous episode might be followed by a straightforward piece of reportage, followed immediately by a farcical anecdote, and so on.*

When the touring party reached the Holy Land a fair amount of sentiment crept in, but a return to humour was never more than a page or so away.

In the following extract the 'innocent' Twain visits the Church of the Holy Sepulchre. He is shown the spot which marks the true centre of the earth and the grave which contains Adam's cadaver. His report deals ironically with wildly specious claims like these and ends with a burst of emotion parodying Laurence Sterne's kind of sentimentalism:

The Greek Chapel is the most roomy, the richest, and the showiest chapel in the Church of the Holy Sepulchre. Its altar, like that of all the Greek churches, is a lofty screen that extends clear across the chapel, and is gorgeous with gilding and pictures. The numerous lamps that hang before it are of gold and silver, and cost great sums.

But the feature of the place is a short column that rises from the middle of the marble pavement of the chapel, and marks the exact *centre of the earth.*

To satisfy himself that this spot was really the centre of the earth, a sceptic once paid well for the privilege of ascending to the dome of the church, to see if the sun gave him a shadow at noon. He came down perfectly convinced. The day was very cloudy, and the sun threw no shadows at all; but the man was satisfied that if the sun had come out and made shadows, it could not have made any for him. Proofs like these are not to be set aside by the idle tongues of cavillers. To such as are not bigoted, and are willing to be convinced, they carry a conviction that nothing can ever shake.

If even greater proofs than those I have mentioned are wanted, to satisfy the headstrong and foolish that this is the centre of the earth, they are here. The greatest of them lies in the fact that from under this very column was taken the *dust from which Adam was made*. This can surely be regarded in the light of a settler. It is not likely that the original man would have been made from an inferior quality of earth, when it was entirely convenient to get first quality from the world's centre. This will strike any reflecting mind forcibly. That Adam was formed of dirt procured in this very spot is amply proven by the fact that in six thousand years no man has ever been able to prove that the dirt was *not* procured here whereof he was made.

It is a singular circumstance that right under the roof of this same great church, and not far away from that illustrious column, Adam himself, the father of the human race, lies buried. There is no question that he is actually buried in the grave which is pointed out as his—there can be none—because it has never yet been proven that that grave is not the grave in which he is buried.

The tomb of Adam! How touching it was, here in a land of strangers, far away from home and friends and all who cared for me, thus to discover the grave of a blood relation! True, a distant one, but still a relation. The unerring instinct of nature thrilled its recognition. The fountain of my filial affection was stirred to its profoundest depths, and I gave way to tumultuous emotion.

I leaned upon a pillar and burst into tears. I deem it no shame to have wept over the grave of my poor dead relative. Let him who would sneer at my emotion close this volume here, for he will find little to his taste in my journeyings through Holy Land. Noble old man—he did not live to see me—he did not live to see his child. And I—I—alas! I did not live to see *him*. Weighed down by sorrow and disappointment, he died before I was born—six thousand brief summers before I was born. But let us try to bear it with fortitude. Let us trust that he is better off where he is. Let us take comfort that his loss is our eternal gain.

                                                                                    Ibid.

The Innocents Abroad brought Twain fame and enough money to get married. He moved to New England and settled down in a mansion in Hartford, Connecticut. As the years passed he continued to be a prolific writer and lecturer, always with humour, although his early optimism and faith in frontier virtues evaporated and he later described mankind as 'creatures to be ashamed of in all their aspects'.

As an old man, with a splendid mane of white hair and a drooping moustache, he was a distinguished literary lion, with a Hon. D.Litt. from Oxford and an international reputation for wit and trenchant humour. His best-known off-the-cuff remark was made when he was in England (where he dined with such figures as Marie Corelli, Anthony Trollope, Elinor Glyn, and the young Winston Churchill). A report was cabled to American journals that Samuel Clemens was dying or dead.

It was, in fact, another Clemens, a cousin, who had been taken ill. American editors cabled their London representatives to rush round to the Clemens apartment and send back the full sensational story:

There was nothing the matter with me and each in his turn was astonished, and not gratified, to find me reading and smoking in my study and worth next to nothing as a text for transatlantic news. One of these men was a gentle and kindly and grave and sympathetic Irishman, who hid his disappointment the best he could and tried to look glad and told me that his paper, the *Evening Sun*, had cabled him that it was reported in New York that I was dead. What should he cable in reply? I said, 'Say the report is exaggerated'.

He never smiled, but went solemnly away and sent the cable in those exact words. The remark hit the world pleasantly. *Mark Twain in Eruption* (1922).

➤ Twain was curious as to the wording of the cablegrams which the reporters arrived clutching. He managed to read the cable held by the *New York World*'s man, which read 'If Mark Twain dying send five hundred words. If dead send a thousand.'

During his lifetime, and long after, Mark Twain was the United States's most famous humorist; he was called 'the Dickens of America', 'the Lincoln of literature'. His art was the hinge which swung the old ante-bellum humour into the modern world. His prose style had the vigour and directness of the frontier humour on which it was nourished, but it also had some of the subtleties and depths of a new nation rapidly becoming more united and complex. T. S. Eliot wrote of his style, 'he purified the dialect of the tribe'.

He began mining his memories in 1872, three years after publishing The Innocents Abroad, *when he decided to write a play about his own boyhood in a sleepy little Missouri river-town way back in the 1830s. He then changed his mind and wrote it as a book, which he called* The Adventures of Tom Sawyer.

Twain wrote it for adults but his friend William Dean Howells advised him that if he removed the considerable amount of naturalistic schoolboy profanity it would become 'the best boy story ever written'.

The character of the hero, Tom Sawyer, was an innovation. Instead of being a pious goody or a colourful little tearaway, Twain made him a kind of juvenile version of Fielding's Tom Jones; an ordinary flesh-and-blood boy with a boy's human failings and qualities; Tom was resourceful, mischievous, and vain, always looking for a chance to show off.

The fence-painting scene in the book is a classic episode in juvenile literature. It seems that the world has to thank a British actor and a British playwright for being its unwitting midwives. Twain wrote later that one evening in London when dining with Henry Irving and W. G. Wills, probably at the Garrick Club, he told a story—almost certainly an old traditional story—about boys being tricked into whitewashing a fence. It went down well so, encouraged, he went back to his hotel and immediately wrote it out in full as a chapter for his book.

As ever with Twain, the manner of telling the story and the richness of seemingly irrelevant detail are as important as the plot: note the concentration with which the boy Ben Rogers, playing at being a steamboat, docks himself before talking.

Tom's nasty brother Sid has told their kind Aunt Polly that Tom has played hookey from school. As punishment Tom is made to spend his Saturday white-washing the front fence:

Saturday morning was come, and all the summer world was bright and fresh, and brimming with life. There was a song in every heart; and if the heart was young the music issued at the lips. There was cheer in every face and a spring in every step. The locust-trees were in bloom, and the fragrance of the blossoms filled the air. Cardiff Hill, beyond the village and above it, was green with vegetation, and it lay just far enough away to seem a Delectable Land, dreamy, reposeful, and inviting.

Tom appeared on the sidewalk with a bucket of whitewash and a long-handled brush. He surveyed the fence, and all gladness left him and a deep melancholy settled down upon his spirit. Thirty yards of board fence nine feet high! Life to him seemed hollow, and existence but a burden. Sighing, he dipped his brush and passed it along the topmost plank; repeated the operation; did it again; compared the insignificant whitewashed streak with the far-reaching continent of unwhitewashed fence, and sat down on a tree-box discouraged. Jim came skipping out at the gate with a tin pail, and singing 'Buffalo Gals'. Bringing water from the town pump had always been hateful work in Tom's eyes before, but now it did not strike him so. He remembered that there was company at the pump. White, mulatto, and negro boys and girls always were there waiting their turns, resting, trading playthings, quarrelling, fighting, skylarking. And he remembered that, although the pump was only a hundred and fifty yards off, Jim never got back with a bucket of water under an hour—and even then somebody generally had to go after him. Tom said:

'Say, Jim, I'll fetch the water if you'll whitewash some.'

Jim shook his head and said:

'Can't, Mars Tom. Ole missis, she tole me I got to go an' git the water an' not stop foolin' roun' wid anybody. She say she spec' Mars Tom gwine to ax me to whitewash, an' she tole me to go 'long an' 'tend to my business—she 'lowed *she'd* 'tend to de whitewashin'.'

'Oh, never mind what she said, Jim. That's the way she talks. Gimme the bucket—I won't be gone only a minute. *She* won't ever know.'

'Oh, I dasn't, Mars Tom. Ole missis she'd take an' tar de head off'n me. 'Deed she would.'

'*She!* She never licks anybody—whacks 'em over the head with her thimble—and who cares for that, I'd like to know? She talks awful, but talk don't hurt—anyways, it don't if she don't cry. Jim, I'll give you a marvel. I'll give you a white alley!'

Jim began to waver.

'White Alley, Jim! And its a bully taw!'

'My! Dat's a mighty gay marvel, *I* tell you! But, Mars Tom, I's powerful 'fraid old missis—'

'And besides, if you will I'll show you my sore toe.'

Jim was only human—this attraction was too much for him. He put down his pail, took the white alley, and bent over the toe with absorbing interest while the bandage was being unwound. In another moment he was flying down the street with his pail and a tingling rear, Tom was whitewashing with vigour, and Aunt Polly was retiring from the field with a slipper in her hand and triumph in her eye.

But Tom's energy did not last. He began to think of the fun he had planned for this day, and his sorrows multiplied. Soon the free boys would come tripping along on all sorts of delicious expeditions, and they would make a world of fun of him for having to work—the very thought of it burnt him like fire. He got out his worldly wealth and examined it—bits of toys, marbles, and trash; enough to buy an exchange of *work*, maybe, but not half enough to buy as much as half an hour of pure freedom. So he returned his straightened means to his pocket, and gave up the idea of trying to buy the boys. At this dark and hopeless moment an inspiration burst upon him! Nothing less than a great, magnificent inspiration.

He took up his brush and went tranquilly to work. Ben Rogers hove in sight presently—the very boy, of all boys, whose ridicule he had been dreading. Ben's gait was hop-skip-and-jump—proof enough that his heart was light and his anticipations high. He was eating an apple, and giving a long, melodious whoop, at intervals, followed by a deep-toned ding-dong-dong, for he was personating a steamboat. As he drew near he slackened speed, took the middle of the street, leaned far over to starboard, and rounded to ponderously and with laborious pomp and circumstance—for he was personating the *Big Missouri*, and considered himself to be drawing nine feet of water. He was boat and captain and engine-bells combined, so he had to imagine himself standing on his own hurricane-deck giving the orders and executing them:

'Stop her, sir! Ting-a-ling-ling!' The headway ran almost out, and he drew up slowly towards the sidewalk.

'Ship up to back! Ting-a-ling-ling!' His arms straightened and stiffened down his sides.

'Set her back on the stabbord! Ting-a-ling-ling! Chow! Ch-chow-wow! Chow!' His right hand, meantime, describing stately circles—for it was representing a forty-foot wheel.

'Let her go back on the labbord! Ting-a-ling-ling! Chow-ch-chow-chow!' The left hand began to describe circles.

'Stop the stabbord! Ting-a-ling-ling! Stop the labbord! Come ahead on the stabbord! Stop her! Let your outside turn over slow! Ting-a-ling-ling!

Chow-ow-ow! Get out that headline! *Lively* now! Come on—out with your spring-line—what're you about there! Take a turn round that stump with the bight of it! Stand by that stage, now—let her go! Done with the engines, sir! Ting-a-ling-ling! *Sh't! sh't! sh't!*' (trying the gauge-cocks).

Tom went on whitewashing—paid no attention to the steamboat. Ben stared a moment, and then said:

'Hi-*yi*! *You're* up a stump, ain't you?'

No answer. Tom surveyed his last touch with the eye of an artist; then he gave his brush another gentle sweep and surveyed the result, as before. Ben ranged up alongside of him. Tom's mouth watered for the apple, but he stuck to his work. Ben said:

'Hello, old chap, you got to work, hey?'

Tom wheeled suddenly and said:

'Why, it's you, Ben! I warn't noticing.'

'Say—I'm going in a-swimming, *I* am. Don't you wish you could? But of course you'd druther *work*—wouldn't you? Course you would!'

Tom contemplated the boy a bit, and said:

'What do you call work?'

'Why, ain't *that* work?'

Tom resumed his whitewashing, and answered carelessly:

'Well, maybe it is, and maybe it ain't. All I know is, it suits Tom Sawyer.'

'Oh come, now, you don't mean to let on that you *like* it?'

The brush continued to move.

'Like it? Well, I don't see why I oughtn't to like it. Does a boy get a chance to whitewash a fence every day?'

This put the thing in a new light. Ben stopped nibbling his apple. Tom swept his brush daintily back and forth—stepped back to note the effect—added a touch here and there—criticised the effect again—Ben watching every move and getting more and more interested, more and more absorbed. Presently he said:

'Say, Tom. Let me whitewash a little.'

Tom considered, was about to consent; but he altered his mind.

'No—no—I reckon it wouldn't hardly do, Ben. You see Aunt Polly's awful particular about this fence—right here on the street, you know—but if it was the back fence I wouldn't mind, and *she* wouldn't. Yes, she's awful particular about this fence; it's got to be done very careful; I reckon there ain't one boy in a thousand, maybe two thousand, that can do it the way it's got to be done.'

'No—is that so? Oh, come, now—lemme just try. Only just a little—I'd let *you*, if you was me, Tom.'

'Ben, I'd like to, honest injun; but Aunt Polly—well, Jim wanted to do it but she wouldn't let him. Sid wanted to do it, and she wouldn't let Sid. Now don't you see how I'm fixed? If you was to tackle this fence, and anything was to happen to it—'

'Oh, shucks, I'll be just as careful. Now, lemme try. Say—I'll give you the core of my apple.'

'Well, here—No, Ben, now don't. I'm afeared—'

'I'll give you *all* of it!'

Tom gave up the brush, with reluctance in his face but alacrity in his heart. And while the late steamer *Missouri* worked and sweated in the sun, the retired artist sat on a barrel in the shade close by, dangled his legs, munched his apple, and planned the slaughter of more innocents. There was no lack of material; boys happened along every little while; they came to jeer, but remained to whitewash. By the time Ben was fagged out, Tom had traded the next chance to Billy Fisher for a kite, in good repair; and when *he* played out, Johnny Miller bought in for a dead rat and a string to swing it with—and so on, and so on, hour after hour. And when the middle of the afternoon came, from being a poor poverty-stricken boy in the morning, Tom was literally rolling in wealth. He had, besides the things before mentioned, twelve marbles, part of a jew's harp, a piece of blue bottle-glass to look through, a spool cannon, a key that wouldn't unlock anything, a fragment of chalk, a glass stopper of a decanter, a tin soldier, a couple of tadpoles, six fire-crackers, a kitten with only one eye, a brass door-knob, a dog-collar—but no dog—the handle of a knife, four pieces of orange-peel, and a dilapidated old window-sash.

The Adventures of Tom Sawyer (1876).

O N an evening in July 1862, when the young Samuel Clemens was beginning his career as a newspaperman in the mining boom-town of Virginia City, Nevada, and the American Civil War was in its second year, a young English clergyman and a friend took three little girls, the Liddell sisters, on a boating trip up the River Thames from Oxford to the water meadows at Godstow. To amuse the girls and to please his favourite, the 10-year-old middle sister Alice, the clergyman made up a long, dream-like story about a White Rabbit who popped down a hole and a girl named Alice who fell down the hole after him.

The Revd Charles Lutwidge Dodgson was not a practising clergyman but a mathematics tutor at Christ Church, Oxford. It seems that his lectures were rather boring but for him to lecture at all was a personal triumph as he was painfully shy and suffered from an awkward stammer. He had always been mildly eccentric—as a child he once armed some worms in his garden with miniature weapons to enable them to fight off the birds—and an element of personal eccentricity stayed with him when he became a somewhat solitary bachelor don. Among his interests, deemed at the time a little unsuitable for a bachelor don, were opera, theatre, the acting of Miss Ellen Terry, the then complicated and smelly process of taking photographs—and the company of little girls.

By all accounts his obsession with young and pretty girls was innocent. In those pre-Freudian days nobody thought it odd that a clergyman found the company of small girls so delightful and their bodies so beautiful that, with their parents' permission and observing the proprieties, he took to drawing them and photographing them while they were naked. He also loved telling them stories.

Three years after inventing for Alice Liddell and her sisters the story of Alice and the White Rabbit he decided, at Alice's suggestion, to write it up into a children's book, with illustrations by the Punch *cartoonist John Tenniel. It was published in 1865 as* Alice's Adventures in Wonderland. *He had already published mathematical works as Charles Lutwidge Dodgson so he concocted a pseudonym for the author of* Alice *by transposing Charles and Lutwidge and transforming Lutwidge via Ludovicus into Lewis, and Charles via Carolus into Carroll.*

Alice in Wonderland, *as the book is now usually known, was an instantaneous success and must be among the best-known and best-liked children's books in the English-speaking world. And among the most quoted.*

It worked on at least two levels. To adults it was an extraordinary and tantalizing mixture of invention, parody, irony, symbolism, punning, word-play and contemporary allusion; for instance it is thought likely that 'Twinkle, twinkle, little bat! How I wonder what you're at!' referred to Bartholomew Price, known as 'Bat', the extremely active Professor of Natural Philosophy at Oxford and Secretary to the Delegates of the University Press, among a dozen other appointments, who was notable in Lewis Carroll's day for always seeming to be hurtling from one committee meeting to another.

Grown-ups tended to be puzzled by the games which Carroll played with logic. He seemed to twist it and bend it, stand it on its head, give it a mirror-image; do everything fanciful with it but destroy it.

Children had no such problems; they accepted Carroll's logical play as easily and naturally as modern children accept computers. To young readers Alice *was just fun, a nimble-minded story with colourful, original characters and bizarre adventures, and with a likeable and resourceful heroine.*

It was the first great children's book which did not preach or aim to improve the young reader's morals. Lewis Carroll understood children. He was much easier in the company of young people than he ever was with adults and he knew how to make children laugh and feel involved in his stories.

At the Mad Tea-Party, Alice, puzzled by it all but plucky, has not only to cope with some odd logic but also with that maddening kind of thoughtless authority which adults so often impose upon children:

There was a table set out under a tree in front of the house, and the March Hare and the Hatter were having tea at it: a Dormouse was sitting between them, fast asleep, and the other two were using it as a cushion, resting their elbows on it, and talking over its head. 'Very uncomfortable for the Dormouse,' thought Alice; 'only as it's asleep, I suppose it doesn't mind.'

The table was a large one, but the three were all crowded together at one corner of it. 'No room! No room!' they cried out when they saw Alice coming. 'There's *plenty* of room!' said Alice indignantly, and she sat down in a large arm-chair at one end of the table.

'Have some wine,' the March Hare said in an encouraging tone.

Alice looked all round the table, but there was nothing on it but tea. 'I don't see any wine,' she remarked.

'There isn't any,' said the March Hare.

'Then it wasn't very civil of you to offer it,' said Alice angrily.

'It wasn't very civil of you to sit down without being invited,' said the March Hare.

'I didn't know it was *your* table,' said Alice: 'it's laid for a great many more than three.'

'Your hair wants cutting,' said the Hatter. He had been looking at Alice for some time with great curiosity, and this was his first speech.

'You should learn not to make personal remarks,' Alice said with some severity: 'it's very rude.'

The Hatter opened his eyes very wide on hearing this; but all he *said* was 'Why is a raven like a writing desk?'

'Come, we shall have some fun now!' thought Alice. 'I'm glad they've begun asking riddles—I believe I can guess that,' she added aloud.

'Do you mean that you think you can find out the answer to it?' said the March Hare.

'Exactly so,' said Alice.

'Then you should say what you mean,' the March Hare went on.

'I do,' Alice hastily replied; 'at least—at least I mean what I say—that's the same thing, you know.'

'Not the same thing a bit!' said the Hatter. 'Why, you might just as well say that "I see what I eat" is the same thing as "I eat what I see"!'

'You might just as well say,' added the March Hare, 'that "I like what I get" is the same thing as "I get what I like"!'

'You might just as well say,' added the Dormouse, which seemed to be talking in its sleep, 'that "I breathe when I sleep" is the same thing as "I sleep when I breathe"!'

'It *is* the same thing with you,' said the Hatter, and here the conversation dropped, and the party sat silent for a minute, while Alice thought over all she could remember about ravens and writing-desks, which wasn't much.

The Hatter was the first to break the silence. 'What day of the month is it?' he said, turning to Alice: he had taken his watch out of his pocket, and was looking at it uneasily, shaking it every now and then, and holding it to his ear.

Alice considered a little, and then said, 'The fourth'.

'Two days wrong!' sighed the Hatter. 'I told you butter wouldn't suit the works!' he added, looking angrily at the March Hare.

'It was the *best* butter,' the March Hare meekly replied.

'Yes, but some crumbs must have got in as well,' the Hatter grumbled: 'you shouldn't have put it in with the bread-knife.'

The March Hare took the watch and looked at it gloomily: then he dipped it into his cup of tea, and looked at it again: but he could think of nothing better to say than his first remark, 'It was the *best* butter, you know'.

Alice had been looking over his shoulder with some curiosity. 'What a funny watch!' she remarked. 'It tells the day of the month, and doesn't tell what o'clock it is!'

'Why should it?' muttered the Hatter. 'Does *your* watch tell you what year it is?'

'Of course not,' Alice replied very readily: 'but that's because it stays the same year for such a long time together.'

'Which is just the case with *mine*,' said the Hatter.

Alice felt dreadfully puzzled. The Hatter's remark seemed to her to have no sort of meaning in it, and yet it was certainly English. 'I don't quite understand you,' she said, as politely as she could.

'The Dormouse is asleep again,' said the Hatter, and he poured a little hot tea upon its nose.

The Dormouse shook its head impatiently, and said, without opening its eyes. 'Of course, of course: just what I was going to remark myself.'

'Have you guessed the riddle yet?' the Hatter said, turning to Alice again.

'No, I give it up,' Alice replied. 'What's the answer?'

'I haven't the slightest idea,' said the Hatter.

'Nor I,' said the March Hare.

Alice sighed wearily. 'I think you might do something better with the time,' she said, 'than wasting it in asking riddles that have no answers.'

'If you knew Time as well as I do,' said the Hatter, 'you wouldn't talk about wasting *it*. It's *him*.'

'I don't know what you mean,' said Alice.

'Of course you don't!' the Hatter said, tossing his head contemptuously. 'I dare say you never even spoke to Time!'

'Perhaps not,' Alice cautiously replied; 'but I know I have to beat time when I learn music.'

'Ah! That accounts for it,' said the Hatter. 'He won't stand beating. Now, if you only kept on good terms with him, he'd do almost anything you liked with the clock. For instance, suppose it were nine o'clock in the morning, just time to begin lessons: you'd only have to whisper a hint to Time, and round goes the clock in a twinkling! Half-past one, time for dinner!'

('I only wish it was,' the March Hare said to itself in a whisper.)

'That would be grand, certainly,' said Alice thoughtfully; 'but then— I shouldn't be hungry for it, you know.'

'Not at first, perhaps,' said the Hatter: 'but you could keep it to half-past one as long as you liked.'

'Is that the way *you* manage?' Alice asked.

The Hatter shook his head mournfully. 'Not I!' he replied. 'We quarrelled last March—just before *he* went mad, you know—' (pointing with his teaspoon at the March Hare,) '—it was at the great concert given by the Queen of Hearts, and I had to sing

> *"Twinkle, twinkle, little bat!*
> *How I wonder what you're at!"*

You know the song, perhaps?'

'I've heard something like it,' said Alice.

'It goes on, you know,' the Hatter continued, 'in this way:

> *"Up above the world you fly,*
> *Like a tea-tray in the sky.*
> *Twinkle, twinkle—"'*

Here the Dormouse shook itself, and began singing in its sleep '*Twinkle, twinkle, twinkle, twinkle—*' and went on so long that they had to pinch it to make it stop.

'Well, I'd hardly finished the first verse,' said the Hatter, 'when the Queen bawled out "He's murdering the time! Off with his head!"'

'How dreadfully savage!' exclaimed Alice.

'And ever since that,' the Hatter went on in a mournful tone, 'he won't do a thing I ask! It's always six o'clock now.'

A bright idea came into Alice's head. 'Is that the reason so many tea-things are put out here?' she asked.

'Yes, that's it,' said the Hatter with a sigh: 'it's always tea-time, and we've no time to wash the things between whiles.'

'Then you keep moving round, I suppose?' said Alice

'Exactly so,' said the Hatter: 'as the things get used up.'

'But what happens when you come to the beginning again?' Alice ventured to ask.

'Suppose we change the subject,' the March Hare interrupted, yawning. 'I'm getting tired of this. I vote the young lady tells us a story.'

'I'm afraid I don't know one,' said Alice, rather alarmed at the proposal.

Then the Dormouse slowly opened its eyes. 'I wasn't asleep,' it said in a hoarse, feeble voice, 'I heard every word you fellows were saying.'

'Tell us a story!' said the March Hare.

'Yes, please do!' pleaded Alice.

'And be quick about it,' added the Hatter, 'or you'll be asleep again before it's done.'

'Once upon a time there were three little sisters,' the Dormouse began in a great hurry; 'and their names were Elsie, Lacie, and Tillie; and they lived at the bottom of a well—'

'What did they live on?' said Alice, who always took a great interest in questions of eating and drinking.

'They lived on treacle,' said the Dormouse, after thinking a minute or two.

'They couldn't have done that, you know,' Alice gently remarked. 'They'd have been ill.'

'So they were,' said the Dormouse; '*very* ill.'

Alice tried a little to fancy to herself what such an extraordinary way of living would be like, but it puzzled her too much: so she went on: 'But why did they live at the bottom of a well?'

'Take some more tea,' the March Hare said to Alice, very earnestly.

'I've had nothing yet,' Alice replied in an offended tone: 'so I can't take more.'

'You mean you can't take *less*,' said the Hatter: 'it's very easy to take *more* than nothing.'

'Nobody asked *your* opinion,' said Alice.

'Who's making personal remarks now?' the Hatter asked triumphantly.

Alice did not quite know what to say to this: so she helped herself to some tea and bread-and-butter, and then turned to the Dormouse, and repeated her question. 'Why did they live at the bottom of a well?'

The Dormouse again took a minute or two to think about it, and then said 'It was a treacle-well.'

'There's no such thing!' Alice was beginning very angrily, but the Hatter and the March Hare went 'Sh! Sh!' and the Dormouse sulkily remarked 'If you can't be civil, you'd better finish the story for yourself.'

'No, please go on!' Alice said very humbly. 'I won't interrupt you again. I dare say there may be *one*.'

'One, indeed!' said the Dormouse indignantly. However, he consented to go on. 'And so these three little sisters—they were learning to draw, you know—'

'What did they draw?' said Alice, quite forgetting her promise.

'Treacle,' said the Dormouse, without considering at all, this time.

'I want a clean cup,' interrupted the Hatter: 'let's all move one place on.'

He moved on as he spoke, and the Dormouse followed him; the March Hare moved into the Dormouse's place, and Alice rather unwillingly took the place of the March Hare. The Hatter was the only one who got any advantage from the change; and Alice was a good deal worse off than before, as the March Hare had just upset the milk-jug into his plate.

Alice did not wish to offend the Dormouse again, so she began very cautiously: 'But I don't understand. Where did they draw the treacle from?'

'You can draw water out of a water-well,' said the Hatter; 'so I should think you could draw treacle out of a treacle-well—eh, stupid?'

'But they were in the well,' Alice said to the Dormouse, not choosing to notice this last remark.

'Of course they were,' said the Dormouse: 'well in.'

This answer so confused poor Alice, that she let the Dormouse go on for some time without interrupting it.

'They were learning to draw,' the Dormouse went on, yawning and rubbing its eyes, for it was getting very sleepy; 'and they drew all manner of things—everything that begins with an M—'

'Why with an M?' said Alice.

'Why not?' said the March Hare.

Alice was silent.

The Dormouse had closed its eyes by this time, and was going off into a doze; but, on being pinched by the Hatter, it woke up again with a little shriek, and went on: '—that begins with an M, such as mouse-traps, and the moon, and memory, and muchness—you know you say things are "much of a muchness"—did you ever see such a thing as a drawing of a muchness?'

'Really, now you ask me,' said Alice, very much confused, 'I don't think—'

'Then you shouldn't talk,' said the Hatter.

This piece of rudeness was more than Alice could bear: she got up in great disgust, and walked off: the Dormouse fell asleep instantly, and neither of the others took the least notice of her going, though she looked back once or twice, half hoping that they would call after her: the last time she saw them, they were trying to put the Dormouse into the teapot.

'At any rate I'll never go *there* again!' said Alice, as she picked her way through the wood. 'It's the stupidest tea-party I ever was at in all my life!'

'Lewis Carroll' (Charles Lutwidge Dodgson (1832–98)), *Alice's Adventures in Wonderland* (1865).

Two of Lewis Carroll's more conventional hobbies were inventing and playing chess. Such was his enthusiasm for chess that inevitably he wanted the Liddell girls to play it too so he taught them by telling them amusing stories to illustrate the rules and the moves. A year or so later he worked these chess stories up into a book and in 1872 published it as Through the Looking Glass and what Alice Found There.

The second Alice book proved to be even more popular than the first. Its frontispiece was a chess-problem and the action of the story was worked out as a game of chess. The tone of the book was a shade more purposeful than Alice in Wonderland; *Alice no longer wandered from one scene to another but was firmly propelled—a chess-piece moved on by a superior force from square to square. And Carroll touched on contemporary issues, such as the way that industrial prosperity was encouraging petty officialdom and regimentation, two forms of bullying disliked by all children:*

'Tickets, please!' said the Guard, putting his head in at the window. In a moment everybody was holding out a ticket: they were about the same size as the people, and quite seemed to fill the carriage.

'Now then! Show your ticket, child!' the Guard went on, looking angrily at Alice. And a great many voices all said together ('like the chorus of a song,' thought Alice) 'Don't keep him waiting, child! Why, his time is worth a thousand pounds a minute!'

'I'm afraid I haven't got one,' Alice said in a frightened tone: 'there wasn't a ticket-office where I came from.' And again the chorus of voices went on. 'There wasn't room for one where she came from. The land there is worth a thousand pounds an inch!'

'Don't make excuses,' said the Guard: 'you should have bought one from the engine-driver.' And once more the chorus of voices went on with 'The man that drives the engine. Why, the smoke alone is worth a thousand pounds a puff!'

Alice thought to herself 'Then there's no use in speaking.' The voices didn't join in, this time, as she hadn't spoken, but, to her great surprise, they all *thought* in chorus (I hope you understand what *thinking in chorus* means—for I must confess that *I* don't), 'Better say nothing at all. Language is worth a thousand pounds a word!'

'I shall dream about a thousand pounds to-night, I know I shall!' thought Alice.

All this time the Guard was looking at her, first through a telescope, then through a microscope, and then through an opera-glass. At last he said 'You're travelling the wrong way,' and shut up the window, and went away.

Through the Looking Glass and what Alice Found There (1872).

One of the book's most delightful episodes is the scene in which Alice meets the White Knight.

It is thought that Carroll wrote the White Knight as a whimsical caricature of himself (Tenniel's drawing of the White Knight was not a portrait of Carroll but of the sub-editor of Punch, Horace Mayhew*). Carroll made the White Knight, like himself, an unsuccessful inventor. In fact Carroll did have one success; besides the weaponry for worms and other splendid failures he invented a portable chess-set for travellers which worked very well.*

Significantly, Carroll made Alice declare that her meeting with the White Knight was the one episode which she remembered most clearly:

Years afterwards she could bring the whole scene back again, as if it had been only yesterday—the mild blue eyes and kindly smile of the Knight—the setting sun gleaming through his hair, and shining on his armour in a blaze of light that quite dazzled her.

Ibid.

That is perhaps how Carroll wanted to be remembered, because his affection for Alice never wavered, even when she was mature and happily married. He ended Through the Looking Glass *with a nostalgic poem recalling the dream-like boat trip on the Thames when he first told the story of* Alice *to the three small girls. The poem was an acrostic: the initial letters of the first words of each line spelt out* ALICE PLEASANCE LIDDELL.

The meeting with the White Knight begins with Alice captured by the Red

Knight. The White Knight gallops up in Don Quixote fashion and releases her after a brief fight which ends, true to the Rules of Battle, with both knights falling off their horses on to their heads. The Red Knight climbs back on and gallops away leaving Alice alone in the wood with her rescuer:

'It was a glorious victory, wasn't it?' said the White Knight, as he came up panting.

'I don't know,' Alice said doubtfully. 'I don't want to be anybody's prisoner. I want to be a Queen.'

'So you will, when you've crossed the next brook,' said the White Knight. 'I'll see you safe to the end of the wood—and then I must go back, you know. That's the end of my move.'

'Thank you very much,' said Alice. 'May I help you off with your helmet?' It was evidently more than he could manage by himself; however, she managed to shake him out of it at last.

'Now one can breathe more easily,' said the Knight, putting back his shaggy hair with both hands, and turning his gentle face and large mild eyes to Alice. She thought she had never seen such a strange-looking soldier in all her life.

He was dressed in tin armour, which seemed to fit him very badly, and he had a queer-shaped little deal box fastened across his shoulders, upside-down, and with the lid hanging open. Alice looked at it with great curiosity.

'I see you're admiring my little box,' the Knight said in a friendly tone. 'It's my own invention—to keep clothes and sandwiches in. You see I carry it upside-down, so that the rain can't get in.'

'But the things can get *out*,' Alice gently remarked. 'Do you know the lid's open?'

'I didn't know it,' the Knight said, a shade of vexation passing over his face. 'Then all the things must have fallen out! And the box is no use without them.' He unfastened it as he spoke, and was just about to throw it into the bushes, when a sudden thought seemed to strike him, and he hung it carefully on a tree. 'Can you guess why I did that?' he said to Alice.

Alice shook her head.

'In hopes some bees may make a nest in it—then I should get the honey.'

'But you've got a bee-hive—or something like one—fastened to the saddle,' said Alice.

'Yes, it's a very good bee-hive,' the Knight said in a discontented tone, 'one of the best kind. But not a single bee has come near it yet. And the other thing is a mouse-trap. I suppose the mice keep the bees out—or the bees keep the mice out, I don't know which.'

'I was wondering what the mouse-trap was for,' said Alice. 'It isn't very likely there would be any mice on the horse's back.'

'Not very likely, perhaps,' said the Knight; 'but, if they *do* come, I don't choose to have them running all about.'

'You see,' he went on after a pause, 'it's as well to be provided for *every-thing*. That's the reason the horse has all those anklets round his feet.'

'But what are they for?' Alice asked in a tone of great curiosity.

'To guard against the bites of sharks,' the Knight replied. 'It's an invention of my own. And now help me on. I'll go with you to the end of the wood—What's that dish for?'

'It's meant for plum-cake,' said Alice.

'We'd better take it with us,' the Knight said. 'It'll come in handy if we find any plum-cake. Help me to get it into this bag.'

This took a long time to manage, though Alice held the bag open very carefully, because the Knight was so *very* awkward in putting in the dish: the first two or three times that he tried he fell in himself instead. 'It's rather a tight fit, you see,' he said, as they got it in at last; 'there are so many candlesticks in the bag.' And he hung it to the saddle, which was already loaded with bunches of carrots, and fire-irons, and many other things.

'I hope you've got your hair well fastened on?' he continued, as they set off.

'Only in the usual way,' Alice said, smiling.

'That's hardly enough,' he said, anxiously. 'You see the wind is so *very* strong here. It's as strong as soup.'

'Have you invented a plan for keeping the hair from being blown off?' Alice enquired.

'Not yet,' said the Knight. 'But I've got a plan for keeping it from *falling* off.'

'I should like to hear it, very much.'

'First you take an upright stick,' said the Knight. 'Then you make your hair creep up it, like a fruit-tree. Now the reason hair falls off is because it hangs down—things never fall *upwards*, you know. It's a plan of my own invention. You may try it if you like.'

It didn't sound a comfortable plan, Alice thought, and for a few minutes she walked on in silence, puzzling over the idea, and every now and then stopping to help the poor Knight, who certainly was *not* a good rider.

Whenever the horse stopped (which it did very often), he fell off in front; and, whenever it went on again (which it generally did rather suddenly), he fell off behind. Otherwise he kept on pretty well, except that he had a habit of now and then falling off sideways; and, as he generally did this on the side on which Alice was walking, she soon found that it was the best plan not to walk *quite* close to the horse.

'I'm afraid you've not had much practice in riding,' she ventured to say, as she was helping him up from his fifth tumble.

The Knight looked very much surprised, and a little offended at the remark. 'What makes you say that?' he asked, as he scrambled back into the saddle, keeping hold of Alice's hair with one hand, to save himself from falling over on the other side.

'Because people don't fall off quite so often, when they've had much practice.'

'I've had plenty of practice,' the Knight said very gravely: 'plenty of practice!'

Alice could think of nothing better to say than 'Indeed?' but she said it as heartily as she could. They went on a little way in silence after this, the Knight with his eyes shut, muttering to himself, and Alice watching anxiously for the next tumble.

'The great art of riding,' the Knight suddenly began in a loud voice, waving his right arm as he spoke, 'is to keep—' Here the sentence ended as suddenly as it had begun, as the Knight fell heavily on the top of his head exactly in the path where Alice was walking. She was quite frightened this time, and said in an anxious tone, as she picked him up, 'I hope no bones are broken?'

'None to speak of,' the Knight said, as if he didn't mind breaking two or three of them. 'The great art of riding, as I was saying, is—to keep your balance properly. Like this, you know—'

He let go of the bridle, and stretched out both his arms to show Alice what he meant, and this time he fell flat on his back, right under the horse's feet.

'Plenty of practice!' he went on repeating, all the time that Alice was getting him on his feet again. 'Plenty of practice!'

'It's too ridiculous!' cried Alice, losing all her patience this time. 'You ought to have a wooden horse on wheels, that you ought!'

'Does that kind go smoothly?' the Knight asked in a tone of great interest, clasping his arms round the horse's neck as he spoke, just in time to save himself from tumbling off again.

'Much more smoothly than a live horse,' Alice said, with a little scream of laughter, in spite of all she could do to prevent it.

'I'll get one,' the Knight said thoughtfully to himself. 'One or two—several.'

There was a short silence after this, and then the Knight went on again. 'I'm a great hand at inventing things. Now, I daresay you noticed, the last time you picked me up, that I was looking rather thoughtful?'

'You *were* a little grave,' said Alice.

'Well, just then I was inventing a new way of getting over a gate—would you like to hear it?'

'Very much indeed,' said Alice politely.

'I'll tell you how I came to think of it,' said the Knight. 'You see, I said to myself "The only difficulty is with the feet: the *head* is high enough already." Now, first I put my head on the top of the gate—the head's high enough—then I stand on my head—then the feet are high enough, you see—then I'm over, you see.'

'Yes, I suppose you'd be over when that was done,' Alice said thoughtfully: but don't you think it would be rather hard?'

'I haven't tried it yet,' the Knight said, gravely; 'so I can't tell for certain—but I'm afraid it would be a little hard.'

He looked so vexed at the idea, that Alice changed the subject hastily.

'What a curious helmet you've got,' she said cheerfully. 'Is that your invention too?'

The Knight looked down proudly at his helmet, which hung from the saddle. 'Yes,' he said; 'but I've invented a better one than that—like a sugar-loaf. When I used to wear it, if I fell off the horse, it always touched the ground directly. So I had a *very* little way to fall, you see—but there was the danger of falling into it to be sure. That happened to me once—and the worst of it was, before I could get out again, the other White Knight came and put it on. He thought it was his own helmet.'

The Knight looked so solemn about it that Alice did not laugh. 'I'm afraid you must have hurt him,' she said in a trembling voice, 'being on the top of his head.'

'I had to kick him, of course,' the Knight said, very seriously. 'And then he took his helmet off again—but it took hours and hours to get me out. I was as fast as—as lightning, you know.'

'But that's a different kind of fastness,' Alice objected.

The Knight shook his head. 'It was all kinds of fastness with me, I can assure you!' he said. He raised his hands in some excitement as he said this, and instantly rolled out of the saddle, and fell headlong into a deep ditch.

Alice ran to the side of the ditch to look for him. She was rather startled by the fall, as for some time he had kept on very well, and she was afraid that he really was hurt this time. However, though she could see nothing but the soles of his feet, she was much relieved to hear that he was talking on in his usual tone, 'All kinds of fastness,' he repeated: 'but it was careless of him to put on another man's helmet—with the man in it, too.'

'How *can* you go on talking so quietly, head downwards?' Alice asked, as she dragged him out by the feet, and laid him in a heap on the bank.

The Knight looked surprised at the question. 'What does it matter where my body happens to be?' he said. 'My mind goes on working all the same. In fact, the more head-downwards I am, the more I keep inventing new things.'

'Now the cleverest thing of the sort that I ever did,' he went on after a pause, 'was inventing a pudding during the meat-course.'

'In time to have it cooked for the next course?' said Alice. 'Well, that *was* quick work, certainly!'

'Well, not the *next* course,' the Knight said in a slow thoughful tone: 'no, not the next *course*.'

'Then it would have to be next day. I suppose you wouldn't have two pudding-courses in one dinner?'

'Well, not the *next* day,' the Knight repeated as before: 'not the next *day*. In fact,' he went on, holding his head down, and his voice getting lower and lower, 'I don't believe that pudding ever *was* cooked! In fact, I don't believe that pudding ever *will* be cooked! And yet it was a very clever pudding to invent.'

'What did you mean it to be made of?' asked Alice, hoping to cheer him up, for the poor Knight seemed quite low-spirited about it.

'It began with blotting-paper,' the Knight answered with a groan.

'That wouldn't be very nice, I'm afraid—'

'Not very nice *alone*,' he interrupted, quite eagerly: 'but you've no idea what a difference it made, mixing it with other things—such as gunpowder and sealing-wax. And here I must leave you.' They had just come to the end of the wood.

Alice could only look puzzled: she was thinking of the pudding.   Ibid.

———

W HEN *John—later Sir John—Tenniel was asked by Lewis Carroll to illustrate* Alice in Wonderland, *he had just been appointed leading cartoonist of a humorous magazine which had by then been going for twenty or so years and was well on its way to becoming the most successful British humorous magazine ever, a national institution—*Punch.

If the founding of the modern New Yorker *magazine eighty years after* Punch, *the result of the single-minded determination of Harold Ross to publish a sophisticated magazine for New Yorkers, had an almost clinically straightforward birth, then the haphazard arrival on the scene of* Punch *back in 1841 could be described as a ditch-delivery.*

The origins of Punch *are still a matter of debate, but it seems probable that the magazine was the not-very-original idea of one or more of a small bunch of young artists, printers, and scribblers who hoped thereby to make some money. The prime mover seems to have been either the engraver, Ebenezer Landells, or one of the original three co-editors, the journalist Henry Mayhew. Or, again, the writer Douglas Jerrold might have been the key figure.*

It was hardly an original idea because at that time new comical magazines were popping up all over the place; most of them, like playful dolphins, enjoying only a brief moment in the sun before sinking out of sight beneath the waves.

Even the name 'Punch' had already been used in such previous publications as 'Punchinello', 'Punch in London', and 'Punch in Cambridge.'

The proposed style of the magazine, far from being something new, was cribbed from a successful Parisian satirical weekly, Charivari *(Fr. n., Cacophonous noise made in derision of some unpopular person).* Charivari *featured a full-page political cartoon—printed on one side of the paper only so that it could be cut out and kept—and a mixture of radical political invective and jokes.*

The first edition of Britain's new humorous magazine came on the streets on Saturday, 17 July 1841. It cost 3d. and was called PUNCH. THE LONDON CHARIVARI. *Advertisements claimed 'This Guffawgraph is intended to form a refuge for destitute wit—an asylum for the thousands of orphan jokes.'*

Punch *as an infant was sickly and its life frequently despaired of: one of its original co-editors, Mark Lemon, was also a playwright (the staff and contributors all did other things, many of them wrote or drew for rival publications) and several times Lemon had to add his royalties to the kitty to keep the enterprise going. But the magazine hung on and gradually its circulation rose until it became a profitable venture. And its circulation continued to rise. And rise.*

The magazine's remarkable metamorphosis from an ailing Guffawgraph to the most universally respected humorous magazine ever can be attributed to a number of factors which, by both chance and design, made it different and eventually very much better than its rivals.

It was never dirty. Yet it began publication at a period in the first years of Victorian Britain when almost all the comic and political sheets were crude and violent in their satire and near-pornographic in their jokes (which most of them still were at the end of the century). The lower-middle-classes were Punch's *readership and it became the one weekly which the rising and increasingly domestic lower-middle-class bread-winner could take home and share with his family.*

It was not party-political, at least to start with. It did not espouse political causes but mocked all politicians and parties, as it did all social evils and distresses.

Intellectually it bridged the gap between the great monthlies with their critic-barons thundering away at current literature, and the semi-literate 'comic cuts'.

The founder-figures of Punch *must have had something a little bit special about them because perhaps the most important reason for the magazine's success was that it attracted to it the best of the writing and drawing talent available, and, just as important, a number of extremely good and timely editors.*

And the magazine began with one very considerable asset: among its founder-members was perhaps the best humorous journalist of the day, Douglas Jerrold.

Jerrold was a short, burly figure, bent with rheumatism. He had been a mid-shipman in the navy and his grandmother, knowing his susceptibility to chills, had written to the captain of his ship asking him to make sure personally that her grandson wore his pattens when the deck was damp. The Captain took this in his stride (he was Jane Austen's brother) and lent the lad his Shakespeare and many books, which were of great help in the development of the young journalist-to-be.

Punch *writers were expected to turn their hand to whatever was required to fill that week's edition: satirical squibs, jokes, topical comments. It was Jerrold who suggested in* Punch *that the glass hall housing the Great Exhibition should be dubbed 'The Crystal Palace'.*

Jerrold wrote many powerful and funny political pieces before, in 1845, be-ginning a series of humorous sketches which he called Mrs Caudle's Curtain Lectures. *These became so popular that the arrival in the magazine of Mrs Caudle did for the circulation of* Punch *what the introduction of Sam Weller did for sales of* The Pickwick Papers. *It was said (though by his son, Blanchard) that in the early 1850s Jerrold had become a more popular writer than Charles Dickens.*

Mrs Caudle's Curtain Lectures *was an important innovation. It was the first great* Punch *series and the first ever comic series of magazine sketches to depict, compassionately, an aspect of ordinary living: the lack of self-confidence of a lower middle-class wife in the status-conscious, materialistic London of the 1840s.*

They were frame stories, with Mr Caudle as the narrator and commentator. In his Introduction to the collected edition Jerrold explained that after the death of Mrs Caudle, Mr Caudle missed her nightly tirade so much that he could not get to sleep. To lay the ghost he committed to paper one curtain lecture of his late wife each night, after which he slept like a child.

Mr Caudle was a small businessman, a toy-man and doll merchant. He worked long hours. The only chance Mrs Caudle had to air her grievances was when the two of them were in bed. Then the hapless Job Caudle was captive and she was able to harangue him at length and with vigour on his latest wife-provoking devilment, like staying downstairs until after midnight with a crony; becoming a Mason and going off for evenings without Mrs Caudle; losing the family umbrella.

Or committing a selfish act of generosity:

MR CAUDLE HAS LENT FIVE POUNDS TO A FRIEND

'You ought to be very rich, Mr Caudle. I wonder who'd lend you five pounds! But so it is: a wife may work and may slave! Ha, dear! the many things that might have been done with five pounds! As if people picked up money in the street! But you always were a fool, Mr Caudle! I've wanted a black satin gown these three years, and that five pounds would have pretty well bought it. But it's no matter how I go,—not at all. Everybody says I don't dress as becomes your wife—and I don't; but what's that to you, Mr Caudle? Nothing. Oh, no! you can have fine feelings for everybody but those belonging to you. I wish people knew you, as I do—that's all. You like to be called liberal— and your poor family pays for it.

'All the girls want bonnets, and when they're to get 'em I can't tell. Half five pounds would have bought 'em—but now they must go without. Of course, *they* belong to you; and anybody but your own flesh and blood, Mr Caudle.

'The man called for the water-rate, to-day; but I should like to know how people are to pay taxes, who throw away five pounds to every fellow that asks them.

'Perhaps you don't know that Jack, this morning, knocked his shuttle-cock through his bed-room window. I was going to send for the glazier to mend it; but after you lent that five pounds I was sure we couldn't afford it. Oh, no! the window must go as it is;. and pretty weather for a dear child to sleep with a broken window. He's got a cold already on his lungs, and I shouldn't at all wonder if that broken window settled him—if the dear boy dies, his death will be upon his father's head; for I'm sure we can't now pay to mend windows. We might though, and do a good many more things, if people didn't throw away their five pounds.

'Next Tuesday the fire-insurance is due. I should like to know how it's to be paid! Why, it can't be paid at all. That five pounds would have just done it—and now, insurance is out of the question. And there never were so many fires as there are now. I shall never close my eyes all night,—but what's that to you, so people can call you liberal Mr Caudle! Your wife and children may all be burnt alive in their beds—as all of us to a certainty shall be, for the insurance *must* drop. And after we've insured for so many years! But how, I should like to know, are people to insure who make ducks and drakes of their five pounds?

'I did think we might go to Margate this summer. There's poor little Caroline, I'm sure she wants the sea. But no, dear creature! she must stop at home—all of us must stop at home—she'll go into a consumption, there's no doubt of that; yes—sweet little angel!—I've made up my mind to lose her, *now*. The child might have been saved; but people can't save their children and throw away their five pounds, too.

'I wonder where poor little Cherub is! While you were lending that five pounds, the dog ran out of the shop. You know, I never let it go into the street, for fear it should be bit by some mad dog, and come home and bite all the children. It wouldn't now at all astonish me if the animal was to come back with the hydrophobia, and give it to all the family. However, what's your family to you, so you can play the liberal creature with five pounds?

'Do you hear that shutter, how it's banging to and fro? Yes,—I know what it wants as well as you, it wants a new fastening. I was going to send for the blacksmith to-day. But now it's out of the question: *now* it must bang of nights, since you've thrown away five pounds.

'Well, things are come to a pretty pass! This is the first night I ever made my supper off roast beef without pickles. But who is to afford pickles, when folks are always lending five pounds?

'Ha! there's the soot falling down the chimney. If I hate the smell of anything, it's the smell of soot. And you know it; but what are my feelings to you? Sweep the chimney! Yes, it's all very fine to say, sweep the chimney— but how are chimneys to be swept—how are they to be paid for by people who don't take care of their five pounds?

'Do you hear the mice running about the room? *I* hear them. If they were only to drag you out of bed, it would be no matter. Set a trap for them! Yes, it's easy enough to say—set a trap for 'em. But how are people to afford the cheese, when every day they lose five pounds?

'Hark! I'm sure there's a noise down stairs. It wouldn't at all surprise me if there were thieves in the house. Well, it *may* be the cat; but thieves are pretty sure to come in some night. There's a wretched fastening to the back-door; but these are not times to afford bolts and bars, when fools won't take care of their five pounds.

'Mary Anne ought to have gone to the dentist's to-morrow. She wants three teeth taken out. Now, it can't be done. Three teeth that quite disfigure the child's mouth. But there they must stop, and spoil the sweetest face that was ever made. Otherwise, she'd have been a wife for a lord. Now, when she grows up, who'll have her? Nobody. We shall die, and leave her alone and unprotected in the world. But what do you care for that? Nothing; so you squander away five pounds.

'And now, see Mr Caudle, what a misery you've brought upon your wretched family! I can't have a satin gown—the girls can't have new bonnets—the water-rate must stand over—Jack must get his death through a broken window—our fire-insurance can't be paid, so we shall all fall victims to the devouring element—the dog will come home and bite us all mad—that shutter will go banging for ever—the soot will always fall—the mice never let us have a wink of sleep—thieves be always breaking in the house—and our dear Mary Anne be for ever left an unprotected maid,—and all, all Mr Caudle, because YOU WILL GO ON LENDING FIVE POUNDS!'

Douglas Jerrold (1803–57), *Mrs Caudle's Curtain Lectures* (1846).

WILLIAM MAKEPEACE THACKERAY, *illustrator and scribbler, was another of the likely, rather louche, lads who were in at the conception of* Punch. *To look at, Thackeray could hardly have been less like his colleague Douglas Jerrold. Thackeray was six feet three inches tall with an enormous head and a broken nose, the result of a fight at school with his best friend. Carlyle, not much of an admirer of novelists, described him as 'a half-monstrous Cornish giant, kind of painter, Cambridge man . . . who is now writing for his life in London'.*

Thackeray was born into a rich middle-class family—his father had made a fortune with the East India Company—but he suddenly dropped a class or two when as a young man he lost his inheritance, probably through bad investments and gambling. He was naturally indolent but the need to earn a living and regain his position in the fashionable world concentrated his mind wonderfully and he set about exercising his talents for sketching and painting, and for writing amusing articles. Having failed to get the job of illustrating Pickwick Papers, *he joined the band of immensely prolific free-lance literary drudges who supplied the magazines with much of their output of humorous caricatures and prose.*

He first began to make a name for himself in 1838 with a successful series of stories for Fraser's Magazine *which were supposedly the autobiography of a cockney footman named Charles Yellowplush.*

This was that period, tedious to modern readers, when authors in Britain, as in America, became fascinated with trying to capture the real speech of people on paper by the use of almost unreadable dialect. They also aimed to raise a laugh by the use of skilful yet painful comical misspelling. Thackeray's early pieces had both of these in abundance. Yet his humour has an ease and freshness to it and a touch of irony and social satire which give a hint of what he was going to go on to achieve as a novelist.

Charles Yellowplush begins his autobiography:

I was born in the year one of the present or Christian hera, and am, in consquints, seven-and-thirty years old. My mamma called me Charles James

Harrington Fitzroy Yellowplush, in compliment to several noble families, and
to a sellybrated coachmin whom she knew, who wore a yellow livry, and
drove the Lord Mayor of London.

Why she gev me this genlmn's name is a diffiklty, or rayther the name of
a part of his dress; however, it's stuck to me through life, in which I was, as
it were, a footman by buth.

Praps he was my father—though on this subjict I can't speak suttinly, for
my ma wrapped up my buth in a mistry. I may be illygitmut, I may have
been changed at nuss; but I've always had genlmnly tastes through life, and
have no doubt that I come of a genlmnly origum.

The less I say about my parint the better, for the dear old creatur was very
good to me, and, I fear, had very little other goodness in her. Why, I can't
say; but I always passed as her nevyou. We led a strange life; sometimes ma
was dressed in sattn and rooge, and sometimes in rags and dutt; sometimes
I got kisses, and sometimes kix; sometimes gin, and sometimes shampang;
law bless us! how she used to swear at me, and cuddle me; there we were,
quarreling and making up, sober and tipsy, starving and guttling by turns,
just as ma got money or spent it. But let me draw a vail over the seen, and
speak of her no more—it's sfishant for the public to know, that her name
was Miss Montmorency, and we lived in the New Cut.

My poor mother died one morning, Hev'n bless her! and I was left in this
wide, wicked wuld, without so much money as would buy me a penny roal
for my brexfast. But there was some amongst our naybours (and let me tell
you there's more kindness among them poor disreppable creaturs than in
half-a-dozen lords or barrynets) who took pity upon poor Sal's orfin (for they
bust out laffin when I called her Miss Montmorency), and gev me bred and
shelter. I'm afraid, in spite of their kindness, that my *morrils* wouldn't have
improved if I'd stayed long among 'em. But a benny-violent genlmn saw me,
and put me to school. The academy which I went to was called the Free
School of Saint Bartholomew's the Less—the young genlmn wore green baize
coats, yellow leather whatsisnames, a tin plate on the left arm, and a cap
about the size of a muffing. I stayed there sicks years; from sicks, that is to
say, till my twelfth year, during three years of witch I distinguished myself
not a little in the musicle way, for I bloo the bellus of the church horgin, and
very fine tunes we played too.

Well, it's not worth recording my jewvenile follies (what trix we used to
play the applewoman! and how we put snuff in the old clark's Prayer-book—
my eye!); but one day, a genlmn entered the school-room—it was on the
very day when I went to subtraxion—and asked the master for a young lad
for a servant. They pitched on me glad enough; and nex day found me
sleeping in the sculry, close under the sink, at Mr Bago's country-house at
Pentonville.

Bago kep a shop in Smithfield market, and drov a taring good trade in the
oil and Italian way. I've heard him say, that he cleared no less than fifty

pounds every year by letting his front room at hanging time. His winders looked right opsit Newgit, and many and many dozen chaps has he seen hanging there. Laws was laws in the year ten, and they screwed chaps' nex for nex to nothink. But my bisniss was at his country-house, wher I made my first *ontray* into fashnabl life. I was knife, errant, and stable-boy then, and an't ashamed to own it; for my merits have raised me to what I am—two livries, forty pound a year, malt-licker, washin, silk-stocking, and wax candles—not counting wails [vails = tips], which is somethink pretty considerable at *our* house, I can tell you.

William Makepeace Thackeray (1811–63), Yellowplush Papers (1838–9).

When Punch *began publication Thackeray was anxious to become a contributor (and earn some money). This was not difficult to achieve as both the senior cartoonist, John Leech, and its main writer, Douglas Jerrold, were his friends. Thackeray contributed hundreds of short prose items and drawings to* Punch *in its early years. These attracted little notice except for one drawing: this became famous because nobody then or since has been able to see the point of it. A rival magazine helpfully offered five hundred pounds to anybody who could explain the drawing. Nobody could.*

Then, in 1842, Thackeray realised his potential with a series of Punch *pieces which made him famous and more popular than even Douglas Jerrold; The Snobs of England, by One of Themselves.*

The word 'snob' always had a connotation of 'lowly'. It was originally village slang for a cobbler's apprentice, then it became Cambridge slang for a person who was not in the university, i.e. a townsman rather than a gownsman. It became the word used for a scab or black-leg who worked during a strike. It was also applied to any low, vulgar person, i.e. the opposite of 'nob'. Then in early Victorian times, and almost certainly helped on its way by Thackeray's Punch *pieces, the meaning of 'snob' took on its modern meaning of somebody with social ambitions 'who vulgarly admires, emulates, and seeks to associate with, social or financial superiors'.*

Ironically, Snobs *reflected a little of Thackeray's own ambitions, but its frontal attack on social climbers was what* Punch *readers wanted to read and it indicated the course which* Punch *was to follow for something like a hundred years. From forceful political satire* Punch *moved to providing comfort and amusement to its middle-class readers by mocking the things which they feared.*

In the following piece Thackeray describes with quite vicious irony the marriage-broking which went on between impoverished aristocracy and self-made City tycoonery with social ambitions:

Our City Snobs have a mania for aristocratic marriages. I like to see such. I am of a savage and envious nature,—I like to see these two humbugs which, dividing, as they do, the social empire of this kingdom between them, hate each other naturally, making truce and uniting, for the sordid interests of either. I like to see an old aristocrat, swelling with pride of race, the descendant of illustrious Norman robbers, whose blood has been pure for centuries, and who looks down upon common Englishmen as a free-born American does on a nigger,—I like to see old Stiffneck obliged to bow down his head and swallow his infernal pride, and drink the cup of humiliation poured out by Pump and Aldgate's butler. 'Pump and Aldgate,' says he, 'your grandfather was a bricklayer, and his hod is still kept in the bank. Your pedigree begins in a workhouse; mine can be dated from all the royal palaces of Europe. I came over with the Conqueror; I am own cousin to Charles Martel, Orlando Furioso, Philip Augustus, Peter the Cruel, and Frederick Barbarossa. I quarter the Royal Arms of Brentford in my coat. I despise you, but I want money; and I will sell you my beloved daughter, Blanche Stiffneck, for a hundred thousand pounds, to pay off my mortgages. Let your son marry her, and she shall become Lady Blanche Pump and Aldgate.'

Old Pump and Aldgate clutches at the bargain. And a comfortable thing it is to think that birth can be bought for money. So you learn to value it. Why should we, who don't possess it, set a higher store on it than those who do? Perhaps the best use of that book, the 'Peerage', is to look down the list, and see how many have bought and sold birth,—how poor sprigs of nobility somehow sell themselves to rich City Snobs's daughters, how rich City Snobs purchase noble ladies—and so to admire the double baseness of the bargain.

Old Pump and Aldgate buys the article and pays the money. The sale of the girl's person is blessed by a Bishop at St George's, Hanover Square, and next year you read, 'At Roehampton, on Saturday, the Lady Blanche Pump, of a son and heir.'

After this interesting event, some old acquaintance, who saw young Pump in the parlour at the bank in the City, said to him, familiarly, 'How's your wife, Pump, my boy?'

Mr Pump looked exceedingly puzzled and disgusted, and, after a pause, said '*Lady Blanche Pump* is pretty well, I thank you.'

'*Oh, I thought she was your wife!*' said the familiar brute, Snooks, wishing him good-bye; and ten minutes after, the story was all over the Stock Exchange, where it is told, when young Pump appears, to this very day.

We can imagine the weary life this poor Pump, this martyr to Mammon, is compelled to undergo. Fancy the domestic enjoyments of a man who has a wife who scorns him; who cannot see his own friends in his own house; who having deserted the middle rank of life, is not yet admitted to the higher; but who is resigned to rebuffs and delay and humiliation, contented to think that his son will be more fortunate.

It used to be the custom of some very old-fashioned clubs in this city, when a gentleman asked for change for a guinea, always to bring it to him in *washed silver*: that which had passed immediately out of the hands of the vulgar being considered 'as too coarse to soil a gentleman's fingers'. So, when the City Snob's money has been washed during a generation or so;

has been washed into estates, and woods, and castles, and town-mansions, it is allowed to pass current as real aristocratic coin. Old Pump sweeps a shop, runs messages, becomes a confidential clerk and partner. Pump the Second becomes chief of the house, spins more and more money, marries his son to an Earl's daughter. Pump Tertius goes on with the bank; but his chief business in life is to become the father of Pump Quartus, who comes out a full-blown aristocrat, and takes his seat as Baron Pumpington, and his race rules hereditarily over this nation of Snobs.

The Snobs of England, by One of Themselves (1846–7).

IN *between the highly popular and long-running series like* Mrs Caudle's Curtain Lectures *and* Thackeray's Snobs, Punch *filled up the pages with such short and ephemeral items as topical paragraphs, single jokes (e.g. 'Advice to Persons About to Marry. Don't.' 1845), and vast numbers of puns, most of them dreadful but a few of them very good indeed (e.g. when Sir Charles Napier conquered the important province of Sind during the war in India,* Punch *suggested that he sent a dispatch reading 'Peccavi', i.e. 'I have sinned'. 1844).*

Punch *was not entirely responsible, but must take its share of the blame, for the proliferation of puns which reached epidemic proportions by the second half of the century. The reason for this extraordinary mania might simply have been that Victorians liked puns, but perhaps another reason was that more widespread primary education had produced a new unsophisticated readership to whom a pun, however feeble and strained, might well have come as a thing of wonder and delight. The pun may be the lowest form of wit but it is a form of wit, and the intellectual effort required to line up the two meanings of a pun might have given those readers much pleasure and satisfaction.*

Whatever the reason, puns abounded. They were not only a staple ingredient of virtually all humorous magazines and newspaper columns, but collections of them were published as complete books, the shining example being Puniana, *270 pp., edited by the Hon. Hugh Rowley, 1867 ('with nearly one hundred designs from his pencil').*

What manner of man, one wondered, was the Hon. Hugh Rowley? What background of experience had this person of quality to qualify him to edit a substantial volume of assorted puns?

After difficult (and increasingly obsessive) research it emerged that the Hon. Hugh's credentials for the task were impeccable. He was the son of the second Baron Langford, went to Eton, on to Sandhurst, served in the XVI Lancers, married twice, retired to Brighton, painted a picture which was exhibited at the Royal Academy, and held the Diploma of the Fanmakers' Company.

The Hon. Hugh Rowley's Puniana *is a fascinating volume on many counts, one*

being that it was so popular with the public that the same publisher launched
W. S. Gilbert's The Bab Ballads *by advertising it as one of the items in 'The New*
"Puniana" Series of Humorous Works'.

But the book's main claim to some kind of permanent literary renown is that
just about every pun in its two hundred and seventy pages is, to twentieth-century
eyes at least, desperately unfunny:

Why was it a mistake to imagine that Robinson Crusoe's island was
uninhabited?

> *Because the very first thing he saw upon landing was a great*
> *swell a pitchin' into a little 'cove' on the shore.*

Pray tell us, apropos of this amusing Crusoe-fiction, what piece of music the
Romans, in the time of the early Christians, most enjoyed?

> *A stab at martyr!*

> [Can't you fancy some old Roman Rossini with a Rose-in-'is button-hole—
> if he had a button-hole in his toga-ry—looking on and beating time; the
> old beast!]

What kind of a book might a man wish his wife to resemble?

> *An almanack; for then he could have a new one every year.*

> [By Jingo! what a job he would have with the seedy-vuns,—*ci-devants* we
> mean, especially if they all stuck to his name!]

Why is Punch like the aerial ship?

> *Because he hasn't made a trip yet.*

> [Punch being emery paper (a merry paper), is very useful for brightening
> up dull things!]

Why is the summary of to-day's paper like a 'sweet thing in cloaks?'

> *Because it's the bare-noos!*

> [A Scotch friend suggests that what with Burn-ooses and deevil-ope'd skirts,
> he wonders the ladies don't burn'ouses all down over their heads: as for
> myself, when I see a young lady going along with her greasy curls hanging
> on to the hood of her burnouse, my heart throbs, vain regrets sadden
> me, and I dream of halcyon days for ever gone; in fact, I think of—of
> much-oil'd-hood (my childhood).]

Why must a Yankee speculator be very subject to water on the brain?

> *Because he has always an ocean (a notion) in his head.*

> [We think we are correct in saying that water on the brain makes a man
> silly or soft; probably it is so because it must b'rain water. Alas and alas,
> how much worse than water on the brain is brandy and water on the
> brain!]

Why is a man looking for the philosopher's stone like Neptune?

> *Because he's a sea-king what never was!*

What's the difference between the sea and soap liniment?

> *One is a beautiful ocean for ships and a cruise or two, the other a beautiful lotion for chips and a bruise hurt too.*

> [It was whilst reading our Pliny that we made this riddle, as some of his descriptions of the sea, when correctly translated, clearly showed us it was so (soap liniment) Pliny meant.]

Etc. Etc. Etc. Etc. Etc. . . .

Hon. Hugh Rowley (1833–1908), *Puniana* (1867).

━━━━━━

PUNCH'S *most prolific punster ever was Francis Cowley Burnand. Burnand first contributed humorous pieces in 1863, was almost immediately asked to join the staff, became editor in 1880, was the first* Punch *editor to be knighted, and was he who replied, when informed that under his editorship* Punch *was not as good as it used to be—'It never was.'*

Burnand, like many of his fellow convivial funsters, was a barrister and a playwright. His plays, mostly farces and burlesques, were stuffed with puns. He wrote for Punch *for over forty years and almost every piece he wrote sprouted puns, mostly poor, mechanical specimens. He seemed unable to rid his work of them, as though they were a form of literary acne.*

Yet Burnand rose above his petty farces and punny columns to write for Punch *its most popular series ever,* Happy Thoughts. *In book form this lived on for years as a minor classic of nineteenth-century humour but is now virtually unknown.*

Happy Thoughts *was the first humorous series to describe everyday predicaments suffered by its author rather than by a third party.*

With it Burnand—with perhaps a nod towards Edward Nares and his Thinks-I-to-Myself *which also told of its author's adventures, although it was a novel and was in many ways different—had invented the 'I' humorous column, the first-person-singular account of happenings.*

In Happy Thoughts, *mercifully almost pun-free and not meant to be satirical or political but just a bit of fun for the whole family, Burnand, the 'I' of the stories, paints himself as a middle-class Pooter: decent, kind, and quite ineffectual at coping with ordinary living. He is a self-appointed intellectual whose mental energy is concentrated on planning and, very occasionally, and only a word or two at a time, on writing a massive philosophical work entitled* Typical Developments.

The Great Thinker always carries a notebook with him so that he can jot down absolutely everything that happens. Nothing is too unimportant for him to record. Sometimes he has a flash of inspiration and this he notes down as a 'Happy Thought'.

It is pages from this personal notebook that we are privileged to read.

Our man does not seem to have a job but he appears to have plenty of money.

This enables him to rent a villa for a while where he can pursue his literary work without petty interruptions:

Being in need of quiet, in order to commence my great work on *Typical Developments*, I have found a charming retreat on the banks of the Thames, somewhere about Twickenham, or Teddington, or Richmond, or Kingston, and all that part.

Capital fishing here. In punts, with a man, and worms: average sport, one tittlebat in ten hours.

First Happy Day.—Charming; perfect quiet. See a man in punt, fishing. Ask him how long he had been there? He says, 'Three hours.' Caught anything? 'Nothing.' He is quite cheerful. Full of happy thoughts, and commence my *Typical Developments*. In the evening catch an earwig; not a bit frightened of him. *The pincers in an earwig's tail don't bite.*

To bed early. Leave the man fishing; his man with the bait asleep. Been there all day? 'Yes.' Caught anything? 'Nothing.' Quite contented.

Second Happy Day.—Up early. Same man in punt; new man with bait. Ask him how long he has been there? 'All night.' Caught anything? 'Nothing.' Not at all irritable. * * * Kill two earwigs in my bath. Sit in my parlour to write.

Before me is my little lawn: at the foot of the lawn runs the river.

9 a.m.—I commence my *Typical Developments*, and note the fact, keeping by me this journal of observation in case anything turns up. Something has turned up; an earwig. Distracting for a moment, but now defunct. All is peace. I walk down the lawn. Caught anything? 'Nothing.' His voice is, I fancy, getting weaker. I am meditating, and my soul is rising to sublime heights . . .

A request has been forwarded to me from the drawing-room to the effect that I would step in and kill an earwig or two. I step in and kill five. Ladies in hysterics. The punt has reappeared: he only put in for more bait. Caught anything? 'Nothing.' Had a bite? 'Once, I think.'

He is calm, but not in any way triumphant.

Our man's life as a Great Writer seeking a peaceful haven takes him from one country house to another and he is caught up in various sporting and social activities which bring him much embarrassment but little time to work on his manuscript, for which he has great plans but in which seems to be stuck permanently at Book 1., Chap 1., Para 2.

All this travelling means that he is frequently in the hands of the new, busy, and brash railway system. On one journey to friends at Chopford he dozes off and finds that he has arrived at somewhere called Slumborough:

My lot, as I have before remarked, seems to be cast among railway officials. I am obliged to get out at Slumborough, and I have to go back to Chopford, which we passed while I was asleep.

Memorandum for suggestion to Railway Authorities.—At any station if the guards see a passenger asleep, they ought to wake him. Or, there might be,—a very *Happy Thought* this,—there might be a set of officials, called Shakers, attached to every train, whose duty, whenever it stopped, should be to go into all the carriages, shake any one they might find asleep, and ask him where he's going?

Happy and Poetical Thought.—Female shakers might wake the gentlemen, and win gloves. No shaker to be eligible over six-and-twenty.

In the Waiting Room.—Dreary. Wonder if Boodel's butler packed up my sponge? Hate uncertainty in these matters, but don't like to unpack in the station. I'll go into the office, and see if my portmanteau is there. No. Where? Of course taken out at Chopford. I shall see it there, at least, I hope so. The pigeon-hole suddenly opens, and the Station-master appears. Now's the time for conversation, and picking up character and materials. I have several questions to ask him. I say, 'I want to know first—' He catches me up impulsively, 'First, where for?' 'Chopford,' I answer, and before I can explain the accident which has brought me to Slumborough, he has dashed at a blue ticket, thumped it in one machine, banged it in another, and has produced it cut, printed, double-stamped, and all complete for authorizing me to go to Chopford. 'One and a penny,' says he. I explain that 'I don't want it, because—' He listens to nothing more, but sits down at his desk, pounces upon a large book, which he opens and shoves aside, then seizes a pen, and begins adding up something on one sheet of paper, and putting down the result on another. While he is engaged in this, I see the telegraphic needles working. He is too absorbed to notice it. 'Twill be only kindness on my part to direct his attention to it. I say, 'Do you know, Sir—' He is up in an instant, with a pen behind his ear. He evidently doesn't recognize me. 'Eh, First? where for?' I can't help saying 'Yes, Chopford—but—' when he dashes at the stamping machines, and produces, like a conjuring trick, another ticket for Chopford. That's two tickets for Chopford, and a third I've got in my pocket. I tell him I don't want it, and am adding 'I don't know if you observed the telegraph needles—' when he sits down, evidently in a temper, growling something about 'if you want to play the fool, go somewhere else'. I'd say something sharp if he wasn't at work, but I never like disturbing a man at work. Stop, I might ask him, it wouldn't take a second, how far is it from Chopford to Furze? I approach the pigeon-hole; I say, mildly, 'If you would oblige me, Sir, for one second—' He is up again more impulsively than ever. 'One, Second. Thought you said, One First,' and before I can point out his mistake he has banged, thumped, and produced for the third time a ticket to Chopford, only now he says, 'Tenpence', that being the reduction on Second Class. I am really afraid of making him very violent, so I buy the ticket. What a sad thing to have such a temper, and be a station-master!

Francis Cowley Burnand (1836–1917), Happy Thoughts (1866).

I N *the circle of amiable young gentlemen who contributed occasional drawings and articles to* Punch *in the 1850s was an extremely pale, 26-year-old clergyman. When introduced to Douglas Jerrold as 'Mr Verdant Green', Jerrold looked at him and said, 'Mr Verdant Green? I should have thought it was Mr Blanco White'.*

The very pale curate's name was really Edward Bradley. He had been introduced as 'Mr Verdant Green' because that was the name of the hero of a novel just published, which he had written and illustrated, entitled The Adventures of Mr Verdant Green.

This turned out to be the first really successful comic novel of university life. By the end of the century a quarter of a million copies had been sold. It depicted an Oxford undergraduate's existence so convincingly that Hippolyte Taine, the French philosopher and historian, used it as source material for parts of his Notes sur l'Angleterre, *a tribute to Bradley's skill as a writer of fiction because he had not been to Oxford—he had taken his degree at Durham University (his pseudonym 'Cuthbert Bede' was formed from the names of Durham's two patron saints).*

The novel describes the arrival at Brazenface College of young Verdant Green and the various near-catastrophes which he suffers during his progress from Freshman to Graduate. Verdant comes from an old Warwickshire family. He is an eager innocent, a mixture of a youthful Mr Pickwick and Candide, and he wears spectacles which clearly is unusual in his college and earns him the nickname of 'Gig-lamps'. His friends include the extrovert Bouncer, son of a sporting squire, and Charles Larkyns, the elegant and whimsical son of Verdant's local vicar.

In this episode, which happens soon after Verdant's arrival, he is the guest at a boisterous undergraduate party at which much tobacco is smoked and much milkpunch drunk. Verdant is unused to milk-punch.

Bradley's phonetic reproduction of the slurred speech of an extremely drunk young man is a little difficult to read but masterly :

There was an immediate hammering of tables and jingling of glasses, accompanied with loud cries of 'Mr Green for a song! Mr Green! Mr Gig-lamps' song!' cries which nearly brought our hero to the verge of idiocy.

Charles Larkyns saw this, and came to the rescue. 'Gentlemen,' he said, addressing the company, 'I know that my friend Verdant can sing, and that, like a good bird, he *will* sing. But while he is mentally looking over his numerous stock of songs, and selecting one for our amusement, I beg to fill up our valuable time, by asking you to fill up a bumper to the health of our esteemed host Smalls (*vociferous cheers*),—a man whose private worth is only to be equalled by the purity of his milk-punch and the excellence of his weeds (*hear, hear*) . . .

Charles Larkyns' friendly diversion in our hero's favour had succeeded, and Mr Verdant Green had regained his confidence, and had decided upon one of those vocal efforts which, in the bosom of his own family, and to the pianoforte accompaniment of his sisters, was accustomed to meet with great applause. And when he had hastily tossed off another glass of milk-punch (merely to clear his throat), he felt bold enough to answer the spirit-rappings which were again demanding 'Mr Green's song!' It was given much in the following manner:

Mr Verdant Green (*in low, plaintive tones, and fresh alarm at hearing the sounds of his own voice*). 'I dreamt that I dwe-elt in mar-arble halls, with'—

Mr Bouncer (*interrupting*). 'Spit it out, Gig-lamps! Dis child can't hear whether it's Maudlin Hall you're singing about, or what.'

Omnes. 'Order! or-*der!* Shut up, Bouncer!'

Charles Larkyns (*encouragingly*). 'Try back, Verdant: never mind.'

Mr Verdant Green (*tries back, with increased confusion of ideas, resulting principally from the milk-punch and tobacco*). 'I dreamt that I dwe-elt in mar-arble halls, with vassals and serfs at my si-hi-hide; and—and—I beg your pardon, gentlemen, I really forgot—oh, I know!—and I also dre-eamt, which ple-eased me most—no, that's not it'—

Mr Bouncer (*who does not particularly care for the words of a song, but only appreciates the chorus*)—'That'll do, old feller! We ain't pertickler,—(*rushes with great deliberation and noise to the chorus*) 'That you lo-oved me sti-ill the sa-ha-hame—chorus, gentlemen!'

Omnes (*in various keys and time*). 'That you lo-oved me sti-ill the same.'

Mr Bouncer (*to Mr Green, alluding remotely to the opera*). 'Now, my Bohemian gal, can't you come out to-night? Spit us out a yard or two more, Gig-lamps.'

Mr Verdant Green (*who has again taken the opportunity to clear his throat*). 'I dreamt that I dwe-elt in mar-arble—no! I beg pardon! sang that (*desperately*)—that sui-uitors sou-ought my hand, that knights on their (*hic*) ben-ended kne-e-ee—had (*hic*) riches too gre-eat to!—(*Mr Verdant Green smiles benignantly upon the company*)—Don't rec'lect anymo.

Mr Bouncer (*who is not to be defrauded of the chorus*). 'Chorus, gentlemen!— That you'll lo-ove me sti-ill the sa-a-hame!'

Omnes (*ad libitum*). 'That you'll lo-ove me sti-ill the same!'...

When the chorus had been sung over three or four times, and Mr Verdant Green's name had been proclaimed with equal noise, that gentleman rose (with great difficulty), to return thanks. He was understood to speak as follows:—

'Genelum anladies (*cheers*),—I meangenelum. ('*That's about the ticket, old feller!' from Mr Bouncer.*) Customd syam plic speakn, I—I—(*hear, hear*)—feel bliged drinkmyel. I'm fresman, genelum, and prow title (*loud cheers*). Myfren Misserboucer, fallowme callm myfren! ('*In course, Gig-lamps, you do me proud, old feller.*') Myfren Misserboucer seszime fresman—prow title, sure you (*hear, hear*). Genelmun, werall jolgoodfles, anwe wogohotill-morrin! ('*We won't, we won't not a bit of it!*') Gelmul, I'm freshmal, an namesgreel, gelmul (*cheers*). Fanyul dousmewor, herescardinpock 'lltellm! Misser Verdalgreel, Braseface, Oxul fresmal, anprowtitle! (*Great cheering and rattling of glasses, during which Mr Verdant Green's coat-tails are made the receptacles for empty bottles, lobsters' claws, and other miscellaneous articles.*) Misserboucer said was fresmal. If Misserboucer wantsultme ('*No, no!*'), herescardinpocklltellmenamesverdalgreel, Braseface! Not shameofitgelmul! prowttitle! (*Great applause.*) I doewaltilsul Misserboucer! thenwhysee sultme? thaswaw Iwaltknow! (*Loud cheers, and roars of laughter, in which Mr Verdant Green suddenly joins to the best of his ability.*) I'm anoxful fresmal, gelmul, 'fmyfrel Misserboucer loumecallimso. (*Cheers and laughter, in which Mr Verdant Green feebly joins.*) Anweer all jolgoodfles, anwe wogohotilmorril, an I'm fresmal, gelmul, anfanyul dowsmewor—an I—doefeel quiwell!'

This was the termination of Mr Verdant Green's speech, for after making a few unintelligible sounds, his knees suddenly gave way, and with a benevolent smile he disappeared beneath the table.

> 'Cuthbert Bede' (Edward Bradley) (1827–89), *The Adventures of Mr Verdant Green* (1853–7).

Hᴜᴍᴏʀᴏᴜs *writers down the years wrote some odd things but what they wrote was not, generally speaking, nonsense. Even Lewis Carroll's writing, bizarre, playful, an intricate pattern of word-plays and tricks with logic, was not nonsense; one suspects that he could have given a detailed and reasoned explanation for every word that he wrote.*

The man for writing pure nonsense (very few women attempted it) was Edward Lear, an unhappy and unhealthy landscape painter who taught Queen Victoria to draw. Lear virtually invented this new and deceptively easy literary form when in 1842 he published his Book of Nonsense, *a collection of mainly meaningless yet wholly delightful pieces which he had written to amuse the Earl of Derby's grandchildren.*

Most of Lear's nonsense was expressed in verse but he frequently wrote nonsensical prose in letters to his aristocratic young friends.

Such a letter from Mr Lear could hardly be described as newsy:

Thrippy Pilliwinx,—

Inkly tinky pobblebockle able-squabs? Flosky! Beebul trimble flosky! Okul scratch abibblebongibo, viddle squibble tog-a-tog, ferry moyassity amsky flamsky crocklefether squiggs.

> Flinky wisty pomm.
> Slushypipp

> Edward Lear (1812–88), Letter to Evelyn Baring, Lord Cromer (1850).

THERE is a term, 'kitchen-table writer', which might reasonably be applied to Edward Lear in that writing was neither his profession nor his vocation but a way of expressing himself, which he enjoyed indulging from time to time and for which he had a considerable gift.

The same might be said of a contemporary of Lear, except that to call the Hon. Emily Eden a 'kitchen-table writer' would be most inappropriate; 'ormulu-escritoire writer' would be nearer the mark. The Hon. Emily Eden was of the nobility; sister of the second Baron Auckland and a direct ancestor of the late Anthony Eden, the British politician and one-time Prime Minister. She was regarded as one of the most delightful women of her time. She might have married Lord Melbourne but went instead to India for seven years to act as official hostess for her unmarried brother, who was Governor-General until he was recalled for instigating the first Afghan War (it ended in the massacre of virtually the entire British garrison).

Back home the Hon. Emily became one of the grand Whig hostesses. When her brother died in 1849 she was released from official duties and could spend more time at her escritoire, writing letters and assembling for publication various accounts of life in India.

But she also wrote a novel in the hope of making a little pin-money. This novel, The Semi-detached House, was published—anonymously, of course—in 1859. It was such a huge success that she dusted off the manuscript of another novel, written thirty years previously, changed its name to The Semi-attached Couple, and sent it off to the publisher. This, too, sold extremely well.

It is not surprising that these two novels were plucked from the shelves of Victorian bookshops and circulating libraries as quickly as they were put up. They were light social comedies: warmly sentimental (all the nice but unwed characters were married off in the last chapters), briskly paced, observant, genteel, and humorous; combining something of the styles of Fanny Burney, Jane Austen, and our own Barbara Cartland.

The Semi-detached House must have been the first prominent novel to be set in 'commuterland'; country villages near enough to London for businessmen to commute to the City by carriage or on the new railway trains.

And the novel's title was the first recorded use in literature of the word 'semi-detached'. 'Double-cottages' built with a shared party wall had been common in the eighteenth century, but it seems that it was not until the nineteenth century, when there was a passion for inventing nonce compounds with the prefix 'semi-', that somebody, no doubt a wily estate agent, coined 'semi-detached' as a good word to accentuate 'detachment' and divert the buyer's mind from the fact that his villa and his neighbour's were in fact as attached as Siamese twins.

At the end of the book there is mention of an advertisement in The Times which reads: 'Dulham.—To be let, a Semi-detached House.' It seems likely that the idea for the book came to the Hon. Emily Eden when she read a similar advertisement, found out what a 'semi-detached house' was, and realized that *there was a story to be made from, say, the predicament of an aristocratic couple finding themselves living cheek-by-jowl with a family from the middle classes.*

All the Hon. Emily's heroes and heroines are, understandably, lords and ladies. In this case her heroine is Blanche, the young and pregnant wife of Lord Chester. Blanche's newly-wed husband, Arthur, has had to go abroad on an important mission and there is nowhere for Blanche to have her baby in peace and comfort. Her kindly and sensible aunt, Lady Sarah, has come to the resue and has rented for Blanche a Thames-side villa called 'Pleasance':

'The only fault of the house is that it is semi-detached.'

'Oh, Aunt Sarah! you don't mean that you expect me to live in a semi-detached house?'

'Why not, my dear, if it suits you in other respects?'

'Why, because I should hate my semi-detachment, or whatever the occupants of the other half of the house may call themselves.'

'They call themselves Hopkinson,' continued Aunt Sarah coolly.

'I knew it,' said Blanche triumphantly. 'I felt certain their name would be either Tomkinson or Hopkinson—I was not sure which—but I thought the chances were in favour of Hop rather than Tom.'

Aunt Sarah did not smile, but drew the mesh out of her netting and began a fresh row.

'Go on, Aunt Sarah,' said Blanche demurely.

'I am going on, thank you, my dear, very nicely; I expect to finish this net this week.'

Blanche looked at her aunt to ascertain if she looked angry, or piqued, or affronted; but Aunt Sarah's countenance was totally incapable of any expression but that of imperturbable stolid sense and good-humour. She did not care for Blanche's little vivacities.

'Do you know the Hopkinsons, Aunt Sarah?'

'No, my dear.'

'Nor their history, nor their number, nor their habits? Recollect, Aunt Sarah, they will be under the same roof with your own pet Blanche.'

'I have several pets, my dear—Tray, and Poll, and your sister, and—'

'Well, but she will be there, too, for I suppose the Lees will let Aileen come to me, now that I am to be deserted by Arthur,' and Blanche's voice quivered, but she determined to brave it through. 'Did you see any of the Hopkinsons when you went to look at the house?'

'Yes, they went in at their door just as I went in at yours. The mother, as I suppose, and two daughters, and a little boy.'

'Oh dear me! a little boy, who will always be throwing stones at the palings and making me jump; daughters who will always be playing *Partant pour la Syrie ;* and the mother—'

'Well, what will she do to offend your Highness?'

'She will be immensely fat, wear mittens—thick, heavy mittens—and contrive to know what I have for dinner every day.'

There was a silence, another row of netting and a turn of the mesh, and then Aunt Sarah said in her most composed tone:

'I often think, my dear, that it is a great pity you are so imaginative, and a still greater pity that you are so fastidious. You would be happier if you were as dull and as matter-of-fact as I am.'

'Dear Aunt Sarah, don't say you are dull. There is nobody I like so much to talk to. You bring out such original remarks, such convincing truths, and in a quiet way, so that they do not make the black bruises which *les vérités dures* generally produce. But *am* I fastidious and imaginative?'

'Yes, my dear, very painfully so. Now, just consider, Blanche; you began this week by throwing yourself into a fever because Arthur was to leave you, on a mission that may be of great future advantage to him. He is to be away only three months, and is as much grieved as you are at the separation it involves. You immediately assert that he is going for a year at least, that he is to forget you instantly, and fall in love with any and every other woman he sees.'

'No, only with that woman with the unpronounceable name that he used to dance with; a very dangerous woman, Aunt Sarah.'

'That he is to be smashed in the railroad to Folkestone, drowned off Antwerp, and finally die of a fever at Berlin; and that in the meanwhile you are to have a dead child immediately, twins soon after, a very bad confinement, besides dying of consumption, and various other maladies,' pursued Aunt Sarah in her steadiest tone.

'Now, if those things are not vain imaginings, Blanche, I do not know what are.'

'They sound plausible, though; and, I assure you, Aunt, I did not imagine them; they suggested themselves, and they look very like the ordinary facts of life. However, I grant it is a bad habit to look forward to evils that may not occur; but then, you know, I am ill. I never had these grey thoughts when I was strong, and Arthur's going away has turned them all black. And now as to my fastidiousness.'

'You always were fastidious, my child, easily jarred by the slightest want of tact and refinement, and I am not much surprised,' added Aunt Sarah, as she looked fondly at her niece. There was something startling in the mobility of Blanche's beautiful features; every thought that passed through her mind might be read in her kindling eyes and expressive lips; she looked too ethereal for contact with the vulgar ills of life.

'I will allow you have some right to be fastidious, darling; and it is only because it interferes with your comfort that I object to it. But you say you cannot go and stay with Lord Chesterton, because he calls you "Blanket", and thinks it a good joke; nor with your sister-in-law, Lady Elinor, because Sir William is fond of money, and you foresee he will say that you cost him at least seventeen shillings and fourpence a day; nor with your Aunt Carey, because the doctor who would attend you wears creaking boots, and calls you my Lady; and now you object to a house that all your friends and your doctor recommend, because it is possible that your next-door neighbour may play on the pianoforte and wear black mittens. Dear Blanche, this is what I call over-fastidiousness; and now I have finished my ten rows, and said all the disagreeable things I could think of, so I will go, and leave you to think how officious and particular old Aunt Sarah is.'

Blanche, accompanied by her lovely sister Aileen (extremely nice: first of the cast to be married off; to a Colonel), moves into their half of 'Pleasance'.

The good Mrs Hopkinson, in the other half, is at first also much agitated at the prospect of sharing her party wall with a family in high-society, but such is the sunny nature of all the girls that the two families find that they like each other more and more.

Then a sudden dramatic turn of the plot metaphorically melts the party wall and transforms the two semi-detached residences into one happy household.

The large cast milling about in this heart-warming scene includes Mrs Hopkinson, her husband, Captain Jack, Blanche's husband Arthur (Lord Chester) back in the very nick of time from abroad, their French maid Mademoiselle Justine, sister Aileen, the Duchess of St Maur, Mr Duckett the local doctor, Mrs Smith the 'month nurse,' Aunt Sarah, and Arthur's gruff but kindly father, Lord Chesterton:

At five in the morning the Hopkinsons were awakened by a loud peal from their door bell.

'Ah, there they are,' said Mrs Hopkinson, jumping up in a fright. 'Oh, John, what shall we do? I knew they would come to us in our turn.'

'Who would come, Jane?' said Captain Hopkinson, who was half asleep.

'Why, the burglars, of course! What will become of us! Where's my purse? I always keep a purse ready to give them, it makes them so good-humoured. Oh, dear, what a noise they make, and they will be quite savage if they are kept waiting,' she said, as another violent ringing was heard. 'John, John, you must not go down to them, they will knock you down. Let me go.'

'I don't see,' said John, laughing, 'why I should let you go and be knocked down instead of me; but, my dear, there is no danger; burglars do not come and ring the bell and ask to be let in like morning visitors. It must be the policeman.'

'Ah, poor man! I daresay, with his head knocked to pieces with a life-preserver, and all over kicks and bites. But, perhaps, he is only come to tell us that the house is on fire,' said Mrs Hopkinson, with a sudden access of cheerfulness. I should not mind that—anything is better than robbers. Oh, John, now don't put your head out so far, those ticket-of-leave men fire in all directions. And do keep calling out Thomas and James, and I will answer with a gruff voice,' said poor Mrs Hopkinson, who was so terrified her whisper could scarcely be heard.

'My dear,' said John, withdrawing his head, 'there is nothing to be alarmed at, it is Lord Chester; Lady Chester is taken ill, and he wants you to go to her.'

'And so that is all,' said Mrs Hopkinson, instantly beginning to dress. 'Ah, poor soul! of course I will. Well now, this *is* neighbourly of them, and I take it very kindly their sending for me. Why, they are two babies themselves, and they can't know what to do with a third.'

And so when Lord Chester met her with the humblest apologies, he found her in a warm fit of gratitude for having been called out of her bed and frightened out of her senses, and delighted to find that her experience as a mother and a nurse was to be made available to her neighbours at a most inconvenient hour.

Pleasance did not wear its usual cheerful aspect that morning; the drawing-room had that deplorable 'last night' look belonging to rooms that have not received the morning attentions of the housemaid. The chairs looked as if they had been dancing all night, and had rumpled their chintz covers, the books seemed to have fallen off the table in their sleep, and the music appeared to have quarrelled with the pianoforte in an attempt to place itself on the music stand. Only one shutter had been partially unclosed, and through the crack there came that struggling ray that ought to be light, but looks very much like dust.

Aileen came the moment she heard of Mrs Hopkinson's arrival, looking pale and frightened, and she immediately hurried her neighbour upstairs, explaining that Blanche had been taken ill sooner than they expected, so that the nurse was not in the house. Arthur had sent for Dr Ayscough, but in the mean time they had all become very nervous, and Blanche thought she should be happier if Mrs Hopkinson was with her, and so they had taken the great liberty of asking her to come to them at that undue hour, &c., &c.

'My dear, don't say another word about it; what are we all sent into the world for, but to be of use to each other? and I am quite pleased that your dear little sister, bless her, fancies having me with her; and now, Miss Grenville, don't you go to her with that frightened face, there is nothing to be frightened about. There is no want of babies coming safely into the world, thank goodness, but go into the room with your usual smiles, and tell her I'm come; and I'll just take off my bonnet, and then go and stay with her until the doctor comes.'

And very serviceable Mrs Hopkinson was. She found Aileen still with tears in her eyes, Mademoiselle Justine occasionally proffering to Blanche a little *tisane de fleur d'orange*, and watching an opportunity to slip out and dress herself in a *petite robe de percale*, and a *bonnet à barbes*, that she had prepared for the particular occasion; and which were not only becoming in themselves, but so appropriate that the Doctor and the nurse must, she thought, be struck by her wonderfully good taste in dress. Arthur was fidgeting up and down the room, one minute looking out of the window and wondering the doctor did not come—the next assuring Blanche that she was better, that she looked better, felt better, and requesting her to agree with him, a complete impossibility under the circumstances, so that poor Blanche became only more nervous. Mrs Hopkinson wisely hurried them all out of the room, advised Justine that the basket with the doll's caps, and the absurd pin-cushion with its 'Welcome, little stranger', were all ready; and told Arthur and Aileen to go and have some breakfast, and to send some to her; and she gave an every day turn to the state of affairs that was soothing.

An hour after, Arthur came with a face of consternation: Dr Ayscough had been telegraphed off to the other side of England, and the nurse could not possibly leave the place she was in till the afternoon.

'What are we to do, Mrs Hopkinson? it is really too bad; what business had that woman in Yorkshire to telegraph for our doctor? and then that other woman detaining Mrs Smith—so selfish! and my poor darling will have no doctor and no nurse—she will die!'

'Oh no, she won't,' said Mrs Hopkinson, half laughing, 'unless you put it into her head to do so. I hope I am as good a month nurse as any in the kingdom; and you had better send for Mr Duckett; of course he is not to be compared to Doctor Ayscough, but he is in good practice at Dulham, and we may as well have him in the house.'

Mr Duckett had always felt that Lady Chester ought to be his property; he had occasionally attended at Pleasance, and during the last week his slumbers had been unusually light, and his attention to the sound of the night bell was unremitting. He came instantly; Lady Sarah arrived from London; and finally, the important Mrs Smith appeared in a hack cab that was almost concealed under a mass of trunks and cap boxes. The Duchess of St Maur came to pay an early visit connected with Aileen's trousseau, and of course the end of Blanche's troubles. Everybody was more or less in a fuss; it was curious, considering that the birth of a baby is not a very unusual circumstance, to see the immense interest that the expectation of a young Chester created. Lady Sarah abandoned her netting; and she, and the Duch-ess, and Aileen whispered and cried, and talked and laughed, and drank tea and coffee at odd hours, and put on *peignoirs*, and did what Shakespeare calls 'the gossips' to perfection. Arthur walked up and down stairs unceasingly; the tread-mill would have been repose to him that day, and he tried to cut little failures of jokes to Duckett on the useless fidgets of the ladies, who were models of quiescence as compared with himself. Duckett assumed a grand attitude of composure, repeated every half hour 'we are going on admirably', and then tried to *égayer* Lord Chester by some horrible surgical anecdote, which in the best of times would have made him shudder, and now that he was nervous and frightened, made him feel that he was undergoing the actual operation described. He was certain that nobody had ever had such a wife as his, and that no woman had ever endured so much with so much fortitude. He went from Lady Sarah to the Duchess to be soothed, and when their matronly experience failed to console him, he turned to Aileen, and as for the brusque word or two which Mrs Hopkinson occasionally found time to bestow on him, he accepted it as an oracle from heaven.

At last, there came the joyful whisper, 'a fine boy'; perhaps the only moment of a fine boy's existence in which his presence is more agreeable than his absence, so let him make the most of it. But if in the whole course of a woman's life there is one moment of happiness more keen, blissful, bright, than another, it is that in which the husband of her choice thanks her for his firstborn child. It was with heartfelt gratitude that Blanche whispered, 'I thank God, love, that He has not taken me from you', for she felt, as Arthur pressed her to his heart, as with tears he thanked her for being so patient, so good—as he blessed her, not so much that she was the mother of his child, as that she was still his own, his wife, his Blanche; yes, she felt that life was indeed to her most precious. 'It would have been hard to die,' she murmured, 'I could not have left all these', and she kissed the hands of her aunt, her sister, and her friend; and quiet tears of gratitude fell as she listened to the short prayer of thanksgiving which Aileen read as she knelt at her sister's bedside.

But there the pathos of the scene ended, then the bustling Mrs Smith assumed her rights. 'Come, come, we must have no more of this reading and talking, and all this crying. Now, my Lord, if you'll just go quite away I'll be particularly obliged to you; and I must make bold to turn all you ladies out of the room, except this good lady,' she added, turning to Mrs Hopkinson, whose *savoir faire* had inspired her with confidence, 'and, Miss Grenville, will you please to see that there is no noise made up those stairs, and I'll just shut the door after you, my Lord, if you will go.'

'I must go to my father, who is down stairs,' said Arthur; 'he is so delighted with his grandson, Blanche.'

'Oh! may I not see him before I settle for the night?' asked Blanche.

'Oh, dear no, my Lady, not on any account,' said Mrs Smith, colouring up as if the mere suggestion was a personal affront. 'As sure as I am alive, not another word shall be spoken here this blessed night. Tell Lady Blanche's papa, my Lord, that her Ladyship wishes him good night, and is very sorry that she is not able to see him. No, no grandpapas indeed,' she muttered, as she bustled about the room, and established that rustling disturbed sort of quiet which is the peculiar result of a regular nurse's exertions, and which is—strange to say—less irritating to the nerves of an invalid than the finished quiet of a lady-like attendant.

Lord Chesterton was extremely pleased with the birth of his grandson, for Arthur was the only heir to his old title and large estates—two possessions which he valued almost equally. He was informed of it at the House of Lords, and actually left that lively assembly in order to drive down to Pleasance, before the important debate on the Trawl and Seine herring fishing nets was brought to a close, a dereliction of public duty which weighed on his conscience; but he tried to atone for it by filling his carriage with red boxes containing minutes about Hospodars, and statements of the wrongs of De-darkham Bux in the well known case of the Jaghire of Munnydumdum. Public men keep up to this day the farce of saying that they read these papers. However, the absorbing interest they possessed did not prevent Lord Chesterton from entering heartily into the private rejoicings at Pleasance.

'I wish you had seen my father,' Arthur afterwards said to Blanche; 'he thought it right to see the baby, because he looks upon that mite as a young earl and a sucking Secretary of State, but he was afraid of touching it, and contented himself with stroking it with the end of his gold pencil case.'

Emily Eden (1797–1869), The Semi-detached House (1859).

———

ANOTHER 'kitchen-table', i.e. part-time, novelist of that period was Anthony Trollope, but the description woefully misrepresents probably the most in-dustrious and professional writer of fiction of the century. Trollope wrote not for pin-money but in the hope of dragging himself up and away from his miserable and impoverished childhood by making a lot of money, and by tremendous application he achieved this: by 1879, he noted, his books had earned him £70,000.

He regarded himself as a workman rather than an artist who depended upon inspiration, and his awesome, self-imposed regime was to rise at 5.30 a.m.—wherever he was—and write 2,500 words of his current book before breakfast. For the rest of the day he was an employee of the General Post Office, originally a clerk but eventually an important official travelling the British Isles as Inspector of Postal Deliveries. He hunted twice a week. Somewhere in between he found time to invent the pillar-box.

During one of his tours of the South-West he loitered for a while among the quiet houses close to Salisbury Cathedral and an idea came to him for the subject of his next attempt to write a successful novel. This attempt succeeded: The Warden, published in 1855, was the beginning of the 'Barchester' series of novels which made his reputation and fortune.

Trollope, the boisterous, burly, extremely busy civil servant had hit upon a quite new subject for humour; the conflicts and romances which disturb a placid ecclesiastical community living in the shadow of an ancient cathedral.

His touch is mostly light and sure; for example, the bishop's reaction to the warden's news that Mr Bold, the warden's enemy in a dispute, has taken to making social visits to the warden's house:

'Indeed, I like Mr Bold much, personally,' continued the disinterested victim; 'and to tell you the "truth",'—he hesitated as he brought out the dreadful tidings,—'I have sometimes thought it not improbable that he would be my second son-in-law.' The bishop did not whistle. We believe that they lose the

power of doing so on being consecrated; and that in these days one might as
easily meet a corrupt judge as a whistling bishop; but he looked as though
he would have done so; but for his apron.

Anthony Trollope (1815–82), The Warden (1855).

*A lawyer has to be retained to give an opinion on the warden's dispute and it is the
Attorney-General himself, Sir Abraham Haphazard. In describing this successful,
important, pompous man, Trollope wrote 'he never quarrelled with his wife, but
he never talked to her. He never had time to talk, he was so taken up with speaking.'*

*It is clear that Trollope enjoyed writing about Sir Abraham, and this might well
have encouraged him to write more about politicians, which he later managed to
do most successfully with his series of political novels about the Palliser family.*

Trollope's gift for light satire bubbles up whenever the lawyer-politician appears:

Sir Abraham Haphazard was deeply engaged in preparing a bill for the
mortification of papists, to be called the 'Convent Custody Bill', the purport
of which was to enable any Protestant clergyman over fifty years of age to
search any nun whom he suspected of being in possession of treasonable
papers, or jesuitical symbols: and as there were to be a hundred and thirty-
seven clauses in the bill, each clause containing a separate thorn for the side
of the papist, and as it was known the bill would be fought inch by inch, by
fifty maddened Irishmen, the due construction and adequate dovetailing of it
did consume much of Sir Abraham's time. The bill had all its desired effect.
Of course it never passed into law; but it so completely divided the ranks of
the Irish members, who had bound themselves together to force on the
ministry a bill for compelling all men to drink Irish whiskey, and all women
to wear Irish poplins, that for the remainder of the session the Great Poplin
and Whiskey League was utterly harmless. Thus it happened that Sir Abraham's opinion was not at once forthcoming, and the uncertainty, the expectation, and suffering of the folk of Barchester were maintained at a high
pitch.

Ibid.

Two years after The Warden *appeared, Trollope published a sequel,* Barchester
Towers, *the second novel in what was to be the 'Barchester' series. Some fresh
characters were introduced, notably the new, sorely henpecked bishop and his
formidable wife, Mrs Proudie.*

*And the bishop's private chaplain—the enemy of Mrs Proudie in a power-struggle
for control of the diocese—the ambitious, hypocritical, dreadful Mr Slope:*

Mr Slope is tall, and not ill-made. His feet and hands are large, as has ever
been the case with all his family, but he has a broad chest and wide shoulders
to carry off these excrescences, and on the whole his figure is good. His
countenance, however, is not specially prepossessing. His hair is lank, and
of a dull pale reddish hue. It is always formed into three straight lumpy
masses, each brushed with admirable precision, and cemented with much

grease; two of them adhere closely to the sides of his face, and the other lies at right angles above them. He wears no whiskers, and is always punctiliously shaven. His face is nearly of the same colour as his hair, though perhaps a little redder: it is not unlike beef,—beef, however, one would say, of a bad quality. His forehead is capacious and high, but square and heavy, and unpleasantly shining. His mouth is large, though his lips are thin and blood-less; and his big, prominent, pale brown eyes inspire anything but confidence. His nose, however, is his redeeming feature: it is pronounced, straight, and well-formed; though I myself should have liked it better did it not possess a somewhat spongy, porous appearance, as though it had been cleverly formed out of a red coloured cork.

I could never endure to shake hands with Mr Slope. A cold, clammy perspiration always exudes from him, the small drops are ever to be seen standing on his brow, and his friendly grasp is unpleasant.

Barchester Towers (1857).

The Warden was quite short, a single volume, but the publishers wanted Bar-chester Towers to be a 'three-decker' (their best customers were the circulating libraries who charged their customers a fee for each volume borrowed, so many a good but slim Victorian novel was padded out to three tedious volumes to suit the libraries). In the event Trollope settled for two volumes, which at least gave him room to expand his scenes: his writing now had the confidence of an author who had found a congenial subject and was enjoying his work.

Here is one of Trollope's extremely well-controlled humorous set-pieces. Mr Slope and Mrs Proudie have instigated a Reign of Terror in order to bring to heel the 'comfortable prebendaries, gentlemanlike clerical doctors, well-used, well-fed minor canons' who had enjoyed such a calm, sleepy existence under the previous bishop. This had resulted in the recall to Barchester of Dr Vesey Stanhope who was rich enough to pay a curate to do his work while he, pleading a sore throat, lived with his family on the sunny shores of Lake Como, Italy.

Mrs Proudie decides to give a grand evening reception to impress the clergy and gentry of Barchester. Dr Stanhope, newly dragged back, is invited, together with his somewhat unconventional children. These include his daughter Madeline, called 'the signora' after her disastrous marriage to an Italian. The signora has a mys-teriously injured foot which requires her to be carried into the room by male volunteers and lowered upon a sofa.

Also present is Dr Stanhope's louche son, Ethelbert (Bertie), an easy-going, charming layabout with an Italianate sense of dress.

Bishop Proudie does not know the Stanhope family by sight:

Ethelbert Stanhope was dressed in light blue from head to foot. He had on the loosest possible blue coat, cut square like a shooting coat, and very short.

It was lined with silk of azure blue. He had on a blue satin waistcoat, a blue neck-handkerchief which was fastened beneath his throat with a coral ring, and very loose blue trowsers which almost concealed his feet. His soft glossy beard was softer and glossier than ever.

The bishop, who had made one mistake, thought that he also was a servant, and therefore tried to make way for him to pass. But Ethelbert soon corrected the error.

'Bishop of Barchester, I presume?' said Bertie Stanhope, putting out his hand, frankly; 'I am delighted to make your acquaintance. We are in rather close quarters here, a'nt we?'

In truth, they were. They had been crowded up behind the head of the sofa: the bishop in waiting to receive his guest, and the other in carrying her; and they now had hardly room to move themselves.

The bishop gave his hand quickly, and made his little studied bow, and was delighted to make —. He couldn't go on, for he did not know whether his friend was a signor, or a count, or a prince.

'My sister really puts you all to great trouble,' said Bertie.

The bishop was delighted to have the opportunity of welcoming the Signora Vicinironi—so at least he said—and attempted to force his way round to the front of the sofa. He had, at any rate, learnt that his strange guests were brother and sister. The man, he presumed, must be Signor Vicinironi—or count, or prince, as it might be. It was wonderful what good English he spoke. There was just a twang of foreign accent, and no more.

'Do you like Barchester, on the whole?' asked Bertie.

The bishop, looking dignified, said that he did like Barchester.

'You've not been here very long, I believe,' said Bertie.

'No—not long,' said the bishop, and tried to make his way between the back of the sofa and a heavy rector, who was staring over it at the grimaces of the signora.

'You weren't a bishop before, were you?'

Dr Proudie explained that this was the first diocese he had held.

'Ah—I thought so,' said Bertie; 'but you are changed about sometimes, a'nt you?'

'Translations are occasionally made,' said Dr Proudie; 'but not so frequently as in former days.'

'They've cut them all down to pretty nearly the same figure, haven't they?' said Bertie.

To this the bishop could not bring himself to make any answer, but again attempted to move the rector.

'But the work, I suppose, is different?' continued Bertie. 'Is there much to do here, at Barchester?' This was said in exactly the same tones that a young Admiralty clerk might use in asking the same question of a brother acolyte at the Treasury.

'The work of a bishop of the Church of England,' said Dr Proudie, with considerable dignity, 'is not easy. The responsibility which he has to bear is very great indeed.'

'Is it?' said Bertie, opening wide his wonderful blue eyes. 'Well, I was never afraid of responsibility. I once had thoughts of being a bishop, myself.'

'Had thoughts of being a bishop!' said Dr Proudie, much amazed.

'That is, a parson—a parson first, you know, and a bishop afterwards. If I had once begun, I'd have stuck to it. But on the whole, I like the Church of Rome best.'

The bishop could not discuss the point, so he remained silent.

'Now, there's my father,' continued Bertie; 'he hasn't stuck to it. I fancy he didn't like saying the same thing over so often. By the by, Bishop, have you seen my father?'

The bishop was more amazed than ever. Had he seen his father? 'No,' he replied; 'he had not yet had the pleasure: he hoped he might'; and, as he said so, he resolved to bear heavy on that fat, immovable rector, if ever he had the power of doing so.

'He's in the room somewhere,' said Bertie, 'and he'll turn up soon. By the by, do you know much about the Jews?'

At last the bishop saw a way out. 'I beg your pardon,' said he; 'but I'm forced to go round the room.'

'Well—I believe I'll follow in your wake,' said Bertie. 'Terribly hot— isn't it?' This he addressed to the fat rector with whom he had brought himself into the closest contact. 'They've got this sofa into the worst possible part of the room; suppose we move it. Take care, Madeline.'

The sofa had certainly been so placed that those behind it found great difficulty in getting out;—there was but a narrow gangway, which one person could stop. This was a bad arrangement, and one which Bertie thought it might be well to improve.

'Take care, Madeline,' said he; and turning to the fat rector, added, 'Just help me with a slight push.'

The rector's weight was resting on the sofa, and unwittingly lent all its impetus to accelerate and increase the motion which Bertie intentionally originated. The sofa rushed from its moorings, and ran half-way into the middle of the room. Mrs Proudie was standing with Mr Slope in front of the signora, and had been trying to be condescending and sociable, but she was not in the very best of tempers; for she found that, whenever she spoke to the lady, the lady replied by speaking to Mr Slope. Mr Slope was a favourite, no doubt; but Mrs Proudie had no idea of being thought less of than the chaplain. She was beginning to be stately, stiff, and offended, when unfortunately the castor of the sofa caught itself in her lace train, and carried away there is no saying how much of her garniture. Gathers were heard to go, stitches to crack, plaits to fly open, flounces were seen to fall, and breadths to expose themselves;—a long ruin of rent lace disfigured the carpet, and still clung to the vile wheel on which the sofa moved.

So, when a granite battery is raised, excellent to the eyes of warfaring men, is its strength and symmetry admired. It is the work of years. Its neat embrasures, its finished parapets, its casemated stories, show all the skill of modern science. But, anon, a small spark is applied to the treacherous fusee— a cloud of dust arises to the heavens—and then nothing is to be seen but dirt and dust and ugly fragments.

We know what was the wrath of Juno when her beauty was despised. We know to what storms of passion even celestial minds can yield. As Juno may have looked at Paris on Mount Ida, so did Mrs Proudie look on Ethelbert Stanhope when he pushed the leg of the sofa into her lace train.

'Oh, you idiot, Bertie!' said the signora, seeing what had been done, and what were to be the consequences.

'Idiot!' re-echoed Mrs Proudie, as though the word were not half strong enough to express the required meaning; 'I'll let him know —'; and then looking round to learn, at a glance, the worst, she saw that at present it behoved her to collect the scattered *débris* of her dress.

Bertie, when he saw what he had done, rushed over the sofa and threw himself on one knee before the offended lady. His object, doubtless, was to liberate the torn lace from the castor; but he looked as though he were imploring forgiveness from a goddess.

'Unhand it, sir!' said Mrs Proudie. From what scrap of dramatic poetry she had extracted the word cannot be said; but it must have rested on her memory, and now seemed opportunely dignified for the occasion.

'I'll fly to the looms of the fairies to repair the damages, if you'll only forgive me,' said Ethelbert, still on his knees.

'Unhand it, sir!' said Mrs Proudie, with redoubled emphasis, and all but furious wrath. The allusion to the fairies was a direct mockery, and intended to turn her into ridicule. So at least it seemed to her. 'Unhand it, sir!' she almost screamed.

'It's not me; it's the cursed sofa!' said Bertie, looking imploringly in her face, and holding up both his hands to show that he was not touching her belongings, but still remaining on his knees.

Hereupon the signora laughed; not loud, indeed, but yet audibly. And as the tigress bereft of her young will turn with equal anger on any within reach, so did Mrs Proudie turn upon her female guest.

'Madam!' she said—and it is beyond the power of prose to tell of the fire which flashed from her eyes. Ibid.

THE *Victorians tended not to rate Trollope very highly, dismissing the accuracy of his character-drawing and his powers of realistic description as photographic rather than creative.*

The fact was that Trollope had no experience whatever of what life was like either in a cathedral close or in the world of politics: it was all invention of a high order.

Mrs Elizabeth Gaskell, on the other hand, kept invention to a minimum and used her memory to the maximum in the amusing stories which she wrote for Charles Dickens's magazine Household Words *about life in a small town in Cheshire. These stories were published in book form in 1853 under the name which she had given the town,* Cranford.

Mrs Gaskell was happily married to a nonconformist minister who looked after a poor parish in Manchester and she wrote several successful novels dealing sympathetically with the social problems afflicting the industrial poor. She also wrote a life of her friend Charlotte Brontë.

But it was Cranford *which brought her to notice as the writer of a work of unusual charm, delicacy, and humour: Lord Houghton, impressed, called it, 'the purest piece of humoristic description that has been added to British literature since Charles Lamb'.*

'Cranford' was actually Knutsford, then a sleepy little country town near Manchester. Mrs Gaskell was brought up there when her mother died, first by an aunt in a tiny cottage and then by an uncle in a rather more splendid house, and she had many years of childhood memories and a store of local stories to draw upon.

The Cranford saga is not feminist but it is firmly feminine:

In the first place, Cranford is in possession of the Amazons; all the holders of houses, above a certain rent, are women. If a married couple come to settle in the town, somehow the gentleman disappears; he is either fairly frightened to death by being the only man in the Cranford evening parties, or he is accounted for by being with his regiment, his ship, or closely engaged in business all the week in the great neighbouring commercial town of Drumble, distant only twenty miles on a railroad. In short, whatever does become of the gentlemen, they are not at Cranford. What could they do if they were there? The surgeon has his round of thirty miles, and sleeps at Cranford; but every man cannot be a surgeon. For keeping the trim gardens full of choice flowers without a weed to speck them; for frightening away little boys who look wistfully at the said flowers through the railings; for rushing out at the geese that occasionally venture into the gardens if the gates are left open; for deciding all questions of literature and politics without troubling themselves with unnecessary reasons or arguments; for obtaining clear and correct knowledge of everybody's affairs in the parish; for keeping their maidservants in admirable order; for kindness (somewhat dictatorial) to the poor; and real tender good offices to each other whenever they are in distress, the ladies of Cranford are quite sufficient. 'A man,' as one of them observed to me once, 'is *so* in the way in the house!'

Elizabeth Gaskell (1810–65), *Cranford* (1853).

The middle and upper-middle class ladies of Cranford did not regard the possession of money as an essential qualification for membership of their circle: Gentility was All and it was not so much a game with the good ladies of Cranford as an obsession.
    It made life a little complicated when juicy fruit was in season:

When oranges came in, a curious proceeding was gone through. Miss Jenkyns did not like to cut the fruit; for, as she observed, the juice all ran out nobody knew where; sucking (only I think she used some more recondite word) was in fact the only way of enjoying oranges; but then there was the unpleasant association with a ceremony frequently gone through by little babies; and so, after dessert, in orange season, Miss Jenkyns and Miss Matty used to rise up, possess themselves each of an orange in silence, and withdraw to the privacy of their own rooms, to indulge in sucking oranges.   Ibid.

The book is presented as memoirs and Mrs Gaskell wrote the scenes as though she had been there at the time. She sometimes led into the scenes by musing on the little personal eccentricities clung to by some Cranfordians—including herself:

String is my foible. My pockets get full of little hanks of it, picked up and twisted together, ready for uses that never come. I am seriously annoyed if any one cuts the string of a parcel, instead of patiently and faithfully undoing it fold by fold. How people can bring themselves to use Indian-rubber rings, which are a sort of deification of string, as lightly as they do, I cannot imagine. To me an Indian-rubber ring is a precious treasure. I have one which is not new; one that I picked up off the floor, nearly six years ago. I have really tried to use it; but my heart failed me, and I could not commit the extravagance.
    Small pieces of butter grieve others. They cannot attend to conversation, because of the annoyance occasioned by the habit which some people have of invariably taking more butter than they want. Have you not seen the anxious look (almost mesmeric) which such persons fix on the article? They would feel it a relief if they might bury it out of their sight, by popping it into their own mouths, and swallowing it down; and they are really made happy if the person on whose plate it lies unused, suddenly breaks off a piece of toast (which he does not want at all) and eats up his butter. They think that this is not waste.   Ibid.

When Cranford *was published, the townsfolk of Knutsford recognized the characters and the stories and pronounced the book to be a true and accurate portrait.*

One old lady wrote in to say that she used to be Miss Barker's maid and she remembered well when the cow fell into the lime pit:

An old lady had an Alderney cow, which she looked upon as a daughter. You could not pay the short quarter-of-an-hour call, without being told of the wonderful milk or wonderful intelligence of this animal. The whole town knew and kindly regarded Miss Betty Barker's Alderney; therefore great was the sympathy and regret when, in an unguarded moment, the poor cow tumbled into a lime-pit. She moaned so loudly that she was soon heard, and rescued; but meanwhile the poor beast had lost most of her hair, and came out looking naked, cold, and miserable, in a bare skin. Everybody pitied the animal, though a few could not restrain their smiles at her droll appearance. Miss Betty Barker absolutely cried with sorrow and dismay; and it was said she thought of trying a bath of oil. This remedy, perhaps, was recommended by some one of the number whose advice she asked; but the proposal, if ever it was made, was knocked on the head by Captain Brown's decided 'Get her a flannel waistcoat and flannel drawers, Ma'am, if you wish to keep her alive. But my advice is, kill the poor creature at once.'

Miss Betty Barker dried her eyes, and thanked the Captain heartily; she set to work, and by-and-by all the town turned out to see the Alderney meekly going to her pasture, clad in dark grey flannel. I have watched her myself many a time. Do you ever see cows dressed in grey flannel in London?

Ibid.

The warm, uncritical, domestic humour of much of Cranford *is well represented by the story of how Mrs Forrester, now not at all well-off, had to resort to desperate measures to rescue from oblivion one of the last remnants of her better days.*

The grand Lady Glenmire is admiring a scrap of fine old lace adorning Mrs Forrester's collar:

'Yes,' said that lady, 'such lace cannot be got now for either love or money; made by the nuns abroad they tell me. They say that they can't make it now, even there. But perhaps they can now they've passed the Catholic Emancipation Bill. I should not wonder. But, in the meantime, I treasure up my lace very much. I daren't even trust the washing of it to my maid' (the little charity school-girl I have named before, but who sounded well as 'my maid'). 'I always wash it myself. And once it had a narrow escape. Of course, your ladyship knows that such lace must never be starched or ironed. Some people wash it in sugar and water; and some in coffee, to make it the right yellow colour; but I myself have a very good receipt for washing it in milk, which stiffens it enough, and gives it a very good creamy colour. Well, ma'am, I had tacked it together (and the beauty of this fine lace is, that when it is wet, it goes into a very little space), and put it to soak in milk, when, unfortunately, I left the room; on my return I found pussy on the table, looking very like a thief, but gulping very uncomfortably, as if she was half-choked with something she wanted to swallow, and could not. And, would you believe it? At first I pitied her, and said, "Poor pussy! poor pussy!" till, all at once, I looked and saw the cup of milk empty—cleaned out! "You naughty cat!" said I; and I believe I was provoked enough to give her a slap, which did no good, but only helped the lace down—just as one slaps a choking child on the back. I could have cried, I was so vexed; but I determined I would not give the lace up without a struggle for it. I hoped the lace might disagree with her at any rate; but it would have been too much for Job, if he had seen, as I did, that cat come in, quite placid and purring, not a quarter of an hour after, and almost expecting to be stroked. "No, pussy!" said I; "if you have any conscience, you ought not to expect that!" And then a thought struck me; and I rang the bell for my maid, and sent her to Mr Hoggins with my compliments, and would he be kind enough to lend me one of his top-boots for an hour? I did not think there was anything odd in the message; but Jenny said, the young men in the surgery laughed as if they would be ill, at my wanting a top-boot. When it came, Jenny and I put pussy in, with her fore-feet straight down, so that they were fastened, and could not scratch, and we gave her a teaspoonful of currant-jelly, in which (your ladyship must excuse me) I had mixed some tartar emetic. I shall never forget how anxious I was for the next half-hour. I took pussy to my own room, and spread a clean towel on the floor. I could have kissed her when she returned the lace to sight, very much as it had gone down. Jenny had boiling water ready, and we soaked it and soaked it, and spread it on a lavender bush in the sun, before I could touch it again, even to put it in milk. But now, your ladyship would never guess that it had been in pussy's inside.'   Ibid.

MARY ANN EVANS, *daughter of an estate manager in Warwickshire, was brought up among the farms bordering the River Severn, went to London to work for magazines as an editor and reviewer, began to write books under the pseudonym 'George Eliot' and is now regarded as one of the great nineteenth-century novelists.*

She was formidably intellectual, intuitive, and emotional, and it might be thought unlikely that anything she wrote could ever fit happily alongside the domestic humour of Mrs Caudle's curtain lectures or Mrs Forrester's lace-eating cat. Yet, not so.

The following extract from The Mill on the Floss *is but one example of how many 'serious' novelists of wide general powers, like George Eliot, could, when she or he needed to, write humour as observant and amusing as that written by professional funny folk.*

The Mill on the Floss is a sombre story with a tragic conclusion. But it is

partly autobiographical, and in this early scene George Eliot calls on the memory
of her early and happy rural life in Warwickshire to describe a Meeting of Aunts.
The aunts are assembling for a family dinner at the home of Mrs Tulliver, mother
of the book's main characters, the children Maggie and Tom. Mrs Tulliver is mild
of manner.

    The first aunt to arrive is Mrs Tulliver's formidable sister, Mrs Glegg. Mrs Glegg
is a disapprover; she disapproves of almost everything that poor Mrs Tulliver
wears or says or does. The third sister is Mrs Pullet, a somewhat nervous hypo-
chondriac who has Married Well, i.e. her husband has more money than his
brothers-in-law:

The Dodsons were certainly a handsome family, and Mrs Glegg was not the least handsome of the sisters. As she sat in Mrs Tulliver's arm-chair, no impartial observer would have denied that for a woman of fifty she had a very comely face and figure, though Tom and Maggie considered their Aunt Glegg as the type of ugliness. It is true she despised the advantages of costume, for though, as she often observed, no woman had better clothes, it was not her way to wear her new things out before her old ones. Other women, if they liked, might have their best thread-lace in every wash; but when Mrs Glegg died, it would be found that she had better lace laid by in the right-hand drawer of her wardrobe, in the Spotted Chamber, than ever Mrs Wooll of St Ogg's had bought in her life, although Mrs Wooll wore her lace before it was paid for. So of her curled fronts [a 'front' was a little false hair-piece which it was the female fashion to wear tucked under a ribbon or the front of the cap so that shiny curls dangled fetchingly over the forehead]: Mrs Glegg had doubtless the glossiest and crispest brown curls in her drawers, as well as curls in various degrees of fuzzy laxness; but to look out on the week-day world from under a crisp and glossy front, would be to introduce a most dreamlike and unpleasant confusion between the sacred and the secular. Occasionally, indeed, Mrs Glegg wore one of her third-best fronts on a week-day visit, but not at a sister's house; especially not at Mrs Tulliver's, who, since her marriage, had hurt her sister's feelings greatly by wearing her own hair, though, as Mrs Glegg observed to Mrs Deane, a mother of a family, like Bessy, with a husband always going to law, might have been expected to know better. But Bessy was always weak!

    So if Mrs Glegg's front today was more fuzzy and lax than usual, she had a design under it: she intended the most pointed and cutting allusion to Mrs Tulliver's bunches of blond curls, separated from each other by a due wave of smoothness on each side of the parting. Mrs Tulliver had shed tears several times at sister Glegg's unkindness on the subject of these unmatronly curls, but the consciousness of looking the handsomer for them, naturally ad-ministered support. Mrs Glegg chose to wear her bonnet in the house to-day—untied and tilted slightly, of course—a frequent practice of hers when she was on a visit, and happened to be in a severe humour: she didn't know what draughts there might be in strange houses. For the same reason she wore a small sable tippet, which reached just to her shoulders, and was very far from meeting across her well-formed chest, while her long neck was protected by a *chevaux-de-frise* of miscellaneous frilling. One would need to be learned in the fashions of those times to know how far in the rear of them Mrs Glegg's slate-coloured silk-gown must have been; but from certain constellations of small yellow spots upon it, and a mouldy odour about it suggestive of a damp clothes-chest, it was probable that it belonged to a stratum of garments just old enough to have come recently into wear.

Mrs Glegg held her large gold watch in her hand with the many-doubled chain round her fingers, and observed to Mrs Tulliver, who had just returned from a visit to the kitchen, that whatever it might be by other people's clocks and watches, it was gone half-past twelve by hers.

'I don't know what ails sister Pullet,' she continued. 'It used to be the way in our family for one to be as early as another,—I'm sure it was so in my poor father's time—and not for one sister to sit half an hour before the others came. But if the ways o' the family are altered, it shan't be *my* fault—I'll never be the one to come into a house when all the rest are going away. I wonder *at* sister Deane—she used to be more like me. But if you'll take my advice, Bessy, you'll put the dinner forrard a bit, sooner than put it back, because folks are late as ought to ha' known better.'

'Oh dear, there's no fear but what they'll be all here in time, sister,' said Mrs Tulliver, in her mild-peevish tone. 'The dinner won't be ready till half-past one. But if it's long for you to wait, let me fetch you a cheesecake and a glass o' wine.'

'Well, Bessy!' said Mrs Glegg, with a bitter smile, and scarcely perceptible toss of her head, 'I should ha' thought you'd know your own sister better. I never *did* eat between meals, and I'm not going to begin. Not but what I hate that nonsense of having your dinner at half-past one, when you might have it at one. You was never brought up in that way, Bessy.'

'Why, Jane, what can I do? Mr Tulliver doesn't like his dinner before two o'clock, but I put it half an hour earlier because o' you.'

'Yes, yes, I know how it is with husbands—they're for putting everything off—they'll put the dinner off till after tea, if they've got wives as are weak enough to give in to such work; but it's a pity for you, Bessy, as you haven't got more strength o' mind. It'll be well if your children don't suffer for it. And I hope you haven't gone and got a great dinner for us— going to expense for your sisters, as 'ud sooner eat a crust o' dry bread nor help to ruin you with extravagance. I wonder you don't take pattern by your sister Deane—she's far more sensible. And here you've got two children to provide for, and your husband's spent your fortin i' going to law, and's likely to spend his own too. A boiled joint, as you could make broth of for the kitchen,' Mrs Glegg added, in a tone of emphatic protest, 'and a plain pudding with a spoonful o' sugar, and no spice, 'ud be far more becoming.'

With sister Glegg in this humour, there was a cheerful prospect for the day. Mrs Tulliver never went the length of quarrelling with her, any more than a water-fowl that puts out its leg in a deprecating manner can be said to quarrel with a boy who throws stones. But this point of the dinner was a tender one, and not at all new, so that Mrs Tulliver could make the same answer she had often made before.

'Mr Tulliver says he always will have a good dinner for his friends while he can pay for it,' she said; 'and he's a right to do as he likes in his own house, sister.'

'Well, Bessy, I can't leave your children enough out o' my savings, to keep 'em from ruin. And you mustn't look to having any o' Mr Glegg's money, for it's well if I don't go first—he comes of a long-lived family; and if he was to die and leave me well for my life, he'd tie all the money up to go back to his own kin.'

The sound of wheels while Mrs Glegg was speaking was an interruption highly welcome to Mrs Tulliver, who hastened out to receive sister Pullet—it must be sister Pullet, because the sound was that of a four-wheel.

Mrs Glegg tossed her head and looked rather sour about the mouth at the thought of the 'four-wheel'. She had a strong opinion on that subject.

Sister Pullet was in tears when the one-horse chaise stopped before Mrs Tulliver's door, and it was apparently requisite that she should shed a few more before getting out, for though her husband and Mrs Tulliver stood ready to support her, she sat still and shook her head sadly, as she looked through her tears at the vague distance.

'Why, whatever is the matter, sister?' said Mrs Tulliver. She was not an imaginative woman, but it occurred to her that the large toilet-glass in sister Pullet's best bedroom was possibly broken for the second time.

There was no reply but a further shake of the head, as Mrs Pullet slowly rose and got down from the chaise, not without casting a glance at Mr Pullet to see that he was guarding her handsome silk dress from injury. Mr Pullet was a small man with a high nose, small twinkling eyes, and thin lips, in a fresh-looking suit of black and a white cravat, that seemed to have been tied very tight on some higher principle than that of mere personal ease. He bore about the same relation to his tall, good-looking wife, with her balloon sleeves, abundant mantle, and large be-feathered and be-ribboned bonnet, as a small fishing-smack bears to a brig with all its sails spread.

It is a pathetic sight and a striking example of the complexity introduced into the emotions by a high state of civilization—the sight of a fashionably drest female in grief. From the sorrow of a Hottentot to that of a woman in large buckram sleeves, with several bracelets on each arm, an architectural bonnet, and delicate ribbon-strings—what a long series of gradations! In the enlightened child of civilization the abandonment characteristic of grief is checked and varied in the subtlest manner, so as to present an interesting problem to the analytic mind. If, with a crushed heart and eyes half blinded by the mist of tears, she were to walk with a too devious step through a door-place, she might crush her buckram sleeves too, and the deep consciousness of this possibility produces a composition of forces by which she takes a line that just clears the doorpost. Perceiving that the tears are hurrying fast, she unpins her strings and throws them languidly backward—a touching gesture, indicative, even in the deepest gloom, of the hope in future dry moments when cap-strings will once more have a charm. As the tears subside a little, and with her head leaning backward at the angle that will not injure her bonnet, she endures that terrible moment when grief, which has made all things else a weariness, has itself become weary; she looks down pensively at her bracelets, and adjusts their clasps with that pretty studied fortuity which would be gratifying to her mind if it were once more in a calm and healthy state.

Mrs Pullet brushed each doorpost with great nicety, about the latitude of her shoulders (at that period a woman was truly ridiculous to an instructed eye if she did not measure a yard and a half across the shoulders), and having done that, sent the muscles of her face in quest of fresh tears as she advanced into the parlour where Mrs Glegg was seated.

'Well, sister, you're late; what's the matter?' said Mrs Glegg, rather sharply, as they shook hands.

Mrs Pullet sat down—lifting up her mantle carefully behind, before she answered—

'She's gone,' unconsciously using an impressive figure of rhetoric.

'It isn't the glass this time, then,' thought Mrs Tulliver.

'Died the day before yesterday,' continued Mrs Pullet; 'an' her legs was as thick as my body,' she added, with deep sadness, after a pause. 'They'd tapped her no end o' times, and the water—they say you might ha' swum in it, if you'd liked.'

'Well, Sophy, it's a mercy she's gone, then, whoever she may be,' said Mrs Glegg, with the promptitude and emphasis of a mind naturally clear and decided; 'but I can't think who you're talking of, for my part.'

'But I know,' said Mrs Pullet, sighing and shaking her head; 'and there isn't another such a dropsy in the parish. I know as it's old Mrs Sutton o' the Twentylands.'

'Well, she's no kin o' yours, nor much acquaintance as I've ever heard of', said Mrs Glegg, who always cried just as much as was proper when anything happened to her own 'kin', but not on other occasions.

'She's so much acquaintance as I've seen her legs when they was like bladders . . . And an old lady as had doubled her money over and over again, and kept it all in her own management to the last. There isn't many old parish'ners like her, I doubt.'

'And they say she's took as much physic as 'ud fill a wagon,' observed Mr Pullet.

'Ah!' sighed Mrs Pullet, 'she'd another complaint ever so many years before she had the dropsy, and the doctors couldn't make out what it was. And she said to me, when I went to see her last Christmas, she said, "Mrs Pullet, if ever you have the dropsy, you'll think of me." She did say so,' added Mrs Pullet, beginning to cry bitterly again; 'those were her very words. And she's to be buried o' Saturday, and Pullet's bid to the funeral.'

'Sophy,' said Mrs Glegg, unable any longer to contain her spirit of rational remonstrance—'Sophy, I wonder *at* you, fretting and injuring your health about people as don't belong to you. Your poor father never did so, nor your aunt Frances neither, nor any o' the family as I ever heard of. You couldn't fret no more than this, if we heard as our cousin Abbott had died suddenly without making his will.'

Mrs Pullet was silent, having finished her crying, and rather flattered than indignant at being upbraided for crying too much. It was not everybody who could afford to cry so much about their neighbours who had left them nothing; but Mrs Pullet had married a gentleman farmer, and had leisure and money to carry her crying and everything else to the highest pitch of respectability.

'George Eliot' (Mary Ann Evans) (1819–80), *The Mill on the Floss* (1860).

———

BOOKS *proliferated during the nineteenth century. By its end, the total of published works had quadrupled from two million at the end of the eighteenth century to eight million. Mechanization made them cheaper to produce and distribute, while popular education provided millions of potential readers and free public libraries lent them books to read. Inevitably, only a fraction of published fiction could be called literature. The majority of the output consisted of minor novels by minor writers, romances, 'orrible murders' and the like, and however much they were enjoyed at the time of publication, once the editions had been sold out the books and their authors slipped into oblivion.*

Henry Kingsley is a worthy representative of that lost army of Victorian minor authors. Both his brothers were writers ; George, a personal physician to important men, wrote travel pieces, and the famous Charles, a parson and advocate of muscular Christianity—he tussled with Cardinal Newman about Truth—was the author of over thirty books, including The Water Babies. *Henry dug for gold in Australia for five years, wrote a little, too, and was popular over there as a person but found no gold so returned home and became a newspaper editor and war-correspondent.*

He also wrote some twenty novels which were much admired in their day, the most popular being Ravenshoe.

Here is a scene which shows Kingsley's skill in writing about the behaviour of young boys and girls.

At a wedding, the narrator unwisely decides to help a nursemaid to look after the three small children in her charge:

I waited till the procession had gone in, and then I found that the tail of it was composed of Gus, Flora, and Archy, with their nurse. If a bachelor is worth his salt, he will make himself useful. I saw that nurse was in distress and anxious, so I stayed with her.

Archy was really as good as gold till he met with his accident. He walked up the steps with nurse as quiet as possible. But even at first I began to get anxious about Gus and Flora. They were excited. Gus wouldn't walk up the steps; but he put his two heels together, and jumped up them one at a time, and Flora walked backwards, looking at him sarcastically. At the top step but one Gus stumbled; whereupon Flora said, 'Goozlemy, goozlemy, goozlemy.'

And Gus said, 'You wait a minute, my lady, till we get into church,' after which awful speech I felt as if I was smoking in a powder magazine.

I was put into a pew with Gus, and Flora, and Archy. Nurse, in her modesty, went into the pew behind us.

I am sorry to say that these dear children, with whom I had no previous acquaintance, were very naughty. The ceremony began by Archy getting too near the edge of his hassock, falling off, pitching against the pew door, bursting it open, and flying out among the free seats, head foremost. Nurse, a nimble and dexterous woman, dashed out, and caught him up, and actually got him out of the church door before he had time to fetch his breath for a scream. Gus and Flora were left alone with me.

Flora had a great scarlet and gold church service. As soon as she opened it, she disconcerted me by saying aloud, to an imaginary female friend, 'My dear, there is going to be a collection; and I have left my purse on the piano.'

At this time, also, Gus, seeing that the business was well begun, removed to the further end of the pew, sat down on the hassock, and took from his trousers' pocket a large tin trumpet.

I broke out all over in a cold perspiration as I looked at him. He saw my distress, and putting it to his lips, puffed out his cheeks. Flora administered comfort to me. She said, 'You are looking at that foolish boy. Perhaps he won't blow it, after all. He mayn't if you don't look at him. At all events, he probably won't blow it till the organ begins; and then it won't matter so much'. . .

I wish those dear children (not meaning them any harm) had been, to put it mildly, at play on the village green, that blessed day.

When I looked at Gus again, he was still on the hassock, threatening propriety with his trumpet. I hope for the best. Flora had her prayer-book open, and was playing the piano on each side of it, with her fingers. After a time she looked up at me, and said out loud—

'I suppose you have heard that Archy's cat has kittened?'

I said, 'No.'

'Oh, yes, it has,' she said. 'Archy harnessed it to his meal cart, which turns a mill, and plays music when the wheels go round; and it ran downstairs with the cart; and we heard the music playing as it went; and it kittened in the wood-basket immediately afterwards; and Alwright says she don't wonder at it; and no more do I; and the steward's-room boy is going to drown some. But you mustn't tell Archy, because, if you do, he won't say his prayers; and if he don't say his prayers, he will—etc., etc.' Very emphatically, and in a loud tone of voice.

This was very charming. If I could only answer for Gus, and keep Flora busy, it was wildly possible that we might pull through. If I had not been a madman, I should have noticed that Gus had disappeared.

He had. And the pew door had never opened, and I was utterly unconscious. Gus had crawled up, on all fours, under the seat of the pew, until he was opposite the calves of his sister's legs, against which calves, *horresco referens*, he put his trumpet and blew a long shrill blast. Flora behaved very well and courageously. She only gave one long, wild shriek, as from a lunatic in a padded cell at Bedlam, and then, hurling her prayer-book at him, she turned round and tried to kick him in the face.

This was the culminating point of my misfortunes. After this, they behaved better . . . Gus only made an impertinent remark about Flora's garters, and Flora only drew a short, but trenchant, historical parallel between Gus and Judas Iscariot.

Henry Kingsley (1830–76), *Ravenshoe* (1862).

By an odd little twist of fate, Henry Kingsley's *Ravenshoe*, published in England, seems to have achieved a kind of immortality in Australia.

'A.T.', writing in the Melbourne *Age* on 2 June 1945 about the origins of strange place-names in the State of Victoria, declared that the little town of Ravenshoe 'was so named because someone found a copy of Henry Kingsley's *Ravenshoe* in a tree there'.

THE *vast output of Victorian non-fiction was not, on the whole, a fertile field for humour, consisting as it did mainly of religious works, critical essays, 'penny cyclopaedias', and books on etiquette and manners for those trying to navigate the unfamiliar and dangerous waters of a higher social status than they were accustomed to.*

But there were exceptions: travel books, for one. Abroad, the unfamiliar food and the alien and unspeakable habits to be faced inculcated either fury or amusement in the breasts of British travellers and a good number of Victorian writers chose to be amused. And some of the best of these books were by amateur writers.

A fair specimen of the nineteenth-century amateur humorous travel book was Three in Norway. By Two of Them, *published in 1882. The 'Two' who wrote the book were James Lees and Walter Clutterbuck. Travel then was a leisurely business reckoned in months rather than days, and could only be undertaken by those with plenty of time and money to spend, so it comes as no surprise to learn that James Lees was an old-Etonian lawyer.*

The English are sportsmen and are on a Norwegian train on their way through the mountains to their camp:

A railway journey is not interesting, anywhere, and less so in Norway than in other countries, as there is not even the sensation of speed to divert your mind, and keep you excited in momentary expectation of a smash. Uphill the pace is slow because it cannot be fast; downhill it is slow for fear of the train running away.

There are only two trains a day, one very early, one rather late, but timed to arrive at its destination before dark, for there is no travelling by night. Directly darkness comes on the train is stopped, and the passengers turn out into an hotel, where they remain to rest till dawn. From Christiana to Eidsvold is about a three-hour journey, and during that time the guard came to look at our tickets 425 times. He wanted to incite us to commit a breach of the peace, or to catch us offending against some of his by-laws, and was always appearing at a new place; first at one door, then the other, anon peeping at us through the hole for the lamp, and again blinking from the next carriage through the ice-water vessel. But we were aware of his attention, and did nothing to annoy him, and always showed the same tickets till they were worn out, and then we produced strawberry jam labels, which seemed to be quite satisfactory.

Later on, comfortably housed in an ancient log chalet, they receive a visitor who does not speak English. The scene where they make desperate attempts at small talk through an interpreter is painful even to read:

After dinner, when we were all buried in our respective letters and papers, occasionally reading out particularly interesting scraps of news, Ragnild came in and informed us that a certain Norwegian, whom we may call Mr Fox, had come there to fish. This was a man who had done some business for us here two years ago, and we had had a little correspondence with him before coming out this year. Thinking we might have given him some trouble, and not having any great liking for his character, we naturally wished to be especially civil to him; so we asked Ragnild to bring him in and stay to interpret for us.

Presently he entered the room, and after greeting us sat down and refused to have anything to drink: this astonished us so much that it completely drove our small stock of smaller talk out of our heads. The commonplaces of polite conversation sound perfectly ridiculous when gravely uttered to an interpreter for transmission to the proper recipient, and so Ragnild seemed to think, for her translation always sounded much shorter than our flowery sentences. We tried a variety of feeble questions to which we already knew the answers, somewhat in the following style:—

'We presume, Mr Fox, that you like Norwegian cheese?'

'Does your brother also like Norwegian cheese?'

'Do you speak German?'

'No? but your brother, we believe, plays the Norwegian german-flute?'

'The friends of your sister's children are also our friends. They live in England, but we believe they still like Norwegian cheese.'

'We like much the cheese of the country, and have never suffered asphyxia from it.'

'We shall take a small quantity with us to England for the destruction of rats,' and so forth.

Presently Esau, getting impatient, suggested in a loud voice that we should 'ask him some questions out of Bennett's Phrase-book'. Then he was covered with shame, as he feared that Ragnild would immediately translate this to Mr Fox; but fortunately she did not.

On reference later to the said Phrase-book we find that some very appropriate and useful sentences may be gleaned from its fertile pages. For instance, 'Who are you? What sort of weather is it to-day?' (these two remarks are introductory, as it were, and to inspire confidence in the person addressed). Then we come to the point: 'Will you lend me a dollar? Be quick! Thank you, you are very kind.' Here the speaker would turn to Ragnild and proceed thus: 'Put this in my carpet bag. Make haste and bring me a light, open, four-wheeled phaeton carriage, drawn by one horse.' Then to Mr Fox, 'Good morning; I must go, but I shall return in a month.' Then the speaker might wink at John and depart.

Now came the most awful pause that the history of the world in its darkest moments can yet point to. We coughed and glared at each other, and felt in our pockets as if we might find something to say there; and then the Skipper had a brilliant idea, and said, 'Ask Mr Fox how long he intends to stay here.' But Ragnild at once replied, 'Only two days,' without referring the question to him at all; so that remark was wasted, and our embarrassment became worse than ever; for now not only had we to invent subjects of conversation, but also to put them in such a form that Ragnild should not be able to answer them without taking Mr Fox into her confidence. He all the time was annoying, as he would do literally nothing to keep up his end of the conversation, and replied to our lengthiest and most brilliant efforts of exuberant verbosity by monosyllables and inarticulate grunts.

At last, in desperation we presented him with a very nice new English knife, for which he did not seem to care at all.

Anon. (James Lees and Walter Clutterbuck), *Three in Norway: By Two of Them* (1882).

V ICTORIAN *memoirs provided a fruitful source of humour. Many distinguished old gentlemen were compelled by their profession or rank to maintain the dignified, unfrivolous front required of Victorian men of affairs but were only too happy to unbutton in print once they had retired.*

The Very Revd Samuel Reynolds Hole, dean of Rochester, only partly came into this category because he had more than a touch of the eighteenth-century squire-parson about him and had led a lively life even when in office: he was a friend of Thackeray, member of the Garrick Club, a pioneer rose-grower, and an occasional contributor to Punch.

In his memoirs Dean Hole describes his first attempts at authorship:

I brought out my first tragedy when I was about eight years of age, and, with a remarkable anticipation and prescience of the sensational incidents which would be most acceptable to the popular taste, I did not weary my audience with preliminary explanations and dull details, but I conducted them at once to scenes of wild excitement and to situations of terrible distress. My drama began, 'Act I, Scene I—*enter a man swimming for his life*'; . . . Our audience, consisting of parents, sisters, and nurses, looked on admiringly; if they had laughed, we should have cried.

The chief merit of my plays was brevity. They occupied about seven minutes, and I have seen nothing so concise in dramatic performances except in a booth of strolling players at a fair in Newark, when, owing to the numerous attendance, a tragedy and comedy, with an interlude of singing and dancing, were executed in a quarter of an hour. I have forgotten the name of the tragedy, but the details were these:—

Woodland scene. Small chapel in the distance, with bell-turret.

Enter GREGORY

GREGORY. 'Ark! I 'ear the chapel bell. [*Bell tolls at intervals.*] It is the signal that tells me my Hemmeline is no more! 'Ere comes Constantius to tell the 'orrid news.

Enter CONSTANTIUS, *on wrong side, and salutes.*

GREGORY [*turning with a scowl of disgust*]. Constantius, thy looks betray the 'orrid news—my Hemmeline is no more!

CONSTANTIUS [*with a broad grin*]. Cheer up, bold Gregory! thine Hemmeline liveth, and Hedmund, thine henemy, lies dead at the chapel door!

GREGORY. Then must I to the forest of Hawleens, and when victory has crowned my harms with triumph I shall return, and claim her for my bride.

Bell. Curtain.

But when I quoted this example of compressed genius to Mr Standing, the

actor, whom I met on board the *Orient* on his way to Australia, he repeated
to me the tragedy, yet more brief, of

'THE EMIGRANT'S RETURN'
In one Act.

Scene—a cottage in Ireland. Enter EMIGRANT, *who surveys the dwelling with
emotion, and knocks at door. Door opens. Enter* INMATE.

EMIGRANT. Is my father alive?
INMATE. He is not.
EMIGRANT. Is my mother living?
INMATE. She is not.
EMIGRANT. Is there any whisky in this house?
INMATE. There is not.
EMIGRANT [*sighs heavily*]. This is indeed a woeful day!   [*Dies*]

Slow music. Curtain.

I improvised scenes off the stage. When the sister aforesaid was contumacious, I pretended to be her lover, just returned from India (I don't know
why, but I was fond of returning from India, also from the field of battle),
and, surveying her with an expression of intense disappointment, sorrowfully
sighed, 'Alas, I left her a blooming girl; I find her a withered maniac!' My
elder sisters, I am afraid, encouraged me in this and similar duettos, and
there was something irresistibly comic in the serious resentment with which
the 'withered maniac', with her golden hair, blue eyes, and roseate cheeks,
invariably heard the allegation.

I must have been nearly ten years old before I became a poet. I could not
hear distinctly the words of the aged vicar, under whom I sat in my early
child days, and that which I heard I could not understand, therefore I feel no
shame in confessing that my first and great epic, on 'The Battle of Waterloo',
was composed during his sermon. I only remember the first verse, but it will
suffice, like some fragment of exquisite sculpture, to suggest the beauty of
the whole:—

> 'We heard the rumbling of Great Gallia's drum,
> Onward we saw the hostile army come;
> Nearer and nearer to the plain we sped,
> Where many a veteran, many a stripling, bled.'

I consider 'the rumbling of Great Gallia's drum' to be one of the most
striking lines in the language and I have often wished, when in Paris and
other cities of France, that she had only one drum to rumble!

Samuel Reynolds Hole (1819–1904), *The Memories of Dean Hole* (1892).

AUGUSTUS HARE, *a contemporary of Dean Hole, was less robust a character. Unmarried, a collector of* objets d'art, *he spent his life writing travel-guides and paying long, comfortable visits to his many friends in fashionable society, whom he cultivated and, no doubt, amused. It is recorded that once, when he was having tea in a grand country-house, his hostess recommended him to try her honey, which was made on the estate. Hare exclaimed: 'Oh, what a good idea to keep a bee!'*

In 1896 Hare began publishing his memoirs. The DNB *called them 'long, tedious, and indiscreet', but they were interesting for their amusing recollections of life in an older, different England.*

Augustus Hare was only 6 years of age in 1840, when his home, the Rectory, was the centre of village social life and his mildly eccentric Grannie effortlessly dominated the house and her family (and the village). And everybody had to go to hear Uncle Julius preach:

The curates always came to luncheon at the Rectory on Sundays. They were always compelled to come in ignominiously at the back door, lest they should dirty the entrance; only Mr Egerton was allowed to come in at the front door, because he was 'a gentleman born'. How Grannie used to bully the curates! They were expected not to talk at luncheon, if they did they were soon put down. 'Tea-table theology' was unknown in those days. As soon as the curates had swallowed a proper amount of cold veal, they were called upon to 'give an account to Mrs Leycester' of all that they had done in the week in the four quarters of the parish—Eton, Ollerton, Wistanswick, and Stoke—and soundly were they rated if their actions did not correspond with her intentions. After the curates, came the school-girls to practise their singing, and my mother was set down to strum the piano by the hour together as an accompaniment, while Grannie occupied herself in seeing that they opened their mouths wide enough, dragging the mouths open by force, and, if they would not sing properly, putting her fingers so far down their throats that she made them sick. One day, when she was doing this, Margaret Beeston bit her violently. Mr Egerton was desired to talk to her afterwards about the wickedness of her conduct. 'How could you be such a naughty girl, Margaret, as to bite Mrs Leycester?'—'What'n her put her fingers down my throat for? oi'll boite she harder next time,' replied the impenitent Margaret.

Grannie used to talk of chaney (china), laylocks (lilacs), and gould (gold): of the Prooshians and the Rooshians: of things being plaguey dear or 'plaguey bad'. In my childhood, however, half my elders used such expressions, which now seem to be almost extinct. 'Obleege me by passing the cowcumber', Uncle Julius always used to say . . .

Grannie was quite devoted to Grandpapa, yet as she was twenty years younger, his great age could not but accustom her to the thought of his death, and she constantly talked before him, to his great amusement, of what she should do as a widow. Judge Leycester ('Uncle Hugh'), my grandfather's brother, had left her a house in New Street, Spring Gardens, and whenever Mary Stanley went to Stoke, she used to make her write down the different stages and distances to London to be ready for her removal. Frequently the family used to be startled by a tremendous 'rat-a-tat-tat-tat', on the dining-room door. Grannie had ordered Richard, the young footman, up, and was teaching him how to give 'a London knock'—it was well he should be prepared. One day the party sitting in the drawing-room were astonished to see the family carriage drive up to the door, with Spragg the butler on the box. 'I was only seeing how Spragg will look as coachman when your Grandpapa is dead,' said Grannie, and Grandpapa looked on at the arrangements and enjoyed them heartily . . .

We went to Hastings for Uncle Julius's Charge to the clergy, which produced much enthusiasm amongst them, very different from his lengthy sermons in Hurstmonceaux, under which the whole congregation used quietly to compose themselves to sleep, probably well aware that they would not understand a word, if they tried to attend. The effect was sometimes most ridiculous of the chancel filled with nodding heads, or of heads which had long since done nodding, and were resting on their elbows locked in fastest slumber. I believe Mrs Sherwood describes a similar scene in one of her stories. Aunt Esther and the curate would try in vain to keep themselves awake with strong lavender lozenges during Uncle Julius's endless discourses. And then 'There's Mrs Hare asleep on one side of the Archdeacon and the curate on the other,' the people would say, and he would go droning on with a sermon preached fifty times before. There were, however, days on which Uncle Julius would emerge from the vestry with clenched hands and his face full of pale enthusiasm, and then I would whisper to my mother! 'Look, Uncle Julius is going to do Lady Macbeth!' There were no slumbers then, but rapt attention, as Uncle Julius in his most thrilling (and they were *thrilling*) tones went through the whole of the sleep-walking scene, wrung his hands over the pulpit-cushion, unable to wash out the 'accursed spot' of sin. This was generally about once a year. Though Hurstmonceaux did not comprehend them, there are, however, many fragments, especially similes, in Uncle Julius's ordinary parish sermons which will always have an effect, especially that of grief at a death—the heavy plunge when the person goes down, and the circles vividly apparent at first, then gradually widening, till they are lost and disappear altogether. And though they did not understand him, his parishioners loved Uncle Julius, for he always acted up to his own answer to a question as to the value of a living—'Heaven or hell, according as the occupier does his duty.'

Uncle Julius had published a versified edition of the Psalms. He thought his Psalter would be adopted by the whole Church, and it was never used in a single church except Hurstmonceaux. During the service, he had the oddest way of turning over the pages with his nose. 'The sixteenth morning of the month,' he gave out one day. 'No, 'tain't' called the voice of Martin the clerk from below, "'tis the seventeenth.' 'Oh, the seventeenth morning of the month.'

Augustus Hare (1834–1903), *The Story of my Life* (1896).

———————

M EMOIR *writers like Dean Hole and Augustus Hare looked back upon their pasts from a serene and comfortable present. They had done well, and in their old age they recalled, with sentimental humour, the quirky but lovable characters and happenings of their youth.*

Thomas Hardy, the poet and novelist, also remembered the past with great affection but bitterly resented the present. The old life had been corrupted and soured for him by 'the ache of modernity'.

The theme of most of Hardy's novels and poetry was the tragedy of how ordinary country folk, brought up in the old traditions and taught to live their lives according to the laws of nature, became victims of the new urban, materialistic, industrialized society and its Victorian middle-class morality.

The novels, like those of George Eliot, are powerful and sombre works but they are lit by a good deal of humour, mostly provided by sundry Wessex villagers. Hardy was born and brought up in Higher Bockhampton, a hamlet near Dorchester ('Casterbridge' in the novels) in Dorset ('Wessex'). As with Mark Twain, the rustic characters he met in his early days and the stories they told were to be invaluable to him later as a writer. Hardy's Wessex rustics were much like Shakespeare's 'rude mechanicals' in their simplicity and exuberance, and Hardy had the Shakespearian gift of being able to move from the dramatic to the comic without the join showing.

As in this extract. A mysterious stranger arrives in the village and asks the local carter to drive him to the Rectory. On the way they pass a mansion:

'That's Endelstow House, Lord Luxellian's,' said the driver.

'Endelstow House, Lord Luxellian's,' repeated the other mechanically. He then turned himself sideways, and keenly scrutinized the almost invisible house with an interest which the indistinct picture itself seemed far from adequate to create. 'Yes, that's Lord Luxellian's,' he said yet again after a while, as he still looked in the same direction.

'What, are we going there?'

'No, Endelstow Rectory, as I have told you.'

'Thought you m't have altered your mind, sir, as ye have stared that way at nothing so long.'

'O no; I am interested in the house, that's all.'

'Most people be, as the saying is.'

'Not in the sense that I am.'

'Ah! . . . Well, his family is no better than my own, 'a b'lieve.'

'How is that?'

'Hedgers and ditchers by rights. But once in ancient times one of 'em, when he was at work, changed clothes with King Charles the Second, and saved the king's life. King Charles came up to him like a common man, and said off-hand, "Man in the smock-frock, my name is Charles the Second; will you lend me your clothes?" "I don't mind if I do," said Hedger Luxellian; and they changed there and then. "Now mind ye," King Charles the Second said, like a common man, as he rode away, "if ever I come to the crown, you come to court, knock at the door, and say out bold, 'Is King Charles the Second at home?' Tell your name, and they shall let you in, and you shall be made a lord." Now, that was very nice of Master Charley?'

'Very nice indeed.'

'Well, as the story is, the king came to the throne; and some years after that, away went Hedger Luxellian, knocked at the king's door, and asked if King Charles the Second was in. "No, he isn't," they said. "Then, is Charles the Third?" said Hedger Luxellian. "Yes," said a young feller standing by like a common man, only he had a crown on, "my name is Charles the Third." And—'

'I really fancy that must be a mistake. I don't recollect anything in English history about Charles the Third,' said the other in a tone of mild remonstrance.

'O that's right history enough, only 'twasn't prented; he was rather a queer-tempered man, if you remember.'

'Very well; go on.'

'And, by hook or by crook, Hedger Luxellian was made a lord, and everything went on well till some time after, when he got into a most terrible row with King Charles the Fourth—'

'I can't stand Charles the Fourth. Upon my word, that's too much.'

'Why? There was a George the Fourth, wasn't there?'

'Certainly.'

'Well, Charleses be as common as Georges. However I'll say no more about it . . . Ah, well! 'tis the funniest world ever I lived in—upon my life 'tis.'

Thomas Hardy (1840–1928), A Pair of Blue Eyes (1873).

Hardy's grandfather and his father were the village stone-masons and builders and Hardy grew up in a family which deeply appreciated nature and music. He learnt to play the violin as a child and happily scraped away at village parties and local festivities. He had a remarkable memory and must have stored up many odd sights and sounds during his fiddling to be used later in one of his character sketches.

Hardy's good ear for music might also have made him sensitive to unusual noises.

Like those emanating from Susan Nunsuch when she danced round the bonfire at the village Fifth-of-November party:

'Susy, dear, you and I will have a jig—hey, my honey?—before 'tis quite too dark to see how well-favoured you be still, though so many summers have passed since your husband, a son of a witch, snapped you up from me.'

This was addressed to Susan Nunsuch; and the next circumstance of which the beholders were conscious was a vision of the matron's broad form whisking off towards the space whereon the fire had been kindled. She was lifted bodily by Mr Fairway's arm, which had been flung round her waist before she had become aware of his intention. The site of the fire was now merely a circle of ashes flecked with red embers and sparks, the furze having burnt completely away. Once within the circle he whirled her round and round in a dance. She was a woman noisily constructed; in addition to her enclosing framework of whalebone and lath, she wore pattens summer and winter, in wet weather and in dry, to preserve her boots from wear; and when Fairway began to jump about with her, the clicking of the pattens, the creaking of the stays, and her screams of surprise, formed a very audible concert.

The Return of the Native (1876).

When the village menfolk got together the conversation usually turned, quite rapidly, to the ever-interesting topic of marriage. It would then move on to women both in general and in particular and how best to cope with them:

'This deceiving of folks is nothing new in matrimony,' said Farmer Cawtree. 'I know'd a man and wife—faith, I don't mind owning, as there's no strangers here, that the pair were my own relations—they'd be at it hot one hour that you'd hear the poker, and the tongs, and the bellows, and the warming-pan, flee across the room with the movements of their vengeance; and the next hour you'd hear 'em singing "The Spotted Cow" together, as peaceable as two holy twins; yes, and very good voices they had, and would strike in like street ballet-singers to one another's support in the high notes.'

' 'Tis so with couples: they do make up differences in all manner of queer ways,' said the bark-ripper. 'I knowed a woman; and the husband o' her went away for four-and-twenty year. An one night he came home when she was sitting by the fire, and thereupon he sat down himself on the other side of the chimney-corner. "Well," says she, "have ye got any news?" "Don't know as I have," says he; "have you?" "No," says she, "except that my daughter by the husband that succeeded 'ee was married last month, which was a year after I was made a widow by him." "Oh! Anything else?" he says. "No," says she. And there they sat, one on each side of that chimney-corner, and were found by the neighbours sound asleep in their chairs, not having known what to talk about at all.'

'Well, I don't care who the man is,' said Creedle, 'it took a good deal to interest 'em, and that's true . . .'

'What women do know nowadays!' observed the hollow-turner. 'You can't deceive 'em as you could in my time.'

'What they knowed then was not small,' said John Upjohn. 'Always a good deal more than the men! Why, when I went courting my wife that is now, the skilfulness that she would show in keeping me on her pretty side as she walked was beyond all belief. Perhaps you've noticed that she's got a pretty side to her face as well as a plain one?'

'I can't say I've noticed it particular much,' said the hollow-turner blandly.

'Well,' continued Upjohn, not disconcerted, 'she has. All women under the sun be prettier one side than t'other. And, as I was saying, the pains she would take to make me walk on the pretty side were unending! I warrant that whether we were going with the sun or against the sun, uphill or downhill, in wind or in lewth, that wart of hers was always towards the hedge, and that dimple towards me.'

The Woodlanders (1887).

Hardy set some of his most lively comedy scenes in churches. It was the music-making which interested him as much as anything.

Here at choir practice the parson strives to improve the choir's accent and tries to introduce the new, scientific system of sight-reading notation, the 'tonic sol-fa':

The parson announced Psalm fifty-third to the tune of 'Devizes', and his voice burst forth with

> 'The Lord look'd down from Heav'n's high tower
> The sons of men to view,'

in notes of rigid cheerfulness.

In this start, however, he was joined only by the girls and boys, the men furnishing but an accompaniment of ahas and hems. Mr Torkingham stopped, and Sammy Blore spoke,—

'Beg your pardon sir,—if you'll deal mild with us a moment. What with the wind and walking, my throat's as rough as a grater; and not knowing you were going to hit up that minute, I hadn't hawked, and I don't think Hezzy and Nat had, either,—had ye, souls?'

'I hadn't got thorough ready, that's true,' said Hezekiah.

'Quite right of you, then to speak,' said Mr Torkingham. 'Don't mind explaining; we are here for practice. Now clear your throats, then, and at it again.'

There was a noise as of atmospheric hoes and scrapers, and the bass contingent at last got under way with a time of its own:

> 'The Lard looked down vrom Heav'n's high tower!'

'Ah, that's where we are so defective the pronunciation,' interrupted the parson. 'Now repeat after me: "The Lord look'd down from Heav'n's high tower."'

The choir repeated like an exaggerative echo: 'The Lawd look'd daown from Heav'n's high towah!'

'Better!' said the parson, in the strenuously sanguine tones of a man who got his living by discovering a bright side in things where it was not very perceptible to other people. 'But it should not be given with quite so extreme an accent; or we may be called affected by other parishes. And, Nathanial Chapman, there's a jauntiness in your manner of singing which is not quite becoming. Why don't you sing more earnestly?'

'My conscience won't let me, sir. They say every man for himself: but, thank God, I'm not so mean as to lessen old fokes' chances by being earnest at my time o' life, and they so much nearer the need o't.'

'It's bad reasoning, Nat, I fear. Now, perhaps we had better sol-fa the tune. Eyes on your books, please. *Doe! doe-ray-mee'* —

'I can't sing like that, not I!' said Sammy Blore, with condemnatory astonishment. 'I can sing genuine music, like F and G; but not anything so much out of the order of nater as that.'

'Perhaps you've brought the wrong book, sir?' chimed in Haymoss, kindly. 'I've knowed music early in life and late—in short, ever since Luke Sneap broke his new fiddle-bow in the wedding psalm, when Pa'son Wilton brought home his bride (you can mind the time, Sammy?—when we sung "His wife, like a fair fertile vine, her lovely fruit shall bring", when the young woman turned as red as a rose, not knowing 'twas coming). I've knowed music ever since then, I say, sir, and never heard the like o' that. Every martel note had his name of A, B, C, at that time.'

'Yes, yes, men; but this is a more recent system!'

'Still, you can't alter a old-established note that's A or B by nater,' rejoined Haymoss, with yet deeper conviction that Mr Torkingham was getting off his head. 'Now sound A, neighbour Sammy, and let's have a slap at Heav'n's high tower again, and show the Pa'son the true way!'   *Two on a Tower* (1882).

The childhood recollections which probably gave Hardy most pleasure were the stories his father told him of the church orchestras which used to play for services.

Hardy's grandfather and father were both much-respected leaders of their local parish church orchestra. Until the early nineteenth century these small bands, or 'quires', consisting perhaps of fiddle, bass-viol, serpent, flute, and clarinet, rehearsed in each other's houses, played for village celebrations, and each Sunday clumped twice or more up the wooden stairs to the church's west gallery, usually built on specially for the quire during the eighteenth century. Church orchestras were replaced with more modern, mechanical means of producing music about the time that Hardy was born.

In one of his stories, perhaps an oral folk-tale retold, Hardy describes a church orchestra's unfortunate, but understandable, lapse from grace. In its comic way it is an epitome of Hardy's defence of human nature, with all its faults, against Victorian notions of virtue:

'They could hardly sit in the gallery; for though the congregation down in the body of the church had a stove to keep off the frost, the players in the gallery had nothing at all. So Nicholas said at morning service, when 'twas freezing an inch an hour, "Please the Lord I won't stand this numbing weather no longer: this afternoon we'll have something in our insides to make us warm, if it cost a king's ransom."

'So he brought a gallon of hot brandy and beer, ready mixed, to church with him in the afternoon, and by keeping the jar well wrapped up in Timothy Thomas's bass-viol bag it kept drinkably warm till they wanted it, which was just a thimbleful in the Absolution, and another after the Creed, and the remainder at the beginning o' the sermon. When they'd had the last pull they felt quite comfortable and warm, and as the sermon went on—most unfortunately for 'em it was a long one that afternoon—they fell asleep, every man jack of 'em; and there they slept on as sound as rocks.

''Twas a very dark afternoon, and by the end of the sermon all you could see of the inside of the church were the pa'son's two candles alongside of him in the pulpit, and his spaking face behind 'em. The sermon being ended at last, the pa'son gie'd out the Evening Hymn. But no quire set about sounding up the tune, and the people began to turn their heads to learn the reason why, and then Levi Limpet, a boy who sat in the gallery, nudged Timothy and Nicholas, and said, "Begin! begin!"

'"Hey? what?" says Nicholas, starting up; and the church being so dark and his head so muddled he thought he was at the party they had played at all the night before, and away he went, bow and fiddle, at "The Devil among the Tailors", the favourite jig of our neighbourhood at that time. The rest of the band, being in the same state of mind and nothing doubting, followed their leader with all their strength, according to custom. They poured out that there tune till the lower bass notes of "The Devil among the Tailors" made the cobwebs in the roof shiver like ghosts; then Nicholas, seeing nobody moved, shouted out as he scraped (in his usual commanding way at dances when the folk didn't know the figures), "Top couples cross hands! And when I make the fiddle squeak at the end, every man kiss his pardner under the mistletoe!"

'The boy Levi was so frightened that he bolted down the gallery stairs and out homeward like lightning. The pa'son's hair fairly stood on end when he heard the evil tune raging through the church, and thinking the quire had gone crazy he held up his hand and said: "Stop, stop, stop! Stop, stop! What's this?" But they didn't hear'n for the noise of their own playing, and the more he called the louder they played.

'Then the folks came out of their pews, wondering down to the ground, and saying: "What do they mean by such wickedness! We shall be consumed like Sodom and Gomorrah!"

'And the squire, too, came out of his pew lined wi' green baize, where lots of lords and ladies visiting at the house were worshipping along with him, and went and stood in front of the gallery, and shook his fist in the musicians' faces, saying, "What! In this reverent edifice! What!"

'And at last they heard'n through their playing, and stopped.

''"Never such an insulting, disgraceful thing—never!" says the squire, who couldn't rule his passion.

''"Never!" says the pa'son, who had come down and stood beside him.

''"Not if the Angels of Heaven," says the squire (he was a wickedish man, the squire was, though now for once he happened to be on the Lord's side)— "not if the Angels of Heaven come down," he says, "shall one of you villainous players ever sound a note in this church again."''

A Few Crusted Characters (1891).

➥ The squire disbanded the orchestra and installed a barrel organ in the church.

━━━━━━━━━

A FEW CRUSTED CHARACTERS *was one of several volumes of short stories by Hardy. But the pieces were mainly expanded anecdotes and character sketches and barely qualified as 'short stories'.*

The short story was a recent phenomenon, emerging in the early part of the nineteenth century following the rise of the modern novel during the eighteenth century. Surprisingly, the term 'short story' did not come into use until the late nineteenth century ; until then short pieces of fiction were called 'tales', 'sketches', or 'articles'.

Edgar Allan Poe, one of its pioneers and advocates, insisted that the modern short story (he still called it 'tale') was a wholly American invention, brought about by the need of the American popular magazine industry for huge quantities of short fiction. The first true American short story was considered to be Washington Irving's Rip Van Winkle, *published in 1819.*

There was not the same hunger for short magazine fiction in Britain so few writers in this country were stimulated into extending the scope of the short story beyond its use as a frame for a longish anecdote or pious reflection or character-sketch. The advances were made in other countries by writers such as Nathaniel Hawthorne in the USA, Honoré de Balzac in France, and Ivan Turgenev in Russia, who proved that the short story could be a subtle and distinct form of literature.

Britain was put back on the map by, appropriately, Rudyard Kipling.

The best of Kipling's fiction is found in his short stories. He took the British form, dusted it off, and made it a vehicle for skilful plotting, polished prose, colour, vigour, and striking literary effects.

Here is a complete Kipling short story. Not this time set in India but in the streets of London. The narrator, Kipling himself, has dined on board a ship anchored in the Pool of London as guest of his friend the first officer. It is time to make his way home. But the chief engineer has also been entertaining a friend. Very thoroughly:

'BRUGGLESMITH'

The first officer of the *Breslau* asked me to dinner on board, before the ship went round to Southampton to pick up her passengers. The *Breslau* was lying below London Bridge, her fore-hatches opened for cargo, and her deck littered with nuts and bolts, and screws and chains. The Black M'Phee had been putting some finishing touches to his adored engines, and M'Phee is the most tidy of chief engineers. If the leg of a cockroach gets into one of his slide-valves the whole ship knows it, and half the ship has to clean up the mess.

After dinner, which the first officer, M'Phee, and I ate in one little corner of the empty saloon, M'Phee returned to the engine-room to attend to some brass-fitters. The first officer and I smoked on the bridge and watched the lights of the crowded shipping till it was time for me to go home. It seemed, in the pauses of our conversation, that I could catch an echo of fearful bellowings from the engine-room, and the voice of M'Phee singing of home and the domestic affections.

'M'Phee has a friend aboard to-night—a man who was a boiler-maker at Greenock when M'Phee was a 'prentice,' said the first officer. 'I didn't ask him to dine with us because—'

'I see—I mean I hear,' I answered. We talked on for a few minutes longer, and M'Phee came up from the engine-room with his friend on his arm.

'Let me present ye to this gentleman,' said M'Phee. 'He's a great admirer o' your wor-rks. He has just hearrd o' them.'

M'Phee could never pay a compliment prettily. The friend sat down suddenly on a bollard, saying that M'Phee had understated the truth. Personally, he on the bollard considered that Shakespeare was trembling in the balance solely on my account, and if the first officer wished to dispute this he was prepared to fight the first officer then or later, 'as per invoice'. 'Man, if ye only knew,' said he, wagging his head, 'the times I've lain in my lonely bunk reading *Vanity Fair* an' sobbin'—ay, weepin' bitterly at the pure fascination of it.'

He shed a few tears for guarantee of good faith, and the first officer laughed. M'Phee resettled the man's hat, that had tilted over one eyebrow.

'That'll wear off in a little. It's just the smell o' the engine-room,' said M'Phee.

'I think I'll wear off myself,' I whispered to the first officer. 'Is the dinghy ready?' The dinghy was at the gangway, which was down, and the first officer went forward to find a man to row me to the bank. He returned with a very sleepy Lascar, who knew the river.

'Are you going?' said the man on the bollard. 'Well, I'll just see ye home. M'Phee, help me down the gangway. It has as many ends as a cat-o'-nine-tails, and—losh!—how innumerable are the dinghies!'

'You'd better let him come with you,' said the first officer. 'Muhammad Jan, put the drunk Sahib ashore first. Take the sober Sahib to the next stairs.'

I had my foot in the bow of the dinghy, the tide was making up-stream, when the man cannoned against me, pushed the Lascar back on the gang-way, cast loose the painter, and the dinghy began to saw, stern-first, along the side of the *Breslau*.

'We'll have no exter-r-raneous races here,' said the man. 'I've known the Thames for thirty years—'

There was no time for argument. We were drifting under the *Breslau*'s stern, and I knew that her propeller was half out of water, in the middle of an inky tangle of buoys, low-lying hawsers, and moored ships, with the tide ripping through them.

'What shall I do?' I shouted to the first officer.

'Find the Police Boat as soon as you can, and for God's sake get some way on the dinghy. Steer with the oar. The rudder's unshipped and—'

I could hear no more. The dinghy slid away, bumped on a mooring-buoy, swung round and jigged off irresponsibly as I hunted for the oar. The man sat in the bow, his chin on his hands, smiling.

'Row, you ruffian,' I said. 'Get her out into the middle of the river—'

'It's a preevilege to gaze on the face o' genius. Let me go on thinking. There was "Little Barnaby Dorrit" and "The Mystery o' the Bleak Druid". I sailed in a ship called the *Druid* once—badly found she was. It all comes back to me so sweet. It all comes back to me. Man, ye steer like a genius.'

We bumped round another mooring-buoy and drifted on to the bows of a Norwegian timber-ship—I could see the great square holes on either side of the cut-water. Then we dived into a string of barges and scraped through them by the paint on our planks. It was a consolation to think that the dinghy was being reduced in value at every bump, but the question before me was when she would begin to leak. The man looked ahead into the pitchy darkness and whistled.

'Yon's a Castle liner; her ties are black. She's swinging across stream. Keep her port light on our starboard bow, and go large,' he said.

'How can I keep anything anywhere? You're sitting on the oars. Row, man, if you don't want to drown.'

He took the sculls, saying sweetly: 'No harm comes to a drunken man. That's why I wished to come wi' you. Man, ye're not fit to be alone in a boat.'

He flirted the dinghy round the big ship, and for the next ten minutes I enjoyed—positively enjoyed—an exhibition of first-class steering. We threaded in and out of the mercantile marine of Great Britian as a ferret threads a rabbit-hole, and we, he that is to say, sang joyously to each ship till men looked over bulwarks and cursed us. When we came to some moderately clear water he gave the sculls to me, and said:

'If ye could row as ye write, I'd respect you for all your vices. Yon's London bridge. Take her through.'

We shot under the dark ringing arch, and came out the other side, going up swiftly with the tide chanting songs of victory. Except that I wished to get home before morning, I was growing reconciled to the jaunt. There were one or two stars visible, and by keeping into the centre of the stream, we could not come to any very serious danger.

The man began to sing loudly:—

> 'The smartest clipper that you could find,
>   Yo ho! Oho!
> Was the *Marg'ret Evans* of the Black X Line,
>   A hundred years ago!

Incorporate that in your next book, which is marvellous.' Here he stood up in the bows and declaimed:—

> 'Ye Towers o' Julia, London's lasting wrong,
>   By mony a foul an' midnight murder fed—
> Sweet Thames, run softly till I end my song—
>   And yon's the grave as little as my bed.

I'm a poet mysel' an' I can feel for others.'

'Sit down,' said I. 'You'll have the boat over.'

'Ay, I'm settin'—settin' like a hen.' He plumped down heavily, and added, shaking his forefinger at me—

> 'Lear-rn, prudent, cautious self-control
> Is wisdom's root.

How did a man o' your parts come to be so drunk? Oh, it's a sinfu' thing, an' you may thank God on all fours that I'm with you. What's yon boat?'

We had drifted far up the river, and a boat manned by four men, who rowed with a soothingly regular stroke, was over-hauling us.

'It's the River Police,' I said, at the top of my voice.

'Oh ay! If your sin do not find you out on dry land, it will find you out in the deep water. Is it like they'll give us drink?'

'Exceedingly likely. I'll hail them.' I hailed.

'What are you doing?' was the answer from the boat.

'It's the *Breslau*'s dinghy broken loose,' I began.

'It's a vara drunken man broke loose,' roared my companion, 'and I'm taking him home by water, for he cannot stand on dry land.' Here he shouted my name twenty times running, and I could feel the blushes racing over my body three deep.

'You'll be locked up in ten minutes, my friend,' I said, 'and I don't think you'll be bailed either.'

'H'sh, man, h'sh. They think I'm your uncle.' He caught up a scull and began splashing the boat as it ranged alongside.

'You're a nice pair,' said the sergeant at last.

'I am anything you please so long as you take this fiend away. Tow us in to the nearest station, and I'll make it worth your while,' I said.

'Corruption—corruption,' roared the man, throwing himself flat in the bottom of the boat. 'Like unto the worms that perish, so is man! And all for the sake of a filthy half-crown to be arrested by the River Police at my time o'life!'

'For pity's sake, row,' I shouted. 'The man's drunk.'

They rowed us to a flat—a fire or a police station; it was too dark to see which. I could feel that they regarded me in no better light than the other man. I could not explain, for I was holding the far end of the painter, and feeling cut off from all respectability.

We got out of the boat, my companion falling flat on his wicked face, and the sergeant asked us rude questions about the dinghy. My companion washed his hands of all responsibility. He was an old man; he had been lured into a stolen boat by a man—probably a thief—he had saved the boat from wreck (this was absolutely true), and now he expected salvage in the shape of hot whisky and water. The sergeant turned to me. Fortunately I was in evening dress, and had a card to show. More fortunately still, the sergeant happened to know the *Breslau* and M'Phee. He promised to send the dinghy down next tide, and was not beyond accepting my thanks, in silver.

As this was satisfactorily arranged, I heard my companion say angrily to a constable, 'If you will not give it to a dry man, ye maun to a drookit.' Then he walked deliberately off the edge of the flat into the water. Somebody stuck a boat-hook into his clothes and hauled him out.

'Now,' said he triumphantly, 'under the rule o' the R-royal Humane Society, ye must give me hot whisky and water. Do not put temptation before the laddie. He's my nephew an' a good boy i' the main. Tho' why he should masquerade as Mister Thackeray on the high seas is beyond my comprehension. Oh, the vanity o' youth! M'Phee told me ye were as vain as a peacock. I mind that now.'

'You had better give him something to drink and wrap him up for the night. I don't know who he is,' I said desperately, and when the man had settled down to a drink supplied on my representations, I escaped and found that I was near a bridge.

I went towards Fleet Street, intending to take a hansom and go home. After the first feeling of indignation died out, the absurdity of the experience struck me fully, and I began to laugh aloud in the empty streets, to the scandal of a policeman. The more I reflected the more heartily I laughed, till my mirth was quenched by a hand on my shoulder, and turning I saw him who should have been in bed at the river police-station. He was damp all over; his wet silk hat rode far at the back of his head, and round his shoulders hung a striped yellow blanket, evidently the property of the State.

'The crackling o' thorns under a pot,' said he, solemnly. 'Laddie, have ye not thought o' the sin of idle laughter? My heart misgave me that ever ye'd get home, an' I've just come to convoy you a piece. They're sore uneducate down there by the river. They wouldna listen to me when I talked o' your worrks, so I e'en left them. Cast the blanket about you, laddie. It's fine and cold.'

I groaned inwardly. Providence evidently intended that I should frolic through eternity with M'Phee's infamous acquaintance.

'Go away,' I said; 'go home, or I'll give you in charge!'

He leaned against a lamp-post and laid his finger to his nose—his dishonourable, carnelian neb.

'I mind now that M'Phee told me ye were vainer than a peacock, an' your castin' me adrift in a boat shows ye were drunker than an owl. A good name is as a savoury bakemeat. I ha' nane.' He smacked his lips joyously.

'Well, I know that,' I said.

'Ay, but ye have. I mind now that M'Phee spoke o' your reputation that ye're so proud off. Laddie, if ye gie me in charge—I'm old enough to be your father—I'll bla-ast your reputation as far as my voice can carry; for I'll call you by name till the cows come hame. It's no jestin' matter to be a friend to me. If you discard my friendship, ye must come to Vine Street wi' me for stealin' the *Breslau's* dinghy.'

Then he sang at the top of his voice:—

> 'In the mornin'—
> I' the mornin' by the black van—
> We'll toddle up to Vine Street i' the mornin'!

Yon's my own composeetion, but *I'm* not vain. We'll go home together, laddie, we'll go home together.' And he sang 'Auld Lang Syne' to show that he meant it.

A policeman suggested that we had better move on, and we moved on to the Law Courts near St Clement Danes. My companion was quieter now, and his speech, which up till that time had been distinct—it was a marvel to hear how in his condition he could talk dialect—began to slur and slide and slummock. He bade me observe the architecture of the Law Courts and linked himself lovingly to my arm. Then he saw a policeman and before I could shake him off, whirled me up to the man singing:—

> 'Every member of the Force
> Has a watch and chain of course—'

and threw his dripping blanket over the helmet of the Law. In any other country of the world we should have run an exceedingly good chance of being shot, or dirked, or clubbed—and clubbing is worse than being shot. But I reflected in that wet-cloth tangle that this was England, where the police are made to be banged and battered and bruised, that they may the better endure a police-court reprimand next morning. We three fell in a festoon, he calling on me by name—that was the tingling horror of it—to sit on the policeman's head and cut the traces. I wriggled clear first and shouted to the policeman to kill the blanket-man.

Naturally, the policeman answered; 'You're as bad as 'im,' and chased me, as the smaller man, round St Clement Danes into Holywell Street, where I ran into the arms of another policeman. That flight could not have lasted more than a minute and a half, but it seemed to me as long and as wearisome as the foot-bound flight of a nightmare. I had leisure to think of a thousand things as I ran; but most I thought of the great and god-like man who held a sitting in the north gallery of St Clement Danes a hundred years ago. I know that he at least would have felt for me. So occupied was I with these considerations, that when the other policeman hugged me to his bosom and said: 'What are you tryin' to do?' I answered with exquisite politeness: 'Sir, let us take a walk down Fleet street.' 'Bow Street 'll do *your* business, I think,' was the answer, and for a moment I thought so too, till it seemed I might scuffle out of it. Then there was a hideous scene, and it was complicated by my companion hurrying up with the blanket and telling me—always by name—that he would rescue me or perish in the attempt.

'Knock him down,' I pleaded. 'Club his head open first and I'll explain afterwards.'

The first policemen, the one who had been outraged, drew his truncheon and cut at my companion's head. The high silk hat crackled and the owner dropped like a log.

'Now you've done it,' I said. 'You've probably killed him.'

Holywell Street never goes to bed. A small crowd gathered on the spot, and some one of German extraction shrieked: 'You haf killed the man.'

Another cried: 'Take his bloomin' number. I saw him strook cruel 'ard. Yar!'

Now, the street was empty when the trouble began, and, saving the two policemen and myself, no one had seen the blow. I said, therefore, in a loud and cheerful voice:—

'The man's a friend of mine. He's fallen down in a fit. Bobby, will you bring the ambulance?' Under my breath I added: 'It's five shillings apiece, and the man didn't hit you.'

'No, but 'im and you tried to scrob me,' said the policeman.

This was not a thing to argue about.

'Is Dempsey on duty at Charing Cross?' I said.

'Wot d'you know of Dempsey, you bloomin' garrotter?' said the policeman.

'If Dempsey's there, he knows me. Get the ambulance quick, and I'll take him to Charing Cross.'

'You're coming to Bow Street, you are,' said the policeman crisply.

'The man's dying'—he lay groaning on the pavement—'get the ambulance,' said I.

There is a ambulance at the back of St Clement Danes, whereof I know more than most people. The policeman seemed to possess the keys of the box in which it lived. We trundled it out—it was a three-wheeled affair with a hood—and we bundled the body of the man upon it.

A body in an ambulance looks very extremely dead. The policemen softened at the sight of the stiff boot-heels.

'Now then,' said they, and I fancied that they still meant Bow Street.

'Let me see Dempsey for three minutes if he's on duty,' I answered.

'Very good. He is.'

Then I knew that all would be well, but before we started I put my head under the ambulance hood to see if the man were alive. A guarded whisper came to my ear.

'Laddie, you maun pay me for a new hat. They've broken it. Dinna desert me now, laddie. I'm o'er old to go to Bow Street in my grey hairs for a fault of yours. Laddie, dinna desert me.'

'You'll be lucky if you get off under seven years,' I said to the policeman.

Moved by a very lively fear of having exceeded their duty, the two police-men left their beats, and the mournful procession wound down the empty Strand. Once west of the Adelphi, I knew I should be in my own country; and the policemen had reason to know that too, for as I was pacing proudly a little ahead of the catafalque, another policeman said 'Good-night, sir' to me as he passed.

'Now, you see,' I said, with condescension. 'I wouldn't be in your shoes for something. On my word, I've a great mind to march you two down to Scotland Yard.'

'If the gentleman's a friend o' yours, per'aps—?' said the policeman who had given the blow, and was reflecting on the consequences.

'Perhaps you'd like me to go away and say nothing about it,' I said. Then there hove into view the figure of Constable Dempsey, glittering in his oilskins, and an angel of light to me. I had known him for months; he was an esteemed friend of mine, and we used to talk together in the early mornings. The fool seeks to ingratiate himself with Princes and Ministers; and courts and cabinets leave him to perish miserably. The wise man makes allies among the police and the hansoms, so that his friends spring up from the round-house and the cab-rank, and even his offences become triumphal processions.

'Dempsey,' said I, 'have the police been on strike again? They've put some things on duty at St Clement Danes that want to take me to Bow Street for garrotting.'

'Lor, sir!' said Dempsey indignantly.

'Tell them I'm not a garrotter, nor a thief. It's simply disgraceful that a gentleman can't walk down the Strand without being manhandled by these roughs. One of them has done his best to kill my friend here; and I'm taking the body home. Speak for me, Dempsey.'

There was no time for the much misrepresented policemen to say a word.

Dempsey spoke to them in language calculated to frighten. They tried to explain, but Dempsey launched into a glowing catalogue of my virtues, as noted by gas in the early hours. 'And', he concluded vehemently, ' 'e writes for the papers, too. How'd *you* like to be written about in the papers—in verse, too, which is 'is 'abit. You leave 'im alone. 'Im an' me have been friends for months.'

'What about the dead man?' said the policeman who had not given the blow.

'I'll tell you,' I said relenting, and to the three policemen under the lights of Charing Cross assembled, I recounted faithfully and at length the adventures of the night, beginning with the *Breslau* and ending at St Clement Danes. I described the sinful old ruffian in the ambulance in words that made him wriggle where he lay, and never since the Metropolitan Police was founded did three policemen laugh as those three laughed. The Strand echoed to it, and the unclean birds of the night stood and wondered.

'Oh lor'!' said Dempsey, wiping his eyes, 'I'd ha' given anything to see that old man runnin' about with a wet blanket an' all! Excuse me, sir, but you ought to get took up every night for to make us 'appy.' He dissolved into fresh guffaws.

There was a clinking of silver and the two policemen of St Clement Danes hurried back to their beats, laughing as they ran.

'Take 'im to Charing Cross,' said Dempsey between shouts. 'They'll send the ambulance back in the morning.'

'Laddie, ye've misca'ed me shameful names, but I'm o'er old to go to a hospital. Dinna desert me, laddie. Tak me home to my wife,' said the voice in the ambulance.

'He's none so bad. 'Is wife'll comb 'is hair for 'im proper,' said Dempsey, who was a married man.

'Where d'you live?' I demanded.

'Brugglesmith,' was the answer.

'What's that?' I said to Dempsey, more skilled than I in portmanteau-words.

'Brook Green, 'Ammersmith,' Dempsey translated promptly. 'Of course,' I said. 'That's just the sort of place he would choose to live in. I only wonder that it was not Kew.'

'Are you going to wheel him 'ome, sir?' said Dempsey.

'I'd wheel him home if he lived in—Paradise. He's not going to get out of this ambulance while I'm here. He'd drag me into a murder for tuppence.'

'Then strap 'im up an' make sure,' said Dempsey, and he deftly buckled two straps that hung by the side of the ambulance over the man's body. Brugglesmith—I know not his other name—was sleeping deeply. He even smiled in his sleep.

'That's all right,' said Dempsey, and I moved off, wheeling my devil's perambulator before me. Trafalgar Square was empty except for the few that slept in the open. One of these wretches ranged alongside and begged for money, asserting that he had been a gentleman once.

'So have I,' I said. 'That was long ago. I'll give you a shilling if you'll help me to push this thing.'

'Is it a murder?' said the vagabond, shrinking back. 'I've not got to *that* yet.'

'No, it's going to be one,' I answered. 'I have.'

The man slunk back into the darkness and I pressed on, through Cockspur Street and up to Piccadilly Circus, wondering what I should do with my treasure. All London was asleep, and I had only this drunken carcase to bear me company. It was silent—silent as chaste Piccadilly. A young man of my acquaintance came out of a pink brick club as I passed. A faded carnation drooped from his button-hole; he had been playing cards, and was walking home before the dawn, when he over-took me.

'What are you doing?' he said.

I was far beyond any feeling of shame. 'It's for a bet,' said I. 'Come and help'.

'Laddie, who's yon?' said the voice beneath the hood.

'Good Lord!' said the young man, leaping across the pavement. Perhaps card-losses had told on his nerves. Mine were steel that night.

'The Lord, The Lord?' the passionless, incurious voice went on. 'Dinna be profane, laddie. He'll come in His ain good time.'

The young man looked at me with horror.

'It's all part of the bet,' I answered. 'Do come and push!'

'W—where are you going to?' said he.

'Brugglesmith,' said the voice within. 'Laddie, d'ye ken my wife?'

'No,' said I.

'Well, she's just a tremenjus wumman. Laddie, I want a drink. Knock at one o' those braw houses, laddie, an'—an'—ye may kiss the girrl for your pains.'

'Lie still, or I'll gag you,' I said savagely.

The young man with the carnation crossed to the other side of Piccadilly, and hailed the only hansom visible for miles. What he thought I cannot tell.

I pressed on—wheeling, eternally wheeling—to Brook Green, Hammersmith. There I would abandon Brugglesmith to the gods of that desolate land. We had been through so much together that I could not leave him bound in the street. Beside, he would call after me, and oh! it is a shameful thing to hear one's name ringing down the emptiness of London in the dawn.

So I went on, past Apsley House, even to the coffee-stall, but there was no coffee for Brugglesmith. And into Knightsbridge—respectable Knightsbridge—I wheeled my burden, the body of Brugglesmith.

'Laddie, what are ye going to do wi' me?' he said when opposite the barracks.

'Kill you,' I said briefly, 'or hand you over to your wife. Be quiet.'

He would not obey. He talked incessantly—sliding in one sentence from clear-cut dialect to wild and drunken jumble. At the Albert Hall he said that I was the 'Hattle Gardle buggle', which I apprehend is the Hatton Garden burglar. At Kensington High Street he loved me as a son, but when my weary legs came to the Addison Road Bridge he implored me with tears to unloose the straps and to fight against the sin of vanity. No man molested us. It was as though a bar had been set between myself and all humanity till I had cleared my account with Brugglesmith. The glimmering of light grew in the sky; the cloudy brown of the wood pavement turned to heather-purple; I made no doubt that I should be allowed vengeance on Brugglesmith ere the evening.

At Hammersmith the heavens were steel-grey, and the day came weeping. All the tides of the sadness of an unprofitable dawning poured into the soul of Brugglesmith. He wept bitterly, because the puddles looked cold and houseless. I entered a half-waked public-house—in evening dress and an ulster, I marched to the bar—and got him whisky on condition that he should cease kicking at the canvas of the ambulance. Then he wept more bitterly, for that he had ever been associated with me, and so seduced into stealing the *Breslau*'s dinghy.

The day was white and wan when I reached my long journey's end, and, putting back the hood, bade Brugglesmith declare where he lived. His eyes wandered disconsolately round the red and grey houses till they fell on a villa in whose garden stood a staggering board with the legend 'To Let'. It needed only this to break him down utterly, and with the breakage fled his fine fluency in his guttural northern tongue; for liquor levels all.

'Olely lil while,' he sobbed. 'Olely lil while. Home—falmy—besht of falm-ies—wife too—you dole know my wife! Left them all a lil while ago. Now everything's sold—all sold. Wife—falmy—all sold. Lemmegellup!'

I unbuckled the straps cautiously. Brugglesmith rolled off his resting-place and staggered to the house.

'Wattle I do?' he said.

Then I understood the baser depths in the mind of Mephistopheles.

'Ring,' I said; 'perhaps they are in the attic or the cellar.'

'You do' know my wife. She shleeps on soful in the dorlin' room, waiting meculhome. *You* do' know my wife.'

He took off his boots, covered them with his tall hat, and craftily as a Red Indian picked his way up the garden path and smote the bell marked 'Visitors' a severe blow with the clenched fist.

'Bell sole too. Sole electick bell! Wassor bell this? I can't riggle bell,' he moaned despairingly.

'You pull it—pull it hard,' I repeated, keeping a wary eye down the road. Vengeance was coming and I desired no witness.

'Yes, I'll pull it hard.' He slapped his forehead with inspiration. 'I'll pull it out.'

Leaning back he grasped the knob with both hands and pulled. A wild ringing in the kitchen was his answer. Spitting on his hands he pulled with renewed strength, and shouted for his wife. Then he bent his ear to the knob, shook his head, drew out an enormous yellow and red handkerchief, tied it round the knob, turned his back to the door, and pulled over his shoulder.

Either the handkerchief or the wire, it seemed to me, was bound to give way. But I had forgotten the bell. Something cracked in the kitchen, and Brugglesmith moved slowly down the doorsteps, pulling valiantly. Three feet of wire followed him.

'Pull, oh, pull!' I cried. 'It's coming now.'

'Qui'ri,' he said. 'I'll riggle bell.'

He bowed forward, the wire creaking and straining behind him, the bell-knob clasped to his bosom, and from the noises within I fancied the bell was taking away with it half the woodwork of the kitchen and all the basement banisters. 'Get a purchase on her,' I shouted, and he spun round, lapping that good copper wire about him. I opened the garden gate politely, and he passed out, spinning his own cocoon. Still the bell came up, hand over hand, and still the wire held fast. He was in the middle of the road now, whirling like an impaled cockchafer, and shouting madly for his wife and family. There he met with the ambulance, the bell within the house gave one last peal, and bounded from the far end of the hall to the inner side of the hall-door, where it stayed fast. So did not my friend Brugglesmith. He fell upon his face, embracing the ambulance as he did so, and the two turned over together in the toils of the never-sufficiently-to-be-advertised copper wire.

'Laddie,' he gasped, his speech returning, 'have I a legal remedy?'

'I will go and look for one,' I said, and, departing, found two policemen. These I told that daylight had surprised a burglar in Brook Green while he was engaged in stealing lead from an empty house. Perhaps they had better take care of that bootless thief. He seemed to be in difficulties.

I led the way to the spot, and behold! in the splendour of the dawning, the ambulance, wheels uppermost, was walking down the muddy road on two stockinged feet—was shuffling to and fro in a quarter of a circle whose radius was copper wire, and whose centre was the bell-plate of the empty house.

Next to the amazing ingenuity with which Brugglesmith had contrived to lash himself under the ambulance, the thing that appeared to impress the constables most was the fact of the St Clement Danes ambulance being at Brook Green, Hammersmith.

They even asked me, of all people in the world, whether I knew anything about it!

They extricated him; not without pain and dirt. He explained that he was repelling boarding-attacks by a 'Hattle Gardle buggle' who had sold his house, wife, and family. As to the bell-wire, he offered no explanation, and was borne off shoulder-high between the two policemen. Though his feet were not within six inches of the ground, they paddled swiftly, and I saw that in his magnificent mind he was running—furiously running.

Sometimes I have wondered whether he wished to find me.

Rudyard Kipling (1865–1936), *Brugglesmith* (1891).

W HEN *Thomas Hardy submitted his first novel to the publishers Chapman and Hall it was accepted, but the publisher's reader asked for a meeting first, told Hardy he must concentrate more on plot, and advised the firm not to publish. The reader was the poet, novelist, and journalist George Meredith (he also turned down* East Lynne *and Samuel Butler's* Erewhon).

Running up against Meredith must have been a daunting experience for the young Hardy, then working as an architect on church restoration and hoping to make some extra money by writing fiction.

George Meredith was a handsome, powerful man, a prey to flatulence and addicted to hurling into the air and catching a heavy iron weight for exercise (this gave him back trouble which eventually confined him to a wheelchair). He worked hard all his life and ended up by joining Hardy and Kipling as a Grand Old Man of Edwardian literature. All three were peppered with honorary degrees and all three were awarded the Gold Medal of the Royal Society of Literature. Hardy and Meredith also received the Order of Merit but Kipling was slightly one-up on them as he was offered the honour but refused it three times. Kipling also declined to be Poet Laureate, but did bring himself to accept the Nobel Prize for Literature.

Meredith's career as a man of letters took some time to get under way. At the age of 21 he had his first poem published and on the strength of that gave up his job as a solicitor's clerk and married the widowed daughter of Thomas Love Peacock. Eight years later he was still struggling along as a poet and literary journalist, and to earn a little extra he was persuaded by the artist Henry Wallis to sit (or more accurately, to lie) for a picture Wallis was painting of the tragic suicide of a young poet which he was going to call The Death of Chatterton. *The two results of this episode were that the painting became one of the best-known of all the popular Victorian every-picture-tells-a-story paintings, and Meredith's wife ran off with Henry Wallis.*

Meredith's sales continued to be disappointingly small during the first half of his long writing life but he was never an easy read. His prose style was peculiarly complex, rich in epigrams, wit, and metaphor, and delivered from an Olympian height with a God-like but rather cheerful air of omniscience; a considerable achievement for a poor journalist born above his father's naval outfitter's shop in Portsmouth.

The importance of Meredith's humorous prose is not that it was as amusing, or even half as amusing, as either Hardy's or Kipling's but that it was significantly different.

It was wholly unsentimental.

For a century and a half sentimental humour had dominated literature and drama. During all those years the social and critical attitudes towards humour were that it was essentially trivial and had no business with important issues; its function was to be whimsical entertainment, to act as a kind of aspirin (or, in those days, tincture of opium) to soothe away anxiety and boredom. Used as such, humour was pronounced harmless and perfectly safe to be taken in small doses by even those citizens required by the society of the day to be relentlessly serious-minded, e.g. politicians and mothers.

The break-out from this strait-jacket and the re-entry into humorous writing of wit, scepticism, effrontery, the comedy of ideas, and all the other cutting edges of modern humour, did not begin with but coincided with a lecture given by Meredith in 1877: On the Idea of Comedy and the Uses of the Comedy Spirit.

Meredith loathed sentimental humour. His belief was that real humour should engage the mind as much as, or even more than, the heart, and that far from being trivial it was vitally important to the human race.

What set Meredith and many others thinking furiously were the implications contained in Darwin's On the Origin of Species by means of Natural Selection, or the Preservation of Favoured Races in the Struggle for Life, *summed up by Herbert Spencer in his famous phrase, 'the survival of the fittest'.*

Meredith's lecture, later printed, was written in prose even more complex than that of his novels, and his meaning is often by no means clear; but his starting-point (I think) was that if Darwin was right, then the human beings who would survive would inevitably be those who were more selfish, ruthless, and bent on self-preservation than their more civilized brothers and sisters. Thus mankind was bound to consist of more and more dreadful people and fewer and fewer nice people.

But there was a solution. Meredith suggested that the awful people could be brought to heel and the balance between worthy and unworthy citizens maintained by mankind developing the Comic Spirit. 'Luminous and watchful', with the 'sunny malice of a faun lurking at the corners of the half-closed lips drawn in an idle wariness of half tension', the Comic Spirit would hover above 'pretentious, bombastic, overblown' people, and when they 'offend sound reason, fair justice; are false in humility or mined with conceit', the Spirit overhead would swing into action, 'look humanely malign and cast an oblique light on them, followed by volleys of silvery laughter'.

The lecture was a plea for a return to the old pre-sentimental function of humour as a means of mocking the inadequacies of our betters and retaining a sense of proportion. It called for the re-introduction of critical, intellectual, witty humour, and pleaded that humour must be taken seriously.

Much of this quickly came about. In fact changes were beginning to take place when Meredith sat down to write his lecture. All through the eighteenth and well into the nineteenth century the possession of a sense of humour was still regarded as an unfortunate flaw in a person's character: the Revd Sydney Smith, one of the century's greatest natural humorists in private, stated in public that in his view 'a sense of humour is incompatible with a kind and generous nature'. But by the last quarter of the century a sense of humour was not merely welcomed in a friend or a public figure, it was almost obligatory; and so it has remained. Nowadays most people can tolerate being called a sex-maniac or a drunkard—there is an oblique compliment to virility lurking beneath the words—but nobody will happily admit that they have no sense of humour.

The sense of humour gained so much social status towards the end of the nineteenth century that for the first time in history, according to Sir Harold Nicolson, a British dignitary was publicly denounced for not having one—William Ewart Gladstone.

Two years after giving the lecture, Meredith wrote a witty, rather odd novel which described the fate of a humourless, selfish gentleman who was quite determined to survive, and on his own terms.

The Comic Spirit hovers expectantly above Sir Willoughby. He is not a nice man at all:

A MINOR INCIDENT, SHOWING AN HEREDITARY APTITUDE IN THE USE OF THE KNIFE

There was an ominously anxious watch of eyes visible and invisible over the infancy of Willoughby, fifth in descent from Simon Patterne, of Patterne Hall, premier of this family, a lawyer, a man of solid acquirements and stout ambition, who well understood the foundation-work of a House, and was endowed with the power of saying No to those first agents of destruction, besieging relatives. He said it with the resonant emphasis of death to younger sons. For if the oak is to become a stately tree, we must provide against the crowding of timber. Also the tree beset with parasites prospers not. A great House in its beginning, lives, we may truly say, by the knife. Soil is easily got, and so are bricks, and a wife, and children come of wishing for them, but the vigorous use of the knife is a natural gift and points to growth. Pauper Patternes were numerous when the fifth head of the race was the hope of his country. A Patterne was in the Marines.

The country and the chief of this family were simultaneously informed of the existence of one Lieutenant Crossjay Patterne, of the corps of the famous hard fighters, through an act of heroism of the unpretending cool sort which kindles British blood, on the part of the modest young officer, in the storming of some eastern riverain stronghold, somewhere about the coast of China. The officer's youth was assumed on the strength of his rank, perhaps likewise from the tale of his modesty: 'he had only done his duty.' Our Willoughby was then at College, emulous of the generous enthusiasm of his years, and strangely impressed by the report, and the printing of his name in the newspapers. He thought over it for several months, when, coming to his title and heritage, he sent Lieutenant Crossjay Patterne a cheque for a sum of money amounting to the gallant fellow's pay per annum, at the same time showing his acquaintance with the first, or chemical, principles of generosity, in the remark to friends at home, that 'blood is thicker than water'. The man is a Marine, but he is a Patterne. How any Patterne should have drifted into the Marines, is of the order of questions which are senselessly asked of the great dispensary. In the complimentary letter accompanying his cheque, the lieutenant was invited to present himself at the ancestral hall, when convenient to him, and he was assured that he had given his relative and friend a taste for a soldier's life. Young Sir Willoughby was fond of talking of his 'military namesake and distant cousin, young Patterne—the Marine'. It was funny; and not less laughable was the description of his namesake's deed of valour: with the rescued British sailor inebriate, and the hauling off to captivity of the three braves of the black dragon on a yellow ground, and the tying of them together back to back by their pigtails, and driving of them into our lines upon a newly devised dying-top style of march that inclined to the oblique, like the astonished six eyes of the celestial prisoners, for straight they could not go. The humour of gentlemen at home is always highly excited by such cool feats. We are a small island, but you see what we do. The ladies at the Hall, Sir Willoughby's mother, and his aunts Eleanor and Isabel, were more affected than he by the circumstance of their having a Patterne in the Marines. But how then! We English have ducal blood in business: we have, genealogists tell us, royal blood in common trades. For all our pride we are a queer people; and you may be ordering butcher's meat of a Tudor, sitting on the cane-bottom chairs of a Plantagenet. By and by you may . . . but cherish your reverence. Young Willoughby made a kind of shock-head or football hero of his gallant distant cousin, and wondered occasionally that the fellow had been content to despatch a letter of effusive thanks without availing himself of the invitation to partake of the hospitalities of Patterne.

He was one afternoon parading between showers on the stately garden terrace of the Hall, in company with his affianced, the beautiful and dashing Constantia Durham, followed by knots of ladies and gentlemen vowed to fresh air before dinner, while it was to be had. Chancing with his usual happy fortune (we call these things dealt to us out of the great hidden dispensary, chance) to glance up the avenue of limes, as he was in the act of turning on his heel at the end of the terrace, and it should be added, discoursing with passion's privilege of the passion of love to Miss Durham, Sir Willoughby, who was anything but obtuse, experienced a presentiment upon espying a thick-set stumpy man crossing the gravel space from the avenue to the front steps of the Hall, decidedly not bearing the stamp of gentlemen 'on his hat, his coat, his feet, or anything that was his', Willoughby subsequently observed to the ladies of his family in the Scriptural style of gentlemen who do bear the stamp. His brief sketch of the creature was repulsive. The visitor carried a bag, and his coat-collar was up, his hat was melancholy; he had the appearance of a bankrupt tradesman absconding; no gloves, no umbrella.

As to the incident we have to note, it was very slight. The card of Lieutenant Patterne was handed to Sir Willoughby, who laid it on the salver, saying to the footman: 'Not at home.'

He had been disappointed in the age, grossly deceived in the appearance of the man claiming to be his relative in this unseasonable fashion; and his acute instinct advised him swiftly of the absurdity of introducing to his friends a heavy unpresentable senior as the celebrated gallant Lieutenant of Marines, and the same as a member of his family! He had talked of the man too much, too enthusiastically, to be able to do so. A young subaltern, even if passably vulgar in figure, can be shuffled through by the aid of the heroical story humorously exaggerated in apology for his aspect. Nothing can be done with a mature and stumpy Marine of that rank. Consideratedness dismisses him on the spot, without parlay. It was performed by a gentleman supremely advanced at a very early age in the art of cutting.

Young Sir Willoughby spoke a word of the rejected visitor to Miss Durham, in response to her startled look: 'I shall drop him a cheque,' he said.

George Meredith (1828–1909), *The Egoist: A Comedy in Narrative* (1879).

I T *was hardly surprising that Meredith turned down Samuel Butler's* Erewhon *for publication if he was looking for strong plots; * Erewhon *had hardly any plot at all. Yet in other ways the book represented the sort of humour which Meredith was trying to encourage; it was utterly unsentimental, intellectual, witty, provocative and, in the manner of Swift, it mocked a great many of the received opinions which the society of the time held sacrosanct, like the superiority of science over art, earnestness, the sentimentality attached to parenthood, and genteel codes of morality.*

Erewhon *was an important book, a pioneer contribution to that vein of modern iconoclastic comedy later to be developed by Bernard Shaw, Oscar Wilde, and others. Shaw wrote in the preface to* Major Barbara *that Samuel Butler, 'was, in his own department, the greatest English writer of the latter half of the nineteenth century'.*

Butler was an odd fish. He deeply detested his father, a clergyman of rigid principles who demanded unquestioning obedience from his gifted but, to him, peculiar son. Young Samuel was not allowed to study art so emigrated to New Zealand. He doubled his money breeding sheep which enabled him to return to England and begin a life of painting—he had eleven pictures hung in the Royal Academy—composing Handel-like pieces of music, quarrelling with his father, and writing travel pieces and semi-novels, really philosophical jeux-d'esprits, the first of which was Erewhon.*

In this extract the narrator, having crossed a range of mountains in some far-distant colony and discovered a strange country called Erewhon (an anagram of 'nowhere'), finds out more about the Erewhonian system, under which, for example, illness is a criminal offence (a man is tried in court for being constipated) and crime is treated as a disease:

The fact, therefore, that the Erewhonians attach none of that guilt to crime which they do to physical ailments, does not prevent the more selfish among them from neglecting a friend who has robbed a bank, for instance, till he has fully recovered; but it does prevent them from even thinking of treating criminals with that contemptuous tone which would seem to say, 'I, if I were you, should be a better man than you are,' a tone which is held quite reasonable in regard to physical ailment. Hence, though they conceal ill-health by every cunning and hypocrisy and artifice which they can devise, they are quite open about the most flagrant mental diseases, should they happen to exist, which to do the people justice is not often. Indeed, there are some who are, so to speak, spiritual valetudinarians, and who make themselves exceedingly ridiculous by their nervous supposition that they are wicked, while they are very tolerable people all the time. This, however, is exceptional; and on the whole they use much the same reserve or unreserve about the state of their moral welfare as we do about our health.

Hence all the ordinary greetings among ourselves, such as, How do you do? and the like, are considered signs of gross ill-breeding; nor do the politer classes tolerate even such a common complimentary remark as telling a man that he is looking well. They salute each other with, 'I hope you are good this morning'; or 'I hope you have recovered from the snappishness from which you were suffering when I last saw you'; and if the person saluted has not been good, or is still snappish, he says so at once and is condoled with accordingly. Indeed, the straighteners have gone so far as to give names from the hypothetical language (as taught at the Colleges of Unreason) to all known forms of mental indisposition, and to classify them according to a system of their own, which, though I could not understand it, seemed to work well in practice; for they are always able to tell a man what is the matter with him as soon as they have heard his story, and their familiarity with the long names assures him that they thoroughly understand his case.

The reader will have no difficulty in believing that the laws regarding ill-health were frequently evaded by the help of recognized fictions, which every one understood, but which it would be considered gross ill-breeding to even seem to understand. Thus, a day or two after my arrival at the Nosni-bors', one of the many ladies who called on me made excuses for her husband's only sending his card, on the ground that when going through the public market-place that morning he had stolen a pair of socks. I had already been warned that I should never show surprise, so I merely expressed my sympathy, and said that though I had only been in the capital so short a time, I had already had a very narrow escape from stealing a clothesbrush, and that though I had resisted temptation so far, I was sadly afraid that if I saw any object of special interest that was neither too hot nor too heavy, I should have to put myself in the straightener's hands.

Mrs Nosnibor, who had been keeping an ear on all that I had been saying, praised me when the lady had gone. Nothing, she said, could have been more polite according to Erewhonian etiquette. She then explained that to have stolen a pair of socks, or 'to have the socks' (in more colloquial language), was a recognized way of saying that the person in question was slightly indisposed . . .

Returning to Erewhonian customs in connection with death, there is one which I can hardly pass over. When anyone dies, the friends of the family write no letters of condolence, neither do they attend the scattering, nor wear mourning, but they send little boxes filled with artificial tears, and with the name of the sender painted neatly upon the outside of the lid. The tears vary in number from two to fifteen or sixteen, according to degree of intimacy or relationship; and people sometimes find it a nice point of etiquette to know the exact number which they ought to send. Strange as it may appear, this attention is highly valued, and its omission by those from whom it might be expected is keenly felt. These tears were formerly stuck with adhesive plaster to the cheeks of the bereaved, and were worn in public for a few months after the death of a relative; they were then banished to the hat or bonnet, and are now no longer worn.

The birth of a child is looked upon as a painful subject on which it is kinder not to touch.   Samuel Butler (1835–1902), *Erewhon: or Over the Range* (1872).

Butler's brilliant and sceptical mind could accept no important theory, however acceptable it was to everyone else without first prodding it and picking at it and turning it upside down to see if it worked that way up. He picked a fearful quarrel with Darwin because he believed that Darwin's theory of evolution diminished the role of intelligence. He made a study of the Odyssey *and proved to his own satisfaction that Homer was a woman. He published* Shakespeare's Sonnets Reconsidered *in which he reasoned that the sonnets were dedicated to a man of lowly birth (the DNB said 'a speculation which has found extremely few adherents').*

Butler made a practice of keeping notebooks in which he jotted down little incongruencies which he had observed, ideas for inclusion in later books, and stories which attracted him.

A selection from these notes gives a taste of Butler's sense of irony and of his eccentric charm:

THE CORPSE'S BROTHER

At a funeral the undertaker came up to a man and said to him, 'If you please, sir, the corpse's brother would be happy to take a glass of sherry with you.'

QUILTER'S ENTRY IN 'WHAT'S WHAT'

He professes to give an article on 'Samuel Butler and his work.' I glanced at it and saw that I need not read unless I wished to be annoyed. He concludes his article:

He lived when we first knew him, and probably does still, the queerest hermit-like life in an old Inn of Court attended only by a boy called Alfred, who was at once servant, friend and a butt for his master's good-humoured pleasantries. Butler used to tell with great delight the story of having left this youth to catalogue some photographs taken by his master on a foreign trip, and how he gave to each in which he had been introduced as a foregound figure, his own name, followed by that of the famous place—'Alfred on the Field of Waterloo', 'Alfred at the Falls of the Rhine'.

It is true that I have lived at 15 Clifford's Inn ever since August 1864, but it is not true that I have lived a 'hermit-like life'. I avoided the Quilters as far as I could because I disliked them. I have always avoided people whom I disliked, but never those whom I liked.

As for Alfred, he had been brought up from childhood by the woman who was my laundress. His mother and father had both died when he was only 2 years old; my laundress, a sister of his mother, had taken to him and his sister—and right well had she done for them. My old servant Robert had died in August 1886, aged 70, and I was then too poor to get a substitute. When my father died at the end of December 1886, times were changed, and I wanted someone whom I could trust, who should be half clerk and accountant, half private secretary, and also generally useful. My laundress asked if Alfred would do. He was just then out of a situation, and was about 23 or 24 years. He came to me January 18, 1887, and has remained with me to the present time, as I trust he will continue to do till I die. He was about 26 or 27 when Quilter first saw him, I suppose in 1890.

So much for my being attended only by a boy. It is quite true that Alfred was almost from the very day he came to me at once servant and friend; that he was ever a butt for any pleasantries on my part I utterly deny. I began to feel almost immediately that I was like a basket that had been entrusted to a dog. I had Alfred and myself in view when I used this simile in *Erewhon Revisited*. He liked to have someone who appreciated him, and whom he could run and keep straight. I was so much older, that to him I was a poor old thing with one foot in the grave, who but for his watchful eye and sustaining hand might tumble into it at any moment.

Did I want a new hat? Alfred knew very well that I should rub on with the old one unless I was kept up to getting a new one.

Here, Sir, is a reminder for you. You must keep it in your waistcoat pocket and keep on repeating it to yourself.

—and the reminder was slipped by him into my waistcoat pocket. It ran:

I am to buy a new hat, and a new pair of boots.

On another like occasion I received the following:

This is the last notice from Alfred to the effect that Samuel Butler Esqr. is to buy himself a new Hat on Wednesday morning the 8th November, 1893. Failing to do so there will be an awful scene on his return to Clifford's Inn—Alfred.

Here are others:

You are to work here to-morrow (Tuesday) until 12 o'clock, then you are to go to Peele's or Wilkinson's and get your dinner. Then reach Drury Lane by 5 to 1 (not later). Pit early door 2s 6d. When you are inside and cannot get a seat in the middle, go to the left hand side and you will see better—Feb. 8, 1892.

March 15, 1893. I have taken a great fancy to the plant we bought at Peckham on Tuesday and should be very pleased and gratified if you gave it to me, and get yourself a geranium when next we go down there—Alfred.

Dec. 20, 1894. Please you are to change your flannels and socks to-morrow morning.—Alfred.

In 1895 I spent several mornings in the Manuscript Room of the British Museum, rubbing out pencil marks I had made on many of Dr Butler's letters, while I was writing my *Life of Dr Butler*. Before giving the letters to the Museum I wanted these marks rubbed out, and the letters being already in the keeping of the Museum (though not yet their property), it was arranged that Alfred and I should have a quiet corner in the Manuscript Room and rub out marks till we had cleaned up the letters. Alfred and I sat side by side and presently I found the following scrap thrust under my notice:

You cannot rub out half so nice as Alfred can.

SOLOMON IN ALL HIS GLORY

But, in the first place, the lilies do toil and spin after their own fashion, and, in the next, it was not desirable that Solomon should be dressed like a lily of the valley.

MARRIAGE

In matrimony, to hesitate is sometimes to be saved.

MR DARWIN IN THE ZOOLOGICAL GARDENS

Frank Darwin told me his father was once standing near the hippopotamus cage when a little boy and girl, aged four and five, came up. The hippopotamus shut his eyes for a minute.

'That bird's dead,' said the little girl; 'come along.'

The Note-Books of Samuel Butler, ed. Henry Festing Jones (1912).

S AMUEL BUTLER *never married. He was what used to be called 'a confirmed bachelor'. He shared his interests and his travels with his close friend, also 'a confirmed bachelor', Henry Festing Jones, a solicitor with musical and literary gifts who became Butler's executor and biographer.*

But Butler had one lady friend. He met Miss Eliza Mary Ann Savage at a School of Art and they began a correspondence, with occasional meetings, which lasted for fourteen years. She might have been in love with him but he was unable, or unwilling, to deepen the relationship and was stricken with remorse when she suddenly died.

Miss Savage was the daughter of an architect. She led a genteel life, first working as a governess and later as assistant secretary of the Society of Lady Artists. She was a cripple and was not beautiful. It was perhaps typical of Butler that in one of the three sonnets which he wrote regretting her death he should describe her as:

> '. . . plain and lame and fat and short,
> Forty and over-kind.'

Butler's friend Festing Jones was not impressed with her appearance when he met her. He wrote that she had 'that kind of dowdiness which I used to associate with ladies who had been at school with my mother'. But even he was won over by her 'friendliness and good-humour'.

Butler consulted Miss Savage on all aspects of his work and took her advice seriously, an extraordinary thing for such an egoist to do, and he kept all her letters to him. They reveal a sharp, clear, original, and humorous mind.

Here Miss Savage recommends a play:

> 22 Beaumont Street, W.
> Wednesday [probably 15 Sept. 1880]

Dear Mr Butler,

. . . I am glad you are so well; if you have not quite got rid of the spleen you must go and see *The World* at Drury Lane. I went last week; it is a wonderful play. The hero is a delightful man; who could help being charmed with a young man, who, for the sake of making the voyage with the girl he loves, starts from the Cape of Good Hope at a moment's notice, without any other baggage than a bouquet of artificial flowers?

But he is a man of astonishing resources, for in the second scene he appears dressed in a beautiful suit of flannels, which he could not have borrowed as the passengers and crew are all undersized, meagre, little men, whereas the hero is a fine fellow, standing about 5 ft. 11 in. and measuring at least 45 in. round the waist. Later on he escapes from a lunatic asylum, knocking down a dozen or so of keepers, as if they were rag dolls. The asylum is indeed admirably planned for escaping from—the principal entrance being about two feet from the river's brink, and there is a punt kept quite handy into which the hero springs.

This scene is greatly applauded, and well it may be, for I never before saw a punt going at the rate of 20 miles per hour, and it is a sight I am glad to have seen. In the last scene but one the hero shows himself to be of exceeding subtlety, for he goes to the three archvillains who are carousing together and makes them confess, having taken the precaution to bring two shorthand writers with him. They are hidden behind the door, and the audience see them taking notes of all the villains say.

The third scene is rather an uncomfortable one. Four men on a raft in mid ocean—one of them dies of starvation and sticks out his arms and legs, in a really ghastly manner. The survivors fall to fighting, and every minute we expect the portly hero to go plump upon the dead man, who will of course jump up with a yell, and spoil the tragedy of the scene, for the raft is only ten feet square, if that. However they keep clear of the corpse in the most skilful manner; and it is like dancing on eggs. Do go and see this play; there are ever so many more scenes all equally good . . .

Yours very truly,
E. M. A. Savage

Butler has lost his umbrella. Miss Savage tries to console him:

48 Gt. Marlborough Street, W.
Thursday [23 Mar. 1882]

[Post card]

No trace of the umbrella here. I am sorry for you, but I dare say you will get it back. My umbrellas always come back persistently. I have never been able to lose one, and when one, by reason of its infirmities, has become unbearable, I have to cast it loose upon society at dead of night, or pitch it into the river. There is one of my umbrellas floating to this day in the Bay of Biscay. I set it floating down the Vilaine in the year '67. It was seen only the year before last.

Miss Savage shared Butler's violent dislike of people whose views did not agree with his. High on both their lists were Darwin and the Prime Minister:

New Berners Club, 64 Berners Street, W.
Dec. 4th, 1880

Dear Mr Butler,

. . . by the by apropos of o.c's I saw Mr Gladstone last week. He came out of Lord Selborne's house in Portland Place. He was looking fearfully cross and very yellow. He seemed very undecided as to where he should cross the street, and he stared at me in a helpless sort of way, as if he expected me to offer him some advice on the matter, but as there was no possibility of putting him in the way of being run over, I refrained from giving an opinion. The crossings about Portland Place are so stupidly safe . . .

Yours very truly,
E. M. A. Savage

Lower down on Butler's list, but still strongly disliked, were Thomas Carlyle and his wife. Miss Savage has a comment on their sometimes prickly union:

22 Beaumont Street
Tuesday [18 Nov. 1884]

Dear Mr Butler,

. . . Are you not glad that Mr and Mrs Carlyle were married to one another, and not to other people? They certainly were justly formed to meet by nature. I was provoked last night by the nonsense some people were talking about him, and as they went on to excuse his bad temper on account of his bad digestion, I said that probably his bad digestion should be excused on account of his bad temper, as probably he had been born with a bad temper, but that bad digestions were generally made (I remember *Erewhon* you see) . . .

Yours very truly,
E. M. A. Savage

Miss Savage's comment on the Carlyles is an example of how a remark from an amateur can be transformed by a professional. Butler took it and reshaped it, then shaved it down, added another thought, and returned it to Miss Savage as a witty and eminently quotable line:

15 Clifford's Inn, E.C.
Friday, Nov. 21st, 1884

Dear Miss Savage,

. . . Yes it was very good of God to let Carlyle and Mrs Carlyle marry one another and so make only two people miserable instead of four.

Believe me, Yours very truly,
S. Butler

Henry Festing Jones (1851–1928), *Samuel Butler, a Memoir* (1920).

———————

ALTHOUGH *wit now had a foothold, good old simple, sentimental comedy was more in demand than ever as the century moved to its end. Education had become compulsory and free and the eight-hour day had arrived so there were even more readers and more time for them in which to read. The 1880s and 1890s saw the rise of mass-appeal newspapers, more penny comics, and humorous weekly magazines and a healthy market for amusing, undemanding books to while away an hour or so.*

It was not the Golden Era of English Humour, but by the sheer volume of humour published it might perhaps qualify as the Electro-Plated Nickel-Silver Era. And not all of it was hack journalism: two books were published in those two decades which have become classics of English humour. The first was Three Men in a Boat, *by Jerome K. Jerome.*

Jerome had a miserable childhood, first in Walsall and then in the East End of

London. He left his first job as a clerk to try his luck at acting but it was with a Vincent Crummles-like touring company and was a wretched life. He tried journalism, put together a book called On the Stage and Off, *and thereafter was in demand. In 1889 he published* Three Men in a Boat *which was an instant success, going into endless editions and being translated into several European languages (for some curious reason both Jerome and George Formby were found particularly hilarious by Russians).*

Jerome went on to write more books and also plays, his big success being The Passing of the Third Floor Back, *a serious drama about Christ turning up as a stranger in a boarding-house and sorting out everybody's lives, etc. With Sir Johnston Forbes-Robertson playing the leading part it was rapturously received by audiences. Max Beerbohm reviewed it and called it 'twaddle and vulgarity unrelieved'.*

Three Men in a Boat *might also have contained a great deal of unrelieved twaddle and vulgarity if Jerome had had his way; he was prone to bouts of solemn moralizing and Fine Descriptive Writing, both of which he thought were important elements in his work and neither of which he was much good at. Happily, serendipity intervened. The book began as a suggestion from Jerome to the editor of a magazine,* Home Chimes, *that he write him a serial about the River Thames, which Jerome knew very well and loved, perhaps calling it 'The Story of the Thames', with fulsome descriptions of the river's scenery and history and some humorous relief thrown in. When the editor read the first episodes he instructed Jerome to delete the fulsome descriptions and stick to the funny bits.*

Jerome's funny bits, which now took up almost the whole of the book, offered little that was new in humour. The notion of describing the high jinks of a trio of amiable young sparks had been used many times before, for instance, in The Adventures of Mr Verdant Green *and* Three in Norway.

But Jerome did it better. Besides contriving many memorably funny episodes, he captured the feeling of male camaraderie and temporary freedom enjoyed by the three young men, George, Harris, and the narrator (not forgetting the dog Montmorency), as, cheerfully irresponsible, and gauche, and physically clumsy, they set out on the river together for their summer holiday.

One aspect of the boating life which they had not foreseen was the amount of physical effort involved.

But a fair division of labour need be no problem between friends:

We woke late the next morning, and, at Harris's earnest desire, partook of a plain breakfast, with 'non dainties'. Then we cleaned up, and put everything straight (a continual labour, which was beginning to afford me a pretty clear insight into a question that had often posed me—namely, how a woman with the work of only one house on her hands manages to pass away her time), and, at about ten, set out on what we had determined should be a good day's journey.

We agreed that we would pull this morning, as a change from towing;

and Harris thought the best arrangement would be that George and I should scull, and he steer. I did not chime in with this idea at all; I said I thought Harris could have been showing a more proper spirit if he had suggested that he and George should work, and let me rest a bit. It seemed to me that I was doing more than my fair share of the work on this trip, and I was beginning to feel strongly on the subject.

It always does seem to me that I am doing more work than I should do. It is not that I object to the work, mind you; I like work: it fascinates me. I can sit and look at it for hours. I love to keep it by me: the idea of getting rid of it nearly breaks my heart.

You cannot give me too much work; to accumulate work has almost become a passion with me: my study is so full of it now, that there is hardly an inch of room for any more. I shall have to throw out a wing soon.

And I am careful of my work, too. Why, some of the work that I have by me now has been in my possession for years and years, and there isn't a finger-mark on it. I take a great pride in my work; I take it down now and then and dust it. No man keeps his work in a better state of preservation than I do.

But, though I crave for work, I still like to be fair. I do not ask for more than my proper share.

Jerome K. Jerome (1859–1927), *Three Men in a Boat* (1889).

The three men who were in the boat were based upon real people. 'J', the narrator, was Jerome himself. 'George' was George Wingrave, a bank clerk whose rooms in Tavistock Place Jerome shared when he had given up acting and was trying to break into journalism. 'George' is the cheerful optimist of the boating party.

'Harris' was based upon a photographer named Carl Hentschel whom Jerome met when they both worked for the same magazine. Jerome, George Wingrave, and Carl Hentschel became friends and knocked about together as a trio of gregarious young bachelors.

The course of Jerome's story-telling was as meandering as the progress of the boat up the river. Sometimes he left the three men alone in their boat and wrote about something else, faintly relevant, which he thought would make an interesting diversion.

Like the saga of the cheeses:

I remember a friend of mine, buying a couple of cheeses at Liverpool. Splendid cheeses they were, ripe and mellow, and with a two hundred horse-power scent about them that might have been warranted to carry three miles, and knock a man over at two hundred yards. I was in Liverpool at the time, and my friend said that if I didn't mind he would get me to take them back with me to London, as he should not be coming up for a day or two himself, and he did not think the cheeses ought to be kept much longer.

'Oh, with pleasure, dear boy,' I replied, 'with pleasure.'

I called for the cheeses, and took them away in a cab. It was a ramshackle affair, dragged along by a knock-kneed, broken-winded somnambulist, which his owner, in a moment of enthusiasm, during conversation, referred to as a horse. I put the cheeses on the top, and we started off at a shamble that would have done credit to the swiftest steam-roller ever built, and all went merry as a funeral bell, until we turned the corner. There, the wind carried a whiff from the cheeses full on to our steed. It woke him up, and, with a snort of terror, he dashed off at three miles an hour. The wind still blew in his direction, and before we reached the end of the street he was laying himself out at the rate of nearly four miles an hour, leaving the cripples and stout old ladies simply nowhere.

It took two porters as well as the driver to hold him in at the station; and I do not think they would have done it, even then, had not one of the men had the presence of mind to put a handkerchief over his nose, and to light a bit of brown paper.

I took my ticket, and marched proudly up the platform, with my cheeses, the people falling back respectfully on either side. The train was crowded, and I had to get into a carriage where there were already seven other people. One crusty old gentleman objected, but I got in, notwithstanding; and, putting my cheeses upon the rack, squeezed down with a pleasant smile, and said it was a warm day. A few moments passed, and then the old gentleman began to fidget.

'Very close in here,' he said.

'Quite oppressive,' said the man next him.

And then they both began sniffing, and, at the third sniff, they caught it right on the chest, and rose up without another word and went out. And then a stout lady got up, and said it was disgraceful that a respectable married woman should be harried about in this way, and gathered up a bag and eight parcels and went. The remaining four passengers sat on for a while, until a solemn-looking man in the corner, who, from his dress and general appearance, seemed to belong to the undertaker class, said it put him in mind of dead baby; and the other three passengers tried to get out of the door at the same time, and hurt themselves.

I smiled at the black gentleman, and said I thought we were going to have the carriage to ourselves; and he laughed pleasantly, and said that some people made such a fuss over a little thing. But even he grew strangely depressed after we had started, and so, when we reached Crewe, I asked him to come and have a drink. He accepted, and we forced our way into the buffet, where we yelled, and stamped, and waved our umbrellas for a quarter of an hour; and then a young lady came, and asked us if we wanted anything.

'What's yours?' I said, turning to my friend.

'I'll have half-a-crown's worth of brandy, neat, if you please, miss,' he responded.

And he went off quietly after he had drunk it and got into another carriage, which I thought mean.

From Crewe I had the compartment to myself, though the train was crowded. As we drew up at the different stations, the people, seeing my empty carriage, would rush for it. 'Here y' are, Maria; come along plenty of room.' 'All right, Tom; we'll get in here,' they would shout. And they would run along, carrying heavy bags, and fight round the door to get in first. And one would open the door and mount the steps, and stagger back into the arms of the man behind him; and they would all come and have a sniff, and then droop off and squeeze into other carriages, or pay the difference and go first.

From Euston, I took the cheeses down to my friend's house. When his wife came into the room she smelt round for an instant. Then she said:

'What is it? Tell me the worst.'

I said:

'It's cheeses. Tom bought them in Liverpool, and asked me to bring them up with me.'

And I added that I hoped she understood that it had nothing to do with me; and she said that she was sure of that, but that she would speak to Tom about it when he came back.

My friend was detained in Liverpool longer than he expected; and, three days later, as he hadn't returned home, his wife called on me. She said:

'What did Tom say about those cheeses?'

I replied that he had directed they were to be kept in a moist place, and that nobody was to touch them.

She said:

'Nobody's likely to touch them. Had he smelt them?'

I thought he had, and added that he seemed greatly attached to them.

'You think he would be upset,' she queried, 'if I gave a man a sovereign to take them away and bury them?'

I answered that I thought he would never smile again.

An idea struck her. She said:

'Do you mind keeping them for him? Let me send them round to you.'

'Madam,' I replied, 'for myself I like the smell of cheese, and the journey the other day with them from Liverpool I shall ever look back upon as a happy ending to a pleasant holiday. But, in this world, we must consider others. The lady under whose roof I have the honour of residing is a widow, and, for all I know, possibly an orphan too. She has a strong, I may say an eloquent, objection to being what she terms "put upon". The presence of your husband's cheeses in her house she would, I instinctively feel, regard as a "put upon"; and it shall never be said that I put upon the widow and the orphan.'

'Very well, then,' said my friend's wife, rising, 'all I have to say is, that I shall take the children and go to an hotel until those cheeses are eaten. I decline to live any longer in the same house with them.'

She kept her word, leaving the place in charge of the charwoman, who, when asked if she could stand the smell, replied, 'What smell?' and who, when taken close to the cheeses and told to sniff hard, said she could detect a faint odour of melons. It was argued from this that little injury could result to the woman from the atmosphere, and she was left.

The hotel bill came to fifteen guineas; and my friend, after reckoning everything up, found that the cheeses had cost him eight-and-sixpence a pound. He said he dearly loved a bit of cheese, but it was beyond his means; so he determined to get rid of them. He threw them into the canal; but had to fish them out again, as the bargemen complained. They said it made them feel quite faint. And, after that, he took them one dark night and left them in the parish mortuary. But the coroner discovered them, and made a fearful fuss.

He said it was a plot to deprive him of his living by waking up the corpses.

My friend got rid of them, at last, by taking them down to a sea-side town, and burying them on the beach. It gained the place quite a reputation. Visitors said they had never noticed before how strong the air was, and weak-chested and consumptive people used to throng there for years afterwards.

Ibid.

On the boat-trip it is Harris who is the knowledgeable one, who knows how a thing should be done although it does not work when he does it, which comes as a surprise to him.

One of his errors of self-confidence produced one of the book's most memorable episodes: Harris in the maze at Hampton Court.

It is Jerome's humorous story-telling at its best; realistic, non-jokey, understated, and beautifully constructed:

Harris asked me if I'd ever been in the maze at Hampton Court. He said he went in once to show somebody else the way. He had studied it up in a map, and it was so simple that it seemed foolish—hardly worth the twopence charged for admission. Harris said he thought that map must have been got up as a practical joke, because it wasn't a bit like the real thing, and only misleading. It was a country cousin that Harris took in. He said:

'We'll just go in here, so that you can say you've been, but it's very simple. It's absurd to call it a maze. You keep on taking the first turning to the right. We'll just walk round for ten minutes, and then go and get some lunch.'

They met some people soon after they had got inside, who said they had been there for three-quarters of an hour, and had had about enough of it. Harris told them they could follow him if they liked; he was just going in, and then should turn round and come out again. They said it was very kind of him, and fell behind, and followed.

They picked up various other people who wanted to get it over, as they went along, until they had absorbed all the persons in the maze. People who had given up all hopes of ever getting either in or out, or of ever seeing their home and friends again, plucked up courage, at the sight of Harris and his party, and joined the procession, blessing him. Harris said he should judge there must have been twenty people following him, in all; and one woman with a baby, who had been there all the morning, insisted on taking his arm, for fear of losing him.

Harris kept on turning to the right, but it seemed a long way, and his cousin said he supposed it was a very big maze.

'Oh, one of the largest in Europe,' said Harris.

'Yes, it must be,' replied the cousin, 'because we've walked a good two miles already'.

Harris began to think it rather strange himself, but he held on until, at last, they passed the half of a penny bun on the ground that Harris's cousin swore he had noticed there seven minutes ago. Harris said: 'Oh, impossible!' but the woman with the baby said, 'Not at all,' as she herself had taken it from the child, and thrown it down there, just before she met Harris. She also added that she wished she never had met Harris, and expressed an opinion that he was an impostor. That made Harris mad, and he produced his map, and explained his theory.

'The map may be all right enough,' said one of the party, 'if you know whereabouts in it we are now.'

Harris didn't know, and suggested that the best thing to do would be to go back to the entrance, and begin again. For the beginning again part of it there was not much enthusiasm; but with regard to the advisability of going back to the entrance there was complete unanimity, and so they turned, and trailed after Harris again, in the opposite direction. About ten minutes more passed, and then they found themselves in the centre.

Harris thought at first of pretending that that was what he had been aiming at; but the crowd looked dangerous, and he decided to treat it as an accident.

Anyhow, they had got something to start from then. They did know where they were, and the map was once more consulted, and the thing seemed simpler than ever, and off they started for the third time.

And three minutes later they were back in the centre again.

After that they simply couldn't get anywhere else. Whatever way they turned brought them back to the middle. It became so regular at length, that some of the people stopped there, and waited for the others to take a walk round, and come back to them. Harris drew out his map again, after a while, but the sight of it only infuriated the mob, and they told him to go and curl his hair with it. Harris said that he couldn't help feeling that, to a certain extent, he had become unpopular.

They all got crazy at last, and sang out for the keeper, and the man came and climbed up the ladder outside, and shouted out directions to them. But all their heads were, by this time, in such a confused whirl that they were incapable of grasping anything, and so the man told them to stop where they were, and he would come to them. They huddled together, and waited; and he climbed down, and came in.

He was a young keeper, as luck would have it, and new to the business; and when he got in, he couldn't get to them, and then he got lost. They caught sight of him every now and then, rushing about the other side of the hedge, and he would see them, and rush to get to them, and they would wait there for about five minutes, and then he would reappear again in exactly the same spot, and ask them where they had been.

They had to wait until one of the old keepers came back from his dinner before they got out.

Harris said he thought it was a very fine maze, so far as he was a judge; and we agreed that we would try to get George to go into it, on our way back.
Ibid.

────────

JEROME K. JEROME *was an actor before he became a writer. So too, by a small coincidence, were the Grossmiths, authors of the other big success of the last quarter of the century,* The Diary of a Nobody. *The difference between them was that while Jerome saw no future in acting and gave it up, the Grossmith brothers went on to become successful and respected performers.*

George Grossmith began work as a police-court reporter for The Times*; not a bad training for writing character humour. But he had a pleasant voice, could dance and act, and write songs ('See Me Dance the Polka'), and he set up a one-man show giving 'penny-readings' of his own comic monologues and songs at the piano; a highly profitable enterprise. In 1877 Richard D'Oyly Carte offered him a part in Gilbert and Sullivan's comic opera* The Sorcerer, *and George stayed with the company for twelve years, creating many of Gilbert and Sullivan's major comic roles.*

George's younger brother, Weedon, studied painting at the Royal Academy school and the Slade and exhibited at the Royal Academy, but in 1885 he too took to the stage. Weedon's comic speciality was playing rather Pooter-ish characters, sad, pompous men who stood on their dignity and made fools of themselves. He was a popular actor and appeared with Beerbohm Tree and for Sir Henry Irving's company.

In 1888 the Grossmith brothers began to write a humorous series for Punch, *illustrated by Weedon. It was a typical* Punch *idea: a burlesque of the many books of memoirs then being published by self-important personages whom nobody had ever heard of. The excellent title,* The Diary of a Nobody, *was suggested by* Punch's *editor, F. C. Burnand. The diary was supposedly written by Mr Pooter, a middle-aged clerk in a mercantile office who lived quietly in a suburban house in Holloway. Mr Pooter's diary did not consist of the usual stuff of memoirs:*

recollections of the writer's participation in important events, meetings with the mighty, and so on, because none of those things had happened to Mr Pooter. Instead, he meticulously recorded the events which were of equal importance in his life: painting the bath, receiving a disagreeable Christmas card, and so on.

The Diary of a Nobody *was a great success in* Punch *and in 1892 it was published, slightly expanded, as a book. It became apparent when the pieces were put together and the diary read as one continuous story that the whole was much greater than the sum of the parts, that there was a touch of genius in the creation of Mr Pooter, and the book deserved to be regarded as a humorous work of art.*

As Mr Pooter unfolds the story of his eventful days we come to know him well and he is rather more complex a character than he appears at first glance. Although he is naïve almost to the point of being downright stupid, gullible, prim, with only a faint glimmering of humour (although he works hard on the little he has), he is nevertheless a man with high standards, and he is honest and loyal. Mr Pooter's petty concerns are really the same worries that everybody has, though on a different scale. Underneath it all he is a thoroughly decent man.

Mr Pooter opens his diary by recounting, in full and frank detail, the dramas which he and his wife Carrie encounter when they settle into their new home:

My dear wife Carrie and I have just been a week in our new house. 'The Laurels', Brickfield Terrace, Holloway—a nice six-roomed residence, not counting basement, with a front breakfast-parlour. We have a little front garden; and there is a flight of ten steps up to the front door, which, by-the-by, we keep locked with the chain up. Cummings, Gowing, and our other intimate friends always come to the little side entrance, which saves the servant the trouble of going up to the front door, thereby taking her from her work. We have a nice little back garden which runs down to the railway. We were rather afraid of the noise of the trains at first, but the landlord said we should not notice them after a bit, and took £2 off the rent. He was certainly right; and beyond the cracking of the garden wall at the bottom, we have suffered no inconvenience.

After my work in the City, I like to be at home. What's the good of a home, if you are never in it? 'Home, Sweet Home', that's my motto. I am always in of an evening. Our old friend Gowing may drop in without ceremony; so may Cummings, who lives opposite. My dear wife Caroline and I are pleased to see them, if they like to drop in on us. But Carrie and I can manage to pass our evenings together without friends. There is always something to be done: a tin-tack here, a Venetian blind to put straight, a fan to nail up, or part of a carpet to nail down—all of which I can do with my pipe in my mouth; while Carrie is not above putting a button on a shirt, mending a pillowcase, or practising the 'Sylvia Gavotte' on our new cottage piano (on the three years' system), manufactured by W. Bilkson (in small letters), from Collard and Collard (in very large letters). It is also a great comfort to us to know that our boy Willie is getting on so well in the Bank at Oldham. We should like to see more of him. Now for my diary:

APRIL 4. Tradesmen still calling: Carrie being out, I arranged to deal with Horwin, who seemed a civil butcher with a nice clean shop. Ordered a shoulder of mutton for tomorrow, to give him a trial. Carrie arranged with Borset, the butterman, and ordered a pound of fresh butter, and a pound and a half of salt ditto for kitchen, and a shilling's worth of eggs. In the evening, Cummings unexpectedly dropped in to show me a meerschaum pipe he had won in a raffle in the City, and told me to handle it carefully, as it would spoil the colouring if the hand was moist. He said he wouldn't stay, as he didn't care much for the smell of the paint, and fell over the scraper as he went out. Must get the scraper removed, or else I shall get into a scrape. I don't often make jokes.

APRIL 5. Two shoulders of mutton arrived, Carrie having arranged with another butcher without consulting me. Gowing called, and fell over scraper coming in. Must get that scraper removed.

APRIL 6. Eggs for breakfast simply shocking; sent them back to Borset with my compliments, and he needn't call any more for orders. Couldn't find umbrella, and though it was pouring with rain, had to go without it. Sarah said Mr Gowing must have took it by mistake last night, as there was a stick in the 'all that didn't belong to nobody. In the evening, hearing someone talking in a loud voice to the servant in the downstairs hall, I went out to see who it was, and was surprised to find it was Borset, the butterman, who was both drunk and offensive. Borset, on seeing me, said he would be hanged if he would ever serve City clerks any more—the game wasn't worth the candle. I restrained my feelings, and quietly remarked that I thought it was possible for a City clerk to be a gentleman. He replied he was very glad to hear it, and wanted to know whether I had ever come across one, for he hadn't. He left the house, slamming the door after him, which nearly broke the fanlight; and I heard him fall over the scraper, which made me feel glad I hadn't removed it. When he had gone, I thought of a splendid answer I ought to have given him. However, I will keep it for another occasion.

APRIL 7. Being Saturday, I looked forward to being home early, and putting a few things straight; but two of our principals at the office were absent through illness, and I did not get home till seven. Found Borset waiting. He had been three times during the day to apologize for his conduct last night. He said he was unable to take his Bank Holiday last Monday, and took it last night instead. He begged me to accept his apology, and a pound of fresh butter. He seems, after all, a decent sort of fellow; so I gave him an order for some fresh eggs, with a request that on this occasion they should be fresh. I am afraid we shall have to get some new stair-carpets after all; our old ones are not quite wide enough to meet the paint on either side. Carrie suggests that we might ourselves broaden the paint. I will see if we can match the colour (dark chocolate) on Monday.

APRIL 8, Sunday. After Church, the Curate came back with us, I sent Carrie in to open the front door, which we do not use except on special occasions. She could not get it open, and after all my display, I had to take the Curate (whose name, by-the-by, I did not catch) round the side entrance. He caught his foot in the scraper, and tore the bottom of his trousers. Most annoying, as Carrie could not well offer to repair them on a Sunday. After dinner, went to sleep. Took a walk round the garden, and discovered a beautiful spot for sowing mustard-and-cress and radishes. Went to Church again in the evening: walked back with the Curate. Carrie noticed he had got on the same pair of trousers, only repaired. He wants me to take round the plate, which I think a great compliment.

The social importance in the 1890s of having a sense of humour is not lost on Mr Pooter, who would dearly love to be dubbed a wit. He has humour but it is a tiny, frail shoot which he has to cultivate carefully. He is immensely pleased when he produces a bloom. Sometimes his merry shafts of wit are appreciated by others: sometimes not:

APRIL 12. . . . Gowing began his usual sniffing, so, anticipating him, I said: 'You're not going to complain of the smell of paint again?' He said: 'No, not this time; but I'll tell you what, I distinctly smell dry rot.' I don't often make jokes, but I replied: 'You're talking a lot of *dry rot* yourself.' I could not help roaring at this, and Carrie said her sides quite ached with laughter. I never was so immensely tickled by anything I had ever said before. I actually woke up twice during the night, and laughed till the bed shook.

APRIL 14. Spent the whole of the afternoon in the garden, having this morning picked up at a bookstall for fivepence a capital little book, in good condition, on *Gardening*. I procured and sowed some half-hardy annuals in what I fancy will be a warm, sunny border. I thought of a joke, and called out Carrie. Carrie came out rather testy, I thought. I said: 'I have just discovered we have got a lodging-house.' She replied: 'How do you mean?' I said: 'Look at the *boarders*.' Carrie said: 'Is that all you wanted me for?'

MAY 25. Carrie brought down some of my shirts and advised me to take them to Trillip's round the corner. She said: 'The fronts and cuffs are much frayed.' I said without a moment's hesitation: 'I'm *frayed* they are.' Lor! how we roared. I thought we should never stop laughing. As I happened to be sitting next the driver going to town on the 'bus, I told him my joke about the 'frayed' shirts. I thought he would have rolled off his seat. They laughed at the office a good bit too over it.

MAY 26. Left the shirts to be repaired at Trillip's. I said to him: 'I'm *'fraid* they are *frayed.*' He said, without a smile: 'They're bound to do that, sir.' Some people seem to be quite destitute of a sense of humour.

The diarist is not physically adroit. Little clumsinesses occasionally mar his day:

MAY 30. As I heard the 'bus coming, I left with a hurried kiss—a little too hurried, perhaps, for my upper lip came in contact with Carrie's teeth and slightly cut it. It was quite painful for an hour afterwards.

Mr Pooter, with that physical awkwardness and tattered dignity later captured so well on film by Jacques Tati, foolishly buys his Christmas cards in a busy shop:

DECEMBER 20. Went to Smirksons', the drapers, in the Strand, who this year have turned out everything in the shop and devoted the whole place to the sale of Christmas cards. Shop crowded with people, who seemed to take up the cards rather roughly, and, after a hurried glance at them, throw them down again. I remarked to one of the young persons serving, that carelessness appeared to be a disease with some purchasers. The observation was scarcely out of my mouth, when my thick coat-sleeve caught against a large pile of expensive cards in boxes one on top of the other, and threw them down. The manager came forward, looking very much annoyed, and picking up several cards from the ground, said to one of the assistants, with a palpable side-glance at me: 'Put these amongst the sixpenny goods; they can't be sold for a shilling now.' The result was, I felt it my duty to buy some of these damaged cards.

I had to buy more and pay more than intended. Unfortunately I did not examine them all, and when I got home I discovered a vulgar card with a picture of a fat nurse with two babies, one black and the other white, and the words: 'We wish Pa a Merry Christmas.' I tore up the card and threw it away. Carrie said the great disadvantage of going out in Society and increasing the number of our friends was, that we should have to send out nearly two dozen cards this year.

Mr Pooter hopes for a quiet and emotional Christmas spent with his family, but fate once again arranges some disquieting moments:

CHRISTMAS DAY. We caught the 10.20 train at Paddington, and spent a pleasant day at Carrie's mother's. The country was quite nice and pleasant, although the roads were sloppy. We dined in the middle of the day, just ten of us, and talked over old times. If everybody had a nice, uninterfering mother-in-law, such as I have, what a deal of happiness there would be in the world. Being all in good spirits, I proposed her health; and I made, I think, a very good speech.

I concluded, rather neatly, by saying: 'On an occasion like this—whether relatives, friends, or acquaintances—we are all inspired with good feelings towards each other. We are of one mind, and think only of love and friendship. Those who have quarrelled with absent friends should kiss and make up. Those who happily have not fallen out, can kiss all the same.'

I saw the tears in the eyes of both Carrie and her mother, and must say I felt very flattered by the compliment. That dear old Reverend John Panzy Smith, who married us, made a most cheerful and amusing speech, and said he should act on my suggestion respecting the kissing. He then walked round the table and kissed all the ladies, including Carrie. Of course one did not object to this: but I was more than staggered when a young fellow named Moss, who was a stranger to me, and who had scarcely spoken a word through dinner, jumped up suddenly with a sprig of mistletoe, and exclaimed: 'Hulloh! I don't see why I shouldn't be in on this scene.' Before one could realize what he was about to do, he kissed Carrie and the rest of the ladies.

Fortunately the matter was treated as a joke, and we all laughed; but it was a dangerous experiment, and I felt very uneasy for a moment as to the result. I subsequently referred to the matter to Carrie, but she said: 'Oh, he's not much more than a boy.' I said that he had a very large moustache for a boy. Carrie replied: 'I didn't say he was not a nice boy.'

Of all Mr Pooter's gentle absurdities perhaps the one which invokes most sympathy, certainly from house-proud readers, is his sudden manic urge to brighten up his home.

It happens when Mr Pooter discovers the amazing versatility of Pinkford's enamel paint:

APRIL 25. In consequence of Brickwell telling me his wife was working wonders with the new Pinkford's enamel paint, I determined to try it. I bought two tins of red on my way home. I hastened through tea, went into the garden and painted some flower-pots. I called out Carrie, who said: 'You've always got some new-fangled craze'; but she was obliged to admit that the flower-pots looked remarkably well. Went upstairs into the servant's bedroom and painted her washstand, towel-horse, and chest of drawers. To my mind it was an extraordinary improvement, but as an example of the ignorance of the lower classes in the matter of taste, our servant, Sarah, on seeing them, evinced no sign of pleasure, but merely said 'she thought they looked very well as they was before'.

APRIL 26. Got some more red enamel paint (red, to my mind, being the best colour), and painted the coal-scuttle, and the backs of our *Shakespeare*, the binding of which had almost worn out.

APRIL 27. Painted the bath red, and was delighted with the result. Sorry to say Carrie was not, in fact we had a few words about it. She said I ought to have consulted her, and she had never heard of such a thing as a bath being painted red. I replied: 'It's merely a matter of taste.'. . .

Another ring at the bell; it was Gowing, who said he 'must apologize for coming so often, and that one of these days we must come round to him'. I said: 'A very extraordinary thing has struck me.' 'Something funny, as usual,' said Cummings. 'Yes,' I replied; 'I think even you will say so this time. It's concerning you both; for doesn't it seem odd that Gowing's always coming and Cummings always going?' Carrie, who had evidently quite forgotten about the bath, went into fits of laughter, and as for myself, I fairly doubled up in my chair, till it cracked beneath me. I think this was one of the best jokes I have ever made.

Then imagine my astonishment on perceiving both Cummings and Gowing perfectly silent, and without a smile on their faces. After rather an unpleasant pause, Cummings, who had opened a cigar-case, closed it up again and said: 'Yes—I think, after that, I shall be going, and I am sorry I fail to see the fun of your jokes.' Gowing said he didn't mind a joke when it wasn't rude, but a pun on a name, to his thinking, was certainly a little wanting in good taste. Cummings followed it up by saying, if it had been said by anyone else but myself, he shouldn't have entered the house again. This rather unpleasantly terminated what might have been a cheerful evening. However, it was as well they went, for the charwoman had finished up the remains of the cold pork.

APRIL 28. Went home early and bought some more enamel paint—black this time—and spent the evening touching up the fender, picture-frames, and an old pair of boots, making them look as good as new. Also painted Gowing's walking-stick, which he left behind, and made it look like ebony.

APRIL 29, Sunday. Woke up with a fearful headache and strong symptoms of a cold. Carrie, with a perversity which is just like her, said it was 'painter's colic', and was the result of my having spent the last few days with my nose over a paint-pot. I told her firmly that I knew a great deal better what was the matter with me than she did. I had got a chill, and decided to have a bath as hot as I could bear it. Bath ready—could scarcely bear it so hot. I persevered, and got in; very hot, but very acceptable. I lay still for some time. On moving my hand above the surface of the water, I experienced the greatest fright I ever received in the whole course of my life; for imagine my horror on discovering my hand, as I thought, full of blood. My first thought was that I had ruptured an artery, and was bleeding to death, and should be discovered, later on, looking like a second Marat, as I remember seeing him in Madame Tussaud's. My second thought was to ring the bell, but remembered there was no bell to ring. My third was, that it was nothing but the enamel paint, which had dissolved with boiling water. I stepped out of the bath, perfectly red all over, resembling the Red Indians I have seen depicted at an East-End theatre. I determined not to say a word to Carrie, but to tell Farmerson to come on Monday and paint the bath white.

George and Weedon Grossmith (1847–1912, 1854–1919), *The Diary of a Nobody* (1892).

──────────

During the *1880s and 1890s, when* Three Men in a Boat *and* The Diary of a Nobody *were recounting the jollities and adversities of lower middle-class London clerks, indigenous humour of a somewhat different style was, at last, coming into full flower in Australia.*

Written humour took a while to get going Down Under. Prose, like everything else, had to start from scratch, that is, 1788 when the first fleet arrived from England and the first convict settlement and township were founded.

The early colonial settlers—administrators, soldiers, prison guards, shopkeepers, farmers—had little time or talent to devote to the arts, and, ironically, it was the transported convicts who laid the seeds of Australia's distinctive style of humour.

During those oppressive times stealing a sheep was a hanging matter in Britain so, besides the hard-core petty criminals and thugs, transportation to the colonies was often the sentence for lesser crimes, such as poaching (over half the prisoners crowding British jails were poor countrymen arrested for poaching), forgery, petty swindling, debt, or keeping a bawdy-house.

Transportation was also favoured by judges for middle-class transgressors whom they were inclined to be less anxious to hang. One of these semi-fortunates was Mr William Hunt, an ex-actor, who used his thespian skills to effect his escape from Port Arthur prison disguised as a kangaroo (the guards gave chase and caught him, hoping for supper). Others included Thomas Muir, poet and 'Scottish Martyr', and Mr George Barrington, ex-actor and pickpocket, who survived to speak the witty prologue to a play acted by convicts at the opening in Sydney of Australia's first theatre.

But during the early years of the 1800s the penal laws of England began to become more liberal which resulted in petty criminals now being given small punishments at home and much more hardened criminals being sentenced to transportation. Hard-living has always tended to produce humour, usually sardonic, and as prison life in Australia became tougher and more sadistic so jail-humour began to emerge from the horrors, beginning with ironic nicknames for aspects of prison life:

Scrubbing brushes: Bread containing more chaff and bran than flour [noted in 1802].

Red shirt: Back scarified by flogging.

Botany Bay dozen: Twenty-five lashes.

Old fake: A convict on his second probation.

A clean potato: A free man.

Pinchgut Island: Small island in Sydney Harbour where troublesome convicts were confined on a diet of stale bread and water.

Quoted by Sidney J. Baker, *The Australian Language* (1945).

➤ Inventing apt and brief nicknames was a peculiarly Australian compulsion (and still is). Early in the 1800s, workers on the sheep stations, who much enjoyed a sing-song, adapted an Irish phrase and invented the fine word 'comollyer'. A 'comollyer' was one of those old ballads which began 'Come all you . . .'

─────────────

THE *convicts, in working gangs or as ticket-of-leave men, provided cheap labour for the sheep and cattle stations. Even when they were freed they usually went to work on the stations; there was nowhere else for most of them to go. Girls were in very short supply but many freed men, 'emancipists', married women convicts. There was a reception centre for these at Parramatta, known as the Female Factory, where the girls, many only petty offenders, were put on hard labour until they were released to become servants or to be married.*

The word 'squatters' is nowadays applied to homeless people who occupy empty buildings, or to landless farmers who settle on territory which belongs to somebody else. In the early years of Australia the word was used, perhaps ironically, to describe those original settlers who were granted enormous tracts of land by the crown. Sheep and cattle proved to be the nation's wealth and the squatters and graziers became an extremely rich and powerful group, controlling most of the affairs of New South Wales and Victoria including the legislature.

By the 1850s the transportation of convicts to Australia decreased and the squatter's supply of cheap labour began to dry up so the colony revived an Assisted Passage scheme to attract immigrant workers (even Charles Dickens believed the squatters' claims that Australia was the Land of Opportunity. He used emigration to the colony as a device to make Magwitch rich and to give Mr Micawber a happy ending as a respected Australian alderman).

The scheme was never a great success but thousands of young hopefuls set out from Britain and Ireland over the years to make a better life. The Australian stockmen and sheep-men were more amused than impressed by the immigrants' Britishness and dubbed them 'new-chums' and 'jackaroos'.

The squatters ran into more labour problems when gold was discovered in the early 1850s and a huge proportion of their work force downed tools and headed for the gold-fields. Would-be prospectors arrived by the shipload from Europe and America and made for the diggings, frequently accompanied by the ship's crew.

Australia and its gold was now so attractive a proposition that being sent there was no longer a punishment but almost a privilege. In 1868 the transportation of convicts from Britain was brought to an end.

During the gold-rush, which lasted less than ten years, the population of New South Wales and Victoria rose from a quarter of a million to nearly a million, but only a small proportion worked on the nation's sheep stations.

The squatters did what they could to discourage digging for gold. They made it compulsory for prospectors to take out an expensive licence, which was a heavy burden for unsuccessful diggers, the vast majority. And they enforced their regulations by installing a tough and notably brutal police force. One abiding result was that the ordinary Australian, since the 'ticket-of-leave' days a conformist and lover of law and order, began to develop a deep antipathy towards 'bosses' and any kind of imposed authority.

A more immediate result was a rebellion of diggers at the Eureka Stockade, Ballarat, who burnt their licences and demanded political reform. Soldiers crushed the uprising but it was a moral victory for the rebels. Reforms were instituted and Eureka Stockade marked the beginning of the end of autocratic rule in Australia. And, indeed, the end of rural Australia as a kind of Feudal System with the land owned by sheep and beef 'barons' and worked by near-slave labour.

Very little in the way of Australian humour appeared in print during those early years. Books were were mainly non-fiction tomes with an occasional Australian novel on a serious theme and reprints of British popular successes—Pickwick Papers *was published in a pirated edition as early as 1838. If people read at all they mainly read journals. In 1856 a writer was moved to remark in his* History of the Colony of Victoria, *'The newspaper press represents the only literature published in the Australian colonies'.*

As in America, every pioneer town soon had one or more small newspapers enjoyed mainly for their vigorous reporting of the details of local marriages, murders, and unfortunate drownings of residents attempting to cross swollen rivers.

Until well into this century, Australians spoke of Britain as 'home' and British influence in the early years of Australia was overwhelming. Over 90 per cent of the population was British-born, or Australian-born from British parents. Almost all early Australian writing was modelled on the British style. Magazines were usually copies of British favourites such as Punch, *of which there was one spectacularly successful imitation, the* Melbourne Punch, *which ran from 1885 to 1925, and a score of dismal failures, including* Humbug, *which burst upon the literary scene in 1869 and fell dead in 1870, four months later.*

The editor of Humbug, *Marcus Clarke, was perhaps typical of the earlier immigrant writers. He was born in England in 1846, went to school at Highgate where he was a friend of Gerard Manley Hopkins, emigrated to Melbourne at the age of 16 to join his brother, a County Court Judge, and became a successful freelance journalist. He died at the age of 35.*

During his brief life Marcus Clarke maintained a huge and varied output of poems, stories, and sketches, some of them humorous, and he wrote a fine (deeply unfunny) story about the horrors of convict life in Tasmania entitled For the Term of his Natural Life *which has been called 'the first great Australian novel'. Yet his writing style, even in pieces about Australia, was English. Apart from the mention of a few colonial place-names like Bendigo and the convict settlement of Norfolk Island, the following literary parody could have come straight from* Punch.

It is clear from this sketch that in Australia, as in Britain, there was a flourishing sub-culture, distinct from the world of 'literature', which relished exciting, undemanding blood-and-thunder romances:

THE HAUNTED AUTHOR

'What can I do for you, sir?' I asked blandly, astonished. He was a tall broad-shouldered man in a rough pea-jacket, and scowled portentously.

'Put me into an honest livelihood,' he answered. It was such a strange request that I could only stare. 'Don't you understand?' he said, seating himself with rough vehemence, 'I want to become a reputable member of society. I want some honest employment.'

'But, my good sir, why do you come to me? Your motive is most excellent, but an honest employment is the last thing at *my* disposal.'

'That be blowed!' said he, 'you could give me a fortune if you liked, you know you could. But I don't want that. No, I'm fly to that game! You'll have some blessed elder brother, that nobody knowed of, coming back from New Zealand and succeeding to the ancestral mansion; or you'll get me pitched out of my gilded chariot at the church door, and marry my wife, that ought to be, to somebody else. I know you. I only want a modest competence, nobody interferes with that.'

'Your language is even more mysterious than your appearance, my friend,' I said.

'Pshaw!' said he (I never heard a man outside a book say 'pshaw'—never), 'don't you know me?'

I looked at him steadily, and it seemed that I ought to know him, that hat, that pea-jacket, that knotted scarf around his muscular throat, those fierce eyes—all were familiar to me . . .

'You don't happen to have any marks about you?' I asked, while a cold sweat broke out upon my brow.

He laughed—that bitter laugh which I had described so often.

'I have a peculiar mole on the back of my neck, the tip of my left ear is shot away, my right side still bears the mark of Pompey's claws when he defended his young mistress Alice in the lonely swamp. I have lost the little finger of my right hand, and have three pear-shaped wens, besides the usual allowance of strawberry marks.'

There was no mistaking him. It was my Villain! I knew his bloodthirsty nature, and dreaded the tremendous struggle which experience told me was to follow.

'But why come here?' I urged.

'I am sick of it,' said my villain, doggedly. 'I ain't to be badgered any more.

It ain't a repectable business. First I was Jabez Jamrack, then Black Will the Smuggler, then Curlewis Carleyon, then a Poacher, then a Burglar, then an Unjust Steward, and now I'm an Escaped Convict.'

It was true. The unhappy creature before me had figured—in my world-renowned novels—in all those capacities . . .

'It ain't because I'm out all nights in all sorts of weathers, mostly thunderous. It ain't because I'm often drunk, always in debt, and totally disreputable. It ain't because I've murdered a large variety of mothers, and brought the grey 'airs of a corresponding number of aged fathers with sorrow to the grave. It ain't because my langwidge is altogether ridiculous, and I leave out more "h"'s' and put in more oaths in my conversation than any natural man did yet. It ain't that. No!' he cried, waxing wroth, 'it's because I'm always left at the end of the third volume, if I'm still alive, without hope of mercy or promise of repentance.'

I shuddered.

'Take some brandy,' I said, and pushed him the decanter. He took it, and filling half-a-tumber with neat spirit drained it at a gulp. I knew he would. The Beast—under my direction—invariably took his liquor in that fashion . . .

'Is it right? Is it just, guvernor? . . . Your comic servant winds up with the chambermaid. Your aristocratic villain, the Marquis, my master, who poisons his niece, and shoots his aunt with an air-gun, he's *all right* . . . he's never hung in chains, or tuk to Newgate, or starved to death in a deserted drive on the diggings of Bend-i-go . . . But why waste words? Are we not alone here? No sound but the whistling of the wind in the wide chimneys of the moated grange; no footsteps but that of the midnight mouser as she creeps stealthily to her prey. Ha, ha! Thou art mine, and—'. . .

Ha, ha indeed! I guessed how it would happen. My experience as a novel-writer told me as much. Just as the enraged ruffian advanced to seize me . . . a new-comer appeared upon the scene.

By his wavy hair, square-toed Wellingtons, massive watch chain, and handkerchief that hung from the right hand pocket of his shooting coat, I knew him at once.

He was Sir Aubrey de Briancourt.

'Assist me!' I exclaimed.

The look of scorn he gave me was sufficient to daunt a bolder man, but I knew of a spell by which I could compel him.

'Hist!' I said, in a thrilling whisper. 'Proud scion of a lordly house, there is another Sir Aubrey. Refuse to aid me, and young Fairfield will assume your name and title. These minions are beyond my power, but remember you are to be *continued in our next.*'

The threat made pale the cheek even of one whose ancestors had bled on Bosworth, and the baronet waved a white hand towards the back door.

'Take my cabriolet, dog!' he said, with that courtesy which characterizes the British aristocrat . . .

I need scarcely remark that I leapt into the cabriolet, and was soon driving with the rapidity of lightning towards Goodman's Gully.

Fast behind came the echo of hooves. The lightning flashed incessantly, and the negro who held the reins was white with fear.

All at once a man clad in a red shirt jumped from behind a bush and seized the head of the mare.

'Who are you?' I cried.

'The most abused of all,' said he. 'I am the Typical Digger! I am the man whom you and the others of your tribe have made eat banknotes as sandwiches. I have shod my horse with gold, and swilled champagne—which I detest—out of stable buckets . . . Am I to pass my life in finding repeatedly gigantic nuggets, and being perpetually robbed of the same? Must I never shave? Shall the tyranny of the fictionmonger compel me to *sleep* in boots?'

'Calm yourself, my friend,' I said, 'There is not much harm done. I know of some poor fellows whom the fictionmongers have treated much more rudely.'

At that instant, the demoniac howls of my pursuers were borne upon the blast.

'That may be,' roared the Digger of Romance, 'But I will be revenged on *thee*. Come!'

The cabriolet disappeared in the distance—there was never a cabriolet yet that did not do so under such circumstances—and my captor led me away.

He paused at the door of the usual bush inn (how well I knew it), and striking three loud blows upon the door (they invariably struck three loud blows), we were admitted into a long apartment. I beheld with astonishment that all the personages whom I had imagined the creatures of my own too fertile brain were there.

'Wretch!' cried the fair Madeline, 'why did you not unite me to the Duke? You know you only changed your mind at the last moment.'

'Monster,' said the lovely Violet, 'You made me pass three nights of horror in the Red Farm, when one stroke of your pen would have freed me.' . . .

'Christian dog!' roared Mordecai the Jew, 'I was born with charitable impulses, and should have lent in peace the humble shilling upon the ragged coat of poverty, had not your felon soul plunged me into crime to gratify the tastes of a blood-and-thunder loving public.'

'And I,' remarked Henry Mortimer, with that cynical smile that I had so often depicted, curling his proud lip, 'did I wish to throw my elder brother down a well in order to succeed to his name and heritage? No! I loved him fondly, madly, as you took pains to state in your earlier chapters.' . . .

'Away with him!' hissed Lady Millicent, the Poisoner. 'I knew not of the deadly power of strychnine until he told me.' . . .

' 'Twas he that let me linger in consumption for forty pages folio!' cried Coralie de Belleisle, the planter's daughter.

' 'Twas he that blighted my voluptuous contours with an entirely un-necessary railway accident!' wept the lovely Geraldene.

'Away with him!'

'Mercy!' I cried, gazing in terror on their well-known lineaments.

'Mercy!' cried the Lost Heiress, Isabella Beaumanoir, 'when for two long hours you deliberated whether my sainted mother or the poacher's wife should give me birth! Mercy for *thee*! Oh, no, no, no!' . . .

I trembled over the abyss.

'Why seek to dispel my *ennui* with this *espièglerie*, *mon ami*,' said the soft tones of the Count in his native tongue. '*Sacré*, let the *pauvre petit* escape, my *déjeuner* at the *fourchette* awaits. The *coup d'œil* is superb, the *tout ensemble* all that could be desired. *Voilà*.'

The digger swung me over the yawning grave. All the buttons in my waistcoat gave way, and for an instant my life hung literally by a thread.

'Will you make me respectable?' said the Villain.

'Never.'

The button cracked. I was going, going—gone, when the alarm-bell sounded, the door was burst open, and

.   .   .

Bridget entered.

'It is the boy from the printers' for the proofs,' said she.

'Tell him to wait,' said I; and wiping the sweat from my intellectual brow, I seized my pen, and in ten lines had got my Villain comfortably in irons at Norfolk Island.

Marcus Clarke (1846–81), *The Marcus Clarke Memorial Volume* (1884).

════════════

B Y *the late 1850s the surface gold had begun to run out and few diggers had enough capital to sink shafts and mine the quartz which now lay deep underground, so a considerable number of independent-minded, tough men and women, used to hard living, were let loose with nowhere to go and nothing to do.*

Under considerable pressure the government acted and from 1861 a series of acts were passed designed to 'unlock the land' and allow would-be farmers to select tiny parcels of land from the squatters' vast runs.

The squatters were up to all sorts of dodges to keep the water-holes and the fertile areas to themselves and release only unproductive acres. On many of the selections the soil was so poor that the only tree which would grow was the unlovely stringybark gum tree, and if the farmer did manage to raise a crop he would awake one morning to see his ground white with cockatoos busily eating it. Those unfortunate selectors were christened 'stringybark cockatoos', or 'cockies'.

But at last it was possible for ordinary folk to make a life on the land. In the

first five years after the 'unlocking' more than 17,000 families had a selection of their own to farm.

From the 1860s to Federation in 1901 the original small, independent colonies grew into a nation.

The expansion and prosperity did not dim the Australian urge to touch things lightly rather than pompously. Even when it came to giving official names to new townships which had sprung up in Victoria, one district surveyor refused to be solemn about it:

Surveyor Willmott's habit of punning was responsible for some quaint names. He is said to have named such places as Katamatite (because an earlier settler driving home drunk kept asking his wife, 'Kate, am I tight?'); Miepoll (after a police magistrate who had a habit of saying 'My Poll says this . . .' and 'My Poll says that . . .'); he might even have been responsible for naming Bandiana, named after a bandy-legged lubra [aboriginal woman] named Anna.

> Article in Melbourne *Age* (1945), quoted by Bill Wannan in *The Australian* (1954).

The second half of the nineteenth century was Australia's golden age. It was a rural economy and more and more of the outback was being made profitable as pastureland.

Many jobs on the sheep stations were seasonal and the shearers, graders, cooks, fencers, and others moved across the country to where the work was, travelling usually in pairs for company. Hospitality was traditional, as it is in most hard-living parts of the world, and any pair of 'rovers' turning up at sundown would be given a night's lodgings and 'rations', their 'tucker' for the next day's march, which would be some tea, flour, and sugar. This, together with a couple of old blue blankets and bits of clothing would be rolled into a kind of horse collar and was known variously as the 'bluey', 'swag', 'drum', 'matilda', and so on; and to set off into the bush carrying it was known amongst other things as 'humping the bluey' or 'waltzing the matilda'.

It was also the age of the bushrangers, the 'wild colonial boys' like Ned Kelly, poor whites from unworkable selections who took off into the bush and waged war on squatters and the police, usually briefly and disastrously.

In the 1870s a number of Education Acts were passed and there was a dramatic rise in literacy. The arrival of the bullock-wagon or the paddle-steamer with the weekly newspaper from Sydney or Melbourne became a big event for all hands on the sheep station.

The 1880s and 1890s saw what has been called 'the genesis of Australian culture'. There was a new self-confidence and a surge of nationalism; a popular slogan was 'Australia for the Australians'. There was a thriving publishing trade and a growing demand in both towns and rural areas for stories and anecdotes of gold-rush days and outback life in the pioneer 60s.

The turning-point for Australian humorous prose was 1880 when a modest, radical newspaper was founded called the Sydney Bulletin. *The editors announced that they would be happy to print stories about Australian life and folklore written by anybody, whether they were professional authors, journalists, or raw amateurs. And they did just that. The* Bulletin *became hugely popular, particularly in the outback where it was widely read and known as 'the Bushman's Bible': many of Australia's finest humorists had their first work printed in its pages.*

One of those authors was Henry Lawson, one of the great Australian literary spirits of the late nineteenth and early twentieth century. He was born in a tent on a goldfield and drifted through a number of poorly paid jobs until his verses and stories about pioneer life began to attract attention and he turned to freelance writing.

The following is probably Lawson's best-known 'sketch'. It is a fine and justly famous example of true Australian humour; realistic, unpretentious and warm-hearted:

THE LOADED DOG

Dave Regan, Jim Bently, and Andy Page were sinking a shaft at Stony Creek in search of a rich gold quartz reef which was supposed to exist in the vicinity. There is always a rich reef supposed to exist in the vicinity; the only questions are whether it is ten feet or hundreds beneath the surface, and in which direction. They had struck some pretty solid rock, also water which kept them bailing. They used the old-fashioned blasting-powder and time-fuse. They'd make a sausage or cartridge of blasting-powder in a skin of strong calico or canvas, the mouth sewn and bound round the end of the fuse; they'd dip the cartridge in melted tallow to make it watertight, get the drill-hole as dry as possible, drop in the cartridge with some dry dust, and wad and ram with stiff clay and broken brick. Then they'd light the fuse and get out of the hole and wait. The result was usually an ugly pot-hole in the bottom of the shaft and half a barrow-load of broken rock.

There was plenty of fish in the creek, fresh-water bream, cod, scat-fish, and tailers. The party were fond of fish, and Andy and Dave of fishing. Andy would fish for three hours at a stretch if encouraged by a nibble or a bite now and then—say once in twenty minutes. The butcher was always willing to give meat in exchange for fish when they caught more than they could eat; but now it was winter, and these fish wouldn't bite. However, the creek was low, just a chain of muddy waterholes, from the hole with a few bucket-fuls in it to the sizeable pool with an average depth of six or seven feet, and they could get fish by bailing out the smaller holes or muddying up the water in the larger ones till the fish rose to the surface. There was the cat-fish, with spikes growing out of the sides of its head, and if you got pricked you'd know it, as Dave said. Andy took off his boots, tucked up his trousers, and went into a hole one day to stir up the mud with his feet, and he knew it. Dave scooped one out with his hand and got pricked, and he knew it too; his arm swelled, and the pain throbbed up into his shoulder, and down into his stomach, too, he said, like a toothache he had once, and kept him awake for two nights—only the toothache pain had a 'burred edge', Dave said.

Dave got an idea.

'Why not blow the fish up in the big waterhole with a cartridge?' he said. 'I'll try it.'

He thought the thing out and Andy Page worked it out. Andy usually put Dave's theories into practice if they were practicable, or bore the blame for the failure and the chaffing of his mates if they weren't.

He made a cartridge about three times the size of those they used in the rock. Jim Bently said it was big enough to blow the bottom out of the river. The inner skin was of stout calico; Andy stuck the end of a six-foot piece of fuse well down in the powder and bound the mouth of the bag firmly to it with whipcord. The idea was to sink the cartridge in the water with the open end of the fuse attached to a float on the surface, ready for lighting. Andy dipped the cartridge in melted bees-wax to make it watertight. 'We'll have to leave it some time before we light it,' said Dave, 'to give the fish time to get over their scare when we put it in, and come nosing round again; so we'll want it well watertight.'

Round the cartridge Andy, at Dave's suggestion, bound a strip of sail canvas—that they used for making water-bags—to increase the force of the explosion, and round that he pasted layers of stiff brown paper—on the plan of the sort of fireworks we called 'gun-crackers'. He let the paper dry in the sun, then he sewed a covering of two thicknesses of canvas over it, and bound the thing from end to end with stout fishing-line. Dave's schemes were elaborate, and he often worked his inventions out to nothing. The cartridge was rigid and solid enough now—a formidable bomb; but Andy and Dave wanted to be sure. Andy sewed on another layer of canvas, dipped the cartridge in melted tallow, twisted a length of fencing-wire round it as an afterthought, dipped it in tallow again, and stood it carefully against a tent-peg, where he'd know where to find it, and wound the fuse loosely round it. Then he went to the camp-fire to try some potatoes which were boiling in their jackets in a billy, and to see about frying some chops for dinner. Dave and Jim were at work in the claim that morning.

They had a big black young retriever dog—or rather an overgrown pup, a big, foolish, four-footed mate, who was always slobbering round them and lashing their legs with his heavy tail that swung round like a stockwhip. Most of his head was usually a red, idiotic slobbering grin of appreciation of his own silliness. He seemed to take life, the world, his two-legged mates, and his own instinct as a huge joke. He'd retrieve anything; he carted back most of the camp rubbish that Andy threw away. They had a cat that died in hot weather, and Andy threw it a good distance away in the scrub; and early one morning the dog found the cat, after it had been dead a week or so, and carried it back to camp, and laid it just inside the tent-flaps, where it could best make its presence known when the mates should rise and begin to sniff suspiciously in the sickly smothering atmosphere of the summer sunrise. He used to retrieve them when they went in swimming; he'd jump in after them, and take their hands in his mouth, and try to swim out with them, and scratch their naked bodies with his paws. They loved him for his good-heartedness and his foolishness, but when they wished to enjoy a swim they had to tie him up in camp.

He watched Andy with great interest all the morning making the cartridge, and hindered him considerably, trying to help; but about noon he went off to the claim to see how Dave and Jim were getting on, and to come home to dinner with them. Andy saw them coming, and put a panful of mutton-chops on the fire. Andy was cook today; Dave and Jim stood with their backs to the fire, as bushmen do in all weathers, waiting till dinner should be ready. The retriever went nosing round after something he seemed to have missed.

Andy's brain still worked on the cartridge; his eye was caught by the glare of an empty kerosene-tin lying in the bushes, and it struck him that it wouldn't be a bad idea to sink the cartridge packed with clay, sand, or stones in the tin, to increase the force of the explosion. He may have been all out, from a scientific point of view, but the notion looked all right to him. Jim Bently, by the way, wasn't interested in their 'damned silliness'. Andy noticed an empty treacle-tin—the sort with the little tin neck or spout soldered on to the top for the convenience of pouring out the treacle—and it struck him that this would have made the best kind of cartridge-case: he would only have had to pour in the powder, stick the fuse in through the neck, and cork and seal it with beeswax. He was turning to suggest this to Dave, when Dave glanced over his shoulder to see how the chops were doing—and bolted. He explained afterwards that he thought he heard the pan spluttering extra, and looked to see if the chops were burning. Jim Bently looked behind and bolted after Dave. Andy stood stock-still, staring after them.

'Run, Andy! Run!' they shouted back at him. 'Run! Look behind you, you fool!' Andy turned slowly and looked, and there, close behind him, was the retriever with the cartridge in his mouth—wedged into his broadest and silliest grin. And that wasn't all. The dog had come round the fire to Andy, and the loose end of the fuse had trailed and waggled over the burning sticks into the blaze; Andy had slit and nicked the firing end of the fuse well, and now it was hissing and spitting properly.

Andy's legs started with a jolt; his legs started before his brain did, and he made after Dave and Jim. And the dog followed Andy.

Dave and Jim were good runners—Jim the best—for a short distance; Andy was slow and heavy, but he had the strength and the wind and could last. The dog capered round him, delighted as a dog could be to find his mates, as he thought, on for a frolic. Dave and Jim kept shouting back, 'Don't foller us! Don't foller us, you coloured fool!' But Andy kept on, no matter how they dodged. They could never explain, any more than the dog, why they followed each other, but so they ran, Dave keeping in Jim's track in all its

turnings, Andy after Dave, and the dog circling round Andy—the live fuse
swishing in all directions and hissing and spluttering and stinking. Jim yelling
to Dave not to follow him, Dave shouting to Andy to go in another direction—
to 'spread out', and Andy roaring at the dog to go home. Then Andy's brain
began to work, stimulated by the crisis: he tried to get a running kick at the
dog, but the dog dodged; he snatched up sticks and stones and threw them
at the dog and ran on again. The retriever saw that he'd made a mistake
about Andy, and left him and bounded after Dave. Dave, who had the
presence of mind to think that the fuse's time wasn't up yet, made a dive
and grab for the dog, caught him by the tail, and as he swung round snatched
the cartridge out of his mouth and flung it as far as he could; the dog
immediately bounded after it and retrieved it. Dave roared and cursed at the
dog, who, seeing that Dave was offended, left him and went after Jim, who
was well ahead. Jim swung to a sapling and went up it like a native bear; it
was a young sapling, and Jim couldn't safely get more than ten or twelve
feet from the ground. The dog laid the cartridge, as carefully as if it were a
kitten, at the foot of the sapling, and capered and leaped and whooped
joyously round under Jim. The big pup reckoned that this was part of the
lark—he was all right now—it was Jim who was out for a spree. The fuse
sounded as if it were going a mile a minute. Jim tried to climb higher and the
sapling bent and cracked. Jim fell on his feet and ran. The dog swooped on
the cartridge and followed. It all took but a very few moments. Jim ran to a
digger's hole, about ten feet deep, and dropped down into it—landing on soft
mud—and was safe. The dog grinned sardonically down on him, over the
edge, for a moment, as if he thought it would be a good lark to drop the
cartridge down on Jim.

'Go away, Tommy,' said Jim feebly, 'go away.'

The dog bounded off after Dave, who was the only one in sight now; Andy
had dropped behind a log, where he lay flat on his face, having suddenly
remembered a picture of the Russo-Turkish war with a circle of Turks lying
flat on their faces (as if they were ashamed) round a newly-arrived shell.

There was a small hotel or shanty on the creek, on the main road, not far
from the claim. Dave was desperate, the time flew much faster in his stimulated imagination than it did in reality, so he made for the shanty. There
were several casual bushmen on the veranda and in the bar; Dave rushed
into the bar, banging the door to behind him. 'My dog!' he gasped, in reply
to the astonished stare of the publican, 'the blanky retriever—he's got a live
cartridge in his mouth—'

The retriever, finding the front door shut against him, had bounded round
and in by the back way, and now stood smiling in the doorway leading from
the passage, the cartridge still in his mouth and the fuse spluttering. They
burst out of that bar; Tommy bounded first after one and then after another,
for, being a young dog, he tried to make friends with everybody.

The bushmen ran round corners, and some shut themselves in the stable.

There was a new weatherboard and corrugated-iron kitchen and wash-house on piles in the backyard, with some women washing clothes inside. Dave and the publican bundled in there and shut the door—the publican cursing Dave and calling him a crimson fool, in hurried tones, and wanting to know what the hell he came here for.

The retriever went in under the kitchen, amongst the piles, but, luckily for those inside, there was a vicious yellow mongrel cattle-dog sulking and nursing his nastiness under there—a sneaking, fighting, thieving canine, whom neighbours had tried for years to shoot or poison. Tommy saw his danger—he'd had experience from this dog—and started out and across the yard, still sticking to the cartridge. Half-way across the yard the yellow dog caught him and nipped him. Tommy dropped the cartridge, gave one terrified yell, and took to the bush. The yellow dog followed him to the fence and then ran back to see what he had dropped. Nearly a dozen other dogs came from round all the corners and under the buildings—spidery, thievish, cold-blooded kangaroo-dogs, mongrel sheep and cattle-dogs, vicious black and yellow dogs—that slip after you in the dark, nip your heels, and vanish without explaining—and yapping, yelping small fry. They kept at a respectable distance round the nasty yellow dog, for it was dangerous to go near him when he thought he had found something which might be good for a dog or cat. He sniffed at the cartridge twice, and was just taking a third cautious sniff when—

It was very good blasting-powder—a new brand that Dave had recently got up from Sydney; and the cartridge had been excellently well made. Andy was very patient and painstaking in all he did, and nearly as handy as the average sailor with needles, twine, canvas and rope.

Bushmen say that that kitchen jumped off its piles and on again. When the smoke and dust cleared away, the remains of the nasty yellow dog were lying against the pailing fence of the yard looking as if he had been kicked into a fire by a horse and afterwards rolled in the dust under a barrow, and finally thrown against the fence from a distance. Several saddle-horses, which had been 'handing-up' round the veranda, were galloping wildly down the road in clouds of dust, with broken bridle-reins flying; and from a circle round the outskirts, from every point of the compass in the scrub, came the yelping of dogs. Two of them went home, to the place where they were born, thirty miles away, and reached it the same night and stayed there; it was not till towards evening that the rest came back cautiously to make inquiries. One was trying to walk on two legs, and most of 'em looked more or less singed; and a little, singed, stumpy-tailed dog, who had been in the habit of hopping the back half of him along on one leg, had reason to be glad that he'd saved up the other leg all those years. For he needed it now. There was one old one-eyed cattle-dog round that shanty for years afterwards, who couldn't stand the smell of a gun being cleaned. He it was who had taken an interest, only second to that of the yellow dog, in the cartridge. Bushmen said that it was amusing to slip up on his blind side and stick a dirty ramrod under his nose: he wouldn't wait to bring his solitary eye to bear—he'd take to the bush and stay out all night.

For half an hour or so after the explosion there were several bushmen round behind the stable who crouched, doubled up, against the wall, or rolled gently on the dust, trying to laugh without shrieking. There were two white women in hysterics at the house, and a half-caste rushing aimlessly round with a dipper of cold water. The publican was holding his wife tight and begging her between her squawks, to 'Hold up for my sake, Mary, or I'll lam the life out of ye!'

Dave decided to apologize later on, 'when things had settled a bit', and went back to camp. And the dog that had done it all, Tommy, the great, idiotic mongrel retriever, came slobbering round Dave and lashing his legs with his tail, and trotted home after him, smiling his broadest, longest, and reddest smile of amiability, and apparently satisfied for one afternoon with the fun he'd had.

Andy chained the dog up securely, and cooked some more chops, while Dave went to help Jim out of the hole.

And most of this is why, for years afterwards, lanky, easygoing bushmen, riding lazily past Dave's camp, would cry, in a lazy drawl and with just a hint of the nasal twang:

'Ello, Da-a-ve! How's the fishin' getting on, Da-a-ve?'

Henry Lawson (1867–1922), Joe Wilson and his Mates (1901).

———

ANOTHER *outstanding Australian writer whose work was first printed in the Bulletin was Andrew Barton Paterson, known as 'Banjo' Paterson because he signed his early work 'The Banjo'.*

Banjo Paterson became world-famous for giving Australia its unofficial national anthem, 'Waltzing Matilda'. The origins of the ballad are something of a mystery still but it seems likely that the tune was adapted by Paterson from a song brought over from England by one of the gaoler-regiments. Paterson wrote a new lyric for it including many splendidly Australian words. 'Waltzing' meant 'stepping out along the road in a sprightly manner', and 'matilda' was a word used by a swagman to describe the rolled-up blue blanket in which he carried his worldly possessions: the word almost certainly derived from German infantry slang via German gold-rush immigrants: in the German army the word mathilde *was a trooper's pet name for a female camp-follower, and then, by understandable association, the blanket which kept him warm at nights.*

It seems that in its early days 'Waltzing Matilda' was just another colourful ditty of the outback, but then Paterson had a stroke of luck. The song was taken up by a wholesale grocer anxious to associate his product with the Real Australia, and was given away free in an advertising leaflet wrapped round packets of 'Billy Tea'. The song then became immensely popular with Australian tea-drinkers, i.e. everybody.

Paterson was born on a farm owned by his parents in New South Wales and became a solicitor in Sydney, writing bush ballads for the Bulletin *in his spare time. With the success of a book of narrative poems and ballads which he called* The Man from Snowy River, *he became a full-time writer, and later a war-correspondent and newspaper editor.*

Paterson also wrote prose pieces about life in the outback; many of these were rewritten versions of the tall stories, yarns, and ballads which he had heard as a young man.

Here is one of 'Banjo' Paterson's tall stories, almost certainly based upon an old oral yarn. It is built around two of Australia's traditional male preoccupations— the comparative performance of horses, and gambling:

BILL AND JIM NEARLY GET TAKEN DOWN

'You see, it was this way,' said Bill reflectively, as we sat on the rails of the horseyard, 'me and Jim was down at Buckatowndown show with that jumpin' pony Jim has, and in the high jump our pony jumped seven feet, so they gave the prize to Spondulix that only jumped six foot ten. You know what these country shows are; a man can't get no sort of fair play at all. We asked the stooards why the prize was give to Spondulix, and they said he jumped better style than the pony. So Jim ups and whips the saddle and bridle off the pony, and he says to the cove at the jump, "Put the bar up to seven foot six," he says, and he rides the pony at it without saddle or bridle, and over he goes, never lays a toe on it, and Spondulix was afraid to come at it. And we offered to jump Spondulix for a hundred quid any time. And I went to the stooards and I offered to back the pony to run any horse on the ground two miles over as many fences as they could put up in the distance, and the bigger the better; and Jim, he offered to fight as many of the stooards as he could get into a room with him. And even then they wouldn't get fair play in a country show. But what I wanted to tell you about was the way we almost got took down afterwards. By gum, it was a near thing!

'We went down from the show to the pub, and there was a lot o' toffs at the pub was bettin' Jim a pound here and a pound there that he wouldn't ride the pony at this fence and at that fence, and Jim picked up a few quid jumpin' 'em easy, for most of the fences weren't no more than six feet high, and, of course, that was like drinkin' tea to the pony. And at last one cove he points to a big palin' fence, and he says: "I'll bet you a fiver your horse won't get over that one"—being seven feet solid palin's—but we knew the pony could do it all right, and Jim wheels round to go at it. And just as he sails at it, I runs up to the fence and pulls myself up with my hands and looks over, and there was a great gully the other side a hundred feet deep and all rocks and stones. So I yelled out at Jim to stop, but it was too late, for he had set the pony going and once that pony went at a fence you couldn't stop him with a block and tackle. And the pony rose over the fence, and when Jim saw what was on the other side, what do you think he did! Why, he turned the pony round in the air and came back to the same side he started from! My oath, it astonished those toffs. You see, they thought they would take us down about getting over safely, but they had to pay up because he went over the fence and back again as safe as a church. Did you say Jim must have been a good rider—well, not too bad, but that was nothin' to— hello, here comes the boss; I must be off. So long!'

A. B. (Banjo) Paterson (1864–1941), the *Bulletin* (3 Apr. 1897).

━━━━━━━━━

Telling *tall stories and boasting were seemingly as compulsive an activity in outback Australia as they had been in frontier America, although the Australian versions were perhaps less cruel, and funnier.*

Seeking out these old traditional Australian forms of humour was very much the task of the 'local colourist' writers of the last quarter of the nineteenth century and the first quarter of this.

One of the most amusing pieces based on genuine old tall stories was written by Alan Marshall. Marshall was born in 1902, contracted polio when young but managed to overcome this disability enough to live in a caravan in various areas of the outback, collecting bushmen folklore and writing articles and stories based upon his researches.

According to Alan Marshall, perhaps the best but certainly the tallest of Australian tall stories were centred on a mythical sheep station known as 'the Speewah':

THEY WERE TOUGH MEN ON THE SPEEWAH

Firstly, there is 'Crooked Mick' who tried to strangle himself with his own beard in the Big Drought. He was a gun shearer; 500 a day was nothing to him. Once, the boss, annoyed because of Crooked Mick's rough handling of some wethers, strode up to him on the board and barked, 'You're fired.' Crooked Mick was shearing flat out at the time. He was going so fast that he shore fifteen sheep before he could straighten up and hang his shears on the hook.

His later days were saddened by a serious accident. He was washing sheep when he slipped and fell into a tank of boiling water. Big Bill, who was standing beside him, whipped him out, tore off his clothes, then seized two wethers and cut their throats. He ripped the hides off the wethers and wrapped them, flesh side in, round Crooked Mick's body and legs. When they got him to a doctor three weeks later the doctor took one look at him then said, 'Boys, you've made a wonderful job of him. It would take a major operation to remove these skins. They're grafted to him.'

According to Big Bill they took Crooked Mick back to the Speewah and shore him every year after that.

'He made twenty-two pounds of wool,' Bill said. 'Not bad.'

Big Bill, who built the barbed wire fence, was the strongest man on the Speewah, they say. He made his fortune on the Croydon goldfields cutting up mining shafts and selling them for post holes. He was originally put on to fence the Speewah but gave it up after a day digging post holes. He left his lunch at the first hole when he started in the morning, then at midday he put down his crowbar and set off to walk back for his lunch. He had sunk so many holes he didn't reach his lunch till midnight. That finished him.

'A bloke'd starve going at that rate,' he said.

Then there was Uncle Harry who rode the crowbar through Wagga without giving it a sore back. He was a modest man who had carted five tons of tin whistles through country that was practically unknown at the time. Once, when Big Bill was boasting about his strength, someone asked Uncle Henry had he ever done any heavy lifting.

'No,' he said modestly, 'I can't claim that I'm a strong man. Weight-lifting was never in my line. However, I once carried a very awkward load off the barge owned by the *Tolarno*. It was near the Tintinnalogy shed and, mind you, I'm not claiming this load was heavy, only that it was very awkward. I carried, and the banks were steep, too, a double-furrow plough, a set of harrows and eight loose melons. As I say, it wasn't the weight, only the awkwardness of it that makes it worth telling.'

Slab-face Joe was the bullocky on the Speewah. He drove a team so long he had a telephone fitted on the leaders with a line going back to the polers. When he wanted to pull up he rang through to the black boy he paid to ride the lead, and told him to stop the leaders. Half an hour afterwards Slab-face would stop the polers. Once when he rang through he got the wrong number and wasted a day trying to raise 'Complaints'.

His team was as strong as they come. When Slab-face Joe was shifting a shed from the Speewah out-station it got bogged in the Speewah Creek. Then Slab-face really got that team into it. They pulled so hard they pulled a two-mile bend in the creek and they weren't extended.

'The Boss' featured in many tales of the Speewah. He had a snout on cockatoos and covered an old red gum with bird lime to catch the flock that was eating his grain. After they landed on the tree he yelled out, 'Got you,' and they all took off at once. They tore that tree out by the roots and the last he saw of it, it was two miles up making south.

Hundreds of men worked on the Speewah. In fact, there were so many they had to mix the mustard with a long-handled shovel and the cook and his assistant had to row out in a boat to sugar the tea. When shearing was on the boss had to ride up and down the board on a motor-bike.

The Speewah holding itself was a tremendous size. When Uncle Harry was sent out to close the garden gate he had to take a week's rations with him, and a jackeroo, going out to bring in the cows from the horse paddock, was gone for six months.

It was mixed country. There were mountains, salt-bush plains, and thick forests of enormous trees. Crooked Mick, bringing in a mob of 3,000 sheep through the big timber, suddenly found himself in pitch darkness. For three days and nights that wretched man punched those sheep along without being able to see one of them. Then daylight snapped on again and Crooked Mick looked back. He had come through a hollow log.

Some of the hills were so steep on the Speewah that when a man rode a horse down one of them the horse's tail hung over his shoulder and down the front of his chest, giving him the appearance of having a lank, black beard.

The Speewah was cursed with every plague. Rabbits were there in millions. They were so thick you had to pull them out of the burrows to get the ferrets in and trappers had to brush them aside to set their traps. On some of the paddocks they had to drive them out to get room to put the sheep in.

Galahs, too, were bad. When the Big Drought broke, the Speewah remained dry as a bone though the rain fell in torrents above it. The first clap of thunder had scared the galahs into flight and they were so thickly packed as they winged over the station that not a drop reached the ground. A mob of them, swooping under Crooked Mick's hut to avoid a hawk, lifted it off the ground with the wind of their wings and carried it for thirty miles. Mick finished his breakfast while going through a belt of cloud at twenty thousand feet, the galahs still pounding along just beneath him.

The kangaroos were as big as elephants on the Speewah—some were bigger. They say that Crooked Mick and Big Bill were once climbing a hill of fur grass when they slipped and fell into a kangaroo's pouch. The hill got up and made off with Crooked Mick and Big Bill arguing the toss as to how they would get out.

For six months those two men lived on kangaroo meat and water they got by sinking a bore in the sand that had collected in the bottom of the pouch. Then some silly cow, out with a gun, shot that kangaroo when it was in the middle of a leap. Crooked Mick and Big Bill, who were ploughing at the time, left that pouch like meteors. They were thrown fifty miles and the skid they made when they hit the earth gouged the bed of the Darling.

Women never feature in the Speewah tales. I have only heard one story in which a woman was supposed to have worked on the Speewah and I'm inclined to think it was a lie. She was a cook and her name was Gentle Annie.

The story was told to me by an old man with pale watery eyes who lived in a hut on the Murray, and, in the telling of it, he kept glancing uneasily over his shoulder towards his hut in which I could hear a woman banging pots around and singing in a husky voice.

According to this old man the Speewah had gone, disappeared, been burnt off the map, and all because of the one and only woman who had ever worked there. Gentle Annie, so he told me, had limbs like a grey box and a frame like the kitchen of a pub. She was always singing and when she sang there was always a change for the worse in the weather. She cooked jam rolls a hundred yards long and her suet puddings had killed twenty shearers.

Once, at the shearing shed dance, she seized Crooked Mick by the beard as she was dancing the waltz cotillion with him, and kissed that horrified man squarely somewhere about where his mouth lay concealed in hair.

What a kiss that was! Its like has never been seen before or since. The whole shed rocked upon its foundations and a blue flame streaked away from the point of contact and tore three sheets of galvanized iron off the roof. A thunderous rumble rolled away across the plains and the air was full of the smell of sulphur, dynamite, gunpowder and Jockey Club perfume.

Ten fires started up at once and the roar of them was like a thousand trains going through a thousand tunnels.

For three months men fought that bushfire without a wink of sleep. They were famished for a drink of tea. As soon as they lit a camp fire to boil the billy the flames of the bushfire engulfed it.

As a last, desperate measure, Crooked Mick ran ahead of the fire at sixty miles an hour holding a billy of water back over the flames till it boiled. The tea he made saved the men but not the Speewah.

Then Big Bill came galloping up on Red Ned, the wildest brumby ever foaled. He drew one enormous breath, then gave one enormous spit and the fire went out with a sizzle.

'What happened to Gentle Annie?' I asked the old man.

'I married her,' he said with that uneasy glance at his hut.

I knew then he was a liar. No man who worked on the Speewah ever got married. It was too sissy.

Alan Marshall (b. 1902), *How's Andy Going?* (1956).

—————

HUMOROUS *accounts of the early days were by no means confined to yarns about mates waltzing their matildas, or trying to avoid work or win bets. There was also domestic humour, in which women featured strongly.*

Oddly, although Australia had the reputation of being a strongly male chauvinistic society, Australian women were written about sympathetically. They could be mates but not 'mates' and they worked hard so it was slyly acknowledged that they were the ones who kept the family and the home going.

Gavin Casey came from Kalgoorlie in Western Australia. He became a journalist in Perth and then began to write short stories for the Bulletin *about life in the*

gold-fields of Western Australia, many of them about family life there. He wrote
about the second phase of the gold-fields, when the old panhandlers had been
superseded by lease-holding mining companies who sunk deep shafts. Gold was no
longer found as dust or as nuggets but in the form of a metallic ore known as
'telluride' which had to be crushed and processed to extract its 'value'.

One thing that had not changed was the presence of the dreaded gold-fields Police
Force. Constables were all around, as ever, waiting to spoil things when a poor
digger had a little bit of semi-honest luck:

RICH STEW

Among the leases cold and cheerless night was sponging out the harsh
colours and contours that daylight revealed as the workings of the mines.
Men working on the surface were heading toward boiler-houses with their
billies, stamping feet and swinging arms and for once envying their mates
snugly tucked away in the warm depths. It was wintry weather, with a
high wind wailing between the poppets, and the Thompsons, who were at
the moment gathered comfortably in their warm kitchen in a happy little
domestic party, were lucky.

Mrs Thompson, lean, hard and active, was engaged in the occupation
suited to the hour, her age, her sex and her status; she leaned over the stove,
with her head almost up the sooty chimney, stirring, and from her vicinity
came savoury odours which spread peace and a sense of well-being among
the other inhabitants of the room. At the table Ted lounged, pulling skin off
the corns of his hands with an elongated fingernail kept specially for the
purpose. In the corner near the cupboard Jimmy, the schoolboy, was seated
on a box with his nose in a 'Deadwood Dick'. On the floor rolled a mixture of
arms and legs that occasionally resolved itself into two separate beings—the
dog and the baby.

Jenny, with leisurely good nature, was placing dishes out on the table,
leaving a clear space around Ted's elbows. And on the sofa, a strange and
aged kitchen furnishing which years of hard service had moulded at last to
the shape of the human body, sprawled the Old Man himself, positively
purring with pleasure.

'Well,' said the Old Man, 'the luck's changed. I ain't seen nothin' but dirt
f'r so long I hardly reckernized this when I seen it.' And he forthwith emptied
into the palm of his hand from a small, screw-topped bottle a stream of tiny,
greyish-silver, undistinguished-looking chips of rock.

'Telluride!' said Ted. 'The dinkum stuff! Gosh, it's good for the eyes. None
of it where I am, worse luck!'

'Well,' contributed Jenny, with an eye to the main chance, 'if there's as
much at the nine hundred as dad says, we ought to all start havin' a bit o'
fun agin soon, anyway.'

'Fun!' snorted Mrs Thompson. 'There's plenty o' things needed about this
place afore you brats start slingin' money around on y'r fun. There's allus

bin two bobs f'r pitchers an' beer. Now, p'raps, there'll be some f'r linos an clothes.'

'There'll be some f'r everthin',' announced the Old Man with confidence and enthusiasm. 'I never seen such a vein. Y' jist got to leave it to y'r old pa. Wot've y' got f 'r tea, Mary?'

'A stoo,' answered the missus. 'A nice rich stoo to celebrate a bit o' luck at last.'

And on this note of optimism and joy the family made a concerted move toward the table.

'That's the stuff t' stick y'r ribs together!' commented Ted, pulling a set of crockery and cutlery into position in front of him. 'Deal it out, ma.'

The Old Man, spilling his grains of precious stone from one hand to the other contentedly, lumbered toward the head of the festive board. Jenny retrieved the baby after a struggle. Even Jimmy showed interest, stuffing his paper into a capacious pocket and shuffling forward. The lid came off the big saucepan and the powerful odour of its savoury contents flowed forth, intensified, tickling the nostrils of an assemblage in fine humour to eat their fill and enjoy it.

'Gosh!' rumbled the Old Man, politely appreciative of the culinary skill of his spouse, 'that's the smell to make a man's belly think his throat's cut!'

And then, cutting through the tranquillity like a reminder of all unpleasant things, startling everybody except the dog and the baby into frozen immobility, came upon the door the thundering knock of Authority.

'Open it up, Thompson,' demanded the voice of the Law. 'Straight away, now, an' no nonsense.'

'Gawd!' said Ted. 'The cops!'

The Old Man tottered. Pride and satisfaction left him, like the air leaving a blown-out tyre. His jaw sagged, and his big, hard paw, full of that telltale kind of ore that could have come only from far underground, waved helplessly in the air. But the missus, bony, practical and quickwitted, was equal to any emergency. Wordlessly, and swiftly as a panther defending its young or a bailiff springing at a rapidly-shrinking three inches of open doorway, she leapt at her lord and master. While the family collected its wits she had possession of the ore, and faster than it can be told, she dropped it into the great pot of stew.

'Open it y'self!' she snapped, with a warning glance at the astonished family. 'It ain't locked.'

Obediently, Sergeant O'Malley, of the Gold-stealing Investigation staff, opened it and stepped blinking into the light. Not without cause he felt that his entry lacked something of impressiveness and he was already in a mood to be nasty. These Thompsons were all 'up to the eyes' in the business that it was his job to stop, and now, with rich dirt uncovered that very day in the level where the Old Man worked, was certainly the time to catch them at it. But he had battered on the door in the manner of a resolute sleuth, and he was entering the room more like a Simple Simon than anything else. It made him pessimistic.

Mrs Thompson, he saw, was stirring at a big pot on the fire with an air of complete indifference. The Old Man looked less normal, but there was an air of triumph about him that boded ill for the success of the sergeant. Ted looked like the village idiot. Jenny was a picture of outraged righteousness. Young Jimmy, with the superiority of his years, seemed to regard the whole business with bored disdain. The dog and the baby, who had come to grips again in the excitement, were hard to sort out and could be disregarded in any case.

'I'll just take a look around, Thompson,' said O'Malley. 'Expectin' nothin' o' course, but just makin' sure there isn't anything in this nice little place o' yours that shouldn't be.'

'Sure, sergeant,' agreed the Old Man expansively, 'you'll find what you say you're expectin', but I know it ain't much use tryin' to stop you fellers when you gits set on a idea.'

The sergeant's heart sank a little further, but that did not prevent him from making a thorough search, with the assistance of Constable Murray. Between them they reduced the potential life of the old sofa by half, brought several pounds of soot down out of the chimney, broke two cups, tramped on the baby three times and on the dog once, and reduced the virtuously indignant Jenny to a state of hissing wrath. But it was fruitless. With every nook and corner examined, the sergeant at last stood in front of the stove, baffled, but still in a mood to be nasty.

'Now p'raps you'll out an' let us have some tea,' said Jenny venomously. 'Disgraceful, I call it, the way you great louts do what you like in honest people's houses.'

The Old Man, too, was inclined to gloat, but he wisely went no further than meaning leers, keeping his mouth shut. It was the missus, triumphant and so far showing it least of all, who could not resist the temptation to turn the knife in the wound.

'Now, Jenny,' she said, 'y've got to let bygones be bygones. The sergeant's got to do his duty, an' very unpleasant it must be sometimes. Most uncomfortable for him, I should say, besides bein' kept late for his own meal. But perhaps he'd stay an' have a bite o' nice rich stoo with us?'

And to their horror the sergeant accepted.

'Don't mind if I do,' he announced gruffly to the accompaniment of glares directed at the missus by the whole family.

What followed is painful to relate. O'Malley, a big man and a messy eater, planted himself in a chair with a dreadful air of permanence and, after sending Murray home, expanded into horrifying joviality. Mrs Thompson, 'dishing up', suffered tortures skimming the surface from the stew with her ladle, and yet having to stir it a little, for fear the bottom would burn out of the pot. Ted's resemblance to the village idiot became more pronounced. The Old Man was in a state of almost complete collapse. Jenny, serving, trembled.

Except for the dog and the baby, only Jimmy was unconcerned; his lofty detachment was colossal.

'Good stoo!' said O'Malley, ladling it into his mouth with vigour.

The first to encounter something hard in a mouthful was Ted, and the mental strain of deciding whether it was bone, which could be removed, or telluride, which must be swallowed, became visible. His brow beaded with sweat, and his eyes goggled. He clenched his teeth on the hard substance, and cast an appealing look at his father. The Old Man frowned. His eyes entreated his mother. She glared. Then he gulped, and, whatever it was, it was gone. He tittered foolishly, and the family frowned blackly at him. But the sergeant was too busy to notice.

Then a crunching like a mine cracker on a mammoth rock informed the coldly perspiring family that the policeman's turn had come.

'Little bit o' bone,' announced the sleuth between his teeth. 'Hard to keep out of a stoo.' Without further ceremony he turned his head, pursed his lips and spat. On the floor, behind him and out of sight, landed an ounce or so of gravy and a small fragment of solid. The family sighed with relief.

The dog, ever appreciative of small offerings, pounced happily from beneath the table, and licked up the gravy with enthusiasm. But it betrayed a fastidiousness it had never before exhibited. It refused the solid, after it had licked it clean. The little slug of telluride was left, glittering in the light, and the family began to fidget.

Then the baby crawled out, and, with intelligence beyond its years, picked up the incriminating evidence and immediately swallowed it. The family sighed with relief again. The baby and the dog licked their chops.

By the time every plate was clean, the Old Man estimated that the family would assay over ten ounces to the ton, with himself showing top value, worth £5 or more, and the baby ready to crush for a little over expenses. But the sergeant had enjoyed his meal, suspecting nothing, and everybody was beginning to be happy again.

'Good stoo!' said O'Malley for the fifth time. 'Damn' good stoo! Never git anythin' like it at the boardin'-house. Could you spare a little more, Mrs Thompson?'

The sergeant's mean mood had passed. He was fed and happy, and he bore no venom toward the Thompsons. But had he drawn his official revolver and slain the dog and the baby and any reasonable number of the family's adult members, he could not have created greater consternation.

'I-I-I'll see if there's any left,' quavered the missus, blue with fright.

'Jist the dregs'll do,' comforted O'Malley. 'A bit of gravy from the bottom o' the pot. It's the rich gravy a man likes after livin' on hash-house tucker for so long. Good, rich gravy!' He smacked his lips.

The family had thought that they had already suffered the ultimate in torture. But when the sergeant set to work on the rich gravy from 'the bottom o' the pot', they realized that what had gone before was as nothing to the excruciating misery of sitting helpless, watching him mop up the thick brown liquid that was positively riddled with 'values'. As has been said, the sergeant was a messy eater, and by and by a heavy stream of the gravy commenced to trickle down his chin. Petrified with fright, the family saw that, borne strongly down this current of nourishment, was a tiny speck of telluride.

It fascinated them. Owlishly they watched while it coursed through the stubbly hairs and eventually dropped off on to his shirt-front. There it stuck, gleaming dully like the head of a nugget tiepin. The family variously and according to their sexes and temperaments, wanted urgently to scream, murder, commit hara-kiri and sink into the bowels of the earth (not in search of telluride).

When the sergeant, now affable and talkative, had mopped up the last of his gravy with a crust of bread his strange and interesting ornament still clung to his bosom, and the family was limp with terror.

'Well, Mrs Thompson,' said O'Malley, rising, 'I hope there's no ill-will. Sure there's not on my part, after such a good feed.'

Becoming aware of something soft beneath his feet, he looked down and, for the first time since the search, saw the baby. He picked it up in a manner masterly for a bachelor policemen.

'Hello, young 'un,' he said. 'Fine little bloke, ain't you?'

But the baby, unused to flattery though it was, was now in no mood to appreciate it. Its eyes, all its attention and all its hopes were fixed upon a small object in the middle of the sergeant's mighty chest.

'Goo!' it said, and reached for the attractive edible. The family found breathing painful.

The baby, however, proved itself to be a true Thompson. Its chubby palm closed over the slug, and remained very much a fist until it was somewhere in the neighbourhood of its tonsils. Then it opened, and, simultaneously with a rise to almost double in the treatment value of the infant, the last scrap of evidence against the family disappeared.

'Cripes!' said the sergeant. 'I believe he's eatin' me shirt buttons. Tackle anythin',' these kids, won't they?'

Lighthearted in their relief the family agreed. They dithered until the sergeant stared, and worried not, for dithering was now safe. They fussed over the baby as it had never been fussed over before. And as soon as the sergeant had gone they kicked the dog with one accord (for causing them that indescribable moment when the first piece of telluride had been exposed) and turned upon Mrs Thompson with impassioned reproaches (for having opened her mouth and put her foot in it).

'Well, damn you,' said the missus, who was quite capable of defending herself, 'if it'd bin left to you half-wits, he'd 'ave found th' lot in y'r dad's hand, anyway. We're safe, thanks to me an' the baby, an' I've got a pain in me stummick that's quite enough without you mob yellin'.'

'So've I,' said Ted. 'Jist a little bit of a one.'

'Don't feel so good meself,' said Jenny. 'Comes of eatin' telluride. I s'pose it makes a stoo too rich altogether. Hope the flatfoot gits one, too.'

'I'll never eat no telluride agin,' swore the missus.

'My oath you won't,' said the Old Man, still sweating with relief. 'There ain't never goin' to be no more in this house, to eat or anythin' else—not if we never has no linos or noo clothes or pitchers or beer neither.'

The baby cooed happily. It's digestive powers seemed to be remarkable. But, on the principle that prevention is better than cure, Mrs Thompson tucked it wearily under her arm and headed for the castor-oil bottle on the mantelpiece.

Gavin Casey (1907–64), It's Harder for Girls (1942).

MOTHERS *and daughters featured even more strongly in the humorous stories written by Sumner Locke, which is not surprising as the author's real christian name was Elizabeth. No doubt 'Sumner Locke', like 'Henry Handel Richardson', and 'Miles (My Brilliant Career) Franklin', found it easier in those days to get her work published under a name which made her sound like a man.*

Elizabeth Sumner Locke set her stories on a poor selection where cattle were raised. The farm is worked by Old Man Dawson and the children but the real boss is Mum Dawson.

In the following episode the Dawson family bravely faces a bereavement when Old Man Dawson decides to die.

WHEN DAWSON DIED

One day Old Man Dawson took to his bed and refused to budge even when the tongue of his wife oscillated at double the usual swing. He said he was going to die; so, after arguing the point with him, she said he could; and daily the family waited, believing that the old man really meant to do as he said. They knew by experience that he seldom went back on his word; and the novel situation of having him do a thing that was altogether foreign to them held them in an excitement worthy of a more stimulating cause.

The two girls used to stand over the skim-buckets and commune as to the future development of things. They wondered if Mum could run the show without Dad, or if Will would be deputed boss. They felt certain there would be fire somewhere—Will was wayward and Mum always did rule the old man. Annie the elder girl was not bad looking—someone had told her that four years ago at the local show; Annie remembered that day because it never came again—and she felt she deserved a better fate than the daily fowl-run and the skim-buckets. There never was enough water to wash the buckets properly; and the old man said the yard dam wasn't to be used for waste water. Perhaps when he'd been dead a bit they might use it when they liked. Mary thought they might sell out and go to the town; and the chance of seeing a bit of life like that pictured in the coloured catalogue that a through traveller had presented them with two years ago was a moment of exquisite pain to them. That day the buckets looked different; they had got twice the amount of slushing during the debate; and Mum was sleeping off a war that she and the old man had had that morning over changing the mattress. The old man wouldn't move for a moment, and the woman had howled with grief at the unturned straw bed.

One of the boys who attended to the special department of pigs suggested at dinner that the doctor had better see the old man, whereat the woman smashed two plates over his head in passing.

'D'yer think old Mill's goin' inter harness again today?' she said wrathfully.

'I kin ride the Yonk for 'im,' protested the small attribute.

'No, yaou can't,' bellowed the woman. 'Wen I was bad with Flora he was twenty minutes too late. D'yer think we want 'im comin' late again?'

'Is father goin' ter die ter-day?' came from the end of the board table, where the second last edition of the family was blowing bubbles into a cup of yesterday's skim.

'Go and ask 'im!' shouted his mother in return. Then she slapped the nearside of her fourth, who was dabbling fingers in a flat tin of milk and pushing the dead flies under to see if they would rise again. 'Take yer dirty 'ands outer that dish. If yer father *did* die, all that milk'd be wanted for the comp'ny comin' round.'

'Kin we invite Jack, Mum?' This from the promoter of the milk bubbles, with wide eyes on his parent.

'Can't invite no one!' snapped the woman. 'And don't you go talkin about it, neither—he mightn't go for years yet; I don't want no bakin' and things for nothin'.'

Annie looked at her confidant of the milk buckets; and a telegraphic anticipation shot in a telepathic way from mind to mind. After dinner the two girls looked out their Show dresses of four years ago, and decided that if company came to call there would be something doing, and maybe Mr Walker, of Horse Gulley, might come along. They had passed him on the road once, and he had said good-day; and they had giggled fit to kill themselves.

When the eldest of the tribe got home that night he was told to 'swaller his tea quick 'cause the old man was dying and had some work he wanted doin' before he died.'

Also the last three numbers of the male portion of the family were in-structed from the depths of the blue-grey blanket bed, where the head of the family lay sunk in his own iniquity, to fetch home some of the cattle which had strayed into a paddock ten miles away. The old man said he didn't want a summons before he died—the brutes better be branded or ear-marked in the morning—he'd like to see it done at once. And so it was—with the pruning knife and a jab of kitchen salt to stop the blood.

About five o'clock next day the general family had assorted themselves round the place. Some of the boys had gone to the paddock dam to wash. The woman had thought it wiser, in case of anything happening; and after consulting the old man he had agreed to allow them to use the dam water, and the boys had raced there, shouting with the inflated lungs of young Australians well in condition.

The second eldest was nailing the prop-roost in the shed where the fowls shared a rest with the milk cans. A board served as a protecting lid for the milk, and some of the older birds roosted there in a crouched attitude, and squawked tones of melancholy into the coming night. Will, the elder, was secreted with his father. The old man spoke from the uncovered pillow of faded dress material:

'What'd yer do? Did yer catch Miller?'

'Yes. I got 'im. Fourteen quid for the bull.'

'That's a better deal—gimme the paper. Did he sign it? . . . And the bull's gone?'

'I'm thinkin',' went on William, 'that them young heifers could go next trip. No good keepin' them?'

'What's the price?' wheezed the old man.

'Dunno,' said Will. 'I'm puttin' a lot on Johnson's chance there. I'll see him ter-morrow.'

'Maybe,' said Mr Dawson from the bed-well. 'I'd like to know what's doin' with them before I'm under.'

'Yes, I'll get fixed for Narragoon ter-morrow. Ye'd better have a sleep now.'

When he had gone out the old man turned to a slit of window where the blind had been looped aside and nailed tight. The blue vapour was settling on the hills right out, and to him looked like white mists. He rubbed his hands over his eyes, but still he saw it; then he called suddenly to the woman, and she came in with a light.

Half an hour after, the dark had come. The boys hadn't returned from the bath in the dam, and the two girls were down at the sheds still talking. Across the yard the voice of the woman burst like a cannon on the right. She called the entire family by name, and, getting no answer, wailed in a mournful tone that ended in a break of bad temper:

'Carn't yer answer, Will? Where are yer? Yer father's dead! Annie, Annie!'

Across the paddock the shriek rent; and animals that sought to sleep raised languid eyes towards the house. The girls came from the shed as Will turned in at the door, rushing past the woman roughly. She waited.

'Yer'd better go down and bring yer brothers out've the mudhole,' she said in a flurry. 'Tell 'em their father's dead; and they's better hurry if they want to see 'im warm.'

The girls began to run, and the woman lit the kitchen lamp and began tidying up the place a bit. Presently the general troops rushed in, breathless.

'Is 'e in bed, Mum?'

'Did you think 'e was in the fowlhouse?'

Then they pushed into the bedroom; and an awesome silence dropped over everything.

Never before, in their mean existence, had they known such a thing! Absolute calm was on each face, calm that was due to a great wonderment. The lamp shed a weak sort of glow that reached across the old man's face so that it was outlined against the coarse pillow. It was ghastly in the half-light; and round the room the family stood, waiting as if some great phenomenon was about to burst upon them.

'Better put out the light,' began the woman, dropping into a frightened calm after the storm of her temper. 'No good wastin' karosine.'

Will was hanging half over the bed. He was sorry the old man had gone before he had fixed up about the cattle. He'd have liked to have brought that bit of business off first.

'Get outer here,' said the woman, in a stifled, strange voice. 'He ain't going to do nothin' more.'

One by one the family turned in the silence; but a sudden disturbance from the bed, together with a shriek from the woman, brought them back with a turn, and a new look in their faces.

'E's movin', I declare!'

Will came again to the bed; and the eyes of the old man suddenly blinked in the dim light.

'Ain't gorn yet?' said the woman, bringing the lamp nearer, while the family climbed about the bed with wary whispers.

The old man sat up. He stared at his fourth child quite squarely.

'Take your dirty feet off the bed,' he said in a strong, vibrating voice. Then he turned to Will. 'Not this time, son; I'm going to get up. Want to look at them heifers—think—they're worth—more'n Johnson will—pay for 'em. Where's me boots?'

In the interval, when the family simmered down into their normal state, the old man could be heard giving Will a hundred injunctions about the place.

In the kitchen the woman and the girls were putting up an amount of hurry and work in preparation of the tea. The woman's tongue got loose again.

'Just as I said. 'E never knows 'is own mind one minute; put that bacon back in the pot, Annie. 'E's sure to be fit for a big feed after dyin' so long. Lord! I never seen 'im so white in 'is natural before. Just as well 'e never died tonight; them heifers wants fixin' up, and Will don't understand— besides, it ain't good buryin' in this hot weather—no rain fer a month by the look of things.'

The old man shuffled through the kitchen, his bootlaces trailing on the floor.

'Joanna, where's the tin dish?' he said, turning at the outer door; 'ain't
'ad a wash since I took bad.'

'Annie, tip that milk into the bucket an' give your father that dish,' said
the woman, glaring dubiously at him. 'Hurry up, too; he wants to wash the
death off him before we sets down.'

And Old Man Dawson, well washed, sat down once more at the family
board and discussed the profits of the coming season.

(Elizabeth) Sumner Locke (1881–1917), Mum Dawson, 'Boss' (1911).

———

ARTHUR HOEY DAVIS *was born in 1868 on his father's selection in Southern
Queensland and left school when he was 12. At the age of 27 he began to
contribute humorous stories based on the hard life on his father's farm to the
Bulletin under the pseudonym 'Steele Rudd' (originally 'Steele Rudder' from his
liking for the eighteenth-century English essayist and for mucking about in boats).*

*At the turn of the century the Bulletin published an illustrated collection of
these stories in a book entitled On Our Selection and this was a big success. More
collections of Rudd family stories followed, ten books in all, plus three silent films,
four sound features, and three plays. Throughout the Depression and the First
World War these nostalgic stories of plucky, funny, rural survival, exemplified by
'Dad' and one of his sons 'Dave', became enormously popular throughout Australia.
They are still popular, but in recent years 'Dad and Dave' have become stereotypes
on which country bumpkin jokes are hung; in the original stories they were also
hard-working and resourceful pioneers.*

*Steele Rudd had little formal education but in those days only a few selection
folk had much of a schooling. Those bright children who could actually write and
do sums were looked up to with respect by the rest of the family:*

One night after the threshing. Dad lying on the sofa, thinking, the rest of us
sitting at the table. Dad spoke to Joe.

'How much,' he said, 'is seven hundred bushels of wheat at six shillings?'

Joe, who was looked upon as the brainy one of our family, took down his
slate with a hint of scholarly ostentation.

'What did y'say, Dad—seven 'undred *bags*?'

'Bushels! *Bushels*!'

'Seven 'un-dered bush-els of wheat. *Wheat* was it, Dad?'

'Yes, *wheat*!'

'Wheat at . . . at *what*, Dad?'

'Six shillings a bushel.'

'Six shillings a . . . *A*, Dad? We've not done any *a*; she's on'y shown us
per!'

'*Per* bushel, then!'

'Per bush-el. That's seven 'undred bushels of wheat at six shillin's per bushel. An' y' wants ter know, Dad— ?'

'How much it'll be, of course.'

'In money, Dad, or—er ?'

'Dammit, yes. *Money*!' Dad raised his voice.

For a while, Joe thought hard, then set to work figuring and rubbing out, figuring and rubbing out. The rest of us eyed him, envious of his learning.

Joe finished the sum.

'Well?' from Dad.

Joe cleared his throat. We listened.

'Nine thousan' poun'.'

Dave laughed aloud. Dad said, 'Pshaw!'—and turned his face to the wall. Joe looked at the slate again.

'Oh, I see,' he said, 'I didn't divide by twelve t'bring t'pounds,' and laughed himself.

More figuring and rubbing out.

Finally, Joe, in loud, decisive tones, announced, '*Four* thousand, *no* 'undred an' twenty poun,' fourteen shillin's an'—'

'Bah! *You* blockhead!' Dad blurted out, and jumped off the sofa and went to bed.

We all turned in.

Steele Rudd (Arthur Hoey Davis) (1868–1935), *On Our Selection* (1899).

AN *extraordinary, and many readers would think merciful, feature of the Australian language is that there are virtually no regional dialects. Unlike a good deal of the provincial humour of the United States and Britain, the reader does not have to wrestle with the unfamiliar words and strange sentence constructions. Probably due to the fact that there was such a huge population of itinerant workers constantly on the move and that almost everybody came originally from either Great Britain or Ireland anyway, most Australians speak and write in the same idiom and always have done.*

Edward Dyson was Steele Rudd's exact contemporary but was born down south in the gold-fields of Ballarat in Victoria. Like Rudd he went to work at the age of 12, and drifted around doing various jobs until the Bulletin *published one of his stories and he found his feet as a free-lance writer.*

The following Dyson sketch, one of his most memorable, is about a shepherd, tired and a bit scratchy after work, who quarrels with his mate over how their supper is to be shared out. Tempers flare, accusations are hurled, blows are aimed, then it all dies down and the two are mates again.

An ordinary little story. Except that the shepherd's mate is his dog:

A DOMESTIC DIFFERENCE

The day had been particularly and peculiarly trying. Never had the contumaciousness of the local ewe and the pigheaded pertinacity of our Australian wether been so poignantly manifested; never had it been borne in upon Daniel Patsey with such convincing force that there are no distances in the Commonwealth but those that divide breakfast and sundown.

In the hut the shepherd sullenly speared a 'leg-o'mutton' steak, and slapped it in the pan, dexterously threw another after it, and then spiked the third and last.

Philp, the iron-grey dog, hit his tail on the clay floor in sudden alarm, and uttered a whine of gentle expostulation.

Dan Patsey paused, and looked severely at the dog. 'Wha's that?' he snapped.

Philp whined again, and swept up considerable dust with his apprehensive tail. His white eye was full of solicitude.

'I s'pose a man can do what he likes with his own?' snorted the shepherd.

Philp jumped back apace, and uttered three little yaps of half-petulant protestation.

'Oh, he can't, can't he?' Patsey's temper was rising. 'Well, well, we'll blessed well see.' He simply hurled the third steak into the pan. 'Now what yer gotter say?'

The dog backed half his length under Dan's bunk, and barked noisily.

'Don' you say that!' cried Daniel, now simply beside himself. 'That what you're sayin' I don't allow no man t'say t' me.'

The dog barked again, his bark ending in an appealing and conciliatory whine.

'Yes, I will cook it, and, wha's more, I'll dash well eat it.'

Patsey seized the pan, and threw it on the fire. Philp emerged from the bunk, and barked with a threatening note.

'So, I'm a liar now, am I?' Daniel was rapidly losing his small remaining self-control. 'Call a man a liar in his own house to his own face! It's somethin' if I've come t'this, that I can't cook me tucker without consultin' a crazy, wall-eyed mongrel what I picked outer the gutter.'

The dog jumped towards Dan showing his teeth and growling.

'Yes, picked outer the gutter! There—yiv got it straight.'

Philp crouched down and sprang up, repeating the operation several times, growling all the while.

Dan Patsey hurled the pan aside in a fury. 'Look here,' he cried, 'I won't put up with no dog talkin' t' me like that. Out o' me house!'

He went swiftly to the corner for a stick; and Philp backed under the bunk again. Only one eye was visible. He barked clamorously.

'Now yiv blessed well done it,' stormed the shepherd. He struck under the bunk. 'Liar, am I? Thief, you sez? Skunk, eh?—me what nursed yeh, 'n' fed yeh, 'n' brought yeh up proper?'

With every sentence the shepherd struck at Philp and the dog ducked and edged away, growling and barking savagely.

'Drunken swiper, eh? Mean, low glutton? Take that, and that.'

The dog barked more wildly, dodging the blows, snapping and snarling.

'Run away from me lawful wife, did I? Left me children to starve?' Daniel was literally roaring now. 'Stole pigs? That settles it. Outer me hut!' Dan made a mad rush, and heaved a mighty kick that just skimmed Philp as he shot through the door.

Dan's kick smote the door-post fearfully, and having hurled the stick and a weird remark after his dog, the shepherd went down, caught up his toe, and hugged it to him lovingly, revolving on the dirt floor, and uttering poignant sounds like a man supping very hot soup.

Philp put his nose in at the door and yapped insultingly.

'Yeh lie,' cried Daniel Patsy, dropping his toe. 'Yeh lie, you dog! It never hurt at all. Out o' me sight. I'm done with yeh.'

Patsey went for another stick, and Philp ran in a scattering way to a distance of about twenty yards. The stick missed him, and he turned and barked defiantly at his master.

'Done with yeh, I am,' roared the shepherd. 'Get off me property. Go 'n' see if you can get any one else fool enough t' do ez well by yez es I done. A sweep like you t' throw in a man's teeth about a bit o' horse-stealin'. Get out, yeh loafer!'

Dan went in to his cooking, and Philp moved in a semi-circle about the door, uttering a desultory, peevish barking. Suddenly Dan appeared again, and Philp fell over his own tail in his hurry to get away.

'If I stole the sheep at Barengower, who helped t' eat it? Tell me that, yeh low hound. Yah-h-h! Get outer me sight. This comes of a man lettin' a dirty dog know his bizness.'

Dan ducked in again, and the savory smell of frying mutton floated into the open. The dog sat on his tail and put up a passionate cry mingling a howl and a growl.

Patsey poked his head out of the calico window. 'Who will?' he snorted. 'You will? You? you? I'd like t' see yeh do it, that's all.'

Philp repeated his cry with greater poignancy.

'Do it! Do it!' sneered the shepherd. 'Why don't yeh do it! Oh, I know your sort. I'd fight a paddockful like you before breakfast.'

The head was withdrawn, and Philp resumed his semi-circle trot and his angry yapping. There was no response for three minutes; and then Patsey appeared at the door, with a fork in his hand. Inside the pan was playing a merry tune.

'Off me land!' cried Dan. 'Comin' here, callin' a man everythin' you can lay your tongue to, 'n' not fit t' black his boots, neither.'

Philp gave a little pitiful yap, and wagged his tail and half his body.

'Miserable cur!' said Dan. 'Abusin' a bloke.'

The dog ventured nearer in a crouching attitude. His yaps were decidedly pitiful and explanatory.

'Bloke what's bin ez good ez a father to yeh,' said Dan in fading tones.

Philp went down on his stomach, and clawed his way to his master's feet, where he lolled out his tongue and looked abject.

'Of course, if yeh apologise,' said Dan doubtingly.

The dog pushed his nose up the right leg of Dan's trousers and whined tenderly.

'Well, yeh know,' said Dan, 'you started it.'

The man went inside, and dug the steak out of the pan on to a plate, two pieces. 'Come in!' he called gruffly. Philp entered with meekness, and went prone in the middle of the hut.

'Yeh know well in yer own heart 'twas you started it,' said Dan; 'but I don't want no trouble with nobody.'

The dog whined, and Dan continued, 'Very well, let it drop. Maybe, ez you say, there was faults on both sides.'

Dan threw the third steak to Philp. It was uncooked. The man and the dog ate. Ten minutes later, sitting by the fire, Daniel Patsey filled his pipe. The dog approached convulsively, and placed his nose on Patsey's knee. Patsey stroked him affectionately.

'There ain't no better dog livin',' not nowhere,' he said.

Philp pig-jumped ecstatically, and then sat up, and beamed lovingly on his boss. The *entente cordiale* was re-established.

Edward Dyson (1865–1931), Below and on Top (1898).

Dyson was different from the other writers of humorous sketches in one important respect. As a young man he had worked in a factory in Melbourne and he was, if not the first, the first successful writer to explore the humour to be found in the factories and mean streets of Australia's industrial towns.

This marked the point at which Australian humorists began to stop writing local-colour stories about Australia's pioneer rural past and to concentrate on the humour of modern urban social life, an area of subject-matter which was not only no longer uniquely Australian but had been busily worked-over for years by city-bred humorists elsewhere. This urban trend was to accelerate as the new century began and manufacturing overtook sheep- and cattle-farming as Australia's main source of wealth.

Here are some extracts from an early Dyson story about high jinks with a lugubrious new chum called Levi Goss in the packing department of Spats' paper-bag factory in Melbourne.

It is quite a long way away from Old Man Dawson's selection in Queensland:

LEVI'S TROUSERS

''Tain't in 'uman nature t' respect a man what lets his missus make his trowsis,' said the head packer. Feathers had the new man in the off corner of his left eye, but was chewing deliberately, and scattering his philosophy for the use of the globe. There was something very impressive about his chewing at moments like this, it lent a ruminating profundity to his disclosure. He swept the brown paper neatly into the end of his parcel, and paused again, leaning on his job.

'No man that wore 'ome-made round-th'-'ouses ever done wonders in this world,' Mills continued. 'Napoleon's missus never made his trowsis, 'n' iv Julius Caesar's ole lady 'd tried t' push a brace iv pants cut off a set iv father's on t' him, he'd 'a' shown her some new hits, take it from me. Straight, there ain't no call fer two opinions 'bout the bloke in breeches with all the fullin' in front, 'n' legs like rusty tin cylinders . . .'

The trousers were Dutch-rigged and wonderful. They were of a thick, hard, brown material, and looked as if they might have stood alone had not one leg been so much shorter than the other: they were extremely baggy fore and aft, and were corrugated up the seams, and had a decided list to port; but the criticism did not seem to reach the wearer. He found no personal significance in the conversation, but was absorbed in the effort to get the paper around his parcel without spilling everything . . .

These trousers were a source of great uneasiness to Levi; they were always on his mind. It was not the eccentricity of their style that worried him—he was plainly unconscious of their imperfections—but fear that an injury should come to them. His care that no stain should sully their well-preserved newness, was not merely the natural anxiety of a careful man. There was terror in it. For a time his little attentions were secret. He would fearfully inspect his nether garments by the lift windows behind the piled bales. He went under cover to brush them many times a day, and before leaving of an evening cautiously removed every particle of factory dust.

Later, when his pants became an object of open ridicule and a target for scorn, Goss's distress about them was open and undisguised, and still the Beauties harried him with heathenish relish. Clots of paste attached themselves to his trousers in ways inconceivable to the wearer; adhesive papers were picked up from every seat; flour bespattered them, and they were defiled with dust and printer's ink and gum. Levi grew haggard in his devotion to them, and wore the look of a hunted animal.

The factory was never without a stock joke or two, and for a fortnight Levi's trousers usurped the honour . . .

One afternoon, eight or nine days later, a short, stout, neat-looking Methodistical woman of about 30, with a very businesslike expression in her eye, came up the back stairs and stood for a moment regarding Levi Goss silently, severely. Levi's work slid from his hand; he cowered under the stern gaze like a criminal. Feathers, looking from one to the other whistled down the scale.

'Goss's sorrer, fer a dollar!' he said.

The woman advanced to Levi. 'So, Mr Goss, this is your quiet little job, is it?' Her eyes went over the factory taking inventory of the girls, and classifying them, and her lips tightened, and her colour rose. 'You dissipated devil!' she hissed. 'You abominable rake! you have deceived me. This is why you have lied to me.'

''Pon my soul, Louisa, I—' Levi's attitude was humble, but the woman cut him short.

'Yes,' she cried, 'you are in your element here with all these hussies, you wretch. Oh, but you shall pay for this.' Nobody seeing Louisa's face could doubt it for a moment. 'To think after all the care I have taken of you, you should have been here unwatched, unguarded. You brute, I'll divorce you.'

The truth dawned upon the factory. Louisa was jealous—jealous of her Levi. It seemed too utterly grotesque, but there was no doubting it. Bella Coleman had marked the word 'hussies', and the contemptuous flashes in Louisa's grey eyes, and she approached diffidently with an anxious expression, seeking vengeance.

'Who—who are you, woman?' she asked in agonized Theatre Royal accents.

'I am this man's wife, that's who I am!' said Louisa, fiercely.

'Great Heavings!' gasped Bella, staggering. 'Great Heavings; and he never told us he was a married man.'

Then she passed on with bowed head and a faltering step, the picture of a blighted life.

Louisa turned on Goss, and for half-a-minute she was speechless. Then she seized him by the shoulder. 'Get your coat!'. . . A tear rolled down Levi's cheek.

Feathers took the matter in hand with judicious gravity. He assured Mrs Goss that her husband's conduct had been most exemplary during his stay in the factory, that he had been blind to beauty and deaf to the voice of tempter. He produced witnesses in proof, Bella Coleman among the rest, and this young lady admitted that Goss's not having told her he was a married man might reasonably have been ascribed to the fact that he had never spoken to her at all. 'I wouldn't have one like him if they gave 'em away with a gold mine,' added Miss Coleman, with convincing emphasis.

Levi looked happier as he went away, and Feathers called a bit of advice after them.

'Take it from me, missus,' he said, 'give the pore man a charnce. Let him buy his own trowsis.'

'Fact'ry 'Ands' (1912).

AUSTRALIAN *humour up to the end of the First World War had some charac-teristics peculiar to the nation. A tiny population was trying to scratch a living on an enormous continent of plains and deserts and mountains and there was much loneliness. Companionship—'mateship'—was very highly valued. A good mate was trustworthy and companionable, but—and this was most im-portant—did not disturb the peace with idle chatter:*

THE GREAT AUSTRALIAN JOKE

Two swagmen who had been mates for a long time were tramping out west in the wheat country. There were good young crops on either side of them.

Harry took his pipe from his mouth and pointed to one of the paddocks. 'Nice crop of wheat,' he grunted.

Five hours later, when they were seated by their campfire, Bill broke the silence. 'Wasn't wheat. 'Twas oats.' Then he rolled up in his blankets and went to sleep. The sun was well up when he woke next morning. Harry and his swag were gone. Bill found a roughly-scribbled note under a stone at the foot of the nearest tree. 'Too much bloody argyment in this camp', it said.

Quoted by Bill Wannan, *The Australian* (1954).

The importance to old-timers of plenty of silence between mates was confirmed in a modern newspaper report:

THE MAGGER

The old yarn about those bush mates, travelling, who parted for ever because one of them said there was too much sugar in the tea, and the other said there was too much conversation in the camp, is better than gospel truth. You can live mates with a murderer, but you can't live mates with a magger.

Ibid., quoting Thomas Dodd, *Australian Worker* (21 Mar. 1928).

🕿 Magger = a person who never stops talking.

The outback life produced a race which was lean, tough, and laconic; not con-temptuous of book-learning as American frontiersmen tended to be, but disliking anything which smacked of pomposity or formality or needed fancy words to express:

THE OLD-TIME SHEARER'S GRACE

'One word's as good as ten.
Wire in. Amen.'

Ibid.

Much early Australian humour was surprisingly kind and dealt affectionately with those aspects of pioneer life held to be good things, like mateship, taciturnity, dogs, colourful lying, betting, and so on. But there was also a radical area of humour which was unmercifully unkind to rich squatters, politicians ('pollies'), the police, unmanly immigrants, and pretentious Englishmen. And the national sense of humour never lost its original sardonic edge, an irreverent, independent-minded

jokiness in the face of calamity which is well illustrated by another favourite
Australian story—perhaps the archetypal (relatively clean) Aussie joke—of the
two Diggers in action in the First World War:

A wounded soldier was being carried across No Man's Land on the back of a
perspiring comrade. Machine-gun fire was heavy.

''Ere,' suddenly exclaimed the wounded Digger, 'what about turning
round and walking backwards for a spell? You're getting the VC, but I'm
getting all the f-----' bullets!'

Ibid.

—————

*A*CROSS *the Pacific, a writer in the USA struck lucky in much the same way as*
did Banjo Paterson with his 'Waltzing Matilda' and the packets of tea.

Ellis Parker Butler was born in Iowa in 1869, five years after Paterson, and
died four years before him. Both of them were country boys with little education
and both became free-lance writers after having a piece published by a popular
journal; with Banjo Paterson this was the Sydney Bulletin *and in Butler's case it*
was The American Magazine.

In 1905 the magazine printed an amusing sketch written by Butler, a piece of
character humour based on a good comedy idea. It might well have remained just
that, a funny piece in the American, *but it was bought by the Railway Appliances*
Company, and reprinted in the form of a pamphlet: ten thousand were given away
by the firm as an advertisement, a book version followed in 1906 and the little
story grew to become a nation-wide favourite, a classic of American humour.

Mr Fannery, an Irishman who works as an agent for a firm which delivers
parcels by wagon, is pig-obstinate in abiding by his rule-book:

PIGS IS PIGS

Mike Flannery, the Westcote agent of the Interurban Express Company,
leaned over the counter of the express office and shook his fist. Mr Morehouse,
angry and red, stood on the other side of the counter, trembling with rage.
The argument had been long and heated, and at last Mr Morehouse had
talked himself speechless. The cause of the trouble stood on the counter
between the two men. It was a soap box across the top of which were nailed
a number of strips, forming a rough but serviceable cage. In it two spotted
guinea-pigs were greedily eating lettuce leaves.

'Do as you loike, then!' shouted Flannery, 'pay for thim an' take thim, or
don't pay for thim and leave thim be. Rules is rules, Misther Morehouse, an'
Mike Flannery's not goin' to be called down fer breakin' of thim.'

'But you everlastingly stupid idiot!' shouted Mr Morehouse, madly shaking
a flimsy book beneath the agent's nose, 'can't you read it here—in your own

plain printed rates? "Pets, domestic, Franklin to Westcote, if properly boxed, twenty-five cents each."' He threw the book on the counter in disgust. 'What more do you want? Aren't they pets? Aren't they domestic? Aren't they properly boxed? What?'

He turned and walked back and forth rapidly, frowning ferociously.

Suddenly he turned to Flannery, and forcing his voice to an artificial calmness spoke slowly but with intense sarcasm.

'Pets,' he said. 'P-e-t-s! Twenty-five cents each. There are two of them. One! Two! Two times twenty-five are fifty! Can you understand that? I offer you fifty cents.'

Flannery reached for the book. He ran his hand through the pages and stopped at page sixty-four.

'An' I don't take fifty cints,' he whispered in mockery. 'Here's the rule for ut. "Whin the agint be in anny doubt regardin' which of two rates applies to a shipment, he shall charge the larger. The consign-ey may file a claim for the overcharge." In this case, Misther Morehouse, I be in doubt. Pets thim animals may be, an' domestic they be, but pigs I'm blame sure they do be, an' me rules says plain as the nose on yer face, "Pigs Franklin to Westcote, thirty cints each." An, Misther Morehouse, by me arithmetical knowledge two times thirty comes to sixty cints.'

Mr Morehouse shook his head savagely. 'Nonsense!' he shouted, 'confounded nonsense, I tell you! Why, you poor ignorant foreigner, that rule means common pigs, domestic pigs, not guinea-pigs!'

Flannery was stubborn.

'Pigs is pigs,' he declared firmly. 'Guinea-pigs or dago or pigs or Irish pigs is all the same to the Interurban Express Company an' to Mike Flannery. Th' nationality of the pig creates no differentiality in the rate, Misther Morehouse! 'Twould be the same was they Dutch pigs or Rooshun pigs. Mike Flannery,' he added, 'is here to tind to the expriss business and not to hould conversation wid dago pigs in sivinteen languages fer to discover be they Chinese or Tipperary by birth an' nativity.'

Mr Morehouse hesitated. He bit his lip and then flung out his arms wildly.

'Very well!' he shouted, 'you shall hear of this! Your president shall hear of this! It is an outrage! I have offered you fifty cents, You refuse it! Keep the pigs until you are ready to take the fifty cents, but, by George, sir, if one hair of those pigs' heads is harmed I will have the law on you!'

He turned and stalked out, slamming the door. Flannery carefully lifted the soap box from the counter and placed it in a corner. He was not worried. He felt the peace that comes to a faithful servant who has done his duty and done it well.

Mr Morehouse went home raging. His boy, who had been awaiting the guinea-pigs, knew better than to ask him for them. He was a normal boy and therefore always had a guilty conscience when his father was angry. So the boy slipped quietly around the house. There is nothing so soothing to a guilty conscience as to be out of the path of the avenger.

Mr Morehouse stormed into the house. 'Where's the ink?' he shouted at his wife as soon as his foot was across the doorsill.

Mrs Morehouse jumped guiltily. She never used ink. She had not seen the ink, nor moved the ink, nor thought of the ink, but her husband's tone convicted her of the guilt of having borne and reared a boy, and she knew that whenever her husband wanted anything in a loud voice the boy had been at it.

'I'll find Sammy,' she said meekly.

When the ink was found Mr Morehouse wrote rapidly, and he read the completed letter and smiled a triumphant smile.

'That will settle that crazy Irishman!' he exclaimed. 'When they get that letter he will hunt another job, all right!'

A week later Mr Morehouse received a long official envelope with the card of the Interurban Express Company in the upper left corner. He tore it open eagerly and drew out a sheet of paper. At the top it bore the number A6754. The letter was short. 'Subject—Rate on guinea-pigs,' it said. 'Dear Sir,—We are in receipt of your letter regarding rate on guinea-pigs between Franklin and Westcote, addressed to the president of this company. All claims for overcharge should be addressed to the Claims Department.'

Mr Morehouse wrote to the Claims Department. He wrote six pages of choice sarcasm, vituperation and argument, and sent them to the Claims Department.

A few weeks later he received a reply from the Claims Department. Attached to it was his last letter.

'Dear Sir,' said the reply. 'Your letter of the 16th inst., addressed to this Department, subject rate on guinea-pigs from Franklin to Westcote, rec'd. We have taken up the matter with our agent at Westcote, and his reply is attached herewith. He informs us that you refused to receive the consignment or to pay the charges. You have therefore no claim against this company, and your letter regarding the proper rate on the consignment should be addressed to our Tariff Department.'

Mr Morehouse wrote to the Tariff Department. He stated his case clearly, and gave his arguments in full, quoting a page or two from the encyclopedia to prove that guinea-pigs were not common pigs.

With the care that characterizes corporations when they are systematically conducted, Mr Morehouse's letter was numbered, O.K.'d and started through the regular channels. Duplicate copies of the bill of lading, manifest, Flannery's receipt for the package and several other pertinent papers were pinned to the letter, and they were passed to the head of the Tariff Department.

The head of the Tariff Department put his feet on his desk and yawned. He looked through the papers carelessly.

'Miss Kane,' he said to his stenographer, 'take this letter. "Agent, Westcote, N.J. Please advise why consignment referred to in attached papers was refused domestic pet rates."'

Miss Kane made a series of curves and angles on her notebook and waited with pencil poised. The head of the department looked at the papers again.

'Huh! Guinea-pigs!' he said. 'Probably starved to death by this time! Add this to that letter: "Give condition of consignment at present."'

He tossed the papers on to the stenographer's desk, took his feet from his own desk and went out to lunch.

When Mike Flannery received the letter he scratched his head.

'Give prisint condition,' he repeated thoughtfully. 'Now what do thim clerks be wantin' to know, I wonder! Prisint condition, is ut? Thim pigs, praise St Patrick, do be in good health, so far as I know, but I niver was no veternairy surgeon to dago pigs. Mebby thim clerks wants me to call in the pig docther an' have their pulses took. Wan thing I do know, howiver, which is, they've glorius appytites for pigs of their soize. Ate? They'd ate the brass padlocks off of a barn door! If the paddy pig, by the same token, ate as hearty as these dago pigs do, there'd be a famine in Ireland.'

To assure himself that his report would be up to date, Flannery went to the rear of the office and looked into the cage. The pigs had been transferred to a larger box—a dry goods box.

'Wan,—two,—t'ree,—four,—foive,—six,—sivin,—eight!' he counted. 'Sivin spotted an' wan all black. All well an' hearty an' all eatin' loike ragin' hippypottymusses.' He went back to his desk and wrote.

'Mr Morgan, Head of Tariff Department,' he wrote, 'why do I say dago pigs is pigs because they is pigs and will be til you say they ain't which is what the rule book says stop your jollying me you know it as well as I do. As to the health they are all well and hoping you are the same. P.S. There are eight now the family increased all good eaters. P.S. I paid out so far two dollars for cabbage which they like shall I put in bill for same what?'

Morgan, head of the Tariff Department, when he received this letter, laughed. He read it again and became serious.

'By George!' he said, 'Flannery is right, "pigs is pigs". I'll have to get authority on this thing. Meanwhile, Miss Kane, take this letter: "Agent, Westcote, N.J. Regarding shipment guinea-pigs, File No.AA6754. Rule 83, General Instructions to Agents, clearly states that agents shall collect from consignee all costs of provender, etc., etc., required for live stock while in transit or storage. You will proceed to collect same from consignee."'

Flannery received this letter next morning, and when he read it he grinned.

'Proceed to collect,' he said softly. 'How thim clerks do loike to be talkin'! *Me* proceed to collect two dollars and twenty-foive cints off Misther Morehouse! I wonder do thim clerks *know* Misther Morehouse? I'll git it! Oh, yes! "Misther Morehouse, two an' a quarter, plaze." "Cert'nly, me dear frind Flannery. Delighted!" *Not!*'

Flannery drove the express wagon to Mr Morehouse's door. Mr Morehouse answered the bell.

'Ah, ha!' he cried as soon as he saw it was Flannery. 'So you've come to your senses at last, have you? I thought you would! Bring the box in.'

'I hev no box,' said Flannery coldly. 'I hev a bill agin Misther John C. Morehouse for two dollars and twinty-foive cints for kebbages aten by his dago pigs. Wud you wish to pay ut?'

'Pay—Cabbages—!' gasped Mr Morehouse. 'Do you mean to say that two little guinea-pigs—'

'Eight!' said Flannery. 'Papa an' mamma an' the six childer. Eight!'

For answer Mr Morehouse slammed the door in Flannery's face. Flannery looked at the door reproachfully.

'I take ut the con-*sign*-y don't want to pay for thim kebbages,' he said, 'If I know signs of refusal, the con-*sign*-y refuses to pay for wan dang kebbage leaf an' be hanged to me!'

Mr Morgan, the head of the Tariff Department, consulted the president of the Interurban Express Company regarding guinea-pigs, as to whether they were pigs or not pigs. The president was inclined to treat the matter lightly.

'What is the rate on pigs and on pets?' he asked.

'Pigs thirty cents, pets twenty-five,' said Morgan.

'Then of course guinea-pigs are pigs,' said the president.

'Yes,' agreed Morgan, 'I look at it that way, too. A thing that can come under two rates is naturally due to be classed as the higher. But are guinea-pigs, pigs? Aren't they rabbits?'

'Come to think of it,' said the president, 'I believe they are more like rabbits. Sort of half-way station between pig and rabbit. I think the question is this— are guinea-pigs of the domestic pig family? I'll ask Professor Gordon. He is authority on such things. Leave the papers with me.'

The president put the papers on his desk and wrote a letter to Professor Gordon. Unfortunately the Professor was in South America collecting zoo-logical specimens, and the letter was forwarded to him by his wife. As the Professor was in the highest Andes, where no white man had ever penetrated, the letter was many months in reaching him. The president forgot the guinea-pigs, Morgan forgot them, Mr Morehouse forgot them. But Flannery did not. One half of his time he gave to the duties of his agency; the other half was devoted to the guinea-pigs. Long before Professor Gordon received the president's letter Morgan received one from Flannery.

'About them dago pigs,' it said, 'what shall I do they are great in family life, no race suicide for them, there are thirty-two now shall I sell them do you take this express office for a menagerie, answer quick.'

Morgan reached for a telegraph blank and wrote:

'Agent, Westcote. Don't sell pigs.'

He then wrote Flannery a letter calling his attention to the fact that the pigs were not the property of the company but were merely being held during a settlement of a dispute regarding rates. He advised Flannery to take the best possible care of them.

Flannery, letter in hand, looked at the pigs and sighed. The dry goods box cage had become too small. He boarded up twenty feet of the rear of the express office to make a large and airy home for them, and went about his business. He worked with feverish intensity when out on his rounds, for the pigs required attention and took most of his time. Some months later, in desperation, he seized a sheet of paper and wrote '160' across it and mailed it to Morgan. Morgan returned it asking for explanation. Flannery replied:

'There be now one hundred sixty of the dago pigs, for heaven's sake let me sell off some, do you want me to go crazy, what?'

'Sell no pigs,' Morgan wired.

Not long after this the president of the express company received a letter from Professor Gordon. It was a long and scholarly letter, but the point was that the guinea-pig was the *Cavia aparoca*, while the common pig was the genus *Sus* of the family *Suidae*. He remarked that they were prolific and multiplied rapidly.

'They are not pigs,' said the president, decidedly, to Morgan. 'The twenty-five cent rate applies.'

Morgan made the proper notation on the papers that had accumulated in File A6754, and turned them over to the Audit Department. The Audit Department took some time to look the matter up, and after the usual delay wrote Flannery that as he had on hand one hundred and sixty guinea-pigs, the property of consignee, he should deliver them and collect charges at the rate of twenty-five cents each.

Flannery spent a day herding his charges through a narrow opening in their cage so that he might count them.

'Audit Dept.,' he wrote, when he had finished the count, 'you are way off there may be was one hundred and sixty dago pigs once, but wake up don't be back number. I've got even eight hundred, now shall I collect for eight hundred or what, how about sixty-four dollars I paid out for cabbages.'

It required a great many letters back and forth before the Audit Department was able to understand why the error had been made of billing one hundred and sixty instead of eight hundred, and still more time for it to get the meaning of the 'cabbages'.

Flannery was crowded into a few feet at the extreme front of the office. The pigs had all the rest of the room and two boys were employed constantly attending to them. The day after Flannery had counted the guinea-pigs there were eight more added to his drove, and by the time the Audit Department gave him authority to collect for eight hundred Flannery had given up all attempts to attend to the receipt or the delivery of goods. He was hastily building galleries around the express office, tier above tier. He had four thousand and sixty-four guinea-pigs to care for. More were arriving daily.

Immediately following its authorization the Audit Department sent another letter, but Flannery was too busy to open it. They wrote another and then they telegraphed:

'Error in guinea-pig bill. Collect for two guinea-pigs, fifty cents. Deliver all to consignee.'

Flannery read the telegram and cheered up. He wrote out a bill as rapidly as his pencil could travel over paper and ran all the way to the Morehouse home. At the gate he stopped suddenly. The house stared at him with vacant eyes. The windows were bare of curtains and he could see into the empty rooms. A sign on the porch said, 'To Let'. Mr Morehouse had moved! Flannery ran all the way back to the express office. Sixty-nine guinea-pigs had been born during his absence. He ran out again and made feverish inquiries in the village. Mr Morehouse had not only moved, but he had left Westcote. Flannery returned to the express office and found that two hundred and six guinea-pigs had entered the world since he left it. He wrote a telegram to the Audit Department.

'Can't collect fifty cents for two dago pigs consignee has left town address unknown what shall I do? Flannery.'

The telegram was handed to one of the clerks in the Audit Department, and as he read it he laughed.

'Flannery must be crazy. He ought to know that the thing to do is to return the consignment here,' said the clerk. He telegraphed Flannery to send the pigs to the main office of the company at Franklin.

When Flannery received the telegram he set to work. The six boys he had engaged to help him also set to work. They worked with the haste of desperate men, making cages out of soap boxes, cracker boxes, and of all kinds of boxes, and as fast as the cages were completed they filled them with guinea-pigs and expressed them to Franklin. Day after day the cages of guinea-pigs flowed in a steady stream from Westcote to Franklin, and still Flannery and his six helpers ripped and nailed and packed—relentlessly and feverishly. At the end of the week they had shipped two hundred and eighty cases of guinea-pigs, and there were in the express office seven hundred and four more pigs than when they began packing them.

'Stop sending pigs. Warehouse full,' came a telegram to Flannery. He stopped packing only long enough to wire back, 'Can't stop,' and kept on sending them. On the next train up from Franklin came one of the company's inspectors. He had instructions to stop the stream of guinea-pigs at all hazards. As his train drew up at Westcote station he saw a cattle-car standing on the express company's siding. When he reaching the express office he saw the express wagon backed up to the door. Six boys were carrying bushel baskets full of guinea-pigs from the office and dumping them into the wagon. Inside the room Flannery, with his coat and vest off, was shovelling guinea-pigs into bushel baskets with a coal scoop. He was winding up the guinea-pig episode.

He looked up at the inspector with a snort of anger.

'Wan wagonload more an' I'll be quit of thim, an' niver will ye catch Flannery wid no more foreign pigs on his hands. No, sur! They near was the death o' me. Nixt toime I'll know that pigs of whativer nationality is domestic pets—an' go at the lowest rate.'

He began shovelling again rapidly, speaking quickly between breaths.

'Rules may be rules, but you can't fool Mike Flannery twice wid the same th'rick—whin ut comes to live stock, dang the rules. So long as Flannery runs this expriss office—pigs is pets—an' cows is pets—an' horses is pets—an' lions an' tigers an' Rocky Mountain goats is pets—an' the rate on thim is twinty-foive cints.'

He paused long enought to let one of the boys put an empty basket in the place of the one he had just filled. There were only a few guinea-pigs left. As he noted their limited number his natural habit of looking on the bright side returned.

'Well, anyhow,' he said cheerfully, ''tis not so bad as ut might be. What if thim dago pigs had been elephants!'

Ellis Parker Butler (1869–1937), Pigs is Pigs (1905).

As in Australia, economic emphasis in the United States was shifting from farming to manufacturing. Pigs is Pigs was not a story about pigs but about guinea-pigs, town-dweller's pets. It was also about the problems which the guinea-pigs raised in the offices of a company. Writers were now concerning themselves with city rather than rural activities.

Finley Peter Dunne achieved great success at the turn of the century with his 'Mr Dooley' pieces, which were firmly rooted in the streets, not even in the soil, of Chicago. They appeared in book form from 1899 to 1919 and were so popular that 'Mr Dooley' and his pronouncements became a national institution.

Dunne was a newspaperman all his life. When a young man he was a member of the Whitechapel Club where writers and cartoonists boozed and played macabre practical jokes on each other and deplored the state of the Union. It was a kind of hearty, cynical, rowdy Chicago version of New York's later and more sophisticated Algonquin Round Table. A fellow member of the club was George Ade, but whereas Ade's theme was the decay of country and small town values, Dunne in 'Mr Dooley' satirized metropolitan incompetence, to be found in government sham and corruption, state education, journalism, religion, business, and so on.

Like the old satirists, Dunne used the device of a foreigner seeing everyday events from a detached viewpoint and made his Mr Dooley Irish. Very Irish. The heavy brogue spoken by Mr Dooley and his naïve friend Hennessy—invented by the author and not to be found in nature—which greatly amused readers when the sketches first appeared, now rather gets in the way, but it is still possible to enjoy

*Mr Dooley's 'cracker-barrel' scepticism and appreciate why he was a landmark in
American humour.*

*Hennessy, permanent customer in the saloon, notices something of interest in
the newspaper:*

'I see,' said Mr Hennessy, 'that wan iv thim New York joods says a man in
pollytics oughtn't to be married.'

'Oh, does he?' said Mr Dooley. 'Well, 'tis little he knows about it. A man
in pollytics has got to be married. If he ain't marrid where'll he go f 'r another
kind iv throuble? An' where'll he find people to support? An unmarrid man
don't get along in pollytics because he don't need th' money. Whin he's in
th' middle iv a prim'ry, with maybe twinty or thirty iv th' opposite party on
top iv him, thinks he to himsilf: "What's th' good iv fightin' f 'r a job?
They'se no wan depindent on me f 'r support," an' he surrinders. But a
marrid man says: "What'll happen to me wife an' twelve childher if I don't
win out here today?" an' he bites his way to th' top iv th' pile an' breaks
open th' ballot box f 'r home and fireside. That's th' thruth iv it, Hinnissy.
Ye'll find all th' big jobs held be marrid men an' all th' timpry clerkships be
bachelors.

'Th' reason th' New York jood thinks marrid men oughtn't to be in pollytics
is because he thinks pollytics is spoort. An' so it is. But it ain't amachoor
spoort, Hinnissy. They don't give ye a pewter mug with ye'er name on it f 'r
takin' a chanst on bein' kilt. 'Tis a proffisional sport, like playin' base-ball
f 'r a livin' or wheelin' a thruck. Ye niver see an amachoor at annything that
was as good as a profissional. Th' best amachoor ball team is beat be a bad
profissional team; a profissional boxer that thrains on bock beer an' Swiss
cheese can lam the head off a goold medal amachoor champeen that's been
atin' moldy bread an' dhrinkin' wather f 'r six months, an' th' Dago that
blows th' cornet on th' sthreet f 'r what annywan 'll throw him can cut the
figure eight around Dinnis Finn, that's been takin' lessons f 'r twinty year.
No, sir, pollytics ain't dhroppin' into tea, an' it ain't wurrukin' a scroll saw,
or makin' a garden in a back yard. 'Tis gettin' up at six o'clock in th' mornin'
an' r-rushin' off to wurruk, an' comin' home at night tired an' dusty. Double
wages f 'r overtime an' Sundahs.

'So a man's got to be married to do it well. He's got to have a wife at home
to make him oncomfortable if he comes in dhrunk, he's got to have little
prattlin' childher that he can't sind to th' Young Ladies' academy onless he
stuffs a ballotbox properly, an' he's got to have a sthrong desire f 'r to live in
th' av'noo an' be seen dhrivin' downtown in an open carredge with his wife
settin' beside him undher a r-red parasol. If he hasn't these things he won't
succeed in pollytics—or packin' port. Ye niver see a big man in pollytics that
dhrank hard, did ye? Ye never will. An' that's because they're all marrid.
Th' timptation's sthrong, but fear is sthronger.

'Th' most domestic men in th' wurruld ar-re pollyticians, an' they always

marry early. An' thats th' sad part iv it, Hinnissy. A pollytician always
marries above his own station. That's wan sign that he'll be a successful
pollytician. Th' throuble is, th' good woman stays planted just where she
was, an' he goes by like a fast thrain by a whistlin' station. D'ye mind
O'Leary, him that's a retired capitalist now, him that was aldherman, an'
dhrainage thrustee, an' state sinitor f 'r wan term? Well, whin I first know
O'Leary he wurruked down on a railroad section tampin' th' thrack an
wan-fifty a day. He was a sthrong, willin' young fellow, with a stiff righthand
punch an' a schamin' brain, an' anny wan cud see that he was intinded to
go to th' fr-ront. Th' aristocracy iv th' camp was Mrs Cassidy, th' widdy lady
that kept th' boordin'-house. Aristocracy, Hinnissy, is like rale estate, a
matther iv location. I'm aristocracy to th' poor O'Briens back in th' alley, th'
brewery agent's aristocracy to me, his boss is aristocracy to him, an' so it
goes, up to the czar of Rooshia. He's th' pick iv th' bunch, th' high man iv
all, th' Pope not goin' in society. Well, Mrs Cassidy was aristocracy to O'Leary.
He niver see such a stylish woman as she was whin she turned out iv a
Sundah afthernoon in her horse an' buggy. He'd think to himsilf, "If I iver
can win that I'm settled f 'r life," an' iv coorse he did. 'Twas a gran' weddin';
manny iv th' guests didn't show up at wurruk f 'r weeks.

'O'Leary done well, an' she was a good wife to him. She made money an'
kept him straight an' started him for constable. He won out, bein' a sthrong
man. Thin she got him to r-run f 'r aldherman, an' ye shud've seen her th'
night he was inaugurated! Be hivins, Hinnissy, she looked like a fire in a
pawnshop, fair covered with dimons an' goold watches an' chains. She was
cut out to be an aldherman's wife, and it was worth goin' miles to watch
her leadin' th' gran' march at th' Ar-rchy Road Dimmycratic Fife an' Dhrum
Corps ball.

'But there she stopped. A good woman an' a kind wan, she cudden't go
th' distance. She had th' house an' th' childher to care f 'r an' her eddycation
was through with. They isn't much a woman can learn afther she begins to
raise a fam'ly. But with O'Leary 'twas diff 'rent. I say 'twas diff 'rent with
O'Leary. Ye talk about ye'er colleges, Hinnissy, but pollytics is th' poor man's
college. A la-ad without enough book larnin' to r-read a meal-ticket, if ye
give him tin years iv polly-tical life, has th' air iv a statesman an' th' manner
iv a jook, an' cud take anny job fr'm dalin' faro bank to r-runnin' th' treasury
iv th' United States. His business brings him up again' th' best men iv th'
com-munity, an' their customs an' ways iv speakin' an' thinkin' an' robbin'
sticks to him. Th' good woman is at home all day. Th' on'y people she sees is
th' childher an' th' neighbors. While th' good man in a swallow-tail coat is
addhressin' th' Commercial club on what we shud do f 'r to reform pollytics,
she's discussin' th' price iv groceries with th' plumber's wife an' talkin' over
th' back fince to the milkman. Thin O'Leary moves up on th' boolyvard. He
knows she'll get along all r-right on th' boolyvard. Th' men'll say: 'They'se
a good deal of rugged common sinse in that O'Leary. He may be a robber,

but they's mighty little that escapes him.' But not wan speaks to Mrs O'Leary. No wan asts her opinion about our foreign policy. She sets day in an' day out behind th' dhrawn curtains iv her three-story brownstone risidence prayin' that somewan'll come in an' see her, an' if annywan comes she's frozen with fear. An' 'tis on'y whin she slips out to Ar-rchey r-road an' finds th' plumber's wife, an' sets in th' kitchen over a cup iv tay, that peace comes to her. By an' by they offer O'Leary th' nommynation f 'r congress. He knows he's fit for it. He's sthronger thin th' young lawyer they have now. People'll listen to him in Wash'nton as they do in Chicago. He says: "I'll take it." An' thin he thinks iv th' wife an' they's no Wash'nton f 'r him. His pollytical career is over. He wud niver have been constable if he hadn't marrid, but he might have been sinitor if he was a widower.

'Mrs O'Leary was in to see th' Dargans th' other day. "Ye mus'be very happy in ye'er gran' house, with Mr O'Leary doin' so well," says Mrs Dargan. An' th' on'y answer th' foolish woman give was to break down an' weep on Mrs Dargan's neck.'

'Yet ye say a pollytician oughtn't to get marrid,' said Mr. Hennessy.

'Up to a certain point,' said Mr Dooley, 'he must be marrid. Afther that— well, I on'y say that, though pollytics is a gran' career f 'r a man, 'tis a tough wan f 'r his wife.'

Finley Peter Dunne (1867–1936), *Mr Dooley's Philosophy* (1900).

———————

AN *extremely successful writer of big-city stories was 'O. Henry'.*
*Until the beginning of the twentieth century the centre of humorous journ-
alism was Chicago. 'O. Henry' was one of the first highly rated authors to write
about New York—Baghdad-on-the-Subway he called it—and the people who lived
and worked there: the shopgirls, clerks, policemen, boarding-house keepers, actresses.*

*O. Henry's real name was William Sydney Porter. He was born in North
Carolina and worked at various jobs in Texas, writing funny pieces for local papers
on the side. He started a humorous weekly,* The Rolling Stone, *but unlike the
modern magazine of the same title it failed. Then he married and took a job in a
bank in Austin, but a smallish sum of money for which he was responsible went
missing; he was suspected of the theft, accepted bad advice and fled to Honduras.
When he heard that his wife was dying he returned to see her and was sent to
prison for three years.*

*The imprisonment was his turning point (it was like an O. Henry story). While
in jail he began to write short stories about his wanderings in Texas and Honduras.
On his release he moved to New York, decided to become an author rather than a
journalist, and was soon the most popular humorous magazine writer of his day.*

O. Henry's development of the short story form influenced generations of later writers. *He wrote about ordinary men and women; he made them funny but wrote about them compassionately; he had a fine eye for the ironic coincidence, he was sentimental, which suited the taste of the times and he perfected what became his trademark—the surprise ending.*

An O. Henry trick ending is like the denouement of a good mystery story. If it catches you unawares you cannot believe that you have been so easily misled and turn back the pages to check the beginning. But O. Henry did not cheat the reader any more than did Agatha Christie or Ellery Queen; all the clues to the ending are there.

Here is a typical little O. Henry sketch about a day in the life of a New York stockbroker. And his stenographer:

THE ROMANCE OF A BUSY BROKER

Pitcher, confidential clerk in the office of Harvey Maxwell, broker, allowed a look of mild interest and surprise to visit his usually expressionless countenance when his employer briskly entered at half-past nine in company with his young lady stenographer. With a snappy 'Good morning, Pitcher,' he dashed at his desk as though he were intending to leap over it, and then plunged into a great heap of letters and telegrams waiting there for him.

The young lady had been Maxwell's stenographer for a year. She was beautiful in a way that was decidedly unstenographic. She forwent the pomp of the alluring pompadour. She wore no chains, bracelets or lockets. She had not the air of being about to accept an invitation to luncheon. Her dress was grey and plain, but it fitted her figure with fidelity and discretion. In her neat black turban hat was the gold-green wing of a macaw. On this morning she was softly and shyly radiant. Her eyes were dreamily bright, her cheeks genuinely peachblow, her expression a happy one, tinged with reminiscence.

Pitcher, still mildly curious, noticed a difference in her ways this morning. Instead of going straight into the adjoining room, where her desk was, she lingered, slightly irresolute, in the outer office. Once she moved over by Maxwell's desk, near enough for him to be aware of her presence.

The machine sitting at that desk was no longer a man; it was a busy New York broker, moved by buzzing wheels and uncoiling springs.

'Well—what is it? Anything?' asked Maxwell sharply. His mail lay like a bank of stage snow on his desk. His keen grey eye, impersonal and brusque, flashed upon her half impatiently.

'Nothing,' replied the stenographer, moving away with a little smile.

'Mr Pitcher,' she said to the confidential clerk, 'did Mr Maxwell say anything yesterday about engaging another stenographer?'

'He did,' answered Pitcher. 'He told me to get another one. I notified the agency yesterday afternoon to send over a few samples this morning. It's 9.45 o'clock, and not a single picture hat or piece of pineapple chewing gum has showed up yet.'

'I will do the work as usual,' then, said the young lady, 'until someone comes to fill the place.' And she went to her desk at once and hung the black turban hat with the gold-green macaw wing in its accustomed place.

He who has been denied the spectacle of a busy Manhattan broker during a rush of business is handicapped for the profession of anthropology. The poet sings of the 'crowded hour of glorious life'. The broker's hour is not only crowded, but the minutes and seconds are hanging to all the straps and packing both front and rear platforms.

And this day was Harvey Maxwell's busy day. The ticker began to reel out jerkily its fitful coils of tape, the desk telephone had a chronic attack of buzzing. Men began to throng into the office and call at him over the railing, jovially, sharply, viciously, excitedly. Messenger boys ran in and out with messages and telegrams. The clerks in the office jumped about like sailors during a storm. Even Pitcher's face relaxed into something resembling animation.

On the Exchange there were hurricanes and landslides and snowstorms and glaciers and volcanoes, and those elemental disturbances were reproduced in miniature in the broker's offices. Maxwell shoved his chair against the wall and transacted business after the manner of a toe-dance. He jumped from ticker to 'phone, from desk to door with the trained agility of a harlequin.

In the midst of this growing and important stress the broker became suddenly aware of a high-rolled fringe of golden hair under a nodding can of velvet and ostrich tips, an imitation sealskin sacque and a string of beads as large as hickory nuts, ending near the floor with a silver heart. There was a self-possessed young lady connected with these accessories; and Pitcher was there to construe her.

'Lady from the Stenographer's Agency to see about the position,' said Pitcher.

Maxwell turned half around, with his hands full of papers and ticker tape.

'What position?' he asked, with a frown.

'Position of stenographer,' said Pitcher. 'You told me yesterday to call them up and have one sent over this morning.'

'You are losing your mind, Pitcher,' said Maxwell. 'Why should I have given you such instructions? Miss Leslie has given perfect satisfaction during the year she has been here. The place is hers as long as she chooses to retain it. There's no place open here, madam. Countermand that order with the agency, Pitcher, and don't bring any more of 'em in here.'

The silver heart left the office, swinging and banging itself independently against the office furniture as it indignantly departed. Pitcher seized a moment to remark to the bookkeeper that the 'old man' seemed to get more absent-minded and forgetful every day of the world.

The rush and pace of business grew fiercer and faster. On the floor they were pounding half a dozen stocks in which Maxwell's customers were investors. Orders to buy and sell were coming and going as fast as the flight of swallows. Some of his own holdings were imperilled, and the man was working like some high-geared, delicate, strong machine—strung to full tension, going at full speed, accurate, never hesitating, with the proper word and decision and act ready and prompt as clockwork. Stocks and bonds, loans and mortgages, margins and securities—here was a world of finance, and there was no room in it for the human world or the world of nature.

When the luncheon hour drew near there came a slight lull in the uproar.

Maxwell stood by his desk with his hands full of telegrams and memoranda, with a fountain pen over his right ear and his hair hanging in disorderly strings over his forehead. His window was open, for the beloved janitress Spring had turned on a little warmth through the waking registers of the earth.

And through the window came a wandering—perhaps a lost—odour—a delicate, sweet odour of lilac that fixed the broker for a moment immovable. For this odour belonged to Miss Leslie; it was her own, and hers only.

The odour brought her vividly, almost tangibly before him. The world of finance dwindled suddenly to a speck. And she was in the next room—twenty steps away.

'By George, I'll do it now,' said Maxwell, half aloud. 'I'll ask her now. I wonder I didn't do it long ago.'

He dashed into the inner office with the haste of a short trying to cover. He charged upon the desk of the stenographer.

She looked up with a smile. A soft pink crept over her cheek, and her eyes were kind and frank. Maxwell leaned one elbow on her desk. He still clutched fluttering papers with both hands and the pen was above his ear.

'Miss Leslie,' he began hurriedly, 'I have but a moment to spare. I want to say something in that moment. Will you be my wife? I haven't had time to make love to you in the ordinary way, but I really do love you. Talk quickly, please—those fellows are clubbing the stuffing out of Union Pacific.'

'Oh, what are you talking about?' exclaimed the young lady. She rose to her feet and gazed at him, round-eyed.

'Don't you understand?' said Maxwell restively, 'I want to marry you. I love you, Miss Leslie. I wanted to tell you, and I snatched a minute when things had slackened up a bit. They're calling me for the 'phone now. Tell 'em to wait a minute, Pitcher. Won't you, Miss Leslie?'

The stenographer acted very queerly. At first she seemed overcome with amazement; then tears flowed from her wondering eyes; and then she smiled sunnily through them, and one of her arms slid tenderly round the broker's neck.

'I know,' she said softly. 'It's this old business that has driven everything else out of your head for the time. I was frightened at first. Don't you remember, Harvey? We were married last evening at eight o'clock in the Little Church Around the Corner.'

O. Henry (William Sydney Porter) (1867–1910), *The Best of O. Henry*, ed. 'Sapper'.

Not all O. Henry's stories were about New York; he also wrote a great many set in the small townships of the South-West which he knew well.

Most of the country stories featured the machinations of various pairs of likeable rogues, the sort of small-time con-men whose ruses had fascinated American readers since the days of the Yankee clock sellers.

The following shows how an O. Henry short story is not just an anecdote with a strong punch line but a good story all the way through—the surprise ending is a bonus:

JEFF PETERS AS A PERSONAL MAGNET

Jeff Peters has been engaged in as many schemes for making money as there are recipes for cooking rice in Charleston, S.C.

Best of all I like to hear him tell of his earlier days when he sold liniments and cough cures on street corners, living hand to mouth, heart to heart, with the people, throwing heads or tails with fortune for his last coin.

'I struck Fisher Hill, Arkansaw,' said he, 'in a buckskin suit, moccasins, long hair and a thirty-carat diamond ring that I got from an actor in Texarkana. I don't know what he ever did with the pocket-knife I swapped him for it.

'I was Dr Waugh-hoo, the celebrated Indian medicine man. I carried only one best bet just then, and that was Resurrection Bitters. It was made of life-giving plants and herbs accidentally discovered by Ta-qua-la, the beautiful wife of the chief of the Choctaw Nation, while gathering truck to garnish a platter of boiled dog for the annual corn dance.

'Business hadn't been too good at the last town, so I only had five dollars. I went to the Fisher Hill druggist and he credited me for half a gross of eighteen ounce bottles and corks. I had the labels and ingredients left over from the last town. Life began to look rosy again after I got in my hotel room with the water running from the tap, and the Resurrection Bitters lining up on the table by the dozen.

'Fake? No, sir. There was two dollars' worth of fluid extract of cinchona and a dime's worth of aniline in that half-gross of bitters. I've gone through towns years after and had folks ask for 'em again.

'I hired a wagon that night and commenced selling the bitters on Main Street. Fisher Hill was a low, malarial town; and a compound hypothetical pneumocardiac anti-scorbutic tonic was just what I diagnosed the crowd as needing. The bitters started off like sweetbreads-on-toast at a vegetarian dinner. I had sold two dozen at fifty cents apiece when I felt somebody pull my coat tail. I knew what that meant; so I climbed down and sneaked a five-dollar bill into the hand of a man with a German silver star on his lapel.

'"Constable," says I, "it's a fine night."

'"Have you got a city license," he asks, "to sell this illegitimate essence of spooju that you flatter by the name of medicine?"

'"I have not," says I. "I didn't know you had a city. If I can find it tomorrow I'll take one out if it's necessary."

'"I'll have to close you up till you do," says the constable.

'I quit selling and went back to the hotel. I was talking to the landlord about it.

'"Oh, you won't stand no show in Fisher Hill," says he. "Dr Hoskins, the only doctor here, is a brother-in-law of the Mayor, and they won't allow no fake doctor to practice in town."

'"I don't practice medicine," says I, "I've got a State pedlar's license, and I take out a city one whenever they demand it."

'I went to the Mayor's office the next morning and they told me he hadn't showed up yet. They didn't know when he'd be down. So Doc Waugh-hoo hunches down again in a hotel chair and lights a jimpson-weed regalia, and waits.

'By and by a young man in a neck-tie slips into the chair next to mine and asks the time.

'"Half-past ten," says I, "and you are Andy Tucker. I've seen you work. Wasn't it you that put up the Great Cupid Combination package on the Southern States? Let's see, it was a Chilian diamond engagement ring, a wedding-ring, a potato masher, a bottle of soothing syrup and Dorothy Vernon—all for fifty cents."

'Andy was pleased to hear that I remembered him. He was a good street man; and he was more than that—he respected his profession, and he was satisfied with 300 per cent profit. He had plenty of offers to go into the illegitimate drug and garden seed business; but he was never to be tempted off the straight path.

'I wanted a partner; so Andy and me agreed to go out together. I told him about the situation in Fisher Hill and how finances was low on account of the local mixture of politics and jalap. Andy had just got in on the train that morning. He was pretty low himself, and was going to canvass the town for a few dollars to build a battleship by popular subscription at Eureka Springs. So we went out and sat on the porch and talked it over.

'The next morning at eleven o'clock, when I was sitting there alone, an Uncle Tom shuffles into the hotel and asked for the doctor to come and see Judge Banks, who, it seems, was the mayor and a mighty sick man.

'"I'm no doctor," says I, "Why don't you go and get the doctor?"

'"Boss," says he, "Doc Hoskins am done gone twenty miles in de country to see some sick persons. He's de only doctor in de town, and Massa Banks am powerful bad off. He sent me to ax you to please, suh, come."

'"As man to man," says I, "I'll go and look him over." So I put a bottle of Resurrection Bitters in my pocket and goes up on the hill to the Mayor's mansion, the finest house in town, with a mansard roof and two cast-iron dogs on the lawn.

'This Mayor Banks was in bed all but his whiskers and feet. He was making internal noises that would have had everybody in San Francisco hiking for the parks. A young man was standing by the bed holding a cup of water.

'"Doc," says the Mayor, "I'm awful sick. I'm about to die. Can't you do nothing for me?"

'"Mr Mayor," says I, "I'm not a regular pre-ordained disciple of S. Q. Lapius. I never took a course in a medical college," says I, "I've just come as a fellow-man to see if I could be of assistance."

'"I'm deeply obliged," says he. "Doc Waugh-hoo, this is my nephew, Mr Biddle. He has tried to alleviate my distress, but without success. Oh, Lordy! Ow-ow-ow!!" he sings out.

'I nods at Mr Biddle and sets down by the bed and feels the Mayor's pulse. "Let me see your liver—your tongue, I mean," says I. Then I turns up the lids of his eyes and looks closely at the pupils of 'em.

'"How long have you been sick?" I asks.

'"I was taken down—ow-ouch—last night," says the Mayor. "Gimme something for it, doc, won't you?"

'"Mr Fiddle," says I, "raise the window shade a bit, will you?"

'"Biddle," says the young man. "Do you feel like you could eat some ham and eggs, Uncle James?"

'"Mr Mayor," says I, after laying my ear to his right shoulder-blade and listening, "you've got a bad attack of super-inflammation of the right clavicle of the harpsichord!"

'"Good Lord!" says he, with a groan. "Can't you rub something on it, or set it or anything?"

'I picks up my hat and starts for the door.

'"You ain't going, doc?" says the Mayor with a howl, "You ain't going away to leave me to die with this—superfluity of the clapboards, are you?"

'"Common humanity, Dr Whoa-ha," says Mr Biddle, "ought to prevent your deserting a fellow-human in distress."

'"Dr Waugh-hoo, when you get through ploughing," says I. And then I walks back to the bed and throws back my long hair.

'"Mr Mayor," says I, "there is only one hope for you. Drugs will do you no good. But there is another power higher yet, although drugs are high enough," says I.

'"And what is that?" says he.

'"Scientific demonstrations," says I. "The triumph of mind over sarsaparilla. The belief that there is no pain and sickness except what is produced when we ain't feeling well. Declare yourself in arrears. Demonstrate."

'"What is this paraphernalia you speak of, doc?" says the Mayor. "You ain't a Socialist, are you?"

'"I am speaking," says I, "of the great doctrine of psychic financiering—

of the enlightened school of long-distance, subconscientious treatment of fallacies and meningitis—of that wonderful indoor sport known as personal magnetism."

'"Can you work it, doc?" asks the Mayor.

'"I'm one of the Sole Sanhedrims and Ostensible Hooplas of the Inner Pulpit," says I. "The lame talk and the blind rubber whenever I make a pass at 'em. I am a medium, a coloratura hypnotist and a spirituous control. It was only through me at the recent seances at Ann Arbor that the late president of the Vinegars Bitters Company could revisit the earth to communicate with his sister Jane. You see me peddling medicine on the streets," says I, "to the poor. I don't practice personal magnetism on them. I do not drag it in the dust," says I, "because they haven't got the dust."

'"Will you treat my case?" asks the Mayor.

'"Listen" says I, "I've had a good deal of trouble with medical societies everywhere I've been. I don't practice medicine. But, to save your life, I'll give you the psychic treatment if you'll agree as mayor not to push the license question."

'"Of course I will," says he. "And now get to work, doc, for them pains are coming on again."

'"My fee will be $250.00, cure guaranteed in two treatments," says I.

'"All right," says the Mayor. "I'll pay it. I guess my life's worth that much."

'I sat down by the bed and looked him straight in the eye.

'"Now," says I, "get your mind off the disease. You ain't sick. You haven't got a heart or a clavicle or a funny-bone or a brain or anything. You haven't got any pain. Declare error. Now you feel the pain you didn't have leaving, don't you?"

'"I do feel some little better, doc," says the Mayor, "darned if I don't. Now state a few lies about my not having this swelling in my left side, and I think I could be propped up and have some sausage and buckwheat cakes."

'I made a few passes with my hands.

'"Now," says I, "the inflammation's gone. The right lobe of the perihelion has subsided. You're getting sleepy. You can't hold your eyes open any longer. For the present the disease is checked. Now, you are asleep."

'The Mayor shut his eyes slowly and began to snore.

'"You observe, Mr Tiddle," says I, "the wonders of modern science."

'"Biddle," says he. "When will you give uncle the rest of the treatment, Dr Pooh-pooh?"

'"Waugh-hoo," says I. "I'll come back at eleven tomorrow. When he wakes up give him eight drops of turpentine and three pounds of steak. Good morning."

'The next morning I went back on time. "Well, Mr Riddle," says I, when he opened the bedroom door, "and how is uncle this morning?"

'"He seems much better," says the young man.

'The Mayor's colour and pulse was fine. I gave him another treatment, and he said the last of the pain left him.

'"Now," I says, "You'd better stay in bed for a day or two, and you'll be all right. It's a good thing I happened to be in Fisher Hill, Mr Mayor," says I, "for all the remedies in the cornucopia that the regular schools of medicine use couldn't have saved you. And now that error has flew and pain proved a perjurer, let's allude to a cheerfuller subject—say the fee of $250. No cheques, please; I hate to write my name on the back of a cheque almost as bad as I do on the front."

'"I've got the cash here," says the Mayor, pulling a pocket-book from under his pillow.

'He counts out five fifty-dollar bills and holds 'em in his hand.

'"Bring the receipt," he says to Biddle.

'I signed the receipt and the Mayor handed me the money. I put it in my inside pocket careful.

'"Now do your duty, officer," says the Mayor, grinning much unlike a sick man.

'Mr Biddle lays his hand on my arm.

'"You're under arrest, Dr Waugh-hoo, alias Peters," says he, "for practicing medicine without authority under the State law."

'"Who are you?" I asks.

'"I'll tell you who he is," says Mr Mayor, sitting up in bed. "He's a detective employed by the State Medical Society. He's been following you over five counties. He came to me yesterday and we fixed up this scheme to catch you. I guess you won't be doing any more doctoring round these parts, Mr Faker. What was it you said I had, doc?" the Mayor laughs, "compound—well, it wasn't softening of the brain, I guess, anyway."

'"A detective," says I.

'"Correct," says Biddle. "I'll have to turn you over to the sheriff."

'"Let's see you do it," says I, and I grabs Biddle by the throat and half throws him out of the window, but he pulls a gun and sticks it under my chin, and I stand still. Then he puts handcuffs on me, and takes the money out of my pocket.

'"I witness," says he, "that they're the same bills that you and I marked, Judge Banks. I'll turn them over to the sheriff when we get to his office, and he'll send you a receipt. They'll have to be used as evidence in the case."

'"All right, Mr Biddle," says the Mayor. "And now, Doc Waugh-hoo," he goes on, "why don't you demonstrate? Can't you pull the cork out of your magnetism with your teeth and hocus-pocus them handcuffs off?"

'"Come on, officer," says I, dignified. "I may as well make the best of it." And then I turns to old Banks and rattles my chains.

'"Mr Mayor," says I, "the time will come soon when you'll believe that personal magnetism is a success. And you'll be sure that it succeeded in this case, too."

'And I guess it did.

'When we got nearly to the gate, I says: "We might meet somebody now, Andy. I reckon you better take 'em off, and—' Hey? Why, of course it was Andy Tucker. That was his scheme: and that's how we got the capital to go into business together.'

Ibid.

THE *head of the Department of Economics and Political Science at McGill University, Montreal, described O. Henry as 'an amazing genius', and went on to call him 'one of the greatest masters of modern literature'.*

But then the head of the department was Professor Stephen Leacock, and both phrases equally well describe his own standing in the field of pre-First World War humorous prose.

Both men were prolific writers; O. Henry left some two hundred and seventy short stories, Leacock some thirty books, and the contribution which both men made to humorous prose is commemorated to this day by the presentation of the 'O. Henry Memorial Award Prizes' in the USA and 'The Leacock Medal for Humor' in Canada.

Like Canada's only previous internationally famous humorist, Thomas 'Sam Slick' Haliburton, Leacock was born in England, on the Isle of Wight, but was taken to live on a farm in Canada at the age of 6. His family was poor but his education was paid for by a legacy and Leacock became a classical scholar, a teacher and lecturer, and then a professor at McGill. His university work was important to him, he was furious when he was forced to retire at, to him, the absurdly early age of 65. He was not all that funny in private; he was quick-tempered, easily frustrated and a little vain, but the intelligence he brought to humorous and comic writing, his wide range of subject-matter and the sunniness of his deceptively simple style lifted him above the heads of most of the other funny men of his day.

Sometimes he was able to combine his two careers, as in the following piece about boarding-houses.

Boarding-houses in those days were much more a part of ordinary living than they are today, particularly in North America. Clerks, shop-assistants, actors and actresses, students, commercial travellers, those who were on the lower rungs of the ladder or had dropped off the higher rungs, could seldom afford to rent apartments and lived, temporarily they hoped, in a boarding-house, which every city and town then had in plenty.

To help those unfortunates unfamiliar with life in a boarding-house and about to face it, Professor Leacock compiled a scholarly paper of accepted mathematical principles:

BOARDING-HOUSE GEOMETRY

Definitions and Axioms

All boarding-houses are the same boarding-house.

Boarders in the same boarding-house and on the same flat [floor] are equal to one another.

A single room is one which has no parts and no magnitude.

The landlady of a boarding-house is a parallelogram—that is, an oblong angular figure, which cannot be described, but which is equal to anything.

A wrangle is the disinclination for each other of two boarders that meet together but are not in the same line.

All the other rooms being taken, a single room is said to be a double room.

Postulates and Propositions

A pie may be produced any number of times.

The landlady can be reduced to her lowest terms by a series of propositions.

A bee line may be made from any boarding-house to any other boarding-house.

The clothes of a boarding-house bed, though produced ever so far both ways, will not meet.

Any two meals at a boarding-house are together less than two square meals.

If from the opposite ends of a boarding-house a line be drawn passing through all the rooms in turn, then the stovepipe which warms the boarders will lie within that line.

On the same bill and on the same side of it there should not be two charges for the same thing.

If there be two boarders on the same flat, and the amount of side of the one be equal to the amount of side of the other, each to each, and the wrangle between one boarder and the landlady be equal to the wrangle between the landlady and the other, then shall the weekly bills of the two boarders be equal also, each to each.

For if not, let one bill be the greater.

Then the other bill is less than it might have been—which is absurd.

Stephen Leacock (1869–1944), *Literary Lapses* (1910).

Leacock was something of a satirist but his satire was amiable. He mocked what he disliked in a good-humoured sort of way but he did not hate and lash out.

In this piece he has a little go, in his own way, at that kind of inverted snobbery— already noted by Charles Dickens in the character of Mr Bounderby in Hard

*Times—whereby men who have become rich feel the need to accentuate how deep
were the depths from which they had so valiantly hoisted themselves:*

SELF-MADE MEN

They were both what we commonly called successful business men—men
with well-fed faces, heavy signet rings on fingers like sausages, and broad,
comfortable waistcoats, a yard and a half round the equator. They were
seated opposite each other at a table of a first-class restaurant, and had fallen
into conversation while waiting to give their order to the waiter. Their talk
had drifted back to their early days and how each had made his start in life
when he first struck New York.

'I tell you what, Jones,' one of them was saying, 'I shall never forget my
first few years in this town. By George, it was pretty uphill work! Do you
know, sir, when I first struck this place, I hadn't more than fifteen cents to
my name, hadn't a rag except what I stood up in, and all the place I had to
sleep in—you won't believe it, but it's a gospel fact just the same—was an
empty tar barrel. No, sir,' he went on, leaning back and closing up his eyes
into an expression of infinite experience, 'no, sir, a fellow accustomed to
luxury like you has simply no idea what sleeping out in a tar barrel and all
that kind of thing is like.'

'My dear Robinson,' the other man rejoined briskly 'if you imagine I've
had no experience of hardship of that sort, you never made a bigger mistake
in your life. Why, when I first walked into this town I hadn't a cent, sir, not
a cent, and as for lodging, all the place I had for months and months was
an old piano box up a lane, behind a factory. Talk about hardship, I guess
I had it pretty rough! You take a fellow that's used to a good warm tar
barrel and put him into a piano box for a night or two, and you'll see mighty
soon—'

'My dear fellow,' Robinson broke in with some irritation, 'you merely show
that you don't know what a tar barrel's like. Why, on winter nights, when
you'd be shut in there in your piano box just as snug as you please, I used to
lie awake shivering, with the draught fairly running in at the bunghole at
the back.'

'Draught!' sneered ithe other man, with a provoking laugh, 'draught!
Don't talk to me about draughts. This box I speak of had a whole darned
plank right off it, right on the north side too. I used to sit there studying in
the evenings, and the snow would blow in a foot deep. And yet, sir,' he
continued more quietly, 'though I know you'll not believe it, I don't mind
admitting that some of the happiest days of my life were spent in that same
old box. Ar, those were good old times! Bright, innocent days, I can tell you.
I'd wake up there in the mornings and fairly shout with high spirits. Of
course, you may not be able to stand that kind of life—'

'Not stand it!' cried Robinson fiercely; 'me not stand it! By gad! I'm made
for it. I just wish I had a taste of the old life again for a while. And as for

innocence! Well, I'll bet you you weren't one-tenth as innocent as I was; no, nor one-fifth, nor one-third! What a grand old life it was! You'll swear this is a darned lie and refuse to believe it—but I can remember evenings when I'd have two or three fellows in, and we'd sit round and play pedro by a candle half the night.'

'Two or three!' laughed Jones; 'why, my dear fellow, I've known half a dozen of us to sit down to supper in my piano box, and have a game of pedro afterwards; yes, and charades and forfeits, and every other darned thing. Mighty good suppers they were too! By Jove, Robinson, you fellows round this town who have ruined your digestions with high living, have no notion of the zest with which a man can sit down to a few potato peelings, or a bit of broken pie crust, or—'

'Talk about hard food,' interrupted the other, 'I guess I know all about that. Many's the time I've breakfasted off a little cold porridge that somebody was going to throw away from a back-door, or that I've gone round to a livery stable and begged a little bran mash that they intended for the pigs. I'll venture to say I've eaten more hog's food—'

'Hog's food!' shouted Robinson, striking his fist savagely on the table, 'I tell you hog's food suits me better than—'

He stopped speaking with a sudden grunt of surprise as the waiter appeared with the question:

'What may I bring you for dinner, gentlemen?'

'Dinner!' said Jones, after a moment of silence, 'dinner! Oh, anything, nothing—I never care what I eat—give me a little cold porridge, if you've got it, or a chunk of salt pork—anything you like, it's all the same to me.'

The waiter turned with an impassive face to Robinson.

'You can bring me some of that cold porridge too,' he said, with a defiant look at Jones; 'yesterday's, if you have it, and a few potato peelings and a glass of skim milk.'

There was a pause. Jones sat back in his chair and looked hard across at Robinson. For some moments the two men gazed into each other's eyes with a stern, defiant intensity. Then Robinson turned slowly round in his seat and beckoned to the waiter, who was moving off with the muttered order on his lips.

'Here, waiter,' he said with a savage scowl, 'I guess I'll change that order a little. Instead of that cold porridge I'll take—um, yes—a little hot partridge. And you might as well bring me an oyster or two on the half shell, and a mouthful of soup (mock-turtle, consommé, anything), and perhaps you might fetch along a dab of fish, and a little peck of Stilton, and a grape, or a walnut.'

The waiter turned to Jones.

'I guess I'll take the same,' he said simply, 'and added, and you might bring a quart of champagne at the same time.'

And nowadays, when Jones and Robinson meet, the memory of the tar barrel and the piano box is buried as far out of sight as a home for the blind under a landslide.

Ibid.

Leacock's best-known pieces are probably his literary parodies of the stereotyped plots and characters of the popular novels of his day. They show an aspect of humour at which Leacock excelled: cheerful nonsense.

Jack Benny recalled hearing laughter coming from Groucho Marx's dressing-room and finding his fellow comic reading a book of Leacock stories. One can see Leacock's parodies appealing to Groucho Marx as both men took pleasure in creating a kind of semi-logical preposterousness, but Jack Benny, a very different kind of comedian, was an equally enthusiastic admirer.

Here is Leacock's version of one of those romantic Silver Fork novels about aristocratic goings-on, where young love, with the help of a thumping coincidence or two, triumphs over villainy.

Early in the story occurs one of the two best-known lines in humorous prose; the one where Lord Ronald flings himself upon a horse and gallops off:

GERTRUDE THE GOVERNESS; OR SIMPLE SEVENTEEN

Synopsis of Previous Chapters:
There are no Previous Chapters.

It was a wild and stormy night on the West Coast of Scotland. This, however, is immaterial to the present story, as the scene is not laid in the West of Scotland. For the matter of that the weather was just as bad on the East Coast of Ireland.

But the scene of this narrative is laid in the South of England and takes place in and around Knotacentinum Towers (pronounced as if written No-sham Taws), the seat of Lord Knotacent (pronounced as if written Nosh).

But it is not necessary to pronounce either of these names in reading them.

Nosham Taws was a typical English home. The main part of the house was an Elizabethan structure of warm red brick, while the elder portion, of which the Earl was inordinately proud, still showed the outlines of a Norman Keep, to which had been added a Lancastrian Jail and a Plantagenet Orphan Asylum. From the house in all directions stretched magnificent woodland and park with oaks and elms of immemorial antiquity, while nearer the house stood raspberry bushes and geranium plants which had been set out by the Crusaders.

About the grand old mansion the air was loud with the chirping of thrushes, the cawing of partridges and the clear sweet note of the rook, while deer, antelope, and other quadrupeds strutted about the lawn so tame as to eat off the sun-dial. In fact the place was a regular menagerie.

From the house downwards through the park stretched a beautiful broad avenue laid out by Henry VII.

Lord Nosh stood upon the hearthrug of the library. Trained diplomat and statesman as he was, his stern aristocratic face was upside down with fury.

'Boy,' he said, 'you shall marry this girl or I disinherit you. You are no son of mine.'

Young Lord Ronald, erect before him, flung back a glance as defiant as his own.

'I defy you,' he said. 'Henceforth you are no father of mine. I will get another. I will marry none but a woman I can love. This girl that we have never seen—'

'Fool,' said the Earl, 'would you cast aside our estate and name of a thousand years? The girl, I am told, is beautiful; her aunt is willing; they are French; pah! they understand such things in France.'

'But your reason—'

'I give no reason,' said the Earl. 'Listen, Ronald, I give you one month. For that time you remain here. If at the end of it you refuse me, I cut you off with a shilling.'

Lord Ronald said nothing; he flung himself from the room, flung himself upon his horse and rode madly off in all directions.

As the door of the library closed upon Ronald the Earl sank into a chair. His face changed. It was no longer that of a haughty nobleman, but of the hunted criminal. 'He must marry the girl,' he muttered. 'Soon she will know all. Tutchemoff has escaped from Siberia. He knows and will tell. The whole of the mines pass to her, this property with it, and I—but enough.' He rose, walked to the sideboard, drained a dipper full of gin and bitters, and became again a high-bred English gentleman.

It was at this moment that a high dogcart, driven by a groom in the livery of Earl Nosh, might have been seen entering the avenue of Nosh Taws. Beside him sat a young girl, scarce more than a child, in fact not nearly so big as the groom.

The apple-pie hat which she wore, surmounted with black willow plumes, concealed from view a face so face-like in its appearance as to be positively facial.

It was—need we say it—Gertrude the Governess, who was this day to enter upon her duties at Nosham Taws.

At the same time that the dogcart entered the avenue at one end there might have been seen riding down it from the other a tall young man, whose long, aristocratic face proclaimed his birth and who was mounted upon a horse with a face even longer than his own.

And who is this tall young man who draws nearer to Gertrude with every revolution of the horse? Ah, who indeed? Ah, who, who? I wonder if any of my readers could guess that this was none other than Lord Ronald.

The two were destined to meet. Nearer and nearer they came. And then still nearer. Then for one brief moment they met. As they passed, Gertrude raised her head and directed towards the young nobleman two eyes so eye-like in their expression as to be absolutely circular, while Lord Ronald directed towards the occupant of the dogcart a gaze so gaze-like that nothing but a gazelle, or a gas-pipe, could have emulated its intensity.

Was this the dawn of love? Wait and see. Do not spoil the story.

Let us speak of Gertrude. Gertrude DeMongmorenci McFiggin had known neither father nor mother. They had both died years before she was born. Of her mother she knew nothing, save that she was French, was extremely beautiful, and that all her ancestors and even her business acquaintances had perished in the French Revolution.

Yet Gertrude cherished the memory of her parents. On her breast she wore a locket in which was enshrined a miniature of her mother, while down her neck inside at the back hung a daguerreotype of her father. She carried a portrait of her grandmother up her sleeve and had pictures of her cousins tucked inside her boot, while beneath her—but enough, quite enough.

Of her father Gertrude knew even less. That he was a high-born English gentleman who had lived as a wanderer in many lands, this was all she knew. His only legacy to Gertrude had been a Russian grammar, a Roumanian phrase-book, a theodolite, and a work on mining engineering.

From her earliest infancy Gertrude had been brought up by her aunt. Her aunt had carefully instructed her in Christian principles. She had also taught her Mohammedanism to make sure.

When Gertrude was seventeen her aunt had died of hydrophobia.

The circumstances were mysterious. There had called upon her that day a strange bearded man in the costume of the Russians. After he had left, Gertrude had found her aunt in a syncope from which she passed into an apostrophe and never recovered.

To avoid scandal it was called hydrophobia. Gertrude was thus thrown upon the world. What to do? That was the problem that confronted her.

It was while musing one day upon her fate that Gertrude's eye was struck with an advertisement.

'Wanted a governess; must possess a knowledge of French, Italian, Russian, and Roumanian, Music, and Mining Engineering. Salary, £1, 4 shillings and 4 pence half-penny per annum. Apply between half-past eleven and twenty-five minutes to twelve at 41 A Decimal Six, Belgravia Terrace. The Countess of Nosh.'

Gertrude was a girl of great natural quickness of apprehension, and she had not pondered over this announcement more than half an hour before she was struck with the extraordinary coincidence between the list of items desired and the things that she herself knew.

She duly presented herself at Belgrave Terrace before the Countess, who advanced to meet her with a charm which at once placed the girl at her ease.

'You are proficient in French?' she asked.

'Oh, oui,' said Gertrude modestly.

'And Italian?' continued the Countess.

'*Oh, si,*' said Gertrude.

'And German?' said the Countess in delight.

'*Ah, ja,*' said Gertrude.

'And Russian?'

'*Yaw.*'

'And Roumanian?'

'*Jep.*'

Amazed at the girl's extraordinary proficiency in modern languages, the Countess looked at her narrowly. Where had she seen those lineaments before? She passed her hand over her brow in thought, and spat on the floor, but no, the face baffled her.

'Enough,' she said, 'I engage you on the spot; tomorrow you go down to Nosham Taws and begin teaching the children. I must add that in addition you will be expected to aid the Earl with his Russian correspondence. He has large mining interests in Tschminsk.'

Tschminsk! why did the simple word reverberate upon Gertrude's ears? Why? Because it was the name written in her father's hand on the title page of his book on mining. What mystery was here?

It was on the following day that Gertrude had driven up the avenue.

She descended from the dogcart, passed through a phalanx of liveried servants drawn up seven-deep, to each of whom she gave a sovereign as she passed and entered Nosham Taws.

'Welcome,' said the Countess, as she aided Gertrude to carry her trunk upstairs.

The girl presently descended and was ushered into the library, where she was presented to the Earl. As soon as the Earl's eye fell upon the face of the new governess he started visibly. Where had he seen those lineaments? Where was it? At the races? or the theatre? on a bus? No. Some subtler thread of memory was stirring in his mind. He strode hastily to the sideboard, drained a dipper and a half of brandy, and became again the perfect English gentleman.

While Gertrude has gone to the nursery to make the acquaintance of the two tiny golden-haired children who are to be her charges, let us say something here of the Earl and his son.

Lord Nosh was the perfect type of the English nobleman and statesman. The years he had spent in the diplomatic service at Constantinople, St Petersburg, and Salt Lake City had given to him a peculiar finesse and noblesse, while his long residence at St Helena, Pitcairn Island, and Hamilton, Ontario, had rendered him impervious to external impressions. As deputy paymaster of the militia of the country he had seen something of the sterner side of the military life, while his heriditary office of Groom of the Sunday Breeches had brought him into contact with Royalty itself. His passion for outdoor sports endeared him to his tenants. A keen sportsman, he excelled in foxhunting, doghunting, pig-killing, bat-catching and the pastimes of his class.

In this latter respect Ronald took after his father. From the start the lad had shown the greatest promise. At Eton he had made a splendid showing at battledore and shuttlecock, and at Cambridge had been first in his class at needlework. Already his name was being whispered in connection with the All England ping-pong championship, a triumph which would undoubtedly carry with it a seat in Parliament.

Thus was Gertrude the Governess installed at Nosham Taws.

The days and the weeks sped past.

The simple charm of the beautiful orphan girl attracted all hearts. Her two little pupils became her slaves. 'Me loves oo,' the little Rasehellfrida would say, leaning her golden head in Gertrude's lap. Even the servants loved her. The head gardener would bring a bouquet of beautiful roses to her room before she was up, the second gardener a bunch of early cauliflowers, the third a spray of late asparagus, and even the tenth and eleventh a sprig of mangel-wurzel or an armful of hay. Her room was full of gardeners all the time, while at evening the aged butler, touched at the friendless girl's lone-liness, would tap softly at her door to bring her a rye whisky and seltzer or a box of Pittsburg Stogies. Even the dumb creatures seemed to admire her in their own dumb way. The dumb rooks settled on her shoulder and every dumb dog around the place followed her.

And Ronald! Ah, Ronald! Yes, indeed! They had met. They had spoken.

'What a dull morning,' Gertrude had said. '*Quel triste matin! Was für ein allerverdamnter Tag!*'

'Beastly,' Ronald had answered.

'Beastly!' The word rang in Gertrude's ear all day.

After that they were constantly together. They played tennis and ping-pong, and in the evening, in accordance with the stiff routine of the place, they sat down with the Earl and Countess to twenty-five-cent poker, and later still they sat together on the verandah and watched the moon sweeping in great circles around the horizon.

It was not long before Gertrude realized that Lord Ronald felt towards her a warmer feeling than that of mere ping-pong. At times in her presence he would fall, especially after dinner, into a fit of profound subtraction.

Once at night, when Gertrude withdrew to her chamber and before seeking her pillow, prepared to retire as a preliminary to disrobing—in other words, before going to bed, she flung wide the casement (opened the window) and perceived (saw) the face of Lord Ronald. He was sitting on a thorn bush beneath her, and his upturned face wore an expression of agonized pallor.

Meantime the days passed. Life at the Taws moved in the ordinary routine of a great English household. At 7 a gong sounded for rising, at 8 a horn blew for breakfast, at 8.30 a whistle sounded for prayers, at 1 a flag was run up at half-mast for lunch, at 4 a gun was fired for afternoon tea, at 9 a bell sounded for dressing, at 9.15 a second bell for going on dressing, while at 9.30 a rocket was sent up to indicate that dinner was ready. At midnight dinner was over, and at 1 a.m. the tolling of a bell summoned the domestics to evening prayers.

Meanwhile the month allotted by the Earl to Lord Ronald was passing away. It was already July 15, then within a day or two it was July 17, and, almost immediately afterwards, July 18.

At times the Earl, passing Ronald in the hall, would say sternly, 'Remember, boy, your consent, or I disinherit you.'

And what were the Earl's thoughts of Gertrude? Here was the one drop of bitterness in the girl's cup of happiness. For some reason that she could not divine the Earl showed signs of marked antipathy.

Once as she passed the door of the library he threw a bootjack at her. On another occasion at lunch alone with her he struck her savagely across the face with a sausage.

It was her duty to translate to the Earl his Russian correspondence. She sought it in vain for the mystery. One day a Russian telegram was handed to the Earl. Gertrude translated it to him aloud.

'Tutchemoff went to the woman. She is dead.'

On hearing this the Earl became livid with fury, in fact this was the day that he struck her with the sausage.

Then one day while the Earl was absent on a bat hunt, Gertrude, who was turning over his correspondence, with that sweet feminine instinct of interest that rose superior to ill-treatment, suddenly found the key to the mystery.

Lord Nosh was not the right owner of the Taws. His distant cousin of the older line, the true heir, had died in a Russian prison to which the machinations of the Earl, while Ambassador at Tschminsk, had consigned him. The daughter of this cousin was the true owner of Nosham Taws.

The family story, save only that the documents before her withheld the name of the rightful heir, lay bare to Gertrude's eye.

Strange is the heart of a woman. Did Gertrude turn from the Earl with spurning? No. Her own sad fate had taught her sympathy.

Yet still the mystery remained! Why did the Earl start perceptibly each time that he looked into her face? Sometimes he started as much as four centimetres, so that one could distinctly see him do it. On such occasions he would hastily drain a dipper of rum and vichy water and become once again the correct English gentleman.

The denouement came swiftly. Gertrude never forgot it.

It was the night of the great ball at Nosham Taws. The whole neighbourhood was invited. How Gertrude's heart had beat with anticipation, and with what trepidation she had overhauled her scant wardrobe in order to appear not unworthy in Lord Ronald's eyes. Her resources were poor indeed, yet the inborn genius for dress that she inherited from her French mother stood her in good stead. She twined a single rose in her hair and contrived herself a dress out of a few old newspapers and the inside of an umbrella that would have graced a court. Round her waist she bound a single braid of bagstring, while a piece of old lace that had been her mother's was suspended to her ear by a thread.

Gertrude was the cynosure of all eyes. Floating to the strains of the music she presented a picture of bright girlish innocence that no one could see undisenraptured.

The ball was at its height. It was away up!

Ronald stood with Gertrude in the shrubbery. They looked into one another's eyes.

'Gertrude,' he said, 'I love you.'

Simple words, and yet they thrilled every fibre in the girl's costume.

'Ronald!' she said, and cast herself about his neck.

At this moment the Earl appeared standing beside them in the moonlight. His stern face was distorted with indignation.

'So!' he said, turning to Ronald, 'it appears that you have chosen!'

'I have,' said Ronald with hauteur.

'You prefer to marry this penniless girl rather than the heiress I have selected for you?'

'Yes,' said Ronald.

'Be it so,' said the Earl draining a dipper of gin which he carried. 'Then I disinherit you. Leave this place, and never return to it.'

'Come, Gertrude,' said Ronald tenderly, 'let us flee together.'

Gertrude stood before them. The rose had fallen from her head. The lace had fallen from her ear and the bagstring had come undone from her waist. Her newspapers were crumpled beyond recognition. But dishevelled and illegible as she was, she was still mistress of herself.

'Never,' she said firmly. 'Ronald, you shall never make this sacrifice for me.' Then to the Earl, in tones of ice, 'There is a pride, sir, as great even as yours. The daughter of Metschnikoff McFiggin need crave a boon from no one.'

With that she hauled from her bosom the daguerreotype of her father and pressed it to her lips.

The Earl started as if shot. 'That name!' he cried, 'that face! that photograph! stop!'

There! There is no need to finish; my readers have long since divined it. Gertrude was the heiress.

The lovers fell into one another's arms, The Earl's proud face relaxed. 'God bless you,' he said. The Countess and the guests came pouring out upon the lawn. The breaking day illuminated a scene of gay congratulations.

Gertrude and Ronald were wed. Their happiness was complete. Need we say more? Yes, only this. The Earl was killed in the hunting-field a few days after. The Countess was struck by lightning. The two children fell down a well. Thus the happiness of Gertrude and Ronald was complete.

Nonsense Novels (1911).

THE *English theatre has been fortunate down the centuries in having an Irish writer of wit arrive on the scene just when English drama was about to droop into the mud and, like a clothes-prop, push it back up again: Farquhar at the end of the seventeenth century, Goldsmith and Sheridan in the eighteenth, Oscar Wilde and Bernard Shaw at the end of the nineteenth.*

George Bernard Shaw's first successes were in prose. As a young man he wrote five novels (only one eventually printed), political pamphlets for the Fabian Society and bits and pieces of literary and art criticism for various journals. Then in 1888, when he was 32, he was appointed music critic of The Star, *a regular job, at two guineas a week. Shaw, who knew a great deal about music, adopted the pseudonym 'Corno di Bassetto' and set about standing criticism on its ear.*

Up to that time criticism of music and the other arts had been ponderous, and deeply respectful of its subject. Shaw's style was irreverent, witty, full of his own personality, and frequently very funny. The musical establishment was infuriated but Shaw had arrived at a time when wit and amusing scepticism were once again becoming socially acceptable to readers, and he began to make his name.

Over the Christmas period of 1889 Shaw needed a rest. If only from singers of carols:

. . . to hear *Venite adoremus*, more generally known as Ow, cam let Haz adore Im, welling forth from a cornet (English pitch), a saxhorn (Society of Arts pitch, or thereabouts), and a trombone (French pitch), is the sort of things that breaks my peace and destroys my good will towards men . . .

So he decided to go away for Christmas to Broadstairs. His account of a seaside holiday in late December must have bemused his Star *readers who were probably expecting something like a review of the Christmas Eve Carol Service in St John's, Smith Square, but Shaw was quite happy to criticize anything.*

The piece ends with an early glimpse of that self-mocking stance of arrogance which Shaw later used devastatingly, partly one suspects to amuse himself but mostly to disconcert his readers:

Obviously the thing to do was to escape from the magnetic atmosphere of London, and slow down in some empty-headed place where I should be thoroughly bored. Somebody suggested Broadstairs. I had always supposed Broadstairs to be a show place at Wapping; but I found that it was half-way between Margate and Ramsgate, in neither of which famous watering-places had I ever set foot.

Let no man henceforth ever trifle with Fate so far as actually to seek boredom. Before I was ten minutes here, I was bored beyond description. The air of the place is infernal. In it I hurry about like a mouse suffocating in oxygen. The people here call it 'ozone' and consider it splendid; but there is a visible crust over them, a sort of dull terra-cotta surface which they pretend to regard as a sign of robust health. As I consume in the ozone, this terrible limekiln crust is forming on me too; and they congratulate me already on 'looking quite different'. As a matter of fact I can do nothing but eat; my brain refuses its accustomed work. The place smells as if someone had spilt a bottle of iodine over it. The sea is absolutely dirtier than the Thames under Blackfriars Bridge; and the cold is hideous. I have not come across a grave-yard yet; and I have no doubt that sepulture is unnecessary, as the houses are perfect refrigerating chambers, capable of preserving a corpse to the remotest posterity.

I am staying in Nuckell's Place; and they tell me that Miss Nuckell was the original of Betsy Trotwood in *David Copperfield*, and that the strip of green outside is that from which she used to chase the donkeys. A house down to the left is called Bleak House; and I can only say that if it is any bleaker than my bedroom, it must be a nonpareil freezer. But all this Dickens-mania is only hallucination induced by the ozone. This morning a resident said to me, 'Do you see that weather-beaten old salt coming along?' 'Yes,' I replied; 'and if you will excuse my anticipating your reply, I may say that I have no doubt that he is the original of Captain Cuttle. But, my dear madam, I myself am Corno di Bassetto; and in future Broadstairs anecdotage will begin to revolve round Me.'

'Corno di Bassetto' (George Bernard Shaw) (1856–1950), *The Star* (27 Dec. 1889).

In *1895 Shaw was lured away from* The Star *by Frank Harris to be drama critic of* The Saturday Review, *the leading literary magazine, for six pounds per week. This came as a great relief to the makers of music and it was now the turn of the actors and playwrights to suffer. For them to get bad but dignified reviews was one thing but when the reviews were not only unfavourable but funny they found it mighty offensive: James Barrie said to Shaw 'You ought to be roasted alive, not that even well-cooked you would be to my taste.' Arthur Pinero ended letters to Shaw with 'Yours, with detestation.'*

There was much in the drama of the nineties which Shaw detested: 'society' comedies, which he described as 'a tailor's advertisement making sentimental remarks to a milliner's advertisement in the middle of an upholsterer's and deco-rator's advertisement'; flashy melodramas; productions of Shakespeare with the text truncated to leave time for massive stage effects and virtuoso performances by the great actor-managers.

Shaw had no time for the kind of production in which, as in many a modern Hollywood television or film production, text and style are mainly concerned with showing off the star performer to best advantage.

In 1895 Mr Johnston Forbes Robertson, the ascetic, fine-featured, and highly successful actor-manager, gave London his Romeo:

Unless an actor is capable of a really terrible explosion of rage, he had better let Romeo alone. Unfortunately, the 'fire-eyed fury' before which Tybalt falls lies outside the gentlemanly limits of Mr Forbes Robertson's stage instinct; and it may be that his skill as an actor is not equal to the task of working-up the audience to the point at which they will imagine an explosion which cannot, of course, be real. At all events the duel scene has none of the murderous excitement which is the whole dramatic point of it: it is tamed down to a mere formal pretext for the banishment of Romeo. Mr Forbes Robertson has evidently no sympathy with Shakespeare's love of a shindy: you see his love of law and order coming out in his stage management of the fighting scenes. Nobody is allowed to enjoy the scrimmage: Capulet and Montague are silenced; and the spectators of the duel are women—I should say ladies—who look intensely shocked to see gentlemen of position so grossly forgetting themselves. Mr Forbes Robertson himself fights with unconcealed repugnance: he makes you feel that to do it in that disorderly way, without seconds, without a doctor, shewing temper about it, and actually calling his adversary names, jars unspeakably on him. Far otherwise have we seen him as Orlando wrestling with Charles. But there the contest was in the presence of a court, with measured ground and due formality—under Queensberry rules, so to speak. For the rest, Mr Forbes Robertson is very handsome, very well dressed, very perfectly behaved. His assortment of tones, of gestures, of facial expressions, of attitudes, are limited to half a dozen apiece; but they are carefully selected and all of the best. The arrangements in the last scene are exceedingly nice: the tomb of the Capulets is beautifully kept, well lighted, and conveniently accessible by a couple of broad steps—quite like a new cathedral chapel. Indeed, when Romeo, contemplating the bier of Juliet (which reflected the utmost credit on the undertaker), said:

> I still will stay with thee,
> And never from this palace of dim night
> Depart again,

I felt that the sacrifice he was making in doing without a proper funeral was greatly softened. Romeo was a gentleman to the last. He laid out Paris after killing him as carefully as if he were folding up his best suit of clothes. One remembers Irving, a dim figure dragging a horrible burden down through the gloom 'into the rotten jaws of death', and reflects on the differences of imaginative temperament that underlie the differences of acting and stage-managing.

The Saturday Review (1895).

During the nineties various bodies were lobbying for a tightening of the laws controlling dramatic productions. Stronger censorship in the theatre was being called for. This was anathema to Shaw, who was trying to persuade playwrights and playgoers to concern themselves with drama which dealt with ideas; he wanted the theatre to be concerned with modern dilemmas.

He happened upon a cry of moral outrage made by the National Vigilance Society about a music-hall performance called 'Living Pictures', which featured young ladies in simulated nudity posing in tableaux representing famous paintings.

Shaw decided to take a look:

I have been to see the Living Pictures at the Palace Theatre. The moment Lady Henry Somerset called public attention to the fact that they were obnoxious to the National Vigilance Association, I resolved to try whether they would offend me. But this, like many other good resolutions of mine, remained unfulfilled until I was reminded of it by the address recently delivered by Mr William Alexander Coote, the secretary of the Association, to the Church and Stage Guild, as reported verbatim in that excellent little paper the Church Reformer. In this address, Mr Coote said that he considered the Living Pictures 'the ideal form of indecency'. I at first supposed this to mean an ideally desirable form of indecency; but later on I found Mr Coote denouncing the pictures as 'shameful productions, deserving the condemnation of all right-thinking people'. That cured my procrastination, and incidentally brought five shillings into the till of the Palace Theatre. For I hurried off to see the Living Pictures at once, not because I wanted to wallow in indecency—no man in his senses would go to a public theatre with that object even in the most abandoned condition of public taste, privacy being a necessary condition of thorough-going indecency—but because, as a critic, I at once perceived that Mr Coote had placed before the public an issue of considerable moment: namely, whether Mr Coote's opinion is worth anything or not. For Mr Coote is a person of real importance, active, useful, convinced, thoroughly respectable, able to point to achievements which we must all admit honorable to him, and backed by an Association strong enough to enable him to bring his convictions to bear effectively on our licensing authorities. But all this is quite compatible with Mr Coote being in artistic matters a most intensely stupid man, and on sexual questions something of a monomaniac.

I sat out the entire list of sixteen Living Pictures. Half a dozen represented naiads, mountain sprites, peris, and Lady Godiva, all practically undraped, and all, except perhaps Lady Godiva, who was posed after a well-known picture by Van Lerius (who should have read Landor's imaginary conversation between Lady Godiva and her husband), very pretty. I need hardly say that the ladies who impersonated the figures in these pictures were not actually braving our climate without any protection. It was only too obvious to a practised art critic's eye that what was presented as flesh was really spun silk. But the illusion produced on the ordinary music-hall frequenter was that of the undraped human figure, exquisitely clean, graceful, and, in striking contrast to many of the completely draped and elaborately dressed ladies who were looking at them, perfectly modest. Many of the younger and poorer girls in the audience must have gone away with a greater respect for their own persons, a greater regard for the virtues of the bath, and a quickened sense of the repulsiveness of that personal slovenliness and gluttony which are the real indecencies of popular life, in addition to the valuable recreation of an escape for a moment into the enchanted land to which

naiads and peris belong. In short, the living pictures are not only works of
art: they are excellent practical sermons; and I urge every father of a family
who cannot afford to send his daughters the round of the picture galleries in
the Haymarket and Bond Street, to take them all (with their brothers) to the
Palace Theatre.

The Saturday Review (1895).

Shaw's most famous piece of dramatic criticism was his review of a production of
Cymbeline, *which he called 'Blaming the Bard'. The article appeared in the autumn
of 1886, just after the pheasant-shooting season had opened.*

*The truth was that Shaw fully recognized the genius of Shakespeare but was
infuriated by the fawning attitude towards the Bard then prevalent. It seemed to
Shaw that it was frequently the wrong aspects of the plays which were praised and
no breath of criticism was allowed of features which were by no means above
criticism, which seemed to him to be a dishonest and unhealthy attitude. So, in the
hope of getting playgoers to begin thinking for themselves, he gave the pot a terrific
stir:*

I confess to a difficulty in feeling civilized just at present. Flying from the
country, where the gentlemen of England are in an ecstasy of chicken-
butchering, I return to town to find the higher wits assembled at a play
three hundred years old, in which the sensation scene exhibits a woman
waking up to find her husband reposing gorily in her arms with his head
cut off.

Pray understand, therefore, that I do not defend Cymbeline. It is for the
most part stagey trash of the lowest melodramatic order, in parts abominably
written, throughout intellectually vulgar, and judged in point of thought
by modern intellectual standards, vulgar, foolish, offensive, indecent, and
exasperating beyond all tolerance. There are moments when one asks despairingly why our stage should ever have been cursed with this 'immortal'
pilferer of other men's stories and ideas, with his monstrous rhetorical fustian,
his unbearable platitudes, his pretentious reduction of the subtlest problems
of life to commonplaces against which a Polytechnic debating club would
revolt, his incredible unsuggestiveness, his sententious combination of ready
reflection with complete intellectual sterility, and his consequent incapacity
for getting out of the depth of even the most ignorant audience, except when
he solemnly says something so transcendently platitudinous that his more
humble-minded hearers cannot bring themselves to believe that so great a
man really meant to talk like their grandmothers. With the single exception
of Homer, there is no eminent writer, not even Sir Walter Scott, whom I can
despise so entirely as I despise Shakespear when I measure my mind against
his.

The Saturday Review (1896).

*After three and a half years as a dramatic critic Shaw bowed out to concentrate on
playwriting, handing over to Max Beerbohm.*

His farewell article, 'Valedictory', was in character:

The English do not know what to think until they are coached laboriously and insistently for years, in the proper and becoming opinion. For ten years past, with an unprecedented pertinacity and obstination, I have been dinning into the public head that I am an extraordinarily witty, brilliant, and clever man. That is now part of the public opinion of England; and no power in heaven or on earth will change it . . .

Then there are the managers. Are *they* grateful? No: they are simply forbearing. Instead of looking up at me as their guide, philosopher, and friend, they regard me merely as the author of a series of weekly outrages on their profession and privacy. Worse than the managers are the Shakespeareans. When I began to write, William was a divinity and a bore. Now he is a fellow-creature; and his plays have reached an unprecedented pitch of popularity. And yet his worshippers overwhelm my name with insult . . .

Still, the gaiety of nations must not be eclipsed. The long string of beautiful ladies who are at present in the square without, awaiting, under the supervision of two gallant policemen, their turn at my bedside, must be reassured when they protest, as they will, that the light of their life will go out if my dramatic articles cease. To each of them I will present the flower left by her predecessor, and assure her that there are as good fish in the sea as ever came out of it. The younger generation is knocking at the door; and as I open it there steps spritely in the incomparable Max.

For the rest, let Max speak for himself. I am off duty for ever, and am going to sleep.   *The Saturday Review* (1898).

———

'THE *incomparable Max' was indeed the younger generation, but he was not so much stepping spritely through Shaw's door as reluctantly sauntering in. He was more interested in literature than drama.*

Max Beerbohm, son of a Lithuanian-born corn merchant, and three-quarters-brother of the actor-manager Herbert Beerbohm Tree (they shared the same father and their mothers were sisters), was 26 when he took over from Shaw. He had already made a reputation as an essayist and caricaturist of unusual elegance and wit in such magazines as the Yellow Book, *and with typical cheek had called his first book, a collection of essays published when he was 23,* The Works of Max Beerbohm.

Max—as everybody called him—was a very different kettle of fish from Shaw. Shaw fizzed with intellectual vigour; there was much that he had to say and a great deal that he wanted to do to change society, and writing came to him easily. Max watched the world from the wings; he found the very act of writing a burden and had no ambitions to better the world—he declared at the age of 23: 'I shall write no more. Already I find myself outmoded. I belong to the Beardsley period. Younger men, with months of activity before them, with fresher schemes and notions, with newer enthusiasms, have pressed forward since then.' 'Months of activity before them' is pure Max Beerbohm.

Yet Max followed the formidable Shaw and wrote brilliant dramatic criticism for the Saturday Review *for twelve years. He then married an American actress and retired again—he was always retiring—and went to live in Rapallo in Italy, returning to England for the two wars, writing essays and parodies in between, and finding a new talent as a broadcaster. In 1939 'the first gentleman of irony' was knighted for services to literature.*

His main concern in the chore of arranging thoughts on paper was 'beauty of expression'. He laboured to achieve an impeccable prose style and at his best he achieved a lightness and enchantment which has rarely been matched.

In the following sympathetic piece, as elegant a humorous literary essay as one could wish to find, he speaks up, as he often did, for the underdog. He muses upon the fate of that unknown clergyman, preserved like a fly in amber in Boswell's Life, *who ventured to pass a comment while the great Samuel Johnson was holding the floor:*

'A CLERGYMAN'

Fragmentary, pale, momentary; almost nothing; glimpsed and gone; as it were, a faint human thrust up, never to reappear, from beneath the rolling waters of Time, he forever haunts my memory and solicits my weak imagination. Nothing is told of him but that once, abruptly, he asked a question, and received an answer.

This was on the afternoon of April 7th, 1778, at Streatham, in the well-appointed house of Mr Thrale. Johnson, on the morning of that day, had entertained Boswell at breakfast in Bolt Court, and invited him to dine at Thrale Hall. The two took coach and arrived early. It seems that Sir John Pringle had asked Boswell to ask Johnson 'what were the best English sermons for style'. In the interval before dinner, accordingly, Boswell reeled off the names of several divines whose prose might or might not win commendation. 'Atterbury?' he suggested. 'JOHNSON: Yes, Sir, one of the best. BOSWELL: Tillotson? JOHNSON: Why, not now. I should not advise any one to imitate Tillotson's style; though I don't know; I should be cautious of censuring anything that has been applauded by so many suffrages.—South is one of the best, if you except his peculiarities, and his violence, and sometimes coarseness of language.—Seed has a very fine style; but he is not very theological. Jortin's sermons are very elegant. Sherlock's style, too, is very elegant, though he has not made it his principal study.—And you may add Smalridge. BOSWELL: I like Ogden's Sermons on Prayer very much, both for neatness of style and subtility of reasoning. JOHNSON: I should like to read all that Ogden has written. BOSWELL: What I want to know is, what sermons afford the best specimen of English pulpit eloquence. JOHNSON: We have no sermons addressed to the passions, that are good for anything; if you mean that kind of eloquence. A CLERGYMAN, whose name I do not recollect: Were not Dodd's sermons addressed to the passions? JOHNSON: They were nothing, Sir, be they addressed to what they may.'

The suddenness of it! Bang!—and the rabbit that had popped from its burrow was no more.

I know not which is the more startling—the debut of the unfortunate clergyman, or the instantaneousness of his end. Why hadn't Boswell told us there was a clergyman present? Well, we may be sure that so careful and acute an artist had some good reason. And I suppose the clergyman was left to take us unawares because just so did he take the company. Had we been told he was there, we might have expected that sooner or later he would join in the conversation. He would have had a place in our minds. We may assume that in the minds of the company around Johnson he had no place. He sat forgotten, overlooked; so that his self-assertion startled every one just as on Boswell's page it startles us. In Johnson's massive and magnetic presence only some very remarkable man, such as Mr Burke, was sharply distinguishable from the rest. Others might, if they had something in them, stand out slightly. This unfortunate clergyman may have had something in him, but I judge that he lacked the gift of seeming as if he had. That deficiency, however, does not account for the horrid fate that befell him. One of Johnson's strongest and most inveterate feelings was his veneration for the Cloth. To any one in Holy Orders he habitually listened with a grave and charming deference. To-day moreover, he was in excellent good humour. He was at the Thrales', where he so loved to be; the day was fine; a fine dinner was in close prospect; and he had had what he always declared to be the sum of human felicity—a ride in a coach. Nor was there in the question put by the clergyman anything likely to enrage him. Dodd was one whom Johnson had befriended in adversity; and it had always been agreed that Dodd in his pulpit was very emotional. What drew the blasting flash must have been not the question itself, but the manner in which it was asked. And I think we can guess what that manner was.

Say the words aloud: 'Were not Dodd's sermons addressed to the passions?' They are words which, if you have any dramatic and histrionic sense *cannot* be said except in a high, thin voice.

You may, from sheer perversity, utter them in a rich and sonorous baritone or bass. But if you do so, they sound utterly unnatural. To make them carry the conviction of human utterance, you have no choice: you must pipe them.

Remember, now, Johnson was very deaf. Even the people whom he knew well, the people to whose voices he was accustomed, had to address him very loudly. It is probable that this unregarded, young, shy clergyman, when at length he suddenly mustered courage to 'cut in', let his high, thin voice soar *too* high, insomuch that it was a kind of scream. On no other hypothesis can

we account for the ferocity with which Johnson turned and rended him.
Johnson didn't, we may be sure, mean to be cruel. The old lion, startled, just
struck out blindly. But the force of paw and claws was not the less lethal.
We have endless testimony to the strength of Johnson's voice; and the very
cadence of those words, 'They were nothing, Sir, be they addressed to what
they may,' convinces me that the old lion's jaws never gave forth a louder
roar. Boswell does not record that there was any further conversation before
the announcement of dinner. Perhaps the whole company had been temporarily deafened. But I am not bothering about them. My heart goes out to
the poor dear clergyman exclusively.

I said a moment ago that he was young and shy; and I admit that I slipped
those epithets in without having justified them to you by due process of
induction. Your quick mind will have already supplied what I omitted. A
man with a high, thin voice, and without power to impress any one with a
sense of his importance, a man so null in effect that even the retentive mind
of Boswell did not retain his very name, would assuredly not be a self-
confident man. Even if he were not naturally shy, social courage would
soon have been sapped in him, and would in time have been destroyed, by
experience. That he had not yet given himself up as a bad job, that he still
had faint wild hopes, I proved by the fact that he did snatch the opportunity
for asking that question. He must, accordingly, have been young. Was he
the curate of the neighbouring church? I think so. It would account for his
having been invited. I see him as he sits there listening to the great Doctor's
pronouncement on Atterbury and those others. He sits on the edge of a chair
in the background. He has colourless eyes, fixed earnestly, and a face almost
as pale as the clerical bands beneath his somewhat receding chin. His forehead is high and narrow, his hair mouse-coloured. His hands are clasped
tight before him, the knuckles standing out sharply. This constriction does
not mean that he is steeling himself to speak. He has no positive intention of
speaking. Very much, nevertheless, is he wishing in the back of his mind
that he could say something—something whereat the great Doctor would
turn on him and say, after a pause for thought, 'Why yes, Sir. That is most
justly observed' or 'Sir, this has never occurred to me. I thank you—' thereby
fixing the observer for ever high in the esteem of all. And now in a flash the
chance presents itself. 'We have,' shouts Johnson, 'no sermons addressed to
the passions, that are good for anything.' I see the curate's frame quiver with
sudden impulse, and his mouth fly open, and—no, I can't bear it, I shut my
eyes and ears. But audible, even so, is something shrill, followed by something
thunderous.

Presently I re-open my eyes. The crimson has not yet faded from that
young face yonder, and slowly down either cheek falls a glistening tear.
Shades of Atterbury and Tillotson! Such weakness shames the Established
Church. What would Jortin and Smalridge have said?—what Seed and
South? And, by the way, who were they, these worthies? It is a solemn

thought that so little is conveyed to us by names which to the palaeo-Georgians conveyed so much. We discern a dim, composite picture of a big man in a big wig and a billowing black gown, with a big congregation beneath him. But we are not anxious to hear what he is saying. We know it is all very elegant. We know it will be printed and be bound in finely-tooled full calf, and no palaeo-Georgian gentleman's library will be complete without it. Literate people in those days were comparatively few; but, bating that, one may say that sermons were as much in request as novels are to-day. I wonder, will mankind continue to be capricious? It is a very solemn thought indeed that no more than a hundred-and-fifty years hence the novelists of our time, with all their moral and political and sociological outlook and influence, will perhaps shine as indistinctly as do those old preachers, with all their elegance, now. 'Yes, Sir,' some great pundit may be telling a disciple at this moment, 'Wells is one of the best. Galsworthy is one of the best, if you except his concern for delicacy of style. Mrs Ward has a very firm grasp of problems but is not very creational.—Caine's books are very edifying. I should like to read all that Caine has written. Miss Corelli, too, is very edifying.—And you may add Upton Sinclair.' 'What I want to know,' says the disciple, 'is, what English novels may be selected as specially enthralling.' The pundit answers: 'We have no novels addressed to the passions that are good for anything, if you mean that kind of enthralment.' And here some poor wretch (whose name the disciple will not remember) inquires: 'Are not Mrs Glyn's novels addressed to the passions?' and is in due form annihilated. Can it be that a time will come when readers of this passage in our pundit's Life will take more interest in the poor nameless wretch than in all the bearers of those great names put together, being no more able or anxious to discriminate between (say) Mrs Ward and Mr Sinclair than we are to set Ogden above Sherlock, or Sherlock above Ogden? It seems impossible. But we must remember that things are not always what they seem.

Every man illustrious in his day, however much he may be gratified by his fame, looks with an eager eye to posterity for a continuance of past favours, and would even live the remainder of his life in obscurity if by so doing he could insure that future generations would preserve a correct attitude towards him forever. This is very natural and human, but, like so many very natural and human things, very silly. Tillotson and the rest need not, after all, be pitied for our neglect of them. They either know nothing about it, or are above such terrene trifles. Let us keep our pity for the seething mass of divines who were not elegantly verbose, and had no fun or glory while they lasted. And let us keep a specially large portion for one whose lot was so much worse than merely undistinguished. If that nameless curate had not been at the Thrales' that day, or, being there, had kept the silence that so well became him, his life would have been drab enough, in all conscience. But at any rate an unpromising career would not have been nipped in the bud. And that is what in fact happened. I'm sure of it. A robust man might

have rallied under the blow. Not so our friend. Those who knew him in
infancy had not expected that he would be reared. Better for him had they
been right. It is well to grow up and be ordained, but not if you are delicate
and very sensitive, and shall happen to annoy the greatest, the most stentorian and roughest of contemporary personages. 'A Clergyman' never held
up his head or smiled again after the brief encounter recorded for us by
Boswell. He sank into a rapid decline. Before the next blossoming of Thrale
Hall's almond trees he was no more. I like to think that he died forgiving
Dr Johnson.

Max Beerbohm (1872–1956), first printed in The Owl (1919).

———————

M AX BEERBOHM *wrote of the great fictional detective Sherlock Holmes, 'I
was at an impressionable age when he burst upon the world; and so he
became part of my life, and will never, I suppose, be utterly dislodged. I cannot
pass through Baker Street, even now, without thinking of him.'*

*The creator of Sherlock Holmes, Arthur Conan Doyle, wrote the first Holmes
story to supplement his small income as a doctor in general practice in Southsea.
The story created little interest in England but* Lippincott's Magazine *in America
commissioned more, the stories were taken up by the* Strand Magazine, *and
became immensely popular. They also became a burden to Conan Doyle who
preferred writing historical romances and adventure stories, so in 1893 he killed
off Holmes by having him fall to his death over the Reichenbach Falls in Switzerland
locked in the embrace of his deadly rival Moriarty. However, popular demand for
the return of Sherlock Holmes was overpowering and Conan Doyle had to resuscitate
the great detective eight years later to solve the mystery of* The Hound of the
Baskervilles.

*In the intervening years Conan Doyle much enjoyed writing about another hero
he had invented for the* Strand Magazine, *Brigadier Gerard. The Brigadier was a
masterly comic invention: a gallant Frenchman fighting against the British in the
Napoleonic Wars; a dandy, a duellist, a petty aristocrat, a man of honour.*

And not a man tortured by feelings of inadequacy:

No doubt you have heard my name mentioned as being the beau-ideal of a
soldier, and that not only by friends and admirers like our fellow-townsfolk,
but also by old officers of the great wars who have shared the fortunes of
those famous campaigns with me. Truth and modesty compel me to say,
however, that this is not so. There are some gifts which I lack—very few, no
doubt—but, still, amid the vast armies of the Emperor there may have been
some who were free from those blemishes which stood between me and
perfection. Of bravery I say nothing. Those who have seen me in the field are
best fitted to speak about that. I have often heard the soldiers discussing
round the camp-fires as to who was the bravest man in the Grand Army.

Some said Murat, and some said Lasalle, and some Ney; but for my own part, when they asked me, I merely shrugged my shoulders and smiled. It would have seemed mere conceit if I had answered that there was no man braver than Brigadier Gerard. At the same time, facts are facts, and a man knows best what his own feelings are.

Arthur Conan Doyle (1859–1930), *The Exploits of Brigadier Gerard* (1896).

Conan Doyle was an imperialist and a patriot, as were most of his readers, and the basic humour of Gerard lay in the Frenchman's ignorance of good old British customs and traditions; but Conan Doyle gave this an extra, ironic twist by having Gerard completely misunderstand what is going on and believe that he is behaving more like an Englishman than the English.

The Brigadier is captured and put in the new jail built on Dartmoor to house French prisoners of war. He escapes, and until his repatriation can be completed is offered hospitality by Lord Rufton at his country house, a normal sort of arrangement then between gentlemen whose countries were at war with each other.

The dashing Frenchman, of course, has no difficulty at all in mastering his host's national sports and beating the Englishmen at their own games:

HOW THE BRIGADIER TRIUMPHED IN ENGLAND

I have told you, my friends, how I triumphed over the English at the fox-hunt when I pursued the animal so fiercely that even the herd of trained dogs was unable to keep up, and alone with my own hand I put him to the sword . . .

I could tell you many stories of English sport, for I saw much of it during the time that I was the guest of Lord Rufton, after the order for my exchange had come to England. There were months before I could be sent back to France, and during that time I stayed with this good Lord Rufton at his beautiful house at High Combe, which is at the northern end of Dartmoor . . .

Ah! what thoughts of sport it brings back to me, the very name of High Combe! I can see it now, the long, low, brick house, warm and ruddy, with white plaster pillars before the door. He was a great sportsman this Lord Rufton, and all who were about him were of the same sort. But you will be pleased to hear that there were few things in which I could not hold my own, and in some I excelled. Beyond the house was a wood in which pheasants were reared, and it was Lord Rufton's joy to kill these birds, which was done by sending in men to drive them out while he and his friends stood outside and shot them as they passed. For my part I was more crafty, for I studied the habits of the birds, and stealing out in the evening I was able to kill a number of them as they roosted in the trees. Hardly a single shot was wasted, but the keeper was attracted by the sound of the firing, and he implored me in his rough English fashion to spare those that were left. That night I was able to place twelve birds as a surprise upon Lord Rufton's supper table, and he laughed until he cried, so overjoyed was he to see them. 'Gad, Gerard, you'll be the death of me yet!' he cried. Often he said the same thing, for at every turn I amazed him by the way in which I entered into the sports of the English.

There is a game called cricket which they play in the summer, and this also I learned. Rudd, the head gardener, was a famous player of cricket, and so was Lord Rufton himself. Before the house was a lawn, and there it was that Rudd taught me the game. It is a brave pastime, a game for soldiers, for each tries to strike the other with the ball, and it is but a small stick with which you may ward it off. Three sticks behind show the spot beyond which you may not retreat. I can tell you that it is no game for children, and I will confess that, in spite of my nine campaigns, I felt myself turn pale when first the ball flashed past me. So swift was it that I had not time to raise my stick to ward it off, but by good fortune it missed me and knocked down the wooden pins which marked the boundary. It was for Rudd then to defend himself and for me to attack. When I was a boy in Gascony I learned to throw both far and straight, so that I made sure that I could hit this gallant Englishman. With a shout I rushed forward and hurled the ball at him. It flew as swift as a bullet towards his ribs, but without a word he swung his staff and the ball rose a surprising distance in the air. Lord Rufton clapped his hands and cheered. Again the ball was brought to me, and again it was for me to throw. This time it flew past his head, and it seemed to me that it was his turn to look pale. But he was a brave man this gardener, and again he faced me. Ah, my friends, the hour of my triumph has come! It was a red waistcoat that he wore, and at this I hurled the ball. You would have said that I was a gunner, not a hussar, for never was so straight an aim. With a despairing cry—the cry of the brave man who is beaten—he fell upon the wooden pegs behind him, and they all rolled upon the ground together. He was cruel, this English milord, and he laughed so that he could not come to the aid of his servant. It was for me, the victor, to rush forwards to embrace this intrepid player, and to raise him to his feet with words of praise, and encouragement, and hope. He was in pain and could not stand erect, yet the honest fellow confessed that there was no accident in my victory. 'He did it a-purpose! He did it a-purpose!' Again and again he said it. Yes, it is a great game this cricket, and I would gladly have ventured upon it again but Lord Rufton and Rudd said that it was late in the season, and so they would play no more . . .

It is pleasant to think that five years afterwards, when Lord Rufton came to Paris after the peace, he was able to assure me that my name was still a famous one in the north of Devonshire for the fine exploits that I had performed. Especially, he said, that they still talked over my boxing match with the Honourable Baldock. It came about in this way. Of an evening many sportsmen would assemble at the house of Lord Rufton, whereby they would drink much wine, make wild bets, and talk of their horses and their foxes. How well I remember those strange creatures. Sir Barrington, Jack Lupton of Barnstaple, Colonel Addison, Johnny Miller, Lord Sadler, and my enemy, the Honourable Baldock. They were of the same stamp all of them, drinkers, madcaps, fighters, gamblers, full of strange caprices and extraordinary whims. Yet they were kindly fellows in their rough fashion, save only this Baldock, a fat man who prided himself on his skill at the box-fight. It was he who, by his laughter against the French because they were ignorant of sport, caused me to challenge him in the very sport at which he excelled. You will say that it was foolish, my friends, but the decanter had passed many times, and the blood of youth ran hot in my veins. I would fight him, this boaster; I would show him that if we had not skill, at least we had courage. Lord Rufton would not allow it. I insisted. The others cheered me on and slapped me on the back. 'No, dash it, Baldock, he's our guest,' said Rufton. 'It's his own doing,' the other answered. 'Look here, Rufton, they can't hurt each other if they wear the mawleys,' cried Lord Sadler. And so it was agreed.

What the mawleys were I did not know; but presently they brought out four great puddings of leather, not unlike a fencing-glove, but larger. With these our hands were covered after we had stripped ourselves of our coats and our waistcoats. Then the table, with the glasses and decanters, was pushed into the corner of the room, and behold us, face to face! Lord Sadler sat in the armchair with a watch in his open hand. 'Time!' said he.

I will confess to you, my friends, that I felt at that moment a tremor such as none of my many duels have ever given me. With sword or pistol I am at home; but here I only understood that I must struggle with this fat Englishman and do what I could, in spite of these great puddings upon my hands, to overcome him. And at the very outset I was disarmed of the best weapon that was left to me. 'Mind, Gerard, no kicking!' said Lord Rufton in my ear. I had only a pair of thin dancing slippers, and yet the man was fat, and a few well-directed kicks might have left me the victor. But there is an etiquette just as there is in fencing, and I refrained. I looked at this Englishman and I wondered how I should attack him. His ears were large and prominent. Could I seize them I might drag him to the ground. I rushed in, but I was betrayed by this flabby glove, and twice I lost my hold. He struck me, but I cared little for his blows, and again I seized him by the ear. He fell, and I rolled upon him and thumped his head upon the ground. How they cheered and laughed, these gallant Englishmen, and how they clapped me on the back!

'Even money on the Frenchman,' cried Lord Sadler.

'He fights foul,' cried the enemy, rubbing his crimson ears. 'He savaged me on the ground.'

'You must take your chance of that,' said Lord Rufton coldly.

'Time,' cried Lord Sadler, and once again we advanced to the assault.

He was flushed, and his small eyes were as vicious as those of a bulldog. There was hatred on his face. For my part I carried myself lightly and gaily. A French gentleman fights, but he does not hate. I drew myself up before him, and I bowed as I have in the duello. There can be grace and courtesy as well as defiance in a bow; I put all three into this one, with a touch of ridicule in the shrug which accompanied it. It was at this moment that he struck me. The room spun round with me. I fell upon my back. But in an instant I was on my feet again and had rushed to a close combat. His ear, his hair, his nose, I seized them each in turn. Once again the mad joy of the battle was in my veins. The old cry of triumph rose to my lips. 'Vive l'Empereur!' I yelled as I drove my head into his stomach. He threw his arm round my neck, and holding me with one hand he struck me with the other. I buried my teeth in his arm, and he shouted with pain. 'Call him off, Rufton!' he screamed. 'Call him off, man! He's worrying me!' They dragged me away from him. Can I ever forget it?—the laughter, the cheering, the congratulations! Even my enemy bore me no ill will, for he shook me by the hand. For my part I embraced him on each cheek.

Five years afterwards I learned from Lord Rufton that my noble bearing upon that evening was still fresh in the memory of my English friends.

Adventures of Gerard (1903).

ANOTHER *steady contributor to the* Strand Magazine *was W. W. Jacobs, who was a clerk in the Post Office Savings Bank until his early short stories were published as a book and earned him enough to encourage him to become a full-time writer.*

Jacobs's stories were mainly about sailors aboard small cargo ships or hanging around the London dock area on shore leave. This was a small, colourful, enclosed world which he knew well as he was born in dockside Wapping and his father was a wharfinger. He also wrote a number of serious tales—including that splendid spine-chiller, The Monkey's Paw—*but it was the humorous short stories about the escapades of old sailormen such as Peter Russet, Sam Small, and Ginger Dick which made his name.*

The docks were guarded by night-watchmen in those days and a dockside night-watchman knew all the seamen and everything that they got up to. What is more he had the whole, long night to tell you all about it:

TRUST MONEY

The night-watchman set his lips and shook his head.

'You can't learn people,' he said firmly; 'it ain't to be done. They all know better than wot you do, and the more iggernerant they are the more they are satisfied with themselves. I once wasted a whole morning telling my missus 'ow to make a steak-pudding, and arter it was done we 'ad to give it to the people next door. She's never forgot it, and to hear 'er talk—if you didn't know her—you'd think it was my fault. The way she twists things round would surprise anybody as wasn't married.'

He gazed meditatively at a passing tug with its string of barges, and shook his head again before continuing:

'Even experience don't learn people. One chap I know used to save 'is money in a little tin money-box. He 'ad 'arf a ounce o' baccy a week and no beer. The box was so full o' sixpences he was thinking of getting another, when his wife's brother lost 'is job and didn't get another till the box was empty.

'You'd ha' thought that would 'ave learned 'im a lesson, but it didn't, and he'd pretty near got another box full when 'is wife 'ad the artfulness to break her leg and 'ad to go to the seaside for a fortnight to get well. He's saving up agin now for wot 'e calls a rainy day. He'll get it all right, and somebody else'll get the money.

'Sailormen never learn anything. If they did they wouldn't be sailormen. They're like children that never grow up. It don't matter where they go ashore with their money, they always go back aboard agin without it.

'I remember one time when old Sam Small was ashore with Peter Russet and Ginger Dick 'aving wot they called a rest; their idea of a rest being spending 'arf the day in bed and the other 'arf leaning up agin the bar of a public-'ouse telling fairytales to the barmaid. They was like three twins for the fust few days, and then Sam wouldn't 'ave nothing more to do with 'em owing to them telling the barmaid at the "Turk's Head"—a very nice gal with yeller 'air and black eyes—that he 'ad got a wife and thirteen children at Melbourne.

'He walked 'ome in front of 'em as if they wasn't there, and when 'e shut the front door he seemed to 'ave the same idea. Ginger noticed it most— being just behind 'im. They 'ad words abut it when they got upstairs, and Sam told 'em plain that he never wanted to see their faces agin; not even if they washed 'em.

'He purtended to be asleep while they was dressing next morning. His eyes was screwed up tight, and it didn't seem as if anything could open 'em, till Ginger said 'e thought he 'ad passed away in 'is sleep and asked Peter to get a pin and make sure. Sam woke up then, and, arter he 'ad finished speaking, Ginger and Peter said they never wanted to see *his* face agin.

'They went off by theirselves, and arter a time Sam got up and went off by 'imself. He didn't see anything of Peter or Ginger at all that day, but from wot the barmaid 'ad to say about 'is grandchildren 'e found they 'ad spent a lot o' time drinking beer and telling more lies at the "Turk's Head".

'He sat up in bed and spoke to 'em about it when they came in that night, but they wouldn't listen to 'im. They said that 'is troubles didn't concern them and they'd be thankful if he'd take 'em somewhere else.

'"We've done with you," ses Ginger.

'"For ever," ses Peter. "And my advice to you, Sam, is to leave off afore you bursts a blood-vessel. Anybody might think the 'ouse was on fire."

'Sam didn't speak to them at all arter that and they didn't speak to 'im, but they 'ad a great deal to say about 'im to each other when 'e was in the room. It was wot Ginger called a nasty subjeck, but they never seemed to get tired of it.

'Sam 'ad made up 'is mind to leave 'em and go off on his own, and then 'e came 'ome one night so full of excitement 'e forgot all about it. He came into the room like a schoolboy and gave 'em such a nice smile they thought he 'ad lost 'is reason. Then he done a little dance all by 'imself in the middle of the room and sat down on 'is bed and laughed.

'"I've come into a forchin," he ses to Peter as the two of 'em stood staring at 'im. "Leastways, I shall to-morrer night."

'Ginger coughed. But not a disagreeable cough, mind you.

'"Come into a forchin?" he ses. "'Ow?"

'Old Sam didn't seem to hear 'im. He sat on 'is bed all rosy with smiles and looking straight at the chest o' drawers as though 'e saw a pile of gold on top of it.

'"And I owe it all to you and Peter, Ginger," he ses, bending down to undo 'is boots. "If you 'adn't been misbe'aved, and carrying on like a couple of bald-faced monkeys purtending to be men, I shouldn't 'ave gone off on my own, and if I 'adn't ha' gone off on my own I shouldn't 'ave met 'em."

'"Met who?" ses Ginger, who was too excited to take any notice of wot he 'ad said about monkeys.

'"Two o' the best," ses Sam; "two gentlemen whose on'y objeck in life is to do good to their fellow-creechers. They told me so theirselves."

'"Did you stand 'em drinks?" ses Peter, catching Ginger's eye.

'"You've got a low mind, Peter," ses Sam, shaking his 'ead; "you ought to be more careful who you go about with. I've 'ad six drinks to-night, or maybe more, and I didn't pay for one of 'em. They wouldn't let me."

'"You don't always try very 'ard," ses Peter, who was beginning to lose his temper.

'"Wot 'ave they got to do with your forchin?" ses Ginger.

'"It's coming through them," ses Sam, "and if you and Peter was diff'rent, if you was on'y 'arf men instead of—of being wot you are, I would get forchins for you too. There's plenty more where mine's coming from."

'"Where's that?" ses Ginger, trying to speak off-hand.

'Sam turned deaf agin, and was just going to get into bed when Ginger stopped 'im gentle-like and turning down the bed-clo'es took out a 'air-brush, an old horse-shoe, a lump o' soap, and a few other things wot 'im and Peter 'ad put there.

'"The 'orse-shoe was for luck, Sam," he ses, with a smile. "P'r'aps it's through that you got your forchin."

'Sam looked at 'im as if he was looking at a dust-bin with a bad smell, and then without a word got into bed and, putting his 'ead on the pillar, shut 'is eyes and went straight off to sleep. Ginger woke up the next morning dreaming that the 'ouse was on fire. The room was full o' smoke, but the moment 'e got 'is eyes open he saw that it was made by Sam, who was sitting up in bed smoking an enormous cigar with a red-and-gold band stuck on it. He purtended not to see that Ginger was looking at 'im, and the airs and graces he see fit to give 'imself with that cigar nearly made Ginger choke. Peter Russet woke up then, and arter he 'ad sniffed and sniffed as if 'e couldn't believe his nose, 'e asked Sam in a nasty voice where he 'ad pinched it from.

'"It was give to me by one o' the gentlemen I was speaking of," ses Sam, knocking the ash off down 'is neck by mistake. "He's got a gold case full of 'em."

'"Gold case?" ses Ginger.

'"With dimonds on it," ses Sam. "He said 'e would 'ave liked to give it to me, on'y it was a birthday present from 'is little boy wot died of whooping-cough."

'Ginger scratched his 'ead, and 'e kept on scratching it till Sam said as 'ow it was vulgar, and asked 'im to go out of the room to do it.

'"But who are they?" ses Peter Russet, arter Ginger 'ad quieted down a bit.

'"Two gentlemen," ses Sam; "two gentlemen wot knows another gentleman when they sees 'im."

'He laid down on 'is back and blew smoke up to the ceiling, until Ginger and Peter sat down on Ginger's bed and tried to swaller their pride and ask him to tell 'em all about it. Ginger tried fust, but he 'adn't swallered enough, and when Sam sat up in bed and told 'im part of wot he thought of 'im, Peter took his side and said that if Ginger 'ad on'y been born without a mouth it 'ud be much better for 'imself and everybody else. He gave Ginger a poke in the ribs with 'is elbow to keep 'im quiet, and said that if anybody deserved to 'ave a forchin given 'im it was Sam Small.

'"One o' the best," he ses, giving Ginger another poke with 'is elbow.

'"We all 'ave our faults, Peter," ses Sam, with a kind smile, "else we should all be angels."

'"There ain't no fat angels," ses Ginger, pushing Peter's elbow away. "They wouldn't look nice. All the angels I've seen in pikchers 'ave got beautiful figgers."

'Peter gave it up then, and arter telling Ginger in a whisper wot a fool 'e was, he picked up 'is trousers off of the floor and began to dress. Neither of 'em took any more notice o' Sam, and arter laying still for a time watching 'em wash and telling Ginger that the soap wouldn't bite 'im he began talking to 'em of 'is own free will.

'He told 'em of a nice, comfortable little pub in a turning off the Mile End Road wot he 'ad found on the evening before. A little pub—clean as a new pin, and as quiet and respectable as a front-parlour. Everybody calling the landlady "Ma", and the landlady calling most of 'em by their Christian names and asking arter their families. There was two poll parrots in cages, with not a bad word between 'em—except once when a man played the cornet out-side—and a canary that almost sang its little 'art out.

'"Wot about the two gentlemen that took a fancy to you?" ses Ginger.

'Sam looked at 'im for a moment as if he was surprised at 'im speaking to 'im.

'"There was on'y one at fust," he ses at last, very slow, "a thin gentleman with a little black moustache, a beautiful white collar, and a silk necktie with a gold pin in it. He was drinking port wine when I went in, and arter looking me up and down, just for a moment, 'e asked me to 'ave one with 'im."

'"Wot for?" ses Ginger.

'"He told me arterwards," ses Sam. "He said as 'ow I was the living image of a cousin of 'is wot 'ad lost his life at sea—saving others. He said at fust he thought I was 'is ghost. There was on'y me and 'im in that bar, and the tears came into his eyes when 'e spoke of 'im."

'"But wot about the forchin, Sam?" ses Ginger, arter waiting a bit. "Wot's the ugly cousin got to do with it?"

'Sam sat up in bed and looked at 'im. Then 'e snapped his lips tight as if 'e was never going to open 'em agin and laid back on the piller.

'"Go on, Sam, old man," ses Peter Russet; "if Ginger had 'arf your looks 'e wouldn't be so bad-tempered. He's got a jealous dispersition. You was just telling us about 'ow the tears came into 'is eyes."

'"We 'ad a long talk," ses Sam, arter looking very 'ard at Ginger, "and arter standing me another glass o' port wine 'e began to tell me all about 'is troubles. He 'ad got hard up through 'elping a friend, and 'e didn't know where to turn for money. He went into that little pub with fourpence ha'penny in 'is pocket and went out with five 'undred pounds."

'"Ow?" ses Peter and Ginger, both speaking at the same time.

'"While 'e was 'aving a fit of the miserables in there and wondering wot 'e was going to do," ses Sam, in a solemn voice, "the door opened and a gentleman came in. A gentleman wot goes about looking for feller-creechers to do good to. That was 'ow the gentleman as was standing me port wine got 'is five 'undred pounds."

'"Did you see it?" ses Ginger, in a nasty voice.

'"I see more than that, Ginger," ses Sam, speaking very low; "I see enough money last night to make the three of us gentlemen for life. And Mr Cooper—that's the gentleman wot 'as it—goes about giving it away. He gave the other gentleman, Mr Jackson by name, five 'undred pounds for trusting 'im. He got talking to 'im and told 'im that a friend of 'is had left 'im a forchin, and as he was a rich man and didn't want it 'e was giving it away. But on'y to people that deserved it, mind yer. And 'e said that the people 'e could trust was them as trusted others."

'"I can't make 'ead or tail of it," ses Ginger.

'"He took a good 'ard look at Mr Jackson," ses Sam, "and then 'e put a thousand pounds into his 'and and told 'im to go for a walk with it while 'e waited for 'im in the pub. When Mr Jackson came back he asked 'im whether *he* could trust 'im, and Mr Jackson, not 'aving any money, trusted 'im with 'is gold watch and chain, two rings, and a tie-pin. When 'e came back he patted 'im on the back and gave 'im five 'undred pounds. Mr Jackson said 'e cried like a child."

"'Cos he 'adn't gone off with the thousand pounds, d'ye mean?" ses Ginger, staring.

"'While he was telling me this," ses Sam to Peter Russet, "who should come in but Mr Cooper 'imself—a short, fat gentleman with blue eyes like a innercent child's and one o' the kindest faces I ever see. It done me good to look at 'im. He was a bit stand-offish at fust, but arter a time we was all 'aving drinks together like brothers. And then Mr Jackson took 'im a bit to one side and whispered to 'im, and I could see plain that 'e was talking about me."

"'Cut it short," ses Ginger, fidgeting.

"'I ain't talking to you," ses Sam. "Ten minutes arterwards *I* was going for a walk with a thousand pounds in my pocket in bank-notes, *and* the gold cigar-case. I couldn't trust '*im* when I came back as I 'ad on'y got four bob in my pocket, but to-night I'm going to meet 'im agin and trust 'im with all I've got. And Mr Jackson told me 'e wouldn't be surprised if I got a thousand pounds. He said Mr Cooper told 'im that he 'ad took a partikler fancy to me."

"'Can't make 'ead or tail of it," ses Ginger, "but mark my words, Sam, there's a catch in it somewhere. Nobody 'ud take a fancy to you unless they was going to get something out of it."

'Sam didn't take no notice of 'im. He got up and dressed 'imself, and when they asked 'im wot he was going to do till evening, he told 'em that was 'is business. Peter Russet and Ginger spent the day together, both of 'em wondering, if Sam did get a forchin, whether they couldn't get one the same way. At last, arter they had 'ad a few pints apiece, they made up their minds to hang about till Sam came 'ome and then follow 'im, unbeknownst, to the pub.

'They didn't wait for 'im in their room 'cos they thought 'e might tumble to it, and he was so late turning up that they began to think 'e wasn't coming 'ome fust arter all. Then about ha'-past six they see 'im come round the corner and go straight into the 'ouse.

'It seemed ages afore he came out agin, and when 'e did they see that he 'ad got 'is best clo'es on and a new cap. They let 'im get a good start, and then follered in a drizzling rain which made the Minories and Whitechapel full of umbrellas that kept getting in between them and Sam, especially one that nearly put Ginger's eye out. It wasn't till he 'ad turned into a quiet street off the Mile End Road that they felt sure of 'im.

'They follered, very careful, and then at last they saw 'im stop at the door of a quiet little pub at the corner of a dark little street. There wasn't a soul about, and, arter stopping a moment to pull 'is cap straight, Sam pushed open the door and stepped inside. Ginger and Peter, arter pinching each other's arms in their excitement, stood in a doorway a little way off and waited.

'"I s'pose he's drinking glasses and glasses o' port wine while we're out 'ere in the wet," ses Ginger, arter about ten minutes.

'"Why don't they make 'aste?" ses Peter Russet. "I believe there's a catch in it somewhere."

'"H'sh!" ses Ginger, all of a sudden.

'They drew back into the doorway and just poked their 'eads out as they saw the pub door open and a man come out. He stood a moment waving his 'and to Sam, who they could see standing near the bar, and then walked off slow down the road.

'"Come on," ses Ginger. "Let's see where he goes."

'They follered as quiet as they could, and then all at once they found themselves going quicker and quicker to keep up with 'im. Twice 'e went round corners, and when they got round they found 'e was ever so far in front.

'"He's been running," ses Ginger. "Come on! He's going off with Sam's money!"

'He started running as 'ard as he could, with Peter just be'ind, and the man in front, wot 'ad begun to run 'imself, left off—and began to walk agin.

'"Wot d'ye want?" he ses, as Ginger caught 'old of 'im, and afore Ginger could answer 'im he gave 'im a fearful bang in the face and a kick in the leg that pretty near broke it.

'Ginger gave two grunts, one for the smack in the face and the other for the kick, and then 'e sailed in at 'im like a madman, and knocked 'im all over the place. His last punch got 'im fair on the chin, and 'e went down in the gutter like a lamb that 'as been pole-axed, and hit 'is 'ead on the kerb.

'"You've killed 'im," ses Peter, staring.

'"Good job, too," ses Ginger, thinking of 'is pore leg. "Come on, let's get Sam's money back."

'Peter looked be'ind 'im, and then, seeing there was nobody about, 'elped Ginger to empty the chap's pockets. In less than a minute they 'ad picked 'im as clean as a bone and was hurrying off, Peter 'olding a watch and chain in his 'and and Ginger stuffing things into 'is pockets and saying that it wasn't robbing to rob a thief. Especially a thief wot kicked.

'They lost their way for a bit, but Ginger didn't mind. He said the more they got lost the 'arder it would be for anybody to find 'em, but they got 'ome at last and, arter shutting the bedroom door careful, emptied out their pockets on to the bed and stood staring at each other.

'"We've got the forchin, Peter," ses Ginger. "Count it agin to make sure."

'"Twenty-seven pounds fourteen shillings and threepence," ses Peter, "two watches and chains—that one is Sam's—"

'"One clasp knife," ses Ginger, "a bit o' lead-pencil, a gold cigar-case made o' something else, and a bundle of imitation bank-notes. That's wot 'e trusted Sam with, I expect, Peter."

'"I wonder 'ow much of the twenty-seven pounds is Sam's?" ses Peter Russet.

'"I forgot that," ses Ginger. "He ought to pay something for that kick on the leg I got, though."

'Peter Russet, wot 'ad seen the leg, nodded. "I wouldn't 'ave 'ad that kick for ten pounds," he ses, in a kind voice. "If you 'ave to lose your leg, Ginger, I wouldn't have 'ad it for fifty."

'Ginger 'ad another look at his leg, and then, to prevent losing it, 'e bathed it with a little cold water and put a bit o' butter on it. Arter which they went out as far as the Town of Ramsgate public-'ouse to drink each other's 'ealths.

'It took 'em a long time, both of 'em being very pleased with each other, but at last, arter the landlord 'ad been holding the door open for 'em till 'is jaws ached, they went back 'ome. They both of 'em thought it was earlier than wot it was, so they was quite surprised when they found Sam 'ad got 'ome before them and gone to bed.

'"Did—did you get the forchin, Sam?" ses Ginger, going over to the wash-stand and sousing 'is face with cold water.

'Sam gave a smile that made 'im look as if he was 'aving a fit.

'"No, Ginger," he ses, very soft. "I remembered your advice, old pal."

'"Advice?" ses Ginger, staring.

'"You said as 'ow there might be a catch in it," ses Sam, "and knowing wot a clever 'ead-piece you've got, Ginger, I thought it over and made up my mind not to trust 'im."

'Peter Russet made a noise that an elephant with the hiccups might ha' been proud of, and then Ginger went over and led 'im across to the wash-stand.

'"You 'old your noise," he ses, pushing Peter's face into the water. "You didn't lose your money arter all, then?" he ses, turning to Sam.

'"No," ses Sam. "At least, not that way, but arter I left the pub to come 'ome and see you and Peter, I—I 'ad a misforchin."

'"Misforchin?" ses Ginger, staring at 'im.

'"I—I 'ad my p-pocket picked," ses Sam, stuttering.

'Peter Russet made another noise afore Ginger could stop 'im, and then they both stood up staring at Sam.

'"A lady asked me the time," ses Sam, shutting his eyes so as 'e couldn't see 'em, "and while I was telling 'er one of 'er pals come up and choked me, and two others helped themselves out o' my pockets."

'Ginger looked at Peter—just in time. Then he looked at Sam again.

'"'Ow much was it?" he ses.

'"Eleven pounds and my watch and chain," ses Sam; "if it wasn't for seven shillings they didn't find, in another pocket, I should be starving. 'Ow long do you think a man could live on seven shillings?"

'"Me or you?" ses Ginger, considering.

'"Me," ses pore Sam.

'"Week or ten days—with care," ses Ginger.

'Sam thanked 'im, but not very loud, and arter saying 'e didn't care wot become of 'im and he didn't suppose 'is pals did neither, he punched 'is piller as if it was somebody 'e didn't like and laid down and shut 'is eyes.

'He was up fust next morning counting 'is seven shillings over and over agin, and Peter and Ginger purtending not to notice it. They didn't see 'im agin till night-time 'cos, when Peter spoke to Ginger about giving 'im his eleven pounds back, Ginger said 'e ought to be made to suffer a little for 'is foolishness fust, to be a lesson to 'im.

'"We're saving it up for 'im," he ses. "While we've got it he can't be spending it."

'"Or trusting people with it," ses Peter.

'Both of 'em felt quite kind to Sam, thinking 'ow good they was going to be to 'im, but Sam 'ardly spoke a word to 'em and was up and out next morning a'most afore they 'ad got their eyes open. Twice they came back to their room that day to see whether he 'ad turned up, and when night-time came and 'e was still missing, Peter Russet said as 'ow he was getting uneasy about 'im.

'"Wot's 'e doing?" he ses. "He ain't got any money to go to pubs with, and there's nowhere else for 'im to go."

'They sat on their beds smoking and drinking some whisky they 'ad brought in with 'em, and Ginger was just helping 'imself to 'is third glass when 'e put the bottle down and sat listening.

'"Somebody coming upstairs," he ses.

'"He's a long time about it," ses Peter, "He *as* been sitting in a pub."

'Somebody was coming up the stairs so slow it seemed as if 'e would never get to the top, and the banisters was creaking as if they would break. Then they 'eard a shuffling on the landing, and as the door opened they both jumped up and called out at the same time:

'"Lor' lumme!" ses Ginger. "'Ave you been run over, Sam?"

'Sam looked at 'im for a moment and then 'e gave a stagger and tumbled on to 'is bed.

'"Mr Cooper!" he ses, in a faint voice.

'"Wot about 'im?" ses Ginger.

'"He done it," ses Sam, "'im and 'is pals. I went round to the pub to see if I could find 'im, thinking 'e might 'ave been took ill the other night, and this is wot I got. He said I'd robbed 'im. Me! He goes off with my money and then 'arf kills me. Wot for? That's wot I want to know."

'"It's a mystery," ses Ginger, shaking his 'ead.

'"I thought you said you didn't give 'im the money," ses Peter.

'Sam didn't answer 'im, and arter drinking a glass o' whisky Ginger gave 'im he 'eld his 'ead in his 'ands and said 'e thought 'e was dying. When they offered to undress 'im he said 'e didn't think it was worth while, but they got 'is clo'es off arter a bit and put 'im into bed.

'"Wot did 'e do it *for*?" he ses, arter he had 'ad two more whiskies. "D'ye think 'e's mad? His 'ead was all bandaged up."

'Ginger shook his 'ead. "It's a mystery," he ses agin.

'He went acrost the room and came back with something tied up in a handkerchief and put it on Sam's bed. Sam looked at it a moment and then 'e picked it up and out tumbled eleven pounds, a watch and chain, and a imitation gold cigar-case.

'"He's fainted," ses Peter Russet.'

W. W. Jacobs (1863–1943), Sea Whispers (1926).

THE Edwardian decade in England was a fertile period for the humorous short story. As well as the large-circulation magazines such as the Strand *which published popular writers of robust humour like W. W. Jacobs, there were many small literary magazines which were happy to publish any writing of merit, particularly from beginners who were more interested in being published than in being paid.*

One of the most prestigious of those political/literary journals was Alfred Orage's The New Age, *which George Bernard Shaw helped Orage set up in 1907, originally as a bulletin for socialist culture. The magazine found a readership and Orage was responsible for the first appearance in print of some formidably gifted new writers, including Katherine Mansfield.*

Miss Mansfield had been born Kathleen Beauchamp in Wellington, New Zealand. She came to London to study at Queen's College and decided to stay and try to make a career as a writer. She led what might fairly be called 'a Bohemian life'. At the age of 21 she met a singing teacher eleven years her senior and three weeks later married him. She abandoned him the following morning.

She then discovered that she was pregnant by somebody else. Her mother hurried over from New Zealand and installed her daughter in a small hotel in Bavaria where she could give birth to her child comfortably and discreetly. The baby was stillborn. But during the months of waiting Katherine Mansfield had filled in her time by writing a series of sketches describing life in a modest, rural Bavarian guest-house.

Back in London she was sheltered by her estranged husband who persuaded her to send her sketches to Orage's New Age, or 'No Wage' as it was known to its regular contributors.

The stories were published and appreciated; readers and critics in Britain decided that a new, original, and delicate talent had emerged, and Miss Mansfield's reputation grew to international stature. She later lived with and eventually married John Middleton Murry, and died of tuberculosis at the age of 34.

The early stories set in the Bavarian hotel show why Katherine Mansfield's style has been called Chekhovian. Like Chekhov's early short stories they were intended to amuse the reader; they were told simply, with clear and realistic detail and considerable psychological insight, and they explored the humour of the self-deceptions, moods, and pretences in human behaviour.

Nothing needs to be said to introduce the following story, one of the Bavarian Pension sketches; the style, the tone of voice is set in the first few lines:

THE MODERN SOUL

'Good-evening,' said the Herr Professor, squeezing my hand; 'wonderful weather! I have just returned from a party in the wood. I have been making music for them on my trombone. You know, these pine-trees provide most suitable accompaniment for a trombone! They are sighing delicacy against sustained strength, as I remarked once in a lecture on wind instruments in Frankfort. May I be permitted to sit beside you on this bench, *gnädige* Frau?'

He sat down, tugging at a white-paper package in the tail pocket of his coat.

'Cherries,' he said, nodding and smiling. 'There is nothing like cherries for producing free saliva after trombone playing, especially after Grieg's "*Ich Liebe Dich*". Those sustained blasts on "*liebe*" make my throat as dry as a railway tunnel. Have some?' He shook the bag at me.

'I prefer watching you eat them.'

'Ah, ha!' He crossed his legs, sticking the cherry bag between his knees, to leave both hands free. 'Psychologically I understood your refusal. It is your innate feminine delicacy in preferring etherealised sensations . . . Or perhaps you do not care to eat the worms. All cherries contain worms. Once I made a very interesting experiment with a colleague of mine at the university. We bit into four pounds of the best cherries and did not find one specimen without a worm. But what would you? As I remarked to him afterwards—dear friend, it amounts to this: if one wishes to satisfy the desires of nature one must be strong enough to ignore the facts of nature . . . The conversation is not out of your depth? I have so seldom the time or opportunity to open my heart to a woman that I am apt to forget.'

I looked at him brightly.

'See what a fat one!' cried the Herr Professor. 'That is almost a mouthful in itself; it is beautiful enough to hang from a watch-chain.' He chewed it up and spat the stone an incredible distance—over the garden path into the flower bed. He was proud of the feat. I saw it. 'The quantity of fruit I have eaten on this bench,' he sighed; 'apricots, peaches, and cherries. One day that garden bed will become an orchard grove, and I shall allow you to pick as much as you please, without paying me anything.'

I was grateful, without showing undue excitement.

'Which reminds me'—he hit the side of his nose with one finger—'the manager of the pension handed me my weekly bill after dinner this evening.

It is almost impossible to credit. I do not expect you to believe me—he has charged me extra for a miserable little glass of milk I drink in bed at night to prevent insomnia. Naturally, I did not pay. But the tragedy of the story is this: I cannot expect the milk to produce somnolence any longer; my peaceful attitude of mind towards it is completely destroyed. I know I shall throw myself into a fever in attempting to plumb this want of generosity in so wealthy a man as the manager of a pension. Think of me to-night'—he ground the empty bag under his heel—'think that the worst is happening to me as your head drops asleep on your pillow.'

Two ladies came on the front steps of the pension and stood, arm in arm, looking over the garden. The one, old and scraggy, dressed almost entirely in black bead trimming and a satin reticule; the other, young and thin, in a white gown, her yellow hair tastefully garnished with mauve sweet peas.

The Professor drew in his feet and sat up sharply, pulling down his waistcoat.

'The Godowskas,' he murmured. 'Do you know them? A mother and daughter from Vienna. The mother has an internal complaint and the daughter is an actress. Fräulein Sonia is a very modern soul. I think you would find her most sympathetic. She is forced to be in attendance on her mother just now. But what a temperament! I have once described her in her autograph album as a tigress with a flower in the hair. Will you excuse me? Perhaps I can persuade them to be introduced to you.'

I said, 'I am going up to my room.' But the Professor rose and shook a playful finger at me. 'Na,' he said, 'we are friends, and, therefore, I shall speak quite frankly to you. I think they would consider it a little "marked" if you immediately retired to the house at their approach, after sitting here alone with me in the twilight. You know this world. Yes, you know it as I do.'

I shrugged my shoulders, remarking with one eye that while the Professor had been talking the Godowskas had trailed across the lawn towards us. They confronted the Herr Professor as he stood up.

'Good-evening,' quavered Frau Godowska. 'Wonderful weather! It has given me quite a touch of hay fever!' Fräulein Godowska said nothing. She swooped over a rose growing in the embryo orchard, then stretched out her hand with a magnificent gesture to the Herr Professor. He presented me.

'This is my little English friend of whom I have spoken. She is the stranger in our midst. We have been eating cherries together.'

'How delightful,' sighed Frau Godowska. 'My daughter and I have often observed you through the bedroom window. Haven't we, Sonia?'

Sonia absorbed my outward and visible form with an inward and spiritual glance, then repeated the magnificent gesture for my benefit. The four of us sat on the bench, with that faint air of excitement of passengers established in a railway carriage on the qui vive for the train whistle. Frau Godowska sneezed. 'I wonder if it is hay fever,' she remarked, worrying the satin reticule for her handkerchief, 'or would it be the dew? Sonia, dear, is the dew falling?'

Fräulein Sonia raised her face to the sky, and half closed her eyes. 'No, mamma, my face is quite warm, Oh, look, Herr Professor, there are swallows in flight; they are like a little flock of Japanese thoughts—*nicht wahr?*'

'Where?' cried the Herr Professor. 'Oh, yes, I see, by the kitchen chimney. But why do you say "Japanese"? Could you not compare them with equal veracity to a little flock of German thoughts in flight?' He rounded on me. 'Have you swallows in England?'

'I believe there are some at certain seasons. But doubtless they have not the same symbolical value for the English. In Germany—'

'I have never been to England,' interrupted Fräulein Sonia, 'but I have many English acquaintances. They are so cold!' She shivered.

'Fish-blooded,' snapped Frau Godowska. 'Without soul, without heart, without grace. But you cannot equal their dress materials. I spent a week in Brighton twenty years ago, and the travelling cape I bought there is not yet worn out—the one you wrap the hot-water bottle in, Sonia. My lamented husband, your father, Sonia, knew a great deal about England. But the more he knew about it the oftener he remarked to me, "England is merely an island of beef flesh swimming in a warm gulf sea of gravy". Such a brilliant way of putting things. Do you remember, Sonia?'

'I forget nothing, mamma,' answered Sonia.

Said the Herr Professor: 'That is the proof of your calling, *gnädiges* Fräulein. Now I wonder—and this is a very interesting speculation—is memory a blessing or—excuse the word—a curse?'

Frau Godowska looked into the distance, then the corners of her mouth dropped and her skin puckered. She began to shed tears.

'*Ach Gott!* Gracious lady, what have I said?' exclaimed the Herr Professor.

Sonia took her mother's hand. 'Do you know,' she said, 'tonight it is *stewed carrots and nut tart* for supper. Suppose we go in and take our places,' her sidelong, tragic stare accusing the Professor and me the while.

I followed them across the lawn and up the steps. Frau Godowska was murmuring, 'Such a wonderful, beloved man'; with her disengaged hand Sonia was arranging the sweet pea 'garniture'.

A concert for the benefit of afflicted Catholic infants will take place in the salon at 8.30 p.m. Artists: Fräulein Sonia Godowska, from Vienna; Herr Professor Windberg and his trombone; Frau Oberlehrer Weidel, and others.

The notice was tied round the neck of the melancholy stag's head in the dining-room. It graced him like a red and white 'dinner bib' for days before the event, causing the Herr Professor to bow before it and say 'good appetite' until we sickened of his pleasantry and left the smiling to be done by the waiter, who was paid to be pleasing to the guests.

On the appointed day the married ladies sailed about the pension dressed like upholstered chairs, and the unmarried ladies like draped muslin dressing-table covers. Frau Godowska pinned a rose in the centre of her reticule; another blossom was tucked in the mazy folds of a white anti-macassar thrown across her breast. The gentlemen wore black coats, white silk ties and ferny buttonholes tickling the chin.

The floor of the salon was freshly polished, chairs and benches arranged, and a row of little flags strung across the ceiling—they flew and jigged in the draught with all the enthusiasm of family washing. It was arranged that I should sit beside Frau Godowska, and that the Herr Professor and Sonia should join us when their share of the concert was over.

'That will make you feel quite one of the performers,' said the Herr Professor genially. 'It is a great pity that the English nation is so unmusical. Never mind! Tonight you shall hear something—we have discovered a nest of talent during the rehearsals.'

'What do you intend to recite, Fräulein Sonia?'

She shook back her hair. 'I never know until the last moment. When I come on the stage I wait for one moment and then I have the sensation as though something struck me here'—she placed her hand upon her collar brooch—'and . . . words come!'

'Bend down a moment,' whispered her mother. 'Sonia, love, your skirt safety-pin is showing at the back. Shall I come outside and fasten it properly for you, or will you do it yourself?'

'Oh, mamma, please don't say such things.' Sonia flushed and grew very angry. 'You know how sensitive I am to the slightest unsympathetic impression at a time like this . . . I would rather my skirt dropped off my body—'

'Sonia—my heart!'

A bell tinkled.

The waiter came in and opened the piano. In the heated excitement of the moment he entirely forgot what was fitting, and flicked the keys with the grimy table napkin he carried over his arm. The Frau Oberlehrer tripped on the platform followed by a very young gentleman, who blew his nose twice before he hurled his handkerchief into the bosom of the piano.

> 'Yes, I know you have no love for me,
> And no forget-me-not.
> No love, no heart, and no forget-me-not,'

sang the Frau Oberlehrer, in a voice that seemed to issue from her forgotten thimble and have nothing to do with her.

'Ach, how sweet, how delicate,' we cried, clapping her soothingly. She bowed as though to say, 'Yes, isn't it?' and retired, the very young gentleman dodging her train and scowling.

The piano was closed, an arm-chair was placed in the centre of the platform. Fräulein Sonia drifted towards it. A breathless pause. Then, presumably, the winged shaft struck her collar brooch. She implored us not to go into the woods in trained dresses, but rather as lightly draped as possible, and bed with her among the pine needles. Her loud, slightly harsh voice filled the salon. She dropped her arms over the back of the chair, moving her lean hands from the wrists. We were thrilled and silent. The Herr Professor, beside me, abnormally serious, his eyes bulging, pulled at his moustache ends. Frau Godowska adopted that peculiarly detached attitude of the proud parent. The only soul who remained untouched by her appeal was the waiter, who leaned idly against the wall of the salon and cleaned his nails with the edge of a programme. He was 'off duty' and intended to show it.

'What did I say?' shouted the Herr Professor under cover of tumultuous applause, 'tem-per-ament! There you have it. She is a flame in the heart of a lily. I know I am going to play well. It is my turn now. I am inspired. Fräulein Sonia'—as that lady returned to us, pale and draped in a large shawl—'you are my inspiration. Tonight you shall be the soul of my trombone. Wait only.'

To right and left of us people bent over and whispered admiration down Fräulein Sonia's neck. She bowed in the grand style.

'I am always successful,' she said to me. 'You see, when I act I *am*. In Vienna, in the plays of Ibsen we had so many bouquets that the cook had three in the kitchen. But it is difficult here. There is so little magic. Do you not feel it? There is none of that mysterious perfume which floats almost as a visible thing from the souls of the Viennese audiences. My spirit starves for want of that.' She leaned forward, chin on hand. 'Starves,' she repeated.

The Professor appeared with his trombone, blew into it, held it up to one eye, tucked back his shirt cuffs and wallowed in the soul of Sonia Godowska. Such a sensation did he create that he was recalled to play a Bavarian dance, which he acknowledged was to be taken as a breathing exercise rather than an artistic achievement. Frau Godowska kept time to it with a fan.

Followed the very young gentleman who piped in a tenor voice that he loved somebody, 'with blood in his heart and a thousand pains'. Fräulein Sonia acted a poison scene with the assistance of her mother's pill vial and the arm-chair replaced by a 'chaise longue'; a young girl scratched a lullaby on a young fiddle; and the Herr Professor performed the last sacrificial rites on the altar of the afflicted children by playing the National Anthem.

'Now I must put mamma to bed,' whispered Fräulein Sonia. 'But afterwards I must take a walk. It is imperative that I free my spirit in the open air for a moment. Would you come with me, as far as the railway station and back?'

'Very well, then, knock on my door when you're ready.'

Thus the modern soul and I found ourselves together under the stars.

'What a night!' she said. 'Do you know that poem of Sappho about her hands in the stars . . . I am curiously sapphic. And this is so remarkable— not only am I sapphic, I find in all the works of all the greatest writers, especially in their unedited letters, some touch, some sign of myself—some resemblance, some part of myself, like a thousand reflections of my own hands in a dark mirror.'

'But what a bother,' said I.

'I do not know what you mean by "bother"; is it rather the curse of my genius . . .' She paused suddenly, staring at me. 'Do you know my tragedy?' she asked.

I shook my head.

'My tragedy is my mother. Living with her I live with the coffin of my unborn aspirations. You heard that about the safety-pin tonight. It may seem to you a little thing, but it ruined my three first gestures. They were—'

'Impaled on a safety-pin,' I suggested.

'Yes, exactly that. And when we are in Vienna I am the victim of moods, you know. I long to do wild, passionate things. And mamma says, "Please pour out my mixture first." Once I remember I flew into a rage and threw a washstand jug out of the window. Do you know what she said? "Sonia, it is not so much throwing things out of windows, if only you would—"'

'Choose something smaller?' said I.

'No . . . "tell me about it beforehand." Humiliating! And I do not see any possible light out of this darkness.'

'Why don't you join a touring company and leave your mother in Vienna?'

'What! Leave my poor, little, sick, widowed mother in Vienna! Sooner than that I would drown myself. I love my mother as I love nobody else in the world—nobody and nothing! Do you think it is impossible to love one's tragedy? "Out of my great sorrows I make my little songs," that is Heine or myself.'

'Oh, well, that's all right,' I said cheerfully.

'But it is not all right!'

I suggested we should turn back. We turned.

'Sometimes I think the solution lies in marriage,' said Fräulein Sonia. 'If I find a simple, peaceful man who adores me and will look after mamma—a man who would be for me a pillow—for genius cannot hope to mate—I shall marry him . . . You know the Herr Professor has paid me very marked attentions.'

'Oh, Fräulein Sonia,' I said, very pleased with myself, 'why not marry him to your mother?' We were passing the hairdresser's shop at the moment. Fräulein Sonia clutched my arm.

'You, you,' she stammered. 'The cruelty. I am going to faint. Mamma to marry again before I marry—the indignity. I am going to faint here and now.'

I was frightened. 'You can't,' I said, shaking her.

'Come back to the pension and faint as much as you please. But you can't faint here. All the shops are closed. There is nobody about. Please don't be so foolish.'

'Here and here only!' She indicated the exact spot and dropped quite beautifully, lying motionless.

'Very well,' I said, 'faint away; but please hurry over it.'

She did not move. I began to walk home, but each time I looked behind me I saw the dark form of the modern soul prone before the hairdresser's window. Finally I ran, and rooted out the Herr Professor from his room. 'Fräulein Sonia has fainted,' I said crossly.

'*Du lieber Gott!* Where? How?'

'Outside the hairdresser's shop in the Station Road.'

'Jesus and Maria! Has she no water with her?' he seized the carafe— 'nobody beside her?'

'Nothing.'

'Where is my coat? No matter, I shall catch a cold on the chest. Willingly, I shall catch one . . . You are ready to come with me?'

'No,' I said; 'you can take the waiter.'

'But she must have a woman. I cannot be so indelicate as to attempt to loosen her stays.'

'Modern souls oughtn't to wear them,' said I. He pushed past me and clattered down the stairs.

When I came down to breakfast next morning there were two places vacant at table. Fräulein Sonia and the Herr Professor had gone off for a day's excursion in the woods.

I wondered.

Katherine Mansfield (1888–1923), In a German Pension (1911).

———

KATHERINE MANSFIELD *had a cousin, Mary Beauchamp, known as Elizabeth, who was born in New Zealand twenty-two years earlier than Katherine. Elizabeth too moved to Europe, studied music, and became a writer.*

Elizabeth's subsequent private life may have lacked the tragic touches of la vie bohème *which dogged her cousin Katherine, but for a nice girl from New Zealand it was fairly spectacular. At the age of 25 she met a Prussian widower on a train in Italy, married him, and became the Countess von Arnim with an enormous estate in Pomerania. She had four daughters and a son, who were tutored at various times by (Sir) Hugh Walpole and E. M. Forster. She did not like her husband (in her first book he was referred to always as The Man of Wrath) and when he died she married Bertrand Russell's brother, the second Earl Russell, also not nice. In between she was H. G. Wells's mistress.*

In his Postscript to an Experiment in Autobiography, *Wells recalls a moment on a walking tour when he and Elizabeth von Arnim took their clothes off under some pine-trees, opened out a copy of* The Times *at a page featuring a letter to the editor from a highly respectable lady author denouncing the immoral tone of younger writers, and then, as Mr Wells put it, 'made love all over Mrs Humphry Ward'.*

The poet Alice Meynell thought that Elizabeth was one of the three wittiest women of the age.

Elizabeth von Arnim, tiny, tough, a survivor, uninterested in her own children but keenly interested in lovers, flowers, and the exact and funny use of words, wrote twenty-two books. The first, her most charming and best-remembered, described her life on the estate in Pomerania and her chief source of pleasure there: Elizabeth and her German Garden.

Seven novels later, in 1909, she tried something quite different, a humorous, ironic story of a deeply un-humorous Prussian officer who takes his wife on a caravanning holiday in England. Unnoticed by him, his obedient little wife is affected by the liberated behaviour of the English couples who share the trip with them and begins to think for herself.

Our hero, the Prussian officer Baron von Ottringel who serves with an obscure regiment in a small provincial town, narrates the story whilst understanding very little of what is happening. He writes the journal so that on his return he can read it aloud to impress selected friends (in quite small groups, because of the sandwiches which he will have to provide).

The Baron is a fine comic invention: vain as Brigadier Gerard but without the charm; mean, stupid, a bully, a snob and utterly selfish.

Here he gives his rationale for embarking on a holiday with his second wife Edelgard in order to commemorate the years he spent with his first wife Marie-Luise:

I should like to explain why we, an officer and his wife who naturally do not like spending money, should have contemplated so costly a holiday as a trip abroad. The fact is, for a long time past we had made up our minds to do so in the fifth year of our marriage, and for the following reason. Before I married Edelgard I had been a widower for one year, and before being a widower I was married for no fewer than nineteen years. This sounds as though I must be old, but I need not tell my readers who see me constantly that I am not. The best of all witnesses are the eyes; also, I began my marrying unusually young. My first wife was one of the Mecklenburg Lunewitzes, the elder (and infinitely superior) branch. If she had lived, I would last year have been celebrating our silver wedding on August 1st, and there would have been much feasting and merry-making arranged for us, and many gifts in silver from our relations, friends, and acquaintances. The regiment would have been obliged to recognize it, and perhaps our two servants would have clubbed together and expressed their devotion in a metal form.

All this I feel I have missed, and through no fault of my own. I fail to see why I should be deprived of every benefit of such a celebration, for have I not, with an interruption of twelve months forced upon me, been actually married twenty-five years? And why, because my poor Marie-Luise was unable to go on living, should I have to attain to the very high number of (practically) five and twenty years' matrimony without the least notice being taken of it?

I had been explaining this to Edelgard for a long time, and the nearer the date drew on which in the natural order of things I would have been reaping a silver harvest and have been in a position to gauge the esteem in which I was held, the more emphatic did I become. Edelgard seemed at first unable to understand, but she was very teachable, and gradually found my logic irresistible. Indeed, once she grasped the point she was even more strongly of opinion than I was that something ought to be done to mark the occasion, and quite saw that if Marie-Luise failed me it was not my fault, and that I at least had done my part and gone on steadily being married ever since. From recognizing this to being indignant that our friends would probably take no notice of the anniversary was but, for her, a step; and many were the talks we had together on the subject, and many the suggestions we made for bringing our friends round to our point of view.

We finally decided that, however much they might ignore it, we ourselves would do what was right, and accordingly we planned a silver-honeymoon trip.

Elizabeth von Arnim's book was published at the height of the bitter debate as to whether women should be legally recognized as people and be promoted from third-class citizenship to second-class. Elizabeth might well have been the first female novelist to write feminist books which were also funny and The Caravaners *became popular among the many British wives who were treated by their husbands in much the same way as the Baron treated Edelgard.*

As the Baron prepares to leave for England, more little details build up of the depths of his male-chauvinist piggishness:

We left our home on August 1st, punctually as we had arranged, after some very hard-worked days at the end during which the furniture was beaten and strewn with naphthalin (against moths), curtains, etc., taken down and piled neatly in heaps, pictures covered up in newspapers, and groceries carefully weighed and locked up. I spent these days at my club, for my leave had begun on the 25th of July and there was nothing for me to do. And I must say, though the discomfort in our flat was intense, when I returned to it in the evening in order to go to bed I was never anything but patient with the unappetizingly heated and dishevelled Edelgard. And she noticed it and was grateful.

In England the Baron is disconcerted to find that the party will consist of three caravans and a number of English folk: the attractive young German widow who suggested the trip, whom he lusts after (unknowingly); a rich elderly couple named Menzies-Legh; a couple of schoolgirls; and two scruffily dressed young men. He is

*offensively chilly to one of the scruffy young men only to find that he is a lord, and
so rapidly changes his tone to one of fawning obsequiousness.*

*Despite heavy rain on their first evening on the road and the problems of getting
a supper together, Edelgard is thoroughly enjoying her first experience of the
English love of 'mucking-in' when on holiday.*

To the noble Baron all is humiliating confusion:

As for Edelgard, I completely lost control over her. She seemed to slip through
my fingers like water. She was everywhere, and yet nowhere. I do not know
what she did, but I know that she left me quite unaided, and I found myself
performing the most menial tasks, utterly unfit for an officer, such as fetching
cups and saucers and arranging spoons in rows. Nor, if I had not witnessed
it, would I ever have believed that the preparation of eggs and coffee was so
difficult . . .

There were hardly enough scrambled eggs to go round, most of them
having been broken in the jolting up the lane on to the common, and after
the meal, instead of smoking a cigar in the comparative quiet and actual
dryness of one's caravan, I found that everybody had to turn to and—will it
be believed?—wash up.

'No servants, you know—so free, isn't it?' said Mrs Menzies-Legh, pressing
a cloth into one of my hands and a fork into the other, and indicating a
saucepan of hot water with a meaning motion of her forefinger.

Well, I had to. My hearers must not judge me harshly. I am aware that it
was conduct unbecoming in an officer, but the circumstances were unusual.
Menzies-Legh and the young men were doing it too, and I was taken by
surprise. Edelgard, when she saw me thus employed, first stared in astonishment and then said she would do it for me.

'No, no, let him do it,' quickly interposed Mrs Menzies-Legh, almost as
though she liked me to wash up in the same saucepan as herself.

But I will not dwell on the forks. We were still engaged in the amazingly
difficult and distasteful work of cleaning them when the rain suddenly descended with renewed fury.

*The caravaners have to walk beside the horses so progress is tiring. Edelgard hacks
a length off her conventionally long German skirt so that she can walk more easily,
and loosens her hair. She is now as casually and suitably dressed as the English
ladies of the party.*

The gallant Baron trudges wearily behind, trying to keep up:

Well, I was often glad at this time that my poor Marie-Luise was spared her
silver-wedding journey, and that a more robust and far less deserving wife
went through it in her stead. Marie-Luise was a most wifely wife, with no
whalebone (if I may so express it) either about her clothes or her character.
All was soft, womanly, overflowing. Touch her, and you left a dimple. Bring

pressure, even the slightest, to bear anywhere on her mind, and it immediately gave way.

'But do you *like* that sort of thing?' asked Mrs Menzies-Legh, to whom, as we plodded along that day, I was talking in this reminiscent strain for want of a better companion.

Ahead walked Edelgard, visibly slimmer, younger, moving quickly and easily in her short skirt and new activity. It was this figure—hardly now at a distance to be distinguished from the figures of the scanty sisters—walking before me that made me think with tenderness of Marie-Luise. Edelgard was behaving badly, and when I told her so at night in our caravan she did not answer.

At home she used to express immediate penitence; here she either said nothing, or said short things that reminded me of Mrs Menzies-Legh, little odd sentences quite unlike her usual style and annoyingly difficult to reply to. And the more she behaved in this manner the more did my thoughts go back regretfully to my gentle and yielding first wife.

Sometimes, I recollect, those twenty years with her had seemed long; but that was because, firstly, twenty years are long, and secondly, because we are none of us perfect, and thirdly, because a wife, unless she is careful, is apt to get on one's nerves.

But how preferable is gentleness to an aggressive activity of mind and body. How annoying to see one's wife striding on ahead with an ease I could not imitate and therefore in itself a slight on her husband. A man wants a wife who sits still, and not only still but on the same chair every day so that he knows where to find her should he happen to want anything. Marie-Luise was a very calm sitter . . . only her hands moved, in a tireless guiding of the needle through those of my undergarments which had become defective.

Many small adventures befall the party; the Baron's behaviour grows worse; he takes to hiding when there is washing-up to be done, harangues the party about the perfidy of England, wonders whether, because the gentleman rise to their feet when his wife joins them, help her down the caravan steps, and generally treat her as a friend, something might be going on between them and her.

Eventually the Baron's behaviour becomes unbearable and after only a week the English make polite and most tactful excuses and depart. The holiday finishes prematurely.

But not before Edelgard—the new Edelgard—finds her voice:

My wife was mending, and did not look up when I came in. How differently she behaved at home. She not only used to look up when I came in, she got up, and got up quickly too, hastening at the first sound of my return to meet me in the passage, and greeting me with the smiles of a dutiful and accordingly contented wife.

Shutting the [caravan] windows I drew her attention to this.

'But there isn't a passage,' said she, still with her head bent over a sock.

Really Edelgard should take care to be specially feminine, for she will certainly never shine on the strength of her brains.

'Dear wife,' I began—then the complete futility of trying to thresh any single subject out in that airy, sound-carrying dwelling stopped me. I sat down on the yellow box instead, and remarked that I was extremely fatigued.

'So am I,' said she.

'My feet ache so,' said I, 'that I fear there may be something serious the matter with them.'

'So do mine,' said she.

This, I may observe, was a new and irritating habit she had got into: whatever I complained of in the way of unaccountable symptoms in divers portions of my frame, instead of sympathizing and suggesting remedies she said hers (whatever it was) did it too.

'Your feet cannot possibly', said I, 'be in the terrible condition mine are in. In the first place mine are bigger, and accordingly offer more scope for disorders. I have shooting pains in them resembling neuralgia, and no doubt traceable to some nervous source.'

'So have I,' said she.

'I think bathing might do them good,' I said, determined not to become angry. 'Will you get me some hot water please?'

'Why?' said she.

She had never said such a thing to me before. I could only gaze at her in a profound surprise.

'Why?' I repeated at length, keeping studiously calm. 'What an extraordinary question. I could give you a thousand reasons if I chose, such as I desire to bathe them; that hot water—rather luckily for itself—has no feet, and therefore has to be fetched; and that a wife has to do as she is told. But I will, dear Edelgard, confine myself to the counter enquiry, and ask why not?'

'I too, my dear Otto,' said she—and she spoke with great composure, her head bent over her mending, 'could give you a thousand answers to that if I chose, such as that I desire to get this sock finished—yours, by the way— that I have walked exactly as far as you have, that I see no reason why you should not as there are no servants here fetch your own hot water, and that your wishing or not to bathe your feet has really if you come to think of it nothing to do with me. But I will confine myself just to saying that I prefer not to go.'

It can be imagined with what feelings—not mixed but unmitigated—I listened to this. And after five years! Five years of patience and guidance.

'Is this my Edelgard?' I managed to say, recovering speech enough for those four words but otherwise struck dumb.

'Your Edelgard?' she repeated musingly as she continued to mend, and not even looking at me. 'Your boots, your handkerchief, your gloves, your socks—yes—'

I confess I could not follow, and could only listen amazed.

'But not your Edelgard. At least, not more than you are my Otto.'

'But—my boots?' I repeated, really dazed.

'Yes,' she said, folding up the finished sock, 'they really are yours. Your property. But you should not suppose that I am a kind of living boot, made to be trodden on. I, my dear Otto, am a human being, and no human being is another being's property.'

A flash of light illuminated my brain. 'Jellaby!' I cried.

'Hullo?' was the immediate answer from outside. 'Want me, Baron?'

'No, no! No, *no!* No, NO!' I cried, leaping up and dragging the door curtain to, as though that could possibly deaden our conversation. 'He's been infecting you,' I continued, in a whisper so much charged with indignation that it hissed, 'with his poisonous—'. . .

'It's true,' she said, not even looking at me but staring out of the window; 'It's true about the boots.'

Elizabeth von Arnim (1866–1941), The Caravaners (1909).

E DWARDIAN *Britain also saw the flowering of another pair of literary cousins, whose success against all odds in a masculine world would have infuriated the Baron of* The Caravaners *and delighted Edelgard.*

Edith Somerville and 'Martin Ross' (real name Violet Martin, of Ross, County Galway) were two ladies of the Anglo-Irish gentry. They lived in and wrote about a period in Irish history when the ascendancy of the ancient Anglo-Irish families had almost disappeared and was about to be replaced by the rising Irish middle class; meanwhile the impoverished Anglo-Irish gentry and the now better-off Irish locals coexisted in a kind of suspended animation.

Edith Somerville lived with her family in a once great house, Drishane, in Co. Cork. She was attractive, high-spirited and a talented artist.

Cousin Martin Ross, a little plainer and much quieter than Edith, was of an equally ancient family and was engaged in trying to keep her ancestral home going by journalism, writing thoughtful pieces for magazines and newspapers.

The cousins met, found that they both had unquenchable—and slightly different—senses of humour and decided to try to write some profitable fiction together. Their first four novels were well received but their fifth book, a collection of humorous sketches of Irish life published in 1899 and titled Some Experiences of an Irish R.M.*, was a great success and won them an international reputation. Two more collections of 'Experiences' followed.*

There was a Celtic Revival going on at the time. Writers such as Lady Gregory and J. M. Synge were emphasizing the poetry and beauty of the Irish language, but Somerville and Ross were no part of this. Their Irish dialogue neither leant on poetic expression, nor on the boozy, truculent style which might be termed the

*Sodom and Begorrah school. Their dialogue was natural, the native Irish phrases
and expressions which they had grown up listening to.*

*The following story comes from the second collection of 'Irish R.M.' stories. An
R.M. was a Resident Magistrate, often an ex-Army Officer, who dispensed justice
in a given rural area, where he was required to live.*

*Our man is Major Sinclair Yates, an Englishman with Irish blood who gets his
wife Philippa's relations to wangle him the appointment so that they can both live
a comfortable, sporting life in Ireland. He finds that he has overestimated the
comfort and available sport and seriously underestimated the rural Irishman's
capacity for avoiding anything which smacks of justice, but bemused by the Irish
way of doing things and whimsically resigned to being outwitted at almost every
turn, he is happy enough.*

*The Major has to catch a ferry back to England to join his wife for a family
wedding, which means making a long train journey across Ireland.*

He is to bring a salmon with him:

POISSON D'AVRIL

The atmosphere of the waiting-room set at naught at a single glance the
theory that there can be no smoke without fire. The station-master, when
remonstrated with, stated, as an incontrovertible fact, that any chimney in
the world would smoke in a south-easterly wind, and further, said there
wasn't a poker, and that if you poked the fire the grate would fall out. He
was, however, sympathetic, and went on his knees before the smouldering
mound of slack, endeavouring to charm it to a smile by subtle proddings
with the handle of the ticket-punch. Finally, he took me to his own kitchen
fire and talked politics and salmon-fishing, the former with judicious attention
to my presumed point of view, and careful suppression of his own, the latter
with no less tactful regard for my admission that for three days I had not
caught a fish, while the steam rose from my wet boots, in witness of the ten
miles of rain through which an outside car had carried me.

Before the train was signalled I realized for the hundredth time the magnificent superiority of the Irish mind to the trammels of official-dom, and the
inveterate supremacy in Ireland of the Personal Element.

'You might get a foot-warmer at Carrig Junction,' said a species of lay
porter in a knitted jersey, ramming my suit-case upside down under the seat.
'Sometimes they're in it, and more times they're not.'

The train dragged itself rheumatically from the station, and a cold spring
rain—the time was the middle of a most inclement April—smote it in flank
as it came into the open. I pulled up both windows and began to smoke;
there is, at least, a semblance of warmth in a thoroughly vitiated atmosphere.

It is my wife's habit to assert that I do not read her letters, and being now
on my way to join her and my family in Gloucestershire, it seemed a sound
thing to study again her latest letter of instructions.

'I am starting today, as Alice wrote to say we must be there two days before the wedding, so as to have a rehearsal for the pages. Their dresses have come, and they look too delicious in them—'

(I here omit profuse particulars not pertinent to this tale)—

'It is sickening for you to have had such bad sport. If the worst comes to the worst, couldn't you buy one?—'

I smote my hand upon my knee. I had forgotten the infernal salmon! What a score for Philippa! If these contretemps would only teach her that I was not to be relied upon, they would have their uses, but experience is wasted upon her; I have no objection to being called an idiot, but, that being so, I ought to be allowed the privileges and exemptions proper to idiots. Philippa had, no doubt, written to Alice Hervey, and assured her that Sinclair would be only too delighted to bring her a salmon, and Alice Hervey, who was rich enough to find much enjoyment in saving money, would reckon upon it, to its final fin in mayonnaise.

Plunged in morose meditations, I progressed through a country parcelled out by shaky and crooked walls into a patchwork of hazel scrub and rocky fields, veiled in rain. About every six miles there was a station, wet and windswept; at one the sole occurrence was the presentation of a newspaper to the guard by the station-master; at the next the guard read aloud some choice excerpts from the same to the porter. The Personal Element was potent on this branch of the Munster and Connaught Railway. Routine, abhorrent to all artistic minds, was sheathed in conversation; even the engine-driver, a functionary ordinarily as aloof as the Mikado, alleviated his enforced isolation by sociable shrieks to every level crossing, while the long row of public-houses that formed, as far as I could judge, the town of Carrig, received a special and, as it seemed, humorous salutation.

The time-table decreed that we were to spend ten minutes at Carrig Junction; it was fifteen before the crowd of market people on the platform had been assimilated; finally, the window of a neighbouring carriage was flung open, and a wrathful English voice asked how much longer the train was going to wait. The station-master, who was at the moment engrossed in conversation with the guard and a man who was carrying a long parcel wrapped in newspaper, looked around, and said gravely—

'Well now, that's a mystery!'

The man with the parcel turned away, and convulsively studied a poster. The guard put his hand over his mouth.

The voice, still more wrathfully, demanded the earliest hour at which its owner could get to Belfast.

'Ye'll be asking me next when I take me breakfast,' replied the station-master, without haste or palpable annoyance.

The window went up again with a bang, the man with the parcel dug the guard in the ribs with his elbow, and the parcel slipped from under his arm and fell on the platform.

'Oh my! oh my! Me fish!' exclaimed the man, solicitously picking up a remarkably good-looking salmon that had slipped from its wrapping of newspaper.

Inspiration came to me, and I, in my turn, opened my window and summoned the station-master.

Would his friend sell me the salmon? The station-master entered upon the mission with ardour, but without success.

No; the gentleman was only just after running down to the town for it in the delay, but why wouldn't I run down and get one for myself? There was half-a-dozen more of them below at Coffey's selling cheap; there would be time enough, the mail wasn't signalled yet.

I jumped from the carriage and doubled out of the station at top speed, followed by an assurance from the guard that he would not forget me.

Congratulating myself on the ascendancy of the Personal Element, I sped through the soapy limestone and towards the public-houses. En route I met a heated man carrying yet another salmon, who, without preamble, informed me that there were three or four more good fish in it, and that he was after running down from the train himself.

'Ye have whips o'time!' he called after me. 'It's the first house that's not a public-house. Ye'll see boots in the window—she'll give them for tenpence a pound if ye're stiff with her!'

I ran past the public-houses.

'Tenpence a pound!' I exclaimed inwardly, 'at this time of year! That's good enough.'

Here I perceived the house with boots in the window, and dived into its dark doorway.

A cobbler was at work behind a low counter. He mumbled something about Herself, through lengths of waxed thread that hung across his mouth, a fat woman appeared at an inner door, and at that moment I heard, appallingly near, the whistle of the incoming mail. The fat woman grasped the situation in an instant, and with what appeared but one movement, snatched a large fish from the floor of the room behind her and flung a newspaper round it.

'Eight pound weight!' she said swiftly. 'Ten shillings!'

A convulsive effort of mental arithmetic assured me that this was more than tenpence a pound, but it was not the moment for stiffness. I shoved a half-sovereign into her fishy hand, clasped my salmon in my arms, and ran.

Needless to say it was uphill, and at the steepest gradient another whistle stabbed me like a spur; above the station roof successive and advancing puffs of steam warned me that the worst had probably happened, but still I ran. When I gained the platform my train was already clear of it, but the Personal Element held good. Every soul in the station, or so it seemed to me, lifted up his voice and yelled. The station-master put his fingers in his mouth and sent after the departing train an unearthly whistle, with a high trajectory and a serrated edge. It took effect; the train slackened, I plunged from the platform and followed it up the rails, and every window in both trains blossomed with the heads of deeply interested spectators. The guard met me on the line, very apologetic and primed with an explanation that the gentleman going for the boat-train wouldn't let him wait any longer, while from our rear came an exultant cry from the station-master.

'Ye *told* him ye wouldn't forget him!'. . .

The journey passed cheerlessly into evening, and my journey did not conspicuously thrive with me. Somewhere in the dripping twilight I changed trains, and again later on, and at each change the salmon moulted some more of its damp raiment of newspaper, and I debated seriously the idea of interring it, regardless of consequences, in my portmanteau. A lamp was banged into the roof of my carriage, half an inch of orange flame, poised in a large glass globe, like a gold-fish, and of about as much use as an illuminant. Here also was handed in the dinner basket that I had wired for, and its contents, arid though they were, enabled me to achieve at least some measure of mechanical distension, followed by a dreary lethargy that was not far from drowsiness.

At the next station we paused long; nothing whatever occurred, and the rain drummed patiently upon the roof. Two nuns and some schoolgirls were in the carriage next door, and their voices came plaintively and in snatches through the partition; after a long period of apparent collapse, during which I closed my eyes to evade the cold gaze of the salmon through the netting, a voice in the next carriage said resourcefully:

'Oh, girls, I'll tell you what we'll do! We'll say the Rosary!'

'Oh, that will be lovely!' said another voice; 'well, who'll give it out? Theresa Condon, you'll give it out.'

Theresa Condon gave it out, in a not unmelodious monotone, interspersed with the responses, always in a lower cadence; the words were in-distinguishable, but the rise and fall of the western voices was lulling as the hum of bees. I fell asleep.

I awoke in total darkness; the train was motionless, and complete and profound silence reigned. We were at a station, that much I discerned by the light of the dim lamp at the far end of a platform glistening with wet. I struck a match and ascertained that it was eleven o'clock, precisely the hour at which I was to board the mail train. I jumped out and ran down the platform; there was no one in the train; there was no one even on the engine, which was forlornly hissing to itself in the silence. There was not a human being anywhere. Every door was closed, and all was dark. The nameboard of the station was faintly visible; with a lighted match I went along it letter by letter. It seemed as if the whole alphabet were in it, and by the time I had got to the end I had forgotten the beginning. One fact I had, however, mastered, that it was not the junction at which I was to catch the mail.

I was undoubtedly awake, but for a moment I was inclined to entertain the idea that there had been an accident, and that I had entered upon existence in another world. Once more I assailed the station house and the appurtenances thereof, the ticket-office, the waiting room, finally, and at some distance, the goods store, outside which the single lamp of the station commented feebly on the drizzle and the darkness. As I approached it a crack of light under the door became perceptible, and a voice was suddenly uplifted within.

'Your best now agin that! Throw down your Jack!'

I opened the door with pardonable violence, and found the guard, the station-master, the driver, and the stoker, seated on barrels round a packing case, on which they were playing a game of cards.

To have too egregiously the best of a situation is not, to a generous mind, a source of strength. In the perfection of their overthrow I permitted the driver and stoker to wither from their places, and to fade away into the outer darkness without any suitable send-off; with the guard and the station-master, I dealt more faithfully, but the pleasure of throwing water on drowned rats is not a lasting one. I accepted the statements that they thought there wasn't a Christian in the train, that a few minutes here or there wouldn't signify, that they would have me at the junction in twenty minutes, and it was often the mail was late.

Fired by this hope I hurried back to my carriage, preceded at an emulous gallop by the officials. The guard thrust in with me the lantern from the card table, and fled to his van.

'Mind the goods train, Tim!' shouted the station-master, as he slammed the door, 'she might be coming anytime now!'

The answer travelled magnificently back from the engine.

'Let her come! She'll meet her match!' A war-whoop upon the steam whistle fittingly closed the speech, and the train sprang into action.

We had about fifteen miles to go, and we banged and bucketed over it in what was, I should imagine, record time. The carriage felt as if it were galloping on four wooden legs, my teeth chattered in my head, and the salmon slowly churned its way forth from its newspaper, and moved along the netting with dreadful stealth.

All was of no avail.

'Well,' said the guard, as I stepped forth on to the deserted platform of Loughranny, 'that owld Limited Mail's th' unpunctualest thrain in Ireland! If you're a minute late she's gone from you, and may be if you were early you might be half-an-hour waiting for her!'

On the whole the guard was a gentleman. He said he would show me the best hotel in the town, though he feared I would be hard set to get a bed anywhere because of the 'Feis' (a Feis, I should explain, is a Festival devoted to competitions in Irish songs and dances). He shouldered my portmanteau, he even grappled successfully with the salmon, and, as we traversed the empty streets, he explained to me how easily I could catch the morning boat from Rosslare, and how it was, as a matter of fact, quite the act of Providence that my original scheme had been frustrated.

All was dark at the uninviting portals of the hotel favoured by the guard. For a full five minutes we waited at them, ringing hard: I suggested that we should try elsewhere.

'He'll come,' said the guard, with the confidence of the Pied Piper of Hamelin, retaining an implacable thumb upon the button of the electric bell. 'He'll come. Sure it rings in his room!'

The victim came, half awake, half dressed, and with an inch of dripping candle in his fingers. There was not a bed there, he said, nor in the town neither.

I said I would sit in the dining-room till the time for the early train.

'Sure there's five beds in the dining-room,' replied the boots, 'and there's mostly two in every bed.'

His voice was firm, but there was a wavering look in his eye.

'What about the billiard-room, Mike?' said the guard, in wooing tones.

'Ah, God bless you! we have a mattress on the table this minute!' answered the boots, wearily, 'and the fellow that got the First Prize for Reels asleep on top of it!'

'Well, and can't ye put the palliasse on the floor under it, ye omadhawn?' said the guard, dumping my luggage and the salmon in the hall, 'sure there's no snugger place in the house! I must run away home now, before Herself thinks I'm dead altogether!'

His retreating footsteps went lightly away down the empty street.

'Annything don't trouble *him!*' said the boots bitterly.

As for me, nothing save the Personal Element stood between me and destitution.

It was in the dark of the early morning that I woke again to life and its troubles. A voice, dropping, as it were, over the edge of some smothering over-world, had awakened me. It was the voice of the First Prize for Reels, descending through a pocket of the billiard-table.

'I beg your pardon, sir, are ye going on the 5 to Cork?'

I grunted a negative.

'Well, if ye were, ye'd be late,' said the voice.

I received this useful information in indignant silence, and endeavoured to wrap myself again in the vanishing skirts of a dream.

'I'm going on the 6:30 meself,' proceeded the voice, 'and it's unknown to me how I'll put on me boots. Me feet is swelled the size o' three-pound loaves with the dint of the little dancing-shoes I had on me in the competition last night. Me feet's delicate that way, and I'm a great epicure about me boots.'

I snored aggressively, but the dream was gone. So, for all practical purposes, was the night.

The First Price for Reels arose, presenting an astonishing spectacle of grass-green breeches, a white shirt, and pearl-grey stockings, and accomplished a toilet that consisted of removing these and putting on ordinary garments, completed by the apparently excruciating act of getting into his boots. At any other hour of the day I might have been sorry for him. He then removed himself and his belongings to the hall, and there entered upon a resounding conversation with the boots, while I crawled forth from my lair to renew the strife with circumstances and to endeavour to compose a telegram to Alice Hervey of explanation and apology that should cost less than seven and sixpence. There was also the salmon to be dealt with.

Here the boots intervened, opportunely, with a cup of tea, and the intelligence that he had already done up the salmon in straw bottlecovers and brown paper, and that I could travel Europe with it if I liked. He further informed me that he would run up to the station with the luggage now, and that maybe I wouldn't mind carrying the fish myself; it was on the table in the hall.

My train went at 6:15. The boots had secured for me one of many empty carriages, and lingered conversationally till the train started; he regretted politely my bad night at the hotel, and assured me that only for Jimmy Durkan having a little drink taken—Jimmy Durkan was the First Prize for Reels—he would have turned him off the billiard table for my benefit. He finally confided to me that Mr Durkan was engaged to his sister, and was a rising baker in the town of Limerick, indeed, he said, any girl might be glad to get him. He dances like whalebone, and he makes grand bread!

Here the train started.

It was late that night, when, stiff, dirty, with tired eyes blinking in the dazzle of electric light, I was conducted by the Herveys' beautiful footman into the Herveys' baronial hall, and was told by the Herveys' imperial butler that dinner was over, and the gentlemen had just gone into the drawing-room. I was in the act of hastily declining to join them there, when a voice cried—

'Here he is!'

And Philippa, rustling and radiant, came forth into the hall, followed in shimmers of satin, and flutterings of lace, by Alice Hervey, by the bride elect, and by the usual festival rout of exhilarated relatives, male and female, whose mission it is to keep things lively before a wedding.

'Is this a wedding present for me, Uncle Sinclair?' cried the bride elect, through a deluge of questions and commiserations, and snatched from under my arm the brown paper parcel that had remained there from force of direful habit.

'I advise you not to open it!' I exclaimed; 'It's a salmon!'

The bride elect, with a shriek of disgust, and without an instant of hesitation, hurled it at her nearest neighbour, the head bridesmaid. The head bridesmaid, with an answering shriek, sprang to one side, and the parcel that I had cherished with a mother's care across two countries and a stormy channel, fell, with a crash, on the flagged floor.

Why did it crash?

'A salmon?' screamed Philippa, gazing at the parcel, round which a pool was already forming, 'why, that's whisky! Can't you smell it?'

The footman here respectfully interposed, and kneeling down, cautiously extracted from folds of brown paper a straw bottle cover full of broken glass and dripping with whisky.

'I'm afraid the other things are rather spoiled, sir,' he said seriously, and drew forth, successively, a very large pair of high-low shoes, two long grey worsted stockings, and a pair of grass-green breeches.

They brought the house down, in a manner doubtless familiar to them when they shared the triumphs of Mr Jimmy Durkan, but they left Alice Hervey distinctly cold.

'You know, darling,' she said to Philippa afterwards, 'I don't think it was very clever of dear Sinclair to take the wrong parcel. I *had* counted on that salmon.'

> Edith Somerville and Martin Ross (1858–1949; 1862–1915), *Further Experiences of an Irish R.M.* (1908).
>
> ➤ When Miss Ross died after a bad fall from a horse, Miss Somerville, who was keen on spiritualism, carried on the partnership by contacting Miss Ross on the Other Side and taking dictation. By this method the co-authors produced thirteen more books.

———

THE *works of Somerville and Ross have never been out of print, have been made into a successful television series and have undoubtedly delighted and amused millions of readers for nearly a century. Yet the books of a contemporary of theirs, an Irish lady author whose readership could be reckoned only in hundreds, probably induced many more wild guffaws and much more uncontrollable, helpless laughter.*

Unhappily that was not her intention.

Amanda McKittrick Ros, wife of the stationmaster of Larne, in Co. Antrim, was a serious novelist (her visiting cards read 'Authoress. At Home always to the honourable'). What distinguished her work, apart from its most peculiar prose, was its author's positively Olympian lack of any vestige of a sense of humour. She could be described as a kind of female, prose McGonagall.

Mrs Ros did not for a moment doubt her own literary genius and took any whiff of criticism as a personal insult. If she heard that an English journal had had the temerity to offer an opinion on one of her books she chased up the review through friends:

I would be glad to see the critique you mentioned which appeared in the 'Daily Express', no matter how bad the beast described his effortless effort to sting the Author, who loves to see she can wring from the critic crabs their biting little bits of buggery. Every critique you see, cut it out and let me have it, please.   Amanda McKittrick Ros (1860–1939), letter to Norman Carrothers. Quoted by Jack Loudan; *O Rare Amanda!*

One humorist and critic, Barry Pain, wrote a funny piece about Mrs Ros's first novel Irene Iddesleigh *for the magazine* Black and White. *He gave his review the ironic title of 'The Book of the Century'.*

Somebody sent Mrs Ros a copy of it. Every formidable inch of her a fighter, she came back at him all guns firing in the preliminary pages of her next book, thus winning Barry Pain a footnote in literary history as being the first reviewer to be attacked by an author for an unfavourable review of her first novel in the preface to her second:

CRITICISM OF BARRY PAIN ON 'IRENE IDDESLEIGH'

By Amanda M. Ros

This so-called Barry Pain, by name, has taken upon himself to criticise a work the depth of which fails to reach the solving power of his borrow'd, and, he'd have you believe, varied talent . . .

'*I have called it The Book of the Century!*' I care not what Barry calls the book I have written. I care not for the opinion of half-starved upstarts, who don the garb of a shabby genteel, and would fain feed the minds of the people with the worthless scraps of stolen fancies . . .

When Barry was swelling his head with the idea he thought to press into universal persuasion, but in which he has experienced a defeat for at least once in his famous life-time, I wonder if he failed to experience a sense of shame, a sense of ignorance, strongly indulged in by his professional brothers, at the great presumption he manifested in laying before the public a page of such balderdash, only attributable to a ranting schoolboy; and one has just to read *Black and White*, page 249, of 19th February, to endorse my pungent remark.

Never in the knowledge of man has there been such a downpour of expression, such a page of kindliness, as that found in *Black and White*, page 249, of 19th February, 1898, entitled '*The Book of the Century*', by (I'm off in a swoon!)—by (ah, the thought is too great, it is too much!)—Bar—(Almighty Father, my brain is in a whizz!)—Barry—(I'm tremendous sick!)—P—(Holy of Holies!)—Pa—(the heart's pulsations are about to stop!)—Pain!—(not a bit of them! I've got relief, by heavens! relief at last!), and good-bye, Barry dear . . .   Preface to *Delina Delaney* (1898).

❉ There was twenty pages of it.

As well as her novels Mrs Ros also published two slim volumes of verse; Poems of Puncture *and* Fumes of Fermentation (*a feature of Mrs Ros's writing style was her devotion to alliteration*). *Many of the poems were slashing denunciations of local Belfast solicitors and clergymen who had done something to arouse her wrath, but there were also one or two whose subjects called for a more reflective and elegaic treatment:*

ON VISITING WESTMINSTER ABBEY A 'REDUCED DIGNITY' INVITED ME TO MUSE ON ITS MERITS.

> Holy Moses! Have a look!
> Flesh decayed in every nook!
> Some rare bits of brain lie here
> Mortal loads of beef and beer . . .

Fumes of Fermentation (1933).

After Barry Pain's piece in Black and White, *Mrs Ros and her works became something of an hilarious in-joke among the young intellectuals of the day. Aldous Huxley wrote an essay on her which he called 'Euphues Redivivus', and her* Irene Iddesleigh *had a band of admirers in Britain which included Osbert Sitwell, Lord Beveridge, Desmond MacCarthy, and E. V. Lucas. The book was published in Belfast and copies were hard to come by in London so copies were passed round between friends, although it was said that the Prime Minister, Lord Salisbury, had one to himself.*

Amanda Ros clubs were formed and parties were held at which everybody had to talk like an Amanda Ros character.

The following sample of Mrs Ros's dialogue will indicate how difficult it must have been to sustain for a whole evening, even if you were Aldous Huxley. The extract is taken from her third novel, Helen Huddleson, *published posthumously in 1969. It is the proposal scene (a highly-charged, emotional passage if ever there was one, yet Mrs Ros manages to squeeze in a quick side-swipe at critics).*

Helen, lovely but poor and vulnerable, is cornered by his lordship, rotten to the core:

'Now Helen, my darling, my queen, my all, had I not loved you as never woman before, I'd have allowed you to go on your way rejoicing, but, I can never, NEVER, I say, see you the wife of any other man save myself.' Helen still remaining laconic as he continued:

'The illimitable love I possess for you within this heart of mine can never suffer that blow you fain would strike it. Truly, it would kill me outright were you to reject an offer hundreds of society shams grieve because they cannot grasp. I have travelled through many foreign climes, I have seen the fairest daughters Nature can produce—or critic-crabs denounce—but none so fair as you, my Helen.'

Still spurnfull, he went on:

'You may think it dishonourable of me trying to wreck the happiness of him to whom you have plighted your vow but there is nothing unfair in love and war, the mightiness of two such strongholds banish all faintness from the human heart. I can't live without you, Helen Huddleson. Say no. I die. Say yes. I will live for you, love you, worship you, cherish you while this life lasts.'

He gazed at her wan face moulded in rigidity, a face immersed in indecision that gave him a thread of hope. He pressed her ruby lips to his, her colour grew white and red alternately, through force of her thoughts.

'Will you love me, my fond girl?' he panted. 'Will you?'

She remained immobile—taciturn.

'Ah, darling—speak,' he pleaded plaintively. 'I am mad with excitement, wild with expectancy, awaiting those sweet lips of yours to open and act their part in conveying to me that for which I have yearned for years.'

He pressed his hot forehead with his hand.

'Will you be my wife, Helen Huddleson?' the sweat drops pebbling his brow as he anxiously awaited her reply.

She trembled violently until at last the answer came.

'Sir—I cannot,' wringing her small hands as the negative dropped from her parched lips . . .

'Then, by heaven, I'll end the scene,' drawing from his jacket pocket a pistol. 'I shall shoot you first—myself after,' holding the weapon menacingly to sever the soul and body of her he could never bear to see the wife of another.

Helen rose, rushed forward towards him screaming:

'Why, oh why, sir, damn your soul forever by such savage acts?'. . .

He looked upon her where she stood gasping, her bleached lips quivering, her hand upon the weapon she still regarded with awe. He gave her a murderous stare, exclaiming in frenzy:

'Helen, Helen, 'tis all your fault. I'll give you another minute to decide, another minute to aid this acheing heart of mine you have so cruelly stabbed by your refusal to own it.'

He counted the seconds and on reaching fifty-nine she clasped him in her trembling arms—shouting:

'I will—I will marry you, Lord Rasberry.'

She then fell fainting at his feet.

Helen Huddleson (1969).

➤ Other characters in the novel were Cherry, Duchess of Greengage; a lady steeped in vice named Madam Pear; a fallen wife called Mrs Strawberry; the Earl of Grape; Sir Christopher Currant; Sir Peter Plum; and the maid Lentil. Over tea, Mrs Ros's biographer, Jack Loudan, asked the author why she had named her principal male character 'Rasberry'. 'Her hand stopped as she was about to put the cup to her lips. There was a puzzled expression on her face as she looked at me. "What else *would* I call him?" she asked.'

Perhaps it was all summed up best by Mark Twain. A friend presented him with a copy of Irene Iddesleigh. *Twain wrote back, 'I find the book enchanting . . . many years ago I began to collect "hogwash" literature, and I am glad of the chance to add to it the extraordinary book which you have sent me.'*

H. G. WELLS *had one foot in humour but at least four more feet in other literary
forms; one in the novel of ideas, another in scientific romances, another in
social comedies, and yet another in encyclopaedic social and scientific histories. In
spite of the huge success of his comic novels such as* Kipps; the Story of a Simple
Soul *and* The History of Mr Polly, *and of his science-fiction novels like* The
Invisible Man *and* The War of the Worlds, *Wells did not look upon himself as a
novelist at all but as a journalist, a 'prophet and spokesman for progress'.*

*Wells first made his mark at the end of the nineteenth century with a series of
highly popular science-fiction stories. Jules Verne was the pioneer of this kind of
imaginative fiction but Wells, the first successful writer of science-fiction in Britain,
extended the form. Verne's stories were adventure yarns based on feasible scientific
developments but Wells's stories, which he called 'fantastic romances', were fables
about real people, with real social problems, caught up in a scientific fantasy.*

*He had always been fascinated by science. After a miserable time as a young boy
working in a draper's shop and as an apprentice pharmacist he won a scholarship
to the Normal School of Science (a 'Normal' school trained teachers. This one was
later more happily renamed the Imperial College of Science and Technology). Wells
much enjoyed himself under the tutelage of the leading biologist of the day T. H.
Huxley. While he was studying he became deeply involved in socialism and he also
fell in love with his cousin and married her, but later ran away with one of his
students (he enjoyed an unusually fervent love-life). He failed his finals. Back he
went as an external student and won his B.Sc. with honours, thus becoming within
a few years the first major novelist (and humorist) to have a sound background of
scientific knowledge.*

*Joseph Conrad called Wells the 'realist of the fantastic'. The following short
story shows how skilfully he made use of realistic detail to heighten the fantasy.*

*Pyecraft is not only the fattest member of the narrator's London club, and the
club's number one bore, but he also shares with the narrator a bizarre secret:*

THE TRUTH ABOUT PYECRAFT

He sits not a dozen yards away. If I glance over my shoulder I can see him.
And if I catch his eye—and usually I catch his eye—it meets me with an
expression—

It is mainly an imploring look—and yet with suspicion in it.

Confound his suspicion! If I wanted to tell on him I should have told
long ago. I don't tell and I don't tell, and he ought to feel at his ease. As if
anything so gross and fat as he could feel at ease! Who would believe me if I
did tell?

Poor old Pyecraft! Great, uneasy jelly of substance! The fattest clubman
in London.

He sits at one of the little club tables in the huge bay by the fire, stuffing.
What is he stuffing? I glance judiciously and catch him biting at a round of
hot buttered teacake, with his eyes on me. Confound him!—with his eyes on
me!

That settles it, Pyecraft! Since you *will* be abject, since you *will* behave as though I was not a man of honour, here, right under your embedded eyes, I write the thing down—the plain truth about Pyecraft. The man I helped, the man I shielded, and who has requited me by making my club unendurable, absolutely unendurable, with his liquid appeal, with the perpetual 'don't tell' of his looks.

And, besides, why does he keep on eternally eating?

Well, here goes for the truth, the whole truth, and nothing but the truth!

Pyecraft—. I made the acquaintance of Pyecraft in this very smoking-room. I was a young, nervous new member, and he saw it. I was sitting all alone, wishing I knew more of the members, and suddenly he came, a great rolling front of chins and abdomina, towards me, and grunted and sat down in a chair close by me and wheezed for a space, and scraped for a space with a match and lit a cigar, and then addressed me. I forget what he said— something about the matches not lighting properly, and afterwards as he talked he kept stopping the waiters one by one as they went by, and telling them about the matches in that thin, fluty voice he has. But, anyhow, it was in some such way we began our talking.

He talked about various things and came round to games. And thence to my figure and complexion. '*You* ought to be a good cricketer,' he said. I suppose I am slender, slender to what some people would call lean, and I suppose I am rather dark, still—I am not ashamed of having a Hindu great-grandmother, but, for that, I don't want casual strangers to see through me at a glance to her. So that I was set against Pyecraft from the beginning.

But he only talked about me in order to get to himself.

'I expect,' he said, 'you take no more exercise than I do, and probably you eat no less.' (Like all excessively obese people he fancied he ate nothing.) 'Yet'—and he smiled an oblique smile—'we differ.'

And then he began to talk about his fatness and his fatness; all he did for his fatness and all he was going to do for his fatness; what people had advised him to do for his fatness and what he had heard of people doing for fatness similar to his. '*A priori*,' he said, 'one would think a question of nutrition could be answered by dietary and a question of assimilation by drugs.' It was stifling. It was dumpling talk. It made me feel swelled to hear him.

One stands that sort of thing once in a way at a club, but a time came when I fancied I was standing too much. He took to me altogether too conspicuously. I could never go into the smoking-room but he would come wallowing towards me, and sometimes he came and gormandised round and about me while I had my lunch. He seemed at times almost to be clinging to me. He was a bore, but not so fearful a bore as to be limited to me; and from the first there was something in his manner—almost as though he knew, almost as though he penetrated to the fact that I *might*—that there was a remote, exceptional chance in me that no one else presented.

'I'd give anything to get it down,' he would say—'anything,' and peer at me over his vast cheeks and pant.

Poor old Pyecraft! He has just gonged, no doubt to order another buttered tea-cake!

He came to the actual thing one day. 'Our Pharmacopoeia,' he said, 'our Western Pharmacopoeia, is anything but the last word of medical science. In the East, I've been told—'

He stopped and stared at me. It was like being at an aquarium.

I was quite suddenly angry with him. 'Look here,' I said, 'who told you about my great-grandmother's recipes?'

'Well,' he fenced.

'Every time we've met for a week,' I said—'and we've met pretty often— you've given me a broad hint or so about that little secret of mine.'

'Well,' he said, 'now the cat's out of the bag, I'll admit, yes, it is so. I had it—'

'From Pattison?'

'Indirectly,' he said, which I believe was lying, 'yes'.

'Pattison,' I said, 'took that stuff at his own risk.'

He pursed his mouth and bowed.

'My great-grandmother's recipes,' I said, 'are queer things to handle. My father was near making me promise—'

'He didn't?'

'No. But he warned me. He himself used one—once.'

'Ah! . . . But do you think—? Suppose—suppose there did happen to be one—'

'The things are curious documents,' I said. 'Even the smell of 'em . . . No!'

But after going so far Pyecraft was resolved I should go farther. I was always a little afraid if I tried his patience too much he would fall on me suddenly and smother me. I own I was weak. But I was also annoyed with Pyecraft. I had got to that state of feeling for him that disposed me to say, 'Well, *take* the risk!' The little affair of Pattison to which I have alluded was a different matter altogether. What it was doesn't concern us now, but I knew, anyhow, that the particular recipe I used then was safe. The rest I didn't know so much about, and, on the whole, I was inclined to doubt their safety pretty completely.

Yet even if Pyecraft got poisoned—

I must confess the poisoning of Pyecraft struck me as an immense undertaking.

That evening I took that queer, odd-scented sandalwood box out of my safe and turned the rustling skins over. The gentleman who wrote the recipes for my great-grandmother evidently had a weakness for skins of a miscellaneous origin, and his handwriting was cramped to the last degree. Some of the things are quite unreadable to me—though my family, with its Indian Civil Service associations, has kept up a knowledge of Hindustani from generation to generation—and none are absolutely plain sailing. But I found the one that I knew was there soon enough, and sat on the floor by my safe for some time looking at it.

'Look here,' said I to Pyecraft next day, and snatched the slip away from his eager grasp.

'So far as I can make it out, this is a recipe for Loss of Weight. ("Ah!" said Pyecraft.) I'm not absolutely sure, but I think it's that. And if you take my advice you'll leave it alone. Because, you know—I blacken my blood in your interest, Pyecraft—my ancestors on that side were, so far as I can gather, a jolly queer lot. See?'

'Let me try it,' said Pyecraft.

I leant back in my chair. My imagination made one mighty effort and fell flat within me.

'What in Heaven's name, Pyecraft,' I asked, 'do you think you'll look like when you get thin?'

He was impervious to reason. I made him promise never to say a word to me about his disgusting fatness again whatever happened—never, and then I handed him that little piece of skin.

'It's nasty stuff,' I said.

'No matter,' he said, and took it.

He goggled at it. 'But—but—' he said.

He had just discovered that it wasn't English.

'To the best of my ability,' I said, 'I will do you a translation.'

I did my best. After that we didn't speak for a fortnight. Whenever he approached me I frowned and motioned him away, and he respected our compact, but at the end of the fortnight he was as fat as ever. And then he got a word in. 'I must speak,' he said. 'It isn't fair. There's something wrong. It's done me no good. You're not doing your great-grandmother justice—'

'Where's the recipe?'

He produced it gingerly from his pocket-book.

I ran my eye over the items. 'Was the egg addled?' I asked.

'No. Ought it have been?'

'That,' I said, 'goes without saying in all my poor dear great-grandmother's recipes. When condition or quality is not specified you must get the worst. She was drastic or nothing. . . . And there's one or two possible alternatives to some of these other things. You've got *fresh* rattlesnake venom?'

'I got a rattlesnake from Jamrach's. It cost—it cost—'

'That's your affair, anyhow. This last item—'

'I know a man who—'

'Yes. H'm. Well, I'll write the alternatives down. So far as I know the language, the spelling of this recipe is particularly atrocious. By-the-bye, dog here probably means pariah dog.'

For a month after that I saw Pyecraft constantly at the club and as fat and anxious as ever. He kept our treaty, but at times broke the spirit of it by shaking his head despondently. Then one day in the cloakroom he said, 'Your great-grandmother—'

'Not a word against her,' I said; and he held his peace.

I could have fancied he had desisted, and I saw him one day talking to three new members about his fatness as though he was in search of other recipes. And then, quite unexpectedly, his telegram came.

'Mr Formalyn!' bawled a page-boy under my nose, and I took the telegram and opened it at once.

'*For Heaven's sake come.—Pyecraft.*'

'H'm,' said I, and to tell the truth I was so pleased at the rehabilitation of my great-grandmother's reputation this evidently promised that I made a most excellent lunch.

I got Pyecraft's address from the hall porter. Pyecraft inhabited the upper half of a house in Bloomsbury, and I went there so soon as I had done my coffee and Trappistine. I did not wait to finish my cigar.

'Mr Pyecraft?' said I, at the front door.

They believed he was ill; he hadn't been out for two days.

'He expects me,' said I, and they sent me up.

I rang the bell at the lattice-door upon the landing.

'He shouldn't have tried it, anyhow,' I said to myself. 'A man who eats like a pig ought to look like a pig.'

An obviously worthy woman, with an anxious face and a carelessly placed cap, came and surveyed me through the lattice.

I gave my name and she let me in a dubious fashion.

'Well?' said I, as we stood together inside Pyecraft's piece of the landing.

''E said you was to come in if you came,' she said, and regarded me, making no motion to show me anywhere. And then, confidentially, ''E's locked in, sir.'

'Locked in?'

'Locked himself in yesterday morning and 'asn't let any one in since, sir. And ever and again *swearing*. Oh, my!'

I stared at the door she indicated by her glances. 'In there?' I said.

'Yes, sir.'

'What's up?'

She shook her head sadly. ''E keeps on calling for vittles, sir. 'Eavy vittle 'e wants. I get 'im what I can. Pork 'e's 'ad, sooit puddin', sossiges, noo bread. Everythink like that. Left outside, if you please, and me go away. 'E's eatin,' sir, somethink *awful*.'

Then came a piping bawl from inside the door: 'That Formalyn?'

'That you, Pyecraft,' I shouted, and went and banged the door.

'Tell her to go away.'

I did.

Then I could hear a curious pattering upon the door, almost like some one feeling for the handle in the dark, and Pyecraft's familiar grunts.

'It's all right,' I said, 'she's gone.'

But for a long time the door didn't open.

I heard the key turn. Then Pyecraft's voice said, 'Come in.'

I turned the handle and opened the door. Naturally I expected to see Pyecraft.

Well, you know, he wasn't there!

I never had such a shock in my life. There was his sitting-room in a state of untidy disorder, plates and dishes among the books and writing things, and several chairs overturned, but Pyecraft—

'It's all right, o' man; shut the door,' he said, and then I discovered him.

There he was right up close to the cornice in the corner by the door, as though some one had glued him to the ceiling. His face was anxious and angry. He panted and gesticulated. 'Shut the door,' he said. 'If that woman gets hold of it—'

I shut the door, and went and stood away from him and stared.

'If anything gives way and you tumble down,' I said, 'you'll break your neck, Pyecraft.'

'I wish I could,' he wheezed.

'A man of your age and weight getting up to kiddish gymnastics—'

'Don't,' he said, and looked agonized.

'I'll tell you,' he said, and gesticulated.

'How the deuce,' said I, 'are you holding on up there?'

And then abruptly I realized that he was not holding on at all, that he was floating up there—just as a gas-filled bladder might have floated in the same position. He began a struggle to thrust himself away from the ceiling and to clamber down the wall to me. 'It's that prescription,' he panted, as he did so. 'Your great-gran—'

He took hold of a framed engraving rather carelessly as he spoke and it gave way, and he flew back to the ceiling again, while the picture smashed on to the sofa. Bump he went against the ceiling, and I knew then why he was all over white on the more salient curves and angles of his person. He tried again more carefully, coming down by way of the mantel.

It was really a most extraordinary spectacle, that great, fat, apoplectic-looking man upside down and trying to get from the ceiling to the floor. 'That prescription,' he said. 'Too successful.'

'How?'

'Loss of weight—almost complete.'

And then, of course, I understood.

'By Jove, Pyecraft,' said I, 'what you wanted was a cure for fatness! But you always called it weight. You would call it weight.'

Somehow I was extremely delighted. I quite liked Pyecraft for the time. 'Let me help you!' I said, and took his hand and pulled him down. He kicked about, trying to get a foothold somewhere. It was very like holding a flag on a windy day.

'That table,' he said, pointing, 'is solid mahogany and very heavy. If you can put me under that—'

I did, and there he wallowed about like a captive balloon, while I stood on his hearthrug and talked to him.

I lit a cigar. 'Tell me,' I said, 'what happened?'

'I took it,' he said.

'How did it taste?'

'Oh, *beastly!*'

I should fancy they all did. Whether one regards the ingredients or the probable compound or the possible results, almost all my great-grandmother's remedies appear to me at least to be extraordinary uninviting. For my own part—

'I took a little sip first.'

'Yes?'

'And as I felt lighter and better after an hour, I decided to take the draught.'

'My dear Pyecraft!'

'I held my nose,' he explained. 'And then I kept on getting lighter and lighter—and helpless, you know.'

He gave way suddenly to a burst of passion.

'What the goodness am I to *do?*' he said.

'There's one thing pretty evident,' I said, 'that you mustn't do. If you go out of doors you'll go up and up.' I waved an arm upward.

'They'd have to send Santos-Dumont after you to bring you down again.'

'I suppose it will wear off?'

I shook my head. 'I don't think you can count on that,' I said.

And then there was another burst of passion, and he kicked out at adjacent chairs and banged the floor. He behaved just as I should have expected a great, fat, self-indulgent man to behave under trying circumstances—that is to say, very badly. He spoke of me and of my great-grandmother with an utter want of discretion.

'I never asked you to take the stuff,' I said.

And generously disregarding the insults he was putting upon me, I sat down in his armchair and began to talk to him in a sober, friendly fashion.

I pointed out to him that this was a trouble he had brought upon himself, and that it had almost an air of poetical justice. He had eaten too much. This he disputed, and for a time we argued the point.

He became noisy and violent, so I desisted from this aspect of his lesson. 'And then,' said I, 'you committed the sin of euphemism. You called it, not Fat, which is just and inglorious, but Weight. You—'

He interrupted to say that he recognized all that. What was he to *do?*

I suggested he should adapt himself to his new conditions. So we came to the really sensible part of the business. I suggested that it would not be difficult for him to learn to walk about on the ceiling with his hands—

'I can't sleep,' he said.

But that was no great difficulty. It was quite possible, I pointed out, to make a shake-up under a wire mattress, fasten the under things on with tapes, and have a blanket, sheet, and coverlet to button at the side. He would have to confide in his housekeeper, I said; and after some squabbling he agreed to that. (Afterwards it was quite delightful to see the beautifully matter-of-fact way with which the good lady took all these amazing inversions.) He could have a library ladder in his room, and all his meals could be laid on the top of his bookcase. We also hit on an ingenious device by which he could get to the floor whenever he wanted, which was simply to put the *British Encyclopaedia* (tenth edition) on the top of his open shelves. He just pulled out a couple of volumes and held on, and down he came. And we agreed there must be iron staples along the skirting, so that he could cling to those whenever he wanted to get about the room on the lower level.

As we got on with the thing I found myself almost keenly interested. It was I who called in the housekeeper and broke matters to her, and it was I chiefly who fixed up the inverted bed. In fact, I spent two whole days at his flat. I am a handy, interfering sort of man with a screwdriver, and I made all sorts of ingenious adaptations for him—ran a wire to bring his bells within reach, turned all his electric lights up instead of down, and so on. The whole affair was extremely curious and interesting to me, and it was delightful to think of Pyecraft like some great, fat blow-fly, crawling about on his ceiling and clambering round the lintel of his doors from one room to another, and never, never, never coming to the club any more . . .

Then, you know, my fatal ingenuity got the better of me. I was sitting by his fire drinking his whisky, and he was up in his favourite corner by the cornice, tacking a Turkey carpet to the ceiling, when the idea struck me. 'By Jove, Pyecraft!' I said, 'all this is totally unnecessary.'

And before I could calculate the complete consequences of my notion I blurted it out. 'Lead underclothing,' said I, and the mischief was done.

Pyecraft received the thing almost in tears. 'To be right ways up again—' he said.

I gave him the whole secret before I saw where it would take me. 'Buy sheet lead,' I said, 'stamp it into discs. Sew 'em all over your underclothes until you have enough. Have lead-soled boots, carry a bag of solid lead, and the thing is done! Instead of being a prisoner here you may go abroad again, Pyecraft; you may travel—'

A still happier idea came to me. 'You need never fear a shipwreck. All you need do is just slip off some or all of your clothes, take the necessary amount of luggage in your hand, and float up in the air—'

In his emotion he dropped the tack-hammer within an ace of my head. 'By Jove!' he said, 'I shall be able to come back to the club again.'

The thing pulled me up short. 'By Jove!' I said, faintly. 'Yes. Of course—you will.'

He did. He does. There he sits behind me now, stuffing—as I live!—a third go of buttered tea-cake. And no one in the whole world knows—except his housekeeper and me—that he weighs practically nothing; that he is a mere boring mass of assimilatory matter, mere clouds in clothing, *niente*, *nefas*, the most inconsiderable of men.

There he sits watching until I have done this writing. Then, if he can, he will waylay me. He will come billowing up to me . . .

He will tell me over again all about it, how it feels, how it doesn't feel, how he sometimes hopes it is passing off a little. And always somewhere in that fat, abundant discourse he will say, 'The secret's keeping, eh? If any one knew of it—I should be so ashamed . . . Makes a fellow look such a fool, you know. Crawling about on a ceiling and all that . . .'

And now to elude Pyecraft, occupying, as he does, an admirable strategic position between me and the door.   H. G. Wells (1866–1946), *Twelve Stories* (1903).

At the turn of the century Wells turned away for the time being from 'Wellsian' science-fiction and began a series of four warmly humorous and satirical stories of English class and society, Love and Mr Lewisham, Kipps, Tono-Bungay, *and* The History of Mr Polly, *which stand comparison with Dickens in their descriptive gusto and their sympathy with the problems of the shabby-genteel class. Like some of Dickens's books, Wells's novels were partly autobiographical. His parents, like Dickens's, were shabby-genteel. His father kept a small, unprofitable shop in Bromley, Kent, and made a few pounds on the side as a professional cricketer (he is in the record books as the first bowler to take four wickets in first-class cricket with four successive balls). When things became difficult his mother went back to her old job as a housekeeper and Wells, aged 14, was sent out to work in a draper's shop.*

Kipps, in Kipps; the Story of a Simple Soul, *is also a draper's assistant, and the girl he loves is in domestic service, but whereas Wells broke out of his background by studying hard, the young Kipps in the book unexpectedly inherits a fortune. He sets out to live the life of a wealthy gentleman but eventually abandons his pretensions and thankfully returns to the simple life and his girl. He finds that trying to behave like a rich man brings problems.*

Like coping with the complexities of dining in the magnificent Royal Grand Hotel:

Safe in his room, Kipps pulled himself together for dinner. He had learnt enough from young Walshingham to bring his dress clothes, and now he began to assume them. Unfortunately in the excitement of his flight from his Aunt and Uncle he had forgotten to put in his other boots, and he was some time deciding between his purple cloth slippers with a golden marigold and the prospect of cleaning the boots he was wearing with the towel, but finally, being a little footsore, he took the slippers.

Afterwards, when he saw the porters and waiters and the other guests catch sight of the slippers, he was sorry he had not chosen the boots.

However, to make up for any want of style at that end, he had his crush hat under his arm.

He found the dining-room without excessive trouble. It was a vast and splendidly decorated place, and a number of people, evidently quite *au fait*, were dining there at little tables lit with electric red-shaded candles, gentlemen in evening dress, and ladies with dazzling astonishing necks. Kipps had never seen evening dress in full vigour before, and he doubted his eyes. And there were also people not in evening dress, who no doubt wondered what noble family Kipps represented. There was a band in a decorated recess, and the band looked collectively at the purple slippers, and so lost any chance they may have had of a donation so far as Kipps was concerned. The chief drawback to this magnificent place was the excessive space of floor that had to be crossed before you got your purple slippers hidden under a table.

He selected a little table—not the one where a rather impudent-looking waiter held a chair, but another—sat down, and, finding his gibus [collapsible silk opera-hat] in his hand, decided after a moment of thought to rise slightly and sit on it. (It was discovered in his abandoned chair at a late hour by a supper-party and restored to him next day.)

He put the napkin carefully on one side, selected his soup without difficulty, 'Clear please,' but he was rather floored by the presentation of a quite splendidly bound wine-card. He turned it over, discovered a section devoted to whisky, and had a bright idea.

''Ere,' he said to the waiter, with an encouraging movement of the head; and then in a confidential manner, 'You 'aven't any Old Methuselah Three Stars, 'ave you?'

The waiter went away to inquire, and Kipps went on with his soup with an enhanced self-respect. Finally, Old Methuselah being unattainable, he ordered a claret from about the middle of the list. 'Let's 'ave some of this,' he said. He knew claret was a good sort of wine.

'A half bottle?' said the waiter.

'Right you are,' said Kipps.

He felt he was getting on. He leant back after his soup, a man of the world, and then slowly brought his eyes round to the ladies in evening dress on his right . . .

He couldn't have thought it!

They were scorchers. Just a bit of black velvet over the shoulders!

He looked again. One of them was laughing with a glass of wine half raised—wicked-looking woman she was; the other, the black velvet one, was eating bits of bread with nervous quickness and talking fast.

He wished old Buggins could see them.

He found a waiter regarding him and blushed deeply. He did not look again for some time, and became confused about his knife and fork over the fish. Presently he remarked a lady in pink to the left of him eating the fish with an entirely different implement.

It was over the *vol au vent* that he began to go to pieces. He took a knife to it; then saw the lady in pink was using a fork only, and hastily put down his knife, with a considerable amount of rich creaminess on the blade, upon the cloth. Then he found that a fork in his inexperienced hand was an instrument of chase rather than capture. His ears became violently red, and then he looked up to discover the lady in pink glancing at him, and then smiling, as she spoke to the man beside her.

He hated the lady in pink very much.

He stabbed a large piece of the *vol au vent* at last, and was too glad of his luck not to make a mouthful of it. But it was an extensive fragment, and pieces escaped him. Shirt-front! 'Dash it!' he said, and had resort to his spoon. His waiter went and spoke to two other waiters, no doubt jeering at him. He became very fierce suddenly. ''Ere!' he said, gesticulating; and then, 'Clear this away!'

The entire dinner-party on his right, the party of the ladies in advanced evening dress, looked at him. . . . He felt that every one was watching him and making fun of him, and the injustice of this angered him. After all, they had had every advantage he hadn't. And then, when they got him there doing his best, what must they do but glance and sneer and nudge one another. He tried to catch them at it, and then took refuge in a second glass of wine.

Suddenly and extraordinarily he found himself a Socialist. He did not care how close it was to the lean years when all these things would end.

Mutton came with peas. He arrested the hand of the waiter. 'No peas,' he said. He knew something of the danger and difficulty of eating peas. Then, when the peas went away, he was embittered again. . . . Echoes of Masterman's burning rhetoric began to reverberate in his mind. Nice lot of people these were to laugh at any one! Women half undressed—It was that made him so beastly uncomfortable. How could one eat one's dinner with people about him like that? Nice lot they were. He was glad he wasn't one of them anyhow. Yes, they might look. He resolved, if they looked at him again, he would ask one of the men who he was staring at. His perturbed and angry face would have concerned any one. The band, by an unfortunate accident, was playing truculent military music. The mental change Kipps underwent was, in its way, what psychologists call a conversion. In a few moments all Kipps' ideals were changed. He who had been 'practically a gentleman', the sedulous pupil of Coote, the punctilious raiser of hats, was instantly a rebel, an outcast, the hater of everything 'stuck up', the foe of Society and the social order of today. Here they were among the profits of their robbery, these people who might do anything with the world. . . .

'No thanks,' he said to a dish.

He addressed a scornful eye at the shoulders of the lady to his left.

Presently he was refusing another dish. He didn't like it—fussed-up food! Probably cooked by some foreigner. He finished up his wine and his bread . . .

'No, thanks.'

'No, thanks.'. . .

He discovered the eye of a diner fixed curiously upon his flushed face. He responded with a glare. Couldn't he go without things if he liked?

'What's this?' said Kipps, to a great green cone.

'Ice,' said the waiter.

'I'll 'ave some,' said Kipps.

He seized fork and spoon and assailed the bombe. It cut rather stiffly. 'Come up!' said Kipps, with concentrated bitterness, and the truncated summit of the bombe flew off suddenly, travelling eastward with remarkable velocity. Flop, it went upon the floor a yard away, and for a while time seemed empty.

At the adjacent table they were laughing altogether.

Shy the rest of the bombe at them?

Flight?

At any rate, a dignified withdrawal.

'No!' said Kipps, 'no more,' arresting the polite attempt of the waiter to serve him with another piece. He had a vague idea he might carry off the affair as though he meant the ice to go on the floor—not liking ice, for example, and being annoyed at the badness of his dinner. He put both hands on the table, thrust back his chair, disengaged a purple slipper from his napkin, and rose. He stepped carefully over the prostrate ice, kicked the napkin under the table, thrust his hands deep into his pockets, and marched out—shaking the dust of the place as it were from his feet. He left behind him a melting fragment of ice upon the floor, his gibus hat, warm and compressed in his chair, and, in addition, every social ambition he had ever entertained in the world.

Kipps; the Story of a Simple Soul (1905).

ONE *of the earliest writers this century to break away successfully from tra-ditional British sentimental comedy and prove that the public was quite prepared to enjoy an entirely different form of humour was Hector Hugh Munro, whose pseudonym was 'Saki' (origin unproved. Could have been derived from a small Amazonian monkey or the cup-bearer in Omar Khayyam's* Rubaiyat: *the latter seems more literary).*

Saki was born in Bengal, the son of the Inspector-General of Police, but was brought up by two maiden aunts in Devon. He tried to make a career in the Bengal police but his health failed and he returned to England and became a newspaper foreign correspondent and short-story writer. His first collection of stories, Regi-nald, *was published in 1904. When the war broke out he enlisted though over-age, refused a commission, and was killed on the Western Front in 1916.*

Saki's upbringing by his aunts was austere and preached the worthiness of leading a conventional life. It did not take. His stories, seemingly frivolous, were elegant but biting social satires which showed his contempt for what he saw as the silly, selfish life led by Edwardian society. Saki's humour was wholly unsentimental and laced with a deft, rather black wit.

A quotation from a Saki story joins Stephen Leacock's 'rode madly off in all directions' as being one of the best-known lines in humorous prose:

'The cook was a good cook, as cooks go; and as cooks go she went.'

> 'Saki' (H. H. Munro) (1870–1916), 'Reginald on Besetting Sins', *Reginald* (1904).

Here are some more examples of Saki's skill in making witty and quotable comments. He usually put them into the mouths of his two main characters Reginald and Clovis, who are amusingly cynical and have more than a touch of what has come to be called 'high camp':

'The Duchess suppressed a sniff. She was one of those people who regard the Church of England with patronizing affection, as if it were something that had grown up in their kitchen garden.'

> 'Reginald at the Theatre'.

'I got up the next morning at early dawn—I know it was dawn, because there were lark-noises in the sky, and the grass looked as if it had been left out all night.'

> Ibid.

'Henry Deplis was by birth a native of the Grand Duchy of Luxemburg. On maturer reflection he became a commercial traveller.'

> 'The Background', *The Chronicles of Clovis* (1911).

'The country's looking very green, but after all, that's what it's there for,' he remarked to his wife two days later.

'That's very modern, and I dare say very clever, but I'm afraid it's wasted on me,' she observed coldly.

> 'The Jesting of Arlington Stringham'.

'Waldo is one of those people who would be enormously improved by death.'

> 'The Feast of Nemesis'.

Death, touched lightly, frequently occurred in Saki's stories, most of which were black comedies and many of which featured animals. In Saki's fictional world the function of animals was not to be cuddly pets but to act as his agents of revenge.

For instance, Tobermory, a cat. At a stuffy house-party an extremely clever guest unwisely teaches the cat Tobermory to talk:

TOBERMORY

It was a chill, rain-washed afternoon of a late August day, that indefinite season when partridges are still in security or cold storage, and there is nothing to hunt—unless one is bounded on the north by the Bristol Channel, in which case one may lawfully gallop after fat red stags. Lady Blemley's house-party was not bounded on the north by the Bristol Channel, hence there was a full gathering of her guests round the tea-table on this particular afternoon. And, in spite of the blankness of the season and the triteness of the occasion, there was no trace in the company of that fatigued restlessness which means a dread of the pianola and a subdued hankering for auction bridge. The undisguised open-mouthed attention of the entire party was fixed on the homely negative personality of Mr Cornelius Appin. Of all her guests, he was the one who had come to Lady Blemley with the vaguest reputation. Some one had said he was 'clever', and he had got his invitation in the moderate expection, on the part of his hostess, that some portion at least of his cleverness would be contributed to the general entertainment. Until tea-time that day she had been unable to discover in what direction, if any, his cleverness lay. He was neither a wit nor a croquet champion, a hypnotic force nor a begetter of amateur theatricals. Neither did his exterior suggest the sort of man in whom women are willing to pardon a generous measure of mental deficiency. He had subsided into mere Mr Appin, and the Cornelius seemed a piece of transparent baptismal bluff. And now he was claiming to have launched on the world a discovery beside which the invention of gunpowder, of the printing-press, and of steam locomotion were inconsiderable trifles. Science had made bewildering strides in many directions during recent decades, but this thing seemed to belong to the domain of miracle rather than to scientific achievement.

'And do you really ask us to believe,' Sir Wilfrid was saying, 'that you have discovered a means for instructing animals in the art of human speech, and that dear old Tobermory has proved your first successful pupil?'

'It is a problem at which I have worked for the last seventeen years,' said Mr Appin, 'but only during the last eight or nine months have I been rewarded with glimmerings of success. Of course I have experimented with thousands of animals, but latterly only with cats, those wonderful creatures which have assimilated themselves so marvellously with our civilization while retaining all their highly developed feral instincts. Here and there among cats one comes across an outstanding superior intellect, just as one does among the ruck of human beings, and when I made the acquaintance of Tobermory a week ago I saw at once that I was in contact with a "Beyond-cat" of extraordinary intelligence. I had gone far along the road to success in recent experiments; with Tobermory, as you call him, I have reached the goal.'

Mr Appin concluded his remarkable statement in a voice which he strove to divest of a triumphant inflection. No one said 'Rats', though Clovis's lips moved in a monosyllabic contortion, which probably invoked those rodents of disbelief.

'And do you mean to say,' asked Miss Resker, after a slight pause, 'that you have taught Tobermory to say and understand easy sentences of one syllable?'

'My dear Miss Resker,' said the wonder-worker patiently, 'one teaches little children and savages and backward adults in that piecemeal fashion; when one has once solved the problem of making a beginning with an animal of highly developed intelligence one has no need for those halting methods. Tobermory can speak our language with perfect correctness.'

This time Clovis very distinctly said, 'Beyond-rats!' Sir Wilfrid was more polite, but equally sceptical.

'Hadn't we better have the cat in and judge for ourselves?' suggested Lady Blemley.

Sir Wilfrid went in search of the animal, and the company settled themselves down to the languid expectation of witnessing some more or less adroit drawing-room ventriloquism.

In a minute Sir Wilfrid was back in the room, his face white beneath its tan and his eyes dilated with excitement.

'By Gad, it's true!'

His agitation was unmistakably genuine, and his hearers started forward in a thrill of wakened interest.

Collapsing into an armchair he continued breathlessly:

'I found him dozing in the smoking-room, and called out to him to come for his tea. He blinked at me in his usual way, and I said, "Come on, Toby; don't keep us waiting" and, by Gad! he drawled out in a most horribly natural voice that he'd come when he dashed well pleased! I nearly jumped out of my skin!'

Appin had preached to absolutely incredulous hearers; Sir Wilfrid's statement carried instant conviction. A Babel-like chorus of startled exclamation arose, amid which the scientist sat mutely enjoying the first fruit of his stupendous discovery.

In the midst of the clamour Tobermory entered the room and made his way with velvet tread and studied unconcern across the group seated round the tea-table.

A sudden hush of awkwardness and constraint fell on the company. Somehow there seemed an element of embarrassment in addressing on equal terms a domestic cat of acknowledged dental ability.

'Will you have some milk, Tobermory?' asked Lady Blemley in a rather strained voice.

'I don't mind if I do,' was the response, couched in a tone of even indifference. A shiver of suppressed excitement went through the listeners, and Lady Blemley might be excused for pouring out the saucerful of milk rather unsteadily.

'I'm afraid I've spilt a good deal of it,' she said apologetically.

'After all, it's not my Axminster,' was Tobermory's rejoinder.

Another silence fell on the group, and then Miss Resker, in her best district-visitor manner, asked if the human language had been difficult to learn. Tobermory looked squarely at her for a moment and then fixed his gaze serenely on the middle distance. It was obvious that boring questions lay outside his scheme of life.

'What do you think of human intelligence?' asked Mavis Pellington lamely.

'Of whose intelligence in particular?' asked Tobermory coldly.

'Oh, well, mine for instance,' said Mavis, with a feeble laugh.

'You put me in an embarrassing position,' said Tobermory, whose tone and attitude certainly did not suggest a shred of embarrassment. 'When your inclusion in this house-party was suggested Sir Wilfrid protested that you were the most brainless woman of his acquaintance, and that there was a wide distinction between hospitality and the care of the feeble-minded. Lady Blemley replied that your lack of brain-power was the precise quality which had earned you your invitation, as you were the only person she could think of who might be idiotic enough to buy their old car. You know, the one they call "The Envy of Sisyphus", because it goes quite nicely up-hill if you push it.'

Lady Blemley's protestations would have had greater effect if she had not casually suggested to Mavis only that morning that the car in question would be just the thing for her down at her Devonshire home.

Major Barfield plunged in heavily to effect a diversion.

'How about your carryings-on with the tortoise-shell puss up at the stables, eh?'

The moment he had said it every one realized the blunder.

'One does not usually discuss these matters in public,' said Tobermory frigidly. 'From a slight observation of your ways since you've been in this house I should imagine you'd find it inconvenient if I were to shift the conversation on to your own little affairs.'

The panic which ensued was not confined to the Major.

'Would you like to go and see if cook has got your dinner ready?' suggested Lady Blemley hurriedly, affecting to ignore the fact that it wanted at least two hours to Tobermory's dinner-time.

'Thanks,' said Tobermory, 'not quite so soon after my tea. I don't want to die of indigestion.'

'Cats have nine lives, you know,' said Sir Wilfrid heartily.

'Possibly,' answered Tobermory; 'but only one liver.'

'Adelaide!' said Mrs. Cornett, 'do you mean to encourage that cat to go out and gossip about us in the servants' hall?'

The panic had indeed become general. A narrow ornamental balustrade ran in front of most of the bedroom windows at the Towers, and it was recalled with dismay that this had formed a favourite promenade for Tobermory at all hours, whence he could watch the pigeons—and heaven knew what else besides. If he intended to become reminiscent in his present outspoken strain the effect would be something more than disconcerting. Mrs Cornett, who spent much time at her toilet table, and whose complexion was reputed to be of a nomadic though punctual disposition, looked as ill

at ease as the Major. Miss Scrawen, who wrote fiercely sensuous poetry
and led a blameless life, merely displayed irritation; if you are methodical
and virtuous in private you don't necessarily want everyone to know it.
Bertie van Tahn, who was so depraved at 17 that he had long ago given up
trying to be any worse, turned a dull shade of gardenia white, but he did
not commit the error of dashing out of the room like Odo Finsberry, a young
gentleman who was understood to be reading for the Church and who was
possibly disturbed at the thought of scandals he might hear concerning other
people. Clovis had the presence of mind to maintain a composed exterior;
privately he was calculating how long it would take to procure a box of
fancy mice through the agency of the *Exchange and Mart* as a species of
hush-money.

Even in a delicate situation like the present, Agnes Resker could not endure
to remain too long in the background.

'Why did I ever come down here?' she asked dramatically.

Tobermory immediately accepted the opening.

'Judging by what you said to Mrs Cornett on the croquet-lawn yesterday,
you were out for food. You described the Blemleys as the dullest people to
stay with that you knew, but said they were clever enough to employ a
first-rate cook; otherwise they'd find it difficult to get any one to come down
a second time.'

'There's not a word of truth in it! I appeal to Mrs Cornett—' exclaimed
the discomfited Agnes.

'Mrs Cornett repeated your remark afterwards to Bertie van Tahn,' continued Tobermory, 'and said, "That woman is a regular Hunger Marcher;
she'd go anywhere for four square meals a day," and Bertie van Tahn said—'

At this point the chronicle mercifully ceased. Tobermory had caught a
glimpse of the big yellow tom from the Rectory working his way through the
shrubbery towards the stable wing. In a flash he had vanished through the
open French window.

With the disappearance of his too brilliant pupil Cornelius Appin found
himself beset by a hurricane of bitter upbraiding, anxious inquiry, and
frightened entreaty. The responsibility for the situation lay with him, and he
must prevent matters from becoming worse. Could Tobermory impart his
dangerous gift to other cats? was the first question he had to answer. It was
possible, he replied, that he might have initiated his intimate friend the stable
puss into his new accomplishment, but it was unlikely that his teaching
could have taken a wider range as yet.

'Then,' said Mrs Cornett, 'Tobermory may be a valuable cat and a great
pet; but I'm sure you'll agree, Adelaide, that both he and the stable cat must
be done away with without delay.'

'You don't suppose I've enjoyed the last quarter of an hour, do you?' said
Lady Blemley bitterly. 'My husband and I are very fond of Tobermory—at
least, we were before this horrible accomplishment was infused into him;

but now, of course, the only thing is to have him destroyed as soon as possible.'

'We can put some strychnine in the scraps he always gets at dinner-time,' said Sir Wilfrid, 'and I will go and drown the stable cat myself. The coachman will be very sore at losing his pet, but I'll say a very catching form of mange has broken out in both cats and we're afraid of it spreading to the kennels.'

'But my great discovery!' expostulated Mr Appin; 'after all my years of research and experiment—'

'You can go and experiment on the short-horns at the farm, who are under proper control,' said Mrs Cornett, 'or the elephants at the Zoological Gardens. They're said to be highly intelligent, and they have this recommendation, that they don't come creeping about our bedrooms and under chairs, and so forth.'

An archangel ecstatically proclaiming the Millennium, and then finding that it clashed unpardonably with Henley and would have to be indefinitely postponed, could hardly have felt more crestfallen than Cornelius Appin at the reception of his wonderful achievement. Public opinion, however, was against him—in fact, had the general voice been consulted on the subject it is probable that a strong minority vote would have been in favour of including him in the strychnine diet.

Defective train arrangements and a nervous desire to see matters brought to a finish prevented an immediate dispersal of the party, but dinner that evening was not a social success. Sir Wilfrid had had rather a trying time with the stable cat and subsequently with the coachman. Agnes Resker ostentatiously limited her repast to a morsel of dry toast, which she bit as though it were a personal enemy; while Mavis Pellington maintained a vindictive silence throughout the meal. Lady Blemley kept up a flow of what she hoped was conversation, but her attention was fixed on the doorway. A plateful of carefully dosed fish scraps was in readiness on the sideboard, but sweets and savoury and dessert went their way, and no Tobermory appeared either in the dining-room or kitchen.

The sepulchral dinner was cheerful compared with the subsequent vigil in the smoking-room. Eating and drinking had at least supplied a distraction and cloak to the prevailing embarrassment. Bridge was out of the question in the general tension of nerves and tempers, and after Odo Finsberry had given a lugubrious rendering of 'Melisande in the Wood' to a frigid audience, music was tacitly avoided. At eleven the servants went to bed, announcing that the small window in the pantry had been left open as usual for Tobermory's private use. The guests read steadily through the current batch of magazines, and fell back gradually on the 'Badminton Library' and bound volumes of *Punch*. Lady Blemley made periodic visits to the pantry, returning each time with an expression of listless depression which forestalled questioning.

At two o'clock Clovis broke the dominating silence.

'He won't turn up tonight. He's probably in the local newspaper office at the present moment, dictating the first instalment of his reminiscences. Lady What's-her-name's book won't be in it. It will be the event of the day.'

Having made this contribution to the general cheerfulness, Clovis went to bed. At long intervals the various members of the house-party followed his example.

The servants taking round the early tea made a uniform announcement in reply to a uniform question. Tobermory had not returned.

Breakfast was, if anything, a more unpleasant function than dinner had been, but before its conclusion the situation was relieved. Tobermory's corpse was brought in from the shrubbery, where a gardener had just discovered it. From the bites on his throat and the yellow fur which coated his claws it was evident that he had fallen in unequal combat with the big Tom from the Rectory.

By midday most of the guests had quitted the Towers, and after lunch Lady Blemley had sufficiently recovered her spirits to write an extremely nasty letter to the Rectory about the loss of her valuable pet.

Tobermory had been Appin's one successful pupil, and he was destined to have no successor. A few weeks later an elephant in the Dresden Zoological Garden, which had shown no previous signs of irritability, broke loose and killed an Englishman who had apparently been teasing it. The victim's name was variously reported in the papers as Oppin and Eppelin, but his front name was faithfully rendered Cornelius.

'If he was trying German irregular verbs on the poor beast,' said Clovis, 'he deserved all he got.'

                                    'Tobermory', *The Chronicles of Clovis* (1911).

━━━━━━━━

M OST *authors tended to be primarily novelists or short-story writers, or both, or professional humorists writing for journals, but there was also another group; the 'men of letters', men—and women—who did not specialize in any one branch of literature but expressed themselves in various forms, essays, fiction, poetry, plays, and literary criticism.*

Three Edwardian men of letters—a now almost extinct branch of authorship—were G. K. Chesterton, Maurice Baring, and Lord Dunsany.

Chesterton was quite happy to be regarded as a journalist but he was also a successful writer of fiction (The Napoleon of Notting Hill, *the* Father Brown *stories, and others), a biographer, historian, critic, parodist, and poet. He and his close friend Hilaire Belloc—Shaw lumped them together as 'Chesterbelloc'—became part of the new school of Georgian poetry which praised the open air and the virtues of country life. The spectacle of the massive Chesterton and the chunky*

Belloc briskly striding the white Sussex lanes and quaffing stoups of ale at wayside inns moved the more lyrical poet T. Sturge Moore to call them 'two buttocks of one bum'.

Chesterton wrote a vast number of literary essays, popular in their day for their vigour, optimism and humour. He was an enjoyer of life, an anti-Puritan and a devout Catholic. In spite of the frolicsome mood of many of his essays they were invariably built round a grain of wisdom. One of his recurring themes was that if a thing is worth doing it is worth doing badly, that is, a game is worth playing, however unskilfully, purely for the pleasure of playing it.

This typical Chesterton essay dwells upon the pleasures of being in bed: it then goes on to argue that it is quite right and proper to stay in bed in the morning as long as you like: until, in fact, you feel like getting up:

ON LYING IN BED

Lying in bed would be an altogether perfect and supreme experience if only one had a coloured pencil long enough to draw on the ceiling. This, however, is not generally a part of the domestic apparatus on the premises. I think myself that the thing might be managed with several pails of Aspinall and a broom. Only if one worked in a really sweeping and masterly way, and laid on the colours in great washes, it might drip down again on one's face in floods of rich and mingled colour like some strange fairy rain; and that would have its disadvantages. I am afraid it would be necessary to stick to black and white in this form of artistic composition. To that purpose, indeed, the white ceiling would be of the greatest possible use; in fact it is the only use I think of a white ceiling being put to.

But for the beautiful experiment of lying in bed I might never have discovered it. For years I have been looking for some blank spaces in a modern house to draw on. Paper is much too small for any really allegorical design; as Cyrano de Bergerac says: 'Il me faut des géants.' But when I tried to find these fine clear spaces in the modern rooms such as we all live in I was continually disappointed. I found an endless pattern and complication of small objects hung like a curtain of fine links between me and my desire. I examined the walls; I found them to my surprise to be already covered with wall-paper, and I found the wall-paper to be already covered with very uninteresting images, all bearing a ridiculous resemblance to each other. I could not understand why one arbitrary symbol (a symbol apparently entirely devoid of any religious or philosophical significance) should thus be sprinkled all over my nice walls like a sort of small-pox. The Bible must be referring to wall-papers, I think, when it says, 'Use not vain repetitions, as the Gentiles do'. I found the Turkey carpet a mass of unmeaning colours, rather like the Turkish Empire, or like the sweetmeat called Turkish Delight. I do not exactly know what Turkish Delight really is; but I suppose it is Macedonian Massacres. Everywhere that I went with my pencil or my paint brush, I found that others had unaccountably been before me, spoiling the walls, the curtains, and the furniture with their childish and barbaric designs.

Nowhere did I find a really clear space for sketching until this occasion when I prolonged beyond the proper limit the process of lying on my back in bed. Then the light of that white heaven broke upon my vision, that breadth of mere white which is indeed almost the definition of Paradise, since it means purity and also means freedom. But alas! like all heavens, now that it is seen it is found to be unattainable: it looks more austere and more distant than the blue sky outside the window. For my proposal to paint on it with the bristly end of a broom has been discouraged—never mind by whom; by a person debarred from all political rights—and even my minor proposal to put the other end of the broom into the kitchen fire and turn it into charcoal has not been conceded. Yet I am certain that it was from persons in my position that all the original inspiration came for covering the ceilings of palaces and cathedrals with a riot of fallen angels or victorious gods. I am sure that it was only because Michael Angelo was engaged in the ancient and honourable occupation of lying in bed that he ever realised how the roof of the Sistine Chapel might be made into an awful imitation of a divine drama that could only be acted in the heavens.

The tone now commonly taken towards the practice of lying in bed is hypocritical and unhealthy. Of all the marks of modernity that seem to mean a kind of decadence, there is none more menacing and dangerous than the exaltation of very small and secondary matters of conduct at the expense of very great and primary ones, at the expense of eternal ties and tragic human morality. If there is one thing worse than the modern weakening of major morals it is the modern strengthening of minor morals. Thus it is considered more withering to accuse a man of bad taste than of bad ethics. Cleanliness is not next to godliness nowadays, for cleanliness is made an essential and godliness is regarded as an offence. A playwright can attack the institution of marriage so long as he does not misrepresent the manners of society, and I have met Ibsenite pessimists who thought it wrong to take beer but right to take prussic acid. Especially this is so in matters of hygiene; notably such matters as lying in bed. Instead of being regarded, as it ought to be, as a matter of personal convenience and adjustment, it has come to be regarded by many as if it were a part of essential morals to get up early in the morning. It is, upon the whole, part of practical wisdom; but there is nothing good about it or bad about its opposite.

Misers get up early in the morning; and burglars, I am informed, get up the night before. It is the great peril of our society that all its mechanism may grow more fixed while its spirit grows more fickle. A man's minor actions and arrangements ought to be free, flexible, creative; the things that should be unchangeable are his principles, his ideals. But with us the reverse is true;

our views change constantly; but our lunch does not change. Now, I should like men to have strong and rooted conceptions, but as for their lunch, let them have it sometimes in the garden, sometimes in bed, sometimes on the roof, sometimes in the top of a tree. Let them argue from the same first principles, but let them do it in a bed, or a boat, or a balloon. This alarming growth of good habits really means a too great emphasis on those virtues which mere custom can ensure, it means too little emphasis on those virtues which custom can never quite ensure, sudden and splendid virtues of inspired pity or of inspired candour. If ever that abrupt appeal is made to us we may fail. A man can get used to getting up at five o'clock in the morning. A man cannot very well get used to being burnt for his opinions; the first experiment is commonly fatal. Let us pay a little more attention to these possibilities of the heroic and the unexpected. I dare say that when I get out of this bed I shall do some deed of an almost terrible virtue.

For those who study the great art of lying in bed there is one emphatic caution to be added. Even for those who can do their work in bed (like journalists), still more for those whose work cannot be done in bed (as, for example, the professional harpooners of whales), it is obvious that the indulgence must be very occasional. But that is not the caution I mean. The caution is this: if you do lie in bed, be sure you do it without any reason or justification at all. I do not speak, of course, of the seriously sick. But if a healthy man lies in bed, let him do it without a rag of excuse; then he will get up a healthy man. If he does it for some secondary hygienic reason, if he has some scientific explanation, he may get up a hypochondriac. G. K. Chesterton (1874–1936), *Tremendous Trifles* (1909).

M AURICE BARING, *novelist, poet, and man of letters, was a friend of Chesterton and like him a convert to Catholicism. Born in Mayfair, educated at Eton, Hildesheim, Cambridge, and Oxford (and always hard up), he was a young man of immense culture and even whilst working in the diplomatic service and as the* Morning Post's *correspondent in Manchuria and Russia—he had a hand in introducing Chekhov's works to the West—he was writing verse plays, eight volumes on contemporary Russia, literary criticism, pranks, and pastiches. His works eventually filled some fifty volumes.*

In some early playful pieces he examined familiar historical scenes from a modern point of view. For example, King Lear. *Baring defends the girls, stressing*

the domestic problems which must suddenly have faced Goneril when her old and
dotty father decided to retire and move in with her:

KING LEAR'S DAUGHTER

Letter from Goneril, Daughter of King Lear, to her sister Regan

'I have writ my sister.'

King Lear, Act I, Scene iv.

The Palace, November.

Dearest Regan,

I am sending you this letter by Oswald. We have been having the most
trying time lately with Papa, and it ended today in one of those scenes which
are so painful to people like you and me, who hate scenes. I am writing now
to tell you all about it, so that you may be prepared. This is what has
happened.

When Papa came here he brought a hundred knights with him, which is
a great deal more than we could put up, and some of them had to live in the
village. The first thing that happened was that they quarrelled with our
people and refused to take orders from them, and whenever one told anyone
to do anything it was either—if it was one of Papa's men—'not his place to
do it'; or if it was one of our men, they said that Papa's people made work
impossible. For instance, only the day before yesterday I found that blue vase
which you brought back from Dover for me on my last birthday broken to
bits. Of course I made a fuss, and Oswald declared that one of Papa's knights
had knocked it over in a drunken brawl. I complained to Papa, who flew into
a passion and said that his knights, and in fact all his retainers, were the
most peaceful and courteous people in the world, and that it was my fault,
as I was not treating him or them with the respect which they deserved. He
even said that I was lacking in filial duty. I was determined to keep my
temper, so I said nothing.

The day after this the chief steward and the housekeeper and both my
maids came to me and said that they wished to give notice. I asked them
why. They said they couldn't possibly live in a house where there were such
'goings-on'. I asked them what they meant. They refused to say, but they
hinted that Papa's men were behaving not only in an insolent but in a
positively outrageous manner to them. The steward said that Papa's knights
were never sober, that they had entirely demoralised the household, and that
life was simply not worth living in the house; it was *impossible* to get anything
done, and they couldn't sleep at night for the noise.

I went to Papa and talked to him about it quite quietly, but no sooner had
I mentioned the subject than he lost all self-control, and began to abuse me.
I kept my temper as long as I could, but of course one is only human, and
after I had borne his revilings for some time, which were monstrously unfair
and untrue, I at last turned and said something about people of his age being

trying. Upon which he said I was throwing up his old age at him, that I was a monster of ingratitude—and he began to cry. I cannot tell you how painful all this was to me. I did everything I could to soothe him and quiet him, but the truth is, ever since Papa has been here he has lost control of his wits. He suffers from the oddest kind of delusions. He thinks that for some reason he is being treated like a beggar; and although he has a hundred knights—a hundred, mind you! (a great deal more than we have)—in the house, who do nothing but eat and drink all day long, he says he is not being treated like a King! I do hate unfairness.

When he gave up the crown he said he was tired of affairs, and meant to have a long rest; but from the very moment that he handed over the management of affairs to us he never stopped interfering, and was cross if he was not consulted about everything, and if his advice was not taken.

And what is still worse is this: ever since his last illness he has lost not only his memory but his control over language, so that often when he wants to say one thing he says just the opposite, and sometimes when he wishes to say some quite simple thing he uses bad language quite unconsciously. Of course we are used to this, and we don't mind, but I must say it is very awkward when strangers are here. For instance, the other day before quite a lot of people, quite unconsciously, he called me a dreadful name. Everybody was uncomfortable and tried not to laugh, but some people could not contain themselves. This sort of thing is constantly happening. So you will understand that Papa needs perpetual looking after and management. At the same time, the moment one suggests the slightest thing to him he boils over with rage.

But perhaps the most annoying thing which happened lately, or, at least, the thing which happens to annoy me most, is Papa's Fool. You know, darling, that I have always hated that kind of humour. He comes in just as one is sitting down to dinner, and beats one on the head with a hard, empty bladder, and sings utterly idiotic songs, which make me feel inclined to cry. The other day, when we had a lot of people here, just as we were sitting down in the banqueting hall, Papa's Fool pulled my chair from behind me so that I fell sharply down on the floor. Papa shook with laughter, and said: 'Well done, little Fool,' and all the courtiers who were there, out of pure snobbishness, of course, laughed too. I call this not only very humiliating for me, but undignified in an old man and a king; of course Albany refused to interfere. Like all men and all husbands, he is an arrant coward.

However, the crisis came yesterday. I had got a bad headache, and was lying down in my room, when Papa came in from the hunt and sent Oswald to me, saying that he wished to speak to me. I said that I wasn't well, and that I was lying down—which was perfectly true—but that I would be down to dinner. When Oswald went to give my message Papa beat him, and one of his men threw him about the room and really hurt him, so that he has now got a large bruise on his forehead and a sprained ankle.

This was the climax. All our knights came to Albany and myself, and said that they would not stay with us a moment longer unless Papa exercised some sort of control over his men. I did not know what to do, but I knew the situation would have to be cleared up sooner or later. So I went to Papa and told him frankly that the situation was intolerable; that he must send away some of his people, and choose for the remainder men fitting to his age. The words were scarcely out of my mouth than he called me the most terrible names, ordered his horses to be saddled, and said that he would shake the dust from his feet and not stay a moment longer in this house. Albany tried to calm him, and begged him to stay, but he would not listen to a word, and said he would go and live with you.

So I am sending this by Oswald, that you may get it before Papa arrives and know how the matter stands. All I did was to suggest he should send away fifty of his men. Even fifty is a great deal, and puts us to any amount of inconvenience, and is a source of waste and extravagance—two things which I cannot bear. I am perfectly certain you will not be able to put up with his hundred knights any more than I was. And I beg you, my dearest Regan, to do your best to make Papa listen to sense. No one is fonder of him that I am. I think it would have been difficult to find a more dutiful daughter than I have always been. But there is a limit to all things, and one cannot have one's whole household turned into a pandemonium, and one's whole life into a series of wrangles, complaints, and brawls, simply because Papa in his old age is losing the control of his faculties. At the same time, I own that although I kept my temper for a long time, when it finally gave way I was perhaps a little sharp. I am not a saint, nor an angel, nor a lamb, but I do hate unfairness and injustice. It makes my blood boil. But I hope that you, with your angelic nature and your tact and your gentleness, will put everything right and make poor Papa listen to reason.

Let me hear at once what happens.

Your loving
Goneril

P.S.—Another thing Papa does which is most exasperating is to throw up Cordelia at one every moment. He keeps on saying: 'If only Cordelia were here', or 'How unlike Cordelia!' And you will remember, darling, that when Cordelia was here Papa could not endure the sight of her. Her irritating trick of mumbling and never speaking up used to get terribly on his nerves. Of course, I thought he was even rather unfair on her, trying as she is. We had a letter from the French Court yesterday, saying that she is driving the poor King of France almost mad.

P.P.S.—It is wretched weather. The poor little ponies on the heath will have to be brought in.

Maurice Baring (1884–1945), *Dead Letters* (1910).

THE third man of letters, Edward John Moreton Drax Plunkett, eighteenth Baron of Dunsany, tall, handsome, bearded, athletic, eccentric, was a prolific essayist, novelist, short-story writer, poet, and playwright. His family was Anglo-Irish, and when still a young man Lord Dunsany found it necessary to make money with his pen—a goose-quill, incidentally, with which he produced beautiful handwriting, rapidly, with never a blotted line.

His short plays, highly popular in America, his short stories, and in fact most of his works were distinguished by his use of fantasy and by his humorous and original turn of mind.

Here is a fine Dunsany piece; a fable, with an ending worthy of O. Henry:

THE TRUE HISTORY OF THE HARE AND THE TORTOISE

For a long time there was doubt with acrimony among the beasts as to whether the Hare or the Tortoise could run the swifter. Some said the Hare was the swifter of the two because he had such long ears, and others said that the Tortoise was the swifter because anyone whose shell was so hard as that should be able to run hard too. And lo, the forces of estrangement and disorder perpetually postponed a decisive contest.

But when there was nearly war among the beasts, at last an arrangement was come to and it was decided that the Hare and the Tortoise should run a race of five hundred yards so that all should see who was right.

'Ridiculous nonsense!' said the Hare, and it was all his backers could do to get him to run.

'The contest is most welcome to me,' said the Tortoise. 'I shall not shirk it.'

Oh, how his backers cheered.

Feeling ran high on the day of the race; the goose rushed at the fox and nearly pecked him. Both sides spoke loudly of the approaching victory up to the very moment of the race.

'I am absolutely confident of success,' said the Tortoise. But the Hare said nothing, he looked bored and cross. Some of his supporters deserted him then and went to the other side, who were loudly cheering the Tortoise's inspiriting words. But many remained with the Hare. 'We shall not be disappointed in him,' they said. 'A beast with such long ears is bound to win.'

'Run hard,' said the supporters of the Tortoise.

And 'run hard' became a kind of catch-phrase which everybody repeated to one another. 'Hard shell and hard living. That's what the country wants. Run hard,' they said. And these words were never uttered but multitudes cheered from their hearts.

Then they were off, and suddenly there was a hush.

The Hare dashed off for about a hundred yards, then he looked around to see where his rival was.

'It is rather absurd,' he said, 'to race with a Tortoise.' And he sat down and scratched himself. 'Run hard! Run hard!' shouted some.

'Let him rest,' shouted others. And 'let him rest' became a catch-phrase too.

And after a while his rival drew near to him.

'There comes that damned Tortoise,' said the Hare, and he got up and ran as hard as he could so that he should not let the Tortoise beat him.

'Those ears will win,' said his friends. 'Those ears will win; and establish upon an incontestable footing the truth of what we have said.' And some of them turned to the backers of the Tortoise and said: 'What about your beast now?'

'Run hard,' they replied. 'Run hard.'

The Hare ran on for nearly three hundred yards, nearly in fact as far as the winning-post, when it suddenly struck him what a fool he looked running races with a Tortoise who was nowhere in sight, and he sat down again and scratched.

'Run hard. Run hard,' said the crowd, and 'Let him rest.'

'Whatever is the use of it?' said the Hare, and this time he stopped for good. Some say he slept.

There was desperate excitement for an hour of two, and then the Tortoise won.

'Run hard. Run hard,' shouted his backers. 'Hard shell and hard living: that's what has done it.' And then they asked the Tortoise what his achievement signified, and he went and asked the Turtle. And the Turtle said: 'It is a glorious victory for the forces of swiftness.' And then the Tortoise repeated it to his friends. And all the beasts said nothing else for years. And even to this day 'a glorious victory for the forces of swiftness' is a catch-phrase in the house of the snail.

And the reason that his version of the race is not widely known is that very few of those that witnessed it survived the great forest-fire that happened shortly after. It came up over the weald by night with a great wind. The Hare and the Tortoise and a very few of the beasts saw it far off from a high bare hill that was at the edge of the trees, and they hurriedly called a meeting to decide what messenger they should send to warn the beasts in the forest.

They sent the Tortoise.

Lord Dunsany (1878–1957), *Fifty-One Tales* (1915).

———

*I*F *there is one book which more than any other evokes nostalgia for Edwardian days, when the pace of life was slower and the countryside and rivers were unpolluted and the woods were still wild and explorable, it is* The Wind in the Willows *by Kenneth Grahame.*

The Wind in the Willows *began as little entertaining stories which Grahame*

*told his son at bedtime and then wrote down in letters when the boy went away to
school. An American publisher pressed Grahame into working the stories into a
book and then rejected the manuscript, but it was eventually published and very
slowly became established as a children's classic. It became one of those rare
children's books (Alice in Wonderland was another), which appealed equally to
grown-ups.*

*The story is about animals and Grahame manages to give each of them a human
character without taking away their animal identity. The river-bankers, little
Ratty, Mole, old wise Badger, even* nouveau riche *but kind Mr Toad with his
sudden crazes and his self-importance, are the goodies. The baddies, the weasels
and stoats, live in the dark Wild Wood.*

*In the opening chapter Mole stops whitewashing his house to take a stroll. It is
one of those hot, summer days of which the Edwardian era, in myth, entirely
consisted. The scene produces what is perhaps the third-best-known quotation in
humorous prose when Ratty messes about in his boat.*

Mole's stroll takes him to the river-bank, where he decides to rest:

As he sat on the grass and looked across the river, a dark hole in the bank
opposite, just above the water's edge, caught his eye, and dreamily he fell to
considering what a nice snug dwelling-place it would make for an animal
with few wants and fond of a bijou riverside residence, above flood level and
remote from noise and dust. As he gazed, something bright and small seemed
to twinkle down in the heart of it, vanished, then twinkled once more like a
tiny star. But it could hardly be a star in such an unlikely situation; and it
was too glittering and small for a glow-worm. Then, as he looked, it winked
at him, and so declared itself to be an eye; and a small face began gradually
to grow up round it, like a frame round a picture.

A little brown face, with whiskers.

A grave round face, with the same twinkle in its eye that had first attracted
his notice.

Small neat ears and thick silky hair.

It was the Water Rat!

Then the two animals stood and regarded each other cautiously.

'Hullo, Mole!' said the Water Rat.

'Hullo, Rat!' said the Mole.

'Would you like to come over?' inquired the Rat presently.

'Oh, it's all very well to talk,' said the Mole, rather pettishly, he being new
to a river and riverside life and its ways.

The Rat said nothing, but stooped and unfastened a rope and hauled on
it; then lightly stepped in a little boat which the Mole had not observed. It
was painted blue outside and white within, and was just the size for the two
animals; and the Mole's whole heart went out to it at once, even though he
did not yet fully understand its uses.

The Rat sculled smartly across and made fast. Then he held up his fore-paw as the Mole stepped gingerly down. 'Lean on that!' he said. 'Now then, step lively!' and the Mole to his surprise and rapture found himself actually seated in the stern of a real boat.

'This has been a wonderful day!' said he, as the Rat shoved off and took to the sculls again. 'Do you know, I've never been in a boat before in all my life.'

'What?' cried the Rat, open-mouthed: 'Never been in a—you never—well, I—what have you been doing, then?'

'Is it so nice as all that?' asked the Mole shyly, though he was quite prepared to believe it as he leant back in his seat and surveyed the cushions, the oars, the rowlocks, and all the fascinating fittings, and felt the boat sway lightly under him.

'Nice? It's the only thing,' said the Water Rat solemnly, as he leant forward for his stroke. 'Believe me, my young friend, there is nothing—absolutely nothing—half so much worth doing as simply messing about in boats. Simply messing,' he went on dreamily: 'messing—about—in—boats; messing—'

'Look ahead, Rat!' cried the Mole suddenly.

It was too late. The boat struck the bank full tilt. The dreamer, the joyous oarsman, lay on his back at the bottom of the boat, his heels in the air.

'—about in boats—or with boats,' the Rat went on composedly, picking himself up with a pleasant laugh. 'In or out of 'em, it doesn't matter. Nothing seems really to matter, that's the charm of it. Whether you get away, or whether you don't; whether you arrive at your destination or whether you reach somewhere else, or whether you never get anywhere at all, you're always busy, and you never do anything in particular; and when you've done it there's always something else to do, and you can do it if you like, but you'd much better not. Look here! If you've really nothing else on hand this morning, supposing we drop down the river together, and have a long day of it?'

The Mole waggled his toes from sheer happiness, spread his chest with a sigh of full contentment, and leaned back blissfully into the soft cushions. 'What a day I'm having!' he said. 'Let us start at once!'

'Hold hard a minute, then!' said the Rat. He looped the painter through a ring in his landing-stage, climbed up into his hole above, and after a short interval reappeared staggering under a fat, wicker luncheon-basket.

'Shove that under your feet,' he observed to the Mole, as he passed it down into the boat. Then he untied the painter and took the sculls again.

'What's inside it?' asked the Mole, wriggling with curiosity.

'There's cold chicken inside it,' replied the Rat briefly; 'coldtonguecoldham-coldbeefpickledgherkinssaladfrenchrollscresssandwichespottedmeatginger-beerlemonadesodawater—

'O stop, stop,' cried the Mole in ecstasies: 'This is too much!'

'Do you really think so?' inquired the Rat seriously. 'It's only what I always take on these little excursions; and the other animals are always telling me that I'm a mean beast and cut it very fine!'

The Mole never heard a word he was saying. Absorbed in the new life he was entering upon, intoxicated with the sparkle, the ripple, the scents and the sounds and the sun-light, he trailed a paw in the water and dreamed long waking dreams. The Water Rat, like the good little fellow he was, sculled steadily on and forbore to disturb him.

'I like your clothes awfully, old chap,' he remarked after some half hour or so had passed. 'I'm going to get a black velvet smoking suit myself some day, as soon as I can afford it.'

Into the story comes Mr Toad, owner of Toad Hall, a magnificent mansion suited to a gentleman of means. Mr Toad is an enthusiast. When he fixes his mind on something new and exciting he goes at it bald-headed, it is the only thing in his world worth living for. Until something even newer comes along whereupon the first fad is instantly abandoned.

Mr Toad has seen a gypsy caravan and in seconds has convinced himself that life on the open road is the only existence for him. He buys a caravan and an old grey horse and persuades Ratty and Mole to join him in his new life. Travelling in a caravan is harmless enough, even with Mr Toad in charge.

But before long a new, modern, and much more perilous enthusiasm takes over:

They were strolling along the high road easily, the Mole by the horse's head, talking to him, since the horse had complained that he was being frightfully left out of it, and nobody considered him in the least; the Toad and the Water Rat walking behind the cart talking together—at least Toad was talking, and Rat was saying at intervals, 'Yes, precisely; and what did *you* say to *him?*'— and thinking all the time of something very different, when far behind them they heard a faint warning hum, like the drone of a distant bee. Glancing back, they saw a small cloud of dust, with a dark centre of energy, advancing on them at incredible speed, while from out the dust a faint 'Poop-poop!' wailed like an uneasy animal in pain. Hardly regarding it, they turned to resume their conversation, when in an instant (as it seemed) the peaceful scene was changed, and with a blast of wind and a whirl of sound that made them jump for the nearest ditch, it was on them! The 'poop-poop' rang with a brazen shout in their ears, they had a moment's glimpse of an interior of glittering plate and rich morocco, and the magnificent motor-car, immense, breath-snatching, passionate, with its pilot tense and hugging his wheel, possessed all earth and air for the fraction of a second, flung an enveloping cloud of dust that blinded and enwrapped them utterly, and then dwindled to a speck in the far distance, changed back into a droning bee once more.

The old grey horse, dreaming, as he plodded along, of his quiet paddock, in a new raw situation such as this simply abandoned himself to his natural emotions. Rearing, plunging, backing steadily, in spite of all the Mole's efforts at his head, and all the Mole's lively language directed at his better feelings, he drove the cart backwards towards the deep ditch at the side of the road. It wavered an instant—then there was a heart-rending crash—and the canary-coloured cart, their pride and their joy, lay on its side in the ditch, an irredeemable wreck.

The Rat danced up and down in the road, simply transported with passion. 'You scoundrels, you highwaymen, you—you—road-hogs!—I'll have the law on you! I'll report you! I'll take you through the Courts!' His home-sickness had quite slipped away from him, and for the moment he was the skipper of the canary-coloured vessel driven on a shoal by the reckless jock-eying of rival mariners, and he was trying to recollect all the fine and biting things he used to say to masters of steam-launches when their wash, as they drove too near the bank, used to flood his parlour carpet at home.

Toad sat straight down in the middle of the dusty road, his legs stretched out before him, and stared fixedly in the direction of the disappearing motor-car. He breathed short, his face wore a placid, satisfied expression, and at intervals he faintly murmured 'Poop-poop!'

The Mole was busy trying to quiet the horse, which he succeeded in doing after a time. Then he went to look at the cart, on its side in the ditch. It was indeed a sorry sight. Panels and windows smashed, axles hopelessly bent, one wheel off, sardine-tins scattered over the wide world, and the bird in the bird-cage sobbing pitifully and calling to be let out.

The Rat came to help him, but their united efforts were not sufficient to right the cart. 'Hi! Toad!' they cried. 'Come and bear a hand, can't you!'

The Toad never answered a word, or budged from his seat in the road; so they went to see what was the matter with him. They found him in a sort of trance, a happy smile on his face, his eyes still fixed on the dusty wake of their destroyer. At intervals he was still heard to murmur 'Poop-poop!'

The Rat shook him by the shoulder. 'Are you coming to help us, Toad?' he demanded sternly.

'Glorious, stirring sight!' murmured Toad, never offering to move. 'The poetry of motion! The *real* way to travel! The *only* way to travel! Here today—in next week tomorrow! Villages skipped, towns and cities jumped—always somebody else's horizon! O bliss! O poop-poop! O my! O my!'

So Mr Toad finds another craze, the new-fangled motor-car. After buying and crashing several, Water Rat and the Mole lock him in Toad Hall for his own good. He escapes down knotted sheets and makes off:

The sign of The Red Lion, swinging across the road halfway down the main street, reminded him that he had not breakfasted that day, and that he was exceedingly hungry after his long walk. He marched into the inn, ordered the best luncheon that could be provided at so short a notice, and sat down to eat it in the coffee-room.

He was about half-way through his meal when an only too familiar sound, approaching down the street, made him start and fall a-trembling all over.

The poop-poop! drew nearer and nearer, the car could be heard to turn into the inn-yard and come to a stop, and Toad had to hold on to the leg of the table to conceal his overmastering emotion. Presently the party entered the coffee-room, hungry, talkative, and gay, voluble on their experiences of the morning and the merits of the chariot that had brought them along so well. Toad listened eagerly, all ears, for a time; at last he could stand it no longer. He slipped out of the room quietly, paid his bill at the bar, and as soon as he got outside sauntered round quietly to the inn-yard. 'There cannot be any harm,' he said to himself, 'in my only just *looking* at it!'

The car stood in the middle of the yard, quite unattended, the stable-helps and other hangers-on being all at their dinner. Toad walked slowly round it, inspecting, criticizing, musing deeply.

'I wonder,' he said to himself presently, 'I wonder if this sort of car *starts* easily?'

Next moment, hardly knowing how it came about, he found he had hold of the handle and was turning it. As the familiar sound broke forth, the old passion seized on Toad and completely mastered him, body and soul. As if in a dream he found himself, somehow, seated in the driver's seat; as in a dream, he pulled the lever and swung the car round the yard and out through the archway; and, as if in a dream, all sense of right and wrong, all fear of obvious consequences, seemed temporarily suspended. He increased his pace, and as the car devoured the street and leapt forth on the high road through the open country, he was only conscious that he was Toad once more, Toad at his best and highest, Toad the terror, the traffic-queller, the Lord of the lone trail, before whom all must give way or be smitten into nothingness and everlasting night. He chanted as he flew, and the car responded with sonorous drone; the miles were eaten up under him as he sped he knew not whither, fulfilling his instincts, living his hour, reckless of what might come to him.

Mr Toad is arrested for stealing the motor-car but escapes and after some hair-raising adventures including being a stowaway on a canal boat and hijacking a horse, he returns home only to find that Toad Hall has been captured by an army of stoats and weasels from the Wild Wood. But Ratty, Mole and the Badger devise a plan and with the help of the other river-side animals the enemy is routed.

At the celebratory banquet given afterwards by Mr Toad, he at last promises his friends to turn over a new leaf, and agrees to abandon the modest programme of events he had put together to entertain his guests:

SPEECH . . . . By TOAD
(There will be other speeches by TOAD during
the evening)

ADDRESS . . . . By TOAD
SYNOPSIS—Our Prison System—The Water-
ways of Old England—Horse-dealing, and

how to deal—Property, its rights and its
duties—Back to the Land—A Typical
English Squire.

SONG . . . .   By TOAD

(*Composed by himself*)

OTHER COMPOSITIONS . . .   By TOAD

will be sung in the course of the
evening by the . . . COMPOSER

Kenneth Grahame (1859–1932), *The Wind in the Willows* (1908).

---

*I*N *spite of humour in the USA becoming city-bred during the early years of the twentieth century and producing a migration of writers from the smaller cities into New York, there was one notable non-migrant: the journalist, editor, and critic, H. L. Mencken, 'The Sage of Baltimore'.*

Apart from reluctant trips to New York when he and George Jean Nathan were editing the Smart Set *magazine and* The American Mercury, *Mencken preferred to stay in Baltimore, and for most of his working life wrote an iconoclastic column for the Baltimore* Evening Sun *pouring blistering scorn on those aspects of America which he detested, which were many (and they included Baltimore).*

He was in many ways the American prose equivalent of his contemporary George Bernard Shaw, whom he much admired. Like Shaw, his aim was to shock readers out of complacency and to set them thinking. He deplored America's lack of writers like Shaw and Ibsen, who exposed the bent ethics and sham in European society, and he championed such new young American writers as Sherwood Anderson, Theodore Dreiser, and Sinclair Lewis.

Walter Lippmann was one of Mencken's many admirers and in the Saturday Review of Literature *called him 'the most powerful personal influence on this whole generation of educated people'. His opponents, who were those millions of citizens of a conservative nature, loathed him almost beyond words: one comment, milder than most, came from the Revd Dr Charles E. Jones, who wrote in the* Gospel Call: *'If a buzzard had laid an egg in a dunghill and the sun had hatched a thing like Mencken, the buzzard would have been justly ashamed of its offspring.'*

Mencken's prose, tough, erudite, polished, the inspiration for much fine journalism to come later from columnists such as Britain's Cassandra and Bernard Levin, also had humour. Here are some typical Mencken pensées:

On American culture:

There may come a time when the composer of string quartettes is paid as much as a railway guard, but it is not yet.

H. L. Mencken (1880–1956), *Prejudices* (six vols., 1919–27)

A definition of adultery:
Democracy applied to love.

A Book of Burlesques (1916).

A sobering thought:
Puritanism—the haunting fear that someone, somewhere, may be happy.

Ibid.

Concerning the conscience:
Conscience is the inner voice that warns us that somebody may be looking.

A Mencken Chrestomathy (1949).

And the epitaph he chose for himself:
If, after I depart this vale, you ever remember me and have thought to please my ghost, forgive some sinner and wink your eye at some homely girl.

Smart Set (1921).

In 1916 he wrote an extraordinary piece for his column suggesting the truth behind the façade of a conventional wedding in prosperous Baltimore.

What was interesting was his pioneer use of a technique of satire whereby the attack is not made frontally but by steadily piling up small, realistic details to give an effect of documentary truth.

None of the details of the following wedding report are particularly significant in themselves, but the completed picture makes a formidable indictment of what Mencken considered to be a complacent, hypocritical society:

THE WEDDING: A STAGE DIRECTION

The scene is a church in an American city of about half a million population, and the time is about eleven o'clock of a fine morning in early spring. The neighbourhood is well-to-do, but not quite fashionable. That is to say, most of the families of the vicinage keep two servants (alas, more or less intermittently!), and eat dinner at half-past six, and about one in four boasts a coloured butler (who attends to the fires, washes windows and helps with the sweeping), and a last year's automobile. The heads of these families are merchandise brokers; jobbers in notions, hardware and drugs; manufacturers of candy, hats, badges, office furniture, blank books, picture frames, wire goods and patent medicines; managers of steamboat lines; district agents of insurance companies; owners of commercial printing offices, and other such business men of substance—and the prosperous lawyers and popular family doctors who keep them out of trouble. In one block lives a Congressman and two college professors, one of whom has written an unimportant textbook and got himself into 'Who's Who in America'. In the block above lives a man who once ran for Mayor of the city, and came near being elected.
The wives of these householders wear good clothes and have a liking for a reasonable gayety, but few of them can pretend to what is vaguely called social

standing, and, to do them justice, not many of them waste any time lamenting it. They have, taking one with another, about three children apiece, and are good mothers. A few of them belong to women's clubs or flirt with the suffragettes, but the majority can get all of the intellectual stimulation they crave in the Ladies' Home Journal *and the* Saturday Evening Post, *with* Vogue *added for its fashions. Most of them, deep down in their hearts, suspect their husbands of secret frivolity, and about ten per cent of them have the proofs, but it is rare for them to make rows about it, and the divorce rate among them is thus very low. Themselves indifferent cooks, they are unable to teach their servants the art, and so the food they set before their husbands and children is often such as would make a Frenchman cut his throat. But they are diligent housewives otherwise; they see to it that the windows are washed, that no one tracks mud into the hall, and that the servants do not waste coal, sugar, soap and gas, and that the family buttons are always sewn on. In religion these estimable wives are pious in habit but somewhat nebulous in faith. That is to say, they regard any person who specifically refuses to go to church as a heathen, but they themselves are by no means regular in attendance, and not one in ten of them could tell you whether transubstantiation is a Roman Catholic or a Dunkard doctrine* ['Dunkards' were members of a Baptist sect which believed in total immersion]. *About two per cent of them have dallied more or less gingerly with Christian Science, their average period of belief being one year.*

The church we are in is like the neighbourhood and its people; well-to-do but not fashionable. It is Protestant in faith and probably Episcopalian. The pews are of thick, yellow-brown oak, severe in pattern and hideous in colour. In each there is a long, removable cushion of a dark, purplish, dirty hue, with here and there some of its hair stuffing showing. The stained-glass windows, which were all bought ready-made and depict scenes from the New Testament, commemorate the virtues of departed worthies of the neighbourhood, whose names appear, in illegible black letters, in the lower panels. . . .

The organist arrives:

The organist is a tall, thin man of melancholy and uraemic aspect, wearing a black slouch hat with a wide brim and a yellow overcoat that barely reaches to his knees. A pupil, in his youth, of a man who had once studied (irregularly and briefly) with Charles-Marie Widor, he acquired thereby the artistic temperament, and with it a vast fondness for malt liquor. His mood this morning is acidulous and depressed, for he spent yesterday evening in a Pilsner ausschank with two former members of the Boston Symphony Orchestra, and it was 3 a.m. before they finally agreed that Johann Sebastian Bach, all things considered, was a greater man than Beethoven, and so parted amicably. Sourness is the precise sensation that wells within him. He feels vinegary; his blood runs cold; he wishes he could immerse himself in bicarbonate of soda. But the call of his art is more potent than the protest of his poisoned and quaking liver, and so he manfully climbs the spiral staircase to his organ-loft.

Once there, he takes off his hat and overcoat, stoops down to blow the dust off the organ keys, throws the electrical switch which sets the bellows going, and then proceeds to take off his shoes. This done, he takes his seat, reaches for the pedals with his stockinged feet, tries an experimental 32-foot CCC, and then wanders gently into a Bach toccata. It is his limbering-up piece: he always plays it as a prelude to a wedding job. It thus goes very smoothly and even brilliantly, but when he comes to the end of it and tackles the ensuing fugue he is quickly in difficulties, and after four or five stumbling repetitions of the subject he hurriedly improvises a crude coda and has done. Peering down into the church to see if his flounderings have had an audience, he sees two old maids enter, the one very tall and thin and the other somewhat brisk and bunchy.

They constitute the vanguard of the nuptial throng, and as they proceed; hesitatingly up the centre aisle, eager for good seats but afraid to go too far, the organist wipes his palms upon his trouser legs, squares his shoulders, and plunges into the program that he has played at all weddings for fifteen years past. It begins with Mendelssohn's Spring Song, pianissimo. Then comes Rubenstein's Melody in F, with a touch of forte towards the close, and then Nevin's 'Oh, That We Two Were Maying', and then the Chopin waltz in A flat 69, No. 1, and then the Spring Song again, and then a free fantasia upon 'The Rosary' and then a Moszkowski mazurka, and then the Dvořák Humoresque (with its heart-rending cry in the middle), and then some vague and turbulent thing (apparently the disjecta membra of another fugue), and then Tschaikowsky's 'Autumn', and then Elgar's 'Salut d'Amour', and then the Spring Song a third time, and then something or other from one of the Peer Gynt suites, and then an hurrah or two from the Hallelujah chorus, and then Chopin again, and Nevin, and Elgar, and—

But meanwhile there is a growing activity below. First comes a closed automobile bearing the six ushers and soon after it another automobile bearing the bridegroom and his best man. The bridegroom and the best man disembark before the side entrance of the church and make their way into the vestry-room, where they remove their hats and coats, and proceed to struggle with their cravats and collars before a mirror which hangs on the wall. The room is very dingy. A baize-covered table is in the centre of it, and around the table stand six or eight chairs of assorted designs. One wall is completely covered by a bookcase, through the glass doors of which one may discern piles of cheap Bibles, hymn-books and back numbers of the parish magazine. In one corner is a small washstand. The best man takes a flat flask of whiskey from his pocket, looks around him for a glass, finds it on the washstand, rinses it at the tap, fills it with a policeman's drink, and hands it to the bridegroom. The latter downs it at a gulp. Then the best man pours out one for himself. . . .

It is now a quarter to twelve, and of a sudden the vestibule fills with wedding guests. Nine-tenths of them, perhaps even nineteen-twentieths, are women, and most of them are beyond thirty-five. Scattered among them, hanging on to their skirts, are about a dozen little girls—one of them a youngster of eight or thereabouts, with spindle shanks and shining morning face, entranced by her first wedding. Here and there lurks a man. Usually he wears a hurried, unwilling, protesting look. He has been dragged from his office on a busy morning, forced to rush home and get into his cutaway coat, and then marched to the church by his wife. One of these men, much hustled, has forgotten to have his shoes shined. He is intensely conscious of them, and tries to hide them behind his wife's skirt as they walk up the aisle. Accidentally he steps upon it, and gets a look over the shoulder which lifts his diaphragm an inch and turns his liver to water. This man will be court-martialed when he reaches home, and he knows it. He wishes that some foreign power would invade the United States and burn down all the churches in the country, and that the bride, the bridegroom and all the other persons interested in the present wedding were dead and in hell. . . .

To the damp funeral smell of the flowers of the altar, there has been added the cacodorous scents of forty or fifty different brands of talcum and rice paper. It begins to grow warm in the church, and a number of women open their vanity bags and duck down for stealthy dabs at their noses. Others, more reverent, suffer the agony of augmenting shines. One, a trickster, has concealed powder in her pocket handkerchief, and applies it dexterously while pretending to blow her nose.

The bridegroom in the vestry-room, entering on the second year (or is it the third?) of his long and ghastly wait, grows increasingly nervous, and when he hears the organist pass from the Spring Song into some more sonorous and stately thing he mistakes it for the wedding march from 'Lohengrin', and is hot for marching upon the altar at once. The best man, an old hand, restrains him gently, and administers another sedative from the bottle. The bridegroom's thoughts turn to gloomy things. He remembers sadly that he will never be able to laugh at benedicts [newly married men] *again; that his days of low, rabelaisian wit and carefree scoffing are over; that he is now the very thing he mocked so gaily but yesteryear. Like a drowning man, he passes his whole life in review—not, however, that part which is past, but that which is to come. Odd fancies throng upon him. He wonders what his honeymoon will cost him, what there will be to drink at the wedding breakfast, what a certain girl in Chicago will say when she hears of his marriage. . . .*

The organist plunges into 'Lohengrin' and the wedding procession gets under way:

The bride and her father march first. Their step is so slow (about one beat to

*two measures) that the father has some difficulty in maintaining his equi-
librium, but the bride herself moves steadily and erectly, almost seeming to
float. Her face is thickly encrusted with talcum in its various forms, so that
she is almost a dead white. She keeps her eyelids lowered modestly, but is still
acutely aware of every glance fastened upon her—not in the mass, but every
glance individually. For example, she sees clearly, even through her eyelids,
the still, cold smile of a girl in Pew 8 R—a girl who once made an unwomanly
attempt upon the bridegroom's affections, and was routed and put to flight by
superior strategy. And her ears are open, too: she hears every 'How sweet!'
and 'Oh, lovely!' and 'Ain't she pale!' from the latitude of the last pew to
the very glacis of the altar of God. . . .*

> The bride arrives beside the bridegroom at the altar rail
> and they stand together, silently looking down at their
> feet.

*Then the music, having died down to a faint murmur and a hush having fallen
upon the assemblage, they look up.*

*Before them, framed by foliage, stands the reverend gentleman of God who will
presently link them in indissoluble chains—the estimable rector of the parish.
He has got there just in time; it was, indeed, a close shave. But no trace of
haste or of anything else of a disturbing character is now visible upon his
smooth, glistening, somewhat feverish face. That face is wholly occupied by
his official smile, a thing of oil and honey all compact, a balmy, unctuous
illumination—the secret of his success in life. Slowly his cheeks puff out,
gleaming like soap-bubbles. Slowly he lifts his prayer-book from the prie-dieu
and holds it droopingly. Slowly his soft caressing eyes engage it. There is an
almost imperceptible stiffening of his frame. His mouth opens with a faint
click. He begins to read.*

The Ceremony of Marriage has begun.

A Book of Burlesques (1916).

*As a journalist Mencken was 'the Thinking Man's reporter'. The prose of his essays
and reports was trenchant yet amusing and his reasoning was first rate (even when
he was backing the wrong horse).*

*Like G. K. Chesterton, Mencken argued clearly and he was an enjoyer of life,
but he attacked with relish those aspects of American life which he did not enjoy.
These included most organized religion and especially the Methodists (he came from
a German family of Protestants), middle-class morality, politicians, European
patronage of American culture, complacency, stupidity, and the majority of his
fellow Americans (whom he called 'the booboisie'). But he loved good music (which
to him was all German music), good writing—and a good drink when work was
over.*

*Mencken's essay on the importance of alcohol to mankind is as persuasive now
as it was when he first published it—in the middle of Prohibition:*

MEDITATIONS IN THE METHODIST DESERT

Portrait of an Ideal World

That alcohol in dilute aqueous solution, when taken into the human organism, acts as a depressant, not as a stimulant, is now so much a commonplace of knowledge that even the more advanced varieties of physiologists are beginning to be aware of it. The intelligent layman no longer resorts to the jug when he has important business before him, whether intellectual or manual; he resorts to it after his business is done, and he desires to release his taut nerves and reduce the steam-pressure in his spleen.

Alcohol, so to speak, unwinds us. It raises the threshold of sensation and makes us less sensitive to external stimuli, and particularly to those that are unpleasant. It reduces and simplifies the emotions. Putting a brake upon all the qualities which enable us to get on in the world and shine before our fellows—for example, combativeness, shrewdness, diligence, ambition—it releases the qualities which mellow us and make our fellows love us—for example, amiability, generosity, toleration, humor, sympathy.

A man who has taken aboard two or three cocktails is less competent than he was before to steer a battleship down the Ambrose Channel, or to cut off a leg, or to draw up a deed of trust, or to conduct Bach's B minor mass, but he is immensely more competent to entertain a dinner party, or to admire a pretty girl, or to *hear* Bach's B minor mass. The harsh, useful things of the world, from pulling teeth to digging potatoes, are best done by men who are as starkly sober as so many convicts in the death-house, but the lovely and useless things, the charming and exhilarating things, are best done by men with, as the phrase is, a few sheets in the wind. *Pithecanthropus erectus* was a teetotaller, but the angels, you may be sure, know what is proper at 5 p.m.

All this is so obvious that I marvel that no utopian has ever proposed to abolish all the sorrows of the world by the simple device of getting and keeping the whole human race gently stewed. I do not say drunk, remember; I say simply gently stewed—and apologize, as in duty bound, for not knowing how to describe the state in a more seemly phrase. The man who is in it is a man who has put all of his best qualities into his showcase. He is not only immensely more amiable than the cold sober man; he is immeasurably more decent. He reacts to all situations in an expansive, generous and humane manner. He has become more liberal, more tolerant, more kind. He is a better citizen, husband, father, friend. The enterprises that make human life on this earth uncomfortable and unsafe are never launched by such men. They are not makers of wars; they do not rob and oppress anyone; they invent no such plagues as high tariffs, 100 per cent Americanism and Prohibition.

All the great villainies of history, from the murder of Abel to the Treaty of Versailles, have been perpetuated by sober men, and chiefly by teetotallers.

But all the charming and beautiful things, from the Song of Songs to terrapin *à la* Maryland, and from the nine Beethoven symphonies to the Martini cocktail, have been given to humanity by men who, when the hour came, turned from well water to something with colour in it, and more in it than mere oxygen and hydrogen.

Prejudices: Fourth Series (1924).

A s *the century grew older, the rise of New York as the centre of entertainment and journalistic humour became unstoppable.*

New York had more theatres than any other city and more were being built, magazines had potentially a vastly bigger readership, there were twelve flourishing daily newspapers in Manhattan alone and five more in Brooklyn most of which had show-biz pages and columns which brought in items of humour and backstage gossip (the Morning Telegraph *was so full of theatrical chit-chat that it was known as 'the chorus girl's breakfast').*

It was the city where writers could become rich and famous more quickly and spectacularly than anywhere else.

The bright young wits from out-of-town moved in; Alexander Woollcott from New Jersey, George S. Kaufman from the Mid-West, Franklin P. Adams from Chicago, Robert Benchley from New England, and the editor who was to have the greatest influence on the style and shape of New York humour, Harold Ross from Aspen in the Rocky Mountains. An exception was Dorothy Parker who was born in New York City.

Humour having become urban was now to become urbane. New York in 1919 was self-confident; there was plenty of money about; a network of friendly neighbourhood bootleggers had eased the pangs of Prohibition and speakeasies brought a new social democracy with rich men-about-town happy to rub shoulders at the bar with boxers, chorus-girls, and gangsters. It was the era of Flaming Youth, jazz, hip-flasks, press-agents and wisecracks: sophistication was the thing.

The amoral ethos of New York in the twenties was brilliantly captured by Anita Loos in her novel Gentlemen Prefer Blondes *(1925), which purports to be the diary of a pert, blonde, naïve 'actress' named Lorelei Lee.*

The book is delicately sub-titled 'The Illuminating Diary of A Professional Lady'.

March 16th:

A gentleman friend and I were dining at the Ritz last evening and he said that if I took a pencil and a paper and put down all of my thoughts it would make a book. This almost made me smile as what it would really make would be a whole row of encyclopedias. I mean I seem to be thinking practically all of the time. I mean it is my favorite recreation and sometimes I sit for hours and do not seem to do anything else but think. So this gentleman said a girl with brains ought to do something else with them besides think. And he said he ought to know brains when he sees them, because he is in the senate and he spends quite a great deal of time in Washington, d.c., and when he comes into contact with brains he always notices it. So it might have all blown over but this morning he sent me a book. And so when my maid brought it to me, I said to her, 'Well, Lulu, here is another book and we have not read half the ones we have got yet.' But when I opened it and saw that it was all a blank I remembered what my gentleman acquaintance said, and so then I realized that it was a diary. So here I am writing a book instead of reading one.

But now it is the 16th of March and of course it is too late to begin with January, but it does not matter as my gentleman friend, Mr Eisman, was in town practically all of January and February, and when he is in town one day seems to be practically the same as the next day.

I mean Mr Eisman is in the wholesale button profession in Chicago and he is the gentleman who is known practically all over Chicago at Gus Eisman the Button King. And he is the gentleman who is interested in educating me, so of course he is always coming down to New York to see how my brains have improved since the last time. But when Mr Eisman is in New York we always seem to do the same thing and if I wrote down one day in my diary, all I would have to do would be to put quotation marks for all other days. I mean we always seem to have dinner at the Colony and see a show and go to the Trocadero and then Mr Eisman shows me to my apartment. So of course when a gentleman is interested in educating a girl, he likes to stay and talk about the topics of the day until quite late, so I am quite fatigued the next day and I do not really get up until it is time to dress for dinner at the Colony.

The book was an immediate best-seller which it remained for many years. It was made into a play and eventually, with added songs, into a successful film.

Rumour had it that part of the popularity of the book was due to young women buying it as a Do-it-Yourself manual on how a girl could get rich quick:

March 22nd:

Well my birthday has come and gone but it was really quite depressing. I mean it seems to me a gentleman who has a friendly interest in educating a girl like Gus Eisman, would want her to have the biggest square-cut diamond in New York. I mean I must say I was quite disappointed when he came to the apartment with a little thing you could hardly see. So I told him I thought it was quite cute, but I had quite a headache and I had better stay in a dark room all day and I told him I would see him the next day, perhaps. Because even Lulu thought it was quite small and she said, if she was I, she really would do something definite and she said she always believed in the old adage, 'Leave them while you're looking good'. But he came in at dinner time with really a very very beautiful bracelet of square cut diamonds so I was quite cheered up. So then we had dinner at the Colony and we went to a show and supper at the Trocadero as usual whenever he is in town. But I will give him credit that he realized how small it was. I mean he kept talking about how bad business was and the button profession was full of bolshevicks who make nothing but trouble. Because Mr Eisman feels that the country is really on the verge of the bolshevicks and I become quite worried. I mean if the bolshevicks do get in, there is only one gentleman who could handle them and that is Mr D. W. Griffith. Because I will never forget when Mr Griffith was directing Intolerance. I mean it was my last cinema before Mr Eisman made me give up my career and I was playing one of the girls that fainted at the battle when all of the gentlemen fell off the tower. And when I saw how Mr Griffith handled all of those mobs in Intolerance I realized that he could do anything, and I really think the government of America ought to tell Mr Griffith to get all ready if the bolshevicks start to do it.

March 30th:

At last Mr Eisman has left on the 20th Century and I must say I am quite fatigued and a little rest will be quite welcome . . .

But before Mr Eisman went to Chicago he told me that he is going to Paris this summer on professional business and I think he intends to present me with a trip to Paris as he says there is nothing so educational as traveling. I mean it did worlds of good to Dorothy when she was abroad last spring and I never get tired of hearing her telling how the merry-go-rounds in Paris have pigs instead of horses.

Anita Loos (1893–1981), *Gentlemen Prefer Blondes* (1925).

IT *was to the fun-chasing New York of Lorelei Lee that the fighting troops returned from France after the Armistice. The non-fighting troops too, including Captain Franklin P. Adams, Sergeant Alexander Woollcott, and Private Harold Ross, who were on the staff of the weekly army paper* Stars and Stripes *and spent the few months of their war in Paris: their rations, Woollcott recalled with relish, were seven-course meals in restaurants, 'partridge and rabbit, beef-steaks and perfect omelettes, patisserie . . .'.*

Back to their newspaper columns and magazine writings went Woollcott, Adams, and Ross, picking up their old friendships and contacts and often meeting for lunch at a small hotel near the Hippodrome theatre called the Algonquin.

Woollcott was a relentless self-publicist. It seems that one day at the Algonquin he airily waved aside a story which two press-agents, John Peter Toohey and Murdock Pemberton, were trying get him to listen to and embarked on yet another of his lengthy lies which began 'when I was in the theatre of war . . .'. Toohey and Pemberton plotted revenge; they mounted a lunch party at the Algonquin to which they invited the New York theatre journalists, including Robert Benchley, Dorothy Parker, Harold Ross, and George S. Kaufman. Their idea was to ridicule Woollcott's endless harping on his war-effort by putting up military banners everywhere with Woollcott's name spelt just slightly wrongly, calling on him for army reminiscences, etc.

The wheeze did not work as Woollcott happily obliged with endless war stories, but at the end of the communal lunch, which the assembled writers seemed to enjoy, John Peter Toohey said 'Why don't we do this every day?' And they did.

The Algonquin lunches became an established part of the writers' lives. The talk was witty, and as the best put-downs and quips were fed by John Peter Toohey to the newspaper columnists the group began to achieve a kind of celebrity.

In the following year the hotel's owner, Frank Case, recognizing a good thing, gave the group a round table to themselves in the centre of the Algonquin's Rose Room. The columnists began to refer to the group as 'The Algonquin Round Table'. They called themselves 'The Vicious Circle'.

The larking around, the all-night parties, the irreverence of the group was understandable in talented people so young (one editor dubbed them 'the amazing whelps'): in 1919 Dorothy Parker was aged 26 and drama critic of Vanity Fair *(she took over from P. G. Wodehouse, who left to write musicals with Jerome Kern and Guy Bolton); Benchley, 29, was the journal's managing editor, and Robert Sherwood was writing pieces for it at the age of 24.*

One of the older members of the Circle—often at their parties but seldom, if at all, at the Round Table (he was too tongue-tied)—was Ring Lardner, already an established and much admired humorous writer.

Lardner began as a sports-writer but achieved his first success with a series of short stories about a failing baseball player which were both funny and bitter. He became, to his surprise and disbelief, one of the most sought-after humorous short-story writers of his generation.

Part of Lardner's odd, original talent was his gift for writing about the kind of dull, commonplace, stupid people whom he particularly disliked. He had an extraordinarily accurate ear for the way they spoke.

As, for instance, when two of them are locked in mindless small-talk:

ON CONVERSATION

The other night I had to be coming back from Wilmington, Del. to wherever I was going and was sitting in the smoking compartment or whatever they now call the wash room and overheard a conversation between two fellows who we will call Mr Butler and Mr Hawkes. Both of them

seemed to be from the same town and I only wished I could repeat the conversation verbatim but the best I can do is report from memory. The
fellows evidently had not met for some three to fifteen years as the judges
say.

'Well,' said Mr Hawkes, 'if this isn't Dick Butler!'

'Well,' said Mr Butler, 'if this isn't Dale Hawkes!'

'Well, Dick,' said Hawkes, 'I never expected to meet you on this train.'

'No,' replied Butler. 'I generally take Number 28. I just took this train this
evening because I had to be in Wilmington today.'

'Where are you headed for?' asked Hawkes.

'Well, I am going to the big town,' said Butler.

'So am I, and I am certainly glad we happened to be in the same car.'

'I am glad too, but it is funny we happened to be in the same car.'

It seemed funny to both of them but they successfully concealed it so far
as facial expression was concerned. After a pause Hawkes spoke again:

'How long since you been back in Lansing?'

'Me?' replied Butler. 'I ain't been back there for twelve years.'

'I ain't been back there either myself for ten years. How long since you
been back there?'

'I ain't been back there for twelve years.'

'I ain't been back there myself for ten years. Where are you heading
for?'

'New York,' replied Butler. 'I have to get there about once a year. Where
are you going?'

'Me?' asked Hawkes. 'I am going to New York too. I have got to go down
there every little while for the firm.'

'Do you have to go there very often?'

'Me? Every little while. How often do you have to go there?'

'About once a year. How often do you get back to Lansing?'

'Last time I was there was ten years ago. How long since you was
back?'

'About twelve years ago. Lots of changes there since we left there.'

'That's the way I figured it. It makes a man seem kind of old to go back
there and not see nobody you know.'

'You said something. I go along the streets there now and don't see nobody
I know.'

'How long since you was there?'

'Me?' said Hawkes. 'I only get back there about once every ten years. By
the way what became of old man Kelsey?'

'Who do you mean, Kelsey?'

'Yes, what became of him?'

'Old Kelsey? Why he has been dead for ten years.'

'Oh, I didn't know that. And what became of his daughter? I mean
Eleanor?'

'Why Eleanor married a man named Forster or Jennings or something like that from Flint.'

'Yes, but I mean the other daughter, Louise.'

'Oh, she's married.'

'Where are you going now?'

'I am headed for New York on business for the firm.'

'I have to go there about once a year—for the firm.'

'Do you get back to Lansing very often?'

'About once in ten or twelve years. I hardly know anybody there now. It seems funny to go down the street and not know nobody.'

'That's the way I always feel. It seems it was not like my old home town at all. I go up and down the street and don't know anybody and nobody speaks to you. I guess I know more people in New York now than I do in Lansing.'

'Do you get to New York often?'

'Only about once a year. I have to go there for the firm.'

'No, it is changing all the time. Just like Lansing. I guess they all change.'

'I don't know much about Lansing any more. I only get there about once in ten or twelve years.'

'What are you reading there?'

'Oh, it is just a little article in Asia. There's a good many interesting articles in Asia.'

'I only seen a couple copies of it. This thing I am reading is a little article on "Application" in the American.'

'Well, go ahead and read and don't let me disturb you.'

'Well, I just wanted to finish it up. Go ahead and finish what you're reading yourself.'

'All right. We will talk things over later. It is funny we happened to get on the same car.'

Ring Lardner (1885–1933), First and Last (1934).

Lardner was probably the heaviest drinker of the Vicious Circle set, a formidable achievement, and a participant in their wilder party pranks. Dinners of the newly formed Authors' League were boisterous affairs where it was customary for some of the more extrovert members to perform a cabaret. For one of those evenings Lardner wrote a nonsense playlet, I Gaspiri. This was a great success and was reprinted in magazines and newspapers; in Paris the Transatlantic Review *hailed it as an intellectual triumph, a model for European dadaists and surrealists. Its original success was more likely to have been due to the fact that the author when writing it and the actors and audience during the performance were almost certainly well and truly stewed, but it was one of the earliest successful examples of wild fantasy, what Benchley called 'the* dementia praecox *school of writing' (Freud was all the rage then).*

I Gaspiri was performed at the Author's League dinner by Marc Connelly,

Robert Sherwood, and Robert Benchley, though how they managed to perform it is mind-boggling:

I GASPIRI—'THE UPHOLSTERERS'

A Drama in Three Acts

Adapted from the Bukovinian of Casper Redmonda

Characters

Ian Obry, *a blotter salesman.*
Johan Wasper, *his wife.*
Greta, *their daughter.*
Herbert Swope [then the important editor of the *World*], *a nonentity.*
Ffena, *their daughter, later their wife.*
Egso, *a Pencil Guster.*
Tono, *a typical Wastebasket.*

Act I

(*A public street in a bathroom. A man named Tupper has evidently just taken a bath. A man named Brindle is now taking a bath. A man named Newburn comes out of the faucet which has been left running. He exits through the exhaust. Two strangers to each other meet on the bath mat.*)

FIRST STRANGER

Where were you born?

SECOND STRANGER

Out of wedlock.

FIRST STRANGER

That's a mighty pretty country around there.

SECOND STRANGER

Are you married?

FIRST STRANGER

I don't know. There's a woman living with me but I can't place her.
(*Three outsiders named Klein go across the stage three times. They think they are in a public library. A woman's cough is heard off-stage left.*)

A NEW CHARACTER

Who is that cough?

TWO MOORS

That is my cousin. She died a little while ago in a haphazard way.

A GREEK

And what a woman she was!
(*The curtain is lowered for seven days to denote the lapse of a week.*) . . .

Act III

(*The Lincoln Highway. Two bearded glue lifters are seated at one side of the road.*)

(Translator's Note: *The principal industry in Phlace is hoarding hay. Peasants sit alongside of a road on which hay wagons are likely to pass. When a hay wagon does pass, the hay hoarders leap from their points of vantage and help themselves to a wisp of hay. On an average a hay hoarder accumulates a ton of hay every four years. This is called Mah Jong.*)

FIRST GLUE LIFTER

Well, my man, how goes it?

SECOND GLUE LIFTER

(*Sings 'My Man' to show how it goes.*)

(*Eight realtors cross the stage in a friendly way. They are out of place.*)

CURTAIN

Ibid.

THE *Vicious Circle was not all that vicious when it began. A tougher note developed later, in the middle-twenties, when the Round Table lunches were a part of New York's smart scene and the swapping of quotable insults round the table, by then more or less in public, had become competitive and merciless. In the early days shy guests could be invited, and those members like George S. Kaufman and Robert Benchley who were rarely without temporary girl-friends could bring along their equivalents of Lorelei Lee without fear of them being humiliated—as long as they were positioned as far away as possible from the table's self-appointed centrepiece, Alexander Woollcott.*

Woollcott, an out-of-towner bedazzled by the glamorous myth of New York, was a literary and dramatic critic, essayist and latterly radio personality. He insulted everybody freely and with rancour; it was an important part of the character he had invented for himself and was such a successful piece of self-promotion that the offensive main character of the play, The Man Who Came to Dinner, *was a portrait of Woollcott. He was also caricatured in two Broadway plays by S. N. Behrman and in Charles Brackett's novel* Entirely Surrounded. *Not at all abashed by this public exposure of his personal character he played the part of himself in various productions of all three plays.*

Woollcott's prose reflected his own persona; flamboyant, plump, egocentric, bitchy, occasionally witty, invariably deeply sentimental (Howard Dietz called him 'Louisa M. Woollcott'). James Thurber took a harder view; in a letter to Groucho Marx he referred to Woollcott as 'old Vitriol and Violets, a man as fragile as nails and as sweet as death'. But unlovable though he could be socially with all that bullying and domination of friends and social snobbery, his writing style, a kind of soft-centred, mandarin baroque, brought a different kind of sophistication to American humorous prose.

Here is one of the popular pieces which helped to make his reputation. Like many of his stories it is an old anecdote reworked in the Woollcott manner:

ENTRANCE FEE

This, then, is the story of Cosette and the Saint-Cyrien, much as they tell it (and these many years have been telling it) in the smoky *popotes* of the French army.

In the nineties, when one heard less ugly babel of alien tongues in the sidewalk cafes, the talk at the *apéritif* hour was sure to turn sooner or later on Cosette—Mlle Cosette of the *Variétés*, who was regarded by common consent as the most desirable woman in France. She was no hedged-in royal courtesan, as her possessive fellow-citizens would point out with satisfaction, but a distributed du Barry, the *chère amie* of a republic.

Her origins were misty. Some said she had been born of fisher folk at Ploubazlanec on the Brittany coast. Others preferred the tale that she was the love-child of a famous actress by a very well-known king. In any case, she was now a national legend, and in her pre-eminence the still-bruised French people found in some curious way a balm for their wounded self-esteem. Her photographs, which usually showed her sitting piquantly on a café table, were cut from *L'Illustration* and pinned up in every barracks. Every French lad dreamed of her, and every right-minded French girl quite understood that her sweetheart was saying in effect, 'Since I cannot hope to have Cosette, will you come to the river's edge at sundown?' Quite understood, and did not blame him.

Everyone had seen the pictures of Cosette's tiny, vine-hung villa at Saint-Cloud, with its high garden wall and its twittering aviary. And even those for whom that wall was hopelessly high took morbid pride in a persistent detail of the legend which said that no man was ever a guest there for the night who could not bring five thousand francs with him. This was in the nineties, mind you, when francs were francs, and men—by a coincidence then more dependable—were men.

The peasant blend of charm and thrift in Cosette filled the cadets at Saint-Cyr with a gentle melancholy. In their twilight hours of relaxation they talked it over, and all thought it a sorrowful thing that, so wretched is the soldier's pittance, not one of those who must some day direct the great *Revanche* would ever carry into battle a memory of the fairest woman in France. For what cadet could hope to raise five thousand francs? It was very sad. But, cried one of their number, his voice shaking, his eyes alight, there were a thousand students at Saint-Cyr, and not one among them so lacking in resource that he could not, if given time, manage to raise at least five francs.

That was how the Cosette Sweepstakes were started. There followed then all the anxious distraction of ways and means, with such Spartan exploits in self-denial, such Damon-and-Pythias borrowings, such flagrant letters of perjured appeal to unsuspecting aunts and godmothers as Saint-Cyr had never known. But by the appointed time the last man had his, or somebody's, five francs.

The drawing of numbers was well under way when a perplexed instructor stumbled on the proceedings and reported his discovery to the Commandant. When the old General heard the story he was so profoundly moved that it was some time before he spoke.

'The lad who wins the lottery,' he said at last, 'will be the envy of his generation. But the lad who conceived the idea—ah, he, my friend, will some day be a Marshal of France!'

Then he fell to laughing at the thought of the starry-eyed youngster arriving at the stage door of the *Variétés* with nothing but his youth and his entrance fee. The innocent budget had made no provision for the trip to Paris, none for a carriage, a bouquet, perhaps a supper party. The Commandant said that he would wish to meet this margin of contingency from his own fatherly pocket.

'There will be extras,' he said. 'Let the young rascal who wins be sent to me before he leaves for Paris.'

It was a cadet from the Vendée who reported to the Commandant next afternoon—very trim in his red breeches and blue tunic, his white gloves spotless, his white cockade jaunty, his heart in his mouth. The Commandant said no word to him, but put a little purse of gold *louis* in his hand, kissed him on both cheeks in benediction, and stood at his window, moist-eyed and chuckling, to watch until the white cockade disappeared down the avenue of trees.

The sunlight, latticed by the *jalousies*, was making a gay pattern on Cosette's carpet the next morning when she sat up and meditated on the day which stretched ahead of her. Her little cadet was cradled in a sweet, dreamless sleep, and it touched her rather to see how preposterously young he was. Indeed, it quite set her thinking of her early days, and how she had come up in the world. Then she began speculating on *his* early days, realized with a pang that he was still in the midst of them, and suddenly grew puzzled. Being a woman of action, she prodded him.

'Listen, my old one,' she said, 'how did a cadet at Saint-Cyr ever get hold of five thousand francs?'

Thus abruptly questioned, he lost his head and blurted out the tale of the sweepstakes. Perhaps he felt it could do no harm now, and anyway she listened so avidly, with such flattering little gasps of surprise and such sunny ripples of laughter, that he quite warmed to his story. When he came to the part about the Commandant, she rose and strode up and down, the lace of her peignoir fluttering behind her, tears in her violet eyes.

'Saint-Cyr has paid me the prettiest compliment I have ever known,' she said, 'and I am the proudest woman in France this day. But surely I must do my part. You shall go back and tell them all that Cosette is a woman of sentiment. When you are an old, old man in the Vendée you shall tell your grandchildren that once in your youth you knew the dearest favors in France, and they cost you not a sou. Not a sou.'

At that she hauled open the little drawer where he had seen her lock up the lottery receipts the night before.

'Here,' she said, with a lovely gesture. 'I give you back your money.' And she handed him his five francs.

Alexander Woollcott (1887–1943), While Rome Burns 1934.

----

*O*NE *member of the Vicious Circle who was entirely without malice (perhaps the only one) was Robert Benchley. As a writer of humorous prose he was the most diversely talented of them all; also probably the one most admired by his colleagues, certainly the one best loved.*

Benchley came from an old New England family; his grandfather had been Lieutenant-Governor of Massachusetts. He went, of course, to Harvard, edited the Harvard Lampoon, *and graduated in 1912. Later he made a list of everything he had learned during his first year at Harvard:*

1. Charlemagne either died or was born or did something with the Holy Roman Empire in 800.

2. By placing one paper bag inside another paper bag you can carry home a milk shake in it.

3. There is a double 'l' in the middle of 'parallel'.

4. Powder rubbed on the chin will take the place of a shave if the room isn't very light.

5. French nouns ending in 'aison' are feminine.

6. Almost everything you need to know about a subject is in the encyclopedia.

Robert Benchley (1889–1945), Quoted in The Algonquin Wits, ed. Robert E. Drennan (1985).

Benchley married young, moved to New York and got a job on the Tribune, *lost it, refused an offer to write subtitles for silent films, and was taken on by* Vanity Fair *together with Robert Sherwood and Dorothy Parker. All three took to lunching at the Algonquin Round Table. They were fired from* Vanity Fair *for too much larking about and all three joined* Life, *Benchley as drama critic.*

All the time he was turning out, seemingly effortlessly, a stream of funny pieces which were published by various papers and journals and collected from time to time into the books which earned him a growing reputation. He was so prolific and

*his work was of such high quality that other writers despaired; years later James
Thurber wrote '. . . one of the greatest fears of the humorous writer is that he has
spent three weeks writing something done faster and better by Benchley in 1919'.*

*Benchley was extremely versatile, with a considerable range of subjects and
styles from topical 'quickies' to playful but erudite parodies of authors such as
Oscar Wilde and Proust.*

*The following, written in 1921, is a literary satire on the kind of myopic,
over-academic textual critic who nit-picks away at a line of Shakespeare until it
comes apart in his hands and he has to put it back together again:*

SHAKESPEARE EXPLAINED

Carrying on the system of footnotes to a silly extreme

PERICLES
ACT II SCENE III

Enter FIRST-LADY-IN-WAITING. *Flourish,*[1] *Hautboys,*[2] *and*[3] *torches.*[4]

FIRST-LADY-IN-WAITING: What[5] ho![6] Where[7] is[8] the[9] music?[10]

NOTES

[1] *Flourish.* The stage direction here is obscure. Clarke claims it should read
'flarish', thus changing the meaning of the passage to 'flarish' (that is, the
King's), but most authorities have agreed that it should remain 'flourish',
supplying the predicate which is to be flourished. There was at this time a
custom in the countryside of England to flourish a mop as a signal to the
passing vendor of berries, signifying that in that particular household there
was a consumer-demand for berries, and this may have been meant in this
instance. That Shakespeare was cognizant of this custom of flourishing the
mop for berries is shown in a similar passage in the second part of King
Henry IV, where he has the Third Page enter and say 'Flourish'. Cf. also
Hamlet, IV, 7:4.

[2] *Hautboys,* from the French *haut,* meaning high and the Eng. *boys,* meaning 'boys'. The word here is doubtless used in the sense of 'high boys',
indicating either that Shakespeare intended to convey the idea of spiritual
distress on the part of the First Lady-in-Waiting, or that he did not. Of this
Rolfe says: 'Here we have one of the chief indications of Shakespeare's
knowledge of human nature, his remarkable insight into the petty foibles of
this work-a-day world.' Cf. T.N. 4:5. 'Mine eye hath play'd the painter, and
hath stell'd thy beauty's form in table of my heart.'

[3] *and.* A favourite conjunctive of Shakespeare's in referring to the need
for a more adequate navy for England. Tauchnitz claims that it should be
pronounced 'und', stressing the antipenult. This interpretation, however,
has found disfavour among most commentators because of its limited significance. We find the same conjunctive in A.W.T.E.W. 6:7. 'Steel-boned,

unyielding *and* uncomplying virtue', and here there can be no doubt that Shakespeare meant that if the King should consent to the marriage of his daughter the excuse of Stephano, offered in Act II, would carry no weight.

⁴ *Torches.* The interpolation of some foolish player and never the work of Shakespeare (Warb.). The critics of the last century have disputed whether or not this has been misspelled in the original, and should read 'trochies' or 'troches'. This might well be since the introduction of tobacco into England at this time had wrought havoc with the speaking voices of the players, and we might well imagine that at the entrance of the First Lady-in-Waiting there might be perhaps one of the hautboys mentioned in the preceeding passage bearing a box of 'troches' or 'trognies' for the actors to suck. Of this entrance Clarke remarks: 'The noble mixture of spirited firmness and womanly modesty, fine sense and true humility, clear sagacity and absence of conceit, passionate warmth and sensitive delicacy, generous love and self-diffidence with which Shakespeare has endowed this First Lady-in-Waiting renders her in our eyes one of the most admirable of his female characters.' Cf. M.S.N.D. 8:9, 'That solder'st close impossibilities and mak'st them kiss.'

⁵ *What*—What.

⁶ *ho!* In conjunction with the preceding word doubtless means 'What ho!' changed by Clarke to 'what hoo!' In the original MS. it reads 'What hi!' but this has been accredited to the tendency of the time to write 'What hi' when 'What ho!' was meant. Techner alone maintains that it should read 'What humpf!' Cf. Ham. 5:0, 'High-ho!'

⁷ *Where.* The reading of the folio, retained by Johnson, the Cambridge editors and others, but it is not impossible that Shakespeare wrote 'why', as Pope and others give it. This would make the passage read 'Why the music?' instead of 'Where is the music?' and would be a much more probable interpretation in view of the music of that time. Cf. George Ade. Fable No.15, 'Why the gunny-sack?'

⁸ *is*—is not. That is, would not be.

⁹ *the.* Cf. Ham. 4:6, M.S.N.D. 3:5, A.W.T.E.W. 2:6, T.N. 1:3 and Macbeth 3:1, 'that knits up *the* raveled sleeves of care'.

¹⁰ *music.* Explained by Malone as 'the art of making music' or 'music that is made'. If it has but one of these meanings we are inclined to think it is the first; and this seems to be favoured by what precedes, '*the* music!' Cf. M. of V. 4:2, 'The man that hath no music in himself.'

The meaning of the whole passage seems to be the First Lady-in-Waiting has entered, concomitant with a flourish, hautboys and torches, and says, 'What ho! Where is the music?'

The Benchley Roundup, ed. Nathaniel Benchley (1954).

Benchley was one of the pioneers and one of the finest exponents of the newly popular nonsensical humour.

Particularly notable, and much imitated later, were his versions of the pro-gramme notes provided by concert-hall managements for those of their audience who had not the faintest idea what the foreign singers were singing about.

Benchley parodies the clichés and the somewhat daft other-worldliness of this kind of translated prose:

(1) ¿VOY VIEN?
(Am I Going in the Right Direction?)

When the acorns begin dropping in Spain there is an old legend that for every acorn which drops there is a baby born in Valencia. This is so silly that no one pays any attention to it now, not even the gamekeeper's daughter, who would pay attention to anything. She goes from house to house, ringing doorbells and then running away. She hopes that some day she will ring the right doorbell and will trip and fall, so that Prince Charming will catch her. So far, no one has even come to the door. Poor Pepita! if that is her name.

(2) CAMISETAS DE FLANELA
(Flannel Vests)

Princess Rosamonda goes nightly to the Puerta del Sol to see if the early morning edition of the papers is out yet. If it isn't she hangs around humming to herself. If it is, she hangs around humming just the same. One night she encounters a young matador who is returning from dancing school. The finches are singing and there is Love in the air. Princess Rosamonda ends up in the Police Station.

(3) LA GUIA
(The Time-Table)

It is the day of the bull fight in Madrid. Everyone is cock-eyed. The bull has slipped out by the back entrance to the arena and has gone home disgusted. Nobody notices that the bull has gone except Nina, a peasant girl who has come to town that day to sell her father. She looks with horror at the place in the royal Box where the bull ought to be sitting and sees there instead her algebra teacher whom she had told that she was staying at home on account of a sick headache. You can imagine her feelings!

(4) NO PUEDO COMER ESO
(I Can Not Eat That!)

A merry song of the Alhambra—of the Alhambra in the moonlight—of a girl who danced over the wall and sprained her ankle. Lititia is the ward of grouchy old Pampino, President of the first National Banco. She has never been allowed further away than the edge of the piazza because she teases people so. Her lover has come to see her and finds that she is fast asleep. He considers that for once he has the breaks, and tiptoes away without waking her up. Along about eleven o'clock she awakes, and is sore as all get-out.

(5) LA LAVANDERA
(The Laundryman)

A coquette, pretending to be very angry, bites off the hand of her lover up to the wrist. Ah, naughty Cirinda! Such antics! However does she think she can do her lessons if she gives up all her time to love-making? But Cirinda does not care. Heedless, heedless Cirinda!

(6) ABRA VD. ESA VENTANA
(Open That Window)

The lament of a mother whose oldest son is too young to vote. She walks the streets singing: 'My son can not vote! My son is not old enough!' There seems to be nothing that can be done about it.　　　　　*The Early Worm (1927).*

An event occured on 30 April 1922 which changed Benchley's career and sent it off in a direction which he never wanted it to go.

The Vicious Circle decided that it would be a lark to hire a theatre for a Sunday and amuse their theatrical friends with a revue of songs and sketches written by themselves. The printed programme called the show 'An Anonymous Entertainment by the Vicious Circle of the Algonquin Hotel'. The show was entitled No Sirree! *(the Broadway hit at the time was a song-and-dance show called* Yes Sirree!*)*

Benchley had written many funny magazine pieces featuring himself as an inadequate bungler unable to cope with life's little problems, and for the revue he performed an act (which he later claimed to have partly extemporized) as a man standing in for a friend who was ill and giving the Treasurer's Report at a local social-club meeting. The act was the hit of the show and Irving Berlin, a frequent visitor to the Round Table and in the audience that night, persuaded Benchley to perform the act on-stage in Berlin's long-running Broadway show, Music Box Revue.

So Benchley took to the professional theatre and performed 'The Treasurer's Report' nightly for nine months at $500 a week. He then went to Hollywood and an experimental film was made of 'The Treasurer's Report'—sometimes claimed to be the first all-talking film ever made. Eventually he began making short films playing the same character caught up in small domestic predicaments. He made forty-six of the shorts and one of them, How to Sleep, *won him an Oscar. He became more and more in demand to play the good-natured bumbler in major feature films and he wrote less and less.*

He died at the age of 56, perhaps the most versatile and original of all modern humorous journalists, beloved by millions of readers and filmgoers throughout the world, rich, unhappy, his death hastened by alcohol and despair.

Here is the text of the piece which began it all.

THE TREASURER'S REPORT

The report is delivered by an Assistant Treasurer who has been called in to pinch-hit for the regular Treasurer who is ill. He is not a very good public-speaker, this assistant, but after a few minutes of confusion is caught up by the spell of his own oratory and is hard to stop.

I shall take but a very few moments of your time this evening, for I realize that you would much rather be listening to this interesting entertainment than to a dry financial statement . . . but I *am* reminded of a story—which you have probably all of you heard.

It seems that there were these two Irishmen walking down the street when they came to a—oh, I should have said in the first place that the parrot which was hanging out in *front* of the store—or rather belonging to one of these two fellows—the *first* Irishman, that is—was—well, *anyway*, this parrot—

(*After a slight cogitation, he realizes that, for all practical purposes, the story is as good as lost ; so he abandons it entirely and, stepping forward, drops his facile, story-telling manner and assumes a quite spurious business-like air.*)

Now, in connection with reading this report, there are one or two points which Dr Murnie wanted brought up in connection with it, and he has asked me to bring them up in connect—to bring them up.

In the first place, there is the question of the work which we are trying to do up there at our little place at Silver Lake, a work which we feel not only fills a very definite need in the community but also fills a very definite need—er—in the community. I don't think that many members of the Society realize just how big the work is that we are trying to do up there. For instance, I don't think that it is generally known that most of our boys are between the age of fourteen. We feel that, by taking the boy at this age, we can get closer to his real nature—for a boy *has* a very real nature, you may be sure—and bring him into closer touch not only with the school, the parents, and with each other, but also with the town in which they live, the country to whose flag they pay allegiance, and to the—ah—(*trailing off*) town in which they live.

Now the fourth point which Dr Murnie wanted brought up was that in connection with the installation of the new furnace last Fall. There seems to have been considerable talk going around about this not having been done quite as economically as it might—have—been—done, when, as a matter of fact, the whole thing *was* done just as economically as possible—in fact, even *more* so. I have here a report of the Furnace Committee, showing just how the whole thing was handled from start to finish.

(*Reads from report, with considerable initial difficulty with the stiff covers.*)

Bids were submitted by the following firms of furnace contractors, with a clause stating that if we did not engage a firm to do the work for us we should pay them nothing for submitting the bids. This clause alone saved us a great deal of money.

The following firms, then, submitted bids:

Merkle, Wybigant Co., the Eureka Dust Bin and Shaker Co., The Elite Furnace Shop, and Harris, Birnbauer and Harris. The bid of Merkle, Wybigant being the lowest, Harris, Birnbauer were selected to do the job.

(Here a page is evidently missing from the report, and a hurried search is carried on through all the pages, without result.)

Well, that pretty well clears up that end of the work.

Those of you who contributed so generously last year to the floating hospital have probably wondered what became of the money. I was speaking on this subject only last week at our up-town branch, and, after the meeting, a dear little old lady, dressed all in lavender, came up on the platform, and, laying her hand on my arm, said: 'Mr So-and-so' (calling me by name) 'Mr So-and-so, what the hell did you do with all the money we gave you last year?' Well, I just laughed and pushed her off the platform, but it has occurred to the committee that perhaps some of you, like that little old lady, would be interested in knowing the disposition of the funds.

Now, Mr Rossiter, unfortunately our treasurer—or rather Mr Rossiter our *treasurer, unfortunately* is confined at his home tonight with a bad head-cold and I have been asked (*he hears someone whispering at him from the wings, but decides to ignore it*) and I have been asked if I would (*the whisperer will not be denied, so he goes over to the entrance and receives a brief message, returning beaming and laughing to himself*). Well, the joke seems to be on *me!* Mr Rossiter has *pneumonia!*

Following, then, is a summary of the Treasurer's Report:

(Reads, in a very businesslike manner.)

During the year 1929—and by that is meant 1928—the Choral Society received the following in donations:

B.L.G.	$500
G.K.M.	500
Lottie and Nellie W—	500
In memory of a happy summer at Rye Beach	10
Proceeds of a sale of coats and hats left in the boat-house	14.55
And then the Junior League gave a performance of 'Pinafore' for the benefit of the Fund which, unfortunately, resulted in a deficit of	$300
Then, from dues and charges	2,354.75
And, following the installation of the new furnace, a saving in coal amounting to $374.75—which made Dr Murnie very happy, you may be sure.	
Making a total of receipts amounting to	$3,645.75

This is all, of course, reckoned as of June.

In the matter of expenditures, the Club has not been so fortunate. There was the unsettled condition of business, and the late Spring, to contend with, resulting in the following—er—rather discouraging figures, I am afraid.

Expenditures	$23,574.70
Then there was a loss, owing to—several things—of	3,326.70
Car-fare	4,452.25
And then, Mrs Rawlins' expense account, when she went down to see the work they are doing in Baltimore, came to $256.50, but I am sure that you will all agree that it was worth it to find out—er—what they are doing in Baltimore.	
And then, under the general head of Odds and Ends	2,537.50
Making a total disbursement of . . . (hurriedly)	$416,546.75

or a net deficit of—ah—several thousand dollars.

Now, these figures bring us down only to October. In October my sister was married, and the house was all torn up, and in the general confusion we lost track of the figures for May and August. All those wishing the *approximate* figures for May and August, however, may obtain them from me in the vestry after the dinner, where I will be with pledge cards for those of you who wish to subscribe over and above your annual dues, and I hope that each and every one of you here tonight will look deep into his heart and (*archly*) into his pocketbook, and see if he can not find it there to help us to put this thing over with a bang (*accompanied by a wholly ineffectual gesture representing a bang*) and to help and make this just the biggest and best year the Armenians have ever had . . . I thank you.

(*Exits, bumping into proscenium*).

The Treasurer's Report and Other Aspects of Community Singing (1930).

———

B ENCHLEY'S *closest associate in the Algonquin Round Table's bunch of flowering talents, which John Peele Bishop called 'the first literary generation of America' but which Edmund Wilson saw as 'the all-star literary vaudeville', was Dorothy Parker.*

Mr Benchley and Mrs Parker (as they liked to address each other) more or less began their writing careers together on Vanity Fair, *once rented an office together which Benchley said was so tiny that 'one cubic foot less of space and it would have constituted adultery' (they gave it the telegraphic address 'Parkbench'), and even shared a bedroom at Robert Sherwood's house after parties, but almost certainly platonically, if only because they were both heavy drinkers and Dorothy Parker, unlike Robert Benchley, did not pursue casual affairs but endured long and ultimately unhappy attachments: she had three unsuccessful marriages (two to the same man) and made three attempts to commit suicide (after one attempt to slash her wrists, Benchley visited her in hospital and said 'Dottie, if you don't stop this sort of thing, you'll make yourself sick').*

Mrs Parker, tiny, dark, huge-eyed, quiet and rather demure, described by Alexander Woollcott as 'a combination of Little Nell and Lady Macbeth,' was undoubtedly the wittiest member of the Algonquin Circle. George S. Kaufman may have been funnier, Woollcott more spiteful, Benchley more whimsical, but Dorothy Parker's repartee epitomized Aristotle's definition of wit as 'educated insult'. Her concise, astringent, sardonic bon-mots, uttered at Round Table sittings and end-lessly quoted, also emerged in her writings, such as her comment in a review for Vanity Fair *of a performance by Katherine Hepburn: 'She ran the whole gamut of emotions, from A to B.' And her comment on A. A. Milne's* Winnie the Pooh *which she was reviewing under the pseudonym Constant Reader: 'Tonstant Weader frowed up.' The trouble was that those Americans who worshipped wisecracks assumed that waspish put-downs made at the Algonquin Round Table were the extent of Mrs Parker's talent, to her understandable fury. She had never been all that frequent a visitor to Vicious Circle lunches, and late in life she even pretended that she had never been to them at all.*

Mrs Parker, a deeply unhappy woman, cared little about life and made a tragic muddle of her own but she cared very much indeed about writing and was pains-taking and very hard-working in her work.

Her short stories, laconic and accurate portraits of life in urban America in the twenties and thirties helped to further the movement towards freeing the short story from 'the burden of plot' and allowing the author to illuminate just one small aspect of human behaviour.

A predicament, very Dorothy Parker, very 1920s, forms the subject of the following story; the morning after the night before for a young man who cannot wholly recall what happened the previous night:

YOU WERE PERFECTLY FINE

The pale young man eased himself carefully into the low chair, and rolled his head to the side, so that the cool chintz comforted his cheek and temple.

'Oh, dear,' he said. 'Oh, dear, oh, dear, oh, dear. Oh.'

The clear-eyed girl, sitting light and erect on the couch, smiled brightly at him.

'Not feeling so well today?' she said.

'Oh, I'm great,' he said. 'Corking, I am. Know what time I got up? Four o'clock this afternoon, sharp. I kept trying to make it, and every time I took my head off the pillow, it would roll under the bed. This isn't my head I've got on now. I think this is something that used to belong to Walt Whitman. Oh, dear, oh, dear, oh, dear.'

'Do you think maybe a drink would make you feel better?' she said.

'The hair of the mastiff that bit me?' he said. 'Oh, no, thank you. Please never speak of anything like that again. I'm through. I'm all, all through. Look at that hand; steady as a humming-bird. Tell me, was I very terrible last night?'

'Oh, goodness,' she said, 'everybody was feeling pretty high. You were all right.'

'Yeah,' he said. 'I must have been dandy. Is every body sore at me?'

'Good heavens, no,' she said. 'Everyone thought you were terribly funny. Of course, Jim Pierson was a little stuffy, there, for a minute at dinner. But people sort of held him back in his chair, and got him calmed down. I don't think anybody at the other tables noticed it at all. Hardly anybody.'

'He was going to sock me?' he said. 'Oh, Lord. What did I do to him?'

'Why, you didn't do a thing,' she said. 'You were perfectly fine. But you know how silly Jim gets, when he thinks anybody is making too much fuss over Elinor.'

'Was I making a pass at Elinor?' he said. 'Did I do that?'

'Of course you didn't,' she said. 'You were only fooling that's all. She thought you were awfully amusing. She was having a marvelous time. She only got a little tiny bit annoyed just once, when you poured the clam-juice down her back.'

'My God,' he said. 'Clam-juice down that back. And every vertebra a little Cabot. Dear God. What'll I ever do?'

'Oh, she'll be all right,' she said. 'Just send her some flowers, or something. Don't worry about it. It isn't anything.'

'No, I won't worry,' he said. 'I haven't got a care in the world. I'm sitting pretty. Oh, dear, oh, dear. Did I do any other fascinating tricks at dinner?'

'You were fine,' she said. 'Don't be so foolish about it. Everybody was crazy about you. The maitre d'hotel was a little worried because you wouldn't stop singing, but he really didn't mind. All he said was, he was afraid they'd close the place again, if there was so much noise. But he didn't care a bit himself. I think he loved seeing you have such a good time. Oh, you were just singing away, there, for about an hour. It wasn't so terribly loud, at all.'

'So I sang,' he said. 'That must have been a treat. I sang.'

'Don't you remember?' she said. 'You just sang one song after another. Everybody in the place was listening. They loved it. Only you kept insisting that you wanted to sing some song about some kind of fusiliers or other, and everybody kept shushing you, and you'd keep trying to start it again. You were wonderful. We were all trying to make you stop singing for a minute, and eat something, but you wouldn't hear of it. My, you were funny.'

'Didn't I eat any dinner?' he said.

'Oh, not a thing,' she said. 'Every time the waiter would offer you something, you'd give it right back to him, because you said that he was your long-lost brother, changed in the cradle by a gypsy band, and that anything you had was his. You had him simply roaring at you.'

'I bet I did,' he said. 'I bet I was comical. Society's Pet, I must have been. And what happened then, after my overwhelming success with the waiter?'

'Why, nothing much,' she said. 'You took a sort of dislike to some old man with white hair, sitting across the room, because you didn't like his necktie and you wanted to tell him about it. But we got you out, before he got really mad.'

'Oh, we got out,' he said. 'Did I walk?'

'Walk! Of course you did,' she said. 'You were absolutely all right. There was that nasty stretch of ice on the sidewalk, and you did sit down awfully hard, you poor dear. But good heavens, that might have happened to anybody.'

'Oh, sure,' he said. 'Louisa Alcott or anybody. So I fell down on the sidewalk. That would explain what's the matter with my—Yes, I see. And then what, if you don't mind?'

'Ah, now, Peter!' she said. 'You can't sit there and say you don't remember what happened after that! I did think that maybe you were just a little tight at dinner—oh, you were perfectly all right, and all that, but I did know you were feeling pretty gay. But you were so serious, from the time you fell down—I never knew you to be that way. Don't you know, how you told me I had never seen your real self before? Oh, Peter, I just couldn't bear it, if you didn't remember that lovely long ride we took together in the taxi! Please, you do remember that, don't you? I think it would simply kill me, if you didn't.'

'Oh, yes,' he said. 'Riding in the taxi. Oh, yes, sure. Pretty long ride, hmm?'

'Round and round and round the park,' she said. 'Oh, and the trees were shining so in the moonlight. And you said you never knew before that you really had a soul.'

'Yes,' he said. 'I said that. That was me.'

'You said such lovely, lovely things,' she said. 'And I'd never known, all this time, how you had been feeling about me, and I'd never dared to let you see how I felt about you. And then last night—oh, Peter dear, I think that taxi ride was the most important thing that ever happened to us in our lives.'

'Yes,' he said. 'I guess it must have been.'

'And we're going to be so happy,' she said. 'Oh, I just want to tell everybody! But I don't know—I think maybe it would be sweeter to keep it all to ourselves.'

'I think it would be,' he said.

'Isn't it lovely?' she said.

'Yes,' he said. 'Great.'

'Lovely!' she said.

'Look here,' he said, 'do you mind if I have a drink? I mean, just medi-
cinally, you know. I'm off the stuff for life, so help me. But I think I feel a
collapse coming on.'

'Oh, I think it would do you good,' she said. 'You poor boy, it's a shame
you feel so awful. I'll make you a whisky and soda.'

'Honestly,' he said, 'I don't see how you could ever want to speak to me
again, after I made such a fool of myself, last night. I think I'd better go join
a monastery in Tibet.'

'You crazy idiot!' she said. 'As if I could ever let you go away now! Stop
talking like that. You were perfectly fine.'

She jumped up from the couch, kissed him quickly on the forehead, and
ran out of the room.

The pale young man looked after her and shook his head long and slowly,
then dropped it in his damp and trembling hands.

'Oh dear,' he said. 'Oh, dear, oh, dear, oh, dear.'

Dorothy Parker (1893–1967), *Here Lies* (1939).

*It was in character for Dorothy Parker to go off to the Spanish Civil War as a
somewhat untidy and alcoholic Republican war correspondent. She was the poet of
the loser and the luckless, but many of her short stories were about New York's
undeservedly fortunate rich, like plump and none-too-bright matrons married to
wealthy businessmen living in brownstone mansions along the more fashionable
avenues.*

*In the following story, which as usual does not seem to contain a superfluous
word nor a word which could be changed for a better one, a rich New York society
lady attends a reception especially to meet the guest of honour, a distinguished
singer of negro spirituals.*

He is black:

ARRANGEMENT IN BLACK AND WHITE

The woman with the pink velvet poppies twined round the assisted gold of
her hair traversed the crowded room at an interesting gait combining a skip
with a sidle, and clutched the lean arm of her host.

'Now I got you!' she said. 'Now you can't get away!'

'Why, hello,' said her host. 'Well. How are you?'

'Oh, I'm finely,' she said. 'Just simply finely. Listen. I want you to do me
the most terrible favor. Will you? Will you please? Pretty please?'

'What is it?' said her host.

'Listen,' she said. 'I want to meet Walter Williams. Honestly, I'm just
simply crazy about that man. Oh, when he sings! When he sings those
spirituals! Well, I said to Burton, "It's a good thing for you Walter Williams
is colored," I said, "or you'd have lots of reason to be jealous." I'd really
love to meet him. I'd like to tell him I've heard him sing. Will you be an
angel and introduce me to him?'

'Why, certainly,' said her host. 'I thought you'd met him. The party's for him. Where is he, anyway?'

'He's over there by the bookcase,' she said. 'Let's wait till those people get through talking to him. Well, I think you're simply marvelous, giving this perfectly marvelous party for him, and having him meet all these white people, and all. Isn't he terribly grateful?'

'I hope not,' said her host.

'I think it's really terribly nice,' she said. 'I do. I don't see why on earth it isn't perfectly all right to meet colored people. I haven't any feeling at all about it—not one single bit. Burton—oh, he's just the other way. Well, you know, he comes from Virginia, and you know how they are.'

'Did he come tonight?' said her host.

'No, he couldn't,' she said. 'I'm a regular grass widow tonight. I told him when I left, "There's no telling what I'll do," I said. He was just so tired out, he couldn't move. Isn't it a shame?'

'Ah,' said her host.

'Wait till I tell him I met Walter Williams!' she said. 'He'll just about die. Oh, we have more arguments about colored people. I talk to him like I don't know what, I get so excited. "Oh, don't be so silly," I say. But I must say for Burton, he's heaps more broader-minded that lots of these Southerners. He's really awfully fond of colored people. Well, he says himself, he wouldn't have white servants. And you know, he had this old colored nurse, this regular old nigger mammy, and he just simply loves her. Why, every time he goes home, he goes out in the kitchen to see her. He does, really, to this day. All he says is, he says he hasn't got a word to say against colored people as long as they keep their place. He's always doing things for them—giving them clothes and I don't know what all. The only thing he says, he says he wouldn't sit down at the table with one for a million dollars. "Oh," I say to him, "you make me sick, talking like that." I'm just terrible to him. Aren't I terrible?'

'Oh, no, no, no,' said her host. 'No, no.'

'I am,' she said. 'I know I am. Poor Burton! Now, me, I don't feel that way at all. I haven't the slightest feeling about colored people. Why, I'm just crazy about some of them. They're just like children—just as easygoing, and always singing and laughing and everything. Aren't they the happiest things you ever saw in your life? Honestly, it makes me laugh just to hear them. Oh, I like them. I really do. Well, now, listen. I have this colored laundress, I've had her for years, and I'm devoted to her. She's real character. And I want to tell you, I think of her as my friend. That's the way I think of her. As I say to Burton, "Well, for heaven's sakes, we're all human beings!" Aren't we?'

'Yes,' said her host. 'Yes, indeed.'

'Now this Walter Williams,' she said. 'I think a man like that's a real artist. I do. I think he deserves an awful lot of credit. Goodness, I'm so crazy about music or anything, I don't care what color he is. I honestly think if a person's an artist, nobody ought to have any feeling at all about meeting them. That's absolutely what I say to Burton. Don't you think I'm right?'

'Yes,' said her host. 'Oh, yes.'

'That's the way I feel,' she said. 'I just can't understand people being narrow-minded. Why, I absolutely think it's a privilege to meet a man like Walter Williams. Yes, I do. I haven't any feeling at all. Well, my goodness, the good Lord made him, just the same as He did any of us. Didn't He?'

'Surely,' said her host. 'Yes, indeed.'

'That's what I say,' she said, 'Oh, I get so furious when people are narrow-minded about colored people. It's just all I can do not to say something. Of course, I do admit when you get a bad colored man, they're simply terrible. But as I say to Burton, there are some bad white people, too, in this world. Aren't there?'

'I guess there are,' said her host.

'Why, I'd really be glad to have a man like Walter Williams come to my house and sing for us, some time,' she said. 'Of course, I couldn't ask him on account of Burton, but I wouldn't have any feeling about it at all. Oh, can't he sing! Isn't it marvelous, the way they all have music in them? It just seems to be right in them. Come on, let's us go on over and talk to him. Listen, what shall I do when I'm introduced? Ought I to shake hands? Or what?'

'Why, do whatever you want,' said her host.

'I guess maybe I'd better,' she said. 'I wouldn't for the world have him think I had any feeling. I think I'd better shake hands, just the way I would with anybody else. That's just exactly what I'll do.'

They reached the tall young Negro, standing by the bookcase. The host performed introductions; the Negro bowed.

'How do you do?' he said.

The woman with the pink velvet poppies extended her hand at the length of her arm and held it so for all the world to see, until the Negro took it, shook it, and gave it back to her.

'Oh, how do you do, Mr Williams,' she said. 'Well, how do you do. I've just been saying, I've enjoyed your singing so awfully much. I've been to your concerts, and we have you on the phonograph and everything. Oh, I just enjoy it!'

She spoke with great distinctness, moving her lips meticulously, as if in parlance with the deaf.

'I'm so glad,' he said.

'I'm just simply crazy about that "Water Boy" thing you sing,' she said. 'Honestly, I can't get it out of my head. I have my husband nearly crazy, the way I go around humming it all the time. Oh, he looks just as black as the ace of—Well. Tell me, where on earth do you ever get all those songs of yours? How do you ever get hold of them?'

'Why,' he said, 'there are so many different—'

'I should think you'd love singing them,' she said. 'It must be more fun. All those darling old spirituals—oh, I just love them! Well, what are you doing, now? Are you still keeping up your singing? Why don't you have another concert, some time?'

'I'm having one the sixteenth of this month,' he said.

'Well, I'll be there,' she said. 'I'll be there, if I possibly can. You can count on me. Goodness, here comes a whole raft of people to talk to you. You're just a regular guest of honor! Oh, who's that girl in white? I've seen her some place.'

'That's Katherine Burke,' said her host.

'Good Heavens,' she said, 'is that Katherine Burke? Why, she looks entirely different off the stage. I thought she was much better-looking. I had no idea she was so terribly dark. Why, she looks almost like—Oh, I think she's a wonderful actress! Don't you think she's a wonderful actress, Mr Williams? Oh, I think she's marvelous. Don't you?'

'Yes, I do,' he said.

'Oh, I do, too,' she said. 'Just wonderful. Well, goodness, we must give someone else a chance to talk to the guest of honor. Now, don't forget, Mr Williams, I'm going to be at that concert if I possibly can. I'll be there applauding like everything. And if I can't come, I'm going to tell everybody I know to go, anyway. Don't you forget!'

'I won't,' he said. 'Thank you so much.'

The host took her arm and piloted her into the next room.

'Oh, my dear,' she said. 'I nearly died! Honestly, I give you my word, I nearly passed away. Did you hear that terrible break I made? I was just going to say Katherine Burke looked almost like a nigger. I just caught myself in time. Oh, do you think he noticed?'

'I don't believe so,' said her host.

'Well, thank goodness,' she said, 'because I wouldn't have embarrassed him for anything. Why, he's awfully nice. Just as nice as he can be. Nice manners, and everything. You know, so many colored people, you give them an inch, and they walk all over you. But he doesn't try any of that. Well, he's got more sense, I suppose. He's really nice. Don't you think so?'

'Yes,' said her host.

'I liked him,' she said. 'I haven't any feeling at all because he's a colored man. I felt just as natural as I would with anybody. Talked to him just as naturally, and everything. But honestly, I could hardly keep a straight face. I kept thinking of Burton. Oh, wait till I tell Burton I called him "Mister"!'

Ibid.

WHEREAS *in Britain humour more or less carried on after the 1914–18 war where it left off, American humour sped off and away in all sorts of new directions, but the contribution made by the Vicious Circle as a whole to this upsurge in modern American humour was, apart from the writers already applauded, minimal.*

Membership of the Vicious Circle was by no means confined to brilliant and quotable humorists. Many of the members were playwrights, impresarios, or musicians, and some were not connected with the arts at all. Yet the Circle as a whole did manage to make one huge, if oblique, contribution to the future of American humour: its gambling arm helped to bring about the founding of the flagship of modern American humorous prose, the New Yorker *magazine.*

In common with a great many writers and theatre people, the members of the Circle were compulsive Saturday-night poker players. In 1921 Frank Case of the Algonquin allocated the Circle a free suite on the second floor of his hotel and thus was born the Thanatopsis Literary and Inside Straight Club, whose weekend sessions and outbursts of wit were gleefully reported by the gossip columnists in Monday's newspapers. By 1925 the activities of the Thanatopsis poker sessions were almost as well known to New Yorkers as the goings-on at the Round Table lunches. The stakes became high and guest players tended to be wealthy.

One of the unlikeliest members of the Vicious Circle was Harold Ross, the young man from the Rocky Mountains, a shock-haired, simian figure who as Private Ross had edited the army paper Stars and Stripes. *Ross, a born outsider, was somehow in the gregarious Circle from the start, as vigorous a practical joker and partygoer as any of them but no wit and a terrible poker player (George S. Kaufman decided that Ross was 'a complete misfit with a good chance of starving to death').*

Ross, who turned out to be a magazine editor of near-genius, was determined to start his own journal 'for and about New York' but lacked the capital. A member of the Thanatopsis (according to some accounts it was Alexander Woollcott, according to others it was, by accident, George S. Kaufman) arranged a poker game so that Ross could meet a rich businessman, Raoul Fleishmann of the Fleishmann bakery family. Fleishmann agreed to put up the money for the new magazine. A title, the New Yorker, *was suggested by the ubiquitous John Peter Toohey, and on Thursday, 19 February 1925, the first issue of the* New Yorker *went on sale.*

Although five of the Vicious Circle lent their names to the new magazine and were claimed to be 'advisory editors' ('the most dishonest thing I ever did' Ross later admitted), the Algonquin wits were of little practical help; they were too busy with their own affairs and only contributed an occasional poem, short story, or sketch.

To begin with, the most original aspect of the New Yorker *was Ross's decision to tailor its style and contents to the tastes of the middle-class, 'sophisticated' citizens of New York. Other magazines aimed to appeal to a general readership of all levels of intelligence (including that mythical lowest-common-denominator of literary awareness, 'the little old lady in Dubuque') and so had a less definable character.*

At the start, New Yorker *humour struck no new note: it was much the same humour as that published by its established rivals like* Judge, The Harvard Lampoon, Life, *and* Vanity Fair, *and it was mostly written by the same writers, but a distinctive* New Yorker *school of humour, which eventually influenced humorous prose almost everywhere to the good, was not long in arriving.*

It was partly the product of Ross's fanatical obsession with clarity and good grammar and of his qualities as an editor—it was said later that under his guidance 'satire and parody flourished, reporting became light-hearted and searching and humor was allowed to infect everything'—but much of the credit must go to the gifted young team of editors and regular contributors which Ross quickly gathered round him, selecting them seemingly by a mixture of magical intuition and plain luck.

E. B. White was one of the earliest recruits to the New Yorker *staff, late in 1926, taken on to write cartoon captions (Mother: 'It's broccoli, dear.' Child: 'I say it's spinach and I say the hell with it.') and to rewrite submitted news items. He proved to be one of the best of all the great American paragraphists and a superb stylist.*

*It was White who came up with the humorous editorial voice which the magazine needed. One of his most important functions was to write, or rewrite 'Notes and Comment' for the 'Talk of the Town' feature (Ross's instructions were 'if you can't be funny, be interesting'). The notion of working up news items into amusing paragraphs was not a new idea—*Punch *had been doing it for over a hundred years as had most other humorous journals—but E. B. White in the* New Yorker *brought to it a dry sophistication and an attitude, which Thomas Mann called 'blithe scepticism', which made 'Talk of the Town' the magazine's most popular running feature.*

Here is how 'Talk of the Town' reported the arrival in New York of the brother of the celebrated 'free-flow' dancer, Isadora Duncan:

ISADORA'S BROTHER

Raymond Duncan is in town with the idea of starting a branch of his academy here. He serves tea every afternoon in his studio in West Seventy-fifth Street, surrounded by his fabrics, his poems, his shepherdess, and his disciples. Reclining on a couch, he talks with you about the future, which he believes must be prepared for by throwing off the past and learning to perform the simple motions of life, such as digging and making sandals. His poems are five dollars, his 'Eternal Beauty' is two dollars, and his fabrics run from four dollars on up. The couch is very hard.

The little brother of Isadora is getting on in years, and looks more like a witch than a shepherd. His long gray locks are held back by a ribbon, his tunic flows classically from his shoulders, and his chubby little arms that have woven so many yards of piece goods look rather flabby and old. After years of tending donkeys and goats on the Acropolis with Penelope, organizing refugees, rebuilding a city in Albania, weaving rugs, digging holes, dyeing linen, writing poems, and administering academies and temples of art, always clinging tight to the immortal and somewhat elusive spirit of his inspired sister, he is still hopeful. He hasn't had on a pair of pants in nineteen years, man and boy.

While we were reclining with him, doing our best to look like a goatherd despite our sack suit, a lady entered the room and asked him 'if it would brutalize him if she suggested a cup of tea'. 'My dear Julia,' he replied, 'the whole world is trying to brutalize me.'

Brute that we were, we drank the tea, bought a small doily, and departed, our sandals clinking merrily along the pave.

'Talk of the Town,' *The New Yorker* (7 Dec. 1929).

E. B. White was one of the founding fathers of another New Yorker *speciality, the 'casual'. The 'casual' was Ross's name for one-off stories and essays written in an easygoing, conversational style which looked simple but was in practice murderously difficult to get right.*

A White casual, indeed everything that he wrote, was marked not only by his lean, straightforward prose style but also by his poet's ear for precisely the right word, and a whiff of wisdom. His unforced humour was a mile away from the 'Phunny Phellow' comicality of the post Civil-War literary comedians and their modern counterparts whose pieces were hilarious to the reader or they were nothing. Some of White's best essays were hardly funny at all but he was incapable of writing an ugly sentence or a paragraph that was not a pleasure to read. Humour, White once wrote, was 'a sly and almost imperceptible ingredient that sometimes gets into writing'.

A characteristic example of White's sly and almost imperceptible humour is the following New Yorker *casual, a classic example of the form.*

The author takes reluctant leave of an old and very dear friend:

FAREWELL MY LOVELY!

(An Aging Male Kisses an Old Flame Goodbye, Circa 1936)

I see by the new Sears Roebuck catalogue that it is still possible to buy an axle for a 1909 Model T Ford, but I am not deceived. The great days have faded, and the end is in sight. Only one page in the current catalogue is devoted to parts and accessories for the Model T; yet everyone remembers springtimes when the Ford gadget section was larger than men's clothing, almost as large as household furnishings. The last Model T was built in 1927, and the car is fading from what scholars call the American scene—which is an understatement, because to a few million people who grew up with it, the old Ford practically *was* the American scene.

It was the miracle that God had wrought. And it was patently the sort of thing that could only happen once. Mechanically uncanny, it was like nothing that had ever come to the world before. Flourishing industries rose and fell with it. As a vehicle, it was hard-working, commonplace, heroic; and it often seemed to transmit those qualities to the person who rode in it. My own generation identifies it with Youth, with its gaudy, irretrievable excitements; before it fades into the mist, I would like to pay it the tribute of the sigh that is not a sob, and set down random entries in a shape somewhat less cumbersome than a Sears Roebuck catalogue.

The Model T was distinguished from all other makes of cars by the fact that its transmission was of a type known as planetary—which was half metaphysics, half sheer fiction. Engineers accepted the word 'planetary' in its epicyclic sense, but I was always conscious that it also meant 'wandering', 'erratic'. Because of the peculiar nature of this planetary element, there was always, in Model T, a certain dull rapport between engine and wheels, and even when the car was in a state known as neutral, it trembled with a deep imperative and tended to inch forward. There was never a moment when the bands were not faintly egging the machine on. In this respect it was like a horse, rolling the bit on its tongue, and country people brought to it the same technique they used with draft animals.

Its most remarkable quality was its rate of acceleration. In its palmy days the Model T could take off faster than anything on the road. The reason was simple. To get under way, you simply hooked the third finger of the right hand around a lever on the steering column, pulled down hard, and shoved your left foot forcibly against the low-speed pedal. These were simple, positive motions; the car responded by lunging forward with a roar. After a few seconds of this turmoil, you took your toe off the pedal, eased up a mite on the throttle, and the car, possessed of only two forward speeds, catapulted directly into high with a series of ugly jerks and was off on its glorious errand. The abruptness of this departure was never equalled in other cars of the period. The human leg was (and still is) incapable of letting in the clutch with anything like the forthright abandon that used to send Model T on its way. Letting in a clutch is a negative, hesitant motion, depending on delicate nervous control; pushing down the Ford pedal was a simple, country motion—an expansive act, which came as natural as kicking an old door to make it budge.

The driver of the old Model T was a man enthroned. The car, with top up, stood seven feet high. The driver sat on top of the gas tank, brooding it with his own body. When he wanted gasoline, he alighted, together with everything else in the front seat; the seat was pulled off, the metal cap unscrewed, and a wooden stick thrust down to sound the liquid in the well. There was always a couple of these sounding sticks kicking around in the ratty sub-cushion regions of a flivver. Refuelling was more of a social function then, because the driver had to unbend, whether he wanted to or not. Directly in front of the driver was the windshield—high, uncompromisingly erect. Nobody talked about air resistance, and the four cylinders pushed the car through the atmosphere with a simple disregard of physical law.

There was this about a Model T; the purchaser never regarded his purchase as a complete, finished product. When you bought a Ford, you figured you had a start—a vibrant, spirited framework to which could be screwed an almost limitless assortment of decorative and functional hardware. Driving away from the agency, hugging the new wheel between your knees, you were already full of creative worry. A Ford was born naked as a baby, and a flourishing industry grew up out of correcting its rare deficiencies and combating its fascinating diseases. Those were the great days of lily-painting. I have been looking at some old Sears Roebuck catalogues, and they bring everything back so clear.

First you bought a Ruby Safety Reflector for the rear, so that your posterior would glow in another car's brilliance. Then you invested thirty-nine cents in some radiator Moto Wings, a popular ornament which gave the Pegasus touch to the machine and did something godlike to the owner. For nine cents you bought a fan-belt guide to keep the belt from slipping off the pulley.

You bought a radiator compound to stop leaks. This was as much a part of everybody's equipment as aspirin tablets are of a medicine cabinet. You bought special oil to stop chattering, a clamp-on dash light, a patching outfit, a tool box which you bolted on the running board, a sun visor, a steering-column brace to keep the column rigid, and a set of emergency containers for gas, oil and water—three thin, disc-like cans which reposed in a case on the running board during long, important journeys—red for gas, gray for water, green for oil. It was only a beginning. After the car was about a year old, steps were taken to check the alarming disintegration. (Model T was full of tumors, but they were benign.) A set of anti-rattlers (ninety-eight cents) was a popular panacea. You hooked them on to the gas and spark rods, to the brake pull rod, and to the steering-rod connections. Hood silencers, of black rubber, were applied to the fluttering hood. Shock-absorbers and snubbers gave 'complete relaxation'. Some people bought rubber pedal pads, to fit over the standard metal pedals. (I didn't like these, I remember.) Persons of a suspicious or pugnacious turn of mind bought a rear-view mirror; but most Model T owners weren't worried by what was coming from behind because they would soon enough see it out in front. They rode in a state of cheerful catalepsy. Quite a large mutinous clique among Ford owners went over to a foot accelerator (you could buy one and screw it to the floor board), but there was a certain madness in these people, because the Model T, just as she stood, had a choice of three foot pedals to push, and there were plenty of moments when both feet were occupied in the routine performance of duty and when the only way to speed up the engine was with the hand throttle.

Gadget bred gadget. Owners not only bought ready-made gadgets, they invented gadgets to meet special needs. I myself drove my car directly from the agency to the blacksmith's, and had the smith affix two enormous iron brackets to the port running board to support an army trunk.

People who owned closed models builded along different lines: they bought ball grip handles for opening doors, window anti-rattlers, and de-luxe flower vases of the cut-glass anti-splash type. People with delicate sensibilities garnished their car with a device called the Donna Lee Automobile Disseminator—a porous vase guaranteed, according to Sears, to fill the car with 'a faint clean odor of lavender'. The gap between open cars and closed cars was not as great then as it is now: for $11.95, Sears Roebuck converted your touring car into a sedan and you went forth renewed. One agreeable quality of the old Fords was that they had no bumpers, and their fenders softened and wilted with the years and permitted the driver to squeeze in and out of tight places.

Tires were $30 \times 3\frac{1}{2}$, cost about twelve dollars, and punctured readily. Everybody carried a Jiffy patching set, with a nutmeg grater to roughen the tube before the goo was spread on. Everybody was capable of putting on a patch, expected to have to, and did have to.

During my association with Model T's, self-starters were not a prevalent accessory. They were expensive and under suspicion. Your car came equipped with a serviceable crank, and the first thing you learned was how to Get Results. It was a special trick, and until you learned it (usually from another Ford owner, but sometimes by a period of appalling experimentation) you might as well have been winding up an awning. The trick was to leave the ignition switch off, proceed to the animal's head, pull the choke (which was a little wire protruding through the radiator) and give the crank two or three nonchalant upward lifts. Then, whistling as though thinking about something else, you would saunter back to the driver's cabin, turn the ignition on, return to the crank, and this time, catching it on the downstroke, give it a quick spin with plenty of That. If this procedure was followed, the engine almost always responded—first with a few scattered explosions, then with a tumultuous gunfire, which you checked by racing around to the driver's seat and retarding the throttle. Often, if the emergency brake hadn't been pulled all the way back, the car advanced on you the instant the first explosion occured and you would hold it back by leaning your weight against it. I can still feel my old Ford nuzzling me at the curb, as though looking for an apple in my pocket.

In zero weather, ordinary cranking became an impossibility, except for giants. The oil thickened, and it became necessary to jack up the rear wheels, which for some planetary reason, eased the throw.

The lore and legend that governed the Ford were boundless. Owners had their own theories about everything; they discussed mutual problems in that wise, infinitely resourceful way old women discuss rheumatism. Exact knowledge was pretty scarce, and often proved less effective than superstition. Dropping a camphor ball into the gas tank was a popular expedient; it seemed to have a tonic effect both on man and machine. There wasn't much to base exact knowledge on. The Ford driver flew blind. He didn't know the temperature of his engine, the speed of his car, the amount of his fuel, or the pressure of his oil (the old Ford lubricated itself by what was amiably described as the 'splash system'). A speedometer cost money and was an extra, like a windshield-wiper. The dashboard of the early models was bare save for an ignition key; later models, grown effete, boasted an ammeter which pulsated alarmingly with the throbbing of the car. Under the dash was a box of coils, with vibrators which you adjusted, or thought you adjusted. Whatever the driver learned of his motor, he learned not through instruments but through sudden developments. I remember that the timer was one of the vital organs about which there was ample doctrine. When everything else had been checked, you had a look at the timer. It was an extravagantly odd little device, simple in construction, mysterious in function. It contained a roller, held by a spring, and there were four contact points on the inside of the case against which, many people believed, the roller rolled. I have had a timer apart on a sick Ford many times. But I never really knew what I was up to—I was just showing off before God. There were almost as many schools of thought as there were timers. Some people, when things went wrong, just clenched their teeth and gave the timer a smart crack with a wrench. Other people opened it up and blew on it. There was a school that held that the timer needed large amounts of oil; they fixed it by frequent baptism. And there was a school that was positive it was meant to run dry as a bone; these people were continually taking it off and wiping it. I remember once spitting into a timer; not in anger, but in a spirit of research. You see, the Model T driver moved in the realm of metaphysics. He believed his car could be hexed.

One reason the Ford anatomy was never reduced to an exact science was that, having 'fixed' it, the owner couldn't honestly claim that the treatment had brought about the cure. There were too many authenticated cases of Fords fixing themselves—restored naturally to health after a short rest. Farmers soon discovered this, and it fitted nicely with their draft-horse philosophy: 'Let 'er cool off and she'll snap into it again.'

A Ford owner had Number One Bearing constantly in mind. This bearing, being at the front end of the motor, was the one that always burned out, because the oil didn't reach it when the car was climbing hills. (That's what I was always told, anyway.) The oil used to recede and leave Number One dry as a clam flat; you had to watch that bearing like a hawk. It was like a weak heart—you could hear it start knocking, and that was when you stopped to let her cool off. Try as you would to keep the oil supply right, in the end Number One always went out. 'Number One Bearing burned out on me and I had to have her replaced,' you would say, wisely; and your companions always had a lot to tell about how to protect and pamper Number One to keep her alive.

Sprinkled not too liberally among the millions of amateur witch doctors who drove Fords and applied their own abominable cures were the heaven-sent mechanics who could really make the car talk. These professionals turned up in undreamed-of spots. One time, on the banks of the Columbia River in Washington, I heard the rear end go out of my Model T when I was trying to whip it up a steep incline onto the deck of a ferry. Something snapped; the car slid backwards into the mud. It seemed to me like the end of the trail. But the captain of the ferry, observing the withered remnant, spoke up.

'What's got her?' he asked.

'I guess it's the rear end,' I replied listlessly. The captain leaned over the rail and stared. Then I saw that there was a hunger in his eyes that set him off from other men.

'Tell you what,' he said casually, trying to cover up his eagerness, 'let's pull the son of a bitch up onto the boat, and I'll help you fix her while we're going back and forth on the river.'

We did just this. All that day I plied between the towns of Pasco and Kenniwick, while the skipper (who had once worked in a Ford garage) directed the amazing work of resetting the bones of my car.

Springtime in the heyday of the Model T was a delirious season. Owning a car was still a major excitement, roads were still wonderful and bad. The Fords were obviously conceived in madness: any car which was capable of going from forward into reverse without any perceptible mechanical hiatus was bound to be a mighty challenging thing to the human imagination. Boys used to veer them off the highway into a level pasture and run wild with them, as though they were cutting up with a girl. Most everybody used the reverse pedal quite as much as the regular foot brake—it distributed the wear over the bands and wore them all down evenly. That was the big trick, to wear all the bands down evenly, so that the final chattering would be total and the whole unit scream for renewal.

The days were golden, the nights were dim and strange. I still recall with trembling those loud, nocturnal crises when you drew up to a signpost and raced the engine so the lights would be bright enough to read destinations by. I have never been really planetary since. I suppose it's time to say goodbye. Farewell, my lovely!

E. B. White (1899–1985), *The New Yorker* (1936), reprinted: *The Second Tree from the Corner* (1954).

IN 1927, *in its second year of publication, the* New Yorker *was still thin and too short of advertising to be profitable but it was doing slightly better and needed more staff. E. B. White met a newspaperman whose work he liked and recommended him to Ross who hired him on the spot.*

And so, casually, James Thurber began the literary career which was to make him the most widely admired American humorist since Mark Twain.

In line with Ross's somewhat ad hoc *approach to appointing staff, he hired Thurber as an editor and not as a writer ('writers are a dime a dozen, Thurber'). Thurber was 33 when he joined the* New Yorker *and he needed the job. He was unhappily married and had just returned from France where he had been working in Paris and Nice as a poorly paid hack for the* Chicago Tribune. *His prose style to begin with rather justified Ross's decison to make him an editor ; it was headlong journalese with occasional rhythms and constructions borrowed from the writer whom he, unfortunately, particularly admired—Henry James. After a few months of hard work being a very bad editor he was gently relieved of the post, put in a tiny room which he had to share with E. B. White, and given the role which he was to adorn and lend distinction to for many years, that of a* New Yorker *staff writer.*

Thurber and White got on extremely well. Thurber always acknowledged White's influence on his writing style. He very quickly learned from White how to slow down his pace and consider more carefully every word he wrote (as White put it: 'it's turning on a mind, not a faucet'), and he began to get his work past Ross without it being returned for rewriting covered with Ross's famous editorial scrawls in the margin, such as, 'Don't get', 'Who he?', 'Transcends credulence' ('credulence' is a splendid Ross word—not to be found in the dictionary), and the much used 'Given facts will fix.'

In 1929 Thurber and White found that they had both been tinkering with the same idea for a book and decided to write it together. The idea was to satirize the quasi-scientific, heavily psychological treatises on sex which had just become fashionable (White said that the heavy writers had got sex down and were breaking its arm). They called their book Is Sex Necessary? or Why You Feel the Way You Do.

In those days a whole book parodying a genre was unusual enough to be a doubtful starter and it was published only nine days after the Wall Street Crash so its chances looked minimal, but in its first five months the book went through eleven printings and sold forty-five thousand copies. The success gave Thurber and White their first whiff of literary fame.

Is Sex Necessary? *is probably the only book on sex ever written which never mentions the act itself: as the chapters unfold it becomes clear that much of the book, although echoing the phraseology of sex instruction, is in fact ironic advice to women on how to bring their menfolk to heel and keep them there.*

One chapter, warning of the psychological disturbances which can afflict husbands if their training is too harsh, gives useful hints to wives on how to develop a more humane approach:

A wife should strive at all times to give her husband at least the *illusion* that he is free to come and go. She should remember that it is the little things that count, that claustrophobia is brought on by an accumulation of small details, that it is, in fact, a tragedy of the trivial. If a husband uses a guest towel, he should be quietly reprimanded, but under no circumstances sent to his room. After pointing out, briefly, that the guest towels are not to be used, the wife might even give him a piece of bread and butter with sugar on it, or a kind word. Too many wives do not consider it important to explain the facts of the guest towel to their husbands. A wife expects her husband to pick up his knowledge in the gutter or from other husbands, who know as little about the actual truth as he does himself. If a husband uses a guest towel, he should be gently reproved and then told where guest towels come from, in clear, simple language. The wife should lead him to the drawer where she keeps the guest towels and show him wherein they differ from ordinary towels—the kind he may use. The average guest towel can be identified by curious markings, either elaborate initials or picturesque designs in one corner or running all the way around the border. The husband should also be told that the use of such towels is not pleasurable, because of the discomfort caused by the hemstitching, the rough embroidery, and the like. He should be made to understand that no man ever uses a guest towel, either in his own home or when he is a guest somewhere else, that they are hung up for lady guests to look at and are not to be disturbed. If he is told these simple truths in a calm, unexcited way, the chances are that he will never use a guest towel again and that he won't worry unduly over the consequences of his having used one once or twice.

> James Thurber and E. B. White (1894–1961, 1899–1985), *Is Sex Necessary?* (1929).

Is Sex Necessary? was illustrated by Thurber, at E. B. White's insistence, and marked the first appearance in print of those strange, haunting little pen drawings of resigned animals (particularly dogs of a breed seemingly designed by Thurber), small, balding, docile men, and women who were either predators or viragos.

Dorothy Parker thought that the people in Thurber drawings had 'the outer semblance of unbaked cookies'.

Thurber himself, who drew as easily and naturally as he blinked, was amused by the intellectualizing which his little sketches were subjected to, and joined in: 'My drawings have been described as pre-intentionalist,' he wrote, 'meaning that they were finished before the ideas for them occurred to me. I shall not argue the point.'

Ross, who could see no merit at all in Thurber's sketches ('how the hell did you get the idea you could draw?'), was forced by their success in the book to begin publishing them in his magazine.

The first to appear in the New Yorker was the famous 'seal' cartoon. This was originally a seal leaning on a rock and looking at two distant dots, with the caption 'Hm, explorers', but the rock came out looking more like the head of a bed, so Thurber changed the picture to a seal leaning over a bedhead, drew in the rest of

the bed, put a husband and wife in it and wrote a new caption 'All right, have it
your way—you heard a seal bark!' It became the best-known and most reprinted
cartoon of the century and, to Thurber's great delight, provoked a telegram of
congratulations and appreciation from the man Thurber considered to be the master
of humorous prose, Robert Benchley.

Many of Thurber's funniest early pieces were in the Benchley tradition but
the domestic predicaments which Thurber wrote about became sharper and the
humiliations more painful: whereas Benchley's bumbling inefficiency exasperated
the normal people around him, Thurber's disasters were, he believed, not of his
own making; he was the innocent victim of the essentially malicious nature of the
world about him:

NINE NEEDLES

One of the most spectacular minor happenings of the past few years which I
am sorry that I missed took place in the Columbus, Ohio, home of some
friends of a friend of mine. It seems that a Mr Albatross, while looking for
something in his medicine cabinet one morning, discovered a bottle of a kind
of patent medicine which his wife had been taking for a stomach ailment.
Now, Mr Albatross is one of those apprehensive men who are afraid of
patent medicines and of almost everything else. Some weeks before he had
encountered a paragraph in a Consumers' Research bulletin which announced that this particular medicine was bad for you. He had thereupon
ordered his wife to throw out what was left of her supply of the stuff and
never to buy any more. She had promised, and here now was another bottle
of the perilous liquid. Mr Albatross, a man given to quick rages, shouted the
conclusion of the story at my friend: 'I threw the bottle out of the bathroom
window and the medicine chest after it!' It seems to me that must have been
a spectacle worth going a long way to see.

I am sure that many a husband has wanted to wrench the family medicine
cabinet off the wall and throw it out of the window, if only because the
average medicine cabinet is so filled with mysterious bottles and un-
identifiable objects of all kinds that it is a source of constant bewilderment
and exasperation to the American male. Surely the British medicine cabinet
and the French medicine cabinet and all the other medicine cabinets must
be simpler and better ordered than ours. It may be that the American habit
of saving everything and never throwing anything away, even empty bottles,
causes the domestic medicine cabinet to become as cluttered in its small way
as the American attic becomes cluttered in a major way. I have encountered
few medicine cabinets in this country which were not pack-jammed with
something between a hundred and fifty and two hundred different items,
from dental floss to boracic acid, from razor blades to sodium perborate, from
adhesive tape to coconut oil. Even the neatest wife will put off clearing out
the medicine cabinet on the ground that she has something else to do that is
more important at the moment, or more diverting. It was in the apartment

of such a wife and her husband that I became enormously involved with a medicine cabinet one morning not long ago.

I had spent the week-end with this couple—they live on East Tenth Street near Fifth Avenue—such a week-end as left me reluctant to rise up on Monday morning with bright and shining face and go to work. They got up and went to work, but I didn't. I didn't get up until about two-thirty in the afternoon. I had my face all lathered for shaving and the wash-bowl was full of hot water when suddenly I cut myself with the razor. I cut my ear. Very few men cut their ears with razors, but I do, possibly because I was taught the old Spencerian free-wrist movement by my writing teacher in the grammar grades. The ear bleeds rather profusely when cut with a razor and is difficult to get at. More angry than hurt, I jerked open the door of the medicine cabinet to see if I could see a styptic pencil, and out fell, from the top shelf, a little black paper packet containing nine needles. It seems that this wife kept a little packet containing nine needles on the top shelf of the medicine cabinet. The packet fell into the soapy water of the wash-bowl, where the paper rapidly disintegrated, leaving nine needles at large in the bowl. I was, naturally enough, not in the best condition, either physical or mental, to recover nine needles from a wash-bowl. No gentleman who has lather on his face and whose ear is bleeding is in the best condition for anything, even something involving the handling of nine large blunt objects.

It did not seem wise to me to pull the plug out of the wash-bowl and let the needles go down the drain. I had visions of clogging up the plumbing system of the house, and also a vague fear of causing short circuits somehow or other (I know very little about electricity and I don't want to have it explained to me). Finally I groped very gently around the bowl and eventually had four of the needles in the palm of one hand and three in the palm of the other—two I couldn't find. If I thought quickly and clearly I wouldn't have done that. A lathered man whose ear is bleeding and who has four wet needles in one hand and three in the other may be said to have reached the lowest known point of human efficiency. There is nothing he can do but stand there. I tried transferring the needles in my left hand to the palm of my right hand, but I couldn't get them off my left hand. Wet needles cling to you. In the end I wiped the needles off on to a bath-towel which was hanging on a rod above the bath-tub. It was the only towel that I could find. I had to dry my hands afterwards on the bath-mat. Then I tried to find the needles in the towel. Hunting for seven needles in a bath-towel is the most tedious occupation I have ever engaged in. I could find only five of them. With the two that had been left in the bowl, that meant there were four needles in all missing—two in the wash-bowl and two others lurking in the towel or lying in the bath-tub under the towel. Frightful thoughts came to me of what might happen to anyone who used that towel or washed his face in the bowl or got into the tub, if I didn't find the missing needles. Well, I didn't find them. I sat down on the edge of the tub to think, and I decided finally that the only thing to do was wrap up the towel in a newspaper and take it away with me. I also decided to leave a note for my friends explaining as clearly as I could that I was afraid there were two needles in the bath-tub and two needles in the wash-bowl, and that they better be careful.

I looked everywhere in the apartment, but I could not find a pencil, or a pen, or a typewriter. I could find pieces of paper, but nothing with which to write on them. I don't know what gave me the idea—a movie I had seen, perhaps, or a story I had read—but I suddenly thought of writing a message with a lipstick. The wife might have an extra lipstick lying around and, if so, I concluded it would be in the medicine cabinet. I went back to the medicine cabinet and began poking around in it for a lipstick. I saw what I thought looked like the metal tip of one, and I got two fingers around it and began to pull gently—it was under a lot of things. Every object in the medicine cabinet began to slide. Bottles broke in the wash-bowl and on the floor; red, brown, and white liquids spurted; nail files, scissors, razor blades, and miscellaneous objects sang and clattered and tinkled. I was covered with perfume, peroxide, and cold cream,

It took me half an hour to get the debris all together in the middle of the bathroom floor. I made no attempt to put anything back in the medicine cabinet. I knew it would take a steadier hand than mine and a less shattered spirit. Before I went away (only partly shaved) and abandoned the shambles, I left a note saying that I was afraid there were needles in the bath-tub and the wash-bowl and that I had taken their towel and that I would call up and tell them everything—I wrote it in iodine with the end of a toothbrush. I have not called up yet, I am sorry to say. I have neither found the courage nor thought up the words to explain what happened. I suppose my friends believe that I deliberately smashed up their bathroom and stole their towel. I don't know for sure, because they have not yet called me up, either.

Let Your Mind Alone (1937).

Thurber's stories of his early life show a kind of buoyant resignation to his lot.

His eyesight was bad throughout his life because when he was aged 6 one of his brothers accidentally blinded him in one eye with a bow and arrow and this also weakened the remaining eye. His father was a badly-paid clerk who spent his leisure hours entering magazine word-puzzle competitions for the prize money and his mother came from a well-off Ohio family who were notable eccentrics; she herself was locally famous when young for a string of practical jokes. Her grandfather, who was devoted to being photographed, had all his teeth capped with gold and Carmen-like, went about with a red rose gripped between his teeth.

With that kind of domestic history, Thurber's account of the occasion when the family's sleep was disturbed might well have been the simple truth:

THE NIGHT THE BED FELL

I suppose that the high-water mark of my youth in Columbus, Ohio, was the night the bed fell on my father. It makes a better recitation (unless, as some friends of mind have said, one has heard it five or six times) than it does a piece of writing, for it is almost necessary to throw furniture around, shake doors, and bark like a dog, to lend the proper atmosphere and verisimilitude to what is admittedly a somewhat incredible tale. Still it did take place.

It happened, then, that my father had decided to sleep in the attic one night, to be away where he could think. My mother opposed the notion strongly because, she said, the old wooden bed up there was unsafe: it was wobbly and the heavy headboard would crash down on father's head in case the bed fell, and kill him. There was no dissuading him, however, and at a quarter past ten he closed the attic door behind him and went up the narrow twisting stairs. We later heard ominous creakings as he crawled into bed. Grandfather, who usually slept in the attic bed when he was with us, had disappeared some days before. (On these occasions he was usually gone six or eight days and returned growling and out of temper, with the news that the federal Union was run by a passel of blockheads and that the Army of the Potomac didn't have any more chance than a fiddler's bitch.)

We had visiting us at this time a nervous first cousin of mine named Briggs Beall, who believed that he was likely to cease breathing when he was asleep. It was his feeling that if he were not awaked every hour during the night, he might die of suffocation. He had been accustomed to setting an alarm clock to ring at intervals until morning, but I persuaded him to abandon this. He slept in my room and I told him that I was such a light sleeper that if anybody quit breathing in the same room with me, I would wake instantly. He tested me the first night—which I had suspected he would—by holding his breath after my regular breathing had convinced him I was asleep. I was not asleep, however, and called to him. This seemed to allay his fears a little, but he took the precaution of putting a glass of spirits of camphor on a little table at the head of his bed. In case I didn't arouse him until he was almost gone, he said he would sniff the camphor, a powerful reviver. Briggs was not the only member of his family who had his crotchets. Old Aunt Melissa Beall (who could whistle like a man, with two fingers in her mouth) suffered under the premonition that she was destined to die on South High Street, because she had been born on South High Street and married on South High Street. Then there was Aunt Sarah Shoaf, who never went to bed at night without the fear that a burglar was going to get in and blow chloroform under her door through a tube. To avert this calamity—for she was in greater dread of anaesthetics than of losing her household goods—she always piled her money, silverware, and other valuables in a neat stack just outside her bedroom, with a note reading, 'This is all I have. Please take it and do not use your chloroform, as this is all I have.' Aunt Gracie Shoaf also had a burglar phobia, but she met it with more fortitude. She was confident that burglars had been getting into her house every night for forty years. The fact that she never missed anything was to her no proof to the contrary. She always claimed that she scared them off before they could take anything, by throwing shoes down the hallway. When she went to bed she piled, where she could get at them handily, all the shoes there were about her house. Five minutes after she had turned off the light, she would sit up in bed and say 'Hark!' Her husband, who had learnt to ignore the whole situation as long ago as 1903, would either be sound asleep or pretend to be sound asleep. In either case he would not respond to her tugging and pulling, so that presently she would arise, tiptoe to the door, open it slightly and heave a shoe down the hall in one direction, and its mate down the hall in the other direction. Some nights she threw them all, some nights only a couple of pairs.

But I am straying from the remarkable incidents that took place during the night that the bed fell on Father. By midnight we were all in bed. The layout of the rooms and the disposition of their occupants is important to an understanding of what later occurred. In the front room upstairs (just under Father's attic bedroom) were my mother and my brother Herman, who sometimes sang in his sleep, usually 'Marching Through Georgia' or 'Onward Christian Soldiers'. Briggs Beall and myself were in a room adjoining this one. My brother Roy was in a room across the hall from ours. Our bull terrier, Rex, slept in the hall.

My bed was an army cot, one of those affairs which are made wide enough to sleep on comfortably only by putting up, flat with the middle section, the two sides which ordinarily hang down like the sideboards of a drop-leaf table. When these sides are up, it is perilous to roll too far towards the edge, for then the cot is likely to tip completely over, bringing the whole bed down on top of one, with a tremendous banging crash. This, in fact, is precisely what happened, about two o'clock in the morning. (It was my mother who, in recalling the scene later, first referred to it as 'the night the bed fell on your father'.)

Always a deep sleeper, slow to arouse (I had lied to Briggs), I was at first unconscious of what had happened when the iron cot rolled me on to the floor and toppled over on me. It left me still warmly bundled up and unhurt, for the bed rested over me like a canopy. Hence I did not wake up, only reached the edge of consciousness and went back. The racket, however, awakened my mother, in the next room, who came to the immediate conclusion that her worst dread was realized: the big wooden bed upstairs had fallen on father. She therefore screamed, 'Let's go to your poor father!' It was this shout, rather than the noise of my cot falling that awakened Herman, in the same room with her. He thought that mother had become, for no apparent reason, hysterical. 'You're all right, Mamma!' he shouted, trying to calm her. They exchanged shout for shout for perhaps ten seconds: 'Let's go to your poor father!' and 'You're all right!' That woke up Briggs. By this time I was conscious of what was going on, in a vague way, but did not yet realize that I was under my bed instead of on it. Briggs, awakening in the midst of loud shouts of fear and apprehension, came to the quick conclusion that he was suffocating and that we were all trying to 'bring him out'. With a low moan, he grasped the glass of camphor at the head of his bed and instead of sniffing it poured it over himself. The room reeked of camphor. 'Ugf, ahfg,' choked Briggs, like a drowning man, for he had almost succeeded in stopping his breath under the deluge of pungent spirits. He leaped out of bed and groped towards the open window, but he came up against one that was closed. With his hand, he beat out the glass, and I could hear it crash and tinkle on the alleyway below. It was at this juncture that I, in trying to get up, had the uncanny sensation of feeling my bed above me! Foggy with sleep, I now suspected, in my turn, that the whole uproar was being made in a frantic endeavour to extricate me from what must be an unheard-of and perilous situation. 'Get me out of this!' I bawled, 'get me out!' I think I had the nightmarish belief that I was entombed in a mine. 'Gugh,' gasped Briggs, floundering in his camphor.

By this time my mother, still shouting, pursued by Herman, still shouting, was trying to open the door to the attic in order to go up and get my father's body out of the wreckage. The door was stuck, however, and wouldn't yield. Her frantic pulls on it only added to the general banging and confusion. Roy and the dog were now up, the one shouting questions, the other barking.

Father, farthest away and soundest sleeper of all, had by this time been awakened by the battering on the attic door. He decided that the house was on fire. 'I'm coming. I'm coming!' he wailed in a slow, sleepy voice—it took him many minutes to regain full consciousness. My mother, still believing he was caught under the bed, detected in his 'I'm coming' the mournful, resigned note of one who is preparing to meet his Maker. 'He's dying!' she shouted. 'I'm all right!' Briggs yelled to reassure her. 'I'm all right!' He still believed that it was his own closeness to death that was worrying Mother. I found at last the light switch in my room, unlocked the door, and Briggs and I joined the others at the attic door. The dog, who never did like Briggs, jumped for him—assuming that he was the culprit in whatever was going on—and Roy had to throw Rex and hold him. We could hear Father crawling out of bed upstairs. Roy pulled the attic door open, with a mighty jerk, and Father came down the stairs, sleepy and irritable but safe and sound. My mother began to weep when she saw him. Rex began to howl. 'What in the name of God is going on here?' asked Father.

The situation was finally put together like a gigantic jigsaw puzzle. Father caught a cold from prowling around in his bare feet but there were no other bad results. 'I'm glad,' said Mother, who always looked on the bright side of things, 'that your grandfather wasn't here.'   *My Life and Hard Times* (1933).

Thurber wrote a great many fables. The form probably suited him particularly well as it not only meant that he could often do one of his little drawings but it also used his experience of succinct paragraph-writing, and he loved puns and animals:

THE SHRIKE AND THE CHIPMUNKS

Once upon a time there were two chipmunks, a male and a female. The male chipmunk thought that arranging nuts in artistic patterns was more fun than just piling them up to see how many you could pile up. The female was all for piling up as many as you could. She told her husband that if he gave up making designs with the nuts there would be room in their large cave for a great many more and he would soon become the wealthiest chipmunk in the woods. But he would not let her interfere with his designs, so she flew into a rage and left him. 'The shrike will get you,' she said, 'because you are helpless and cannot look after yourself.' To be sure, the female chipmunk had not been gone three nights before the male had to dress for a banquet and could not find his studs or shirt or suspenders. So he couldn't go to the banquet, but that was just as well, because all the chipmunks who did go were attacked and killed by a weasel.

The next day the shrike began hanging around outside the chipmunk's cave, waiting to catch him. The shrike couldn't get in because the doorway was clogged up with soiled laundry and dirty dishes. 'He will come out for a walk after breakfast and I will get him then,' thought the shrike. But the chipmunk slept all day and did not get up and have breakfast until after dark. Then he came out for a breath of air before beginning work on a new design. The shrike swooped down to snatch up the chipmunk, but could not see very well on account of the dark, so he batted his head against an alder branch and was killed.

A few days later the female chipmunk returned and saw the awful mess the house was in. She went to the bed and shook her husband. 'What would you do without me?' she demanded. 'Just go on living, I guess,' he said. 'You wouldn't last five days,' she told him. She swept the house and did the dishes and sent out the laundry, and then she made the chipmunk get up and wash and dress. 'You can't be healthy if you lie in bed all day and never get any exercise,' she told him. So she took him for a walk in the bright sunlight and they were both caught and killed by the shrike's brother, a shrike named Stoop.

Moral: Early to rise and early to bed makes a male healthy and wealthy and dead.

Fables in our Time (1940).

Thurber's humour increasingly reflected his conviction that American wives had an instinctive urge to subdue their husbands and break their spirits, if necessary to the point of destruction.

He had no doubt at all that wives were unbeatable in this war of attrition but he was prepared, occasionally, to let a husband win just one battle:

THE UNICORN IN THE GARDEN

Once upon a sunny morning a man who sat in a breakfast nook looked up from his scrambled eggs to see a white unicorn with a golden horn quietly cropping the roses in the garden. The man went up to the bedroom where his wife was still asleep and woke her. 'There's a unicorn in the garden,' he said, 'Eating roses.' She opened one unfriendly eye and looked at him. 'The unicorn is a mythical beast,' she said, and turned her back on him. The man walked slowly downstairs and out into the garden. The unicorn was still there; he was now browsing among the tulips. 'Here, unicorn,' said the man, and he pulled up a lily and gave it to him. The unicorn ate it gravely. With a high heart, because there was a unicorn in his garden, the man went upstairs and roused his wife again. 'The unicorn,' he said, 'ate a lily.' His wife sat up in bed and looked at him, coldly. 'You are a booby,' she said, 'and I am going to have you put in the booby-hatch.' The man, who had never liked the words 'booby' and 'booby-hatch', and who liked them even less on a shining morning when there was a unicorn in the garden, thought for a moment. 'We'll see about that,' he said. He walked over to the door. 'He has a golden horn in the middle of his forehead,' he told her. Then he went back to the garden to watch the unicorn; but the unicorn had gone away. The man sat down among the roses and went to sleep.

As soon as the man had gone out of the house, the wife got up and dressed as fast as she could. She was very excited and there was a gloat in her eye. She telephoned the police and she telephoned a psychiatrist; and she told them to hurry to her house and bring a strait-jacket. When the police and the psychiatrist arrived they sat down in chairs and looked at her, with great interest. 'My husband,' she said, 'saw a unicorn this morning.' The police looked at the psychiatrist and the psychiatrist looked at the police. 'He told me it ate a lily,' she said. The psychiatrist looked at the police and the police looked at the psychiatrist. 'He told me it had a golden horn in the middle of its forehead,' she said. At a solemn signal from the psychiatrist, the police leaped from their chairs and seized the wife. They had a hard time subduing her, for she put up a terrific struggle, but they finally subdued her. Just as they got her into the strait-jacket, the husband came back into the house.

'Did you tell your wife you saw a unicorn?' asked the police. 'Of course not,' said the husband. 'The unicorn is a mythical beast.' 'That's all I wanted to know,' said the psychiatrist. 'Take her away. I'm sorry, sir, but your wife is as crazy as a jay bird.' So they took her away, cursing and screaming, and shut her up in an institution. The husband lived happily ever after.

Moral: Don't count your boobies until they are hatched.   Ibid.

Thurber later used much the same plot in a story which was one of his own favourites, The Catbird Seat. *But a triumphant male was a rarity in Thurber's world.*

Thurber's output, and fame, grew during the 1930s. For the New Yorker *he wrote and illustrated stories, sketches, fables, essays, parables, and reminiscences which were published as collections in five best-selling books between 1931 and 1939. More stories and books were to follow during the forties and fifties, plus fantasy stories for children and a successful play,* The Male Animal, *which he wrote with his oldest friend Elliott Nugent, but the zenith of Thurber's creative career came on 18 March 1939 when the* New Yorker *published* The Secret Life of Walter Mitty, *perhaps the nearest any writer has yet come to the perfect post-Freud humorous story.*

The story's success was immediate and on a colossal scale. It was reprinted by a host of journals including Reader's Digest *which took it round the world; American servicemen on both fronts formed Walter Mitty clubs. The name 'Walter Mitty' passed into the language: in a learned article the British medical journal the* Lancet *dubbed persistent day-dreaming 'the Walter Mitty syndrome'. Newspapermen and radio commentators began using, and still use, phrases like 'he's suffering from a Walter Mitty complex', or, 'he is going through a Walter Mitty phase'. Metro-Goldwyn-Mayer bought the story, rewrote it almost out of existence and mangled the remains into a screen vehicle for Danny Kaye. It was made into an opera by the composer Charles Hamm. It was almost made into a musical by Rodgers and Hammerstein. It became, mercifully briefly, an awful off-Broadway musical with lyrics like 'Hello, I Love You, Goodbye'. In 1944 it was successfully adapted into a radio play with the role of Mitty beautifully performed by—a happy eventuality—Robert Benchley.*

Perhaps the most touching comment came to Thurber in a letter from Harold ('writers are a dime a dozen, Thurber') Ross, who wrote 'in your way you are just about the master of them all, by Jesus'.

It has been said that The Secret Life of Walter Mitty *earned its author more money per word than any other story in the history of literature. This seems highly likely as, despite its great impact and influence, it was surprisingly short. Thurber, in a letter to Alastair Cooke, spoke of '4,000 words' but his biographer Burton Burstein insisted that it was only 2,500 words long. (It seems to have shrunk. Using the text of the story as reprinted in* My World—and Welcome to it, *I make it 2,065 words. If all the hyphens are removed and words like 'ta-pocketa-pocketa-pocketa-pocketa-pocketa' are counted as 6 and not 1, I still only make it 2,097 words.)*

In 1961 Thurber died, aged 67. During the last years his sight weakened and then failed completely; he became increasingly bitter, he drank hard, and he was a considerable trial to his friends (though, on his last tour of Europe, still able to come up with such remarks as 'A woman's place is in the wrong', and when a lady in Paris remarked that she had all his books in English and in French translations and really rather preferred reading them in French: 'Yes, I'm afraid my work does lose a little in the original.')

The American literary world had lost in Thurber a true original, a craftsman in words who used them as both ammunition and toys, who had created, and shared,

a private world occupied by fantasy animals, machinery which he did not under-
stand, dogs with wrinkled foreheads, situations beyond his control, the oddest of
relations, eccentric maidservants, conventional little men, ferocious women, and
much else. E. B. White said in his memorial of Thurber: 'he wrote the way a child
skips rope, the way a mouse waltzes.'

One of Thurber's last requests was that his obituary in the New Yorker *should*
be a reprinting of the story which of all his humorous pieces he was most pleased
to have written:

THE SECRET LIFE OF WALTER MITTY

'We're going through!' The Commander's voice was like thin ice breaking. He wore his full-dress uniform, with the heavily braided white cap pulled down rakishly over one cold gray eye. 'We can't make it, sir. It's spoiling for a hurricane, if you ask me.' 'I'm not asking you, Lieutenant Berg,' said the Commander. 'Throw on the power lights! Rev her up to 8,500! We're going through!' The pounding of the cylinders increased: ta-pocketa-pocketa-pocketa-*pocketa-pocketa.* The Commander stared at the ice forming on the pilot window. He walked over and twisted a row of complicated dials. 'Switch on No. 8 auxiliary!' he shouted. 'Switch on No. 8 auxiliary!' repeated Lieutenant Berg. 'Full strength in No. 3 turret!' shouted the Commander. 'Full strength in No. 3 turret!' The crew, bending to their various tasks in the huge, hurtling eight-engined Navy hydroplane, looked at each other and grinned. 'The Old Man'll get us through,' they said to one another. 'The Old Man ain't afraid of Hell!' . . .

'Not so fast! You're driving too fast!' said Mrs Mitty. 'What are you driving so fast for?'

'Hmm?' said Walter Mitty. He looked at his wife, in the seat beside him, with shocked astonishment. She seemed grossly unfamiliar, like a strange woman who had yelled at him in a crowd. 'You were up to fifty-five,' she said. 'You know I don't like to go more than forty. You were up to fifty-five.' Walter Mitty drove on toward Waterbury in silence, the roaring of the SN202 through the worst storm in twenty years of Navy flying fading in the remote, intimate airways of his mind. 'You're tensed up again,' said Mrs Mitty. 'It's one of your days. I wish you'd let Dr Renshaw look you over.'

Walter Mitty stopped the car in front of the building where his wife went to have her hair done. 'Remember to get those overshoes while I'm having my hair done,' she said. 'I don't need overshoes,' said Mitty. She put her mirror back into her bag. 'We've been all through that,' she said, getting out of the car. 'You're not a young man any longer.' He raced the engine a little. 'Why don't you wear your gloves? Have you lost your gloves?' Walter Mitty reached in a pocket and brought out the gloves. He put them on, but after she had turned and gone into the building and he had driven on to a red light, he took them off again. 'Pick it up, brother!' snapped a cop as the light changed, and Mitty hastily pulled on his gloves and lurched ahead. He drove around the streets aimlessly for a time, and then he drove past the hospital on his way to the parking lot.

. . . 'It's the millionaire banker, Wellington McMillan,' said the pretty nurse. 'Yes?' said Walter Mitty, removing his gloves slowly. 'Who has the case?' 'Dr Renshaw and Dr Benbow, but there are two specialists here, Dr Remington from New York and Mr Pritchard-Mitford from London. He flew over.' A door opened down a long, cool corridor and Dr Renshaw came out. He looked distraught and haggard. 'Hello, Mitty,' he said. 'We're having the devil's own time with McMillan, the millionaire banker and close personal friend of Roosevelt. Obstreosis of the ductal tract. Tertiary. Wish you'd take a look at him.' 'Glad to,' said Mitty.

In the operating room there were whispered introductions: 'Dr Remington, Dr Mitty. Mr Pritchard-Mitford, Dr Mitty.' 'I've read your book on strep-tothricosis,' said Pritchard-Mitford, shaking hands. 'A brilliant performance, sir.' 'Thank you,' said Walter Mitty. 'Didn't know you were in the States, Mitty,' grumbled Remington. 'Coals to Newcastle, bringing Mitford and me up here for a tertiary.' 'You are very kind,' said Mitty. A huge, complicated machine, connected to the operating table, with many tubes and wires, began at this moment to go pocketa-pocketa-pocketa. 'The new anesthetizer is giving way!' shouted an intern. 'There is no one in the East who knows how to fix it!' 'Quiet, man!' said Mitty, in a low, cool voice. He sprang to the machine, which was now going pocketa-pocketa-queep-pocketa-queep. He began fingering delicately a row of glistening dials. 'Give me a fountain pen!' he snapped. Someone handed him a fountain pen. He pulled a faulty piston out of the machine and inserted the pen in its place. 'That will hold for ten minutes,' he said. 'Get on with the operation.' A nurse hurried over and whispered to Renshaw, and Mitty saw the man turn pale. 'Coreopsis has set in,' said Renshaw nervously. 'If you would take over, Mitty?' Mitty looked at him and at the craven figure of Benbow, who drank, and at the grave, uncertain faces of the two great specialists. 'If you wish,' he said. They slipped a white gown on him; he adjusted a mask and drew on thin gloves; nurses handed him shining . . .

'Back it up, Mac! Look out for that Buick!' Walter Mitty jammed on the brakes. 'Wrong lane, Mac,' said the parking-lot attendant, looking at Mitty closely. 'Gee. Yeh,' muttered Mitty. He began cautiously to back out of the lane marked 'Exit Only'. 'Leave her sit there,' said the attendant. 'I'll put her away.' Mitty got out of the car. 'Hey, better leave the key.' 'Oh,' said Mitty, handing the man the ignition key. The attendant vaulted into the car, backed it up with insolent skill, and put it where it belonged.

They're so damn cocky, thought Walter Mitty, walking along Main Street; they think they know everything. Once he had tried to take his chains off, outside New Milford, and he had got them wound around the axles. A man had had to come out in a wrecking car and unwind them, a young, grinning garageman. Since then Mrs Mitty always made him drive to a garage to have the chains taken off. The next time, he thought, I'll wear my right arm in a sling; they won't grin at me then. I'll have my right arm in a sling and they'll see I couldn't possibly take the chains off myself. He kicked at the slush on the sidewalk. 'Overshoes,' he said to himself, and he began looking for a shoe store.

When he came out into the street again, with the overshoes in a box under his arm, Walter Mitty began to wonder what the other thing was his wife had told him to get. She had told him, twice, before they set out from their house for Waterbury. In a way he hated these weekly trips to town—he was always getting something wrong. Kleenex, he thought, Squibb's, razor blades? No. Toothpaste, toothbrush, bicarbonate, carborundum, initiative and referendum? He gave it up. But she would remember it. 'Where's the what's-its-name?' she would ask. 'Don't tell me you forgot the what's-its-name.' A newsboy went by shouting something about the Waterbury trial.

... 'Perhaps this will refresh your memory.' The District Attorney suddenly thrust a heavy automatic at the quiet figure on the witness stand. 'Have you ever seen this before?' Walter Mitty took the gun and examined it expertly. 'This is my Webley-Vickers 50.80,' he said calmly. An excited buzz ran around the courtroom. The Judge rapped for order. 'You are a crack shot with any sort of firearms, I believe?' said the District Attorney, insinuatingly. 'Objection!' shouted Mitty's attorney. 'We have shown that the defendant could not have fired the shot. We have shown that he wore his right arm in a sling on the night of the fourteenth of July.' Walter Mitty raised his hand briefly and the bickering attorneys were stilled. 'With any known make of gun,' he said evenly, 'I could have killed Gregory Fitzhurst at three hundred feet *with my left hand*.' Pandemonium broke loose in the courtroom. A woman's scream rose above the bedlam and suddenly a lovely, dark-haired girl was in Walter Mitty's arms. The District Attorney struck at her savagely. Without rising from his chair, Mitty let the man have it on the point of the chin. 'You miserable cur!'...

'Puppy biscuit,' said Walter Mitty. He stopped walking and the buildings of Waterbury rose up out of the misty courtroom and surrounded him again. A woman who was passing laughed. 'He said "puppy biscuit"', she said to her companion. 'That man said "puppy biscuit" to himself.' Walter Mitty hurried on. He went into an A & P, not the first one he came to but a smaller one farther up the street. 'I want some biscuit for small, young dogs,' he said to the clerk. 'Any special brand, sir?' The greatest pistol shot in the world thought a moment. 'It says "Puppies Bark for It" on the box,' said Walter Mitty.

His wife would be through at the hairdresser's in fifteen minutes, Mitty saw in looking at his watch, unless they had trouble drying it; sometimes they had trouble drying it. She didn't like to get to the hotel first; she would want him to be there waiting for her as usual. He found a big leather chair in the lobby, facing a window, and he put the overshoes and the puppy biscuit on the floor beside it. He picked up an old copy of *Liberty* and sank down into the chair. 'Can Germany Conquer the World Through the Air?' Walter Mitty looked at the pictures of bombing planes and of ruined streets.

'The cannonading has got the wind up in young Raleigh, sir,' said the sergeant. Captain Mitty looked up at him through tousled hair. 'Get him to bed,' he said wearily. 'With the others. I'll fly alone.' 'But you can't, sir,' said the sergeant anxiously. 'It takes two men to handle that bomber and the Archies are pounding hell out of the air. Von Richtman's circus is between here and Saulier.' 'Somebody's got to get that ammunition dump,' said Mitty. 'I'm going over. Spot of brandy?' He poured a drink for the sergeant and one for himself. War thundered and whined around the dugout and battered at the door. There was a rending of wood and splinters flew through the room. 'A bit of a near thing,' said Captain Mitty carelessly. 'The box barrage is closing in,' said the sergeant. 'We only live once, Sergeant,' said Mitty, with his faint, fleeting smile. 'Or do we?' He poured another brandy and tossed it off. 'I never see a man could hold his brandy like you, sir,' said the sergeant. 'Begging your pardon, sir.' Captain Mitty stood up and strapped on his huge Webley-Vickers automatic. 'It's forty kilometers through hell, sir,' said the sergeant. Mitty finished one last brandy. 'After all,' he said softly, 'what isn't?' The pounding of the cannon increased; there was the rat-tat-tatting of machine guns, and from somewhere came the menacing pocketa-pocketa-pocketa of the new flame-throwers. Walter Mitty walked to the door of the dugout humming 'Auprès de Ma Blonde'. He turned and waved to the sergeant. 'Cheerio!' he said . . .

Something struck his shoulder. 'I've been looking all over this hotel for you,' said Mrs Mitty. 'Why do you have to hide in this old chair? How did you expect me to find you?' 'Things close in,' said Walter Mitty vaguely. 'What?' Mrs Mitty said. 'Did you get the what's-its-name? The puppy biscuit? What's in that box?' 'Overshoes,' said Mitty. 'Couldn't you have put them on in the store?' 'I was thinking,' said Walter Mitty. 'Does it ever occur to you that I am sometimes thinking?' She looked at him. 'I'm going to take your temperature when I get you home,' she said.

They went out through the revolving doors that made a faintly derisive whistling sound when you pushed them. It was two blocks to the parking lot. At the drugstore on the corner she said, 'Wait here for me. I forgot something. I won't be a minute.' She was more than a minute. Walter Mitty lighted a cigarette. It began to rain, rain with sleet in it. He stood up against the wall of the drugstore smoking . . . He put his shoulders back and his heels together. 'To hell with the handkerchief,' said Walter Mitty scornfully. He took one last drag on his cigarette and snapped it away. Then, with that faint, fleeting smile playing about his lips, he faced the firing squad; erect and motionless, proud and disdainful, Walter Mitty the Undefeated, inscrutable to the last.

My World—and Welcome to it (1942).

———

THREE *of the Round Table wits, Woollcott, Benchley, and Dorothy Parker, joined E. B. White and Thurber on the* New Yorker *as resident columnists towards the end of the 1920s but the trio were by now famous writers, social celebrities, and much in demand. Their contributions to the magazine were not distinguished.* New Yorker *humour was moving in a new direction and it was away from the old Vicious Circle style.*

Dorothy Parker got off a few splendid quips in her book column but her wit needed bad books on which to feed; she had little relish for praising. On the other hand, Woollcott thrived on writing fulsome encomiums so his column 'Shouts and Murmers' was equally one-sided in the other direction.

Robert Benchley, caught up in his rising film career, tried to commute by train between Hollywood and New York but finally had to be replaced as drama critic by one of the New Yorker's *young, up-and-coming group of staff writers, Wolcott Gibbs.*

Gibbs was a small, handsome, shy, dapper man who wrote well in all the forms which the magazine called for. As well as contributing items to 'The Talk of the Town', editing, reviewing plays, movies, and books, he was a brilliant parodist and writer of casuals.

In one of Wolcott Gibbs's casuals he recalls his first appearance on stage as a Shakespearian actor:

RING OUT, WILD BELLS

When I finally got around to see Max Reinhardt's cinema version of 'A Midsummer-Night's Dream', and saw a child called Mickey Rooney playing Puck, I remembered suddenly that long ago I had taken the same part.

Our production was given on the open-air stage at the Riverdale Country School, shortly before the war. The scenery was only the natural scenery of that suburban dell, and the cast was exclusively male, ranging in age from eleven to perhaps seventeen. While we had thus preserved the pure, Elizabethan note of the original, it must be admitted that our version had its drawbacks. The costumes were probably the worst things we had to bear, and even Penrod, tragically arrayed as Launcelot in his sister's stockings and his father's drawers, might have been embarrassed for us. Like Penrod, we were costumed by our parents, and like the Schofields, they seemed on the whole a little weak historically. Half of the ladies were inclined to favor the Elizabethan, and they had constructed rather bunchy ruffs and farthingales for their offspring; others, who had read as far as the stage directions and learned that the action took place in an Athenian wood, had produced something vaguely Athenian, usually beginning with a sheet. Only the fairies had a certain uniformity. For some reason their parents had all decided on cheesecloth, with here and there a little ill-advised trimming with tinsel.

My own costume was mysterious, but spectacular. As nearly as I have ever been able to figure things out, my mother found her inspiration for it in a Maxfield Parrish picture of a court jester. Beginning at the top, there was a cap with three stuffed horns; then, for the main part, a pair of tights that covered me to my wrists and ankles; and finally slippers with stuffed toes that curled up at the ends. The whole thing was made out of silk in alternate green and red stripes, and (unquestionably my poor mother's most demented stroke) it was covered from head to foot with a thousand tiny bells. Because all our costumes were obviously perishable, we never wore them in rehearsal, and naturally nobody knew that I was invested with these peculiar sound effects until I made my entrance at the beginning of the second act.

Our director was a man who had strong opinions about how Shakespeare should be played, and Puck was one of his favorite characters. It was his theory that Puck, being 'the incarnation of mischief', never ought to be still a minute, so I had been coached to bound onto the stage, and once there to dance up and down, cocking my head and waving my arms.

'I want you to be a little whirlwind,' this man said.

Even as I prepared to bound onto the stage, I had my own misgivings about those dangerously abundant gestures, and their probable effect on my bells. It was too late, however, to invent another technique for playing Puck, even if there had been room for anything but horror in my mind. I bounded onto the stage.

The effect, in its way, must have been superb. With every leap I rang like a thousand children's sleighs, my melodies foretelling God knows what worlds of merriment to the enchanted spectators. It was even worse when I came to the middle of the stage and went into my gestures. The other ringing had been loud but sporadic. This was persistent, varying only slightly in volume and pitch with the vehemence of my gestures. To a blind man, it must have sounded as though I had recklessly decided to accompany myself on a xylophone. A maturer actor would probably have made up his mind that an emergency existed, and abandoned his gestures as impracticable under the circumstances. I was thirteen, and incapable of innovations. I had been told by responsible authorities that gestures went with this part, and I continued to make them. I also continued to ring—a silvery music, festive and horrible.

If the bells were hard on my nerves, they were even worse for the rest of the cast, who were totally unprepared for my new interpretation. Puck's first remark is addressed to one of the fairies, and it is mercifully brief.

I said, 'How now, spirit! Whither wander you?'

This unhappy child, already embarrassed by a public appearance in cheesecloth and tinsel, was also burdened with an opening speech of sixteen lines in verse. He began bravely:

'Over hill, over dale,
    Thorough bush, thorough brier,
Over park, over pale,
    Thorough flood, thorough fire . . .'

At the word 'fire,' my instructions were to bring my hands up from the ground in a long, wavery sweep, intended to represent fire. The bells pealed. To my startled ears, it sounded more as if they exploded. The fairy stopped in his lines and looked at me sharply. The jingling, however, had diminished; it was no more than as if a faint wind stirred my bells, and he went on:—

'I do wander every where,
    Swifter than the moone's sphere . . .'

Here again I had another cue, for a sort of swoop and dip indicating the swiftness of the moone's sphere. Again the bells rang out, and again the performance stopped in its tracks. The fairy was clearly troubled by these interruptions. He had, however, a child's strange acceptance of the inscrutable, and was even able to regard my bells as a last-minute adult addition to the program, nerve-racking but not to be questioned. I'm sure it was only this that got him through that first speech.

My turn, when it came, was even worse. By this time the audience had succumbed to a helpless gaiety. Every time my bells rang, laughter swept the spectators, and this mounted and mingled with the bells until everything else was practically inaudible. I began my speech, another long one, and full of incomprehensible references to Titania's changeling.

'Louder!' said somebody in the wings. 'You'll have to talk louder.'

It was the director, and he seemed to be in a dangerous state.

'And for heaven's sake, stop that jingling!' he said.

I talked louder, and I tried to stop the jingling, but it was no use. By the time I got to the end of my speech, I was shouting and so was the audience. It appeared that I had very little control over the bells, which continued to jingle in spite of my passionate efforts to keep them quite.

All this had a very bad effect on the fairy, who by this time had many symptoms of a complete nervous collapse. However, he began his next speech:

'Either I mistake your shape and making quite,
Or else you are that shrewd and knavish sprite
Call'd Robin Goodfellow: are you not he
That . . .'

At this point I forgot that the rules had been changed and I was supposed to leave out the gestures. There was a furious jingling, and the fairy gulped.

'Are you not he that, that . . .'

He looked miserably at the wings, and the director supplied the next line, but the tumult was too much for him. The unhappy child simply shook his head.

'Say anything!' shouted the director desperately. 'Anything at all!'

The fairy only shut his eyes and shuddered.

'All right!' shouted the director. 'All right, Puck. You begin your next speech.'

By some miracle, I actually did remember my next lines, and had opened my mouth to begin on them when suddenly the fairy spoke. His voice was a high, thin monotone, and there seemed to be madness in it, but it was perfectly clear.

'Fourscore and seven years ago,' he began, 'our fathers brought forth on this continent a new nation, conceived . . .'

He said it right through to the end, and it was certainly the most successful speech ever made on that stage, and probably one of the most successful speeches ever made on any stage. I don't remember, if I ever knew, how the rest of us ever picked up the dull, normal thread of the play after that extraordinary performance, but we must have, because I know it went on. I only remember that in the next intermission the director cut off my bells with his penknife, and after that things quieted down and got dull.

Wolcott Gibbs (b. 1902), A Bed of Neuroses (1937).

———

THE *first few years of the* New Yorker *had been difficult for Ross but by the end of the 1920s the work of Thurber, White, and his other staff writers had edged the magazine a little nearer to Ross's ambition to achieve an immaculate literary style. In spite of the Depression, the* New Yorker *went into the thirties in good shape. It had earned a reputation for sophistication and innovation and was attracting contributions from the best young cartoonists and fiction writers. What the magazine now needed was what* Punch *had lacked in its early days, a popular humorous series with such wide appeal that it would set the town talking and make the magazine required reading for anybody who wanted to stay in the conversation.* Punch *managed it with Douglas Jerrold's 'Mrs Caudle's Curtain Lectures', and Ross did the same with Clarence Day's* Life with Father.

Clarence Day, son of a Wall Street broker, a Yale graduate, retired ill from the navy and became a journalist and essayist. He also drew cartoons in a simplistic, naïve style which anticipated James Thurber. In the early 1930s he sent to the New Yorker *some stories of his home life as the child of a rich New York family in the late 1800s. Ross printed them as a series and the response was dramatic. They really did become a talking point among New Yorkers and the magazine's circulation leaped up and continued to rise from then on.*

Life with Father, *as the stories came to be called, was probably the most successful American domestic humour written between the two wars. The resultant book was a best-seller, a dramatized version became Broadway's longest-running play, Hollywood made it into an enjoyable film, then came a television series ...*

The humour did not fit at all into the developing and distinctive New Yorker *schools of calm sophistication. The stories, sentimental and cosy, could well have been published by any magazine. They were, in effect, a return to the tradition of 'local colour' writing; a nostalgic evocation of simpler, quieter times when America seemed somehow to be more American.*

Life with Father *was set in a wealthy part of New York in the 1880s, and told of how young Clarence, with his mother and his brother, coped with their domineering, very* Victorian *paterfamilias, who held strong views on practically everything. When he made up his mind that something should be done, he not only did it but invariably overdid it.*

Father has taken a house for the summer on a hill overlooking the Hudson River:

FATHER WAKES UP THE VILLAGE

One of the most disgraceful features of life in the country, Father often declared, was the general inefficiency and slackness of small village tradesmen. He said he had originally supposed that such men were interested in business, and that that was why they had opened their shops and sunk capital in them, but no, they never used them for anything but gossip and sleep. They took no interest in civilized ways. Hadn't heard of them, probably. He said that of course if he were camping out on the veldt or the tundra, he would expect few conveniences in the neighbourhood and would do his best to forgo them, but why should he be confronted with the wilds twenty miles from New York?

Usually, when Father talked this way, he was thinking of ice. He strongly objected to spending even one day of his life without a glass of cold water beside his plate at every meal.

Then one very hot summer day, disaster strikes. The ice is not delivered to accompany Father's dinner when he arrives hot and tired from the city: the ice-man would not make his horse toil up the hill just for 60 cents-worth of ice and the ice had melted in the heat anyway.

The arrival home of Father is not looked forward to with pleasure by his small son, the narrator:

It was a long afternoon.

At five o'clock Brownie was hitched up again. The coachman and I drove back to the village. We had to meet Father's train. We also had to break the bad news to him that he would have no ice-water for dinner, and that there didn't seem to be any way to chill his Rhine wine.

The village was as sleepy as ever, but when Father arrived and learned what the situation was, he said it would have to wake up. He told me that he had had a long, trying day at the office, the city was hotter than the Desert of Sahara, and he was completely worn out, but that if any ice-man imagined for a moment he could behave in that manner, he, Father, would take his damned head off. He strode into the Coal & Ice Office.

When he came out, he had the clerk with him, and the clerk had put on his hat and was trying to calm Father down. He was promising that he himself would come with the ice-wagon if the driver had left, and deliver all the ice we could use, and he'd be there inside an hour.

Father said, 'Inside of an hour be hanged; you'll have to come quicker than that!'

The clerk got rebellious. He pointed out that he would have to go to the stables and hitch up the horses himself, and then get someone to help him hoist a block of ice out of the ice-house. He said it was 'most time for his supper and he wasn't used to such work. He was only doing it as a favour to Father. He was just being neighbourly.

Father said he'd have to be neighbourly in a hurry, because he wouldn't stand it, and he didn't know what the ice company meant by such actions.

The clerk said it wasn't his fault, was it? It was the driver's.

This was poor tactics, of course, because it wound Father up again. He wasn't interested in whose fault it was, he said. It was everybody's. What he wanted was ice and plenty of it, and he wanted it in time for his dinner. A small crowd which had collected by this time listened admiringly as Father shook his finger at the clerk and said he dined at six-thirty.

The clerk went loping off towards the stables to hitch up the big horses. Father waited till he'd turned the corner.

Followed by the crowd, Father marched to the butcher's.

After nearly a quarter of an hour, the butcher and his assistant came out, unwillingly carrying what seemed to be a coffin wrapped in a black mackintosh. It was a huge cake of ice.

Father got in, in front, sat on the box seat beside me, and took up the reins. We drove off. The coachman was on the back seat, sitting back-to-back to us, keeping the ice from sliding out with the calves of his legs. Father went a few doors up the street to a little house-furnishing shop and got out again.

I went in the shop with him this time. I didn't want to miss any further scenes of this performance. Father began proceedings by demanding to see all the man's ice-boxes. There were only a few. Father selected the largest he had. Then, when the sale seemed arranged, and when the proprietor was smiling broadly with pleasure at this sudden windfall, Father said he was buying the refrigerator only on two conditions.

The first was that it had to be delivered at his home before dinner. Yes, now. Right away. The shopkeeper explained over and over that this was impossible, but that he'd have it up the next morning, sure. Father said, no, he didn't want it the next morning, he had to have it at once. He added that he dined at six-thirty, and that there was no time to waste.

The shopkeeper gave in.

The second condition, which was then put to him firmly, was staggering. Father announced that the ice-box must be delivered to him full of ice.

The man said he was not in the ice business.

Father said, 'Very well then. I don't want it.'

The man said obstinately that it was an excellent ice-box.

Father made a short speech. It was the one that we had heard so often at home about the slackness of village tradesmen, and he put such strong emotion and scorn in it that his voice rang through the shop. He closed it by saying, 'An ice-box is of no value to a man without ice, and if you haven't the enterprise, the gumption, to sell your damned goods to a customer who wants them delivered in condition to use, you had better shut up your shop and be done with it. Not in the ice business, hey? You aren't in business at all!' He strode out.

The dealer came to the door just as Father was getting into the dog-cart, and called out anxiously, 'All right, Mr Day. I'll get that refrigerator filled for you and send it up right away.'

Father drove quickly home. A thunderstorm seemed to be brewing, and this had waked Brownie up, or else Father was putting some of his own supply of energy into him. The poor old boy probably needed it as again he climbed the steep hill. I got out at the foot, and as I walked along behind I saw that Morgan was looking kind of desperate, trying to sit in the correct position with his arms folded while he held in the ice with his legs. The big cake was continually slipping and sliding around under the seat and doing its best to plunge out. It had bumped around his calves all the way home. They must have got good and cold.

When the dog-cart drew up at our door, Father remained seated a moment while Morgan, the waitress, and I pulled and pushed at the ice. The mackintosh had come off by this time. We dumped it out on the grass. A little later, after Morgan had unharnessed and hurriedly rubbed down the horse, he ran back to help us boys break the cake up, push the chunks around to the back door, and cram them into the ice-box while Father was dressing for dinner.

Mother had calmed down by this time. The Rhine wine was cooling. 'Don't get it too cold,' said Father.

Then the ice-man arrived.

The old clerk was with him, like a warden in charge of a prisoner. Mother stepped out to meet them, and at once gave the ice-man the scolding that had been waiting for him all day.

The clerk asked how much ice we wanted. Mother said we didn't want any now. Mr Day had brought home some, and we had no room for more in the ice-box.

The ice-man looked at the clerk. The clerk tried to speak, but no words came.

Father put his head out of the window. 'Take a hundred pounds, Vinnie,' he said. 'There's another box coming.'

A hundred-pound block was brought into the house and heaved into the washtub. The waitress put the mackintosh over it. The ice-wagon left.

Just as we all sat down to dinner the new ice-box arrived, full.

Mother was provoked. She said, 'Really, Clare!' crossly. 'Now what am I to do with that piece that's waiting out in the washtub?'

Father chuckled.

She told him he didn't know the first thing about keeping house, and went out to the laundry with the waitress to tackle the problem. The thunderstorm broke and crashed. We boys ran around shutting the windows upstairs.

Father's soul was at peace. He dined well, and he had his coffee and cognac served to him on the piazza. The storm was over by then. Father snuffed a deep breath of the sweet-smelling air and smoked his evening cigar.

'Clarence,' he said, 'King Solomon had the right idea about these things. "Whatsoever thy hand findeth to do," Solomon said, "do thy damnedest".'

Mother called me inside. 'Whose mackintosh is that?' she asked anxiously. 'Katie's torn a hole in the back.'

I heard Father say contentedly on the piazza, 'I like plenty of ice.'

Clarence Day (1874–1935), Life With Father (1935).

━━━━━━━━

M ANY *more series of stories based upon a single situation or character landed on the* New Yorker *editors' desks in the thirties.*

One of these, another big success, came from Leo Rosten, a Polish-born lecturer, political scientist, and author of economic analyses. At one time Rosten had earned his living teaching English to a class of adult immigrants. Using a pen-name, 'Leonard Q. Ross', he wrote and submitted a series of sketches based upon the colourful characters in his old class. The stories were centred upon the keenest student, Mr Hyman Kaplan (Evelyn Waugh called him 'the magnificent Mr Kaplan' and thought the stories 'immensely funny').

Mr Kaplan, portly, perpetually smiling, optimistic, is tireless in his determination to overcome the initial difficulties and, as soon as possible, speak perfect English:

THE EDUCATION OF H*Y*M*A*N K*A*P*L*A*N

In the third week of the new term, Mr Parkhill was forced to the conclusion that Mr Kaplan's case was rather difficult. Mr Kaplan first came to his special attention, out of the thirty-odd adults in the beginners' grade of the American Night Preparatory School for Adults ('English—Americanization—Civics—Preparation for Naturalization'), through an exercise the class had submitted. The exercise was entitled 'Fifteen Common Nouns and Their Plural Forms'. Mr Parkhill came to one paper which included the following:

house	makes	.... houses
dog	„	.... dogies
library	„	.... Public library
cat	„	.... Katz

Mr Parkhill read this over several times, very thoughtfully. He decided that here was a student who might, unchecked, develop into a 'problem case'. It was clearly a case that called for special attention. He turned the page over and read the name. It was printed in large, firm letters with red crayon. Each letter was outlined in blue. Between every two letters was a star, carefully drawn, in green. The multi-colored whole spelled, unmistakably, H*Y*M*A*N K*A*P*L*A*N.

This Mr Kaplan was in his forties, a plump, red-faced gentleman, with wavy blond hair, two fountain pens in his outer pocket, and a perpetual smile. It was a strange smile, Mr Parkhill remarked: vague, bland, and consistent in its monotony. The thing that emphasized it for Mr Parkhill was that it never seemed to leave the face of Mr Kaplan, even during Recitation and Speech period. This disturbed Mr Parkhill considerably, because Mr Kaplan was particularly bad in Recitation and Speech.

Mr Parkhill decided he had not applied himself as conscientiously as he might to Mr Kaplan's case. That very night he called on Mr Kaplan first.

'Won't you take advantage of Recitation and Speech practice, Mr Kaplan?' he asked, with an encouraging smile.

Mr Kaplan smiled back and answered promptly, 'Vell, I'll tell abot Prazidents United States. Fife Prazidents United States is Abram Lincohen, he vas freeink de neegers; Hodding, Coolitch, Judge Vashington, an' Banjamin Frenklin.'

Further encouragement revealed that in Mr Kaplan's literary Valhalla the 'most famous tree american wriders' were Jeck Laundon, Valt Viterman, and the author of 'Hawk L. Barry-Feen', one Mock-tvain. Mr Kaplan took pains to point out that he did not mention Relfvaldo Amerson because 'He is a poyet, an' I'm talkink abot wriders.'

Mr Parkhill diagnosed the case as one of 'inability to distinguish between "a" and "e"'. He concluded that Mr Kaplan *would* need special attention. He was frankly, a little disturbed.

Mr Kaplan's English showed no improvement during the next hard weeks. The originality of his spelling and pronunciation, however, flourished—like a sturdy flower in the good, rich earth. A man to whom 'Katz' is the plural of 'cat' soon soars into higher and more ambitious endeavor. As a one-paragraph 'Exercise in Composition', Mr Kaplan submitted:

When people is meating on the boulvard, on going away one is saying, 'I am glad I mat you,' and the other is giving answer, 'Mutual.'

Mr Parkhill felt that perhaps Mr Kaplan had overreached himself, and should be confined to the simpler exercises.

Mr Kaplan was an earnest student. He worked hard, knit his brows regularly (albeit with that smile), did all his homework, and never missed a class. Only once did Mr Parkhill feel that Mr Kaplan might, perhaps, be a little more *serious* about his work. That was when he asked Mr Kaplan to give a noun.

'Door,' said Mr Kaplan, smiling.

It seemed to Mr Parkhill that 'door' had been given only a moment earlier, by Miss Mitnick.

'Y-es,' said Mr Parkhill. 'Er—and another noun?'

'Another door,' Mr Kaplan replied promptly.

Mr Parkhill put him down as a doubtful 'C'. Everything pointed to the fact that Mr Kaplan might have to be kept on an extra three months before he was ready for promotion to Composition, Grammar, and Civics, with Miss Higby.

One night Mrs Moskowitz read a sentence, from 'English for Beginners', in which 'the vast deserts of America' were referred to. Mr Parkhill soon discovered that poor Mrs Moskowitz did not know the meaning of 'vast'. 'Who can tell us the meaning of "vast?"' asked Mr Parkhill lightly.

Mr Kaplan's hand shot up, volunteering wisdom. He was all proud grins. Mr Parkhill, in the rashness of the moment, nodded to him.

Mr Kaplan rose, radiant with joy. '"Vast!" It's commink from *diraction*. Ve have four diractions: de naut, de sot, de heast, and de vast.'

Mr Parkhill shook his head. 'Er—that is "west", Mr Kaplan.' He wrote 'vast' and 'west' on the blackboard. To the class he added, tolerantly, that Mr Kaplan was apparently thinking of 'west', whereas it was 'vast' which was under discussion.

This seemed to bring a great light into Mr Kaplan's inner world. 'So is "vast" vat you eskink?'

Mr Parkhill admitted that it was 'vast' for which he was asking.

'Aha!' cried Mr Kaplan. 'You minn "*vast*" not'—with scorn—'"*vast*."'

'Yes,' said Mr Parkhill, faintly.

'Hau Kay!' said Mr Kaplan, essaying the vernacular. 'Ven I'm buyink a suit clothes, I'm gattink de cawt, de pents, an' de vast!'

Stunned, Mr Parkhill shook his head, very sadly. 'I'm afraid that you've used still another word, Mr Kaplan.'

Oddly enough, this seemed to give Mr Kaplan great pleasure.

Several nights later Mr Kaplan took advantage of Open Questions period.

This ten-minute period was Mr Parkhill's special innovation in the American Night Preparatory School for Adults. It was devoted to answering any questions which the students might care to raise about any difficulties which they might have encountered during the course of their adventures with the language. Mr Parkhill enjoyed Open Questions. He liked to clear up *practical* problems. He felt he was being ever so much more constructive that way. Miss Higby had once told him that he was a born Open Questions teacher.

'Plizz, Mr Pockheel,' asked Mr Kaplan as soon as the period opened. 'Vat's de minnink fromm—'. It sounded, in Mr Kaplan's rendition, like 'a big department'.

'"A big department", Mr Kaplan?' asked Mr Parkhill, to make sure.

'Yassir!' Mr Kaplan's smile was beauteous to behold. 'In de stritt, ven I'm valkink, I'm hearink like "I big de pottment".'

It was definitely a pedagogical opportunity.

'Well, class,' Mr Parkhill began. 'I'm sure that you have all—'

He told them that they had all probably done some shopping in the large downtown stores. (Mr Kaplan nodded.) In these large stores, he said, if they wanted to buy a pair of shoes, for example, they went to a special *part of* the store, where only shoes were sold—a *shoe* department. (Mr Kaplan nodded.) If they wanted a table, they went to a different *part* of the store, where *tables* were sold. (Mr Kaplan nodded.) If they wanted to buy, say, a goldfish, they went to still another part of the store, where goldfish ... (Mr Kaplan frowned; it was clear that Mr Kaplan had never bought a goldfish.)

'Well, then,' Mr Parkhill summed up hastily, 'each article is sold in a different *place*. These different and special places are called *departments*.' He printed 'D-E-P-A-R-T-M-E-N-T' on the board in large, clear capitals. And a *big* department, Mr Kaplan, is merely such a department which is large—*big!*'

He put the chalk down and wiped his fingers.

'Is that clear now, class?' he asked, with a little smile. (It was rather an ingenious explanation, he thought; it might be worth repeating to Miss Higby during the recess.)

It *was* clear. There were thirty nods of approval. But Mr Kaplan looked uncertain. It was obvious that Mr Kaplan, a man who would not compromise with truth, did *not* find it clear.

'Isn't that clear *now*, Mr Kaplan?' asked Mr Parkhill anxiously.

Mr Kaplan pursed his lips in thought. 'It's a *fine* haxplination, Titcher,' he said generously, 'but I don' unnistand vy I'm hearink de voids de vay I do. Simms to me it's used in annodder minnink.'

'There's really only one meaning for "a big department".' Mr Parkhill was definitely worried by this time. '*If* that's the phrase you mean.'

Mr Kaplan nodded gravely. 'Oh, dat's de phrase—ufcawss! It sonds like dat—or maybe a lettle more like "I big de pottment".'

Mr Parkhill took up the chalk. ('*I* big department' was obviously a case of

Mr Kaplan's own curious audition.) He repeated the explanation carefully, this time embellishing the illustrations with a shirt department, a victrola section, and 'a separate part of the store where, for example, you buy canaries, or other birds'.

Mr Kaplan sat entranced. He followed it all politely, even the part about 'canaries, or other birds'. He smiled throughout with consummate reassurance.

Mr Parkhill was relieved, assuming, in his folly, that Mr Kaplan's smiles were a testimony to his exposition. But when he had finished, Mr Kaplan shook his head once more, this time with a new and superior firmness.

'Is the explanation *still* not clear?' Mr Parkhill was genuinely concerned by this time.

'Is de haxplination clear!' cried Mr Kaplan with enthusiasm. 'Ha! I should live so! Soitinly! Clear like *gold*! So clear! An' netcheral too! But Mr Pockheel—'

'Go on, Mr Kaplan,' said Mr Parkhill, studying the white dust on his fingers. There was, after all, nothing more to be done.

'Vell! I think it's more like "I big depottment".'

'Go on, Mr Kaplan, go on.' (*Domine, dirige nos.*)

Mr Kaplan rose. His smile was broad, luminous, transcendent; his manner was regal.

'I'm hearink it in de stritt. Somtimes I'm stendink in de stritt, talkink to a frand, or mine vife, mine brodder—or maybe only stendink. An' somvun is pessink arond me. An' by hexident he's givink me a bump you know, a *poosh*! Vell, he says, "Axcuse me!" no? But sometimes, an' *dis* is vat I minn, he's sayink "*I big de pottment!*"'

Mr Parkhill studied the picture of 'Abram Lincohen' on the back wall, as if reluctant to face reality. He wondered whether he could reconcile it with his conscience if he were to promote Mr Kaplan to Composition, Grammar, and Civics—at once. Another three months of Recitation and Speech might, after all, be nothing but a waste of Mr Kaplan's valuable time.

> 'Leonard Q. Ross' (Leo Rosten) (b.1908), *The Education of H*y*m*a*n K*a*p*l*a*n* (1937).

As the the New Yorker's *prestige rose, so it was increasingly bombarded with unsolicited contributions from hopeful young humorists. Most of these pieces were, in the nature of things, useless, but in one or two rare instances the writers had real talent and a style which suited the* New Yorker, *and the combination of healthy seedling in the right soil produced some fine results.*

The most spectacularly successful humorist so nourished was S. J. Perelman, arguably the most original—and funniest—comic prose stylist of the present century, who wrote his best work from 1935 on when he became a regular contributor to the magazine.

Sidney (really Simeon) Joseph Perelman first had a submitted piece accepted by the New Yorker *in 1930. It was a typical Perelman idea based on a newspaper item about a woman who claimed that the oddest sight she had ever seen was a drunk kissing the statue of a horse in the middle of a fountain. Perelman claimed to be the man in question and wrote the lady an aggrieved open letter: 'Things have come to a pretty pass indeed when a taxpayer can't step into a park without a covey of spies like yourself skulking in the shrubbery . . . I suppose you were sitting up with a sick rhododendron . . .'*

Perelman was then aged 26 and had already published two books, a collection of humorous pieces mainly written for Judge *magazine, and an awful comic novel, which he wrote with Quentin Reynolds, called* Parlor, Bedlam and Bath. *This last was Perelman's only attempt at a long, sustained piece of writing.*

His parents were immigrant Russian Jews and he was born in Brooklyn. When he was still young the family moved to Providence, Rhode Island. He worked at various manual jobs and went on to Brown University where he became cartoonist of the college magazine. In later years he lived in a country house in Erwinna, Pennsylvania, where he wrote numerous prose pieces and some unsuccessful Broadway plays.

Perelman's part-time jobs while he was at school, which became useful source material later, provided him with the pocket money he needed to haunt the local cinema and buy magazines and books, which were his escape from life on the run-down chicken farm which was slowly ruining his father.

His main interest was in drawing cartoons. At Brown University, an establishment for the sons of wealthy men, he was a day student, which was cheaper, and in his spare time he worked in an electroplating works and in various shops to help support his family. Being a Jew he was ineligible for election to a college fraternity. Unlike most other students he became deeply impressed with European literature, particularly the works of Joseph Conrad and James Joyce, and he became a fervent Anglophile. So in a rich, sports-conscious university the shy, shabby, literary Perelman was something of an outsider. His best friend, and a lasting influence, was another Jewish outsider, the (temporarily) rich, stylish, fellow-intellectual Nathan Weinstein, who was later to change his name and become the novelist 'Nathaniel West'.

Weinstein was a snappy dresser. Later on, when Perelman was working and able to afford such luxuries, he bought himself well-cut English tweeds and good brogue shoes, sported a perfectly tied tie (with a Windsor knot) and was a noticeably dapper figure for the rest of his life.

Perelman provided many of the cartoons and designs for the university magazine, The Brown Jug, *and in his last year became its editor, which meant that he had to write more. This came relatively easily because since a child he had been fascinated by words for their own sake; they had become a kind of hobby. He did not speak Yiddish—his family was not religious—but he began to memorize Yiddish words for the sheer enjoyment of them. At Brown he took courses in Italian, German, Latin, and French, and went on collecting words and phrases as keenly as his fellow students set about accumulating sports trophies, sorority pins, and virginities.*

Trigonometry was beyond Perelman, and his case was not helped by upsetting the college authorities with his vigorous editorials championing the anti-Philistine views of the dreaded H. L. Mencken, so he left Brown without a degree and set out to make his living as a cartoonist. He got a job with Judge *magazine providing two cartoons and one humour piece a week. The cartoons were mostly mock woodcuts of 1890s sentimentality or somewhat surreal drawings of men doing odd things like sitting on sheep, with even odder captions ('I've Got Bright's Disease and He's Got Mine'). His written humour was much influenced by George Ade and Ring Lardner (he admitted later in life 'I was such a Lardner thief I should have been arrested'). In 1929 he married Nathaniel West's sister Laura and published his first book, a collection of forty-nine pieces from* Judge *which he called* Dawn Ginsbergh's Revenge *(he later became ashamed of it, refused to let it be republished and it is now virtually a collector's item.)*

A knockabout vaudeville act made up of four brothers had been such a sensation on Broadway that the publishers sent them a proof copy of Perelman's book in the hope of getting a quote which could be printed on the cover. Back came: 'From the moment I picked up your book until I laid it down, I was convulsed with laughter. Someday I intend reading it. Groucho Marx.'

The book did not do well but Groucho invited Perelman and another cartoonist whose humour he liked, Will Johnstone, to write an original scenario for the Marx Brothers' next movie. Johnstone and the Perelmans moved to California to work on the script of this film, Monkey Business, *and Perelman hated Hollywood on sight ('a dreary industrial town controlled by hoodlums of enormous wealth, the ethical sense of a pack of jackals, and taste so degraded that it befouled everything it touched').*

Perelman's opinion of the movie capital was not sweetened when he returned to work on his second (and for him his last) Marx Brothers film, Horse Feathers. *But, the pay was good in Hollywood and he and his wife worked together for years, on and off, as studio contract writers, contributing anonymously to a string of undistinguished gangster movies, comedy thrillers, and musicals.*

His experiences of the Hollywood production-machine in operation prompted him to write a satirical piece, 'Scenario', for a short-lived little arts magazine called Contact *co-edited by his brother-in-law Nathaniel West.*

The humour of 'Scenario' is bitter and the structure of the piece is quite different from Perelman's later work. He illustrates the materialism and the uncreative, second-hand thinking of studio story-conferences mainly through the use of movie clichés, which he weaves into an extraordinary flow of James Joyce-inspired free association:

SCENARIO

Fade in, exterior grassy knoll, long shot. Above the scene the thundering measures of Von Suppe's 'Light Cavalry Overture'. Austerlitz? The Plains of

Abraham? Vicksburg? The Little Big Horn? Cambrai? Steady on, old son; it is Yorktown. Under a blood-red setting sun yon proud crest is Cornwallis. Blood and 'ouns, proud sirrah, dost brush so lightly past an exciseman of the Crown? Lady Rotogravure's powdered shoulders shrank from the highwayman's caress; what, Jermyn, footpads on Hounslow Heath? A certain party in the D.A.'s office will hear of this, you bastard. There was a silky insolence in his smile as he drew his greatcoat about his face and leveled his shooting-stick at her dainty puss. Leave go that lady or I'll smear yer. No quarter, eh? Me, whose ancestors scuttled stately India merchantmen of their comfits and silken stuffs and careened their piratical craft in the Dry Tortugas to carouse with bumboat women till the cock crew? Yuh'll buy my booze or I'll give yuh a handful of clouds. Me, whose ancestors rode with Yancey, Jeb Stuart, and Joe Johnston through the dusty bottoms of the Chickaumaga? Oceans of love, but not one cent for tribute. Make a heel out of a guy whose grandsire, Olaf Hasholem, swapped powder and ball with the murderous Sioux through the wheels of a Conestoga waggon, who mined the yellow dirt with Sutter and slapped nuggets across the rude bars of Leadville and Goldfield? One side, damn your black hide, suh, or Ah'll send mo' dirty Litvak to the boneyard. It's right up the exhibitor's alley, Mr Biberman, and you got to hand it to them on a platter steaming hot. I know, Stanley, but let's look at this thing reasonable; we've been showing the public Folly Larrabee's drawers two years and they been cooling off. Jeez Crize—it's a hisTORical drama, Mr Biberman, it'll blow 'em outa the back of the houses, it's the greatest thing in the industry, it's dynamite! Pardon me, officer, is that General Washington? Bless yer little heart, mum, and who may yez be, savin' yer prisince? Honest old Brigid the applewoman of Trinity, is it? How dégagé he sits on his charger, flicking an infinitesimal speck of ash from his plumcoloured waistcoat! Gentlemen, I give you Martha Custis, hetman of the Don Cossacks, her features etched with the fragile beauty of a cameo. And I walked right in on her before she had a chance to pull the god-damned kimono together . . . Got you in the groin that time, General! Mine host, beaming genially, rubbing his hands and belching. Get Anderson ready with the sleighbells and keep that snow moving. Hit 'em all! Hotter on eighty-four, Joe Devlin! Are we up to speed? Quiet, please, we're turning! Chicago, hog-butcher to the world, yclept the Windy City. BOOZE AND BLOOD, he oughta know, running a drugstore for eleven years on Halstead Street. You cut to the back of the Big Fellow, then three lap dissolves of the presses— give 'em that Ufa stuff, then to the street—a newsbody, insert of the front page, the El roaring by—Kerist, it's the gutsiest thing in pictures! Call you back, chief. Never mind the Hays office, this baby is censor-proof! Call you back, chief. We'll heave the telephone through the glass door and smack her in the kisser with the grapefruit, they liked it once and they'll love it twice. Call you back, chief. The gat in the mesh-bag. A symbol, get me? . . . A warm, vivid and human story with just that touch of muff the fans enjoy . . . You didn't know that she was the morganatic wife of Prince Rupprecht, *did* you? That her affairs with men were the talk of Vienna, *did* you? That—Vanya, is this true? Bowed head, for her man. His boyish tousled head clean-cut against the twilight. Get out. *Get out.* GET OUT! Oh, mumsie, I want to die. That hooker's gotta lay off that booze, Mr Metz, once more she comes on the set stinking and I take the next boat back to Buda-Pesth. But in a great tangled garden sits a forlorn, tragic-eyed figure; the face a mask of carved ivory, the woman nobody knows—Tilly Bergstrom. What lies behind her shattered romance with Grant Snavely, idol of American flaps? Turn 'em over, you punks, I'll stay on this set till I get it right. Cheese it, de nippers! The jig is up, long live the jig—ring out the old, ring in the new. For love belongs to everyone, the best things in life are free.

S. J. Perelman (1904–79), Contact, reprinted: Crazy Like a Fox (1944).

By now Perelman had given up being a cartoonist and was a full-time professional writer; very professional, in fact, in that his sole ambition was to become extremely rich as quickly as possible ('I loathe writing,' he once said, 'but I'm a great believer in money').

His career as a hack movie scenarist was getting nowhere so he tried to write a hit Broadway play to augment his adequate but unspectacular income from radio and theatre sketches and magazine pieces. He and Laura wrote several plays which were produced, but none of them succeeded. One of the problems was that he had no gift for natural dialogue. The people in his plays tended to speak like cartoon characters, in funny parodies of real speech.

But Perelman's pastiche dialogue, agony though it must have been for actors to play, worked beautifully on the printed page and he used it effectively in his prose pieces, frequently switching styles from one character to another and back again. These dialogue sequences were usually in the form of a playlet dramatizing some loony situation which he had read about in a newspaper such as the predicament of the Woolworths heiress, Barbara Hutton, whose estranged husband, in a moment of pique, infuriated her by revealing to their son Lance that the family fortune came from the Woolworths chain of stores.

Perelman ponders how young Lance took the shameful news that his mother's money came from forty or fifty thousand ten-cent stores. Did he force his father to his knees and demand retraction of the slur? Did he fling himself, with a choked cry, into his mummy's lap, all tears and disillusion?:

HOW SHARPER THAN A SERPENT'S TOOTH

SCENE: *The library of the luxurious Park Avenue triplex of Mr and Mrs Leotard Allardyce DuPlessis Weatherwax. The furnishings display taste but little ostentation: a couple of dozen Breughels, fifteen or twenty El Grecos, a sprinkling of Goyas, a smidgen of Vermeers. The room has a lived-in air: a fistful of loose emeralds lies undusted in an ash tray, and the few first folios in evidence are palpably dog-eared. The curtain rises on a note of marital discord. Octavia*

*Weatherwax, a chic, poised woman in her mid-forties, has just picked up a bust
of Amy Lowell by Jacob Epstein and smashed it over her husband's head. Milo,
a portly, well-groomed man of fifty, spits out a tooth, catches up a bust of
Epstein by Amy Lowell, and returns the compliment.*

OCTAVIA (*brushing plaster from her coiffure*): Listen, Milo, we can't go on this
way.

MILO: Why not? I've still got this left. (*He picks up a bust of Amy Epstein by
Lowell Thomas.*)

OCTAVIA: No, no, this is the handwriting on the wall. Our marriage is washed
up—napoo—*ausgespielt.*

MILO: Maybe you're right. I've felt for some time that things haven't been
the same between us.

OCTAVIA: Oh, well, the fat's in the fire. How are we to break the news to
Rapier?

MILO: Rapier? What Rapier is that?

OCTAVIA: Why, our nineteen-year-old son, whom he's home from Yale on
his midyears and don't suspicion that his folks are rifting.

MILO: Oh, yes. Where is our cub at the present writing?

OCTAVIA: In the tack room, furbishing up the accouterments of his polo
ponies.

MILO (*acidly*): Far better off to be furbishing up on his Euclid, lest he drag the
name of Weatherwax through the scholastic mire.

OCTAVIA: Shhhh, here he comes now. (*The sound of expensive Scotch brogues
approaching on a parquet floor is heard, an effect achieved by striking two
coconut shells together.*) If you need me, I shall be laying down on my lounge
with a vinegar compress. (*She exits as Rapier enters—a rather awkward bit
of stagecraft, as they trip over each other, but if the play runs, the property man
can always saw another door in the set. Rapier, albeit somewhat spoiled, is a
blueblood to his finger tips, carries his head and feet as though to the manner
born.*)

RAPIER: Hiya, Jackson. What's buzzin' cousin?

MILO: Humph. Is that some of your new-fangled college slang?

RAPIER: Don't be a sherbert, Herbert. (*Lighting a gold-monogrammed Egyptian
Prettiest*) What's cookin', good-lookin'?

MILO (*gravely*): Son, I'm not going to mince words with you.

RAPIER: Don't mince, quince. I'm waitin', Satan.

MILO: My boy, the Weatherwax union has blown a gasket. Our frail matri-
monial bark, buffeted by the winds of temperament, has foundered on the
shoals of incompatability.

RAPIER: Get in the groove, fatso. I don't latch on to that long-hair schmaltz.

MILO: To employ the vulgate, your mother and I have pphhht.

RAPIER (*with quick sympathy*): That's rum, chum.

MILO: Yes, it's hard on us oldsters, but it isn't going to be easy for you,
either.

RAPIER (*frightened*): You mean I've got to go to work?

MILO: Certainly not. As long as there's a penny of your mother's money left, we'll make out somehow.

RAPIER: Look, guv'nor . . . that is, me . . . aw, cripes, can I ask you something man to man?

MILO (*aside*): I was afraid of this.

RAPIER: Well, I've been running with a pretty serious crowd up at New Haven—lots of bull sessions about swing and stuff—and I've been wondering. Where does our money come from?

MILO (*evasively*): Why—er—uh—the doctor brings it. In a little black bag.

RAPIER: Aw, gee, Dad, I'm old enough to know. *Please.*

MILO: There, there. Now run along and play with your ponies.

RAPIER: Wouldn't you rather tell me than have me learn it in the gutter?

MILO: We-e-ell, all right, but my, you children grow up quick nowadays. Have you ever heard of the Weatherwax All-Weather Garbage Disposal Plan?

RAPIER: You—you mean whereby garbage is disposed of in all weathers by having neatly uniformed attendants call for and remove it?

MILO: Yes. That is the genesis of our scratch.

RAPIER (*burying his face in his hands*): Oh, Daddy, I want to die!

MILO: Steady on, lad. After all, think of the millions which their flats would be a welter of chicken bones, fruit peels, and old teabags were it not for our kindly ministrations.

RAPIER (*sobbing*): I'll never be able to hold my head up in Bulldog circles again.

MILO: Nonsense. Why, you wear the keenest threads on the campus and are persona grata to myriad Eli frats.

RAPIER (*his face drawn and a new maturity in his voice*): No, Father, this is the end of halcyon days in the groves of Academe. I'm going away.

MILO: Where?

RAPIER: Somewhere beyond the horizon—to fabled Cathay or Samarkand and Ind, if needs be. Anywhere I can find other values than the tinkle of money and the clang of refuse cans.

MILO (*his eyes shining*): There speaks a Weatherwax, my boy. Here, I want you to have this little keepsake.

RAPIER: What is it?

MILO: A letter of credit for seven hundred grand. It won't buy much except dreams, but it belonged to your mother.

RAPIER: Thank you, sir. (*He starts out.*)

MILO: Wait a minute, I can't let you go like this. You'll need money, introductions, shelter—

RAPIER: I'll patch up that old private railroad car of mine—the one underneath the Waldorf-Astoria.

MILO: Take ours, too. It's only using up steam.

RAPIER (*simply*): I'm sorry, Dad. From now on I walk alone.

Good-bye. (*He exits, colliding with his mother—there simply* must *be two doors in this set. Octavia looks back at him, puzzled.*)

OCTAVIA: Why, goodness, what ails the child? What's that exalted look on his face?

MILO: That, Octavia, is what a very great Russian named Louis Tolstoy once called 'redemption'.

OCTAVIA: Milo! You didn't tell—you couldn't—

MILO (*his shoulders bowed*): It just soaked in through his pores. (*Octavia, her eyes tragic, picks up a bronze caryatid, smashes it over his head, and exits. He shrugs, picks up a Greek bacchante loitering in the wings, and consoles himself.*)

CURTAIN

The New Yorker, reprinted: *Keep It Crisp* (1946).

By the middle 1930s, Perelman's reputation as a humorist had grown considerably through his magazine pieces. The pot of gold which a Broadway hit represented still eluded him and he was reluctant to work any more in Hollywood; life as a hack writer was too depressing to justify the salary and working on the Marx Brothers movies had not been a happy experience; he was not used to writing in committee, nor of having his lines changed or thrown out because it was thought that they were too clever for audiences to understand. Although Perelman must have made a telling contribution to the two films it is also true that much of his work had gone for nothing. The Marx Brothers tended to treat a script as a basis upon which they themselves would build. Their preferred way of working was to agree upon an idea and have a scenario blocked out by experienced Broadway vaudeville writers like Morris Ryskind and Harry Ruby. The brothers, chiefly Groucho, would then alter the lines endlessly in rehearsal, often try out key scenes in a vaudeville theatre and rewrite them again, even give the completed film a sneak preview and make further changes.

Perelman was a precise and fastidious writer (he called himself a 'bleeder'). He liked to work alone, in silence, usually in a tiny bare room with a typewriter (and a photograph of James Joyce), no view from the window, hours 10 a.m.–6 p.m., six days a week. He selected his words with immense care and arranged them exactly. He claimed to rewrite a piece at least thirty times and when he made even a small correction he retyped the whole page. His rate of output averaged 1,000 words a working week (compare Anthony Trollope: 2,500 words before breakfast).

But for magazine humorists the wells were beginning to dry up. The public's appetite for humour was now being increasingly satisfied by radio and film comedy, and during the 1930s many of the old-established humour magazines went out of business, including Judge *and* College Humor, *both of which Perelman had worked on as a staff writer,* Life, Vanity Fair, *and* Ballyhoo.

Perelman was delighted and no doubt relieved when in 1935 he came to a working arrangement with the New Yorker *and became one of its regular contributors: the income was good and he could now concentrate on writing his comic essays, the only form of writing which he even remotely enjoyed.*

For the next thirty years S. J. Perelman's pieces in the New Yorker *were one of its most popular features. His work was circulated to a world-wide readership and he became internationally famous. His humour was particularly appreciated by British readers which, Anglophile that he was, pleased him. He had an understanding editor who did not fiddle with his prose or want him to tone down the erudite references and foreign phrases which bothered Broadway and the Marx Brothers but were an essential part of his idiosyncratic style. His work matured.*

In some of his pieces he had to appear as himself and for these he invented a comic persona. The fictional Perelman was, inevitably, inadequate, but in a new, very Perelman way; he was not a bumbler in the Benchley manner, nor a henpecked dreamer like Mitty, but a puny, cowardly, aggressive poseur, a would-be boulevardier whose trendy, intellectual patter ill-concealed a born loser.

Here we meet the fictional Perelman with a domestic problem; he has engaged a new cook:

KITCHEN BOUQUET

. . . The first reckless crocus of March was nosing up through the lawn as I sprang from the driver's seat, spread my cloak across a muddy spot, and obsequiously handed down Philomène Labruyère—colored, no laundry. Philomène was a dainty thing, built somewhat on the lines of Lois De Fee, the lady bouncer. She had the rippling muscles of a panther, the stolidity of a water buffalo, and the lazy insolence of a shoe salesman. She stood seventy-five inches in her stocking feet, which I will take my Bible oath were prehensile. As she bent down to lift her suitcase, she picked up the car by mistake and had it halfway down the slope before I pointed out her mistake. She acknowledged her mistake with a look of such sheer hatred that I knew at once I should have kept my lip buttoned. After all, perhaps the woman wanted my automobile in her bedroom for some purpose of her own.

'You—you can take it up with you if you want,' I stammered, thinking to retrieve her esteem. 'I've got plenty of others—I mean I've got plenty of nothing—I mean.' With my ears glowing, I attempted to conceal my *gaffe* by humming a few bars of 'Summertime', but her cold, appraising glance told me that Philomène had me pegged.

'Whuh kine place *is* this?' she rumbled suspiciously. 'You mus' be crazy.'

'But aren't we all?' I reminded her with a charming smile. '*C'est la maladie du temps*—the sickness of the times—don't you think? *Fin-de-siècle* and lost generations, in a way. "I should have been a pair of ragged claws scuttling across the floors of silent seas." How well Eliot puts it! D'ye ever see anything of the old *transition* crowd?' I skipped along doing my best to lighten her mood, carried her several hatboxes, and even proferred a reefer, but there was no doubt in either of our minds who had the upper hand.

That Philomène was a manic-depressive in the downhill phase was, of course, instantly apparent to a boy of five. Several boys of five, who happened to be standing around and were by way of being students of psychopathology, stated their belief to me in just those words: 'Manic-depressive, downhill phase.' At the close of business every evening, Philomène retired to her room armed with a sixteen-inch steak knife, doubtless to ward off an attack by her Poltergeist. She then spent the best part of an hour barricading her door with dressers, armoires, and other heavy furniture, preparatory to sleeping with the lights on. I say 'sleeping' utterly without conviction; she undoubtedly molded lead statues of her employer and crooned to them over a slow fire.

But if her behaviour was erratic, there was no lack of consistency in Philomène's cuisine. Meat loaf and cold fried chicken succeeded each other with the deadly precision of tracer bullets. At last, when blood and sinew could stand no more and I was about to dissolve the union, I suddenly discovered that this female Paul Bunyon had grown to womanhood under the bright skies of Martinique, and I knew a moment of elation. I let it be bruited through the servants' hall that I would look tolerantly on fried plantain, yams, and succulent rice dishes. That afternoon the kitchen was a hive of activity. The air was heavy with saffron, pimento, and allspice. I heard snatches of West Indian calypsos, caught a glimpse of Philomène's head swathed in a gay bandanna. With the care befitting a special occasion, I dressed negligently but with unimpeachable taste in whites and cummerbund, mixed myself several excellent stengahs, and sauntered to dinner for all the world like an up-country tea planter. A few moments later, Philomène entered with what might be called a smoking salver except for the circumstance that it was stone cold. On it lay the wing and undercarriage of an even colder chicken, flanked by two segments of meat loaf.

After five minutes of reflection, during which, I am told, my features closely resembled a Japanese print, I arose and, throwing out my tiny chest, marched into the kitchen. The maledictions withered on my lips. Seated at the table, my black hibiscus blossom was tucking in a meal consisting of *potage Parmentier avec croûtons*, a crisp *gigot*, *salade fatiguée*, and *pot de crème au chocolat*.

'You—thing,' I said at length, and five minutes later Philomène was on her way back to St Pierre.   *The New Yorker*, reprinted: *Crazy Like a Fox*

A Perelman speciality, soon taken up by other humorists and now commonplace, was to give his prose pieces funny punning titles.

Here are a representative few to give the flavour, chosen almost at random from hundreds:

> Beat me, Post-Impressionist Daddy
> Nothing but the Tooth
> Is there an Osteosynchrondroitrician in the House?
> Methinks He Doth Protein Too Much
> Carry Me Back to Old Pastrami
> No Starch in the Dhoti, *S'il Vous Plait*

De Gustibus Ain't What Dey Used to Be
The Yanks Are Coming, in Five Brilliant Colors
Personne Ici Except Us Chickens
It's Not the Heat, It's the Cupidity
Nothin' Could Be Finer Than to Dine from Manny's
      China in the Mornin'
Pale Hands I Loathe

Perelman once wrote that there was no such thing as 'kindly' humour and that he wrote his pieces from a sense of anger. It is true that his work was a long way from the old British tradition of sentimental comedy but it was not all that angry either. With a few exceptions, like 'Scenario', his subjects tended to be aspects of modern American life too trivial to warrant biting satire; it was enough for him to hold them up to our notice with a kind of wondering disbelief that such fatuity could exist.

In the following piece he is full of ironic praise for a peculiarly American phenomenon, the pulp magazine. His assumed delight knows no bounds when he happens upon a publication which combines the two most popular elements of pulp novelettes: sexually suggestive prose and violence:

SOMEWHERE A ROSCOE . . .

This is the story of a mind that found itself. About two years ago I was moody, discontented, restless, almost a character in a Russian novel. I used to lie in bed for days drinking tea out of a glass (I was one of the first in this country to drink tea out of a glass; at that time fashionable people drank from their cupped hands). Underneath, I was still a lively, fun-loving American boy who liked nothing better than to fish with a bent pin. In short, I had become a remarkable combination of Rashkolnikov and Mark Todd.

One day I realized how introspective I had grown and decided to talk to myself like a Dutch uncle. 'Luik here, Mynheer,' I began (I won't give you the accent, but honestly it was a riot), 'you're over-trained. Open up a few new vistas—go out and get some fresh air!' Well, I bustled about, threw some things into a bag—orange peel, apple cores and the like—and went out for a walk. A few minutes later I picked up from a park bench a tattered pulp magazine called *Spicy Detective*. . . . Talk about your turning points!

I hope nobody minds my making love in public, but if Culture Publications, Inc., of 900 Market Street, Wilmington, Delaware, will have me, I'd like to marry them. Yes, I know—call it a schoolboy crush, puppy love, the senseless infatuation of a callow youth for a middle-aged, worldly-wise publishing house; I still don't care. I love them because they are the publishers of not only *Spicy Detective* but also *Spicy Western* and *Spicy Adventure*. And I love them because their prose is so soft and warm.

'Arms and the man I sing', sang Vergil some twenty centuries ago, preparing to celebrate the wanderings of Aeneas. If ever a motto was tailor-made for the masthead of Culture Publications, Inc., it is 'Arms and the Woman', for in *Spicy Detective* they have achieved the sauciest blend of libido and murder this side of Gilles de Rais. They have juxtaposed the steely automatic and the frilly panty and found that it pays off. Above all, they have given the world Dan Turner, the apotheosis of all private detectives. Out of Ma Barker by Dashiell Hammett's Sam Spade, let him characterize himself in the opening paragraph of 'Corpse in the Closet', from the July 1937 issue:

I opened my bedroom closet. A half-dressed female corpse sagged into my arms . . . . It's a damned screwy feeling to reach for pyjamas and find a cadaver instead.

Mr Turner, you will perceive, is a man of sentiment, and it occasionally gets him into a tight corner. For example, in 'Killer's Harvest' (July 1938) he is retained to escort a young matron home from the Cocoanut Grove in Los Angeles:

Zarah Trenwick was a wow in a gown of silver lamé that stuck to her lush curves like a coating of varnish. Her make-up was perfect; her strapless dress displayed plenty of evidence that she still owned a cargo of allure. Her bare shoulders were snowy, dimpled. The upper slopes of her breast were squeezed upward and partly overflowed the tight bodice, like whipped cream.

To put it mildly, Dan cannot resist the appeal of a pretty foot, and disposing of Zarah's drunken husband ('I clipped him on the button. His hip pockets bounced on the floor'), he takes this charlotte russe to her apartment. Alone with her, the policeman in him succumbs to the man, and 'she fed me a kiss that throbbed all the way down my fallen arches', when suddenly:

From the doorway a roscoe said 'Kachow!' and a slug creased the side of my noggin. Neon lights exploded inside my think-tank . . . She was as dead as a stuffed mongoose . . . I wasn't badly hurt. But I don't like to be shot at. I don't like dames to be rubbed out when I'm flinging woo at them.

With an irritable shrug, Dan phones the homicide detail and reports Zarah's passing in this tender obituary: 'Zarah Trenwick just got blasted to hellangone in her tepee at the Gayboy. Drag your underwear over here—and bring a meat-wagon.' Then he goes in search of the offender:

I drove over to Argyll; parked in front of Fane Trenwick's modest stash . . . I thumbed the bell. The door opened. A Chink house-boy gave me the slant-eyed focus. 'Missa Tenwick, him sleep. You go way, come tomollow. Too late fo' vlisito'.' I said 'Nerts to you, Confucius,' and gave him a shove on the beezer.

Zarah's husband, wrenched out of bed without the silly formality of a search warrant, establishes an alibi depending upon one Nadine Wendell. In a trice Dan crosses the city and makes his gentle way into the lady's boudoir, only to discover again what a frail vessel he is *au fond*:

The fragrant scent of her red hair tickled my smeller; the warmth of her slim young form set fire to my arterial system. After all, I'm as human as the next gazebo.

The next gazebo must be all too human, because Dan betrays first Nadine and then her secret; namely that she pistoled Zarah Trenwick for reasons too numerous to mention. If you feel you must know them, they appear on page 110, cheek by jowl with some fascinating advertisements for loaded dice and wealthy sweethearts, either of which will be sent to you in plain wrapper if you'll forward a dollar to the Majestic Novelty Company of Janesville, Wisconsin.

The deeper one goes into the Dan Turner saga, the more one is struck by the similarity between the case confronting Dan in the current issue and those in the past. The murders follow an exact, rigid pattern almost like the bullfight or a classic Chinese play. Take 'Veiled Lady', in the October 1937 number of *Spicy Detective*. Dan is flinging some woo at a Mrs Brantham in her apartment at the exclusive Gayboy Arms, which apparently excludes everybody but assassins:

> From behind me a roscoe belched 'Chow-Chow!' A pair of slugs buzzed past my left ear, almost nicked my cranium. Mrs Brantham sagged back against the pillow of the lounge . . . She was as dead as an iced catfish.

Or this vignette from 'Falling Star', out of the September 1936 issue:

> The roscoe said 'Chow!' and spat a streak of flame past my shoulder . . . The Filipino cutie was lying where I'd last seen her. She was as dead as a smoked herring.

And again, from 'Dark Star of Death', January 1938:

> From a bedroom a roscoe said: 'Whr-r-rang!' and a lead pill split the ozone past my noggin . . . Kane Fewster was on the floor. There was a bullet-hole through his think-tank. He was as dead as a fried oyster.

And still again, from 'Brunette Bump-off ', May 1938:

> And then, from an open window beyond the bed, a roscoe coughed 'Ka-chow!'. . . I said, 'What the hell—!' and hit the floor with my smeller . . . A brunette jane was lying there, half out of the mussed covers . . . She was as dead as vaudeville.

The next phase in each of these dramas follows with all the cold beauty and inevitability of a legal brief. The roscoe has hardly spoken, coughed, or belched before Dan is off through the cornbrake, his nostrils heavy with the scent of Nuit de Noël. Somewhere, in some dimly lit boudoir, waits a voluptuous parcel of womanhood who knows all about the horrid deed. Even if she doesn't, Dan makes a routine check anyway. The premises are invariably guarded by an Oriental whom Dan is obliged to expunge. Compare the scene at Fane Trenwick's modest stash with this one from 'Find That Corpse' (November 1937):

> A sleepy chink maid in pajamas answered my ring. She was a cute little slant-eyed number. I said 'Is Mr Polznak home?' She shook her head. 'Him up on location in Flesno. Been gone two week.' I said 'Thanks. I'll have a gander for myself.' I pushed

past her. She started to yip . . . 'Shut up!' I growled. She kept on trying to make a noise. So I popped her on the button. She dropped.

It is a fairly safe bet that Mr Polznak has forgotten the adage that a watched pot never boils and has left behind a dewy-eyed coryphée clad in the minimum of chiffon demanded by the postal authorities. The poet in Dan ineluctably vanquishes the flatfoot ('Dark Star of Death'): 'I glued my glims on her blond loveliness; couldn't help myself. The covers had skidded down from her gorgeous, dimpled shoulders; I could see plenty of delishful, she-male epidermis.' The trumpets blare again; some expert capework from our *torero*, and ('Brunette Bump-off'): 'Then she fed me a kiss that sent a charge of steam past my gozzle . . . Well, I'm as human as the next gink.'

From then on, the author's typewriter keys infallibly fuse in a lump of hot metal and it's all over but the shouting of the culprit and '*Look, Men: One Hundred Breezy Fotos!*' Back in his stash, his roscoe safely within reach, Dan Turner lays his weary noggin on a pillow, resting up for the November issue. And unless you're going to need me for something this afternoon, I intend to do the same. I'm *bushed.*

The New Yorker, reprinted: *Crazy Like a Fox.*

Perelman extended his range with a number of travel pieces (the form was extremely well paid and he enjoyed travelling), a batch of excellent essays on the somewhat well-worn theme of a townee moving to the country, and a New Yorker *series under the title 'Cloudland Revisited' in which he re-examined, with dismay, the old best-selling novels and silent films which had given him so much pleasure as a boy.*

'Cloudland Revisited' proved to be the most popular of all his series ideas. The pieces had a pattern. He began each with appropriate reminiscences of his boyhood, introduced the old book or film, then, as it were, shook the dust out of it and held it up for our critical inspection, pointing out to us the twists the plot was taking and what the main characters were getting up to.

Alas, on revisiting the old silent epic The Four Horsemen of the Apocalypse *after a lapse of thirty years, the magic of Rudolph Valentino's acting and the relentless drama of the story did not quite exert the same grip on Perelman as they had done the first time round:*

CLOUDLAND REVISITED: IT TAKES TWO TO TANGO, BUT ONLY ONE TO SQUIRM

By current standards, the needs of a young man-about-town in Providence, Rhode Island, in 1921 were few—an occasional pack of straw-tipped Melachrinos, an evening of canoeing on the Ten Mile River, with its concomitant aphrodisiac, a pail of chocolate creams, and a mandatory thirty-five cents daily for admission to the movies. My fluctuating resources (most of the family's money evaporated in visionary schemes like a Yiddish musical-comedy production of *The Heart of Midlothian*) often forced me to abjure tobacco and amour, but I would sooner have parted with a lung than missed such epochal attractions as *Tol'able David* or Rudolph Valentino in *The Four Horsemen of the Apocalypse*, and I worked at some very odd jobs indeed to feed my addiction to the cinema. One of them, I recall, was electroplating radiators in a small, dismal factory that turned out automobile parts. It was an inferno of dust and noise; half a dozen presses, operated by as many scorbutic girls whose only diet seemed to be pork pies, were kept busy turning out the honeycomb radiators used in several cars at that time, and it was my task to baptize these artefacts in a huge vat filled with boiling acid. The fumes that rose from the immersion were so noisome that I lost eleven pounds and developed nightmares during which I shrieked like a brain-fever bird. Compelled under parental pressure to resign, I wheedled a job as clerk at the baked-goods counter of Shepard's, a department store that dealt in fancy groceries. Overnight my anemia magically vanished. Cramming myself with cinnamon buns, broken cookies, jelly doughnuts, ladyfingers, brownies, macaroons—anything I could filch while the floorwalker's back was turned— I blew up to fearful proportions. When not folding boxes or discomposing customers, I transported fresh stock from the bakery on the top floor of the building, a function that eventually led to my downfall. One afternoon, spotting a beguiling tureen, I snatched a heaping ladleful of what I thought was whipped cream but which proved to be marshmallow. Just as I was gagging horribly, I heard behind me the agonized whisper, 'Cheese it, here comes Mr Madigan!' and the floorwalker appeared, his mustache aquiver. He treated me to a baleful scrutiny, enquired whether I was subject to fits, and made a notation on his cuff. The following payday, my envelope contained a slip with a brief, unemotional dispatch. It stated that due to a country-wide shortage of aprons, the company was requisitioning mine and returning me to civilian life.

After a fortnight of leisure, my bloat had disappeared but so had my savings, and, unable to wangle credit or passes from the picture houses, I reluctantly took a job selling vacuum cleaners from door to door. The equipment that graced my particular model must have weighed easily three hundred pounds, and I spent a hideous day struggling on and off streetcars with it and beseeching suburban matrons to hold still for a demonstration. I was met everywhere by a vast apathy, if not open hostility; several prospects, in fact, saw fit to pursue me with brooms. Finally, a young Swedish housewife, too recent an immigrant to peg a tyro, allowed me to enter her bungalow. How I managed to blow all the fuses and scorch her curtains, I have no idea, but it happened in an *Augenblick*. The next thing I knew, I was fleeing through an azalea bed under a hail of Scandinavian cusswords, desperately hugging my appliance and coils of hose. The coup de grace came upon my return to the warehouse. It transpired that I had lost a nozzle and various couplings, elbows, and flanges, the cost of which I had to make good by pawning the household samovar.

*

It was more or less inevitable these early travails should return from limbo when, as happened recently, I settled myself into a projection room at the Museum of Modern Art with a print of *The Four Horsemen of the Apocalypse*. Actually, I would have much preferred to reinspect another vehicle of Valentino's called *Blood and Sand*, which co-starred Nita Naldi, down whom it used to be my boyhood ambition to coast on a Flexible Flyer, but the ravages of time had overtaken it. (Miss Naldi, *mirabile dictu*, is as symmetrical as ever.) *The Four Horsemen*, however, provided the great lover with a full gamut for his histrionic talents, and a notable supporting cast, containing among others, Alice Terry, Wallace Beery, Alan Hale, Stuart Holmes, Joseph Swickard, and Nigel de Brulier. It was difficult to believe that only thirty-two years before—only yesterday, really, I told myself comfortingly—it had kept me on the edge of my chair. Ah, well, the chairs were narrower in those days. You positively get lost in the ones at the Museum.

The Four Horsemen, as any nonagenarian will remember, was based on Vicente Blasco Ibañez's best seller. It was released on the heels of the First World War, and its pacifist theme was unquestionably responsible for a measure of its success, but Valentino's reptilian charm, his alliances with Winifred Hudnut and Natacha Rambova, the *brouhaha* about his excesses and idiosyncracies were the real box-office lure. An interminable, narcotic genealogy precedes his appearance in the film, establishing a complex hierarchy of ranchers in the Argentine dominated by his maternal grandfather, an autocratic Spanish hidalgo. Julio Desnoyers (Valentino) is French on his father's side and the patriarch's favourite; he has German cousins being groomed as legatees of the family fortunes, and the sequence pullulates with murky domestic intrigue. Petted and indulged by the old man, Julio grows up into a sleek finale hopper who tangoes sinuously, puffs smoke into the bodices of singsong girls, and generally qualifies as a libertine. In the fullness of time, or roughly six hundred feet of minutiae that remain a secret between the cameraman and the cutter, Julio's mother inherits half the estate and removes her son, daughter and husband to Paris, where they take up residence in a Gallic facsimile of Kaliski and Gabay's auction rooms. Julio dabbles at painting—at least, we behold him before an easel in the manner of those penny-arcade tableaux called 'What the Butler Saw Through the Keyhole' sighting off lickerishly at some models dressed in cheesecloth—and, in more serious vein, applies himself to seducing Margeurite Laurier (Alice Terry), the wife of a French senator. The role must have been a nerve-wracking one for Valentino. Not only did he have to keep an eye peeled for the senator but the production was being directed by Miss Terry's husband, Rex Ingram. No wonder the poor cuss fell apart when he did.

To provide Valentino with a setting for his adagios, the affair gets under way at a fashionable temple of the dance called the Tango Palace, packed with gigolos and ladies in feathered turbans swaying orgiastically; then Margeurite, apprehensive of gossip, makes surreptitious visits to her lover's atelier. He, intent on steam-rolling her into the Turkish corner, is oblivious of all else, and there is a portentous moment, embroidering the favourite movie theme that mankind always exhibits unbridled sensuality just prior to Armageddon, when his male secretary tries to show him a newspaper head-line reading, 'ARCHDUKE FERDINAND ASSASSINATED AT SARAJEVO', only to have Julio petulantly brush it aside. The symbolism now starts to pile up thick and fast. The secretary, croaking ominously, exits to consult a mysterious bearded philosopher in a Russian tunic (Nigel de Brulier), who, it has been planted, dwells upstairs. No reliable clue to this character's identity is anywhere given, but he seems to be a melange of Prince Myshkin, Savanarola, and Dean Inge, possesses the gift of tongues, and is definitely supernatural. His reaction to the murder is much more immediate, possibly because he doesn't have a girl in his room. 'This is the beginning of the end,' he announces somberly. 'The brand that will set the world ablaze.' Downstairs, meanwhile, Margeurite's scruples are melting like hot marzipan under Julio's caresses, and it is mani-fest that she is breaking up fast. The camera thereupon cuts back to the oracle extracting an apple from a bowl of fruit. 'Do you wonder that the apple, with its coloring, was chosen to represent the forbidden fruit?' he asks the secretary, with a cryptic smile. 'But when peeled, how like woman without her cloak of virtue!' I don't know how this brand of rhetoric affected other people of my generation but it used to make me whinny. I secretly compared it to the insupportable sweetness of a thousand violins.

Before very long, Margeurite's husband ferrets out her peccadillo, wrath-fully announces his intention of divorcing her, and challenges Julio to a duel. The scandal never eventuates, happily; in response to a general mobilization order, the senator joins his regiment, the Fifth Calvados Fusiliers, and his wife, seeking to make atonement for her guilt, enrolls as a nurse. 'The flames of war had singed the butterfly's wings,' explains a Lardnerian subtitle, 'and in its place there was—a woman, awakening to the call of France.' Excused from military service because of his nationality, Julio dawdles around Paris making an apathetic pitch for Margeurite, which she priggishly rejects on the ground that venery is unseemly while the caissons roll—a view diametrically opposed to that of another nurse in the same conflict described in *A Call to Arms*. Throughout the preceding, the soothsayer in the attic had been relentlessly conjuring up double-exposure shots of the apocalyptic horsemen and their sinister baggage, and a funereal pall descends on the action—not that it had been a Mardi Gras thus far, by any means. Julio's father (Joseph Swickard) has been taken prisoner at his country house by a detachment of uhlans commanded by Wallace Beery, who proceeds to stage one of those classic Hearst-Sunday-supplement revels with bemonocled Prussians singing '*Ach, du lieber Augustin*', girls running around in their teddies, etc. At the height of the debauch, a frosty-eyed general (Stuart Holmes) enters and is revealed as Desnoyer's own nephew; i.e., a cousin of Julio's from the Argen-tine. Touched by the old man's plight, the officer displays unusual clemency and has him confined to a small, airy dungeon all his own; then, unbuckling his sword, he broaches an especially choice jeroboam of his uncle's champagne for the staff. Julio and Margeurite, in the meantime, continue their marathon renunciation in, of all places, the grotto at Lourdes, where she is nursing her husband, now blind and, of course, totally unaware of her identity. With a tenacity verging on monomania, Julio still hopes to con his sweetheart back to the ostermoor, but she is adamant. At length, he sickens of the whole enterprise—a process one has anticipated him in by a good half hour—castigates himself as a coward unworthy of her love, and rushes off to enlist. And just in the nick, it may be added, for what scenery hasn't been blasted by the foe has been chewed beyond recognition by the actors. Next to Mary Miles Minter laundering a kitten, nobody in the history of the silent screen could induce mal-de-mer as expertly as Valentino when he bit his knuckles to portray heartbreak.

The ensuing sequence is a bit choppy, occupying itself with Julio's heroism under fire and his parent's vicissitudes, though the only indication we get of the former is a shot of him, in a poilu helmet, fondling a monkey at a first-aid station. (However, the animal may conceivably have been afflicted with rabies.) Papa Desnoyers eludes his captors and visits the young man at the front with news that Margeurite pines for him but is devoting herself unsparingly to the senator, which can hardly be described as an ingenious plot twist. There obviously remains but one situation to be milked to dramatize the irony of war—a battlefield encounter between Julio and his German cousin—and, blithely skipping over the mechanics of how a general falls into a shell hole in No Man's Land, the scenario maneuvers the relatives into a death grapple. I rather suspect that at this point a hurried story conference was called on the set to debate the propriety of allowing Valentino to be strangled. No doubt it was argued that the spectacle might cause mixed emotions in the audience, and a compromise was evolved wherein, before the outcome is resolved, we whisk to Margeurite's bedroom as she prepares to abandon her husband for Julio. Suddenly her lover's image materializes, suffused with an unearthly radiance, and she realizes the issue is academic. The rest of the picture is a lugubrious wash-up of the incidentals, climaxed by a graveside meeting between the elder Desnoyers and Julio's former upstairs neighbour, the apparition in the fright wig. Their conclusion, as I understood it, was that things were going to be a great deal worse before they came any better, but confidentially I found it hard to keep from whistling as I raced the projectionist to a *bourbonnerie*, around the corner from the museum. After all, come sunshine or sorrow, it was extremely unlikely that I would ever have to see *The Four Horsemen of the Apocalypse* a third time.

With the fatuity of middle age, I imagined that I had exorcised the ghost of Valentino for keeps, but in some inexplicable fashion his aura must have clung to my person or otherwise put a hex on me. An evening or so later,

my wife exhumed from the attic a Spanish shawl and several filigree combs
she had been hoarding until she could get the right offer from a thrift shop.
As she was executing an impromptu fandango to the strains of 'Siboney',
employing a pair of coasters as castanets, I was jealously impelled to demonstrate my superior co-ordination. 'Watch this, everybody!' I sang out,
flourishing a roll of shelf paper. 'My impression of a matador winding himself
in his sash, as created by the immortal Rudy Valentino in *Blood and Sand!*' I
wrapped one end of the paper around my midriff, ordered a teen-age vassal
to pay out some twenty feet and steady the roll, and, with a wild '*Olé!*' spun
gyroscopically in her direction. Halfway, I ran full tilt into a peculiar blizzard
of white specks and, to weather it, grabbed at a student lamp for support.

I got the lamp, all right, and plenty of time to regret my impetuosity. Lazing
around the house with my tweezers, subsequently probing for slivers of glass,
it occured to me all at once that maybe Valentino used a double in moments
of hazard. Maybe I should have, beginning way back around 1921.

The New Yorker, reprinted, *The Most of S. J. Perelman* (1978).

*Perelman never achieved his ambition to become magnificently rich but did not do
too badly. He managed at last to have a hit show on Broadway with* One Touch
of Venus, *a musical for which he co-wrote the libretto with Ogden Nash (they
wanted Marlene Dietrich to play the lead and went to her hotel suite to persuade
her but she declined, indicating the interview was at an end by wedging a musical
saw between her lovely knees, taking up a bow, and losing herself in music). And
he also won his battle with Hollywood by winning an Oscar for his work on the
script of* Round the World in Eighty Days (*a traumatic experience with the
whizz-kid impresario Mike Todd which Perelman described in a piece entitled*
Round the Bend in Eighty Days).*

*He never attempted to write a novel, nor did he write an autobiography. He was
a private person, prepared to use memories of his boyhood for comic material but,
unlike most humorists, not prepared to reveal anything of his real self as an adult,
a married man, a father of two children. This was probably because his personal
life was not very happy. Although for a change he was not a heavy drinker, he was
obsessed with his work and himself and this put a strain on his marriage which
from the beginning was punctuated with infidelities on both sides. And his children
were a bother to him. He preferred animals which he could silence more easily
when he wanted to work. The result, not surprisingly, was that his son grew away
from him and behaved foolishly, eventually criminally.*

*Quietly and nattily dressed, looking sometimes like a Savile Row version of
Rudyard Kipling, he spoke softly and thoughtfully. He could be very funny with
friends but others found him remote, melancholy, and disagreeable. He never wrote
about love and tenderness, or emotional human relationships, or beauty, or politics,
or religion, or indeed any serious subject. He did not aim to preach, like Mark
Twain, but to write the sort of prose which he himself found funny. Like most
humorists he found it easier to be funny about things which he disliked.*

But what prose it was. As well as what he called his 'preoccupation with clichés, baroque language and elegant variation', and the fastidious balance and rhythm of his sentences, he also brought to comic writing a new verbal agility and erudition. His use of words was dazzling: as E. B. White said, 'Perelman commanded a vocabulary that is the despair (and joy) of every writing man. Sid is like a Roxy organ that had three decks, fifty stops and a pride of pedals under the bench. When he wants a word, it's there.'

About his Joycean free associations and his excursions into wild Benchley-like fantasy, Benchley himself wrote, 'Perelman took over the dementia praecox *field and drove us all to writing articles on economics for the* Commentator. *Any further attempts to garble thought-process sounded like imitation-Perelman. He did to our weak little efforts at "crazy stuff" what Benny Goodman has done to middle-period jazz. He swung it. To use a swing phrase, he took it "out of the world" and there he remains, all by himself.'*

Perelman began by imitating Lardner and a great many modern humorists have returned the compliment by being inspired and influenced by Perelman; his effect on present humour on both sides of the Atlantic has been profound. Alan Coren, then editor of Punch, *wrote in his obituary of Perelman, 'It took me long years to control the writing hold he had over me, and I wasn't alone, God knows, in that; there's a lot of Perelman in a lot of humorists, how could there not be.'*

Of all Perelman comic essays (or feuilletons, *as he liked to call them), the one which displays the most of his gifts is* Strictly From Hunger, *which originally appeared in the old humour magazine* Life; *he rewrote it at the height of his powers in the late thirties to become the title piece of his second book.*

The narrative is a succession of parodies, beginning in the style of an all-American boy starting out on an exciting adventure, moving on to the more elegant tones of a Victorian gentleman-traveller in an Anthony Hope novel, branching out into jokes, word-play, clichés dismantled and reassembled, finally dissolving into a glorious, inane, tinsel town montage complete with happy-ever-after fade-out.

And beneath it all lies a deadly accurate picture of what it felt like to work in Hollywood in 1931:

STRICTLY FROM HUNGER

Yes I was excited, and small wonder. What boy wouldn't be, boarding a huge, mysterious, puffing steam train for golden California? As Mamma adjusted my reefer and strapped on my leggings, I almost burst with impatience. Grinning redcaps lifted my luggage into the compartment and spat on it. Mamma began to weep into a small pillowcase she had brought along for the purpose.

'Oh, son, I wish you hadn't become a scenario writer!' she sniffled.

'Aw, now, Moms,' I comforted her, 'it's no worse than playing the piano in a call house.' She essayed a brave little smile, and, reaching into her reticule, produced a flat package which she pressed into my hands. For a moment I was puzzled, then I cried out with glee.

'Jelly sandwiches! Oh, Moms!'

'Eat them all, boy o' mine,' she told me, 'they're good for boys with hollow little legs.' Tenderly she pinned to my lapel the green tag reading 'To Plushnick Productions, Hollywood, California.' The whistle shrilled and in a moment I was chugging out of Grand Central's dreaming spires followed only by the anguished cries of relatives who would now have to go to work. I had chugged only a few feet when I realized that I had left without the train, so I had to run back and wait for it to start.

As we sped along the glorious fever spots of the Hudson I decided to make a tour of inspection. To my surprise I found that I was in the only passenger car of the train; the other cars were simply dummies snipped out of cardboard and painted to simulate coaches. Even 'passengers' had been cunningly drawn in colored crayons in the 'windows', as well as ragged tramps clinging to the blinds below and drinking Jamaica ginger. With a rueful smile I returned to my seat and gorged myself on jelly sandwiches.

At Buffalo the two other passengers and I discovered to our horror that the conductor had been left behind. We finally decided to divide up his duties; I punched his tickets, the old lady opposite me wore a conductor's hat and locked the washroom as we came into stations, and the young man who looked as if his feet were not mates consulted a Hamilton watch frequently. But we missed the conductor's earthy conversation and it was not until we had exchanged several questionable stories that we began to forget our loss.

A flicker of interest served to shorten the trip. At Fort Snodgrass, Ohio, two young and extremely polite road-agents boarded the train and rifled us of our belongings. They explained that they were modern Robin Hoods and were stealing from the poor to give to the rich. They had intended to rape all the women and depart for Sherwood Forest, but when I told them that Sherwood Forest as well as the women were in England, their chagrin was comical in the extreme. They declined my invitation to stay and take a chance on the train's pool, declaring that the engineer had fixed the run and would fleece us, and got off at South Bend with every good wish.

The weather is always capricious in the Middle West, and although it was midsummer, the worst blizzard in Chicago's history greeted us on our arrival. The streets were crowded with thousands of newsreel cameramen trying to photograph each other bucking the storm on the Lake Front. It was a novel idea for the newsreels and I wished them well. With only two hours in Chicago I would be unable to see the city, and the thought drew me into a state of composure. I noted with pleasure that a new coat of grime had been given to the Dearborn Street station, though I was hardly vain enough to believe that it had anything to do with my visit. There was the usual ten-minute wait while the porters withdrew with my portable typewriter to a side room and flailed it with hammers, and at last I was aboard the 'Sachem', a crack train of the B.B.D. & O. lines.

It was as if I had suddenly been transported into another world. 'General

Crook', in which I was to make my home for the next three days, and his two neighbours, 'Lake Tahoe' and 'Chief Malomai', were everything that the word 'Pullman' implies; they were Pullmans. Uncle Eben, in charge of the 'General Crook', informed me that the experiment of air-cooling the cars had been so successful that the road intended to try heating them next winter.

'Ah suttinly looks fo'd to dem roastin' ears Ah's gwine have next winter, he, he, he!' he chuckled, rubbing soot into my hat.

The conductor told me he had been riding on trains for so long that he had begun to smell like one, and sure enough, two brakemen waved their lanterns at him that night and tried to tempt him down a siding in Kansas City. We became good friends and it came as something of a blow when I heard the next morning that he had fallen off the train during the night. The fireman said that we had circled about for an hour trying to find him but that it had been impossible to lower a boat because we did not carry a boat.

The run was marked by only one incident out of the ordinary. I had ordered breaded veal cutlet the first evening, and my waiter, poking his head into the kitchen, had repeated the order. The cook. unfortunately, understood him to say '*dreaded* veal cutlet,' and resenting the slur, sprang at the waiter with drawn razor. In a few seconds I was the only living remnant of the shambles, and at Topeka I was compelled to wait until a new shambles was hooked on and I proceeded with dinner.

It seemed only a scant week or ten days before we were pulling into Los Angeles. I had grown so attached to my porter that I made him give me a lock of his hair. I wonder if he still has the ten-cent piece I gave him? There was a gleam in his eye which could only have been insanity as he leaned over me. Ah, Uncle Eben, faithful old retainer, where are you now? Gone to what obscure ossuary? If this should chance to meet your kindly gaze, drop me a line care of *Variety*, won't you? They know what to do with it.

II

The violet hush of twilight was descending over Los Angeles as my hostess, Violet Hush, and I left its suburbs headed towards Hollywood. In the distance a glow of huge piles of burning motion-picture scripts lit up the sky. The crisp tang of frying writers and directors whetted my appetite. How good it was to be alive, I thought, inhaling deep lungfuls of carbon monoxide. Suddenly our powerful Gatti-Cazazza slid to a stop in the traffic.

'What is it, Jenkin?' Violet called anxiously through the speaking-tube to the chauffeur (played by Lyle Talbot).

A *suttee* was in progress by the roadside, he said—did we wish to see it? Quickly Violet and I elbowed our way through the crowd. An enormous funeral pyre composed of thousands of feet of film and scripts, drenched with Chanel Number 5, awaited the torch of Jack Holt, who was to act as master of ceremonies. In a few terse words Violet explained this unusual custom, borrowed from the Hindus and never paid for. The worst disgrace that can

befall a producer is an unkind review from a New York reviewer. When this
happens, the producer becomes a pariah in Hollywood. He is shunned by his
friends, thrown into bankruptcy, and like a Japanese electing hara-kiri, he
commits *suttee*. A great bonfire is made of the film, and the luckless producer,
followed by directors, actors, technicians, and the producer's wives, immolate
themselves. Only the scenario writers are exempt. These are tied between the
tails of spirited Caucasian ponies, which are then driven off in opposite
directions. This custom is called 'a conference'.

Violet and I watched the scene breathlessly. Near us Harry Cohl, head of
Moribund Studios, was being rubbed with huck towels preparatory to throwing himself into the flames. He was nonchalantly smoking a Rocky Ford
five-center, and the man's courage drew a tear to the eye of even the most
callous. Weeping relatives besought him to eschew his design, but he stood
adamant. Adament Eve, his plucky secretary, was being rubbed with crash
towels preparatory to flinging herself into Cohl's embers. Assistant directors
busily prepared spears, war bonnets and bags of pemmican which the Great
Chief would need on his trip to the 'Happy Hunting Grounds'. Wampas and
beads to placate the Great Spirit (played by Will Hays) were piled high about
the stoical tribesman.

Suddenly Jack Holt (played by Edmund Lowe) raised his hand for silence.
The moment had come. With bowed head Holt made a simple invocation
couched in one-syllable words so that even the executives might understand.
Throwing his five-center to a group of autograph hunters, the great man
poised himself for the fatal leap. But from off-scene came the strident clatter
of cocoanut shells, and James Mohl, Filmdom's fearless critic, wearing the
uniform of a Confederate guerilla and the whiskers of General Beauregard,
galloped in on a foam-flecked pinto. It was he who had sent Cohl into
Coventry. It was a dramatic moment as the two stood pitted against each
other—Cohl against Mohl, the Blue against the Gray. But with true Southern
gallantry Mohl was the first to extend the hand of friendship.

'Ah reckon it was an unworthy slur, suh,' he said in manly tones. 'Ah-all
thought you-all's pictuah was lousy but it opened at the Rialto to sensational
grosses, an' Ah-all 'pologizes. Heah, have a yam.' And he drew a yam from
his tunic. Not to be outdone in hospitality, Cohl drew a yam from his tunic,
and soon they were exchanging yams and laughing over the old days.

When Violet and I finally stole away to our waiting motor, we felt that we
were somehow nearer to each other. I snuggled luxuriously into the buffalo
laprobe Violet had provided against the treacherous night air and gazed out
at the gleaming neon lights. Soon we would be in Beverley Hills, and already
the quaint native women were swarming alongside in their punts urging us
to buy their cunning beadwork and mangoes. Occasionally I threw a handful
of coppers to the Negro boys, who dove for them joyfully. The innocent
squeals of the policemen as the small blackamoors pinched them were irresistible. Unable to resist them, Violet and I were soon pinching each other

till our skins glowed. Violet was good to the touch, with a firm fleshy texture like a winesap or pippin. It seemed but a moment before we were sliding under the porte-cochere of her home, a magnificent rambling structure of beaverboard patterned after an Italian ropewalk of the sixteenth century. It had recently been remodelled by a family of wrens who had introduced chewing-gum into the left wing, and only three or four obscure Saxon words could do it justice.

I was barely warming my hands in front of the fire and watching Jimmy Fidler turn on a spit when my presence on the Pacific Slope made itself felt. The news of my arrival had thrown international financial centers into an uproar, and sheaves of wires, cables, phone messages, and even corn began piling up. An ugly rumour that I might reorganize the motion-picture industry was being bruited about in the world's commodity markets. My brokers, Whitelipped and Trembling, were beside themselves. The New York Stock Exchange was begging them for assurances of stability and Threadneedle Street awaited my next move with drumming pulses. Film shares ricocheted sharply, although wools and meats were sluggish, if not downright sullen. To the reporters who flocked around me I laughingly declaimed that this was a business trip. I was simply a scenario writer to whom the idea of work was abhorrent. A few words murmured into the transatlantic telephone, the lift of an eyebrow here, the shrug of a shoulder there, and equilibrium was soon restored. I washed sparsely, curled my mustache with a heated hairpin, flicked a drop of Sheik Lure on my lapel, and rejoined my hostess.

After a copious dinner, melting-eyed beauties in lacy black underthings fought with each other to serve me kümmel. A hurried apology, and I was curled up in bed with the Autumn 1927 issue of *The Yale Review*. Halfway through an exciting symposium on St Thomas Aquinas' indebtedness to Professors Whitehead and Spengler, I suddenly detected a stowaway blonde under the bed. Turning a deaf ear to her heartrending entreaties and burning glances, I sent her packing. Then I treated my face to a feast of skin food, buried my head in the pillow and went bye-bye.

III

Hollywood Boulevard! I rolled the rich syllables over on my tongue and thirstily drank in the beauty of the scene before me. On all sides nattily attired boulevardiers clad in rich stuffs strolled nonchalantly, inhaling cubebs and exchanging epigrams stolen from Martial and Wilde. Thousands of scantily draped but none the less appetizing extra girls milled past me, their mouths a scarlet wound and their eyes clearly defined in their faces. Their voluptuous curves set my blood on fire, and as I made my way down Mammary Lane, a strange thought began to invade my brain: I realized that I had not eaten breakfast yet. In a Chinese eatery cunningly built in the shape of an old shoe I managed to assuage the inner man with a chopped glove salad topped off with frosted cocoa. Charming platinum-haired hostesses in red pajamas and peaked caps added a note of color to the surroundings, whilst a gypsy orchestra played selections from Victor Herbert's operettas on musical saws. It was a bit of old Vienna come to life, and the sun was a red ball in the heavens before I realized with a start that I had promised to report at the Plushnick studios.

Commandeering a taxicab, I arrived at the studio just in time to witness the impressive ceremony of changing the guard. In the central parade ground, on a snowy white charger, sat Max Plushnick, resplendent in a producer's uniform, his chest glittering with first mortgage liens, amortizations, and estoppels. His personal guard, composed of picked vice-presidents of the Chase National Bank, was drawn up stiffly about him in a hollow square.

But the occasion was not a happy one. A writer had been caught trying to create an adult picture. The drums rolled dismally, and the writer, his head sunk on his chest, was led out amid a ghastly silence. With the aid of a small stepladder Plushnick slid lightly from his steed. Sternly he ripped the epaulets from the traitor's tunic, broke his sword across his knee, and in a few harsh words demoted him to the mail department.

'And now,' began Plushnick, 'I further condemn you to eat . . .'

'No, no!' screamed the poor wretch, falling to his knees and embracing Plushnick's jackboots. 'Not that, not that!'

'Stand up, man,' ordered Plushnick, his lip curling; 'I condemn you to eat in the studio restaurant for ten days and may God have mercy on your soul.' The awful words rang out on the still evening air and even Plushnick's hardened old mercenaries shuddered. The heartrending cries of the unfortunate were drowned in the boom of the sunset gun.

In the wardrobe department I was photographed, fingerprinted, and measured for the smock and Windsor tie which were to be my uniform. A nameless fear clutched at my heart as two impassive turnkeys herded me down a corridor to my supervisor's office. For what seemed hours we waited in an anteroom. Then my serial number was called, the leg-irons were struck off, and I was shoved through a door into the presence of Diana ffrench-Mamoulian.

How to describe what followed? Diana ffrench-Mamoulian was accustomed to having her way with writers, and my long lashes and peachblow mouth seemed to whip her to insensate desire. In vain, time and again, I tried to bring her attention back to the story, only to find her gem-incrusted fingers straying through my hair. When our interview was over, her cynical attempt to 'date me up' made every fibre of my being cry out in revolt.

'P-please,' I stammered, my face burning. 'I—I wish you wouldn't. . . . I'm engaged to a Tri Kappa at Goucher—'

'Just one kiss,' she pleaded, her breath hot against my neck. In desperation I granted her boon, knowing full well that my weak defenses were crumbling before the onslaught of this love tigress. Finally she allowed me to leave, but only after I had promised to dine at her penthouse apartment and have an intimate chat about the script. The basket of slave bracelets and marzipan I found awaiting me on my return home made me realize to what lengths Diana would go.

I was radiant that night in blue velvet tails and a boutonniere of diamonds from Cartier's, my eyes starry and the merest hint of cologne at my ear-lobes. An inscrutable Oriental served the Lucullan repast and my vis-a-vis was as sparkling as the wine.

'Have a bit of the wing, darling?' queried Diana solicitously, indicating the roast Long Island airplane with applesauce. I tried to turn our conversation from the personal note, but Diana would have none of it. Soon we were exchanging gay banter over the mellow Vouvray, laughing as we dipped fastidious fingers into the Crisco parfait for which Diana was famous. Our meal finished, we sauntered into the rumpus room and Diana turned on the radio. With a savage snarl the radio turned on her and we slid over the waxed floor in the intricate maze of the jackdaw strut. Without quite knowing why, I found myself hesitating before the plate of liquer candies Diana was pressing on me.

'I don't think I should—really, I'm a trifle faint—'

'Oh, come on,' she urged masterfully. 'After all, you're old enough to be your father—I mean I'm old enough to be my mother. . . .' She stuffed a brandy bonbon between my clenched teeth. Before long I was eating them thirstily, reeling about the room and shouting snatches of coarse drunken doggerel. My brain was on fire, I tell you. Through the haze I saw Diana ffrench-Mamoulian, her nostrils dilated, groping for me. My scream of terror only egged her on, overturning chairs and tables in her bestial pursuit. With superhuman talons she tore off my collar and suspenders. I sank to my knees, choked with sobs, hanging on to my last shirt-stud like a drowning man. Her Svengali eyes were slowly hypnotizing me; I fought like a wounded bird—and then, blissful unconsciousness.

When I came to, the Oriental servant and Diana were battling in the centre of the floor. As I watched, Yen Shee Gow drove a well-aimed blow to her mid-section, following it with a right cross to the jaw. Diana staggered and rolled under a table. Before my astonished eyes John Chinaman stripped the mask from his face and revealed the features of Blanche Almonds, a little seamstress I had long wooed unsuccessfully in New York. Gently she bathed my temples with Florida water and explained how she had followed me, suspecting Diana ffrench-Mamoulian's intentions. I let her rain kisses over my face as beaming Ivan tucked us in and cracked his whip over the prancing bays. In a few seconds our sleigh was skimming over the hard crust toward Port Arthur and freedom, leaving Plushnick's discomfited officers gnashing one another's teeth. The wintry Siberian moon glowed over the tundras, drenching my hair with moonbeams for Blanche to kiss away. And so, across the silvery steppes amid the howling of wolves, we rode into a new destiny, purified in the crucible that men call Hollywood.

Life, rewritten for *The New Yorker*, reprinted: *Strictly From Hunger* (1937).

―――――――

LUDWIG BEMELMANS *was a contemporary of S. J. Perelman but apart from the fact that they both contributed to the* New Yorker *and both were artists as well as writers (it is extraordinary how many humorists were, from Thackeray on), they had little in common.*

Bemelmans was not a cartoonist but a painter of decorative, witty watercolours of considerable merit; he had several exhibitions and painted some famous New Yorker *covers, and he illustrated his own three dozen or so books.*

He came to New York in 1914 *from the Tyrol district of Austria and worked his way up in the hotel trade, which he loathed. A gregarious man who should have been born in Vienna, he was a sparkling raconteur and conversationalist and eventually made enough money from writing and painting and owning a restaurant to travel widely and to live the life of a modest* bon vivant.

Apart from his Madeleine *books for children, almost all his humour was partly or wholly autobiographical. The most popular of his pieces were his descriptions of backstage, or rather backrestaurant, life in the grand hotels in which he worked. There was something peculiarly fascinating about his insights into the secret workings of luxury establishments which in those days were not, like most newly built modern hotels, multi-storey people-parks but were palaces in their own right: Grand Hotels, Majestic Hotels, and Splendide Hotels which were truly grand, majestic, and splendid.*

Fascinating, too, were his revelations of the strict, quasi-military system of command and discipline traditional in the catering profession; a bus boy was terrified of the waiter for whom he dashed to and from the kitchen with dishes; the waiter was frightened of the captain who supervised his table; the captain trembled lest he incurred a frown from the maître d'hôtel *in charge of the restaurant, and everybody was deeply in awe of the hotel's general manager.*

Bemelmans gave us glimpses of this alien world in a series of charming, acutely perceptive character sketches which included his story of Fritzl, the new bus boy in the restaurant at the Splendide Hotel.

Fritzl desperately misses his hometown of Regensburg, Austria, from which he has so recently been wrenched, and he is a lonely and shy lad:

THE HOMESICK BUS BOY

In a corner of the main dining room of the Splendide, behind an arrangement of screens and large palms that were bedded in antique Chinese vases, six ladies of uncertain age used to sit making out luncheon and dinner checks. When a guest at the Splendide called for the bill, it was brought to him in

longhand—contrary to the practice in most other hotels in New York City—
in purple ink, on fine paper decorated with the hotel crest. The six ladies,
seated at a long desk near the exit to the kitchen, attended to that. And since
there were periods when they had little to do, one of them, a Miss Tappin,
found time to befriend the bus boy Fritzl, from Regensburg.

Fritzl was not much more than a child. He wore a white jacket and a long
white apron, and he carried in his pocket a comb which he had brought all
the way from Regensburg. A scene of the city was etched on the side of it.
Fritzl's hair stood up straight, moist, and yellow, and he had the only red
cheeks in the dining room. When anyone spoke to him, his ears also turned
red, and he looked as if he had just been slapped twice in the face.

Miss Tappin was very English. She had seen better days and in her youth
had travelled on the Continent. She detested the maître d'hôtel, the waiters,
and the captains, but she was drawn to the lonesome bus boy, who seemed
to be of nice family, had manners, and was shy. Fritzl did not like the maître
d'hôtel, the waiters, or the captains either. Least of all he liked the waiter he
worked for, a nervous wreck of a Frenchman who was constantly coming
behind the screens and palms, saying 'Psst!' and dragging Fritzl out onto the
floor of the restaurant to carry away some dirty dishes.

When Fritzl was thus called away, Miss Tappin would sigh and then look
into the distance. She called Fritzl 'a dear', and said that he was the living
image of a nephew of hers who was at Sandhurst—the son, by a previous
marriage, of her late sister's husband, a Major Graves. 'What a pity!' Miss
Tappin would say whenever she thought of Fritzl. 'He's such a superior type,
that boy. Such a dear. So unlike the bobtail, ragtag, and guttersnipes around
him. I do hope he'll come through all right!' Then she would sigh again and
go back to her bills. Every time Fritzl passed the long desk, whether with
butter, water bottles, or dirty dishes, a quick signal of sympathy passed
between them.

The conversations with Fritzl afforded Miss Tappin an exquisite weapon
with which to irritate the other five ladies who shared the desk—women
who came from places like Perth Amboy, Pittsburg, and Newark. With Fritzl
leaning on her blotter, she could discuss such topics as the quaintness of
Munich and its inhabitants and the charm and grandeur of the Bavarian
Alps. These beautiful mountains neither Fritzl nor Miss Tappin had ever seen.
Regensburg is not far away from the Alps but Fritzl's parents were much too
poor ever to have sent him there. Miss Tappin's stay in Munich had been
limited to a half-hour wait between trains at the railroad station while she
was on her way to visit her sister in Budapest.

Regensburg, however, she soon came to know thoroughly from Fritzl, who
often spread a deck of pocket-worn postcards and calendar pictures on the
desk in front of her. These views showed every worthwhile street corner and
square of his beloved city. He acquainted her with Regensburg's history and
described its people and the surrounding countryside. He read her all the

letters he received from home, and gradually Miss Tappin came to know everybody in Regensburg.

'Dear boy,' she would say, touching his arm, 'I can see it all clearly. I can picture your dear mother sitting in front of her little house on the banks of the Danube—the little radish garden, the dog, the cathedral, and the wonderful stone bridge. What a lovely place it must be!' Then her eyes would cloud, for Miss Tappin had the peculiar British addiction to scenes that are material for postcards . . . Into the middle of these flights always came the nervous 'Psst!' of the old French waiter. Then Fritzl would lift his apron, stow the postcards away in the back pocket of his trousers, and run. When he passed that way later with a tray of dirty dishes, he sent her his smile, and again when he came back with an armful of water bottles or a basin of cracked ice and a basket of bread. They recognized each other as two nice people do, walking their dogs in the same street.

Fritzl's service station stood in another corner of the restaurant, and near it was another palm in another Chinese vase. When he was not at Miss Tappin's desk or in the kitchen or busy with his dirty dishes, Fritzl hid behind this palm. He was afraid of everyone, even the guests. He came out from behind his palm only when his waiter called him, or when the orchestra played Wagner, Weber, or Strauss music, or when I, his other friend in the hotel, passed by.

By this time I was assistant manager in the banquet department, but Fritzl was not afraid of me. I was his friend because I, too, came from Regensburg. Sometimes when I appeared in the restaurant, Fritzl would lean out from behind his palm and say in a hoarse whisper, '*Du*, Ludwig, have you a minute for me?' Once he put his arm round my neck and started to walk with me through the dining room as if we were boys in Regensburg. When I told him this was not done, he looked hurt, but later, in the pantry, he forgave me and told me all the latest and most important news of Regensburg.

Another time he showed me a little book he had made out of discarded menus. In this book he had written down what he earned and what he spent. His income was eight dollars a week, and his expenses, including an English lesson at one dollar, were seven. In three years, he calculated, he would have enough money to go back to Regensburg. I told him he could make much more money if he attended to his job and got to be a waiter, and he said he would try. But Fritzl was very bad dining room material. He was slow, earnest, and awkward. A good waiter jumps, turns fast, and has his eyes everywhere. One can almost tell by watching a new man walk across the room whether he will be a good or an indifferent waiter. One can also tell, as a rule, whether he will last . . .

We sometimes took a walk together, Fritzl and I, usually up or down Fifth Avenue, in the lull between luncheon and dinner. One day, in the upper window of a store building near Thirty-fourth Street, Fritzl saw an advertisement that showed a round face smoking a cigar. Under the face was written 'E. Regensburg and Sons, Havana Cigars'. From that day on, Fritzl always wanted to walk downtown towards Thirty-fourth Street. He would point up at the window as we passed and say, 'Look, Ludwig— Regensburg.'. . .

When I asked Fritzl why he loved Regensburg so much, his answer sounded like Heinrich Heine. 'Do you remember the seven stone steps,' he said, 'the worn stones that lead down from the Street of St Pancraz to the small fish market? The old ivy-covered fountain whose water came from the mouth of two green dolphins? The row of tall oaks with a bench between every other pair of trees? The sand pit next to the fountain where children play, where young girls walk arm in arm, where the lamplighter arrives at seven, and where, sitting on a bench, I can see, between the leaning walls of two houses, a wide strip of moving water—the Danube—and beyond it my parent's house? There I grew up. There every stone is known to me. I know the sound of every bell, the name of every child, and everyone greets me.'. . .

When we returned to the hotel from an afternoon walk, Fritzl always disappeared into the Splendide's basement, where the dressing rooms for the bus boys were, and changed his clothes. The other bus boys' lockers were lined with clippings from *La Vie Parisienne* and with pictures of cyclists and boxers. The door of Fritzl's was covered with views of Regensburg.

One evening Fritzl came up from his locker to assist at a dinner party given by Lord Rosslare, who had ordered a fairly good dinner, long and difficult to serve. He was a moody client, gay one day, unbearable the next. When he complained, his voice could be heard out on the street. Rosslare's table was in the center of the room, and next to it was a smaller table on which to ladle out the soup, divide the fish into portions, and carve the rack of lamb. The maître d'hôtel and his assistants supervised all this. Fritzl's waiter was moist with nervousness and fear. Everything went well, however, until the rack of lamb was to be carved.

The lamb had arrived from the kitchen and stood on an electric heater on Fritzl's table behind the palm. Next to Lord Rosslare stood the maître d'hôtel, who intended to carve. He had the knife in one hand and a large fork in the other. He looked along the edge of the knife and tested its sharpness. The old waiter polished the hot plates in which the lamb was to be served and then carried the stack of them and the sauce to the table. Because the maître d'hôtel was shouting at him to hurry up, he told Fritzl to follow him with the rack of lamb. All Fritzl had to do was to take the copper casserole and follow him. To save time, they walked across the dance floor instead of round it. Rosslare leaned back and complained about the slowness of the service. The maître d'hôtel stamped his feet and waved the carving knife. With his mouth stretched, he signaled to the old waiter and Fritzl so they could read his lips: 'Dépêchez-vous, salauds.'

All this made Fritzl nervous, and in the middle of the dance floor he tripped and fell. The rack of lamb jumped out of the casserole. Then an even more terrible thing happened. Fritzl, on all fours, crept over to the lamb, picked it up calmly and put it back in the casserole, licked his slippery fingers, got to his feet, and, to everyone's horror, carried it over to the table to be carved.

Rosslare laughed. The whole dining room laughed. Only Monsieur Victor, the maître d'hôtel, was not amused. He retired to his office and bit into his fist. Next day the captain at the station got a severe reprimand. The old waiter was to be laid off for two weeks and Fritzl was to be discharged.

In a hotel that employed hundreds of people, there were always changes in personnel. And fortunately an old Greek who had been attendant in the men's washroom in the banquet department left on that day for his homeland. His job was vacant and Fritzl got it.

In the washroom, Fritzl was his own master. There were no maîtres d'hôtel, captains, and waiters to be afraid of. No one said 'Psst!' and 'Come here!' to him. He began to be more cheerful. One of his uncles, he told me, a veteran of the war of 1870, had, in recognition of his services, been given the washroom concession at the Walhalla, a national shrine built of marble, like the washroom in the banquet department of the Splendide, and situated not far from Regensburg.

Every morning Fritzl went down to the storeroom and got his supply of brushes, soap, ammonia, and disinfectants. Next he went to the linen room and exchanged his dirty towels for clean ones. Then he put his washroom in order. He whistled while he polished the knobs and handles and water faucets, and when everything was shining he conscientiously flushed all the toilets and pressed the golden buttons that released a spray of water into the porcelain basins, to see that they were working. If any of the plumbing was out of order, he telephoned down to the engineers. At noon he reported to the banquet office and was told whether any parties would take place during the afternoon or evening. If the banquet rooms were not engaged, he was free for the rest of the day.

When Fritzl worked, he made good money. He soon learned to brush the guests off and to hold them up at the narrow door so that none escaped without producing a dime or a quarter. In busy seasons he sometimes made as much as thirty dollars a week . . .

Late at night, after he had locked up the men's room, Fritzl arranged his coins in neat stacks and entered the total in his book. He often came into the banquet office when everyone else was gone, and asked to use my typewriter. On this machine, using two fingers, he slowly composed glowing prospectuses of the hotel—letters that his mother would proudly show around. On the hotel's stationery, he wrote that the Splendide was the most luxurious hotel in the world; that it was twenty-two stories high; that it had seven hundred apartments, any one of which was better furnished than the rooms in the castle of the Duke of Thurn und Taxis in Regensburg; that in these apartments lived the richest people in America; that he was employed at a lucrative

income in the Department of Sanitation; and that he would probably come
home for a short visit in the summer.

Ludwig Bemelmans (1898–1962), Hotel Splendide (1940).

> Fritzl was a real person. He was Bemelmans's younger brother, Oscar.

────────────

*IT seems only right and proper that Damon Runyon, the chronicler of Broadway
and its seamier citizens, should have been born in Manhattan. By an odd fluke
of fate, though, it was not the Manhattan of New York City but another one,
Manhattan, Kansas.*

*Runyon was first and foremost a newspaperman. After fighting for two years in
the Spanish–American War he started work as a journalist with a newspaper in
Colorado. He was then aged 16. In 1911 he moved to New York and became a
sports writer, and eventually what was known in the trade as 'a colyamist' on the
New York* American. *In the 1920s he began to write stories using his knowledge
of the mean streets around Broadway and the sporting community whose members
congregated there; the Guys—illegal bookies, crap-game impresarios, Big Wheels,
small-time crooks—and their various Dolls.*

*Runyon's humorous pieces were not comic essays, nor were they character
sketches—his characters were merely types; big, angry crook; small, frightened
crook; loving but simple chorus-girl; spotty mug-punter, and so on—he wrote
conventional short stories in the good old American tradition, tales told in the
vernacular. The plots were, in the manner of O. Henry, neatly constructed with
good, professionally wrought endings. Their distinction lay in the manner of their
telling. Runyon invented a peculiar argot for his characters to speak; a kind of
pseudo-Broadway/Brooklyn patois which everybody, including the narrator, spoke
in the present tense with an occasional foray into the hopeful future.*

*His cast of muscle-bound, pea-brained delinquents with names like Harry the
Horse, Society Max, and Big Nig, were professional villains, party to murder and
all manner of mayhem, but Runyon wrote about them when they were, as it were,
off-duty; the stories were not violent but deeply sentimental and as soft-centred as
a box of violet chocolate creams.*

*An early story tells of The Brain and a complication which he has with his
accumulation of Dolls, which surprises his friends somewhat on account of when
The Brain accumulates a Doll she usually remains accumulated and he never picks
a crow:*

THE BRAIN GOES HOME

One night The Brain is walking me up and down Broadway in front of
Mindy's Restaurant, and speaking of this and that, when along comes a
red-headed raggedy doll selling apples at five cents per copy, and The Brain,

being very fond of apples, grabs one out of her basket and hands her a five-dollar bill.

The red-headed raggedy doll, who is maybe thirty-odd and is nothing but a crow as far as looks are concerned, squints at the finnif, and says to The Brain like this:

'I do not have change for so much money,' she says, 'but I will go and get it in a minute.'

'You keep the change,' The Brain says, biting a big hunk out of the apple and taking my arm to start me walking again.

Well, the raggedy doll looks at the Brain again, and it seems to me that all of a sudden there are large tears in her eyes as she says:

'Oh, thank you, sir! Thank you, thank you, and God bless you, sir!'

And then she goes on up the street in a hurry, with her hands over her eyes and her shoulders shaking, and The Brain turns around very much astonished, and watches her until she is out of sight.

'Why, my goodness!' The Brain says. 'I give Doris Clare ten G's last night, and she does not make half as much fuss over it as this doll does over a pound note.'

'Well,' I say, 'maybe the apple doll needs a pound note more than Doris needs ten G's.'

'Maybe so,' The Brain says. 'And of course, Doris gives me much more in return than just an apple and a God bless me. Doris gives me her love. I guess,' The Brain says, 'that love costs me about as much dough as any guy that ever lives.'

'I guess it does,' I say, and the chances are we both guess right, because off-hand I figure that if The Brain gets out on three hundred G's per year for love, he is running his love business very economically indeed, because it is well known to one and all that The Brain has three different dolls, besides an ever-loving wife.

In fact, The Brain is sometimes spoken of by many citizens as the 'Love King', but only behind his back, because The Brain likes to think his love affairs are a great secret to all but maybe a few, although the only guy I ever see in this town who does not know all about them is a guy who is deaf, dumb, and blind.

I once read a story about a guy by the name of King Solomon who lives a long time ago and who has a thousand dolls all at once, which is going in for dolls on a very large scale indeed, but I guarantee that all of King Solomon's dolls put together are not as expensive as any one of The Brain's dolls. The overhead on Doris Clare alone will drive an ordinary guy daffy, and Doris is practically frugal compared to Cynthia Harris and Bobby Baker.

Then there is Charlotte, who is The Brain's ever-loving wife and who has a society bug and needs plenty of coconuts at all times to keep her a going concern. I once hear The Brain tell Bobby Baker that his ever-loving wife is a bit of an invalid, but as a matter of fact there is never anything the matter with Charlotte that a few bobs will not cure, although of course this goes for nearly every doll in this world who is an invalid.

When a guy is knocking around Broadway as long as The Brain, he is bound to accumulate dolls here and there, but most guys accumulate one at a time, and when this one runs out on him, as Broadway dolls will do, he accumulates another, and so on, and so on, until he is too old to care about such matters as dolls, which is when he is maybe a hundred and four years old, although I hear of several guys who beat even this record.

But when The Brain accumulates a doll he seems to keep her accumulated, and none of them ever run out on him, and while this will be a very great nuisance to the average guy, it pleases The Brain no little because it makes him think he has a very great power over dolls.

'They are not to blame if they fall in love with me,' The Brain says to me one night. 'I will not cause one of them any sorrow for all the world.'

Well, of course, it is most astonishing to me to hear a guy as smart as The Brain using such language, but I figure he may really believe it, because The Brain thinks very good of himself at all times. However, some guys claim that the real reason The Brain keeps all his dolls is because he is too selfish to give them away, although personally I will not take any of them if The Brain throws in a cash bonus, except maybe Bobby Baker.

Anyway, The Brain keeps his dolls accumulated, and furthermore he spends plenty of dough on them, what with buying them automobiles and furs and diamonds and swell places to live in—especially swell places to live in. One time I tell The Brain he will save himself plenty if he hires a house and bunches his dolls together in one big happy family, instead of having them scattered all over town, but The Brain says this idea is no good.

'In the first place,' he says, 'they do not know about each other, except Doris and Cynthia and Bobby know about Charlotte, although she does not know about them. They each think they are the only one with me. So if I corral them all together they will be jealous of each other over my love. Anyway,' The Brain says, 'such an arrangement will be very immoral and against the law. No,' he says, 'it is better to have them in different spots, because think of the many homes it gives to me to go to in case I wish to go home. In fact,' The Brain says, 'I guess I have more homes to go to than any other guy on Broadway.'

Well, this may be true, but what The Brain wants with a lot of different homes is a very great mystery on Broadway, because he seldom goes home, anyway, his idea in not going home being that something may happen in this town while he is at home that he is not in on. The Brain seldom goes anywhere in particular. He never goes out in public with any one of his dolls, except maybe once or twice a year with Charlotte, his ever-loving wife, and finally he even stops going with her because Doris Clare says it does not look good to Doris's personal friends.

The Brain marries Charlotte long before he becomes the biggest guy in gambling operations in the East, and a millionaire two or three times over, but he is never much of a hand to sit around home and chew the fat with his ever-loving wife, as husbands often do. Furthermore, when he is poor he has to live in a neighbourhood which is too far away for it to be convenient for him to go home, so finally he gets out of the habit of going there.

But Charlotte is not such a doll as cares to spend more than one or two years looking at the pictures on the wall, because it seems the pictures on her wall are nothing but pictures of cows in the meadows and houses covered with snow, so she does not go home any more than necessary, either, and has her own friends and is very happy indeed, especially after The Brain gets so he can send in right along.

I will say one thing about The Brain and his dolls: he never picks a crow. He has a very good eye for faces and shapes, and even Charlotte, his ever-loving wife, is not a crow, although she is not as young as she used to be. As for Doris Clare, she is one of the great beauties on the Ziegfeld roof in her day, and while her day is by no means yesterday, or even the day before, Doris holds on pretty well in the matter of looks. Giving her a shade the best of it, I will say that Doris is thirty-two or three, but she has plenty of zing left in her, at that, and her hair remains very blonde, no matter what.

In fact, The Brain does not care much if his dolls are blonde or brunette, because Cynthia Harris's hair is as black as the inside of a wolf, while Bobby Baker is betwixt and between, her hair being a light brown. Cynthia Harris is more of a Johnny come-lately than Doris, being out of Mr Earl Carroll's 'Vanities', and I hear she first comes to New York as Miss Somebody in one of these beauty contests which she will win hands down if one of the judges does not get a big wink from a Miss Somebody Else.

Of course, Cynthia is doing some winking herself at this time, but it seems that she picks a guy to wink at thinking he is one of the judges, when he is nothing but a newspaperman and has no say whatever about the decision.

Well, Mr Earl Carroll feels sorry for Cynthia, so he puts her in the 'Vanities' and lets her walk around raw, and The Brain sees her, and the next thing anybody knows she is riding in a big foreign automobile the size of a rum chaser, and is chucking a terrible swell.

Personally, I always consider Bobby Baker the smartest of all The Brain's dolls, because she is just middling as to looks and she does not have any of the advantages of life like Doris Clare and Cynthia Harris, such as jobs on the stage where they can walk around showing off their shapes to guys such as The Brain. Bobby Baker starts off as nothing but a private secretary to a guy in Wall Street, and naturally she is always wearing clothes, or anyway, as many clothes as an ordinary doll wears nowadays, which is'nt so many, at that.

It seems that The Brain once has some business with the guy Bobby works for and happens to get talking to Bobby, and she tells him how she always wishes to meet him, what with hearing and reading about him, and how he is just as handsome and romantic-looking as she always pictures him to herself.

Now I wish to say I will never call any doll a liar, being at all times a gentleman, and for all I know, Bobby Baker may really think The Brain is handsome and romantic-looking, but personally I figure if she is not lying to him, she is at least a little excited when she make such a statement to The Brain. The best you can give The Brain at this time is that he is very well dressed.

He is maybe forty years old, give or take a couple of years, and he is commencing to get a little bunchy about the middle, what with sitting down at card-tables so much and never taking any exercise outside of walking guys such as me up and down in front of Mindy's for a few hours every night. He has a clean-looking face, always very white around the gills, and he has nice teeth and a nice smile when he wishes to smile, which is never at guys who owe him dough.

And I will say for The Brain he has what is called personality. He tells a story well, although he is always the hero of any story he tells, and he knows how to make himself agreeable to dolls in many ways. He has a pretty fair sort of education, and while dolls such as Cynthia and Doris, and maybe Charlotte, too, will rather have a charge account at Cartier's than all the education in Yale and Harvard put together, it seems that Bobby Baker likes highbrow gab, so naturally she gets plenty of same from The Brain.

Well, pretty soon Bobby is riding around in a car bigger than Cynthia's, though neither is as big as Doris's car, and all the neighbours' children over in Flatbush, which is where Bobby hails from, are very jealous of her and running around spreading gossip about her, but keeping their eyes open for big cars themselves. Personally, I always figure The Brain lowers himself socially by taking up with a doll from Flatbush, especially as Bobby Baker soon goes in for literary guys, such as newspaper scribes and similar characters around Greenwich Village.

But there is no denying Bobby Baker is a very smart little doll, and in the four or five years she is one of The Brain's dolls, she gets more dough out of him than all the others put together, because she is always telling him how much she loves him, and saying she cannot do without him, while Doris Clare and Cynthia Harris sometimes forget to mention this more than once or twice a month.

Now what happens early one morning but a guy by the name of Daffy Jack hauls off and sticks a shiv in The Brain's left side. It seems that this is done at the request of a certain party by the name of Homer Swing, who owes The Brain plenty of dough in a gambling transaction, and who becomes very indignant when The Brain presses him somewhat for payment. It seems that Daffy Jack, who is considered a very good shiv artist, aims at The Brain's heart, but misses it by a couple of inches, leaving The Brain with a very bad cut in his side which calls for some stitching.

Big Nig, the crap shooter, and I are standing at Fifty-second Street and Seventh Avenue along about 2 a.m., speaking of not much, when The Brain comes stumbling out of Fifty-second Street, and falls in Big Nig's arms, practically ruining a brand-new topcoat which Big Nig pays sixty bucks for a few days back with the blood that is coming out of the cut. Naturally, Big Nig is indignant about this, but we can see that it is no time to be speaking to The Brain about such matters. We can see that The Brain is carved up quite some, and is in a bad way.

Of course, we are not greatly surprised at seeing The Brain in this condition, because for years he is practically no price around this town, what with this guy and that being anxious to do something or other to him, but we are never expecting to see him carved up like a turkey. We are expecting to see him with a few slugs in him, and both Big Nig and me are very angry to think that there are guys around who will use such instruments as a knife on anybody.

But while we are thinking it over, The Brain says to me like this:

'Call Hymie Weissberger, and Doc Frisch,' he says, 'and take me home.'

Naturally, a guy such as The Brain wishes his lawyer before he wishes his doctor, and Hymie Weissberger is The Brain's mouthpiece, and a very sure-footed guy, at that.

'Well,' I say, 'we better take you to a hospital where you can get good attention at once.'

'No,' The Brain says. 'I wish to keep this secret. It will be a bad thing for me right now to have this get out, and if you take me to a hospital they must report it to the coppers. Take me home.'

Naturally, I say which home, being somewhat confused about The Brain's homes, and he seems to study a minute as if this is a question to be well thought out.

'Park Avenue,' The Brain says finally, so Big Nig stops a taxi-cab, and we help The Brain into the cab and tell the jockey to take us to the apartment house on Park Avenue near Sixty-fourth where The Brain's ever-loving wife Charlotte lives.

When we get there, I figure it is best for me to go up first and break the news gently to Charlotte, because I can see what a shock it is bound to be to any ever-loving wife to have her husband brought home in the early hours of the morning all shivved up.

Well, the doorman and the elevator guy in the apartment house give me an argument about going up to The Brain's apartment, saying a blow out of some kind is going on there, but after I explain to them that The Brain is sick, they let me go. A big fat butler comes to the door of the apartment when I ring, and I can see there are many dolls and guys in evening clothes in the apartment, and somebody is singing very loud.

The butler tries to tell me I cannot see Charlotte, but I finally convince him it is best, so by and by she comes to the door, and a very pleasant sight she is, at that, with jewellery all over her. I stall around awhile, so as not to alarm her too much, and then I tell her The Brain meets with an accident and that we have him outside in a cab, and ask her where we shall put him.

'Why,' she says, 'put him in a hospital, of course. I am entertaining some very important people to-night, and I cannot have them disturbed by bringing in a hospital patient. Take him to a hospital, and tell him I will come and see him to-morrow and bring him some broth.'

I try to explain to her that The Brain does not need any broth, but a nice place to lie down in but finally she gets very testy with me and shuts the door in my face, saying as follows:

'Take him to a hospital, I tell you. This is a ridiculous hour for him to be coming home, anyway. It is twenty years since he comes home so early.'

Then as I am waiting for the elevator, she opens the door again just a little bit and says:

'By the way, is he hurt bad?'

I say we do not know how bad he is hurt, and she shuts the door again, and I go back to the cab again, thinking what a heartless doll she is, although I can see where it will be very inconvenient for her to bust up her party, at that.

The Brain is lying back in the corner of the cab, his eyes half-closed, and by this time it seems that Big Nig stops the blood somewhat with a handkerchief, but The Brain acts somewhat weak to me. He sort of rouses himself when I climb in the cab, and when I tell him his ever-loving wife is not home he smiles a bit and whispers:

'Take me to Doris.'

Now Doris lives in a big apartment house away over on West Seventy-second Street near the Drive, and I tell the taxi jockey to go there while The Brain seems to slide off into a doze. Then Big Nig leans over to me and says to me like this:

'No use taking him there,' Big Nig says. 'I see Doris going out to-night all dressed up in her ermine coat with this actor guy, Jack Walen, she is struck on. It is a very great scandal around and about the way they carry on. Let us take him to Cynthia,' Nig says. 'She is a very large-hearted doll who will be very glad to take him in.'

Now Cynthia Harris has a big suite of rooms that cost fifteen G's a year in a big hotel just off Fifth Avenue, Cynthia being a doll who likes to be downtown so if she hears of anything coming off anywhere she can get there very rapidly. When we arrive at the hotel I call her on the house 'phone and tell her I must see her about something very important, so Cynthia says for me to come up.

It is now maybe three-fifteen, and I am somewhat surprised to find Cynthia home, at that, but there she is, and looking very beautiful indeed in a negligee with her hair hanging down, and I can see that The Brain is no chump when it comes to picking them. She gives me a hello pleasant enough, but as soon as I explain what I am there for, her kisser gets very stern and she says to me like this:

'Listen,' she says, 'I got trouble enough around this joint, what with two guys getting in a fight over me at a little gathering I have here last night and the house copper coming in to split them out, and I do not care to have any more. Suppose it gets out that The Brain is here? What will the newspapers print about me? Think of my reputation!'

Well, in about ten minutes I can see there is no use arguing with her, because she can talk faster than I can, and mostly she talks about what a knock it will be to her reputation if she takes The Brain in, so I leave her standing at the door in her negligee, still looking very beautiful, at that.

There is now nothing for us to do but take The Brain to Bobby Baker, who lives in a duplex apartment in Sutton Place over by the East River, where the swells set up a colony of nice apartments in the heart of an old tenement-house neighbourhood, and as we are on our way there with The Brain lying back in the cab just barely breathing, I say to Big Nig like this:

'Nig,' I say, 'when we get to Bobby's, we will carry The Brain in without asking her first and just dump him on her so she cannot refuse to take him in, although', I say, 'Bobby Baker is a nice little doll, and I am pretty sure she will do anything she can for him, especially', I say, 'since he pays fifty G's for this apartment we are going to.'

So when the taxi-cab stops in front of Bobby's house, Nig and I take The Brain out of the cab and lug him between us up to the door of Bobby's apartment, where I ring the bell. Bobby opens the door herself, and I happen to see a guy's legs zip into a room in the apartment behind her, although of course there is nothing wrong in such a sight, even though the guy's legs are in pink pyjamas.

Naturally, Bobby is greatly astonished to see us with The Brain dangling between us, but she does not invite us in as I explain to her that The Brain is stabbed and that his last words are for us to take him to his Bobby. Furthermore, she does not let me finish my story which will be very sad indeed, if she keeps on listening.

'If you do not take him away from here at once,' Bobby says, before I am down to the pathetic part, 'I will call the cops and you guys will be arrested on suspicion that you know something about how he gets hurt.'

Then she slams the door on us, and we lug The Brain back down the stairs into the street, because all of a sudden it strikes us that Bobby is right, and if The Brain is found in our possession all stabbed up, and he happens to croak, we are in a very tough spot, because the cops just naturally love to refuse to believe guys like Big Nig and me, no matter what we say.

Furthermore, the same idea must hit the taxi-cab jockey after we lift The Brain out of the cab, because he is nowhere to be seen, and there we are away over by the East River in the early morning, with no other taxis in sight, and a cop liable to happen along any minute.

Well, there is nothing for us to do but get away from there, so Big Nig and I start moving, with me carrying The Brain's feet, and Big Nig his head. We get several blocks away from Sutton Place, going very slow and hiding in dark doorways when we hear anybody coming, and now we are in a section of tenement houses, when all of a sudden up out of the basement of one of these tenements pops a doll.

She sees us before we can get in a dark place, and she seems to have plenty of nerve for a doll, because she comes right over to us and looks at Big Nig and me, and then looks at The Brain, who loses his hat somewhere along the line, so his pale face is plain to be seen by even the dim street light.

'Why,' the doll says, 'it is the kind gentleman who gives me the five dollars for the apple—the money that buys the medicine that saves my Joey's life. What is the matter?'

'Well,' I say to the doll, who is still raggedy and still red-headed, 'there is nothing much the matter except if we do not get him somewhere soon, this guy will up and croak on us.'

'Bring him into my house,' she says, pointing to the joint she just comes out of. 'It is not much of a place, but you can let him rest there until you get help. I am just going over here to a drug store to get some more medicine for Joey, although he is out of danger now, thanks to this gentleman.'

So we lug The Brain down the basement steps with the doll leading the way, and we follow her into a room that smells like a Chinese laundry and seems to be full of kids sleeping on the floor. There is only one bed in the room, and it is not much of a bed any way you look at it, and there seems to be a kid in this bed, too, but the red-headed doll rolls this kid over to one side of the bed and motions us to lay The Brain alongside of the kid. Then she gets a wet rag and starts bathing The Brain's noggin.

He finally opens his eyes and looks at the red-headed raggedy doll, and she grins at him very pleasant. When I think things over afterward, I figure The Brain is conscious of much of what is going on when we are packing him around, although he does not say anything, maybe because he is too weak. Anyway, he turns his head to Big Nig, and says to him like this:

'Bring Weissberger and Frisch as quick as you can,' he says. 'Anyway, get Weissberger. I do not know how bad I am hurt, and I must tell him some things.'

Well, The Brain is hurt pretty bad, as it turns out, and in fact he never gets well, but he stays in the basement dump until he dies three days later, with the red-headed raggedy doll nursing him alongside her sick kid Joey, because the croaker, old Doc Frisch, says it is no good moving The Brain, and may only make him pop off sooner. In fact, Doc Frisch is much astonished that The Brain lives at all, considering the way we lug him around.

I am present at The Brain's funeral at Wiggin's Funeral Parlours, like everybody else on Broadway, and I wish to say I never see more flowers in all my life. They are all over the casket and knee-deep on the floor, and some of the pieces must cost plenty, the price of flowers being what they are in this town nowadays. In fact, I judge it is the size and cost of the different pieces that makes me notice a little bundle of faded red carnations not much bigger than your fist that is laying alongside a pillow of violets the size of a horse blanket.

There is a small card tied to the carnations, and it says on this card, as follows: 'To a kind gentleman', and it comes to my mind that out of all the thousands of dollars' worth of flowers there, these faded carnations represent the only true sincerity. I mention this to Big Nig, and he says the chances are I am right, but that even true sincerity is not going to do The Brain any good where he is going.

Anybody will tell you that for off-hand weeping at a funeral The Brain's ever-loving wife Charlotte does herself very proud indeed, but she is not one-to-seven with Doris Clare, Cynthia Harris, and Bobby Baker. In fact, Bobby Baker weeps so loud that there is some talk of heaving her out of the funeral altogether.

However, I afterwards hear that loud as they are at the funeral, it is nothing to the weep they all put on when it comes out that The Brain has Hymie Weissberger draw up a new will while he is dying and leaves all his dough to the red-headed raggedy doll, whose name seems to be O'Halloran, and who is the widow of a bricklayer and has five kids.

Well, at first all the citizens along Broadway say it is a wonderful thing for The Brain to do, and serves his ever-loving wife and Doris and Cynthia and Bobby just right; and from the way one and all speaks you will think they are going to build a monument to The Brain for his generosity to the red-headed raggedy doll.

But about two weeks after he is dead, I hear citizens saying the chances are the red-headed raggedy doll is nothing but one of The Brain's old-time dolls, and that maybe the kids are his and that he leaves them the dough because his conscience hurts him at the finish, for this is the way Broadway is. But personally I know it cannot be true, for if there is one thing The Brain never has it is a conscience.

Damon Runyon (1884–1946), *Guys and Dolls* (1932).

———

O NE *of the more interesting oddities of between-the-wars American humorous prose was the publication in 1930 of a slim volume entitled* The Specialist.

It is indisputably a small masterpiece. Only about three thousand words long, about the length of a New Yorker *casual, it is in the rose-growers' sense of the word, a 'sport', a one-off piece of mild eccentricity nothing to do with the main root-system of prose humour.*

Its author, Charles 'Chick' Sale, was not even a writer but a character comedian who specialized in making appearances as an after-dinner entertainer, in those days a profitable form of work for vaudeville performers. Chick Sale's most popular act was his portrayal of an old country carpenter named Lem Putt, a craftsman whose speciality, and love, was the building of privies.

Piracy and plagiarism were great problems to character comedians in the early part of this century. Original music-hall acts were constantly being stolen by uninventive performers and it was impossible for Chick Sale to get legal protection for a theatrical character like 'Lem Putt' but somebody advised him that he should commit his act to print whereupon it might be protected by the laws of literary copyright, which were effective.

In 1929 he did this by forming a token publishing company and setting in type his act exactly as he performed it (even leaving in his occasional references to his after-dinner audience, like, 'And I tell you, gentlemen, there ain't nothin'. . .'). In 1930 he printed off a few copies for legal purposes and offered the spare copies for sale.

Over fifty years later, a million copies of The Specialist *have been sold, hardback, in ten languages, and it is still in print and going strong.*

The book was illustrated by William Kermode who put on the cover a drawing of an old farmer, Elmer Ridgway, sitting patiently on his Lem Putt family three-holer. George Bernard Shaw sent the author one of his famous postcards: it read 'The illustrations are excellent but the frontispiece fails in courage. Clearly it should represent the Elmer family in situ. *G.B.S.'*

The indelicate subject-matter would doubtless have helped to make Chick Sales's act popular at gentlemen's dinners but the indelicacies were handled so delicately that even in England the Times Literary Supplement *was able to report: 'Lem, we gather, is an artist in his own way . . . his observations are shrewd and amusing, but since to appreciate their humour one must submit to a slight violation of the reticence and modesty which Lem understands but does not profess, we cannot recommend this book to fastidious people. For our part we find it too genial to be offensive.'*

The shock effect of a humorous book being based upon such a taboo subject as lavatories has evaporated with the years, leaving behind the real strengths of Chick Sales's humour: the nostalgic invocation of peaceful rural life in Illinois and the character of Lem himself, gentle, good, a self-appointed master-craftsman for whom the expression 'job-satisfaction' might have been invented:

THE SPECIALIST

You've heerd a lot of pratin' and prattlin' about this bein' the age of specialization. I'm a carpenter by trade. At one time I could of built a house, barn, church or chicken coop. But I seen the need of a specialist in my line, so I studied her. I got her; she's mine. Gentlemen, you are face to face with the champion privy builder of Sangamon County.

Luke Harkins was my first customer. He heerd about me specializin' and decided to take a chance. I built for him just the average eight family three holer. With that job my reputation was made, and since then I have devoted all my time and thought to that special line. Of course, when business is slack, I do do a bit of paper-hangin' on the side. But my heart is just in privy buildin'.

Elmer Ridgway needs an estimate for a new privy on the old Robinson property which Elmer and family are moving into.

Lem's specialized knowledge and experience is never so brilliantly displayed as when he is advising a customer on the planning of his privy:

Elmer comes out and we get to talkin' about a good location. He was all fer puttin' her right alongside a jagged path runnin' by a big Northern Spy.

'I wouldn't do it, Elmer,' I sez; 'and I'll tell you why. In the first place, her bein' near a tree is bad. There ain't no sound in nature so disconcertin' as the sound of apples droppin' on the roof. Then another thing, there's a crooked path runnin' by that tree and the soil ain't adapted to absorbin' moisture. Durin' the rainy season she's likely to be slippery. Take your grandpappy—goin' out there is about the only recreation he gets. He'll go out some rainy night with his nighties flappin' around his legs, and like as not when you come out in the mornin' you'll find him prone in the mud, or maybe skidded off one of them curves and wound up in the corn crib. No, sir,' I sez, 'put her in a straight line with the house and, if it's all the same to you, have her go past the wood-pile. I'll tell you why.

'Take a woman, fer instance—out she goes. On the way back she'll gather five sticks of wood, and the average woman will make four or five trips a day. There's twenty sticks in the wood box without any trouble. On the other hand, take a timid woman, if she sees any men folks around, she's too bashful to go direct out, so she'll go to the wood-pile, pick up the wood, go back to the house and watch her chance. The average timid woman—especially a new hired girl—I knowed to make as many as ten trips to the wood-pile before she goes in, regardless. On a good day you'll have your wood box filled by noon . . .'

On the question of economy versus durability Lem is staunchly on the side of strength. And he backs up his recommendation with a sober warning of what can happen if his advice is ignored:

'When it come to construction,' I sez, 'I can give you joists or beams. Joists make a good job. Beams cost a bit more, but they're worth it. Beams, you might say, will last forever. 'Course, I could give you joists, but take your Aunty Emmy, she ain't gettin' a mite lighter. Some day she might be out there when them joists give way and there she'd be—catched. Another thing you've got to figger on, Elmer,' I sez, 'is that Odd Fellows picnic in the fall. Them boys is goin' to get in there in fours and sixes, singin' and drinkin' and the like, and I want to tell you there's nothin' breaks up an Odd Fellows picnic quicker than a diggin' party . . .'

There is a telling moment when Lem asks Elmer what he wants in the way of ablutionary aids. The choice is 'catalogue' or 'cobs'. There was little waste paper on a farm so it was traditional to use as loo paper the enormous Sears Roebuck mail order catalogue which went to every rural household. A hole was drilled in the corner, a loop of string was added and it was hung in the privy on a nail. The terrible alternative, particularly in frosty weather, was the old frontier method in use before the days of free catalogues—dry corn cobs:

'Now, about her furnishin's. I can give you a nail or hook for the catalogue, and besides, a box for cobs. You take your pa, for instance; he's of the old school and naturally he'd prefer the box; so we put 'em both in, Elmer. Won't cost you a bit more for the box and keeps peace in the family. You can't teach an old dog new tricks,' I sez . . .

➜ The farmlands of the USA used to be called 'the cob and catalog belt'.

And so Lem goes on with the planning, asking for decisions all the way, leaving nothing to chance; the poet of the privy:

'Now,' I sez, 'how do you want that door to swing? Openin' in or out?' He said he didn't know. So I sez it should open in. This is the way it works out: 'Place yourself in there. The door openin' in, say, about forty-five degree. This gives you air and lets the sun beat in. Now, if you hear anybody comin', you can give it a quick shove with your foot and there you are. But if she swings out, where are you? You can't run the risk of havin' her open for air or sun, because if anyone comes, you can't get up off that seat, reach way round and grab 'er without gettin' caught, now can you?' He could see I was right.

So I built his door like all my doors, swingin' in, and, of course, facing east, to get the full benefit of th' sun. And I tell you, gentlemen, ther ain't nothin' more restful than to get out there in the mornin,' comfortably seated, with th' door about three-fourths open. The old sun, beatin' in on you, sort of relaxes a body—makes you feel m-i-g-h-t-y, m-i-g-h-t-y r-e-s-t-f-u-l . . .

Chick (Charles) Sale (1885–1935), *The Specialist* (1930).

———

A T the time when the wits of America were moving to New York there was no similar migration of provincial humorists to London, nor was there in Britain any marked shift in emphasis to match the great American switch from the old homely story-telling to a new urban literacy and sophistication.

In 1919, the year when members of the Algonquin's Vicious Circle were *beginning to sharpen their wits on each other for the pleasure of New York's newspaper readers, one of Britain's most successful humorous publications was a late-Victorian romantic novelette written by a 9-year-old schoolgirl.*

The manuscript of The Young Visiters, *ill-spelt, almost without punctuation, was submitted to the publishers Chatto and Windus with a note explaining that it had been written when the authoress was only 9.*

Chatto and Windus decided to publish and asked the distinguished playwright, Sir James Barrie, to write a preface. Barrie, somewhat prudently since he had built his reputation on writing about winsome children like Sentimental Tommy, Peter Pan, *and* Alice Sit-by-the-Fire, *agreed on condition that he could meet the authoress and verify for himself that 'Daisy Ashford' was not in reality George Bernard Shaw in skittish mood, or a literary bricklayer.*

Daisy Ashford turned out to be quite genuine; an agreeable lady in her late thirties who really had written the story in pencil in a twopenny notebook when she was 9 and then left it forgotten in a drawer.

In recent years The Young Visiters *has come to be recognized as a small comic masterpiece. The story, a compound of every Silver Fork romance since* Evelina, *is freshly told with a child's naïvety and innocence. The authoress's picture of the grown-up world of rich men is exciting in her own, childlike terms; her rich hero Bernard can tip 2s. 6d. without even thinking about it, her heroine Ethel is old enough to put on rouge whenever she feels like it (which is frequently: 'she carried . . . a green silk bag containing a few stray hairpins a clean handkerchief five shillings and a pot of ruge in case.') And in Mr Salteena, Ethel's admirer, the young authoress has created one of literature's most memorable and likeable losers.*

In only one sentence does the authoress let the mask slip and reveal the little girl beneath: 'After he had finished his meal he got down . . .'

The story, which drives along at a cracking pace, begins at the house of Mr Salteena, a middle-sized man aged 42 with whom our heroine is staying for a few days. (No chaperone. Perhaps unnecessary because of Mr Salteena's great age.) Mr Salteena, whose father was a butcher, is not quite a gentleman but is trying hard to become one. His friend Bernard is very gentlemanly ('rather bent in the middle with very nice long legs') and when he invites Mr Salteena to stay for a few days he tactfully encloses a fashionable top hat for Mr Salteena to wear so that he won't look so common:

Chapter One

QUITE A YOUNG GIRL

Mr Salteena was an elderly man of 42 and was fond of asking people to stay with him. He had quite a young girl staying with him of 17 named Ethel Monticue. Mr Salteena had dark short hair and mustache and wiskers which were very black and twisty. He was middle size and he had very pale blue eyes. He had a pale brown suit but on Sundays he had a black one and he had a topper every day as he thorght it more becoming. Ethel Monticue had fair hair done on the top and blue eyes. She had a blue velvit frock which had grown rarther short in the sleeves. She had a black straw hat and kid gloves.

One morning Mr Salteena came down to brekfast and found Ethel had come down first which was strange. Is the tea made Ethel he said rubbing his hands. Yes said Ethel and such a quear shaped parcel has come for you. Yes indeed it was a quear shape parcel it was a hat box tied down very tight and a letter stuffed between the string. Well well said Mr Salteena parcels do turn quear I will read the letter first and so saying he tore open the letter and this is what it said

MY DEAR ALFRED.

I want you to come for a stop with me so I have sent you a top hat wraped up in tishu paper inside the box. Will you wear it staying with me because it is very uncommon. Please bring one of your young ladies whichever is the prettiest in the face.

I remain Yours truely
BERNARD CLARK.

Well said Mr Salteena I shall take you to stay Ethel and fancy him sending me a top hat. Then Mr S. opened the box and there lay the most splendid top hat of a loverly rich tone rarther like grapes with a ribbon round compleat.

Well said Mr Salteena peevishly I dont know if I shall like it the bow of the ribbon is too flighty for my age. Then he sat down and eat the egg which Ethel had so kindly laid for him. After he had finished his meal he got down and began to write to Bernard Clark he ran upstairs on his fat legs and took out his blotter with a loud sniff and this is what he wrote

MY DEAR BERNARD

Certinly I shall come and stay with you next Monday I will bring Ethel Monticue commonly called Miss M. She is very active and pretty. I do hope I shall enjoy myself with you. I am fond of digging in the garden and I am parshial to ladies if they are nice I suppose it is my nature. I am not quite a gentleman but you would hardly notice it but cant be helped anyhow. We will come by the 3-15.

Your old and valud friend
ALFRED SALTEENA.

And so Ethel and Mr Salteena prepare to set off on their visit. This next chapter produces what is probably the twelfth most famous line in humorous prose when Ethel comments on the drains:

Chapter Two

STARTING GAILY

When the great morning came Mr Salteena did not have an egg for his brekfast in case he should be sick on the jorney.

What top hat will you wear asked Ethel.

I shall wear my best black and white alpacka coat to keep off the dust and flies replied Mr Salteena.

I shall put some red ruge on my face said Ethel because I am very pale owing to the drains in this house.

You will look very silly said Mr Salteena with a dry laugh.

Well so will you said Ethel in a snappy tone and she ran out of the room with a very superier run throwing out her legs behind and her arms swinging in rithum.

Well said the owner of the house she has a most idiotick run.

Presently Ethel came back in her best hat and a lovly velvit coat of royal blue. Do I look nice in my get up she asked.

Mr Salteena survayed her. You look rarther rash my dear your colors dont quite match your face but never mind I am just going up to say goodbye to Rosalind the housemaid.

Well dont be long said Ethel. Mr S. skipped upstairs to Rosalinds room. Good-bye Rosalind he said I shall be back soon and I hope I shall enjoy myself.

I make no doubt of that sir said Rosalind with a blush as Mr Salteena silently put 2/6 on the dirty toilet cover.

Take care of your bronkitis said Mr S. rarther bashfully and he hastilly left the room waving his hand carelessly to the housemaid.

Come along cried Ethel powdering her nose in the hall let us get into the cab. Mr Salteena did not care for powder but he was an unselfish man so he dashed into the cab. Sit down said Ethel as the cabman waved his whip you are standing on my luggage. Well I am paying for the cab said Mr S. so I might be allowed to put my feet were I like.

They traveled 2nd class in the train and Ethel was longing to go first but thought perhaps least said soonest mended. Mr Salteena got very excited in the train about his visit. Ethel was calm but she felt excited inside. Bernard has a big house said Mr S. gazing at Ethel he is inclined to be rich.

Oh indeed said Ethel looking at some cows flashing past the window . . .

Ethel has shown that she can be a bit of a little madam but she recovers her girlish spirits in the grandeur of Bernard Clark's mansion and she and the slightly-common Mr Salteena thoroughly enjoy their taste of High Life. The big excitement is being brought morning tea in bed; this happens several times in the book and clearly represents to the young authoress the ultimate in self-indulgence:

Chapter Four

MR SALTEENAS PLAN

Mr Salteena woke up rarther early next day and was surprised and delighted to find Horace the footman entering with a cup of tea.

Oh thankyou my man said Mr Salteena rolling over in the costly bed. Mr

Clark is nearly out of the bath sir announced Horace I will have great plesure in turning it on for you if such is your desire. Well yes you might said Mr Salteena seeing it was the idear and Horace gave a profound bow.

Ethel are you getting up shouted Mr Salteena.

Very nearly replied Ethel faintly from the next room.

I say said Mr Salteena excitedly I have had some tea in bed.

So have I replied Ethel . . .

Mr Salteena seizes his soap and wanders off to find the bathroom which is 'most sumpshous':

It had a lovly white shiny bath and sparkling taps and several towels arrayed in readiness by thourghtful Horace. It also had a step for climbing up the bath and other good dodges of a rich nature . . .

After breakfast Mr Salteena corners Bernard in his study to ask his advice on an important personal matter:

Fire away said Bernard lighting his pipe. Well I cant exactly do that said Mr Salteena in slow tones it is a searious matter and you can advise me as you are a thorugh gentleman I am sure.

Well yes said Bernard what can I do for you eh Alf? . . .

Alf Salteena reveals all. He is desperate to become a gentleman, clearly in order to make himself more attractive in Ethel's eyes. Bernard, ever kindly, gives Mr Salteena a letter of recommendation to his friend the earl of Clincham who has 'a compartment at Crystal pallace' (the door is labelled 'Clincham Earl of' in big letters) where, for a fee, he teaches common people to behave like gentlemen.

The middle section of the book follows poor Mr Salteena in his struggle to become a member of polite society. Clincham takes him to a levee where 'on a golden chair was seated the prince of Wales in a lovely ermine cloak and a small but costly crown'.

But it was unwise of Mr Salteena to leave Bernard alone with Ethel. In a trice the besotted Bernard has whisked her up to London for a week's fun (still no chaperone but one feels that Bernard can be trusted under all circumstances).

The happy young lovers book in at the luxurious Gaierty hotel:

Chapter Seven

BERNARDS IDEAR

. . . Ethel was spellbound at the size of the big hall—Bernard poked his head into the window of the pay desk. Have you a coupple of bedrooms for self and young lady he enquired in a lordly way.

A very handsome lady with golden hair and a lace apron glanced at a book and hastily replied Oh yes sir two beauties on the 1st floor number 9 and 10.

Thankyou said Bernard we will go up if you have no objection.

None whatever sir said the genial lady the beds are well aired and the view is quite pleasant.

Come along Ethel cried Bernard this sounds alright eh.

Oh quite said Ethel with a beaming smile.

They went upstairs and entered number 9 a very fine compartment with a large douny bed and white doors with glass handles leading into number 10 an equally dainty room but a trifle smaller.

Which will you have Ethel asked Bernard.

Oh well I would rarther you settled it said Ethel. I am willing to abide by your choice.

The best shall be yours then said Bernard bowing gallantly and pointing to the biggest room.

Ethel blushed at his speaking look. I shall be quite lost in that huge bed she added to hide her embarassment.

Yes I expect you will said Bernard . . . .

This steamy little scene sets the mood for the next few days during which Bernard falls even more firmly in love with Ethel and she with him.

They meet Mr Salteena at a society party and he, now a gent, proposes to Ethel who promptly rejects him. He takes it badly at first but then philosophically resigns himself to the inevitable:

This is agony cried Mr Salteena clutching hold of a table my life will be sour grapes and ashes without you.

Be a man said Ethel in a gentle whisper and I shall always think of you in a warm manner.

Well half a loaf is better than no bread responded Mr Salteena in a gloomy voice . . .

Bernard and Ethel are eventually married in Westminster Abbey and depart on honeymoon to Egypt (Ethel in 'a very chick toque', Bernard in 'clean under clothing').

But not before the authoress has concentrated all her formidable skills as a storyteller on making Bernard's proposal to Ethel the great romantic climax of her extraordinary novel:

Chapter Nine
A PROPOSALE

Next morning while imbibing his morning tea beneath his pink silken quilt Bernard decided he must marry Ethel with no more delay. I love the girl he said to himself and she must be mine but I somehow feel I can not propose in London it would not be seemly in the city of London. We must go for a day in the country and when surrounded by the gay twittering of the birds and the smell of the cows I will lay my suit at her feet and he waved his arm wildly at the gay thought. Then he sprang from bed and gave a rat tat at Ethel's door.

Are you up my dear he called.

Well not quite said Ethel hastilly jumping from her downy nest.

Be quick cried Bernard I have a plan to spend a day near Windsor Castle and we will take our lunch and spend a happy day.

Oh Hurrah shouted Ethel I shall soon be ready as I had my bath last night so wont wash very much now.

No dont said Bernard and added in a rarther fervent tone through the chink of the door you are fresher than the rose my dear no soap could make you fairer.

Then he dashed off very embarrased to dress. Ethel blushed and felt a bit excited as she heard the words and she put on a new white muslin dress in a fit of high spirits. She looked very beautiful with some red roses in her hat and the dainty red ruge in her cheeks looked quite the thing. Bernard heaved a sigh and his eyes flashed as he beheld her and Ethel thorght to herself what a fine type of manhood he reprisented with his nice thin legs in pale broun trousers and well fitting spats and a red rose in his button hole and rarther a sporting cap which gave him a great air with its quaint check and little flaps to pull down if necessary. Off they started the envy of all the waiters.

They arrived at Windsor very hot from the jorney and Bernard at once hired a boat to row his beloved up the river. Ethel could not row but she much enjoyed seeing the tough sunburnt arms of Bernard tugging at the oars as she lay among the rich cushions of the dainty boat. She had a rarther lazy nature but Bernard did not know of this. However he soon got dog tired and suggested lunch by the mossy bank.

Oh yes said Ethel quickly opening the sparkling champaigne.

Dont spill any cried Bernard as he carved some chicken.

They eat and drank deeply of the charming viands ending up with merangs and choclates.

Let us now bask under the spreading trees said Bernard in a passiunate tone.

Oh yes lets said Ethel and she opened her dainty parasole and sank down upon the long green grass. She closed her eyes but she was far from asleep. Bernard sat beside her in profound silence gazing at her pink face and long wavy eye lashes. He puffed at his pipe for some moments while the larks gaily caroled in the blue sky. Then he edged a trifle closer to Ethels form.

Ethel he murmered in a trembly voice.

Oh what is it said Ethel hastily sitting up.

Words fail me ejaculated Bernard horsly my passion for you is intense he added fervently. It has grown day and night since I first beheld you.

Oh said Ethel in supprise I am not prepared for this and she lent back against the trunk of the tree.

Bernard placed one arm tightly round her. When will you marry me Ethel he uttered you must be my wife it has come to that I love you so intensly that if you say no I shall perforce dash my body to the brink of yon muddy river he panted wildly.

Oh don't do that implored Ethel breathing rarther hard.

Then say you love me he cried.

Oh Bernard she sighed fervently I certinly love you madly you are to me like a Heathen god she cried looking at his manly form and handsome flashing face I will indeed marry you.

How soon gasped Bernard gazing at her intensly.

As soon as possible said Ethel gently closing her eyes.

My Darling whispered Bernard and he seiezed her in his arms we will be marrid next week.

Oh Bernard muttered Ethel this is so sudden.

No no cried Bernard and taking the bull by both horns he kissed her violently on her dainty face. My bride to be he murmered several times.

Ethel trembled with joy as she heard the mistick words.

Oh Bernard she said little did I ever dream of such as this and she suddenly fainted into his out stretched arms.

Oh I say gasped Bernard and laying the dainty burden on the grass he dashed to the waters edge and got a cup full of the fragrant river to pour on his true loves pallid brow.

She soon came to and looked up with a sickly smile take me back to the Gaierty hotel she whispered faintly.

With pleasure my darling said Bernard I will just pack up our viands ere I unloose the boat.

Ethel felt better after a few drops of champagne and began to tidy her hair while Bernard packed the remains of the food. Then arm in arm they tottered to the boat.

I trust you have not got an illness my darling murmered Bernard as he helped her in.

Oh no I am very strong said Ethel I fainted from joy she added to explain matters.

Oh I see said Bernard handing her a cushon well some people do he added kindly and so saying they rowed down the dark stream now flowing silently beneath a golden moon. All was silent as the lovers glided home with joy in their hearts and radiunce on their faces only the sound of the mystearious water lapping against the frail vessel broke the monotony of the night.

So I will end my chapter.

Daisy Ashford (1881–1972), *The Young Visiters* (1919).

Another comic novelist who made an early impact on post-First World War Britain was E. F. Benson. Unlike Daisy Ashford, Fred Benson (as he was always known) was not the sort of person to give up writing once he had enjoyed a touch of the divine itch. His first novel Dodo, published when he was aged 26, was a huge success and he spent his next forty-seven years mixing with the witty sector of society and happily scribbling light fiction and collections of reminiscences at the rate of nearly two volumes a year; he wrote ninety-three books, all of them amusing and successful in their day. He was, as Michael Sadleir noted sadly in the Dictionary of National Biography, uncontrollably prolific.

Fred's two distinguished brothers and remarkable sister all wrote voluminously and with distinction (one brother, A. C. Benson, wrote the poem which, set to pulse-stirring music by Elgar, became 'Land of Hope and Glory').

Perhaps it was something in the Benson blood which made them into such compulsive authors; certainly the family was a little unconventional even for late-Victorian theological/intellectual circles.

Their father was Archbishop of Canterbury and he had proposed to their mother when she was 11. She was his second cousin, Mary Sidgwick, a formidably brainy lady decribed by Gladstone as 'the cleverest woman in Europe'. After bearing the archbishop six children she decided that enough was enough and left Lambeth Palace to live with her lesbian lover, Lucy Tait, daughter of the previous Archbishop of Canterbury. The surviving children, three brothers and their sister, were homosexual, if anything.

What distinguished Fred's stories from most other contemporary comedies of manners was that he disliked most of the characters he wrote about. He did not invite us to smile at the whimsical behaviour of charming eccentrics but at the absurd conduct of self-absorbed and vain fools. Members of the general public in his stories were usually mildly oafish and ladies of the minor aristocracy were invariably domineering and repellant. He was particularly hard on middle-class ladies with social ambitions—but he clearly had very little respect for women of any description.

A typical example of Fred Benson's skilfully malicious froth is Paying Guests, a novel published in 1929.

It is set in a superior boarding-house, 'Wentworth' (gardens—kitchen and flower, tennis courts—hard and soft, a croquet lawn—hard or soft according to the state of the weather. And two bathrooms) in the small town of Bolton Spa.

Wentworth has a shifting population of well-to-do hypochondriacs and malingerers, there to take the spa waters, but it also has some regular healthy residents including Miss Howard, a permanent virgin of 40 who skips everywhere, laughing. Miss Howard paints water-colours and plays the piano. This being a Fred Benson novel, she is also deceitful, pretending to own a country estate which is only a semi-detached house and practising for hours her 'extemporary' piano pieces. Colonel Chase, ex-Indian Army, dominates the bridge table and impressively ad-libs the answers to The Times crossword to any guests who are having trouble with it (he has already worked on it for a long time in his room).

There is to be a concert in the town in aid of the Children's Hospital. Mr Graves, masseur at the thermal baths and raconteur, has gone down with flu and the Revd H. Banks persuades the Colonel to appear instead, to tell those ghost stories, set in India, with which the Colonel has so frequently curdled the blood of Wentworth residents. Miss Howard has agreed to provide suitably eerie piano music on cue ('when I saw—in the far corner . . .'):

Dinner was early that night for the entertainment began at a quarter to eight for eight, whatever that meant. Colonel Chase had pinned a quantity of medals and ribands to his evening coat, among which Mrs Holders swore she detected an ordinary shilling with a hole in it. The assembly room was packed, all but the front row where seats were reserved for the party from Wentworth, and the four centre ones, so Mr Banks excitedly told them, for the Dowager Duchess of Appledore and her party. She had sent in from the Grange that afternoon to order them, with the intimation that she might be a few minutes late. As she was patroness of the Children's Hospital Mr Banks was sure that the entertainment was not to begin without her and her party. He and Town Councillor Bowen had arranged to receive her at the door, and he hoped that Colonel Chase would assist them. So they all three waited for the august arrivals in a strong draught for a quarter of an hour. Then the glad word went about that the motor from the Grange had arrived, and an awed silence settled on the rest of the front row.

The reception committee bowed and smiled and an icy blast swept Lady Appledore and party into the hall. In number and splendour her party was disappointing, for it consisted of two women so wrapped up in cloaks and scarves and capes and woolies that nothing whatever could be seen of them. They were then partially unwound by the reception committee and the bleak and wintry features of Lady Appledore, whose face resembled a frost-bitten pansy with all its markings huddled up together in the middle, were disclosed. 'Party' was her companion, Miss Jobson, whose life was spent in holding skeins of wool for her, reading books to her, and sitting opposite to her in the motor. Lady Appledore then nodded to Mr Banks to signify that she was ready, and the choir of St Giles sang a lullaby and a drinking song amid indescribable apathy.

Colonel Chase's moment had arrived: Miss Howard had slipped into her place behind the piano, and Mr Banks introduced the gallant Colonel whose stories were so well known by repute (and, he might have added, to Wentworth by repetition). The gallant Colonel like Horatio of old had thrown himself into the breach caused by the lamented absence of Mr Graves and so they were going to taste what he might call the choicest of Colonel Chase's anecdotal vintage for themselves.

Wentworth violently led the otherwise tame applause and Colonel Chase's ruddy face had faded to the hue of the cheapest pink blotting paper as he told them about the Curate's egg. Wentworth rocked with laughter but Mrs

Oxney heard Lady Appledore say to her companion, 'I am never amused, Miss Jobson, at jokes about the Church', and she remembered with dismay that the story of the Dean was coming and that her ladyship was the daughter of one. She whispered her apprehensions to her sister who felt sure that Colonel Chase would substitute the story of the little boy and his father's whisky. That would be far more suitable for Lady Appledore was a savage teetotaller.

The narrator embarked upon his story of 'My encounter with the Man-eater', which had so often frozen the blood of Wentworth. But the audience, with the curious unanimity of crowds, had made up their minds, after the Curate's egg, that he was a comic, pure and simple, and the crack-jaw Indian names and allusions to tiffin and Chota-hazzi produced little titters of delighted laughter. They became more and more certain of it when he bade them follow him into the pathless solitary jungle with the kites whistling overhead (here some dramatic boy at the back whistled piercingly between his fingers) and up the dry nullah-wallah. 'All at once,' said the Colonel, pointing at Mrs Oxley, 'I heard a rustle in the bushes close by me, and turning I saw within a few yards of me the gleaming eyes and flashing teeth of the man-eater.' He whisked round, making the movement of putting his rifle to his shoulder, and at that moment, the performing dog which had escaped from its master, leaped on to the stage and sat up and begged. So loud a roar of delighted laughter went up from the entire hall that no one ever knew whether the man killed the man-eater or the man-eater the man. As it slowly subsided amid sporadic cackles, a yelp or two from the performing dog denoted that somebody was 'larning' it to be a tiger.

The story of the little boy and the whisky followed and pleased Lady Appledore very much. 'A teetotaller for life, I expect,' she said to Miss Jobson, 'I should like some more stories of that sort.'

Colonel Chase sat down for a moment after this, and drank a little water out of the glass in which he had pretended as a little boy to put back the whisky. This took the audience's fancy tremendously, and he couldn't conceive why. He was in so strange a mental state that even Mrs Bliss, the interpreter of Mind, would have found him hard to treat. He was simmering with fury at the story of the man-eater having been received with those ribald gusts of laughter, and felt sure that he would have gripped his audience and made them catch their breath with suspense, had not that wretched mongrel bounded on to the stage at the climax. On the other hand, the roars of laughter which had greeted him went to his head like wine, and he hardly knew whether to be elated or indignant. He rose to tell his ghost story, and little did they think what terrors and goose-flesh were coming: then as the *encore*, he would restore them with the tale of the grocer.

The little boy with the whisky had rather damped the spirits of his audience, but on the announcement of 'My own ghost' they brightened up again, and cheerfully beat time to the first few bars of 'On the Road to Mandalay'.

'In the year 1895,' said Colonel Chase, 'I was stationed at Futiput-Sekri, and by the order of his Excellency the Viceroy—'

The quicker-witted portion of his audience began to laugh. It was like George Robey saying 'The last time I had tea with the King'. They knew the sort of thing that was coming. Colonel Chase drew himself up and fingered his medals.

'By the order of his Excellency the Viceroy,' said Colonel Chase, rather severely, 'I was sent into the district of Astmetagaga to make a report of the discontent among the Bizributmas. Bellialonga, the capital of the Bizributma tribe was a three-days journey from Futipur-Sekri, and I had to sleep at two dak-bungalows on the way. Just before sunset on the day of which I am speaking I came in sight of the dak-bungalow of Poona-padra, and sent my khitmagar on with a couple of coolies to cook my dinner, and deal with superfluous cobras.'

'Really very good,' said Lady Appledore to Miss Jobson, 'a perfect parody of Mr Kipling. I am sure something very comical is coming.'

Colonel Chase could not hear what she said but he saw that both she and Miss Jobson had their eyes fixed on him with avid attention.

'The khitmagar was in the cook-house when I arrived,' said he, turning slightly towards the piano to show Miss Howard that her cue was imminent, 'and night was at hand. My table was laid and I was just about to light the lamp, when I saw at the other end of the room—I mean, *in the far corner*—'

The piano punctually emitted a wailing moan, and Colonel Chase raised his voice a little.

'—a grey shape forming itself into the semblance of a man. As the lamp burned brighter—'

'You 'aven't lit it yet, mister,' said some precisian from the back.

'—burned brighter,' repeated Colonel Chase, 'I saw the dread form with greater distinctness, and my heart stood still. It was clothed in ragged garments, sparse elfin-locks hung over its forehead—forehead,' said he, looking wildly round for the man whose duty it was at this particular moment to switch off all the lights in the hall except one close above the platform, by which the audience could see his face of horror surrounded by darkness, 'and blood dripped from a jagged wound in its throat. Slowly it detached itself from the wall and advanced on me—'

Every single light went out, including that above the platform, and the man at the switches, seeing his mistake, put them all on again. The laughter became general, but, as it were, expectant, holding itself in for the climax.

'—towering ever higher as it approached. Cold sweat broke out on my forehead, my throat was dry as dust—'

''Ave a drink,' said a delighted voice.

'—my knees trembled, and I knew that the powers of Hell were loose. "Avaunt," I cried, "In the name of God avaunt"... The phantom shrieked—'

Miss Howard, whose hands were poised above the keys, struck a tremendous ascending arpeggio, the end of which was drowned in a roar of laughter. The hall hooted with inextinguishable joy: never was there such a comic as the Colonel.

E. F. Benson (1867–1940), *Paying Guests* (1929).

Fred's most popular humorous books were the 'Lucia' stories, the first of which, Queen Lucia, was published in 1920. The later stories were set in the small Sussex town of Rye (renamed Tilling). Fred lived there in Lamb House, once the home of Henry James, and was mayor of Rye for three years.

The Lucia books told of the two ladies locked in combat over which of them was to be Tilling society's First Lady: Miss Elizabeth Mapp, fiftyish, unscrupulous, frumpish, insanely jealous, or the splendid Mrs Emmeline Lucas, known as 'Lucia' (pronounced in the Italian fashion), a widow, fiftyish, lean, arty, hyperactive and venomously ambitious (perhaps the one female character for whom Fred seems to have had a sneaking admiration).

Lucia's ally in the village social skirmishing is Georgie, an effete, fastidious figure in a ginger wig who plays duets with her on the piano and does charming embroidery.

The mundane day-to-day details of living are managed for them by their house-maids, their 'treasures', who are always addressed by their surnames: Lucia is looked after by Grosvenor and Georgie by Foljambe.

Lucia has bought Miss Mapp's big house, Mallards, and what with her new work on Tilling Town Council and settling into the house, she and Georgie are pleasantly surprised one evening to find themselves, for a change, alone:

'Hurrah, for one of our quiet evenings again,' said he.

It was with a sense of restored well-being that they sank into their chairs, too content in this relief from strain to play duets. Georgie was sewing a border of lace on to some new doilies for finger-bowls, and Lucia found the 'Characters of Theophrastus', and read to him in the English version the sketch of Benjy's prototype. As their content worked inside them both, like tranquil yeast, they both became aware that a moment of vital import to them, and hardly less so to Tilling, was ticking its way nearer. A couple of years ago only, each had shuddered at the notion that the other might be thinking of matrimony, but now the prospect of it had lost its horror. For Georgie had stayed with her when he was growing his shingles-beard and she had stayed with him when she was settling into Mallards, and those days of domestic propinquity had somehow convinced them both that nothing was further from the inclination of either than any species of dalliance. With that nightmare apprehension removed they could recognise that for a considerable portion of the day they enjoyed each other's society more than their own solitude: they were happier together than apart. Again, Lucia was beginning to feel that, in the career which was opening for her in Tilling, a husband would give her a certain stability: a Prince Consort, though emphatically not for dynastic purposes, would lend her weight and ballast.

Georgie with kindred thoughts in his mind could see himself filling that eminent position with grace and effectiveness.

Georgie, not attending much to his sewing, pricked his finger: Lucia read a little more Theophrastus with a wandering mind and moved to her writing-table, where a pile of letters was kept in place by a pretty paper-weight consisting of a small electroplate cricket bat propped against a football, which had been given her jointly by the two clubs of which she was President. The clock struck eleven: it surprised them both that the hours had passed so quickly: eleven was usually the close of their evening. But they sat on, for all was ready for the vital moment, and if it did not come now, when on earth could there be a more apt occasion? Yet who was to begin, and how?

Georgie put down his work, for all his fingers were damp, and one was bloody. He remembered that he was a man. Twice he opened his mouth to speak, and twice he closed it again. He looked up at her, and caught her eye, and that gimlet-like quality in it seemed not only to pierce but to encourage. It bored into him for his good and for his eventual comfort. For the third time, and now successfully, he opened his mouth.

'Lucia, I've got something I must say, and I hope you won't mind. Has it ever occurred to you that—well—that we might marry?'

She fiddled for a moment with the cricket bat and the football, but when she raised her eyes again, there was no doubt about the encouragement.

'Yes, Georgie: unwomanly as it may sound,' she said, 'it has. I really believe it might be an excellent thing. But there's a great deal for us to think over first, and then talk over together. So let us say no more for the present. Now we must have our talk as soon as possible: some time to-morrow.'

She opened her engagement book. She had bought a new one, since she had become a Town Councillor, about as large as an ordinary blotting-pad.

'*Dio*, what a day!' she exclaimed. 'Town Council at half-past ten, and at twelve I am due at the slope by the Norman tower to decide about the planting of my almond trees. Not in lines, I think, but scattered about: a little clump here, a single one there. . . . Then Diva comes to lunch. Did you hear? A cinder from a passing engine blew into her cook's eye as she was leaning out of the kitchen window, poor thing. Then after lunch my football team are playing their opening match and I promised to kick off for them.'

'My dear, how wonderfully adventurous of you!' exclaimed Georgie. 'Can you?'

'Quite easily and quite hard. They sent me up a football and I've been practising in the *giardino segreto*. Where were we? Come to tea, Georgie— no, that won't do: my Mayor is bringing me the plans for the new artisan dwellings. It must be dinner then, and we shall have time to think it all over. Are you off? *Buona notte, caro: tranquilli*—dear me, what is the Italian for "sleep"? How rusty I am getting!'

Lucia did not go back with him into the house, for there were some ends for the meeting at half-past ten to be looked through. But just as she heard the front door shut on his exit, she remembered the Italian for sleep, and hurriedly threw up the window that looked on the street.

'*Sonni*,' she called out, '*Sonni tranquilli*.' Georgie understood: and he answered in Italian. '*I stessi a voi*, I mean, *te*,' he brilliantly shouted.

The half-espoused couple had all next day to let simmer in their heads the hundred arrangements and adjustments which the fulfilment of their romance would demand. Again and again George cast his doily from him in despair at the magnitude and intricacy of them. About the question of connubialities, he meant to be quite definite: it must be a *sine qua non* of matrimony, the first clause in the marriage treaty, that they should be considered absolutely illicit, and he need not waste thought over that. But what was to happen to his house, for presumably he would live at Mallards? And if so, what was to be done with his furniture, his piano, his bibelots? He could not bear to part with them, and Mallards was already full of Lucia's things. And what about Foljambe? She was even more inalienable than his Worcester china, and Georgie felt that though life might be pretty much the same with Lucia, it could not be the same without Foljambe. Then he must insist on a good deal of independence with regard to the companionship his bride would expect from him. His mornings must be inviolably his own and also the time between tea and dinner as he would be with her from then till bed-time severed them. Again two cars seemed more than two people should require, but he could not see himself without his Armaud. And what if Lucia, intoxicated by her late success on the Stock Exchange, took to gambling and lost all her money? The waters on which they thought of voyaging together seemed sown with jagged reefs, and he went across to dinner the next night with a drawn and anxious face. He was rather pleased to see that Lucia looked positively haggard, for that showed that she realised the appalling conundrums that must be solved before any irretraceable step was taken. Probably she had got some more of her own.

They settled themselves in the chairs where they had been so easy with each other twenty-four hours ago and Lucia with an air of determination, picked up a paper of scribbled memoranda from her desk.

'I've put down several points we must agree over, Georgie,' she said.

'I've got some, too, in my head,' said he.

Lucia fixed her eyes on a corner of the ceiling, as if in a music-face, but her knotted brow showed it was not that.

'I thought of writing to you about the first point, which is the most important of all,' she said, 'but I found I couldn't. How can I put it best? It's this, Georgie. I trust that you'll be very comfortable in the oak bedroom.'

'I'm sure I shall,' interrupted Georgie eagerly.

'—and all that implies,' Lucia went on firmly. 'No caresses of any sort: none of those dreadful little dabs and pecks Elizabeth and Benjy used to make at each other.'

'You needn't say anything more about that,' said he. 'Just as we were before.'

The acuteness of her anxiety faded from Lucia's face.

'That's a great relief,' she said. 'Now what is my next point? I've been in such a whirl all day and scribbled them down so hastily that I can't read it. It looks like "Frabjious".'

'It sounds as if it might be Foljambe,' said Georgie. 'I've been thinking a lot about her. I can't part with her.'

'Nor can I part with Grosvenor, as no doubt you will have realised. But what will their respective positions be? They've both bossed our houses for years. Which is to boss now? And will the other one consent to be bossed?'

'I can't see Foljambe consenting to be bossed,' said Georgie.

'If I saw Grosvenor consenting to be bossed,' said Lucia, 'I merely shouldn't believe my eyes.'

'Could there be a sort of equality?' suggested Georgie. 'Something like King William III and Queen Mary?'

'Oh, Georgie, I think there might be a solution there,' said Lucia. 'Let us explore that. Foljambe will only be here during the day, just as she is now with you, and she'll be your valet, and look after your rooms, for you must have a sitting-room of your own. I insist on that. You will be her province, Georgie, where she's supreme. I shall be Grosvenor's. I don't suppose either of them wants to leave us, and they are friends. We'll put it to them to-morrow, if we agree about the rest.'

'Won't it be awful if they don't come to terms?' said Georgie. 'What are we to do then?'

'Don't let's anticipate trouble,' said Lucia. 'Then let me see. "Mallards Cottage" is my next entry. Naturally we shall live here.'

'I've been worrying terribly about that,' said Georgie. 'I quite agree we must live here, but I can't let the Cottage with all my things. I don't wish other people to sleep in my bed and that sort of thing. But if I let if unfurnished, what am I to do with them? My piano, my pictures and embroideries, my sofa, my particular armchair, my bed, my bibelots? I've got six occasional tables in my sitting-room, because I counted them. There's no room for them here, and things go to pot if one stores them. Besides there are a lot of them which I simply can't get on without. Heart's blood.'

A depressed silence followed, for Lucia knew what his household goods meant to Georgie. Then suddenly she sprang up, clapping her hands, and talking so weird a mixture of baby-language and Italian that none but the most intimate could have understood her at all.

'Georgino!' she cried. 'Ickle me vewy clever. Lucia's got a *molto bella* idea. Lucia knows how Georgino loves his *bibelotine*. Tink a minute: shut oo eyes and tink! Well, Lucia no tease you any more . . . Georgino will have booful night-nursery here, bigger nor what he had in Cottagino. And booful *salone* bigger nor *salone* there. Now do you see?'

'No, I don't,' said Georgie firmly.

Lucia abandoned baby and foreign tongues.

'I'll send all the furniture in your bedroom and sitting-room here across to Mallards Cottage, and you shall fill them with your own things. More than enough room for the curtains and pictures and occasional tables which you really love. You wouldn't mind letting the Cottage if you had all your special things here?'

'Well, you are clever!' said Georgie.

An appreciative pause followed instead of that depressed silence, and Lucia referred to her notes.

'"Solitude" is my next entry,' she said. 'What can—Oh, I know. It sounds rather as if I was planning that we should see as little as possible of each other if and when we marry, but I don't mean that. Only, with all the welter of business which my position in Tilling already entails (and it will get worse rather than better) I must have much time to myself. Naturally we shall entertain a good deal: those quaint Bridge parties and so on, for Tilling society will depend on us more than ever. But ordinarily, when we are alone, Georgie, I must have my mornings to myself, and a couple of hours at least before dinner. Close times. Of course nothing hard or fast about it; very likely we shall often make music together then. But you mustn't think me unsociable if, as a rule, I have those hours to myself. My municipal duties, my boards and committees already take a great deal of time, and then there are all my private studies. A period of solitude every day is necessary for me. Is it not Goethe who says that we ripen in solitude?'

'I quite agree with him if he does,' said Georgie. 'I was going to speak about it myself if you hadn't.'. . .

It was late now, and Georgie went to bed. A random idea of kissing Lucia once, on the brow, entered his mind, but after what had been said about caresses, he felt she might consider it a minor species of rape.

Lucia's Progress (1935).

━━━━━━━

AFTER *the First World War there was worry about the decline in purity of the English language (there usually is) and in 1919 some mutually concerned gentlemen, including the poet Robert Bridges, formed* The Society for Pure English *to fight a rearguard action. A co-founder was Logan Pearsall Smith, an American man-of-letters who had written on* The English Language *in 1912 and had become a naturalized Briton in 1913.*

Logan Pearsall Smith lived quietly with his mother—he was not the marrying kind—and applied himself to literature, developing almost an obsession for seeking out and trying to achieve perfection in prose. His ambition was to live on after his funeral in a perfect phrase.

He began work on a slim volume of thoughts—pensées, *maxims, aphorisms* (*the English language does not have an exact word for them; Logan suggested* illuminations), *which he constantly rewrote and worked over and polished until the prose was lapidary, passionless, and said exactly what he wanted it to say.*

He had the volume published privately in 1903, calling it Trivia. *Nobody thought much of it, least of all his mother, who was a best-selling author of vigorous, improving yarns featuring ardently religious heroes.*

'*It is certainly quaint and interesting,*' *she wrote, giving the impression that she was holding her son's friendless little book at arm's length and peering at it through a lorgnette,* '*but it is what I suppose would be called very "precious", as it begins nowhere and ends nowhere and leads to nothing.*'

But Pearsall Smith persevered. He added more illuminations, *constantly polished each item, and in 1918 a new and much enlarged version of* Trivia *was published by a real publisher. It became a great success on both sides of the Atlantic and was followed by* More Trivia *in 1922 and* Afterthoughts *in 1931.*

Logan Pearsall Smith's work seems to be lasting; the critic Edmund Wilson admitted that there was something in Pearsall Smith's prose which was '*dry, independant, even tough*'.

His illuminations *do tend to stick in the memory:*

SOCIAL SUCCESS

The servant gave me my coat and hat, and in a glow of self-satisfaction I walked out into the night. 'A delightful evening,' I reflected, 'the nicest kind of people. What I said about finance and philosophy impressed them; and how they laughed when I imitated a pig squealing.'

But soon after, 'God, it's awful,' I muttered, 'I wish I was dead.'

AGE AND DEATH

What's more enchanting than the voice of young people, when you can't hear what they say?

IN THE WORLD

You cannot be both fashionable and first-rate.

If you want to be thought a liar, always tell the truth.

ART AND LETTERS

A best-seller is the gilded tomb of a mediocre talent.

What sight in the world is sadder than the sight of a lady we admire admiring a nauseating picture?

MYSELF

People say that life is the thing, but I prefer reading.

How often my soul visits the National Gallery, and how seldom I go there myself!

LAST WORDS

Thank heavens, the sun has gone in, and I don't have to go out and enjoy it.

And a final encouraging thought:

An improper mind is a perpetual feast.

Logan Pearsall Smith (1865–1946), *Afterthoughts* (1931).

===

ANOTHER *brilliant collector of brief but telling remarks was James Agate who for the two decades between the wars was Britain's most vigorous, colourful, and popular theatre critic.*

Agate was a very hard worker and had a huge output of critical prose and theatre journalism but he was also a terrific spender and all his life only just managed to keep one step ahead of financial disaster. Although discreetly homosexual, very well-read and steeped in the arts he was no tender aesthete but a stocky Mancunian who dressed like a Newmarket vet.

He loved harness ponies, which he bought and exhibited, also champagne, golf, great acting, music, paintings, stimulating dinner-parties, and all aspects of good living; he hated Shaw's plays, mime, the acting in British films, all movies featuring skaters, and anything at all by Walt Disney.

In 1935 Agate decided to bestow upon posterity a record of his daily life, a running autobiography in the form of a detailed diary. He went at the task as diligently as he went at everything and between 1935 and 1948 published nine large volumes. He called the first volume EGO *and numbered the subsequent volumes* EGO 2, EGO 3, *and so on.*

The EGOS *are causeries; mixed in with diary events are random observations and scraps of reported conversation but also little odditities and incongruities of human behaviour and speech which he found funny, and for these he had a very finely tuned ear indeed:*

February 20. 1933.

Lunched with Lionel Fielden and Cecil Maddan, both of the B.B.C. Fielden told me of a lively bit of dialogue at a dinner-party an evening or two ago.

A BRIGADIER. There must always be righteous wars.

FIELDEN. What in your opinion, sir, would be a righteous war?

BRIGADIER. Damn it, a war to prevent naked savages raping one's womenfolk!

FIELDEN. The first time a naked savage lays a finger on Mrs Culverin I give you my word, General, I'll enlist!

True story: The Mayor of some Lancashire town being presented with a pair of statues for the Town Hall remarked after inspecting the nude figures: 'Art is art, and nothing can be done to prevent it. But there is the Mayoress's decency to be considered!'

James Agate (1877–1947), EGO (1935).

September 25 Wednesday

Lunched at the Ivy with Curt Dehn, my lawyer, who asked the name of the man lunching opposite. I said, 'John Gielgud.' Dehn said, 'It's a rum sort of head. The profile's Roman Emperor, but the rest is still at Eton.'

August 8 Sunday

So Lady Tree has gone. A kindly soul and a delicious wit. It is always said that the line in Barrie's play apropos of boiler-scraping—'What fun men have!'—was one of her dress-rehearsal impromptus. I remember how, about to recite at a charity matinee, she advanced to a gold chair, and, swathed in heliotrope tulle, said smilingly, 'I want you all to imagine I'm a plumber's mate!' In her early years her extreme plainness was a handicap. In later life her face became her fortune; it was that of a benevolent horse.

September 12 Sunday

Made a jaunt to Canterbury. I asked the verger if Becket was buried in the Cathedral. He replied. 'He was. But in Henry the Eighth's time they dug the swine up and scattered the bones outside.' I went away making a note of this extraordinary utterance.

November 5 Saturday

Motored to Windermere and decided that I am like Wordsworth, who, according to Miss Mitford, expected his admirers to 'admire *en masse*—all, every page, every line, every word, every comma; to admire nothing else, and to admire all day long'.

November 25 Friday

Luncheon party at the Garrick to Hamish Hamilton, off to America. Actually it was H.H.'s party, given to see himself off . . . Eddie [Marsh] told us of a magnificent rebuke to a late-comer at a luncheon party, the host being Lord Brougham and the guest a famous society leader arriving half an hour late and pleading she had been buying a chandelier. Lord B., looking straight ahead, said, 'I once knew a man who bought a chandelier after luncheon.'

July 25 Tuesday

Nouveaux Contes Scabreux, No.7. This is a tale of a rosy-cheeked schoolboy who turns to the master flogging him and winningly remarks, 'Excuse me, sir, but this is pleasing me more than it is hurting you!'

October 10 Tuesday

Brother Edward sends me this from York:

'There are those who can move their ears, one or both, as they please; there are those that can move all their hair towards their forehead, and back again, and never move their heads. There are those that can counterfeit the voices of birds and of other men, cunningly: and there are some that can break wind backward continuously, that you would think they sung'.—St Augustine. *De Civitate Dei.*

December 22 Friday

Letter from a friend in the country: 'There are six evacuated children in our house. My wife and I hate them so much that we have decided to *take away* something from them for Christmas!' *EGO 4* (1940).

October 4 Friday

Oxford is not the hub of modern culture I expected to find it. Seeing two ladies vainly exhorting a dog to get into a motor-car, I prodded it with my stick, repeating Cyrano's command to Christian: 'Monte donc, animal!' The elder lady gave me a severe look and said, 'I think that was most uncalled for.' *EGO 5* (1942).

July 11 Thursday

Vignette. Hermione Gingold at the Ivy wearing a hat like a Martello tower with cascades of veiling, putting a bunch of carnations in her mouth à la Carmen, and saying with an atrocious leer, 'Any gentleman like to strip to the waist?' *EGO 9* (1948).

E ARLIER *in the century the demand for funny reading matter was brisk enough to support a surprising number of publications from* Alley Sloper's (*rather saucy*) Half Holiday *to the* Strand *and* Pearson's *and, in between,* Nash's, *the* Story-teller, *the* London, *the* Royal, *the* Red, *the* Yellow, Cassell's, *the* New, *the* Novel, *the* Grand, *the* Pall Mall, *the* Windsor, Blackwells, *the* Cornhill, Chamber's, *the* Happy Mag, *and the* Humorist, *among others.*

The Humorist *printed stories and lots of jokes which all seemed to begin:* 'Smith, Brown, and Robertson went into a gents' outfitters in the Strand one day and Jones said to the girl behind the braces counter . . .' *The funny magazine market then was big enough, and the general standard of humour undistinguished enough, for any bright lad with a quick wit and a facility with words to make himself a reasonable living; the magazine world supported a small army of semi-successful professionals.*

A writer named Dudley Clark was a thorough professional of that period, a hard-working humorist who contributed widely to a number of magazines, including Punch, *without becoming very famous. He was writing and writing well in 1922 when yet another magazine* Gaiety ('A Magazine of Humour') *was launched: it lasted only a few months.*

Dudley Clark's contribution to Gaiety, vol. 1, no. 4. *March, 1922, was not on*

*a very original theme—the idea of parodying newspaper correspondence columns
had whiskers on it even then—but he worked the idea so well that it is reprinted
here to represent, and celebrate, all those writers whose run-of-the-mill (but good
run-of-the mill) contributions kept magazines going:*

OUR HELPFUL LETTER-WRITERS

(From the correspondence column of the 'Daily Stunter'.)

Sir,

   Could any of your numerous readers enlighten me as to the precise locality
where the late Dr Watts was inspired to write his beautiful and moving little
poem about the busy bee? I am desirous of raising funds for a monument to
be erected on the spot, as the poem was a great favourite with my late
husband.

Yours, etc.,

ANGELICA RAMSBOTTOM

*

Sir,

   With reference to your correspondent's letter regarding the outburst of
putrid nonsense about the bee, which was written by the late Dr Watts, it is
easy to see that the misguided poet in question never kept a bee. I have, and
I say—'Give me rabbits!'

Yours, etc.,

DISGUSTED APIARIST

*

Sir,

   'Disgusted Apiarist' may prefer keeping rabbits to keeping bees, but it is
quite evident that enormous fortunes are being made from the latter. The
price of bees-wax in this village is nothing short of scandalous, and yet the
government does nothing. I suppose it is too timid, or else some *Society woman
is pulling the wires.* Could not you start a 'Cheaper bees-wax' campaign in
your invaluable columns?

   I enclose a letter from my son-in-law who is a bushranger in Australia.
This will show you what they think out there about the Coalition. I think his
letter should be printed: you could alter the adjectives.

Yours, etc.,

COUNTRY READER

*

Sir,

   The letter in your columns from 'Country Reader' concerning the price of
bees-wax, stimulates me to draw your attention to the serious decline in the
ant-egg industry. My late uncle (in whose warehouse I was a packer for
thirty years) was wholesale purveyor of ants' eggs, and by skill and discrimination built up an enormous business. The inexplicable decision of the

Government not to make use of ants' eggs during the recent war hit us severely, as our intricate plant was not adaptable to the making of munitions. At the moment it looks as though yet another typically British industry is about to disappear owing to the criminal slothfulness and ineptitude of Whitehall.

Yours, etc.,
ONE OF THE HAS BEENS

*

Sir,

The crisis in the ant-egg industry is simply a sign of the times. Cinemas and chars-a-banc offer so much excitement nowadays that people are not keeping gold-fish to anything like the same extent to which their forefathers did in the good old days.

Intellectual pursuits are indeed on the wane. Is it that we are becoming less aesthetic?

Yours, etc.,
ANOTHER HAS BEEN

*

Sir,

Modern England does not know the meaning of the word 'aesthetic'. Our railway stations prove this. Could not you use your powerful influence to start a campaign for 'Brighter Booking-offices'?

Yours, etc.,
FED-UP

*

Sir,

What does 'One of the Has Beens' expect from the present Government? Look at Mesopotamia! Look at Kamchooka and the Suckanspit Settlements! In fact, look anywhere! Government education in India, for example, is a blot on our escutcheon. There is scarcely a modern native servant who knows how to prepare a decent curry. The stability of the empire is being steadily undermined by inefficient wastrels, and it is costing us *six shillings in the pound*.

Yours, etc.,
MAJOR (LATE BENGAL L.I.).

*

Sir,

My great-aunt used to make magnificent curry. I fancy she got the recipe from a Devonshire gipsy, unless I am thinking of wortleberry wine.

Yours, etc.,
TABITHA MUGWUMP

Sir,

My grandfather ate curry on his ninety-seventh birthday, and died shortly afterwards with a smile on his face. Can any of your readers beat this?

Yours, etc.,
X. Y. Z.

*

Sir,

My great-grandfather, to settle a bet, imbibed the entire contents of a bottle of Tomato Chutney at the age of 102. This is mentioned in the 'Reminiscences of Bishop D . . . . .' who was much impressed by the feat, over which he lost half-a-sovereign.

Yours, etc.,
ONE OF THE OLD SCHOOL

*

Sir,

My great-grandfather, to show his contempt for Benjamin Disraeli, devoured seven pork chops in succession when he was 105 years of age. Those were indeed the days of robust and sincere politics.

Yours, etc.,
PIG LOVER

(*The correspondence regarding the late Dr Watts is now closed*—Ed.)

Dudley Clark, *Gaiety*, 1922.

---

*P*UNCH *in the early 1920s was little different from* Punch *in the early 1910s, in spite of a war in between. If anything it had become slighty more reactionary; the younger members of the staff had gone off to the war and the older men who had replaced them were still in charge.*

Even the success of Ross's New Yorker *in the middle twenties had little effect. In fact it encouraged* Punch's *old guard to close ranks and resist the influences of the* New Yorker's *innovations—it was not until late in the 1930s that* Punch *began to use brief,* New Yorker *style captions beneath joke drawings instead of up to five or six lines of dialogue.* Punch, *unlike the* New Yorker, *retained its strongly political stance; its criticism of books and plays remained serious, sensible, and reliable but it retained its pre-eminence as a humorous journal by once again attracting brilliant contributors; humorists of the calibre of A. P. Herbert.*

A. P. Herbert's first piece in Punch *was written while he was still at school. After serving in the Navy during the Great War and then becoming a barrister-at-law (he never practised), he joined the staff of* Punch *in 1924 and set about mocking the out-of-date pre-War regulations that post-War Britain was heir to, absurd police methods, the idiocies of the Licensing Laws, Town Council busybodies, the neglect of the River Thames as a thoroughfare, the farcical charades necessary to obtain a divorce, and so on.*

This was campaigning journalism, not at all the kind of thing which the editor, Owen Seaman, was happy with but he permitted it, probably because everything that A. P. Herbert wrote, be it prose or verse, was direct, thoughtful, funny, and had a kind of intelligent charm that was unique and unmistakable.

From 1935 to 1950 A.P.H. sat in the House of Commons as Independent Member of Parliament for Oxford University where he carried on the campaigns which he had initiated in Punch, *notably getting a Private Member's Bill through Parliament reforming the divorce laws.*

He continued to write prolifically; besides his Punch *pieces there were novels, musical shows for the theatre, and revues.*

In 1945 he was knighted.

A.P.H.'s greatest contribution to Punch *was his superb series of 'Misleading Cases', based upon some of the more asinine aspects of British law. These pieces took the form of counsel's pleadings, or the summing-up and judgment of the presiding magistrate or judge, in formal legal language, of an action before the court. The action was brought by or against a Mr Albert Haddock (i.e. 'A.P.H.' A. P. Herbert himself).*

Mr Haddock deeply resents being bullied by government officials. When some unwise bureaucrat puts the pressure on Mr Haddock, that upholder of freedom responds by practising passive resistance. The hapless bureaucrat then takes Mr Haddock to court.

BOARD OF INLAND REVENUE V. HADDOCK; REX V. HADDOCK

The Negotiable Cow

'Was the cow crossed?'

'No, your worship, it was an open cow.'

These and similar passages provoked laughter at Bow Street today when the Negotiable Cow case was concluded.

Sir Joshua Hoot, KC (appearing for the Public Prosecutor): Sir Basil, these summonses, by leave of the Court, are being heard together, an unusual but convenient arrangement.

The defendant, Mr Albert Haddock, has for many months, in spite of earnest endeavours on both sides, been unable to establish harmonious relations between himself and the Collector of Taxes. The Collector maintains that Mr Haddock should make over a large part of his earnings to the Government. Mr Haddock replies that the proportion demanded is excessive, in view of the inadequate services or consideration which he himself has received from the Government. After an exchange of endearing letters, telephone calls, and even cheques, the sum demanded was reduced to fifty-seven pounds; and about this sum the exchange of opinions continued.

On the 31st of May the Collector was diverted from his respectable labours by the apparition of a noisy crowd outside his windows. The crowd, Sir Basil, had been attracted by Mr Haddock, who was leading a large white cow of malevolent aspect. On the back and sides of the cow were clearly stencilled in red ink the following words:

> *To the London and Literary Bank, Ltd.*
>
> Pay the Collector of Taxes, who is no gentleman, or Order,
> the sum of fifty-seven pounds (and may he rot!).
>
> £57/0/0   ALBERT HADDOCK

Mr Haddock conducted the cow into the Collector's office, tendered it to the Collector in payment of income-tax and demanded a receipt.

Sir Basil String: Did the cow bear the statutory stamp?

Sir Joshua: Yes, a twopenny stamp was affixed to its dexter horn. The Collector declined to accept the cow objecting that it would be difficult or even impossible to pay the cow into the bank. Mr Haddock, throughout the interview, maintained the friendliest demeanour; and he now remarked that the Collector could endorse the cow to any third party to whom he owed money, adding that there must be many persons in that position. The Collector then endeavoured to endorse the cheque—

Sir Basil String: Where?

Sir Joshua: On the back of the cheque, Sir Basil, that is to say, on the abdomen of the cow. The cow, however, appeared to resent endorsement and adopted a menacing posture. The Collector, abandoning the attempt, declined finally to take the cheque. Mr Haddock led the cow away and was arrested in Trafalgar Square for causing an obstruction. He has also been summoned by the Board of Inland Revenue for non-payment of income-tax.

Mr Haddock, in the witness-box, said that he had tendered a cheque in payment of income-tax, and if the Commissioners did not like his cheque they could do the other thing. A cheque was only an order to a bank to pay money to the person in possession of the cheque or a person named on the cheque. There was nothing in statute or customary law to say that that order must be written on a piece of paper of specified dimensions. A cheque, it was well known, could be written on a piece of notepaper. He himself had drawn cheques on the backs of menus, on napkins, on handkerchiefs, on the labels of wine-bottles; all these cheques had been duly honoured by his bank and passed through the Bankers' Clearing House. He could see no distinction in law between a cheque written on a napkin and a cheque written on a cow. The essence of each document was a written order to pay money, made in the customary form and in accordance with statutory requirements as to stamps, etc. A cheque was admittedly not legal tender in the sense that it could not lawfully be refused; but it was accepted by custom as a legitimate form of payment. There were funds in his bank sufficient to meet the cow; the Commissioners might not like the cow, but, the cow having been tendered, they were estopped from charging him with failure to pay. (Mr Haddock here cited *Spowers v. The Strand Magazine, Lucas v. Finck, and Wadsworth v. The Metropolitan Water Board.*)

As to the action of the police, Mr Haddock said it was a nice thing if in the heart of the commercial capital of the world a man could not convey a negotiable instrument down the street without being arrested. He had instituted proceedings against Constable Boot for false imprisonment.

Cross-examined as to motive, witness said that he had no cheque-forms available and, being anxious to meet his obligations promptly, had made use of the only material to hand. Later he admitted that there might have been present in his mind a desire to make the Collector of Taxes ridiculous. But why not? There was no law against deriding the income-tax.

Sir Basil String (after the hearing of further evidence): This case has at least brought to the notice of the Court a citizen who is unusual both in his clarity of mind and integrity of behaviour. No thinking man can regard those parts of the Finance Act which govern the income-tax with anything but contempt. There may be something to be said—not much—for taking from those who have inherited wealth a certain proportion of that wealth for the service of the State and the benefit of the poor and needy; and those who by their own ability, industry, and exertion have earned money may reasonably be invited to surrender a small portion of it towards the maintenance of those public services by which they benefit, to wit, the Police, the Navy, the Army, the public sewers, and so forth. But to compel such individuals to bestow a large part of their earnings upon other individuals, whether by way of pensions, unemployment grants, or education allowances, is manifestly barbarous and indefensible. Yet this is the law. The original and only official basis of taxation was that individual citizens, in return for their money, received collectively some services from the State, the defence of their property and persons, the care of their health or the education of their children. All that has now gone. Citizen A, who has earned money, is commanded simply to give it to Citizens B, C, and D, who have not, and by force of habit this has come to be regarded as a normal and proper proceeding, whatever the comparative industry or merits of Citizens A, B, C, and D. To be alive has become a virtue, and the mere capacity to inflate the lungs entitled Citizen B to a substantial share in the laborious earnings of Citizen A. The defendant, Mr Haddock, repels and resents this doctrine, but, since it has received the sanction of Parliament, he dutifully complies with it. Hampered by practical difficulties, he took the first steps he could to discharge his legal obligations to the State. Paper was not available, so he employed instead a favourite cow. Now, there can be nothing obscene, offensive, or derogatory in the presentation of a cow by one man to another. Indeed, in certain parts of our Empire the cow is venerated as a sacred animal. Payment in kind is the oldest form of payment, and payment in kind meant more often than not meant payment in cattle. Indeed, during the Saxon period, Mr Haddock tells us, cattle were described as *viva pecunia*, or 'living money', from their being received as payment on most occasions, at certain regulated prices. So that, whether the cheque was valid or not, it was impossible to doubt the validity of the cow; and whatever the Collector's distrust of the former it was at least his duty to accept the latter and credit Mr Haddock's account with its value. But, as Mr Haddock protested in his able argument, an order to pay is an order to pay, whether it is made on the back of an envelope or on the back of a cow. The evidence of the bank is that Mr Haddock's account was in funds, therefore, the Collector of Taxes did wrong, by custom if not by law, in refusing to take the proferred animal, and the summons issued at his instance will be discharged.

As for the second charge, I hold again that Constable Boot did wrong. It cannot be unlawful to conduct a cow through the streets of London. The horse, at the present time a much less useful animal, constantly appears in those streets without protest, and the motor-car, more unnatural and unattractive still, is more numerous than either animal. Much less can the cow be regarded as an improper or unlawful companion when it is invested (as I have shown) with all the dignity of a bill of exchange.

If people choose to congregate in one place upon the apparition of Mr Haddock with a promissory cow, then Constable Boot should arrest the people, not Mr Haddock. Possibly, if Mr Haddock had paraded Cockspur Street with a paper cheque for one million pounds made payable to bearer, the crowd would have been as great, but that is not to say that Mr Haddock would have broken the law. In my judgment Mr Haddock has behaved throughout in the manner of a perfect knight, citizen, and taxpayer. The charge brought by the Crown is dismissed; and I hope with all my heart that in his action against Constable Boot Mr Haddock will be successful. What is the next case, please?

A. P. Herbert (1890–1971), *Punch*, reprinted: *Misleading Cases in the Common Law* (1929).

———

ONE Punch *series which had the mark of success upon it from the beginning was the work of two somewhat ill-assorted semi-professional humorists. The series appeared in* Punch *in 1929, was published as a book in 1930, has been in print ever since, is rediscovered by each new generation of schoolchildren, was adapted into a long-running stage show, is now accepted as a classic of English humour (although one of the authors, Sellar, was a Scot), and is included in just about every anthology of humour in the Western world. It is W. C. Sellar and R. J. Yeatman's extraordinary* jeu d'esprit, 1066 and All That.

Walter Sellar and Julian Yeatman met at Oriel College, Oxford, just after the First World War. Both had fought and been wounded in the war and at Oriel they became lifelong friends.

Sellar's wounds were only light but he suffered from poor health most of his life and died at the age of 52.

Yeatman was severely wounded, so badly shot-up by shellfire that his body was perforated like a colander, but he continued to play strenuous outdoor sports during a long life.

Sellar was a quiet man with a melancholy streak but, as was sometimes the case with deeply serious men, he took great delight in Lear-like nonsense.

Yeatman was witty and convivial. His family was connected with Taylor's Port (Taylor, Fladgate, and Yeatman Ltd.), he was comfortably well off and he knocked about London with a fox-terrier, Jim, never more than eight inches away from his right ankle (even at an audience with King George V); he painted, was a good musician, did some writing for films and seemed to know and be liked by everybody: when Clark Gable filmed in Britain he preferred to relax with the Yeatmans at their home rather than in his suite at the Connaught (Yeatman's son remembers Clark Gable looking into a mirror, taking his dentures out, and saying softly and sadly: 'America's sweetheart!').

In the late 1920s, when the two friends were still in their late twenties, they decided that it would be fun to write something for Punch *and they hit upon a brilliantly original idea: a series of pieces parodying history lessons as taught in school from history textbooks. The touch of genius came in their conviction that history really consisted of the names and dates and bits of action which were memorable; the rest, being forgotten, did not exist. So the book's sub-title was:*

A Memorable History of England,
comprising all the parts you can remember,
including 103 Good Things,
5 Bad Kings and
2 Genuine Dates

They began to exchange notes and ideas for their Memorable History. As one author was a schoolmaster in Surrey and the other a London-bound advertising man they worked mainly by post. When they had finally completed the book version Yeatman left it in a taxi and they had to start again from the beginning.

They went on to write three more comic works; And Now All This, Horse Nonsense *(mainly by Yeatman, Sellar disliked horses), and* Garden Rubbish *(mainly by Sellar, Yeatman loathed gardening). These were good fun and contained many Sellar-and-Yeatman felicities (such as in* Horse Nonsense, *a comment on hunting: 'One man's Meet is another man's poison.' And a reminder that the horse is the only animal you can knock nails into.) But the sequels did not have the genius of the first book.*

Sellar and Yeatman's achievement was managing in 1066 and All That *to write only about those aspects of history which almost every Britisher just remembered; those few names and places and dates and historical phrases like 'ravaging the north' which somehow penetrated the natural defences of a schoolchild and stuck in the mind for ever.*

It is a peculiarly difficult book to quote from because almost every line in it is equally quotable. Also the exuberance of the book, the mad punning, the running jokes, the freshness of the humour, make it difficult to resist the temptation to reprint the whole thing.

However. Herewith a generous sample:

CHAPTER I

Caesar Invades Britain

The first date in English History is 55 BC (for the other date see Chapter 11, *William the Conqueror*), in which year Julius Caesar (the *memorable* Roman Emperor) landed, like all other successful invaders of these islands, at Thanet. This was in the Olden Days, when the Romans were top nation on account of their classical education, etc.

Julius Caesar advanced very energetically, throwing his cavalry several thousands of paces over the River Flumen; but the Ancient Britons, though all well over military age, painted themselves true blue, or *woad*, and fought as heroically under their dashing queen, Woadicea, as they did later in thin red lines under their good queen, Victoria.

Julius Caesar was therefore compelled to invade Britain again the following year (54 BC, not 56, owing to the peculiar Roman method of counting), and having defeated the Ancient Britons by unfair means, such as battering-rams, tortoises, hippocausts, centipedes, axes, and bundles, set the memorable Latin sentence, 'Veni, Vidi, Vici', which the Romans, who were all very well educated, construed correctly.

The Britons, however, who of course still used the old pronunciation, understanding him to have called them 'Weeny, Weedy, and Weaky', lost heart and gave up the struggle, thinking that he had already divided them All into Three Parts.

CHAPTER 3

The Conversion of England

Noticing some fair-headed children in the slave market one morning, Pope Gregory, the memorable Pope, said (in Latin), 'What are those?' and on being told that they were Angels, made the memorable joke—'*Non Angli, sed Angeli*' ('*not* Angels, but *Anglicans*') and commanded one of his Saints called St Augustine to go and convert the rest.

The conversion of England was thus effected by the landing of St Augustine in Thanet and other places, which resulted in the country being overrun by a Wave of Saints. Among these were St Ive, St Pancras, the great St Bernard (originator of the clerical collar), St Bee, St Ebb, St Neot (who invented whisky), St Kit and St Kin, and the Venomous Bead (author of *The Rosary*).

England was now divided into seven kingdoms and so ready were the English to become C. of E. that on one memorable occasion a whole Kingdom was easily converted by a sparrow.

Wave of Egg-Kings

Soon after this event Egg-Kings were found on the thrones of all these kingdoms, such as Eggberd, Eggbreth, Eggfroth, etc. None of them, however, succeeded in becoming memorable—except in so far as it is difficult to forget such names as Eggbirth, Eggbred, Eggbear, Eggfish, etc. Nor is it even remembered by what kind of Eggdeath they perished.

CHAPTER I I

William I: A Conquering King

In the year 1066 occurred the other memorable date in English History, viz. *William the Conqueror, Ten Sixty-six.* This is also called *The Battle of Hastings,* and was when William I (1066) conquered England at the Battle of Senlac (*Ten Sixty-six*).

When William the Conqueror landed he lay down on the beach and swallowed two mouthfuls of sand. This was his first conquering action and was in the South; later he ravaged the North as well.

The Norman Conquest was a Good Thing, as from this time onwards England stopped being conquered and thus was able to become top nation.

CHAPTER 20

Robin Hood and his Merrie Men

About this time the memorable hero Robin Hood flourished in a romantic manner. Having been unjustly accused by two policemen in Richmond Park, he was condemned to be an outdoor and went and lived with a maid who was called Marion, and a band of Merrie Men, in Greenwood Forest, near Sherborne. Amongst his Merrie Men were Will Scarlet (*The Scarlet Pimpernel*), Black Beauty, White Melville, Little Red Riding Hood (probably an outdaughter of his) and the famous Friar Puck who used to sit in a cowslip and suck bees, thus becoming so fat that he declared he could put his girdle round the Earth.

Robin Hood was a miraculous shot with the long-bow and it is said that he could split a hare at 400 paces and a Sheriff at 800. He therefore spent his time blowing a horn and shooting at the Sheriff of Nottingham (who was an outwit). He always used to sound his horn first, particularly when shooting round a corner; this showed his sportsmanship and also enabled him to shoot the Sheriff running, which was more difficult.

Robin Hood was also very good at socialism and often took money away from rich clergymen and gave it to the poor, who loved him for his generosity. He died very romantically. Having taken some medicine supplied by his Wicked Aunt and feeling his strength going, he blew a dying blast on his horn and with his dying breath fired a last shot out of his bedroom window, and *hit the Sheriff of Nottingham again.*

CHAPTER 61

Causes of the Great War

The Great War was between Germany and America and was thus fought in Belgium.

The War

The War lasted three years or the duration, the Americans being 100% victorious. At the beginning the Russians rendered great assistance to the American cause by lending them their memorable steam-roller and by passing silently through England one Sunday morning before breakfast with snow on their boots. The Americans were also assisted by the Australians (AZTECS) and some Canadians, and 51 Highlanders.

CHAPTER 62

A Bad Thing

America was thus clearly top nation, and History came to a .

TEST PAPER V

Up to the End of History

1. Sketch vaguely, with some reference to the facts:
   (1) The Southsea Bubble, (2) the Ramillies Wig.

2. Would it have been a Good Thing if Wolfe had succeeded in writing Gray's Elegy instead of taking Quebec?

3. Analyse and distinguish between The Begums of Oudh. Would they have been deceived by the Banana Sahib?

4. 'An Army marches on its stomach' (Napoleon). Illustrate and examine.

5. Account (loudly) for the success of Marshal Ney as a leader of horse.

6a. 'What a city to boot!' Who said this, Wellington or Blucher or Flora McNightingown?

6b. Did anybody say 'I know that no one can save this country and that nobody else can'? If not, who did say it?

7. Ruminate fearlessly on (1) Lord Cardigan, (2) Clapham.

8. Do not attempt to remember what Mr Gladstone said in 1864 but account for the paramountcy of (1) Milk Puddings, (2) Bags, in his political career.

9. Comment *Quietly* on (a) Tariff Reform.
                          (b) Mafeking Night.
                          (c) The Western Front.

10. Refrain from commenting on the Albert Memorial, The September Massacres, the Dardanelles, The O.B.E., or any other subjects that you consider too numerous to mention. (The better the fewer.)

11. Write not more than two lines on The Career of Napoleon Buonapart, *or* the Acquisition of our Indian Empire, *or* The Prime Ministers of England.

12. What price Glory?

N.B.—Do not on any account attempt to write on both sides of the paper at once.

W. C. Sellar (1898–1951) and R. J. Yeatman (1897–1968), *1066 and All That* (1930).

PUNCH *was good at finding women contributors and one of its best lady humorists between the wars was Miss E. M. Delafield, who reported for them astringently on various aspects of female human nature on the wing.*

E. M. Delafield (an anglicized version of her real name, E. M. de la Pasture) was a prolific novelist and contributor to magazines. During the twenties she wrote a series for Punch *of sharply observed conversation-pieces between ladies, entitled* As Others Hear Us. *As was inevitable in feminine contributions to humorous magazines in the twenties, most of the the ladies written about lived leisurely lives in Kensington or in middle-class comfort in a pretty village.*

But in this series Miss Delafield was not so much interested in Kensington and Sussex ladies being charming as equally nicely brought-up ladies being quietly beastly to each other or subtly bitchy about somebody else.

In the following dialogue sketch describing the pick-over following a fiancée being introduced to the young man's family, Miss Delafield's ear is so accurate and merciless that one feels that had she been a man, some zealous feminist might well have lain in wait for the author behind the Albert Hall one dark Kensington night and revenged womanhood with a hat-pin:

DISCUSSING THE FIANCÉE

'Well, what did you think of her?'

'Of course, they've all got this terrific poise nowadays, haven't they?'

'Yes, I noticed that too. But I quite liked her.'

'Oh, I quite liked her too. The hat was a mistake.'

'The hat was a mistake but the frock was good. Would you say it was a perm, or natural, when she took off her hat?'

'A frightfully good perm.'

'Well, dear, I can only say that poor Tony won't be able to afford things like that kind when they're married, and I only hope she understands it, that's all.'

'Oh, Aunt Catherine, did you hate her?'

'Aunt Catherine thought she was utterly mouldy. I'm certain she did.'

'No, dear, I haven't said I didn't like her. On the contrary. I daresay she's a very nice girl indeed, though I think she looks a good deal older than dear Tony.'

'Six months.'

'Is that what she says, dear? I hope she'll lose that irritating little *cough* of hers. It quite got on my nerves.'

'It would be a great mistake if she were delicate. Poor darling Tony isn't at all strong, and I never think it does for husband and wife *both* to be delicate.'

'Mother, Tony's *perfectly* strong.'

'Darling, you're too young to remember what a time I had with him when he was cutting his second teeth.'

'I must say, I never thought Tony would choose that *kind* of wife, did you? I mean—well—she's so sort of tall, isn't she?'

'Oh, huge. Though I must say, she's got good eyes. Did you hear what she said?'

'Which?'

'About wanting to be near the fire. I thought that was rather funny, I must say. Tony does so hate a hot room.'

'I'm thankful to say I brought up *all* my children to like the fresh air.'

'She wasn't an only child or anything, was she?'

'No, because she said "My little niece" or something. I didn't much like her voice, did you?'

'Oh my dear, they all talk like that nowadays. In that sort of voice, I mean, so that you can't hear a single word, and when you do it's all American slang.'

'What's that, what's that? Don't tell me Tony's going to be married to an American!'

'Oh, Uncle Tom, are you awake? No, it's all right—we're only talking about Tony's *fiancée*.'

'Is that the girl he used to go to all those concerts with before Christmas?'

'No, no, no. That was all over *ages* ago, Uncle Tom. Besides, there was nothing in that at all. This one is terrifically good at games. Nothing to do with concerts.'

'Oh. Nothing to do with concerts. Well, that's a good thing, anyhow. Where's the newspaper, somebody?'

'Naturally, Tony's my only son, and I feel very, very anxious about the future. I've always said that my children must go their own way; no one can ever say I've interfered with them, and I'm not going to say *one word* now.'

'Mother, do you think she's frightful?'

'No, dear, I don't want to say that. I'm old-fashioned, I suppose. To my mind, a man must choose his wife for himself, without advice from anybody. As I said to Tony before he ever proposed to this girl: Make sure that she's *good*, and a *lady*, and *healthy*, and *intelligent*, and that she's going to get on with your friends and relations, and you with hers—and then, my dear boy, if you feel that you can afford to marry—then I suppose there's no help for it.'

'Well, they won't have a bean between them, that's one thing.'

'I shouldn't have thought—I daresay I'm quite wrong—but I shouldn't have *thought*, somehow, that this was quite the kind of girl to manage on a very small income.'

'Oh, she doesn't know a thing about house-keeping. She said so. I must say I thought it was frightfully funny.'

'Oh, the whole thing's *funny*.'

'Yes, that's what I thought. I thought it was funny altogether.'

'Well, dears, we may not quite understand what poor dear Tony *sees* in this poor girl, but at least we can welcome her and make her feel how ready we all are to make the best of it.'

E. M. Delafield (1890–1943), Punch, reprinted: As Others Hear Us (1937).

E. M. Delafield's most widely read series was Diary of a Provincial Lady, *originally written as short pieces for the magazine* Time and Tide. *She published them in book form in 1931 and eventually wrote three sequels.*

It was socially and economically a different world in the 1930s: in her Diary *the Provincial Lady pleads poverty yet she has pleasantly comical difficulties with her cook, maid, and French governess, has a daughter at home and a son away at public school, and her husband at moments of crisis dozes behind* The Times.

In later books the Provincial Lady's preoccupations grow less those of village gentlefolk and more and more like the everyday domestic problems facing ordinary women, culminating in the Second World War when the Provincial Lady finds it most difficult even keeping her end up amongst a team of mixed volunteer ladies running the local Army Canteen:

October 3rd.—Old Mrs Winter-Gammon develops tendency, rapidly becoming fixed habit, of propping herself against Canteen counter, smoking cigarettes and chattering merrily. She asserts that she can do without sleep, without rest, without food and without fresh air. Am reluctantly forced to the conclusion that she can.

Conversation of Mrs W.-G. is wholly addressed to me, since Mrs. Peacock—leg in no way improved—remains glued to her box from which she can manipulate Cash-register—and leave Debutante to do one end of the counter, Colonial young creature with blue eyes in the middle, and myself at the other end.

Custom goes entirely to Debutante, who is prettyish, and talks out of one corner of tightly-shut mouth in quite unintelligible mutter, and Colonial, who is amusing. Am consequently left to company of Granny Bo-Peep.

She says roguishly that we old ones must be content to put up with one another and before I have time to think out civil formula in which to tell her that I disagree, goes on to add that, really, it's quite ridiculous the way all the boys come flocking round her. They like, she thinks, being mothered— and yet, at the same time, she somehow finds she can keep them laughing. It isn't that she's specially witty, whatever some of her clever men friends— such as W. B. Yeats, Rudyard Kipling and Lord Oxford and Asquith—may have said in the past. It's just that she was born, she supposes, under a dancing star. Like Beatrice.

(If Granny Bo-Peep thinks that I am going to ask her who Beatrice was, she is under a mistake. Would willingly submit to torture rather than do so, even if I didn't know, which I do.)

She has the audacity to ask, after suitable pause, if I know my Shakespeare.

Reply No not particularly, very curtly, and take an order for two Welsh rarebits and one Bacon-and-sausage to the kitchen. Have barely returned before Granny Bo-Peep is informing me that her quotation was from that lovely comedy *Much Ado About Nothing*. Do I know *Much Ado About Nothing*?

Yes, I do—and take another order for Sausages-and-mashed. Recollection comes before me, quite unnecessarily, of slight confusion which has always been liable to occur in my mind, as to which of Shakespeare's comedies is called *As You like It* and which *Much Ado About Nothing*. Should be delighted to tell old Mrs W. G. that she has made a mistake, but am not sufficiently positive myself.

Moreover, she gives me no opportunity.

Have I heard, she wants to know, from poor Blanche? I ask Why poor? and try to smile pleasantly so as to show that I am not being disagreeable— which I am. Well, says Granny Bo-Peep indulgently, she always thinks that poor Blanche—perfect dear though she is—is a wee bit lacking in *fun*. Granny Bo-Peep herself has such a keen sense of the ridiculous that it has enabled her to bear all her troubles where others, less fortunately endowed, would almost certainly have gone to pieces. Many, many years ago her doctor— one of the best-known men in Harley Street—said to her: Mrs Winter-Gammon, by rights you ought not to be alive to-day. You ought to be dead. Your health, your sorrows, your life of hard work for others, all should have killed you long, long ago. What has kept you alive? Nothing but your wonderful spirits.

And I am not, says Mrs W. G., to think for one instant that she is telling me this in a boastful spirit. Far from it. Her vitality, her gaiety, her youth-fulness and her great sense of humour have all been bestowed upon her from Above. She has had nothing to do but rejoice in the possession of these attributes and do her best to make others rejoice in them too.

Could well reply to this that if she has succeeded with others no better than she has with me, all has been wasted—but do not do so.

Shortly afterwards Commandant comes in, at which Mrs Peacock rises from her box, blue-eyed young Colonial drops a Beans-on-Toast on the floor, and Society Deb. pays no attention whatever.

Granny Bo-Peep nods at me very brightly, lights her fourteenth cigarette and retires to trestle-table on which she perches swinging her legs, and is instantly surrounded—to my fury—by crowd of men, all obviously delighted with her company.

Commandant asks what we have for supper—averting eyes from me as she speaks—and on being handed list goes through items in tones of utmost contempt.

She then orders two tomatoes on toast. Friend—known to me only as Darling—materialises behind her, and cries out that surely, surely, darling, she's going to have more than *that*. She must. She isn't going to be allowed to make her supper on tomatoes—it isn't *enough*.

Commandant makes slight snarling sound but no other answer, and I retire to kitchen with order, leaving Darling still expostulating.

Previously ordered Sausages-and-mashed, Welsh rarebit, Bacon-and-sausage are now ready, and I distribute them, nearly falling over distressed young Colonial who is scraping up baked beans off the floor. She asks madly what she is to do with them and I reply briefly: Dustbin.

Commandant asks me sharply where her tomatoes are and I reply, I hope equally sharply, In the frying-pan. She instantly takes the wind out of my sails by replying that she didn't say that she wanted them fried. She wants the *bread* fried, and the tomatoes uncooked . . .

Time and Tide, reprinted: *The Provincial Lady in War-time* (1940).

———

J AN STRUTHER (*another example of the feminine gift for thinking up logical pen-names; real name J. Anstruther*) *was a frequent contributor to* Punch *and, like E. M. Delafield, wrote about village gentry and Kensington ladies, but Jan Struther's work was in the old British tradition of sentimental comedy, inviting us to smile at the idiosyncratic ways of rather nice people.*

In 1939 Jan Struther published a gently humorous novel about a middle-aged wife coping with the outbreak of war which she called Mrs Miniver.

In 1942 this was made into a major Hollywood tear-jerker saluting the British middle class under fire. The picture, starring Greer Garson and Walter Pidgeon, dragged in the Battle of Britain and Dunkirk which had not happened when the book was written, added a great deal of tight-lipped courage and bitten-back emotion and ended with a wondrously kitsch scene in which the principal actors stood in a bombed church singing 'Onward Christian Soldiers'.

The film won five Oscars. The distinguished critic Pauline Kael called it 'one of the most scandalously smug of all Academy Award winners'.

In adapting the novel to the screen many things in the book had to be sacrificed to make room for the action scenes which Hollywood required. Most unhappily, one of the finer things to be sacrificed was the character of Mrs Miniver. The Mrs Miniver of the book was transformed into a film heroine, Greer Garson, calm and defiant in the face of whatever hell the Hun could throw at her, a paragon of feminine grit.

Which is a pity, because the character of Mrs Miniver was not at all like that. In creating the gentle, delightful Mrs Miniver, Jan Struther demonstrated her command of the humour of realistic domestic detail, of the almost Proustian accumulation of life's small discomforts, problems, and obsessions which Mrs Miniver observed, endured, and, on the whole, rather enjoyed.

Take the matter of the sound made by her car's windscreen wipers:

One of the minor arts of life, thought Mrs Miniver at the end of a long day's Christmas shopping, was the conservation of energy in the matter of swing doors. With patience and skilful timing it was very seldom necessary to use your strength on them. You could nearly always follow close behind some masterful person who had already done the pushing; and if you were too late for that and the door had begun to swing towards you, then it was well worth pausing for a second until it swung away again and needed only a gentle encouragement. This seemed obvious enough; but there was an astounding number of people who seemed to glory in taking the line of most resistance, hurling themselves against an approaching door and reversing its direction by brute force, as though there were virtue in the act. They must lead, she reflected, very uncomfortable lives.

Placing herself neatly in the wake of a bull-necked woman in tweeds, she slipped out of the shop. There was a raw wind; sleety rain was beginning to fall, blurring the lamplight; the pavements were seal-sleek; it was settling down into one of those nasty wet evenings which the exiled Londoner longs for with a quite unbearable nostalgia.

She tumbled all her parcels into the back of the car, slid, happy but exhausted, into the driving-seat, and set off; for home. The double screen-wiper wagged companionably, uttering over and over again the same faint wheedling word, which she could never quite make out. It was a dissyllable, something like 'receive' or 'bequeath'. She was glad, at any rate, that they now had a screen-wiper which moved at a constant speed. Their last had been one of those which work off the induction: lively and loquacious when you are at a standstill, sulky and slow as soon as you get going and really need its help—like the very worst type of human being.

She felt a little guilty: it was the first time she had caught herself comparing the beloved old car unfavourably in any way with the usurping new one.

Getting home was evidently going to be a long job. The usual six o'clock home-going stream was in spate with Christmas crowds, and Oxford Street was a solid jam. It was her own fault, she had to admit, as she sat back and waited for the lights to change. Every year the same thing happened. At the beginning of November she made up her mind that this time, for once, she would get her Christmas shopping done early. She went as far as writing out a list—and there, for several weeks, the matter rested. At intervals she tried to pretend that Christmas Day fell on the fifth of December, or, alternatively, that all her friends and relations lived in South Africa and that she had to catch an early mail; but it was no use. The feeling of temporal urgency cannot be artificially produced, any more than the feeling of financial distress. The rich young man who determines to work his way round the world may gain many things, but the experience of poverty is not one of them. He knows that in the ultimate emergency he can always cable home for funds; and Mrs Miniver knew perfectly well that Christmas was not until the twenty-fifth of December, and that all the people on her list lived in England.

(The screen-wiper wagged steadily. 'Sea-green . . . sea-green . . .' Perhaps that was nearer the mark?)

Besides, successful present-choosing depends very largely upon the right atmosphere, upon the contagious zest of crowds, upon sudden inspirations and perceptions, heightened rather than otherwise by a certain sense of pressure in space and time. To do it cold-bloodedly, in a half-empty shop, without any difficulty or competition, is as joyless as a *mariage de convenance*. So perhaps it was just as well, she told herself consolingly, that she had, as usual, left it till the middle of December.

('Wee Free . . . Wee Free . . .' Warmer. She'd get it yet.)

The lights changed. She put the car into bottom gear, paused, then let in the clutch. It occurred to her as she did so that it was not only people's physical reactions to those three colours that had become automatic but their mental ones as well. Red, yellow, green—frustration, hope, joy: a brand-new conditioned reflex. Give it a few more years to get established, and psychiatrists would be using coloured rays, projected in that sequence, for the treatment of melancholia; and to future generations green would no longer suggest envy, but freedom. In such haphazard ways are symbolisms born and reborn.

At the next crossing, red again. Frustration—but somehow one accepted it without resentment, simply because it was not imposed by a human hand. One could be annoyed with a policeman, but not with a tin hollyhock. The same was true of automatic telephones; ever since the dialling system had come in, the world's output of irritation must have been halved. It was an argument for the mechanisation of life which had not previously struck her.

She got home at last. Clem was already in, with his legs stretched out in front of the fire.

'Successful?' he asked, seeing her festooned with parcels.

'Look here,' she said, 'that screen-wiper—I think what it says is "Beef Tea".'

'My goodness,' said Clem. 'I believe you're right.'

Jan Struther (1901–53), Mrs Miniver (1939).

M ARY DUNN *was a professional humorist who for a time was quietly successful at writing bland, comedy-of-manners pieces for magazines until she found touch with material of a much more combustible nature, a book of spoof high-society memoirs,* Lady Addle Remembers, *published in 1936.*

Miss Dunn's own life was a little like something remembered by Lady Addle; her consort, Andrew Shirley, was an impecunious art historian and younger son (i.e. no inheritance) of the Earl Ferrers, one of whose ancestors had been the last aristocrat in Britain to be hanged by a silken rope. Also Shirley, echoing the hero of Somerset Maugham's Of Human Bondage, *had seduced a tradesman's daughter when he was an undergraduate at Oxford and had done the decent thing and married her, so Andrew and Mary Dunn had to begin their life together Living in Sin.*

Lady Addle Remembers *was a success, going into three editions. In 1944 Mary Dunn reversed the usual pattern and based a series of pieces for* Punch *on the characters she had created in her book. These* Punch *pieces, in their turn, were collected into two more Lady Addle books,* The Memoirs of Mipsie *(1945) and* Lady Addle at Home *(1947), which did not do as well.*

The Lady Addle memoirs were a well-deserved satire on the dreary, name-dropping, high-society memoirs which proliferated in the 1920s and 30s. Lady Addle, like some of the Duchesses and Countesses who inspired her, had not an atom of self-criticism in her nature. Instead she had a wealth of mindless complacency and a bullet-proof conviction that Position was All, that if you are Titled your behaviour is above criticism:

CHAPTER I

How dear to this heart are the scenes of my childhood
When fond recollection presents them to view.
Samuel Woodsworth: 'The Old Oaken Bucket'

Childhood at Coots Balder! What memories it brings back to one! The fine old grey building with its stately towers—its Gothic brewhouse—its Restoration still-room, and its bathrooms built in what I still hold to be the best and purest era of plumbing—the late 'eighties. Nowadays people calling themselves 'decorators' design bathrooms of black looking glass and chromium plate. But to my mind there is nothing to touch old tiles of cabbage green, with the mahogany bath tops worn almost white by the splashings of many noble visitors . . . polished, one might say, by the seats of the mighty.

Then the gardens, with their smooth green lawns, their picturesque, sloping tennis courts and splendid clock golf courses. Ah, what spacious days those were! The interior of the house was just fine, from the state bedroom containing the magnificent bed, slept in by two emperors, with four carved legs and fringed pelmets, down to the vast pantry with its marble floor.

I happen particularly to remember that marble floor because it was the cause of a charming incident. One of the footmen—I think his name was Giles—had slipped on it and broken his leg, which necessitated his being removed to hospital just when we had a house party, which was most inconvenient for my mother. Nevertheless, with all her usual graciousness and consideration she went the very next month to the cottage where his mother lived to inquire after the boy. Dear old Mrs Hummick was a great friend of ours and would never let us pass her door without begging us to come in and take a cup of nettle tea or a glass of gherkin wine. On this occasion she had an extra little present of a jar of tadpole jelly—a delicious recipe of her own—and when my dear mother thanked her (she had the most beautiful manners of any woman I have ever known and almost invariably thanked for any present she was given) Mrs Hummick curtsied and said: 'You're very welcome, m'lady, and as for the boy's leg, he couldn't have broked it in a better house.' I always think that remark epitomizes the perfect relationship existing between employer and employee in the last century.

It is a great moment for Lady Addle when her brother Crainiham, of whom she is rightly proud, falls for a most delightful—and suitable—girl:

The prettiest of all the pretty girls of that date, my own family excepted, was dear, vivacious, enchanting Dorothy Divott [Hon. Dorothy Divott, second daughter of Lord Foozle]—'Duckie' as she was always called, and what a duck she was! The life and soul of any party, always the leading spirit of dumb crambo—the daredevil in beggar-my-neighbour. So it is not to be wondered at that when my eldest brother Crainiham openly showed his admiration it was looked upon with nothing but favour from our parents.

I shall always remember their first meeting. Crainy was always rather quiet and reserved, though not from any lack of brains, because he passed fifty-first into Sandhurst after only two years at his crammers—this being a record in our family. But he very seldom spoke in sentences of more than one or at the most two words, and practically never expressed an opinion on anything at all. This was due not to any cowardice, but rather to a rare and splendid honesty which I know made him hold—though I never, of course, actually heard him say so—that no man should express an opinion on any subject unless he previously had an opinion to express. Imagine our surprise, therefore, when on first being introduced to Ducky at a garden party, after barely ten minutes silence, we clearly heard Crainy say: 'It's a lovely day, isn't it, Miss Divott?'

Well, anyone who could make Crainy sparkle like that was a genius and my romantic mind was made up on the spot. Crainy and Duckie should marry—nothing should stop it. Unless, I suddenly thought with horror, the rather exacting bridegroom's part of several sentences should prove too great a strain for him. But we'll take that fence when it comes, I decided, lapsing into a metaphor culled from my well-loved sport.

Lady Addle's account of how her bike sprang a puncture and she met the man she was destined to marry must be one of the most idyllic of modern love stories, in spite of the phallic symbolism of his lordship's bicycle pump at the end (of which, in her innocence, Lady Addle could not possibly have been aware):

I had scarcely passed ten minutes in weighing the pros and cons of walking back over the road on which I had come, or walking on over the road ahead of me—both routes would have led me to Coots Balder in about the same time—when suddenly round the corner came a bicycle. It was a man's bicycle, and seated on it was—a man! That man was my future husband.

Immediately he recognized me he sprang off his machine with a charming look of concern on his handsome face. I shall never forget his first words.

'I say, can I help you?' Then with a quickness of perception which I learnt later on to know and love: 'I see your back tyre is flat. Perhaps you have a puncture?'

In a moment he had whisked out his own pump and was bending over my back wheel, while I watched admiringly the strong young shoulders and noted the ease with which he pumped the tyre up without once having to pause for breath. Then he straightened himself and felt the rubber with a master hand.

'I think that's all right now,' he said. 'It was just flat—not a puncture as far as I can see.'

Then came words that sent the hot blood coursing into my cheeks: 'We are both fond of bicycling, aren't we?'

What I answered I scarcely knew. I murmured some conventional reply in a whirl of embarrassment and happiness to think that he had remembered those other rides too, and the next thing I knew was that he was gone. Only when he was round the corner and out of earshot, did I discover that he had left his pump behind.

There was never any doubt in my mind but that it was a deliberate act on his part and no accident. He wanted to leave me protected and safeguarded against any possible future deflation, while he deliberately exposed himself to the same risk. That was Addle all over.

Modern girls will laugh at me for being sentimental, but I am not ashamed to confess that for five nights running I slept with that pump under my pillow, and woke each day to find myself holding fast to the handle. We Victorians may be considered old-fashioned, but we had our glorious moments of real romance.

Unhappily life for Lady Addle is not all love and bicycle pumps. She has a cross to bear in the spectacular shape of her sister Mipsie. It might seem to an insensitive reader that Mipsie was simply a high-class whore (many noble families had one or two) but Lady Addle insists that poor Mipsie was a Victim of Life:

It was in spring of 1902 that I first began to realize that things were not going right between her and Oxo [her current husband], chiefly through his fault, I must say. While he was fighting in South Africa, Mipsie had done the obviously sensible thing which was to save the vast expense of Brisket Castle by shutting it up and taking a house in Paris instead. He raised no objection at the time, yet on his return, although Mipsie came home within six months, which was as soon as she could manage to wind up her affairs in France, he was furious and practically refused to pay her Paris debts. He actually seemed to expect her to have existed there on the same money as she would have lived on at Brisket, which was frankly ridiculous. That was the beginning of the rift. The next quarrel was over the children. There were two, a girl and a boy, whom Mipsie worshipped and made a point of seeing at least twice a week. But she was always adorably vague and one day when Soppy and her family of eight were staying there Mipsie lifted up little Archie Hogshead and said to a caller: 'This is my baby.' It was a very natural mistake to make—they were, after all, first cousins—but Oxo chose to take umbrage and accused her of not knowing which were her own children. Mipsie, with her flashing wit, tried to ease matters by a playful rejoinder: 'Well, how do you know which are yours?' but he was too angry to be soothed. The breach widened.

The end came over a stupid misunderstanding. Mipsie was expected back from Brussels, where she had been on a visit, to act as hostess to a large shooting party at Brisket, but was taken suddenly ill and telegraphed: 'Cannot return. In bed with *migraine*.' Oxo, who was always a very poor French scholar, had never heard of the word, so completely misconstruing the contents of the message rushed frantically to Brussels, where, as bad luck would have it, Mipsie's attack had suddenly subsided and she was trying to revive her strength for the journey by a quiet little dinner with an old friend in the private room of an hotel. Explanations were all in vain. After a distressing scene of violent recriminations on both sides Oxo left for England, and we learnt that they had separated.

Poor darling brave Mipsie! What she must have suffered during the divorce proceedings, losing not only her good name but her children and the famous Brisket pearls as well as having her allowance cut down to a beggarly £3,000 a year, I dread to think. She was always so sensitive and so proud—the pride of a thoroughbred—and hated to fall short of any standard or ideal she had set for herself. That was the reason why she accepted the offer of Fr. 50,000 a year as an allowance from another old friend, the Marquis de Pelouse. It was to enable her to live as Oxo, in the days when he had loved her, would have liked her to. It was amazing loyalty for a woman who had been treated as Mipsie had; yet the world said malicious and bitter things even about that.

She soon married again.

Mary Dunn (1900–58), *Lady Addle Remembers* (1936).

───────

*D*URING *the early* 1930*s the older generation of* Punch *staff-writers, survivors from pre-war, began to give way to a new breed of younger, post-war humorists with less entrenched attitudes. Several of these new men (no women) began as casual contributors and were eventually invited to join the staff. It was this influx of fresh minds and talents to the* Punch *management which did as much as anything to maintain the standards of the magazine during the thirties and forties.*

There was H. F. Ellis (known as 'H. F. E.', Humphry, or, due to the colour of his hair, Copper); Double First in Classics, Magdalen College; vigorous player of Rugby football for his University, for the town of Richmond, Surrey, and for the county of Kent; briefly a schoolmaster; first piece accepted by Punch *in* 1931; *joined the staff in* 1933; *appointed Deputy Editor* 1949; *contributor to the* New Yorker *from* 1954.

Ellis's work for Punch *was mainly in the middle-of-the-road* Punch *tradition of the worked-up domestic incident or personal experience but he elevated the genre by the quality of his humour and by his writing style; his English English is as precise and beautiful as E. B. White's American English.*

'H. F. E.' faced the world not as a bumbler or a boaster but as a perfectly normal, amiable chap, the sort of chap who would subscribe to Punch, *reasonably intelligent, nimble enough with his fingers. The fault was not in himself but in his stars. He was constantly bemused to find how unfairly and unreasonably the little things of life arraigned themselves against him.*

The following piece, a classic of its kind, became the hit of an immediately post-war stage revue when given as a monologue by the actor George Benson. It was one of a Punch *series entitled* For Men in Aprons *in which Ellis gave expert advice to the new underprivileged, that is, those middle-class gentlemen who returned from the war to homes bereft of servants or household help and for the first time in their lives found themselves expected to lend a hand with the domestic chores:*

WASHING-UP

Of the disappointingly few letters I have received in response to my offer, made a month ago in this paper, to help you with your household problems, perhaps the most interesting is one which deals with the vexed questions of getting cold porridge out of the crevices of saucepans. But before I answer this point in detail, may I permit myself the luxury of a general reflection on saucepans?

In the old pre-war days, it will be remembered, when in some sudden emergency we offered our assistance at the sink, it was always clearly understood that we men did not concern ourselves with saucepans—nor indeed with any cooking utensil likely to have dried foodstuffs adhering tenaciously to its sides and bottom. We did the plates and cutlery and we held the glasses momentarily under the tap. But the rest was women's work; somebody would do it in the morning. Those spacious days are over. Nothing, literally nothing, is nowadays considered too revolting for a man to touch. When I say that men have been known to tackle those brown earthenware jars used for Lancashire hot-pot, from the rims of which (for this is not the place to speak of the unimaginable interiors) the jagged ridges of caked and blackened gravy must be chipped off with a chisel, when I mention this simple fact returning husbands will, I think, gain some notion of the pass to which we have come.

Very well then. Now to my correspondent, whose name I decipher as Brandsop or (more improbably) Brushoff. He writes:

'I can get most of the porridge out all right with the scratcher, but it won't do the corners or the part where the handle joins the top of the saucepan. Poking about with a skewer is fatiguing work and makes me late with the fireplaces, nor does it really do the job properly. I am at my wits' end and would give up porridge altogether, if we could get any eggs, bacon, kidneys or fish.'

Well, this is a problem that has puzzled most of us in our time. Nor is it to be solved by any such drastic expedient as dropping porridge off the menu, because (apart from any other considerations) exactly the same difficulty crops up with boiled milk. So let's face it boldly, shall we?

When Mr Brandsop speaks of the 'scratcher' he is referring undoubtedly to that bundle of twisted wire which is usually kept in a soap-dish on the draining-board or under the plate-rack, and he is absolutely right to use it for the main interior surfaces of the pan. Used fearlessly, with a brisk rotary movement, the scratcher will clear up the most stubborn situation in no time. But it is not designed to penetrate nooks and crannies. For such pockets of resistance as the corners of a saucepan and (as Mr Brandsop well says) the junction of the handle with the main framework, a special instrument has been devised and is to be found in any well-appointed scullery. If Mr Brandsop will look round he may find a piece of apparatus resembling a bundle of twigs bound about the middle with a metal clasp. It is often balanced behind the kitchen taps, where these are close enough together to afford a lodgment, and may have escaped his observation. The correct name for this thing is not known to me; it is referred to in this house as the 'scritcher', and the name, which conveys with some fidelity the greater precision and delicacy with which it scratches, will serve as well as another. Now, having possessed yourself of scratcher and scritcher, here is the way to go to work. First scour out with the scratcher, rinse and put away. Most of the porridge will now be embedded in the scratcher, but that need not concern you. Bad as things are, the time has not yet come when we men are expected to clean the scratcher. Next take the scritcher and scritch lightly but firmly in all the crevices. Rinse again. Finish by whisking round the rim of the saucepan in such a way that half the bristles of the scritcher are inside and half out. Give it a firm rinse, mop out and hang up or hurl under the dresser according to local custom.

Before I leave Mr Brandsop's or (as seen from some angles) Mr Brushoff's letter, I must just sound one rather serious note. He talks of being made 'late with the fireplaces' by his difficulties with the porridge saucepan! If this means, as I fear it does, Mr Brandsop, that you are leaving the fireplaces until after breakfast, I can only say that you are starting the day under a hopeless handicap. Do get the sitting-room at least tidied up and the fire laid first thing in the morning. We were not allowed to be slovenly in the Army. Don't let us be content with a lower standard in the privacy of our own homes.

I have spent so long over this very important problem of saucepans that I have only time now to deal briefly with a point raised by Mr Joseph Twill, of Mole's End, Gloucestershire. He wants to know whether it is possible to stop milk boiling over, and suggests that a really deep saucepan might conceivably be a solution.

I propose to answer Mr Twill's question by enunciating a number of rules for milk-boilers. They are based on common sense and a wide experience of mopping up milk both on gas and electric stoves.

1. Never boil milk. Heat it till turgid and remove.

2. It is impossible to combine the heating of milk with any other pursuit whatsoever. (The same rule applies to the toasting of bread under a grill. Thus to attempt to heat milk and toast bread at the same time—a very common fault—is the height of insanity. The only thing to be said for it is that the milk boiling over puts the toast out.)

3. An unwatched pot boils *immediately*.

4. Half a pint of milk brought to a temperature of 100° Centigrade rises to a height greater than the walls of the saucepan, *irrespective of the dimensions of the saucepan*. To take an extreme case, if a jug of milk were poured into the crater of Vesuvius, Pompei would inevitably be engulfed a second time.

5. The speed at which boiling milk rises from the bottom of the pan to any point beyond the top is greater than the speed at which the human brain and hand can combine to snatch the confounded thing off.

Follow these rules, Mr Twill, and you will be all right. But keep a dish-cloth handy.

H. F. Ellis (b. 1907), Punch (1946).

In the late 1930s Ellis started writing pieces for Punch *which were supposedly episodes from the journals of A. J. Wentworth, BA, assistant master at Burgrove, an imaginary small preparatory school in the country. This was dry humour, wickedly accurate, and as English as baked jam-roll. The stories proved to be even more popular in America than in England.*

A collection of the pieces was published in 1949 as The Papers of A. J. Wentworth, BA, *another volume,* A. J. Wentworth, BA (Retd.) *appeared in 1962, and* Swansong of A. J. Wentworth *in 1982.*

Mr Wentworth was a subtle comic invention with just a whiff of an ex-public-school Pooter about him. He had taught small boys for a great number of years and had no interest whatsoever in modern teaching methods. He was a stickler for discipline in class, a little pompous, a mite touchy and accident-prone. The pupils in Set IIIA, particularly the bright boy Mason, easily out-manœuvred Mr Wentworth who was rarely even conscious that a manœuvre was taking place.

Mr Wentworth had unshakeable faith in the reasonableness of his own conduct. He would never accept that he had ever behaved, or could behave, in any way oddly, or unwisely. The author points out on a dust jacket that one comment 'in the Times Educational Supplement of all places' to the effect that 'we love him in spite of everything' really nettled Mr Wentworth. 'In spite of what, may I ask?' he cried.

The first of the papers from Mr Wentworth's journal is the statement he prepared for the police justifying (not that it needed justifying, of course) a disciplinary measure he felt it necessary to take when teaching Set IIIA:

STATEMENT OF ARTHUR JAMES WENTWORTH, BA

My name is Arthur James Wentworth, I am unmarried and I am by profession an assistant master at Burgrove Preparatory School, Wilminster. The Headmaster is the Reverend Gregory Saunders, MA. He is known to the boys as the Squid—not necessarily, I think, a term of opprobrium. He is a classical scholar of moderate attainments, a generous employer and much given to the use of the expression, 'The School must come first, Wentworth'. I attach no particular meaning to this remark.

At 11.15 on the morning of Saturday 8 July, I entered Classroom 4 for the purpose of instructing Set IIIA in Algebra. There were present Anderson, Atkins, Clarke, Etheridge, Hillman, Hopgood II, Mason, Otterway, Sapoulos, Trench and Williamson. Heathcote, who has, I am told, a boil, was absent. It should be explained that though I have given these names in the alphabetical order in which they appear in the school list, that is not the order in which the boys were sitting on this occasion. It is the custom at Burgrove for boys to sit according to their position in the previous week's mark-lists. Thus in the front row were seated Etheridge, a most promising mathematician, Hillman, Mason, Otterway and Clarke. Hopgood II, the boy whom I am now accused of assaulting, was in the middle of the second row. The third and last row was shared by Sapoulos, a Greek, and Atkins, a cretin. I do not think these facts have any bearing on anything that is to follow, but I give them for the sake of completeness.

'This morning,' I remarked, taking up my *Hall and Knight,* 'we will do problems,' and I told them at once that if there was any more of that groaning they would do nothing but problems for the next month. It is my experience, as an assistant master of some years' standing, that if groaning is not checked immediately it may swell to enormous proportions. I make it my business to stamp on it.

Mason, a fair-haired boy with glasses, remarked when the groaning had died down that it would not be possible to do problems for the next month, and on being asked why not, replied that there were only three weeks more of term. This was true, and I decided to make no reply. He then asked if he could have a mark for that. I said, 'No, Mason, you may not,' and, taking up my book and a piece of chalk, read out, 'I am just half as old as my father and in twenty years I shall be five years older than he was twenty years ago. How old am I?' Atkins promptly replied, 'Forty-two.' I enquired of him how, unless he was gifted with supernatural powers, he imagined he could produce the answer without troubling to do any working-out. He said, 'I saw it in the *Schools Year-book*.' This stupid reply caused a great deal of laughter, which I suppressed.

I should have spoken sharply to Atkins, but at this moment I noticed that his neighbour Sapoulos, the Greek boy, appeared to be eating toffee, a practice which is forbidden at Burgrove during school hours. I ordered him to stand up. 'Sapoulos,' I said, 'you are not perhaps quite used yet to our English ways, and I shall not punish you this time for your disobedience; but please understand that I will not have eating in my class. You did not come here to eat but to learn. If you try hard and pay attention, I do not altogether despair of teaching you something, but if you do not wish to learn I cannot help you. You might as well go back to your own country.' Mason, without being given a permission to speak, cried excitedly, 'He can't, sir. Didn't you know? His father was chased out of Greece in a revolution or something. A big man with a black beard chased him for three miles and he had to escape in a small boat. It's true, sir. You ask him. Sapoulos got hit on the knee with a brick, didn't you, Sappy? And his grandmother—at least I think it was his grandmother—'

'That will do, Mason,' I said. 'Who threw that?'

I am not, I hope, a martinet, but I will not tolerate the throwing of paper darts, or other missiles in my algebra set. Some of the boys make small pellets out of their blotting-paper and flick them with their garters. This sort of thing has to be put down with a firm hand or work becomes impossible. I accordingly warned the boy responsible that another offence would mean an imposition. He had the impertinence to ask what sort of an imposition. I said that it would be a pretty stiff imposition, and if he wished to know more exact details he had only to throw another dart to find out. He thereupon threw another dart.

I confess that at this I lost patience and threatened to keep the whole set in during the afternoon if I had any more trouble. The lesson then proceeded.

It was not until I had completed my working out of the problem on the board that I realized I had worked on the assumption—of course ridiculous—that I was *twice* my father's age instead of *half*. This gave the false figure of minus 90 for my own age. Some boy said, 'Crikey!' I at once whipped round and demanded to know who had spoken. Otterway suggested that it might have been Hopgood II talking in his sleep. I was about to reprimand Otterway for impertinence when I realized that Hopgood actually was asleep and had in fact, according to Williamson, been asleep since the beginning of the period. Mason said, 'He hasn't missed much, anyway.'

I then threw my *Hall and Knight*. It has been suggested that it was intended to hit Hopgood II. This is false. I never wake up sleeping boys by throwing books at them, as hundreds of old Burgrove boys will be able to testify. I intended to hit Mason, and it was by a mischance which I shall always regret that Hopgood was struck. I have had, as I told my Headmaster, a great deal to put up with from Mason, and no one who knows the boy blames me for the attempt to do him some physical violence. It is indeed an accepted maxim in the Common Room that physical violence is the only method of dealing with Mason which produces any results; to this the Headmaster some time ago added a rider that the boy be instructed to remove his spectacles before being assaulted. That I forgot to do this must be put down to the natural agitation of a mathematics master caught out in an error. But I blame myself for it.

I do not blame myself for the unfortunate stunning of Hopgood II. It was an accident. I did all I could for the boy when it was discovered (I think by Etheridge) that he had been rendered unconscious. I immediately summoned the Headmaster and we talked the matter over. We agreed that concealment was impossible and that I must give a full account of the circumstances to the police. Meanwhile the work of the school was to go on as usual; Hopgood himself would have wished it. The Headmaster added that in any case the School must come first.

I have made this statement after being duly cautioned, of my own free will and in the presence of witnesses. I have read it through three times with considerable satisfaction, and am prepared to state on oath that it is a true and full account of the circumstances leading up to the accident to Hopgood II. I wish only to add that the boy is now none the worse for the blow, and has indeed shown increased zeal for his studies since the occurrence.

> (*Signed*) A. J. Wentworth, BA. *Punch*, reprinted: *The Papers of A. J. Wentworth, BA* (1949).

A NOTHER *distinguished* Punch *staff writer was Richard Mallett. Mallett began early, having had his first piece accepted by* Punch *when he was a 16-year-old freelance journalist. He joined the staff of* Punch *from* The Evening News *in 1937 and was Acting Assistant Editor during most of the war.*

Mallett was a highly skilled parodist—he is credited with having invented the trick of reviewing a novel in the style of the novel itself—and a good versifier. More importantly, when films became too important to ignore any longer Mallett became Punch's *first regular, serious reviewer, and very good he was; one American editor thought Mallett one of the world's best film critics.*

His humorous stories about his peculiar aunt were remarkable, if only for having got into Punch *at all. They had a strong whiff about them of that nonsensical humour pioneered by Ring Lardner and Benchley which Mallett's editor, Evoe, considered to be an alien American phenomenon which* Punch *readers could well do without.*

But somehow Mallett got his way, probably because in most other areas his tastes were classical and traditional. The result was the appearance in Punch *at last of a gentle form of* dementia praecox *humour.*

The stories are narrated by the author's kindly old Aunt Tabitha:

DO SOMETHING

'When I was working as a lumberjack, bar-tender and telephone linesman in Old Bond Street, W.,' said my Aunt Tabitha, knocking her pipe out on the cat, 'many of the girls used to bring me their little problems, and the advice I always used to give them was this: Do something. I have never regretted it.'

'Have they?' I asked, gazing round the charming old-world room with its chintz-covered work-basket (full of tobacco) and dainty spittoons.

'I see no reason why they should have,' said Aunt Tabitha. 'It is the best possible advice for a girl with her way to make in the world. I gave it once to a girl named Muriel who was in a jam about some chimneys, and since that day she has never looked back.'

'No?'

'At least I think not. I never caught her looking back, anyhow.'

'Did she look either to the right or to the left?' I inquired.

'No,' said Aunt Tabitha, eyeing the whisky, 'but she looked up, of course, because of the chimneys. It is the bane of a girl's life when she's engaged to an architect—she has to go about with her nose in the air looking at chimneys. This bothered Muriel a lot and she was continually trying to make up her mind to speak to the architect about it, but he was so much wrapped up in his subject that she never could find the opportunity. In the end she dotted him one and got all ready to leap in with her objections to chimneys as soon as he came round.'

Aunt Tabitha paused to clear her throat, or light a cigar, or look out of the window, or something, for she was well aware that I should have to split the narrative up into paragraphs like this when I wrote it out.

'But before he came round,' Aunt Tabitha went on, 'she happened to catch sight of a man in a white coat carrying a cash-register. Taken in by this man's glamour she went off with him; much to his annoyance, for he already had two wives and seven children as well as the cash-register, which was his eye's apple. Often during the cold winter nights he would sit up for hours with his cash-register. This used to bother Muriel a lot. "Oh, I have been blind—blind!" she used to say to him. "I have jumped out of the chimneys into the cash-register! Ha, ha!" (here she used to laugh hysterically). "What a fool I've been! What a blind crazy fool! Oh!" Here,' said Aunt Tabitha, 'she would put the back of her hand to her head about a couple of inches below the hair-line, walk five paces rapidly up and five paces rapidly down, grip the back of a chair with one hand until the knuckles showed white, bite her lip till the blood came, and leave off again until it went. Also a vein would probably be throbbing ominously in her temple.'

'And the man in the white coat,' I said—'what would he reply to that?'

'He generally asked her to get some oil,' said Aunt Tabitha, 'for the cash-register. Then the fit would leave her as suddenly as it had come, which was not suddenly in the least. Well, in due course she asked my advice.'

'Pardon me,' I said courteously, 'you said she asked your advice about the chimneys.'

'I said nothing of the kind,' roared Aunt Tabitha in a passion, throwing her embroidery-frame to the ground. 'I said the gal was in a jam about some chimneys, and so she was, and I said I gave her my advice, and so I did. But the advice I gave her was about the cash-register. "Do something," I said.'

'Subtle.'

'Subtle my eye. She took it as advice to go back to the architect. So there she is again all among the chimneys.'

'And she's still never looked back?'

'Why should she? All there is to look at is the cash-register and a few of this fellow's wives. However,' said Aunt Tabitha, 'the chimneys soon began to get her down again, and before long she came to me. "My dear," I said with a smile as tender as a plump pullet, "I am an old woman. When you are as old as I, or me, or whichever it is," I said, "you will be able to look back and realize that there are chimneys and chimneys." "Which are these?" she murmured through her tears, making a bubble or two. "Chimneys," I replied very quietly. "There, there," I went on pretty nearly as tenderly as before, "have your cry out. You would not think to look at me now that I too, many years ago was—bothered by chimneys?" "Why," said Muriel wonderingly, "what can you know of chimneys, you?" "Ah!" I said, "I too have known chimneys." At this Muriel herself became very tender—about two-thirds as tender as I had been the first time. She said very softly, "What happened to them?" It was some moments,' said Aunt Tabitha, 'before I could speak—we were having tea at the time. Then I said, with a smile that was infinitely sad and wise: "They were all struck by lightning in the great storm of 1888."'

There was a pause. (There always is just before the end, if you notice.)

'And then?' I said.

'Then I rang the bell,' said Aunt Tabitha briskly, 'for some more cake. Ah, me! I remember it all as if it were yesterday. It *was* yesterday,' she added as an afterthought, refilling her pipe.

Richard Mallett (1910–72), *Punch.*

━━━━━━

*I*F *a* Punch *staff writer had to be nominated as the humorist whose work overall best demonstrates modern post-war* Punch *prose humour it is all Lombard Street to a China orange that the vote would go to J. B. (Basil) Boothroyd, tall, debonair, the possessor of Tudor Street's neatest small fawn moustache.*

Basil Boothroyd began adult life working in a bank but was soon winging off to Punch *examples of what he termed 'frivolous journalism'. From 1938 he became a regular contributor, served in the RAF during the War, was made an Assistant Editor in 1952 and in 1955 was honoured by being invited to become, as Humphry Ellis and Richard Mallett already were, a Member of the Punch Table.*

He has written for, and appeared on, radio and television, he adapted The Diary of a Nobody *for BBC Television and Humphry Ellis's* The Papers of A. J. Wentworth, BA *for Independent Television, he wrote an authorized biography of Prince Philip, Duke of Edinburgh, he lectured and gave speeches, he tackled most of the writing jobs on* Punch *over the years including reviewing, supplying topical light verse and writing virtually single-handed the page of topical comments then called* Charivaria, *but it is as the author of over 2,500* Punch *pieces (referred to gloomily by Boothroyd as 'my side-splitters') that he is most admired.*

He was the pro's pro. Although never much of an innovator it only required a nudge—like the annual arrival of Christmas, the despair of less inventive writers— for Boothroyd to deliver an original treatment of a good idea expressed in a lean, nervy, sparkling prose style:

NO SEX PLEASE, I'M SANTA

You might keep this away from the kids. Their Christmas games have been cleaned up since my own formative years. You don't get any mysterious and unsettling urges playing *Vermin*, £17.95 + p&p. Belting electronic moles with a laser-hammer demands full concentration from the pimpliest of boys. Same with the *Hobbit* jigsaw. I don't say Mrs Petworth, kneeling close and helping me trace Bilbo's journey through Eriador and Rhonavion to the huts of the Raftelves, couldn't have wrenched things round to a sexy spin-off, but even she would have been pushed.

She would be in her eighties now, I suppose, if anywhere, but was a strong, gardenia-scented widow when she got me in the Forbes-Stimsons' airing cupboard. She wore stuff on her lips. I'd noticed this during 'Matchboxes'. It isn't much played now, but recreational historians will know it. Contestants have to transfer the outside of a matchbox to each other's noses using no hands. She was next in line to me, and clumsy. You wouldn't believe how often she muffed things and fell against my face. She was rotten at it.

Later, playing 'Sardines' at her own suggestion, she was just as bad, not even grasping the rules. As I had understood it, the object was to cram the greatest number of players into the smallest spaces. Enid Forbes-Stimson, with a dozen or so fellow-guests, was to prove the winner on this occasion. When the whistle went they trooped from the WC with a second go of fudge for prizes.

Mrs Petworth and I were in the cupboard for ages after that. 'It's silly, going in there,' I'd told her. 'There's hardly room for two, even.'

'Just,' she said.

Christmases were white then, but as soon as she let me out I ran home through the snow without my overcoat. 'And your shirt all undone,' my mother said. 'You look feverish.' My father said what had I been thinking about, and I said I didn't know, which was not a lie. I was stubborn about going back for the coat, even next day when Santa had brought me my thick Christmas jersey and strong boots. They both said they didn't understand me.

So that must have been Christmas Eve, the airing cupboard. Next day, the Day, it was my friend Daisy Scotwood's party, where they always had charades. A naturally shy boy, not yet daring to ask to be excused, even when bursting with lemonade, I nevertheless quite fancied myself at the intellectual challange of charades, and could mime individual syllables like port/man/teau with the best. It was disappointing to find on arrival that Daisy had switched to the game's dressing-up version. She was pretty old, probably fifteen, and at least it was flattering when she teamed us together against Bobby and Netta Catchpole.

She thought of our word. Adam/ant. In a bigger house we shouldn't have had to dress up in her bedroom. Or perhaps we should, from the way she went about things. 'You be Adam and I'll be the ant,' she said, and wouldn't hear of what I thought a sensible objection: that she was too big for a convincing ant, but I could have managed it. 'Stupid,' she said. 'I'm a girl. Get your trousers off.' Despite her offer of a fig-leaf, string and a green face-cloth, I wouldn't do this. Then she wanted to wrestle.

'What are you two up to? We're all waiting,' said Mrs Scotwood, rapping on the door and out of breath with the climb.

Daisy threw me on the bed and ran downstairs, shouting back up, 'He won't play. He's a little pansy.'

'What's the matter with you?' said her mother, dropping her hostessy smile and pulling my jersey the right way out.

I said I felt funny, and she said I'd better go home in that case, as they'd got new carpets everywhere. Long after they moved to Horsham I still passed the Scotwoods' house by a detour after that.

Boxing Day, the party was at my house. My parents left us quite early, on church work for the Old Folks. I don't know how it came about that Connie Wilmslow was invited, unless they thought it would be a good thing to have a more-or-less grown-up to oversee the younger guests.

As suffragan host I was in a position to nominate my very favourite game, 'Pepper's Wedding'. This took the form, as some may remember, of readings from a story with words left blank but furnished by other players drawing slips from a hat. Hilarious incongruities resulted, and my ribs used to ache for days after playing it.

I did the reading: 'The bride's dress, which was tastefully ornamented with—'

'Dead fish,' read Netta Catchpole from the hat.

It was some time before I could go on.

'At the wedding breakfast,' I finally got out, but only by thinking of something serious like death, 'Mr Pepper made a brilliantly funny speech about his wife's—'

'Bum,' read Connie Wilmslow. She was sharing the small sofa with me, and though I didn't notice it at the time something she was wearing under her dress made quite a deep mark on my leg.

'That's not right, Connie,' I said, when almost everyone had laughed but me. She said, oh, no, she'd misread it. She should have said suspender-belt. Look. Then she showed me the slip but before I could read it pushed it down the front of her blouse. 'No,' I said. 'I just know those words aren't in there. I've played it heaps of times.'

'Want to bet?' she said, putting my hand on her chest, 'Read it yourself.'

It seemed so silly, and quite spoilt the game.

'Let's play "Passing the Key,"' then,' Connie said.

'Oh yes!' cried Netta and several of the older girls.

In this game, a key on a very long piece of string is passed down inside the clothing of the players looping them together and sometimes getting caught up and having to be . . . the winner is the one who . . . if two of the players find themselves . . . Well, I forget exactly, I know a big boy whom I secretly envied for being called Gerald and having two fountain pens found Connie's slip of paper, and what it actually said was 'wooden leg', and could have been very funny. I don't know, as my father would have said, what she could have been thinking about.

Anyway, I'm only saying that everything's changed now. Even the early developer, with the modern game and puzzle, has to keep his mind on what he's doing. Show me a girl-next-door who shoves her Rubik Cube up a boy's shorts and I'll show you a freakish exception. Instructions to 'fill this mind-bending atomic maze with heavy water and see if you can position the balls', can bring no harm to the growingest of boys.

They might if Mrs Petworth and Daisy Scotwood and Connie Wilmslow were around to join in the fun. But they are all long gone, I regret—though with a reminiscent blush—to say.

Basil Boothroyd (1910–88), *Punch.*

One of the drawbacks of making a career on Punch *was that until recent years the writer's work was published semi-anonymously ; only initials were permitted, e.g. 'A. P. H' for A. P. Herbert, or some twist of the author's name, such as 'Evoe' for E. V. Knox. The result of this was that, unlike star contributors to the* New Yorker *and other successful journals, very few* Punch *writers, if any, became famous for what they wrote in* Punch. *The professional skills of old* Punch *hands like Basil Boothroyd makes this lack of a much wider, international fame seem most unfair, particularly when the quality of Boothroyd's writing remained remarkably high throughout his vast output.*

How many humorous writers, who have been knocking out a funny piece every week for coming up to fifty years, could let their enormous file of material be dipped into and a piece picked out at random, and be fairly confident that it would be just as fresh and inventive as any of the other pieces?

Not Basil Boothroyd, who was far too nervous and modest. Yet here is just such a piece, selected virtually at random from his huge output:

CAN YOU READ MUSIC ?

Rachmaninov, as everyone knows, used to get mad with people who thought his C sharp minor Prelude described a man nailed into his coffin on insufficient medical evidence who kept banging on the lid to attract passers-by. Rachmaninov said this was rubbish. He simply had the idea of writing a prelude, selected a key, and wrote it. Why he couldn't have selected an easier key is neither here nor there, and only opens up that old mystery for halting executants, viz. what have all the other keys got that the key of C hasn't? But I realize that this is the lower criticism, and a subordinate theme at that.

What I'm concerned with at the moment is the man who announced the Egmont Overture on the radio the other day, and told me I was in for 'a thrilling expression of the composer's belief in human rights'. Now, I haven't thought very highly of Beethoven in the past. His work has seemed a bit thick and straining to me, not unlike a dull but efficient exhibition of weight-lifting; nor do I care for his endings, with enough repetitions of the common chord to make me yell 'All right, all *right*'. But this new light on the man sends my respect shooting up. A composer who can juggle the reed, brass and catgut to convey his belief in human rights is fully entitled to have his scaled-down bust on the top of school pianos. The theme isn't an easy one to get over in an orchestral score. You can't even fall back on onomatopoeia, really. Tchaikovsky with his bells of Moscow leaves us in no doubt what's going on. Delius with his cuckoos is instantly interpretable. But getting eighty musicians to sound like the Magna Carta is another kettle of drums.

As a matter of fact, the whole business of getting the musical message worries me. What *are* the musicians saying to us, as we close our eyes and concentrate, trying to forget that the contra-bassoonist looks like Roy Welensky? Works with evocative titles are simple. The Skater's Waltz leaves us in no doubt of Waldteufal's intention, apart from a passing speculation whether the skating is ice or roller. No one mutters 'What the hell is this?' when their programme clearly advertises Night on the Bare Mountain. But there you are, of course. The programme blows the gaff. Can we honestly say that if we didn't know the title in advance we shouldn't sit through Night on the B.M. thinking that Moussorgsky was rhapsodizing about collective farms or men's-wear trends? Even the Skater's Waltz, if loosed upon a non-French-speaking public as *Les Patineurs*, could have them tapping their feet dreamily to private visions of pastry-cooks at work in sun-drenched Provence.

When we come, therefore, to works coldly and academically titled Etude, or Suite for Oboe and Strings, or Concerto No. 47, the whole field of interpretation lies open. They could be telling us about ethics; the Zuyder Zee; the lack of moral fibre among deck-hands on a lentil ship. It's just a matter of taking our pick. What is the Alban Berg violin concert all about, to take a somewhat challenging example? This is the work, as you will recall wryly, in which the soloist appears to select notes at random for a long time and then stop. What is Herr Berg saying to *you*, as you sit there looking rapt, and thinking how well a few bars of 'Bam-Bam-Bammy Shore' would drop in at this point? It's all very well to be told by the programme about the chromatic major ninth suggesting a 'joyous upsurge of the spirit'; as far as I'm concerned, this particular passage has a sharp melancholy, and suggests men trying to drag a tree up a rocky slope, its branches constantly getting snagged up with tough little shrubs (chord of the major thirteenth, very likely) and immense irregular boulders (supertonic seventh to B flat). On the other hand, the lady sitting next to us, who was trying to beat time but has now given up, wears a faint reminiscent smile. To her, perhaps, the music speaks of happy Sheffield tram rides of long ago; or the feeling you get when you hear birds running about in the false roof and wonder if you ought to go up there and get them out.

By what authority—this is what I want to know—by what authority does the programme note on the Tchaikovsky Sixth tell me that in the fourth movement I'm being treated to 'a grim dance between Death and the Neurotic, with a last hysterical protest against the inevitable?' Who spread this story in the first place? Tchaikovsky? I see that the Dvořák No. 8 ('known as No. 4' but what the heck) gives me a picture of the composer 'at first in church, later in his garden'; while his No. 9 ('known as No. 5', if you like documentation) shows him 'filled with sympathy for the oppressed coloured peoples'. All right. If you say so. And thanks for all your help.

But do I need it? Granted, if I'm told about the church and garden and the coloured folk, I can probably make myself hear tombs and outhouses and Uncle Tom's Cabin. But if I'm not told—and I didn't ask to be—what's to prevent me hearing greyhounds being exercised, or heavily photogenic waves crashing on the esplanade at Hove?

I don't mind accepting a tip or two on the technical side. I might easily miss 'the drone-bass on the cellos suggesting bagpipes' (and glad to, actually). In the same way, 'the inverted secondary theme returning a semitone higher' could well elude me, and I welcome these simple aids to added enjoyment. But when it comes to what the composer is *saying*, could I make a few personal decisions? For instance:

Haydn's No. 102 in B flat expresses his lifelong fear of falling through the bottom of a sedan chair.

The greater part of the works of Liszt reflect his advocacy of cheap boots for agricultural workers.

In his variations on the Paganini theme, Brahms is commenting subtly on physics and dynamics, including light-hearted references to Boyle's Law and Fletcher's Trolley.

I'm quite prepared to have these views challenged by people who think they know better. Perhaps they do know better. But if I'm not as free as the next man to express an opinion, then it looks to me as if Beethoven, standing up for me as he did in the Egmont, was more or less wasting his time.

Punch.

———————

THE *Revd Edward Lamburn's elder daughter Richmal was a compulsive writer who made a splendid and, it seems now, lasting contribution to the canon of English humorous short stories.*

Richmal (an old Christian name for girls which had been in the family since the 1700s but was a burden because everybody assumed that somebody called 'Richmal' must be a boy), took a degree in classics at the Royal Holloway College, Egham and in 1917 became classics mistress at Bromley High School for Girls, which enabled her to get going in earnest on her real pleasure in life which was scribbling stories. To save face, and perhaps her job, she tacked her middle name on to her Christian name and wrote under the pseudonym 'Richmal Crompton'.

In 1923 Richmal Crompton was crippled by an attack of polio and had to give up teaching so was able to devote her whole time to writing.

In 1919 Miss Crompton had dashed off a pot-boiler, a short story for the popular family monthly, Home Magazine. *It was called 'Rice-mould' and it featured a tough, small boy whom she called William. She was asked for more William stories and they became a regular feature of the magazine and its successor, the* Happy Mag. *In 1922 the publishers issued two books of William stories entitled* Just— William *and* More William. *She eventually wrote thirty-eight William books with sales of over nine million copies in fourteen languages ; there were also four William*

*films, a radio adaptation, and two television series. William was a great success in
every country he went to except, curiously, the USA.*

*Miss Crompton did not regard herself as a writer for children. 'William' had
been written as an amusing trifle for adults, and she went on, rather doggedly, to
write forty-nine grown-up books, but with never the same success.*

*The point of the William stories is the insight and humour which Richmal
Crompton brings to bear on the character of William himself. He is badly behaved
but not a villain. He is a fiercely independent, unbookish boy, adventurous, happier
in the open air, alert to what is going on and curious (i.e. nosy) about everything;
he is also a romantic and not at all awed by his enemies (i.e. parents and other
grown-ups who want to civilize him).*

*He is, in addition, scruffy, unhygienic, unmindful of others and given to acting
spontaneously without consideration of cause and effect. But although he brings
about considerable havoc and woe it is unintentional, usually happening when
William, in his totally unco-ordinated way, is trying to be helpful.*

*The other resident characters in the William stories are somewhat two-
dimensional with one strong characteristic apiece: Mr Brown, William's father, is
irascible; William's mother is placid to the point of being bovine; William's
brother is always falling in love and being extemely soppy about it, and his sister
Ethel, a flapper, is always being fallen in love with and being equally soppy. There
is a nice little girl next door and William has some friends of his own age, the
Outlaws, who are less interesting than he.*

*The stories, most of which are strongly plotted, are set in stockbroker 'Metroland'
somewhere near London, to which Mr Brown goes daily by train. It is, or was to
begin with, a parlourmaid-cook/housekeeper-gardener sort of comfortable middle-
class existence.*

*The first story in the first collection to be printed tells of the disastrous influence
on the impressionable William of a visit to the cinema.*

In those pioneer days the films were short, silent, and extremely exciting:

WILLIAM GOES TO THE PICTURES

It all began with William's aunt, who was in a good temper that morning,
and gave him a shilling for posting a letter for her and carrying her parcels
from the grocer's.

'Buy some sweets or go to the Pictures,' she said carelessly, as she gave it
to him.

William walked slowly down the road, gazing thoughtfully at the coin.
After deep calculations, based on the fact that a shilling is the equivalent of
two sixpences, he came to the conclusion that both luxuries could be indulged
in.

In the matter of sweets, William frankly upheld the superiority of quantity
over quality. Moreover, he knew every sweetshop within a two mile radius
of his home whose proprietor added an extra sweet after the scale had
descended, and he patronised these shops exclusively. With solemn face and

eager eye, he always watched the process of weighing, and 'stingy' shops were known and banned by him.

He wandered now to his favourite confectioner and stood outside the window for five minutes, torn between the rival attractions of Gooseberry Eyes and Marble Balls. Both were sold at 4 ounces for 2d. William never purchased more expensive luxuries. At last his frowning brow relaxed and he entered the shop.

'Sixpennoth of Gooseberry Eyes,' he said, with a slightly self-conscious air. The extent of his purchases rarely exceeded a penny.

'Hello!' said the shopkeeper, in amused surprise.

'Gotter bit of money this mornin',' explained William carelessly, with the air of a Rothschild.

He watched the weighing of the emerald green dainties with silent intensity, saw with satisfaction the extra one added after the scale had fallen, received the precious paper bag, and, putting two sweets into his mouth, walked out of the shop.

Sucking slowly, he walked down the road towards the Picture Palace. William was not in the habit of frequenting Picture Palaces. He had only been there once before in his life.

It was a thrilling programme. First came the story of desperate crooks who, on coming out of any building, glanced cautiously up and down the street in huddled, crouching attitudes, then crept ostentatiously on their way in a manner guaranteed to attract attention and suspicion at any place and time. The plot was involved. They were pursued by police, they leapt on to a moving train and then for no accountable reason, leapt from that on to a moving motor-car and from that they plunged into a moving river. It was thrilling and William thrilled. Sitting quite motionless, he watched, with wide, fascinated eyes, though his jaws never ceased their rotatory movement and every now and then his hand would go mechanically to the paper bag on his knees and convey a Gooseberry Eye to his mouth.

The next play was a simple country love-story, in which figured a simple country maiden wooed by the squire, who was marked out as the villain by his moustachios.

After many adventures the simple country maiden was won by a simple country son of the soil in picturesque rustic attire, whose emotions were faithfully portrayed by gestures that must have required much gymnastic skill; the villain was finally shown languishing in a prison cell, still indulging in frequent eyebrow-play.

Next came another love-story—this time of a noble-hearted couple, consumed with mutual passion and kept apart not only by a series of misunderstandings possible only in a picture play, but also by maidenly pride and reserve on the part of the heroine and manly pride and reserve on the part of the hero that forced them to hide their ardour beneath a cold and haughty exterior. The heroine's brother moved through the story like a good fairy, tender and protective towards his orphan sister, and ultimately explained to each the burning passion of the other.

It was moving and touching and William was moved and touched.

The next was a comedy. It began by a solitary workman engaged upon the re-painting of a door and ended with a miscellaneous crowd of people, all covered with paint, falling downstairs on top of one another. It was amusing. William was riotously and loudly amused.

Lastly came the pathetic story of a drunkard's downward path. He began as a wild young man in evening clothes drinking intoxicants and playing cards. He had a small child with a pious and superior expression, who spent her time weeping over him and exhorting him to a better life, till, in a moment of justifiable exasperation, he threw a beer bottle at her head. He then bedewed her bed in Hospital with penitent tears, tore out his hair, flung up his arms towards Heaven, beat his waistcoat, and clasped her to his breast, so it was not to be wondered at that, after all that excitement, the child had a relapse and with the words 'Good-bye, Father. Do not think of what you have done. I forgive you,' passed peacefully away.

William drew a deep breath at the end, and still sucking, arose with the throng and passed out.

Once outside, he glanced cautiously around and slunk down the road in the direction of his home. Then he doubled suddenly and ran down a back street to put his imaginary pursuers off his track. He took a pencil from his pocket and, levelling it at the empty air, fired twice. Two of his pursuers fell dead, the rest came on with redoubled vigour. There was no time to be lost. Running for dear life, he dashed down the next street, leaving in his wake an elderly gentleman nursing his toe and cursing volubly. As he neared his gate, William again drew the pencil from his pocket and, still looking back down the road, and firing as he went, he rushed into his own gateway.

William's father, who had stayed at home that day because of a bad headache and a touch of liver, picked himself up from the middle of a rhododendron bush and seized William by the back of his neck.

'You young ruffian,' he roared, 'what do you mean by charging into me like that?'

William gently disengaged himself.

'I wasn't chargin', Father,' he said, meekly. 'I was only jus' comin' in at the gate, same as other folks. I jus' wasn't looking jus' the way you were coming, but I can't look all ways at once, cause—'

'Be *quiet*!' roared William's father.

Like the rest of the family, he dreaded William's eloquence.

'What's that on your tongue? Put your tongue out.'

William obeyed. The colour of William's tongue would have put to shame Spring's freshest tints.

'How many times am I to tell you,' bellowed William's father, 'that I won't have you going about eating filthy poisons all day between meals?'

'It's not filthy poison,' said William. 'It's jus' a few sweets Aunt Susan gave me 'cause I kin'ly went to the post office for her an'—'

'Be *quiet*! Have you got any more of the foul things?'

'They're not foul things,' said William doggedly. 'They're good. Jus' have one, an' try. They're jus' a few sweets Aunt Susan kin'ly gave me an—'

'Be *quiet*! Where are they?'

Slowly and reluctantly William drew forth his bag. His father seized it and flung it far into the bushes. For the next ten minutes William conducted a thorough and systematic search among the bushes and for the rest of the day consumed Gooseberry Eyes and garden soil in fairly equal proportions.

He wandered round to the back garden and climbed on to the wall.

'Hello!' said the little girl next door, looking up.

Something about the little girl's head and curls reminded William of the simple country maiden. There was a touch of the artistic temperament about William. He promptly felt himself the simple country son of the soil.

'Hello, Joan,' he said in a deep, husky voice intended to be expressive of deep affection. 'Have you missed me while I've been away?'

'Didn't know you'd been away,' said Joan. 'What are you talking so funny for?'

'I'm not talkin' funny,' said William in the same husky voice, 'I can't help talkin' like this.'

'You've got a cold. That's what you've got. That's what Mother said when she saw you splashing about in your rain tub this morning. She said "The next thing we shall hear of William Brown will be he's in bed with a cold."'

'It's not a cold,' said William mysteriously. 'It's jus' the way I feel.'

'What are you eating?'

'Gooseberry Eyes. Like one?' He took the packet from his pocket and handed it down to her. 'Go on. Take two—three,' he said in reckless generosity.

'But they're—dirty.'

'Go on. It's only ord'nery dirt. It soon sucks off. They're jolly good.' He poured a shower of them lavishly down to her.

'I say,' he said, reverting to his character of simple country lover. 'Did you say you'd missed me? I bet you didn't think of me as much as I did of you. I jus' bet you didn't.'

His voice had sunk deeper and deeper until it almost died away.

'I say, William, does your throat hurt you awful, that you've got to talk like that?'

Her blue eyes were anxious and sympathetic.

William put one hand to his throat and frowned.

'A bit,' he confessed lightly.

'Oh, William!' she clasped her hands. 'Does it hurt all the time?'

Her solicitude was flattering.

'I don't talk much about it, anyway, do I?' he said manfully.

She started up and stared at him with big blue eyes.

'Oh, William! Is it—is it your—lungs? I've got an aunt that's got lungs and she coughs and coughs,' William coughed hastily, 'and it hurts her and makes her awful bad. Oh, William, I do *hope* you've not got lungs.'

Her tender, anxious little face was upturned to him. 'I guess I have got lungs,' he said, 'but I don't make a fuss about 'em.'

He coughed again.

'What does the doctor say about it?'

William considered a minute.

'He says it's lungs all right,' he said at last. 'He says I gotter be jolly careful.'

'William, would you like my new paintbox?'

'I don't think so. Not now. Thanks.'

'I've got three balls and one's quite new. Wouldn't you like it, William?'

'No—thanks. You see, it's no use my collectin' a lot of things. You never know—with lungs.'

'Oh, *William!*'

Her distress was pathetic.

'Of course,' he said hastily, 'if I'm careful it'll be all right. Don't you worry about me.'

'Joan!' from the house.

'That's Mother. Good-bye, William dear. If Father brings me home any chocolate, I'll bring it in to you. I will—honest. Thanks for the Gooseberry Eyes. Good-bye.'

'Good-bye—and don't worry about me,' he added bravely.

He put another Gooseberry Eye in his mouth and wandered round aimlessly to the front of the house. His grown-up sister, Ethel, was at the front door, shaking hands with a young man.

'I'll do all I can for you,' she was saying earnestly.

Their hands were clasped.

'I know you will,' he said equally earnestly.

Both look and handclasp were long. The young man walked away. Ethel stood at the door, gazing after him, with a far-away look in her eyes. William was interested.

'That was Jack Morgan, wasn't it?' he said.

'Yes,' said Ethel absently and went into the house.

The look, the long handclasp, the words lingered in William's memory. They must be jolly fond of each other, like people are when they're engaged, but he knew they weren't engaged. P'raps they were too proud to let each other know how fond they were of each other—like the man and girl at the pictures. Ethel wanted a brother like the one in the pictures to let the man know she was fond of him. Then a light came suddenly into William's mind and he stood deep in thought.

Inside the drawing-room, Ethel was talking to her mother.

'He's going to propose to her next Sunday. He told me about it because I'm her best friend, and he wanted to ask me if I thought he had any chance. I said I thought he had, and I said I'd try to prepare her a little and put in a good word for him if I could. Isn't it thrilling?'

'Yes, dear. By the way, did you see William anywhere? I do hope he's not in mischief.'

'He was in the front garden a minute ago.' She went to the window. 'He's not there now, though.'

William had just arrived at Mr Morgan's house.

The maid showed him into Mr Morgan's sitting-room.

'Mr Brown,' she announced.

The young man rose to receive his guest with politeness not unmixed with bewilderment. His acquaintance with William was of the slightest.

'Good afternoon,' said William. 'I've come from Ethel.'

'Yes?'

'Yes.' William fumbled in his pocket and at last drew forth a rosebud, slightly crushed by its close confinement in the company of the Gooseberry Eyes, a top and a piece of putty.

'She sent you this,' said William gravely.

Mr Morgan gazed at it with the air of one who is sleep-walking.

'Yes? Er—very kind of her.'

'Kinder keep-sake. Souveneer,' explained William.

'Yes. Er—any message?'

'Oh, yes. She wants you to come in and see her this evening.'

'Er—yes. Of course. I've just come from her. Perhaps she remembered something she wanted to tell me after I'd gone.'

'P'raps.'

Then, 'Any particular time?'

'No. 'Bout seven, I expect.'

'Oh, yes.'

Mr Morgan's eyes were fixed with a fascinated wondering gaze upon the limp, and by no means spotless, rose-bud.

'You say she—sent this?'

'Yes.'

'And any other message?'

'No.'

'Er—well, say I'll come with pleasure, will you?'

'Yes.'

Then, 'She thinks an awful lot of you, Ethel does.'

Mr Morgan passed a hand over his brow.

'Yes? Kind—er—very kind, I'm sure.'

'Always talkin' about you in her sleep,' went on William, warming to his theme. 'I sleep in the next room and I can hear her talkin' about you all night. Jus' sayin' your name over and over again. "Jack Morgan, Jack Morgan, Jack

Morgan".' William's voice was husky and soulful. 'Jus' like that—over an' over again. "Jack Morgan, Jack Morgan, Jack Morgan".'

Mr Morgan was speechless. He sat gazing with horror-stricken face at his young visitor.

'Are you—*sure?*' he said at last. 'It might be someone else's name.'

'No 'tisn't,' said William firmly. 'It's yours. "Jack Morgan, Jack Morgan, Jack Morgan"—jus' like that. An' she eats nothin' now. Always hangin' round the windows to watch you pass.'

The perspiration stood out in beads on Mr Morgan's brow.

'It's *horrible*,' he said at last in a hoarse whisper.

William was gratified. The young man had at last realised his cruelty. But William never liked to leave a task half done. He sat still and calmly and silently considered his next statement. Mechanically he put a hand into his pocket and conveyed a Gooseberry Eye to his mouth. Mr Morgan also sat in silence with a stricken look upon his face, gazing into vacancy.

'She's got your photo,' said William at last, 'fixed up into one of those little round things on a chain round her neck.'

'Are—you—*sure?*' said Mr Morgan desperately.

'Sure's fate,' said William, rising. 'Well, I'd better be goin'. She pertic-ler wants to see you alone tonight. Good-bye.'

But Mr Morgan did not answer. He sat huddled up in his chair staring in front of him long after William had gone jauntily on his way. Then he moistened his dry lips.

'Good Lord,' he groaned.

William was thinking of the pictures as he went home. That painter one was jolly good. When they all got all over paint! And when they all fell downstairs! William suddenly guffawed out loud at the memory. But what had the painter chap been doing at the very beginning before he began to paint? He'd been getting off the old paint with a sort of torch thing and a knife, then he began putting the new paint on. Just sort of melting the old paint and then scraping it off. William had never seen it done in real life, but he supposed that was the way you did get old paint off. Melting it with some sort of fire, then scraping it off. He wasn't sure whether it was that, but he could find out. As he entered the house he took his penknife from his pocket, opened it thoughtfully, and went upstairs.

Mr Brown came home about dinner-time.

'How's your head, Father?' said Ethel sympathetically.

'Rotten!' said Mr Brown, sinking wearily into an arm-chair.

'Perhaps dinner will do it good,' said Mrs Brown, 'it ought to be ready now.'

The housemaid entered the room.

'Mr Morgan, mum. He wants to see Miss Ethel. I've shown him into the library.'

'*Now?*' exploded Mr Brown. 'What the deu—why the dickens is the young idiot coming at this time of day? Seven o'clock! What time does he think we have dinner? What does he mean by coming round and paying calls at dinner-time? What—'

'Ethel, dear,' interrupted Mrs Brown, 'do go and see what he wants and get rid of him as soon as you can.'

Ethel entered the library, carefully closing the door behind her to keep out the sound of her father's comments, which were plainly audible across the hall.

She noticed something wan and haggard on Mr Morgan's face as he rose to greet her.

'Er—good evening, Miss Brown.'

'Good evening, Mr Morgan.'

They then sat in silence, both awaiting some explanation of the visit. The silence became oppressive. Mr Morgan, with an air of acute misery and embarrassment, shifted his feet and coughed. Ethel looked at the clock. Then—

'Was it raining when you came, Mr Morgan?'

'Raining? Er—no. No—not at all.'

Silence.

'I thought it looked like rain this afternoon.'

'Yes, of course. Er—no, not at all.'

Silence.

'It does make the roads so bad round here when it rains.'

'Yes.' Mr Morgan put up a hand as though to loosen his collar. 'Er—very bad.'

'Almost impassable.'

'Er—quite.'

Silence again.

Inside the drawing-room, Mr Brown was growing restive.

'Is dinner to be kept waiting for that youth all night? Quarter past seven! You know it's just what I can't stand—having my meals interfered with. Is my digestion to be ruined simply because this young nincompoop chooses to pay his social calls at seven o'clock at night?'

'Then we must ask him to dinner,' said Mrs Brown, desperately. 'We really must.'

'We must *not*,' said Mr Brown. 'Can't I stay away from the office for one day with a headache, without having to entertain all the young jackasses for miles around.' The telephone bell rang. He raised his hands above his head.

'Oh—'

'I'll go, dear,' said Mrs Brown, hastily.

She returned with a worried frown on her brow.

'It's Mrs Clive,' she said. 'She said Joan has been very sick because of some horrible sweets William gave her, and she said she was so sorry to hear about

William and hoped he'd be better soon. I couldn't make it out, but it seems that William has been telling them that he had to go and see a doctor about his lungs and the doctor said they were very weak and he'd have to be careful.'

Mr Brown sat up and looked at her. 'But—why—on—earth?' he said slowly.

'I don't know, dear,' said Mrs Brown, helplessly. 'I don't know anything about it.'

'He's mad,' said Mr Brown with conviction. 'Mad. It's the only explanation.'

Then came the opening and shutting of the front door and Ethel entered. She was very flushed.

'He's gone,' she said. 'Mother, it's simply horrible! He didn't tell me much, but it seems that William actually went to his house and told him that I wanted to see him alone at seven o'clock this evening. I've hardly spoken to William today. He couldn't have misunderstood anything I said. And he actually took a flower with him—a dreadful-looking rosebud—and said I'd sent it. I simply didn't know where to look or what to say. It was horrible!'

Mrs Brown sat gazing weakly at her daughter.

Mr Brown rose with the air of a man goaded beyond endurance.

'Where *is* William!' he said shortly.

'I don't know, but I thought I heard him go upstairs some time ago.'

William *was* upstairs. For the last twenty minutes he had been happily and quietly engaged upon his bedroom door with a lighted taper in one hand and penknife in the other. There was no doubt about it. By successful experiment he had proved that that was the way you got old paint off. When Mr Brown came upstairs he had entirely stripped one panel of its paint.

*   *   *

An hour later William sat in the back garden on an upturned box sucking, with a certain dogged defiance, the last and dirtiest of the Gooseberry Eyes. Sadly he reviewed the day. It had not been a success. His generosity to the little girl next door had been misconstrued into an attempt upon her life, his efforts to help on his only sister's love affair had been painfully misunderstood, lastly because (among other things) he had discovered a perfectly scientific method of removing old paint he had been brutally assaulted by a violent and unreasonable parent. Suddenly William began to wonder if his father drank. He saw himself, through a mist of pathos, as a Drunkard's child. He tried to imagine his father weeping over him in Hospital and begging his forgiveness. It was a wonder he wasn't there now, anyway. His shoulders drooped—his whole attitude became expressive of extreme dejection.

Inside the house, his father reclining at length in an armchair, discoursed to his wife on the subject of his son. One hand was pressed to his aching brow, and the other gesticulating freely. 'He's insane,' he said, 'stark, raving insane. You ought to take him to a doctor and get his brain examined. Look at him today. He begins by knocking me into the rhododendron bushes—under no provocation, mind you. I hadn't spoken to him. Then he tries to poison that nice little thing next door with some vile stuff I thought I'd thrown away. Then he goes about telling people he's consumptive. He looks it, doesn't he? Then he takes extraordinary messages and love tokens from Ethel to strange young men and brings them here just when we're going to begin dinner, and then goes round burning and hacking at the doors. What's the sense in it—in any of it? They're the acts of a lunatic.'

Mrs Brown cut off her darning wool and laid aside the socks she had just finished darning.

'It certainly sounds very silly, dear,' she said mildly. 'But there might be some explanation of it all, if only we knew. Boys are funny things.'

She looked at the clock and went over to the window. 'William!' she called. 'It's your bedtime, dear.'

William rose sadly and came into the house.

'Good night, Mother,' he said; then he turned a mournful and reproachful eye upon his father.

'Good night, Father,' he said. 'Don't think about what you've done, I for—'

He stopped and decided, hastily but wisely, to retire with all possible speed.

Richmal Crompton (1890–1969), *Just—William* (1922).

❧ The original of William was Richmal Crompton's brother John. When John grew up he left England, joined the Rhodesian police, and during the Second World War served in Iceland under Air Commodore Wigglesworth—who happened to be the original of the fictitious air ace of World War One, Biggles. In William Amos's book *The Originals* in which he traced this sort of thing, Amos pointed out that the War Office, unaware that it had the combined might of *Just—William* and *Biggles in Iceland*, neglected to exploit the situation. He added, 'Imagine the havoc that pair could have caused had Britain allowed them to be captured.'

R ICHMAL CROMPTON's *total output of nearly ninety books is impressive but she seems like a case of writer's block when compared with Charles Harold St John Hamilton. Mr Hamilton wrote himself into the* Guinness Book of Records *as the world's most prolific author with a total output of prose equivalent to a thousand novels.*

Unlike Miss Crompton, Mr Hamilton was happy to write solely for the juvenile market. He was the leading writer of that genre, unique to Britain, of the school story: yarns of adventure, sport, caning, and eating in an ancient, ivy-clad, Eton-like public school. He wrote under a great number of aliases and seems to have invented about thirty boarding schools to write about but to most living Englishmen, and a fair proportion of Englishwomen, it requires only the mention of two of his fictional schools to bring a flood of memories.

For instance, 'St Jim's' in the Gem, *which was published from 1907 to 1939. The entire text of 15,000 to 20,000 words per week was written by Hamilton under the pseudonym of 'Martin Clifford'. Pupils at St Jim's included Tom Merry; 'Gussy', the Honourable Arthur Augustus D'Arcy (who said things like: 'The feahful outsidahs! Weally, I shall be obliged to give you a feahful thwashin'!'); and good old reliable Jack Blake.*

An even more famous school was 'Greyfriars' in the Magnet, *also written weekly in its entirety from 1908 until its closure in 1940 by Hamilton, this time under his favourite* nom de plume, *which he came to regard as his real name, Frank Richards. Greyfriars pupils included Harry Wharton; Bob Cherry; Frank Nugent (a self-portrait); the Bounder, Vernon-Smith, who played billiards and smoked cigarettes; the 'dusky nabob' Inky, Hurree Jamsett Ram Singh ('Let dogs delight in the barkfulness and bitefulness, but the soft answer is the cracked pitcher that goes longest to a bird in the bush, as the English proverb remarks'); and, of course, Billy Bunter, the Fat Owl of the Remove, perhaps the most famous schoolboy in fiction.*

The magazines themselves ceased publication at the beginning of the war but during the 1940s and 1950s the demand for more stories about Billy Bunter and the Famous Five was so strong that Frank Richards began them again, this time as books and a television series. He carried on writing them until he died at his villa in Kingsgate, near Broadstairs, at the age of 85, a frail, old-fashioned old bachelor, occasionally glimpsed pottering about in a skull-cup, dressing-gown, and bicycle clips.

In 1940 George Orwell wrote a famous essay in Horizon *reviewing the world of Boys' Weeklies, or 'Penny Dreadfuls' (most of them were at least twopence) and he severely criticized the* Gem *and the* Magnet *for being 'sodden in the worst illusions of 1910', these illusions being, he believed, the Conservative view that (a) nothing ever changes, and (b) foreigners are funny (i.e. inferior). To Orwell's surprise, Frank Richards, whom he had assumed by the enormous output to be a syndicate of writers beavering away under the one pseudonym, wrote a reply stoutly defending his* Magnet *and its values.*

Richards pointed out that his aim was to amuse his 12- to 15-year-old readers by giving them a diverting and often exciting read, not to dismay them with intimations of how beastly their grown-up life would almost certainly turn out to be. And the stories had their own code of ethics.

Here is a short extract which, in Frank Richard's oddly repetitive but vigorous prose, reminds us that Billy Bunter, cadger, liar, scrounger, the epitome of sloth and gluttony, never actually gets away with it.

In fact, the Fat Owl has rather a thin time:

BAT FOR BUNTER!

'Bunter!'
  No reply.
  'Bunter!'

Still no reply.

The door of No. 7 Study, in the Remove passage at Greyfriars, was half-open. Billy Bunter was in his study. Undoubtedly he heard Harry Wharton's voice calling in the passage.

But if he heard, he heeded not.

Bunter was busy.

Billy Bunter had lines on hand for Mr Quelch, his form-master. But he was not busy on those lines. He had a translation to do for Monsieur Charpentier, the French master. But he was not busy on that translation.

Such things as these, Billy Bunter was wont to put off till the last minute: or even a little later.

But he was busy; much too busy to heed a calling voice in the passage. He was eating!

On the study table was a large cake: or, more accurately, what had been a large cake. It had been large when it arrived in No. 7 Study, ten minutes ago, under a fat arm. Since then the work of demolition had been proceeding without pause.

Slice after slice, transferred to the most capacious mouth in the Greyfriars Remove, had disappeared on the downward path.

But much remained. And so long as a plum or a crumb remained, Billy Bunter was not likely to heed calling voices. What the captain of the Remove wanted, he did not know. Neither did he care. He concentrated on cake! From No. 7 Study, a sound of steady munching floated out into the passage. And it went on, uninterrupted, as Harry Wharton called along the passage from the landing.

Wharton's voice was heard again.

'Seen Bunter about, Smithy? Nugent said he came up to the studies.'

There was a chuckle: then Smithy's voice.

'I haven't seen him—'

'Oh! Bother!'

'But I've heard him! Unless there's a geegee in No. 7 champing corn.'

'The fat ass! If he's in his study, why can't he answer?' Tramping footsteps came up the passage to the door of No. 7.

Still Billy Bunter did not heed. He was not interested in Harry Wharton or what he might happen to want. He did not even blink round through his big spectacles as the door was kicked wider open, and the captain of the Remove looked in.

Munch! munch! munch!

Bunter did not take the trouble to reply. Indeed he would have found it a little difficult, at the moment, to become vocal, through a barrage of cake. He went on munching.

'You're wanted, fathead.'

Munch! munch! munch!

'Quelch wants you in his study,' hooted Wharton. 'He's just told me to send you in.'

'Oh!'

Billy Bunter's musical effect ceased, at that. He turned his spectacles on the captain of the Remove, with a startled and alarmed blink.

'Oh!' he repeated. 'Did—did you say Quelch?'

'Yes, I did say Quelch, fathead, and you'd better not keep him waiting.' With that, Harry Wharton turned from the door. The captain of the Remove was due for nets after class, and he was in flannels, with his bat under his arm. His friends were waiting for him below: and possibly he was not too pleased to be sent in search of a fat Owl.

'I—I say, hold on a minute!' exclaimed Bunter. He rose from the table, for the moment almost forgetful of even cake. 'I—I say, what does Quelch want?'

'How should I know, ass?'

'I—I mean, is—is it anything about a cake?' gasped Bunter.

Harry Wharton stared at him: and then burst into a laugh.

'You fat villain—'

'Oh, really, Wharton—'

'Whose cake is that you are scoffing?'

'It's mine, of course, it—it came from Bunter Court this morning,' answered Bunter, hastily. 'But—but did Quelch say anything about a cake? I—I mean, if the House-dame's missed a cake, Quelch might think—'

'He might!' agreed Harry Wharton. 'Very likely, I fancy.'

'Well, I never had it! I haven't been down the kitchen stairs since class—why should I? But—but Mrs Kebble might think I had—'

'Why should she, if you haven't?'

'Well, she saw me coming up, you know: and you know what women are—suspicious—!'

'Oh, my hat!'

'So—so if Quelch said anything about a cake—'

'He didn't say anything, except send you to his study at once.'

'Oh! Perhaps it's only my lines, then,' said Bunter. 'He asked me for my lines in form, you know, and I said I'd left them in my study, and he said take them to him after class—'

'Better take them with you, then!'

'Only—only I haven't done them!' explained Bunter. 'I—I'd rather not see Quelch yet. He might think I told him a crammer about leaving the lines in my study, if he found out that I hadn't done them. You know Quelch!'

'Hallo, hallo, hallo!' came a roar from the landing at the end of the Remove passage. 'You coming, Wharton?'

'Coming!' called back Harry.

'I say, hold on a minute!' exclaimed Bunter. 'I say, I don't want to see Quelch just yet. I've got to finish this cake—I mean, I've got to get my lines done. I say, you cut back, and tell him you haven't been able to find me.'

'Wha-a-t?'

'That will keep him quiet!' explained Bunter. 'He will think I went out of gates after class, if you can't find me. That will be all right.'

'But I have found you!' howled Harry Wharton.

'For goodness sake, keep to the point!' said Bunter, peevishly 'The point is that I don't want to see Quelch just yet, see? That's important. You go and tell Quelch that you can't find me anywhere—'

Harry Wharton gazed at the fat Owl of the Remove from the doorway. His bat, under his arm, slipped down into his hand. That was a danger-signal, if Bunter had heeded it. But Billy Bunter's fat thoughts were concentrated on cake, lines, and Quelch, and he was oblivious of danger-signals.

'Tell him you've looked everywhere, and nobody's seen me anywhere,' he went on. 'That will do for Quelch. You might mention that you saw me going out of gates after class—that would be better, really. See?'

'You fat, frabjous, footling fibber—'

'Oh, really, Wharton—'

'Get a move on!' Harry Wharton came into the study, bat in hand.

'I tell you I don't want to see Quelch yet! You go to him and say— Yarooooh! Keep that bat away, you beast! Whooooop!'

Harry Wharton did not keep the bat away. Having prodded the business-end of the bat at the plumpest ribs in Gretyfriars School, he prodded again, and yet again. Billy Bunter, with a series of breathless squeaks, dodged round the table.

'Wow! Beast! Will you keep that bat away?' he roared. 'I—I say, old chap, have some of the cake! Have a slice of—yow-ow-ow-ow-ow! Wow! If you don't stop prodding that bat at me, I'll jolly well—whooooooooop!'

'Are you going?'

'No—I—I—I mean, yes! Wow!'

Billy Bunter rolled out of the study. Really, there was no arguing with a cricket bat, in an energetic hand, prodding at his plump ribs. He rolled down the Remove passage to the landing, the captain of the Remove following him, still prodding. A surprised stare from Bob Cherry greeted them as they arrived on the landing.

'Hallo, hallo, hallo! What's this game?' inquired Bob.

'Yaroooh!'

'Quelch wants Bunter,' explained Wharton. 'And Bunter wants me to tell Quelch that he's gone out of gates. I'm going to prod him as far as Masters' Studies.'

'Good egg!' exclaimed Bob Cherry, heartily. 'I'll help!'

'Yooo-hoooooop!'

Billy Bunter did the staircase in record time.

Frank Richards (Charles Hamilton) (1876–1961), *Backing Up Billy Bunter* (1955).

IN *May 1924 a humorous book by an anonymous author was published which did not sell particularly well but was much enjoyed by a small coterie of readers. In 1954 it was republished, again with modest sales. Then in 1965 Anthony Burgess wrote a piece in the* Times Literary Supplement *asking for information about the book and its author and was astonished at the response; letters arrived from all over the English-speaking world expressing delight—and surprise—that somebody else had discovered the virtually unknown work.*

In his introduction to the 1966 reprint, Anthony Burgess described the book as 'one of the great comic novels of the twentieth century': Robert Robinson went even further and declared: 'I think it is the funniest unknown book in the world. I place it without hesitation in the same class as Diary of a Nobody, *a work which I believe it surpasses.'*

Strong sentiments, but then Augustus Carp Esq. by Himself *is an extraordinary book. Its subtitle,* Being the Autobiography of a Really Good Man *gives a hint of the sardonic irony which abounds as the dreadful Augustus Carp, a humourless, self-righteous prig, recounts the story of his life as a practising Evangelical hypocrite.*

In 1965, in response to Anthony Burgess's appeal in the TLS, *the identity of the anonymous author was revealed after much family agonizing by the author's daughter, his literary executor. Burgess thought it might well have been a frolic written by some luminary of the Savile Club but the author turned out to be a distinguished doctor, Sir Henry Howarth Bashford, Kt., MD, FRCP, Chief Medical Officer to the Post Office, Medical Adviser to the Treasury, and Hon. Physician to King George V.*

Sir Henry had led a genteel but impoverished childhood, brought up by his widowed mother in Bedford. He left home at the age of 15 to become a farmer in Canada but eighteen months later he was back again hoping to borrow enough money to buy a farm; his friends persuaded him to stay in England and become a medical student instead.

He prospered as a civil service physician and wrote a number of books under his own name; middle-of-the-road library titles like Vagabonds in Perigord *and* Tommy Wideawake; *'doctor' books with titles like* The Harley Street Calendar, The Corner of Harley Street; *and a volume of children's stories called* Half-past Bedtime.

There had been one peculiarly strong influence in Sir Henry Bashford's early life: the Evangelical movement. His mother was a devout participator and Henry was brought up to live a rigid, Evangelical life. The turning-point came when he was a medical student and fell among enthusiasts; he got in with a group of muscular Christians who were zealous and bigoted and from then on he developed a loathing for all religious extremism, particularly the grim puritanism from which he had suffered. He seems to have bottled this up successfully,—he was a most amiable man who tried to be on good terms with everybody—but at the age of 44 he finally rid his system of his private anger by sitting down and writing, anonymously, Augustus Carp Esq., *perhaps the severest, almost certainly the funniest satire yet on low-church religious hypocrisy.*

The story is set back in the 1910s. In the opening words Augustus Carp lets us know exactly the sort of man he is proud to be:

It is customary, I have noticed, in publishing an autobiography to preface it with some sort of apology. But there are times, and surely the present is one of them, when to do so is manifestly unnecessary. In an age when every standard of decent conduct has either been torn down or is threatened with destruction; when every newspaper is daily reporting scenes of violence, divorce, and arson; when quite young girls smoke cigarettes and even, I am assured, sometimes cigars; when mature women, the mothers of unhappy children, enter the sea in one-piece bathing-costumes; and when married men, the heads of households, prefer the flicker of the cinematograph to the Athanasian Creed—then it is obviously a task, not to be justifiably avoided, to place some higher example before the world . . .

We are introduced to Augustus's father, a 'civic official in a responsible position' (he is a debt-collector for the Metropolitan Water Board):

Although my father had numerous faults, as I afterwards discovered and was able to point out to him, he yet brought to bear on me the full force of a frequently noble character . . .

Somewhat under lower middle height, my father, even as a boy, had been inclined to corpulence, a characteristic, inherited by myself, that he succeeded in retaining to the end of his life. Nor did he ever lose—or not to any marked extent—either the abundant hair that grew upon his scalp, his glossy and luxurious moustache, or his extraordinarily powerful voice. This was a deep bass that in moments of emotion became suddenly converted into a high falsetto, and he never hesitated, in a cause that he deemed righteous, to employ it to its full capacity. Always highly coloured, and the fortunate possessor of a large and well-modelled nose, my father's eyes were of a singular pale, unwinking blue, while in his massive ears, with their boldly outstanding rims, resided the rare faculty of independent motion . . .

Both Augustus and his father treat his mother, whose tiny dowry they used to buy their house, as an unpaid skivvy:

From the time of his marriage to the day of my birth, and as soon thereafter as the doctor had permitted her to rise, my father had been in the habit of enabling my mother to provide him with an early cup of tea. And this he had done by waking her regularly a few minutes before six o'clock. In view of the fact, however, that he was now occupying a different bedroom, and that, owing to my indisposition, she was awake most of the night, he offered to excuse her should she chance to be asleep at that hour, from the per-formance of this wifely duty. Needless to say, it was not an offer that she could accept. Indeed, in his heart he had not expected her to do so. And I have even considered the incident, in later years, as illustrative of a certain weakness in my father's character.

As well as his indigestion and his skin disease, our hero also manages whilst still a child to contract, and retain for life, a few extras:

. . . several forms of neurasthenia, a marked tendency to eczema, occipital headaches, sour eructations, and flatulent distension of the abdomen [also the odd boil and a bout of acne].

Nor do Augustus's devout friends escape the black humour. Dr Sir Henry Bashford doles out his medicine in easy-to-swallow doses but nevertheless it is bitter stuff in its quiet way. On the whole, the devouter the friend the more revolting the affliction which Sir Henry inflicts upon him or her.
    It could be just a small accident of birth, as with Augustus's distant relation and playmate Emily:

Happy as I was, however, with . . . a pound or two of chocolates, and my rabbit Isaiah, or to settle down for a long summer afternoon with the Hymnal Companion to the Book of Common Prayer, I was not averse from an occasional ramble in the company of my father, or even from exercise of a more vehement order with younger and suitable comrades. The chief of these latter was Emily Smith, the granddaughter of Mrs Emily Smith, my mother's aunt, a gentle child, who was unfortunately an albino, but of a deeply religious and sympathetic nature.

A little stronger are the speech defects suffered by Augustus's deeply pious young friends, Simeon and Silas Whey:

Xtian [Augustus's way of writing the word 'Christian'] lads of about my own age, and each with an impediment in his speech, both were destined on this account for eventual ordination in the Church of England . . . Reticent in the extreme, partly, in the case of Silas, owing to an initial difficulty in articulating anything at all, and in the case of Simeon, owing to a kind of laryngeal click from which he is still unfortunately a sufferer, they appeared to find a comfort in my own natural eloquence that I was glad to bestow upon them. In return for this, their ample pocket-money was always entirely at my disposal and many a pound of toffee and Turkish Delight was I able to enjoy at their expense . . . What knitted us together, however, at this painful juncture was the curious fact that, in addition to others, both of them were suffering like myself from an invasion of the ring-worm.

Ezekiel Stool, rich young man, founder of the Anti-Dramatic and Saltatory [saltation = dancing] Union and son of Abraham Stool, inventor of Stool's Adult Gripe Water and a prominent religious maniac, is more seriously devout and so his sufferings are more of Old Testament severity. Like 'my brother Esau', Ezekiel is a hairy man:

No taller than myself, and weighing considerably less, he [Ezekiel] had suffered all his life from an inherent dread of shaving, and the greater portion of his face was in consequence obliterated by a profuse but gentle growth of hair. His voice too, owing to some developmental defect, had only partially broken; and indeed his father Abraham (afterwards removed to an asylum) had on more than one occasion attempted to sacrifice him, under the mistaken impression that he was some sort of animal that would be suitable as a burnt offering.

Ezekiel has five young sisters who would be well off when the mad old man died, a point of riveting interest to Augustus. But when he meets the sisters at dinner he finds that their physical beauty could hardly be described as flawless:

Simply divided into twins and triplets, these were all younger than Ezekiel himself, the triplets being then twenty-four, and the twins three years younger. None of them was married, and indeed, as regarded the triplets, this was scarcely perhaps to be wondered at. For though they had been interestingly named by their father as Faith, Hope, and Charity, they were plain girls, deeply marked by the smallpox, and of rather less than the average intelligence. Nor indeed were the twins, Tact and Understanding, at all remarkable for personal beauty, and the toes of one of them, as I was afterwards to discover, were most unfortunately webbed.

It is November and the small, hairy Ezekiel is mistaken by small boys for a Guy Fawkes. Augustus rescues him (at no danger to himself) and is taken to meet Ezekiel's family, including Ezekiel's unhinged father, Abraham:

As Ezekiel said, I had probably twice saved his life, and during the evening meal, to which he at once invited me, both his parents and his five sisters repeatedly expressed their satisfaction. Mr Abraham Stool indeed, who had not then been segregated, but who was already under the impression that he was the Hebrew patriarch, several times insisted on my approaching him and placing my hand under his left thigh, after which he would offer me, in addition to Mrs Stool, a varying number of rams and goats.

Augustus discovers his headmaster being indiscreet and is able to blackmail the unfortunate man into getting him a job in a small but fervently devotional publishing house (their big gun is the Revd Eustace Cake whose new religious novel, Gnashers of Teeth, bids fair to being even more powerful than his last, Without are Dogs). Here at work Augustus, who seems to put on about a stone in weight per year, watches his diet carefully:

At eleven o'clock . . . I would despatch Miss Botterill to a neighbouring branch of the Aerated Bread Company for a glass of hot milk and a substantial slice of a cake appropriately known as lunch cake. I would then, at twelve-thirty, repair in person to the same branch of this valuable company, where I would generally order from one of the quieter waitresses a double portion of sausages and mashed potatoes, accompanied by a cup of coffee, and followed by an apple dumpling or a segment of baked jam roll. This was the more necessary because the hour from one to two was usually the busiest of the working day, while from two to three, when my subordinates lunched in turn, I had, of course, only one of them to assist me.

By three o'clock, however, they had both returned, and I would take the opportunity, five minutes later, of again sending Miss Botterill to the Aerated Bread Company for my mid-afternoon cup of tea. This I would drink, un-thickened by food, but at half-past four I would send her out for another cup, and with this I would eat a roll and butter, a small dish of honey, and perhaps a single doughnut. Thus fortified I would then continue at work until six o'clock, when the showroom closed, and at half-past six I was sitting down at home to the chief meal of the evening. Taken somewhat earlier than had been my father's custom in the days of my boyhood and adolescence, I had found myself obliged to insist on the alteration in view of the many demands upon my evening hours. Most of my active work, for example, at the doors of public-houses, required an attendance from seven to nine, while few of the local prayer-meetings began at a later hour than half-past seven or eight.

Early as was this meal, however, it was none the less welcome, consisting as it usually did of a joint and two vegetables followed by a wholesome pudding, tea, bread and jam, and perhaps a slice or two of home-made cake. Then after evening prayers, I would embrace my father, who was now always in bed by a quarter to nine, and leave the house upon some such holy errand as I have described in the previous paragraph. I did not fail, however, on returning home, to drink a bowl of arrowroot and eat some digestive biscuits, and whenever possible, in the interests of my health, I would retire to my bedroom at ten-fifteen.

The plot of Augustus Carp, Esq. *is rich and thick and swiftly moving. Ezekiel Stool offers Augustus one of his five ugly but well-off sisters in marriage. Augustus recoils. Ezekiel says he will keep the offer open knowing that it is the only chance they are likely to get.*

Then things go disastrously wrong. Augustus is fired from his job. No reference. No source of income. His father dies. His mother rebels and goes off to live with a friend in the South of France on the money she has saved from the housekeeping ('But you don't know the language!' 'Pas trop,' she said, 'mais ça suffit'). As a last resort Augustus goes to Ezekiel, who has gone off religion and now is a man-about-town with chambers in Albany, Piccadilly, and pleads with Ezekiel to let him have one of his plain, rich sisters in marriage, as once promised:

He was silent for a moment, but in so far as it was visible, his expression was far from reassuring. Then he rang the bell, and Tact entered the room. She was the less attractive of the two twins.

'That's the one,' he said. 'I made them draw lots. But you can only marry her on one condition—that you sign an agreement to live north of the Thames and make a home for her four sisters.'

He tilted his chin a little and put his hands in his pockets. A distant dog barked three times. With a supreme effort I clung to my senses.

'Do you mean all,' I whispered, 'including Faith?'

Faith was the least attractive of the three triplets.

'All or none,' he said.

He pulled out his watch.

I could hear it ticking.

'Why did you do that?' I asked.

'I'm giving you a minute,' he said, 'in which to decide.'

Faint though I was, I staggered to my feet.

'Then as a Xtian,' I said, 'no less than a gentleman—'

'Thirty seconds,' he said.

'I'll take her.'

He replaced his watch, and I took Tact's hand. All the female Stools have poor circulations.

'So we'll be getting married,' I said, 'in due course.'

'Yes,' she said. 'That'll be very nice.'

> Anon. (Sir Henry Howarth Bashford) (1880–1961), *Augustus Carp Esq. by Himself: Being the Autobiography of a Really Good Man* (1924).

☜ Tact turned out to be the sister with webbed feet.

IN 1932 *a masterpiece of humour was published: Stella Gibbons's* Cold Comfort Farm.

In its first year, Cold Comfort Farm *won the Femina Vie Hereuse prize and had very good sales indeed; more than fifty years later it is still firmly in print.*

Stella Gibbons was at first educated at home, which was in a rather dreary part of North London where her father was a doctor, and she began to write by scribbling down stories and verses in Woolworths notebooks to read out later to cheer up her two brothers. Her first job was as secretary to an editor but soon she was a contributing writer and for ten years she turned out verses and short stories.

She also reviewed books. And in reviewing half-a-dozen books per week she must have had her fill of what might be termed the Of-The-Earth-Earthy school of fiction, novels of rural passion and rustic pessimism which were then at the height of their vogue. Thomas Hardy had metaphorically broken up the old ground of the countryside-as-arcadia and younger novelists such as Mary Webb and D. H. Lawrence were diligently working away at the mud with their breast-ploughs, lamenting the loss to mankind of the old rural virtues like the simple life and making love with boots on.

This was the genre of fiction which Stella Gibbons parodied so brilliantly in Cold Comfort Farm. *It was her first novel. 'A minor classic,' wrote Hugh Walpole. The* Times Literary Supplement *described Miss Gibbons as 'one of the most brilliant satirists and parodists of the day . . . possessor of a wicked and witty pen'. She went on to write two sequels to* Cold Comfort Farm *and twenty-three other books, all distinguished by her cool, intelligent humour.*

Cold Comfort Farm *is more than just a comical parody of rustic writing which could well have grown tedious over a whole book. Only the Starkadder family and the life they lead on Cold Comfort Farm are parodied, the rest of the characters are ordinary, rational people, especially the book's strong-minded, unusual, and delightful heroine, Flora Poste. An odd feature of the book is that it is set 'in the near future', hence some of the telephones have television screens attached, and the postman delivers the mail by plane.*

Flora Poste, quite a bossy-boots but tolerably so, is aged 19 and has just been orphaned by Spanish Flu. From her parents she has inherited a strong will, a slender ankle, and a hundred pounds per annum. Rather than go to work she decides to write to her four remaining relations in the hope that one of them will give her a home in exchange for her 'beautiful eyes and a hundred pounds a year'.

Flora decides that the Starkadders of Cold Comfort Farm badly need her to tidy up their lives.

The day she is due to arrive at Cold Comfort Farm, life starts as usual at 6.30, with old Adam Lambsbreath, the cowman, milking his beloved herd, and one of the Starkadder sons, the magnificently sexual animal Seth, up early for once to join his mother Judith for breakfast:

The beasts stood with heads lowered dejectedly against the wooden hoot-pieces of their stalls. Graceless, Pointless, Feckless and Aimless awaited their turn to be milked. Sometimes Aimless ran her dry tongue, with a rasping sound sharp as a file through silk, awkwardly across the bony flank of Feckless, which was still moist with the rain that had fallen upon it through the roof during the night, or Pointless turned her large dull eyes sideways as she swung her head upwards to tear down a mouthful of cobwebs from the wooden runnet above her head. A lowering, moist, steamy light, almost like that which gleams below the eyelids of a man in fever, filled the cowshed.

Suddenly a tortured bellow, a blaring welter of sound that shattered the quiescence of the morning, tore its way across the yard, and died away in a croak that was almost a sob. It was Big Business, the bull, wakening to another day, in the clammy darkness of his cell.

The sound woke Adam. He lifted his head from the flank of Feckless and looked around him in bewilderment for a moment; then slowly his eyes, which looked small and wet and lifeless in his primitive face, lost their terror as he realised that he was in the cowshed, that it was half-past six on a winter morning, and that his gnarled fingers were about the task which they had performed at this hour and in this place for the past eighty years and more.

He stood up, sighing, and crossed over to Pointless, who was eating Graceless's tail. Adam, who was linked to all dumb brutes by a chain forged in soil and sweat, took it out of her mouth and put into it, instead, his neckerchief—the last he had. She mumbled it, while he milked her, but stealthily spat it out so soon as he passed on to Aimless, and concealed it under the reeking straw with her hoof. She did not want to hurt the old man's feelings by declining to eat his gift. There was a close bond: a slow, deep, primitive, silent down-dragging link between Adam and all living beasts; they knew each other's simple needs. They lay close to the earth, and something of earth's old fierce simplicities had seeped into their beings.

Suddenly a shadow fell athwart the wooden stanchions of the door. It was no more than a darkening of the pallid paws of the day which were now embracing the shed, but all the cows instinctively stiffened, and Adam's eyes, as he stood up to face the new-comer, were again piteously full of twisted fear.

'Adam,' uttered the woman who stood in the doorway, 'how many pails of milk will there be this morning?'

'I dunnamany,' responded Adam, cringingly; ''tes hard to tell. If so be as our Pointless has got over her indigestion, mayby 'twill be four. If so be as she hain't, maybe three.'

Judith Starkadder made an impatient movement. Her large hands had a quality which made them seem to sketch vast horizons with their slightest gesture. She looked a woman without boundaries as she stood wrapped in a crimson shawl to protect her bitter, magnificent shoulders from the splintery cold of the early air. She seemed fitted for any stage, however enormous.

'Well, get as many buckets as you can,' she said, lifelessly, half-turning away. 'Mrs Starkadder questioned me about the milk yesterday. She has been comparing our output with that from other farms in the district, and she says we are five-sixteenths of a bucket below what our rate should be, considering how many cows we have.'

A strange film passed over Adam's eyes, giving him the lifeless primeval look that a lizard has, basking in the swooning Southern heat. But he said nothing.

'And another thing,' continued Judith, 'you will probably have to drive down into Beershorn to-night to meet a train. Robert Poste's child is coming to stay with us for a while. I expect to hear some time this morning what time she is arriving. I will tell you later about it.'

Adam shrank back against the gangrened flank of Pointless.

'Mun I?' he asked, piteously. 'Mun I, Miss Judith? Oh, dunna send me. How can I look into her liddle flower-face, and me knowin' what I know? Oh, Miss Judith, I beg of 'ee not to send me. Besides,' he added, more practically, ''tes close on sixty-five years since I put hands to a pair of reins, and I might upset the maidy.'

Judith, who had slowly turned from him while he was speaking, was now half-way across the yard. She turned her head to reply to him with a slow, graceful movement. Her deep voice clanged like a bell in the frosty air:

'No, you must go, Adam. You must forget what you know—as we all must, while she is here. As for the driving, you had best harness Viper to the trap, and drive down into Howling and back six times this afternoon, to get your hand in again.'

'Could not Master Seth go instead o' me?'

Emotion shook the frozen grief of her face. She said low and sharp:

'You remember what happened when he went to meet the new kitchen-maid . . . No. You must go.'

Adam's eyes, little blind pools of water in his primitive face, suddenly grew cunning. He turned back to Aimless and resumed his mechanical stroking of the teat, saying in a sing-song rhythm:

'Ay, then I'll go, Miss Judith. I dunnamany times I've thought as how this day might come. . . . And now I mun go to bring Robert Poste's child back to Cold Comfort. Ay, 'tes strange. The seed to the flower, the flower to the fruit, the fruit to the belly. Ay, so 'twill go.'

Judith had crossed the muck and rubble of the yard, and now entered the house by the back door.

In the large kitchen, which occupied most of the middle of the house, a sullen fire burned, the smoke of which wavered up the blackened walls and over the deal table, darkened by age and dirt, which was roughly set for a meal. A snood full of coarse porridge hung over the fire, and standing with one arm resting upon the high mantel, looking moodily down into the heaving contents of the snood, was a tall young man whose riding-boots were splashed with mud to the thigh, and whose coarse linen shirt was open to his waist. The firelight lit up his diaphragm muscles as they heaved slowly in rough rhythm with the porridge.

He looked up as Judith entered, and gave a short, defiant laugh, but said nothing. Judith slowly crossed over until she stood by his side. She was tall as he. They stood in silence, she staring at him, and he down into the secret crevasses of the porridge.

'Well, mother mine,' he said at last, 'here I am, you see. I said I would be in time for breakfast, and I have kept my word.'

His voice had a low, throaty, animal quality, a sneering warmth that wound a velvet ribbon of sexuality over the outward coarseness of the man.

Judith's breath came in long shudders. She thrust her arms deeper into her shawl. The porridge gave an ominous, leering heave; it might almost have been endowed with life, so uncannily did its movements keep pace with the human passions that throbbed above it.

'Cur,' said Judith, levelly, at last. 'Coward! Liar! Libertine! Who were you with last night? Moll at the mill or Violet at the vicarage? Or Ivy, perhaps, at the ironmongery? Seth—my son . . .' Her deep, dry voice quivered, but she whipped it back, and her next words flew out at him like a lash.

'Do you want to break my heart?'

'Yes,' said Seth, with an elemental simplicity.

The porridge boiled over.

Flora arrives, settles in and meets the family one by one as they lurch in from the fields or down from upstairs.

In case the reader is one of those busy people who is not always sure whether a sentence is Literature or is in fact not very well written, Miss Gibbons helpfully marked her finest prose passages with one, two, or three stars, ★, ★★, ★★★, in the manner perfected by the late Herr Baedeker for indicating the merits of cathedrals.

Reuben Starkadder's first meeting with Flora is a three-star job:

At four o'clock she came downstairs to look for some tea.

She did not bother to glance into her little parlour to see if her own tea were on the table. She went straight into the kitchen.

Of course, there were no preparations for tea in the kitchen; she realised, as soon as she saw the ashy fire and the crumbs and fragments of carrot left on the table from dinner, that it was rather optimistic of her to have expected any.

But she was not daunted. She filled the kettle, put some wood on the fire and set the kettle on it, flicked the reminders of dinner off the table with Adam's drying-up towel (which she held in the tongs), and set out a ring of cups and saucers about a dented pewter teapot. She found a loaf and some butter, but no jam, of course, or anything effeminate of that sort.

Just as the kettle boiled and she darted forward to rescue it, a shadow darkened the door and there stood Reuben, looking at Flora's gallant preparations with an expression of stricken amazement mingled with fury.

'Hullo,' said Flora, getting her blow in first. 'I feel sure you must be Reuben. I'm Flora Poste, your cousin, you know. How do you do? I'm so glad to see somebody has come in for some tea. Do sit down. Do you take milk? (No sugar . . . of course . . . or do you? I do, but most of my friends don't.')

★★★ The man's big body, etched menacingly against the bleak light that stabbed in from the low windows, did not move. His thoughts swirled like a beck in spate behind the sodden grey furrows of his face. A woman. . . . Blast! Blast! Come to wrest away from him the land whose love fermented in his veins like slow yeast. She-woman. Young, soft-coloured, insolent. His gaze was suddenly edged by a fleshy taint. Break her. Break. Keep and hold and hold fast the land. The land, the iron furrows of frosted earth under the rain-lust, the fecund spears of rain, the swelling, slow burst of seed-sheaths, the slow smell of cows and cry of cows, the trampling bride-pride of the bull in his hour. All his, his . . .

'Will you have some bread and butter?' asked Flora, handing him a cup of tea.

A favourite character in back-to-the-soil novels was the fey, elfin girl-child, glimpsed running through the dewy grass in bare feet, hair streaming out behind her, etc., and, of course, Cold Comfort Farm *has one.*

Flora meets her when she is watching Amos coping with dirty breakfast dishes in the time-honoured country way:

Adam ... had gone out into the yard, where a thorn-tree grew, and returned with a long thorn-spiked twig torn from its branches. Flora watched him with interest while he turned the cold water on to the crusted plates, and began picking at the incrustations of porridge with his twig.

She bore it as long as she could, for she could hardly believe her own eyes, and then she said:

'What on earth are you doing?'

'Cletterin' the dishes, Robert Poste's child.'

'But surely you could do it much more easily with a little mop? A nice little mop with a handle? Cousin Judith ought to get you one. Why don't you ask her? It could get the dishes cleaner, and it would be so much quicker, too.'

'I don't want a liddle mop wi' a handle. I've used a thorn twig these fifty years and more, and what was good enough then is good enough now. And I don't want to cletter the dishes more quickly, neither. It passes the time away, and takes me thoughts off me liddle wild bird.'

'But,' suggested the cunning Flora, remembering the conversation which had roused her that morning at dawn, 'if you had a little mop and could wash the dishes more quickly, you could have more time in the cowshed with the dumb beasts.'

Adam stopped his work. This had evidently struck home. He nodded once or twice, without turning round, as though he were pondering, and Flora hastily followed up her advantage.

'Anyway, I shall buy one for you when I go into Beershorn tomorrow.'

At this moment there came a soft rap at the closed door which led out into the yard; and a second later it was repeated. Adam shuffled across to the door, muttering 'My liddle wennet!' and flung it wide.

A figure which stood outside, wrapped in a long green cloak, rushed across the room and up the stairs so quickly that Flora only had the merest glimpse of it.

She raised her eyebrows. 'Who was that?' she asked, though she was sure that she knew.

'My cowdling—my liddle Elfine,' said Adam, listlessly picking up his thorn twig, which had fallen into the snood of porridge on the hearth.

'Indeed, and does she always charge about like that?' enquired Flora, coldly; she considered her cousin deficient in manners.

'Ay. She's as wild and shy as a Pharisee of the woods. Days she'll be away from home, wanderin' on the hills, wi' only the wild birds and the liddle rabbits an' the spying' maggies for company. Ay, and o' nights, too . . .' His face darkened. 'Ay, she's away then, too, wanderin' far from those that loves her and cowdled her in their bosoms when she was a mommet. She'll break my heart into liddle sippets, so she will.'

'Does she go to school?' asked Flora, looking distastefully in a cupboard for a rag with which to dust her shoes. 'How old is she?'

'Seventeen. Nay, niver talk o' school for my wennet. Why, Robert Poste's child, ye might as soon send the white hawthorn or the yellow daffydowndilly to school as my Elfine. She learns from the skies an' the wild marsh-tiggets, not out o' books.'

'How trying,' observed Flora, who was feeling lonely and rather cross. 'Look here, where is everybody this morning? I want to see Miss Judith before I go out for a walk.'

'Mus' Amos, he's down seein' the well drained for Sairy-Lucy's Polly we think she's fallen into it; Mus' Reuben, he's down Nettle Flitch, ploughin'; Mus' Seth, he's off a-mollocking somewheres in Howling; Miss Judith, she's upstairs a-layin' out the cards.'

'Well, I shall go up and find her. What does mollocking mean? . . . No, you need not tell me. I can guess.'

Flora has plans for the farm, which badly needs reorganizing. It has potential but is being neglected by Amos, the senior Starkadder, who is not at all interested in agriculture.

Amos's enthusiasm lies in being a preacher with a small but zealous religious sect whose credo could be described as a less jolly version of Calvinism. Flora, in a famous scene (which must have delighted the heart of Sir Henry Howarth Bashford) tries to get to know the weird Amos better by going with him to one of his meetings and watching him in action:

'Are you going down into Beershorn to preach to the Brethren to-night?'

Amos looked at her, as though seeing her for the first, or perhaps the second time. ★★★ His huge body, rude as a wind-tortured thorn, was printed darkly against the thin mild flame of the declining winter sun that throbbed like a sallow lemon on the westering lip of Mockuncle Hill, and sent its pale, sharp rays into the kitchen through the open door. The brittle air, on which the fans of the trees were etched like ageing skeletons, seemed thronged by the bright, invisible ghosts of a million dead summers. The cold beat in glassy waves against the eyelids of anybody who happened to be out in it. High up, a few chalky clouds doubtfully wavered in the pale sky that curved over against the rim of the Downs like a vast inverted *pot-de-chambre*. Huddled in the hollow like an exhausted brute, the frosted roofs of Howling, crisp and purple as broccoli leaves, were like beasts about to spring.

'Ay,' said Amos, at last.

'Well, may I come too?'. . .

He did not seem surprised. Indeed, she caught in his eye a triumphant light, as though he had long been expecting her to see the error of her ways and come to him and the Brethren for spiritual comfort.

'Git up,' said Amos to Flora.

'Is there a rug?' she asked, hanging fire.

'Nay. The sins burnin' in yer marrow will keep yer warm.'

But Flora thought otherwise, and darting into the kitchen, she returned with her leather coat, in the lining of which she had been mending a tiny tear.

'It must be so interesting to preach to the Brethren, Cousin Amos, I quite envy you. Do you prepare your sermon beforehand or do you just make it up as you go along?'

An apparent increase in Amos's looming bulk, after this question had had time to sink in, convinced her in the midst of a disconcerting and ever-lengthening pause that he was swelling with fury. Cautiously she glanced over the side of the trap to see if she could jump out should he attempt to smite her. The ground looked disagreeably muddy and far off; and she was relieved when Amos at last replied in a tolerably well-controlled voice:

'Doan't 'ee speak o' the word o' the Lord in that godless way, as though 'twere one o' they pagan tales in the *Family Herald*. The word is not prepared beforehand; it falls on me mind like the manna fell from heaven into the bellies of the starving Israelites.'

'Really! How interesting. Then you have no idea what you are going to say before you get there?'

'Ay . . . I allus knows 'twill be summat about burnin' . . . or the eternal torment . . . or sinners comin' to judgment. But I doan't know exactly what the words will be until I gets up in me seat and looks round at all their sinful faces, awaitin' all eager for to hear me. Then I knows what I mun say, and I says it.'

'Does anyone else preach, or are you the only one?'

'Oanly me. Deborah Checkbottom, she tried onceways to get up and preach. But 'tweren't no good. Her couldn't.'

'Wouldn't the spirit work or something?'

'Nay, it worked. But I wouldn't have it. I reckoned the Lord's ways is dark and there'd been a mistake, and the spirit that was meant for me had fallen on Deborah. So I just struck her down wi' the gurt old Bible, to let the devil out of her soul.'

'And did it come out?' asked Flora, endeavouring with some effort to maintain the proper spirit of scientific enquiry.

'Ay, he came out. We heard no more o' Deborah's tryin' to preach. Now I preaches alone. No one else gets the word like I do.'

They stopped in front of a building which Flora at first took to be an usually large dog-kennel. The doors were open, and inside could be seen the seats and walls of plain pitch-pine. Some of the Brethren were already seated, and others were hurrying in to take their places.

The dog-kennel was nearly full.

Somebody was playing a shocking tune on the poor little wheezy organ near the door. Except for this organ, Flora observed, peering over Amos's shoulder, the chapel looked like an ordinary lecture hall, with a little round platform at the end farthest from the door, on which stood a chair.

'Is that where you preach, Cousin Amos?'

'Ay.'

'Does Judith or either of the boys ever come down to hear you preach?' She was making conversation because she was conscious of a growing feeling of dismay at what lay before her, and did not wish to give way to it.

Amos frowned.

'Nay. They struts like Ahab in their pride and their eyes drips fatness, nor do they see the pit digged beneath their feet by the Lord. Ay, 'tes a terrible wicked family I'm cursed wi', and the hand o' the Lord it lies heavy on Cold Comfort, pressin' the bitter wine out o' our souls.'

'Then why don't you sell it and buy another farm on a really *nice* piece of land, if you feel like that about it?'

'Nay . . . there have always been Starkadders at Cold Comfort,' he answered, heavily. ''Tes old Mrs Starkadder—Ada Doom as was, before she married Fig Starkadder. She's sot against our leavin' the farm. She'd never see us go. 'Tes a curse on us. And Reuben sits awaitin' for me to go, so as he can have the farm. But un shall niver have un. Nay I'll leave it to Adam first.'

Before Flora could convey to him her lively sense of dismay at the prospect indicated in this threat, he moved forward saying, ''Tes nearly full. We mun go in,' and in they went.

Flora took a seat at the end of a row near the exit; she thought it would be as well to sit near the door in case the double effect of Amos's preaching and no ventilation became more than she could bear.

Amos went to a seat almost directly in front of the little platform, and sat down after directing two slow and brooding glances, laden with promise of terrifying eloquence to come, upon the Brethren sitting in the same row.

The dog-kennel was now packed to bursting, and the organ had begun to play something like a tune. Flora found a hymn-book being pressed into her hand by a female on her left.

'It's number two hundred, "Whatever Shall We Do, O Lord",' said the female, in a loud conversational voice.

Flora had supposed, from impressions gathered during her wide reading, that it was customary to speak only in whispers in a building devoted to the act of worship. But she was ready to learn otherwise, so she took the book with a pleasant smile and said, 'Thank you so much.'

The hymn went like this:

> Whatever shall we do, O Lord,
> When Gabriel blows o'er sea and river,
> Fen and desert, mount and ford?
> The earth may burn, but we will quiver.

Flora approved of this hymn, because its words indicated a firmness of purpose, a clear plan in the face of a disagreeable possibility, which struck an answering note in her own character. She sang industriously in her pleasing soprano. The singing was conducted by a surly excessively dirty old man with long, grey hair who stood on the platform and waved what Flora, after the first incredulous shock, decided was a kitchen poker.

'Who is that?' she asked her friend.

''Tes Brother Ambleforth. He leads the quiverin' when we begins to quiver.'

'And why does he conduct the music with a poker?'

'To put us in mind o' hell fire' was the simple answer, and Flora had not the heart to say that as far as she was concerned, at any rate, this purpose was not achieved.

After the hymn, which was sung sitting down, everybody crossed their legs and arranged themselves more comfortably, while Amos rose from his seat with terrifying deliberation, mounted the little platform and sat down.

For some three minutes he slowly surveyed the Brethren, his face wearing an expression of the most profound loathing and contempt, mingled with a divine sorrow and pity. He did it quite well. Flora had never seen anything to touch it except the face of Sir Henry Wood when pausing to contemplate some late-comers into the stalls at the Queen's Hall just as his baton was raised to conduct the first bar of the 'Eroica'. Her heart warmed to Amos. The man was an artist.

At last he spoke. His voice jarred the silence like a broken bell. 'Ye miserable, crawling worms, are ye here again, then? Have ye come like Nimshi, son of Rehoboam, secretly out of yer doomed houses to hear what's comin' to ye? Have ye come, old and young, sick and well, matrons and virgins (if there is any virgins among ye, which is not likely, the world bein' in the wicked state it is), old men and young lads to hear me tellin' o' the great crimson lickin' flames o' hell fire?'

A long and effective pause, and a further imitation of Sir Henry. The only sound (and it, with the accompanying smell, was quite enough) was the whickering hissing of the gas flares which lit the hall and cast sharp shadows from their noses across the faces of the Brethren.

Amos went on:

'Ay, ye've come.' He laughed shortly and contemptuously. 'Dozens of ye.

Hundreds of ye. Like rats to a granary. Like field-mice when there's harvest home. And what good will it do ye?'

Second pause, and more Sir Henry stuff.

'Nowt. Not the flicker of a whisper of a bit o' good.'

He paused and drew a long breath, and suddenly he leaped from his seat and thundered at the top of his voice:

'Ye're all damned!'

An expression of lively interest and satisfaction passed over the faces of the Brethren, and there was a general rearranging of arms and legs as though they wanted to sit as comfortably as possible while listening to the bad news.

'Damned,' he repeated, his voice sinking to a thrilling and effective whisper. 'Oh, do ye ever stop to think what that word *means* when ye use it every day, so lightly, o'yer wicked lives? No. Ye doan't. Ye never stop to think what anything means, do ye? Well, I'll tell ye. It means endless horrifyin' torment, with yer poor sinful bodies stretched out on hot grid-irons in the nether-most fiery pit of hell, and demons mockin' ye while they waves cooling jellies in front of ye, and binds ye down tighter on yer dreadful bed. Ay, an' the air'll be full of the stench of burnt flesh and the screams of your nearest and dearest . . .'

He took a gulp of water, which Flora thought he more than deserved. She was beginning to feel that she could do with a glass of water herself.

Amos's voice now took on a deceptively mild and conversational note. His protruding eyes ranged slowly over his audience.

'Ye know, doan't ye, what it feels like when ye burn yer hand in takin' a cake out of the oven or wi' a match when ye're lightin' one of they godless cigarettes? Ay. It stings wi' a fearful pain, doan't it? And ye run away to clap a bit o' butter on it to take the pain away. Ah, but' (an impressive pause) 'there'll be no butter in hell! Yer whoal body will be burnin' and stingin' wi' that unbearable pain, and yer blackened tongues will be stickin' out of yer mouth, and yer cracked lips will try to scream out for a drop of water, but no sound woan't come because yer throat is drier nor the sandy desert and yer eyes will be beatin' like great red hot balls against yer shrivelled eye-lids . . .'

It was at this point that Flora quietly rose and with an apology to the woman sitting next to her, passed rapidly across the narrow aisle to the door.

The most memorable Starkadder is the dreaded matriarch of the family, Aunt Ada Doom, who spends all her days behind the locked door of her bedroom, seeing hardly anybody except the hired woman who staggers upstairs five times a day with enormous meals on trays: memorable if only because most of Aunt Ada's conversation consists of reiteration of what must be about the fifth most famous line in humorous prose, the one about 'something nasty . . .'.

Here is a passage from the emotional scene when Flora returns to the farm late at night to find that Aunt Ada Doom, whom she has never met, has chosen this night to make her annual descent downstairs for the Counting, the ceremony of finding out how many Starkadders have survived their violent way of life for another year:

The great kitchen was full of people. They were all silent, and all painted over by the leaping firelight with a hellish red glow. Flora could distinguish Amos, Judith, Meriam, the hired girl; Adam, Ezra, and Harkaway; Caraway, Luke and Mark and several of the farm-hands. They were all grouped, in a rough semi-circle, about someone who sat in a great high-backed chair by the fire. The dim gold lamplight and the restless firelight made Rembrandt shadows in the remoter corners of the kitchen, and threw the dwarf and giant shadows of the Starkadders across the ceiling . . .

Everybody was staring at the door. The silence was terrific. It seemed the air must burst with its pressure, and the flickering movement of the light and the fireglow upon the faces of the Starkadders was so restlessly volatile that it emphasised the strange stillness of their bodies. Flora was trying to decide just what the kitchen looked like, and came to the conclusion it was the Chamber of Horrors at Madame Tussaud's.

'Well, well,' she said, amiably, stepping over the doorstep and drawing off her gloves, 'the gang *is* all here, isn't it! Is that Big Business I see there in the corner? Oh, I beg your pardon, it's Micah. I suppose there aren't any sandwiches?'

This cracked the social ice a bit. Signs of life were observed.

'There's food on the table,' said Judith, lifelessly, coming forward, with her burning eyes fixed upon Seth; 'but first, Robert Poste's child, you must greet your Aunt Ada Doom.'

And she took Flora's hand (Flora was very bucked that she had shed her clean gloves) and led her up to the figure which sat in the high-backed chair by the fire.

'How d'ye do, Aunt Ada?' said Flora, pleasantly, putting out her hand. But Aunt Ada made no effort to take it. She folded her own hands a little more closely upon a copy of the 'Milk Producers' Weekly Bulletin and Cowkeepers' Guide', which she held on her lap, and observed, in a low, toneless, voice:

'I saw something nasty in the woodshed.'

Flora turned to Judith, with raised and enquiring eyebrows. A murmer came from the rest of the company, which was watching closely.

''Tis one of her bad nights,' said Judith, whose gaze kept wandering in the direction of Seth (he was wolfing beef in a corner). 'Mother,' she said, louder, 'don't you know me? It's Judith. I have brought Flora Poste to see you— Robert Poste's child.'

'Nay. . . . I saw something nasty in the woodshed,' said Aunt Ada Doom, fretfully moving her head from side to side, ' 'Twas a burnin' noonday . . . sixty-nine years ago. And me no bigger than a titty wren. And I saw something na—'

'Well, perhaps she likes it better that way,' said Flora, soothingly. She had been observing Aunt Ada's firm chin, clear eyes, tight little mouth and close grip upon the 'Milk Producers' Weekly Bulletin and Cowkeepers' Guide', and she came to the conclusion that if Aunt Ada was mad, then she, Flora, was one of the Marx Brothers.   Stella Gibbons (b. 1902), *Cold Comfort Farm* (1932).

A YEAR *after* Cold Comfort Farm, *another first novel was published, A. G. Macdonnell's* England, Their England, *which contained what is generally agreed to be quite simply the funniest description of a village cricket match in literature. A large and rash claim, but there it is.*

It came about in this manner. After the 1914–18 war a literary journalist, Georgian poet and critic named John Squire—later Sir John Squire—founded a magazine called the London Mercury *to nurture Georgian poetry and new authors, which he managed to do quite well in every respect except financially. He was no businessman but he was a tremendous enthusiast, not only for poetry of the hearty, 'foaming tankard' school, but also for architecture and cricket. And he was— almost literally—mad about cricket.*

In the spring of 1920 he set up his own amateur cricket team consisting of similarly cricket-mad friends, mostly in the literary world. He originally christened his team the Old Age Pensioners but as this seemed a little unkind to some of the members he changed it to the Invalids. Regular members of the Invalids included W. A. Darlington, the critic; A. D. Peters, the literary agent; Alec Waugh, the novelist and brother of Evelyn; Clifford Bax, the playwright; Edmund Blunden, the poet; and J. M. Hone, the Irish philosopher. Squire was not at all a good bowler but being captain gave him the right to put himself on to bowl whenever he felt like it, which was often. He frequently fielded in the slips although he was extremely short-sighted: one bowler remembers Squire dropping thirty-nine catches off his bowling in one game.

Neville Cardus, the great cricket writer and Squire's friend, told of one match when the opposing batsman hit an easy catch high in the sky. Six Invalids ran to get under it and jostled for position. The authoratitive voice of Squire boomed out, 'Leave it to Thompson!' As the ball thudded into the grass they remembered that Thompson wasn't playing that week.

The extent of Squire's flair for organizing can also be judged from a note containing vital information which he sent to Clifford Bax: 'Dear Bax, the match on May 15th is with the Morning Post *and at Wimbledon, or Putney, or some such place.'*

Most of their matches were played either on the village greens of Fordcombe in Kent or of Rodmell in Sussex and are lovingly remembered still by surviving members of the Invalids: Alec Waugh recalls one game at Rodmell when they were

two men short so Squire made up the team with a schoolboy of 11 and the
taxi-driver who had driven latecomers from the station.

Into the offices of the London Mercury *in the early thirties strolled a huge,*
dapper, amiable Scot, looking for work. He was a would-be novelist named A. G.
Macdonnell. He played cricket. Squire gave him a job on the Mercury *(and a place*
on the team) and Macdonnell set about collecting material for a social satire he
was planning about a young Scotsman (i.e. himself) who sets out to find the true
England and the real English. In 1933 the book was published and was a great
success: England, Their England.

In Macdonnell's exciting as well as funny village cricket match in England,
Their England, *some of the Invalids appear, lightly disguised, as fictitious players*
in Hodge's team. John Squire himself appears, libellously undisguised, as Hodge.
Surviving members of the Invalids swear that the incidents which occur in the
story were neither invented nor much exaggerated; they claim that everything
depicted had actually happened in one or another of the Invalids' matches and the
whole thing reads to them like a fairly normal Sunday game.

In the story, Donald Cameron, the foreigner from Scotland, arrives in good time,
eager to learn much from his first glimpse of Sunday village cricket, perhaps the
most idiosyncratic of all English public pleasures:

The entire scene was perfect to the last detail . . . There was the forge, with
the blacksmith, his hammer discarded, tightening his snake-buckled belt for
the fray and loosening his braces to enable his terrific bowling-arm to swing
freely in its socket. There on a long bench outside the Three Horseshoes sat a
row of elderly men, facing a row of pint tankards, and wearing either long
beards or clean-shaven chins and long whiskers. Near them, holding pint
tankards in their hands, was another group of men, clustered together and
talking with intense animation. Donald thought that one or two of them
seemed familiar, but it was not until he turned back to the char-à-banc to
ask if he could help with the luggage that he realised that they were Mr
Hodge and his team already sampling the proprietor's wares (a notice above
the door of the inn stated that the proprietor's name was A. Bason and that
he was licensed to sell wines, spirits, beers, and tobacco).

All round the cricket field small parties of villagers were patiently waiting
for the great match to begin—a match against gentlemen from London is an
event in a village—and some of them looked as if they had been waiting for
a good time. But they were not impatient. Village folk are very seldom
impatient. Those whose lives are occupied in combating the eccentricities of
God regard as very small beer the eccentricities of Man.

Blue-and-green dragonflies played at hide-and-seek among the thistle-
down and a pair of swans flew overhead. An ancient man leaned upon a
scythe, his sharpening-stone sticking out of a pocket in his velveteen waistcoat. A magpie flapped lazily across the meadows. The parson shook hands
with the squire. Doves cooed. The haze flickered. The world stood still.

At twenty minutes to 3, Mr Hodge [who has mislaid two members of his team] had completed his rather tricky negotiations with the Fordenden captain, and had arranged that two substitutes should be lent by Fordenden in order that the visitors should field eleven men, and that nine men on each side should bat. But just as the two men on the Fordenden side, who had been detailed for the unpleasant duty of fielding for both sides and batting for neither, had gone off home in high dudgeon, a motor-car arrived containing not only Mr Hodge's two defaulters but a third gentleman in flannels as well, who swore stoutly that he had been invited by Mr Hodge to play and affirmed that he was jolly well going to play. Whoever stood down, it wasn't going to be him. Negotiations therefore had to be reopened, the pair of local Achilles had to be recalled, and at ten minutes to 3 the match began upon a twelve-a-side basis.

Mr Hodge, having won the toss by a system of his own founded upon the differential calculus and the Copernican theory, sent in his opening pair to bat. One was James Livingstone, a very sound club cricketer, and the other one was called, simply Boone. Boone was a huge, awe-inspiring colossus of a man, weighing at least eighteen stone and wearing all the majestic trappings of a Cambridge Blue. Donald felt that it was hardly fair to loose such cracks upon a humble English village until he fortunately remembered that he, of all people, a foreigner, admitted by courtesy to the National Game, ought not to set himself up to be a judge of what is, and what is not, cricket.

The Fordenden team ranged themselves at the bidding of their captain, the Fordenden baker, in various spots of vantage amid the daisies, buttercups, dandelions, vetches, thistle-down, and clumps of dark-red sorrel; and the blacksmith having taken in, just for luck as it were, yet another reef in his snake-buckle belt, prepared to open the attack. It so happened that, at the end at which he was to bowl, the ground behind the wicket was level for a few yards and then sloped away rather abruptly, so that it was only during the last three or four intensive, galvanic yards of his run that the blacksmith, who took a long run, was visible to the batsman or indeed to anyone on the field of play except the man stationed in the deep field behind him. This man saw nothing of the game except the blacksmith walking back dourly and the blacksmith running up ferociously, and occasionally a ball driven smartly over the brow of the hill in his direction.

The sound club player having taken guard, having twiddled his bat round several times in a nonchalant manner, and having stared arrogantly at each fieldsman in turn, was somewhat surprised to find that, although the field was ready, no bowler was visible.

His doubts however, were resolved a second or two later, when the blacksmith came up, breasting the slope superbly like a mettlesome combination of Vulcan and Venus Anadyomene. The first ball which he delivered was a high full-pitch to leg, of appalling velocity. It must have lighted upon a bare patch among the long grass near long-leg, for it rocketed, first bounce, into the hedge and four byes were reluctantly signalled by the village umpire. The row of gaffers on the rustic bench shook their heads, agreed that it was many years since four byes had been signalled on that ground, and called for more pints of old-and-mild. The other members of Mr Hodge's team blanched visibly and called for more points of bitter. The youngish professor of ballistics, who was in next, muttered something about muzzle velocities and started to do a sum on the back of an envelope.

The second ball went full-pitch into the wicket-keeper's stomach and there was a delay while the deputy wicket-keeper was invested with the pads and gloves of office. The third ball, making a noise like a partridge, would have hummed past Mr Livingstone's left ear had he not dexterously struck it out of the ground for six, and the fourth took his leg bail with a bullet-like full-pitch. Ten runs for one wicket, last man six. The professor got the fifth ball on the left ear and went back to the Three Horseshoes, while Mr Harcourt had the singular misfortune to hit his wicket before the sixth ball was even delivered. Ten runs for two wickets and one man retired hurt. A slow left-hand bowler was on at the other end, the local rate-collector, a man whose whole life was one of infinite patience and guile. Off his first ball the massive Cambridge Blue was easily stumped, having executed a movement that aroused the professional admiration of the Ancient who was leaning upon his scythe. Donald was puzzled that so famous a player should play so execrable a stroke until it transpired, later on, that a wrong impression had been created and that the portentous Boone had gained his Blue at Cambridge for rowing and not for cricket. Ten runs for three wickets and one man hurt.

The next player was a singular young man. He was small and quiet, and he wore perfectly creased white flannels, white silk socks, a pale-pink silk shirt, and a white cap. On the way down in the char-à-banc he had taken little part in the conversation and even less in the beer-drinking. There was a retiring modesty about him that made him conspicuous in that cricket eleven, and there was a gentleness, an almost finicky gentleness about his movements which hardly seemed virile and athletic. He looked as if a fast ball would knock the bat out of his hands. Donald asked someone what his name was, and was astonished to learn that he was the famous novelist, Robert Southcott himself [a combined portrait of the two novelists William Gerhardie and Alec Waugh].

Just as this celebrity, holding his bat as delicately as if it was a flute or a fan, was picking his way through the daisies and thistle-down towards the wicket, Mr Hodge rushed anxiously, tankard in hand, from the Three Horseshoes and bellowed in a most unpoetical voice: 'Play carefully, Bobby. Keep your end up. Runs don't matter.'

'Very well, Bill' replied Mr Southcott sedately.

Donald was interested by this little exchange. It was the Team Spirit at work—the captain instructing his man to play a type of game that was demanded by the state of the team's fortunes, and the individual loyally suppressing his instincts to play a different type of game.

Mr Southcott took guard modestly, glanced furtively round the field as if it was an impertinence to suggest that he would survive long enough to make a study of the fieldsmen's positions worth while and hit the rate-collector's first ball over the Three Horse-shoes into a hay-field. The ball was retrieved by a mob of screaming urchins, handed back to the rate collector, who scratched his head and then bowled his fast yorker, which Mr Southcott hit into the saloon bar of the Shoes, giving Mr Harcourt such a fright that he required several pints before he fully recovered his nerve. The next ball was very slow and crafty, endowed as it was with every iota of finger-spin and brain-power which a long-service rate-collector could muster. In addition, it was delivered at the extreme end of the crease so as to secure a background of dark laurels instead of a dazzling white screen, and it swung a little in the air; a few moments later the urchins, by this time delirious with ecstasy, were fishing it out of the squire's trout stream with a bamboo pole and an old bucket.

The rate-collector was bewildered. He had never known such a travesty of the game. It was not cricket. It was slogging; it was wild, unscientific bashing; and furthermore, his reputation was in grave danger. The instalments would be harder than ever to collect and Heaven knew they were hard enough to collect as it was, what with bad times and all. His three famous deliveries had been treated with contempt—the leg-break, the fast yorker, and the slow, swinging off-break out of the laurel bushes. What on earth was he to try now? Another six and he would be laughed out of the parish. Fortunately the village umpire came out of a trance of consternation to the rescue. Thirty-eight years of umpiring for the Fordenden Cricket Club had taught him a thing or two and he called 'Over' firmly and marched off to square-leg. The rate-collector was glad to give way to a Free Forester, who had been specially imported for this match. He was only a moderate bowler, but it was felt that it was worth while giving him a trial, if only for the sake of the scarf round his waist and his cap. At the other end the fast bowler pounded away grimly until an unfortunate accident occurred. Mr Southcott had been treating with apologetic contempt those of his deliveries which came within reach, and the blacksmith's temper had been rising for some time. An urchin had shouted, 'Take him orf!' and the other urchins, for whom Mr Southcott was by now a firmly established deity, had screamed with delight. The captain had held one or two ominous consultations with the wicket-keeper and other advisers, and the blacksmith knew that his dismissal was at hand unless he produced a supreme effort.

It was the last ball of the over. He halted at the wicket before going back for this run, glared at Mr Harcourt, who had been driven out to umpire by his colleagues—greatly to the regret of Mr Bason, the landlord of the Shoes— glared at Mr Southcott, took another reef in his belt, shook out another inch in his braces, spat on his hand, swung his arm three or four times in a meditative sort of way, grasped the ball tightly in his colossal palm, and then turned smartly about and marched off like a Pomeranian grenadier and vanished over the brow of the hill. Mr Southcott, during these proceedings, leant elegantly upon his bat and admired the view. At last, after a long stillness, the ground shook, the grasses waved violently, small birds arose with shrill clamours, a loud puffing sound alarmed the butterflies, and the blacksmith, looking more like Venus Anadyomene than ever, came thundering over the crest. The world held its breath. Among the spectators conversation was suddenly hushed. Even the urchins, understanding somehow that they were assisting at a crisis in affairs, were silent for a moment as the mighty figure swept up to the crease. It was the charge of Von Bredow's Dragoons at Gravelotte over again.

But alas for human ambitions! Mr Harcourt [a portrait of the poet Hugh Mackintosh], swaying slightly from leg to leg, had understood the menacing glare of the bowler, had marked the preparation of a titanic effort, and—for he was not a poet for nothing—knew exactly what was going on. And Mr Harcourt sober had a very pleasant sense of humour, but Mr Harcourt rather drunk was a perfect demon of impishness. Sober, he occasionally resisted a temptation to try to be funny. Rather drunk, never. As the giant whirlwind of vulcanic energy rushed past him to the crease, Mr Harcourt, quivering with excitement and internal laughter, and wobbling uncertainly upon his pins, took a deep breath and bellowed, 'No ball!'

It was too late for the unfortunate bowler to stop himself. The ball flew out of his hand like a bullet and hit third-slip, who was not looking, full pitch on the knee-cap. With a yell of agony third-slip began hopping about like a stork until he tripped over a tussock of grass and fell on his face in a bed of nettles, from which he sprang up again with another drum-splitting yell. The blacksmith himself was flung forward by his own irresistible momentum, startled out of his wits by Mr Harcourt's bellow in his ear, and thrown off his balance by his desperate effort to prevent himself from delivering the ball, and the result was that his gigantic feet got mixed up among each other and he fell heavily in the centre of the wicket, knocking up a cloud of dust and dandelion-seed and twisting his ankle. Rooks by hundreds arose in protest from the vicarage cedars. The urchins howled like intoxicated banshees. The gaffers gaped. Mr Southcott gazed modestly at the ground. Mr Harcourt did not think the world had ever been, or could ever be again, quite such a capital place, even though he had laughed internally so much that he had got hiccups.

Mr Hodge, emerging at that moment from the Three Horseshoes, surveyed the scene and then the scoreboard with an imperial air. Then he roared in the same rustic voice as before:

'You needn't play safe any more, Bob. Play your own game.'

'Thank you, Bill,' replied Mr Southcott as sedately as ever, and, on the resumption of the game, he fell into a kind of cricketing trance, defending his wicket skilfully from straight balls, ignoring crooked ones, and scoring one more run in a quarter of an hour before he inadvertently allowed, for the first time during his innings, a ball to strike his person.

'Out!' shrieked the venerable umpire before anyone had time to appeal.

The score at this point was sixty-nine for six, last man fifty-two.

The only other incident in the innings was provided by an Amercian journalist, by name Shakespeare Pollock—an intensely active, alert, on-the-spot young man. Mr Pollock had been roped in at the last moment to make up the eleven, and Mr Hodge and Mr Harcourt had spent quite a lot of time on the way down trying to teach him the fundamental principles of the game. Donald had listened attentively and had been surprised that they made no reference to the Team Spirit. He decided in the end that the reason must have been simply that everyone knows all about it already, and that it is therefore taken for granted.

Mr Pollock stepped up to the wicket in the lively manner of his native mustang, refused to take guard, on the ground that he wouldn't know what to do with it when he had got it, and, striking the first ball he received towards square leg, threw down his bat, and himself set off at a great rate in the direction of cover-point. There was a paralysed silence. The rustics on the bench rubbed their eyes. On the field no one moved. Mr Pollock stopped suddenly, looked round, and broke into a genial laugh.

'Darn me—' he began, and then he pulled himself up and went on in refined English, 'Well, well! I thought I was playing baseball.' He smiled disarmingly round.

'Baseball is a kind of rounders, isn't it, sir?' said cover-point sympathetically.

Donald thought he had never seen an expression change so suddenly as Mr Pollock's did at this harmless, and true, statement. A look of concentrated, ferocious venom obliterated the disarming smile. Cover-point, simple soul, noticed nothing, however, and Mr Pollock walked back to the wicket in silence and was out next ball.

The next two batsmen, Major Hawker, the team's fast bowler, and Mr Hodge himself, did not score, and the innings closed at sixty-nine, Donald not-out nought. Opinion on the gaffers' bench which corresponded in years and connoisseurship very closely with the Pavilion at Lord's, was sharply divided on the question whether sixty-nine was, or was not, a winning score.

After a suitable interval for refreshment, Mr Hodge led his men, except Mr Harcourt who was missing, out into the field and placed them at suitable positions in the hay.

The batsmen came in. The redoubtable Major Hawker, the fast bowler, thrust out his chin and prepared to bowl. In a quarter of an hour he had terrified seven batsmen, clean bowled six of them, and broken a stump. Eleven runs, six wickets, last man two.

After the fall of the sixth wicket there was a slight delay. The new batsman, the local rate-collector, had arrived at the crease and was ready. But nothing happened. Suddenly the large publisher [based on the portly Cecil Harmer], who was acting as wicket-keeper, called out, 'Hi! Where's Hawker?'

The words galvanised Mr Hodge into portentous activity.

'Quick!' he shouted. 'Hurry, run, for God's sake! Bob, George, Percy, to the Shoes!' and he set off at a sort of gallop towards the inn, followed at intervals by the rest of the side except the pretty youth in the blue jumper, who lay down; the wicket-keeper, who did not move; and Mr Shakespeare Pollock, who had shot off the mark and was well ahead of the field.

But they were all too late, even Mr Pollock. The gallant Major, admitted by Mr Bason through the back door, had already lowered a quart and a half of mild-and-bitter, and his subsequent bowling was perfectly innocuous, consisting, as it did, mainly of slow, gentle full-pitches to leg which the village baker and even, occasionally, the rate-collector hit hard and high into the long grass. The score mounted steadily.

Disaster followed disaster. Mr Pollock, presented with an easy chance of a run-out, instead of lobbing the ball back to the wicket-keeper, had another reversion to his college days and flung it with appalling velocity at the unfortunate rate-collector and hit him in the small of the back, shouting triumphantly as he did so, 'Rah, rah, rah!' Mr Livingstone, good club player, missed two easy catches off successive balls. Mr Hodge allowed another easy catch to fall at his feet without attempting to catch it, and explained afterwards that he had been all the time admiring a particularly fine specimen of oak in the squire's garden. He seemed to think that this was a complete justification of his failure to attempt, let alone bring off, the catch. A black spot happened to cross the eye of the ancient umpire just as the baker put all his feet and legs and pads in front of a perfectly straight ball, and, as he plaintively remarked over and over again, he had to give the batsman the benefit of the doubt, hadn't he? It wasn't as if it was his fault that a black spot had crossed his eye just at that moment. And the stout publisher seemed to be suffering from the delusion that the way to make a catch at the wicket was to raise both hands high in the air, utter a piercing yell, and trust to an immense pair of pads to secure the ball. Repeated experiments proved that he was wrong.

The baker lashed away vigorously and the rate-collector dabbed the ball hither and thither until the score—having once been eleven runs for six wickets—was marked up on the board at fifty runs for six wickets. Things were desperate. Twenty to win and five wickets—assuming that the blacksmith's ankle and third-slip's knee-cap would stand the strain—to fall. If the lines on Mr Hodge's face were deep, the lines on the faces of his team when he put himself on to bowl were like plasticine models of the Colorado Canyon. Mr Southcott, without any orders from his captain, discarded his silk sweater from the Rue de la Paix, and went away into the deep field, about a hundred and twenty yards from the wicket. His beautifully brushed head was hardly visible above the daisies. The professor of ballistics sighed deeply. Major Hawker grinned a colossal grin, right across his jolly red face, and edged off in the direction of the Shoes. Livingstone, loyal to his captain, crouched alertly. Mr Shakespeare Pollock rushed about enthusiastically. The remainder of the team drooped.

But the remainder of the team was wrong. For a wicket, a crucial wicket, was secured off Mr Hodge's very first ball. It happened like this. Mr Hodge was a poet, and therefore a theorist, and an idealist. If he was to win a victory at anything, he preferred to win by brains and not by muscle. He would far sooner have his best leg-spinner miss the wicket by an eighth of an inch than dismiss a batsman with a fast, clumsy full-toss. Every ball that he bowled had brain behind it, if not exactness of pitch. And it so happened that he had recently watched a county cricket match between Lancashire, a county that he detested in theory, and Worcestershire, a county that he adored in fact. On the one side were factories and the late Mr Jimmy White; on the other, English apples and Mr Stanley Baldwin. And at this particular match, a Worcestershire bowler, by name Root, a deliciously agricultural name, had outed the tough nuts of the County Palatine by placing all his fieldsmen on the leg-side and bowling what are technically known as 'in-swingers'.

Mr Hodge, at heart an agrarian, for all his book-learning and his cadences, was determined to do the same. The first part of the performance was easy. He placed all his men upon the leg-side. The second part—the bowling of the 'in-swingers'—was more complicated, and Mr Hodge's first ball was a slow long-hop on the off-side. The rate-collector, metaphorically rubbing his eyes, felt that this was too good to be true, and he struck the ball sharply into the untenanted off-side and ambled down the wicket with as near an approach to gaiety as a man can achieve who is cut off by the very nature of his profession from the companionship and goodwill of his fellows. He had hardly gone a yard or two when he was paralysed by a hideous yell from the long grass into which the ball had vanished, and still more by the sight of Mr Harcourt, who, aroused from a deep slumber amid a comfortable couch of grasses and daisies, sprang to his feet and, pulling himself together with miraculous rapidity after a lightning if somewhat bleary glance round the field, seized the ball and unerringly threw down the wicket. Fifty for seven, last man twenty-two. Twenty to win: four wickets to fall.

Mr Hodge's next ball was his top-spinner, and it would have, or might have, come very quickly off the ground had it ever hit the ground; as it was, one of the short-legs caught it dexterously and threw it back while the umpire signalled a wide. Mr Hodge then tried some more of Mr Root's stuff and was promptly hit for two sixes and a single. This brought the redoubtable baker to the batting end. Six runs to win and four wickets to fall.

Mr Hodge's fifth ball was not a good one, due mainly to the fact that it slipped out of his hand before he was ready, and it went up and came down in a slow, lazy parabola, about seven feet wide of the wicket on the leg-side. The baker had plenty of time to make up his mind. He could either leave it alone and let it count one run as a wide; or he could spring upon it like a panther and, with a terrific six, finish the match sensationally. He could play the part either of a Quintus Fabius Maximus Cunctator, or of a sort of Tarzan. The baker concealed beneath a modest and floury exterior a mounting ambition. Here was his chance to show the village. He chose the sort of Tarzan, sprang like a panther, whirled his bat cyclonically, and missed the ball by about a foot and a half. The wicket-keeping publisher had also had time in which to think and to move, and he also had covered the seven feet. True, his movements were less like the spring of a panther than the sideways waddle of an aldermanic penguin. But nevertheless he got there, and when the ball had passed the flashing blade of the baker, he launched a mighty kick at it—stooping to grab it was out of the question—and by an amazing fluke kicked it on to the wicket. Even the ancient umpire had to give the baker out, for the baker was still lying flat on his face outside the crease.

'I was bowling for that,' observed Mr Hodge modestly, strolling up the pitch.

'I had plenty of time to use my hands,' remarked the wicket-keeper to the world at large, 'but I preferred to kick it.'

Donald was impressed by the extraordinary subtlety of the game.

Six to win and three wickets to fall.

The next batsman was a schoolboy of about sixteen, an ingenuous youth with pink cheeks and a nervous smile, who quickly fell a victim to Mr Harcourt, now wide awake and beaming upon everyone. For Mr Harcourt, poet that he was, understood exactly what the poor, pink child was feeling, and he knew that if he played the ancient dodge and pretended to lose the ball in the long grass, it was a hundred to one that the lad would lose his head. The batsman at the other end played the fourth ball of Mr Livingstone's next over hard in the direction of Mr Harcourt. Mr Harcourt rushed towards the spot where it had vanished in the jungle. He groped wildly for it, shouting as he did so, 'Come and help. It's lost.' The pink child scuttered nimbly down the pitch. Six runs to win and two wickets to fall. Mr Harcourt smiled demoniacally.

The crisis was now desperate. The fieldsmen drew nearer and nearer to the batsmen, excepting the youth in the blue jumper. Livingstone balanced himself on his toes. Mr Shakespeare Pollock hopped about almost on top of the batsmen, and breathed excitedly and audibly. Even the imperturbable Mr Southcott discarded the piece of grass which he had been chewing so steadily. Mr Hodge took himself off and put on the Major, who had by now somewhat lived down the quart and a half.

The batsmen crouched down upon their bats and defended stubbornly. A snick through the slips brought a single. A ball which eluded the publisher's gigantic pads brought a bye. A desperate sweep at a straight half-volley sent the ball off the edge of the bat over third-man's head and in normal circumstances would have certainly scored one, and possibly two. But Mr Harcourt was on guard at third-man, and the batsmen, by nature cautious men, one being old and the sexton, the other the postman and therefore a Government official, were taking no risks. Then came another single off a mis-hit, and then an interminable period in which no wicket fell and no run was scored. It was broken at last disastrously, for the postman struck the ball sharply at Mr Pollock, and Mr Pollock picked it up and, in an ecstasy of zeal, flung it madly at the wicket. Two overthrows resulted.

The scores were level and there were two wickets to fall. Silence fell. The gaffers, victims simultaneously of excitement and senility, could hardly raise their pint pots—for it was past 7 o'clock, and the front door of the Three Horseshoes was now as wide open officially as the back door had been unofficially all afternoon.

The Major, his red face redder than ever and his chin sticking out almost as far as the Napoleonic Mr Ogilvy's, bowled a fast half-volley on the leg-stump. The sexton, a man of iron muscle from much digging, hit it fair and square in the middle of the bat, and it flashed like a thunderbolt, waist-high, straight at the youth in the blue jumper. With a shrill scream the youth sprang backwards out of its way and fell over on his back. Immediately behind him, so close were the fieldsmen clustered, stood the mighty Boone. There was no chance of escape for him. Even if he had possessed the figure and the agility to perform back-somersaults, he would have lacked the time. He had been unsighted by the youth in the jumper. The thunderbolt struck him in the midriff like a red-hot cannon-ball upon a Spanish galleon, and with the sound of a drumstick upon an insufficiently stretched drum. With a fearful oath, Boone clapped his hands to his outraged stomach and found that the ball was in the way. He looked at it for a moment in astonishment and then threw it down angrily and started to massage the injured spot while the field rang with applause at the brilliance of the catch.

Donald walked up and shyly added his congratulations. Boone scowled at him.

'I didn't want to catch the bloody thing,' he said sourly, massaging away like mad.

'But it may save the side,' ventured Donald.

'Blast the bloody side,' said Boone.

Donald went back to his place.

The scores were level and there was one wicket to fall. The last man in was the blacksmith, leaning heavily upon the shoulder of the baker, who was going to run for him, and limping as if in great pain. He took guard and looked round savagely. He was clearly still in a great rage.

The first ball he received he lashed at wildly and hit straight up in the air to an enormous height. It went up and up and up, until it became difficult to focus it properly against the deep, cloudless blue of the sky, and it carried with it the hopes and fears of an English village. Up and up it went and then at the top it seemed to hang motionless in the air, poised like a hawk, fighting, as it were, a heroic but forlorn battle against the chief invention of Sir Isaac Newton, and then it began its slow descent.

In the meanwhile things were happening below, on the terrestrial sphere. Indeed, the situation was rapidly becoming what the French call *mouvemente*. In the first place, the blacksmith forgot his sprained ankle and set out at a capital rate for the other end, roaring in a great voice as he went, 'Come on, Joe!' The baker, who was running on behalf of the invalid, also set out, and he also roared 'Come on, Joe!' and side by side, like a pair of high-stepping hackneys, the pair cantered along. From the other end Joe set out on his mission, and he roared 'Come on, Bill!' So all three came on. And everything would have been all right, so far as the running was concerned, had it not been for the fact that the blacksmith and the baker, also very naturally, ran with their heads turned not only upwards but also backwards as well, so that they too gazed at the ball, with an alarming sort of squint and a truly terrific kink in their necks. Half-way down the pitch the three met with a magnificent clang, reminiscent of early, happy days in the tournament-ring at Ashby-de-la-Zouche, and the hopes of the village fell with the resounding fall of their three champions.

But what of the fielding side? Things were not so well with them. If there was doubt and confusion among the warriors of Fordenden, there was also uncertainty and disorganisation among the ranks of the invaders. Their main trouble was the excessive concentration of their forces in the neighbourhood of the wicket. Napoleon laid it down that it was impossible to have too many men upon a battlefield, and he used to do everything in his power to call up every available man for a battle. Mr Hodge, after a swift glance at the ascending ball and a swift glance at the disposition of his troops, disagreed profoundly with the Emperor's dictum. He had too many men, far too many. And all except the youth in the blue silk jumper, and the mighty Boone, were moving towards strategical positions underneath the ball, and not one of them appeared to be aware that any of the others existed. Boone had not moved because he was more or less in the right place, but then Boone was not likely to bring off the catch, especially after the episode of the last ball. Major Hawker, shouting 'Mine, mine!' in a magnificently self-confident voice, was coming up from the bowler's end like a battle-cruiser. Mr Harcourt had obviously lost sight of the ball altogether, if indeed he had ever seen it, for he was running round and round Boone and giggling foolishly. Livingstone and Southcott, the two cracks, were approaching competently. Either of them would catch it easily. Mr Hodge had only to choose between them and, coming to a swift decision, he yelled above the din, 'Yours, Livingstone!' Southcott, disciplined cricketer, stopped dead. Then Mr Hodge made a fatal mistake. He remembered Livingstone's two missed sitters, and he reversed his decision and roared 'Yours, Bobby!' Mr Southcott obediently started again, while Livingstone, who had not heard the second order, went straight on. Captain Hodge had restored the *status quo*.

In the meantime the professor of ballistics had made a lightning calculation of angles, velocities, density of the air, barometer-readings and temperatures, and had arrived at the conclusion that the critical point, the spot which ought to be marked in the photographs with an X, was one yard to the north-east of Boone, and he proceeded to take up station there, colliding on the way with Donald and knocking him over. A moment later Bobby Southcott came racing up and tripped over the recumbent Donald and was shot head first into the Abraham-like bosom of Boone. Boone stepped back a yard under the impact and came down with his spiked boot, surmounted by a good eighteen stone of flesh and blood, upon the professor's toe. Almost simultaneously the portly wicket-keeper, whose movements were a positive triumph of the spirit over the body, bumped the professor from behind. The learned man was thus neatly sandwiched between Tweedledum and Tweedledee, and the sandwich was instantly coverted into a ragout by Livingstone, who made up for his lack of extra weight—for he was always in perfect training—by his extra momentum. And all the time Mr Shakespeare Pollock hovered alertly upon the outskirts like a Rugby scrum-half, screaming American University cries in a piercingly high tenor voice.

At last the ball came down. To Mr Hodge it seemed a long time before the invention of Sir Isaac Newton finally triumphed. And it was a striking testimony to the mathematical and ballistical skill of the professor that the ball landed with a sharp report upon the top of his head. Thence it leapt up into the air a foot or so, cannoned on to Boone's head, and then trickled slowly down the colossal expanse of the wicket-keeper's back, bouncing slightly as it reached the massive lower portions. It was only a foot from the ground when Mr Shakespeare Pollock sprang into the vortex with a last ear-splitting howl of victory and grabbed it off the seat of the wicket-keeper's trousers. The match was a tie. And hardly anyone on the field knew it except Mr Hodge, the youth in the blue jumper, and Mr Pollock himself. For the two batsmen and the runner, undaunted to the last, had picked themselves up and were bent on completing the single that was to give Fordenden the crown of victory. Unfortunately, dazed with their falls, with excitement, and with the noise, they all three ran for the same wicket, simultaneously realised their error, and all three turned and ran for the other—the blacksmith, ankle and all, in the centre and leading by a yard, so that they looked like pictures of the Russian *troika*. But their effort was in vain, for Mr Pollock had grabbed the ball and the match was a tie.

And both teams spent the evening at the Three Horseshoes, and Mr Harcourt made a speech in Italian about the glories of England and afterwards fell asleep in a corner, and Donald got home to Royal Avenue at 1 o'clock in the morning, feeling that he had not learnt very much about the English from his experience of their national game.

A. G. Macdonnell (1895–1941), *England, Their England* (1933).

BETWEEN *the World Wars there were two novelists and short story writers whose styles, utterly different, had a strong influence on young readers and writers. One wrote literary novels of power and importance, the other just wrote elegant, amusing, and trivial entertainments.*

The foremost of those widely imitated authors was Ernest Hemingway and the other was Dornford Yates.

Yates's mannered writing, lush, graceful, a little archaic, witty, was as different from Hemingway's as Earl Grey tea in bone china is from a slug of bourbon from the bottle but it was also in its own way, after school set-books, something of a revelation.

Yates's stories had an old-fashioned Edwardian grace and charm and he wrote about a dream-like world, rich and privileged, in which courteous and thoroughly reliable gentlemen with names such as Crispin Willoughby VC, Pomfret Tudor, Surrey Fettering, Lord St Omer of Peerless, and beautiful ladies with names like Madrigal Stukely, Lady Daffodil Malmorey, Belinda Pomeroy, lived on delightful country estates named Brocade, Footman's Hassock, Palfrey, near villages known as Brooch, Poke Abbas, Dimity Green, and Forage (villains had brutish names such as Douglas Bladder, Major von Blodgenbruck, Goat, and Sweaty). It was heady stuff.

'Dornford Yates' was the pen-name of Major Cecil William Mercer, a first cousin of 'Saki' (H. H. Munro). After university Mercer read law—his father was a solicitor—and was called to the Bar in 1909. He was a Captain during the First World War and a Major during the Second but the 1914–18 war left him with painful and permanent rheumatism so he left the Bar and devoted himself to his writing, which he had got off to a good start in 1911 with a short story in Windsor Magazine *about a small group of amusing gentry whose leader was known as Berry.*

Major Mercer was, by all accounts, a somewhat unlovable person who made many of his friends and relations unhappy, including two wives. His thirty-four best-selling books brought him in a fortune, which did nothing to inhibit his latent egoism and intolerance. After living richly for some time in the Biarritz area of the South of France he ended his years in a splendid castle which he had built in Umtali, Southern Rhodesia.

But no loucheness intruded into his books. His heroes were kindly and gentlemanly to an extravagant degree (they tended to address their women as 'my lady' which could have sounded like a footman addressing a dowager-duchess but in fact came out charmingly in the novels) and the women were all enchantingly attractive and as witty as the men.

It is easy to find a reason why the Dornford Yates stories became so immensely popular after the First World War (over two million sold in Britain and the Commonwealth alone). The stories perpetuated the myth that life in Britain was unchanged by the Great War and was still in a state of Edwardian grace; at White Ladies in 1919 the estate was still aglow with pre-war affluence and leisure, the sun was shining, cook was in the kitchen and all was right with the world. At any rate, Berry's world.

But even more important, perhaps, was that much of life in post-war England was dispirited and drab and Dornford Yates wrote high romance in a fresh and colourful style; it was 'escapist' reading at its most charming. In Hemingway, love was described as something which hung on a hook behind the bathroom door: in the Berry books it was the cool adoration as practised at the French Court of Margaret of Navarre. Dornford Yates's lovers exchanged sweet badinage, touched finger-tips, flirted in the back of the Rolls, and managed to make love without actually doing anything.

Another vital factor was the splendidly unrepentant snobbery which drenched the books. It is a fact which seemed to have escaped George Orwell in his condemnation of boys' stories set in public schools that in escapist literature many readers liked to read about, and perhaps dream for a moment that they were in the hand-made shoes of, characters who were much luckier, more attractive, and richer than themselves. Whatever egalitarian attitudes readers might have struck in public, in the privacy of their reading a great many of them clearly enjoyed a wallow in vicarious snobbery, particularly when it was laid on with the Yates style:

We gave him money, and he rose and uncovered and pulled his white forelock with the antique courtesy of his class.

Berry and Co., 'How Jill's Education was Improved'.

One shudders to think what Orwell might have made of some of Yates's comments. The following not only touches upon the loyalty which decent chaps have towards their old school and their regiment but also has a whiff of good old British xenophobia (Yates disliked all forms of foreigner):

Lock, stock and barrel, Merry Down had been sold to the highest bidder. Of that there was no manner of doubt. What was more to the point was that the purchaser, who had paid a good price, was of English blood, and had known Derry Bagot at Eton, and had soldiered with him, first in South Africa and afterwards in France. The place had passed into good, clean hands and was to be well cared for.

Berry and Co., 'Adele Feste Arrives.'

All Dornford Yates stories had strong plots and idiosyncratic punctuation: where most writers would have put a full stop or a semi-colon, Yates put a . . . or a ———, which helped the action to move smoothly amd swiftly. Moreover, Yates was a pioneer of dialogue which reflected the broken nature, the hesitations, repetitions, and interruptions, of ordinary speech.

The following early Berry story begins on a lovely warm Sunday morning at White Ladies in the Summer of 1919, and ends with Berry wildly misquoting the last verse of 'Drink to Me Only With Thine Eyes':

HOW WILL NOGGIN WAS FOOLED, AND BERRY RODE FORTH AGAINST HIS WILL.

'Who's going to church?' said Daphne, consulting her wrist-watch.

There was a profound silence.

My sister turned to Jill.

'Are you coming?' she said. 'Berry and I are.'

'I beg your pardon,' said her husband.

'Of course you're coming,' said Daphne.

'Not in these trousers. This is the first time I've worn them, and I'm not going to kneel in them for any one.'

'Then you'll change,' said his wife. 'You've plenty of time.'

Berry groaned.

'This is sheer Bolshevism,' he said. 'Is not my soul my own?'

'We shall start,' said Daphne, 'in twenty minutes.'

It was nearly half-past ten in the morning of a beautiful summer day, and we were all taking our ease in the sunshine upon the terrace. It was the first Sunday which we had spent all together at White Ladies for nearly five years.

So far as the eye could see, nothing had changed.

At the foot of the steps the great smooth lawn stretched like a fine green carpet, its shadowed patches yet bright with dew. There were the tall elms and the copper beech and all the proud company of spreading giants—what were five years to them? There was the clump of rhododendrons, a ragged blotch of crimson, seemingly spilled upon the green turf, and there the close box hedge that walled away the rose-garden. And beyond the sunk fence a gap showed an acre or so of Bull's Mead—a great deep meadow, and in it two horses beneath a chestnut tree, their long tails a-swish, sleepily nosing each other to rout the flies; while in the distance the haze of heat hung like a film over the rolling hills. Close at hand echoed the soft impertinence of a cuckoo, and two fat wood-pigeons waddled about the lawn, picking and stealing as they went. The sky was cloudless, and there was not a breath of wind.

The stable clock chimed the half-hour.

My sister returned to the attack.

'Are you coming, Boy?'

'Yes,' said I. 'I am.'

Berry sat up and stared at me.

'Don't be silly,' he said. 'There's a service this morning. Besides, they've changed the lock of the poor-box.'

'I want to watch the Vicar's face when he sees you,' said I.

'It will be a bit of a shock,' said Jonah, looking up from the paper. 'Is his heart all right?'

'Rotten,' said Daphne. 'But that doesn't matter. I sent him a note to warn him yesterday.'

'What did you say?' demanded her husband.

'I said, "*We're back at last, and—don't faint—we're all coming to church tomorrow, and you've got to come back to lunch.*" And now, for goodness sake, go and change.'

'But we shall perspire,' said Berry. 'Profusely. To walk half a mile in this sun is simply asking for it. Besides—'

'What's the car done?' said Jonah. 'I'm going, and I can't hurry with this.' He tapped his short leg affectionately. 'We needn't take Fitch. Boy or I can drive.'

'Right oh,' said my sister, rising. 'Is ten-minutes-to early enough?'

Jonah nodded.

'This,' said Berry, 'is a conspiracy for which you will all pay. Literally. I shall take the plate round, and from you four I shall accept nothing but paper. Possibly I shall—'

Here the girls fell upon him and bore him protesting into the house and out of earshot.

'Who's going to look after the car while we're in church?' said I.

'There's sure to be somebody ready to earn a couple of bob,' said Jonah. 'Besides, we can always disconnect the north-east trunnion, or jack her up and put the wheels in the vestry or something.'

'All right. Only we don't want her pinched.' With a yawn I rose to my feet. 'And now I suppose I'd better go and turn her out.'

'Right oh,' said Jonah, picking up his paper again.

I strolled into the house.

We were proud of the car. She was a 1914 Rolls, and we had bought her at a long price less than a week ago. Fresh from the coach-builder's, her touring body was painted silver-grey, while her bonnet was of polished aluminium. Fitted with every conceivable accessory, she was very good-looking, charming alike to ride or drive, and she went like the wind. In a word, she did as handsome as she was.

It was eight minutes to eleven as we slid past the lodge and on to the Bilberry road.

Before we had covered two furlongs, we swung round a corner to see a smart two-seater at rest by the dusty hedgerow, and a slight dark girl in fresh blue and white standing with one foot on the step, wiping her dainty fingers on a handful of cotton-waste.

'Agatha!' cried Daphne and Jill. 'Stop, Boy, stop!'

Obediently I slowed to a standstill, as my lady came running after us.

'You might have told me,' she panted. 'I never knew you were back. And I am so glad.'

'We only arrived on Friday, dear,' said Daphne, and introduced Berry and me. Jonah, it appeared, had met Miss Deriot at tennis in 1914.

'But you had your hair down then,' he said gravely.

'It's a wonder I haven't got it down now,' said Miss Deriot. 'Why didn't you come along five minutes earlier? Then you could have changed my tire.'

'And why are you driving away from church?' said Jill.

'One of the colts has sprained his shoulder, and we're out of embrocation; so I'm going to get some from Brooch.'

'I'll come with you,' said Berry eagerly, preparing to leave the car. 'I don't like to think of you—'

'Nonsense,' said Daphne, detaining him.

'But supposing she has another puncture?'

'Yes, I can see you mending it on a day like this.'

'It's very kind of you,' said Miss Deriot, with a puzzled smile.

'Don't thank the fool,' said my sister. 'If I thought he'd be the slightest use to you, I'd send him; but he only wants an excuse to get out of going to church.'

'Poor jade,' said her husband. 'I am a knight, a simple starlit knight, a Quixote of today. Your brutish instincts—'

'Carry on, Boy,' said Daphne. I let in the clutch. 'And come over this afternoon, Agatha, and we'll tell you all about everything.'

'Yes, do,' cried Jill.

'All right,' said Miss Deriot. 'So long.'

Three minutes later I was berthing the car close to the lich-gate in the shade of sweet-smelling limes, that made a trembling screen of foliage within the churchyard wall.

As luck would have it, Will Noggin, once a groom in our service and now a trooper of the Dragoon Guards, was leaning lazily against the grey wall, taking his ease. As we drew abreast of him, he stood to attention and saluted, a pleased grin of recognition lighting his healthy face. We greeted him gladly.

'Glad to see you're all right, Will,' said Jill.

'Thank you, miss.'

'Aren't you going to church?' said Daphne.

'Not today, m'm. I'm on leave, and I've 'ad my share o' church parades i' the last four years, m'm.'

We all laughed.

'Well, if you're not going,' said I, 'we want some one to keep an eye on the car.'

'I'll do it gladly, sir.'

'Right oh! She's a pretty piece of goods, isn't she?'

'She is that, sir,' said Will, visibly impressed.

As I followed the others into the porch, I glanced back to see our sentinel walking about his charge, bending an appreciative gaze upon her points.

They were singing the *Venite.*

On the ledge of our old pew lay a note addressed to 'Major Pleydell' in the Vicar's handwriting. When Berry had read it he passed it to Daphne, and I was able to read it over her shoulder.

DEAR MAJOR

Sometimes in the old days you used to read the lessons. I think we should all like it if you would do so today; but don't, if you don't want to.

Yours very sincerely

JOHN BAGOT

In a postscript the writer named the appointed passages of Holy Writ.

As soon as the Psalm had started Berry stepped to the lectern, found his places and cast his eye over the text. Before the second Psalm was finished, he was once more in his place . . .

It was just after the beginning of the Second Lesson that we heard the engine start. There was no mistaking the purr of our Rolls-Royce. For a second the girls and Jonah and I stared at one another, panic-stricken. Then with one impulse we all started instinctively to our feet. As I left the pew I heard Daphne whisper, 'Hsh! We can't all—' and she and Jonah and Jill sank back twittering. Berry's eyes met mine for an instant as I stepped into the aisle. They spoke volumes, but to his eternal credit his voice never faltered.

I almost ran to the porch, and I reached the lich-gate to see our beautiful car, piloted by a man in a grey hat, scudding up the straight white road, while in her wake tore a gesticulating trooper, shouting impotently, ridiculously out-distanced. Even as I watched, the car flashed round a bend and disappeared.

For a moment I stood in the middle of the road, stupefied. Then I heard a horn sounded behind me, and I mechanically stepped to one side. Fifty yards away was the two-seater we had encountered on our way to church.

Frantically I signalled to the girl at the wheel. As I did so, a burst of music signified that the Second Lesson had come to an end.

'Whatever's the matter?' cried Miss Deriot, as she pulled up.

'Somebody's pinched the Rolls. Will you—'

'Of course. Get in. Which way did they go?'

'Straight ahead,' said I, opening the door.

We were well under way before I had taken my seat. As we came to the bend I threw a glance over my shoulder, to see four figures that I knew standing without the lich-gate. They appeared to be arguing. As we turned the corner a stentorian voice yelled—

'The Bloodstock road, sir! I can see their blinkin' dust.'

Perched on one of the lower branches of a wayside oak, Will Noggin was pointing a shaking finger in the direction he named . . .

Three miles short of Bloodstock the little two-seater picks up another puncture (a
routine occurrence in 1919 and very useful in plot construction). The spare wheel
has already been used so Boy and Agatha—not one of Dornford Yates's best girl's
names; more that of a P. G. Wodehouse aunt than a young charmer, but no doubt
more acceptable in 1919—set off on foot towards The Thatcher inn at Bloodstock,
taking a short-cut over the hills and flirting delicately the while ('from the crown
of her broad-brimmed hat to the soles of her buckskin shoes she was the pink of
daintiness').

They reach the top of the final hill and look down on the village:

In the little curved space that fronted the inn the Rolls was standing silent
and unoccupied.

I must have exclaimed, for Agatha was over the stile in an instant, and
asking me what was the matter. Then she saw, and the words died on her
lips. Together we stood spell-bound.

The door of the inn was shut, and there was no one in sight.

My first impulse was to dart down the steps, beat upon the door of the
tavern, and confront the thief. But valour yielded to discretion. The great
thing was to recover the car. I had but a slip of a girl with me, the spot was
a lonely one, and it was more than likely that the highwayman was not
working alone. Besides, Agatha must not be involved in any violence.

I turned to my lady.

'You stay here. I'm going to take her and drive straight to the police-station.
I'll pick up some police and come back just as quickly as ever I can.'

Miss Deriot shook her pretty head.

'I'm coming with you,' she said. 'Carry on.'

'But, my dear—'

'I often wish I wasn't so obstinate.' She spoke meditatively. 'But we're all
like that. Mules aren't in it with the Deriots,' she added, with a dazzling
smile.

'Neither, apparently, are cucumbers,' said I, and with that I began to
descend . . .

Gingerly I stepped into the sandy road and started to cross it a-tiptoe.

Facing towards Bloodstock, the car presented her off side to us.

With the utmost caution I proceeded to negotiate the two spare wheels
and clamber into the driver's seat. As I sat down, Miss Deriot slipped in front
the bonnet and round to the other side. She was opening the high side-door
and my foot was on the self-starter, when I heard the murmur of voices.

We were not a second too soon.

The moment I had started the engine there was a cry, followed by the
clattering of heavy shoes upon cobbles, and as the car slid into the road a
man in a grey hat came tearing out of the inn's courtyard, waving his
arms and yelling like one possessed. Hard on his heels came pounding his
supporters, three of them, all bellowing like bulls.

So much I saw for myself. Agatha, kneeling on the seat by my side, kept me informed of their movements till we swept out of sight.

'He's simply dancing. The one in the grey hat, I mean. Now he's shaking his fist at us. Oh, he's mad. He's thrown his hat on the ground. O-o-o, Boy, he's trying to kick one of the others. Oh, I wish you could see . . .' The merry voice dissolved into peals of laughter . . .

They drive to the local police-station but only a comically exasperated station sergeant is present. The rest of the Force is searching for a gang of car thieves who have already stolen four cars that morning.

Agatha finds it is lunchtime so takes Boy to her home, Broadacre ('a fine old place on the edge of the forest itself, and thither we came without incident, just as an old-fashioned gong was summoning the household to meat'), where he meets her parents. Her father served in the Navy. Not, it hardly needs saying, as a three-badge stoker ('Admiral and Mrs Deriot were kindness itself. First I was given a long, cold, grateful drink. Then the old sailor led me to his own chamber and ministered personally to my wants').

After lunch they set off back to White Ladies. Agatha, as a treat, is allowed to drive the Rolls while Boy passes baroque compliments on her personal appearance, including her hair ('at the moment there is a particularly beautiful tress caressing your left shoulder. And I think you ought to know that the wind is kissing it quite openly. I hope I shan't catch it,' I added cheerfully).

They arrive at White Ladies and park the recovered Rolls in the middle of the stable yard:

As we walked round to the front of the house, 'We won't tell the others that we've found her just yet,' said I. 'We'll hear what they've got to say first.'

'Perhaps they're all out looking for her,' said Agatha.

'Not at all. Daphne's sure to be here somewhere.'

As I spoke we rounded a clump of laurels to see the lady in question comfortably ensconced in a deck-chair upon the lawn. By her side was Jill, seated upon a cushion, one little foot tucked under her, nursing the other's instep with her slim, brown hand. On a rug at her feet lay Jonah, his chin propped between his two palms and a pipe in his mouth.

All three were gazing contentedly across the grass to where the drive swept wide to the foot of the broad grey steps. *There stood a handsome Rolls-Royce, the facsimile of the one from which we had just alighted.*

With a great gasp Agatha stopped dead, and I recoiled as from a spectre. Instinctively we clasped one another.

'It's all right,' I whispered. 'I've seen it too. It'll go away in a moment. Shows what imagination will do.'

'But—it's real!' cried Agatha.

'Real enough, my lady,' said Jonah's voice. He seemed to be speaking from a great distance. 'And I bet you never expected to see her again so soon,' he added, looking at me with a smile.

'To tell you the truth,' said I, 'we didn't.'

As in a dream I watched a dazed and stammering Agatha made welcome and set in a chair by my sister's side. Somebody—Jill, I fancy,—led me to the rug and persuaded me to sit down. Mechanically I started to fumble for a cigarette. Then I heard Jonah talking, and I came to my senses.

'We thought you'd be surprised,' he was saying, 'but I didn't think you'd take it like this. After all, there's nothing uncanny about it.'

'But I don't understand—'

'Listen. Will Noggin was sitting in the car when he heard a crash, and there was a fellow lying in the middle of the road, about fifty yards away, with a push-bike beside him. Naturally Will jumped out and ran to his help. The man seemed to be having a fit, and Will was just loosening his collar, when he heard the engine start and saw the Rolls moving. He left the chap in the road and ran like mad, but he was too late. Nobody ever saw the fellow with the push-bike again. Of course he was one of the gang, and his fall was a put-up job to get Will out of the way. Pretty smart—what?

'Well, you hadn't been gone five minutes when Fitch arrived on his motor-bike. He'd come to bring us a can of petrol, for after we'd left he remembered the tank was almost empty.

'That gave me a bit of hope. If they stuck to the main road you were pretty well bound to catch them, for Fitch swore they'd never get five miles. But, of course, they might turn off. So I thought the rest of us had better follow and search the by-roads for all we were worth. So I sat on Fitch's carrier with the can under one arm, and Daphne commandeered the curate's push-bike and sent Berry after us.'

'Isn't he back yet?' said I, looking round.

'Not yet,' said Jonah, with a grin.

'And doesn't he know she's found?'

'That pleasure is still awaiting him. Well, Fitch was right. We left the Bloodstock road for the second time at Dew Thicket, and at the foot of the hill there she was, dry as a bone, but as right as rain.'

'Abandoned?'

'Apparently. Anyway, there was nobody in sight. I sent Fitch after you and drove her home. Fitch had a burst directly he'd left me, and had to walk back to Bilberry.'

'Is that all?' said I.

'Well, it's enough, isn't it?'

'Not nearly,' said I, rising to my feet. 'Kindly accompany me to the stables.'

'What do you mean, Boy?' cried Jill.

'Sh!' said I. 'Come and see.'

In silence I led the way, Agatha treading solemnly by my side. As we turned under the archway that led to the stable-yard—

'You see,' I said, carelessly, 'we, too, have met with some success.'

The Rolls was standing where I had left her, waiting to be backed into the garage.

My sister gave a cry and caught at Jonah's arm. Jonah started violently and smothered an exclamation. Jill put one hand to her eyes, as if to brush away a vision.

There was a long silence.

At length I turned to Jonah.

'I fear that you were hasty, brother. A moment's reflection will show you that you and Fitch have spoiled some poor car-owner's day. Let me suggest that you return your ill-gotten gains to the foot of the hill beyond Dew Thicket without delay. As a matter of fact, I know the police are very concerned about this theft. It was the fourth in the district this morning.'

Fitch came forward, touching his hat.

'It's a mistake anybody might make, sir. They're as like as two peas.' He pointed to the car. 'She's the spit of ours, she is.'

'Don't be silly,' said I. 'I admit they're exactly alike, but that's ours.'

Fitch shook his head.

'Different chassis number, sir, to say nothing of the number-plates.'

I stared at him. Then—

'Nonsense,' I said sturdily.

'It's a fact, sir. The one in the front's ours. I'm afraid you've stole somebody else's car.'

*   *   *

We had returned to the front of the house and were wondering what to do, when our attention was attracted by a sudden outburst of cries and the noise of a car's tires tearing at the road. This lay but a hundred yards away on the farther side of the brown stream by which the lawn was edged. For the length of a cricket pitch the hedgerow bounding the highway was visible from where we stood, and as this was not more than four feet high, we were able to observe a scene which was clearly but the prologue to a drama in which we were presently to appear.

Under the explosive directions of a man in a grey hat, who was standing upright and holding on to the wind-screen, frantic efforts were being made to turn what seemed to be a small touring car. Even as we looked, a savage gesture in our direction suggested that our friend was identifying the Rolls by our side as stolen property for the benefit of four individuals who crouched timorously behind him. To my consternation I observed that these were no less than an inspector and three constables of the County Police.

The next minute the car had been turned round and was being driven rapidly back to our lodge-gates.

'Leave them to me,' said Jonah, quietly. 'Go and sit down on the lawn, all of you. I'll fix them.'

*   *   *

'That's the fellow,' said Grey Hat, in a shaking voice, 'and that's his accomplice.' He pointed a fat hand at myself and Agatha in turn.

'I beg your pardon,' said Jonah. Grey Hat turned and looked him up and
down. 'Were you wanting anything? I mean, I live here.'

'I don't know who you are,' came the reply. 'But that's my car, and those
are the people who stole it.'

'One thing at a time. My name's Mansel.'

'I'm the Chief Constable of the County.'

'Good. Now, about the car. I was under the impression that it was mine.'

'Don't try and bluff me, sir,' roared the other. 'You know perfectly well
that that car was stolen from the outskirts of Bloodstock only a few hours
ago. You're a receiver, sir, a common—' He checked himself with an effort.
'Inspector!' The officer addressed came forward and saluted. 'Caution the
three of them.'

'Hadn't you better identify your property first?' said Jonah. 'I mean, I don't
want to interfere, but if it's a question of our arrest—'

The Inspector hesitated, and the Chief Constable's face took on a darker
shade of red. He was a coarse-looking man, generously designed and expensively over-dressed. For a moment I thought he was going to strike Jonah.
Then he caught a heavy underlip in his teeth, turned on his heel, and strode
to the Rolls-Royce.

He cast a proprietor's eye over her points. Then he stepped behind her as
though to come to her other side. The next second he was back and shaking
his fist in Jonah's face.

'So you've had the infernal audacity to alter the number-plates, have you?'
he yelled. 'Thought to bluff me, I suppose. You impudent—'

'One moment,' said Jonah steadily. 'Without looking at the dash, tell me
your chassis number. Your chauffeur should know it.'

'One double seven eight,' came parrot-fashion from the lips of the gentleman referred to.

'Thank you,' said Jonah.

Grey Hat almost ran to the Rolls, tore open the bonnet, and stared at the
dash—stared . . . .

We waited in a silence so charged with expectancy as to be almost
unbearable.

At last the Chief Constable straightened his back. His eyes were bulging
and his face redder than ever. Twice he essayed to speak without success.
Then—

'I said it was my car,' said Jonah placidly.

For a moment Grey Hat stood looking at him. Then, muttering something
about 'a mistake', he started to lurch towards the police car. As the
officers turned shamefacedly to follow their chief, Jonah's parade voice rang
out.

'Stop!' At the word of command, master and men stood still where they were. 'My friends and I have been openly accused of felony and threatened with arrest.'

The Chief Constable swallowed before replying.

'I was mistaken,' he said thickly. 'I—I apologize.'

'You mean to say you believed that to be your car?'

'I did.'

'Why?'

'It's exactly like it.'

'There must be some difference.'

'There's no difference at all. If mine were here, I'd defy you to tell them apart.'

'Do you seriously suggest that I shouldn't know my own car?'

'I do.'

'And that such a mistake on my part would be excusable?'

'Certainly.'

'Thank you,' said Jonah. 'That excusable mistake was made this morning. My car was stolen and sought for. Your car was found. If you will accompany me to the stables, I shall be happy to restore it to you at once.'

Grey Hat started forward, his face transfigured with excitement and relief.

'You mean to say—' he began.

'Come, sir,' said Jonah icily. 'I feel sure that the ladies will excuse your withdrawal.'

*　　*　　*

It was half an hour later, just when we were finishing tea, that a cry from Jill made us all turn to follow her gaze down the curling drive.

Twenty paces away was Berry, plodding slowly in our direction, wheeling a tired-looking bicycle. His clothes were thick with dust, his collar was like a piece of wet rag, and on his face there was a look of utter and profound resignation.

As we started to our feet—

'Don't touch me,' he said 'I'm leading in the Marathon race. The conditions are fearful. Competitors are required not only to walk, but at the same time to propel a bicycle, the hind tire of which must be deflated. You're only allowed five falls, and I've used four of them.' With a final effort he reached the edge of the lawn and laid the bicycle gently on its side. '"How we brought the good news from Aix to Ghent",' he continued. 'Yes, I see the car, but I'm not interested. During the last five hours my life has been so crowded with incident that there is no room for anything else. Isn't there a cycling club about here I can join? I've always fancied a grey sweater.'

'Did I hear you say that you had fallen, brother?' said I.

'You did. Four times were these noble limbs prostrated in the dust. The first time was when the handle-bars came off. Oh, it's a beautiful machine.' Solemnly he waited for the laughter to subside. 'But she doesn't turn easily.

If my blood counts, there are at least three corners in the County that are forever England. And now will somebody fetch the vicar? I shan't last long. And some drinks.' He stretched himself upon the grass. 'Several drinks. All together in a large vessel.'

Jill fled, weak with laughter, to execute his commands. Berry proceeded to remove his collar and tie.

'I can't think,' he said suddenly, 'why they call them safety bicycles. I suppose it's because they strike only on the box.' He turned to Daphne. 'Since I left you this morning, woman, I have walked with Death. Oh, more than once. Of course I've walked without him, too. Miles and miles.' He groaned. 'I never knew there was so much road.'

'Didn't you do any riding?' said Jonah. 'I know they're called push-bikes, but that's misleading. Lots of people ride them. That's what the saddle's for.'

'Foul drain,' said my brother-in-law, 'your venomous bile pollutes the crystal flood of my narration. Did I ride? That was the undoing of the sage. When he recovered consciousness for the second time, it was to discover that the chain was missing and that the back tire was windless. In my endeavours to find the chain I lost myself. That reminds me. I must put an advertisement in *The Times* to the effect that any one returning a bicycle-chain to White Ladies will be assaulted. I have no desire to be reminded of to-day. If anybody had told me you could cover about fifty miles of open road in England without meeting anything but road-hogs, who not only failed to stop when I hailed them, but choked and blinded me with their filthy dust, I should have prayed for his soul. And not a pub open!'

He stopped to watch with a glistening eye the approach of Jill, bearing a tankard in one hand and a large jug of some beverage in the other.

'What is it?' he said.

'Shandy-gaff.'

'Heaven will reward you, darling, as I shan't.' He took a long draught. 'And yet I don't know. I've got an old pair of riding-breeches I don't want, if they're any use to you.'

There was a shriek from Agatha and Jill.

'Is anybody going to church?' said Daphne, consulting her wrist-watch.

Berry choked.

Gravely I regarded him.

'Run along and change,' said I. 'And you can return the curate his bicycle at the same time. Besides, a walk'll do you good.'

'Don't tempt me,' he replied. 'Two hours ago I registered a vow. I shall drink no water until it is accomplished.'

'Let's hear it,' said I.

'To offer no violence to a fool for six months,' said Berry, refilling his tankard. 'By the way, you'll have to be careful when you take off my boots. They're very full of foot this evening.' He sank back and closed his eyes. 'You know I never look at the almanac, but before I was up this morning I knew that this was a blue-letter day.'

'How?' said his wife.

'I left a stud within the bath, and heard Jonah find it.' He spread out a dramatic arm.

> 'And he thereon did only sit,
>   So blind he couldn't see,
> And then the fat-head yelled and swore,
>   Not at himself, but me.'

Dornford Yates (Major Cecil William Mercer) (1885–1960), *Berry and Co.* (1920).

THE *light comedy-of-manners featuring the well-bred rich was also the province of a lady novelist, Angela Thirkell, of whom something weightier might well have been expected considering her background.*

Mrs Thirkell, later in life a tall, willowy figure swathed either in clouds of lemon tulle or black, was the daughter of the classical scholar, critic, and Oxford Professor of Poetry, J. M. Mackail. Her mother was the only daughter of the Pre-Raphaelite painter, Sir Edward Burne-Jones. Her brother was the novelist and biographer, Denis Mackail, and Stanley Baldwin and Rudyard Kipling were cousins. After being brilliant at school as a gymnast, pianist, and linguist she went to a finishing school in Paris and in 1911, at the age of 21, married a singer, J. Campbell MacInnes and had two sons; one was the brilliant writer and eccentric, Colin MacInnes. The marriage was a disaster and Mr MacInnes was divorced. Mrs MacInnes then fell in love with a Tasmanian engineer, George Thirkell, and took her boys off to live a life of simple domesticity in a small suburban house in Melbourne. Another son was born but that marriage also failed, and in 1930 Mrs Thirkell admitted defeat and returned to her parents' home in Kensington. Here this difficult, erudite, strangely unemotional lady, increasingly formidable and remote even to her own children, began to write tranquil, charming, funny novels.

She wrote over thirty books and the most successful were her country books. These featured more or less the same large cast of characters and were set in her modern version of Trollope's 'Barsetshire'.

Perhaps not surprisingly, the local gentry who pursued such a comfortable, trivial, amusing social round in her books were not the sort of people she liked much. Jan Struther and Dornford Yates wrote of people they would love to have resembled but Angela Thirkell, like E. M. Delafield and E. F. Benson, did not admire her characters.

The picture she painted with such unsympathetic accuracy was of a tranquil, very English way of life which was about to disappear for ever.

For instance, the placid, almost torpid existence lived by Mrs Brandon with her

*daughter, Delia, and her epicene son, Francis, in a lovely old house in the sleepy
village of Pomfret Madrigal (a name worthy of Dornford Yates):*

Mrs Brandon carried her flowers into the little room known as the flower-
room, along one wall of which ran a long marble slab with four basins in it,
relics of a former Brandon with four gardening daughters. She then fetched
yesterday's flowers from the hall and living-rooms, refilled the vases, and
began to arrange her flowers. This she always called 'my housekeeping',
adding that it took more time than all her other duties put together, but she
couldn't bear anyone else to do it, thus giving an impression of one who was
a martyr to her feeling for beauty. As a matter of fact she spoke no more
than the truth, for Cook arranged the menus, and Nurse looked after the
linen and did all the sewing and darning, so that Mrs Brandon would have
been hard put to it to find anything useful to do . . .

*Crises in the Brandon family are on the small side, for example, on which day the
picnic should be held. The young people want to make it Wednesday so that their
friends can come but Mrs Brandon wants to visit rich Aunt Sissie on Wednesday
so the children taunt her for being after Aunt Sissie's money. And then the maid,
Rose, wants to change her afternoon off:*

'Francis, darling,' said Mrs Brandon, who had collected another great bunch
of sweet peas and was holding them thoughfully to her face, 'we *must* go to
Aunt Sissie on Wednesday.'

'Yes, I think we must,' said Francis. 'Anyone who didn't know you would
think you were mercenary, darling, but I know you haven't the wits to
concentrate. You've got a kind heart though, and anyone who looked at you
sympathizing with people would think you really cared. Give me a smell of
those sweet peas.'

Mrs Brandon held up the flowers and Francis sniffed them violently.

'There are few pleasures like really burrowing one's nose into sweet peas,'
he said, much refreshed. 'You're a bit like them, darling, all pinky-purple
colours and a nice smell. Do you want your tall handsome son to help you
to take the flowers to the church? It will look so well if we go together, and
everyone will say what a comfort I am to you and what a wonderful mother
you have been.'

Mrs Brandon laughed with a great good humour and gave Francis a long
basket to fill with tall flowers. Then they walked across the garden, up
a lane, past the Cow and Sickle, and so into the churchyard by the side
gate.

Mrs Brandon could never be thankful enough that her husband had died
at Cannes and been decently buried in the English cemetery. If he had been
buried in Pomfret Madrigal church she would have had to keep his grave
and memory decorated with flowers. If she had undertaken this pious duty
herself she would certainly have forgotten it and left the flowers, a wet mush

of decay, to scandalize the village. If she had told Turpin the gardener to look after it, not only would the village have been scandalized, but he would have chosen the stiffest asters and dahlias like rosettes, bedded out begonias, even cultivated immortelles for the purpose, and given the little plot the air of a County Council Park. The only alternative Mrs Brandon could imagine was to have what might be called an all-weather grave, sprinkled with chips from the stone-mason's yard, or battened down under a granite slab, and to do this to the unconscious Mr Brandon would have seemed to his widow a little unkind. So Mr Brandon reposed at Cannes and a sum of money was paid yearly to keep his memory as green as the climate allowed, while a neat tablet in Pomfret Madrigal church bore witness in excellent lettering to the dates of his birth and death.

Pomfret Madrigal church was of great antiquity, being the remains of the former Abbey of that name. Part of it was supposed to date from the reign of King John, but as that particular part was considered by archaeologists to be buried in the thick chancel walls, everyone was at liberty to have his own opinion. A few years previously the Vicar, Mr Miller, a newcomer and an ardent enthusiast for his new church, had discovered faint traces of colour in a very dark corner high up on the south wall. Mrs Brandon, always pleased to give pleasure, had made a handsome contribution towards a fund for church restoration, a learned professor famed for extracting mural paintings from apparently blank walls had visited the church, and the work had been put in hand. After several months' slow, careful, and to the Vicar maddeningly exciting work, Professor Lancelot had brought to light two square feet of what might have been patterned border, and a figure, apparently standing on its head, which was variously identified as Lucifer, Fulke de Pomfret who had impounded some of the Abbey pigs in revenge for alleged depredations on his lady's herb garden, and Bishop Wyckens who had made himself extremely unpopular with the Abbey about the matter of some waste land over at Starveacres. However, all these differences of opinion were drowned and forgotten in Professor Lancelot's supreme discovery that the fragment of border might almost with certainty be attributed to Nicholas de Hogpen, an extremely prolific artist practically none of whose work was known. Others supported the view that the work should stand to the credit of an unknown monk whose work in Northumberland was described in an imperfect MS. which the owner, Mr Amery P. Otis of Brookline, Mass., would not allow anyone to see. The correspondence on this subject, beginning in the *Journal of the Society of Barsetshire Archaeologists*, had overflowed into the *Sunday Times* and *Observer*, causing several correspondents to write to the Editor about yellow-backed tits who had nested near mural paintings, or the fact that their great-great-grandfather had as a child sat on the knee of a very old man whose grandfather said he remembered someone who said he had heard of the Reformation. The Vicar read every word of correspondence and pasted all the cuttings into an album, as also a photograph from the

Daily Spectrum with the caption 'Rector of Pomfret Madrigal says Mural Paintings unique', and an inset called The Rev. Milker.

Since these eventful doings the paintings had gradually receded into the walls and were now invisible except to the eye of faith, which could often be found in the tourist season, guide book in hand, twisting itself almost upside down in its efforts to make out the inverted figure.

The July morning was now very hot. The little churchyard, on a slope facing the south, was shimmering with heat, and the flowers in the jam jars and Canadian salmon tins on the poorer graves were already wilting. In spite of her shady hat and her parasol of a most becoming shade of pink, Mrs Brandon was glad to get into the coolness of the little church. She slipped into a pew, knelt for a moment, and then emerged, apparently spiritually much refreshed.

'What *do* you say, darling, when you do that?' asked Francis. 'I've often wondered.'

Mrs Brandon looked guilty.

'I never quite know,' she said. 'I try to concentrate, but the only way I can concentrate is to hold my breath very hard, and that stops me thinking. And when I shut my eyes I see all sorts of spokes and fireworks. I always mean to ask to be nicer and kinder, but things like Rose wanting to change her afternoon out, or Aunt Sissie's letter, come into my mind at once. But I did have one very good idea, which was that if Rose changes her afternoon we could have the picnic that day and kill two birds with one stone.'

'People have been excommunicated for less than that,' said Francis.

Angela Thirkell (1890–1961), *The Brandons* (1939).

M ANY *successful writers of humorous prose could express themselves well in verse; Thackeray, Thomas Hardy, Kingsley Amis spring to mind; also the Australian outback writers and the American frontier poets; almost all* Punch *writers, including all the editors and many contributors such as A. P. Herbert and A. A. Milne, and almost all the* New Yorker *staffers, notably Dorothy Parker, E. B. White, Thurber, Peter de Vries, and John Updike.*

Oddly, it rarely worked well the other way round; very few good poets were successful at writing humorous prose. Indeed, very few seem to have tried. Perhaps the two forms of expression were naturally incompatible in the same mysterious way that many trombone players can also play the piano but very few pianists can play the trombone.

A splendid exception (but not as a trombone player) was Dylan Thomas, a poet of colour and power and spiritual depth who could also write exuberant, naturalistic, comic prose.

Dylan Thomas was a writer of poetry from the days when he edited the Swansea Grammar School magazine, but to earn a living he had to write a great deal of prose and dialogue; as a journalist, for the BBC, and as a scriptwriter for films. Eventually he published as many books of prose and dialogue as he did of poetry; seven of each.

In the following autobiographical piece, from Portrait of the Artist as a Young Dog, *Dylan Thomas describes an episode which occurred when he was aged 17 and a reporter on the* South Wales Daily Post.

He is on the last drunken lap of a Christmas-time pub-crawl in Swansea:

OLD GARBO

We crawled down Strand alleys by the side of the mortuary, through a gas-lit lane where hidden babies cried together, and reached the 'Fishguard' door as a man, muffled like Mr Evans, slid out in front of us with a bottle or a black-jack in one gloved hand. The bar was empty. An old man whose hands trembled sat behind the counter, staring at his turnip watch.

'Merry Christmas, Pa.'

'Good evening, Mr F.'

'Drop of rum, Pa.'

A red bottle shook over two glasses.

'Very special poison, son.'

'This'll make your eyes bulge,' said Mr Farr.

My iron head stood high and firm, no sailors' rum could rot the rock of my belly. Poor Leslie Bird the port-sipper, and little Gil Morris who marked dissipation under his eyes with a blacklead every Saturday night. I wished they could have seen me now, in the dark, stunted room with photographs of boxers peeling on the wall.

'More poison, Pa,' I said.

'Where's the company to-night? gone to the Riviera?'

'They're in the snuggery, Mr F., there's a party for Mrs Prothero's daughter.'

In the back room, under a damp royal family, a row of black-dressed women on a hard bench sat laughing and crying, short glasses lined by their Guinnesses. On an opposite bench two men in jerseys drank appreciatively, nodding at the emotions of the women. And on the one chair, in the middle of the room, an old woman, with a bonnet tied under her chins, a feather boa, and white gym shoes, tittered and wept; above the rest. We sat on the men's bench. One of the two touched his cap with a sore hand.

'What's the party, Jack?' asked Mr Farr. 'Meet my colleague, Mr Thomas; this is Jack Stiff, the mortuary keeper.'

Jack Stiff spoke from the side of his mouth. 'It's Mrs Prothero there. We call her Old Garbo because she isn't like her, see. She had a message from the hospital about an hour ago, Mrs Harris's Winifred brought it here, to say her second daughter's died in pod.'

'Baby girl dead, too,'—said the man at his side.

'So all the old girls came round to sympathize, and they made a big collection for her, and now she's beginning to drink it up and treating round. We've had a couple of pints from her already.'

'Shameful!'

The rum burned and kicked in the hot room, but my head felt tough as a hill and I could write twelve books before morning and roll the 'Carlton' barmaid, like a barrel, the length of Tawe sands.

'Drinks for the troops!'

Before a new audience, the women cried louder, patting Mrs Prothero's knees and hands, adjusting her bonnet, praising her dead daughter.

'What'll you have, Mrs Prothero, dear?'

'No, have it with me, dear, best in the house.'

'Well, a Guinness tickles my fancy.'

'And a little something in it, dear.'

'Just for Margie's sake, then.'

'Think if she was here now, dear, singing *One of the Ruins* or *Cockles and Mussels*; she had a proper madam's voice.'

'Oh, don't, Mrs Harris!'

'There, we're only bucking you up. Grief killed the cat, Mrs Prothero. Let's have a song together, dear.'

> 'The pale moon was rising above the grey mountain,
> The sun was declining beneath the blue sea,
> When I strolled with my love to the pure crystal fountain,'

Mrs Prothero sang.

'It was her daugher's favourite song,' said Jack Stiff's friend.

Mr Farr tapped me on the shoulder; his hand fell slowly from a great height and his thin, bird's voice spoke from a whirring circle on the ceiling. 'A drop of out-of-doors for you and me.' The gamps and bonnets, the white gym-shoes, the bottles and the mildew king, the singing mortuary man, the *Rose of Tralee*, swam together in the snuggery; two small men, Mr Farr and his twin brother, led me on an ice-rink to the door, and the night air slapped me down. The evening happened suddenly. A wall slumped over and knocked off my trilby; Mr Farr's brother disappeared under the cobbles. Here came a wall like a buffalo; dodge him, son. Have a drop of angostura, have a drop of brandy, Fernet Branca, Polly, Ooo! the mother's darling! have a hair of the dog.

'Feeling better now?'

I sat in a plush chair I had never seen before, sipping a mothball drink and appreciating an argument between Ted Williams and Mr Farr. Mr Farr was saying sternly: 'You came in here to look for sailors.'

'No, I didn't then,' said Ted. 'I came for local colour.'

The notices on the walls were: '"The Lord Jersey." Prop.: Titch Thomas.'

'No Betting.' 'No Swearing, B—— you.' 'The Lord helps Himself, but you mustn't.' 'No Ladies allowed, except Ladies.'

'This is a funny pub,' I said. 'See the notices?'

'Okay now?'

'I'm feeling upsydaisy.'

'There's a pretty girl for you. Look, she's giving you the glad.'

'But she's got no nose.'

My drink, like winking, had turned itself into beer. A hammer tapped. 'Order! order!' At a sound in a new saloon a collarless chairman with a cigar called on Mr Jenkins to provide *The Lily of Laguna*.

'By request,' said Mr Jenkins.

'Order! order! for Katie Sebastopol Street. What is it, Katie?'

She sang the National Anthem.

'Mr Fred Jones will supply his usual dirty one.'

A broken baritone voice spoiled the chorus; I recognized it as my own, and drowned it.

A girl of the Salvation Army avoided the arms of two firemen and sold them a *War Cry*.

A young man with a dazzling handkerchief round his head, black and white holiday shoes with holes for the toes, and no socks, danced until the bar cried: 'Mabel!'

Ted clapped at my side. 'That's style! "Nijinsky of the Night-world," there's a story! Wonder if I can get an interview?'

'Half a crack,' said Mr Farr.

'Don't make me cross.'

A wind from the docks tore up the street, I heard the rowdy dredger in the bay and a boat blowing to come in, the gas-lamps bowed and bent, then again smoke closed about the stained walls with George and Mary dripping above the women's bench, and Jack Stiff whispered, holding his hand in front of him like the paw of an animal: 'Old Garbo's gone.'

The sad and jolly women huddled together.

'Mrs Harris's little girl got the message wrong. Old Garbo's daugher's right as rain, the baby was born dead. Now the old girls want their money back, but they can't find Garbo anywhere.' He licked his hand. 'I know where she's gone.'

His friend said: 'To a boozer over the bridge.'

In low voices the women reviled Mrs Prothero, liar, adulteress, mother of bastards, thief.

'She got you know what.'

'Never cured it.'

'Got Charlie tattooed on her.'

'Three and eight she owes me.'

'Two and ten.'

'Money for my teeth.'

'One and a tanner out of my Old Age.'

Who kept filling my glass? Beer ran down my cheek and my collar. My mouth was full of saliva. The bench spun. The cabin of the 'Fishguard' tilted. Mr Farr retreated slowly; the telescope twisted, and his face, with wide and hairy nostrils, breathed against mine.

'Mr Thomas is going to get sick.'

'Mind your brolly, Mrs Arthur.'

'Take his head.'

The last tram clanked home. I did not have the penny for the fare. 'You get off here. Careful!' The revolving hill to my father's house reached to the sky. Nobody was up. I crept to a wild bed, and the wallpaper lakes converged and sucked me down.

Sunday was a quiet day, though St Mary's bells, a mile away, rang on, long after church time, in the holes of my head. Knowing that I would never drink again, I lay in bed until midday dinner and remembered the unsteady shapes and far-off voices of the ten o'clock town. I read the newspapers. All news was bad that morning, but an article called 'Our Lord was a Flower-lover' moved me to tears of bewilderment and contrition.

Dylan Thomas (1914–53), *Portrait of the Artist as a Young Dog* (1940).

———

AUSTRALIAN *humorous journalism of the thirties and forties is ably repre-sented by Lennie Lower, a much read, much loved and none too stable Sydney character (he was once fired from the* Australian Women's Weekly *by its owner, Sir Frank Packer, for allegedly writing something saucy about Noel Coward), who one night might be found by his friends in a state of dismal depression and the next night enjoying an eccentric and alcoholic spree.*

Most of Lennie Lower's published books were collections of pieces from his newspaper columns but his first book, published in 1930, was the hugely successful comic novel, Here's Luck.

Here's Luck *recounts the tribulations of Jack Gudgeon, aged 48, a male chau-vinist, rate-owing denizen of one of Sydney's poorer suburbs, whose wife suddenly ups and leaves him. His attempts to look after himself and his layabout adolescent son Stanley result in a series of the sort of drunken catastrophes which Lennie Lower might well have experienced in real life. There is so much boozing, coarse eating, and introspection that the hero Jack Gudgeon could well be described as The Thinking Man's Ocker.*

The story begins with Jack's son Stanley being disappointed in love and revealing to his Jack-disliking mother and his Jack-hating aunt Gertrude that he has decided to go abroad to forget.

Jack tells the story:

I smoked for a while and then went downstairs after salvaging one of my ties which Stanley had borrowed and thrown under the bed with the rest of his discarded clothing. One thing about Stanley, he is a methodical boy and pitches his clothes on the floor in symmetrical heaps where they can be easily turned over with the foot when anything is required. The two women were waiting for me at the foot of the stairs when I came down. I felt like going back. Stanley's aunt folded her arms, shot a glance at the wife, pursed her lips, and shrugged her shoulders. Without speaking she managed to say that this was the plague they had been speaking about. I knew immediately that Stanley had seized his opportunity. He's like that. And his mother will back him up on any fool thing so long as I'm made to look ridiculous.

'What have you been doing to Stanley?' snapped the wife.

'Stanley who?' I asked.

Silly, I know, but I wasn't prepared.

'What's wrong with him?' I added.

'He is going to South Africa to hunt elephants,' she said slowly.

Aunt Gertrude spoke up. She has a voice like a knife that has been left stuck in a lemon too long.

'He is going to South Africa to hunt elephants,' she said slowly in a hanged-by-the-neck-till-you-are-dead tone.

Elephants mind you! But I had got used to this sort of thing.

'Well, well!' I said, 'I suppose he'll need to take his lunch; or perhaps he can get lunch over there. I think they do have that sort of thing. Mealies and kopies and veldts and things. Of course, he'll find it a little different but—'

'John!' said my wife.

If there's anything I hate, it's 'John'.

'The poor boy is going to South Africa to try to forget. His hopes are blasted—'

'Agatha!' I said.

She blushed slightly.

'To think that the wife of my bosom—'

'Bosom your grandmother!'

There are times when the veneer of refinement peels off Agatha.

She led the way into the drawing-room. Stanley was there, standing with arms folded and a look of hopeless determination on his face—or determined hopelessness. Properly blasted. He was gazing out the window as if he already saw the elephants advancing with writhing tentacles.

Agatha sank into a chair, suddenly overcome.

'He is going to South Africa—to hunt elephants!' she whispered brokenly.

'Elephants! He is going to hunt them in South Africa!' she moaned. 'Elephants—Africa—South!'

'Hunt—going—to,' I added, to help her out of the mess.

Aunt Gertrude sniffed.

Her sniffs remind me, somehow, of the dried husk-like skin of a snake, after it has been shed.

'Ah, Stanley!' moaned the wife, warming up to the work.

'Don't go to South Africa!'

It made me mad to see her pretending to take him seriously.

'I will. I am. I shall—must!' said Stanley.

I could see that with all the encouragement he was getting he had become rather taken with the idea.

'But, Stanley—it's so far away! Couldn't you go to the zoo?'

'Zoo!' hooted Stanley. 'Zoo! What zoo!'

It sounded like the war-cry of the Randwick Rovers.

His eye-balls seemed to pop out.

'I don't want those lop-eared, peanut elephants! I want elephants that are wild! That crouch ready to spring and tear one limb from limb with their claws! Elephants!' he concluded with a short of triumph.

'But, Stan; elephants don't have have claws,' said Agatha.

'They'll wish they had before I'm finished with them,' said Stanley fiercely.

'Ah, let him go and hunt elephants if he wants to—the poor boy,' put in Gertrude. If he's brought home mangled beyond recognition perhaps he (me) will see what a heartless brute he is!'

Agatha seemed to think this over for a while and then with an air of comparative cheerfulness straightened her dress and remarked: 'Oh, well; I suppose if he wants to go, he wants to go.'

This seemed to me profound, but sound. There was absolutely no argument against it.

'Elephants!' muttered Stanley, gazing at me and licking his lips.

'Bah!' I exclaimed, turning to him, 'what have elephants ever done to you that you should pick on them like this! Poor little elephants that never said a harsh word—who woke you up to this damned elephant rot, anyhow?'

'Well, Stanley, if you've made up your mind that's all there is about it,' cut in Gertrude.

'Yes, Yes,' sobbed Agatha.

I closed my mouth. It only needed me to object to all this rot; to put my foot down firmly and forbid it, and the pair of them would have bundled him off to South Africa immediately. I know women. That is, I know that much about them. Of course this elephant talk was all damned rot. Stanley's idea of amusement at my expense. Any unpleasantness where I was the goat could always command Agatha's and Gertrude's hearty support. I treated the matter as a joke—fool that I was.

Agatha went out of the room, presumably to cut a few sandwiches for Stanley to take to South Africa.

Gertrude walked over to Stanley and put her hand on his shoulder, 'Stanley,' she said, 'be very careful in South Africa. Don't go rushing in among the elephants and hurting yourself—'

'That's the way. One at a time,' I said heartily. 'I bet they laugh their trunks off when they spot him.'

I got the snake-skin sniff again.

'And always wear your goloshes,' she went on. 'I'm sure those jungles are not properly drained—and flannel next to your skin, and be careful crossing the roads at intersections, and *don't* speak to any strange men.'

'And wash behind your ears and see if you can bring home an ant-eater,' I said.

I pronounced it 'aunt-eater' and, thinking that was good enough to exit on, I exited, with the honours of the last word thick upon me.

The next few hours I spent roaming about the house waiting for dinner. Stanley had gone out. I strolled into the kitchen two or three times. They were both sitting there; Agatha sobbing loudly behind her handkerchief each time I entered, and Gertrude eyeing me as she would a sick python, and saying, 'Poor dear', to Agatha and patting her on the hand. It was impressed upon me that I was as welcome as a leprous gorilla at a wake, but it was some time before it dawned on me that there wasn't going to be any dinner!

This was over the odds! Even if all this tomfoolery was true and Stanley was going to South Africa; and supposing everybody was all torn to shreds with sorrow, and that—a man's dinner is his dinner. A man must eat though the earth collapse and the heavens roll together as a scroll. There is a limit to everything. It struck me that it would be a pretty good idea to go to South Africa and take Stanley. A man could at least fry a slab of elephant to keep him going between meals.

I was beginning to get a bit nasty tempered, when the front door opened and Stanley came in. He looked a bit down in the mouth.

'Look here, Stan,' I said, going up to him. 'Are there enough of these blasted elephants to go round? Couldn't we share them between us? We'd get on all right together, you and I. I could hold the elephants while you shot them.'

'Or,' I added, as he didn't seem to be too enthusiastic, 'we could take a tusk each and tear them apart. I'm sure we could made a do of it. What about it, Stan?'

'I'm not going, dad,' he said mournfully.

'Not going!'

Despite the fact that I knew he hadn't the faintest hope of going, I was surprised and a little disappointed. I had been thinking the matter over and the more I thought about it the better it looked. The thought of getting away from Agatha and snake-skin and living in the decent society of wild elephants had taken hold of me. Then of course, one wouldn't be with the elephants all the time. Most likely they'd have a bar in South Africa. Very likely a billiard-table too. A rough-hewn stone affair, but still a billiard-table. Perhaps one could even teach the natives poker! And here were all my new risen hopes dashed to the ground and trodden on.

'Is that you, Stanley?' came a shrill voice from the kitchen.

'Come upstairs, dad,' whispered Stanley.

We cat-footed up to his room.

'Dad,' he said, as soon as he had shut the door, 'I've just been around to say good-bye to Estelle.'

'Who the hell's Estelle?' I asked. The phrase struck me at the time as a good title for a Fox-Bottom or something.

'Estelle? She's that knobby-kneed, enamel-faced giggling man-eater we were talking about a while ago.'

'Oh!' I said, 'the one with the sky-eyes and the bleeding lips?'

'Where is that dammed thing!' he snapped savagely.

I handed him the poem from the dressing-table and he tore it about in a way that must have strained him from the waist up, and threw the pieces up in the air as if he was having a Venetian carnival all to himself. I waited.

He burst out at last.

'You know that tripe-faced mug Oscar Winthrop?'

I nodded.

He paused and seemed to gather himself together; his eyes narrowed and he leered at me. Then slowly he hissed, 'He's got a motor-bike and side-car!'

'Good God!' I gasped.

To say that I was stunned by this disclosure would be to put if feebly: moreover, it would be a lie.

'Got it day before yesterday,' he explained, 'and she's been riding out in it ever since. The mug!'

'Who?'

'Oscar,' he said, sitting down on the edge of his bed.

'And little Oyster-mouth—what about her?'

'Now that I look back,' he growled, 'I can see that I was her ice-cream fetcher, her target, her door-mat, her picture show ticket. Mug!'

'Who?'

'Me.'

'And elephants are off?' I said regretfully.

He snorted as he wiped the dust off his boots with the quilt.

'Think I'm mad?'

We looked at each other for a while.

'There's no dinner,' I said.

'No dinner!' he cried, staring at me.

'Perhaps you could go down to your mother or your aunt and—'

He stood up and put his hand affectionately on my shoulder.

'Don't be silly, dad.'

'Well,' I said, 'there's a place down in King Street where I usually go when your mother is like this. One can get steak and eggs—'

'Come on,' he said, 'and we'll go to the fight after.'

He looked back as he made for the door.

'Of course, I'm broke, you know.'

'That's all right,' I said, 'I've got a pound or two your mother doesn't know about.'

While I brushed my hair I thought of Stanley. He's got sense, although it's pretty well camouflaged. He gets more like me every day. It was just possible that I might get him a job at Flannery's Crown and Anchor, as a useful. I know Flannery. Stan would be useful all right. It would be pretty hard lines if he wasn't useful to his poor old father in a job like that. At least, that was what I thought.

Still thinking, I got my hat and we sneaked out and headed for steak and eggs and freedom. I said steak and eggs, and freedom. Freedom we understand. It means letting one's beard grow and going without a collar. Freedom is what we wave flags for. But steak and eggs!

Lennie Lower (1903–47), Here's Luck (1930).

Lennie Lower's newspaper column humour was the kind which throve upon news items and very much in the news in the summer of 1930 was cricket; it was the nail-biting Test series in England between England and Australia during which the great Australian batsman Don Bradman made 334 runs, the highest score ever in Test cricket.

Something like half the population of Australia (probably 98 per cent of the male population) stayed up all night during that historic Test series listening to the running commentaries on the wireless, broadcast live from England:

BRADMAN AND THE BURGLAR

It was 2.30 a.m.

The burglar paused outside the window, jemmy in hand. A light filtered through the drawn blind, but it was the dull mumbling from within that held him hesitant for some minutes.

Then he gently, very expertly, opened the window. A harsh, stilted voice said, 'Bradman's score now stands at 301'.

Five people were hunched about the loud speaker. Father, mother, two sons, and a daughter. The floor was littered with half-burnt cigarette ends and dead matches. One of the younger men was dotting down Bradman's hits on the back of a player roll which was already half unrolled.

'McCabe cover-drove another for two,' carked the loud speaker.

'Who's bowling?' said the burglar excitedly, stepping into the room.

'Larwood,' said the whole family, without looking up.

'Goodo!' exclaimed the burglar.

Searching the house, he packed up the most portable valuables and was looking for more when a loud, harmonious groan came from around the loud speaker.

'Wot's up!' he cried, rushing in. 'Is 'e out?'

'Clean bowled by that beast Larwood,' sobbed the mother, dabbing her eyes with her handkerchief.

'That's the front door,' said the father. 'Someone answer it.'

No one answered it. 'Tate bowling,' said the announcer.

'I suppose I'll 'ave to go,' grumbled the burglar. A scream came from the room as he opened the door.

'What's wrong here?' said the policeman sternly.

'Richardson's out for one!' murmured the burglar in a hoarse voice.

'My God!' exclaimed the policeman, rushing in.

And at 3.45 a.m., the blear-eyed family dragged itself to bed, the policeman, nervously gazing about for the sergeant, went back to his beat, and the burglar went home, having forgotten his loot.

'*Any'ow*' he muttered, as he climbed wearily into his bed. '*I don't care. Five 'undred and sixty-six is goin' to take some catchin'.*'
Here's Another (1932).

———

THE *Australian preoccupation with cricket is deeply entrenched, and if any national sport is reacted to as emotionally and taken as seriously as is cricket in Australia then it is a natural target for humour.*

A classic Australian short story about cricket is 'That Barambah Mob' by the novelist and teacher 'David Forrest'; 'classically Australian' because of the laconic manner in which it is told and also because the subject of the humour is the Australian male's obsession with the game both as player and spectator.

The story is about a writer's search for the truth behind the legends surrounding one of Australia's most remarkable cricketing characters of the 1930s, the Aboriginal, Eddie Gilbert, a bowler with a murderously fast delivery of the ball. Eddie Gilbert originally played for a local team based on the small town of Barambah in outback Queensland:

THAT BARAMBAH MOB

'Eddie Gilbert?' said the publican at Murgon. He polished a glass for a moment and eyed us carefully.

'Henry Stulpnagel's your man,' he said.

We went and found Henry Stulpnagel.

We had followed a long trail to find out about Gilbert, and we eyed our new source of information very carefully before we sat down. Mr Stulpnagel somehow reminded us of dairy-farms; and where most people would perspire we thought that Mr Stulpnagel would sweat. He was a big, dopey-looking bloke with a couple of front teeth missing, and not very much hair left on top of his head. When we found him he was sitting on the post-office steps and staring down the Cherbourg Road across the Barambah flats. We said it was a good day, sat down on the steps, and stared across the Barambah flats.

He eyed us very carefully, said that the train was in but that the mail hadn't come over yet. He didn't say what he thought of the day. When he saw our note-book, we knew he was a dairy-farmer, because his eyes classified us with drought, fire, the pear, flood and Noogoora burr.

It appeared he thought we were from the Taxation Department.

'You got the lot last time,' said Mr Stulpnagel gloomily.

We said we had come to find out about Eddie Gilbert, and for a moment Mr Stulpnagel transferred his gaze from the distant line of trees on the Barambah and looked us up and down. Amongst other things, his gaze noted that we would not sweat, but perspire.

'What would you know about Gilbert?'

We said that was the point. We didn't know anything about Gilbert, but we understood that Mr Stulpnagel was an authority on the black and white streak from Barambah.

Mr Stulpnagel said, 'Come from Queensland, ey?'

He went to collect his mail, leaving us to stare down the Cherbourg Road. When he came back, we asked whether it was really true that Mr Stulpnagel had once hit a six into the Barambah from the Murgon Showground. His gaze followed ours, down the Cherbourg Road, out of the town, across the Barambah flats, over several farms and stopped at the line of trees. It was pleasant standing in the sun.

Mr Stulpnagel said, 'The beer come up on the train, too.'

We went back to visit the publican. Mr Stulpnagel had a glass of Four X and switched over to Green Death.

We asked whether it was true that he was the first white man ever to take strike to the bowling of Gilbert.

He surveyed our city clothes and said he believed so.

We wrote that down.

We wanted to know whether Eddie Gilbert was as fast as they said, and Mr Stulpnagel's lip curled as though his beer might have been flat.

'He got Bradman for a duck, didn't he?'

We agreed very hastily that that was so. We made a new approach.

'Speaking of Bradman, Mr Stulpnagel, they say you were no mean slouch with a bat yourself.'

He took the top off his beer.

'I was openin' bat for the district for seven years. Take the shine off the new ball. That was my job.'

Mr Stulpnagel had flogged new-ball bowlers from Kilkivan to Nanango.

We wondered whether this was the reason the touring MCC omitted the South Burnett from its itinerary.

'Ah, there'd be more to it than that,' said Mr Stulpnagel. He rolled a cigarette.

'Mind you,' he said, 'I was pretty fit in them days. Milkin' fifty cows single-handed, twice a day.'

He licked the cigarette and spared us a glance.

'And no machines,' he added.

From his mental eminence, he surveyed our capacity for milking cows, and was reassured of his perspectives.

We drank our beer and pursed our lips. This sixer of Mr Stulpnagel's . . . it really did go into the Barambah, did it?

'Well,' said Mr Stulpnagel. 'That was what the bloke said who had t' go an' fox it.'

We ordered beer all round.

'While he was away,' said Mr Stulpnagel, 'we took lunch. Some of the Goomeri blokes belly-ached about the way I was slowin' up the game, but I made up for it when the ball came back. I carried me bat right through, and after the shine was off the ball I gave their spinners somethin' to belly-ache about.'

We wrote that down.

'I didn't have the polish of a bloke like Bradman,' said Mr Stulpnagel and sipped at his beer. 'But I was quick on me feet. What you call agile.'

Mr Stulpnagel was very agile for a dairy-farmer. He got that way keeping out of the way of bumpers on concrete wickets. Later on when he had begun to slow up, he took to discarding his cap and parting his hair in the middle so that he didn't have to duck so far.

'But it don't make for polish,' said Mr Stulpnagel.

We wrote that down.

We said Rex Rogers was a bit of a slogger, but he had been lucky enough to make the Shield.

That was so, but it wasn't luck that did the trick. It was circumstances.

'It was Gilbert,' said Mr Stulpnagel gloomily. 'Concrete wickets an' Gilbert. Rogers never had t' handle that combination.'

Mr Stulpnagel had never got to play Shield.

'Later on,' he said, 'we used t' go down t' Brisbane t' see Gilbert slippin' into Bradman.'

We straightened up with a bit of a jerk and poised our pencil.

We wondered, with bated breath, whether Mr Stulpnagel had actually seen Gilbert bowl the ball that turned Shield cricket upside down.

He had, indeed!

'Bowled him for a duck!' boomed Mr Stulpnagel. 'They say it wasn't one of Bradman's days, but don't let them kid y'. He got him fair and square and that's in the book for everybody to see.'

We scribbled furiously.

What sort of a ball was it that got him?

'It was a full toss. Bradman played all over it like a schoolkid. Fair on his off-stump. The 'keeper took it inside the fence.'

We finished writing.

We said, 'A bloke in Brisbane said it swerved as it came in.'

'Some blokes'll tell you anything,' said Mr Stulpnagel curtly. 'Did he see that ball bowled?'

'He said he did.'

'Yeh,' said Mr Stulpnagel.

We didn't tell him about the man in Ipswich who said it was an out-swinger; nor about the bloke in Toogoolawah who said it was a yorker, right up in the block-hole.

'Look,' said Mr Stulpnagel, 'Gilbert never swung the ball. Straight up and down.'

We scribbled very fast.

'He didn't have t' swing the ball,' said Mr Stulpnagel. 'He was the fastest bowler the world's ever seen. And when you're that fast, why muck about with the fancy stuff?'

We said that was a good question.

We said that a Mr Meisenhelter had claimed to have batted against swing bowling from Gilbert.

'Meisenhelter?' said Mr Stulpnagel slowly and took another beer.

'You mean old Norm?' he said and shook his head. 'Gilbert was over the hill then. Probably down t' Larwood's standards.'

We said cautiously that some people reckoned Larwood was fast, faster maybe than Miller and Lindwall and the Demon.

Mr Stulpnagel said that these things were relative.

We wrote that down.

Mr Stulpnagel rolled up his sleeve over his biceps and we examined the corrugated and dotted scar imprinted there by the seam of a cricket-ball.

Mr Stulpnagel said, 'It wasn't Larwood done that.'

He inclined his head and we studied the scar on the top of his head. The mark was old and brown and still recognisably a diamond in shape. Enclosed in the diamond, in reverse, were the words, '. . . nufactured in Austra . . .'

Mr Stulpnagel straightened up and said gloomily, 'Larwood never done that, neither.'

'Gilbert?' we whispered.

'Thirty years ago this summer,' said Mr Stulpnagel.

We reached for our beer and changed direction and wrote down what we had been told.

We wanted to know whether all that damage was done in one innings.

Mr Stulpnagel grimaced at our intellect.

'You should try gettin' hold of the idea that Gilbert only bowled one ball t' you in an innings.'

There was a little silence.

We said, 'Just how fast was Gilbert?'

Mr Stulpnagel reckoned it was a hundred mile an hour.

We said that was faster than Larwood and Demon Spofforth and Lindwall and Miller.

Mr Stulpnagel said, 'We've been into that already.'

We stopped writing and asked him how he knew it was a hundred mile an hour.

'You could tell,' said Mr Stulpnagel. 'Mind you, I don't know about them turf wickets, but on the concrete you could tell.'

'How?'

Mr Stulpnagel said, 'You seen tyres smoke on the bitumen when they stand on the brakes?'

We had.

'When that ball hit the concrete,' said Mr Stulpnagel, 'she'd smoke.'

He measured with his finger and thumb. 'You'd see this little wisp of smoke when she come at y', comin' like the hammers o' hell. Hundred mile an hour.'

We wrote that down and supposed that some blokes tried to get out of the way.

'Oh, they tried,' said Mr Stulpnagel.

We wrote that down.

'Mind you,' said Mr Stulpnagel, 'blokes like that shouldn't take the game up.'

We wanted to know whether Gilbert had scared him at all.

'Not the first time,' said Mr Stulpnagel. 'That come afterwards. When you'd see the draw for the season, and see you was down for the first match against Barambah. Bill Ritter who used t' live out on the Windera Road, he was my openin' partner, he sold up and bought a farm over in Barambah.'

'Just to get away from the black and white streak?'

'Mind you, he didn't put it that way,' said Mr Stulpnagel, 'but he played for Barambah that year.'

If Mr Stulpnagel wasn't scared the first time he met Gilbert, just how did he feel.

'Queer,' said Mr Stulpnagel and ordered a glass.

'They batted first that day,' he said. 'They was always bottom in the points table; and then Bill Ritter an' me, went out t' belt a few sixes off them.'

He drank some of his beer.

'We didn't take much notice of the black bloke, because that Barambah always was a queer mob.'

He drank the rest of his beer.

'They give Charlie Schultz the new ball, and we run a couple o' twos and a single. And so I come about t' face the other opener. Everybody started t' walk off, and I thought it must be drinks, so I started t' walk off, too.'

He rolled a cigarette.

'The black bloke was standin' there in his whites, and he said to me, he said, "No, not you. You stay here." I said, "What's goin' on here?" And he said t' me, he said, "I am going to bowl to you, Mr Stulpnagel".'

We ordered Mr Stulpnagel a pot of Green Death.

'I stood there an' I looked around, and by golly it made you feel queer. There was only the black bloke and the umpire in front of me. Ernie Vogel, he was their 'keeper, he was bunched up in front of the grandstand . . . and the rest o' them were scattered about on the fence. Everybody in the stand was as quiet as anything. They were feelin' queer, too. Wonderin' what it was all about. Except a couple of the Barambah women folk who were shiftin' along the stand out of the line o' wicket.'

'It was so quiet you could hear the footsteps of the deep third walkin' up Taylor Street towards the power-house.'

We felt a bit queer ourselves. We ordered Green Death.

'Then,' said Mr Stulpnagel, 'you couldn't hear them footsteps any more.'

He sank some of his beer.

'Then he give it to me,' said Mr Stulpnagel. 'He only run about five yards and I suppose that put me off a bit. But in that last yard or two he went all streaky an' I knew I had real trouble on me hands.'

We wanted to know whether he sighted it well. Mr Stulpnagel looked at us doubtfully.

He heard it.

'It whistled,' said Mr Stulpnagel. 'You could hear it comin'.'

He measured with his finger and thumb. 'And there was this little wisp o' smoke when she come off the mat. That's when he gave me this.'

He inclined his head, and we examined the tip of his ear. There was a scar there but the letters were indecipherable.

'I'm a bit deaf in that ear,' said Mr Stulpnagel.

We thought he was lucky he wasn't clean-bowled first ball.

'It depends on what y' call luck,' said Mr Stulpnagel gloomily. 'He went back his five yards and give me the next one.'

Did it whistle?

'Maybe,' said Mr Stulpnagel, 'I dunno. I didn't hear nothin'. I didn't see too much, neither. I was still waitin' to play it when something cracked behind me . . . and all that Barambah mob started yellin' Howsat.'

We wrote that down.

'They took one bail at deep fine leg and there was me middle stump flat on the ground. In two bits and some splinters.'

He was silent for a while and we wondered what happened to the other bail.

'You hear yarns,' said Mr Stulpnagel slowly . . . he shook his head, 'I dunno what happened to it. Fred Kleinschmidt always reckoned the deep third took it in front of the Powerhouse.'

Was that possible?

'Oh, it was possible,' said Mr Stulpnagel, 'but you don't want to take too much notice of anything old Fred ever tells you.'

We supposed that his averages went to pot after that.

At the end of that season, Mr Stulpnagel didn't have an average.

We said sympathetically that this must have made him feel crook.

'It did and it didn't,' said Mr Stulpnagel. 'It was a bit hard t' take for a while. But then he made that trip to Brisbane t' clean up Bradman, and then Bradman's average didn't look so hot itself. So when you felt miserable you was in good company t' be miserable with.'

'It was all right when he made his trips to Brisbane. But then you'd come into town one day and a bloke'd say t' you, "Gilbert come home on the train this mornin'." And you wouldn't sleep so well as the fixture come up.'

Mr Stulpnagel toyed with his glass.

'That was when it got bad. There you'd be standin' out there. All by y'rself an' only the umpire an' the black bloke in front of y'. And the other umpire a bit toey out there at square leg. And your partner down the other end prayin' t' God you wouldn't hit a single.'

We ordered Mr Stulpnagel another beer.

'And Ernie Vogel, he was their 'keeper; he'd pat you on the shoulder and say "good luck, Henry", and then you were on your own.'

There was a little silence.

We wanted to know whether it was Gilbert who had removed Mr Stulpnagel's front teeth.

'That was the tractor,' said Mr Stulpnagel. 'Startin' handle come back at me.'

We wrote that down.

He leaned forward and tapped the bar with his glass. 'The truth about Gilbert is that in his openin' overs there wasn't a batsman he met ever saw one of his deliveries. It was Gilbert or the game . . . somethin' had t' give. Write that down.'

We wrote that down.

'They had plenty to go on,' said Mr Stulpnagel. 'He made an ape of Bradman, and he was black, and he was born in Queensland, and they didn't like the look o' that whippy wrist of his. They reckoned he wasn't bowlin'.'

We wrote that down.

'They'd have fixed him for keeps, only someone took a slow-motion film and that was that.'

'Yes?' we said.

'He was bowling all right,' said Mr Stulpnagel. 'It's all right about them blokes who was makin' the fuss. They knew the day was comin' when they'd have t' stand out there, an' Ernie Vogel pattin' them on the shoulder before he buried himself under the fence.'

We fetched another beer.

'Not that I blame Ernie, mind you,' said Mr Stulpnagel. 'He had a wife an' six kids t' think about and none of them was old enough t' help with the milkin'.'

We wrote that down.

We wondered what else Mr Stulpnagel could tell us about Edward Gilbert.

He thought about it while he drank his pot.

He shook his head slowly. 'No, I don't think so. There's a bloke out on the Redgate Road might be able t' help y'. Old Augie Schulte. Although I suppose most o' what he knows he got from that Barambah mob, and they always was a queer lot.'

We had one for the road with Mr Stulpnagel and he drove off to Boat Mountain to get stuck into the milkin'.

We got ourselves lost in the main street while we were looking for the Brisbane Road and enquired of a policeman.

As an afterthought, we wanted to know whether he knew anything about Gilbert.

The policeman put his foot on our mudguard and said that as a matter of fact he had seen Gilbert bowl Bradman for a duck.

'He snicked it,' said the policeman. 'It was a shooter.'

We didn't tell him about the bloke in Brisbane who said it swung in, nor about the man in Ipswich who said it swung out. We didn't mention the bloke in Toogoolawah who said it was a yorker, right up in the block-hole; nor Mr. Stulpnagel who said it was a full toss.

Policemen are reliable witnesses. We wrote it down that it was a shooter.

A black bloke walking down the street said, 'G'day.'

The policeman said, 'G'day, Mr Gilbert.'

We scribbled at a tremendous rate of knots.

The policeman took his foot off our mudguard and said, 'Hey, Eddie. Just a minute.'

We met Mr Gilbert. We don't really remember what he looked like.

We wondered whether he would be kind enough to describe the ball that got Bradman for a duck.

Mr Gilbert looked at us very carefully for a while.

'I don't really know,' he said apologetically. 'When I let it go, I didn't see it again till the 'keeper threw it up in the air.'

He looked rather embarrassed.

He said, 'You'd have t' ask someone who was watchin'.'

We looked at Mr Gilbert very carefully for a while.

Then we said good-afternoon to Mr Gilbert, we said good-afternoon to the policeman, and we drove wildly back to Brisbane, anywhere, to get away from that Barambah mob. We ran out of petrol coming through

Toogoolawah, but we had the pace, and we'd have got home all right if it hadn't been for that sharp turn out of Ipswich Road at the 'Gabba'.

That stopped us.

'David Forrest' (David Denham) (b. 1924), 'That Barambah Mob', *Modern Australian Humour* (1963).

———

ALEXANDER MACDONALD, *a well-known and thoroughly professional humorist who worked for years in the early days of ABC radio as a gag-writer for such comedians as Jack Davey and Roy Rene, also developed parallel careers as a radio and television reviewer and as a humorous columnist for papers like the* Daily Telegraph *and the* Sunday Telegraph.

Here is a typical Alexander Macdonald newspaper column, some cautionary advice on the Australian male's third interest in life (cricket being the first):

DR MAC'S SEASONAL SERMON TO PARTYGOERS

We are now approaching the season of the year when the bird is in the bag, the bear is in the fridge and grog-blossoms are in full bloom.

It's the season when every boy's thoughts turn, not a little anxiously, towards the state of Old Man Liver.

(He don't say nuthin'—he gives no warnin'—he grins and bears it—till one fine mornin'—dat ol' Man Liver, he just quits playin' along.)

Meanwhile, speaking with all the bumptious superiority of one who is pledged to drink nothing but buttermilk and creaming soda during the next fortnight, allow me to give you weaklings (who don't possess my iron will-power) a short sermon on the Perils of Partygoing.

(No sneaking out, in the bleachers, there! Back to your pews, sirrahs!)

Text: *The Seven Deadly Gins*: The partygoer's commonest weakness is a form of hallucination in which he imagines he is consuming one drink for everybody else's four. Thus, at the end of seven Martinis he deludes himself that he's only had two, and so on, and so on—until the Sandman finally arrives, armed with the usual blunt instrument.

(I witnessed a classic case of this one morning back in 1937, when I was making a light breakfast on champagne—at 9*d.* a glass—with Mr Peter Finch. After breakfast Finch—who had about seven or eight under his belt—declared, 'Ah, there's nothing like a couple of champagnes to fix a man up for the day.' At which he stepped from his stool and, with the consummate dignity of a born actor fell flat on his face.)

Dr Mac's Counter-ploy—the Mock Middy: Borrowing the principle used by a give-up-smoking agency—which recommends puffing at a plastic dummy cigarette and making believe that you're actually smoking—I have devised a foolproof gimmick for those who Don't Trust Themselves at Parties (and we are legion).

It consists of a middy glass filled with solid amber and topped with a layer of meerschaum (to simulate foam) which you take along to the party under your coat.

Produce your mock middy and pretend to sip from it—with every evidence of lip-smacking relish. *And remember—it's all in the mind!* Simply make *believe* that it's beer. Soon you will find yourself actually *enjoying* the natural hop flavour of the solid amber. You'll wonder what you every saw in *real* beer. '*Liquid* beer? Ugh!' you'll say. 'How did I ever drink it?'

(I am assuming, of course, that you are a congenital idiot, with a file a foot thick at the Reception House.)

Dr Mac's Counsel to Hopeless Cases: Not many of you, alas, will have the strength of character to employ the mock middy system this season. So, for you unfortunates who will almost certainly be greeting Christmas Day with a bleached scowl, allow me to offer one or two time-hallowed words of advice:

On Waking Up: The first thing you will be aware of once the priceless boon of consciousness has been restored to you, will be the metallic thudding of gay gong-notes somewhere behind the ears. Do not panic. These are the Christmas chimes from the neighbouring church, wishing you jollity, joy and goodwill.

On Making Breakfast: Don't!

On Getting Dressed: Choose first, a shirt with no buttons. In your condition, what with the church bells and a curious, humming noise in the frontal lobe of the skull (this last is quite imaginary—ignore it) shirt buttons will assume the magnitude of manhole covers and each buttonhole the abstract unreality of a slit in a marsh-mallow.

The greatest hazard, however, is that exhausting operation, the Putting on of the Shoes. There are some reckless fools who court instant insanity by sitting on the edge of the bed and *bending forward* to perform this feat . . . with the result, of course, that the head falls off and rolls under the bed.

Correct procedure is to *step* into the shoes from an upright posture. If the shoes are too tight fitting to be stepped into, go barefooted for the rest of the day.

But now, at last, you are prepared to face the world!

No, not yet. There is still one little chore to be attended to. Go to the cupboard under the stairs where you keep the radiator, the vacuum-cleaner and last months unpaid bills, and take out your shot-gun.

And now off you go, at a trembling jog-trot, to the Wee Kirk around the corner.

Steady now, lad—you need a keen eye and a cool head for this job! Line the bell-ringer up in your sights. *Bang!* You've potted him.

(Shove the cadaver up the A flat organ pipe. It won't be discovered for weeks.)

Your task is done. You may now face the residue of the year with a clear conscience.

Alexander Macdonald (1915–73), *Don't Frighten the Horses* (1961).

N EW ZEALANDER *Barry Crump in his run-up to becoming a writer of humour was for a time a deer-culler, trapper, bushman, fisherman, safari-guide, crocodile-hunter, and TV comedian. He found touch with the reading public in spectacular fashion in 1960 with a book about his experiences as a deer-culler,* A Good Keen Man.

Crump must now be New Zealand's most successful humorous author; over twenty books published with combined sales of something like a million copies, which works out about one to every three inhabitants.

The humour in his first books tended to be somewhat manic, but by his tenth, No Reference Intended, *Crump's style had calmed down and his humour sprang from character and a fine ear for the terse, lean speech of New Zealand countrymen.* No Reference Intended *tells of a jaded journalist, Cosgrove, who decided to invent a bizarre story in order to get himself fired.*

In the following episode we find Cosgrove in the little one-horse township of Ongapuni. He is there to interview a Mrs Mobberley and get a story out of her as to why she ended a crippled horse's sufferings with an axe. He goes to the local pub in search of a taxi to take him to Mrs Mobberley's place.

He is in a tearing hurry:

Cosgrove asked the publican if he would mind pointing out which was the taxi driver, and the publican, whose both hands were occupied with something in his pockets, nodded his head wisely in the general direction of two men deep in urgent conversation at the far end of the bar.

As he approached these two men Cosgrove saw that they were both so un-taxi-driverish-looking that he was tempted to suspect the publican of having played some kind of joke on him. And when he was close enough to address them they went on talking as though he was invisible.

'Well, as I said at the time, Bert, there's no tellin' how many's goin' t' turn up, and that's a fact.'

'Yeah, there's no tellin' how many of 'em's goin' t' turn up all right. I backed yerrup on that, remember?'

'I think I did 'ear somethin', Bert. But it was me told 'em t' git another twenty tickets extra, above and beyond what they reckoned they was goin' t' need.'

'Yeah, well I mentioned it t' Stew Miller when we first went in in the first place and he said f' me t' bring it up after the meetin' but you got in first. Stew'll tell y'. You arst 'im if I come up to 'im when we first went in . . .'

'Excuse me,' said Cosgrove politely. 'Is one of you gentlemen the taxi driver?'

For a moment it didn't look as though either of them was going to answer him. They didn't turn their heads to look at him, as he had every right to expect them to; they turned their whole bodies, ever so slowly, until they'd about-faced and were leaning with their drinks in their hands and their backs against the bar, looking at him.

For a long time they stood like that and then Cosgrove saw that one of them was actually going to speak. He saw the decision on the whiskery face, the bracing of the lungs, the intake of breath, the pause, the mouth beginning to open . . .

'Yeah. That's right,' he drawled.

It took Cosgrove a moment to remember the question and then relate it to the answer. Then he addressed himself to the talkative one.

'I was wondering if you could run me out to where Mrs Mobberly lives?'

The taxi driver thought it over for a few seconds.

'Not me, mate,' he said. 'I'd like to be able to help y', but I can't. Haven't got a car or anythin'.'

Another pause, this time from Cosgrove.

'Is your taxi not working at the moment?' he enquired.

'S'not *my* taxi, mate, it's me mate 'ere's.'

Cosgrove felt his temper begin to rise alarmingly and then slowly subside as he deftly reduced the consequences of saying what he felt to its lowest probable common denominator . . . a belt in the ear from both sides at once. He turned to the other man, who looked even less like a taxi driver than the other had.

'Could *you* drive me out to Mrs Mobberly's place?' he asked through politely-clenched manners.

The second taxi driver thoughtfully considered the proposition for a few moments. Cosgrove's thumb went through the lining of his pocket with a loud *brip!* that caused both taxi drivers to deepen their looks at him warily.

At last the second taxi driver spoke.

'I s'pose so,' he grunted. 'Don't see why not.'

He turned to his mate for approval of the decision.

'Sure, don't see why not,' his mate agreed.

'Thank you,' said Cosgrove, turning to lead the way out to the footpath.

'I'm going right past Miz' Mobberly's place this afternoon,' went on the real taxi driver. 'I could drop you off on the way if you like,' he added generously.

Cosgrove, frozen in his half-turned-away postion, felt all his pores open and close like anemones. 'I'd really prefer to go now, if you could manage it,' he said. 'I'm in a rather urgent hurry as a matter of fact. I only have a few hours to get a lot of work done. I have to meet a deadline.'

'In a hurry, eh?'

'Yes, I *am* in a hurry.'

'Well, if you're in a hurry I might be able to help you out.' He drank from his glass.

'That's very kind of you,' said Cosgrove, prepared to think a little more kindly of the man, now that he had things moving.

'She's right, mate . . .' He paused as though he'd just made a curious discovery. 'Y' new around here, aren't y'?'

'Yes. Look, could we go now please? I'm in a hurry. It's urgent.'

'In that case I don't see why we shouldn't get away right now,' said the taxi driver actively.

'Well, let's get along, shall we?' urged Cosgrove.

The taxi driver drained his glass and put it on the bar. 'Don't fill that one up again, Bert,' he instructed. 'I've got to dash. Got to get this bloke over to Miz' Mobberly's. He's in a hurry.'

'Okay then,' replied Bert understandingly. 'See y' when y' git back.'

'Righto, see y' when I git back. . . . Will y' be in 'ere?'

'Think so. Either in 'ere or over Sam's place.'

'Okay. If y' not in 'ere I'll 'ave a look over at Sam's place.'

Cosgrove was following the taxi driver out the door when Bert spoke from behind them at the bar. The taxi driver stopped and Cosgrove cannoned into him.

'I'll most likely be in 'ere,' Bert had said.

'Okay,' said the taxi driver. 'I'll look in 'ere first.'

'Righto.'

'See y'.'

And suddenly Cosgrove and his captive taxi driver were out on the foot-path, actually moving towards the taxi, which was parked about a hundred and fifty yards from the hotel.

'Are you very busy at the moment?' Cosgrove enquired pleasantly, to dispel the odd feeling that it had all been too easy and something would yet intervene to prevent him from getting to Mrs Mobberly.

'Comes and goes,' replied the taxi driver. 'As a matter of fact,' he confided, 'I don't know too much about the taxi business. I just took over the outfit.'

'Is that a fact?' said Cosgrove uneasily.

'Yeah, bought Ronnie Wall out. Matter of fact I bin a farmer all me life. The doc made me sell out the farm and take on a lighter caper because of me 'ealth.'

'Really?'

'Yeah. Got a crook ticker on me. Coronary Thrombosis.'

'I'm very sorry to hear it,' said Cosgrove absently, reaching to open the front passenger's door of the taxi.

'Yeah,' agreed the taxi driver sympathetically. 'It's a bit of a blow to a man all right, havin' t' take it easy after workin' 'ard all me life.'

Cosgrove had got into the taxi and closed the door, so the taxi driver went round to his side and opened that door and began to climb in.

'Still, it's no good complainin',' he went on. 'Worries the missus more than me.' He slammed the door. 'Yeah, when a man's time's up he's a gonner, I reckon. No use worryin' about it.'

Cosgrove watched in rising apprehension as the taxi driver fumbled at his pocket openings. The taxi driver sat there in silence for a moment and then he said: 'I'm gunna have t' git out again. I've forgot to take me keys out of me pocket before I got in. Always doin' that. Funny, isn't it?'

Cosgrove didn't think it was funny enough to be worth the strain of making a polite comment. The taxi driver got out and plunged his hands into his cluttered pockets several times each. 'I'm a beggar t' lose things,' he announced with a bashful grin.

This was the final straw. Cosgrove felt his will power begin to smoulder restlessly inside him. If the taxi driver announced the loss of his ignition key Cosgrove wasn't going to be responsible for his words or actions. He half-closed his eyes and waited fearfully for the terrible pronouncement.

'Ah,' said the taxi driver. 'Got 'em. Knew all along they was in me pocket somewhere.'

Cosgrove relaxed. Then the taxi driver bent down to look into the car.

'Just hold the fort 'ere for a mo, will y' mate?' he said. 'Just remembered somethin'. Won't be a tick.'

Cosgrove nodded dumbly. The taxi driver began to cross the street and stopped to look both ways for traffic on the silent thoroughfare, then moved towards the other side. Out of the corner of his eye Cosgrove saw him pause, think, and slowly retrace his steps. He came and opened the door of the cab and looked in again.

'Anything y' want from the shop, mate?' he asked.

'Nup,' was all Cosgrove could say to thank him for his thoughtfulness.

'Okay. Just thought if there was somethin' y' wanted I could have picked it up f' y', seein' as I'm goin' along there meself.'

As Cosgrove couldn't answer he closed the door, looked both empty ways again, crossed the street, and ambled slowly out of sight along the footpath.

When his driver had gone, Cosgrove sighed loudly several times in the hot cab and wondered if he wished he were back in the office. He couldn't decide, so he wondered about Ailsa Mobberly. From a dozen cross-pollinations of the stock that bred men such as the taxi driver, Mrs Mobberly would have sprouted, flowered briefly, and then married back into. Cosgrove had known exactly what kind of woman she was as soon as he'd heard about her. He'd met them in dozens of country places, just like this one. Even the same smells and times of year. He'd met them in hundreds of different interviews in thousands of different shapes and dresses and faces and circumstances. This sounded like a great variety, and it was. In fact Cosgrove had decided that they lacked variety in only two respects. They were all colourless and all ignorant. What other kind of woman would fit into the environs of the country's stately cowsheds and woodsheds? And now this brave member of the tribe had killed a crippled horse with an axe (four-and-a-half-pound-*Plumb*) and was going to get her name in the paper. Cosgrove even knew what she was going to say:

'I had to do it. The poor thing was suffering.' And her husband would come in from his labours and hover within earshot, on hand to see that nothing bad for the family got into the papers. (*I knocked off and went up to the house when that reporter bloke came to get the story off the missus about killing that horse the other day, Jim. You can't trust them bastards as far as you can kick 'em. They put words in your mouth, that's what they do. If he'd tried any of his funny stuff with my missus he'd have been out the gate quicker than he came in, I can tell you!*)

After all, Cosgrove reflected, you can't blame these men. Mrs Mobberly had only done what is expected of the wives of men of this calibre. No strangers to violence, these sturdy fellows. (One of them once punched Cosgrove in the face and split his lip because the typesetter on another paper had got his name wrong in a list of people convicted and fined for after-hours drinking.) Such a man would have finished Ailsa Mobberly's horse off without any of this newspaper nonsense. He would have simply walked up, drawn back his powerful right arm, and pulled out his tobacco in one smooth movement.

Cosgrove was so engrossed in taking out his frustrations on these absent members of the taxi driver's kin that he failed to hear him returning. The sudden rattle of the opening door started Cosgrove's visions into guilty cover.

'Forgot me smokes,' said the taxi driver gravely, settling into his seat and fumbling patiently for the cellophane tag opener on the wrong end of a new packet of cigarettes. 'I'm no good without me smokes.'

He got the packet open and broke the ends of two cigarettes with his clumsy fingers before he succeeded in extracting one. Then he patted his pockets and gazed blankly around the silent cab.

Cosgrove waited for it with the teeth on the blind side of his face gritted and the lips on the taxi driver's side hooked back into the best he could do in the way of a smile. Then the taxi driver turned to him and spoke with all the exasperation of someone whose just been robbed:

'I don't suppose y' got a match on y' by any chance, mate?'

'I'm sorry,' said Cosgrove. 'I don't smoke.'

'Strike,' said the taxi driver. 'I forgot to offer you one. Here, help yourself.'

'I don't smoke,' repeated Cosgrove.

'She's right,' said the taxi driver reassuringly. 'I got plenty.'

'I don't smoke.'

'Take one for later then,' invited the taxi driver encouragingly.

'*I don't smoke.*'

'Don't smoke, eh?' said the taxi driver. His tone suggested that he was quite prepared to believe Cosgrove didn't smoke, but he found it difficult.

'Couldn't do without me smokes meself. Not that I hold it against a joker that doesn't smoke. If they don't want to smoke that's their business. I don't believe in interferin' in anyone's private affairs . . .'

He broke off to reach over and rummage in the glovebox in front of Cosgrove. 'Did you see where I put me matches?' he asked.

'No, as a matter of fact I didn't,' said Cosgrove, leaning back into the seat out of the way of the taxi driver's rummaging.

'I bet that bloody Bert's got them, that's what'll have happened. Bert's lifted 'em. He's a beaut at that caper.'

Cosgrove could see a box of matches between some papers in the glovebox and was about to say so when the taxi driver found another box, all on his own.

'There y'are,' he said triumphantly. 'I knew I had a box of matches in there somewhere'. He lit his cigarette. 'Sure y' won't have one?' he enquired.

'Quite sure, thank you,' said Cosgrove firmly.

'Well, I'll just leave 'em on the seat 'ere so you can bog into 'em if y' change yer mind later on.'

As far as Cosgrove could see there was now no reason why they couldn't set off. He waited to see what would happen. The taxi driver must have had similar thoughts.

'Well, we could get away now,' he said. 'Don't want to hold y' up if yer in a hurry.'

He rummaged at himself for a few moments.

'Looks like I'm goin' t' have to git out again,' he said resignedly. 'I've gone and forgotten to get me keys out a' me pants pocket again. Don't seem to 'ave been doin' anything but get in and out of the bloody car all day. It's tough on a man with a crook ticker, y'know.' He held up the found keys. 'Knew they were there somewhere,' he grinned, getting back into the car and slamming the door.

He put the key in the ignition switch, turned it on and pressed the starter. Incredibly, the car started. And then, even more incredibly, they moved off along the road with a series of gentle jerks. Cosgrove felt an absurd desire to apologise to the taxi driver for his lack of faith in him. Instead he asked:

'Is it very far to Mrs Mobberly's place?'

'No distance at all, mate. No distance at all. Just out this way a bit.'

The vehicle accelerated violently and Cosgrove thought with a slash of panic of the taxi driver's Coronary Thrombosis. He flung a look at the speedometer. They were travelling at fifteen miles an hour in second gear and had covered just under one hundred yards.

A hundred and thirty yards from the last of Ongapuni's shops (Cosgrove idly paced out these distances on a walk later) the taxi rolled gently around a left-hand turn at an elegant ten miles an hour, off the town's bitumen strip and on to a long straight metalled road.

'Don't like goin' too fast just yet,' explained the taxi driver. 'Pays to take it easy at first.'

'Do you mean you're only learning to drive a car?' demanded Cosgrove, his voice harsh with alarm.

'Been at it close on three weeks now,' said the taxi driver proudly. 'Speed's the thing causes all the accidents, y'know. I'm not goin' to do any speedin' till I get used to it.'

'You mean you don't even hold a taxi licence?'

'Nar, the traffic bloke only comes out 'ere every four months or so,' explained the taxi driver. 'If I can catch 'im next time 'e comes I'll hit 'im up for a licence.'

'I certainly hope you do,' said Cosgrove, and he couldn't help adding: 'But you'll probably have to hold him up for it, by the look of things.'

The taxi driver let the car drift to a stop in the centre of the road. Cosgrove mistook the grim look of concentration on his face for anger at Cosgrove's sarcastic remark. He hadn't realised that the man was so sensitive.

'Look, I'm terribly sorry,' he blurted. 'I had no intention of offending you. I had no idea . . .'

He saw by the way the taxi driver was looking at him that something was wrong. 'What's wrong?' he asked, clearing his throat to cover up the quavering in his voice.

'There's nothin' wrong with me, mate,' said the taxi driver.

'Then why have we stopped here like this?'

'This is where y' wanted to go, ain't it? Miz Mobberly's place?'

'Yes, Mrs Mobberly's place. I want to interview her.'

'Well, you're there, mate. That's 'er 'ouse in be'ind them trees there.'

Cosgrove got woodenly out of the car and looked back up the road.

There was the main road they'd turned off a few moments ago, still there. (Two hundred and ten yards.)

And there was the town, Ongapuni, less than a quarter of a mile across the paddocks, two or three hundred yards, a few minutes' walk.

And there was the letterbox, A. MOBBERLY (MISS), painted on it.

And there in the taxi was the taxi driver, happily puffing on that same cigarette, with all the satisfaction of having done a job, and done it well. To him it was perfectly logical for someone to hire a taxi for a journey so short that the vehicle didn't have time to get into top gear.

Cosgrove felt suddenly fond of the fumbling taxi driver; they'd been through so much together. Incredible that it was only an hour and a half since he'd left the hotel in search of Mrs Mobberly. It seemed like weeks. It was crazy.

He walked round to the taxi driver's open window.

'How much do I owe you?' he asked generously.

'Ar, cut it out mate. I wouldn't charge a man fer a bit of a trip like that. Forget it . . .'ere, 'ave a smoke.'

He passed the opened packet out and Cosgrove took the cigarette his taxi driver knew he needed all the time. Then Cosgrove moved towards the side of the road as the taxi driver jerked away with a nod and a 'See y' later,' and drove away at a sedate few miles an hour, not back towards the town, but straight away along the middle of the road in the direction he was facing. It was a long time before he passed out of sight.

To Cosgrove there was only one possible explanation. The taxi driver had obviously decided to drive straight on, right round the world and back into Ongapuni from the other way, rather than go to all the bother of turning his taxi round. Perhaps he didn't know about the reverse gear.

Barry Crump (b. 1935), No Reference Intended (1960).

―――――――――

N EW ZEALAND *continues to be a short-story reading nation. And a short-story writing nation. The North and South Islands probably have a greater proportion of short-story writers per head of population than any other nation. One has the impression that if one were to fling six whitebait fritters out of an Auckland hotel window, the chances are good that at least one of them would fall about the ears of a short-story writer strolling below.*

There is also the Listener, *New Zealand's official broadcasting journal and its most influential literary magazine, which acts as a kind of Kiwi equivalent of the* Sydney Bulletin, *encouraging local writers to write about local life.*

In which case is there perhaps a truly 'New Zealand Short Story'?

Indeed there is, according to A. K. Grant, BA.

Alan Grant was once a 'scribbling barrister' but his scribbling side eventually took over and he left the law to become a full-time writer, contributing satirical pieces to the Christchurch newspapers and the Listener. *His light, literary, gently ironic touch, reminiscent of the* New Yorker's *E. B. White, was recognized and he became a regular columnist for the* NZ Listener *and a writer and editor for New Zealand television.*

In the following piece, Grant considers the anatomy of the New Zealand Short Story:

AN INQUIRY INTO THE CONSTRUCTION AND CLASSIFICATION OF THE NEW ZEALAND SHORT STORY

The short story and the poem are the two forms in which New Zealand writers have achieved the greatest distinction. What is not generally appreciated is that, while on the one hand only a rare spirit can write a good poem, on the other hand almost any literate person can write a good New Zealand short story. The reason for this is that there is a finite number of types of New Zealand short story. Their skeletons have been assembled by pioneers and all the modern writer has to do is flesh them out. In support of my thesis I shall list below a number of basic, irreducible types of New Zealand short story, accompanied by suggestions as to the development of the possibilities with which each is pregnant.

(1) *The sensitive Maori kid who doesn't quite know what is going on short story . . .*

Such short stories, as their categorisation suggests, commonly involve a Maori boy of about ten years of age, around whom things happen which he grasps but dimly. They frequently begin as follows:

Watene sat on the wooden steps of the back door. He could smell the odour of the kumara scones his mother was baking in the kitchen. Outside, his father was tinkering with the engine of the 1937 Ford V8 which his father called The Old Sow. Watene laughed, thinking of his father calling the Old Sow the Old Sow. The sun warmed his limbs. Watene felt good.

Following the opening passages of this type of story, an Event occurs. The Event is followed in due course by its acceptance by the child protagonist, even though he doesn't understand it properly. Alternatively the c.p. accepts and throws his arms around an adult who precipitated or was involved in the event. The whole story should be redolent of the odour of Polynesian sanctity and should condemn by implication the lapsed, unspontaneous nature of the Pakeha, unable to respond to simple events in a simple way.

(2) *The Ordinary Kiwi working bloke short story . . .*

A lot of these were written during the thirties and forties. They are narrated in the first person by an Ordinary Kiwi working bloke who explains why one of his workmates drives him up the wall and tells us what he does about it. One should leap straight into the mise-en-scène when writing such a story:

I knew there was going to be trouble as soon as Fred, our foreman, brought Mortimer over. Mortimer looked a real nong. 'This here is Mortimer,' said Fred. 'He's a pongo, but he can't help it.' He walked away, rolling a smoke between his left ear and the side of his head without using his hands. None of us could work out how he did it. 'Grab hold of that bloody grubber,' I said. 'What's a grubber?' asked Mortimer, like a nong. 'Oh dear, oh bloody dear,' I said to myself.

This type of story can develop in two ways: (*a*) Mortimer proves not to be such a nong after all and is eventually, though grudgingly, accepted by the narrator; (*b*) he really does prove to be trouble and something bad happens— a fight, a work accident—as a consequence of which the gang breaks up and the narrator slopes off back to the big smoke. In order to give the story an historical perspective the incident should occur during the Depression but its narration should be taking place ten or twenty years later. This allows the narrator to append a coda along the following lines:

One afternoon in Queen Street I bumped into Shorty, who had been in the gang with us. I took him to the Prince of Wales, bought him a few pony beers, and we yarned about old times. 'What ever happened to Mortimer?' I asked him. 'Haven't you heard?' said Shorty, incredulous. 'Morty's just landed a $5 million contract selling wood chips to the Japanese.' I didn't say anything. I simply moved on to the top shelf.

(3) *Then if you think you're depressed already just wait till you read this but it may help me to make some sense of my breakdown short story . . .*

This type of short story is directly related to the confessional poetry of Robert Lowell, Anne Sexton and Sylvia Plath. The creative impetus behind it more commonly finds its expression in the form of a novel rather than a short story. However short stories of this type do appear. I shall not give an example of one because I am feeling quite cheerful, a frail mood and one easily dispelled by contemplation of the type of short story I am refusing to contemplate.

(4) *The lovable housewife and mother coping with adolescent kids in the suburbs short story . . .*

This is much the most meritorious type of New Zealand short story because unlike all the others it does not preserve itself in the aspic of its own solemnity. It was developed almost single-handed by Marie Bullock and begins as follows:

I wandered into the front room. George, my eldest, was lying on the sofa eating a Vegemite sandwich with one hand and plucking at the strings of his guitar with the other. 'Have you done your chemistry homework?' I asked. 'No,' said George, 'Chemistry's stupid.' What could I say? I agreed with him. 'Well go and tidy up your bedroom,' I riposted feebly. 'Don't need to,' said George smugly. 'I've given Donny ten cents to do it.' 'Donny!' I cried. 'But he's only three!' 'So what?' said George. 'He still knows what ten cents is worth.'

(5) *The zonked out of one's skull in Ponsonby short story . . .*

The zonked out of one's skull in Ponsonby short story was developed in the sixties and production models appear in our literary magazines to this very day. In such short stories the writer attempts to combine the described sexual and hallucinogenic experience without making sense of either and using words rather than language, for example:

. . . cast off cried the red admiral I put my hands under her buttocks while the heliotrope wall flowed into the Propontis push she cried but I floated bobbing against the stars bobbing prodding oh god oh god yes her heels fused with my calves and we soared into a mauve Van Allen belt while she came out of the unknown I could keep this kind of stuff up forever but you will have taken my point by now . . .

(6) *The sub-Katherine Mansfield 'At the Bay' short story . . .*

The first rays of the sun slid over the peak of Mt Winterslow and stabbed downward to a dew-drop trembling on the tip of a toitoi plume. A faint breeze stirred the top branches of the tall beech tree on the edge of the school playground. Fantails flicked about the branches looking for all the world as though they were attached to the trunk by invisible strands of elastic. An opalescent mist rose—oh so uncertainly!— from the long grass beside the shingle road. The dust of the road had been dampened by the dew and smelled of dew-dampened dust. In the paddock next to the school two horses cropped the wet grass with a sound like pinking shears cutting through velvet. In a corner of the playground stood a square white tent. The flaps on one side had been folded right back. In front of the tent two wooden trestles supported a large flat board. For now the tent was empty, but soon it would be full of teachers noting results and parents inquiring about placings.

It was the day of the school sports.

The above list is not, of course, exhaustive. There are at least four other basic types of short story which I have not listed because I write such stories myself. None have so far been accepted for publication. I am aware of the reason for this. All that stands between my short stories and the acknowledgment of a major new talent is the lack of a suitable non-de-plume. A. K. Grant carries no aura or penumbra with it. O. E. Middleton suggests intelligence, Maurice Shadbolt combines the Gallic artiness of Maurice with the no-nonsense Anglo-Saxon sound of Shadbolt, Frank Sargeson is suitably demotic, Katherine Mansfield is the sort of name you would expect a sensitive upper middle-class spirit to have. A. K. Grant—there's just nothing there. I think I might try Peregrine Ruapehu de Vere Stacpoole Whineray.

A. K. Grant (b. 1941), *NZ Listener Short Stories* (1977).

WOULD-BE *novelists in New Zealand, slumped over typewriters in Windy Welly or jogging miserably round Christchurch wondering what to write about, would be cheered to learn that not only is there a 'New Zealand Short Story' but there is also a 'New Zealand Novel'.*

It is, of course, not just a 'Novel' but a 'Great Novel' and it is yet to be written, but the poet, critic and satirist A. R. D. Fairburn has worked out a simple story-line for it and a cast of characters, and he is confident that his novel will be greeted by his fellow Kiwis with cries of 'Oh, yes, this is the real New Zealand':

SKETCH-PLAN FOR THE GREAT NEW ZEALAND NOVEL

The story is about Tom Shaughnessy, son of an Irish remittance man, who died fighting in an insane asylum six months before our hero is born, and a beautiful young girl of seventeen, an inmate of the Borstal institution. Tom has a childhood in which sunshine and shadow are mingled. He forms a passionate attachment for his mother which is to dominate his life. Leaving school at the age of eighteen after he had finished for good and all with Standard 2, Tom digs post-holes, acts as chucker-out in a tough joint, becomes a jockey but is unsuccessful owing to his shortness of stature, writes short stories, takes to shop-lifting and serves several gaol sentences (during which he makes many new friends), and in general kicks around and is kicked around. As can be seen already, Tom Shaughnessy is an ordinary, simple New Zealander with the dreams, and hopes, the tastes and ambitions, of simple, ordinary people.

Disturbed by his failure to interest, or be interested by, women, Tom broods about life. He passes through a deep spiritual crisis, and seeks the advice and protection of a kindly non-conformist missioner, who has a wife and family of ten boys, all between the ages of 9 and 12. After living with them for a year, Tom is amazed to discover accidentally that the wife is not really the missioner's wife, but is really a man dressed up as a woman. Feeling that the house is too crowded, he is on the point of leaving and running away to sea when, one day, the missioner's wife shoots him (the missioner), and Tom is arrested and charged with the murder. The trial is a long-drawn-out one, in which the whole gamut of human emotions is run through by the lawyers. One afternoon towards the end of the third week, when things are looking black indeed for Tom Shaughnessy, news comes that the missioner's wife has committed suicide, leaving a note of confession in the form of a short autobiographical novel. The trial is abandoned at once, and Tom leaves the Court with hardly a stain on his character.

From this point onward, Tom Shaughnessy really begins to get into his stride, and the story gathers emotional depth and momentum. Tom discovers accidentally that he has an hereditary disease and is going blind, and tries to shoot himself; but, since he has never had any military training, manages only to blow off the lobe of his right ear. He is nursed back to health and sanity by 'Hobson Street Hattie', a woman with a rough exterior but a heart of gold. He begins a novel, but abandons it in despair when he finds that Hattie too is working on a novel, and that there is nobody to cook the meals. We next find Tom taking a correspondence course in sheep-farming. Before many weeks have passed he catches a train and settles down to rural life, striving to save his soul and integrate himself through contact with the simplicities of Nature and Mother Earth.

War breaks out, and an old petty-officer friend in the Navy, who has just published a collection of short stories, persuades Tom to join up in order to fight against tyranny. With the war at last over, the story moves rapidly to its conclusion. The petty-officer, after a profound spiritual crisis, decides to become a missioner; and Tom Shaughnessy, unable to forget the past or to face the future alone, disguises himself as a woman and lives with the ex-petty-officer. They befriend a shy young man of Irish extraction named Shaun Tomassey, who is ambitious to become a writer. Shaun comes to live with them. And so the story ends, with everybody sadder and wiser, but looking forward bravely to the future.

This story gives an unforgettable picture of New Zealand life. But it also has a universal meaning. It is a tale of simple, ordinary people, their joys and their sorrows, their tears and their smiles. It is, as one might say, just life—but life made more vivid and significant by the magic touch of Art.

Above all, it gives us New Zealanders a penetrating study of us as we really are, beneath our shy exteriors.

> A. R. D. Fairburn (1904–57), 'The Great New Zealand Novel' in *The Woman Problem and other Prose* (1967).

―――――――――

IN *Canada, the writing of humorous short stories is stimulated by the annual awarding of the Stephen Leacock Medal and the subsequent publication in book form of the winners. Many of the Leacock Medal winners are primarily humorous columnists, as is Eric Nicol who has won the Stephen Leacock medal for humour three times—a record.*

Nicol took a BA and MA at the University of British Columbia, spent a year at the Sorbonne in Paris looking into the comedy theories of Henri Bergson, wrote comic scripts for the BBC, settled in Vancouver, wrote six stage plays (two for children), was a free-lance writer for radio and television, published many books, and from 1951 has written a syndicated column for the Vancouver Province. *He is probably the most versatile and prolific of the contemporary Canadian journalist/humorists and the most consistent.*

Much of Nicol's humorous column is based upon domestic affairs; frequently upon the yawning gap between the illusion of family life and the reality of it:

PRECIOUS LEAVINGS

The garbage disposer of tomorrow will be a laser beam that makes the waste vanish—pouf!—in one flash of ruby light.

So says David McDermand of Chicago, an appliance industry executive addressing the American Home Economics Association. 'It won't grind, it won't mulch, it won't burn in the sense we think of burning. It will simply, utterly and absolutely disintegrate any substance placed in its path.'

Ha, ha, you're the droll one, McDermand. A laser beam, eh? Garbage simply vaporized, eh? Who does your project planning—Wayne and Shuster?

Only a bachelor who has led a very sheltered life would suggest that garbage can be disposed of like the magician's girl in tinselled tights. If you lived in our house, with small children, you'd know that a girl in tinselled tights is about the only thing that has not, at one time or another, been retrieved from the garbage.

You see, McDermand, the way that garbage works is this: You have the plastic receptacle under the sink, right? When it is heap full of garbage, featuring soggy old teabags and vegetable tops that have started to hum songs of the soil, Mummy discovers that her engagement ring is missing.

You still with me? You have a child aged 13 months to 4 years in the house. Where is the first place you look for Mummy's engagement ring? Correct, in the garbage. Past experience has taught you that to the child 13 months to 4 years all the world is garbage and the place for its manifold wonders is in the garbage receptacle.

So, you spread some newspaper and dump the loaded garbage receptacle onto it and pick over the attractive items one by one. Everything looks so good you just can't make up your mind which one to choose first. Just as you are frisking the last mouldy half of orange peel, Mummy announces that she has found her engagement ring in her jewel case, of all places.

You will note, McDermand, how far we have come from instantaneous disintegration of garbage. Garbage is never really done with, so long as there are little hands to throw into the disposer objects that do not qualify as waste. To name a few, according to records kept at our house: Daddy's left shoe (best pair), keys to front and back doors, crank for oven rack, cutlery (assorted, sterling silver), and the records kept at our house.

Exhuming the kitchen garbage is only Phase One of a search for such articles. Phase Two is to go through the outdoor garbage can, also known as Operation Yeuch. Phase Three—or terminal stage—is to chase the garbage truck all the way to the dump, and leap into the burning pit.

A laser beam simply does not meet the conditions of garbage disposal in the average home. With utter and immediate disintegration, parents returning from a brief absence from the kitchen will find that Little Boy Blue has blown the Wedgwood and his baby sister.

The laser beam certainly has its place in the home of the future. Visitors who come to the door during your favorite TV program, the bra that Daddy has unaccountably found in his jacket pocket—rubbish of this kind begs for instant disintegration. But garbage—oh, no. Leavings are such sweet sorrow.

Eric Nicol (b. 1919).

An area to which Eric Nicol is devoted is the sex war. All it takes is for some sexist remark to be passed in a newspaper article, e.g. that female liberation could lead to women treating men as casual sex-objects, and Nicol is away, the bit between his teeth:

THE NEW WOMAN

News has just reached me of the sexual revolution that is freeing women to be as frivolous as men. Before I adopt my usual position in such a situation— throwing my apron over my head and waiting for it to go away—I wish to make a statement.

It is deplorable that young women should think of a man as a fun object. As we all know, women in beauty parlors ogle photos of men in the women's magazines, pictures that reduce manhood to a mere plaything. But we have always blamed this on the hair-dryer overheating the thyroid gland.

Apparently the New Woman is bolder than this. Basically immature, she fails to understand that to us men sex can only be meaningful as part of the larger experience of love, marriage, children, bills, heavy drinking, fights, divorce and alimony. Only thus enriched does sex have any real meaning.

Granted, some of us men are willing to settle for sex without meaning. But usually such a man has a problem. Like being already married. Thousands of men are willing to settle for something less than the fulfilment that is marriage simply because they already have a wife. Often this makes them so sick they don't even want to talk about it.

But you take a normal man like myself and you have a man who looks upon a curvaceous, ardent, full-lipped girl not as someone to share a brief passionate interlude but as the grandmother of his children's children. That, in my opinion, is why so many young women put those attractive grey streaks in their hair. They know that men, the right kind of men, like to consider them as potential nanas.

Personally, I find it degrading that a woman should view me as the transitory companion of a 'score' or 'make-out', as these girls call it. It hasn't happened yet, but I am fully prepared to resent it when it does.

More frequently the new, liberated female fastens her lickerish gaze on the young male rock'n'roll singer who, though he does not gate-fold in the nude, kindles in the eyes of his feminine audience a light that men reserve for the decent privacy of the barber shop.

The Pill may have emancipated woman from the traditional values she has attached to liaison with a member of the opposite sex, but she must be made to understand that men are not constituted, physically, mentally or morally, to treat intimate relations as a kind of passing tilt on the quilt.

A man is not just a man. He is a future father. Deep within him lie all the responsibilities, the mysteries, of fatherhood. These are the ancestral forces against which today's female libertinism must be measured and, I am confident, be found wanting. A woman may tell you that you are good-looking, witty, considerate, honest, intelligent and sexually thoroughly satisfying, but if she doesn't tell you you're permanent, well, man, you've been insulted.

Speaking of myself, I'd like to see some New Woman try to use me as the object of an idle moment's pleasure. Yes, sir, I'd like to see her try.

Ibid.

———————

IN 1947 a Canadian professor published an extraordinary book which never became well known internationally but in its own modest fashion deserves a place as a fine example of Canadian literary humour: a kind of companion piece, certainly in its originality, to the British eccentric literary inventions such as Augustus Carp, Lady Addle, and the Starkadders.

The book was Sarah Binks, *by Paul Hiebert.*

Hiebert was Professor of Chemistry at the University of Manitoba and he had a party-piece which convulsed many a private party and public concert in Winnipeg in which he gave readings from subtly awful poetry (which he had written), supposedly the work of Sarah Binks (whom he had invented), a Canadian poetess of prairie life whom he christened the 'Sweet Songstress of Saskatchewan'. In 1947 he put some of these poems together and linked them to form a spoof biography.

Hiebert insisted that Sarah Binks *was not a satire but an affectionate parody of primitive rural poetesses and of the sort of painstaking literary biography which is burdened with a wealth of trivial facts but has a subject of minuscule general interest.*

In the book, Sarah first wins fame with a cheery poem, Despond Not, *which was published in* The Horsebreeder's Gazette *during a drought; heavy rain followed immediately:*

DESPOND NOT

... Despond not, for shame such speak,
 Aloft! Aloft!
Tut! Whistle low, with peakered beak,
Soft, soft! Despond not!

In the following passage from her biography, we learn how Sarah Binks became a celebrity throughout Saskatchewan, or some of it, when she went on to win an unfortunate first prize in a literary competition.

Sarah lives on the Binks Farm in the district of Willows, which is near Quagmire and Pelvis, with her father Jacob Binks, grown-up Mathilda, and Ole, the Norwegian hired hand. Her nearest neighbours are the Schwantzhackers, who have thirteen daughters.

The saga of Sarah's sadly all-too-brief literary career continues:

It is the tragedy, the great ironic tragedy of Sarah Binks's life that this first tangible evidence of her success, the horse thermometer, should also have been the instrument of her death, the fatal dagger which stilled her voice for ever. But it is a splendidly fitting tragedy. Sarah would not have had it otherwise. The McCohen and Meyers Stock Conditioner Company may well say, 'If we had known that the horse thermometer was going to carry her off we would have given her instead a hypodermical needle of which we also carry a full line.' But between a hypodermic needle and a horse thermometer, Sarah would have unhesitatingly chosen the horse thermometer. The will to live was strong in her, but the will to self-expression was greater ...

The great literary contest sponsored by the McCohen and Meyers Stock Conditioner Company is history in the annals of the Quagmire Agricultural Society Fair. The exact conditions of the contest as originally outlined, have been preserved in the Binksian Collection whose trustees were fortunate enough to obtain a copy of *Swine and Kine*, where the announcement first appeared. Sarah herself was not a subscriber to *Swine and Kine* and Jacob Binks, as a true dirt farmer, disdained it as a women's magazine. 'The dam thing is all about pigs.' But the self-contained economics of the Schwantz-hacker menage *was* concerned with pigs and they regularly received a copy. Sarah was able to peruse it whenever the thirteen sisters had finished reading the advertisements and Mathilda was permitted to carry it across. The opportunity thus afforded the thirteen Schwantzhacker sisters to express themselves for Sarah's benefit in marginal comments and drawings proved to be a greater literary opportunity for her than for them. She seized at once upon the McCohen and Meyers' announcement, and so great was her preoccupation that she forgot, for once, to cross the eyes of all the illustrations of pigs and their owners in *Swine and Kine* before returning it to the thirteen sisters . . .

Her keen sense of literary values told her also that of all the manuscripts submitted in this competition, ninety-five per cent would undoubtedly deal with horse or cow and she recognized the value of originality in a competition of this kind. For a while she considered the indigenous gopher as a fitting farm animal, but in the end abandoned it as too trivial. As a fur-bearing animal it had some value in the tail, but its economic value had yet to be established.

Sarah eventually wrote about sheep. It seemed to the judges that in her keenly felt poem, the Old West, the sense of a country of big open spaces blew through every line:

HORDES OF SHEEP

'Tis night on the prairie and night on the plain,
And all is still—no sign of rain—
And all is peace, and deep in his teepee
The red man sleeps and his squaw is sleepy;
The red man snores with the red man's cunning;
But hark, what's that? 'tis the sound of running,
'Tis the sound of rushing, of hurrying feet,
And hark, what's that? 'Tis the sound of bleat;
Louder it comes, it rises wild,
Ah, the mother hears it and grabs her child,
Louder still, the frantic mother,
Grabs her child, and another, and another,
And the red man waked by that hurrying tread,
Turns deathly pale beneath his red;
The Indian Brave is roused from sleep;
'Run for your life boys, here come sheep!'. . .

2nd Prize: McCohen and Meyers Stock Conditioner Company Literary Contest.

Sarah submitted *Hordes of Sheep* with every confidence. But her active mind, intent upon a second entry, at once began to cast about for another farm animal. The same difficulty which she had previously experienced presented itself, a shortage of farm animals. She did not like to venture into the field of poultry. 'Poultry and poetry don't mix,' she had once told Mathilda, and this in spite of the success of *The Cursed Duck*. It was therefore a fortunate day for her when the farm skunk whose home was in one of the farther reaches of the coulee, paid one of his infrequent visits to the Binks home and decided to stay over for the week-end. Here was Sarah's inspiration. She had completely forgotten about the skunk and her quick intuition told her at once that she would have a free field, in the matter of literary theme. Few farms in the dry belt were fortunate enough to have one of these quaint animals within their borders and were obliged to depend almost entirely on the pail-smudge to control their mosquitoes. But welcome as was the skunk, it resisted all attempts at domestication, preferring the free life, if hazardous at times, to the security of 'bed and board and the right to mate', for which the once proud sheep had sold its heritage. Sarah admired the skunk for its independence, but also mildly resented its manner of resisting all advances, especially after Ole's friendly overtures had been met with a distant snub. With deft sureness she puts her finger on the one weak spot in the skunk character, its pride.

THE FARM SKUNK

I take it that the skunk is proud,
And uses devious device,
To hold himself aloof from crowd,
Surrounds himself with social ice.

He tends to give himself an air,
And has been known to snub his betters,
His attitude a bored hauteur,
Like those who talk of art and letters.

He lifts his eyebrows to his peers,
Attempts at friendliness annoy him.
No wonder that in course of years
His very best of friends avoid him.

1st Prize: McCohen and Meyers Stock Conditioner Company Literary Contest.

The announcement of the award and the publication of *The Farm Skunk*, by Sarah Binks, of Willows, Saskatchewan, gave Sarah no surprise. She had expected it, and her only doubt had been whether *Hordes of Sheep* or *The Farm Skunk* would be awarded first place.

The big day of the Quagmire Agricultural Society Fair arrived soon after the announcement of the award. Sarah received her exhibitor's badge and was duly notified to be somewhere in the neighbourhood of the grandstand during the middle of the afternoon. The Hon. Grafton Tabernackel himself, who had opened the fair, consented to present the prize in person but was unfortunately engaged at the moment in opening some special exhibits behind the sheep barn when Sarah's name was called. Her appearance when she stepped onto the platform was the signal for tumultuous applause. She had been preceded by a trapeze act and the next item on the list of attractions was to have been a symbolic dance by Lolita, one of the performers from the far end of the midway who had been brought to Quagmire at tremendous expense for this occasion. It was an exceptionally windy day and the grandstand had been looking forward to this act with much anticipation, especially after one of the trapeze artists had just been blown off the trapeze and had landed on the third base of the adjoining baseball diamond where a game was in progress, and from which position of vantage he was able to score for Quagmire.

Sarah herself had some misgivings about the wind when she stepped onto the platform and her attention was occupied with it to such an extent that for some time she was mistaken for Lolita and given round after round of applause. In fact, it was not until Adolf McCohen, rising to the occasion in the absence of the premier, presented Sarah with the bright and shining horse thermometer, that the public was really aware that their new poetess had come among them . . .

A full winter was to pass and its heavy cloak was to 'enfold . . . beneath its blighted snow-banks' the entire Binks farm for many a long month . . . Sarah was happy, profoundly, contentedly happy. The chores were light, the afternoons were long, and Jacob Binks had presented her one Christmas with almost a cubic foot of unused mortgage and auction-sale handbills which he had acquired from the Quagmire printery and upon whose backs Sarah could write and write. Ole chewed his cigars and Mathilda returned from the fair and managed to send word across to the Schwantzhacker farm that she would continue her visit with Sarah until the next chinook. Once a day the two girls took the temperature of all the Binks's horses with Sarah's thermometer, and once at least, Jacob Binks used it when Ole returned through a blizzard from a political meeting, 'to see if the dam' Swede's as hot as he looks'.

Alas, the horse thermometer. That fateful instrument which had so often taken the temperature of the horses and which had been the first step towards renown . . .

Happy Sarah, who could write with this sword of Damocles hanging over her. If she was aware of what lay in store for her she gave no sign. 'To face the fact undismayed' was written upon her shield henceforth.

If she had any premonition, her works during this final year do not show it.

Paul Hiebert (1892–1987), Sarah Binks (1947).

🐦 Those readers who are aware of how, or rather where, a horse thermometer is normally put to use will be immensely relieved to learn that Sarah Binks's death by horse thermometer was in fact caused by her accidentally biting through the glass bulb and swallowing a lethal dose of mercury. There was an epidemic of hives in the area and Sarah attempted to take her own temperature (the human way) whilst at the same time chewing a Scotch mint, of which she was inordinately, indeed fatally, fond.

THE 1920s *saw a burst of inventive humour in British newspapers of such energy and momentum that the wave flowed on for something like fifty years.*

The founding father of this extraordinarily fertile period in Fleet Street newspaper-column humour was Dominic Bevan Wyndham Lewis, FRSL.

D. B. Wyndham Lewis's timing was impeccable in starting this new school of humour except for one awkwardness: he had to share his touch of fame with a much more celebrated contemporary namesake with whom he has been confused ever since.

The other one—Percy Wyndham Lewis, usually known simply as 'Wyndham Lewis'—was an American-born essayist, poet, and novelist, a writer of savagely satirical prose with near-fascist tendencies and a painter, leader of the Vorticist school. His portraits, which had a great influence on many later British painters included a famous study of Edith Sitwell. Miss Sitwell always referred to D. B. the humorist as 'the wrong Wyndham Lewis'.

The two Wyndham Lewis's had virtually nothing in common. D. B., a Francophile who lived in France whenever he could, was educated in Cardiff, was a convert to Catholicism, had great personal charm (and a stutter), was an authority on French history and literature, and a spirited biographer of François Villon, Ronsard, Molière, et cie. He also, with Charles Lee, assembled the classic and magnificently funny anthology of good bad verse, The Stuffed Owl. *The only reference to D. B. to be found in the* Oxford Companion to English Literature *is a sentence in brackets at the end of a longish entry on (Percy) Wyndham Lewis which reads in its entirety: 'He is not to be confused with D. B. Wyndham Lewis, 1894–1969, the Catholic biographer.'*

Even Catholic biographers have to make a living and D. B. earned his crust by becoming a literary journalist. He joined the Daily Express *in 1919, became literary editor and started a humorous column which he called 'By the Way', giving himself the pseudonym of 'Beachcomber'. This column worked so well that from then on he devoted himself to humorous journalism, writing for various newspapers and journals some of the most innovative, witty, and nonsensical columns in modern journalism: from 1925 to 1930 he was 'At the Sign of the*

Blue Moon' in the Daily Mail; *he then became 'Mustard and Cress' in the* Sunday Referee, *went back to the* Daily Mail *in* 1935, *began writing a regular piece as D.B.W.L. for the* Bystander, *and ended a splendid career on a high note as 'Timothy Shy' of the* News Chronicle.

Aficionados *cherish items such as his description of the vastly aged but still vestigially beautiful French cabaret artiste, Mistinguette:*

A rose-red cutie, half as old as time.

A random philosophical thought:

Mayors are born free but everywhere they are in chains.

And a fragment of the autobiography which he appended to a collection of some of his 'Timothy Shy' pieces:

. . . Mr Shy has from time to time been entertained in pre-war days by rich women, but not very much. Today, in uniform, he is Simpson's favourite model. On being nodded to by Professor Joad in the Lavatory of the Athenaeum (3.28 p.m., 18/7/32, Wash-basin no. 5), in mistake, as it turned out later, Mr Shy at once abandoned Literature, resigned from the P.E.N. Club Wolfcub Patrol, and took up thinking in a big way.

'Timothy Shy' (D. B. Wyndham Lewis) (1891–1969).

Whether there was any cross-fertilization in those early days between the London newspaper columnists and the New York wits is not proven, but certainly Wyndham Lewis was practising the new dementia praecox *style of surrealistic humour at much the same time as were Ring Lardner and Robert Benchley, and with equal skill and charm:*

A BALKAN LYRIC

(From the Szlo-Molczchakian of Smorko Kssykvcs.)

It was, then, you?
You!
Gschzzsic!

Ibid.

For a while in the early days Wyndham Lewis's column in the Daily Mail *was weekly, which meant that he had a little more space. The extra hundred or so words occasionally proved a godsend.*

It would have been lamentable if his delicate and moving report of Miss Diana Mulberry's legal action for damages against the Home Secretary had been shorter. By even a sentence:

SCENE WITH HAREBELLS

High Court of Justice, King's Bench Division:

BEFORE Mr JUSTICE CHEESE and a special Jury the hearing was begun of the action Mulberry *v.* Home Secretary.

Mr Roring, KC, said: My Lord, this is an action in which we ask for nominal damages for wrongful imprisonment. The facts pertaining may be stated very briefly. Miss Diana Mulberry is a maiden lady living in South Kensington and justly celebrated as a writer of dainty stories and playlets. On the—

Mr Justice Cheese: Has anybody got a pin?

A Juror: An ordinary pin or a safety-pin, my Lord?

Mr Justice Cheese: Never mind, I can draw things instead. Well, Mr Roring?

Mr Roring: On the night of the third of April, my Lord, towards half-past ten o'clock, Miss Mulberry was returning in a taxicab from a dinner-party in Hampstead. The night was clear and mild and there was a full moon. As her cab skirted the Heath Miss Mulberry perceived in a little distant dell a clump of harebells nodding in the breeze, and the sight suddenly caused her, in her own words, to 'come all over whimsy'. She therefore leaned out and stopped the taxicab, alighted, and, seizing the driver, Jas. Tomlinson, by the hand, ran swiftly towards the harebell clump. On arriving there she blew the harebells a kiss and ran tiptoe behind a tree, crying to Jas. Tomlinson: 'Let's pretend!'

She then peeped from behind the tree, ran out, and kneeling down by the harebells pretended to telephone to Jas. Tomlinson, saying: 'Hello, Prince Wonderful, this is 9908 Fairyland speaking!'

Mr Justice Cheese: And was it?

Mr Roring: Er—no, my Lord. After further indulgence in whimsiness, which the evidence will disclose, Miss Mulberry again took Jas. Tomlinson by the hand and danced with him on tiptoe round the harebells, shouting with elfish glee. It was at this point that Police-Constable Bumpton arrived and took Miss Mulberry, after a slight struggle, into custody.

Mr Justice Cheese: It's odd I can never draw necks properly.

Mr Roring: As y'Ludship pleases.

Mr Justice Cheese: Ears, yes. Necks, no.

Miss Mulberry then gave evidence bearing out counsel's opening.

Mr Roring: Harebells have a decided effect on you, Miss Mulberry?—Yes. They make me feel dancey! I always think the fairies use them for telephones!

Mr Roring: Bluebells have this effect also?—Certainly.

Mr Justice Cheese: And dumb-bells?—I beg your pardon?

Mr Justice Cheese: When I said 'dumb-bells', that was just a little whimsy crack of my own. Proceed, Mr Roring.

Jas. Tomlinson, taxicab-driver, of Little Padge Street, Bermondsey, described the dance by moonlight among the harebells.

Mr Roring: You enjoyed the dance, Mr Tomlinson?—Not so bad.

You ran after Miss Mulberry and blew her a kiss?—Not to the lady I didn't. I never blew kisses to no lady. I got my licence to think of.

Did you blow a kiss to the policeman when he appeared?—Well, I can't rightly say. The lady was telephoning to 'im, like. ''Ullo,' she says, 'is that Prince Winkipop? The darling 'arebells 'ave missed you, Prince!'

Mr JUSTICE CHEESE: And had they?—I couldn't rightly say, melud.

PC Reginald Bumpton, YY709, said that Miss Mulberry was dancing on tiptoe hand in hand with Tomlinson. He requested them to move away. The complainant then said: ''Oo knows but we are all enchanted 'ere tonight, in the moonlight, among the 'arebells?'

Mr RORING: You cautioned her?—I cautioned 'er, and she replied: ''Ush! The fairies are ringing us up!' I cautioned 'er further, and she replied: 'Tinkle, tinkle. Princess 'Oneylocks speaking.' She then 'opped up and down on 'er toes, very excited.

What was the taxicab driver doing?—'E was larfing.

Mr JUSTICE CHEESE (to Miss Mulberry): Were *you* laughing?—Oh, *no*. It was all so beautiful! The harebells were chiming a little cozy cuddly song and a little breeze came dancing in, curtseying to the trees, and—

Mr JUSTICE CHEESE: Can you draw horses' legs?—No.

Mr JUSTICE CHEESE: Nor can I.

Miss MULBERRY: I should like to add that a tiny, wee, winsome baby rabbit peeped out at us!

Mr JUSTICE CHEESE: Can you draw a rabbit?—Oh, no. One doesn't *draw* rabbits, one *thinks* them! Lovely warm tender furry rabbity tricksy thoughts peeping in and out of one's dreams. One thinks harebells, too. Slim, dancey, pale-blue thoughts! Every time a fairy trips over a rainbow a new harebell is born.

Mr JUSTICE CHEESE (to PC Bumpton): Is that true?—I can't say, my Lord.

Mr JUSTICE CHEESE: Is anybody here from the Royal Botanical Society?

Mr BOOMER, KC (for the Home Secretary): The Chief Conservator of Kew will be called, my Lord. He will tell the Court that the complainant's theory with regard to harebells is extremely doubtful.

Mr JUSTICE CHEESE: The Home Secretary is being called also?

Mr BOOMER, KC: Yes, m'lud. Our case is that the whimsy conduct with which the complainant was charged took place after eight p.m.

Mr JUSTICE CHEESE: Oh, Auntie!

The Court adjourned for luncheon.

Ibid.

An occasional treat was a batch of D. B. Wyndham Lewis's parodies of 'gutter press' headlines. He seemed to catch their tone of voice exactly:

NEWS

(*With all due acknowledgements*)

£10,000 WIFE HITS LONE AIRMAN WITH MYSTERY FISH

Amazing West End Drama Sensation.

WEALTHY MAYFAIR MAN'S HAT FILLED WITH LINSEED AS SPORTS GIRL PLEADS FOR
SPLENDID ISOLATION

'Get out of Europe'—£1,500 Mother's Cry

A beautiful sad-faced auburn-haired girl sat to-night in a ☞ Page 9. Col. 1.

And a parody of one of those warmly romantic 'women's interest' columns:

WONDERFUL LONDON YESTERDAY

Sergeant Dawn Vereker, loveliest young policewoman in London, bent wonderingly over the greying, handsome, dissolute head of the baronet who lay
before her in the Piccadilly gutter, ashen-pale, his eyes closed. Her violet eyes
were suddenly wide with dismay under the lamp.

'Frobysher!'

The adorable sergeant's cry had hardly been uttered when into the opening
eyes of the elderly fallen man-about-town in his immaculate evening garb
came an answering look of recognition.

'Mother!'

And soon, unheeding the traffic which roared past them, Titian-haired
mother and erring son were locked in an embrace . . . together . . . a
moment . . . ere duty called her . . . the world forgot . . .

London, London, what a heartbreak old town you are.

Ibid.

———————

O NE *day in the early 1920s, D. B. Wyndham Lewis's room at the* Daily
Express, *the reporter's room, was enlivened by the arrival of a new man, a
failed* Sunday Express *staff-writer whose line had been to supply nature notes and
small poems about birds.*

D. B. Wyndham Lewis recalled the tender moment of their meeting:

The door was burst open and a thick-set, furious, bucolic figure all over
straw and clay, strode in and banged passionately on the floor with a
thick gnarled stick uttering a roar soon known and feared in every pub in
Fleet Street:

'Flaming eggs! Will no one rid me of this stinking town!'

> Quoted in: *Beachcomber. The Works of J. B. Morton* (ed. Richard Ingrams,
> 1974).

*The new man was J. B. Morton, full name John Cameron Audrieu Bingham Michael
Morton, known to his colleagues as Johnny.*

*The extrovert behaviour was habitual. He was forever banging his blackthorn
stick on the bars of pubs and bellowing for ale, as noted in A. G. Macdonnell's*

England, their England, *where Morton appears, thinly disguised if at all, as 'Mr Huggins':*

. . . A man of about thirty-five, a thick-set man of medium height, with a red face and red hands and an irresistible combination of vitality and impertinence . . . In a sudden whirl of rage, he seized an enormously thick walking stick, or rather cudgel, which leant against the counter beside him, and struck the counter a terrific blow which set the glasses jumping and rattling and shouted, 'Stinking fish! Is there no one here to serve a gentleman? . . . Scum,' said the red-faced man; 'Filthy, lousy, herring-gutted, spavin-bellied scum!'

That kind of heartiness would not suit modern pubs; it would be out of keeping with cocktails under paper sunshades, piped pop music, and microwave-ovened quiches, but at the time it would have been enjoyed by the other drinkers and even admired as amusing behaviour. That was the immediate post-First World War era, when Georgian poetry was rejoicing in the countryside and fresh air, and there was a general urge to return to rustic simplicities.

Johnny Morton, who had fought in the Great War and been shell-shocked on the Somme, was really celebrating the pleasures of being alive—as were his contemporaries Chesterton and Belloc and D. B. Wyndham Lewis—but the world Morton was alive in was too modern and sleazy for his tastes and he hankered after an older, merrier England. So he, and many others like him, looked for their pleasures to the few good things which were as yet unspoiled: country walks, wine, beer, playing cricket, making people laugh.

In those early days much of Morton's humour was physical. Notable pranks included bending down to the slot of a pillar-box and calling inside 'Don't cry, my little man, we'll have you out in a jiffy. Be brave . . .' until a large crowd had gathered and a fire engine summoned, whereupon he would slip away.

And covering the front doorstep of Virginia Woolf's cottage with empty quart brown-ale bottles.

Morton, having failed as a writer of nature fillers for the Sunday Express, *proved to be even more incompetent as a reporter on the* Daily Express, *but D. B. Wyndham Lewis, who had become his close friend, knew there was more to Morton than clowning in bars and playing tricks on strangers; he knew that Morton was a fellow-Francophile, erudite and witty, and that he had powers of humorous invention which matched or were even better than his own. When Wyndham Lewis moved to the* Daily Mail *he arranged for Morton to be taken off reporting and tried out on the* Express's *funny column.*

So in 1924 J. B. Morton became 'Beachcomber'. And except for a while at the beginning and the end, when it went out weekly, he wrote a Beachcomber column daily, six days a week, for fifty-one years.

It was an astonishing achievement by any standards, not only because of the quantity of work done but for its remarkable quality.

G. K. Chesterton described Beachcomber as 'a huge thunderous wind of elemental and essential laughter'. Evelyn Waugh said that he had 'the greatest comic fertility of any Englishman'.

Morton picked up the column where D. B. Wyndham Lewis left off, bringing to it the same vigorous dislike of modernism, fuddy-duddyism, pseudo-art, puritanism, and then adding not only new attributes like his own particular kinds of nonsense, his love of hauntingly funny (but not silly) names, and characters who, though insane or criminal, were curiously lovable, but also a marvellous (and, over a span of fifty years, perhaps vital) gift for keeping characters and ideas going, unwilting, seemingly for ever.

Fifty years bridged generations. Children and grandchildren were able to share with their parents the ritual of reading Beachcomber at breakfast, and Beachcomber's characters became part of many families' private culture. Households grew up reciting to each other the inventions of Dr Strabismus (Whom God Preserve) of Utrecht, the names of Huntingdonshire cabmen, advertisements for 'Snibbo', and they talked to each other in the manner of Mrs McGurgle, ambitious and genteel landlady of the seaside boarding-house, Hotel McGurgle (et de l'Univers).

Long-running series are never easy to appreciate from a single sample but the following compilation of random paragraphs and regular features might give new readers an inkling of why the column ran for fifty years.

To older readers it might well bring a reminder of the stickiness of marmalade and the smell of morning steam trains on the up line:

BALLET

Le Spectre du Fromage

Here is modern balletography at its most evocative; a tenuous lyric replete with the *fromagerie* which we have come to expect from the productions of Commissarmutzky. From the opening *pas de cheval*, during which Tumbleova rises dreamily from the Cheese like a sleepy night-watchman on the frontiers of Fairyland, to the closing *ricochet* of the Marquis, who has been thrown against the dungeon wall, the spectacle is a feast for eye, ear, heart, brain, and that aesthetic sixth sense of the *aficionado*. Serge Trouserin, who has little to do but shoot his imaginary arrows at the huge Cheese, contrives to suggest, particularly in his *demi-pas*, his *retroussements*, and his irresistible *chinoiseries*, a spirit out of tune with mundane *affaires*.

(Tomorrow: Chuckusafiva in *L'oiseau sur le Chapeau de Nelly*.)

DR STRABISMUS IS BUSY

Dr Strabismus (Whom God Preserve) of Utrecht, is working hard on about fourteen thousand and fifty new inventions. These include a collapsible salt-bag, a bottle with its neck in the middle, a rice-sifter, a stanchion to prop up other stanchions, a suet-container, a foghorn key, a leather grape, a new method of stencilling on ivory, basalt cubes for roofing swimming baths, a fox-trap, a dummy jellyfish, waterproof onions, false teeth for swordfish, a method of freezing meat-skewers, a hand-woven esparto grass egg cosy which plays Thora when released from the egg, a glass stilt, a revolving wheelbarrow, an iron thumb for postmen, a hash-pricker, a beer-swivel with blunt flanges and a red go-by, a fish detector, a screw for screwing screws into other screws, hot pliers, a plush sausage-sharpener, a rope-soled skate for using in mountain quarries, an oiled cork for use in rabbit-hutches, a cheese anchor and a chivet for screaming radishes.

CAFE DES VACHES, PARIS

I am basking in the Parisian sunshine, drinking my Pernod, and watching the cosmopolitan crowd passing up and down the boulevard.

From my table I can see old *père* Nichaud, the doyen of the Poupouists, and a disciple of the Apollinaris, who taught me how to draw mackerel with my eyes shut.

Ah, Lolotte has just entered. Lolotte, the little dancer from the *Brebis Qui Tousse*, who used to shoot plums off the tree with a rook-rifle—how long ago?

With her is handsome young Fujiyama, the Japanese artist, and Dolmen, the dour Cornish poet who strangled La Folie with his braces at the corner of the Rue des Mauvaises Odeurs.

'Garçon!'

Surely I know that *voix*.

Assurement! It is 'Gop', the wicked caricaturist of the *Calviniste du Nord*, the go-ahead paper that first printed Dubosc's explanation of Proust.

We greet each other.

'*Tiens, mon vieux!*'

'*Et vous?*'

'*Pas mal.*'

'Gop' married the widow Colifichet, because he owed her four months' rent. He and Puant are the authors of '*Bonsoir, Nou-Nou!*' the new review at the Alouette.

He was a wild young man in his youth, this 'Gop', and used to drop eggs from the top of the Eiffel Tower.

At a corner table, in the shade, Manon, from the *Grands Augustins*, is talking to Mathilde Mercredi, the soubrette from the *Samaritaine*. 'Tic' greets them. He is smoking one of his long Cuban cigars at the wrong end, and his trousers are patched with leading articles from the 'Ami du Peuple'.

'*Hé, Manon!*'

The slim girl starts, and looks up.

'*Mais . . . tais toi!*'

Here comes Tric-Trac, who sells his own songs at ten sous the kilo every evening in the Place Pigalle. They say he has written an opera in which he makes use of only three notes.

Ah, now for a real Bohemian—Paradis, in his velvet coat and black trousers, with his pale, dirty face and eyes that burn like live coals. He is dying, they say. He sleeps in the day-time, and drinks all night, but if he cared he could be a great artist.

Paradis was brought up on his father's estate in the Morvan, but he ran away to a publisher's (the modern equivalent of running away to sea) and managed to get a novel published. It failed, and he did no more work.

His father makes him a handsome allowance, and he lives in the Rue Chat Maigre with Tortoise, the poet, and Beaugras, the etcher.

At a table on the pavement I note Van Kuypens, the Dutchman. With him is La Grenouille, who sits for Garnache. When he becomes excited he pours his coffee into his coat-pocket and takes off his boots. They say that he has a crayon frieze running round the lining of his hat, representing a boar-hunt in the forest of Quercy.

La Grenouille sleeps in a canoe which is anchored to the side of a big swimming bath, but she keeps a mole in a fur glove suspended from the ceiling.

The sun sinks. The café teems with life.

Ah, Paris!

A clock in the Rue Manet strikes six-thirty, and I think of those words of de Gourmont.

KNITTING NOTE

Here is a dainty pair of braces for your doggy.

Work on a ribbed welt with two-ply. Cast on eight stitches working in B.3, H.7, Kt. to pawn's fifth and mate in three purl. Rip out six on the third row, ending at back edge in 4. Pick up rep. val. at side to 7, going straight to 14 ins. Then take a half-gill of peptonised milk essence and pour it into a container leaving the armhole hollow, as shown in Fig. 6.

(*Enter the Icebergs, a Jewish family from the Arctic.*)

ALONE WITH NATURE

A cascade of melody from the old larch—in many a ferny dell the shy lesser celandine—A flash of wings announces the arrival of the tiny beercrest—By tilth and loam spring's message, etc.—feathered songsters of this fronded isle, and/or jovial chanticleers of highway and hedge—bits about age-old plough turning up the benignant soil—greystern nesting in old blow-pipe there to lay her mottled eggs—quack-quack from the slime-strewn pond—willow-catkins, etc. Sticky chestnut buds lambs gambolling on many a lea call in at Campbell's about the smell in the attic snakes sloughing winter skins on sunny uplands.

PRODNOSE: It seems to me your rough notes have got mixed up with your copy.

MYSELF: 'Tis no matter. The public likes a glimpse of a writer's workshop.

———————

SEESAW

We three have noticed in your column, if such may we call it, we hope, a number of letters about phenomena in restaurants. Sir, we are the three Persian gentlemen who played seesaw in the lounge of the restaurant. It was upon the belly of the fattest of us, Risamughan, that the plank (from a sugar-melon tree of Kermanshah) was gently but firmly laid. Then Ashura and I, Kazbulagh, sat one at each end of the plank, and the sport, as you English call it, began. Sir, we beg to state that we did not do this to advertise anything except our own extreme happiness. For, sir, we were going home to our own families in Filthistan, the gramophone company for which we had the honour to act as night-watchers having gone burst. So, sir, we played seesaw for fun in the nearest place we could find. And, sir, one day, if we ever return from Persia, we hope to play seesaw again in that most hospitable restaurant. And, sir, P.S., it does not at all hurt Rizamughan's belly, since he wears a thick cork bathmat, with 'Welcome' written on it, under his shirt—a souvenir from our boarding-house, sir, in the Cromwell Road. Astonishing good luck, sir, and remember us as

The Filthistan Trio

———————

GOOD ENOUGH FOR 'PUNCH'

'Do you hone your razors?' asked Liszt.

'Of course I do,' replied Wagner. 'Don't you?'

'No, I borrow them,' retorted the abbé, with a grin.

———————

CARSTAIRS COME TO BHOO

When Carstairs—Big White Carstairs—crossed the unspeakable Wudgi desert that lies between Seringapahaha and Klang-Klang he took with him nothing but a dozen Union Jacks, a dress suit, and a water-pistol.

'And why,' lisps the sub-human reader, 'why a water-pistol?'

Because there are no wells in that desert, ghoulish lout.

'But,' continues the idiot reader, 'a water-pistol holds very little water.'

That is true enough but there are times when very little water may save a man's life, as the bailiff said to the actress when she poured him out a stiff whisky and bade him, with old-world courtesy, say when.

Carstairs allowed himself one drop of water a day from the pistol.

'But,' clamours the footling reader, 'did he meet no wild animals or nomads?'

Of course he did. Filthistan and Stin-King are infested with frightful crea-tures. His method with wild beasts was to choke them to death with bits of Union Jack; for the flags were made of specially coarse material, suitable for hoisting in all weathers, or for making into warm overcoats. As for the nomads, when they saw him in evening dress they knew the Empire was upon them, and they brought him gifts of yak's liver, black rice, and camel's milk cheese.

'And where,' asks the long-eared reader, 'did he finally end up?'

Why, in the walled city of Bhoo, where they worship their dead aunts. And the water-pistol is now in the Museum of Folk-Lore at Wembley, between a letter from Mr Gladstone to the Golden Vale Laundry and half the hoof of a dirtibeeste captured by Cecil Rhodes in Matabeleland, on the occasion when the natives sang, 'Oh, dear, what can the Matabele, Cecil's so long in the kraal'.

STULTITIA'S COMEDY

Here is interesting theatrical news. Stultitia Cabstanleigh has had her little play produced at the Mayfair Theatre. It has no title—a fashion that may spread rapidly—and it is described as a *soufflé*. The first night audience laughed heartily at the witty lines, and the talented authoress herself, sitting on a dais in full view of the auditorium, rang a small bell before each joke or epigram, as a signal for the chattering to die down.

Several young men in the stalls were so enthusiastic that they demanded encores in the case of many of the epigrams. The action of the play was held up many times in this manner, and the authoress made a pretty speech, pointing out that the good lines would occur often during the last two acts— so that there would be no need to encore them.

I really cannot resist printing one or two of the more brilliant lines below:

A cynic is the man who eats the cherry and leaves the martini.
Life is a trifle—but sherry makes it tolerable.
You can't be sure of a woman who sneezes.
She has a Rolls body and a Balham mind.
No woman of forty can afford to be happy.

MORE WIT FROM STULTITIA

My dear, marriage is a vulgar effort on the part of dull people to bring boredom to a fine art.
Every modern poet has his favourite Mews.
Eating foie gras with an unintelligent man is like dancing a tango in diving boots.

THANKS TO SNIBBO

Dear Sir,—For many years I thought there was a little Persian milkman in iron trousers riding a zebra round my room. Then I was recommended to take Snibbo, and I have not seen that little Persian milkman since.—(*Signed*) F. TOGGLETON.

(If you suffer from little Persian milkmen, mice in tartan overcoats, yellow gasworks with bristles all over them, neuralgia, depression, or boils, write for the free Snibbo Booklet, recommended by 123,784 doctors.)

NERVE-WRACKING MASTERPIECE

The third volume in the *Huntingdonshire Cabmen* is published this morning. No higher praise can be given to it than to say that it is worthy of its predecessors. An age devoted to pleasure-seeking and cheap sensation is, perhaps, inclined to underrate the importance of this exhaustive list of cabmen's names. But an attempt has been made in this new volume to counteract any tendency to dullness by abandoning the usual alphabetical order. Thus it is with a pleasant shock of surprise that one finds, on page 231, 'Jelf, E. N., Barlow, D. J.' Such happy juxtapositions as this stimulate the interest of the reader, and give a semblance of narrative to what the undiscerning might call a mere catalogue of names. The volume concludes with 'Henderson, N.', and leaves one wondering whether there will be other Hendersons in Volume IV, promised for the autumn season. One would like to quote the whole book, but perhaps the following excerpt will give a taste of this monumental work:

Chance, B., Harris, Arthur, Kermode, S. S., Vale, P., Manton, W. R., Caldecott, R., Lister, Tom, Robinson, B. L., Robinson, E. T., Prout, V., Garrison, F. J., Sladder, T. W. M.

The juxtaposition of two Robinsons is a masterpiece of style, as daring as it is unexpected. But in justice it must be said that this volume contains nothing as memorable as the amazing 'Baines, H., Baines, L. T.' of Volume II.

FOULENOUGH AND VITA BREVIS

Psychologists have often said that the apparent dislike of Captain Foulenough shown by Miss Vita Brevis masks a kind of involuntary admiration.

He is certainly a persistent wooer, and on his return to England he has once more begun to lay siege to her. He said yesterday: 'If I don't marry her, I won't marry anyone—at least, hardly anyone.' Miss Brevis said yesterday: 'It's his practical jokes I can't stand. He called the other day while my brother the Dean was with me. The maid announced "Mr Claude Thirst", and he bounded in, seized a decanter of sherry, shouting "Thirst come, Thirst served," drained it, and handed it to my brother, saying: "Give me twopence on this empty." My brother was nonplussed.'

IN THE CITY

The Bumblethorpe loan is bad tactics. The early trustee issue, already over-subscribed in some quarters, is to be released for repayment of the special redeemable stock, in short-term loans on ordinary holdings. Securities released on corresponding profits could very easily be used at exchange rates, by covering short falls. But this is not being done. Why? Simply because those who might balance the offering of dollars have not the guts to support at lower levels the demand for cumulative preference releases. It is all part of the mania for sale by tender, and the sooner the surplus is bought back and absorbed by the bears, the sooner some shrewd manipulation will enable the supporters of revaluation to resume aggressive exchange of sterling.

MR JUSTICE COCKLECARROT
HOME LIFE

Cocklecarrot always refers to his retiring and very silent wife as Mrs Justice Cocklecarrot. For the first eight years this raised a wan smile on her face, but the joke has now worn thin, and he gets no encouragement when he trots out the phrase. Since, however, it is his only jest, some of his friends still greet it with a short and insincere burst of laughter. One or two mutter, 'Jolly good!' Others sigh heavily and turn away. And she, the source of the phrase, sits as impassible as a lump of earth, listening, always listening, but taking no part in any conversation. Which explains why the servants were recently staggered to hear her say suddenly, in a loud, clear voice, to her lord and master: 'Wivens fell down a manhole on Christmas Eve.' Cocklecarrot was in the hall about to set out for his club. He turned in astonishment, gazed at his wife, said 'Thank you, my love,' and went out dreamily into the street.

Ten minutes later he returned, with a puzzled frown on his face, and sought his wife in her boudoir. 'What Wivens was it you were speaking of?' he asked. 'E. D. Wivens,' said his wife. 'I see,' said Cocklecarrot, who had never heard of the man. Silence fell. After a quarter of an hour, Cocklecarrot, happy in this new talkativeness of his wife, said pleasantly: 'Did you know him, my dear?' 'No,' said his wife. So Cocklecarrot again set out for his club.

TAIL-PIECE

From that moment she never looked back.

(From Mr Lot's 'Life and Times of Mrs Lot')

MR O. THAKE

Mr Thake is taking a little holiday at a hotel on the Continent. Unhappily, he kindly helped a lady guest to get her sister's article on oranges published in a

newspaper, since when he has been deluged with further requests. And Saunders,
his man-servant at home, will keep forwarding him odd objects:

Hotel Des Fous Du Monde, Deauville

Dear Beachcomber,

Shakespeare says somewhere that there is a destiny that shapes our ends,
no matter how roughly we hew them. How true that is in my case! Wherever
I go, and whatever I do, I seem to meet trouble. I scarcely know which way
to turn at present. My room here is like Bedlam. I have got Miss Barbara
Waveling's confounded article, which isn't even typed. Then there are her
sister's idiotic drawings, Miss Vera Randell's poems, which I don't understand, some young man's puzzle problems, two short stories from some other
young man, a one-act play from a woman called Grabbham, a ballet from
her brother, and an essay on the Patriotism of Byron by an undergraduate.
And all this nonsense started because, in an unguarded moment, I promised
Miss Hester Waveling I would do my best for her sister's writing. The thing
is impossible. She seems to have told everybody that I am a sort of god in the
literary and artistic world. Only this morning a letter arrived from a girl I've
never heard of, asking my advice about contralto songs. Really!

I am forwarding all this stuff to you. For pity's sake use as much of it as
you can, or they will blame me. I simply dread the post now. For all I know,
there may be more members of the Waveling family lurking about. Whenever
I meet the eldest sister she gives me no peace, but at once talks literature. I
flatter myself that I am a cultured man, but I cannot bear being asked, after
breakfast, what I think of Thackeray. There is a time for everything, and this
is overdoing it.

Yours ever,
O. Thake.

P.S.—Tell Saunders he must be mad to send me diving-boots. They are
entirely useless to me. I don't see the point.

DIPLOMATIC COURSE

Quoting a recent dictum that 'There should no longer be any room for
gentlemen in the diplomatic service', Dr Smart-Allick [Headmaster of Nark-
over School] has decided to prepare some of his more promising pupils for a
diplomatic career.

A recent examination paper is worth quoting. One of the questions
was:

How would you, as an Ambassador in a foreign capital, set about procuring an
interview with the Minister for Foreign Affairs of the country to which you are
accredited?

One of the answers was: 'I wood send a beutiful wumman to elure him
into my clutches.'

Here are one or two more answers:

'Sanbag him in a loanly ally.'
'Get old uv some inkeriminating letters and blackmale im.'
'Brake in to his ministery and hold him up at the point of the ruvvolver.'
'Get him into a game of whist behind locked dores.'
'Pertend to be his long lorst unkil.'
'Dissgise meself as a gass inspekter cum to read his metre.'

A FOUL INNUENDO

There have lately been complaints in the newspapers, from Civil Servants, that lodging-house keepers show favouritism to their regular clientele. The accusation roused that well-known seaside landlady, Mrs McGurgle.

Dear Sir,

I treat civil servants just like my other lodgers. No better and no worse. It is rapid eating and not social status that gets a second helping. If I see an empty plate, I fill it, be its owner a big panjandrum in Government circles or only a humble traveller in biscuits. Snobbery, I am thankful to say, has never cast its foul shadow across the threshold of Marine House. For though the late Mr McGurgle, by whom I had the honour to be led to the altar at St. Philip's in this very resort, held an important position in a warehouse, he never to his dying day set up to be better than his fellows. An early decease, due to tainted cocoa partaken of at a French watering-place during a well-earned holiday, robbed me of my guide, philosopher and friend, but I flatter myself that Marine House is run today as it was in his lifetime, without fear or favour.

All are welcome, from dukes to dustmen.

Yours faithfully,
Florence McGurgle.

TAIL-PIECE

One disadvantage of being a hog is that at any moment some blundering fool may try to make a silk purse out of your wife's ear.

'Beachcomber' (J. B. Morton) (1893–1975), extracts from his column 'By the Way' in the *Daily Express* (1924–75).

IN 1930 *a new humorous column appeared in the* Sunday Express *called 'Sitting on the Fence'. It was announced as being by a New Humorist (it was actually by an experienced 37-year-old reporter and occasional dramatic critic) whose name, it said in large letters, was* NATHANIEL GUBBINS. *Below that it said, in almost as large letters,* 'Believe It Or Not This Is a Real Name!' (*it was certainly a real name but only half of it belonged to Mr Gubbins whose Christian name was Norman*).

The column ran for twenty-three years, achieving most success and respect during the Second World War when Gubbins's talent was at its most relevant.

Nat Gubbins's humour was very different from Beachcomber's. There were no great, soaring firework displays of nonsensical invention. Gubbins's gift was for logging the attitudes and speech of the ordinary working people whom he lived amongst and liked, the dwellers in suburbia who bought the Sunday Express, *lived in a semi-detached or terraced house with a pram in the hall, were law-abiding, conventional, and enjoyed a leisurely pint in the pub.*

Nat Gubbins had an extremely accurate ear for the way people talked in pubs:

MAN IN A PUB

'To cut a long story short,' said The Man in the Local, 'me and the wife and the two daughters caught the train by the skin of our teeth, and we was down in Devonshire the same evening. Of course, as you might expect, the train was crowded and the wife couldn't get a seat with her back to the engine, so she was feeling pretty poorly most of the way, though not as bad as my daughter Vi. I think you've met my daughter Vi in here?'

'Is that the one who can't eat fish?' we asked.

'No,' said The Man, 'it's Marge who can't eat fish and Vi who can't eat eggs. One look at an egg and Vi's stomach turns right over, and as for Marge, a mouthful of fish will bring her out in a rash before you can say Jack Robinson. And in that way she takes after her uncle George. I think you've met my uncle George in here?'

We said we didn't remember having the pleasure.

'Get along with you,' said The Man. 'Why, old George was in here last Tuesday. Or was it Wednesday?'

We said we didn't know.

'No. I'm a liar,' said The Man. 'It was on the Thursday, because that was the day the wife's great-aunt came to stay for a long week-end, though any week-end with the wife's great-aunt is a long one. Of course, the old lady's getting on now, and is as deaf as a post and as cunning as a fox. And eat? She never stops from the time she wakes up till the time she goes to bed. Of course, it's no good telling her there's a war on because she's never heard a bomb go off and she thinks you're talking about the Battle of Waterloo. Naturally we did what we could for her on the rations, a nice bit of bacon in the morning, a bit of mutton and two veg. for her lunch, a bit of relish for her supper, so I can tell you we were a bit surprised to hear a noise in the night and find her picking at the larder. And in that way she reminds me of my old pal Charlie, who always had a slice of bread and a pork chop and a spoonful of cold greens by the side of his bed in case he woke up hungry, and died of eating diabetes in 1907. Or was it 1908?'

We shook our head helplessly.

'No. I'm a liar,' said The Man. 'It was nineteen-nought-nine, because that was the year Marge was born as pretty as a picture with a shock of black hair all over her little head, though you'd never believe it if you saw her now, because she's as fair as fair and would have been married years ago if she wasn't so particular. But then that's always been the trouble with Marge. Fellers could take her to dances and theatres, but she always kept them at arm's length and if any one of them so much as said a word out of place she'd go as red as a peony and run like a hare straight back to her mum. She always said to me, "Dad," she said, "I'm waiting for Mr Right to come along!" But then, as I always say, marriage is a lottery and you can't pick and choose when you're in the middle thirties and the first bloom's gone. Now, Vi's a different cup of tea altogether. Fellers are attracted to Vi like bees to a honey-pot. But she never takes them seriously, and, although she's a bit of a tomboy and always ready for a lark, it's so far and no farther with Vi. I remember she once said to me, "Dad," she said, "I don't mind a bit of fun with a feller, but when it comes to stepping over the mark I'm an iceberg".'

We asked The Man what he was going to have.

'Seeing that it's you,' said The Man, 'I don't mind if I have a pint. Well, to cut a long story short . . .'

> Nathaniel Gubbins (1893–1976), 'Sitting on the Fence', *Sunday Express* (1930–53).

One of the long-running features he built up, which he began in 1936, was 'Diary of a Worm'. This was an almost exact modern replica of Douglas Jerrold's 'Mrs Caudle's Curtain Lectures', except that worm's exasperated wife did not wait until she got to bed before pitching into miserable worm.

There is a war on but worm's wife sees this as no excuse for worm humiliating her and generally giving way to moral depravity:

DIARY OF A WORM

Worm and wife are in cafe bar, when in comes worm's old friend, the Bouncing Blonde, now a sergeant in the ATS.

Bouncing Blonde shouts with delight at sight of worm, hits worm great thump on back, and asks 'How's the old trouble and strife?' and on seeing worm's wife roars, 'Why, there's the old ball and chain herself,' sits down next to worm and bangs table for waiter.

Blushing worm, although delighted to see hearty Bouncing Blonde, is embarrassed at wife's stiffening attitude, and when Bouncing Blonde says, 'What about a pint of pig's-ear all round?' worm says half-pint will be enough for him. Bouncing Blonde says, 'Rubbish', and tells waiter to bring three pints of wallop.

When three pints come, Bouncing Blonde blows off froth and, with cry of 'Down the hatch', sinks three-quarters of tankard at gulp. Admiring worm tries to emulate example, but chokes and has to blow nose furiously. Worm's wife tries to wither Bouncing Blonde with cold, penetrating stare, but Bouncing Blonde only finishes pint and orders another round.

After second pint Bouncing Blonde says she has date with American soldier, who is swell guy with oodles of necessary, gives worm hearty kiss and thumps worm's wife on back telling her not to be sour puss and to get on with her gargle. Worm's wife's hat knocked over her eyes by blow and worm trembles in seat as Bouncing Blonde bounces out.

Oh, so this is the new humiliation wife has to put up with, is it? Not content with leaving wife alone every evening for years while worm wastes time and money in low taverns, worm has to take wife out with sole purpose of making her a fool in front of other women? Of course, wife has always known of worm's disgusting habits, but has suffered in silence for sake of home and toddler worm. Although wife is accustomed to neglect, she will never get accustomed to being insulted by great brazen hussy who is nothing but home-breaker in uniform. No wonder bishops are complaining about decline in morals, when even little middle-aged men like worm have no sense of decency. Wife could understand if worm were big, fine man with commanding presence like gas manager, though if wife's experience is any criterion, men like gas manager are open and honourable and do not have sneaking little affairs in third-rate cafes with low-class women.

Of course, after this, wife can never hold up head in Worm's Avenue again and wife only hopes that worm's employers never get to hear of it because that would mean that worm would be sacked and wife and toddler worm end up in gutter.

Worm finishes drink and worm and wife join end of long bus queue in black-out.

                                                                              Ibid.

In another series of pieces Gubbins entirely reversed the roles of worm and wife. He created Sparrow, the original male chauvinist bird, so utterly beastly to his wife that she had a permanently damp beak from always being in tears. At the first sign of a whimper from her, Sparrow flew off and boozed the night away at the dissolute Tree Tops Club. Or much worse, visited the Other Sparrow, a pouting, négligé-clad enchantress who was not so much a bird of easy prey as a fully-fledged Fallen Sparrow.

It was gritty stuff for a Sunday paper:

THE SPARROWS

'What are we doing for Christmas?' asked the Sparrow's wife, looking up from her tiny piece of knitting.

'Eating too much and drinking too much, I hope,' said the Sparrow.

'You don't have to make silly remarks,' said his wife.

'You don't have to ask silly questions,' said the Sparrow.

'It wasn't a silly question at all,' said his wife.

'It's the silliest question in the world,' said the Sparrow. 'Especially in war-time.'

'I can't see that it's silly,' said his wife.

'Of course you don't,' said the Sparrow.

'Well, I suppose we can discuss it,' said his wife.

'Discuss what?'

'Well, we might go somewhere.'

'Where?' asked the Sparrow. 'The south of France?'

'You're just being difficult,' said his wife.

'Or,' said the Sparrow, 'we might hop on to one of those cruise liners. The Grey Funnel Line's still running.'

'Perhaps you'd like an old-fashioned Christmas at home,' said his wife.

'Kissing all your hideous relations under the mistletoe?' asked the Sparrow.

'You don't have to kiss them,' said his wife, a tear starting in her eye.

'The uglier they are, the more they insist,' said the Sparrow.

'If you're talking about my sisters,' said his wife, 'they were once considered beautiful.'

'So was Cleopatra,' said the Sparrow, 'but that's a long time ago.'

'I don't see why I should sit here and listen to insults about my sisters,' said his wife, the tear rolling down her beak.

'Well, stand up and listen.'

'They're always saying nice things about you.'

'But what a pity he drinks,' mimicked the Sparrow.

'Well, it is a pity, isn't it?' asked his wife.

'No, it isn't,' said the Sparrow. 'It's fine.'

'I suppose you'll spend most of Christmas at that awful Tree Tops Club,' said his wife.

'I certainly will,' said the Sparrow.

'I can't think what you talk about there,' said his wife, the tear dropping on to her knitting.

'You don't have to think any longer,' said the Sparrow. 'We talk about sex.'

'It's a pity you don't have anything more interesting to talk about,' said his wife.

'There isn't anything more interesting,' said the Sparrow. 'Ask the sparrows who go to the pictures.'

'I think it's disgusting,' said his wife.

'It's only disgusting to nasty-minded people.'

'I'm sure I haven't got a nasty mind.'

'You haven't got a mind at all,' said the Sparrow.

'With this awful war going on and everything,' said his wife, 'I wonder you're not ashamed of yourself.'

'It's love that makes the world go round,' said the Sparrow, flying straight to the Other Sparrow's Nest.

Ibid.

Gubbins hated dogs and loved cats and the following piece is one of the many which featured Sally, his cat. It is also a demonstration of Gubbins's ability to find humour in the day-to-day trivia of wartime domestic life.

Rationing had just been imposed. Regulations were issued seemingly hourly by the Minister of Food, Lord Woolton. Nat Gubbins mirrored what most ordinary Britons felt about rationing: they were not dismayed—there was always (just) enough food to go round—but it was yet another complex, dispiriting privation for citizens to get used to:

THE PRIVATE LIFE OF NATHANIEL GUBBINS

Being the Diary of Uncle Nat Gubbins alone in The Nest
with a week's rations for one as allowed by Lord Woolton.

Off to grocer's with ration book after sharing morning milk with Sally the Cat and offering her kipper scraps begged from a neighbour. Sally the Cat, accustomed to whole kipper to herself in peace-time, sniffs disdainfully at scraps. Kicks back legs (usual cat's method of registering disgust) and retires to her corner by kitchen stove glaring balefully at Uncle Nat.

Apologise to Sally and promise to go to fishmonger (two miles away) tomorrow. Dirty look from Sally says plainly, 'Why not today?'

At grocer's receive seven neat little packets: 2 oz. butter, 2 oz. lard, $\frac{1}{4}$ lb. margarine, $\frac{1}{2}$ lb. sugar, $\frac{1}{4}$ lb. bacon (three rashers), $\frac{1}{2}$ lb. cheese, and 2 oz. tea.

Ask grocer what about delicious Spam on points? Grocer says family has had all points rations for month. Eggs? Grocer says U.N. is entitled to one egg a week if available. Egg not available.

Return with little packets to Nest terrified to face cat, who thinks U.N. has gone to fishmongers.

Sally, as expected, is waiting on doorstep. Surprised she is not tapping impatient paw. At sight of little packets Sally's tail goes up and purring begins. No man who has arrived home at Christmas without turkey could feel more shamed and humiliated than U.N. as cat sniffs hopefully at packets of lard, margarine, tea, gives one reproachful glance over shoulder and walks with majestic dignity towards garden in search of field mice.

Meat? Oh yes, meat. Ring up butcher (also about two miles away) and ask how much one man is entitled to per week. Butcher says it will be about size of small chop. Oh goody. Can butcher send small chop? Can butcher do what? Can butcher *send* small chop? Why, says sarcastic butcher, nothing could be simpler. Would U.N. like small chop sent in six-wheeled lorry or dropped by plane. U.N. says he doesn't care how it's sent as long as he gets it, and butcher asks U.N. if he knows there's a war on. U.N. replies he has heard about it somewhere and conversation ends by butcher banging down receiver.

Problem now is what for lunch? Shall U.N. dig potatoes from garden and fry rasher or have bread and cheese? Problem solved by fact that U.N. not very good at cooking potatoes. Eat bread and cheese and half week's butter ration.

Supper the same except for embarrassment of eating under reproachful eyes of Sally the Cat, who has had no luck with field mice.

Explain to Sally that Lord Woolton won't allow cats to eat anything fit for human consumption, but if piece of cheese is left on kitchen table by mistake an intelligent cat should know what to do.

Ibid.

W HEN *William Connor joined the* Daily Mirror *in 1935 it was in the process of change. It was then a genteel illustrated newspaper with a drooping circulation, aimed at cooks and governesses. A small, lively group of young journalists was bent on transforming it into a brash, demogogic, innovative tabloid. They succeeded.*

The transformed Mirror *was socialist in policy in the tradition of the old Labour Party and it quickly became the voice of 'working lads and lasses'.*

William Connor was not a journalist at all when he started but a copywriter of sorts with the J. Walter Thompson advertising agency. Connor and a couple of similarly young and restless colleagues had sold to another newspaper an idea for a strip cartoon inspired by (i.e. pinched from), the famous Ripley 'Believe It Or Not' strip, on the strength of which he and his friends contrived to be taken on by the new-style Mirror *as ideas men and writers.*

Connor was deputed to try his hand at writing a daily column. This was published under a pseudonym (normal newspaper practice; the theory was that the newspaper could then fire the columnist and replace him many times over without readers ever knowing). Connor was given the nom-de-plume *'Cassandra', which he had to rush home and look up in a classical dictionary:*

I was a bit surprised to discover that I had changed my sex; was the daughter of the King of Troy; that I could foretell in the stars when the news was going to be bad; that a chap named Apollo had made many a pass at me; that nobody believed me when I spoke the unpleasant truth and that I was going to come to a sticky end by being efficiently murdered by Clytaemnestra, the wife of the mighty King Agamemnon.

So I went out and had a beer to pull myself together.

'Cassandra' (Sir William Connor) (1909–67), *Daily Mirror* (July 1965).

Bill Connor turned out to be a natural columnist; idiosyncratic, a violent hater, sentimental (especially in regard to cats), well read, funny, grandly egotistical, a lover of words. In many ways, particularly in his trenchant, declamatory style, he was England's nearest equivalent to America's Sage of Baltimore, H. L. Mencken.

After the usual hesitant start, the Cassandra column settled and became the most famous, widely read, and influential newspaper column of its day. And its day lasted thirty-two years.

In 1966 Connor became Sir William Connor, the first newspaperman to be knighted for services to journalism.

'Cassandra' was not a funny columnist, for amusement only, in the manner of 'Beachcomber' and Nat Gubbins. Many of the Cassandra pieces were either straight journalism, such as interviews, travel pieces, etc., usually with some humour in them, or they were crusading attacks on some bureaucratic lunacy or government action of which he disapproved.

The column continued to criticize the government after the war had started. The Prime Minister, Sir Winston Churchill, did not approve of this at all and described Cassandra as 'dominated by malevolence'. Connor put the column aside in 1942 and joined the army.

He returned home when the war was over and resumed his column after four years of war-service. The post-war Cassandra columns tended to be more broadly based in subject, more mature and funnier. And he wrote more frequently about food. He loved good food and was merciless on foods which he disliked, one of which was turkey.

Turkey may not be wildly exciting but few of us have the energy to hate it:

What a shocking fraud the turkey is.

In life, preposterous, insulting—that foolish noise they make to scare you away! In death—unpalatable. The turkey has practically no taste except a dry, fibrous flavour reminiscent of a mixture of warmed-up plaster of Paris and horsehair. The texture is like wet sawdust and the whole vast, feathered swindle has the piquancy of a boiled mattress.   *Daily Mirror* (24 Dec. 1953).

Cassandra's dislike of turkey was as nothing compared with his hatred and contempt for cabbage cooked in the English manner.

English boiled cabbage to Cassandra, who was the prince of self-taught, obsessional gourmets, was a provocation. It challenged him to pour upon it his most colourful and awful descriptive prose:

O listen to the words:

'BOILED CABBAGE: Remove the coarse outer leaves of the cabbage and cut off the stalk. Either halve or quarter the cabbage and wash thoroughly in cold water. Drain thoroughly and put in a large saucepan with a plentiful amount of salted boiling water. When the water is again on the boil, allow from ten to fifteen minutes fast boiling, according to size and freshness of the cabbage. Cabbages boiled for longer than this are apt to be flabby and flavourless.'

Flabby and flavourless!

The words are cripples—cripples bleeding to death. Letters hooked and handcuffed together—hamstrung and powerless, flabby and flavourless indeed! The phrase is a crawling compliment.

Boiled cabbage *à l'Anglaise* is something compared with which steamed coarse newsprint bought from bankrupt Finnish salvage dealers and heated over smoky oil stoves is an exquisite delicacy. Boiled British cabbage is something lower than ex-Army blankets stolen by dispossessed Genoese dosshousekeepers who used them to cover busted-down henhouses in the slum district of Karachi, found them useless, threw them in anger in the Indus, where they were recovered by convicted beachcombers with grappling irons, who cut them in strips with shears and stewed them in sheep-dip before they were sold to dying beggars.

Boiled cabbage!

Daily Mirror (30 June 1950).

Bill Connor was one of that dying, or perhaps dead, breed, the Fleet Street 'characters', the famous columnists and newsmen of their era, idiosyncratic in appearance, word, and deed, slumped seemingly all day in one of their natural habitats such as El Vino's in Fleet Street, with a newspaper sticking out of a pocket, a cigarette burning away between the fingers, and a glass rising and falling steadily.

This must have been a way of life well known to Connor if only because one of his earliest Cassandra columns was an accurate and devastating picture of what it is like to experience the inevitable aftermath of heavy drinking—what our forefathers called (a word which should surely never have been lost) a 'crapula':

ON HANGOVERS

A hangover is when your tongue tastes like a tram-driver's glove.

When your boots seem to be steaming and your eyes burn in their sockets like gooseberries.

Your stomach spins slowly on its axis and your head gently swells and contracts like a jelly in a tideway.

Voices sound far off and your hands tremble like those of a centenarian condemned to death.

Slight movements make you sweat, even as you shiver from the deadly cold that is within you.

Bright lights hurt the eyes, and jeering, gibbering people from the night before seem to whisper in your ears, and then fade with mocking horrible laughter into silence.

The finger-nails are brittle and your skin hangs on you like an old second-hand suit.

Your feet appear to be swollen, and walking is like wading through a swamp of lumpy, thick custard.

Your throat is cracked and parched like the bottom of an old saucepan that has boiled dry. The next moment the symptoms change, and your mouth is stuffed with warm cotton wool.

When you brush your hair you are certain that there is no top to your skull, and your brain stands naked and throbbing in the stabbing air.

Your back aches and feels as though someone is nailing a placard to your shoulder blades.

Knee joints have turned to dish-water and eyelids are made of sheets of lead lined with sandpaper.

When you lean on a table it sways gently and you know for certain that you are at sea.

Should you step off a kerb you stumble, for it is a yard deep and the gutter yawns like a wide, quaking trench.

You have no sense of touch and your fingertips feel with all the acuteness of decayed firewood smeared with putty.

The nostrils pulsate and smell the evil air.

You believe that you are in a horrible dream but when you wake up you know it will all be true.

Your teeth have been filed to stumps and are about to be unscrewed one by one from your aching jaw.

You want to sleep, but when you close your eyes you are dizzy, and you keel over like a waterlogged barrel crammed with old, sodden cabbage stalks in the Grand Union Canal.

When you read your eyes follow each letter to try to spell the words, but in vain—no message reaches your empty, sullen brain.

Should you look at a simple thing like a tree, it will appear that the bark is gradually crawling upwards.

Lights flash and crackle before you and innumerable little brown dwarfs start tapping just below the base of your skull with tiny, dainty hammers made of compressed rubber . . .

O Death, where is thy sting?

Daily Mirror (c.1937).

IN 1955 *the* Daily Telegraph, *rather staid and conservative, began a four-days-a-week humorous column, 'The Way of the World' by 'Peter Simple'.*

'Peter Simple' was originally the journalist Colin Welch but for thirty-odd years the column has been written by Michael Wharton. According to the political journalist and editor Anthony Howard, Michael Wharton is 'one of the few British eccentrics left to us—a kind of Evelyn Waugh in aspic'. Kingley Amis speaks of Peter Simple's 'eloquent and versatile hatred', which he repeatedly brings to bear on such targets as progressives, architects, actors and actresses, despoilers of

the countryside, psychologists, ecologists, and anybody or anything to do with television.

Peter Simple's humour differs from that of Timothy Shy, Beachcomber, or Cassandra and the others in being decidedly and sometimes ferociously political, and right wing at that. The column is studded with paragraphs which unashamedly bash leftists and multi-racialists:

PERSONAL

Progressive Woman, 36, experienced demonstrator (six Aldermaston marches, over 300 hours picketing South African Embassy in two years, etc.), would like to meet Anti-fascist Man, about 40, view friendship and marriage. Interest in Communist Chinese nightsoil collection methods desirable. Box 482.

Retired Bengali terrorist, 57, ex-Indian National Army, B.Sc. (Chittagong), sly disposition, experienced amateur explosives expert, permanent curry-stains, wishes contact British Woman second-hand clothing dealer preferably Mancunian, of similar interests and background, view matrimony. Box 483.

One-legged Widower, 65, five foot one inch, 18 stone, chronic indigestion, Left-wing views, reduced circumstances, with large collection of old copies of *New Statesman*, would like to meet beautiful, politically conscious Girl, 18–25, perfect health, amiable disposition, large private income, country house, university degree, driving and pilot's licence, nursing experience, etc., etc., view marriage. Box 484.

Lonely? Repulsive? No friends? Why not join the Brassgrove Park Progressive Circle, Ulbricht Road, London, sw46, and meet others like yourself? Combined teach-in, short-story reading and humanist tea-dance every Sunday. This week: Rhodesian Sanctions Excuse-me Dance. Box 485 for particulars.

'Peter Simple' (Michael Wharton) (b. 1913), 'The Way of the World', *Daily Telegraph* (1955–   ).

The column, like all long-running columns, has a repertoire of permanent characters and situations which pop up regularly.

One of Peter Simple's star performers who makes frequent reappearances is the rich, left-wing intellectual, Mrs Dutt-Pauker:

ROMANCE

Rumours that Mrs Dutt-Pauker, the 53-year-old Hampstead thinker, is thinking of marrying for the third time have caused surprise and some bitterness in Left-wing circles. Surprise, because she has the reputation of being faithful to her second husband's memory; bitterness, because of their impressive financial resources, which, meant for all mankind, may now go to benefit one man.

By inheritance, by 35 years of progressive thinking, by a Left-wing flair for the stockmarket and by sheer forward-looking greed, she has built up a considerable fortune. As well as her large house in Hampstead, she has a country house in Dorset, Beria Garth, another in Wales, Glyn Stalin, and another in the West of Ireland, Leninmore.

Her first husband, whom she met and married during the Spanish Civil War, had to be accidentally liquidated in Barcelona in 1937; at the same time her name became linked with that of Walter Ulbricht, then working in Catalonia, with whom she shared a romantic passion for the techniques of terrorism. Though love faded, as love will, they have always remained good friends. He still sends her a coloured picture postcard of the Berlin Wall every May Day.

But the love of her life was her second husband, bespectacled, four foot ten Ernst Dutt-Pauker, a typical swashbuckling Highlander, stalwart of the Siege of Madrid, hero of a thousand purges, friend of Bela Kun, Yagoda, Beria and Gero, and at one time motoring correspondent of the *Daily Worker*.

His study in Mrs Dutt-Pauker's Hampstead house is still kept just as he left it at his death: on his desk a half-completed plan for a people's re-educational labour camp on Exmoor lies next to the stuffed head of Marshal Tukhachevski and a silver-mounted upper set of Marx's false teeth.

Can any individual man, however bold and resolute, many people are asking, take over, as well as Mrs Dutt-Pauker herself, this glorious but over-powering heritage of progressivism? Isn't there rather a case here for a people's collective, an object lesson in the building of Socialism?

Ibid.

One of Peter Simple's most powerful and effective satires has been his series of descriptions of life on a nightmarish experimental hi-sci agricultural unit:

ON THE OHM FARM

Midsummer on the Ohm Farm! At this crown of the year, what intimations of immortal technology, what synthetized ecstasies and panagnostic longings haunt the agrotechnical, neopastoral scene!

A heat haze, chemical-compounded, deadly to everything that breathes, shimmers on the boundless plain which stretches on every side to what, if it could be seen, might be called the horizon. Here and there, as you watch through protective goggles, a glint of metal appears as the sun strikes, in-dicating the electrified barbed-wire fencing which separates the various ex-perimental areas: the semi-automated pig centre, the 40-foot beet-processing compound, the nuclear-operated bovine forcing sheds.

Far off appear (or is it a mirage, born of some memory of angel infancy?) the dazzling white shapes of the administrative buildings. There gnarled Old Seth Roentgen and his devoted team of research scientists watch the flickering dials on the control consoles and programme the computers which will show, in millionths of a second, the current rate of broiler-egg production, the boiler-calf fattening indices or ratios of lamb-hormone-injection.

A line from Arnold's 'Scholar-Gipsy', written, perhaps, on just such a midsummer day as this, comes into the mind unbidden: 'Go, for they call you, shepherd, from the hill.'

And sure enough there emerges from an electronically operated manhole not far off, the figure of Bert Fishbein the shepherd, muffled in protective clothing. Geiger-counter in hand, he makes his way carefully through the light, poisoned breeze, to where his flock of giant, 60-uddered experimental ewes bleat plaintive thunder in their aluminium cotes. *Ibid.*

But not all Peter Simple's pieces are didactic. On occasions he can be as flippant as any of his comical colleagues:

HAGGARD'S JOURNAL

June 1, 1772: Rain. An American colonist named Franklin reported to have been blown up whilst flying a kite in a thunderstorm in order to study the effects of the Electric Fluid. Ate a capon for dinner but it was bad, so I gave the remains to my wife who presently turned green and was conveyed to her chamber insensible.

June 2, 1772: Thunder and lightning. Amos Hornblower put in the stocks for stealg. an egg. Whilst visitg. Soup Hales in a.m. in order to tear down some cottages, a one-legged person bumped into me and upon my horse-whippg. him complained in the French tongue, whereupon I gave him an extra half-dozen blows for being a canting foreigner. Spent p.m. jumping up and down in front of Amos Hornblower in the stocks, puttg. my fingers to my nose and suchlike merry japes.

Ate a pease pddg. for supper but it was bad, so I sent it to Amos Hornblower. I then called for the cook and dismissed him by the simple expedient of discharging my fowling piece at him as he entered the room.

June 3, 1772: Floods. Amos Hornblower removed to the Spital insensible. Grunge, my butler, left to hire a new cook. Drank a bott. of port for breakfast but Grunge informed me he had hired a cook and a sumptuous meal appeared for dinner. As I was eating Grunge informed me that the new cook was a one-legged Frenchman lately arrived in Soup Hales, whereupon, peering closely into the pie, I percvd. small slivers of glass floatg. in the gravy. ITEM: To emetics, £0 0s. $0\frac{1}{2}d$. *Ibid.*

In 1939 *the Irish Times in Dublin had the good fortune to find and take on a humorist who became to the Irish a near-genius. For twenty-seven years he wrote them a daily, later weekly, column acclaimed in Ireland for its mix of eccentricity, satire, wit, and Irishness.*

S. J. Perelman called him 'the best comic writer I can think of'.

The column was called 'Cruiskeen Lawn'. It was written in Irish to begin with, then for a while it alternated daily between Irish and English, finally appearing entirely in English. Except for a bit of Latin.

The writer had many more names than is usual. He was born Brian O Nuallain (usually anglicized to 'Brian O'Nolan') which was his name while he worked in the Irish Civil Service. He wrote under two other names; for his novels he was 'Flann O'Brien' and for his Irish Times *column he was 'Myles na Gopaleen' (even that had a variation, 'Myles na gCopaleen').*

Myles na Gopaleen's column was rich in original characters. One of the regulars was a Dubliner he supposedly chatted to at a bus stop while they were both waiting for buses. Typically, the leading character of the pieces was not the Dubliner but his brother, whom we never meet.

The Brother knows all there is to be known about absolutely everything:

THE BROTHER

The Brother can't look at an egg.

Is that so?

Can't stand the sight of an egg at all. Rashers, ham, fish, anything you like to mention—he'll eat them all and ask for more. But he can't go the egg. Thanks very much all the same but no eggs. The egg is barred.

I see.

I do often hear him talking about the danger of eggs. You can get all classes of disease from eggs, so the brother says.

That is disturbing news.

The trouble is that the egg never dies. It is full of all classes of microbes and once the egg is down below in your bag, they do start moving around and eating things, delighted with themselves. No trouble to them to start some class of an ulcer on the sides of the bag.

I see.

Just imagine all your men down there walking up and down your stomach and maybe breeding families, chawing and drinking and feeding away there, it's a wonder we're not all in our graves man, with all them hens in the country.

I must remember to avoid eggs.

I chance an odd one meself but one of these days I'll be a sorry man. Here's me Drimnagh 'bus, I'll have to lave yeh, don't do anything when your uncle's with you, as the man said.

Good bye.
Myles na Gopaleen (Brian O'Nolan) (1911–66), 'Cruiskeen Lawn', *The Irish Times* (1939–66).

Myles na Gopaleen had the columnist's trick of keeping an idea going for years, by returning to it now and then and moving it forward just a fraction.

Like his promise to reveal to his readers what he looked like:

A few weeks ago I was interrupted when about to give the public my long-awaited description of my own face. Several anxious readers have written in asking when they might expect it. My answer is that they may expect it to-day. Let us take the features one by one and then stand back, as one stands back from a majestic Titian or Van Gogh, and view the whole magnificent—

The Plain People of Ireland: Is this going to be long?

Myself: Not very.

The Plain People of Ireland: How long roughly?

Myself: Well, say ten lines for the vast Homeric brow, the kingly brow that is yet human wise and mild. Then the eyes, peerless wine-green opal of rare hue, brittle and ebullient against the whiteness of Himalayan snow—

The Plain People of Ireland: Another ten lines?

Myself: Say seven each. That's fourteen altogether.

The Plain People of Ireland: Seven *each*! You don't say there's any difference between them?

Myself: Well, there's not exactly any difference, nothing that could be said to be repugnant or incompatible. Nevertheless, there is some slight divergence of *vivre*, some indefinable yet charming *indépendance*, some enchanting *drôlerie de la paupière*—

The Plain People of Ireland: And how about the gob and the snot?

Myself: If you mean the finely-moulded masterful—

The Plain People of Ireland: Did you ever hear this one: As a beauty I am not a star. There are others more handsome by far—

Myself: I did, I did, Stop!

The Plain People of Ireland: But my face I don't mind it, for I am behind it, It's the people in front get the jar!

Myself: Lord save us!

The Plain People of Ireland: Could we not leave the whole thing over to another time?

Myself: Very well. But heaven knows whom we are disappointing in this matter.   Ibid.

The Irishness of Myles's humour frequently flirted successfully with the dementia praecox *school of writing:*

As regards Mary, the Rose of Tralee, it will be recalled that it was not her beauty alone that won one; oh no, 'twas the truth in her eyes ever dawning. Bearing this in mind, it occurred to the Myles na gCopaleen Research Bureau the other day to try to ascertain whether the truth still dawns in the eyes of the ladies of to-day. An investigator was sent out with instructions to engage a hundred ladies in conversation and examine their eyes for traces of the truth, dawning, fully dawned, declining or otherwise. He was away for a week and then returned to submit the following record of his researches:

> 15% Mild mydriasis, probably caused by the consumption of slimming drugs.
> 21% Ptosis of the lids due to defect in the oculomotor nerve, anisocoria, opthalmia, one or more small chalazions.
> 18% Pronounced hyperthyroidism.
> 14% Evidence of retinal haemorrhages, papillary oedema, exophthalmos.
> 1% Mikulicz's disease.
> 1% Paralysis of the orbicularis oculi.

'No evidence of the truth ever dawning anywhere?' we asked.

'No,' he said, 'and what's more, I'm going to marry one of them.'

'Which one?' we asked.

'Mikulicz's disease,' he said, 'and she has three cute little yellow chalazions too.'

We agreed to put him on the married man's scale and changed the subject by putting that damn lovely thing by Toselli on the gramophone.   Ibid.

Myles's most popular running characters were Keats and Chapman, a brace of poets whom he put through small and improbable adventures so contrived as always to finish on a mind-numbing pun:

Keats and Chapman (in the old days) spent several months in the county Wicklow prospecting for ochre deposits. That was before the days of (your) modern devices for geological divination. With Keats and Chapman it was literally a question of sniffing the stuff out. The two of them sniffed their way into Glenmalure and out of it again, and then snuffled back to Woodenbridge. In a field of turnips near Avoca Keats suddenly got the pungent effluvium of a vast ochre mine and lay for hours face down in the muck delightedly permeating his nostrils with the perfume of hidden wealth. No less lucky was Chapman. He had nosed away in the direction of Newtonmountkennedy and came racing back shouting that he too had found a mine. He implored Keats to come and confirm his nasal diagnosis. Keats agreed. He accompanied Chapman to the site and lay down in the dirt to do his sniffing. Then he rose.

'Great mines stink alike', he said.   Ibid.

And an irresistible tailpiece:

Here is something I bet you did not know—that your second finger (beside the little finger) is longer than the other one beside it, all preconceived notions to the contrary. Lay your hand palm down on the table and measure both fingers carefully along the left edge.   Ibid.

ABOUT *the same time that the 28-year-old Myles na Gopaleen (or Flann O'Brien) was about to begin his important column for the* Irish Times, *a slightly younger Irish lad, a mere junior reporter, was preparing to leave the* Irish Times *to take up a post with Lord Beaverbrook's press in England.*

The younger lad was immensely tall and thin, with sparse hair the colour of a Kellogg's cornflake, eyes set as close together as a pair of cuff-links, a tendency to drift slightly sideways when walking like a young crab in wine, and an appalling stammer. He was the Hon. Patrick Campbell, later to become the 3rd Baron Glenavy.

As a young man Paddy spent most of his time lolling about Dublin, all too aware that his only real interests were playing golf and talking to people in bars, and his chances of building himself any sort of decent career upon these were slight.

In desperation his father persuaded the Irish Times *to take him on as a kind of semi-paid trainee reporter and Paddy realized that he had 'stumbled into the only job that required no degrees, no diplomas, no training and no specialized knowledge of any kind'.*

Paddy's humorous journalism prospered. In 1947 he was writing regular pieces for the British monthly magazine, Lilliput (*they turned out to be his best work*), *and he became its assistant editor. He began to write screenplays and additional dialogue for the Rank Organization's comedies and his last newspaper job was a weekly humorous column for the* Sunday Times.

Paddy Campbell was an 'I'-writer; he wrote subjective pieces telling about some predicament in which he found himself, usually some quite believable and true situation, like his report of setting about seducing a willing girl in his room only to find that the fire brigade practising escape drill below his window was compulsively watchable.

Of all the humorists of his era he probably wrote the purest 'humour' in this book's definition of the word; no jokes or witty word-plays but a bringing to our notice of strange characters he had met whose function seemed to be to break up the greyness of our more humdrum lives. His prose was plain, unpredictable, a little sad at times, with a rare and refreshing grace of style.

As in this memoir of his old editor on the Irish Times:

MR SMYLLIE, SIR

When, in these trying times, it's possible to work on the lower slopes of a national newspaper for several weeks without discovering which of the scurrying executives is the editor, I count myself fortunate to have served under one who wore a green sombrero, weighed twenty-two stone, sang parts of his leading articles in operatic recitative, and grew the nail on his little finger into the shape of a pen nib, like Keats.

Even the disordered band of unemployed cooks, squabbling like crows over the Situations Vacant columns in the front office files, knew that he was Robert Maire Smyllie, Editor of the *Irish Times*, and fell silent as he made his swift rush up the stairs.

He was a classical scholar, at home among the Greek philosophers. He was the incorruptible champion of the fading Protestant cause in holy Ireland. His political and humanitarian views won international respect, and he spent most of his time on the run from the importunities of such characters as Chloral O'Kelly and Twitchy Doyle.

They lay in wait for him every evening in their chosen lairs in the front office and threw themselves in his path, as though to halt a rushing loco-motive, as soon as he appeared at the door.

Chloral O'Kelly was a deeply melancholic youth who drank disinfectant, and was in constant need of 3s. 9d. for another bottle. Twitchy Doyle was a little old man with a straggly, jumping moustache who lived by reviewing reprints of Zane Grey. The moment the Editor burst through the front door they closed on him with urgent appeals, battling for position with Deirdre of the Sorrows, an elderly woman who believed for twelve years that she was being underpaid for her contributions to the Woman's Page. The Editor shot through them, weaving and jinking, crying: 'No—not tonight—tomorrow—goodbye'—and put on an extra burst of speed which carried him up the stairs to the safety of his own room, there to deliver his unforgettable cry: 'Pismires! Warlocks! Stand aside!'

I looked up 'pismire' once in the dictionary and found it meant an ant. It pictured, vividly, the unrelenting tenacity of his hangers-on.

For four years, six nights a week, I worked beside this enormous, shy, aggressive, musical, childlike, cultured and entirely unpredictable human being, separated from him by only a wooden partition, in a monastic life cut off almost completely from the world.

We worked in a high, dusty room topped by an opaque glass dome. There were no outside windows, so that the lights burned day and night. Alec Newman, the Assistant Editor, and Bill Fleming, the theatre critic, shared the outside part. Then came the Editor's office, partitioned off by battered wooden panelling. I had a tiny box jammed between him and the wall, with a sliding hatch between us for the purposes of communication. When it was open I got a portrait view of the great head, hair brushed smoothly back, brick-red face, snub nose supporting glasses and a ginger moustache enclosing the stem of a curved pipe the size of a flower-pot. 'Mr Campbell, we do not wish to be observed', was the signal for the hatch to be closed.

Alec, Bill and I got in about nine-thirty every night and started to scratch around for leader subjects in the English papers. At ten o'clock the Editor burst in like a charging rhino, denounced pismires and warlocks, and went to ground in his own room.

At ten-thirty came the inevitable inquiry: 'Well, gentlemen— ?'

Alec assumed the responsibility of answering for all of us. 'Nothing, Mr Smyllie, sir. All is sterility and inertia.'

The reply was automatic. 'Ten-thirty, and not a strumpet in the house painted! Art is long, gentlemen, but life is shuddering shorter than you think.' 'Shuddering' and 'shudder' were favourite words of complaint.

Alec made his set protest. 'You're hard, Mr Smyllie, sir. Hard!'

'Mr Newman?'

'Sir?'

'Take your King Charles's head outside and suck it.'

I never discovered the origin of this extraordinary injunction, but it meant that some disagreement had taken place between them during the afternoon and that Alec had better be careful from now on. My own orders came floating over the partition.

'Mr Campbell?'

'Sir?'

'Prehensilize some Bosnian peasants.'

'Immediately, sir.'

The cryptic order had a simple origin. The Editor, seeking once to commend a piece of writing that clung closely, without irrelevant deviation, to its theme, had hit upon the word prehensile, which passed immediately into the language of our private, nocturnal life. Somerset Maugham, for instance, was a prehensile writer. Henry James unprehensile in the extreme. From here it was a short step to prehensilizing an untidily written contribution. Reprehensilization covered a second re-write. We didn't even notice we were saying it after a week or two.

The Bosnian peasant came from a discovery of mine on the back page of the *Manchester Guardian*—an exceedingly improbable story about a Balkan shepherd who'd tripped over a railway line and derailed a train with his wooden leg. The shepherd, in addition, had only one eye, and was carrying a live salmon in his arms. I cannot imagine, now, how even a short fourth leader could have been written on such a theme, but for months I was dependent on the *Guardian*'s Balkan correspondent for my ideas. Acceptance of this *argot* led me once to frighten the life out of the Bishop—I think—of Meath.

I'd come in very late and burst straight into the Editor's room. 'I'm sorry I got held up, Mr Smyllie, sir!' I cried. 'I can always reprehensilize some one-eyed Bosnian bastards!' It was only then that I saw the Bishop sitting in the visitors' chair with his top-hat on his knee. I've never seen a man so profoundly affected by a sentence containing only eight words.

If pursuing his personal, King Charles's head war with Alec, the Editor would suddenly give him the first, interminable leader to write on some political theme, while doing the second and shorter one himself.

Silence settled in for about an hour, with the four typewriters rattling away. Sometimes, then, we got: 'Cold—cold—cold—'

Almost anything could start it off, from the mere weather conditions to some philosophic reflection that had entered the Editor's mind. His typewriter stopped. The rest of us paused, too, expectant in our boxes. The voice rose, high and ghostly, from the Editor's compartment:

'Cold—cold—cold—'

We echoed it, still higher and thinner:

'Cold—cold—cold—'

The Editor's voice took on a deeper, tragically declamatory note:

> 'Cold as a frog in an ice-bound pool,
> Cold as a slew of gooseberry fool,
> Colder than charity—'

There was a long pause, while we stuffed our handkerchiefs into our mouths, struggling to remain silent. The next line came out with rasping cynicism:

'And that's pretty chilly—'

He allowed this to sink in, then returned to the dramatic narrative form:

'But it isn't as cold as poor Brother Billy—'

We all joined in, vying with one another to achieve the maximum in greasy self-satisfaction, on the last line:

'Cause *he's DAID!*'

There was another pause, while we savoured the dying echoes. 'Get on with it, gentlemen,' said the Editor, and the four typewriters started again. But now that his appetite for music had been aroused—and he was a profoundly musical man, with a fine baritone voice—he would give us an encore, singing the words of his leader in a long recitative, like a chant:

> 'O, the Dublin Corporation has decided
> In its wis-*dum*—'

We joined in, like a Greek chorus, in the background:

> 'In its wis-*dum* . . . its wis-*dum* . . .'
> 'To sign the death warrant
> 'Of the traam-*ways*—'
> 'Traam-*ways* . . . traam-ways . . .'
> 'A measure with which we find ourselves
> 'In agree-ment—'
> 'In agree-ment . . .agree-ment . . .'

There'd be a sudden break in the mood. The voice came out with a snap. 'Thank you, gentlemen, and give my regards to your poor father, too.'

When he was writing the words poured out of him in a flood, without correction, and at times, indeed, without much thought. He'd been doing it too long. But there were occasions when he bent the whole of his courageous and intelligent mind to denouncing the rising tide of parochial Irish republicanism—notably on the death of George V.

This long-drawn-out decline was being charted much more thoroughly by the *Irish Times*, with its Unionist sympathies, than by the other newspapers. Night after night Smyllie put a new touch to his obituary leader, after the routine inquiry, 'Has the poor old shudderer passed on?' Finally, the King died and the leader was sent out for setting. We were all in the Editor's room when the first edition came off the machines. He tore open the leader page to see how it looked, and gave a scream like a wounded bull when he saw that the second half of it, possibly inadvertently, had been printed upside down. Pismires and warlocks that morning were relegated to the ends of hell.

This concern for the English King got us into scattered forays with the IRA, leading once to the windows of the office in Cork being broken by a shower of stones. When the news reached the Editor he made, taking as his framework, 'They cannot intimidate me by shooting my lieutenants,' one of the most carefully formulated battle-cries I've ever heard in my life.

We were in the office at the time. He instructed me to give him the noggin of brandy, filed under B in his correspondence cabinet, and took a steady pull. 'These shudderers,' said Robert Maire Smyllie, 'cannot intimidate me by throwing half-bricks through the windows of the branch office while my lieutenants are taking a posset of stout in the shebeen next door.'

When we left, round about two o'clock the following morning, however, he was in a noticeable hurry to mount his bicycle. As he swung his massive weight into the saddle one of the pedals snapped off clean. He fell off, sprang up again, shouted, 'Mr Campbell, as your superior officer I order you to give me your velocipede!'—snatched it out of my hand, leaped aboard and sped off into the darkness. I limped after him on the broken one. When we got back to his house we drank Slivovitz until breakfast, in further defiance of 'the porter-slopping shudderers from Ballydehob.'

In the office there was indeed at this time the feeling of a beleaguered garrison, one which prompted all of us to remain in the place until daylight, rather than face the dark streets on our bicycles. Those were the great nights of the domino games that kept us locked in combat over the Editor's desk until the charwomen came in in the morning.

'A little pimping, Mr Smyllie, sir?' Alec would suggest, after the paper had gone to bed.

'A little pimping, Mr Newman, would be acceptable.'

No one could ever remember how it came to be called pimping, with the additional refinement of 'hooring', to describe the act of blocking the game with a blank at both ends, but because of Smyllie's complete purity of mind these technicalities added a notable spice to the game.

I can see him now, his green, wide-brimmed hat set square on his head, the great pipe fuming and a glass of brandy by his side, delicately picking up his tiles with the pen-nib fingernail raised in the air.

The unspoken purpose of the three of us was to do him down by a concerted onslaught, all playing into one another's hands to present him with a blank, when his turn came to play, on both ends.

'Pimp, Mr Newman, pimp,' I would urge Alec, sitting on my right. We always used these formal titles when in play.

Alec would close one end. 'Hoor, Mr Campbell, hoor!'

If, happily, I had a suitable blank I would lose no time in playing it, then we all burst into a triumphant cry:

'Hoored, Mr Smyllie, sir—hoored! Take a little snatch from the bucket!'

With an expressionless face, and the dainty finger-nail raised in the air, the great man would draw some more tiles from the middle, on occasion being lucky enough to find a natural seven, and then play it with an elegant flick of the wrist, like an eighteenth-century gallant. 'That, gentlemen,' he would say, 'should wipe the shuddering grins off your kissers. *Nemo me impune lacessit*—and best wishes to all at home.'

I left the *Irish Times* under rather dubious circumstances, intending, in fact, only to take a week's holiday in London, but I was also writing a column for the Irish edition of the *Sunday Dispatch* at this time, and thought it might be interesting to call in at headquarters. As a result of this I wrote a piece about the English scene which they used in all the editions, and paid me a little more than five times what I was getting for a whole week's work at home. I sent Smyllie a telegram, saying I'd been held up, and hoped to be back soon. He countered with a letter saying he would be delighted to see the last of me if I'd send him a year's salary, in lieu of notice. I replied that I'd see my bank manager about it. I remained on in London, and the correspondence came to an end.

In the next three years I returned fairly frequently to Dublin, without daring to go and call on him, until one day, coming back in an aeroplane, I opened the *Irish Times* and saw a paragraph in his Saturday diary column, which he wrote under the name of Nichevo.

It was very short. 'My spies tell me,' it read, 'that Paddy Campbell is back again in Dublin, after a long safari looking for tsetse fly in the bush. He is now preparing a definitive biography of Schopenhauer, and is doing a lot of field research on the subject in the back bar of Jammet's, and the Dolphin Hotel.'

It was an intimation that peace had been declared. But he was dead before I could say, 'Good evening, Mr Smyllie, sir,' again.

Patrick Campbell (Third Baron Glenavy) (1913–80), *Lilliput*.

In the late 1960s, against all odds considering his stammer, Patrick Campbell became a successful and much loved television performer.

Theoretically the stammer should have been embarrassing to television viewers but this was rarely so, mainly because Paddy was so entirely open about the whole process. He did not trade on it either; he was an Irishman who loved to talk, he had a stammer which spoiled his flow and so he hated it. When he was locked silent by a troublesome initial letter he would show his frustration by banging his knee and muttering, 'Come along! Come along!'

In the following classic piece of modern humour, Paddy Campbell writes of just about the worst nightmare that can befall somebody with a speech impediment:

THE HOT BOX

Once upon a time I was given an assignment to write an article about a load of archaeological remains, dug up by some fool on the outskirts of Waterford.

This was in the days when the newsprint situation allowed us to devote whole columns to fossils, brass rubbings, or even the Franciscan method of illuminating manuscripts.

Caught by the Waterford job, I made a demur. No knowledge of archaeological remains—very busy at the moment with an article about badminton . . .

'Round about 1,200 words,' said the news editor. 'Riordan, in the public library, knows all about it.'

He measured me for a moment. 'You two ought to get on,' he said, 'like a house on fire. Or an ammunition dump exploding,' he added.

I asked him what he meant.

'You mind your own business,' he said.

I went along to the library, already rehearsing, 'Riordan', and 'archaeological remains'. It had, of course, to be Riordan and archaeological remains just at a time when my intermittent stammer was passing through a cycle which left me incapable of dealing with these initial letters.

There were two elderly gentlemen in subdued suits at the desk, both reading.

I chose the one on the right.

'Excuse me,' I said, 'are you Mr M'Reer—M'Reer—M'Reer . . .'

I was full of air, and putting in the intrusive 'm'—a strategy which often worked—but this time nothing happened.

The librarian looked up. He wore half-moon, gold-rimmed glasses, and a black woollen cardigan. He nodded towards his colleague. He also put down his book and prepared to listen—with what seemed to be a disproportionate measure of interest.

I saw why a moment later.

'I'm A'Rah—A'Rah—A'Rah . . .' began the second librarian, with his eyes tightly shut.

I'd walked into another one.

I should, of course, have given it up at once—gone back to the office, and said Riordan was on holiday.

But then the fighting instinct arose in me. My intrusive 'm' against his intrusive 'a'. I'd tried the intrusive 'a' myself, and knew that in careless hands it could bring on strangulation.

I scanned the sentence that lay before me. It contained only a number of minor obstacles.

I shot it out very quickly.

'I believe you know something abow-abow-abowbow—could you tell me what you know of the Waterford arkie-arkie-arkie—the Waterford find?'

It turned out to be rather rougher than I'd expected.

Riordan sat back. 'What was that?' he said.

I looked at him coldly. He knew perfectly well what we'd got ourselves into. It was up to him to pull his weight.

Even Waterford seemed to have collapsed. I took another breath. 'Man found some flints or something down south and I was told you knew something abah-abah . . . You knew something,' I said.

The other librarian had now abandoned all interest in his book, and was leaning forward intently.

'Ah, yes,' said Riordan easily. 'The archaeological remains discovered in Waterford.' You could hear every syllable, clear as a bell.

He stood up. 'I think I can find you the reference, I have aboo-aboo-aboo-aboo . . .'

I let him have it. It was sheer joy.

He'd nearly torn his memo pad in half by the time that I released him.

'You have a book,' I said, 'which will help us.'

'Downstairs,' said Riordan. He loosened his collar. 'Come this way,' he said.

The other librarian half rose in his seat, watching us right to the door. He'd taken his glasses off, and his mouth was open.

We went down into the basement, and along a passage lined with pipes.

'By the way,' I said, 'what's your first name? I think I know a friend of yours.'

I'd seen the card on his desk, in a brass slot: BRIAN RIORDAN. The chances were if he couldn't say book he couldn't say Brian either.

He stopped, as if shot. Convulsively, he gripped the handle of a low, barred door which had appeared in front of us. His neck began to swell. He drew a couple of long, shuddering breaths.

I watched him with interest. One foot came off the ground, and writhed about.

Suddenly, he got it. It came out like a tyre bursting.

'Jack!' said Brian Riordan.

'Can't be the same person,' I said easily. 'The Riordan I was thinking of is—' Everything shut down. I fought it blindly for a second. 'Someone else,' I said.

We went into the cellar with honours approximately even. It was a tiny room, brilliantly whitewashed, about six feet by six. A bare electric light bulb hung from the ceiling at eye level. It was very hot. Pipes ran all round the walls.

Riordan turned round. The light hung between us, very bright and dazzling.

'Where was this find made?' he said.

The stuff had been dug up in a place called Rathally. But as far as I was concerned, what with the heat, and the glare, and the congestion, it might well just have been Czrcbrno, a hamlet in the Balkans.

I tried everything—the finger tapping, the coughing, the intrusive 'm', even a short whistle. Nothing happened. The light, agitated by some truant blast, swayed gently backwards and forwards, Riordan waited, leaning forward politely—exultant.

I thought I was going to faint. I had ceased to breathe. I half-turned my head—intending, perhaps, to jump upon Rathally from the rear—and then I saw Theodore Blake. He was peering through the bars, and from the look of deep peace upon his face, I knew that he, too, was engaged with the priceless gift of speech.

Theodore—of all people!

Riordan opened the gate. 'Well,' he said, 'Mr Bla—Mr Bla—Bla . . .' He gave it up. Theodore came in. We moved back a little to give him room.

Theodore had lately been using an old method of my own. No sound emerged. No hint of expression ever crossed his face. He seemed to be lost in meditation. But it was then you knew that he was really on the griddle.

The three of us, tightly pressed together, the bulb hanging between us, stood there, waiting.

A full minute later Theo said, 'Hello'.

I'd better luck than Riordan. I said, 'What are you doing here?'

Riordan tried to say, 'What can I do for you, Mr Blake?' and nearly made it, until the 'b', as usual, beat him all ends up. He actually struck his head against the books behind him.

All this time Theordore was quietly at work. Suddenly, he got it out. 'Can I have that book on Roman coins?' he said, so careful and expressionlessly that it sounded like Roger, the talking Robot.

'Certainly,' said Riordan, and turned to the bookshelves.

It was certainly unfair. He must have known quite well where the book was, but he began fiddling about, pretending he couldn't find it.

Theo and I looked at one another. It was up to someone to say something. We got down to it together.

Theo won. 'What are *you* doing here?' he said.

I lowered my voice an octave. 'I'm gathering material on the arkie-arkie—.' I couldn't go on. I simply couldn't face 'archaeological' again.

'On coins,' I said. 'M'Roh—M'Roh—the same kind of coins as yourself.'

Riordan swung round from the book-case. I'd forgotten about him.

'You said you wanted the Waterford archaeological remains!' he exclaimed.

'You've got it wrong,' I said. 'I'm doing a story abah—a story on coins.' I was going to add—'through the ages'—and then abandoned it. 'Just coins,' I said.

The awful look of unearthly peace came over Theo's face. I knew what he was going to say. He was going to say that he'd been commissioned to write an article about coins and couldn't understand why I was doing one, too.

We waited for Theodore. I was difficult not to look at him, because we were jammed cheek to cheek, but we did our best.

Theodore looked straight ahead, motionless, carved out of stone.

'But,' he said, three minutes later, 'I'm doing an article about coins. Why are you doing one, too?'

Riordan opened his mouth.

'Ubu-ubu-ubu—' he began, harping on my commitment to archaeological remains.

'It doesn't matter,' I said. 'There has been some confusion. I can easily switch over to the arkie-arkie-arkie-'

'Ubu-ubu-' gasped Riordan, 'you asked me for that boo-boo-boo- that in the first pip-pip-'

It was absolutely indescribable. And suddenly Theodore joined in. On the very first word he slipped right back into his old habit—the wurr-wurr-wurr. God alone knows what he was trying to say. He simply wurred.

I don't know how long it went on for—me busy with arkie-arkie, Riordan pip-pipping, and Theo lost in the throes of wurr.

Steam seemed to be running down the walls. Once the electric light bulb bounced off my forehead with a sharp 'Ponk!'

Something snapped. 'Here,' I said, 'let me—' I couldn't say 'out'. I let it go. I pushed past them, fled along the passage, and a moment later was in the open air.

In my hand was Theo's book about coins.

I sent it back next day, by registered post.

Ibid.

———————

THE Sunday Times's *decision to hire Paddy Campbell might well have been prompted by the success that their traditional rival 'quality' Sunday paper, the* Observer, *was having with their humorous column, 'Oddly Enough', written by an ex-scriptwriter and advertising copywriter named Paul Jennings.*

Paul Jennings's Observer *column lasted for twelve years and a dozen books of collected 'Oddly' pieces were published over the years.*

Much of Jennings's work is autobiographical in inspiration but he has never been a reporter and his prose is not declamatory and journalistic but flexible, erudite, and rather literary. His most important contribution to Thought has been what he calls 'Resistentialism', a philosophic concept in which he argues in print that 'things are against us' and that all inanimate objects are malevolently uncooperative.

Jennings is probably the most scholarly of the humorous columnists and is certainly the most musical. He must be one of the few columnists to have been for years on active service with the New Philharmonia Choir, and is surely the only recorded humorist to list as his main pleasure in life 'madrigal-singing'.

Not surprisingly, Paul Jennings has a particularly sensitive ear. This was not an advantage when he was on the Continent and trying to get to sleep in a small, bad, French provincial hotel:

NUITS BLANCHES 1964

10 p.m. After dinner in basic French hotel (air mild, dense, brackish; shiny old wooden spiral stairs, grey doors with straight handles, giant's-footsteps W.C., potatoey soup, beal or veef, hexagonal coffee cups, other guests all French except one morose English couple, wife wearing glasses, slacks, high heels), in small town reached after whole day bowling over forested ridges. Ask *patronne* what are big buildings above river. One is seminary, one home for old priests.

10.30 p.m. As usual, head too low on long bolster under bottom sheet, but too high on folded pillow—presumably must be folded, because 4 feet square. Why? They obviously know where human shoulder comes, they haven't got square bolster as well. Maybe it not pillow at all? Eiderdown for square child? Huge stomachwarmer, all French carry special tapes for tying warmer to their stomachs?

Own stomach unhappy about veef, or beal, or all those grapes. As though little men inside trying to lift heavy cover off well down which they want to pour something. Suddenly they manage it; *pripple-ipple-ipple gulLOY*, it runs into a kind of lake at bottom. But when turn over there seem to be other little men who want to pour it back again. Elsewhere pioneers digging new wells at right-angles (or blasting? Tiny muffled explosions). Parties of little men quarrelling (anti-bodies?), then uniting to blow up containing walls of several rivers, lakes, etc. Gurgling cataract rushes down smooth new channel, should be all right now; sense of release, peace in allegorical-symbolical landscape, in style of Dürer woodcut: *Das Land der Inner Man, translated from ye German, London 1564. With ye Mappe of Peristaltia.* Peasant reclining by wide lake. But suddenly musket fire, *ping, gromp! Pripple ipple,* start again, lean cavalry scour plain, earthquake, smoke drifts across little low suns—*orblets,* anagram of bolster. Also *lobster, bolters, roblest (roblest Noman of them all), sterbol* (industrial detergent?), *bestrol* (pirate petrol firm) . . .

Jerk awake. *Why* square pillow? Chuck it out, try to sleep against bolster. *Or belts. Or blest.* Pak op *trobles* in ol kit bag . . . Old priests nodding, smiling, long grey hair like Abbé Liszt, in front row of armchairs at Christmas play by seminarists, mumming Trojan War with wooden swords, but one seminarist, dressed as maid, answers telephone in rapid French which understand perfectly, for somehow it is English as well. Suddenly curtains fall, chairs turned over as old priests, seminarists, rush out to belfry and man ropes—12 midnight. Old French hymn on bells in moonlit spire:

> Bong, ting clang bong, clang,
> Ting clang bong bing bang;
> Bong, clang ting bong, clang,
> Ting tong bing bong clang.

No. 19th-century hymn. Much more awake than in daytime not (ROT bels!), have super-consciousness of lacy Gothic 19th-cent. church, full of widows with pursed lips, Gothic bells in huge Dürer–Carolingian landscape, messages from Pope over forested ridges to Cologne, Rome, Aachen, Lindisfarne. Meanwhile 19th-cent. atheists riposte with monster town clock, strikes every hour *twice*. No tunes, just BUENGG, BUENNG. Fiery atheist-syndicalist 19th-cent. mayor in tricolour sash, M. Alphonse Rataplan, unveiling municipal clock. Name of a name, is not pure time the measure of human progress, *mes amis*, rather than the tunes of an ignorant past? Ceremony boycotted by widows. Band of *sapeurs pompiers*, poum poum poum. Battle of the Bells. Dong clang bong . . . *Gromp, pripple ipple* . . .

Try folding pillow then. Where hell it? Grope. Crash. Tinkle. Damn. Knocked over glass of mineral water, specially put on floor in case huge pillow knocked it off bedside table. Lean firmly against pillow now foot high; perhaps French sleep sitting up . . .

1 a.m. *Bong Ting* hymn is played every hour.

2 a.m. How did municipal clock manage to strike *before* Bong Ting this time? Atheist mayor in red night-cap, cackling to himself, climbing up stairs in clock tower with lantern to advance it.

In silence after mighty tintinnabulation, tiny waspish noise, growing louder. It is mo-ped, coming in over lonely moonlit forested ridges. Stops next door to hotel. Huge iron gates creak open, animated conversation. Mo-ped starts up again, no silencer (ridden by Monsignor with urgent message for Rome, not time for repairs), *bwam bwam* off past snoring old priests, dreaming seminarists, lacy spire, into empty forest. What was message? Man next door now creaks gates open wider, starts up huge diesel lorry, shouts for helpers to load it with buckets, planks, bins, angle-iron, bellbuoys, crankcases, billboards, gongs, clang-pots, thundersheets. Urgent, driver impatiently revs up engine, finally roars off, gate creaks shut.

3 a.m. Entire performance repeated, although can't tell whether it is a new Monsignor or same one back from forest. What they *doing*? Resolve to look out of window next time, presumably 4 a.m., and see. Tie great pillow round head with luggage strap, both ears covered. Should probably have slept anyhow, anyway, next thing it is

8 a.m. All quiet as grave except for woman in dressing-gown taking down shutters opposite. Shall never know, now.

Paul Jennings (b. 1918), *Observer*, reprinted: *Golden Oddlies* (1983).

WHEN *Paul Jennings left the* Observer *the paper kept up the intellectual standard he had set by taking on as their resident humorous columnist a brilliant young journalist and columnist from the* Guardian, *Michael Frayn.*

If what the Observer *wanted was humour with a high IQ, their far-sightedness in appointing Frayn was confirmed by his subsequent career. He had already published four novels and from the* Observer *he went straight into writing televison plays and documentaries. In 1970 he began to write a run of what proved to be highly successful stage plays—nine by 1984. He also translated four plays. On the way he collected armfuls of awards.*

Michael Frayn's plays are much concerned with ideas and with structures; many of them are adroit farces, ingeniously manipulated.

His fascination with the geometric patterns which people's lives take on, which interweave with sad or happy results, was in evidence in some of his Observer *pieces, including the following sketch.*

In this he manages to give us a complete and complex domestic comedy entirely in brief messages scribbled on Christmas cards. And these are exchanged by casual acquaintances who barely know each other:

A HAND OF CARDS

Bernard—

> *With all good wishes*
> *for a Merry Christmas*
> *and a Happy New Year!*
>
> —from Charles (Edwards!)

I don't know whether you remember me—we used to prop up the bar of the Rose and Crown together occasionally in the good old days, in dear old London town. How are you keeping back there in England, you old reprobate? Look me up if you're ever passing through New Zealand.

*

Bernard and Jean—

> *Wishing you a Very*
> *Merry Christmas and the*
> *Happiest of New Years*
>
> —from Charles

Congratulations on your marriage—saw it in the *Times* airmail edition. Nice work if you can get it. Meant to write on the spot. Anyway, cheers to you both.

*

Bernard, Jean and Baby Flora (!)—

> *All Best Wishes for*
> *Xmas and the New Year*
>
>> —from Charles and Kitty (!)

Charles took the plunge at last, as you can see! Many congratulations on the Flora effort—saw it in the *Times*—meant to write. You must come out and see us some time.

*

Bernard, Jean, Flora, and Polly (!)—

> *To Wish You a*
> *Joyous Christmas*
>
>> —from Charles, Kitty, Gareth (!),
>> and Luke (!)

Yes, you did hear right—twins! Identical—fair, with Charles's nose and mouth. Born 14 July—same day as Fall of Bastille! Charles had to be revived with brandy. Gareth ate ear-ring last month, otherwise everything OK. Tremendous congrats on Polly. Meant to write.

*

Jean, Flora and Polly—

> *The mail coach dashes thru' the snowy ways*
> *To bring good cheer and news of happy days!*
>
>> —from Charles, Kitty, Gareth, Luke,
>> Lionel (!), and Mother.

Dreadfully sorry about news of you and Bernard, but I'm sure you're usually better off apart in these cases. Great shock when we got your last year's card, meant to write at once, but you know how it is, what with Lionel and all the rest of it. Lionel was a slight mistake, of course! Mother's moved in to help out.

*

Bernard, Jean, Flora, Polly, and Daisy (!)—

> *Peace on Earth, Goodwill to men*
>
>> —from Kitty and Walter
>> (CRAIGIE!), not to mention
>> Gareth, Luke, Lionel, Mother,
>> Victoria and Georgina!

Heartiest congrats on you and Bernard getting together again—further hearty congrats on weighing in so smartly with Daisy! Meant to write as soon as your last Xmas card arrived. Walter and I were married in Auckland on 9 June, reception for 120, two days' honeymoon at Rotorua while mother looked after children. Victoria and Georgina are Walter's children by first marriage, of course! Walter is engineer—low temperature. Poor Charles is coming over to England in New Year, told him to look you up.

*

Bernard, Jean, Flora, Polly, Daisy, and James(!)—

> *Hearty Good Wishes for*
> *a Merry Xmas and a*
> *Prosperous New Year!*

>> —Kitty, Walter, Gareth, Luke, Lionel,
>> Mother, Victoria, Georgina, Murray,
>> Lester and baby Linda.

Congrats on James—my word you keep at it! Victoria and Georgina had lovely joint wedding at St Margaret's, Wanganui, in Feb. Vicky married Murray West (his father's in agricultural machinery down near Christchurch), Georgie married Lester Dewie—nice young man, went to school in England (Thorpehurst—know it?), now learning hotel business. Georgie's baby Linda born (prematurely!) 3 Aug. Did poor Charles ever show up in GB?

*

Charles(!), Jean, Flora, Polly, Daisy, and James—

> *When the Yule log brightly burns*
> *And brings its Christmas cheer,*
> *To days gone by fond Mem'ry turns*
> *And old friends far and near!*

>> —from Kitty, Walter, Gareth, Luke,
>> Lionel, Victoria, Murray, Georgina,
>> Lester, Linda, Sukie, and Simon.

Heartiest congrats from all of us on you and Charles! V. best wishes—all tickled pink. Shameful of me not to write in Summer when I heard news but Vicky just producing Simon, and then Georgie was having Sukie while I looked after Linda, then Mother passed quietly away.

*

Charles, Jean, Flora, Polly, Daisy, James, Dinah(!), Gareth, Luke, and Lionel—

> *Yuletide Greetings!*

>> —from Kitty, Walter, Victoria, Murray,
>> Georgina, Lester, Linda, Sukie, Simon,
>> and Gabriel.

Congratulations on Dinah! Don't know how you do it! Gabriel (Simon's brother) born 7 Oct. in flood. Hope Gareth, Luke, and Lionel are settling down all right with their father for Xmas, seems very quiet here without them, though Lester's mother is coming for Xmas Day (she's just lost her husband, sadly) plus his two sisters Charmian and Henrietta, so house will be quite full. Walter has ulcer.

*

Charles, Jean, Flora, Polly, Daisy, James, Dinah, Gareth, Luke, Lionel, Georgina, Lester, Linda, Sukie, and Jane—

> *Christmas Comes But Once a Year,*
> *and When it Comes it Brings Good Cheer!*

> —from Kitty, Walter, Victoria, Murray, Simon, Gabriel, Nicholas, Charmian, Henrietta, *Bernard*!(!), Cecilia and Timothy.

Hope the boys are enjoying their Xmas jaunt as usual and behaving themselves. So good of you to have Georgie and Lester and the girls for Xmas while they're over in England, hope Charles will be up and about again soon. Guess what, Bernard's here! Coming for Xmas Day with his new wife Cecilia and their baby Timothy (three months). Sends his love—says he doesn't send Xmas cards any more. I know what he means—once you start it never ends.

Michael Frayn (b. 1933), *The Observer*, reprinted: *The Original Michael Frayn* (1983).

———

THERE *are a number of writers whose main work lies in more sober fields but who from time to time come up with a splendidly amusing column or piece.*

Representing these humorous fellow-travellers is P. J. Kavanagh, better known as a poet, novelist, and literary journalist. Here, in a neat piece of anecdote-weaving for his Spectator *column, he pictures for us an episode from his past when he was within spitting distance of fame and luxury (and notice that even poets can succumb to the temptation of using a pun in their title):*

LEAN TIMES

Spring has been arriving incognito this year, in dark and wind. So instead of observing what is nearly invisible I have been thinking about David Lean.

He was in the news recently because of his film *Passage to India*, and this reminded me that I once had a part in his film *Lawrence of Arabia*. This in turn reminds me of the old story about the long-out-of-work Scottish actor who at last landed the part of the doctor in *Macbeth*. At home, asked what *Macbeth* was about, he said 'Well, there's this *doctor* . . .' Well, in *Lawrence of Arabia* there was this adjutant.

After being measured for uniform and riding boots (those, also, bespoke) a chauffeur in a Rolls took me to the airport. He was deferential until we had a puncture, then he began to swear because he did not know where the spare wheel was. He was a mock-chauffeur, and therefore an appropriate part of the whole experience.

I was to fly to Seville first class, which I looked forward to, never having travelled that way. But there turned out to be no first class on my aeroplane. Never mind, there was always the return journey.

We were shooting in a Royal Palace in Seville, which contained rooms the size of aeroplane hangars, with marble floors, and in these we filmed. There was immediately an air of unreality about everything. As I stood next to Peter O'Toole in a freezing corridor, waiting for our cue, I wondered why his eyes were so unnaturally blue, his hair so unnaturally yellow, and why he had had a nose job. It was no surprise that studio gossip reported he had been christened 'Florence of Arabia' by studio executives in the US, but he was not that kind of actor and Lawrence had been rather a plain-looking man; so why?

Then there was a break in the filming, because of some disaster; directorial temper was frayed and we four players, participants in the same scene, sat waiting for two days in a small cold room. O'Toole entertained us with absurd stories, while Donald Wolfit sat implacably waiting his turn to speak and Claude Rains just sat. When Wolfit did speak it was always at length and always, rather endearingly, about himself. 'It was Philadelphia and we opened on the Thursday to a packed house. I myself was playing the Merchant, and I remember . . .' I swear I heard him resonantly ask O'Toole, 'Have *you* ever played The Gloomy One?' After a while I missed Claude Rains and came across him alone in the Throne Room wrapped in a rug in the semi-dark and sitting on the throne: 'I can't stand any more of that man's stories,' he groaned.

At last filming started. I opened the door on cue and announced 'Colonel Lawrence, Sir' to Wolfit–Allenby but the glass in the door had flashed and it had to be dismantled. An hour later I opened it again but my bespoke boots made too much noise on the marble floor and were removed from me to be resoled with felt. (This was a relief because I had had difficulty keeping my balance in front of a hundred pairs of impatient eyes.) An hour later, everyone mad with anxiety by this time, for each hour lost was costing thousands of pounds, I entered again and my bespoke breeches split down the seam. True.

During one of the delays I saw David Lean pick up a family photograph from the Allenby–Wolfit desk and express displeasure. Later I learned that a wig had been flown from England, put on a Spanish actress, a picture taken and the photograph replaced. It was never going to be in shot. O'Toole had praised Lean's attention to detail, but this substitution struck me as megalomania. If he really cared for detail why had he made O'Toole appear as a blond bombshell? More and more it became a film I had no wish to see.

However, there was still the first class flight to look forward to, and the champagne. Several of us settled ourselves luxuriously into our seats. I saw Claude Rains outside on the tarmac, looking sad as usual. An anxious official approached us: 'Mr Rains has the wrong ticket. Would anyone care to change to second class?' His eye caught mine . . . I never did get to travel first class, or see the film.

P. J. Kavanagh (b. 1931), *The Spectator* (27 Apr. 1985).

A N *occasional humorist of wit and a fine writer in other spheres was Paul Dehn.* *Dehn somehow managed to find time to write humorous pieces for* Punch *and others whilst being immersed in other literary activities including film criticism, books of poetry, lyrics for musicals, songs and sketches for West End revues, libretti for operas, the commentaries for award-winning documentaries, and writing or co-writing the screenplays of innumerable films like* Seven Days to Noon (*for which he won an Oscar*), Goldfinger, The Spy Who Came In From The Cold, *four of the* Planet of the Apes *films, and* Murder on the Orient Express.

Glancing through the New Yorker, *Paul Dehn noticed that one advertiser, an importer of French wines into the USA, had the brilliant idea of overcoming the language barrier by translating the names of his French wines into phonetic English.*

To Paul Dehn these invented, phonetic non-words took on a bizarre reality:

SCHOTTO BOTTLED

Advertising in a recent issue of the New Yorker, Messrs Barton and Guestier (Wine Merchants Inc.) have undertaken the enlightened task of introducing their clientele to certain European wines which many an American has either never heard of or (if we may credit rumour) is too frightened to order on the telephone for fear of mispronouncing. The advertisement contains the following list:

So tairn	Shah blee
May dock	Mah kon
Bow Joe lay	Mawn rah shay
Poo yee Fweesay	Poc mahr
Schotto Neff du Pop	Grahv
Sant Ay mee lee on	

Literate Europeans and Orientals will, of course, recognize at once the titles of eleven comparatively well-known Drinking Songs. But I wonder how many Americans will know the words (or, indeed, the meaning) of these 'ditties' that Messrs Barton and Guestier are obviously recommending their clients to sing, while the unfamiliar bottle goes round the table. It is for their benefit that I take the liberty of adding an explanatory 'gloss' on some of the better-known songs.

So tairn became popular in Scotland about 1796:

> So tairn frae yon stuir,
> An' glaur me the tassie.
> Wha helpit the puir
> Nae gowaned a lassie!
>
> Nae gowaned a mither
> Wha whelpit a bairn!
> We'll quecht it thegither,
> So tairn, lassie, tairn!

(*stuir*: mess. *glaur*: toss. *tassie*: utensil. *gowaned*: solicited (*Sc.* for advice). *quecht*: *turpitudinem alicui per vim inferre*)

The ladies (or 'lassies') should courteously *turn* as each man upends his individual utensil. The piece has been translated into Lallans by Sydney Goodsir Smith, but the original is the simpler version.

May dock is a 14th-century English wassail song. The words of these often had very little relevance to the act of drinking, until they resolved into the rollicking chorus that was wassail's happiest convention:

> Sith May dock blowe,
> We schal hav snowe
> When bulluc lowe
> Wid windes snell.
>
> Ac fadeth May dock
> In fold and padock,
> Ne holt ne hadock
> Moun swete smell
>
> *Then troll the boll, boteler . . . etc.*

(*snell*: painful. *hadock*: haycock; not (as Quiller-Couch in the *Oxford Book of English Verse*) haddock.)

Bow Joe Lay is a straight 18th-century drinking shanty:

> 'Twere nor' nor' west from Port o' Brest
> (Yare, yare and away!)
> That hard abaft the scupper-tholes
> Bow Joe lay.
>
> *With a ho, Joe! Blow, Joe!*
> *Row me round the bay.*
> *Fill us a tot and wet the spot*
> *Where Bow Joe lay.*

Bow Joe has never been satisfactorily identified. Some hold that 'bow' refers to the shape of his limbs and is an *ellipsis* for 'bow-legged Joe'; others, that it is a corruption of Fr. beau and that, for a naval man, he was singularly beautiful.

Poo-yee Fweesay is a Chinese *haiku* (circ. 5080 BC) and should strictly be sung only when drinking wine that has been distilled from rice:

> *Poo-yee fweesay,*
> *Ori-tamae!*
> *Nao, nao, hou han shi.*
> *Shan, kuei fweesay, ho tsai yu.*

> Princess Poo-yee
> Come down!
> Nao, nao, blows the autumn wind.
> I long for a royal lady, but dare not speak.

> (tr. Arthur Waley)

The author, Po, is said to have died of drink.

Schotto Neff, du, Pop is a traditional Yiddish lament still sung, over a glass of *klatsch* on the Sabbath, by the descendants of those Jews who were driven from the Great Ghetto of Neff by edict of Czar Nicholas at the turn of the 19th century.

> 'Schotto Neff, du, Pop?
> Schotto Neff, du, Pop?'
> 'Weh, weh, bontsche schnee!
> Schot' woh' Neff dein Pop.'

> 'Dost remember Neff, thou, mine father?
> Dost remember Neff, thou, mine father?'
> 'Woe, woe! Silent snow!
> Remembers well Neff thine father.'

With the words of the remaining songs I am unfamiliar, though any reasonably experienced folklorist will recognize the titles.

Sant Ay, Mee Lee on was first sung in French by a group of 17th-century Catholic missionaries far from their home village ('St. Ay, white-roofed, still calls . . .') and translated by their Hawaiian converts, whose descendants sing it to this very day—though its regional significance has long been forgotten and it is sung chiefly during beach-banquets arranged at moderate cost for the tourist trade. I am indebted to the *Guide Michelin* for a comprehensive note on modern St. Ay:

> ST. AY Loiret [64]—(8)—620 h. Alt. 100—Bouguereau

Shah Blee is a loyal toast from the 4th-century Persian; *Mah Kon*, a popular Siamese love-song; *Mawn Rah Shay*, a ritualistic Hindu invocation to Rah Shay (King Breath), which is not really a drinking song at all, unless Messrs Barton and Guestier have actually bottled the waters of the Ganges; *Poe Mahr* (more correctly *Po Mahr*: 'A little more!'), a *skjemtsang* (joke-song) in which second-year students of Uppsala University induct freshmen into the joys of Aquavit; and *Grahv*, a Latvian dirge.

A good list, on the whole, though there are notable omissions. What of the Tibetan *Ahman Yak?* Or that festive group of Italo-Yugoslav *canzonette della frontiera* compositely called *Romanay Contee* (Tales of the Gipsies)? Or the bitter little Trinidad calypso, *Ma, go!?* Or the evergreen *Arnjew:*

> Arnjew de kutiest
> Butiest frutiest
> Beibi—
> Arnjew?

But this, on second thoughts, is still in current usage among certain irre-dentist minorities all over America. The Vanderbilts are said to sing it in family conclave once yearly. New York (one so easily forgets) used to be Nieuw Amsterdam.

Paul Dehn (1912–76), Punch, reprinted: For Love and Money (1956).

K EITH WATERHOUSE, *a humorist of great flexibility and range, one of our most reliable and brilliant professionals, has written over ten novels (Auberon Waugh considers him to be Britain's most underrated novelist) including the history of the doomed would-be escapologist from suburbia,* Billy Liar. *With the playwright Willis Hall he has written a number of screenplays which were filmed in Hollywood and London, also ten stage plays, two musicals, and numerous TV plays and series.*

He has written columns in the Guardian, Daily Mirror, *and the* Daily Mail, *and over the years has won five national awards for them. And he has been writing regularly for* Punch *for over twenty years.*

Some of the items in his newspaper columns are political and social comment, but many of his pieces are pure humour, like the following which he wrote for a Punch *Christmas edition. On one level it is a funny story of an overtired-and-emotional lad's drunken progress through sleazy Soho pubs and clubs on Christmas Eve in the company of a kind Lady of the Night, who is gently robbing him en route.*

On another level it is a rollicking parody of the Christmas Eve chapter in Dylan Thomas's Portrait of the Artist as a Young Dog *(see p. 751 above):*

A DRUNK'S CHRISTMAS IN SOHO

Years and beers and cheers ago, when I was a boyo, when there was more slag in Old Compton Street than in the valleys, when we swallowed and wallowed all day in caverns that smelt like armpits, and nuzzled and nestled in armpits like taverns, I don't mean taverns, the word I just said, caverns;

back in those sprawling, crawling, falling, your-glasses-please-gentlemen-calling times, it snowed and it snowed.

But here a brass-blonde nursing a gin-and-It like a new born babe says; 'It snowed last year too, dear. I fell on my bum outside the French pub and you kissed it better.'

'But that was not the same snow,' I say. 'Our snow came shawling down and swam and drifted over the bat-black, hat-black, cat-black, mat-black, sat-black, rat-black, fat-black, ha ha ha ha ha ha excuse me ahem.'

'Get on with it, then.'

'Listen, tight lady of the light. As you were, night. Listen to what I am telling you. Listen, because this is very interesting. Listen, because this is the most interesting, winteresting, splinteresting, pinteresting—'

'Oh God, he's off again.'

'One Christmas was so much like another, in those lost boy years spewed up in sawdust and gone out of sight except for the little animals I sometimes see a moment before sleep, that I can never remember whether I was pissed for six days and six nights when I was twenty-five or for twenty-five days and nights when I was who's got my drink?'

'You've got to humour him, you know, Were there drinks then, too?'

'Rivers and oceans of them. I rode in a barrel down a Niagara of rum, then bobbed in a dimpled bottle across the seven C's, Calvados, Crème de menthe, cherry brandy, Charrington's Export and look, I'm not a bloody fool, you know, this is ginger ale.'

'It's Scotch and ginger, dear. Was there singing?'

'Such singing as a child cradled in sleep hears when the lark-choir caged in dreams cries at the dew-drop morning. HO! THIS IS NUMBER ONE, AND THE FUN HAS JUST BEGUN, ROLL ME OVER, LAY ME DOWN AND DO IT AGAIN . . .'

'Come along, dear, the landlord has very kindly invited us to leave. Mind the steps.'

'WE THREE KINGS OF ORIENT ARE, ONE IN A TAXI, ONE IN A CAR . . . Where are we now?'

'In a club, dear. The one you're not barred from. Tell us about the jokes.'

'But I haven't told you about the singing yet. Such singing as a child cradled in sleep—'

'You did mention the singing, dear. You told that policeman in Leicester Square all about the singing, and I said I'd look after you. Tell us about the jokes.'

'In those Christmases gone-by, when the snow-thatched roofs glistened like icing-sugar in the dew-drop morning, and the lark-choir caged in dreams cried at the children cradled in sleep, there was this thick-mick, bog-fog Irishman who was trying to change this electric-light bulb—'

'Keep your voice down, dear, the barman comes from Belfast. And I'm sure you won't mind, but you've just bought my friend a bottle of champagne. I've put the rest of the money in your top pocket.'

'In those chestnut-pulling Christmases gone by, not chestnut-pulling, cracker-pulling, in those chestnut-cracking, cracker-pulling, pulling-cracking, stocking-filling, pillowcase-stuffing, turkey-plucking, stop-me-if-you've-heard-it Christmases gone by, such jokes were told as would set double chins bouncing like jellies and bosoms heaving like chapel-picnic blancmanges, and nipples the size and substance of glacé cherries would balloon from their sequinned moorings and—'

'Were there barmaids in those days?'

'Of course there were barmaids, you stupid ignorant cow! Whose nipples the size and substance of glacé cherries do you think would balloon from their sequinned moorings, if not the double-chin bouncing, bosom-heaving barmaids? And I'll tell you another thing about those triple-Scotch, nipple-touch, tipple-much Christmases gone by, they didn't water the sodding whisky.'

'Come on, dear.'

'Where going now?'

'Back to my place.'

'And when it was rat-black night and the frolicking and rollicking were over, and drunks lay like skittles in the alleys and policemen with fat lips frog-marched poets up the snow-sleet, Bow-Street steps, and the yule frog correction yule log hissed and sighed then crackled into powder like the snow-thatched roofs crumbling like icing-sugar in the dew-drop mornings and the lark-choir, no stuff the lark-choir, you've made me lose my bloody thread now.'

'Sorry, dear, I was just taking a pound note for the taxi fare. I've put the rest of your money in your back pocket.'

'Back-pocket Venuses, slim as Venus pencils, flitted out of that cat-pack night and scrawled and scribbled their indelible kisses over the fat-lipped poet's frog-slobbering cheeks, then with calligraphic fingers scratched copper-plate pothooks across his parchment belly, oh Christ.'

'What's the matter, dear?'

'I'm going to be sick. A Vesuvius of light ale, rum and peppermint, Scotch on the rocks, gin and tonic, and that green stuff we were drinking on the alley-cat-scuttling bomb site, churns and heaves and then erupts, rumbling to the surface like a Rhondda pit-cage and spewing through frog-slobbering lips with the whirling, swirling force of a clogged-up fountain in a vomitarium. Why is there always tomato in it?'

'Out you get, dear.'

'Where going this time?'

'The taxi-driver has very nicely asked us to walk the rest of the way, dear. It's just round the corner.'

'And peeping round the corner of all the years, as a child peeps through church-steeple fingers at the tangerine-smelling tin-toy-promising stocking on the patchwork quilted horizon, I see a young man in his prime staggering through the Notting Hill, Rotting Hill tag-end-and-bobtail of Christmas and bawling at the Yule-frog dawn, 'TWAS ON THE GOOD SHIP VENUS, YOU REALLY SHOULD HAVE SEEN US—'

'Come to the Presents, dear.'

'There were Presents for everyone. There were Turkeys, plucked from the Food Hall at Harrods, and pressed on the doorman at Claridge's as a tip for not letting us in. There were shiny half-crowns for newsvendors, and sweet quires of the *Evening Standard* for the foot-stamping, No. 11-damn-and-blasting bus queues. There were crisp-and-even fivers for the commissionaires of night clubs, and teddy-bears that mooed for the cow-faced hostesses. And in the senseless, Wenceslas-singing evening, all the barmaids with nipples the size and substance of glacé cherries, would smirk and say "You shouldn't have" as they dabbed bedroom-smelling scent on their bouncing, heaving—'

'You've told me about the barmaids already, dear. Get back to the Presents.'

'In a minute. I think I'm going to be sick again. A Vesuvius of—'

'Just lean against the lamp-post, dear. And get back to the Presents, to take your mind off what you've had to drink. Were there Presents for your lady-friends?'

'Oh, yes. The street-girls were paved with gold, those Christmases of so long ago.'

'That's the idea, dear, I've left you enough for your bus fare. It's in your side pocket. I'd ask you in, but my landlady doesn't like it. Merry Christmas, dear,' says the brass-blonde who nursed her gin-and-It all night like a newborn babe.

'Merry Christmas,' I say, and then I lay me down to sleep.

Keith Waterhouse (b. 1929), Punch, reprinted: Fanny Peculiar (1983).

Here is Waterhouse in a different mood.

In this story (his own favourite piece) he tells of the predicament of a trapped man. The man's wife has found what seems to be incriminating evidence and the man has to keep his brain ice-cool and try to talk his way out of it.

He soon realizes that this is impossible and he is doomed, but he must keep trying. And then, as desperation sets in, go on trying harder and harder . . . :

A LIKELY STORY

What knickers in what glove compartment?

It's not my car.

It may well be my car, now that I look at it from this angle, but those are not my knickers. Surely they're your knickers?

Yes, because don't you remember: when the dog chewed up my Kermit Squeezee-Sponge and I asked if you could spare me a bit of wash-leather or something to rub over the windscreen? And you said there was an old blue check duster in that biscuit tin under the sink where we keep the shoe-cleaning things?

I must have absent-mindedly gone to your dressing-table drawer and taken out that pair of red satin knickers, then put it in the glove compartment thinking it was an old blue check duster.

Since you ask, no, I can't really see you wearing red satin knickers in a million years, especially that type. I'd qualify that even further and make it ten million years. Maybe that's one reason why we're not as close as we used to be.

However that doesn't alter the fact that the knickers were in your dressing-table drawer, where, not bothering to switch on the bedside lamp, I mistook them in the gathering dusk for a blue check duster.

How do I know? I expect you put them there yourself, after unwrapping them.

I know you have a short memory but surely you can remember getting a pair of red knickers for Christmas, among other perhaps more suitable items? *I* certainly remember—I can remember your very words. 'Thank you very much but I couldn't wear these in a million years,' you said. 'I'll take them back to Janet Reger's when the shops open again and change them for a cardigan.' Then you must have popped them in your dressing-table drawer and not given them another moment's thought from that day to this.

All right. Joke over. Do you want to know what really happened?

You're not going to like this, I'm warning you.

Because it involves someone whose guts you hate.

Beresford, the office practical joker.

Of course you knew he was the office practical joker. That's why you hate his guts. Because he kept patting your bum at that dinner-dance we went to.

Well, *he* thought it was a practical joke. Surely I'm not to be held responsible for my colleague's off-beat sense of humour?

So. I can't prove anything, but I did notice when I set off home the other night that Beresford, the office practical joker, was hanging round the car-stack, where he had no right to be since he doesn't drive. As you know.

Let me just get this straight. You're saying that if I try to tell you that Beresford, the office practical joker, somehow got into the car, somehow forced open the glove compartment without breaking the lock, planted a pair of red satin knickers that he happened to have in his pocket, then somehow managed to lock the compartment again, you're going to see a solicitor, right?

Then it's very fortunate indeed that that isn't what happened.

Beresford, the office practical joker, is only peripherally involved. The incident really centres on Carmichael.

Carmichael. I don't think you've met him. Has quite a reputation as the office conjuror. I've seen him do tricks with playing cards that would astound you. We all tell him he should take it up professionally. Listen: imagine, if you will, a bowl of goldfish, a wristwatch, an ordinary table napkin, the flags of all nations, an egg—

Did I mention tricks with glove compartments? Or sleight of hand with pairs of red knickers? Then until I do mention tricks with glove compartments and sleight of hand with pairs of red knickers, be so kind as to reserve judgement.

Where was I?

Good heavens.

You know that sensation one sometimes gets? Yes you do—the sensation that you know what someone's about to say? *Déjà vu*, isn't it? Well, I just had it then.

It was when I said 'Where was I?' It suddenly brought something back to me. Sitting in the car and saying those very words, Well, not quite those very words but near enough. It wasn't 'Where was I?,' it was 'Where am I?' or something of that kind. I must have temporarily lost my memory.

No, I know that's not the same thing as *déjà vu*, but you know what I mean. Of course you do. Don't tell me you've never temporarily lost your memory and come round hearing yourself saying, 'Where am I?' or 'Who am I?'

I don't think I like your tone. I wouldn't *dream* of asking you to believe that I came round saying, 'Where am I or who am I, and how did that pair of red knickers find its way into the glove compartment?' Had that been the case I would have mentioned it at the time.

The time I found myself sitting in the car asking, 'Where am I' or 'Who am I?' as the case may be. The time I temporarily lost my memory.

Yes, well I was going to tell you about it but I forgot.

Red knickers don't come into it anywhere. I just got sidetracked by that moment of *déjà vu* or whatever it was.

I *am* getting back to the nitty-gritty. Beresford, the office practical joker, and Carmichael, the office conjuror, were how shall I put it, somewhat the worse for wear. Tired and emotional, as the phrase has it. Stinko. Three sheets in the wind.

You're right up to a point. Beresford, the office practical joker, didn't *used* to drink, but now he drinks like a fish. The only reason you don't know he drinks is that you won't have him in the house, because you hate his guts.

They were hanging round the car-stack. Beresford, the office practical joker, who doesn't drive, although he does now drink, was supporting Carmichael, the office conjuror, who both drives and drinks.

They'd been celebrating.

Does it matter? Actually, since you ask, they'd been celebrating the news that Emerson, the office kleptomaniac, had just been appointed Bristol branch manager.

Didn't you? Oh, yes, the company keeps it hushed up. We've been asked not to talk about it. It's an illness. He takes pills for it.

Yes, that's perfectly correct, he did take charge of the Bristol branch two and a half years ago—in order, I might add in confidence, to save him the humiliation of being kept under surveillance by officers from Bow Street who suspected him of purloining washing from clothes-lines. But it was only a temporary appointment until recently. As Emerson, the office kleptomaniac, will tell you if you ask him, he came back to Head Office to be confirmed as permanent Bristol manager. And promptly got pie-eyed with Beresford, the office practical joker, and Carmichael, the office conjuror.

By all means ring him up to congratulate him, if you know the STD code.

You may mention red knickers if you wish, but I cannot for the life of me see why you should want to. Have I accused Emerson, the office kleptomaniac, of stealing a pair of red knickers from Marks and Spencer's and then stuffing them in the glove compartment when he saw Beresford, the office practical joker, disguised as a policeman?

Very well then.

The only reason Emerson, the office kleptomaniac, comes into the story is that he was spending the night at the home of Carmichael, the office conjuror, before returning to Bristol by train. Carmichael, the office conjuror, was too drunk to drive. Beresford, the office practical joker, does not drive, as has been established. Foolishly, I volunteered to give them all a lift.

Now I am not going to weary you with details of how Carmichael, the office conjuror, threw his latch-key out of the car window while we were crossing Chiswick flyover. He swore that when we arrived at the house he could produce it out of my glove compartment, and he is so damn clever— you know he's a member of the magic circle, don't you? Oh, yes. Vice-president— that's why we believed him, not knowing how sloshed he was.

So. We arrived at Carmichael's, the office conjuror's, and I can see I don't have to tell you what's happened: we open the glove compartment and you've guessed it—no latch-key. Can't get in the house. Beresford, the office practical joker, has by now passed out cold and none of us knows where he lives, so I couldn't dump them all at *his* place. And I couldn't bring them back here because you loathe Beresford's, the office practical joker's, guts.

So.

I'm cruising along Chiswick High Road wondering whether to drive them to a hotel or what the hell to do, when what should I see reflected in my diplights but this ankle length ball-gown. Containing, as it turned out, one stunning blonde, thumbing a lift.

Are you sure I haven't told you this story? I thought I had.

So naturally, being the gent I am, I stop, and in gets this blonde and sits in the front passenger seat, where the glove compartment is. Beresford, the office practical joker, Carmichael the office conjuror, and Emerson, the office kleptomaniac, were all in the back, sleeping it off.

Now as you know, there's a light in the glove compartment, which happened to be open because we'd been searching for Carmichael's, the office conjuror's latch-key; so I was able to get a good look at her face. Hello, I thought, I've seen you before darling.

And do you know who it was?

I can see you're not going to get it. Of all people, it was none other than Jamieson, the office transvestite. Not much of a coincidence, because as you probably know he lives in the same street as Carmichael, the office conjuror, and Bates, the office security manager.

'Thank God it's you four,' says Jamieson, the office transvestite, 'because I'm in dead trouble . . .'

Ibid.

———————

FROM the end of the war until 1978 Punch had four editors, none of whom would have listed in their passports as their principal occupation 'writer of humorous prose'. Kenneth Bird, 1949–52, the cartoonist 'Fougasse', was principally concerned with modernizing the look of the pages; Malcolm Muggeridge, 1953–7, was the well-known journalist and interviewer who dragged the magazine into the post-war world by such devices as bringing in new writers and permitting the inclusion of a little light sex and satire; Bernard Hollowood, 1958–68, was initially an industrial reporter and Punch's first radio and television critic; and William Davis, 1969–78, was a financial journalist.

Then, in 1978, when Davis left, Punch had as its new editor Alan Coren, a true writer of humorous prose and the man whom the Sunday Times called 'the funniest writer in Britain today'.

Coren had never been anything other than a humorous writer. He won a Commonwealth Fellowship at Oxford which took him on to Yale and the University of California, Berkeley, and at the age of 25 he began writing for Punch. Three years later he was made an assistant editor and then literary editor and, in 1969, deputy editor. Whilst at Punch he also wrote funny/critical columns for three national newspapers and many other magazines. In 1987 he resigned from Punch and became a diarist on The Times and for a time, editor of the Listener.

Superficially, Alan Coren's style is remarkably like S. J. Perelman's whose influence he has always gratefully acknowledged (cf. the quotation from Coren's obituary of Perelman in Punch on p. 609 above): Coren almost always uses the same device as Perelman of taking off into a flight of fancy from a press-cutting and he also twists well-known phrases, sometimes adding a pun, to give his pieces Perelman-like titles:

> 'Half a Pound of Tuppeny Vice'
> 'I'm Gonna Sit Right Down and Write The Times a Letter'
> 'A Small Thing but Minoan'
> 'Red Sky at Night, the Refinery's Alight'
> 'If That's the Acropolis, How Come it don't Chime?' [Etc.]

Coren, too, writes in the mixed style which Perelman pioneered and which has had an enormous influence on humorous prose. It is the trick of mixing good prose with *slang and then suddenly bringing in an erudite reference or some recondite or otiose word (like 'recondite' or 'otiose').*

Perelman's style happens to be particularly original and therefore detectable, but the non-Perelman aspects of Coren's writing soon become apparent. One essential difference between the two writers is that Coren's rate of output is very much higher than Perelman's ever was. Perelman rewrote constantly and his prose was finally as dense and rich as a slice of American Pecan Fruit Cake, but he took weeks to write one short piece. Coren, on Punch, *was writing (besides many other things) a piece every week and his prose, a similarly dense mixture of slang and scholarship, bowls along equally fluently.*

Take a typical Coren feuilleton (*Coren rather likes to use Perelman's word to describe his sketches). The piece, incidentally, bears what is surely a near-perfect title.*

Coren considers the implications of a scientific report condemning the effect of booze on the Creative Spirit:

GO EASY, MR BEETHOVEN, THAT WAS YOUR FIFTH!

'Shrunk to half its proper size, leathery in consistency and greenish-blue in colour, with bean-sized nodules on its surface.' Yes, readers, I am of course describing Ludwig van Beethoven's liver, and I do apologize for going over such familiar ground, but I wanted to put the less musical members of my flock in the picture right from the start. I think they also ought to know that his spleen was more than double its proper size: far too many *soi-disant* music-lovers these days, when they drop the pick-up on *Egmont* or the *Eroica* and retire to their *chaise longue* for a quick listen, think to themselves *Poor old sod, he was deaf as a brick,* and leave it at that, entirely neglecting the fact that beneath the deaf-aid on his waistcoat Herr van Beethoven sported as misshapen a collection of offal as you could shake a stick at, including a pancreas the size of a pickled walnut and a length of intestine that could have been mistaken for pipe-lagging by all but the most astute German plumber.

I am reminded of all this internal strife by today's *Guardian*, which, in its copy-hungry turn, quotes from the current issue of the *Journal of Alcoholism*, a periodical of which I had not previously heard. Which is odd, since if I'm not on their mailing-list, who is? At all events, this bizarre broadsheet has clearly decided that it is not going to be outdone in Ludwig's bicentenary year by all the other mags, and has hopped aboard the wagon, if they'll pardon the expression, with a succinct length of verbiage by one Doctor Madden, consultant psychiatrist at a Chester hospital addiction unit. He it is whom I quote at the beginning of this *feuilleton*, and if I may say so, Doctor, as one stylist to another, I have rarely encountered so well-turned a memorial to a great man. Why that sentence was not chiselled on Ludwig van Beethoven's gravestone, I shall never know. I gather you've translated it from the report of his autopsy, and it may be that it reads even better in German, but I doubt it: poetry is what 'bean-sized nodule' is, and don't let anyone tell you otherwise. Indeed, you may well have altered the listening habits of an entire generation: how shall any of us be able to tune in to *Fidelio* again, without the tears springing to our eyes at the memory of the greenish-blue liver behind it? Will our rapture at the *Emperor* not be intensified beyond measure by the thought of that gigantic spleen, throbbing away like a ship's boiler under the composer's vest?

One flaw, however, mars the sunny scholarship of your piece: not content to commemorate the bicentenary merely by your thrilling evocation of distorted bowel and giblet and leaving it at that, you insist, I'm afraid, on going on to moralize. And it's none of your business, Doc. Having broken the unethical news that Ludwig's organs got this way through a daily consumption of booze that could have floated a Steinway down Kaiserstrasse, you then wind up the scoop with the homiletic clincher: 'Beethoven had a brain and mind capable of many years of musical productivity, had his life not been shortened by alcohol.' Now, I realize that this oleaginous aside may have been the result of editorial pressure, and that if you hadn't put it in all your readers might have rushed out immediately and begun hitting the sauce in the hope of coming up with a quartet or two, but couldn't you have turned the sentiment a little less harshly? And aren't you being just a teeny bit demanding? Aren't nine symphonies, thirty-two piano sonatas, seven concertos, two masses, sixteen string quartets, and two suitcasefuls of quintets enough for you and the rest of mankind?

And don't you perhaps feel that, after that lot, posterity owes Ludwig a little snort or two?

I suppose not. All human life is divided between those who order by the crate and those who believe that sherry trifle leads to the everlasting bonfire, and never the twain shall meet except on the sodden salient of the *Journal of Alcoholism* for such brief and bitter skirmishes as the one filleted above. You're on one side, Doc, and Ludwig and I are on the other. My own conclusion would be diametrically different from yours, viz, that if Beethoven had not been a regular supplier of empties to the trade, he wouldn't have written anything at all, and how does that grab you, abstemious musicologists? If the great man had been confined to Lucozade on the advice of Chester's addiction unit, my bet is that he'd have thrown in the towel at *Chopsticks* and gone down in history as a mediocre hosier.

Because it is no accident that all men of creative genius have toiled in the shadow of the corkscrew—how else is a giant to survive among pygmies, make the mundane tolerable, fence himself off from the encroachments of numbing normalcy? How but through regular intakes of fermented anaesthetic are we—there, I've said it—artists to stave off the canvas jacket and the screaming abdab? How must Beethoven have felt of a morning, his head full of whirling crotchets and jangling semi-breves, to have his housekeeper running off at the gob about the price of vermicelli, or shrieking through his blessed deafness in an attempt to bring home to him the immutable truth that if you send six pillow-cases to the laundry, you only ever get five back? Is it any wonder that he followed up his Special K with a few quick chasers of schnapps? Do you for one moment imagine that the Piano Concerto No. 4 in G Major was written by a teetotaller, given the fact that the decorators were in the haus at the time, Beethoven's shoes hadn't come back from the cobblers, he was four months overdue on his Schedule D payment, his mistress had run off with a door-to-door wurst salesman, and the dog had just trodden on his glasses?

And, worst of all, people like you, Doctor Madden, were constantly nagging him to get on with the bloody music, what about a couple of quick symphonies to follow up the 9th, shouldn't take you more than an hour or so to rattle 'em off, mate, and how would you like to address the Rotarians next Wednesday night, dress formal, and isn't it time you did a personal tour of Silesia, and by the way it's the Prime Minister's birthday coming up, so could you see your way clear to knocking out a little celebratory sextet, no fee naturally, oh yes, I nearly forgot, my wife's brother plays the triangle, not professional of course, but we all think he's rather good, so I've arranged a little dinner-party next Friday to give you the chance of hearing him . . .

I'm amazed his nodules didn't get any bigger than beans, all things considered.

It's a dodgy tightrope along which we creators wobble, Doc: enough booze to close the world off and keep us inventing, but not so much that we allow the golden haze to settle on us permanently, while the piano-strings slacken, and the typewriter rusts, and the brushes dry out and go stiff, and the public yawns and goes off in search of fresh fodder, muttering about what an inconsiderate bleeder that Shakespeare was, snuffing it in his fifties and leaving us with little more than *Lear, Hamlet, Macbeth, Othello, Antony and Cleopatra*, well I'm not surprised, you know what they say, he couldn't leave the stuff alone, liver like a dried pea, well that's the trouble with artists, isn't it, hoity-toity, too good for the rest of us, they've got to be different, haven't they, bloody bohemians the lot of them, load of boozers, junkies, fairies, layabouts, I mean to say, only nine symphonies, only thirty plays, *only ten novels*, only ONE Sistine Chapel (they say he was so pissed he couldn't get up the ladder), I mean, what do you expect?

Et in El Vino ego, Doc. In a small way, of course. What might *I* not have done, be doing, were it not for the lure of the barmaid's pinny and the brass-handled pump? Ah, the first chapters I have! What prolegomena! What flyleaf notes! A thousand words of the best, then it's off to the local for a self-congratulatory belt, and when I roll home, in a day or two, all in ashes, forgotten, dead. How was it going to go on, this trilogy, before those bottles intervened? Who was this character, and this, and who cares, now? Ah, those publishers' lunches, yes, I'll do a novel, yes, I have this wonderful idea, he meets her, see, and they go off to Ensenada, and her husband, broken by drugs and a lifetime of inferior diplomacy, kills his mistress, let's have another bottle of this excellent Mouton Cadet, but their son returns from the Congo where his mercenary activities have involved him with none other than, my goodness this is an amicable cognac, oh yes, you should certainly have the first draft by February, as you say, it's a natural, film rights alone should bring us in . . .

And I wake up in a Turkish bath, some time later, and can only remember that I had my umbrella when I left the house, but was it in the cab, or was it in the restaurant, or am I thinking of my raincoat?

Well, that's it, Doc, another thousand words, another bottle. And that's all you'll get from me today. All I ask is that when my liver and I kick off, and the *Journal of Alcoholism* rings up for a few succinct remarks on posterity's loss, you'll recall all this, and understand a little.

It may surprise you, but I'd hate to be remembered as just another greenish-blue liver, shrunk to half its proper size.

Alan Coren (b. 1938), Punch, reprinted: The Sanity Inspector (1974).

Alan Coren's virtuosity of invention is remarkable and deeply admired by his peers (Clive James wrote in an Observer *review 'He has a comic imagination which can actually render your jaded scribe flabbergasted').*

He scours the newspapers for odd stories, but that is standard practice for most humorous columnists; it is what Coren does with a paragraph when he finds one with potential which lifts him above the heads of most of his colleagues. He seems to use it as a kind of launching pad into some quite original orbit.

Like the small newspaper paragraph which revealed that Christopher Robin did not have a happy childhood as A. A. Milne's son. Surely nobody could squeeze anything very funny out of that?

W-e-ll . . .

THE HELL AT POOH CORNER

From Christopher Robin Milne's recent autobiography, it turns out that life in the Milne household was very different from what millions of little readers have been led to believe. But if it was grim for him, what must it have been like for some of the others involved? I went down to Pooh Corner—it is now a tower block, above a discount warehouse—for this exclusive interview.

Winnie-the-Pooh is sixty now, but looks far older. His eyes dangle, and he suffers from terminal moth. He walks into things a lot. I asked him about that, as we sat in the pitiful dinginess which has surrounded him for almost half a century.

'Punchy,' said Winnie-the-Pooh, 'is what I am. I've been to some of the best people, Hamley's, Mothercare, they all say the same thing: there's nothing you can do about it, it's all that hammering you took in the old days.'

Bitterly, he flicked open a well-thumbed copy of *Winnie-the-Pooh*, and read the opening lines aloud:

'Here is Edward Bear, coming downstairs now, bump, bump, bump, on the back of his head, behind Christopher Robin. It is, as far as he knows, the only way of coming downstairs.' He looked at me. 'The hell it was!' he muttered. 'You think I didn't want to walk down, like normal people? But what chance did I stand? Every morning, it was the same story, this brat comes in and grabs me and the next thing I know the old skull is bouncing on the lousy line. Also,' he barked a short bitter laugh, 'that was the last time anyone called me Edward Bear. A distinguished name, Edward. A name with *class*. After the king, you know.'

I nodded. 'I know,' I said.

'But did it suit the Milnes?' Pooh hurled the book into the grate, savagely. 'Did it suit the itsy-bitsy, mumsy-wumsy, ooze-daddy's-ickle-boy-den Milnes? So I was Winnie-the-Pooh. You want to know what it was like when the Milnes hit the sack and I got chucked in the toy-cupboard for the night?'

'What?' I said.

'It was "Hello, sailor!" and "Give us a kiss, Winifred!" and, "Watch out, Golly, I think he fancies you!," not to mention,' and here he clenched his sad, mangy little fists, 'the standard "Oy, anyone else notice there's a peculiar poo in here, ha, ha, ha!"'

'I sympathize,' I said, 'but surely there were compensations? Your other life, in the wood, the wonderful stories of . . .'

'Yeah,' said Pooh, heavily, 'the wood, the stories. The tales of Winnie-the-Schmuch, you mean? Which is your favourite? The one where I fall in the gorse bush? The one where I go up in the balloon and the kid shoots me down? Or maybe you prefer where I get stuck in the rabbit hole?'

'Well, I—'

'Hanging from a bloody balloon,' muttered Pooh, 'singing the kind of song you get put in the funny farm for! Remember?

> "How sweet to be a cloud,
> Floating in the blue!
> Every little cloud
> *Always* sings aloud."

That kind of junk,' said Pooh, 'may suit Rolf Harris. Not me.'

'Did you never sing it, then?' I enquired.

'Oh, I sang it,' said Pooh. 'I sang it all right. It was in the script. *Dumb bear comes on and sings*. It was in the big Milne scenario. But you know what I wanted to sing?'

'I have no idea,' I said.

His little asymmetrical eyes grew even glassier, with a sadness that made me look away.

'*Body and Soul*,' murmured Pooh, 'is what I wanted to sing, *Smoke Gets in*

Your Eyes. Or play the trumpet, possibly. It was,' he sighed, '1926. Jazz, short skirts, nightingales singing in Berkeley Square, angels dancing at the Ritz, know what I mean? A world full of excitement, sex, fun, Frazer-Nash two-seaters and everyone going to Le Touquet! And where was I? Hanging around with Piglet and passing my wild evenings in the heady company of Eeyore! *The Great Gatsby* came out that year,' said Pooh, bitterly. 'The same year as *Winnie-the-Pooh.*'

'I begin to understand,' I said.

'Why couldn't he write that kind of thing about me?' cried the anguished Pooh. 'Why didn't I get the breaks? Why wasn't I a great tragic hero, gazing at the green light on the end of Daisy's dock? Why didn't Fitzgerald write *Gatsby Meets a Heffelump* and Milne *The Great Pooh?*'

'But surely it was fun, if nothing else?' I said. 'Wasn't the Milne household full of laughter and gaiety and—'

'A. A. Milne,' Pooh interrupted, 'was an Assistant Editor of Punch. He used to come home like Bela Lugosi. I tell you, if we wanted a laugh, we used to take a stroll round Hampstead cemetery.'

Desperately, for the heartbreak of seeing this tattered toy slumped among his emotional debris was becoming unendurable, I sought an alternative tack.

'But think,' I said cheerily, 'of all the millions of children you have made happy!'

He was not to be shaken from his gloom.

'I'd rather,' he grunted, 'think of all the bears I've made miserable. After the Pooh books, the industry went mad. My people came off the assembly line like sausages. Millions of little bears marching towards the exact same fate as my own, into the hands of kids who'd digested the Milne rubbish, millions of nursery tea-parties where they were forced to sit around propped against a stuffed piglet in front of a little plastic plate and have some lousy infant smear their faces with jam. "O look, nurse, Pooh's ate up all his cake!" Have you any idea what it's like,' he said, 'having marmalade on your fur? It never,' and his voice dropped an octave, 'happened to Bulldog Drummond.'

'I'm sorry?'

Pooh reached for a grubby notebook, and flipped it open.

'"Suddenly the door burst from its hinges, and the doorway filled with a huge and terrible shape.

'"Get away from that girl, you filthy Hun swine!" it cried.

'"The black-hearted fiend who had been crouched over the lovely Phyllis turned and thrust a fist into his evil mouth.

'"Mein Gott!" he shrieked, "Es ist Edward Bear, MC, DSO!"

'"With one bound, our hero . . ."'

Pooh snapped the notebook shut.

'What's the use?' he said. 'I wrote that, you know. After Milne packed it in, I said to myself, it's not too late, I know where the pencil-box is, I shall come back like Sherlock Holmes, a new image, a . . . I took it to every publisher in London. "Yes, very interesting," they said, "what about putting in a bit where he gets his paw stuck in a honey jar, how would it be if he went off with Roo and fell in a swamp, and while you're at it, could he sing a couple of songs about bathnight?"'

He fell silent. I cleared my throat a couple of times. Far off, a dog barked, a lift clanged. I stood up, at last, since there seemed nothing more to say.

'Is there anything you need?' I said, somewhat lamely.

'That's all right,' said Winnie-the-Pooh. 'I get by. No slice of the royalties, of course, oh dear me no, well, I'm only the bloody bear, aren't I? Tell you what, though, if you're going past an off-licence, you might have them send up a bottle of gin.'

'I'd be delighted to,' I said.

He saw me to the door.

'Funny thing,' he said, 'I could never stand honey.'

Punch, reprinted: Golfing For Cats (1975).

Along with most humorists Alan Coren has deplored in print his incompetence in dealing with mechanical things, his fury at bureaucratic muddle, and so on, but in his Punch pieces he mostly operated in rather less-explored territories. He came up with extraordinary things like a burlesque of Chaucer based on air travel ('Across the aisle two HIPPIES sat entwined, / Hopynge ere longe, to blow their tiny minde / Upon the Golden Road to Samarkand, / Then on across the Kush, through Kashmir, and, / At last drop out in distant Katmandu, / Where grass is not just greene, but cheeper, too'. . .), and an Australian Oedipus (Chorus: 'Our mouths are like the inside of an abbo's trousers. We have all been walking through yesterday's lunch. We are as much use as an earwig's tit. What happened to last Wednesday?').

The following powerful, indeed haunting, feuilleton is a piece which demonstrates three qualities of Coren's work which are not to be found in Perelman: a strong feeling for the magnetic-field-like connections between past and present, a compassionate sense of the idiocy of many sincerely held social and political attitudes, and a near-perfect ear for the nuances of common speech:

LONG AGE AND FAR AWAY

Much talk is talked of the need for the Dunkirk spirit today. But suppose instead that we had had today's spirit at Dunkirk?

Up to his waist in the filthy sea, oil lapping his sodden webbing, bomb-blasted flotsam bobbing about him, he sucked his teeth, and shook his head.

'I'm not bleeding going in that,' he said, 'I'm not bleeding going home in no rowing boat.'

'Right,' said his mate.

'Eighteen blokes in it already,' he said. 'Conditions like that, they're not fit for a pig.'

'Not fit for a pig, conditions like that,' said his mate.

'Got brought here in a troopship, didn't we?' he said. He cupped his hands towards the rowing boat, and the man leaning towards them over its stern, arm outstretched. 'Got brought here in a bleeding troopship!' he shouted, 'Ten square feet of space per man!'

'Regulations,' said his mate, nodding. 'All laid down. Nothing about going back in no bloody rowing-boat. Get away with murder if you let' em, some people.'

A Stuka shrieked suddenly overhead, levelled, veered up out of its dive, back into the flakky sky. Its bomb exploded, drenching the two men.

'Not even got a roof on,' he said. 'What happens if it starts coming down cats and dogs halfway across? You could catch pneumonia.'

'Get a chill on the liver,' said his mate.

'*And* there's seasickness. It's not as if I'm a sailor. I'm not sayin it isn't all right for *sailors*, am I? All right for them, open bloody boat. I mean it's their line, know what I mean? But I'm a gunner. That's what I got took on as, that's what I am. If I'd wanted to be a sailor, I'd have got took on as a sailor.'

'I'm a cook,' said his mate. 'Cook, I said when they asked me up the recruiting. I didn't say bleeding admiral. I didn't say, I want to be a cook on account of I'm interested in the standing up to me waist in water, did I?'

'Course you didn't.'

An Me109 came low over the surface, strafing the scummy sea. A machine-gun bullet took his hat away.

'You'd have got more as an admiral, too,' he said. 'You get compensation, working in filthy conditions. I reckon they owe us special benefits. Nothing about all this in basic training, was there? Prone shooting and a bit of the old bayonet, dry conditions, two bob a day, all meals.'

'When was the last time you had a square meal?' asked his mate.

'I never thought of that!' He took a notepad from his saturated battle-blouse, licked his pencil, scribbled. 'I never thought of that at all. Three days ago, as a matter of fact. Bleeding Cambrai, if you can call two spoons of warm bully a square meal.'

'FOR GOD'S SAKE GET A MOVE ON!' cried the man in the stern.

The two privates waded awkwardly forward.

'Not so bloody fast, mate,' said the first. 'I require a few moments with the brothers here.'

The eighteen stared at him over the gunwales. Red fatigue rimmed their eyes, their bandages were thick with oil, their helmets were gone, leaving their hair to whiten with the salt.

'It has been brought to my attention by Brother Wisley here,' he said, 'that we are being expected to work in conditions unfit for a pig. Not only are we not being allowed to pursue our chosen trade, we have been dumped here in what can only be described as the sea, we have been required to leave our tools behind on the beach, we have not had a square meal for three days, and as for the statutory tea-break, I can't remember when. I won't even go into the overtime question.'

'We won't even go into the overtime question,' said his mate. 'But may I draw the meeting's attention to the fact that members of the Kings Own Yorkshire Light Infantry can be seen on our left climbing into a cabin cruiser?'

The eighteen turned, and looked.

'Bloody hell,' said a corporal.

'Well might you say bloody hell, brother!' said the first private. 'Course, I'm not saying our brothers in the KOYLI are not entitled to what they can get, and good luck, but the anomaly of the heretofore mentioned situation currently under review before the meeting by which we of the Royal Artillery . . .'

'And the Catering Corps.'

'. . . and the Catering Corps, Brother Wisley, thank you, by which we of the Royal Artillery and the Catering Corps do not enjoy parity is one which threatens all we hold most dear.'

'RIGHT!' cried the man in the stern, 'Get in, or shut up, we haven't got all damned day, Jerry's throwing . . .'

The private held up his hand.

'Just a minute, squire,' he said, 'just a minute. After frank and free discussions with my ad hoc executive here, we regret to inform you that deadlock has been reached in the negotiations, and unless you are prepared to furnish us with such basic requirements . . .'

'I'm getting out anyway, brother,' said the corporal. He eased himself over the side. 'Come on, you lot, I have no intention of allowing my brothers on the floor to be manipulated by a cynical management and subjected to actual distress to serve the whim of the bosses.'

'Well said, brother!' cried the private.

The eighteen slid into the icy water.

The rowing boat came about, and sploshed off towards another queue. But a bomb, exploding between it and them, gave the private time to wade up to the head of the line, and the man on crutches leading it.

'I know these are difficult times, brothers,' announced the private, 'but let us not use that as an excuse to allow ourselves to be led like lambs to the slaughter. Solidarity is our watchword, brothers.'

The line hesitated.

'We could be, er, needed back home,' said the man at the front, 'couldn't we?'

The private stared at him bitterly.

'Oh, got a troublemaker, have we?' he said loudly. 'It's amazing, there's always one, isn't there?'

'Always bloody one,' said a voice down the line.

'Thank you, brother.' He poked a finger into the leader's chest. 'You'll get that crutch across your bonce in a minute, son,' he said. He spread his hands to take in the gradually assembling crowd of waterlogged soldiers. 'Got one

of your thinkers! Doesn't know all this scaremongering is just put about by
the gumment to screw the working man, doesn't realize that your real
situation is all very nice, thaank you, doesn't . . .' The private broke off as a
couple of Heinkels came howling in from the dunes, their tracer slicing a red
swathe through the crowd, drowning his words '. . . doesn't appreciate that
gumment propaganda is being cunningly directed to militate public opinion
on the side of nationalistic interests contrary to the welfare of the entire work
force, does he?'

'I think we ought to vote on it,' said a fusilier who had been standing next
to a man dismembered in the last strafe.

'Oh, yes, and I don't think?!' snorted the private. 'You won't catch me
out with no snap show of hands, brother, contrary to the democratic secret
ballot as we know it. I should cocoa!'

The men shifted their feet uneasily. The private had articulated it all so
clearly, and, after all, the men who had brought the little boats were, for the
most part, men of a class they had long learned to mistrust. Nor did they
wish to betray their mates, with whom they had come through no small
adversity; and it could not be denied that it was at just such fraught moments
as this that advantage could be taken of them, with their defences down,
and the odds in favour of those who sought to control them.

And, after all, were things so bad that they should forget all else but
short-term salvation? They were not yet dead, were they, which was rather
more relevant than the emotionally-loaded evidence that others could be
seen to be dying. They had, had they not, stuck it out on the beach up until
then, why should they not continue to stick it out now?

Slowly, but with what certainly appeared to be determination, the entire
waiting army turned, and began to wade back towards the littered dunes,
and the devil they knew.

There were, of course, one or two who glanced over their shoulders in the
direction of England; but, naturally, it was too far away for them to be able
to discern anything, even had the darkness not, by then, been falling.

Ibid.

BESIDES *writing his humorous pieces, Alan Coren is also a critic (television
and books); a double function which is oddly rare.*

*Not many well-known professional humorists in Britain have also been pro-
fessional critics although there have been a number in the USA, who have enlivened
notices of books and plays with some memorably witty comments, like the
humorous columnist of the* Denver Tribune, *Eugene Field (of the actor Creston
Clarke's performance as King Lear: 'He played the King as though under momentary apprehension that someone else was about to play the ace'), Dorothy Parker*

(*'Verlaine was always chasing Rimbauds'*), Alexander Woollcott (*'The play left a taste of warm parsnip juice'*).

One of the few British humorists to become a regular book reviewer was the young Arthur Marshall. Arthur Marshall had been a pupil at Oundle, the public school, and returned there to teach. He had always found the behaviour and conversation of schoolgirls and schoolmistresses peculiarly funny, and in 1932 he began to write and perform little skits about them, taking the part himself of the botany mistress leading the nature ramble or the headmistress giving the girls a bracing talk. His best-known creation was the formidable 'Nurse Dugdale'. Two years later he was spotted by a radio producer and put into a late-night BBC revue called Charlot's Hour, *thus making history as the first drag act to perform on the wireless. Gramophone records followed, and then in 1935 Raymond Mortimer, literary editor of the* New Statesman, *asked Arthur Marshall to apply his undoubted gift for understanding schoolchildren to reviewing a pile of juvenile Christmas books written about girls' schools.*

Arthur Marshall's idiosyncratic but sympathetic round-up of schoolgirl stories became a popular feature of the Christmas-books edition of the New Statesman *and remained so for many years.*

Here is his line-up of what could go into the Christmas stockings of schoolgirls in 1956:

Strange Quest at Cliff House. By Nancy Moss (Chambers).
Valerie of Gaunt Crag. By Elizabeth Hyde (Chambers).
Theo and her Secret Societies. By Margaret Rowan (Chambers).
Two Girls in a Boat. By C. Salter (Blackie).
The New Girl at Melling. By Margaret Biggs (Blackie).

Though this year's schoolgirl stories are milk-and-water when compared with the Brazilian glories of yesteryear, there are indications that the authoresses are once more concentrating on the sensible, basic subjects such as lying, cheating, squabbling, and shinning up and down creepers.

In *Strange Quest at Cliff House*, Miss Nancy Moss gives us the third of her splendid Cliff House yarns. Devilish Irene Fletcher is still head girl and has now instituted fagging, sharply crushing all opposition: 'How dare you raise your voice to me! Another word and I will take you straight to Miss Pusey.' There are still no cricket-pitches or tennis-courts, and the Black Sheep (a chic society of the smarter prefects) are 'dedicated to keeping Cliff House the slack and degenerate school' it had previously been. In pursuit of this unusual aim they watch TV in the boxroom, steam open letters, and lure poor little Violet Starr on to Hermit Island, a naval gunnery practice area, where the startled junior comes in for a brisk bombardment.

The live-wire Miss Bolney arranges co-educational rambles ('"It's official," chortled Ann'), with a Roman pavement one day and two prehistoric stone circles the next, and Christine is all excitement when a sailing club is begun ('There's something in me that answers the call of the sea'). Susan Savage and Cissie Carew go sailing with Miss Bolney and no sooner are they out of harbour than water covers the floorboards ('Why, what's this? We're awash!'), the sail is hauled down ('Girls, you must bale!'), the water rises ('Good gracious!') and they look about for assistance ('Wave to the trawler, Cissie'). At sunrise upon the cliff top, and in a scene of great power, Beatrice Lamont, her face working convulsively, confesses that it was she who was responsible ('It was I who pulled out the bung, Miss Bolney'), Miss Bolney countering with 'In what way have I so gravely offended you?' Poor Beatrice ('Don't get hysterical, Beattie') receives a tremendous wigging from Miss Pusey at prayers, leaving her 'statuesque and stricken' and, understandably, no longer a prefect.

Valerie of Gaunt Crag is chiefly remarkable for the complication of its plot. To Cornish Gaunt Crag, former residence of the rascally Silas Trevase, whose hidden treasure is being unwittingly guarded by a sizeable octopus, comes Valerie Peterson, whose blind, ex-R.N. father, widower of world-famous violinist, Athalie, is living incognito on a local house-boat after a spell of employment with smuggler Cork Dowling, and is now secretly *fiancé* to Miss Lenstead, who shares a photographic interest with Dr Langford, whose son, Murray, 'has a cheery word for everyone' and rescues Valerie when she steers her bicycle ('Golly, I *am* being a bother!') into a pond, if you follow me.

Also prominent is Christine Masters, whose Aunt Cynthia is proprietress of the Half Moon Restaurant ('Aunt Cynthia never serves, as you know').

Last summer, Christine had deliberately damaged Wynne Carter's violin ten minutes before she was due to compete before Sir Miles and Lady Craig and other school governors for the much-coveted Trocambria Trophy . . . Accomplished violinist as Wynne Carter was, being robbed of her beloved instrument at the last moment was a blow from which she was unable to recover.

Valerie, wrongly accused of blabbing to Miss Vaughan, has to parade in a sandwichboard with SNEAK on it, while the Fourth Form recites 'Here comes Valerie, Sneak of the School, the girl who broke the Golden Rule', after which trying experience Valerie blubs in the Marie Curie dorm ('She *is* taking it badly') and has to be calmed with cocoa. Did Valerie compete for the Trocambria Trophy? But of course; 'Miss Waller gave her a chord' and off she went into Wieniawski's *Légende*, raising it from 'the corporeal to the spiritual level', after which Lord (apparently) Craig leapt over the Judges' Table and Valerie, 'physically and emotionally spent', slumped forward in a dead faint, Miss Whiting ('Fish' to the girls) looking sharp with the smelling salts.

Theo and her Secret Societies finds us at Blair Court on the south coast with June Surtees, Sandra Matlock, Cherry Heskwith, and Miss Bellows, Miss Batt and Miss Darkaritt. There is a good deal of hockey under Mrs Kyre ('Pax! Pax! I can do no more!'), study beanos ('That was scrumptious cocoa, Kath'), some forbidden night outings ('I'll drift up to bed earlyish and put a bolster in'), and the Drama comp. with Candy Hoskins in pale sea-green net with a very full ballet-length skirt ('H'm, sounds lovely') and little Alyth Boone as Puck. The new girl, Theo Fleet, finds it all rather tame but she starts a Dare Club and there are other exciting wheezes:

'We could be pixies in the house and get up early to do things when everyone was asleep,' suggested Janet, hesitatingly.
They all turned to her with their eyes alight.
'The very thing!' cried Theo.

Theo has some ups and downs in popularity but eventually wins through ('One of the day girls offered her an open packet of potato crisps').

Two Girls and a Boat takes us into an east coast yachting world where Babs visits Jill who has got a 'simply gorgeous little dinghy' and knows all about gudgeons, pintles, sail tiers and how to rig a new backstay. Similarly well informed are Lady Alicia Bloggs, in a tight-fitting yellow jumper and puce velveteen slacks, and a mysterious Pole called Anton Wladislauw who lost his way in Colchester. A flash of gold teeth, a black beard, and here is a member of the secret police, Feodor Zabrowski, up to no good:

'Hah!' yapped the visitor. 'I wish to buy a yacht. There is yachts to sell here, no?'
'No,' said Jill.
'Pssht!' said the man disgustedly—

and with a final 'Tcha!' he goes off to try his luck in Mersey. Lady Alicia takes the girls sailing and is ready with 'We'll goosewing the jib' in between shrieks of 'Lee-oh!' and 'Port gun'l'. Meanwhile, Zabrowski is seen behaving oddly in Clacton, Babs gets photographic instruction from Bill ('You are inclined to over-expose') and Anton's brother, Stefan, dives into the sea from a passing liner. 'Urr-humph' says Jill's father towards the end. Quite so.

In *The New Girl at Melling* (colours: green and gold), the headmistress, Miss Pickering, is described as being nervous and tender-hearted and is inclined to doodle on her blotting-pad, which really will not do *at all*. However, there is the music mistress, Miss Killegan, who plays 'New every morning is the love' at prayers, with her golden gypsy earrings swinging to the rhythm, and winds up with a sonata 'which she did not know very well'. When not at the keyboard she tends to appear in a duffle coat and tartan trousers. Musical Anne Laurence falls foul of the maths mistress, cardigan-swathed Miss Saunders, and is sent to the library to write out fifty times, 'I must try to control my disgusting rudeness'. Then, her mind awhirl with impots and music ('I played Mozart this evening, you know'), she is discovered sleep-walking in her blue 'jamas'. However, she is fully herself again after a few chromatic scales ('Just stop a mo and hear me play the Beethoven'), and in no time at all is playing the Purcell to Sir Stephen Pearce, fresh from the Proms and all attention: 'You've got something out of the ordinary, you know. Something in the touch—the feel. Can't analyse it, but it's there.'

Arthur Marshall (1910–89) *The New Statesman*, reprinted: *Girls Will Be Girls* (1974).

Arthur Marshall became a Lieutenant-Colonel in Intelligence during the war and afterwards returned to Oundle and schoolmastering for a bit but went on writing reviews for the New Statesman, *of general books now as well as schoolgirl stories, becoming a regular columnist in 1976. He also returned to broadcasting and eventually took the late Patrick Campbell's place on the television word game* Call My Bluff.

Many of his reviews are really not reviews so much as literary essays in the good old-fashioned Desmond MacCarthy/Robert Lynd style, only funnier. He rarely gets to the book under scrutiny until at least three-quarters of the way through the essay. His technique is to backtrack so as to give himself a long, discursive run-up which is often nothing whatsoever to do with the book but perhaps a memoir, or an amusing thought which has occurred, or another glimpse of gracious living at his (fictitious) cottage 'Myrtlebank' ('Earl Grey and a light sponge for tea; a toasted scone if it turns nippy').

The New Statesman *is famous for its literary competitions. A good one might be to read the first page of the following Arthur Marshall book review and then say what book you think he is reviewing. Or if you think that this might be too difficult (which it is), have a wild guess as to what the book could conceivably, on the evidence of the opening page, even be* about:

BOOTS BOOTS BOOTS BOOTS

Invited earlier in the year to appear, if this doesn't seem too much like boasting, on the Russell Harty TV show, lavishly brought to us in glorious colour (I come out predominately beetroot) by London Weekend TV, I was asked a question by this charming interviewer concerning my *New Statesman* work and its possible message and, briskly throwing aside the frivolous mask and speaking in all seriousness and from the heart, I replied immodestly that I regarded myself as being the Jeanette MacDonald of the prose world.

Alas, the unthinking chose to suppose that I was joking but this was far from being so. I did not by this imply an approaching sex-change into another and even naughtier *Naughty Marietta*. I merely meant that, like that toothy songster from the world of celluloid, I too provide harmless, humdrum and airy nothings at regular intervals. I myself, as you'll have long since discovered to your advantage, can easily be ignored and avoided whereas, in her heyday, it was virtually impossible to avoid Miss MacDonald. But then, who wanted to?

Having followed attentively, as I always did, her dazzling career, there is one question to which I have never found a completely satisfactory answer. I mull the problem over from time to time but yet the puzzle remains a puzzle, its solution forever maddeningly hidden. To get at the truth one would need to have all her films shown simultaneously in some vast arena, a musical treat probably too difficult to arrange.

The unanswerable question is, in which of her many films did Jeanette MacDonald actually sing *loudest*.

She was certainly at full voice in both *The Vagabond King* and *Rose Marie*. Sometimes I think that *One Hour With You* was loudest, sometimes *The Merry Widow*. Ah well. Never mind. She provided, in *The Love Parade*, one of my favourite moments in films. She was, I think, a Princess of some foreign kind and, abandoning for the moment her dream lover, Maurice Chevalier, she strode forth, dressed as a Grenadier, to review her troops. They sang, and she, heaven knows, sang right back at them. At one point, facing them all drawn up on parade, she shrieked with no trace of emotion, the line 'My heart is aflame with your loyalty'. Delicious.

How different and exciting prewar life would have been for the boys in the Oundle OTC if we had had tuneful Miss MacDonald to review us. The OTC was periodically 'inspected' but only by Major-Generals with gingery moustaches. The initials OTC stood, of course, for Officers' Training Corps, though I could never quite follow whether this meant that we were all being trained to be officers or were merely a batch of cannon-fodder being marched about by officers to keep *them* in training. As the phrase 'officers and gentlemen' was then popular, I rather fancy that the former of the two explanations is the correct one, much emphasis being laid in our scholastic life on gentlemanly behaviour. To remain in the ranks would then have been far from gentlemanly.

The OTC has been renamed the CCF, which stands for Combined Cadet Force and is much more realistic. I gather that participation in it is nowadays a good bit more enlivening than in my day, when nothing remotely interesting ever happened and total boredom reigned supreme. Our hearts were aflame with nothing whatsoever except resentment. Nobody could have appeared less like dear Jeanette than the officers who commanded us. Deepest depression was their, and indeed our, portion.

But I seldom remained depressed for very long. As with some other occupations in school life, we learnt to remove the mind by inventing a dream world to which we could fly and there was to hand a meaty antidote to the OTC in the shape of the enormously popular Foreign Legion yarns of P. C. (Percival Christopher) Wren. When marching endlessly down the dusty, winding roads of Northamptonshire (in other circumstances, a county of great charm and beauty), it helped greatly to imagine we were in North Africa and about to be attacked at any moment by rascally Arabs and Touaregs whose age-old customs, after a skirmish, of laying out and paying the last courtesies to their enemy dead left so very much to be desired, not to speak of one or two portions missing. On field days against other schools, our battle cry of 'death to the infidel!' much startled the saintly boys of the opposing forces (usually Rugby or Uppingham). But I fear that none of our officers, in addition to failing to look like Jeanette MacDonald, could manage the faintest resemblance to the tyrannical Sergeant Lejaune (*jaune* my foot) of *Beau Geste* with his thrilling brutalities and insults and cross-patch cries of 'God smite you, you unspeakable corruption!' and 'I'll teach you, you swine!' and 'Silence, dog!' But it is extraordinary to discover that, apart from the really wild improbabilities of Wren's masterpiece (words normally reserved solely for St Paul's but which are here intended for *Beau Geste*), the descriptions of life in the Legion appear to have been little exaggerated.

Simon Murray, late of Bedford School, joined the Foreign Legion in 1960 during the North African upheavals, and his book, *Legionnaire* (Sidgwick and Jackson, £6.95) tells of his five years' service in the breezy manner of a public school prefect showing off a little in the common room. Rigged out in the uniform with the blue cummerbund and bright red epaulettes (which we last saw, I fancy, on Gary Cooper), he knows what to do when some skulking Spaniard pinches his seat on the train ('I yanked him to his feet and threw him the length of the carriage'). Foreigners aren't too greatly admired, especially a swarthy frog ('He's puke-making and has guts made of lime juice') and Lieutenant Lasalle ('little French creep') and Lieutenant Otard ('rather wet-looking'), but how jolly that it's hooray for us all over everywhere ('The English appear to be held in high regard'). And so, with an occasional home-sick thought ('Oh to be in England—parties, friends, *The Times*'), a musing or two about Life ('How quickly turns the wheel of fate') and grapes in abundance ('one hell of a laxative'), he settles down to the extremely Spartan regime interspersed with the comforts provided by tremendous boozing and, in Mr Murray's case, enormous food parcels arriving from Fortnum and Mason.

By way of keeping order, the NCO's laid about them with rifle butts ('Ledermann is down to his last three teeth') but the right sort of chap can always admire here and there 'a certain toughness, indelible in those who are made of the right fibre'. I regret to say, however, that there are some wonky fibres about and there were 136 deserters in the space of four months.

Chaps from comprehensives, I wouldn't be at all surprised.

The New Statesman, reprinted: *Smile Please: Further Musings from Myrtlebank* (1982).

———

A FTER *the Humorist as Critic, the Critic as Humorist—a species much more plentiful. Since Bernard Shaw demonstrated how serious criticism could be made attractive to the general public by adding wit and humour, a high entertainment factor in critical articles has been increasingly demanded by newspaper editors and is now commonplace.*

The father-figure of witty post-war English dramatic criticism was Kenneth Tynan.

Tynan, lean, ever elegant, decided at an early age to make an impact on the world and to make it quickly and colourfully.

When a schoolboy of 18 he invited the foremost drama critic of the day, the formidable James Agate of the Daily Express, *to give a lecture on Theatre to the Sixth Form Conference of his school, King Edward's School, Birmingham. Afterwards Agate was given lunch but, to his fury, nothing alcoholic to drink. He wrote in his diary:*

This annoyed me so much that when K. P. Tynan, my boy-chairman, told me that the programme included a concert, a cricket match, and a performance of *Hamlet* with himself in the title-role, I said, 'And how, pray, will visitors know which entertainment is which?'

James Agate (1877–1947), *Ego 8* (19 July 1945).

Eager to further his career now that he was getting near to beginning one, Tynan sent the famous Agate back to town with a copy of a long and erudite prose poem he had written on the subject of 'L'Art pour L'Art', and a request for an opinion on it.

He got it next day:

My Dear Hamlet,
Of course you can write. You write damned well. You write better than I have ever attempted to write. The mistake you make is the old one of trying to say too much . . . I don't believe George Moore ever thought of Rimbaud as 'a consumptive youth weaving garlands of sad flowers with pale, weak hands'. Rimbaud described himself at that period as 'surly of aspect, ungainly of figure, with huge red hands like a washer-woman'. And I conjure you, now and forever, to put a stop to your punning . . . to say that 'Verlaine was always chasing Rimbauds' is just *common*. Like cheap scent . . .

Ego 8 (20 July 1945).

Did young Tynan, the sixth-former, crib the Verlaine line from Dorothy Parker or did he think of it independently? He was capable of making it up for himself. Dorothy Parker's reaction to Agate's opinion of it as a line would have been interesting.

Precocious and sparklingly intelligent, Tynan went on to be unstoppable, cutting a swathe through undergraduate life at Oxford like a plain, pale, male Zuleika Dobson, and getting himself his first job as a theatre critic for the Evening Standard *by sheer audacity.*

But he was good. He had an obsessional love of the theatre, an uncanny understanding of the acting and writing processes, and wit, and the combination brought him a brilliant career as the drama critic for many newspapers and journals including the Observer *and the* New Yorker. *He became the first Literary*

Director of the National Theatre, under (then) Sir Laurence Olivier, and later its Literary Consultant.

Here is Kenneth Tynan's savagely witty review in the Observer *of an adaptation for the stage of William Faulkner's novel,* Requiem for a Nun. Requiem for a Nun *is a sequel to an earlier novel,* Sanctuary, *a sadistic horror-story verging on pornography which Faulkner wrote to make a lot of money (it did) but which to his surprise was hailed as a work of art.*

The plot of Requiem *tells of the tortured redemption of Temple Drake (one of the best-known of American literature's suffering heroines) who pluckily survived becoming mixed up with a gangster, murder, gainful employment in a brothel, a blackmailer, a homicidal coloured maid who was a dope-fiend . . .*

Tynan uses parody to make his point, a form of which he was the master among the younger critics. The review is in the form of a double-parody: the sense of one play is rendered in the manner of another.

The Stage Manager of Thornton Wilder's Our Town *steps forward and gives his normal comforting chat to the audience, his whole manner a reaffirmation of the simple virtues of American small-town life.*

But the content of his chat is a parody of Faulkner's appalling plot and characters:

JUST PLAIN FOLKS

The curtain has just fallen on William Faulkner's *Requiem for a Nun* (Royal Court). It has been performed with imposing devoutness by Ruth Ford, Bertice Reading, Zachary Scott and John Crawford. The production (by Tony Richardson) and the setting (by Motley) have been austerely hieratic. Let us now imagine that there steps from the wings the Stage Manager of Thornton Wilder's 'Our Town'. Pulling on a corn-cob pipe, he speaks.

S.M.: 'Well, folks, reckon that's about it. End of another day in the city of Jefferson, Yoknapatawpha County, Mississippi. Nothin' much happened. Couple of people got raped, couple more got their teeth kicked in, but way up there, those faraway old stars are still doing their old cosmic criss-cross, and there ain't a thing we can do about it. It's pretty quiet now. Folks hereabouts get to bed early, those that can still walk. Down behind the morgue a few of the young people are roastin' a nigger over an open fire, but I guess every town has its night-owls, and afore long they'll be tucked up asleep like anybody else. Nothin' stirring down at the big old plantation house—you can't even hear the hummin' of that electrified barbed-wire fence, 'cause last night some drunk ran slap into it and fused the whole works. That's where Mr Faulkner lives, and he's the fellow that thought this whole place up, kind of like God. Mr Faulkner knows everybody round these parts like the back of his hand, 'n most everybody round these parts knows the back of Mr Faulkner's hand. But he's not home right now, he's off on a trip round the world as Uncle Sam's culture ambassador, tellin' foreigners about how we've got to love everybody, even niggers, and how integration's bound to happen in a few thousand years anyway, so we might just as well make haste slowly. Ain't a thing we can do about it.

(*He takes out his watch and consults it.*)

Along about now the good folk of Jefferson City usually get around to screamin' in their sleep. Just ordinary people havin' ordinary nightmares, the way most of us do most of the time.

(*An agonised shrieking is briefly heard.*)

Ayeah, there they go. Nothin' wrong there that an overdose of Seconal won't cure.

(*He pockets his watch.*)

Like I say, simple folk fussin' and botherin' over simple, eternal problems. Take this Temple Stevens, the one Mr Faulkner's been soundin' off about. 'Course Mr Faulkner don't pretend to be a real play-writer, 'n maybe that's why he tells the whole story backwards, 'n why he takes up so much time gabbin' about people you never met—and what's more, ain't going to meet. By the time he's told you what happened before you got here, it's gettin' time to go home. But we were talkin' about Temple. Ain't nothin' special about her. Got herself mixed up in an auto accident—witnessed a killin'— got herself locked up in a sportin' house with one of those seck-sual perverts— witnessed another killin'—got herself married up and bore a couple of fine kids. Then, just as she's fixin' to run off with a blackmailer, her maid Nancy— that's the nigger dope-fiend she met in the cathouse—takes a notion to murder her baby boy. That's all about Temple—just a run of bad luck that could happen to anyone. And don't come askin' me why Nancy murders the kid. Accordin' to Mr Faulkner, she does it to keep him from bein' tainted by his mother's sins. Seems to me even an ignorant nigger would know a tainted child was better'n a dead one, but I guess I can't get under their skins the way Mr Faulkner can.

(*He glances up at the sky.*)

Movin' along towards dawn in our town. Pretty soon folks'll start up on the old diurnal round of sufferin' and expiatin' and spoutin' sentences two pages long. One way or another, an awful lot of sufferin' gets done around here. 'Specially by the black folk—'n that's how it should be, 'cause they don't feel it like we do, 'n anyways, they've got that simple primitive faith to lean back on.

(*He consults his watch again.*)

Well, Temple's back with her husband, and in a couple of minutes they'll be hangin' Nancy. Maybe that's why darkies were born—to keep white marriages from bustin' up. Anyway, a lot of things have happened since the curtain went up tonight. Six billion gallons of water have tumbled over Niagara Falls. Three thousand boys and girls took their first puff of marijuana, 'n a puppy-dog in a flying coffin was sighted over Alaska. Most of you out there've been admirin' Miss Ruth Ford's play-actin', 'n a few of you've been wonderin' whether she left her pay-thos in the dressing-room or whether maybe she didn't have any to begin with. Out in Hollywood a big producer's been readin' Mr Faulkner's book and wonderin' whether to buy the rights for Miss Joan Crawford. Right now, all over the world, it's been quite an evening. 'N now Nancy's due for the drop.

(*A thud offstage. The Stage Manager smiles philosophically.*)

Ayeah—that's it—right on time.

(*He re-pockets his watch.*)

That's the end of the play, friends. You can go out and push dope now, those of you that push dope. Down in our town there's a meeting of the Deathwish Committee, 'n a fund-raisin' rally in aid of Holocaust Relief, 'n all over town the prettiest gals're primping themselves up for the big beauty prize—Miss Cegenation of 1957. There's always somethin' happenin'. Why—over at the schoolhouse an old-fashioned-type humanist just shot himself. *You* get a good rest, too. Good-night.'

(*He exits. A sound of Bibles being thumped
momentarily fills the air.*)

Kenneth Tynan (1927–80), *Observer* (1957).

───

THE *double-parody was quite a recent refinement, invented, it seems, after the First World War by Sir John Squire, he of Georgian poetry and that keen but creaky-kneed cricket team of writers and publishers, the Invalids.*

Parody itself, 'the comic imitation of a serious matter', goes back to the Greeks and it has led a healthy life in literary journals as a weapon of critical humour. Punch *printed great numbers of parodies over the years and some of its editors, like Sir Owen Seaman and E. V. Knox, were among the best parodists of their day. But the majority of parodies in Britain were of poetry.*

In the USA, where poetry was a smaller element of the national culture, the parodying of prose, which began with such unlikely examples as Bret Harte's parody of Jane Eyre *written for gold-rush Californians, moved on to become in the 1920s and 1930s a regular feature of popular magazines like the* New Yorker.

One of the earliest New Yorker *prose parodists was Corey Ford, a founder-writer of the magazine (it was Corey Ford who christened the top-hatted and monocled dandy on the cover, Eustace Tilley. It seems that he liked the name 'Eustace' and 'Tilley' was the name of his maiden aunt).*

The Norris Plan is a double-parody, written in the 1920s by Corey Ford as a satire on the fecundity of the then current best-selling authors. Of those who are mentioned in the piece, Edgar Wallace published over 150 novels, Faith Baldwin over 75, Hugh Walpole over 40, Mary Roberts Rinehart nearly 30, and Mazo de la Roche 27.

The expression 'birth control' had been coined about 1914 by the American feminist Margaret Sanger but the Comstock organization for Purity immediately took steps to get the phrase classified as obscene. Then suddenly, in the 1920s, it became legally possible for the first time to mention 'birth control' in a book.

Two prolific popular novelists, Charles G. Norris and his wife Kathleen Norris, immediately seized upon this new legal freedom and made birth control the topical and titillating theme of their latest bids for best-sellerdom, Mrs Norris in a novel which she called Passion Flower *and Charles in a story which he managed to call* Seed—*an explicit title if ever there was one.*

Corey Ford observed all this and put it together. The substance of the parody is 'literary contraception', treating birth control as a means of curtailing literary rather than human over-production. The style is that of a typically emotional, over-adjectival Norris romantic novel:

THE NORRIS PLAN

It was early in the summer that Kathy told him that Edgar Wallace was going to have another novel.

It was a heavenly warm bright shiny clear happy Sunday morning, and the broad green velvety smooth flat rolling croquet field in the middle of Central Park was filled with gay warm yellow sunlight. She and Charles were moving idly among the wickets, swinging their mallets at the smooth fat shiny round balls. Charles had tried for the stake and missed it, and now he sat on his up-turned mallet, his smooth fat shiny round face puckered into a frown.

'Edgar thinks he's going to have another novel, Charlie.'

'Gosh, that's tough!' Charlie commented absently. He was trying to re-member whether he was dead on her.

'He's been typing his eyes out,' Kathy continued in a rather faint voice. 'He says the first two novels aren't so bad, or even the first twenty,' she pursued. 'But when you get to write the fiftieth novel or so, it's terrible.'

Charlie extended his toe, slyly moved his ball an inch or two in front of the wicket, and faced her with a great wholesome happy cheerful laugh.

'What's terrible, honey?' he asked.

'The novel, of course!' she conceded honestly. 'Charlie,' she went on suddenly, deliberately, not looking at him as she knocked her ball into position for the center wicket, 'I wonder how you'd feel if I were going to have another novel?'

'I know how I'd feel,' Charlie said promptly; 'I'd take it out into a vacant lot somewhere and burn it!'

'Oh, Charlie, why?' Kathy asked, widening her big dark round bright eyes reproachfully. 'Everybody writes them.' Her cheeks were suddenly red, and her eyes full of tears. 'Look at Faith Baldwin, or Hugh Walpole, or Mary Roberts Rinehart, or Mazo de la Roche, or Margaret Ayer Barnes—they deliver one every year. Sometimes they even have twins.'

'Well, if I was in Edgar's place,' Charlie said, as he judged his distance and then rapped the stake smartly, 'I'd go to my publishers and have them decide that the public couldn't stand another novel just now, that they'd have to save his reputation by—well, cutting it out.'

'Oh, Charlie! Isn't that a terribly wrong thing to do?'

'What's wrong with it?'

'Well—well—' she stopped, puzzled and a little sick. 'It seems so unfair to the novel. It—it ought to have its little chance.'

'Don't you think the public ought to have a chance, too?'

'But—but there seems to be something so *humiliating* about it,' Kathy faltered, her cheeks burning. 'To have a whole season go by without being on the best-seller lists! To have to give up the first-serial rights—and the second-serial rights—and the movie rights—and the foreign rights—'

'It isn't half as bad, I should think, as writing it,' Charlie argued.

'Oh, no, Charlie, that's natural!'

'I don't know about that,' Charlie began, laying his mallet down and pointing an argumentative forefinger at the woman before him. 'I've been doing a lot of thinking about this whole subject of book-control. Of course, my publishers don't agree with me. They believe that the practice of Literary Contraception profanes the sacrament of Inspiration, and is a frustration of the creative instinct in Art. It is my opinion, however, that reckless breeding should be checked for the sake of the author's reputation. It unquestionably takes the lives of thousands of writers annually, ruins the careers of as many more, and in addition brings hundreds of thousands of diseased, crippled and deformed novels into the world that should never have been written. Some of them die, many linger on in dire poverty, shivering in their paper jackets, while others roam at large, doubtless interbreeding in the movies and producing a weak and imbecile line of sequels that threatens to lower the whole stock of American literature.

'Several authors that you and I know are—or were—examples of such reckless breeding. You may recall, Kathy, an author by the name of John Erskine.'

'Very well.'

'His history came to my attention very forcibly the other day in a Liggett's window. He's confined now in the dollar reprints; but before he was put where he couldn't do any further harm, he had brought a weak and helpless novel into the world named *Unfinished Business*, which was totally unable to exist alone, and was forced to depend on its older sister Helen and its brother Galahad for its entire support. Thus the future happiness of two healthy novels was threatened by this imbecile brother; and the poor author—whose health had been none too good after having *Adam and Eve* and *Uncle Sam*— went into a serious decline.'

He shook his head.

'The saddest case is Emil Ludwig. After writing the life of everyone else, the poor fellow has now produced a biography of himself!'

'Uncle Emil! *Himself?*'

'Pitiful case. A fine talent gone to pot-boiling. He had a publisher in New York, and he bore him one volume after another. After Emil had delivered him six or seven books in rapid succession, however, the public grew tired of him, disappeared at intervals, rejected a couple. You wouldn't know him today; he's beaten in spirit, in substance, in artistic integrity. The biography racket had crushed him body and soul. You can't deny it, legal book-control undoubtedly would have been a blessing to Uncle Emil.'

Kathy leaned weakly on her mallet. The warm bright sunny cheerful Park swam before her, the croquet-wickets, stakes, balls, and idle spectators seemed blurred before her eyes.

'You look kinda white yourself, Kathy,' interrupted Charles curiously.

'I don't know—I'm all right, I guess.'

'You've been having too many novels in the last few years,' he said solicitously. 'Every three months or so. It weakens you, honey. *Passion Flower* was too much for you—let alone *Margaret Yorke.*'

The very title made waves of nausea sweep over her. She clutched her mallet and swung listlessly at the croquet-ball before her. It went short of the wicket.

'A lot of other American authors present interesting phases of this problem,' continued Charlie, hitting his ball deftly between two wickets, and rapping the stake. 'Take the late James Branch Cabell, for instance. He was undoubtedly one of the outstanding figures of our era; but he didn't know the meaning of book-control. Overproduction weakened him, and he died in giving birth to his last novel. If he had practised literary contraception, he might have been alive today. Let me see—are you still for the middle wicket?'

Kathy shook her head vaguely. She was thinking again of her panic-stricken visit to her publisher this very morning and her face burned, and her hands were dry. A business-like man; it was nothing to him. No, there was no question about Mrs Norris's condition; she was scheduled for his fall lists. He was sorry, but he did not know any way out of it now. It would be extremely expensive to remove it at this date. He never advised it.

It was like a nightmare. Her publisher had removed her last doubt. This was no longer fear: it was terrible certainty.

'I'm going to have a novel. In October.'

No, she did not have the courage to tell Charlie. She dragged herself across the court, and swung dizzily again at the ball. Charlie smiled as it wired itself behind the wicket, and he took his turn, grasping the mallet firmly as he elaborated further on his favourite theme: 'There is one thing more I'd like to bring up about this question, and I'm done. It requires approximately three novels a year to sustain our present-day novelists, if they depend on royalties alone. The average number of novels born of literate stock is 2.8; while those of men and women from the pulpwoods is 97.2. You can clearly see where book-control is being practised. In order to save the decent novelists from bringing about a complete suicide of American literature, not only must they publish more, but the fecundity of the illiterate writers must be curtailed. It must be obvious to anyone who stops to consider the situation at all that our intellectual class of writers is dying out, and the cheaper novelists and less mentally fit are on the increase; it must necessarily follow that our standard of national literature will decline and continue to decline.'

He paused and drew out a sheaf of notes from his hip pocket. Kathy saw the scene rapidly growing black before her eyes; she felt herself swaying guiltily as Charlie read the climax of his argument aloud.

'The crux of the whole situation is this: our intelligent writers are not producing, and our ignorant, inferior ones are. Unless book-control is stopped among the upper classes, and its use legalized among the lower classes, the best part of our literature will die off, and the country will be over-run by incompetents and morons—'

There was a little moan, and then a faint thud behind him. Kathy had fainted.

'Kathy! Kathy!'

She found herself stretched upon the wooden bench at the side of the croquet field. Her teeth chattered, and Charlie, who was fumbling about vaguely, pale with concern and sympathy, held her hands.

'You're freezing!'

'Don't look so scared, Charlie!'

She laughed frantically, her teeth still chattering. He stared at her sympathetically.

'Anything I can do for you, Kath?' He was not thinking of what he was saying. Her heart beat fast, and she regarded him steadily, not moving a muscle. Suddenly, in an odd tone, he began, 'Kathy'—

She looked at him, turning over to lie on her back, her face flushed, her hands icy, and her head rocking.

'Kath,' he said, clearing his throat. 'Have you thought—you know, this might be—'

Kath swallowed with a dry throat and patted his hand.

'It is, Charlie,' she whispered, with a little effort.

'How d'you know?' he asked quickly.

'I asked a publisher. Our publisher.'

'And he said—?'

'—Said there was no mistake about it. It is due some time in October.'

'He—What do you know about that?' Charlie stammered, his face lighted with bewilderment and surprise. 'You poor kid,' he added awkwardly.

Kathy's fingers continued to cling tightly to his hand; she watched him anxiously.

'Isn't there some way to—get out of it, Kath?' Charlie asked presently, a little doubtfully. 'You've had thirty-three, you see. I just thought, maybe—well, remember, you're not as strong as you were—you see, the last ten or twelve you've had have all died—'

Her pale face grew whiter, and gripping his hand, with sudden fear and entreaty in her voice, she said:

'Charlie, I won't. It means—no, I couldn't do that. Getting rid of your own novel! That's bad—that's *badder*, to me, than not writing a novel at all. Think of it, dear—not to have the name of Norris on a best-seller list this fall—'

'Well, now, I don't know about that,' said Charlie in a queer strained voice.

'Charlie!' She looked up at him in sudden comprehension. 'You don't mean that *you*—'

Suddenly she was sitting up, her arm tightly about him, her wet cheek pressed against his. He spoke after a long pause, his eyes lowered guiltily.

'It's true, Kathy. My publisher told me today. *I'm going to have a novel in October myself!*'

She was laughing joyfully, exultantly.

'Then all this you were saying about literary contraception, and book-control, and our country being over-run by incompetents and morons— you don't mean a word of it?'

'Of course I mean it,' he affirmed stoutly. 'I'm strongly in favour of book-control—'

She stared at him in bewilderment.

'—for everybody else,' he concluded hastily.

The Norrises embraced together in perfect understanding.

John Riddell (Corey Ford) (1902–69), reprinted: In the Worst Possible Taste (1932).

―――――――

FRANK SULLIVAN *was a regular contributor to the* New Yorker *since the early 1930s and well known to its readers for highly individual contributions over many years. There was his annual poem wishing Merry Christmas to a great number of well-known citizens in a free-wheeling rhyming couplet form which owed much to Ogden Nash, Lord Byron, and William McGonagall.*

And there was his series of dialogues featuring his cliché expert, Mr Arbuthnot:

Q. Mr Arbuthnot, you are, I believe, an expert on the use of the cliché as applied by the tabloids to the recounting of news about love, murder, and other events of violence?

A. I am an alleged expert in that field.

Q. Why 'alleged'?

A. Crime reporters *always* say 'alleged'. . .

Q. Splendid, Mr Arbuthnot. Now tell us what yawns for an alleged murderer.

A. Jail. He *faces* the noose, or chair.

Q. How does he behave at his trial?

A. With complete unconcern, although he may collapse at the verdict, if found guilty. The tabloids rather expect it of him.

Q. What kind of moves does his lawyer makes?

A. Surprise moves.

Q. With what?

A. Surprise witnesses . . .

Q. If convicted of murder in the first, the guilty party does what?

A. He pays the supreme penalty. He pays his debt to society.

Q. And if acquitted?

A. He begins life anew.

> ● The success of the 'cliché expert' was such that Myles na Gopaleen ran the same idea for years in a virtually unchanged form in his *Irish Times* column.

The third of Sullivan's contributions to the canon of New Yorker *prose was his parodies. The Sullivan parodies were rarely critical of anybody or anything specific; they were usually genial, gentle pastiches of styles and genres.*

Here Sullivan gives us a parody of one of those comfortable autobiographies, reeking of cigar smoke, leather, and old brandy, in which a member of one of the grand old New York families looks back on the past with affection and total recall:

MY OWN NEW YORK CHILDHOOD

When I was a boy, Fourteenth Street was where Twenty-third Street is now, and Samuel J. Tilden and I used to play marbles on the lot where the Grand Opera House still stood. Governor Lovelace brought the first marble from England to this country on August 17, 1668, and gave it to my Great-Aunt Amelia van Santvoort, of whom he was enamored. She had several copies made, and Sam Tilden and I used to amuse ourselves with them.

I remember the Sunday afternoons when Governor Lovelace would come to tea at our house, although I could not have been much more than a tad at the time. I can hear the rich clanking of the silver harness as his magnificent equipage, with its twelve ebony outriders in cerise bombazine, rolled up in our house at No. 239 East 174th Street. I was the envy of all the kids on the block because I was allowed to sit in the carriage while the Governor went in to take tea with Great-Aunt Amelia. I always chose Ada Rehan to sit beside me. She was a little golden-haired thing at the time and none of us dreamed she would one day go out from East 174th Street and shoot President Garfield.

Great-Aunt Amelia was a dowager of the old school. You don't see many of her kind around New York today, probably because the old school was torn down a good many years ago; its site is now occupied by Central Park. People used to say that the Queen, as they called Great-Aunt Amelia, looked more like my Aunt Theodosia than my Aunt Theodosia did.

But Aunt Caroline was really the great lady of our family. I can still see her descending the staircase, dressed for the opera in silk hat, satin-lined cape, immaculate shirt, white tie, and that magnificent, purple-black beard.

'Well, boy!' she would boom at me, 'Well!'

'Well, Aunt Caroline!' I would say, doing my best to boom back at her.

She would chuckle and say, 'Boy, I like your spirit! Tell Grimson I said to add an extra tot of brandy to your bedtime milk.'

Oh, those lollipops at Preem's, just around the corner from the corner! Mm-m-m, I can still taste them! After school, we kids would rush home and shout, 'Ma, gimme a penny for a lollipop at Preem's, willya, Ma? Hey, Ma, willya?' Then we would go tease Jake Astor, the second-hand-fur dealer around the corner. I shall never forget the day Minnie Maddern Fiske swiped the mink pelt from Jake's cart and stuffed it under Bishop Potter's cope.

Miss Hattie Pumplebutt was our teacher at P.S.67. She was a demure wisp of a woman, with white hair parted in the middle, pince-nez that were forever dropping off her nose, always some lacy collar high around her throat, and paper cuffs. We adored her. Every once in a while she would climb up on her desk, flap her arms, shout 'Whee-e-e! I'm a bobolink!' and start crowing. Or she would take off suddenly and go skipping about the tops of our desks with a dexterity and sure-footedness truly marvellous in one of her age. When we grew old enough, we were told about Miss Pumplebutt. She took dope. Well, she made history and geography far more interesting than a lot of non-sniffing teachers I have known.

One day, Jim Fisk and I played hooky from school and went to the old Haymarket on Sixth Avenue, which was then between Fifth and Seventh. We had two beers a piece and thought we were quite men about town. I dared Jim to go over and shoot Stanford White, never dreaming the chump would do it. I didn't know he was loaded. I got Hail Columbia from Father for that escapade.

Father was very strict about the aristocratic old New York ritual of the Saturday-night bath. Every Saturday night at eight sharp we would line up: Father, Mother, Diamond Jim Brady; Mrs Dalrymple, the housekeeper;

Absentweather, the butler; Aggie, the second girl; Aggie, the third girl; Aggie, the fourth girl; and twelve of us youngsters, each one equipped with soap and a towel. At a command from Father, we would leave our mansion on East Thirtieth Street and proceed solemnly up Fifth Avenue in single file to the old reservoir, keeping a sharp eye out for Indians. Then, at a signal from Papa, in we'd go. Everyone who was anyone in New York in those days had his Saturday-night bath in the reservoir, and it was there that I first saw and fell in love with the little girl whom I later made Duchess of Marlborough.

My Grandmamma Satterthwaite was a remarkable old lady. At the age of eighty-seven she could skip rope four hundred and twenty-two consecutive times without stopping, and every boy on the block was madly in love with her. Then her father failed in the crash of '87 and in no time she was out of pigtails, had her hair up, and was quite the young lady. I never did hear what became of her.

It rather amuses me to hear the youngsters of today enthusing about the croissants, etc., at Spodetti's and the other fashionable Fifth Avenue patisseries. Why, they aren't a patch on Horan's!

Mike Horan's place was at Minetta Lane and Washington Mews, and I clearly remember my father telling a somewhat startled Walt Whitman that old Mike Horan could bend a banana in two—with his bare hands! But I never saw him do it. We kids used to stand in front of his shop for hours after school waiting for Mike to bend a banana, but he never did. I can still hear the cheerful clang of his hammer on the anvil and the acrid smell of burning hoofs from the Loveland Dance Palace, across the way on Delancey Street, which was then Grand. Then the Civil War came and the property of the Loyalists was confiscated. I still have some old Loyalist property I confiscated on that occasion. I use it for a paperweight. Old Gammer Wilberforce was a Loyalist. We used to chase her down the street, shouting 'Tory!' at her. Then she would chase us up the street, shouting:

> 'Blaine, Blaine, James G. Blaine!
> Continental liar from the State of Maine!'

or:

> 'Ma! Ma! Where's my Pa?'
> 'Gone to the White House, ha, ha ha!'

Of course, very few white people ever went to Chinatown in those days. It was not until the Honorah Totweiler case that people became aware of Chinatown. I venture to say that few persons today would recall Honorah Totweiler, yet in 1832 the Honorah Totweiler case was the sensation of the country. In one day the circulation of the elder James Gordon Bennett jumped seventy-four thousand as a result of the Totweiler case.

One sunny afternoon in the autumn of September 23, 1832, a lovely and innocent girl, twelfth of eighteen daughters of Isaac Totweiler, a mercer, and

Sapphira, his wife, set out from her home in Washington Mews to return a cup of sugar—but let the elder Bennett tell the story:

It is high time (Bennett wrote) that the people of these United States were awakened to the menace in which the old liberties for which our forefathers fought and bled, in buff and blue, by day and night, at Lexington and Concord, in '75 and '76, have been placed as a result of the waste, the orgy of spending, the deliberate falsifications, the betrayal of public trust, and the attempt to set up a bureaucratic and unconstitutional dictatorship, of the current Administration in Washington. Murphy must go, and Tammany with him!

After dinner on Sundays, my Grandpa Bemis would take a nap, with the *Times*, or something, thrown over his face to keep out the glare. If he was in a good humor when he awoke, he would take us youngsters up to Dick Canfield's to play games, but as he was never in a good humor when he awoke, we never went to Dick Canfield's to play games.

Sometimes, when we kids came home from school, Mrs Rossiter, the housekeeper, would meet us in the hall and place a warning finger on her lips. We knew what that meant. We must be on our good behaviour. The wealthy Mrs Murgatroyd was calling on Mother. We would be ushered into the Presence, Mother would tell us to stop using our sleeves as a handkerchief, and then Mrs Murgatroyd would laugh and say, 'Oh, Annie, let the poor children alone. Sure, you're only young once.' Then she would lift up her skirt to the knee, fish out a huge wallet from under her stocking, and give us each $2,000,000. We loved her. Not only did she have a pair of d—d shapely stems for an old lady her age, but she was reputed to be able to carry six schooners of beer in each hand.

I shall never forget the night of the fire. It was about three o'clock in the morning when it started, in an old distaff factory on West Twelfth Street. I was awakened by the crackling. I shivered, for my brother, as usual, had all the bedclothes, and there I was, with fully three inches of snow (one inch powder, two inches crust) on my bare back. The next morning there were seven feet of snow on West Twenty-seventh Street alone. You don't get that sort of winter nowadays. That was the winter the elder John D. Rockefeller was frozen over solid from November to May.

On Saturdays we used to go with Great-Aunt Tib to the Eden Musee to see the wax figure of Lillian Russell. There was a woman! They don't build girls like her nowadays. You can't get the material, and even if you could, the contractors and the plumbers would gyp you and substitute shoddy.

I was six when the riots occurred. No, I was *thirty*-six. I remember because it was the year of the famous Horace Greeley hoax, and I used to hear my parents laughing about it. It was commonly believed that Mark Twain was the perpetrator of the hoax, although Charles A. Dana insisted to his dying day that it was Lawrence Godkin. At any rate, the hoax, or 'sell', originated one night at the Union League Club when Horace chanced to remark to Boss

Tweed that his (Horace's) wife was entertaining that night. The town was agog for days, no one having the faintest notion that the story was not on the level. Greeley even threatened Berry Wall with a libel suit.

Well, that was New York, the old New York, the New York of gaslit streets, and sparrows (and, of course, horses), and cobblestones. The newsboy rolled the *Youth's Companion* into a missile and threw it on your front stoop and the postmen wore uniforms of pink velvet and made a point of bringing everybody a letter every day.

Eheu, fugaces!—

> Frank Sullivan (1892–1976), *The Night the Old Nostalgia Burned Down* (1953).

———

*I*RA WALLACH, *New York-born humorist and playwright, was among the funniest of the magazine parodists, a master of what might be termed the focused parody; the dissection and identification of the component parts of one particular writer's style and the reproduction of that style with critical and comic intent.*

Here is Wallach's almost painfully true parody of one of Erskine Caldwell's stories, God's Little Acre, *which is set among the poor whites scratching a living in the poverty-stricken south. This was one of those novels which, due to continual eruptions of sexual activity, is known fondly in the book trade as a bodice-ripper.*

The weather in an Erskine Caldwell story, like the action, is hot and tacky:

GOD'S LITTLE BEST SELLER

Georgia has more girls with erect breasts than any other state in the Union, and that's a fact.

That's what Luke was thinking. Luke examined the third step on the porch, the broken step. He always said he was going to fix that step. 'Bring me a little closer to the Lord,' he said, 'when the step is finished.' He shaded his eyes and looked over the field. Out on the new ground Spike was planting a cotton seed for the twelfth time. This time it ought to stay down.

'Spike!' Luke hollered, wiping the sweat off his forehead with his shirt-sleeve. He put the shirtsleeve back in his pocket.

Spike laid the cotton seed to one side and ambled towards the porch. Then Tucker came out of the house and sat down next to Luke on the second step. 'Look here, now, boys,' Luke said, 'we ain't agoin' to give up. We been fixin' this step for nine years now and I got a feelin' in my bones we're gonna fix it for good this year, and that's a fact.'

Tucker hefted the broken end of the plank.

'Get the car, boys,' Luke told them. 'We're gone to Wrightstown now and get us a nail.'

Spike walked silently around the house and began filling the tires with air. He didn't have no pump so he just blew them up with his mouth. When the tires were full Spike got up off his knees. 'Ain't no sense gone to Wrightstown afore we eat, is there, boys?'

'They ain't, and that's a fact.'

They went single file into the kitchen where Effie, Luscious Lil, and Gloria Mundy were cooking the grits. Luke stared at his daughters. 'God sure give me a handsome set of girls,' he said to himself. He shook his head admiringly. 'Luscious Lil,' he said out loud, 'every time I look at your rising beauties I get a feelin'!'

'Aw, Paw!' Luscious Lil hid her face in the hominy grit pot. 'Aw, Paw!'

'Never mind that "Aw, Paw" stuff. If I gotta say it, I gotta say it. God give me three fine girls with erect breasts, that's what it looks like, it does, and that's a fact. But them rising beauties—makes me feel like loping around the house!'

'Aw, Paw,' said Luscious Lil, crawling behind the stove.

'Yes, sir,' Luke said, 'the Lord was sure good to me, giving me three daughters with—'

'Eat your grits, Paw,' said Tucker. 'We ain't never gonna get that nail without we get to Wrightstown before sundown.'

Luke ate his grits silently. While they were eating, the door creaked open and Philo Butts waddled in. Philo Butts was the local coke salesman, but he didn't like to sell cokes on hot days. He wiped his flushed red face with a pocket towel. Then he looked at Lucious Lil. His eyes had a hound-dog look.

'I shore would like to marry with you, Luscious Lil,' he said plaintively.

'Set down and eat some grits, Philo,' said Luke.

Philo pulled out a chair and sat down. He ate with one hand. The other was under the table, feeling around Luscious Lil's garter. He got his fingers under the garter.

'That's my garter you got your fingers under,' said Luke. 'Luscious Lil don't wear no garters.'

'They ain't much use without stockings,' said Luscious Lil.

Philo sighed. It was too hot to take his hand away, so he left it there. Then Luscious Lil stuck her tongue out at Philo. 'Stupid!' she said. Then she got undressed and wouldn't pass the coffee pot to Philo. Philo was flustered. He couldn't eat his grits nohow.

'Stop teasing Philo,' said Effie, 'and pass him the coffee pot.' She rumpled Philo's hair. 'Why don't you let Philo alone?'

Luke looked up. 'The Lord sure gave me three beautiful daughters with—'

'Come on, Paw,' said Tucker. 'We got to get to Wrightstown.'

They all started out for the car. On the way Bledsoe, the hired man from the Flacksey place down near to Euphoria, came ambling by. 'Still fixing the third step, Luke?' he asked, his eyes on Effie. Effie stared back at him, her lips quivering a little, the corners of her mouth wet.

'We aim to have it all done this year,' said Luke, 'and that's a fact.'

Effie smiled and Bledsoe smiled back. 'Wait a minute, Paw,' Effie said. 'I got to talk to Bledsoe a bit.'

She took Bledsoe by the arm and led him away. Luke, Spike, Tucker, Philo, Luscious Lil and Gloria Mundy, sat down on the running board.

In a little while, Tucker scratched his head. 'Wonder what's keeping Effie?' he asked. 'Maybe we better all take a look.'

They got up slowly and walked around the barn. Effie and Bledsoe were lying on the ground near Effie's clothes which lay in a heap next to the well.

Luke shook his head. 'You hadn't oughta leave your clothes in the damp, Effie,' he complained. They all stood around in a circle. 'Imagine that!' Luke was querulous. 'Just when we was getting ready to go to Wrightstown.'

'Go away, Paw, and you and Tucker and Spike, too,' said Luscious Lil, pushing them.

'Why, what's the matter with you, Luscious Lil?' asked Luke.

'Effie don't like the menfolk around at a time like this. You ought to be ashamed of yourself, Paw.'

'Me? Why should I be ashamed of myself? Effie ain't thin-skinned like you.'

'Go away, Paw,' insisted Luscious Lil.

Luke turned silently and went back to the car with the boys. Effie came along in a few minutes and got on to the front seat. Bledsoe stood with one foot on the running board while the others got in. He was staring at Luscious Lil. Luscious Lil's lip quivered a little. The corners of her mouth were wet.

'Better hurry up, Paw,' said Tucker, 'or we ain't never gonna get out of here.'

The car's exhaust blew a cloud of dust in Bledsoe's face. Luscious Lil drove fast. The back door of the car rattled and threatened to break the piece of wire that held it to the body. Luke looked around at his family. 'The Lord sure was good to me,' he said to himself, watching Luscious Lil's rising beauties. Luke got down on the floor of the car and barked. 'Aw, Paw!' said Luscious Lil, pressing her cheek against the dashboard.

'Better watch the road, Luscious Lil,' Tucker warned.

Twenty minutes later they reached Jessamyn's house in Wrightstown. Jessamyn was Luke's other daughter. She was married to Brad, and Brad worked in the mill when the mill was working. But there was no work now, and Brad was sitting on the porch, thinking. He was thinking he couldn't live away from the mill, and he was thinking of all the girls he could see from the mill windows, girls with wide mouths and erect breasts and flowery eyes and erect breasts. The men were lean and hard and they waited around the shut gates of the mill where they could see the girls with their erect breasts, not like in the country, but Brad could never be a country man, never leave Wrightstown or the mill, with its big window from which he could look out and see the girls pass with their wide mouths and their erect breasts. Brad glowered. Jessamyn greeted Luke and the girls, but Brad didn't say anything. A girl passed by on the street, and Brad watched her pass, with her wide mouth and her e.b.'s.

Brad finally looked up. 'Hello, folks,' he said.

'Come to town to get a nail,' Luke explained.

'You still on that plank?' Brad asked. 'Nine years and still at it?'

'Thought maybe you and Jessamyn'd come out and help us hammer,' Luke said. 'We're almost done. We sure could use you now to help a mite, and that's a fact.'

Brad rose slowly. He turned to Jessamyn. 'Supper ready?' he asked.

She nodded. They all went into the kitchen. After supper they sat on the porch and watched the sun go down. Brad didn't look at the sun. He looked at the dark silhouette of the mill.

Luke yawned. Then he rose and turned to Tucker and Spike. 'Guess it's too late to get that nail tonight,' he said. 'Let's go.'

The boys nodded and followed Luke to the car. Luke looked back. 'Coming, girls?'

Effie said 'Think we'll stay over, Paw. Pick us up tomorrow when you come back for the nail.'

Luke and the boys drove off.

An hour later the girls walked inside the house. Jessamyn picked up her knitting. Suddenly Brad turned to Luscious Lil. There was something in his face that frightened Jessamyn. Brad looked drunk but he wasn't.

'I got a feelin' inside me,' he muttered, staring at Luscious Lil, 'it's the mill and me, and something that said to me all the time, I got to have Luscious Lil. Your Paw is right, Luscious Lil. Your Paw is absolutely right. I'm mighty powerful now. Nothing is gonna stop me, nothing, and that's as sure as God made little green apples. Don't move none, Luscious Lil!'

Luscious Lil stood silently, her mouth half open, her body shaking like a hog's ear in a high wind.

Brad went on as though he didn't care if anyone were listening or not. 'I've waited for this, Luscious Lil. And now I'm gonna do it. I'm gonna take all the basting outen your dress, and all the basting outen your underwear, and I'm gonna take all the nails outen your shoes, and I'm gonna do it all with my teeth!'

He moved toward her. She stood trembling, waiting. She knew she couldn't move if she wanted to. Effie said, 'Philo Butts is gonna kill you, Brad.' Jessamyn was knitting. She dropped a stitch.

Brad just walked toward Luscious Lil. He leaned over her shoulder. Then he bared his teeth and suddenly, in a spurt of violence, he tore at the basting. Thread by thread the dress dropped off. The shoes took longer. Finally Brad got the last nail between his teeth and the soles flopped off. Silently, he lifted Luscious Lil and carried her to the couch.

Gloria Mundy crawled around the floor while Effie played solitaire. 'Put the black ten on the red jack,' said Jessamyn, looking up from her knitting. There was a beautiful expression on her face.

A few neighbours dropped in and looked around. 'See you got company,' one of them said. He was a lean young fellow with a double thumb. Gloria Mundy crawled over to him and clutched convulsively at his trouser cuff. He leaned over and dragged her into the next room. There was a lot of noise and Jessamyn had to shout when she asked, 'You folks want me to freeze some ice cream?'

'That'd be nice,' Brad murmered. Luscious Lil sat up. She knew now that Paw was right, and Paw and Brad knew something nobody else knew and never would know, and that was a man has to feel with all his power and not care what or who or when or whatever or however or if or why, if it stands in the way, and that's the way it was with Brad. And that was why she would never forget Brad.

Effie ran out of solitaire and then she helped turn the freezer. When the ice cream was done they looked up and saw Philo Butts standing in the doorway. Philo was staring at Brad and levelling a shotgun at him. 'You hadn't ought to have done it, Brad,' he said, 'and that's a fact.'

Brad tried to hide behind Effie, but Effie was in the kitchen dishing out the ice cream. The explosion rattled the wood walls of the house. Luscious Lil screamed. Just then Luke and Spike and Tucker came in the door. Luke stared at Brad, lying next to the ice-cream freezer. 'Strawberry?' he asked.

Luscious Lil, Effie, Gloria Mundy, and Jessamyn kneeled beside Brad's body and wept. They put their arms around each other and they laid their heads against each other's shoulders. Then the women's auxiliary came in with their erect breasts, and kneeled by Brad's body and wept.

Luke turned to Philo. 'The sheriff's gonna hear about this come Sunday,' he said. 'Better take a walk, Philo. Sun's down and walking won't be so hard.'

Philo took the shotgun and stood in the doorway.

'All my life I wanted to keep the peace,' said Luke. 'God blessed me with three fine daughters—'

'Four, Paw,' said Tucker.

'—four fine daughters with erect breasts. Guess the Lord had to give me the sorrows, too.' Luke sat down slowly like a tired man. 'Tucker,' he said, 'I guess we might as well stay in Wrightstown and pick up the nail in the morning.'

Philo opened the door and stared into the darkness. Luscious Lil stood up, Jessamyn next to her. 'Wait for us,' Luscious Lil whispered to Philo. He waited. Luscious Lil got down on the floor and Jessamyn got down on the floor, crawled over to Philo, and hooked on to his legs. Luke looked at Philo, sympathy in his eyes. 'That's gonna make for hard walking,' he said, 'and that's a fact.'

Luke heard the door close. From outside he could hear the faint swoosh-swoosh of Luscious Lil and Jessamyn dragging in the street as they clung to Philo's legs.

In the morning Spike and Tucker went over to the general store and fetched a nail. Effie waited on the porch for them. When they returned they all got in the car. Effie drove. In twenty minutes they were back and they started hammering at the nail like crazy. 'We'll get it fixed this year,' Luke swore.

'Hello, Effie.' The voice came from the porch. Effie saw that it was Bledsoe. Her mouth was wide and moist, and she had erect shoulders. Bledsoe walked down the farm a piece to the tree at the edge of the new ground, and Effie followed.

'What's Effie doing now?' asked Luke complainingly.

'Aw, let her alone, Paw,' said Tucker.

'God was mighty good to me,' said Luke. 'He give me four beautiful daughters with—'

'Pass the hammer, Paw,' said Tucker.

Luke looked at the new nail. This time, he promised himself, this year they'd get that third plank in, and that's a fact.

Ira Wallach (b. 1913), *Hopalong-Freud Rides Again* (1952).

PETER DE VRIES, *poet and humorist, has been a staff-writer on the New Yorker since 1944 and he has written many sparky, sophisticated novels mainly about morals and manners in Connecticut.*

People in his books tend to tell jokes quite a lot; good jokes, too. As if to counter this, he invented a character who was a kind of Thurber Man with a different problem. Whereas Thurber Man was a Milquetoast oppressed by bossy women, de Vries Man was a frustrated wit, a man who could never manage to make his witticisms work for various reasons, usually because he could not think of a riposte quickly enough or nobody was listening anyway.

One of Peter de Vries's New Yorker pieces has become a little classic of this kind of humour-about-humour. It tells of a typical de Vries man who has studied the problem of being witty and found a rational solution:

LAUGHTER IN THE BASEMENT

'She has no mind, merely a mind of her own,' is something I recently said in open conversation, with less profit than I had anticipated. When I say anticipated, I mean over a fairly long stretch, for the remark is one of a repertory of retorts I carry about in my head, waiting for the chance to spring them. This is a form of wit I call prepartee—prepared repartee for use in contingencies that may or may not arise. For instance, I have been waiting for years for some woman to dismiss a dress she has on as 'just something I slipped into', so that I can say, behind my hand, 'Looks more like something she slipped and *fell* into.'

There are two types of prepartee: the kind you can wangle an opening for, and the kind you can't. The sally about the woman who had no mind, merely a mind of her own, required no specific straight line but only a general one, in a context I was able to steer the conversation to after bringing the woman into it myself. But my plan to retort dryly when next I hear somebody say that money doesn't matter, 'No, provided one has it', is something else again. I can, of course, bring up the *subject* of money any time I choose, but though you can lead a stooge to water, you can't make him drink, and unless somebody says, 'Money doesn't matter', in so many words, or virtually that, I will never get to use the riposte.

The chances of my getting a feeder for it are slimmer than you might think. Clichés are like cops, in that you can never find one when you want one. This applies to trite questions as well as trite statements. I have been waiting since 1948 for some poor devil to ask, 'What does a woman want most in a man?' so that I can come back, quick as a flash, with 'Fiscal attraction'. And I have been lying in wait even longer to hear so much as the vaguest reference to current realistic fiction as a reflection of our time, so that I can murmur, 'I had thought it rather a reflection *on* it'.

I almost murmured that one in Cos Cob. I was at a buffet supper in the home of friends there, and found myself in the library with the hostess and a couple of other guests. It was a week after my quip about the woman with no mind, and I had been trying to analyse just why it had failed. I had finally diagnosed my waggeries as, texturally, the suave and underplayed sort, requiring small groups and an intimate, offhand delivery, so I was happy to find myself in the snug library with just a handful of people, well away from the general commotion in the living room, so reminiscent of the previous week's mob. Coffee had been poured and brandy was passed. I began setting up the conversation for my little *mot* about realistic novels. Having lit my pipe, I squeezed from the packed shelves a volume of fiction suited to my design and casually asked the hostess, 'Have you read this?'

She nodded briskly. 'Yes, I thought it pretty good of its kind,' she said.

'Ah, of its kind. But what good is its kind?' I asked.

By dint of such questions, by tirelessly jockeying the discussion this way and that, by nudging, cuing, and tinkering with her responses, I succeeded in maneuvering her to within striking distance of my aphorism. Prepartee is very much like those games in which, over a course beset with delays, digressions, 'penalties', and other pitfalls, one tries to move a disc to a goal marked 'Home'. After a quarter of an hour, I heard the hostess say, 'Well, I mean realistic novels of this sort, whatever you may think of them artistically, do have some value for our time.'

I sat on the edge of my chair. One more jump and I would be Home. Very carefully, very deliberately, I said, 'How do you mean?'

At that moment a hearty character in tweeds boomed into the room. 'Just a minute,' I snapped. 'Ethel here is talking. Go on, Ethel. What was it you were saying? What are these novels in connection with our time?'

'They hold a mirror up to it,' she said.

I sat back in my chair. 'I see,' I said, and reached for my cold cup of coffee.

With Home so hard to gain in manipulable contexts, the chances of scoring with rejoinders depending on straight lines you can't even *begin* to finagle are discouraging indeed. Thus the odds against my ever being told, by a newcomer to my community, 'We'd like to meet some people who count,' in order that I may answer, 'Well, I can introduce you to a couple of bank tellers,' are really astronomical. And I long ago decided not to hold my breath till I hear someone refer to a third party as 'my cousin twice removed,' so I can say, 'I didn't know he was your cousin, but I knew he was twice removed—once as a treasurer of his firm and later to the state prison at Ossining'.

Recognizing all this, I eventually scaled my ambitions down to where I bluntly *asked* people to stooge for me, as you do in putting a riddle. This is a tawdry substitute for the real thing, but better than nothing when you're bent on making an impression, as I was recently at a party where I found myself *à deux* with a toothsome girl, a house guest of the host and hostess. We were sitting together on the floor, through which the sound of laughter from the basement game room occasionally seeped. We sat leaning against chairs, with our elbows hitched up on the seats, having a pleasant chat. I had spotted her from the first as a merry, responsive sort, a kid who could go along with a joke. In no connection, I turned to her and said, 'Did I ever tell you about my cousin twice removed?'

She shook her head, tossing a wealth of black hair. 'No. What about him?' she asked.

'Well, as I say, he was twice removed—once as treasurer of the bank he was connected with and later to the state prison at Ossining.'

She laughed gaily, throwing her head back. 'So you've got a banker in jail in your family?' she said. 'Well, we've got a congressman at large in ours.'

Having failed with large groups, then with small, and finally with a single companion (the less said about that brash chit the better), there seemed nothing left for me to do but talk to myself, a state to which frustration has brought stronger men than I. However, I rallied after making what you might call one more strategic retreat. I thought I would apply the technique I had evolved to the lowest common denominator—the practical joke.

We know a couple, living in one of the suburban towns near Westport,

named Moses. They are of impressive Yankee extraction, and moved down
from Vermont six years ago. One of the nuisances of living in the country is,
of course, power failures, and I got the notion of ringing them up sometime
when the electricity was off, and asking, 'Where was Moses when the lights
went out?' This is admittedly a far cry from my early high ideals for prepartee—so far, indeed, as to be not true prepartee at all. Nevertheless, as
some philosopher or other has said, a difference in quantity, if great enough,
becomes a difference in quality, and this gag depended on such a number of
factors going just right—that is to say, just wrong—that I felt it to be qual-
itatively unique. It required, to begin with, a meteorological mishap of such
extent and duration as to plunge into darkness an area wide enough to
embrace Westport, where I live, and the town where the Moseses' place is, a
good ten miles inland. It called for the most perfect timing, in that it would
have to be pulled when falling limbs had broken the power lines, which are
strung along the tops of the poles, but not yet the telephone connections
underneath. It would depend on the Moseses and ourselves being brought
simultaneously to the same pass. Having met these conditions, it would still
require the phone's being answered by Mrs Moses and not Moses himself. (I
couldn't say, 'Where were you when the lights went out?') So the sporting
odds against my getting Home were actually greater than they had been
across more cerebral courses.

It wasn't until the ice storm early last January, or three and a half years
after the gag's conception, that the necessary factors coincided. I thought I
saw my chance during the big blow of '51, when the winds attained hurricane force, but our power and phone lines were both reduced to spaghetti
before I could get my wits about me. However, in this winter's adventure,
our juice went at dusk, taking with it light, heat, and cooling power. The
phone still worked, but, of course, it was being monopolized for the time
being by housewives on the party line making unnecessary calls.

During dinner, which consisted of shredded wheat crouched over by
candlelight, I mentally reviewed the situation. Everything was in order; it
remained to be seen only whether the Moseses could be got through to by
phone. (That they had no power was a fair certainty, for it had been knocked
out or shut off for miles around.) I vibrated like a scientist for whom every
long-awaited element is fortuitously aligning itself in his favor, hurrying him
toward the exquisite moment of experiment. Dinner over, I slipped into our
dark vestibule and sat down at the phone. I found it alive and free, and, what
was more, the operator got me the number I wanted after only a few
moments' delay. Hearing the ring at the other end, I sat erect, realizing I had
forgotten there was still a final requisite beyond that of the other phone's
working—a woman's voice would have to answer.

I heard the phone picked up. 'Hello?' a voice said. It was a woman's.

'Where was Moses when the lights went out?' I asked.

'In bed,' she said. 'He hasn't been at all well.'

'Aw, gosh, that's too bad. I'm sorry to hear that,' I said. 'What seems to be the trouble?'

'Oh, the usual—flu, grippe, or whatever you want to call it,' Mrs Moses said. 'Who is this?'

I told her. Then I added, 'I've had a cold myself, which is probably why you didn't recognize my voice. Well, we were just wondering how you two were making out over there. Is there anything we can . . .'

Thus prepartee, in either its pure or debased form, is no indolent hobby, no pastime for the weak-nerved. The life of a parlor desperado, with its long hours in ambush, is a hard and often wearing one. It has its midnight post-mortems just like its more familiar counterpart, departee—which is, I think, the proper term for remarks thought up on the way home. I don't know which is the more frustrating, moments to which one has proved unequal or stunners for which no occasion arose, but I have found both abrasive. My little tittup about Moses and the lights came to an end when I hung up to find my wife behind me with a flashlight, a child clinging to either leg. 'Who was that?' she asked, playing the beam on me. I told her. I also told her why I had phoned, and said that I wondered why Mrs Moses hadn't been more on the ball. I asked my wife whether *she* didn't think the line was funny. 'Funny!' she said. 'Don't make me laugh.'

Peter de Vries (b. 1910), New Yorker, reprinted: Without a Stitch in Time
(1950).

H<small>UMOROUS</small> *letter-writing in post-war USA was enlivened by the publication in the 1960s of a collection from the comedian Groucho Marx.*

Any lingering thought that the particular humour of the Marx Brothers was the invention of S. J. Perelman (a widely-held theory which was bitterly resented by both parties) was dispelled with the publication in 1967 of The Groucho Letters, *a demonstration of Groucho's own personal mixture of effrontery, awful jokes, and inspired lunacy.*

Groucho admitted in an interview on BBC television that he was so little interested in comedy for its own sake that he would willingly have given up making films and made raincoats instead if there had been more money in it, but he went on to say that the most gratifying moment of his professional life was when the Library of Congress asked him to donate his personal papers. These included his correspondence, later published as The Groucho Letters.

Here is Groucho's remarkable duel with the Warner Brothers, or rather with their baffled and unamusable legal department.

> When the Marx Brothers were about to make a movie called A Night in Casablanca, *there were threats of legal action from the Warner Brothers, who, five years before, had made a picture called, simply,* Casablanca

(with Humphrey Bogart and Ingrid Bergman as stars). Whereupon Groucho, speaking on behalf of all the brothers, immediately dispatched the following letter:

Dear Warner Brothers:

Apparently there is more than one way of conquering a city and holding it as your own. For example, up to the time that we contemplated making this picture, I had no idea that the city of Casablanca belonged exclusively to Warner Brothers. However, it was only a few days after our announcment appeared that we received your long, ominous legal document warning us not to use the name Casablanca.

It seems that in 1471, Ferdinand Balboa Warner, your great-great-grandfather, while looking for a shortcut to the city of Burbank, had stumbled on the shores of Africa and, raising his alpenstock (which he later turned in for a hundred shares of the common), named it Casablanca.

I just don't understand your attitude. Even if you plan on re-releasing your picture, I am sure that the average movie fan could learn in time to distinguish between Ingrid Bergman and Harpo. I don't know whether I could, but I would certainly like to try.

You claim you own Casablanca and that no one else can use that name without your permission. What about 'Warner Brothers'? Do you own that, too? You probably have the right to use the name Warner, but what about Brothers? Professionally, we were brothers long before you were. We were touring the sticks as The Marx Brothers when Vitaphone was still a gleam in the inventor's eye, and even before us there had been other brothers—the Smith Brothers; the Brothers Karamazov; Dan Brothers, an outfielder with Detroit; and 'Brother, Can You Spare a Dime?' (this was originally 'Brothers, Can You Spare a Dime?' but this was spreading a dime pretty thin, so they threw out one brother, gave all the money to the other one and whittled it down to, 'Brother, Can You Spare a Dime?')

Now Jack, how about you? Do you maintain that yours is an original name? Well, it's not. It was used long before you were born. Offhand, I can think of two Jacks—there was Jack of 'Jack and the Beanstalk', and Jack the Ripper, who cut quite a figure in his day.

As for you, Harry, you probably sign your checks, sure in the belief that you are the first Harry of all time and that all other Harrys are imposters. I can think of two Harrys that preceded you. There was Lighthouse Harry of Revolutionary fame and a Harry Appelbaum who lived on the corner of 93rd Street and Lexington Avenue. Unfortunately, Appelbaum wasn't too well known. The last I heard of him, he was selling neckties at Weber and Heilbroner.

Now about the Burbank studio. I believe this is what you brothers call your place. Old man Burbank is gone. Perhaps you remember him. He was a great man in a garden. His wife often said Luther had ten green thumbs.

What a witty woman she must have been! Burbank was the wizard who crossed all those fruits and vegetables until he had the poor plants in such a confused and jittery condition that they could never decide whether to enter the dining room on the meat platter or the dessert dish.

This is pure conjecture, of course, but who knows—perhaps Burbank's survivors aren't too happy with the fact that a plant that grinds out pictures on a quota settled in their town, appropriated Burbank's name and uses it as a front for their films. It is even possible that the Burbank family is prouder of the potato produced by the old man than they are of the fact that from your studio emerged 'Casablanca' or even 'Gold Diggers of 1931'.

This all seems to add up to a pretty bitter tirade, but I assure you it's not meant to. I love Warners. Some of my best friends are Warner Brothers. It is even possible that I am doing you an injustice and that you, yourselves, know nothing at all about this dog-in-a-Wanger attitude. It wouldn't surprise me at all to discover that the heads of your legal department are unaware of this absurd dispute, for I am acquainted with many of them and they are fine fellows with curly black hair, double-breasted suits and a love of their fellow man that out-Saroyans Saroyan.

I have a hunch that this attempt to prevent us from using the title is the brainchild of some ferret-faced shyster, serving a brief apprenticeship in your legal department. I know the type well—hot out of law school, hungry for success and too ambitious to follow the natural laws of promotion. This bar sinister probably needled your attorneys, most of whom are fine fellows with curly black hair, double-breasted suits, etc., into attempting to enjoin us. Well, he won't get away with it! We'll fight him to the highest court! No pasty-faced legal adventurer is going to cause bad blood between the Warners and the Marxes. We are all brothers under the skin and we'll remain friends until the last reel of 'A Night in Casablanca' goes tumbling over the spool.

Sincerely,
Groucho Marx

For some curious reason this letter seemed to puzzle the Warner Brothers legal department. They wrote—in all seriousness—and asked if the Marxes could give them some idea of what the story was about. They felt that something might be worked out. So Groucho replied:

Dear Warners,

There isn't much I can tell you about the story. In it I play a Doctor of Divinity who ministers to the natives and, as a sideline, hawks can openers and pea jackets to the savages along the Gold Coast of Africa.

When I first meet Chico, he is working in a saloon, selling sponges to bar-flies who are unable to carry their liquor. Harpo is an Arabian caddie who lives in a small Grecian urn on the outskirts of the city.

As the picture opens, Porridge, a mealy-mouthed native girl, is sharpening some arrows for the hunt. Paul Hangover, our hero, is constantly lighting two cigarettes at once. He is apparently unaware of the cigarette shortage.

There are many scenes of splendor and fierce antagonisms, and Color, an Abyssinian boy, runs Riot. Riot, in case you have never been there, is a small night club on the edge of the city.

There's a lot more I can tell you, but I don't want to spoil it for you. All this has been okayed by the Hays Office, Good Housekeeping and the survivors of the Haymarket Riots; and if the times are ripe, this picture can be the opening gun in a new worldwide disaster.

Cordially,
Groucho Marx

Instead of mollifying them, this note seemed to puzzle the attorneys even more; they wrote back and said they still didn't understand the story line and they would appreciate it if Mr Marx would explain the plot in more detail. So Groucho obliged with the following:

Dear Brothers,

Since I last wrote you, I regret to say there have been some changes in the plot of our new picture 'A Night in Casablanca'. In the new version I play Bordello, the sweetheart of Humphrey Bogart. Harpo and Chico are itinerant rug peddlers who are weary of laying rugs and enter a monastery for a lark. This is a good joke on them, as there hasn't been a lark in the monastery for fifteen years.

Across from this monastery, hard by a jetty, is a waterfront hotel, chockfull of apple-cheeked damsels, most of whom have been barred by the Hays Office for soliciting. In the fifth reel, Gladstone makes a speech that sets the House of Commons in an uproar and the King promptly asks for his resignation. Harpo marries a hotel detective; Chico operates an ostrich farm. Humphrey Bogart's girl, Bordello, spends her last years in a Bacall house.

This, as you can see, is a very skimpy outline. The only thing that can save us from extinction is a continuation of the film shortage.

Fondly,
Groucho Marx

After that, the Marxes heard nothing more from the Warner Brothers' legal department.

Groucho Marx (1895–1977), *The Groucho Letters* (1967).

S INCE *the war, few newspapers in the USA have gone in for bizarrely comical columns in the manner of Britain's Beachcomber or Peter Simple, leaning more towards the traditional Broadway showbiz gossip-and-wisecrack style à la Walter Winchell, and humorous journalistic stories of people and places, again mostly showbiz, by writers like H. Allen Smith.*

The most consistently funny of the post-war newspaper columnists, working mainly in the American style of written-up interviews and personal experiences, has been Art Buchwald in the New York Herald Tribune *and syndicated to over 550 other newspapers throughout the world.*

Many of Art Buchwald's stories begin with a seemingly straight assignment, as in the following piece in which he is hustled by a publicity agent into writing about the making of an 'epic' film, Alexander the Great.

Art Buchwald's account of his day on the set, although we know *that almost certainly some of it and conceivably all of it is but highly professional invention, still, curiously, manages to convince us that he really did experience most of what he says he went through and that he did actually meet those he claims to have met:*

I FOUGHT WITH ALEXANDER

Some time ago a United Artists drumbeater called me up and said, 'As you know, Robert Rossen is making *Alexander the Great* and we are arranging a junket of hand-picked journalists to tour Greece with Arnold Toynbee, who will point out all the great battlefields. Are you interested?'

'Has Toynbee said he'll go?' I asked.

'No, but the hand-picked journalists said they would.'

Three months later the same man called me and said that Toynbee had 'chickened out' (a military expression meaning that he wasn't going) and the Greek trip was off. The film was being made in Spain anyway, because Spain looked more like Greece than Greece did. A few weeks afterwards the man called again.

'Rossen is marrying off five thousand virgins in *Alexander the Great* in one of the greatest scenes ever filmed in movie history. A hand-picked group of journalists has been invited to attend the wedding.'

'Who's he marrying them off to?'

'Five thousand Greek soldiers. You see, according to history, Alexander wanted to mate the East with the West, and he decided to make his soldiers marry Persian women—the offspring would be the twain that were never supposed to meet.'

I calculated that even if the press agent was exaggerating by double, that still left a marriage of 2,500 virgins to 2,500 Greek soldiers—a figure that could not very well be ignored.

But when I arrived in Madrid I discovered I had been taken in. Rossen was making a film called *Alexander the Great* but he wasn't marrying off any virgins to Greek soldiers.

'I do have a mass wedding in my picture, but it won't take place for a couple of weeks and as far as I know Alexander never specified what kind of girls he wanted for the wedding, as long as they were Persian.

'This week we are filming battle scenes. As you know, Alexander fought the Persian and Greek mercenaries at Granicus and routed them in his famous human-tank attack. As long as you're here, why don't you fill in as a Greek mercenary?'

'How much does it pay?'

'A dead Greek gets $4.80 a day, a dead Greek lying in the water gets $5.50; a Persian on horseback gets $6.00, a dead Persian gets as much as a dead Greek; one of Alexander's men who doesn't speak gets $3.95; a refugee from a battle gets $3.80. We are using eight hundred soldiers from the Spanish Army and they are getting $1.50 a day. Take your choice.'

I told Rossen I'd rather be a live Greek than a dead Persian floating in the water and he agreed to pay me $3.95. Since I was a hand-picked journalist it was decided to put me next to Alexander in the battle line-up. Alexander was being played by Richard Burton, the Welsh actor who began his epic career in *The Robe*. The battle was to be fought on a plain just outside of Madrid, near the airport.

On the big day I was delivered to a tent at eight o'clock in the morning for make-up and costume. I was thrown a helmet, a spear, a sword, a grey tunic and a shield. Franco's army and cavalry arrived and they were divided up, half to play Persians, half to play Greeks.

Mr Rossen was riding around on a palomino pony getting his shots lined up. Mr Burton was playing cricket behind his tent; the British camera crew was drinking tea. The air was filled with the tenseness that usually precedes a great battle.

I practised throwing a spear at a dead tree trunk (the dead tree trunk was getting $2.50 a day) and I took several swipes with my sword at a chair reserved for Claire Bloom, who was playing the female lead.

At eleven-thirty we started lining up for the battle—Persian and Greek mercenaries on one side of the river, Alexander and good Greeks on the other. The sound of American, English, Italian and Spanish voices rent the air. The horses whinnied and the sheep bleated, three planes took off from the airport in succession. Mr Rossen drew up his palomino pony in front of the CinemaScope camera, dismounted and prepared for action. I aimed my spear at a Greek mercenary and waited for Mr Rossen to give the word.

Mr Burton moved in beside me.

'Be careful of those Spaniards,' he whispered. 'They think they are really fighting a battle and you're liable to get hurt.'

'Fear not, Alexander,' I told him. 'We'll be eating Darius's cavalry for breakfast and we'll be spitting Greek mercenaries out of our teeth in the morning.'

'I'm not talking about Greeks and Persians, I'm talking about the Spaniards.

Those extras are crazy. They start swinging swords and spears and no one knows who's going to get hit. In our last battle they had to carry five men out and the doctors had to put twelve stitches in one of them.'

Rossen was shouting for us to keep quiet. 'Have we got enough blood on the set?' he asked the make-up department.

They said there was enough blood.

'Okay, give Alexander a large wound in the leg.'

I lifted my spear to protect him, but somehow the make-up man fought his way through and splashed blood all over Burton's thigh.

'Somebody tie a bandage around Alexander's leg,' Rossen said. 'You there' (he pointed at me), 'tie a bandage around his leg.'

'Which leg?'

'The one with the wound on it.'

'Do as he says,' said Burton. 'Then maybe we'll be out of the fight. I'll ask for you to stay behind with me to tend the wound.'

'What about the Persians?'

'They're not Persians, I tell you, they're Spanish extras and they're going to make a *paella* out of us.'

'Okay, anything you say.'

Rossen rehearsed a scene with Alexander and General Memnon, the Athenian who was in the pay of the Persian Emperor Darius. In it Memnon, played by Peter Cushing, comes to Alexander and asks for quarter. Alexander refuses to give him quarter and Memnon goes off to fight and die. While Alexander talked to Memnon I was supposed to wipe the blood off Burton's leg.

Just before the scene started I whispered to Burton, 'Why don't you give him quarter? Then maybe the battle will be called off.'

He whispered back, 'Rossen doesn't want me to give the Persian and Greek mercenaries any quarter.'

'That's fine for him. He doesn't have to face those Spanish extras.'

The scene was played beautifully and Memnon rode back across the river to make his last stand. Suddenly Rossen gave the signal for Alexander's men to attack the Persians. About six hundred grim-faced extras on each side started to square off, throwing spears, swinging swords and dropping rocks.

'Come with me!' Burton shouted, and we both jumped down behind a large rock and hid from the director.

'Victor Mature taught me how to do this,' Burton said to me. 'When the scene is over we'll put dirt on each other and Rossen won't even know the difference.'

We threw dirt and some more blood on each other, and by the time Rossen shouted 'Cut!' we looked in pretty bad shape. The battlefield was littered with Spanish extras holding their heads in their hands and moaning and groaning. The Persian cavalry had gone off into the hills, completely routed.

We walked back to where Rossen was standing.

'Nice work boys,' he said.

Burton winked at me. I helped put a Spanish extra on a stretcher and then got in line with some 'dead' Greeks and Persians who were waiting to get paid. It was hard to take, but almost every one of them got more money than I did.

Art Buchwald (b. 1925), Paris edition of *New York Herald Tribune*, reprinted: *I Chose Caviar* (1957).

For fourteen years Art Buchwald was resident in Paris, interpreting Europe to millions of Americans who had no real idea what went on there and could not understand what Europeans said when they spoke. He then moved back to the States and did much the same thing for Washington, DC.

When Europe was his beat, Buchwald covered almost every major post-war international event, including the glittering reopening in 1955 of the Vienna State Opera House. This Buchwald attended via an obligatory visit to the most creamy of Vienna's cream-cake shops, Demel's:

SLOW TORTURE BY *TORTE*

There are many people in Vienna who consider the State Opera House the most important building in the city. But there are others of us, mostly on the higher cultural levels, who would trade three performances of *Fidelio* and two performances of *Lohengrin* for one plate of *Schlag* at Demel's, the grand-mother of all Viennese pastry shops. Demel's is to Austria what the Tower of London is to England. Inside the hallowed mirrored walls are displayed the treasures of the country—foaming mountains of custard, strata upon strata of chocolate cake, bottomless lakes of fruit-flavoured mousse, tunnel after tunnel of apple strudel and glaciers of ice cream and frozen tart.

It has been said that if Austria had an Aga Khan he would be weighed each year at Demel's and given the equivalent in whipped cream and straw-berry icing.

My initial visit to Demel's was an experience that could be put in the same class with the first time I met Ava Gardner or the second time I met Gina Lollobrigida. I went in with my eyes open, but it wasn't long before they became glazed and eventually shut.

The first thing I saw on entering Demel's was a large marble stand filled with homemade candies. On top of the stand was a handwritten sign ad-vertising the speciality of the day. It was strawberry mousse with vanilla cream, grilled almonds and hazelnuts, sherbert and assorted candied fruits.

'A strong man,' said Si Bourgin, an International Food Patrolman, told us, 'would quail at such a dish, but the average Austrian woman can eat three of them.'

As my eyes became used to the light, I saw a room to the right with about twenty tables. The *décor* was late nineteenth century, and very little has been changed since Emperor Franz Josef used to pop in for an apple turnover. In the centre of the shop was the high altar. It was divided into two sections.

One was devoted to sandwiches, cold cuts, salads, aspics and canapés. The other section was piled high with cakes filled with cream, cream filled with cakes, chocolate filled with nuts, nuts filled with chocolate, apples filled with pie crust and pie crust filled with apples. There were pineapple tarts, pecan nut rolls, lemon butter moulds, puff pastes, *Streusel* cakes, sweet crescents, plain *Gugelhupf* and complicated *Gugelhupf*, ladies' doughnuts, devil's doughnuts, *Anna Torten*, *Sacher Torten* and whipped cream in every shape and form.

I started to shake uncontrollably, and Bourgin had to slap me in the face to bring me back to my senses.

The women who wait on people are known as the Sisters of Demel's. They are dressed in shapeless black smocks and have all taken vows never to serve any pastry unless it has been made with butter. 'Death before shortening' is their motto.

I chose five or six pastries as well as the *Anna Torte* (known as the most chocolate cake in the world), a large cup of coffee and a whipped cream.

As I sat at a table and prepared to go to work, I heard a low rumbling, groaning and moaning.

'What's that?' I asked Mr Bourgin.

'That's what is known as the Demel lament. Look around at all the women. You see them mumbling in German? Each afternoon they come here and as they eat they say, "Oh, I can't eat this—it's so fattening. Oh, I can't take another bite, I shouldn't. Tomorrow I will eat nothing all day. I swear this is the last *Sacher Torte* I will touch for a month." And so on. They never stop eating while they're talking. You could compare the Demel lament to a Gregorian chant. If an Austrian woman could not lament she would not come here.'

'What kind of people do come here?'

'The Viennese aristocracy, tourists, beautiful women and people who are trying to forget their unhappy childhoods. You must never talk to a beautiful woman at Demel's. If she strikes your fancy you could send over a pound of butter with your compliments. If she accepts it you can then formally introduce yourself—but it must be done outside the shop. There is a back room known as the Rauch Salon, where you may take a pretty girl or a business acquaintance. But it is very difficult to talk of love or business at Demel's.'

I finished off the six pastries and *Anna Torte* and the coffee with *Schlag*. Before I knew it I was lamenting to myself. Bourgin carried me to the door.

I tried to apologize for my condition, but Bourgin would not hear of it.

'This always happens the first time someone visits Demel's. The *Schlag* just creeps up on you from behind.'

Bourgin rolled me back to the Bristol hotel. The *concierge* looked at me disapprovingly.

'Butterfat poisoning?' he asked Bourgin.

'Demel's,' said Bourgin.

The *concierge* nodded knowingly and rolled me up to my room.

Having survived the ritual trial by *Schlag* at Demel's, I felt ready to face the music. This was offered up on a silver platter with the reopening of the noble Vienna State Opera House. It was the greatest event in Europe since Queen Elizabeth's Coronation. Composers, musicians and many serious patrons of the arts like myself were on hand to participate in this glorious musical occasion.

The most beautiful women in the world, wearing more jewels per square seat than at any opera opening in the last fifty years, and the best-looking men, all in white ties and tails, applauded the opening-night performance of Beethoven's *Fidelio* lustily and with much gusto.

And speaking of white ties and tails, you're probably all wondering how I got mine. Vienna, whose name is synonymous with romance and easy living, does not make too many demands on its visitors. But at the reopening of the opera house, which cost $10,000,000 to rebuild and took nine years of sacrifice and hard work, it was thought that the wearing of a white tie and a tail coat was not asking too much. And it wasn't, if you had one. If you didn't, it was asking a lot.

By the time I arrived in Vienna, the diplomatic corps had raided all the rental agencies, and the closets were bare. You couldn't find a white tie or a black tail for love or money, or both. Vienna may have the greatest opera, but it has nothing to compare with Moss Bros., the impeccable London hiring service.

While pondering this situation a few mornings before the opening, I chanced to order breakfast at the Bristol Hotel. When the waiter arrived, I was startled to see him wearing tails. I jumped up with elation and made the waiter stand at attention while we measured shoulders back-to-back. It was a perfect fit.

I started to negotiate over the rental, but the waiter informed me that his tails had already been promised to an Iron Curtain businessman who lived on the same floor. He did pass on the word, though, that the only tails left in the whole city belonged to a wine steward at Sacher's, and he thought I could get them if I ordered enough wine.

The wine steward, who hadn't been to Demel's for several months, was thinner than I was, but in Vienna there is a saying, 'Opera lovers can't be choosers', and we made a deal.

The next problem was finding medals. You can't go in tails to the Vienna State Opera without medals on your coat. I was fortunate in finding the store that specialized in opera medals. I bought a good-conduct medal for having sat through an entire performance of *Parsifal* without coughing, a distinguished-service medal for seeing *Faust* fifty times, a Purple Heart for my foot's going to sleep during the second act of *The Girl of the Golden West*, and a Legion of Merit for holding the spear in Wagner's *Walküre*. I rented the white tie and vest and borrowed the starched shirt from a stuffed shirt at the American Embassy. Except for the wine card I carried in place of the opera programme, I could easily have been mistaken for Franz Josef's nephew.

So much has been written about the Vienna Opera, and so little about what it is like to go in a white tie and tails after a visit to Demel's! The first feeling I had was of listening to the Beethoven overture in an iron lung. When the curtain went up and I tried to turn my head, the shirt turned with it. As Fidelio entered upon the scene, my coat started to strain and groan. My shoulder blades started to cut a hole in the top of the jacket. When Pizarro made his entrance, a stud pin popped out, but my cuff links held fast.

In the second act, while Rocco and Fidelio were digging a grave for Florestan, one wing of my collar tried to take off, and during the 'Leonora' overture, the vest buttons gave out.

The performance took twenty-one curtain calls, but I didn't have a chance to listen to the applause. I had to get the tails back to Sacher's.

It was a memorable evening for those of us who could be there; Vienna lives again; Beethoven marches on; the opera touched the hearts of all of us; but the wine steward's tails at Sacher's will never be the same again.

Ibid.

E RMA BOMBECK *writes, or wrote, a thrice-weekly humorous column, 'At Wit's End', which was syndicated to, it was claimed, 700 newspapers, and she also appeared twice a week on the networked television breakfast show,* Good Morning America.

Mrs Bombeck was extremely good at what she did, which was to be the leading humorous writer specializing in the funny side of being a mother. This would seem to be a limiting subject but not to Mrs Bombeck. She explored and exploited the humour of bearing children, coping with babies, watching children grow up, suffering teenagers, and in her hands the subject seemed to have no end. It was the very stuff of domestic situation-comedy and it fell from Mrs Bombeck's pen in a warm, bubbling flow, some of it collected in half a dozen or so books with jokey and somewhat irrelevant titles, like Life is a Bowl of Cherries—What am I Doing in the Pits?; I Lost Everything in the Post-Natal Depression; *and* The Grass is Always Greener Over the Septic Tank.

Here is an example of The Bombeck *domestic touch. The Bombeck family, the children mainly teenagers, has moved into a new house. A call comes in and for once it is not for one of the children but for the mother:*

The other night I nearly fell off my chair when a voice said, 'MOM! TELEPHONE!'

I wandered through the house shouting, 'Where! Where!'

'IN HERE!' shouted my daughter. 'IN THE HALL CLOSET!'

I crawled in under a topcoat and felt my way along the cord to the phone.

'Are you going to talk long?' she asked.

'I don't even know who it is,' I answered.

'I didn't ask who it was,' she said, 'I asked if you were going to talk for a long time.'

'I won't know until I know who it is,' I said firmly. I grabbed the receiver and said, 'Hello'.

'Who is it?' she asked impatiently.

'An obscene phone caller,' I whispered.

'Are you going to be long?' she persisted.

'I don't know,' I said, listening intently.

In the small bit of light that was available, I saw my daughter dance up and down in front of me, grabbing her throat while her eyes bugged and her tongue began to swell.

'Pardon me, sir,' I said to the caller. 'Could you hang on just a moment? My daughter, Karen, is in front of me and is trying to tell me one of three things: (a) Her pantyhose are too tight and have cut off the blood supply to her kidneys, (b) she is thirsty and is asking permission to split a soft drink with her brother, or (c) she will die if she does not get the phone within the next minute and a half.'

Covering the phone I said, 'Karen, what do you want?'

'I have to call Celeste,' she said. 'It is a matter of life and death.'

'In a minute,' I said and returned to my caller.

The closet door opened and my son poked his head in and pantomimed, 'Who is it?'

'It's an obscene phone call,' I mouthed back. 'What do you want?'

'Do you have a no. 2 tomato can? Fifteen jelly beans? Four buggy wheels? And a box of cocktail toothpicks?'

'Not on me,' I said.

Another figure crawled into the closet. It was getting crowded. 'Mom, who are you talking to?'

'An obscene phone caller.'

'The dog wants out,' he said. 'What's obscene mean?'

'Get a dictionary.'

'You want the dog to go on a dictionary?'

'I want you to look up obscene.' Into the phone I said, 'Really, I am too paying attention. It's just that . . .'

My daughter crawled in the closet with a poster that read, 'FIVE MINUTES WILL BE TOO LATE.'

My son persisted, 'It can be a no. 2 can of orange juice if you don't have the tomatoes.'

'PLEASE!' I said aloud.

Finally, my husband poked his nose in the closet.

'Is that Grandma from Florida? Why wasn't I called?'

'It's not Grandma,' I said. 'It's an obscene phone caller.'

'Oh. We really oughta call Grandma now that we know where the phone is. We haven't talked with her since Christmas.'

Finally, I said to my caller, 'Look, the timer on the stove is going off because I have been on the phone ten minutes now, my daughter is demonstrating right here in the closet, my son is forcing me to drink down a no. 2 can of orange juice and my husband wants me to call Florida. If it isn't too much trouble, could you call back?'

There was a silence on the other end, then a curt, 'Forget it, lady,' before the click.

Erma Bombeck (b. 1927), *'Just Wait Till You Have Children of Your Own!'* (1971).

In her later work Mrs Bombeck has become a little more reflective. In a different kind of book she dropped the fictional, sit-com way of writing in favour of putting together some brief portraits, drawn from experience, rather in the style of seventeenth-century 'characters'.

These sketches describe various types of motherhood:

WHAT KIND OF MOTHER WOULD . . . ?

WASH A MEASURING CUP WITH SOAP AFTER IT ONLY HELD WATER?

SHARON

Everyone said Sharon was a terrific mother.

Her neighbours said it.

She painted the inside of her garbage cans with enamel, grew her own vegetables, cut her own grass every week, made winter coats for the entire family from remnants, donated blood and baked Barbara Mandrell a doll cake for her birthday.

Her mother said it.

Sharon drove her to the doctor's when she had an appointment, color-co-ordinated the children's clothes and put them in labeled drawers, laundered aluminium foil and used it again, planned family reunions, wrote her Congressman, cut everyone's hair and knew her health insurance policy number by heart.

Her children's teacher said it.

She helped her children every night with their homework, delivered her son's paper route when it rained, packed nutritious lunches with little raised faces on the sandwiches, was homeroom mother, belonged to five car pools and once blew up 234 balloons by herself for the seventh grade cotillion.

Her husband said it.

Sharon washed the car when it rained, saved antifreeze from year to year, paid all the bills, arranged their social schedule, sprayed the garden for bugs, moved the hose during the summer, put the children on their backs at night to make sure they didn't sleep on their faces, and once found a twelve-dollar error in their favour on a tax return filed by H & R Block.

Her best friend said it.

Sharon built a bed out of scraps left over from the patio, crocheted a Santa Claus to cover the extra roll of toilet paper at Christmastime, washed fruit before her children ate it, learned to play the harpsichord, kept a Boston fern alive for a whole year, and when the group ate lunch out always figured out who owed what.

Her minister said it.

Sharon found time to read all the dirty books and campaign against them. She played the guitar at evening services. She corresponded with a poor family in Guatemala . . . in Spanish. She put together a cookbook to raise funds for a new coffee maker for the church. She collected door to door for all the health organizations.

Sharon was one of those women blessed with the knack of being organized. She planned a 'theme party' for the dog's birthday, made her children elaborate Halloween costumes out of old grocery bags, and her knots came out just right on the shoelaces when they broke.

She put a basketball 'hoop' over the clothes hamper as an incentive for good habits, started seedlings in a toilet paper spindle, and insulated their house with empty egg cartons, which everyone else threw away.

Sharon kept a schedule that would have brought any other woman to her knees. Need twenty-five women to chaperone a party? Give the list to Sharon. Need a mother to convert the school library to the Dewey Decimal System? Call Sharon. Need someone to organize a block party, garage sale, or school festival? Get Sharon.

Sharon was a Super Mom!

Her gynecologist said it.

Her butcher said it.

Her tennis partner said it.

Her children . . .

Her children never said it.

They spent a lot of time with Rick's mother, who was always home and who ate cookies out of a box and played poker with them.

Motherhood—The Second Oldest Profession (1983).

―――――――――

ERMA BOMBECK *lived with her three children and husband Bill and wrote her sketches of happy families in her sunny home in Paradise Valley, Arizona. Fran Lebowitz, magazine writer (Andy Warhol's* Interview, Mademoiselle, Vogue) *and wit, lived and wrote in the Greenwich Village area of New York City.*

Ms Lebowitz's writing style is sharply different from Mrs Bombeck's; Ms Lebowitz does not write comic fiction but brief essays which comment brilliantly and usually somewhat acidly on life as she finds it.

The difference of approach between America's two most popular women prose humorists of the 1970s and 1980s is apparent when Ms Lebowitz ventures into Mrs Bombeck's territory and gives us a Lebowitz-eye view of children:

CHILDREN: PRO OR CON?

Moving, as I do, in what would kindly be called artistic circles, children are an infrequent occurence. But even the most artistic of circles includes within its periphery a limited edition of the tenaciously domestic.

As I am generally quite fond of children I accept this condition with far less displeasure than do my more rarified acquaintances. That is not to imply that I am a total fool for a little grin but simply that I consider myself to be in a position of unquestionable objectivity and therefore eminently qualified to deal with the subject in an authoritative manner.

From the number of children in evidence it appears that people have them at the drop of a hat—for surely were they to give this matter its due attention they would act with greater decorum. Of course, until now prospective parents have not had the opportunity to see the facts spelled out in black and white and therefore cannot reasonably be held accountable for their actions. To this end I have carefully set down all pertinent information in the fervent hope that it will result in a future populated by a more attractive array of children than I have thus far encountered.

Pro

I must take issue with the term 'a mere child', for it has been my invariable experience that the company of a mere child is infinitely preferable to that of a mere adult.

*

Children are usually small in stature, which makes them quite useful for getting at those hard-to-reach places.

*

Children do not sit next to you in restaurants and discuss their preposterous hopes for the future in loud tones of voice.

*

Children ask better questions than do adults. 'May I have a cookie?' 'Why is the sky blue?' and 'What does a cow say?' are far more likely to elicit a cheerful response than 'Where's your manuscript?' and 'Who's your lawyer?'

*

Children give life to the concept of immaturity.

*

Children make the most desirable opponents in Scrabble as they are both easy to beat and fun to cheat.

It is still quite possible to stand in a throng of children without once detecting even the faintest whiff of an exciting, rugged after-shave or cologne.

*

Not a single member of the under-age set has yet to propose the word *chairchild*.

*

Children sleep either alone or with small toy animals. The wisdom of such behaviour is unquestionable, as it frees them from the immeasurable tedium of being privy to the whispered confessions of others. I have yet to run across a teddy bear who was harbouring the secret desire to wear a maid's uniform.

*

Con

Even when freshly washed and relieved of all obvious confections, children tend to be sticky. One can only assume that this has something to do with not smoking enough.

*

Children have decidedly little fashion sense and if left to their own devices will more often that not be drawn to garments of unfortunate cut. In this respect they do not differ greatly from the majority of their elders, but somehow one blames them more.

*

Children respond inadequately to sardonic humor and veiled threats.

*

Notoriously insensitive to subtle shifts in mood, children will persist in discussing the color of a recently sighted cement-mixer long after one's own interest in the topic has waned.

*

Children are rarely in the position to lend one a truly interesting sum of money. There are, however, exceptions, and such children are an excellent addition to any party.

*

Children arise at an unseemly hour and are ofttimes in the habit of putting food on an empty stomach.

*

Children do not look well in evening clothes.

*

All too often children are accompanied by adults.

> Fran Lebowitz (b. 1950), *Metropolitan Life* (originally, *A Henry Robbins Book*, (1978).

Fran Lebowitz updated and brought back to popularity the literary one-liner, the self-contained pithy comment, sometimes witty, sometimes merely a wisecrack. Inevitably she has been been compared, not unkindly, to Dorothy Parker.

Her rate of successful strike is pretty high considering the difficulty of this kind of witty, humorous writing; she may not hit a great many bull's-eyes but she hardly ever misses the target altogther, and she scores an impressive number of inners.

Here is a random selection of her bon-mots:

Advice to Teen-agers:
Stand firm in your refusal to remain conscious during algebra. In real life, I assure you, there is no such thing as algebra.

Advice to Parents:
Do not, on a rainy day, ask your child what he feels like doing, because I assure you what he feels like doing you won't feel like watching.

Poetry:
Generally speaking, it is inhumane to detain a fleeting insight.

Pensées:
Violet will be a good color for hair at just about the same time that brunette becomes a good color for flowers.

Despite whatever touch of color or caprice they might indeed impart, I will never, never, *never* embellish my personal written correspondence with droll little crayoned drawings.

Writing Women's Books:
Enroll in medical school and study gynecology. It will not be long before disenchantment sets in and you realize that the literary possibilities of the vulva have been somewhat overestimated.

More Pensées:
Dogs who earn their living by appearing in television commercials in which they constantly and aggressively demand meat should remember that in at least one Far Eastern country they *are* meat.

Polite conversation is rarely either.

People Who Have or Have Had Almost the Exact Same Hairstyle:
William Wordsworth and Frank Lloyd Wright.
W. B. Yeats and David Hockney.
Jean Cocteau and Eli Wallach.
Johan August Strindberg and Katherine Hepburn.

Last Pensées:
Brown rice is ponderous, overly chewy, and possessed of unpleasant religious overtones.

Alas, I do not rule the world and that, I am afraid, is the story of my life— always a godmother, never a God.

Ibid.

———

Humorists *like Fran Lebowitz write for journals but are not strictly speaking 'journalists'; similarly there are a great many journalists who write humorously but could not really be termed 'humorists'. A worthy United States representative of this form of authorship might be Tom Wolfe.*

Tom Wolfe is a founder member and chief exponent of what he named in a book-title as The New Journalism. *The New Journalism was a product of the 1960s along with such phenomena as the Beatles, Flower-Power, and the influential magazine of youth culture,* Rolling Stone, *with its offset litho printing and its look of a folded tabloid newspaper.*

Tom Wolfe's New Journalism was to do with observing with detachment the new freedoms and attitudes of the 1960s and 1970s and chronicling them in a prose style which was colourful, chirpy and frequently very funny:

STIFFENED GIBLETS

For me the 1970s began the moment I saw Harris, on a little surprise visit to the campus, push open the door of his daughter Laura's dormitory room. Two pairs of eyes popped up in one of the beds, blazing like raccoons' at night by the garbage cans . . . illuminating the shanks, flanks, glistening haunches, and cloven declivities of a boy and girl joined mons-to-mons. Harris backed off, one little step after another. He looked as if he were staring down the throat of a snake. He pulled the door shut, ever so gingerly.

The girl in the bed was not his daughter, but that didn't calm him in the slightest. For an hour we lurched around the campus, looking for Laura. Finally we went back to her room, on the chance she might have returned. This time Harris knocked on the door, and a girl's voice said, 'Come in'. Quite a cheery voice it was, too.

'Laura?'

But it wasn't Laura. Inside, in the bed, was the same couple—except that they were no longer *in medias res*. They were sitting with the covers pulled up to about collarbone level, looking perfectly relaxed. At home, as it were.

'Hi,' says the girl. 'Can we help you?'

Their aplomb is more than Harris can deal with. He takes on the look of a man who, unaccountably, feels that he has committed the gaffe. He begins to croak. He sounds ashamed.

'I'm Laura's . . . I'm looking for my . . . I want . . .'

'Laura's at the library,' says the boy. He's just as relaxed and cheery as the girl.

Harris backs out and closes the door once more . . . very diffidently . . . At the library we find his missing daughter. She has long, brown Pre-Raphaelite hair, parted in the middle, a big floppy crew-neck sweater, jeans, and clogs. She's eighteen years old and looks about twelve and is not the least bit embarrassed by what her father tells her.

'Daddy, really. Don't pay any attention to that,' she says. 'I mean, my God, everybody used to have to use the kitchen! There was a mattress on the floor in there, and you used to have to jump over the mattress to get to the refrigerator-sort-of-thing. So we made a schedule, and everybody's room is a Free Room a couple of days a month, and if your room's a Free Room, you just go to the library-sort-of-thing. I mean, the kitchen was . . . so . . . gross!'

All Harris does is nod slowly, as if some complex but irresistible logic is locking into place. In the time it takes us to drive back to New York, Harris works it out in his mind . . . The kitchen was so gross-sort-of-thing . . . That's all . . . By nightfall he has dropped the entire incident like a rock into a lake of amnesia.

By the next morning he has accepted the new order of things as the given, and in that moment he becomes a true creature of the 1970s . . .

The idea of a coed dorm, with downy little Ivy Leaguers copulating in Free Rooms like fox terriers was a lurid novelty even as late as 1968. Yet in the early 1970s the coed dorm became *the standard*. Fathers, daughters, faculty— no one so much as blinked any longer. It was in the 1970s, not in the 1960s, that the ancient wall around sexual promiscuity fell. And it fell like the walls of Jericho; it didn't require a shove.

Tom Wolfe (b. 1931), In Our Time (1980).

Tom Wolfe was an 'old' newspaper journalist and foreign correspondent for some years before striking off into the 'new' journalism, after which he became a frequent contributor to Esquire, Harpers, *and* New York Magazine.

When his pieces of New Journalism were published in book form he gave the books titles which seemed weird but were in fact accurate indications of the style of his writing, like his accounts of some of the wilder aspects of life in the 1960s, he titled The Electric Kool-Aid Acid Test *and* The Kandy-Kolored Tangerine-Flake

Streamline Baby. *He is also an artist and two of his later books are about the art world, the one on architecture being memorably titled* From Bauhaus to Our House.

Much of Tom Wolfe's work is concerned with appraising style; especially the domestic impedimenta, character traits and twinges of snobbery which delineate his contemporary New Yorkers. In one of his best-known pieces he drew a sketch of rich New Yorkers, politically left of centre, whom he christened 'the Radical Chic'.

Here is a sketch of another New Yorker, also well off, who might perhaps be termed one of the city's Cultural Chic:

THE SECRET HEART OF THE NEW YORK CULTURATUS

He's anti-Nuke, like everybody else, but he wishes the movement wasn't so full of earnest California types playing guitars and singing those dreadful Pete Seeger Enlightened Backpacker songs—all those women with snap-around denim skirts and low-heeled shoes and honest calves and their poor wimp husbands with their round eyeglasses and droopy beards and their babies strapped to their chests by some sort of papoose rig and spitting up natural-food mush onto their workshirts.

He's for human rights and he's against repression, but somehow he can't get excited about the Board People: they're a greedy grasping little race that refuses to be assimilated into the new order. Besides, the subject encourages revisionism about the war in Vietnam.

It's tacky to use terms like 'Middle America' and 'the silent majority'. They're so sixties, so out of date. He calls them 'the fly-over people' instead. They're the people you fly over on the way to Los Angeles.

He doesn't start sentences with 'hopefully'. He doesn't wear tennis shirts with stripes on them. He doesn't rent summer places north of Route 27. He stopped buying Bolla wines even before they started advertising on television, and he stopped buying bell-bottomed pants two years ago. 'Christ,' he says to himself, 'my radar is fantastic!'

The other day he and his friends were doing the usual, standing up for gay rights, blah-blah-blah, and he could see the maid staring at him. He was so goddamned embarrassed! She was probably wondering if he was one of them!

He loved the gasoline shortage. All those ethnoproles, who come barreling into Manhattan from Queens in their Coupes de Ville and Monte Carlos with their elephant-collar sport shirts open to the thoracic box, the better to reveal the religious medals twinkling in their chest hair, went back down into the subway where they belonged.

He has an apartment with pure-white walls and a living room with about 4,000 watts worth of R-30 spotlights encased in white cannisters suspended from ceiling tracks and a set of corbusier bentwoods, which no one ever sits in because they catch you like a karate chop in the small of the back but which remain on the premises because they are in the permanent design collection of the Museum of Modern Art. He has a set of Mies van der Rohe S-shaped tubular-steel cane-bottomed dining-room chairs, which are among the most famous chairs of the twentieth century but also among the most disastrously designed, so that at least one guest always pitches face forward into the lobster bisque. The only decorations are the Honest Toiler sort, such as the wood-fire-kiln Swedish pots in the living room and the eighteenth-century toolheads, suitably blackened, mounted on the walls of the kitchen. He has a thin wife, starved to near-perfection. He's very proud of the place and likes to invite people over.   Ibid.

———

S PIKE MILLIGAN, *writer/performer of near genius, was largely responsible for the iconoclastic and influential post-war BBC radio comedy series,* The Goon Show.

The Goon Show, which would have made perfect sense to Laurence Sterne and Lewis Carroll, was a reaction to wartime regimentation and took the form of wild, erratic and very noisy flights of fancy, featuring strange and wonderful comic characters.

Spike had always scribbled bits of verse, limericks, delightfully childlike jokes (On his sixtieth birthday: 'Anybody can be sixty—it takes a bus to be 60A'), and is perfectly at home with humorous prose; his series of books about his wartime experiences, all best-sellers, brought his total of books published to more than thirty-seven.

His first novel was the original and funny Puckoon, *published in 1963 and since curiously neglected. It is the story, with baroque diversions, of Dan Milligan's return after the war to Puckoon, a village on the border with Northern Ireland, and the very Irish shenanigans which take place there (a long time before the later and more deadly troubles).*

In Chapter 2, Dan Milligan is cycling slowly through the countryside, in no great hurry to begin the casual labouring job which his wife has forced him to seek. The day is a scorcher:

'Oh dear, dis weather, I niver knowed it so hot.' It felt as though he could have grabbed a handful of air and squeezed the sweat out of it. 'I wonder,' he mused, 'how long can I go on losin' me body fluids at dis rate before I'm struck down with the dehydration? Ha ha! The answer to me problems,' he said, gleefully drawing level with the front door of the 'Holy Drunkard' pub.

'Hello! Hi-lee, Ho-la, Hup-la!' he shouted through the letter box.

Upstairs, a window flew up like a gun port, and a pig-of-a-face stuck itself out.

'What do you want, Milligan?' said the pig-of-a-face. Milligan doffed his cap.

'Ah, Missis O'Toole, you're looking more lovely dan ever. Is there a chance of a cool libation for a tirsty traveller?'

'Piss off!' said the lovely Mrs O'Toole.

'Oh what a witty tongue you have today,' said Milligan, gallant in defeat. Well, he thought, you can fool some of the people all the time and all the people some of the time, which is just long enough to be President of the United States, and on that useless profundity, Milligan himself pedalled on, himself, himself.

'Caw!' said a crow.

'Balls!' said Milligan.

Father Patrick Rudden paused as he trod the gravel path of the church drive. He ran his 'kerchief round the inside of his holy clerical collar. Then he walked slowly to the grave of the late Miss Griselda Strains and pontifically lowered his ecclesiastical rump on to the worn slab. Muttering a silent apology to the departed lady, but reflecting, it wouldn't be the first time she'd had a man on top of her, least of all one who apologised as he did. He was a tall handsome man touching fifty, but didn't appear to be speeding. His stiff white hair was yellowed with frequent applications of anointment oil. The width of neck and shoulder suggested a rugby player, the broken nose confirmed it. Which shows how wrong you can be as he never played the game in his life. The clock in the church tower said 4.32, as it had done for three hundred years. How old the church was no-one knew. It was, like Mary Brannigan's black baby, a mystery . . .

Money! That was the trouble. Money! The parish was spiritually solvent but financially bankrupt. Money! The Lord will provide, but to date he was behind with the payments. Money! Father Rudden had tried everything to raise funds, he even went to the bank. 'Don't be a fool, Father!' said the manager, 'Put that gun down.' Money! There was the occasion he'd promised to make fire fall from heaven. At the psychological moment the priest had mounted the pulpit and called loudly 'I command fire to fall from heaven!' A painful silence followed. The priest seemed uneasy. He repeated his invocation much louder, 'I COMMAND FIRE TO FALL FROM HEAVEN!' The sibilant voice of the verger came wafting hysterically from the loft. 'Just a minute, Father, the cat's pissed on the matches!'. . .

The sound of a male bicycle frame drew the priest's attention. There coming up the drive was the worst Catholic since Gengis Khan.

'Ah, top of the morning to yez, Father,' Milligan said, dismounting.

'Well, well, Dan Milligan.' There was surprise and pleasure in the priest's voice. 'Tell me, Dan, what are you doing so far from your dear bed?'

'I'm feeling much better, Father.'

'Oh? You been ill then?'

'No, but I'm feeling much better now dan I felt before.'

There was a short pause, then a longer one, but they were so close together you couldn't tell the difference.

'It's unexpectedly hot fer dis time of the year, Father.'

'Very hot, Milligan. Almost hot enough to burn a man's conscience, eh?'

'Ha, ha, yes Father,' he laughed weakly, his eyes two revelations of guilt.

'When did you last come to church, Milligan?'

'Oh, er, I forget—but I got it on my Baptismal certificate.'

The priest gave Milligan a long meaning stare which Milligan did not know the meaning of. Then the Milligan, still holding his bike, sat down next to the priest. 'By Gor, Father, wot you tink of dis weather?'

'Oh, it's hot, all right,' said Father Rudden, relighting his pipe. Producing a small clay decoy pipe, Milligan started to pat his empty pockets. 'Here,' said the priest, throwing him his tobacco pouch.

Together the two men sat in silence; sometimes they stood in silence which after all is sitting in silence only higher up. An occasional signal of smoke escaped from the bowl and scurried towards heaven. 'Now Milligan,' the priest eventually said, 'what is the purpose of this visit?' Milligan knew that this was, as the Spaniards say, '*El Momento de la Verdad*', mind you, he didn't think it in Spanish, but if he had, that's what it would have looked like.

'Well, Father,' he began, puffing to a match, 'well, I'—puff-puff-puff—'I come to see'—puff-puff—'if dis grass cuttin''—job'—puff-puff—'is still goin'.'

The enquiry shook the priest into stunned silence. In that brief moment the Milligan leaped on to his bike with a 'Ah well, so the job's gone, good-bye.' The priest recovered quickly, restraining Milligan by the seat of the trousers.

'Oh, steady Father,' gasped Milligan, 'dem's more than me trousers yer clutchin'.'

'Sorry, Milligan,' said the priest, releasing his grip. 'We celibates are inclined to forget them parts.' 'Well you can forget mine for a start,' thought Milligan. Why in God's name did men have to have such tender genitals? He had asked his grandfather that question. 'Don't worry 'bout yer old genitals lad,' said the old man, 'they'll stand up for themselves.'

What about that terrible, terrible evening so long ago? Dan Milligan was seventeen, he had arrived for his first date with Mary Nolan. Her father had ushered him into the parlour with a forked vermin stick. Alone in the room with him was Mary's youngest brother, a little toddler of four. The little fellow carried in his hand such an innocent thing as a clay lion, but this, plus momentum, and brought unexpectedly into violent contact with Milligan's testicles, caused him to writhe and scream with pain; at which moment the radiant Mary chose to enter the room. To be caught clutching himself was too much for the sensitive Dan. With only the whites of his eyes showing, he disguised his convulsions as a macabre Highland fling. Cross-eyed, bent double and screaming 'Och aye!' he danced from the room and she never saw him again. For many years after, young Dan Milligan wore an outsized cricketer's protective cup; during the mixed bathing season, many ladies made his acquaintance, only to be disappointed later.

'Yes, there's plenty of work to be done, Dan,' the priest was saying. He led Milligan into the gardener's hut. A small wood plank shed tucked in a cluster of cool elms. 'Michael Collins himself hid in here from the Tans,' said the priest proudly, opening the door.

'Did he ever cut the grass?'

'No, but once, when the English were after him he set fire to it. What a blaze! Twenty courtin' couples nearly burnt to death! Them's the tools.' The priest pointed to four sentinel scythes standing in the corner like steel flamingoes.

'Ooh!' Milligan backed away. 'They look awful heavy, Father. Would you like ter lift one to see if me fears are well founded?'

'Saints alive, Milligan, there's no weight in 'em at all, man,' said the priest, lifting one and making long sweeping strokes. 'See? No weight in 'em at all,' he repeated, holding his groin for suspected rupture. He stood at the door and pointed out. 'You can start against that wall and work inwards. If only I was younger.'

So saying the priest made off up the path. As he did, Milligan though he heard supressed laughter coming from the holy man. Carefully Milligan folded his jacket and cap and placed them on the roots of a flowering oak. He turned and faced the ocean of tall waving grass. His unshaven face took on that worried look of responsibility. Spitting in his hands he took hold of the instrument. Placing his feet apart he threw the scythe behind him, then, with a cry of 'Hiayeee! Hoo! Hup-la!' he let go with a mighteous low curling chop; it started way behind him but, never a man of foresight, so great was the initial momentum, by the time the scythe had travelled ninety degrees it was beyond his control. All he could do was to hang on; the great blade flashed past his white terrified face disappearing behind his back, taking both of his arms out of sight and sockets, at the same time corkscrewing his legs which gave off an agonising crackling sound from his knees. For a brief poetic moment he stayed twisted and poised, then fell sideways like a felled ox. 'Must be nearly lunch time,' he thought as he hit the ground. The Lord said: 'Six days shalt thou labour and on the seventh thou shalt rest.' He hadn't reckoned wid the unions. Forty-eight hours a week shalt thou labour and on the seventh thou shalt get double time. Ha. It was more profitable to be in the union.

As Milligan laboured unevenly through the afternoon, long overgrown tombstones came to light,

R.I.P.

TOM CONLON O'ROURKE

Not Dead, just Sleeping

'He's not kiddin' anyone but himself,' Milligan chuckled . . .

The sun bled its scarlet way to the horizon and the skies nodded into evening. The birds flew to their secret somewheres, and bats grew restless at the coming of night. 4.32? Good heavens, it gets dark early round here.

'How are you getting on then, Dan?'

At the sound of the priest's voice, Milligan put on a brief energetic display of hoeing. The priest blew his nose. 'Farnnnn—farnnnnnnnn,' it went, in a deep melodious E♭. 'I think you've done enough for me today, it's nearly seven.'

'Seven?' Milligan cursed in his head. 'Trust me to work to a bloody stopped clock!'

'You mustn't kill yerself, Milligan.'

'I'm in the right place if I do.'

They both laughed.

A cool breeze blew in from the Atlantic, fetching the smell of airborne waves. The first ectoplasms of evening mist were forming over the river. Here and there fishes mouthed an O at the still surface. The Angelus rang out its iron prayer. Murphy, out in his fields, dropped his hoe and joined hands in prayer. 'The Angel of the Lord declared unto Mary.'

The near Godless Milligan trundled his bike towards the Holy Drinker,

'IIIIII—

> Once knew a Judy in Dubleen town
> Her eyes were blue and her hair was brown
> One night on the grass I got her downnnn
> and the . . .'

The rest of the words were lost to view as the song turned a bend in the road.

'I wonder if I'll see him again,' pondered Father Rudden. For that reason he had refrained from paying Milligan by the day.

Spike Milligan (b. 1918), *Puckoon* (1963).

PUNS *continued to please or infuriate during the twentieth century but after the Second World War they began to appear less frequently in humorous prose. This proved only a temporary respite because they then began to emerge, as it were, under new management.*

In the last few years, citizens accustomed to dropping in at restaurants with traditional names like 'Murphy's Fish and Chips', or 'The Copper Kettle ; Morning Coffee and Light Refreshments' have begun to notice that these places have ceased to exist ; eating-houses are nowadays much more fancifully named. It is here that the pun has found a new home and seems to be breeding.

The following is a list of some of the new-style restaurant names, all perfectly genuine eateries in the USA:

> Snax Fifth Avenue.
> Barnum and Bagel.
> Just for the Halibut.
> Lettuce Entertain You.
> The Boston Sea Party.
> Just Desserts.
> The Tower of Pizza.
> Lox, Stock and Bagel.
> Franks-a-Lot.
> Jonathan Livingston Seafood.
> 3.14159 [*it sells pies*].

And this is not the only service industry where puns have established a foothold and are multiplying; they are also spreading like a colourful, contagious and slightly irritating rash among unisex hair-dressing salons.

The old High Street shops proclaiming 'Sid and Ricky, Hair Stylistes (late of Staines)' now boast names like the following, taken at random from the London telephone directory:

> Curl Up and Dye.
> Shear Excitement.
> Hair Today Gone Tomorrow.
> The Clip Joint.
> From Hair to Eternity.
> Blood Sweat and Shears.
> United Hairlines.
> Shylocks.
> Streaks Ahead.
> Sophisticut.
> Hairloom.
> Do Yer Nut.
> Thatchers.

Another breeding ground for the modern pun has proved to be newspaper headlines on the women's pages of newspapers, in Sunday colour supplements, and in glossy magazines.

The Tatler has made a feature of concocting desperate puns to head its articles and is rather proud of them:

Sexy singer Tina Turner at a photo session in Eton College:

DON'T THIGH FOR ME, ARDENT TINA

An investigation into bankruptcy proceedings:

ADVENTURES IN THE SKINT TRADE

A piece about rich grasslands:

PASTURE PRIME

Enquiry into the influence of Freemasonry in Britain:

OF MASON MEN

Picture story about the choirboys of Pilgrims' School:

RUFF TRADE

The Tatler (1985–7).

Surprisingly, there has been a small but regular supply of original, literary puns available to addicts since 1956.

These are part of a BBC radio programme called My Word, *an unserious literary quiz played by four professional writers and broadcast world-wide. At the end of the programme the two male contestants, Frank Muir and Denis Norden, each tell a story which has to end with a pun on a given quotation or proverb.*

Although these puns originated orally, a huge quantity of the stories have since been printed in book form so they now qualify as humorous (or, to taste, not-the-slightest-bit-humorous) prose:

MAUD, BORED, AND DANGEROUS TO GNAW.
'Mad, bad and dangerous to know.'
(Lady Caroline Lamb, about Byron, in her *Journal*)   [Muir]

THE LEASE SAID SAUNA'S MENDED.
'The least said, soonest mended.'
(Charles Dickens, *Pickwick Papers*)   [Norden]

SO HE PASSED DOVER, AND THE STRUMPETS UNDID
FOR HIM ON THE OTHER SIDE.
'So he passed over, and the trumpets sounded for him on the other side.'
(Bunyan, *Pilgrim's Progress*)   [Muir]

DRESSED IN A LITTLE BRIE FOR THORA T.
Dressed in a little brief authority.'
(Shakespeare, *Measure for Measure*)   [Norden]

A ROSE, 'RED SETTER,' ARTHUR SOLD AS THYME.
'A rose-red city half as old as time.'
(Revd John Burgon, 'Petra')   [Muir]

AND IS THEIR ANNIE STILL FORTY?
'And is there honey still for tea?'
(Rupert Brooke, 'The Old Vicarage, Grantchester')   [Norden]

THERE'S MANET, ASLEEP! 'TWIXT THE CARP AND THE LEAP!
'There's many a slip 'twixt the cup and the lip.'
(Proverb).   [Muir]

SWEETHEART, THE HUGHES'S OFFER VERSE AT TEA.
'Sweet are the uses of adversity.'
(Shakespeare, *As You Like It*)   [Norden]

GOOD PIE, MISSED THE CHIPS.
'Good-bye, Mr Chips.'
(James Hilton, title of novel)   [Muir]

HYERES TODAY, GHENT TOMORROW.
'Here today, gone tomorrow'
(Proverb)   [Norden]

TOO MANY KIRKS SPOIL ARBROATH.
'Too many cooks spoil the broth'
(Proverb)   [Muir]

Frank Muir and Denis Norden (b. 1920; 1922), *The Complete and Utter 'My Word' Collection* (1983).

◗ For the reader to be given the pun but not the story which made some kind of sense of it might seem unfair but it is meant as a kindness, like being allowed to taste the roasted apple without first having to eat the brawn.

———————

THE *market for magazine short stories, reduced to a few publications by the strictures of wartime publishing, almost disappeared entirely in Britain during the 1950s. Short story magazines like Argosy sank without trace. The short story survived in post-war Britain as a literary form thanks mainly to H. E. Bates, A. E. Coppard, William Plomer, Graham Greene, William Sansom, Elizabeth Bowen, William Trevor, V. S. Pritchett, Frank O'Connor and other gifted writers to whom the short story had a particular appeal and whose collections the reading public was prepared to buy in book form. Many of these writers were also successful novelists but some, like Frank O'Connor, flourished better within the disciplines of the short story form.*

Frank O'Connor (real name, Michael O'Donovan) was Irish, very Irish. He fought as a Republican in the Civil War, translated from the Gaelic, began writing stories in Gaelic, was compared by W. B. Yeats to Chekhov, and became a director of the Abbey Theatre. He turned to writing stories in English, the best of them being perhaps his character sketches of middle- and lower-class Irish folk and the 'warm dim odorous feckless evasive southern quality' of the life he once lived in his native Cork.

The story of his first shriving must be, in its quiet way, one of the most widely enjoyed short stories of this century:

FIRST CONFESSION

All the trouble began when my grandfather died and my grandmother—my father's mother—came to live with us. Relations in the one house are a strain at the best of times, but, to make matters worse, my grandmother was a real old countrywoman and quite unsuited to the life in town. She had a fat, wrinkled old face, and, to Mother's great indignation, went round the house in bare feet—the boots had her crippled, she said. For dinner she had a jug of porter and a pot of potatoes with—sometimes—a bit of salt fish, and she poured out the potatoes on the table and ate them, slowly, with great relish, using her fingers by way of a fork.

Now, girls are supposed to be fastidious, but I was the one who suffered most from this. Nora, my sister, just sucked up to the old woman for the penny she got every Friday out of the old-age pension, a thing I could not do. I was too honest, that was my trouble; and when I was playing with Bill Connell, the sergeant major's son, and saw my grandmother steering up the path with a jug of porter sticking out from beneath her shawl I was mortified. I made excuses not to let him come into the house, because I could never be sure what she would be up to when we went in.

When Mother was at work and my grandmother made dinner I wouldn't touch it. Nora once tried to make me, but I hid under the table from her and took the bread-knife with me for protection. Nora let on to be very indignant (she wasn't, of course, but she knew Mother saw through her, so she sided with Gran) and came after me. I lashed out at her with the bread-knife, and after that she left me alone. I stayed there till Mother came in from work and made my dinner, but when Father came in later Nora said in a shocked voice: 'Oh, Dadda, do you know what Jackie did at dinner time?' Then, of course, it all came out; Father gave me a flaking; Mother interfered, and for days after that he didn't speak to me and Mother barely spoke to Nora. And all because of that old woman! God knows, I was heart-scalded.

Then, to crown my misfortunes, I had to make my first confession and communion. It was an old woman called Ryan who prepared us for these. She was about the one age with Gran; she was well-to-do, lived in a big house on Montenotte, wore a black cloak and bonnet, and came every day to school at three o'clock when we should have been going home, and talked to us of hell. She may have mentioned the other place as well, but that could only have been by accident, for hell had the first place in her heart.

She lit a candle, took out a new half-crown and offered it to the first boy who would hold one finger—only one finger!—in the flame for five minutes by the school clock. Being always very ambitious I was tempted to volunteer, but I thought it might look greedy. Then she asked were we afraid of holding one finger—only one finger!—in a little candle flame for five minutes and not afraid of burning all over in roasting hot furnaces for all eternity. 'All eternity! Just think of that! A whole lifetime goes by and it's nothing, not even a drop in the ocean of your sufferings.' The woman was really interesting about hell, but my attention was all fixed on the half-crown. At the end of the lesson she put it back in her purse. It was a great disappointment; a religious woman like that, you wouldn't think she'd bother about a thing like a half-crown.

Another day she said she knew a priest who woke one night to find a fellow he didn't recognise leaning over the end of his bed. The priest was a bit frightened—naturally enough—but he asked the fellow what he wanted, and the fellow said in a deep, husky voice that he wanted to go to confession. The priest said it was an awkward time and wouldn't it do in the morning, but the fellow said that the last time he went to confession, there was one sin he kept back, being ashamed to mention it, and now it was always on his mind. Then the priest knew it was a bad case, because the fellow was after making a bad confession and committing a mortal sin. He got up to dress, and just then the cock crew in the yard outside, and—lo and behold! - when the priest looked round there was no sign of the fellow, only a smell of burning timber, and when the priest looked at his bed didn't he see the print of two hands burned in it? That was because the fellow had made a bad confession. This history made a shocking impression on me.

But the worst of all was when she showed us how to examine our conscience. Did we take the name of the Lord, our God, in vain? Did we honour our father and our mother? (I asked her did this include grandmothers and she said it did.) Did we love our neighbours as ourselves? Did we covet our neighbour's goods? (I thought of the way I felt about the penny that Nora got every Friday.) I decided that, between one thing and another, I must have broken the whole ten commandments, all on account of that old woman, and so far as I could see, so long as she remained in the house I had no hope of ever doing anything else.

I was scared to death of confession. The day the whole class went I let on to have a toothache, hoping my absence wouldn't be noticed; but at three o'clock, just as I was feeling safe, along comes a chap with a message from Mrs Ryan that I was to go to confession myself on Saturday and be at the chapel for communion with the rest. To make it worse, Mother couldn't come with me and sent Nora instead.

Now, that girl had ways of tormenting me that Mother never knew of. She held my hand as we went down the hill, smiling sadly and saying how sorry she was for me, as if she were bringing me to the hospital for an operation.

'Oh, God help us!' she moaned. 'Isn't it a terrible pity you weren't a good boy? Oh, Jackie, my heart bleeds for you! How will you ever think of all your sins? Don't forget you have to tell him about the time you kicked Gran on the shin.'

'Lemme go!' I said, trying to drag myself free of her. 'I don't want to go to confession at all.'

'But sure, you'll have to go to confession, Jackie,' she replied in the same regretful tone. 'Sure, if you didn't, the parish priest would be up to the house looking for you. 'Tisn't, God knows, that I'm not sorry for you. Do you remember the time you tried to kill me with the bread-knife under the table? And the language you used to me? I don't know what he'll do with you at all, Jackie. He might have to send you up to the bishop.'

I remember thinking bitterly that she didn't know the half of what I had to tell—if I told it. I knew I couldn't tell it, and understood perfectly why the fellow in Mrs Ryan's story made a bad confession; it seemed to me a great shame that people wouldn't stop criticising him. I remember that steep hill down to the church, and the sunlit hillsides beyond the valley of the river, which I saw in the gaps between the houses like Adam's last glimpse of Paradise.

Then, when she had manœuvred me down the long flight of steps to the chapel yard, Nora suddenly changed her tone. She became the malicious devil she really was.

'There you are!' she said with a yelp of triumph, hurling me through the church door. 'And I hope he'll give you the penitential psalms, you dirty little caffler.'

I knew then I was lost, given up to eternal justice. The door with the coloured-glass panels swung shut behind me, the sunlight went out and gave place to deep shadow, and the wind whistled outside so that the silence within seemed to crackle like ice under my feet. Nora sat in front of me by the confession box. There were a couple of old women ahead of her, and then a miserable-looking poor devil came and wedged me in at the other side, so that I couldn't escape even if I had the courage. He joined his hands and rolled his eyes in the direction of the roof, muttering aspirations in an anguished tone, and I wondered had he a grandmother too. Only a grand-mother could account for a fellow behaving in that heartbroken way, but he was better off than I, for he at least could go and confess his sins; while I would make a bad confession and then die in the night and be continually coming back and burning people's furniture.

Nora's turn came, and I heard the sound of something slamming, and then her voice as if butter wouldn't melt in her mouth, and then another slam, and out she came, God, the hypocrisy of women! Her eyes were lowered, her head was bowed, and her hands were joined very low down on her stomach, and she walked up the aisle to the side altar looking like a saint. You never saw such an exhibition of devotion; and I remembered the devilish malice with which she had tormented me all the way from our door, and wondered were all religious people like that, really. It was my turn now. With the fear of damnation in my soul I went in, and the confessional door closed of itself behind me.

It was pitch-dark and I couldn't see priest or anything else. Then I really began to be frightened. In the darkness it was a matter between God and me, and he had all the odds. He knew what my intentions were before I even started; I had no chance. All I had ever been told about confession got mixed up in my mind and I knelt to one wall and said: 'Bless me, father, for I have sinned; this is my first confession.' I waited for a few minutes, but nothing happened, so I tried it on the other wall. Nothing happened there either. He had me spotted all right.

It must have been then that I noticed the shelf at about one height with my head. It was really a place for grown-up people to rest their elbows, but in my distracted state I thought it was probably the place you were supposed to kneel. Of course, it was on the high side and not very deep, but I was always good at climbing and managed to get up all right. Staying up was the trouble. There was room only for my knees, and nothing you could get a grip on but a sort of wooden moulding a bit above it. I held on to the moulding and repeated the words a little louder and this time something happened all right. A slide was slammed back; a little light entered the box, and a man's voice said: 'Who's there?'

''Tis me, father,' I said for fear he mightn't see me and go away again. I couldn't see him at all. The place the voice came from was under the moulding, about level with my knees, so I took a good grip of the moulding and swung myself down till I saw the astonished face of a young priest looking up at me. He had to put his head on one side to see me, and I had to put mine on one side to see him, so we were more or less talking to one another upside-down. It struck me as a queer way of hearing confessions, but I didn't feel it my place to criticise.

'Bless me, father, for I have sinned; this is my first confession,' I rattled off all in one breath, and swung myself down the least shade more to make it easier for him.

'What are you doing up there?' he shouted in an angry voice, and the strain the politeness was putting on my hold of the moulding, and the shock of being addressed in such an uncivil tone, were too much for me. I lost my grip, tumbled and hit the door an unmerciful wallop before I found myself flat on my back in the middle of the aisle. The people who had been waiting stood up with their mouths open. The priest opened the door of the middle box and came out, pushing his biretta back from his forehead; he looked something terrible. Then Nora came scampering down the aisle.

'Oh, you dirty little caffler!' she said, ' I might have known you'd do it. I might have known you'd disgrace me. I can't leave you out of my sight for one minute.'

Before I could even get to my feet to defend myself she bent down and gave me a clip across the ear. This reminded me that I was so stunned I had even forgotten to cry, so that people might think I wasn't hurt at all, when in fact I was probably maimed for life. I gave a roar out of me.

'What's all this about?' the priest hissed, getting angrier than ever and pushing Nora off me. 'How dare you hit the child like that, you little vixen?'

'But I can't do my penance with him, father,' Nora cried, cocking an outraged eye up at him.

'Well, go and do it, or I'll give you some more to do,' he said, giving me a hand up. 'Was it coming to confession you were, my poor man?' he asked me.

''Twas, father,' said I with a sob.

'Oh,' he said respectfully, 'a big hefty fellow like you must have terrible sins. Is this your first?'

''Tis, father,' said I.

'Worse and worse,' he said gloomily. 'The crimes of a lifetime. I don't know will I get rid of you at all today. You'd better wait now till I'm finished with these old ones. You can see by the looks of them they haven't much to tell.'

'I will, father,' I said with something approaching joy.

The relief of it was really enormous. Nora stuck out her tongue at me from behind his back, but I couldn't even be bothered retorting. I knew from the very moment that man opened his mouth that he was intelligent above the ordinary. When I had time to think, I saw how right I was. It stood to reason that a fellow confessing after seven years would have more to tell than people that went every week. The crimes of a lifetime, exactly as he said. It was only what he expected, and the rest was the cackle of old women and girls with their talk of hell, the bishop and the penitential psalms. That was all they knew. I started to make my examination of conscience, and barring the one bad business of my grandmother it didn't seem so bad.

The next time, the priest steered me into the confession box himself and left the shutter back the way I could see him get in and sit down at the further side of the grill from me.

'Well, now,' he said, 'what do they call you?'

'Jackie, father,' said I.

'And what's a-trouble to you, Jackie?'

'Father,' I said, feeling I might as well get it over while I had him in good humour, 'I had it all arranged to kill my grandmother.'

He seemed a bit shaken by that, all right, because he said nothing for quite a while.

'My goodness,' he said at last, 'that'd be a shocking thing to do. What put that into your head?'

'Father,' I said, feeling very sorry for myself, 'she's an awful woman.'

'Is she?' he asked. 'What way is she awful?'

'She takes porter, father,' I said, knowing well from the way Mother talked of it that this was a mortal sin, and hoping it would make the priest take a more favourable view of my case.

'Oh, my!' he said, and I could see he was impressed.

'And snuff, father,' said I.

'That's a bad case, sure enough, Jackie,' he said.

'And she goes round in her bare feet, father,' I went on in a rush of self pity, 'and she know I don't like her, and she gives pennies to Nora and none to me, and my Da sides with her and flakes me, and one night I was so heart-scalded I made up my mind I'd have to kill her.'

'And what would you do with the body?' he asked with great interest.

'I was thinking I could chop that up and carry it away in a barrow I have,' I said.

'Begor, Jackie,' he said, 'do you know you're a terrible child?'

'I know, father,' I said, for I was just thinking the same thing myself. 'I tried to kill Nora too with a bread-knife under the table, only I missed her.'

'Is that the little girl that was beating you just now?' he asked.

''Tis, father.'

'Someone will go for her with a bread-knife one day, and he won't miss her,' he said rather cryptically. 'You must have great courage. Between ourselves there's a lot of people I'd like to do the same to but I'd never have the nerve. Hanging is an awful death.'

'Is it, father?' I asked with the deepest interest—I was always very keen on hanging. 'Did you ever see a fellow hanged?'

'Dozens of them,' he said solemnly. 'And they all died roaring.'

'Jay!' I said.

'Oh, a horrible death!' he said with great satisfaction. 'Lots of the fellows I saw killed their grandmothers too, but they all said 'twas never worth it.'

He had me there for a full ten minutes talking, and then he walked out the chapel yard with me. I was genuinely sorry to part with him, because he was the most entertaining character I'd ever met in the religious line. Outside, after the shadow of the church, the sunlight was like the roaring of waves on a beach; it dazzled me; and when the frozen silence melted and I heard the screech of trams on the road my heart soared. I knew now I wouldn't die in the night and come back, leaving marks on my mother's furniture. It would be a great worry to her, and the poor soul had enough.

Nora was sitting on the railing, waiting for me, and she put on a very sour puss when she saw the priest with me. She was mad jealous because a priest had never come out of the church with her.

'Well,' she asked coldly, after he left me, 'what did he give you?'

'Three Hail Marys,' I said.

'Three Hail Marys,' she repeated incredulously. 'You mustn't have told him anything.'

'I told him everything,' I said confidently.

'About Gran and all?'

'About Gran and all.'

(All she wanted was to be able to go home and say I'd made a bad confession.)

'Did you tell him you went for me with the bread-knife?' she asked with a frown.

'I did to be sure.'

'And he only gave you three Hail Marys?'

'That's all.'

She slowly got down from the railing with a baffled air. Clearly, this was beyond her. As we mounted the steps back to the main road she looked at me suspiciously.

'What are you sucking?' she asked.

'Bullseyes.'

'Was it the priest gave them to you?'

''Twas.'

'Lord God,' she wailed bitterly, 'some people have all the luck! 'Tis no advantage to anybody trying to be good. I might just as well be a sinner like you.'

'Frank O'Connor' (Michael O'Donovan) (1903–66) *The Stories of Frank O'Connor* (1953).

A*NOTHER master of the short-story form is V. S. Pritchett, one of English literature's few knights. Sir Victor, short-storywriter, critic, novelist, biographer, left the leather trade early to become a writer. He became a columnist and critic in the Hazlitt and Lamb vein for the* New Statesman and Nation (*or* Staggers and Naggers *as it was affectionately known in those days*), *then literary editor in 1946, and finally a director.*

Victor Sawden Pritchett lectured to universities in the USA on comic elements in the English novel and gave readings from Dickens to which his physical appearance lent an appropriate air: the New York Times *described him as 'composed primarily of smile, pipe, wispy hair and glasses'.*

His admiration for Dickens is apparent in his short stories; there is the same affectionate fascination with the middle and lower-middle class semi-eccentrics who make life a little bit less conformist and predictable. And Pritchett found the short story, which Chekhov argued should not have the artificialities of a beginning and an end imposed upon it, the best literary form for his kind of miniaturist character drawing, the sketching of an individual in the course of a small incident.

For example Mr Pritchett's portrait of his dentist at work:

OEDIPUS COMPLEX

'Good morning, Mr P' said Mr Pollfax, rinsing and drying his hands after the last patient. 'How's Mr P?' I was always Mr P until I sat in the chair and he switched the lamp on and had my mouth open. Then I got a peerage.

'That's fine, my lord,' said Mr Pollfax, having a look inside.

Dogged, with its slight suggestion of doggish, was the word for Mr Pollfax. He was a short man, jaunty, hair going thin, with jaunty buttocks and a sway to his walk. He had two lines, from habitual grinning, cut deep from the nostrils, and scores of lesser lines like the fine hair of a bird's nest round his egg-blue eyes. There was something innocent, heroic and determined about Mr Pollfax, something of the English Tommy in tin hat and full pack going up the line. He suggested in a quiet way—war.

He was the best dentist I ever had. He got you into the chair, turned on the light, tapped around a bit with a thing like a spoon and then, dropping his white-coated arm to his side, told you a story. Several more stories followed in his flat Somerset voice, when he had your mouth jacked up. And then, removing the towel and with a final 'Rinse that lot out,' he finished with the strangest story of all and let you go. A month or so later the bill came in. 'Mr Pollfax presents his compliments,' and across the bottom of it, in his hand, 'Be good'. I have never known a dentist like Mr Pollfax.

'Open, my lord,' said Mr Pollfax. 'Let's see what sort of life his Lordship has been leading. Still smoking that filthy pipe, I see. I shall have to do some cleaning up.'

He tapped around and then dropped his arm. A look of anxiety came into his face. 'Did I tell you that one about the girl who went to the Punch and Judy show? No? Nor the one about the engine-driver who was put on sentry duty in Syria? You're sure? When did I see you last? What was the last one I told you? That sounds like last April? Lord, you have been letting things go. Well,' said Mr Pollfax, tipping back my head and squirting something on to a tooth, 'we'll have a go at that root at the back. It's not doing you any good. It was like this. There was a girl sitting on the beach at Barmouth with her young man watching a Punch and Judy show . . .' (Closer and closer came Mr Pollfax's head, lower and lower went his voice.)

He took an instrument and began chipping his way through the tooth and the tale.

'Not bad, eh?' he said, stepping back with a sudden shout of laughter.

'Ah,' I mouthed.

'All right, my lord,' said Mr Pollfax, withdrawing the instrument and relapsing into his dead professional manner. 'Spit that lot out.'

He began again.

There was just that root, Mr Pollfax was saying. It was no good there. There was nothing else wrong; he'd have it out in a couple of shakes.

'Though, my lord,' he said, 'you did grow it about as far back in your throat as you could, didn't you, trying to make it as difficult as you could for Mr Pollfax? What we'll do first of all is to give it a dose of something.'

He swivelled the dish of instruments towards me and gave a tilt to the lamp. I remembered that lamp because once the bulb had exploded, sending glass all over the room. It was fortunate, Mr Pollfax said at the time, that it had blown the other way and none of it had hit me, for someone might have brought a case for damages against someone—which reminded him of the story of the honeymoon couple who went to a small hotel in Aberdeen . . .

'Now,' said Mr Pollfax, dipping things in little pots and coming to me with an injection needle; 'open wide, keep dead still. I was reading Freud the other day. There's a man. Oedipus complex? Ever read about that? Don't move, don't breathe, you'll feel a prick, but for God's sake don't jump. I don't want it to break in your gum. I've never had one break yet, touch wood, but they're thin, and if it broke off you'd be in a nursing-home three weeks and Mr Pollfax would be down your throat looking for it. The trouble about these little bits of wire is they move a bit farther into the system every time you swallow.'

'There now,' said Mr Pollfax.

'Feel anything? Feel it prick?' he said, 'Fine.'

He went to a cupboard and picked out the instrument of extraction and then stood, working it up and down like a gardener's secateurs in his hand. He studied my face. He was a clean-shaven man and looked like a priest in his white coat.

'Some of the stories you hear!' exclaimed Mr Pollfax. 'And some of the songs. I mean where I come from. "The Lot that Lily Lost in the Lottery"— know that one? Is your skin beginning to tingle, do you feel it on the tip of your tongue yet? That's fine, my lord, I'll sing it to you.'

Mr Pollfax began to sing. He'd give it another minute, he said, when he'd done with Lily; he'd just give me the chorus of 'The Night Uncle's Waistcoat Caught Fire'.

'Tra la la,' sang Mr Pollfax.

'I bet,' said Mr Pollfax sadistically, 'one side of his lordship's face has gone dead and his tongue feels like a pincushion.'

'Blah,' I said.

'I think,' he said, 'we'll begin.'

So Mr Pollfax moved round to the side of me, got a grip on my shoulders and began to press on the instrument in my mouth. Pressing and drawing firmly, he worked upon the root. Then he paused and increased the pressure. He seemed to be hanging from a crowbar fixed to my jaw. Nothing happened. He withdrew.

'The Great Flood begins,' said Mr Pollfax, putting a tube in my mouth and taking another weapon from the tray.

The operation began again. Mr Pollfax now seemed to hang and swing on the crowbar. It was not successful.

'Dug himself in, has he?' muttered Mr Pollfax. He had a look at his instruments. 'You can spit, my lord,' he said.

Mr Pollfax now seized me with great determination, hung, swung, pressed and tugged with increased energy.

'It's no good you thinking you're going to stay in,' said Mr Pollfax in mid-air, muttering to the root. But the instrument slipped and a piece of tooth broke off as he spoke.

'So that's the game is it?' said Mr Pollfax, withdrawing. 'Good rinse, my lord, while Mr Pollfax considers the position.'

He was breathing hard.

Oh well, he said, there were more ways than one of killing a cat. He'd get the drill on it. There were two Jews standing outside Buckingham Palace when a policeman came by, he said, coming at me with the drill which made a whistling noise like a fishing line as he drew it through. The tube gargled in my mouth. I was looking, as I always did at Mr Pollfax's, at the cowls busily twirling on the chimneys opposite. Wind or no wind, these cowls always seemed to be twirling round. Two metal cowls on two yellow chimneys. I always remember them.

'Spit, my lord,' said Mr Pollfax, changing to a coarser drill. 'Sorry, old man, if it slipped, but Mr Pollfax is not to be beaten.'

The drill whirred again, skidding and whining; the cowls twirled on the chimneys, Mr Pollfax's knuckles were on my nose. What he was trying to do, he said, was to get a purchase.

Mr Pollfax's movements got quicker. He hung up the drill, he tapped impatiently on the tray, looking for something. he came at me with something like a button-hook. He got it in. He levered like a signalman changing points.

'I'm just digging,' he said. Another piece of tooth broke off.

Mr Pollfax stared when he heard it go and drew back.

'Mr Pollfax is in a dilemma,' he said.

Well, he'd try the other side. Down came the drill again. There were beads of sweat on his brow. His breath was shorter.

'You see,' exclaimed Mr Pollfax suddenly and loudly, looking angrily up at his clock. 'I'm fighting against time. Keep that head this way, hold the mouth. That's right. Sorry my lord, I've got to bash you about, but time's against me.'

'Why, damn this root,' said Mr Pollfax, hanging up again. 'It's wearing out my drill. We'll have to saw. Mr Pollfax is up against it.'

His face was red now, he was gasping and his eyes were glittering. A troubled and emotional look came over Mr Pollfax's face.

'I've been up against it in my time,' exclaimed Mr Pollfax forcefully between his teeth. 'You heard me mention the Oedipus complex to you?'

'Blah,' I managed.

'I started well by ruining my father. I took every penny he had. That's a good start, isn't it?' he said, speaking very rapidly. 'Then I got married. Perfectly happy marriage, but I went and bust it up. I went off with a French girl and her husband shot at us out in the car one day. I was with that girl eighteen months and she broke her back in a railway accident and I sat with her six months watching her die. Six ruddy months. I've been through it. Then my mother died and my father was going to marry again, a girl young enough to be his daughter. I went up and took that girl off him, ran off to Hungary with her, married her and we've got seven children. Perfect happiness at last. I've been through the mill,' said Mr Pollfax, relaxing his chin and shining a torch down my mouth, 'but I've come out in the end.'

'A good rinse, my noble lord,' said Mr Pollfax.

'The oldest's fourteen,' he said, getting the saw. 'Clever girl. Very clever with her hands.'

He seized me again. Did I feel anything? Well, thank God for that, said Mr Pollfax. Here we'd been forty minutes with this dammed root.

'And I bet you're thinking why didn't Mr Pollfax let sleeping dogs lie, like the telephone operator said. Did I tell you that one about the telephone operator? That gum of yours is going to be sore.'

He was standing, legs apart, chin trembling, eyes blinking, hacking with the button-hook, like a wrestler putting on a headlock.

'Mr Pollfax with his back against the wall,' he said, between his teeth.

'Mr Pollfax making a last-minute stand,' he hissed.

'On the burning deck!' he gasped.

'Whence,' he added, 'all but he had fled.'

'Spit,' he said. 'And now let's have another look.' He wiped his brow. 'Don't say anything. Keep dead still. For God's sake don't let it hear you. My lords, ladies and gentlemen, pray silence for Mr Pollfax. It's coming, it isn't. It is. It is. There,' he cried, holding a fragment in his fingers.

He stood gravely to attention.

> '*And his chief beside,*
> *Smiling the boy fell dead,*'

said Mr Pollfax. 'A good and final spit, my lord and prince.'

V. S. Pritchett (b. 1900), *Collected Stories* (1956).

➤ Sir Victor was terrified one day when he was helpless in the chair and Mr Pollfax produced the book which contained the above story. To his surprise Mr Pollfax said cheerfully, 'Very good skit, my lord. You've got me off to a T!' Later, Sir Victor learned that Mr Pollfax was a tremendous womanizer whose practice it was to write pornographic poems to his mistresses and keep copies in his desk drawer. When Mr Pollfax died, his solicitor had the delicate task of asking Mr Pollfax's widow, an accomplished amateur flautist and a woman of religion and innocence, whether she had come across any, well, verses in her late husband's desk. 'Oh, *yes.*' said Mrs Pollfax. 'I set them to music.'

A KIND *of humorous short story different from the realistic account of a personal experience, like 'First Confession', or the character sketch, like 'Oedipus Complex', is the worked-up comic anecdote, the fictional story of a farcical occurrence built up with comical characters and a dramatic shape.*

A most unlikely retailer of this kind of cheerful fun would seem to be the novelist and poet Lawrence Durrell, friend and editor of Henry Miller and brother of the writer, naturalist and founder of Jersey Zoo, Gerald Durrell. Yet Lawrence Durrell had a considerable success in the late 1950s with two books of humorous stories about a British Embassy in the Balkans, Esprit de Corps: Sketches from Diplomatic Life, *and* Stiff Upper Lip.

But Lawrence Durrell was writing from experience. He had always been very much a European and before and during the war had worked as a press officer for the British Council and the Foreign Office in a number of such un-British locations as Egypt, Belgrade, Cyprus, and Yugoslavia.

His stories are supposedly about the British Embassy in Serbia, where the fictional ambassador is a man named Polk-Mowbray. They are frame stories narrated by Antrobus, a career diplomat who knows precisely the rules of that exquisitely tricky game:

JOTS AND TITTLES

'In Diplomacy,' said Antrobus, 'quite small things can be One's Undoing; things which in themselves may be Purely Inadvertent. The Seasoned Diplomat keeps a sharp eye out for these moments of Doom and does what he can to avert them. Sometimes he succeeds, but sometimes he fails utterly—and then Irreparable Harm ensues.

'Foreigners are apt to be preternaturally touchy in small ways and I remember important negotiations being spoilt sometimes by a slip of the tongue or an imagined slight . . .

'Quite the most illuminating example of this sort of thing occurred on the evening when Polk-Mowbray swallowed a moth. I don't think I ever told you about it before. It is the sort of thing one only talks about in the strictest confidence. It was at a dinner party given to the Communist People's Serbian Trade and Timber Guild sometime during Christmas week back in '52. Yugoslavia at that time had just broken with Stalin and was beginning to feel that the West was not entirely populated by "capitalist hyenas" as the press said. They were still wildly suspicious of us, of course, and it was a very hot and embarrassed little group of peasants dressed in dark suits who accepted Polk-Mowbray's invitation to dinner at the Embassy. Most of them spoke only their mother tongue. Comrade Bobok, however, the leader of the delegation, spoke a gnarled embryonic English. He was a huge sweating Bosnian peasant with a bald head. His number two, Pepic, spoke the sort of French that one imagines is learned in mission houses in Polynesia. From a diplomatist's point of view they were Heavy Going.

'I shall say nothing about their messy food habits; Drage the butler kept circling the table and staring at them as if he had gone out of his senses. We were all pretty sweaty and constrained by the time the soup plates were removed. The conversation was early cave-man stuff consisting of growls and snarls and weird flourishes of knife and fork. Bobok and Pepic sat on

Polk-Mowbray's right and left respectively; they were flanked by Spalding the Commercial Attaché and myself. We were absolutely determined to make the evening a success. De Mandeville for some curious reason best known to himself had decreed that we should eat turkey with mustard and follow it up with plum pudding. I suppose it was because it was Christmas week. Comrade Bobok fell foul of the mustard almost at once and only quenched himself by lengthy potations which, however, were all to the good as they put him into a good temper.

'The whole thing might have been carried off perfectly well had it not been for this blasted moth which had been circling the Georgian candlesticks since the start of the dinner-party and which now elected to get burnt and crawl on to Polk-Mowbray's side-plate to die. Polk-Mowbray himself was undergoing the fearful strain of decoding Comrade Bobok's weighty pleasantries which were full of corrupt groups and he let his attention wander for one fatal second.

'As he talked he absently groped in his side-plate for a piece of bread. He rolls bread balls incessantly at dinner, as you know. Spalding and I saw in a flash of horror something happen for which our long diplomatic training had not prepared us. Mind you, I saw a journalist eat a wine-glass once, and once in Prague I saw a Hindu diplomat's wife drain a glass of vodka under the impression that it was water. She let out a moan which still rings in my ears. But never in all my long service have I seen an Ambassador eat a moth—and this is precisely what Polk-Mowbray did. He has a large and serviceable mouth and into it Spalding and I saw the moth disappear. There was a breathless pause during which our poor Ambassador suddenly realized that something was wrong; his whole frame stiffened with a dreadful premonition. His large and expressive eye became round and glassy with horror.

'This incident unluckily coincided with two others; the first was that Drage walked on with a blazing pudding stuck with holly. Our guests were somewhat startled by this apparition, and Comrade Bobok, under the vague impression that the blazing pud must be ushering in a spell of diplomatic toasts, rose to his feet and cried loudly: "to Comrade Tito and the Communist People's Serbian Trade and Timber Guild. *Jiveo!*" His fellow Serbs rose as one man and shouted: "*Jiveo!*"

'By this time, however, light had begun to dawn on Polk-Mowbray. He let out a hoarse jarring cry full of despair and charred moth, stood up, threw up his arms and groped his way to the carafe on the sideboard, shaken by a paroxysm of coughing. Spalding and I rocked, I am sorry to say, with hysterical giggles, followed him to pat him on the back. To the startled eyes of the Yugoslavs we must have presented the picture of three diplomats laughing ourselves to death and slapping each other on the back at the sideboard, and utterly ignoring the sacred toast. Worse still, before any of us could turn and explain the situation Spalding's elbow connected with Drage's spinal cord. The butler missed his footing and scattered the pudding like an incendiary bomb all over the table and ourselves. The Yugoslav delegation sat there with little odd bits of pudding blazing in their laps or on their waistcoats, utterly incapable of constructive thought. Spalding, I am sorry to say, was racked with guffaws now which were infectious to a degree. De Mandeville who was holding the leg of the table and who had witnessed the tragedy also started to laugh in a shrill feminine register.

'I must say Polk-Mowbray rallied gamely. He took an enormous gulp of wine from the carafe and led us all back to table with apologies and excuses which sounded, I must say, pretty thin. What Communist could believe a capitalist hyena when he says that he has swallowed a moth? Drage was flashing about snuffing out pieces of pudding.

'We made some attempt to save the evening, but in vain. The awful thing was that whenever Spalding caught De Mandeville's eye they both subsided into helpless laughter. The Yugoslavs were in an Irremediable Huff and from then on they shut up like clams, and took their collective leave even before the coffee was served.

'It was quite clear that Spalding's Timber Pact was going to founder in mutual mistrust once more. The whole affair was summed up by the *Central Balkan Herald* in its inimitable style as follows: "We gather that the British Embassy organized a special dinner at which the Niece de Resistance was Glum Pudding and a thoroughly British evening was enjoyed by all." You couldn't say fairer than that, could you?'

> Lawrence Durrell (b. 1912), *Esprit de Corps: Sketches from Diplomatic Life* (1957).

The alarming misprints in the Central Balkan Herald, *as quoted above, were a part of the perils of embassy life in Durrell's Serbia and featured in many of Antrobus's reminiscences.*

In fact the wartime history of the Central Balkan Herald *and its editor-proprietors, the Grope sisters, was the subject of one of the most poignant of the* Esprit de Corps *stories:*

FRYING THE FLAG

'Of course, if there had been any justice in the world,' said Antrobus, depressing his cheeks grimly. 'If we ourselves had shown any degree of responsibility, the two old ladies would have been minced, would have been incinerated. Their ashes would have been trampled into some Serbian field or scattered in the sea off some Dalmatian island, like Drool or Snot. Or they would have been sold into slavery to the Bogomils. Or just simply crept up on from behind and murdered at their typewriters. I used to dream about it, old man.'

'Instead of which they got a gong each.'

'Yes. Polk-Mowbray put them up for an MBE. He had a perverted sense of humour. It's the only explanation.'

'And yet time softens so many things. I confess I look back on the old *Central Balkan Herald* with something like nostalgia.'

'Good heavens,' said Antrobus, and blew out his cheeks. We were enjoying a stirrup-cup at his club before taking a turn in the park. Our conversation, turning as it always did upon our common experiences abroad in the Foreign Service, had led us with a sort of ghastly inevitability to the sisters Grope; Bessie and Enid Grope, joint editor-proprietors of the *Central Balkan Herald* (circulation 500). They had spent all their lives in Serbia, for their father had once been Embassy chaplain and on retirement had elected to settle in the dusty Serbian plains. Where, however, they had inherited the old flat-bed press and the stock of battered Victorian faces, I cannot tell, but the fact remains that they had produced between them an extraordinary daily newspaper which remains without parallel in my mind after a comparison with newspapers in more than a dozen countries—THE BALKAN HERALD KEEPS THE BRITISH FLAG FRYING—that was the headline that greeted me on the morning of my first appearance in the Press Department. It was typical.

The reason for a marked disposition towards misprints was not far to seek; the composition room, where the paper was hand-set daily, was staffed by half a dozen hirsute Serbian peasants with greasy elf-locks and hands like shovels. Bowed and drooling and uttering weird eldritch-cries from time to time they went up and down the type-boxes with the air of half-emancipated baboons hunting for fleas. The master printer was called Icic (pronounced Itchitch) and he sat forlornly in one corner living up to his name by scratching himself from time to time. Owing to such laborious methods of composition the editors were hardly ever able to call for extra proofs; even as it was the struggle to get the paper out on the streets was grandiose to watch. Some time in the early thirties it had come out a day late and that day had never been made up. With admirable single-mindedness the sisters decided, so as not to leave gaps in their files, to keep the date twenty-four hours behind reality until such times as, by a superhuman effort, they could produce two newspapers in one day and thus catch up.

Bessie and Enid Grope sat in the editorial room which was known as the 'den'. They were both tabby in colouring and wore rusty black. They sat facing one another pecking at two ancient typewriters which looked as if they had been obtained from the Science Museum or the Victoria and Albert.

Bessie was News, Leaders, and Gossip; Enid was Features, Make-up, and general Sub. Whenever they were at a loss for copy they would mercilessly pillage ancient copies of *Punch* or *Home Chat*. An occasional hole in the copy was filled with a ghoulish smudge—local block-making clearly indicated that somewhere a poker-work fanatic had gone quietly out of his mind. In this way the *Central Balkan Herald* was made up every morning and then delivered to the composition room where the chain gang rapidly reduced it to gibberish. MINISTER FINED FOR KISSING IN PUBIC. WEDDING BULLS RING OUT FOR PRINCESS.

QUEEN OF HOLLAND GIVES PANTY FOR EX-SERVICE MEN. MORE DOGS HAVE BABIES THIS SUMMER IN BELGRADE. BRITAINS NEW FLYING-GOAT.

In the thirties this did not matter so much but with the war and the growth of interest in propaganda both the Foreign Office and the British Council felt that an English newspaper was worth keeping alive in the Balkans if only to keep the flag flying. A modest subsidy and a free news service went a long way to help the sisters, though of course there was nothing to be done with the crew down in the composition room. 'Mrs Schwartkopf has cast off clothes of every description and invites inspection', 'In a last desperate spurt the Cambridge crew, urged on by their pox, overtook Oxford'.

Every morning I could hear the whistles and groans and sighs as each of the secretaries unfolded his copy and addressed himself to his morning torture. On the floor above, Polk-Mowbray kept drawing his breath sharply at every misprint like someone who has run a splinter into his finger. At this time the editorial staff was increased by the addition of Mr Tope, an elderly catarrhal man who made up the news page, thus leaving Bessie free to follow her bent in paragraphs on gardening ('How to Plant Wild Bubs') and other extravagances. It was understood that at some time in the remotest past Mr Tope had been in love with Bessie but he 'had never Spoken'; perhaps he had fallen in love with both sisters simultaneously and had been unable to decide which to marry. At all events he sat in the 'den' busy with the world news; every morning he called on me for advice. 'We want the *Herald* to play its full part in the war effort,' he never failed to assure me gravely. 'We are all in this together.' There was little I could do for him.

At times I could not help feeling that the *Herald* was more trouble than it was worth. References, for example, to 'Hitler's nauseating inversion—the rocket-bomb' brought an immediate visit of protest from Herr Schpunk the German *chargé*, dictionary in hand, while the early stages of the war were greeted with BRITAIN DROPS BIGGEST EVER BOOB ON BERLIN. This caused mild speculation as to whom this personage might be. Attempts, moreover, to provide serious and authoritative articles for the Herald written by members of the Embassy shared the same fate. Spalding, the commercial attaché who was trying to negotiate on behalf of the British Mining Industry, wrote a painstaking survey of the wood resources of Serbia which appeared under the startling banner BRITAIN TO BUY SERBIAN TIT-PROPS, while the military attaché who was rash enough to contribute a short strategic survey of Suez found that the phrase 'Canal Zone' was printed without a 'C' throughout. There was nothing one could do. 'One feels so desperately ashamed,' said Polk-Mowbray, 'With all the resources of culture and so on that we have— that a British newspaper abroad should put out such disgusting gibberish. After all, it's semi-official, the Council has subsidised it specially to spread the British Way of Life . . . It's not good enough.'

But there was nothing much we could do. The *Herald* lurched from one extravagance to the next. Finally in the columns of Theatre Gossip there occurred a series of what Antrobus called Utter Disasters. The reader may be left to imagine what the Serbian compositors would be capable of doing to a witty urbane and deeply considered review of the 100,000th performance of *Charley's Aunt.*

The *Herald* expired with the invasion of Yugoslavia and the sisters evacuated to Egypt where they performed prodigies of valour in nursing refugees. With the return to Belgrade, however, they found a suspicious Communist regime in power which ignored all their requests for permission to refloat the *Herald.* They brought their sorrows to the Embassy, where Polk-Mowbray received them with a stagey but absent-minded sympathy. He agreed to plead with Tito, but of course he never did. 'If they start that paper up again,' he told Chancery darkly, 'I shall resign.' 'They'd make a laughing stork out of you, sir,' said Spalding. (The pre-war mission had been returned almost unchanged.)

Mr Tope also returned and to everyone's surprise had Spoken and had been accepted by Bessie; he was now comparatively affluent and was holding the post which in the old days used to be known as Neuter's Correspondent— aptly or not who can say?

'Well, I think the issue was very well compounded by getting the old girls an MBE each for distinguished services to the British Way of Life. I'll never forget the investiture with Bessie and Enid in tears and Mr Tope swallowing like a toad. And all the headlines Spalding wrote for some future issue of the *Herald*: "Sister Roasted in Punk Champage after solemn investitute."'

'It's all very well to laugh,' said Antrobus severely, 'but a whole generation of Serbs have had their English gouged and mauled by the *Herald.* Believe me, old man, only yesterday I had a letter from young Babic, you remember him?'

'Of course.'

'For him England is peppered with fantastic place-names which he can only have got from the *Herald.* He says he enjoyed visiting Henleg Regatta and Wetminster Abbey; furthermore, he was present at the drooping of the colour; he further adds that the noise of big Bun striking filled him with emotion; and that he saw a film about Florence Nightingale called "The Lade With the Lump". No, no, old man, say what you will the *Herald* has much to answer for. It is due to sinister influences like the Gropes and Topes of this world that the British Council's struggle is such an uphill one. Care for another?'

Ibid.

M EMOIRS *flourished in the post-war years as they usually do after a war, many written by military commanders anxious to clear up a few details for posterity, or ex-politicians also justifying their errors of judgement, or actors with long memories, most of the books serious in tone and written to retrieve respect rather than to amuse.*

A colourful exception was My Grandmothers and I *written by Diana Holman-Hunt, granddaughter of the painter. This was an account of her childhood and, as her parents were in India, of the two grandmothers who brought her up. Her memories, written-up a little, had much the same charm and appeal (but not quite the same commercial success) as the American hit of the* 1920s, Life With Father.

Diana's mother's mother, who was known simply as Grandmother, warm, kind, soft and scented, lived in agreeable comfort in Sussex with her charming and witty husband.

Her other grandmother, whom she called Grand, was her father's mother, Mrs Holman Hunt (the hyphen between Holman and Hunt seems to be a recent addition), widow of William Holman Hunt, the painter of allegorical pictures in realistic detail (he was the first important painter to capture on canvas, exactly, the translucent membrane inside a sheep's ear). He was also co-founder of the pre-Raphaelite Brethren. Grand was a tall, strong, gaunt woman with steel pince-nez spectacles and flowing dresses. She lived in a dusty, gas-lit, chilly house in West Kensington with her slightly loony maid, Helen. The house was crammed with art treasures and memories of the past, a period in which Mrs Holman Hunt mentally dwelt most of the time.

Unlike Grandmother, Grand did not enjoy spending money, nor did she attach much importance to items like personal comfort and food.

When little Diana left Grandmother's lush nest and arrived with her teddy bear Edward to stay with Grand, even going to bed turned out to be a complicated and adventurous procedure:

'Hark, I think I hear Helen with the bells.'

I ran to the hall. Helen stood there, puffing as usual. Lengths of wire, with sharp prongs at each end, were wound round her neck, and bells on metal rings were hanging from her arms. In one hand she held a hammer and in the other a basket full of tins.

'The trip-wires first,' Grand said, briskly, 'bring a candle, dear.'

'Take a candle child to light your mother through the snow!'

I giggled because Helen looked so funny. Grand stretched the wires across the room and hammered the sharp pegs in the floor between the Persian rugs. She made piles of tins here and there about the room.

'What is she doing, Helen?' I asked.

'Them's for trapping the thieves what come in the night,' she whispered. 'We don't want to be murdered in our beds now, do we?'

'I should think not!' I exclaimed, much startled. The old Monk at home was bad enough. 'There aren't any thieves in Bryanston Square—at least we don't set any traps,' I boasted loudly.

'The things there are all very well in their way,' Grand condescended, 'but they don't compare with the treasures here; what with menservants, telephones and electric light, such precautions would be perhaps superfluous: electric light, thanks to Sir Joseph Swan, who was your godfather's father you know. Gabriel Rossetti was once offered a post in a telegraph office. He declined of course. In my opinion the discipline would have done him good. Now for the bells.' She hooked them over the doors.

'You'd better fetch what you need from your box and say goodnight to Helen. Take care not to walk on the paint.'

There was a notice tacked to a tread; 'Edith H-H painted this staircase in 1905'. I picked my way with Edward and my nightgown under my arm, swinging my new check sponge-bag.

In Grand's bedroom the windows were open so that when we opened the door, the curtains billowed like sails. She lit the gas with a pop and said: 'You will sleep on the Chesterfield dear. Do as I do, we can both be modest.' Turning her back, she drew a huge white tent over her head.

I sat down and unlaced my boots. Grand was performing amazing contortions, writhing under her tent and kicking strange garments aside: a pair of stays shot across the room.

I managed to undo my dress and, shaking with cold, fingered the straps of my harness. It was buckled at the back. I saw some scissors on the table, and after a moment's reflection, with two quiet snips, cut through the canvas. I crumpled the contraption in a ball and hid it with Edward under my blanket. I felt wide awake and wicked. It was the slyest thing I'd ever done. I discarded my petticoats, lawn and flannel, my silk vest and my drawers until but for my socks I stood naked.

Grand turned round: 'My dear child! Where is your kimono? The one your father sent you last Christmas from the East?'

I had forgotten to fetch it from my hamper.

She picked up the paisley shawl and draped it round my body. She was still wearing her tent. 'Wait while I turn off the light but bring the candle.'

We climbed another flight of stairs. After much rattling of matches she again lit the gas and turned it very low. An elaborate illuminated notice was nailed over the bath: 'Edith H-H painted this bath with white enamel and varnished the mahogany surround in 1906. After use visitors are requested to clean gently with brush provided and polish with soft cloth hanging on the right. Kindly confirm that taps are not dripping.'

'Stand well back!' she ordered, approaching the geyser, 'just in case it explodes.' A sinister hissing was followed by a violent bang and a roar. 'Keep well away till the water runs. You never know.' She held up a warning finger.

I cowered in the doorway. A thin stream of boiling, rusty water cascaded into the bath, filling the room with steam. My hair clung round my neck in a damp, sweaty mass and my nose felt full.

She shouted out of the fog: 'Stay where you are! Shut your eyes! I'm going to get in when I've turned on the cold.'

I sank to the floor coughing. I couldn't see a thing but I could hear a dragon snorting and then a long agonized sigh, followed by sudden pandemonium: pipes thumping and banging and invisible water gurgling in torrents.

'Look alive!' she cried. 'Your turn next. The water isn't dirty; it's only lather from the Castile soap.'

In a daze I sponged my face and washed myself a little in the narrow bath.

'That's enough!' She pulled out the plug and, blinded by steam, flicked a huckaback towel in my eye. 'I'll scrub, you can polish. Here's the soft rag.'

I wiped with frenzied dabs but water appeared from nowhere; dripping from the ceiling and running down the walls. The faster I mopped the enamel, the wetter it became.

'That'll do! I think you must be tired?'

'I am rather,' I confessed. Pushing my hair off my forehead, I followed her down to the bedroom. She held the candle, which wobbled and threw our grotesque shadows on the walls.

I collapsed on the sofa and drew the scratch blanket up to my chin. The harness was curled up in a nest by Edward.

'But what about your prayers?'

'God bless,' I said, lying where I was, 'God bless . . .' I mumbled the list of names, 'and help me be a good girl. Amen.'

'My pet, you should be reverently on your knees, but perhaps this once . . .'

Although I was tired, I stayed awake, missing my smooth linen sheets, quilt and pillows. No wonder Fowler was reluctant to leave me in such a dangerous place, where hot baths devitalized and geysers exploded; and robbers came in the night to murder one in bed. Grandmother would think it quite unsuitable, possibly disastrous. At this moment, I was sure, at least forty thieves were lurking downstairs. No, not lurking, tumbling about over the wires, stubbing their toes and barking their shins on the sharp corners of Italian tables. Inflamed with rage they would seize weapons off the wall, which Grand had imprudently left at their disposal, and creep up the stairs and come in without knocking. Fowler knew she would never see me again; that was why she was crying. Surely we would have some warning. The bells would ring! Would the bells ring? Would we have time to hide in the cupboard?

I sat up. 'Grand?'

'Yes dear, what is it? Aren't you asleep?'

'When the bells ring, what shall we do?'

'I will tell you,' she said, in a confident tone. 'You will spring out of bed and twirl this large wooden rattle, round and round, out of the window, and

I will blow several short sharp blasts on that whistle tied to the end of my bed.'

'Then what'll happen?' I asked, anxiously clutching at Edward.

'The good police will come to our rescue. The dear, brave men—what admirable patience they show with the smallest problem,—telling foreigners their way about and what omnibus to take . . .'

'I don't think they'll get here in time to catch the thieves.' I was breathing deeply. The trip-wires were wrong and would only make the thieves angry. I could see their eyes smouldering with revenge as they reached for the daggers on the walls.

'It is to be hoped they'll sprain their ankles,' she said with a shrug. 'I assure you we can always rely on the police. I contribute to their funds.'

'Are you sure?' I persisted.

'Quite sure,' she said, reaching to snuff out the candle. She hadn't said her prayers . . .

When I awoke, Edward and my blanket had fallen on the floor. Scattered flies had settled on the ostrich eggs that dangled in a bunch from a plaster rose on the ceiling. The clock struck six.

Grand's head had rolled off her pillow; her mouth was open and formed a dark hole. Her scalp showed pink through her thin white hair. She looked tired and scraggy. It was high time she had a treat. What was the use of all that money in the hall—real silver coins, not just coppers to throw to the gate-boys—unless it would buy delicious food? . . .

'Ah, good morning my pet,' said Grand, rubbing her eyes, and gulping at something that made her face fatter. 'I hope you slept soundly?'

'The sofa's like a canoe, a canoe made of iron.'

'We'd better say our prayers,' she said.

'Prayers in the morning? I never say prayers in the morning, nobody does.'

She knelt on a stool, facing the wall on the right of her bed. 'Dear me, what a heathen.' She gazed at the shelf, on which stood a vase of plaited palm crosses and a framed drawing of hands, lifted in prayer.

'This is Dürer's famous drawing, only a reproduction of course. D'you know,' she asked, turning round, 'Mr Ruskin said that, in his opinion, Holman was the best draughtsman since Dürer? And,' she pointed to a glass case over the shelf, 'this is Holman's Order of Merit and, in that frame, are his palette and brushes.' She closed her eyes and her lips seemed to gibber. She had told me all this before.

'I was thinking,' she said, getting up, 'what a pleasant surprise it would be for your grandmother, if while you were here, you learnt the Lord's prayer in French or even Italian.'

Fowler wouldn't like it. She would call it tommyrot.

'You've outgrown that childish prayer you said to me last night. Really you should put your father first, not last after the pugs and Mrs Hopkins, whoever she may be. I expect Arthur is the Pritchard boy? I noticed he came early on the list and I must confess, I was rather hurt not to hear my name.'

'Oh dear, I didn't think . . .'

'Notre père qui est en ciel,' she murmured, 'it distresses me, your religious education is not, well not exactly . . . Ah, I hear Helen with our breakfast.'

The egg wore a red flannel cap: I attacked its shell with gusto, hammering 'Foreign' into splintered letters. When I dug my spoon in the top, I drew back in disgust: 'It smells!'

'All eggs smell,' said Grand.

'But it smells bad,' I explained, 'like . . .'

She picked it up and sniffed: 'It's not new-laid but it's fresh and perfectly wholesome. It might have been more prudent of Helen to fry it. I should use plenty of salt and pepper.' She set the egg back in its cup and walked round the room, sipping her tea.

'Now what delightful thing shall we choose to do today?' She surveyed the invitation cards stuck in the looking-glass frame, letting some more flop in the fender . . .

What could I do with my egg? Would Helen give me away if I poured my hot milk into the tea-pot?

'Why, I do believe we're free this afternoon. You choose, my pet, we'll do exactly as you like.'

'I should like to go to Selfridges,' I said, without hesitation.

'Selfridges? Who, where and what are Selfridges?'

'It's a wonderful place,' I said, feeling excited. 'Fowler took me there one day to have an ice and you've no idea how interesting it is, and, and . . .' I faltered, seeing her face stiff with disapproval, 'what lovely things they have.' I patted Edward.

'A shop! I scarcely think—no, no. I suggest the Zoological Gardens, if we must indulge plebeian tastes. Your father is a Fellow, indeed he has presented some exhibits so we should be admitted free of charge.'

'I'd rather go to the Serpentine and feed the ducks, if Helen has some crumbs.'

'I'll tell you what,' she exclaimed, as if she'd had a sudden inspiration, 'we will go to the National Gallery or the Tate; and then, if we feel inclined, we'll pay a call. Now there's no time to dawdle, when you're dressed and we've made the bed you can run downstairs to Helen. I'm sure she would appreciate a little help. Later I thought you could put on a pinafore and sweep up the leaves in the garden. Would that appeal to you at all?'

'Yes, that would be nice,' I said, leaning out of the window and throwing my egg at the elm, which had a notice chained to its trunk: 'William Make-peace Thackeray and his children played round this tree.'

'Was it in this garden that Grandpa Holman boiled the horse?' I stripped off my nightgown while she wasn't looking.

'You gruesome child,' she said, making a face in the glass, 'I believe it's your favourite story.'

'Tell me again,' I pleaded, putting on my clothes.

'Well, when Holman was working on the *Flight into Egypt*—which was afterwards called *The Triumph of the Innocents*—I sat at first for the virgin and your father, an adorable babe in my arms, was Jesus—that canvas gave enormous trouble wrinkling and shrinking and . . .'

'Go on about the horse,' I urged, lacing up my boots.

'When we returned from the East he felt that the anatomy of the ass . . .'

'The anatomy of the ass!' I echoed, rejoicing to hear the silly words again.

'. . . presented an insuperable problem,' we chanted together.

'He made endless studies in pencil.'

'Do go on.' I was seized with giggles.

'So he went to a knacker.'

'But the knacker said he hadn't got a donkey,' I recited, swinging my legs to keep time, 'so instead, Grandpa ordered a large dead horse.'

'It seems to be your story,' she said dryly, 'but at last it, the horse I mean, arrived in a cart—somewhat odoriferous . . .'

'Very smelly!' I shrieked, 'like the egg.' I smothered my nose in the blanket.

'The carcase was cut into huge red joints, which we carried through the drawing-room, down the steps, and laid on the grass in the garden . . .'

'You forgot to say you dropped some bits on the rugs,' I interrupted.

'After much confabulation, we went out and bought some bricks, and a large old copper, which we found abandoned in a builder's yard. Holman borrowed a barrow and we wheeled everything home, causing some consternation in the streets—dear Holman was quite unselfconscious. We carried jug after jug of water out of the house . . .'

'You couldn't get the fire to burn. The water wouldn't boil!'

'Indeed it wouldn't. Holman had imagined the flesh would soon fall from the bone and he would assemble the skeleton with ease in his studio.'

'But you couldn't cook it all at once. The head was so big. It didn't have a tail, the knacker had sold it already. It rained; the fire went out; the sticks were damp. You cooked and cooked, day after day and then?'

'And then the police arrived.' This was the incredible fact for which I'd waited.

'I must admit,' she said, 'the stench was indescribable. The whole neighbourhood complained.'

I rocked with laughter. I could see Grand prodding the dead horse with a poker, to test if it were done; her eyes smarting with the smoke.

'Look, here is the engraving.' She reached up and took a picture from the wall.

'There you are, but it isn't very like you as the Virgin on the donkey; and there's Papa as Jesus. He told me you smacked him over and over again because he wriggled. He was cold without any clothes. I'm sure his hair was never curly. It looks awful on a boy. You can't really see the donkey with all those cherubs dancing about. Boiling the horse was just a waste of time.'

'My dear, they're infant spirits, not cherubs. This one examining a tear in her dress is your Aunt Gladys . . .'

There was a knock on our bedroom door and Helen came in with a letter. It was not on a salver.

Diana Holman-Hunt, *My Grandmothers and I* (1960).

━━━━━━━

M ANY *successful non-fiction humorous books published in Britain after the war were based upon one good comic idea. The oddest and most original of those good ideas must surely have been the hoax perpetrated by the now distinguished politician and author, Humphrey Berkeley, when he was an undergraduate at Pembroke College, Cambridge.*

In 1947 the young Berkeley, aged 21, decided to invent for himself a minor public school and a mildly eccentric headmaster (based on Evelyn Waugh's Dr Fagan in Decline and Fall*). The names had to be plausible. After a great deal of thought and market-researching on unsuspecting fellow undergraduates he settled on 'Selhurst School, Near Petworth, Sussex', with its Headmaster, 'H. Rochester Sneath'.*

Berkeley then set to work in earnest, plotting his jape with precision. He had letter-headings printed and he arranged with the Post Office to forward letters addressed to the school to an undergraduate friend at his lodgings, 'Castle Brae', in Cambridge.

Then purporting to be Sneath, he wrote a series of faintly peculiar, slightly insulting letters to the distinguished headmasters of some of Britain's oldest and most respected public schools and sat back to see what would happen. The replies, puzzled, indignant, furious, poured in.

Here are some of Mr Sneath's letters, and the genuine replies which he received:

To the Master of Marlborough College

Selhurst School
Near Petworth
Sussex
March 15th, 1948

Dear Master,

As you are probably aware this summer sees the 300th anniversary of the foundation of Selhurst. In view of our connection with Royalty and the fact that at the beginning we numbered among our pupils the nephew of a Balkan Monarch, I am most anxious to have the honour of entertaining Their Majesties if this is at all feasible.

Perhaps you would be kind enough to let me know how you managed to engineer a visit recently from the King and Queen.

Perhaps you would also give me any tips which you may have learned from your visit as to how Royalty should be treated since Selhurst would certainly wish the scale of its hospitality to be second to none.

With kind regards and all good wishes.

Yours sincerely,
H. *Rochester Sneath*
Headmaster

The College
Marlborough
Wilts
March 19th, 1948

Dear Mr Sneath,

I have your letter of March 15th. I did nothing whatever to engineer the recent Royal visit, I merely received a communication from the King's Private Secretary saying that the King and Queen could visit the school on March 12th if that day would be convenient.

No doubt the fact that the King's Private Secretary, the Lord Chancellor and the Archbishop of Canterbury are all Old Marlburians had something to do with the matter.

I simply made arrangements for the day when I knew that the King and Queen would come.

I am in no position to help you in your request.

Yours truly,
F. *M. Heywood*
Master

Selhurst School
Near Petworth
Sussex
March 26, 1948

Dear Heywood,

I am writing you this letter in the strictest confidence. I understand from a Mr Robert Agincourt who was Senior French Master at Selhurst, for one term two years ago, that he is applying for a post on the staff of Marlborough College.

He has asked me if I could give him a testimonial to present to you and I told him that by no stretching of veracity was I able to do this. You will understand that nothing that I have to say about Mr Agincourt is actuated by any personal malice but I feel it my duty to inform you of the impression that he gave while he was at Selhurst.

During this brief stay no less than five boys were removed from the school as a result of his influence, and three of the Matrons had nervous breakdowns. The pictures on the walls of his rooms made a visiting Bishop shudder and would certainly rule out another Royal visit. His practices were described by the Chairman of the County Hospital as 'Hunnish'. The prominent wart on his nose was wittily described as 'the blot on the twentieth century' by a visiting conjuror.

As you cannot fail to have noticed, his personal appearance is against him, and, after one memorable Carol Service, a titled Lady who was sitting next to him collapsed in a heap. He was once observed climbing a tree in the School Grounds naked at night and on another occasion he threw a flower pot at the wife of the Chairman of the Board of Governors.

Should you wish any further information, I should be glad to furnish it for I could not wish another Headmaster to undergo the purgatory that I suffered that term.

I am staying for some days with my sister Mrs. Harvey-Kelly at Castle Brae, Chesterton, Cambridge and I would be grateful if you would reply to this address.

Yours sincerely,
H. Rochester Sneath
Headmaster

The College
Marlborough
Wilts
March 28th, 1948

Dear Mr Sneath,

The man whom you have mentioned has not made any approach to me and I require no further information about him.

Yours truly,
F. M. Heywood
Master

To the Headmaster of the Oratory

Selhurst School
Near Petworth
Sussex
April 22nd, 1948

Dear Headmaster,

I understand that your School, like mine, had to undergo the troubles of evacuation in the war. I thought, therefore, that you might be interested to know that my Solicitors have discovered that there is a loophole in the existing law that would enable us to claim some quite substantial sums of money from the Government. In these times when every class and interest seems able to plunder the Exchequer, it seems a pity that really deserving causes like the School should be left out in the cold. Also there is the advantage that any sum gained could now be put into something tangible as we have learned that a capital levy is likely to become increasingly severe. If you would care to learn the details we might fix up a meeting and, in all events, I must ask you to keep the matter quiet. My Solicitors assure me that though no charge in the Courts could result, the method might perhaps be thought a trifle dishonest. However, it would be in a good cause, and, surely for a Jesuit like yourself, that would be alright!

Yours very truly,
H. Rochester Sneath
Headmaster

From The Revd the Headmaster
The Oratory School
Woodcote
Nr. Reading
April 24th, 1948

Dear Headmaster,

Very many thanks for your letter of April 22nd. I am interested in what you say of the possibility of making a claim on the Government on account of evacuation of our premises during the war.

I don't know whether it would apply in our case as we decided in the end to sell our former property at Caversham Park outright to the BBC. However, we lost nearly 100 boys by the move, and are now faced with the necessity of considerable extension to the property here, the estimate for which is hair-raising.

I have not the honour to belong to the Jesuits, but I shall none the less be interested to hear any further news on this subject which you may have to impart.

Yours sincerely,
G. A. Tomlinson

Selhurst School
Near Petworth
Sussex
April 29th, 1948

Dear Headmaster,

Thank you for your letter of April 24th. I have consulted my Solicitors again upon your problem and the fact that you have sold your former property without compulsion, unfortunately disqualifies you from any such claim. I regret having raised false hopes, but I was unaware of the full facts. I must also apologise for addressing you as a Jesuit, but I was under the impression that all Catholic Schools were owned by that Order.

Yours sincerely,
H. Rochester Sneath
Headmaster

After some correspondence between Sneath and Dr Gaunt, the Headmaster of Malvern College, that good man mentioned Selhurst to a lady looking for a school for her son.

The unfortunate lady wrote to Sneath asking for details about Selhurst:

To the Headmaster of Selhurst School

18 Canonbury Square
London, N1
March 19th, 1948

Dear Dr Sneath,

I was discussing with my friend Dr Gaunt, the Headmaster of Malvern last week the possibilities of another public school for my younger son Oswald, aged ten years, and he happened to mention the name of Selhurst. My elder son Christopher was at Malvern, is quite emphatic that Malvern would not suit Oswald at all and I am inclined to agree with him.

Although I confess that I have not heard of Selhurst I am anxious to try something quite new as my late husband, Brigadier Jack Worsley was nothing if not modern in his ideas.

Perhaps you would be good enough to give me some details of Selhurst and its varied activities. Oswald is a sensitive child and not unintelligent, although he is very fond of school debating and I have no doubt that you will be able to provide any special treatment which may be desirable for him.

Perhaps I have not made it quite clear that I am anxious for Oswald's name to be put on your waiting list.

Yours sincerely,
Henrietta Worsley

Selhurst School
Near Petworth
Sussex

My dear Mrs Worsley,

I thank you very much for your letter. I am indeed glad that my dear friend Mr H. G. A. Gaunt has mentioned my name to you and that of our illustrious school. I would be delighted to do all that I can for you. I must, however, point out that a school of our standing has few if any vacancies at the best of times and at the moment we have a waiting list which is full until 1962 and I have many tentative offers until 1965. However, the best course for you to adopt is for you to write to the Domestic Bursar, the Reverend Wotan Sneath, sending him a registration fee of £8 which is non-recoverable and your son's name will be placed upon our waiting list for the Waiting List.

I am interested though not entirely surprised to hear that you think that Malvern is unsuitable for your second boy. The day of the conventional public school is now over. At Selhurst we endeavour, and I think with some success, to provide a truer and nobler concept of education. My staff is recruited from a very wide cross section of talent and includes a Doctor of Philosophy from Munich and a man, Mr Digby Groat, who recently forfeited his deposit in a by-election where he was standing as a King's Cavalier. My brother, the Rev

Wotan Sneath, the School Chaplain, has had a career of unusual distinction. He was considered for a fellowship of his college and then was received into the orders of the Roman Catholic Church where he reached the dignity of a minor prelate. Troubled by intellectual doubts he left the Roman fold and became a Congregationalist Minister and in 1929 was Moderator of the Free Church Council. Believing that the unity of the Christian Churches was essential he subsequently took Anglican orders and his promotion has been so rapid that he is now on nodding terms with a Colonial Bishop and numbers among his friends a rural dean and a Canon of the Church of Ireland. He is, as you will appreciate, fully qualified to minister to boys of no less than three religious persuasions.

Should we have a vacancy for your boy he will find Selhurst a vigorous and expanding School. We now have 275 boys and our School clubs include a Communist club and an affiliated branch of the Housewives League. You will therefore see that he will have ample opportunity for debate.

Dear Lady, it was delightful to hear from you and I am wondering whether your late husband was the 'Foxy' Worsley that I used to know many years ago. I could tell you a few things about him!

Yours very sincerely,
H. Rochester Sneath
Headmaster

To the Headmaster of Tonbridge

Selhurst School
Near Petworth
Sussex
March 30th, 1948

Dear Rootie,

You will doubtless remember old 'Tubby' Sneath—well it will give you a helluva shock, you old bounder, because last year I took on the Headship here. Do you remember prophesying my early death in a South American brothel? I must say that I never imagined that you would get muddled up in this racket either, and imagine my surprise when I returned from India to be told that the man whom I had carried home, drunk as a coot seven times a week, should have got a job. At least I presume the Headmaster of Tonbridge is you!

Listen Rootie, quite seriously, Selhurst is having a beano for its three hundredth anniversary on June 19th. Could you come down, old boy, and give us a sermon on the Sunday? I've got the bleeding Minister, Tomlinson I mean, coming down on the Saturday to dole out the pots. Mind you behave yourself and don't start making eyes at the Matron, even though she may remind you of Vera Grant.

Let me know, old boy, and give Phyllis and the kids a kiss from me and please reply to me c/o R. L. Bidwell, Ballyfree House, Glenealy, Co. Wicklow, as I am staying in Ireland for a month.

All the best you old swab and have one on me.

Tubby

The Headmaster
The School House
Tonbridge, Kent
March 31st, 1948
Dear Sir,

I have received from you a letter opening 'Dear Rootie'. It is not intended for me though addressed to the Headmaster of Tonbridge. In view of the contents of the letter I should be obliged if you would send me the name of the person to whom you have written as Headmaster of Tonbridge and on what the incorrect information is based; for if it is widely presumed that he is Headmaster of Tonbridge that needs correcting for reasons obvious to you.

I am going away on Saturday and my address will be:
Long Close
Lyddington, Nr Swindon, Wilts

Yours faithfully,
E. E. A. Whitworth

Amazingly, only two headmasters smelt something fishy about their letter from H. Rochester Sneath and realized it must be a leg-pull.

One was Walter Oakeshott, Headmaster of Winchester, who was told that Selhurst School's founder was his Puritan forebear, Ebenezer Oakshott, so would he come to Selhurst and unveil a plaque. He replied with a letter of regret from his private secretary, Angela Thacklethwycke.

The other, the Revd John Sinnott SJ, Headmaster of Wimbledon College, countered Humphrey Berkeley in fine Jesuitical fashion:

To the Rector of Beaumont College

Selhurst School
Near Petworth
Sussex
April 29th, 1948
Dear Rector of Beaumont,

I am writing to you upon a matter of some delicacy. As you may perhaps have read in one of the more prominent Psychic Journals, we at Selhurst are suffering from a troublesome ghost. In any old foundation such as ours, this is often to be expected, and this particular ghost is generally believed to be the spirit of a Matron who committed suicide at the beginning of the last century, after having been seduced by a Housemaster. I understand that Catholic priests alone are able to exorcise these ghosts with Holy Water, incense etc. I am told that Jesuits are particularly qualified for this owing to some degree they take, and that they would be more discreet than the local clergy. As this Spirit has already caused offence to a visiting Peeress, and, by appearing at dinner, has caused the wife of the Chairman of the Board of Governors to collapse in a heap, we are anxious to lay it as soon as possible, particularly as in a month's time we are to entertain the widow of an Ambassador. If you would consent to come, I should, or course, pay you the usual fee, and perhaps you would preach a sermon in our Chapel.

I shall be staying for about a fortnight with my sister Mrs Harvey-Kelly at Castle Brae, Chesterton, Cambridge and would be grateful if you would reply there.

Yours sincerely,
H. Rochester Sneath
Headmaster

Wimbledon College
Edge Hill
SW 19
May 1st, 1948

Dear Sir,

Your letter has been passed on to me by the Rector of Beaumont College, who is indisposed and unfit for violent exertions. I quite understand the predicament in which you find yourself, and will make a point of coming down to Selhurst School, if you will let me know the date of your return from Chesterton.

It will be necessary for you to have ready for me the usual Bell, Book and Candle, a gallon of holy water and a packet of salt. The latter is required for sprinkling on a certain part of the ghostly anatomy, so it should be loose and capable of being taken up in pinches.

These operations usually take some time, and remuneration is at the rate of a guinea an hour. An essential condition for success is that all present (myself excepted) should be fasting for at least twenty-four hours before the ceremony begins.

Trusting to hear from you in due course.

Yours sincerely,
John Sinnott,
Headmaster

Humphrey Berkeley (b. 1926), *The Life and Death of Rochester Sneath: A Youthful Frivolity* (1974).

🦢 The hoax was revealed when a magazine, *News Review*, sent a reporter to interview Mr Sneath and found that neither he nor the school existed. The trail finally led to the undergraduate Berkeley. He was reprimanded by the Master of Pembroke College and banned from the college for two years for making mock of distinguished headmasters. A friend advised him to deposit with his bank manager the portfolio of letters and replies, wait twenty-five years, and then publish the whole thing as a book. Which is what he did.

IN *1947, the year that the young Humphrey Berkeley was planning his H. Rochester Sneath hoax, a book was published based upon another funny and wholly original idea. The book has now become a classic of modern humour and has originated a new concept and given a new word to the language, or at any rate a new suffix: -manship. This has been much borrowed since, as in Adlai Stevenson's coinage of 'brinkmanship'. The book was* The Theory and Practice of Gamesmanship; or the Art of Winning Games without Actually Cheating *by Stephen Potter.*

On the jacket of one of his -manship books, Potter described himself as 'Failed academic lecturer, failed novelist, failed literary biographer, reasonable compiler, reasonable educational pamphleteer, failed editor, failed book critic, failed rowing blue . . .' But this was pure authormanship. Like his recommendation of how to dedicate your book so as to soften the hearts of antagonistic critics: 'This book is for Tammy, in the hope that the precious gift of eyesight will soon be fully restored to her.' You do not mention that Tammy is your aunt and 97 years old.

In truth Potter was a writer of great erudition, charm and wit who had done great work in bringing those gifts to radio; with Joyce Grenfell he wrote and produced a series of mock feature programmes, the 'How' series, which was the foundation of that particular kind of broadcast humour.

After the great success of Gamesmanship, *Potter followed it up over the years with many more -manships, including* Lifemanship *(1950),* One-Upmanship *(1952), and* Supermanship *(1958). The style of all the books was academic, with prose of an appropriately scholarly seriousness and a profusion of diagrams, graphs, and footnotes.*

In the Introduction to Gamesmanship, *Potter tells of the glorious moment when the revelation came. He was playing tennis with Professor Joad, the philosopher [the people mentioned in the books are mostly real and Potter's friends] against Smith and Brown [fictional characters], two powerful and fit undergraduates:*

Score: forty-love. Smith at S^1 (see p. 12) is about to cross over to serve to me (at P). When Smith gets to a point (K) *not less than one foot and not more than two feet* beyond the centre of the court (I know now what I only felt then—that timing is everything in this gambit), Joad, (standing at J^2) called across the net, in an even tone:

'Kindly say clearly, please, whether the ball was in or out.'

Crude to our ears, perhaps. A Stone-Age implement. But beautifully accurate gamesmanship for 1931. For the student must realize that these two young men were both in the highest degree charming, well-mannered young men, perfect in their sportsmanship and behaviour. Smith (at point K) stopped dead.

Smith: I'm so sorry—I *thought* it was out. (*The ball had hit the back netting twelve feet behind him before touching the ground.*) But what did you think, Brown?

Brown: I *thought* it was out—but do let's have it again.

Joad: No, I don't want to have it again. I only want you to say clearly, if you will, whether the ball is in or out.

There is nothing more putting off to young university players than a slight suggestion that their etiquette or sportsmanship is in question. How well we know this fact, yet how often we forget to make use of it. Smith sent a double fault to me, and another double fault to Joad. He did not get in another ace service until halfway through the third set of a match which incidentally we won.

That night I thought long and hard. Could not this simple gambit of Joad's be extended to include other aspects of the game—to include all games? For me, it was the birth of gamesmanship.

From that simple beginning the science of gamesmanship grew, ever subtler and more effective.

Here is a brief report of a later gamesmanship 'play', developed over the years and now used with precision against Potter's friend 'Wayfarer':

(182) *Distinguished Visitor Play*. J. Strachey [real person: John Strachey, Eton and Magdalen College, Labour politician and Minister of Food] made beautiful use of this gambit in a recent lawn tennis doubles 'friendly' in which 'Wayfarer' was concerned. The game was played at a time when Anglo-****ish relations were cordial, but delicately balanced. 'To my surprise,' writes 'Wayfarer', 'Strachey, asking if he could bring his own partner, astonished us by turning up with the ****ish Ambassador. Before the game began Strachey took me aside to "explain the position". He suggested that the game should be played, "for obvious reasons", without gamesmanship. On the whole (he tipped me the wink) it would be no bad thing if the Ambassador (who was, of course, Strachey's partner) ended up on the winning side. "Someone on the highest level" had hinted as much to him.

'Pleased to comply, my partner and I obediently lost the first set. Before the next set began, however, Strachey let it slip out that he had been pulling our leg, that it was not the ****ish Ambassador at all, but—and here it seemed to me that I recognised the vaguely familiar face—one of the Oval Umpires who in his spare time played lawn tennis as a member of the East Kennington LTC. This silly trick angered me, and my play in the second set was not improved in consequence, particularly as we both drove hard at the Oval man's body but, in our annoyance, usually missed it. Two sets to Strachey.

'In the third set Strachey out-manœuvred us once more. He told us, finally, that in fact his partner really *was* the ****ish Ambassador, who, indeed, he turned out to be. This, of course, completely upset us, the remembrance of our rude behaviour in Set II rendering us almost incapable of returning the simplest ball. This gave Strachey the third set and the match.

'The whole game, which was played on an asphalt court, lasted exactly fifty-eight minutes.'

Stephen Potter (1900–69), *The Theory and Practice of Gamesmanship* (1947).

━━━━━━

CYRIL NORTHCOTE PARKINSON, *MA, Ph.D, F.R.Hist.S.; historian, journalist, novelist, author; Professor of History, University of Malaya; Visiting Professor, University of Harvard; Professor Emeritus and Hon. President, Troy State University, Alabama; and much more, could hardly be described as a typical professional humorist. Yet he, like Stephen Potter, had a good idea and wrote a hugely successful book about it,* Parkinson's Law.

This was the first humorous book to be a best-seller about the science, or whatever it is, of office management.

It was a kind of senior civil servant's vade mecum. *Its style, like Potter's, was cool, and Parkinson too deployed his arguments in a scholarly fashion and with diagrams.*

It was published in 1958 and was a brilliant counterblast to the many quasi-scientific manuals and courses on company organization then being promoted as the golden path to prosperity.

The phrase 'Parkinson's Law' passed into the language and became familiar to millions, most of whom had no idea what the law actually stated.

In the book Professor Parkinson first defines his law and then goes on to justify and extend it:

WORK EXPANDS SO AS TO FILL THE TIME AVAILABLE FOR ITS COMPLETION

General recognition of this fact is shown in the proverbial phrase 'It is the busiest man who has time to spare'. Thus, an elderly lady of leisure can spend the entire day in writing and dispatching a postcard to her niece at Bognor Regis. An hour will be spent finding the postcard, another in hunting for spectacles, half an hour in a search for the address, an hour and a quarter in composition, and twenty minutes in deciding whether or not to take an umbrella when going to the pillar box in the next street. The total effort that would occupy a busy man for three minutes all told may in this fashion leave another person prostrate after a day of doubt, anxiety, and toil.

Granted that work (and especially paperwork) is thus elastic in its demands on time, it is manifest that there need be little or no relationship between the work to be done and the size of the staff to which it may be assigned. A lack of real activity does not, of necessity, result in leisure. A lack of occupation is not necessarily revealed by a manifest idleness. The thing to be done swells in importance and complexity in a direct ratio with the time to be spent. This fact is widely recognized, but less attention has been paid to its wider implications, more especially in the field of public administration. Politicians and taxpayers have assumed (with occasional phases of doubt) that a rising total in the number of civil servants must reflect a growing volume of work to be done. Cynics, in questioning this belief, have imagined that the multiplication of officials must have left some of them idle or all of them able to work for shorter hours. But this is a matter in which faith and doubt seem equally misplaced. The fact is that the number of the officials and the quantity of the work are not related to each other at all. The rise in the total of those employed is governed by Parkinson's Law and would be much the same whether the volume of the work were to increase, diminish, or even disappear. The importance of Parkinson's Law lies in the fact that it is a law of growth based upon an analysis of the factors by which that growth is controlled.

The validity of this recently discovered law must rest mainly on statistical proofs, which will follow. Of more interest to the general reader is the explanation of the factors underlying the general tendency to which this law gives definition. Omitting technicalities (which are numerous) we may distinguish at the outset two motive forces. They can be represented for the present purpose by two almost axiomatic statements, thus: (1) 'An official wants to multiply subordinates, not rivals' and (2) 'Officials make work for each other.'

To comprehend Factor One, we must picture a civil servant, called A, who finds himself overworked. Whether this overwork is real or imaginary is immaterial, but we should observe, in passing, that A's sensation (or illusion) might easily result from his own decreasing energy: a normal symptom of middle age. For this real or imagined overwork there are, broadly speaking, three possible remedies. He may resign; he may ask to halve the work with a colleague called B; he may demand the assistance of two subordinates, to be called C and D. There is probably no instance, however, in history of A choosing any but the third alternative. By resignation he would lose his pension rights. By having B appointed, on his own level in the hierarchy, he would merely bring in a rival for promotion to W's vacancy when W (at long last) retires. So A would rather have C and D, junior men, below him. They will add to his consequence and, by dividing the work into two categories, as between C and D, he will have the merit of being the only man who comprehends them both. It is essential to realize at this point that C and D are, as it were, inseparable. To appoint C alone would have been impossible. Why? Because C, if by himself, would divide the work with A and so assume almost the equal status that has been refused in the first instance to B; a status the more emphasized if C is A's only possible successor. Subordinates must thus number two or more, each being thus kept in order by fear of the other's promotion. When C complains in turn of being overworked (as he certainly will) A will, with the concurrence of C, advise the appointment of two assistants to help C. But he can then avert internal friction only by advising the appointment of two more assistants to help D, whose position is much the same. With this recruitment of E, F, G, and H the promotion of A is now practically certain.

Seven officials are now doing what one did before. This is where Factor Two comes into operation. For these seven make so much work for each other that all are fully occupied and A is actually working harder than ever. An incoming document may well come before each of them in turn. Official E decides that it falls within the province of F, who places a draft reply before C, who amends it drastically before consulting D, who asks G to deal with it. But G goes on leave at this point, handing the file over to H, who drafts a minute that is signed by D and returned to C, who revises his draft accordingly and lays the new version before A.

What does A do? He would have every excuse for signing the thing unread, for he has many other matters on his mind. Knowing now that he is to succeed W next year, he has to decide whether C or D should succeed to his own office. He had to agree to G's going on leave even if not yet strictly entitled to it. He is worried whether H should not have gone instead, for reasons of health. He has looked pale recently—partly but not solely because of his domestic troubles. Then there is the business of F's special increment of salary for the period of the conference and E's application for transfer to the Ministry of Pensions. A has heard that D is in love with a married typist and that G and F are no longer on speaking terms—no one seems to know why. So A might be tempted to sign C's draft and have done with it. But A is a conscientious man. Beset as he is with problems created by his colleagues for themselves and for him—created by the mere fact of these officials' existence—he is not the man to shirk his duty. He reads through the draft with care, deletes the fussy paragraphs added by C and H, and restores the thing to the form preferred in the first instance by the able (if quarrelsome) F. He corrects the English—none of these young men can write grammatically— and finally produces the same reply he would have written if officials C to H had never been born. Far more people have taken far longer to produce the same result. No one has been idle. All have done their best. And it is late in the evening before A finally quits his office and begins the return journey to Ealing. The last of the office lights are being turned off in the gathering dusk that marks the end of another day's administrative toil. Among the last to leave, A reflects with bowed shoulders and a wry smile that late hours, like grey hairs, are among the penalties of success.

C. Northcote Parkinson (b. 1909), *Parkinson's Law: the Pursuit of Progress* (1958).

GEORGE MIKES *had his good idea in the early 1940s. Mikes (pronounced mee-kesh—but his real name was Siklos) was a Hungarian who studied law at Budapest University but preferred journalism as a career. To his dismay his editor sent him to England to cover the Munich crisis but he came to like English life and decided to stay, making a successful career as a humorous writer, broadcaster, and critic.*

The good idea which Mikes had was to write a kind of mock instruction manual for fellow aliens, purporting to help them understand English customs and traditions and the English temperament. Mikes was well equipped to undertake this if only because there is perhaps no continental more alien to English ways than a Hungarian.

How to be an Alien was published by the well-known publishing house of Andre Deutsch (another Hungarian) in 1946. It came out in paperback in 1966 and has been reprinted once a year ever since, except for 1978 and 1981 when it was reprinted twice a year.

Many more How to . . . *books followed, plus other books of humour, a novel, and a political volume or two but none were quite as successful as the first. The humour of national characteristics inevitably involves a deal of generalizing which can become tedious but Mikes managed to keep his touch light and witty.*

His observations on English mores were much enjoyed by English readers:

A WARNING TO BEGINNERS

In England* everything is the other way round.

On Sundays on the Continent even the poorest person puts on his best suit, tries to look respectable, and at the same time the life of the country becomes gay and cheerful; in England even the richest peer or motor-manufacturer dresses in some peculiar rags, does not shave, and the country becomes dull and dreary. On the Continent there is one topic which should be avoided—the weather; in England, if you do not repeat the phrase 'Lovely day, isn't it?' at least two hundred times a day, you are considered a bit dull . . .

On the Continent people have good food; in England people have good table manners . . .

Continental people are sensitive and touchy; the English take everything with an exquisite sense of humour—they are only offended if you tell them that they have no sense of humour. On the Continent the population consists of a small percentage of criminals, a small percentage of honest people and the rest are a vague transition between the two; in England you find a small percentage of criminals and the rest are honest people. On the other hand, people on the Continent either tell you the truth or lie; in England they hardly ever lie, but they would not dream of telling you the truth.

---

* When people say England, they sometimes mean Great Britain, sometimes the United Kingdom, sometimes the British Isles—but never England.

Many continentals think that life is a game; the English think cricket is a game.

TEA

The trouble with tea is that originally it was quite a good drink.

So a group of the most eminent British scientists put their heads together, and made complicated biological experiments to find a way of spoiling it.

To the eternal glory of British science their labour bore fruit. They suggested that if you do not drink it clear, or with lemon or rum and sugar, but pour a few drops of cold milk into it, and no sugar at all, the desired object is achieved. Once this refreshing, aromatic, oriental beverage was successfully transformed into colourless and tasteless gargling-water, it suddenly became the national drink of Great Britain and Ireland—still retaining, indeed usurping, the high-sounding title of tea . . .

I have coffee for breakfast; I drink innumerable cups of black coffee during the day; I have the most unorthodox teas even at tea-time.

The other day, for instance—I just mention this as a terrifying example to show you how low some people can sink—I wanted a cup of coffee and a piece of cheese for tea. It was one of those exceptionally hot days and my wife (once a good Englishwoman, now completely and hopelessly led astray by my wicked foreign influence) made some cold coffee and put it in the refrigerator, where it froze and became one solid block. On the other hand, she left the cheese on the kitchen table, where it melted. So I had a piece of coffee and a glass of cheese.

SEX

Continental people have sex life; the English have hot-water bottles.

George Mikes (1912–87), *How to be an Alien* (1946).

FOR *something like twenty years Caryl Brahms and S. J. Simon wrote a series of comic novels which began with an idea similar to George Mikes's but which they turned on its head.*

The idea, common to the two series of books, was the assumption, the basis of much comedy, that foreigners are funny. George Mikes, being a Hungarian, found the English funny; Brahms and Simon, both of foreign stock, rather surprisingly found the non-English funnier.

Caryl Brahms, ballet critic and a writer on all the visual arts, was born in England but her parents were immigrants; her mother was born in Constantinople. S. J. Simon, real name Skidelsky, was a Russian born in Manchuria. According to Caryl Brahms, all good young Russians want to study agriculture at university and then play bridge all day, which is more or less what Simon managed to do.

After university he became a journalist and writer on bridge, played the game semi-professionally, and in 1948, the year he died, was a member of the British International Bridge Team which won just about everything at Copenhagen.

Brahms and Simon met when they were freelance journalists and the first comic novel which they wrote together was a spoof on Russian ballet, that is to say a spoof on funny Russians and a spoof on a ballet company, on which two subjects each author was an expert. After two more books about funny Russians they moved on to writing funny historical stories ; the titles give the flavour : Don't Mr Disraeli, No Bed for Bacon.

The point about the Brahms/Simon books was their enormous vitality ; they crackled along, sparking off joke after joke like a catherine-wheel at full whirl.

Scenes were brief and flicked backwards and forwards as in the script of a comic film ; and like 1066 and All That *only the bits of history that most of us remember were used, usually plucked skilfully out of context and quoted with accuracy. Above all, a controlled lunacy, a confident dottiness illuminated the pages.*

No Bed for Bacon *told of Sir Francis Bacon's attempts to cadge one of the royal beds which Queen Elizabeth kept gracefully bestowing. The plot brought in Shakespeare, his producer Burbage, and the putting on of plays at the Theatre in the latter part of the sixteenth century.*

At rehearsal one of the players, the effete Master Melody, objects to a line and points out to Burbage that at his last theatre a hack was kept at hand to alter any lines with which the actors were not happy.

Richard Burbage looks round and calls out, 'Is Will Shakespeare in the house ?' :

SHAKSPURE

In a cold dark little room over against the back of the Theatre, Sir Francis Bacon was talking eloquently. Opposite him a melancholy figure sat tracing its signature on a pad.

> *Shakesper*
> *Shakspere*
> *Shekspar*

He always practised tracing his signature when he was bored. He was always hoping that one of these days he would come to a firm decision upon which of them he liked the best.

He looked at them. He considered them. He shook his head.

'Master Will,' said Bacon abruptly, 'I don't believe you're listening.'

Caught out, Shakespeare laid aside his pad. 'I heard every word,' he declared. 'You were saying something about a bed.'

'It is almost mine,' boasted Bacon. 'The next time the Queen goes on a Progress I am to have the first bed she sleeps in. The Master of the Revels has promised it faithfully this time.'

Shakespeare smiled.

'It was not his fault,' protested Bacon, 'that I did not get the bed on the

Progress to Warwick. Sir Philip Sydney,' he explained, 'turned a graceful compliment at a vital moment and the rash Queen gave it him for nothing.'

'And the Progress to Cheltenham?' asked Shakespeare. 'What went wrong there?'

Bacon blushed. 'The arrangements,' he admitted. 'It was delivered to some place in Stratford. It was the second-best bed, too.' He sighed.

Shakespeare looked elaborately out of the window.

'There seems to be quite a mode for Gloriana's bedsteads,' he observed.

'Enormous,' said Bacon. 'Every noble in the land covets one to leave to his children. Prices are soaring daily.'

'Quite an investment,' said Shakespeare.

Bacon looked at him. 'And now to business,' he said coldly. 'I am here, Master Will, upon a delicate errand. Gloriana wants to see a play.'

Shakespeare leapt to his feet. He knocked over his chair. He beamed. He shook Bacon by the hand.

'Which one?'

'Er,' said Bacon.

'I know,' flashed Shakespeare. 'It is *Romeo and Juliet*. We will play her the balcony scene as it has never yet been seen.'

'No,' said Bacon.

'*The Dream*,' said Shakespeare. 'With real nightingales,' he added ambitiously.

Bacon shook his head.

'*The Shrew? Much Ado? Two Gentlemen?*'

Bacon waved them away.

Shakespeare pondered. An awful thought struck him.

'Don't tell me,' he pleaded, 'that she's asked for *Timon of Athens*?'

'No, no,' said Bacon soothingly. 'She did not ask for that. As a matter of fact she did not ask for any of your plays. She did not even,' he added, enjoying his moment, 'specify the author.'

'Oh,' said Shakespeare, dimmed.

'So,' observed Bacon with irritating charm, 'I thought I might trickle it your way.' He made a descriptive gesture.

The curtains parted. A little old man came diffidently into the room. He had the rather lost air of a clown out of his part. Seeing Bacon, he checked, won his victory with a visible effort, and advanced.

'Master Will,' he asked, 'are you busy?'

'He is,' said Bacon coldly.

But Shakespeare smiled. 'What is it, Obadiah?'

The little man studied his toe. 'Just a thing I have been thinking about,' he said.

Bacon stirred restlessly.

'I could be very funny in it,' said the little man wistfully.

'Aha,' said Shakespeare. He leant back. 'Proceed,' he invited.

The little man broke into a babble. A mosaic of words, gestures, and mimicry filled the room, Soon the little man was acting all over it. Bacon looked at him in some disgust. It didn't even make sense. But Shakespeare was listening with that intentness that a wise playwright will never grudge his clown. From time to time he nodded. He did not need adjectives and verbs to translate the thoughts in a player's mind. He did not need rhetoric and couplets to tell him that his clown was offering him not only an interpretation but a creation. He had not yet made friends with this creation, but already he was making room in his mind to receive it. Yet like every author faced with the prospect of more work, his first comment was an objection.

'A grave-digger,' he said. 'How can I be funny about a grave-digger?'

'I will show you,' said Obadiah Croke eagerly. He mouthed a bit more. 'Master Will,' he pleaded, 'only give me a graveyard and together we will work out the business to crack the sides of the groundlings.'

'A graveyard,' said Shakespeare reflectively. He stroked his beard.

'A graveyard,' said Bacon, hoping to cut the argument short, 'is not comical.'

But Shakespeare rounded on him. The opposition had provided just the stimulation he needed.

'But it is hugely funny,' he said. 'A graveyard. Think of it.' He roared with laughter.

Obadiah Croke thought of it. He roared with laughter.

Bacon thought of it ('Men feare *death* as Children feare to goe in the darke'). He looked at the boisterous children in front of him. He marvelled.

'A graveyard,' repeated Shakespeare, wiping his eyes.

'With a grave-digger,' said Obadiah with relish.

'Two grave-diggers,' said Shakespeare, overcome at the thought.

They looked at the marvelling Bacon. They roared again.

Obadiah sobered first.

'That's a fine idea, Master Will,' he said. 'I could use a second grave-digger for a feed. A smaller part, of course.'

'Of course,' said Shakespeare. He pulled up a chair. 'Sit down, my good Obadiah,' he invited, 'I'll tell you how I see it.'

Obadiah sat down. Soon they were immersed in props and business.

Behind them Bacon paced restlessly up and down.

'But,' said Shakespeare some twenty minutes later, 'how do I get him off?'

Player and author looked at one another in dismay.

Bacon seized his opportunity. He took Obadiah Croke firmly by the shoulders and trundled him out of the room.

'Like this,' he said.

He came back. He sat down. He crossed his legs.

But Shakespeare had jumped to his feet and run to the doorway.

'Obadiah,' he shouted. 'I've got it! We won't take you off at all. We'll let you meet the hero. With a skeleton,' he promised.

A confused babble came down the passage.

Rubbing his hands, Shakespeare returned to his desk.

'He likes it,' he told Bacon happily.

Bacon spread his hands to heaven. These players!

'And now,' said Shakespeare cosily, 'what is it we were talking about, my friend?'

Back at the Theatre Shakespeare and Bacon were talking figures.

'A shipwreck,' said Shakespeare, tapping the list in front of him. 'An impersonation, three songs for a baritone, a sorting out, and a happy ending. That,' he decided, 'will be forty pounds.'

'Too much,' said Bacon promptly.

'Too much!' said Shakespeare. 'Forty pounds too much for a new play by Will Shakespeare!'

Bacon remained unmoved. 'Beaumont and Fletcher,' he said, 'would do it for a ten-pound note. What is more,' he pointed out, 'there are two of them.'

'Beaumont and Fletcher!' said Shakespeare. He picked up his quill. *Shakespaw*, he scribbled viciously. Clearly he was about to fly into a passion.

'Master Will,' said Bacon hastily. 'I was speaking only in terms of money. I was not, of course, in any way comparing their work with yours.'

'Ten pounds,' said Shakespeare, only partly mollified. 'It is an affront! Why my Lord of Southampton pays me more than that for a sonnet.'

'No doubt,' Bacon agreed. 'But all the same, forty pounds is too costly for Gloriana.'

Shakespeare got up.

'Master Bacon,' he said, 'you are reasoning like a child. For ten pounds Beaumont and Fletcher will give you any one of a dozen plays—each indistinguishable from the other. They have only to open a drawer—any drawer—and pick the first. But for my forty pounds I will give you,' he smiled, 'Illyria.'

Bacon nodded. 'But all the same,' he said, 'forty pounds.'

'What is more,' said Shakespeare generously, 'I will throw you in, without extra charge, a comic lord. I have a perfect name for him.' He beamed. 'Sir Toby Belch.'

'Good God,' said Bacon.

'Mind you,' said Shakespeare, 'I was reserving him for my Merry Wives, but for Gloriana I will transfer him to Illyria and make do with Falstaff.'

'You killed him off last week,' said Bacon. 'Hal Five,' he reminded him.

'So I did,' said Shakespeare, crestfallen. 'I remember—a' babbled of green fields. But no matter,' he brightened, 'he shall come to life again.' He sat down. 'I think I see how I am to do it.' He picked up his quill. He was immersed.

Bacon took away the quill.

'Master Will,' he said. 'Back to your muttons, I beg. Let me remind you that I have not come here this day to act as audience to your grave-diggers, nor to aid you in resurrecting characters for Master Burbage, nor to stand mute while your genius uses up your paper and my time.'

'Mm,' said Shakespeare. He sighted another quill, pounced on it, and went on scribbling.

'But,' said Bacon, removing this quill also, 'I am here because the Queen has charged me with finding a diversion for my Lord Essex.'

'Essex!' said Shakespeare with strong disapproval. 'Why did you not tell me this earlier, my lord? Now,' he said firmly, 'the price is fifty.'

The curtains parted. Prometheus Melody inserted his head carefully between the folds.

'Your servant, sir,' he said, 'and could you direct me to the hack's room?'

'You have arrived,' said Shakespeare shortly.

'Indeed,' said Master Melody. He advanced into the room. He dusted a chair. He sat down cautiously.

'And which of you gentlemen,' he asked, 'is the author?'

Shakespeare looked at Bacon, but Bacon was looking at the aesthetic Master Melody. Shakespeare smiled.

'I am the author,' he said. 'What is amiss?'

'This,' said Master Melody. He got up, pulled out the part he had refused to read at rehearsal, folded it to the offending lines, and thrust it into the playwright's hands.

'Young man,' he said, 'read me these lines, if you can.'

Shakespeare drew himself up.

'IF I CAN!'

A lesser man would have given ground. But not Prometheus Melody, the Essex of Blackfriars. He was not going to be cowed by a mere hack who did not even bother to wear a ruff in his workroom.

'If you can,' he challenged.

Shakespeare looked at them. He glanced at the lines. He declaimed them.

'This mumbling mongrel,' jeered Master Melody.

'Who,' he appealed to Bacon, 'has ever heard a mongrel mumbling?'

'Who indeed?' agreed Bacon courteously.

Shakespeare looked at them. His anger vanished. He smiled.

'Leave these lines with me,' he said. 'We will see what the hack can do with them.'

He read them over to himself. He tasted the adjectives. Clearly they could be used in that shining play these people would never give him time to write, *Love's Labour's Won*.

'I think,' he said, 'we might cut them out of Romeo altogether.'

But Bacon and Melody had forgotten all about him. They were strolling out together and conversing amiably.

'By the way, Master Melody,' Bacon was saying, 'what are you doing after the play on Friday?'

Shakepeare smiled again. He sat down. He spread a fresh sheet of parchment. He reached for his quill. He wrote:

LOVE'S LABOUR'S WON

A Play in Five Acts by William Shakespere

He crossed out *Shakespere* and wrote *Shakspure*.

The curtains parted. Richard Burbage came in.

'Will,' he said, 'are you busy?'

Shakespeare sighed and pushed his precious foolscap into a drawer.

'No,' he said, resigned. 'Not at all. Only a new part for Master Melody, a new scene for Obadiah, and a new play for Gloriana and my Lord of Essex.'

Burbage brushed these trifles aside.

'I've been thinking,' he said. 'I'd like to play a Dane—young, intellectual—I see him pale, vacillating, but above everything sad and prone to soliloquy.'

'I know,' said Shakespeare. 'Introspective.'

The curtains parted. Bacon had come back. He pulled out a sheaf of papers from his pocket and laid them on the desk.

'By the way, Will,' he said. 'I almost forgot. When you've got a moment to spare, you might polish up this essay . . .'

> Caryl Brahms and S. J. Simon (1901–82); 1902–48, *No Bed for Bacon* (1941).

———

I N the 1940s and 1950s there was a surge of what might be termed 'professional' humour, not professional in the sense that it earned money, though the best of it did this most satisfactorily, but because it was humour based on a profession. Usually that of the writer.

A fine example of professional humour is Richard Gordon's perpetually popular Doctor in the House, an autobiographical novel which tells the story of the training and early experiences of a young medical man, Richard Gordon himself. The success of the book inevitably brought about a swarm of imitations, jolly/grisly reminscences of other blood-letting toilers from dentists to vets. But none equalled the original as a work of humour.

Richard Gordon, real name Dr Gordon Ostlere, was, like Tobias Smollett and Eugene Sue, a member of that small group which managed to succeed in two professions; ship's doctor and author. Gordon had also been an anaesthetist at St Bartholomew's Hospital and assistant editor of the British Medical Journal.

It has been said that anything to do with hospitals and somebody else's suffering is a sure-fire subject for entertainment but Gordon really earned his success; he incorporated a large quantity of traditional medical yarns and students' anecdotes, cunningly edited and shaped, into the Doctor stories, and his characters are not types but rounded and believable people. One of the great strengths of Gordon's humour is that it is so well written.

Sir Lancelot Spratt, the Consulting Surgeon of the books, the Chief, might seem at first glance to be a fraction overdrawn, to be just a bit too autocratic and awesome to be real. But to a young medical student? With no confidence? Having to walk the hospital's surgery wards beside this formidable figure?

The Chief spent two hours examining the candidates for the afternoon's operating list, with whom he illustrated to us the principles of surgery. Sometimes he passed all morning on one case, if the patient contained a lump of sufficient interest to him; on other Tuesdays he would whip round the whole ward, diagnosing like a machine-gun. Sitting was forbidden, and towards lunchtime the students shifted heavily from one foot to the other. Sir Lancelot thought any young man incapable of standing on his own feet for a couple of hours as another disagreeable product of modern life, like socialism.

On our first ward round we were pushed easily into place by the precision with which the rest of the troupe fell in. Sir Lancelot strode across the ward, drew up sharply, and looked over the patients in the two rows of beds, sniffing the air like a dog picking up a scent. He thundered over to the bedside of a small, nervous man in the corner. The firm immediately rearranged itself, like a smart platoon at drill. The Chief towered on the right of the patient's head; Sister stood opposite, her nurses squeezed behind her; the students surrounded the foot and sides of the bed like a screen; and the registrar and housemen stood beyond them, at a distance indicating that they were no longer in need of any instruction in surgery.

Sir Lancelot pulled back the bedclothes like a conjurer revealing a successful trick.

'You just lie still, old fellow,' he boomed cheerfully at the patient. 'Don't you take any notice of what I'm going to say to these young doctors. You won't understand a word of what we're talking about, anyway. Take his pyjamas off, Sister. Now you, my boy,' he continued, gripping me tightly by the arm as I was nearest, 'take a look at that abdomen.'

I stretched out a hand to feel the patient gingerly in the region of the umbilicus. I noticed his skin was covered with goose-pimples and twitched here and there nervously.

'Take your dirty little hand away!' said Sir Lancelot savagely, flicking it off the surface of the abdomen like a fly. He paused solemnly, and continued in a heavy tone, wagging his finger: 'The first rule of surgery, gentlemen— eyes first and most, hands next and least, tongue not at all. Look first and don't chatter. An excellent rule for you to remember all your lives. Now look, boy, look.'

I gazed at the abdomen for a whole minute but it appeared no different from any that might be seen on Brighton beach. When I thought I had inspected it long enough to satisfy the Chief, who rose uncomfortably above me, I diffidently stretched out my arm and prodded about with my finger in search of a lump.

'*Doucemong, doucemong*,' Sir Lancelot began again. 'Gently, boy—you're not making bread. Remember'—his finger came up again warningly—'a successful surgeon must have the eye of a hawk, the heart of a lion, and the hand of a lady.'

'And the commercial morals of a Levantine usurer,' murmured Grimsdyke under his breath.

With a flow of relief, I finally discovered the lump. It was about the size of an orange and tucked under the edge of the ribs. We lined up and felt it one after the other, while Sir Lancelot looked on closely and corrected anyone going about it the wrong way. Then he pulled a red grease-pencil from the top pocket of his coat and handed it to me.

'Where are we going to make the incision?' he asked. By now the patient was forgotten; it was the lump we were after. Sir Lancelot had an upsetting habit of treating the owners of lumps as if they were already rendered unconscious by the anaesthetic.

I drew a modest line over the lesion.

'Keyhole surgery!' said Sir Lancelot with contempt. 'Damnable! Give me the pencil!' He snatched it away. 'This, gentlemen, will be our incision.'

He drew a broad, decisive, red sweep from the patient's ribs to below his umbilicus.

'We will open the patient like *that*. Then we can have a good look inside. It's no good rummaging round an abdomen if you can't get your hand in comfortably. What do we do then? Right—take a better look at the lump we've been feeling. Do you think it's going to be easy to remove?' he asked me, gripping my arm again.

'No, sir.'

'Correct—it's going to be most difficult. And dangerous. There are at least a dozen ways in which we can make a slight error—even though we are experienced surgeons—and kill the patient like that!' He snapped his fingers frighteningly.

'Now!' He tapped the abdomen with his pencil as if knocking for admission. 'When we have cut through the skin what is the next structure we shall meet? Come on, you fellers. You've done your anatomy more recently than I have . . . what's that? Yes, subcutaneous fat. Then, gentlemen, we first encounter the surgeon's worst enemy.' He glared at us all in turn. 'What?' he demanded in general. There was no reply. 'Blood!' he thundered.

At that point the patient restored his personality to the notice of his doctors by vomiting.

In the afternoon the famous surgeon, his assistants, and the troupe of uneasy students assemble in the operating theatre. The students are to see for the first time the famous surgeon actually wielding the healing scalpel.

They gather in a tight group round the operating table, our hero safely tucked away at the back. But the famous surgeon commands our hero to step closer . . . :

The only indication that there was a patient present at all was a pair of feet in thick, coarse-knitted bed-socks that stuck pathetically from one end of the audience.

As soon as Sir Lancelot spoke, the group round the table opened as if he were Aladdin at the mouth of his cave. I walked unhappily into the centre. My companions closed tightly behind me, and I found myself wedged against the table opposite Sir Lancelot with a man who played in the second row of the hospital forwards immediately behind me. Escape was therefore out of the question, on physical as well as moral grounds.

The operation was on the point of starting. The patient was still invisible, as the body was covered with sterile towels except for a clean-shaved strip of lower abdomen on the right-hand side of which the operating light was focused diagnostically. I couldn't even see if it was a young man or a woman.

Having forced me into a ringside seat, Sir Lancelot then appeared to dismiss me from his mind. He paused to adjust the cuff of the rubber glove that stretched over his bony hand. Stubbins and Crate were waiting with gauze dabs, and the theatre sister was threading needles with catgut as unconcernedly as if she was going to darn her stockings.

'Stubbins,' said Sir Lancelot chattily, making a three-inch incision over the appendix, 'remind me to look into Fortnum's on my way home, there's a good lad. My missus'll give me hell if I forget her dried ginger again. I suppose it was all right for me to start?' he asked the anaesthetist.

The *Daily Telegraph* rustled slightly in assent.

I was surprised. Dried ginger in an operating theatre? Shopping lists disturbing the sanctity of surgery? And the *Daily Telegraph*?

'I've got a damn funny story to tell you lads,' went on Sir Lancelot affably, deepening his incision. 'Make you all laugh. Happened to me last week. An old lady turned up in my rooms in Harley Street . . . Sister!' he exclaimed in a tone of sudden annoyance, 'do you expect me to operate with a jam-spreader? This knife's a disgrace.'

He threw it on the floor. Without looking at him she handed him another.

'That's better,' Sir Lancelot growled. Then, in his previous tone, as though he were two people making conversation, he went on: 'Where was I? Oh yes, the old lady. Well, she said she'd come to see me on the advice of Lord—Lord Someoneorother, I can't remember these damn titles—whom I'd operated on last year. She said she was convinced she'd got gallstones.

'Now look here, Stubbins, can't you and Crate keep out of each other's way? Your job is to use that gauze swab sensibly, not wave it around like a Salvation Army banner. How the devil do you think I can operate properly if everything's wallowing in blood? Why am I always cursed with assistants who have a couple of left hands? And I want a clip, Sister. Hurry up, woman, I can't wait all night!'

Sir Lancelot had cut through the abdominal wall while he was talking, like a child impatient to see inside a Christmas parcel.

'Well,' he went on, all affability again, seemingly conducting the operation with the concentration of a gossipy woman knitting a pair of socks, 'I said to this old lady, "Gallstones, eh? Now, my dear, what makes you think you've got gallstones?" And I've never seen anyone look so embarrassed in my life!'

He returned to the operation.

'What's this structure, gentlemen?'

A reply came from under a student's mask on the edge of the crowd.

'Quite correct, whoever you are,' said Sir Lancelot, but without any congratulation in his voice. 'Glad to see you fellers remember a little fundamental anatomy from your two years in the rooms . . . so I wondered what was up. After all, patients don't get embarrassed over gallstones. It's only piles and things like that, and even then it's never the old ladies who are coy but the tough young men. Remember that bit of advice, gentlemen . . . Come on, Stubbins, wake up! You're as useless as an udder on a bull.'

He produced the appendix from the wound like a bird pulling a worm from the ground, and laid it and the attached intestine on a little square of gauze.

'Then the old lady said to me, "As a matter of fact, Sir Lancelot, I've been passing them all month . . ." Don't lean on the patient, Stubbins! If I'm not tired you shouldn't be, and I can give you forty or fifty years, my lad.

'So now we come to the interesting part of the story. She showed me a little box, like those things you sent out pieces of wedding cake in . . . Sister! What in the name of God are you threading your needles with? This isn't catgut, it's rope. What's that, woman?' He leant the red ear that stuck out below his cap towards her. 'Speak up, don't mutter to yourself. I'm not being rude, damn you! I'm never rude in the theatre. All right, tell your Matron, but give us a decent ligature. That's more like it. Swab, man, swab. Stubbins, did I ever tell you about the Matron when she was a junior theatre nurse? She had a terrible crush on a fellow house-surgeon of mine—chap called Bungo Ross, used to drink like a fish and a devil for the women. Became a respected G.P. in Bognor or somewhere. Died last year. I wrote a damn good obituary for him in the *British Medical Journal*. I'm tying off the appendicular artery, gentlemen. See? What's that, Stubbins? Oh, the old lady. Cherry stones.'

He tossed the appendix into a small enamel bowl held for him by Stubbins.

'Looks a bit blue this end, George,' he said in the direction of the anaethetist. 'All right, I suppose?' The anaesthetist was at the time in the corner of the theatre talking earnestly to one of the nurses who had been serving out the instruments. Theatre kit is unfair to nurses; it makes them look like white bundles. But one could tell from the rough shape of this one, from the little black-stockinged ankles below her gown and the two wide eyes above her mask, that the parcel would be worth the unwrapping. The anaesthetist jumped back to his trolley and began to twiddle the knobs on it. Sister, who was already in a wild temper, injected the nurse with a glance like a syringeful of strychnine.

'Forceps, Sister!' bellowed Sir Lancelot. She handed him a pair which he looked at closely, snapping them together in front of his mask. For some reason they displeased him, so he threw them over the heads of the crowd at the opposite wall. This caused no surprise to anyone, and seemed to be one of his usual habits. She calmly handed him another pair.

'Swabs correct, Sister, before I close? Good. Terribly important that, gentlemen. Once you've left a swab inside a patient you're finished for life. Courts, damages, newspapers, and all that sort of thing. It's the only disaster in surgery the blasted public thinks it knows anything about. Cut their throats when they're under the anaesthetic, yes, but leave anything inside and you're in the *News of the World* in no time. Shove in the skin stitches, Stubbins. What's the next case? Tea? Excellent. Operating always makes me thirsty.'

Richard Gordon (b. 1921), *Doctor in the House* (1952).

———

THREE *years after* Doctor in the House *was published*, Brothers in Law *attempted—successfully, as it turned out—to do for young barristers what* Doctor *had done for young medical men.*

The authors were of a somewhat different nature. Brothers in Law *was written by Henry Cecil, whose real name was His Honour Judge Leon, MC. His Honour Judge Leon was known to barristers as a rather quirky and unpredictable judge (bad news to a barrister) but as Henry Cecil the author he was a delightful man, tremendously gregarious and kindly but also sceptical and shrewd. He was a little stage-struck but deeply, to coin a phrase, book-struck.* Doctor in the House *was Richard Gordon's first book but* Brothers in Law *was Henry Cecil's seventh. He was a compulsive maker of books; his final score—impressive for the part-time occupation of a full-time County Court Judge, was 25 novels, 7 books of non-fiction, 8 plays (mostly written in collaboration with experienced dramatists and one,* Settled Out of Court, *with, and it must have been an extraordinary experience for both of them, the American/Armenian novelist, William Saroyan), and two television series (written in collaboration with the less spectacular Frank Muir and Denis Norden).*

Henry Cecil's humour was not read for the quality of his prose and characterization but for his plots and the charm of his dialogue. All his stories were concerned with some odd aspect of the law which he made understandable and funny. His characters were difficult to distinguish one from the other as they all spoke more or less in the same idiom; middle-class lady, racing tout, vicar,

policeman, viscount, burglar, all—apart from an occasional interjection such as
'blimey' to indicate class—spoke with intelligent fluency. His young lovers seemed
to be cut from thin but stiff cardboard, but his court cases were marvellously witty
and funny.

In Brothers in Law, *in place of the young 'doctor in the house', Simon Sparrow,*
there is the young law student, Roger Thursby, now qualified and in court for the
first time. Instead of Simon's dread Consultant Surgeon, Sir Lancelot Spratt, Roger
has his Head of Chambers, the peripatetic Mr Grimes, not an ogre but a bustling,
busy barrister who has to appear in several court cases at the same time (a quite
common and profitable practice amongst busy barristers).

So Roger, instead of sitting peacefully in court watching Mr Grimes pleading, is
unexpectedly left to argue all by himself a case about which he knows nothing.
And, what is more, in front of a wickedly playful judge, Sir Hugo (almost certainly
a fictionalized sketch of His Honour Judge Leon himself):

'Take a note, my dear fellow,' whispered Mr Grimes to Roger.

'What in?' asked Roger.

'A notebook, my dear fellow—I'm sorry, your Honour. I was just arranging
with my learned friend Mr—Mr Thorburn—'

'Yes, yes,' said Sir Hugo, 'but these devilling arrangements should be made
beforehand. I take it that I'm going to be deprived of the pleasure of hearing
your further argument, Mr Grimes.'

'Only for a very short time, your Honour. I'm on my feet before Mr Justice
Nettlefold.'

Sir Hugo removed his spectacles and looked at Mr Grimes, with a puzzled
air for a moment, 'Oh, of course,' he said. 'The prophetic present. Well, I
mustn't keep you, Mr Grimes. Very good of you to come at all and I'm sure
your learned junior will fill your place admirably while you are away.'

'It's very good of your Honour,' said Mr Grimes and with a few whispered
words to Roger—'Ye'll be all right, my dear fellow, just tell him the tale, just
tell him the tale,' Mr Grimes was gone.

It had happened so quickly that Roger had difficulty in realizing that he,
Roger Thursby Esq., barrister-at-law, aged twenty-one, called to the Bar two
days previously, had been left in Court to represent one side or the other (he
did not know which) in a building dispute before a judge called an Official
Referee, of whom he had only vaguely heard. He looked round the Court.
There was not a face he knew. Something inside his head began to go
round and round and the Official Referee's face started to approach him with
alarming swiftness. He realized that he must pull himself together or faint.
Sir Hugo addressed him:

'Now that the wind has dropped, Mr Truefold, would you continue your
learned leader's submission?' Roger wished he had fainted. He rose unsteadily, and looked blankly in front of him.

'Your learned leader was saying,' went on Sir Hugo who, without intending to be unkind, enjoyed this sort of scene immensely, 'let me see—what was he saying? Something about malt, I believe. Strange, in a building dispute. Ah—no, I remember—he was submitting that the onus was on the other side. No doubt you would like to elaborate the submission?'

Roger continued to look blankly in front of him. It was not that the power of speech had left him, but he simply did not know what to say. He had sufficient presence of mind to realize that, if he started, 'Your Honour' and then paused, the Official Referee would, after waiting a decent interval, say, 'Yes, Mr Truefold?' and then he would either have to repeat, 'Your Honour' or lapse into silence again. It was better not to break it at all unless and until he could think of one sentence which meant something. The only sentence he could think of was: 'I want to go home,' and that wouldn't do at all. It flashed through his mind that he could pretend to faint and he cursed himself for having resisted a moment before the genuine impulse to do so. But he had a natural inclination to tell the truth. This was sometimes embarrassing in his relations with Sally and Joy, but they were a long way from his mind at this particular moment. He remained standing and staring and thinking for the thoughts which would not come.

'Come, Mr Trueband,' said Sir Hugo affably, 'it's quite calm now. Shall we proceed?'

There was nothing for it. 'Your Honour,' he began—and then came the inevitable pause. Sir Hugo looked enquiringly at him, and so did counsel on the other side and, indeed, nearly everyone in the Court.

The pause had already passed the stage at which it became unbearable when Sir Hugo duly came in with the expected 'Yes, Mr Truefold?' to which Roger replied with the only words he had so far learned: 'Your Honour,' and again there was that terrible pause. Eventually Sir Hugo broke it with: 'I suppose you say that the defendants, having admitted that the work was done and that it had not been paid for, it is for them to show that parts of it have been properly done?'

With relief which he could not conceal, Roger added a word to his repertoire. 'Yes, Your Honour,' he said, and getting bolder—'I do.' Then, 'Your Honour,' he added, in case the emphasis sounded rude.

'An admirable submission, Mr Truelove,' said Sir Hugo, 'and very succinctly put. But,' and he paused and frowned for a moment. 'But,' he went on, 'isn't it for the plaintiff in the first instance to give evidence that he has performed his contract—and can he do that without showing that the work was properly done?'

Roger's boldness vanished. The only truthful answer he could make would have been: 'I don't know.' But that wouldn't do. So he adopted his first line of defence, of standing and staring, keeping a 'Your Honour' in reserve for use if necessary.

'You can't very well rely,' went on Sir Hugo, 'on the maxim *omnia rite,* etc.—incidentally, I never can remember exactly how it goes.'

'*Omnia rite ac sollemniter esse acta praesumuntur,*' said Roger, thanking his patron saint for making him learn that legal maxim for his Bar examinations.

'Thank you, Mr Tredgold,' said Sir Hugo, 'thank you very much. But you can't rely on that maxim in a case such as the present, can you?'

At any rate, there was an answer to that which made sense.

'I suppose not, Your Honour.'

'Or can you, perhaps?' went on Sir Hugo. 'I'm not sure. Perhaps you could refer me to one or two of the authorities on the point.'

At this juncture, Roger's opponent could not resist getting up and saying:

'Surely, Your Honour, there is no presumption in law that a builder always does the right thing. If there were any presumption I should have thought it would have been the other way about.'

'Well, to whom does the presumption apply, do you think?' said Sir Hugo, mercifully directing his question to Roger's opponent. 'To Official Referees, perhaps?'

At that moment Alec came into Court, although Roger did not see him. Mr Grimes had managed to take over the reins from Charles in the running down case, not without a little obstruction from Mr Justice Nettlefold who disliked Mr Grimes's habit of chopping and changing and who, besides, was now running cheerfully along with the plaintiff. 'Mr Hepplewhite is deputizing very satisfactorily for you, Mr Grimes,' the judge said quite untruthfully—except in the sense that, as the judge was doing all the work for the plaintiff, it was quite satisfactory from that gentleman's point of view. However, eventually the judge allowed himself to be persuaded and Mr Grimes took over. The plaintiff did not do quite so well after that. This was no fault of Mr Grimes. It is just the way things happen. Once Alec had seen Mr Grimes safely into Court before Mr Justice Nettlefold he returned to the Official Referee's Court to see what was happening there, ready to send the junior clerk—who had now come over with him—sprinting round to fetch Mr Grimes if disaster seemed imminent.

'Anyway,' went on Sir Hugo, 'isn't there anything to be done in this case? Is there a Scott Schedule, Mr Trueband?' and he turned pleasantly and enquiringly to Roger. Roger was still standing and the relief when the Official Referee started to address his opponent was so great that he had begun to feel the warm blood moving through his veins again. But at the mention of 'Scott Schedule' it froze again. What on earth was a Scott Schedule? He thought of Sir Walter Scott and Scott the explorer. He thought of Scotland. Perhaps Sir Hugo had said Scotch Schedule. Just as people sometimes have an insane urge to throw themselves in front of tube trains, Roger suddenly had an urge to say: 'No, Your Honour, but I think there's an Irish stew.' That would be the end of his career at the Bar. Short and inglorious. But over. No more standing and staring and freezing and boiling. Which is worse, a cold sweat or a hot sweat? All these thoughts crammed themselves confusedly into his mind as he stood miserably waiting. Then he heard a voice from the ceiling of the Court:

'A Scott Schedule, Your Honour?' it said.

He knew that it was his voice really, but he did not feel himself speak and he never knew his voice sounded like that.

'Yes, Mr Trueglove. Is there one? Or perhaps Mr Grimes ran away with it.'

Roger endeavoured to smile, but it was very difficult. After what seemed an age his opponent came to his rescue.

'I'm afraid there isn't, Your Honour.'

Henry Cecil (Henry Cecil Leon) (1902–76), *Brothers in Law* (1955).

A GENRE *of comedy which was consistently popular in the United States but never had much appeal in Britain was campus humour; fun and games at university.*

Britain had the occasional success, like the Victorian comic novel, The Adventures of Mr Verdant Green, *but perhaps because British universities were until recent years only attended by a privileged minority, they held only a minority interest; there was never in Britain a national and grown-up fascination with the humour and the high jinks of campus life as reflected in the USA by early Hollywood comedy films, books, cartoons and university comic magazines. Many college humour magazines had mass circulations outside the colleges and were the training ground of such writers as Perelman, Benchley, E. B. White, and James Thurber.*

*Max Shulman, the comic novelist, short-story writer, playwright (*The Tender Trap*), and screenplay writer, was the doyen of college humorists, even writing a syndicated campus newspaper column for sixteen years which he called* On Campus. *It all began when he was in the Army Air Force during the war and had a huge success with a farcical novel in which a poor farm-lad told of his experiences at a Mid-West university. The book, which later became a Broadway musical, was named (good title)* Barefoot Boy With Cheek.

It is clear from the opening pages of the book that Shulman's parodical prose-style owes a very great deal to S. J. Perelman, particularly to 'Strictly from Hunger'. But the book is full-length (which was beyond Perelman) and it brims over with bright, frisky, very American gags and comic ideas:

The morning of the big day dawned bright and clear. As the rosy fingers of the sun crept through my window and illuminated the C&H on my homemade bed sheet, I could scarcely contain myself. 'Huzzah!' I shouted. 'Huzzah!'

I bounded joyously from my bed. I bounded right back again. My drop-seat pajamas had become entangled in a bed-spring during the night. Disengaging myself, I ran to wake Mother. 'Mother,' I called. 'Mother, give me to eat.'

But loveable old Mother had anticipated me. She had been up for hours. While I had lain in drowsyland, she had slaughtered the brood sow and bustled about preparing the morning meal. When I came into the kitchen my favourite breakfast was already on the table.

'Mother!' I cried. 'Johnson grass and brala suet. Just for me.'

'Set down and eat, slugabed,' she chided gently. 'You don't want to be late the first day.'

I could not help taking her in my arms and kissing her careworn cheek. A person can choose his friends and select a wife, but he has only one mother, I always say. The trouble with many of us is that we don't appreciate our mothers. I think that a certain day should be set aside each year and dedicated to mothers. It could be called 'Mother's Day'.

'Son,' she said, 'you ain't my baby no more.'

'The hell you say, Mother,' I said. 'The hell you say.'

'You're agoin' off to thet air university and get your haid all full of larnin,' and you're gonna fergit your pore old igerant mother.'

'Aw, you're not so dumb,' I protested.

'Yes, I be,' she declared. 'I don't know no more than your old houn' dog Edmund layin' over there by the stove.'

I jumped up from the table. 'Now just you be careful what you're saying about Edmund. I don't mean to have that dog run down when I'm here. He's a mighty smart dog.' I whistled to him. 'Play dead, Edmund,' I said. 'See,' I said to Mother. 'Look at how he obeys. All four feet sticking up in the air.'

'He ain't playin,' son,' said Mother softly. 'I didn't want to tell you. He's been dead since Friday.'

Edmund dead! I couldn't believe it. Why, only last Friday I had seen him happily flushing grouse. In his excitement he had flushed too many, and we had had to call a plumber. But it was all fixed now, and Edmund was forgiven. Naturally, I had punished him, but—No. No! I couldn't have—

'Mother!' I cried.

'Yes, son,' she said. 'He died right after. That last time you ran over him with the car did it.'

I stumbled over to the window and pressed my hot forehead against the pane. A cloud passed over the sun, and it began to rain. The room was oppressively quiet. A loon cried over the lake.

Father came into the kitchen. 'Good morning, son,' he said. 'I came to say good-by before you went off to the University.'

'Thank you,' I said simply.

'Button your fly,' Mother said.

'Oh, button your lip,' Father exclaimed testily, and hit her in the mouth with a skillet. Mother went to weld her dentures.

Father came over and put his arm around me. 'Son, today you are entering a new phase of your life.'

'Oh, can't you leave me alone?' I snapped. 'Can't anybody leave me alone?'

Father drew back. 'Why son, what's the matter? This should be the happiest day in your life.'

I laughed ironically. 'The happiest day of your life, he says.'

'No, no,' Father interrupted. 'I said the happiest day *in* your life. Not *of*— *in*!'

'Oh. Excuse me. The happiest day in your life, he says.' I lifted my clenched fists. 'Oh, ironical gods! What a mockery you have made of this day.'

'Why, son, what—'

I pointed mutely at Edmund.

'I understand,' said Father simply.

The door opened and two men from the animal rescue league came in. They took Edmund. 'Neighbours been complaining,' one of them explained.

Father put an arm round my shaking shoulders. 'You know, son,' he said, 'I had a dog once. A little Pekingese bitch named Anna May.'

'Is it true what they say about the Pekingese, Father?' I asked.

He winked obscenely and continued: 'She wasn't much of a dog, I guess. She couldn't hunt. She was no good as a watchdog. All she did all day long was lie on a chaise longue reading slim yellow French novels and eating bonbons. But when I came home from a hard day at the egg candlery, Anna May was always waiting, wagging her little tail and being sick on the rug. I— I guess I loved her, that's all,' Father said.

'I understand,' I said simply . . .

The University of Minnesota builds not only minds, it also builds bodies. Before you can enter the University you must undergo a thorough and rigorous examination at the Student Health Centre. Minnesota has one of the finest health centres in the country. Here prominent doctors, serving without compensation, give unstintingly of their time and wisdom that youth of Minnesota might be strong.

I shall always remember, with a mixture of gratitude and admiration, the day I went through the Health Service for my operation. I was extensively examined by not one, but many doctors, each an expert in his particular branch of medicine.

First I was sent to the bone surgeon. He was sitting at his desk reading a copy of *Film Fun*. 'How many arms and legs you got?' he asked, without putting down the *Film Fun*.

'Two,' I answered.

'Two altogether?'

'No sir, two of each.'

'O.K. You're all right. Go ahead,' he said, still looking at the *Film Fun*.

I proceeded to the office of the heart doctors. Because heart examination is a delicate, involved process, two doctors are assigned to that duty. When I came into the office, they were standing by the window dropping paper bags filled with water on pedestrians.

'I had an interesting case the other day,' said one to the other. 'I was listening to a kid's heart and it was the damnedest thing I ever heard. It didn't thump. It chimed in three notes.'

'What do you know?' said the second. 'What caused that?'

'I couldn't find out for a long time,' answered the first. 'It wasn't until I went way back into the kid's history that I found the solution. His mother was frightened by an NBC station break.'

'Well, what do you know?' said the second. 'Say, I heard of another interesting case yesterday. Dr Curette in plastic surgery told me about it. A man came in to see him. The fellow didn't have a nose.'

'No nose?' said the first. 'How did he smell?'

'Terrible,' said the second.

'Oh, Harold,' said the first, 'you're more fun than a barrel of monkeys.'

I cleared my throat. They turned and noticed me for the first time.

'I've come for a heart examination,' I said.

'You look all right. Go ahead,' they said.

They went over to the sink to fill some more bags with water.

My next stop was the weighing room. I stepped on the scale, my weight was recorded, and a doctor said, 'You make friends easily. You are a good worker although you are a little inclined to put things off. You are going to make a long trip on water.'

I gave him a penny and proceeded to the abdominal clinic. The doctor was sitting at a table building a boat in a bottle. 'Ever have to get up in the middle of the night?' he asked.

'Yes sir,' I answered.

'Hmmm,' he said. 'I'm going to have a little trouble with the mizzenmast. Know anything about boats?'

'Some,' I confessed modestly.

'I love boats,' he said, 'I love the sea. Right now I'd like to be on a trim little schooner hauling a cargo of oscars from the Levant. I love the good feel of a stout ship on a rough sea. Perhaps a nor'wester would blow up, and all the hearty mates would be on the deck pulling together while the grizzled old skipper stood on the bridge and yelled his orders: "Keelhaul the bosun! Jettison the supercargo!"'

'My, you certainly know a lot about boats,' I said admiringly.

He lowered his eyes. 'I should. I was cuckold on the Yale crew in 1912. But enough of this. So you have to get up in the middle of the night?'

'Yes, sir. You see, my sister Morningstar keeps company with an engineer on the Natchez, Mobile and Duluth railroad. About a year ago he got put on a night run, and Morningstar never got to see him. She complained so much that he finally had a sidetrack built into our back yard.

'Now when he comes by at night he runs the train into our back yard for a while. I have to get up in the middle of the night and go out and keep his steam up while he comes in the house and trifles with Morningstar.'

But he wasn't listening. He was fiddling with his boat in the bottle.

'Wonder which side is starboard,' he mumbled.

I left quietly for the chiropodist's office.

The doctor was sitting behind his desk playing 'Your Feet's Too Big' on a jews-harp when I came in.

'How did you get here?' he asked.

'Why, I walked.'

'Well, then,' he said, 'your feet are all right. You're lucky. There was a girl in here the other day whose feet were in terrible shape. She had been wearing such high heels that she constantly leaned forward at a forty-five degree angle. Gave the impression of being on a ski slide.'

'What did you do for her?' I asked.

'Cut off her legs, naturally. She's much happier now. She's made a lot of new friends who affectionately call her "Shorty".'

I made as if to go.

'Wait a minute. Know how I got interested in chiropody?'

'No sir,' I said, for I did not.

He giggled. 'I got webbed feet, that's why.' He leaped up from his chair and ran around the room quacking wildly. Water was rolling off his back.

Now I went to the last office, the psychiatrist's. He was driving golf balls through the window. An angry crowd was collecting outside. 'Any insanity in your family?' he asked.

'Oh, not really insanity,' I said. 'Maybe some of them act a little funny sometimes, but I wouldn't call it insanity. Uncle Bert, for instance, he's in Washington now circulating a petition to free Sacco and Vanzetti.

'And Cousin Roger. He's got a little farm in Des Moines. Every day he hauls his produce to Des Moines in a square-wheeled cart.

'And Uncle Donald. He started a million-dollar suit against the Reynolds Tobacco Company last year. He says he got a hump on his back from smoking camels.

'And Aunt Yetta. Every time she needs a little money, she pulls out a tooth and puts it under her pillow.

'And then there's Cousin Booker, who thinks he's got a diamond in his navel, and Aunt Melanie who burns churches, and Uncle Alex who hangs on the wall and says he's a telephone, and Uncle Milton who has been standing in a posthole since 1924.

'But I wouldn't call that insanity exactly, would you, Doctor?'

'Oh, certainly not,' he said. 'They're probably just a little tired. Well, my boy, the examination is all over. Let me congratulate you. You are now a student at the University of Minnesota.'

Tears filled my eyes and my throat was all choked up.

'Don't try to talk,' said the doctor. 'Just hold me tight. I want to remember you always, just like this.'

Max Shulman (b. 1919), *Barefoot Boy With Cheek* (1943).

━━━━━━━━

IN *the category of Second World War novels it is difficult to think of a book by an American, or any other, author which has been as widely read internationally and as much admired for its power and originality as Joseph Heller's* Catch-22.

Joseph Heller served as a bombardier (in Britain, bomb-aimer) in the US Air Force, went on to read literature at the universities of New York, Columbia, and Oxford, and then became a successful magazine executive. In 1961 he published a novel based on his wartime experiences in the Army Air Force. The protagonist was Captain Yossarian, an impulsive bombardier, and the story, set on a small Mediterranean island, told of Yossarian's resistance to his mad commander's willingness to sacrifice his entire squadron to get promotion.

Joseph Heller's Catch-22 *hardly comes under the heading of 'humour'. It is a bitter, surrealistic satire on military illogic and personal greed, but it is also grotesquely comic and its title has passed into the language.*

Early on in the story Yossarian tries to get out of going on any more dangerous bombing missions by getting the airbase doctor to ground him as unfit for flying. But there is a catch to this.

In the Air Force Medical Rule Book it is called 'Catch-22':

Yossarian came to him one mission later and pleaded again, without any real expectation of success, to be grounded. Doc Daneeka snickered once and was soon immersed in problems of his own, which included Chief White Halfoat, who had been challenging him all that morning to Indian wrestle, and Yossarian, who decided right then and there to go crazy.

'You're wasting your time,' Doc Daneeka was forced to tell him.

'Can't you ground someone who's crazy?'

'Oh, sure. I have to. There's a rule saying I have to ground anyone who's crazy.'

'Then why don't you ground me? I'm crazy. Ask Clevinger.'

'Clevinger? Where is Clevinger? You find Clevinger and I'll ask him.'

'Then ask any of the others. They'll tell you how crazy I am.'

'They're crazy.'

'Then why don't you ground them?'

'Why don't they ask me to ground them?'

'Because they're crazy, that's why.'

'Of course they're crazy,' Doc Daneeka replied. 'I just told you they're crazy, didn't I? And you can't let crazy people decide whether you're crazy or not, can you?'

Yossarian looked at him soberly and tried another approach. 'Is Orr crazy?'

'He sure is,' Doc Daneeka said.

'Can you ground him?'

'I sure can. But first he has to ask me to. That's part of the rule.'

'Then why doesn't he ask you to?'

'Because he's crazy,' Doc Daneeka said. 'He has to be crazy to keep flying combat missions after all the close calls he's had. Sure, I can ground Orr. But first he has to ask me to.'

'That's all he has to do to be grounded?'

'That's all. Let him ask me.'

'And then you can ground him?' Yossarian asked.

'No. Then I can't ground him.'

'You mean there's a catch?'

'Sure there's a catch,' Doc Daneeka replied. 'Catch-22. Anyone who wants to get out of combat duty isn't really crazy.'

There was only one catch and that was Catch-22 which specified that a concern for one's own safety in the face of dangers that were real and immediate was the process of a rational mind. Orr was crazy and could be grounded. All he had to do was ask; and as soon as he did, he would no longer be crazy and would have to fly more missions. Orr would be crazy to fly more missions and sane if he didn't, but if he was sane he had to fly them. If he flew them he was crazy and didn't have to; but if he didn't want to he was sane and had to. Yossarian was moved very deeply by the absolute simplicity of this clause of Catch-22 and let out a respectful whistle.

'That's some catch, that Catch-22,' he observed.

'It's the best there is,' Doc Daneeka agreed.

Joseph Heller (b. 1923), *Catch-22* (1961).

———

A STRAIN *of black humour and fantasy ran through much American wartime literature and continued during the post-war years. Night-club and television humour became more aggressive, politically conscious, and socially critical in the fifties and sixties; it was the era which produced Mort Sahl and Lenny Bruce.*

But the pendulum swung. In 1974 a radio show called A Prairie Home Companion *began on the public radio station in St Paul, Minnesota, in the heart of midwest America. The show lasted for two hours and went out live on Saturdays at 5 p.m. Singers sang to guitars, an orchestra played, there was an episode of a comedy serial, and tunes from a Wurlitzer organ in the pit. In the third of the segments of the show a huge young man named Garrison Keillor ambled on and, without notes, talked for about half an hour about the fictitious small prairie town in which he claimed to have been raised, Lake Wobegon.*

Each talk began, 'It has been a quiet week in Lake Wobegon,' and finished, 'That's the news from Lake Wobegon, where all the women are strong, the men are good-looking and all the children are above average.'

Garrison Keillor's weekly monologues grew in fame until he had an enormous coast-to-coast audience of devotees. In 1985 Keillor wrote some of the stories down, arranged them more or less in chronological order, and published the result as a book, Lake Wobegon Days.

The interesting thing is that in the late 1980s this slow and gentle book became a huge success. In competition with the usual list of brick-thick, hyped-up historical novels and steamy knicker-rippers, Lake Wobegon Days *became America's no. 1 best-seller. A year later it was published in Britain and immediately became Britain's no. 1 best-seller as well.*

Keillor's mock reminiscences of Lake Wobegon are not full of jokes or comical incidents but take America back to the humour of Mark Twain; they are not sentimental but kindly and full of regard for the foibles and banalities of American small-town life.

The stories give a clear and colourful picture of a simple, hard-working, poor, farming community, mostly immigrant families from Germany and Norway who had settled by chance on the most unproductive area of prairie in rural Minnesota. Many of the characters are conventional enough as befits life-long Lutherans, Catholics, and worshippers at the Norwegian church, but some of them are distinctly odd.

Like the German, Leon Winkler, who with his powerfully-built brother, Roman Winkler, worked a remote farm some way out of Lake Wobegon:

Roman was the older, a heavy man; he lived in a pair of blue bib-overalls that he stretched fore and aft, belly and shanks, a very admirable figure of a man, with hands big as legs of lamb, a ruddy face, a distinguished band of white across his forehead where the hat left off, and a white dome above the fringe of curly brown hair. He was an admirable horseman in his day, then an admirable mechanic; he was admired for sheer strength, having once lifted a steer and put it on a wagon; he was admired for never being at a loss for words and never wasting any either. He even spat tobacco admirably— pooching his cheeks and putting the thin brown line exactly where he wanted it, not a big blow, just a real nice spit, very graceful and discreet.

Most of all, he was a good worker, *steady* (one of the finest words one man could say about another); he didn't slack off, he was good for twelve, fifteen hours of work a day. He was generous in trading work with his neighbours, he didn't keep a count of it, and when he worked for them, it was the same as working for himself. They called him, he came, and he carried his end and some of theirs. Clarence Bunsen said that Roman Winkler could not be convicted of horse theft anywhere in Mist County if they found the horses in his bedroom.

He had to be a good worker, the farm being as poor as it was, though you couldn't tell it from looking at that clean white house, the red barn and the row of outbuildings (granary, pig barn, chicken coop, tractor shed, and tool shed) which was as trim and well-kept as an Army post though he got no help from his brother Leon.

Neither brother ever married, so far as we know (though Leon spent a few years in the Philippines with the Navy and hinted at other arrangements there). For almost all of Leon's life, they lived under the same roof.

Leon, the younger, was slight of build, had thin wrists and delicate fingers and went around in jeans, a blue sweater, and a stocking cap. He had a faraway look in his eye so that, talking to him, eventually you'd look over your shoulder to see what he saw back there, and he had the ability to look at work for days at a time. Some days he stayed in bed until afternoon. Bed, after all, was where he found himself when he woke up, he felt fine there, and he could think of no reason to get out, because his bookcase was by the bed, and books were all he needed. He could crawl into a book and pull the covers over him and stay until it got dark, and then go back to sleep. He bought books at auctions, he bought them C.O.D., and every week he came to town with Roman and hauled a bagful out of the library.

Being Roman's brother he was not talked about, only a little, and that mostly pretty tolerant, even when he went off on one of his bright ideas, which didn't last more than a day or two. Once he decided to put on *Coriolanus* and talked four people into coming to a rehearsal, which he forgot to attend. Another time he started to build an ocean-going yacht in the barn, then loaded potatoes in the hull. The boat broke up and Roman used the lumber to make a ramp to load hogs on the truck.

Drink wasn't his problem, inspiration was. Once he sat all night under Hazel Bunsen's bedroom window, presumably thinking about her, which frightened Hazel, who was young and practical, but he got over her sometime around breakfast and walked home.

When they were younger, the brothers had some fierce arguments about work and responsibility, but as they got old, they were able to say it all in a few words. 'Oh, *Leon*' 'Ah, Roman'.

Roman farmed, kept house, cooked, did laundry, did everything but make Leon's bed in the morning, though Leon said in his own defence that sometimes he was on the verge of doing chores only to find that Roman had done them already. He also said that Roman was trying to make more of the farm than it was, which was true. Whatever God intended the land to be, it certainly wasn't a showplace for seed corn and purebred Polish hogs. Roman worked, Leon said, as if he could by sheer effort pull the corn up out of the ground and make it grow, Leon said he worked, too. On a book, though he wasn't ready to show it to anyone, which would distill the wisdom of the ages into a single volume. This book, when finished, would change people's minds about him, but he was in no hurry to finish it, knowing that work that lasts comes slow.

Then one day Leon announced that he was leaving home, at the age of sixty-two. Roman had dreams at night in which he rounded up pigs who were loose in the corn, and they kept Leon awake. So he went over the hill and made him a sod house in the meadow. Dug down six feet and put up walls of turf blocks and laid old lumber across the top and laid on a sod roof, and he moved in with his books and bed and a woodstove. 'My brother who lives in the dirt,' Roman said, but he was lonely without him and came down in the evening with Leon's hot supper in a pie tin.

Leon didn't lack for visitors the last few years. He planted flowers on the roof, which bloomed beautifully in the summer and also in the winter, germinated by the heat of the stove. People drove out to see it, a patch of bright colours in the snow, and dropped in to see him. He climbed out of bed, marked his place in the book, snipped off some roots from his ceiling, and boiled up tea. He died in a bed full of books, with an encyclopedia on his chest, open to a page of pictures of flowers. Roman pulled the covers over his face, hauled out the woodstove, hitched the team to the two main timbers, clucked twice, and buried Leon under a ton of dirt. After a couple of years, rains had leveled the mound, and Roman, who was forgetful in his old age, ploughed the meadow and planted corn. In that one patch he got the corn he always wanted, seven and eight feet high, like a squadron of soldiers. 'Ja, that's the best I ever had,' he said. 'I just wish that my brother Leon could be here to see it.'

The religious division in town was between the strict, sombre, low church of the Protestants—the young author and his family belonged to a particularly bleak sect called the Brethren—and the much jollier and more colourful religion of the Catholics. The boy-storyteller secretly admired the more exciting Catholic way of doing things and for a while had an ambition to be burnt at the stake, but this passed.

There is a lot of religion in Lake Wobegon, even in its day-to-day life:

In Lake Wobegon, car ownership is a matter of faith. Lutherans drive Fords, bought from Bunsen Motors, the Lutheran car dealer, and Catholics drive Chevies from Main Garage, owned by the Kreugers, except for Hjalmar Ingqvist, who has a Lincoln. Years ago, John Tollerud was tempted by Chevyship until (then) Pastor Tommerdahl took John aside after church and told him it was his (Pastor Tommerdahl's) responsibility to point out that Fords get better gas mileage and have a better trade-in value. And he knew for a fact that the Kreugers spent a share of the Chevy profits to purchase Asian babies and make them Catholics. So John got a new Ford Falcon. It turned out to be a dud. The transmission went after ten thousand miles and the car tended to pull to the left. In a town where the car ownership is by faith, a person doesn't complain about these things, and John figured there must be a good reason for his car trouble, which perhaps he would fully understand one day.

The Brethren, being Protestant, also drove Fords, of course, but we distinguished ourselves from Lutherans by carrying small steel Scripture plates bolted to the top of our license plates. The verses were written in tiny glass beads so they showed up well at night. We ordered these from the Grace and Truth Scripture Depot in Eerie, Pennsylvania, and the favorites were, 'The wages of sin is death. Rom. 6.23' and 'I am the way, the truth and the life. Jn. 10.6.' The verse from John was made of white beads, the Romans of lurid red, and if your car came up behind a Brethren car on a road at night, that rear verse jumped right out at you . . .

My own purpose was escape, first in my dad's car (a Ford Fairlane station wagon) and then in the car he gave me (a 1956 Tudor sedan). Both these cars had verses bolted to the plates, so I carried pliers with me and pulled over just outside town and removed the evidence of our faith and put it in the trunk. Then I raced off and did what I could to debauch myself, and, on the way back, sometimes reeling from the effects of a couple Grain Belts and half a pack of Pall Malls, I bolted the verses back on.

Opportunities for debauchery in Lake Wobegon were thin on the ground but one year, when the author was 16, a girl from Minneapolis came to town to stay with her cousins, the rich Ingqvists, for a skating and skiing holiday.

She was much older than the author, well into her late teens, and a great deal wiser.

It is a beautifully told romance, finishing with what could be one of the most delicately understated consummations ever written:

Christmas, years later, I got five dollars from Grandma, a big raise from the one dollar she gave to little kids, and bought a bottle of Jade East cologne with it, the kind Chip Ingqvist used, the name of which I found out by making fun of him for smelling like rotten fruit. 'It's Jade East,' he said, smiling his superior Ingqvist smile. 'It's what they wear at the U.' With a splash of it on my neck and wearing the new Christmas sweater, I headed for the skating rink after supper, feeling like I was cut out for romance. I was sixteen. Six feet, three inches tall, and I walked with a peculiar springing stride, like a pogo stick, which sometimes I looked behind me and saw a little kid imitating. The Jade East was supposed to take care of that, and also I tried to saunter . . .

On this cold night, the skating rink was a carnival. The music I could hear when I left my house, and now I saw the long V of colored lights hung out across the rink from the warming house. Its windows blazed white. Pairs of skaters flowed counterclockwise in a great loop to 'The Blue Skirt Waltz', and little kids buzzed round the big slow wheel as it turned. I looked for the girl I loved, who I had met the night before.

She was older, eighteen or nineteen, and had worn bright lipstick and sat down beside me in the warming house and slowly unlaced her leather boots and took them off and then her socks. My face turned red. In the Age of Imagination, before the Age of Full Disclosure, the removal of any article of clothing was inspirational. She was a cousin of the Ingqvists, up from Minneapolis for Christmas break, and had a way about her that set her apart.

Her hair, for example, was jet-black and cut short as a man's. She wore a short skirt and tights, but unlike other girls whose tights were lumpy from long johns, hers were tight. She leaned against me and said, 'Got a cigarette?'

No girl had asked me that before, because I didn't smoke, but for her sake I said, 'Yeah,' thinking I *might* have one—it certainly was worth a look, and who would say no at a time like that?—then said, 'Oh, I just remembered. I forgot mine at home.' She said, 'Oh, well. I think I got two in my purse.' She offered me one. I didn't smoke, but then I was young, I'd been held back, it was time to get started on these things, so I said 'Thanks.' She gave me the book of matches. As I lit one and held it towards her mouth, she held my hand to steady it, and although I knew that you didn't make babies this way, two hands together holding a match, I thought it must be similar. We took deep drags and blew out big clouds of smoke, then she leaned back and inhaled again, and I leaned forward and put my head between my knees. Not sick exactly, I was simply appreciating it more than most people do. I was sixteen, I experienced everything deeply.

This night she was there again, sitting on the bench against the wall, with my friend Jim who was not smoking but who was inhaling her smoke as deeply as he could. 'Dorene's from Minneapolis,' he told me. I ignored him. 'I got to show you something,' I told her. 'Whenever you're done here.'

As we walked up the hill towards Main Street, I wasn't so sure what I could show her in Lake Wobegon that would be interesting, so I made up a story about a woman named Lydia Farrell who had lived here in love with the memory of a boy who had drowned. I picked out Florian Krebsbach's house as the home where Lydia spent fifty years in solitude, cherishing the few brief moments she spent with young Eddie before his boat overturned in a sudden storm. The moral was that we must seize our few bright moments and live deeply. It surprised me, how easily I did this and kept her interested. We walked up to the Ingqvists, both enjoying Lydia's sweet sad life, and then she asked me if I skied. I said, 'Sure.' I never had, but how would I know I couldn't unless I tried? So the next afternoon, I was squeezed next to her in the back seat of the Lingqvists' Lincoln, Chip driving, eight of us in the car, going goodness knows where.

Unbelievable to me, being in the same car with the Ingqvists and that whole Ingqvist crowd, sharp dressers in those Norwegian ski sweaters you couldn't find in town and who never had asked me before so much as to come into their house. But Dorene, who was even finer than they, had seen something in me. She was from Minneapolis but had spotted some personal quality of mine that other people had never seen, and I was determined not to let her down. I imagined her turning to me with a smoky Minneapolis look and saying, 'Kiss me,' and so had practised kissing, using my thumb and forefinger as practice lips. I had also gone to the library and skimmed through a book about skiing. I felt prepared to do either.

A long drive during which they all talked about college and how much harder it was than high school. You have to study six or seven hours a day, Chip said. I said I didn't think it was so hard. They laughed: 'What do you know?' I said I'd read a lot of college books. 'Like *what?*' A lot of different things, I said. Dorene held my hand. She said, 'It isn't hard for everybody. Some people have a harder time in high school, then they do real good in college.'

I was grateful for that, but by the time we got to where we were going, I was much less confident about everything. It was dark. A plywood Swiss chalet sat between two spruce at the end of the parking lot, and beyond it strings of light ascended a hill much steeper than what seemed possible in Minnesota (Maybe we were in Wisconsin.) They got their skis off the car carrier. I was going to say, 'That's all right, you go ahead, I feel like I'm coming down with something. I'll just wait in the building. I'll be okay. You go ahead'—and then she put a pair of skis and ski poles in my hands and said, 'Let's go,' so I went.

I put on the skis, which she refastened so they wouldn't fall off, and showed me where to stand, next to her, holding hands, and the big wheel groaned in the wheel house and the bench came up behind and scooped us up and we rose into the dark. 'I can't ski,' I said; she said 'I know.' We kissed. We slid off at the top and I staggered after her to the edge of the precipice where Chip Ingqvist stood, adjusting his binding. He grinned at me and flung himself off. She told me to relax, stay loose, bend my knees, and if I lost my balance to just sit down—and she jumped over the edge and I did too, and followed her down in a series of short rides. Skiing, sitting down, skiing. I lost momentum in the sittings so at the bottom where other skiers flashed across the flats to the chalet and plowed to a stop, I had to walk. She was gone when I got there. I sat in the chalet with some people who hoped they could make it to Colorado in February, then she appeared, limping. She twisted her ankle while getting off the lift and had made the long trip down in pain. I examined it as if ankles were my specialty, a top ankle man called in from Minneapolis: 'Can you walk on it?' I asked. She said, 'I don't want to sit here with all these people feeling sorry for me,' so we went to the car, her arm around my neck, mine around her waist. We sat in the car for awhile. After a while, I said, 'I never did this before,' but she seemed to be aware of that.

Garrison Keillor (b. 1942), *Lake Wobegon Days* (1985).

THE *arts in England after the First World War were stimulated by a wave of tendencies which was later christened Modernism. Much of this movement, led by Ezra Pound, T. S. Eliot, and James Joyce in literature, was concerned with breaking away from pre-First World War Edwardian naturalism and experimenting with the heightened use of imagery and myth, the use of non-traditional techniques such as stream-of-consciousness writing, and the new avenues opened up by Freud's psychological explanations of human behaviour.*

The comic novel, depending much more on naturalism, was less affected by all this, but in the 1920s it rose to impressive heights just the same with the work of a brilliant batch of young, innovative novelists like Ronald Firbank, with his exotic, dandified stories set in a world of what is now called High Camp; Henry Green, whose books, as plain and unadorned as a monk's cell, were written almost entirely in dialogue; and Anthony Powell, whose brittle, witty novels satirizing the seedier aspects of pleasure-seeking London Society, began with (the title says it all) Afternoon Men *(1931).*

Much of this new writing had a direct and nourishing influence on the work of a fellow author who went on to become arguably the greatest comic novelist of the century, Evelyn Waugh.

The young Evelyn Waugh enjoyed an energetic, epicene, and boozy social life at university, and came down from Hertford College, Oxford, in 1924 with a third-class degree and no clear idea of what to do with his life.

As with many another undetermined possessor of a poor degree in those days, he retreated into the ill-paid refuge of schoolmastering. For the next three years he was moderately unhappy as an assistant master in small, private boarding schools in Wales, Aston Clinton, and Notting Hill. He was so despondent after the joyless experience of his first school, the one in Wales, that on leaving it he walked into the sea to drown himself but met a jellyfish and decided instead to wade rapidly back to the beach and live. Teaching was clearly a waste of time and in 1927 he left the profession without ever really having been in it.

He was good at drawing and making furniture—he always said that he derived greater pleasure from carpentry than from writing—and thought of trying to make a living at one or the other (he began taking evening classes in carpentry and wrote of being instructed to saw a small block of teak in half: when the term ended after three months of sawing he still had a inch left to go). He also quite liked writing but was a little inhibited by the success of his elder brother Alec, who had written a novel about his public school Sherborne, The Loom of Youth, *which had become a scandalous success.*

At this time Waugh had had two items published, an essay, The Pre-Raphaelite Brethren *(1926), and a book on Rossetti (1928), but neither made any money and the young Waugh desperately needed quite a lot of money. He had managed to become part of London's smart set and wanted to marry Evelyn Gardner, daughter of the late Lord Burghclere, whose widow was unenthusiastic about her pretty daughter marrying an unknown, smallish young man who was not mentioned in Debrett, had no family capital, no income, and no job.*

So Waugh (aged 25) set out to make a quick fortune by writing a comic novel illustrated with his own drawings. He based the first half of the story on his experiences teaching at the small preparatory school in Wales. He called the book Decline and Fall, *an Illustrated Novelette.*

It was published in 1928 and was an immense success, financially, critically, and every other way.

Eighteen more novels and stories followed, plus seven idiosyncratic travel books and four other works.

Evelyn Waugh died in 1966. Graham Greene said of him, 'He was the best novelist of my generation. When he died one felt as if one's commanding officer were dead.'

Waugh was in life a kind of walking paradox; everything about him seemed to contradict everything else. Even his friends acknowledged that he could be, and frequently was, a somewhat unpleasant person, truculent, impatient, a great hater; yet his humour could be kindly. He satirized the superficial and selfish Bright Young Things of Mayfair in his second book, Vile Bodies, *published in 1930, yet at the same time was trying to be one himself ('he definitely was not a bright young person at all', a friend at the time, Lady Diana Mosley, recollected later). He was a snob and an aesthete yet he wrote his books to amuse a mass audience and succeeded brilliantly. He handled the tragic with frivolity, a considerable artistic achievement. In later life he contrived to look and behave like an eccentric country gentleman of the old school in boldly checked tweeds and pork-pie hat yet only succeeded in looking like Dylan Thomas dressed as a turf accountant. But his prose was rarely less than beautiful.*

'Prelude', the opening section of Decline and Fall, *gives a synopsis of the themes which he goes on to develop later in the book; in fact, in a good many of his books. There are the snobbish and venal figures of authority who have no business to be either, insensitive academics, constantly bullied aesthetes, baying philistines from good families who can get away with anything, and the ordinary, decent chaps who suffer from the devastating unfairness of everything.*

In Paul Pennyfeather, the protagonist of Decline and Fall, *Waugh sketched the first of his gallery of uncomplaining, incurious non-heroes who were the still centre of bizarre happenings whirling about their ears:*

PRELUDE

Mr Sniggs, the Junior Dean, and Mr Postlethwaite, the Domestic Bursar, sat alone in Mr Sniggs' room overlooking the garden quad at Scone College. From the rooms of Sir Alastair Digby-Vane-Trumpington, two staircases away, came a confused roaring and breaking of glass. They alone of the senior members of Scone were at home that evening, for it was the night of the annual dinner of the Bollinger Club. The others were all scattered over Boar's Hill and North Oxford at gay, contentious little parties, or at other senior common-rooms, or at the meetings of learned societies, for the annual Bollinger dinner is a difficult time for those in authority.

It is not accurate to call this an annual event, because quite often the Club is suspended for some years after each meeting. There is tradition behind the Bollinger; it numbers reigning kings among its past members. At the last dinner, three years ago, a fox had been brought in in a cage and stoned to death with champagne bottles. What an evening that had been! This was the first meeting since then, and from all over Europe old members had rallied for the occasion. For two days they had been pouring into Oxford: epileptic royalty from their villas of exile; uncouth peers from crumbling country seats; smooth young men of uncertain tastes from embassies and legations; illiterate lairds from wet granite hovels in the Highlands; ambitious young barristers and Conservative candidates torn from the London season and the indelicate advances of debutantes; all that was most sonorous of name and title was there for the beano.

'The fines!' said Mr Sniggs, gently rubbing his pipe along the side of his nose. 'Oh, my! the fines there'll be after this evening!'

There is some highly prized port in the senior common-room cellars that is only brought up when the College fines have reached £50.

'We shall have a week of it at least,' said Mr Postlethwaite, 'a week of Founder's port.'

A shriller note could now be heard rising from Sir Alastair's rooms; any who have heard that sound will shrink at the recollection of it; it is the sound of the English county families baying for broken glass. Soon they would all be tumbling out into the quad, crimson and roaring in their bottle-green evening coats, for the real romp of the evening.

'Don't you think it might be wiser if we turned out the light?' said Mr Sniggs.

In darkness the two dons crept to the window. The quad below was a kaleidoscope of barely discernible faces.

'There must be fifty of them at least,' said Mr Postlethwaite. 'If only they were all members of the college! Fifty of them at ten pounds each. Oh my!'

'It'll be more if they attack the Chapel,' said Mr Sniggs. 'Oh, please God, make them attack the Chapel.'

'I wonder who the unpopular undergraduates are this term. They always attack their rooms. I hope they have been wise enough to go out for the evening.'

'I think Partridge will be one; he possesses a painting by Matisse or some such name.'

'And I'm told he has black sheets on his bed.'

'And Sanders went to dinner with Ramsay MacDonald once.'

'And Reading can afford to hunt but collects china instead.'

'And smokes cigars in the garden after breakfast.'

'Austen has a grand piano.'

'They'll enjoy smashing that.'

'There'll be a heavy bill for tonight; just you see! But I confess I should feel easier if the Dean or the Master were in. They can't see us from here, can they?'

It was a lovely evening. They broke up Mr Austen's grand piano, and stamped Lord Reading's cigars into his carpet, and smashed his china, and tore up Mr Partridge's sheets and threw the Matisse into his water-jug; Mr Sanders had nothing to break except his windows, but they found the manuscript at which he had been working for the Newdigate Prize Poem, and had great fun with that. Sir Alastair Digby-Vane-Trumpington felt quite ill with excitement, and was supported to bed by Lumsden of Strathdrummond. It was half-past eleven. Soon the evening would come to an end. But there was still a treat to come.

Paul Pennyfeather was reading for the Church. It was his third year of uneventful residence at Scone. He had come there after a creditable career at a small public school of ecclesiastical temper on the South Downs, where he had edited the magazine, been President of the Debating Society, and had, as his report said, 'exercised a wholesome influence for good' in the House in which he was head boy. At home he lived in Onslow Square with his guardian, a prosperous solicitor who was proud of his progress but abysmally bored by his company. Both his parents had died in India at the time when he won the essay prize at his preparatory school. For two years he had lived within his allowance, aided by two valuable scholarships. He smoked three ounces of tobacco a week—John Cotton, Medium—and drank a pint and a half of beer a day, the half at luncheon and the pint at dinner, a meal he invariably ate in Hall. He had four friends, three of whom had been at school with him. None of the Bollinger Club had ever heard of Paul Pennyfeather, and he, oddly enough, had never heard of them.

Little suspecting the incalculable consequences that the evening was to have for him, he bicycled happily back from a meeting of the League of Nations Union. There had been a most interesting paper on plebiscites in Poland. He thought of smoking a pipe and reading another chapter of the *Forsyte Saga* before going to bed. He knocked at the gate, was admitted, put away his bicycle, and diffidently, as always, made his way across the quad towards his rooms. What a lot of people there seemed to be about! Paul had no particular objection to drunkenness—he had read a rather daring paper to the Thomas More Society on the subject—but he was consumedly shy of drunkards.

Out of the night Lumsden of Strathdrummond swayed across his path like a druidical rocking-stone. Paul tried to pass.

Now it so happened that the tie of Paul's old school bore a marked resemblance to the pale blue and white of the Bollinger Club. The difference of a quarter of an inch in the width of the stripes was not one that Lumsden of Strathdrummond was likely to appreciate.

'Here's an awful man wearing the Boller tie,' said the Laird. It is not for nothing that since pre-Christian times his family had exercised chieftainship over unchartered miles of barren moorland.

Mr Sniggs was looking rather apprehensively at Mr Postlethwaite.

'They appear to have caught somebody,' he said. 'I hope they don't do him any serious harm.'

'Dear me, can it be Lord Reading? I think I ought to intervene.'

'No, Sniggs,' said Mr Postlethwaite, laying a hand on his impetuous colleague's arm. 'No, no, no. It would be unwise. We have the prestige of the senior common-room to consider. In their present state they might not prove amenable to discipline. We must at all costs avoid an *outrage*.'

At length the crowd parted, and Mr Sniggs gave a sigh of relief.

'But it's quite all right. It isn't Reading. It's Pennyfeather—someone of no importance.'

'Well, that saves a great deal of trouble. I am glad, Sniggs; I really am. What a lot of clothes the young man appears to have lost!'

Next morning there was a lovely College meeting.

'Two hundred and thirty pounds,' murmured the Domestic Bursar ecstatically, '*not* counting the damage! That means five evenings with what we have already collected. Five evenings of Founder's port!'

'The case of Pennyfeather,' the Master was saying, 'seems to be quite a different matter altogether. He ran the whole length of the quadrangle, you say, *without his trousers*. It is unseemly. It is more: it is indecent. In fact, I am almost prepared to say that it is flagrantly indecent. It is *not* the conduct we expect from a scholar.'

'Perhaps if we fined him heavily?' suggested the Junior Dean.

'I very much doubt whether he could pay. I understand he is not well off. *Without trousers*, indeed! And at that time of night! I think we should do far better to get rid of him altogether. That sort of man does the college no good.'

Two hours later, while Paul was packing his three suits in his little leather trunk, the Domestic Bursar sent a message that he wished to see him.

'Ah, Mr Pennyfeather,' he said, 'I have examined your rooms and noticed two slight burns, one on the window-sill and the other on the chimney-piece, no doubt from cigarette ends. I am charging you five-and-sixpence for each of them on your battels. That is all, thank you.'

As he crossed the quad Paul met Mr Sniggs.

'Just off?' said the Junior Dean brightly.

'Yes, sir,' said Paul.

And a little farther on he met the chaplain.

'Oh, Mr Pennyfeather, before you go, surely you have my copy of Dean Stanley's *Eastern Church*?'

'Yes. I left it on your table.'

'Thank you. Well, good-bye, my dear boy. I suppose that after that reprehensible affair last night you will have to think of some other profession. Well, you may congratulate yourself that you discovered your unfitness for the priesthood before it was too late. If a parson does a thing of that sort, you know, all the world knows. And so many do, alas! What do you propose doing?'

'I don't really know yet.'

'There is always commerce, of course. Perhaps you will be able to bring to the great world of business some of the ideals you have learned at Scone. But it won't be easy, you know. It's a thing to be lived down with courage. What did Dr Johnson say about fortitude? . . . Dear, dear! *no trousers!*'

At the gates Paul tipped the porter.

'Well, good-bye, Blackall,' he said. 'I don't suppose I shall see you again for some time.'

'No, sir, and very sorry I am to hear about it. I expect you'll be becoming a schoolmaster, sir. That's what most of the gentlemen does, sir, that gets sent down for indecent behaviour.'

'God damn and blast them all to hell,' said Paul meekly to himself as he drove to the station, and then felt rather ashamed, because he rarely swore.

Evelyn Waugh (1903–66), Decline and Fall, an Illustrated Novelette (1928).

The plot of Decline and Fall *gets under way with Paul Pennyfeather trying to be a teacher at a small, wholly incompetent preparatory school in Wales. It then makes a dog's-leg turn and moves to Mayfair where Paul almost marries Margot, the prettiest of the parents he met at the school, a society beauty whose fortune turns out to come from running a chain of brothels in South America. The innocent Paul is arrested and convicted of keeping the bawdy-houses and is sent to prison. Margot marries the Home Secretary.*

Waugh's highly original technique was to give his goldfish bowl of characters a good stir every now and then and bring them round into sight again in new circumstances. Thus the next time we meet the Headmaster, Doctor Fagan, he has sold the school and opened a private nursing home in Worthing; Philbrick, school butler and confidence trickster, turns up regularly as various implausible characters; Captain Grimes, a fellow teacher, becomes a fellow convict, and Mr Prendergast, the school chaplain, arrives as chaplain at Paul's prison and has his head sawn off by a deranged convict.

The casual and unemotional way in which mayhem and death are strewn about is a notable feature of Waugh's early novels. It was a mixture of detached irony and black humour which was then both hair-raising and irresistibly funny.

One remembers the fate of little Lord Tangent, after the incident during the school's first Sports Day. No fuss whatever is made of the accident or its aftermath. The reader is kept up to date with the boy's progress only by a few brief, almost oblique references made later, mainly by Tangent's mother, the formidable Lady Circumference.

The incident begins as Doctor Fagan is trying to get the running races started:

'I am concerned with *style*. I wish, for instance, we had a starting pistol.'

'Would this be any use?' said Philbrick, producing an enormous service revolver. 'Only take care; it's loaded.'

'The very thing,' said the Doctor. 'Only fire into the ground, mind. We must do everything we can to avoid an accident. Do you always carry that about with you?'

'Only when I'm wearing my diamonds,' said Philbrick.

'First race,' said Paul through the megaphone, 'under sixteen. Quarter-mile!' He read out Grimes's list of starters.

'What's Tangent doin' in this race?' said Lady Circumference. 'The boy can't run an inch.'

The silver band stopped playing.

'The course,' said Paul, 'starts from the pavilion, goes round that clump of elms . . .'

'Beeches,' corrected Lady Circumference loudly.

'. . . and ends in front of the bandstand. Starter, Mr Prendergast; time-keeper, Captain Grimes.'

'I shall say, "Are you ready? one, two, three!" and then fire,' said Mr Prendergast. 'Are you ready? One'—there was a terrific report. 'Oh dear! I'm sorry'—but the race had begun. Clearly Tangent was not going to win; he was sitting on the grass crying because he had been wounded in the foot by Mr Prendergast's bullet. Philbrick carried him, wailing dismally, into the refreshment tent, where Dingy helped him off with his shoe. His heel was slightly grazed. Dingy gave him a large slice of cake, and he hobbled out surrounded by a sympathetic crowd.

'That won't hurt him,' said Lady Circumference, 'but I think somebody ought to remove the pistol from that old man before he does anything serious.'

'I knew that was going to happen,' said Lord Circumference.

'A most unfortunate beginning,' said the Doctor.

'Am I going to die?' said Tangent, his mouth full of cake.

'For God's sake look after Prendy,' said Grimes in Paul's ear. 'The man's as tight as a lord, and on one whisky, too.'

'First blood to me!' said Mr Prendergast gleefully.

'How's your young hopeful been doing, Lady Circumference?'

'My boy's been injured in the foot,' said Lady Circumference coldly.

'Dear me! Not badly, I hope? Did he twist his ankle in the jumping?'

'No,' said Lady Circumference, 'he was shot at by one of the assistant masters. But it was kind of you to enquire.'

Six days later the school was given a half-holiday, and soon after luncheon the bigamous union of Captain Edgar Grimes and Miss Florence Selina Fagan was celebrated at the Llanabba Parish Church. A slight injury to his hand prevented Paul from playing the organ. He walked down the church with Mr Prendergast, who, greatly to his dismay, had been instructed by Dr Fagan to give away the bride.

'I do not intend to be present,' said the Doctor. 'The whole business is exceedingly painful to me.' Everybody else, however, was there except little Lord Tangent, whose foot was being amputated at a local nursing-home.

For some reason or other, Paul's marriage seemed to inspire the public as being particularly romantic. Perhaps they admired the enterprise and gallantry with which Margot, after ten years of widowhood, voluntarily exposed herself to a repetition of the hundred and one horrors of a fashionable wedding, or perhaps Paul's sudden elevation from schoolmaster to millionaire struck a still vibrant chord of optimism in each of them, so that they said to themselves over their ledgers and typewriters: 'It may be me next time.' Whatever the reason, the wedding was certainly an unparalleled success among the lower orders. Inflamed by the popular Press, a large crowd assembled outside St Margaret's on the eve of the ceremony equipped, as for a first night, with collapsible chairs, sandwiches, and spirit stoves, while by half past two, in spite of heavy rain, it had swollen to such dimensions that the police were forced to make several baton-charges and many guests were crushed almost to death in their attempts to reach the doors, and the route down which Margot had to drive was lined as for a funeral with weeping and hysterical women.

Society was less certain in its approval, and Lady Circumference, for one, sighed for the early nineties, when Edward Prince of Wales, at the head of *ton*, might have given authoritative condemnation to this ostentatious second marriage.

'It's maddenin' Tangent having died just at this time,' she said, 'People may think that it's my reason for refusin'. I can't imagine that *anyone* will go.'

The Captain Grimes mentioned earlier as entering into a bigamous marriage with the Headmaster's daughter (Grimes already had a wife, a spirited Irish girl who later enlisted with enthusiasm as one of Paul's fiancée's whores) qualifies as the first of the many Waugh characters to lodge themselves forever in the reader's memory.

Grimes had a wooden leg and was homosexual. The first gave him little bother but the latter led him into deep trouble and he was constantly finding himself, as he termed it, in the soup. Yet he was buoyed up in moments of despair by a Micawber-like optimism; not in his case founded upon belief in the ultimate benevolence of fate but in the power of the old-boy network, that freemasonry among ex-public schoolboys which decreed that they looked after their own irrespective of any crimes committed, hearts broken, or other manifestations of manly moral turpitude.

Grimes, briefly not in the soup, explains to Paul how it works:

'This looks like being the first end of term I've seen for two years,' he said dreamily. 'Funny thing, I can always get on all right for about six weeks, and then I land in the soup. I don't believe I was ever meant by Nature to be a schoolmaster. Temperament,' said Grimes, with a far-away look in his eyes—'that's my trouble, temperament and sex.'

'Is it quite easy to get another job—after you've been in the soup?' asked Paul.

'Not at first, it isn't, but they're ways. Besides, you see, I'm a public-school man. That means everything. There's a blessed equity in the British social system,' said Grimes, 'that ensures the public-school man against starvation. One goes through four or five years of perfect hell at an age when life is bound to be hell, anyway, and after that the social system never lets you down.

'Not that I stood four or five years of it, mind; I got the push soon after my sixteenth birthday. But my housemaster was a public-school man. He knew the system. "Grimes," he said, "I can't keep you in the House after what has happened. I have the other boys to consider. But I don't want to be too hard on you. I want you to start again." So he sat down there and then and wrote me a letter of recommendation to any future employer, a corking good letter, too. I've got it still. It's been very useful at one time or another. They may kick you out, but they never let you down.

'I subscribed a guinea to the War Memorial Fund. I felt I owed it to them. I was really sorry,' said Grimes, 'that that cheque never got through.

'After that I went into business. Uncle of mine had a brush factory at Edmonton. Doing pretty well before the war. That put the lid on the brush trade for me. You're too young to have been in the war, I suppose? Those were the days, old boy. We shan't see the like of them again. I don't suppose I was really sober for more than a few hours for the whole of that war. Then I got into the soup again, pretty badly that time. Happened over in France. They said, "Now, Grimes, you've got to behave like a gentleman. We don't want a court-martial in this regiment. We're going to leave you alone for half an hour. There's your revolver. You know what to do. Good-bye, old man," they said quite affectionately.

'Well, I sat there for some time looking at that revolver. I put it up to my head twice, but each time I brought it down again. "Public-school men don't end like this," I said to myself. It was a long half hour, but luckily they had left a decanter of whisky in there with me. They'd all had a few, I think. That's what made them all so solemn. There wasn't much whisky left when they came back, and, what with that and the strain of the situation, I could only laugh when they came in. Silly thing to do, but they looked so surprised, seeing me there alive and drunk.

'"The man's a cad," said the colonel, but even then I couldn't stop laughing, so they put me under arrest and called a court-martial.

'I must say I felt pretty low next day. A major came over from another battalion to try my case. He came to see me first, and bless me if it wasn't a cove I'd known at school.

'"God bless my soul," he said, "if it isn't Grimes of Podger's! What's all this nonsense about a court-martial?" So I told him. "H'm," he said, "pretty bad. Still, it's out of the question to shoot an old Harrovian. I'll see what I can do about it." And next day I was sent to Ireland on a pretty cushy job connected with postal service. That saw me out as far as the war was concerned. You can't get into the soup in Ireland, do what you like. I don't know if all this bores you?'

'Not at all,' said Paul. 'I think it's most encouraging.'

'I've been in the soup pretty often since then, but never quite so badly. Someone always turns up and says, "I can't see a public-school man down and out. Let me put you on your feet again." I should think,' said Grimes, 'I've been put on my feet more often than any living man.'

Philbrick came across the bar parlour towards them.

'Feeling lonely?' he said. 'I've been talking to the stationmaster here, and if either of you wants an introduction to a young lady—'

'Certainly not,' said Paul.

'Oh, all right,' said Philbrick, making off.

'Women are an enigma,' said Grimes, 'as far as Grimes is concerned.'

Ibid.

The year 1928 should have been the beginning of much happiness for Waugh. He had quietly married Evelyn Gardner without her mother scenting it and preventing it, and Decline and Fall *was a success beyond all expectations. But everything did not fall out quite like that and the next two or three years saw some huge upsets in Waugh's life.*

He began work on his next novel, Vile Bodies, *a funny, bitter satire on the capricious, loveless round of pleasure enjoyed by the Bright Young Things of Mayfair, but within months his young wife found Evelyn lacking as a bright young husband and took a lover. Waugh found out and, deeply shocked, started divorce proceedings.*

In 1930 his divorce came through, he was received into the Roman Catholic Church (his successful second marriage did not take place until seven years later), and Vile Bodies *was published to great acclaim. It was now clear that the extraordinary maturity of* Decline and Fall *was not a one-book fluke but that Waugh had a rich talent which was already expanding and moving on to bigger things.*

Waugh began to travel; he went to Abyssinia to report the coronation of the Emperor Haile Selassie for The Times, *which resulted in the high-spirited and colourful novel* Black Mischief, *1932.*

In the following extract from Black Mischief, *Basil Seal, a young white opportunist working for a newspaper in a newly emergent African state, has helped the local Ministry of Modernization to produce a poster bringing home to the tribespeople the perils of over-population:*

Finally there resulted a large, highly coloured poster well calculated to convey to the illiterate the benefits of birth control. It was in many ways the highest triumph of the new Ministry and Mr Youkoumian was the hero. Copies were

placarded all over Debra Dowa; they were sent down the line to every station
latrine, capital and coast; they were sent into the interior to vice-regal lodges
and headmen's huts, hung up at prisons, barracks, gallows and juju trees,
and wherever the poster was hung there assembled a cluster of inquisitive,
entranced Azanians.

It portrayed two contrasted scenes. On one side a native hut of hideous
squalor, overrun with children of every age, suffering from every physical
incapacity—crippled, deformed, blind, spotted and insane; the father prematurely aged with paternity squatted by an empty cook-pot; through the
door could be seen his wife, withered and bowed with child-bearing, desperately hoeing at their inadequate crop. On the other side a bright parlour
furnished with chairs and table; the mother, young and beautiful, sat at her
case eating a huge slice of raw meat; her husband smoked a long Arab
hubble-bubble (still a caste mark of leisure throughout the land), while a
single healthy child sat between them reading a newspaper. Inset between
the two pictures was a detailed drawing of some up-to-date contraceptive
apparatus and the words in Sakuyu: WHICH HOME DO YOU CHOOSE?

Interest in the pictures was unbounded; all over the island woolly heads
were nodding, black hands pointing, tongues clicking against filed teeth in
unsyntactical dialects. Nowhere was there any doubt about the meaning of
the beautiful new pictures.

See: on right hand: there is rich man: smoke pipe like big chief: but his
wife she no good; sit eating meat: and rich man no good: he only one son.

See: on left hand: poor man: not much to eat: but his wife she very good,
work hard in field: man he good too: eleven children: one very mad, very
holy. And in the middle: Emperor's juju. Make you like that good man with
eleven children.

And as a result, despite admonitions from squire and vicar, the peasantry
began pouring into town for the gala, eagerly awaiting initiation to the fine
new magic of virility and fecundity.

Black Mischief (1932).

*Perhaps the best example of another Waugh gift, literary pastiche, occurs in a line
which every Waugh aficionado knows by heart. It is from* Scoop (1938), *Waugh's
satire on Fleet Street and its foreign correspondents, written after his own experiences working for the* Daily Mail *in Abyssinia during Mussolini's invasion.*

The luckless Nature Correspondent of The Beast, *our hero, William Boot, is
accidentally sent to war in place of another Boot who is an* avant-garde *novelist.*

*In the scene where the newspaper chiefs pick the wrong Boot comes the famous
line beginning* 'Feather-footed'—*the epitome of every overwritten Nature Note:*

'Who's Boot?' asked Mr Salter at last.

'I know the name,' said the Managing Editor.

'The Chief wants to send him to Ishmaelia. He's the Prime Minister's
favourite writer.'

'Not the chap I was thinking of,' said the Managing Editor.

'Well, I've got to find him.' He listlessly turned the pages of the morning paper. 'Boot,' he said. 'Boot. Boot. Boot. Why! *Boot*—here he is. Why didn't the chief say he was a staff man?'

At the back of the paper, ignominiously sandwiched between Pip and Pop, the Bedtime Pets, and the recipe for a dish named 'Waffle Scramble', lay the bi-weekly half-column devoted to Nature:

LUSH PLACES, *edited by William Boot, Countryman.*

'Do you suppose that's the right one?'

'Sure of it. The Prime Minister is nuts on rural England.'

'He's supposed to have a particularly high-class style: *Feather-footed through the plashy fen passes the questing vole* . . . would that be it?'

'Yes,' said the Managing Editor. 'That must be good style. At least it doesn't sound like anything else to me.'

Another aspect of Waugh's comic genius was his extraordinary skill in drawing ambiguous characters who might or might not be what they appear to be, and delineating these characters in impeccably subtle and exact dialogue. And no character in the Waugh canon is so ambiguous as the international financier (or is he?) in Scoop.

William Boot, ex-sedentary writer on country matters now transmogrified into a questing vole, i.e. a war correspondent, is rushed to the war zone, Ishmaelia in East Africa.

His journey begins at Croydon Airport where The Beast *has hired him a private plane to cross the Channel on the first stage of his journey to the front:*

He did not leave alone.

The propellors were thundering; the pilot threw away his cigarette and adjusted his helmet; the steward wrapped a rug round William's feet and tenderly laid in his lap a wad of cotton wool, a flask of smelling salts and an empty paper bag; the steps were being wheeled away from the door. At that moment three figures hurried from the shelter of the office. One was heavily enveloped in a sand-coloured ulster; a check cap was pulled low on his eyes and his collar was fastened high against the blast of the engines. He was a small man in a hurry, yet, bustling and buttoned up as he was, a man of unmistakable importance, radiating something of the dignity of a prize Pekingese. This impression was accentuated by the extreme deference with which he was treated by his companions, one a soldierly giant carrying an attaché case, the other wearing the uniform of high rank in the company.

This official now approached William, and, above the engine, asked his permission to include a passenger and his servant. The name was lost in the roar of the propellors. 'Mr . . . I needn't tell you who *he* is . . . only plane available . . . request from a very high quarter . . . infinitely obliged if . . . as far as Le Bourget.'

Boot does not talk to the odd little stranger or to his enormous servant during the flight and then forgets them in the effort of getting through customs all the paraphernalia his newspaper has provided for his stay in East Africa, including an adequate supply of cleft sticks, a cigar humidor, and a collapsible canoe. He catches the Blue Train for the South of France for the next stage of his journey and makes his way to the restaurant car:

Opposite him at the table to which he was directed sat a middle-aged man, at the moment engaged in a homily to the waiter in fluent and apparently telling argot. His head was totally bald on the top and of unusual conical shape; at the sides and back the hair was closely cut and dyed a strong, purplish shade of auburn. He was neatly, rather stiffly dressed for the time of the year, and heavily jewelled; a cabochon emerald, massive and dull, adorned his tie; rubies flashed on his fingers and cuff-links as his hands rose and spread configuring the swell and climax of his arguments; pearls and platinum stretched from pocket to pocket of his waistcoat. William wondered what his nationality could be and thought perhaps Turkish. Then he spoke, in a voice that was not exactly American or Levantine or Eurasian or Latin or Teuton, but a blend of them all.

'The moment they recognise an Englishman they think they can make a monkey out of him,' he said in this voice. 'That one was Swiss; they're the worst; tried to make me buy mineral water. The water in the carafes is excellent. I have drunk quantities of it in my time without ever being seriously affected—and I have a particularly delicate stomach. May I give you some?'

William said he preferred wine.

'You are interested in clarets? I have a little vineyard in Bordeaux—on the opposite slope of the hill to Château Mouton-Rothschild where in my opinion the soil is rather less delicate than mine. I have to have something to give my friends. They are kind enough to find it drinkable. It has never been in the market, of course. It is a little hobby of mine.'

He took two pills, one round and white, the other elliptical and black, from a rococo snuff-box and laid them on the table-cloth beside his plate. He drew a coroneted crêpe de Chine handkerchief from his pocket, carefully wiped his glass, half-filled it with murky liquid from the water bottle, swallowed his medicine and then said:

'You are surprised at my addressing you?'

'Not at all,' said William politely.

'But it *is* surprising. I make a point of never addressing my fellow travellers. Indeed I usually prefer to dine in the coupé. But this is not our first meeting. You were kind enough to give me a place in your aeroplane this afternoon. It was a service I greatly appreciate.'

'Not at all,' said William. 'Not at all. Very glad to have been any help.'

'It was the act of an Englishman—a fellow Englishman,' said the little man simply. 'I hope that one day I shall have the opportunity of requiting it . . . I probably shall,' he added rather sadly. 'It is one of the pleasant if quite onerous duties of a man of my position to requite the services he receives— usually on a disproportionately extravagant scale.'

'Please,' said William, 'do not give the matter another thought.'

'I never do. I try to let these things slip from my mind as one of the evanescent delights of travel. But it has been my experience that sooner or later I am reminded of them by my benefactor . . . You are on your way to the Côte d'Azur?'

'No, only as far as Marseilles.'

'I rejoice in the Côte d'Azur. I try to get there every year, but too often I am disappointed. I have so much on my hands—naturally—and in winter I am much occupied with sport. I have a little pack of hounds in the Midlands.'

'Oh? Which?'

'You might not have heard of us. We march with the Fernie. I suppose it is the best hunting country in England. It is a little hobby of mine, but at times, when there is a frost, I long for my little house at Antibes. My friends are kind enough to say I have made it comfortable. I expect you will one day honour me with a visit there.'

'It sounds delightful.'

'They tell me the bathing is good but that does not interest me. I have some plantations of flowering trees which horticulturists are generous enough to regard with interest, and the largest octopus in captivity. The chef too is, in his simple seaside way, one of the best I have. Those simple pleasures suffice for me . . . You are surely not making a long stay in Marseilles?'

'No, I sail tomorrow for East Africa. For Ishmaelia,' William added with some swagger.

The effect on his companion was gratifying. He blinked twice and asked with subdued courtesy:

'Forgive me; I think I must have misheard you. Where are you going?'

'To Ishmaelia. You know, the place where they say there is a war.'

There was a pause. Finally: 'Yes, the name is in some way familiar. I must have seen it in the newspapers.' And, taking a volume of pre-Hitler German poetry from the rack above him, he proceeded to read, shaping the words with his lips like a woman in prayer, and slowly turning the leaves . . .

With his coffee he swallowed two crimson cachets. Then he closed his book of love poems and nodded across the restaurant car.

The soldierly valet who had been dining at the next table turned to go.

'Cuthbert.'

'Sir?'

He stood attentively at his master's side.

'Did you give my sheets to the *conducteur*?'

'Yes, sir.'

'See that he has made them up properly. Then you may go to bed. You know the time in the morning?'

'Yes, sir; thank you, sir; good-night, sir.'

'Good night, Cuthbert . . .' Then he turned to William and said with peculiar emphasis: 'A very courageous man that. He served with me in the war. He never left my side, so I recommended him for the V.C. He never leaves me now. And he is adequately armed.'

This preposterous figure, now slightly sinister, turns up again on the boat to Africa but Boot hardly notices him: the ship is unbearably uncomfortable, the crossing is miserable and Boot is busy nursing a fellow-journalist, Corker, who has been poisoned by eating the fish at dinner.

Eventually the ship arrives off Steamer Point, Aden, and drops anchor:

Passport officers came on board and sat in judgement in the first-class smoking room. The passengers who were to disembark assembled to wait their turn. William and Corker passed without difficulty. They elbowed their way to the door, through the little knot of many-coloured, many-tongued people who had emerged from the depths of the ship. Among them was a plump, dapper figure redolent of hair-wash and shaving soap and expensive scent; there was a glint of jewellery in the shadows, a sparkle of reflected sunshine on the hairless, conical scalp; it was William's dining companion from the Blue Train. They greeted one another warmly.

'I never saw you on board,' said William.

'Nor I you. I wish I had known you were with us. I would have asked you to dine with me in my little suite. I always maintain a certain privacy on the sea. One so easily forms acquaintances which become tedious later.'

'This is a long way from Antibes. What's brought you here?'

'Warmth,' said the little man simply. 'The call of the sun.'

There was a pause and, apparently, some uncertainty at the official table behind them.

'How d'you suppose this bloke pronounces his name?' asked the first passport officer.

'Search me,' said the second.

'Where's the man with the Costa-Rican passport?' said the first passport officer, addressing the room loudly.

A Hindu who had no passport tried to claim it, was detected and held for further inquiry.

'Where's the Costa-Rican?' said the officer again.

'Forgive me,' said William's friend. 'I have a little business to transact with these gentlemen,' and, accompanied by his valet, he stepped towards the table.

'Who's the pansy?' asked Corker.

'Believe it or not,' William replied, 'I haven't the faintest idea.'

At this stage it must have been abundantly clear even to Boot that his odd little acquaintance had told him a pack of lies and was entirely bogus.

But then, as Boot and Corker disembarked into the ship's overcrowded tender and it rolled and pitched slowly towards the shore . . .

A speed-boat shot past them in a glitter of sunlit spray, bouncing on the face of the sea and swamping their bulwarks in its wash. In it sat Cuthbert the valet, and his enigmatic master.

Scoop: A Novel about Journalists (1938).

Waugh not only made a practice of having useful characters turn up again in the same story but he also recycled them in later books. The dreadful popular newspaper The Beast, *which first appeared in* Scoop, *turned up in later books. One of the upper-class louts who caused Paul Pennyfeather to be sent down in* Decline and Fall, *Sir Alastair Digby-Vane-Trumpington, reappeared with a wife in* Black Mischief, *and yet again, reformed now and virtuous, in* Put Out More Flags. *And in* Put Out More Flags *Waugh went even further and not only revived another character from* Black Mischief, *the charming and thoroughly unreliable Basil Seal, but promoted him to be the 'hero' (Waugh's 'heroes' tend to need quotation marks).*

Basil Seal was the mildly distinguished Seal family's major disappointment. In his mid-thirties he remained a feckless opportunist on the make who, in his search for profitable pleasure, had failed at a succession of employments including being leader-writer for The Beast, *lecturer for the BBC, courier taking a party on a conducted tour of the Italian Lakes (he managed to drop all their tickets and passports into Lake Garda), composer of dialogue for the cinema, champagne salesman on commission, and press agent for a female contortionist.*

The first winter of the war found Basil staying with his sister Barbara in her comfortable house in the remote village of Malfrey. It was the time when schoolchildren were being evacuated from London to the country before the bombing began. Barbara was Malfrey's local billeting officer.

Waugh, never one to show undue affection towards children, including his own, draws what can safely be termed an unsentimental picture of the Connollys, the little family of cockney waifs who are sent to be cared for by the sleepy village of Malfrey:

These had appeared as an act of God apparently without human agency; their names did not appear on any list; they carried no credentials; no one was responsible for them. They were found lurking under the seats of a carriage when the train was emptied on the evening of the first influx . . .

Nothing was ever discovered about the Connollys' parentage. When they could be threatened or cajoled into speaking of their antecedents they spoke, with distaste, of an 'Auntie'. To this woman, it seemed, the war had come as a God-sent release. She had taken her dependants to the railway station, propelled them into the crowd of milling adolescents, and hastily covered her tracks by decamping from home. Enquiry by the police in the street where the Connollys professed to have lived, produced no other information than that the woman had been there and was not there any longer. She owed a little for milk; otherwise she had left no memorial on that rather un-impressionable district.

There was Doris, ripely pubescent, aged by her own varied accounts any-thing from ten years to eighteen. An early and ingenious attempt to have her certified as an adult was frustrated by an inspecting doctor who put her at about fifteen. Doris had dark, black, bobbed hair, a large mouth and dark pig's eyes. There was something of the Esquimo about her head, but her colouring was ruddy and her manner more vivacious than is common among that respectable race. Her figure was stocky, her bust prodigious, and her gait, derived from the cinematograph, was designed to be alluring.

Micky, her junior by the length of a rather stiff sentence for house-breaking, was of lighter build; a scrawny, scowling little boy; a child of few words and those, for the most part, foul.

Marlene was presumed to be a year younger. But for Micky's violent denials she might have been taken for his twin. She was the offspring of unusually prolonged coincident periods of liberty in the lives of her parents which the sociologist must deplore, for Marlene was simple. An appeal to have her certified imbecile was disallowed by the same inspecting doctor, who ex-pressed an opinion that country life might work wonders with the child.

There the three had stood, on the eve of the war, in Malfrey Parish Hall, one leering, one lowering, and one drooling, as unprepossessing a family as could be found in the kingdom . . .

The longest that the Connollys stayed in any place was ten days; the shortest was an hour and a quarter. In six weeks they had become a legend far beyond the parish . . . They were cited in the House of Commons; there were paragraphs about them in official reports.

Barbara tried separating them, but in their first night apart Doris climbed out of her window and was lost for two days, to be found in a barn eight miles away, stupefied with cider; she gave no coherent account of her ad-venture. On the same evening Mick bit the wife of the roadman on whom he was quartered, so that the district nurse had to be called in; while Marlene had a species of seizure which aroused unfulfilled hopes that she might be dead.

After more appalling incidents nobody in the neighbourhood will have anything more to do with the Connollys. Barbara, who is temporarily housing them, does not know what to do next.

Basil gives the matter some thought and a rather beautiful idea, neat, simple and just, suddenly occurs to him.

He tells Barbara that he will take over from her and be the billeting officer for the awful children:

Basil set about the problem of finding a home for the Connollys with zeal and method. He settled himself at a table with an ordnance map, the local newspaper and the little red leather-covered address book which had been one of old Mrs Sothill's legacies to Barbara; in this book were registered all her more well-to-do neighbours for a radius of twenty miles, the majority of whom were marked with the initials G.P.O. which stood for Garden Party Only. Barbara had done her best to keep this invaluable work of reference up to date, and had from time to time crossed out those who had died or left the district and added the names of newcomers.

Presently Basil said, 'What about the Harknesses of Old Mill House, North Grappling?'

'Middle-aged people. He retired from some sort of job abroad. I think she's musical. Why?'

'They're advertising for boarders.' He pushed the paper across to her, where she read in the *Accommodation* column: *Paying Guests accepted in lovely modernized fifteenth-century mill. Ideal surroundings for elderly or artistic people wishing to avoid war worries. All home produce. Secluded old-world gardens. 6 gns weekly. Highest references given and expected. Harkness, Old Mill House, North Grappling.*

'How about that for the Connollys?'

'Basil, you can't'.

'Can't I just? I'll get to work on them at once. Do they allow you extra petrol for your billeting work?'

'Yes, but . . .'

'That's grand. I'll take the Connollys over there this morning. D'you know, this is the first piece of serious war work I've done so far?'

Normally, whenever the car left the garage there was a stampede of evacuees to the running boards crying, 'Give us a ride.' This morning, however, seeing the three forbidding Connollys in the back seat, the other children fell back silently. They were not allowed by their mothers to play with the Connollys.

'Mister, why can't I sit in front with you?'

'You've got to keep the other two in order.'

'They'll be good.'

'That's what you think.'

'They'll be good if I tell them, Mister.'

'Then why aren't they?'

''Cos I tell 'em to be bad. In fun you know. Where are we going?'

'I'm finding a new home for you, Doris.'

'Away from you?'

'Far away from me.'

'Mister, listen. Micky ain't bad really nor Marlene isn't silly. Are you, Marlene?'

'Not very silly,' said Marlene.

'She can be clean if she wants to be, if I tell her. See here, Mister, play fair. You let us stay with you and I'll see the kids behave themselves.'

'And what about you, Doris?'

'I don't have to behave. I'm not a kid. Is it on?'

'It is not.'

'You going to take us away?'

'You bet I am.'

'Then just you wait and see what we give them where we're going.'

'I shan't wait and see,' said Basil, 'but I've no doubt I shall hear about it in good time.'

North Grappling was ten miles distant, a stone-built village of uneven stone tile roofs none of which was less than a century old. It lay off the main road in a fold of the hills; a stream ran through it following the line of its single street and crossing it under two old stone bridges . . .

This morning, half lost in snow, the stones which in summer seemed grey were a golden brown, and the pleached limes, which in their leaf hid the low front, now revealed the mullions and dripstones, the sundial above the long, centre window, and the stone hood of the door carved in the shape of a scallop shell. Basil stopped the car by the bridge.

'Jesus,' said Doris. 'You aren't going to leave us here.'

'Sit tight,' said Basil. 'You'll know soon enough.'

He threw a rug over the radiator of the car, opened the little iron gate and walked up the flagged path, grimly, a figure of doom. The low, winter sun cast his shadow before him, ominously, against the door which Mr Harkness had had painted apple green. The gnarled trunk of a wistaria rose from beside the door-jamb and twisted its naked length between the lines of the windows. Basil glanced once over his shoulder to see that his young passengers were invisible and then put his hand to the iron bell. He heard it ring melodiously not far away, and presently the door was opened by a maid dressed in apple green, with an apron of sprigged muslin and a starched white cap that was in effect part Dutch, part conventual, and wholly ludicrous. This figure of fancy led Basil up a step, down a step and into a living room, where he was left long enough to observe the decorations. The floor was covered in coarse rush matting and in places by bright Balkan rugs. On the walls were Thornton's flower prints (with the exception of his masterpiece, *The Night-Flowering Cercus*), samplers and old maps. The most prominent objects of furniture were a grand piano and a harp.

There were also some tables and chairs of raw looking beech. From an open hearth peat smoke billowed periodically into the room, causing Basil's eyes to water. It was just such a room as Basil had imagined from the advertisement and Mr and Mrs Harkness were just such a couple. Mrs Harkness wore a hand-woven woollen garment, her eyes were large and poetic, her nose was long and red with the frost, her hair nondescript in colour and haphazard in arrangement. Her husband had done all that a man can to disguise the effects of twenty years of club and bungalow life in the Far East. He had grown a little pointed beard; he wore a homespun suit of knickerbockers in the style of the pioneers of bicycling; he wore a cameo ring round his loose silk tie; yet there was something in his bearing which still suggested the dapper figure in white ducks who had stood his round of pink gins, evening after evening, to other dapper white figures, and had dined twice a year at Government House.

They entered from the garden door. Basil half expected Mr Harkness to say 'take a pew', and clap his hands for the gin. Instead they stood looking at him with enquiry and some slight distaste.

'My name is Seal. I came about your advertisement in the *Courier*.'

'Our advertisement. Ah yes,' said Mr Harkness vaguely. 'It was just an idea we had. We felt a little ashamed here, with so much space and beauty; the place is a little large for our requirements these days. We did think that perhaps if we heard of a few people like ourselves—the same simple tastes— we might, er, join forces as it were during the present difficult times. As a matter of fact we have one newcomer with us already. I don't think we *really* want to take anyone else, do we, Agnes?'

'It was just an idle thought,' said Mrs Harkness. 'A green thought in a green place.'

'This is not a Guest House, you know. We take in paying guests. Quite a different thing.'

Basil understood their difficulties with a keenness of perception that was rare to him. 'It's not for myself that I was enquiring,' he said.

'Ah, that's different. I daresay we might take in one or two more if they were, if they were *really* . . .'

Mrs Harkness helped him out. 'If we were sure they were the kind of people who would be happy here.'

'Exactly. It is essentially a *happy* house.'

It was like his housemaster at school. 'We are essentially a keen House, Seal. We may not win many cups but at least we try.'

'I can see it is,' he said gallantly.

'I expect you'd like to look round. It looks quite a little place from the road, but is surprisingly large, really, when you come to count up the rooms.'

A hundred years ago the pastures round North Grappling had all been corn-growing land and the mill had served a wide area. Long before the Harknesses' time it had fallen into disuse and, in the 'eighties, had been turned into a dwelling house by a disciple of William Morris. The stream had been diverted, the old mill pool drained and levelled and made into a sunken garden. The rooms that had held the grindstones and machinery, and the long lofts where the grain had been stored, had been tactfully floored and plastered and partitioned. Mrs Harkness pointed out all the features with maternal pride.

'Are your friends who were thinking of coming here artistic people?'

'No, I don't think you could call them that.'

'They don't write?'

'No, I don't think so.'

'I've always thought this would be an ideal place for someone who wanted
to write. May I ask, what *are* your friends?'

'Well, I suppose you might call them evacuees.'

Mr and Mrs Harkness laughed pleasantly at the little joke.

'Townsfolk in search of sanctuary, eh?'

'Exactly.'

'Well, they will find it here, eh, Agnes?'

They were back in the living room. Mrs Harkness laid her hand on the
gilded neck of the harp and looked out across the sunken garden with a
dreamy look in her large grey eyes. Thus she had looked out across the
Malaya golf course, dreaming of home.

'I like to think of this beautiful old house still being of use in the world.
After all it was built for *use*. Hundreds of years ago it gave bread to the people.
Then with the change of the times it was left forlorn and derelict. Then it
became a home, but it was still out of the world, shut off from the life of the
people. And now at last it comes into its own again. Fulfilling a *need*. You
may think me fanciful,' she said, remote and whimsical, 'but in the last few
weeks I feel sometimes I can see the old house smiling to itself and hear the
old timbers whispering, "They thought we were no use. They thought we
were old stick-in-the-muds. But they can't get on without us, all these busy
go-ahead people. They come back to us when they're in trouble."'

'Agnes was always a poet,' said Mr Harkness. 'I have had to be the practical
housewife. You saw our terms in the advertisement?'

'Yes.'

'They may have seemed to you a little heavy, but you must understand
that our guests live exactly as we do ourselves. We live simply but we like
our comfort. Fires,' he said, backing slightly from the belch of aromatic smoke
which issued into the room as he spoke, 'the garden,' he said, indicating the
frozen and buried enclosure outside the windows. 'In the summer we take
our meals under the old mulberry tree. Music. Every week we have chamber
music. There are certain *imponderabilia* at the Old Mill which, to be crude,
have their market value. I *don't* think,' he said coyly, 'I *don't* think that in
the circumstances'—and the circumstances Basil felt sure were meant to
include a good fat slice of Mrs Harkness' poetic imagination—'six guineas is
too much to ask.'

The moment for which Basil had been waiting was come. This was the
time for the grenade he had been nursing ever since he opened the little,
wrought-iron gate and put his hand to the wrought-iron bell-pull. 'We pay
eight shillings and sixpence a week,' he said. That was the safety pin; the
lever flew up, the spring struck home; within the serrated metal shell the
primer spat and, invisibly, flame crept up the finger's length of fuse. Count
seven slowly, then throw. One, two, three, four . . .

'Eight shillings and sixpence?' said Mr Harkness. 'I'm afraid there's been some misunderstanding.'

Five, six, *seven*. Here it comes. Bang! 'Perhaps I should have told you at once. I am the billeting officer. I've three children for you in the car outside.'

It was magnificent. It was war. Basil was something of a specialist in shocks. He could not recall a better.

Put Out More Flags (1942).

> Basil's simple but beautiful plan was, of course, blackmail. After being snowed in with the Connollys, Mr Harkness turned up, a broken man, and asked Basil tearfully how much he would take to billet them elsewhere. With the willing co-operation of Doris, who was no fool, Basil went on to make a small fortune. When he eventually went into the army he sold the Connolly family to a friend as a going concern.

Waugh's trilogy of the War, Sword of Honour, *was made up of* Men at Arms, *which came from his experiences at the beginning of the war in the Royal Marines,* Officers and Gentlemen, *based upon his service with the Commandos and the unfortunate Allied withdrawal from Crete, and* Unconditional Surrender, *taken from his experiences with the partisans in Yugoslavia. It is his most massive achievement as a novelist.*

Judged as a comic work it contains some of his finest humorous character-drawing and one self-contained episode, Apthorpe and his thunder-box, which is a classic of modern comedy; the confrontation of two irresistible forces each of whom, when pressed, becomes a stubbornly immovable object.

The scene is a rambling private school and its grounds requisitioned in the early days of the war as an officers' training camp for the Halberdiers, an ancient and elite regiment.

The first of the irresistible forces is the new commander of the Halberdiers, the dangerously bloodthirsty, heavily wounded warrior, Lieutenant-Colonel Ritchie-Hook (one of Waugh's best inventions, almost certainly based physically upon General Adrian Carton de Wiart, an extraordinarily brave soldier who had been badly wounded in many campaigns and had had all sorts of bits of himself shot away).

The local administrative officers and their wives have mounted a little luncheon party to welcome their new commander to the camp. The group includes Guy Crouchback, the hero (not this time a non-hero but Waugh's other sort of protagonist, the innocent-as-victim).

Ritchie-Hook's reputation has preceded him:

At five minutes to one Mrs Green and Miss Green, wife and daughter of the Captain-Commandant, rose from their places and collected the guests.

'We mustn't be late,' said Mrs Green. 'Ben Ritchie-Hook is coming. He's a terror if he's kept waiting for his food.'

'I find him rather a terror always,' said Miss Green . . .

'I've heard of him,' said Sarum-Smith as though to be known to him had some sinister connotation like being 'known' to the police . . .

Guy too had heard of him often. He was the great Halberdier *enfant terrible* of the First World War; the youngest company commander in the history of the Corps; the slowest to be promoted, often wounded, often decorated, recommended for the Victoria Cross, twice court-martialled for disobedience to orders in the field, twice acquitted for the brilliance of his independent actions; a legendary wielder of the entrenching tool; where lesser men collected helmets Ritchie-Hook once came back from a raid across no-man's-land with the dripping head of a German sentry in either hand . . .

The three probationary Halberdiers stood back for the ladies to pass and followed them through the garden gate with adolescent misgivings and there before them unmistakably, separated from them only by the plate glass of the drawing-room window, stood Lieutenant-Colonel, shortly to be gazetted Brigadier Ritchie-Hook glaring at them balefully with a single, terrible eye. It was black as the brows above it, this eye, black as the patch which hung on the other side of the lean, skew nose. It was set in a steel-rimmed monocle . . .

'Gin for the lady,' cried Colonel Ritchie-Hook. He stretched out a maimed right hand, two surviving fingers and half a thumb in a black glove, clutched a glass and presented it to Mrs Leonard . . .

In the drawing-room with the coffee Colonel Ritchie-Hook showed the softer side of his character. There was a calendar on the chimney-piece, rather shabby now in November and coming to the end of its usefulness. Its design was fanciful, gnomes, toadstools, hare-bells, pink bare babies and dragonflies.

'I say,' he said. 'That's a lovely thing. My word it *is* lovely. Isn't it lovely?'

Ritchie-Hook settles in within hours and begins hectoring, exercising, and frightening the young ex-civilians under his command into the Ritchie-Hook version of a crack fighting unit of the modern army, i.e. one capable of what he called 'biffing' the enemy at will:

The Training Programme followed no text book. Tactics as interpreted by Brigadier Ritchie-Hook consisted of the art of biffing. Defence was studied cursorily and only as the period of reorganization between two bloody assaults. The Withdrawal was never mentioned. The Attack and the Element of Surprise were all. Long raw misty days were passed in the surrounding country with maps and binoculars. Sometimes they stood on the beach and biffed imaginary invaders into the hills; sometimes they biffed imaginary invaders from the hills into the sea. They invested downland hamlets and savagely biffed imaginary hostile inhabitants. Sometimes they merely collided with imaginary rivals for the use of the main road and biffed them out of the way.

Brigadier Ritchie-Hook's adversary in the affair of the thunder-box was the owner of the box, Apthorpe, who is to many readers Waugh's most satisfyingly amusing creation. Indeed, Apthorpe was so perfect a creature of Waugh's imagination that

he grew in importance of his own accord and eventually Waugh had, most reluct-
antly, to kill him off before he upset the structure of the book.

Apthorpe and Guy Crouchback were the oldest of their batch of recruits, most of
whom were a pale and weedy lot:

Apthorpe alone looked like a soldier. He was burly, tanned, moustached, primed with a rich vocabulary of military terms and abbreviations. Until recently he had served in Africa in some unspecified capacity. His boots had covered miles of bush trail.

Boots were a subject of peculiar interest to Apthorpe.

He and Guy first met on the day they joined. Guy got into the carriage at Charing Cross and found Apthorpe seated in the corner opposite to him. He recognized the badges of the Halberdiers and the regimental horn buttons. His first thought was that he had probably committed some heinous breach of etiquette by travelling with a senior officer.

Apthorpe had no newspaper or book. He stared fixedly at his own feet for mile after mile. Presently by a process of furtive inspection Guy realized that the insignia of rank on Apthorpe's shoulders were not crowns but single stars like his own. Still neither spoke, until after twenty minutes Apthorpe took out a pipe and began carefully filling it from a large rolled pouch. Then he said: 'This is my new pair of porpoises. I expect you wear them too.'

Guy looked from Apthorpe's boots to his own. They seemed very much alike. Was 'porpoise' Halberdier slang for 'boots'?

'I don't know. I just told the man I always go to, to make me a couple of pairs of thick black boots.'

'He may have given you cow.'

'Perhaps he did.'

'A great mistake, old man, if you don't mind my saying so.'

He puffed his pipe for another five minutes, then spoke again: 'Of, course, it's really the skin of the white whale, you know.'

'I didn't know. Why do they call it "porpoise"?'

'Trade secret, old man.'

More than once after their meeting Apthorpe reverted to the topic. Whenever Guy gave evidence of sophistication in other matters, Apthorpe would say: 'Funny you don't wear porpoises. I should have thought you were just the chap who would.'

Apthorpe thought in straight lines and once an idea had penetrated his skull he
clung to it with a naïve and rather impressive tenacity.

It was his refusal to abandon a principle, on principle, that led to confrontation
with his terrifying Commanding Officer and to a mounting series of predicaments
culminating in a moment of high tragedy:

The adventure had begun on the first Sunday afternoon of the new regime.

The school rooms were almost deserted that afternoon; everyone was either upstairs or else in the town. Guy was reading his weekly papers in the hall when he saw through the plate-glass window a taxi drive up and Apthorpe emerge, carrying with the help of the driver, a large square object, which they placed in the porch. Guy went out to offer his help.

'That's all right, thank you,' said Apthorpe stiffly. 'I'm just shifting some of my gear.'

'Where d'you want to put it?'

'I don't quite know yet. I shall manage quite well, thank you.'

Guy returned to the hall and stood in the window gazing idly out. It was getting too dark to read comfortably and the man had not yet appeared to put up the black-out screens. Presently he saw Apthorpe emerge from the front door into the twilight and begin furtively burrowing about in the shrubbery. He watched fascinated until some ten minutes later he saw him return. The front porch opened directly into the hall. Apthorpe entered backwards dragging his piece of gear.

'Are you sure I can't help?'

'Quite sure, thank you.'

There was a large cupboard under the stairs. Into this Apthorpe with difficulty shoved his burden. He removed his gloves and coat and cap and came with an air of unconcern to the fire saying: 'The Commodore sent you his compliments. Says he misses us at the Club.'

'Have you been there?'

'Not exactly. Just dropped in on the old man to fetch something.'

'That piece of gear?'

'Well, yes, as a matter of fact.'

'Is it something private, Apthorpe?'

'Something of no general interest, old man. None at all.'

At that moment the duty servant came in to fix the black-out. Apthorpe said: 'Smethers.'

'Sir.'

'Your name is Smethers, isn't it?'

'No, sir. Crock.'

'Well, never mind. What I wanted to ask you was about the offices, the back-parts of the house.'

'Sir?'

'I need some sort of little shed or store-house, a gardener's hut would do, a wash-house, dairy, anything of that kind. Is there such a place?'

'Was you wanting it just for the moment, sir?'

'No, no, no. For as long as we're here.'

'Couldn't say, I'm sure, sir. That's for the Q.M.'

'Yes. I was only wondering,' and when the man had gone: 'Stupid fellow that. I always thought he was called Smethers.'

Guy turned back to his weekly papers. Apthorpe sat opposite him gazing at his boots. Once he got up, walked to the cupboard, peered in, shut it and returned to his chair.

'I can *keep* it there, I suppose, but I can't possibly *use* it there, can I?'

'Can't you?'

'Well, how *can* I?'

There was a pause during which Guy read an article about the inviolability of the Mikkely Marshes. (These were the brave days before the fall of Finland.) Then Apthorpe said:

'I thought I could find a place for it in the shrubbery but it's all much more open than I realized.'

Guy said nothing and turned a page of the *Tablet*. It was clear that Apthorpe was longing to divulge his secret and would shortly do so.

'It is no good going to the Q.M. *He* wouldn't understand. It's not exactly an easy thing to explain to anyone.'

Then, after another pause, he said: 'Well, if you *must* know, it's my thunder-box.'

This was far above Guy's hopes; his mind had been running on food, medicine, small-arms; at the very best he had hoped for something exotic in footwear.

'May I see it?' he asked reverently.

'I don't see why not,' said Apthorpe. 'As a matter of fact I think it will interest you; it's pretty neat, a type they don't make any more. Too expensive, I suppose.'

He went to the cupboard and dragged out the treasure, a brass-bound, oak cube.

'It's a beautiful piece of work really.'

He opened it, showing a mechanism of heavy cast-brass and patterned earthenware of solid Edwardian workmanship. On the inside of the lid was a plaque bearing the embossed title of *Connelly's Chemical Closet*.

'What do you think of it?' said Apthorpe.

Guy was not sure of the proper terms in which to praise such an exhibit.

'It's clearly been very well looked after,' said Guy.

It seemed Guy had said the right thing.

'I got it from a High Court Judge, the year they put drains into the Government buildings at Karonga. Gave him five pounds for it. I doubt if you could find one for twenty these days. There's not the craftsmanship any more.'

'You must be very proud of it.'

'I am.'

'But I don't quite see why you need it here.'

'Don't you, old man? Don't you?' A curiously solemn and fatuous expression replaced the innocent light of ownership that had until now beamed from Apthorpe. 'Have you never heard of a rather unpleasant complaint called "clap", Crouchback?'

Guy was dumbfounded.

'I say, what a beastly thing. I am sorry. I had no idea. I suppose you picked it up the other night in London when you were tight. But are you having it properly seen to? Oughtn't you to go sick?'

'No, no, no, no. *I* haven't got it.'

'Then who has?'

'Sarum-Smith for one.'

'How do you know?'

'I don't *know*. I simply chose Sarum-Smith as an example. He's just the sort of young idiot who would. Any of them might. And I don't intend to take any risks.'

He shut his box and pushed it away under the stairs. The effort seemed to rile him.

'What's more, old man,' he said, 'I don't much like the way you spoke to me just now, accusing me of having clap. It's a pretty serious thing, you know.'

'I'm sorry. It was rather a natural mistake in the circumstances.'

'Not natural to me, old man, and I don't quite know what you mean by "circumstances". I *never* get tight. I should have thought you would have noticed that. Merry, perhaps, on occasions, but never *tight*. It's a thing I keep clear of. I've seen far too much of it.'

Apthorpe was up at first light next day exploring the outbuildings and before breakfast had discovered an empty shed where the school perhaps had kept bats and pads. There with the help of Halberdier Crock he installed his chemical closet and thither for several tranquil days he resorted for his comfort. It was two days after the fall of Finland that his troubles began.

Back from biffing about the downs, and after a late luncheon inclined for half an hour's rest, Guy was disturbed by Apthorpe. He wore a face of doom.

'Crouchback, a word with you.'

'Well.'

'In private if you don't mind.'

'I do mind. What is it?'

Apthorpe looked round the ante-room. Everybody seemed occupied.

'You've been using my thunder-box.'

'No, I haven't.'

'Someone has.'

'Well, it isn't me.'

'No one else knows of it.'

'How about Halberdier Crock?'

'He wouldn't dare.'

'Neither would I, my dear fellow.'

'Is that your last word?'

'Yes.'

'Very well. But in future I shall keep a look-out.'

'Yes, I should.'

'It's a serious matter, you know. It almost amounts to pilfering. The chemical is far from cheap.'

'How much a go?'

'It isn't the money. It's the principle.'

'And the risk of infection.'

'Exactly.'

For two days Apthrope posted himself in the bushes near his shed and spent every available minute on watch. On the third day he drew Guy aside and said: 'Crouchback, I owe you an apology. It isn't you who has been using my thunder-box.'

'I know that.'

'Yes, but you must admit the circumstances were very suspicious. Anyway I've found out who it is, and it's most disturbing.'

'Not Sarum-Smith?'

'No. Much more disturbing that that. *It's the Brigadier.*'

'Do you think *he's* got clap?'

'No. Most unlikely. Far too much a man of the world. But the question arises, what action ought I to take?'

'None.'

'It's a matter of principle. As my superior officer he has no more right to use my thunder-box than to wear my boots.'

'Well, I'd lend him my boots if he wanted them.'

'Perhaps; but then, if you'll forgive my saying so, you're not very particular about your boots, are you, old man? Anyway you think it is my duty to submit without protest?'

'I think you'll make a tremendous ass of yourself if you don't.'

'I shall have to think about it. Do you think I ought to consult the B.M.?'

'No.'

'You may be right.'

Next day Apthrope reported: 'Things are getting worse.'

It showed how much the thunder-box had occupied Guy's thoughts that he knew at once what Apthorpe meant.

'More intruders?'

'No, not that. But this morning as I was coming out I met the Brigadier going in. He gave me a very odd look—you may have noticed he has rather a disagreeable stare on occasions. His look seemed to suggest that *I* had no business there.'

'He's a man of action,' said Guy. 'You won't have to wait long to know what he thinks about it.'

All day Apthorpe was distracted. He answered haphazardly when asked an opinion on tactics. His solutions of the problems set them were wild. At every pause in the routine he kept vigil by the hut. He missed tea and did not return until ten minutes before the evening lecture. He was red-nosed and blue-cheeked.

'You'll make yourself ill, if this goes on,' said Guy.

'It can't go on. The worst has happened already.'

'What?'

'Come and see. I wouldn't have believed it, if I hadn't seen it with my own eyes.'

They went out into the gloom.

'Just five minutes ago. I'd been on watch since tea and was getting infernally cold, so I started walking about. And the Brigadier came right past me. I saluted. He said nothing. Then he did this thing right under my very eyes. Then he came past me again and I saluted and he positively grinned. I tell you, Crouchback, it was *devilish*.'

They had reached the hut. Guy could just see something large and white hanging on the door. Apthorpe turned his torch on it and Guy saw a neatly inscribed notice: *Out of Bounds to all ranks below Brigadier.*

'He must have had it made specially by one of the clerks,' said Apthorpe awfully.

'It's put you in rather a fix, hasn't it?' said Guy.

'I shall send in my papers.'

'I don't believe you can in war-time.'

'I can ask for a transfer to another regiment.'

'I should miss you, Apthorpe, more than you can possibly believe. Anyway there's a lecture in two minutes. Let's go in.'

The Brigadier himself lectured. Booby traps, it appeared, were proving an important feature of patrol work on the Western front. The Brigadier spoke of trip-wires, detonators, anti-personnel mines. He described in detail an explosive goat which he had once contrived and driven into a Bedouin encampment. Seldom had he been more exuberant.

This was one of the evenings when there was no discussion or night exercise and it was generally accepted that those who wished might dine out.

'Let's go to the Garibaldi,' said Apthorpe. 'I won't sit at the same table with that man. You must dine with me as my guest.'

There, in the steam of *minestrone*, Apthorpe's face became a healthier colour and strengthened by Barolo his despair gave place to defiance . . .

'I don't think,' said Apthorpe, 'it would be any good appealing to the Army Council, do you?'

'No.'

'You could not expect them to meet a case like this with purely open minds. I don't suggest positive prejudice but, after all, it's in their interests to support authority, if they possibly can. If they found a loophole . . .'

'You think there are loopholes in your case?'

'Quite frankly, old man, I do. In a court of honour, of course, the thing would be different, but in its purely legal aspect one has to admit that the Brigadier is within his rights in putting any part of the brigade premises out of bounds. It is also true that I installed my thunder-box without permission. That's just the sort of point the Army Council would jump on.'

'Of course,' said Guy, 'it's arguable that since the thunder-box has not risen to the rank of brigadier, it itself is out of bounds.'

'You've got it, Crouchback. You've hit the nail on the head.' He goggled across the table in frank admiration . . .

'But there's now the question of action. How are we going to get the thunder-box out?'

'The way you got it in, I suppose.'

'Not so easy, old man. There's wheels within wheels. Halberdier Crock and I carried it there. How can we carry it away without going out of bounds? One can't order a man to perform an unlawful action. You must remember that. Besides I shouldn't really care to *ask* him. He was distinctly unco-operative about the whole undertaking.'

'Couldn't you lasso it from the door?'

'Pretty ticklish, old man. Besides, my lariat is with the rest of my gear at the Commodore's.'

'Couldn't you draw it out with a magnet?'

'I say, are you trying to be funny, Crouchback?'

'It was just a suggestion.'

'*Not* a very practical one, if you don't mind my saying so. No. Someone must go in and get it.'

'Out of bounds?'

'Someone who doesn't know, or at least who the Brigadier doesn't know knows, that the hut is out of bounds. If he was caught he could always plead that he didn't see the notice in the dark.'

'You mean me?'

'Well, you're more or less the obvious person, aren't you, old man?'

'All right,' said Guy. 'I don't mind.'

'Good for you,' said Apthorpe, greatly relieved . . .

They returned to Kut-al-Imara. There was no one about. Apthorpe kept *cave* and Guy, without much difficulty, dragged the object into the open.

'Where to now?'

'That's the question. Where do you think will be the best place?'

'The latrines.'

'Really, old man, this is scarcely the time or place for humour.'

'I was only thinking of Chesterton's observation. "Where is the best place to hide a leaf? In a tree."'

'I don't get you, old man. It would be jolly awkward up a tree, from *every* point of view.'

'Well, let's not take it far. It's bloody heavy.'

'There's a potting-shed I found when I was making my recce.'

They took it there, fifty yards away. It was less commodious than the hut, but Apthorpe said it would do. As they were returning from their adventure he paused in the path and said with unusual warmth: 'I shan't forget this evening's work, Crouchback. Thank you very much . . .'

After a few more steps Apthorpe said: 'Look here, old man, if you'd care to use the thunder-box, too, it's all right with me.'

It was a moment of heightened emotion; an historic moment, had Guy recognized it, when in their complicated relationship Apthorpe came nearest to love and trust. It passed, as such moments do between Englishmen.

'It's very good of you but I'm quite content as I am.'

'Sure?'

'Yes.'

'That's all right then,' said Apthorpe, greatly relieved.

Thus Guy stood high in Apthorpe's favour and became with him joint custodian of the thunder-box.

In full retrospect all the last weeks of March resolved themselves into the saga of the chemical closet. Apthorpe soon forgot his original motive for installing it.

He was no longer driven by fear of infection. His right of property was at stake. Waiting to fall in, on the morning after the first translation, Apthorpe drew Guy aside. Their new comradeship was on a different plane from frank geniality; they were fellow conspirators now. 'It's still there.'

'Good.'

'Untouched.'

'Fine.'

'I think, old man, that in the circumstances we had better not be seen talking together too much.'

Later, as they went into the mess for luncheon Guy had the odd impression that someone in the crowd was attempting to hold his hand. He looked about him and saw Apthorpe, with averted face, talking with great emphasis to Captain Sanders. Then he realized that a note was being passed to him.

Apthorpe made for a place at table as far as possible from his. Guy opened the screw of paper and read: '*The notice has been taken down from the hut. Unconditional surrender?*'

Not until tea-time did Apthorpe consider it safe to speak.

'I don't think we've any more to worry about. The Brig. has given us best.'

'It doesn't sound like him.'

'Oh, he's unscrupulous enough for anything, I know that. But he has his dignity to consider.'

Guy did not wish to upset Apthorpe's new, gleeful mood, but he doubted whether these adversaries had an identical sense of dignity. Next day it was apparent that they had not.

Apthorpe arrived for parade (under the new regime there was half an hour's drill and physical training every morning) with a face of horror. He fell in next to Guy. Again there was an odd inter-fumbling of fingers and Guy found himself holding a message. He read it at the first stand-easy while Apthorpe turned ostentatiously away. '*Must speak to you alone first opportunity. Grave developments.*'

An opportunity came half-way through the morning.

'The man's mad. A dangerous, certifiable maniac. I don't know what I ought to do about it.'

'What's he done now?'

'He came within an inch of killing me, that's all. If I hadn't been wearing my steel helmet I shouldn't be here to tell you. He caught me with a bloody great flower-pot, full of earth and a dead geranium, square on the top of my head. That's what he did this morning.'

'He threw it at you?'

'It was on top of the potting-shed door.'

'Why were you wearing your tin-hat?'

'Instinct, old man. Self-preservation.'

'But you said last night you thought the whole thing was over. Apthorpe, do you always wear your tin-hat on the thunder-box?'

'All this is irrelevant. The point is that this man simply isn't responsible. It's a very serious matter for someone in his position—and ours. A time may come when he holds our lives in his hands. What ought I to do?'

'Move the box again.'

'And not report the matter?'

'Well, there's your dignity to consider.'

'You mean there are people who might think it funny?'

'Awfully funny.'

'Damn,' said Apthorpe. 'I hadn't considered that side of the question.'

'I wish you'd tell me the truth about the tin-hat.'

'Well, if you must know, I *have* been wearing it lately. I suppose it really boils down to home-sickness, old man. The helmet has rather the feel of a solar topee, if you see what I mean. It makes the thunder-box more homely.'

'You don't start out wearing it?'

'No, under my arm.'

'And when do you put it on, before or after lowering the costume? I must know.'

'On the threshold, as it happens. Very luckily for me this morning. But, you know, really, old man, I don't quite get you. Why the interest?'

'I must visualize the scene, Apthorpe. When we are old men, memories of things like this will be our chief comfort.'

'Crouchback, there are times when you talk almost as though you found it funny.'

'Please don't think that, Apthorpe. I beg you, anything but that.'

Already after so brief a reconciliation Apthorpe was getting suspicious. He would have liked to be huffy but did not dare. He was pitted against a ruthless and resourceful enemy and must hold fast to Guy or go down.

'Well, what is our next move?' he asked.

That night they crept out to the potting-shed and Apthorpe in silence showed with his torch the broken shards, the scattered mould and the dead geranium of that morning's great fright. In silence he and Guy lifted the box and bore it as they had planned back to its original home in the games-hut.

Next day, the Brigadier appeared at first parade.

'ATM 24, as no doubt you all know, recommends the use of games for training in observation and field-craft. This morning, gentlemen, you will play such a game. Somewhere about these grounds has been concealed an antiquated field latrine, no doubt left here as valueless by the former occupants of the camp. It looks like a plain square box. Work singly. The first officer to find it will report to me. Fall out.'

'His effrontery staggers me,' said Apthorpe. 'Crouchback, guard the shed. I will draw off the hunt.'

New strength had come to Apthorpe. He was master of the moment. He strode off purposefully towards the area of coal-bunkers and petrol dump and, sure enough, the Brigadier was soon seen to follow behind him. Guy made deviously for the games-hut and sauntered near it. Twice other seekers approached and Guy said: 'I've just been in there. Nothing to see.'

Presently the bugle recalled them. The Brigadier received the 'nil report,' mounted his motor-cycle and drove away scowling ominously but without a word; he did not reappear at all that day.

'A bad loser, old man,' said Apthorpe.

But next day the *Out of Bounds* notice was back on the shed.

As Guy foresaw, those mad March days and nights of hide-and-seek drained into a deep well of refreshment in his mind, but in retrospect the detail of alternate ruse and counter-ruse faded and grew legendary. He never again smelled wet laurel, or trod among pine needles, without reliving those encumbered night patrols with Apthorpe, those mornings of triumph or disappointment. But the precise succession of episodes, indeed their very number, faded and were lost among later, less child-like memories.

The climax came in Holy Week at the very end of the course. The Brigadier had been in London for three days on the business of their next move. The thunder-box stood in a corner of the playing-field, unhoused but well hidden between an elm tree and a huge roller. There for the three days Apthorpe enjoyed undisputed rights of property.

The Brigadier returned in alarmingly high spirits. He had bought some trick glasses at the toy-shop which, when raised, spilled their contents down the drinker's chin, and these he secretly distributed round the table before dinner. After dinner there was a long session of Housey-housey. When he had called the last house he said: 'Gentlemen, everyone except the B.M. and I goes on leave tomorrow. We meet under canvas in the lowlands of Scotland where you will have ample time to put into practice the lessons you have learnt here. Details will be posted as soon as the B.M. has sweated them out. You will particularly notice that officer's baggage and equipment is defined by a scale laid down at the War House. Those limits will be strictly observed. I think that's all, isn't it B.M.? Oh, no, one other thing. You are all improperly dressed. You have been promoted as from this morning. Get those second pips up before leaving camp.'

That night there was singing in the dormitories:

> 'This time tomorrow I shall be
> Far from this Acadamee.'

Leonard improvised

> 'No more TEWTS and no more drill,
> No more night ops to cause a chill.'

'I say,' said Guy to Apthorpe. 'That scale of equipment won't allow for your gear.'

'I know, old man. It's very worrying.'

'And the thunder-box.'

'I shall find a place for it. Somewhere quite safe, a crypt, a vault, somewhere like that where I shall know it's waiting for me until the end of the war.'

> 'No more swamps through which to creep,
> No more lectures to make me sleep.'

The cheerful voices reached the room marked '*Bde. HQ*' where the Brigadier was at work with his brigade major.

'That reminds me,' he said. 'I've some unfinished business to attend to outside.'

Next morning as soon as the sun touched the unshaded window of Passchendaele, Apthorpe was up, jabbing his shoulder-straps with a pair of scissors. Then he tricked himself out as a lieutenant. He nothing common did nor mean on their morning of departure. His last act before leaving the dormitory was a friendly one; he offered to lend Guy a pair of stars from a neat leather stud-box which he now revealed to be full of such adornments and of crowns also. Then before Guy had finished shaving, Apthorpe, correctly dressed and bearing his steel helmet under his arm, set out for his corner of the playing field.

The spot was not a furlong away. In less than five minutes an explosion rattled the windows of the schoolhouse. Various jolly end-of-term voices rose from the dormitories: 'Air-raid'; 'Take cover'; 'Gas'.

Guy buckled his belt and hurried out to what he knew must be the scene of the disaster. Wisps of smoke were visible. He crossed the playing field. At first there was no sign of Apthorpe. Then he came upon him, standing, leaning against the elm, wearing his steel helmet, fumbling with his trouser buttons and gazing with dazed horror on the wreckage which lay all around the roller.

'I say, are you hurt?'

'Who is that? Crouchback? I don't know. I simply don't know, old man.'

Of the thunder-box there remained only a heap of smoking wood, brass valves, pinkish chemical powder scattered many yards, and great jags of patterned china.

'What happened?'

'I don't know, old man. I just sat down. There was a frightful bang and the next thing I knew I was on all fours on the grass, right over there.'

'Are you hurt?' Guy asked again.

'Shock,' said Apthorpe. 'I don't feel at all the thing.'

Guy looked more closely at the wreckage. It was plain enough from his memories of the last lecture what had happened.

Apthorpe removed his steel helmet, recovered his cap, straightened his uniform, put up a hand to assure himself that his new stars were still in place. He looked once more at all that remained of his thunder-box; the *mot juste*, thought Guy.

He seemed too dazed for grief.

Guy was at a loss for words of condolence.

'Better come back to breakfast.'

They turned silently towards the house.

Apthorpe walked unsteadily across the wet, patchy field with his eyes fixed before him.

On the steps he paused once and looked back.

There was more of high tragedy than of bitterness in the epitaph he spoke.

'*Biffed.*'

Men at Arms (1952).

————

ALTHOUGH *Evelyn Waugh is widely accepted as the finest comic novelist of this century, the single most important, original, and often infuriatingly complex comic novel of the century was written by somebody else, namely James Joyce. The novel was* Ulysses.

This seemingly odd contradiction makes more sense when it is realized that when talking about Waugh's fiction the word 'comic' tends to be used in its modern meaning of 'giving rise to mirth . . . funny', whereas when describing Joyce's work, 'comic' reverts to its old classical meaning of 'that which is not tragic . . . which has a happy ending'.

Ulysses *first appeared as a book, tentatively, in* 1922. *Some of it had appeared in a little magazine in New York but the book had to be published in Paris because of some unusually frank references to sexual and lavatorial activities and copies brought into the USA and Britain were instantly seized and burned by the authorities before the nation could become irredeemably corrupted.*

It was not until 1934 that an enlightened judge in the USA pronounced the offending passages in the book to be unpleasant but not pornographic. In 1936 Britain followed suit. But by then the book was a sensation in the literary world and had attracted lavish praise from many of the new young writers such as Ernest Hemingway, T. S. Eliot, and Ezra Pound.

It was a kind of Bible to the Modernists as it successfully put into practice many of their aims, like stream-of-consciousness interior monologues and Freudian psychology, mixing fantasy with realism and using several prose styles to tell a story which largely did away with the complications of a plot.

It is perfectly possible for a reader to burst into wild guffaws on reading Ulysses, *or for that matter Rabelais,* The Anatomy of Melancholy, *or the essay on noses in* Tristram Shandy, *but chances are that the reader thus overwhelmed would not be your average reader but one with, say, an educated appreciation of the depth and breadth of discursive medieval literature and one who happens to be in exactly the right, rare, mood for finding classical comedy, i.e. non-tragic prose, rib-tickling.*

Joyce's Ulysses *fulfils the old Greek requirement of comedy by having a happy ending—Molly Bloom, the womanhood-figure, warmly sensual, affirms the human need for love and affection, and in her long and famous soliloquy celebrates having had her share of both from husband and lover—but the comedy is not the kind which easily triggers laughter; it is not the comedy of comical incident or of character but almost entirely the comedy of language, or rather languages. Joyce has written the book in a number of complex, dazzling prose styles, rich in parody, pastiche, puns, allusions, words used as notes of music, echoes of other literature, myths, illusions.*

The frame of the novel is a day in Dublin. A specific day: the 16th of June, 1904, in remembrance of the day when Joyce first walked round Dublin with Nora Barnacle, a quiet, simple, very pretty chambermaid who later lived with him in Zurich and Paris in near poverty, looked after him and loved him without understanding a word he wrote, bore him a son and daughter, and eventually married him.

The chapters which tell the story of the day in Dublin mirror episodes in Homer's Odyssey; *the main characters are Leopold Bloom (Odysseus), husband of Molly, Jewish, sells advertising space for a Dublin newspaper and is impotent from regret over his wife's infidelity; his wife Molly (Penelope); and Stephen Dedalus, impoverished and word-drunk perpetual student (Telemachus).*

Ulysses *is a work of art which should be read as a whole: of all the great books of the world it is one of the volumes least capable of yielding a satisfactory sample. But even if a few pages cannot give a reader new to Joyce much of an indication of the sweep and depth of his imagination, the reader can at least get an inkling of Joyce's several individual, strange, and eventually hypnotic styles of writing.*

In the following extract it is now the evening of July 16th and a display of fireworks is lighting up the sky over Dublin. Bloom is idling on the beach staring at a pretty young girl, Gerty MacDowell, who is sitting on a rock, supposedly minding some children with her friends Cissie and Edy. Gertie is at a dangerously romantic stage and devotes as much time as she can to reading novelettes. She has no intention whatsoever of joining her two friends further along where she can get a better view of the fireworks because she knows that a man, Bloom, is watching her and something beautiful and romantic could very well happen to her at any moment.

The mundane, rather sordid little scene which follows is transformed into something beautiful and delicately erotic by a good deal of wishful thinking from Gertie and from being written in a pastiche of Gertie's personal language; the rich, throbbing prose of late-Victorian romances:

The eyes that were fastened upon her set her pulses tingling. She looked at him a moment, meeting his glance, and a light broke in on her. Whitehot passion was in that face, passion silent as the grave, and it had made her his. At last they were left alone without the others to pry and pass remarks and she knew he could be trusted to the death, steadfast, a sterling man, a man of inflexible honour to his fingertips. His hands and face were working and a tremor went over her. She leaned back far to look up where the fireworks were and she caught her knee in her hands so as not to fall back looking up and there was no-one to see only him and her when she revealed all her graceful beautifully shaped legs like that, supply soft and delicately rounded, and she seemed to hear the panting of his heart, his hoarse breathing, because she knew about the passion of men like that, hotblooded, because Bertha Supple told her once in dead secret and made her swear she'd never about the gentleman lodger that was staying with them out of the Congested Districts Board that had pictures cut out of papers of those skirtdancers and highkickers and she said he used to do something not very nice that you could imagine sometimes in the bed. But this was altogether different from a thing like that because there was all the difference because she could almost feel him draw her face to his and the first quick hot touch of his handsome lips. Besides there was absolution so long as you didn't do the other thing before being married and there ought to be women priests that would understand without your telling out and Cissy Caffrey too sometimes had that dreamy kind of dreamy look in her eyes so that she too, my dear, and Winny Rippingham so mad about actors' photographs and besides it was on account of that other thing coming on the way it did.

And Jacky Caffrey shouted to look, there was another and she leaned back and the garters were blue to match on account of the transparent and they all saw it and shouted to look, look there it was and she leaned back ever so far to see the fireworks and something queer was flying through the air, a soft thing to and fro, dark. And she saw a long Roman candle going up over

the trees up, up, and, in the tense hush, they were all breathless with
excitement as it went higher and higher and she had to lean back more and
more to look up after it, high, high, almost out of sight, and her face was
suffused with a divine, an entrancing blush from straining back and he could
see her other things too, nainsook knickers, the fabric that caresses the skin,
better than those other pettiwidth, the green, four and eleven, on account of
being white and she let him and she saw that he saw and then it went so
high it went out of sight a moment and she was trembling in every limb from
being bent so far back he had a full view high up above her knee no-one ever
not even on the swing or wading and she wasn't ashamed and he wasn't
either to look in that immodest way like that because he couldn't resist the
sight of the wondrous revealment half offered like those skirtdancers behaving
so immodest before gentlemen looking and he kept on looking, looking. She
would fain have cried to him chokingly, held out her snowy slender arms to
him to come, to feel his lips laid on her white brow the cry of a young girl's
love, a little strangled cry, wrung from her, that cry that has rung through
the ages. And then a rocket sprang and bang shot blind and O! then the
Roman candle burst and it was like a sigh of O! and everyone cried O! O! in
raptures and it gushed out of it a stream of rain gold hair threads and they
shed and ah! they were all greeny dewy stars falling with golden, O so lovely!
O so soft, sweet, soft!

Then all melted away dewily in the grey air: all was silent. Ah! She glanced
at him as she bent forward quickly, a pathetic little glance of piteous protest,
of shy reproach under which he coloured like a girl. He was leaning back
against the rock behind. Leopold Bloom (for it is he) stands silent, with bowed
head before those young guileless eyes. What a brute he had been! At it
again? A fair unsullied soul had called to him and, wretch that he was, how
had he answered? An utter cad he had been! He of all men! But there was
an infinite store of mercy in those eyes, for him too a word of pardon even
though he had erred and sinned and wandered. Should a girl tell? No, a
thousand times no. That was their secret, only theirs, alone in the hiding
twilight and there was none to know or tell save the little bat that flew so
softly through the evening to and fro and little bats don't tell.

*Chapter 15 is entirely different in style, a dream-like flow of fantasies and allusions
in the form of a play. In places the work bears a strong resemblance to the
post-Freud* dementia-praecox *sketches which Ring Lardner and Robert Benchley
were writing at that time in the USA and D. B. Wyndham Lewis in England.*

*The evening has become night and Bloom at last catches up with Stephen Dedalus
in a Dublin brothel. Stephen is a little drunker than anybody else. The ghost of
Stephen's mother appears among the whores and their customers:*

THE MOTHER: I pray for you in my other world. Get Dilly to make you that
boiled rice every night after your brain work. Years and years I loved you, O
my son, my firstborn, when you lay in my womb.

ZOE: (*Fanning herself with the grate fan*) I'm melting!

FLORRY: (*Points to Stephen*) Look! He's white.

BLOOM: (*Goes to the window to open it more*) Giddy.

MOTHER: (*With smouldering eyes*) Repent! O, the fire of hell!

STEPHEN: (*Panting*) The corpsechewer! Raw head and bloody bones!

THE MOTHER: *Her face drawing near and nearer, sending out an ashen breath*) Beware! (*She raises her blackened, withered right arm slowly towards Stephen's breast with outstretched fingers*) Beware! God's hand (*A green crab with malignant red eyes sticks deep its grinning claws in Stephen's heart.*)

STEPHEN: (*Strangled with rage*) Shite! (*His features grow drawn and grey and old.*)

BLOOM: (*At the window*) What?

STEPHEN: *Ah non, par exemple!* The intellectual imagination! With me all or not at all. *Non serviam!*

FLORRY: Give him some cold water. Wait. (*She rushes out.*)

THE MOTHER: (*Wrings her hands slowly, moaning desperately*) O Sacred Heart of Jesus, have mercy on him! Save him from hell, O divine Sacred Heart!

STEPHEN: No! No! No! Break my spirit all of you if you can! I'll bring you all to heel!

THE MOTHER: (*In the agony of her deathrattle*) Have mercy on Stephen, Lord, for my sake! Inexpressible was my anguish when expiring with love, grief and agony on Mount Calvary.

STEPHEN: *Nothung!*

(*He lifts his ashplant high with both hands and smashes the chandelier. Time's livid final flame leaps and, in the following darkness, ruin of all space, shattered glass and toppling masonry.*)

THE GASJET: Pwfungg!

BLOOM: Stop!

LYNCH: (*Rushes forward and seizes Stephen's hand*) Here! Hold on! Don't run amok!

BELLA: Police!

(*Stephen, abandoning his ashplant, his head and arms thrown back stark, beats the ground and flees from the room past the whores at the door.*)

BELLA: (*Screams*) After him!

(*The two whores rush to the halldoors. Lynch and Kitty and Zoe stampede from the room. They talk excitedly. Bloom follows, returns.*)

THE WHORES: (*Jammed in the doorway, pointing*) Down there.

ZOE: (*Pointing*) There. There's something up.

BELLA: Who pays for the lamp? (*She seizes Bloom's coattail*) There. You were with him. The lamp's broken.

BLOOM: (*Rushes to the hall, rushes back*) What lamp, woman?

A WHORE: He tore his coat.

BELLA: (*Her eyes hard with anger and cupidity, points*) Who's to pay for that? Ten shillings. You're a witness.

BLOOM: (*Snatches up Stephen's ashplant*) Me? Ten shillings? Haven't you lifted enough off him? Didn't he . . . !

BELLA: (*Loudly*) Here, none of your tall talk. This isn't a brothel. A ten shilling house.

BLOOM: (*His hand under the lamp, pulls the chain. Pulling, the gasjet lights up a crushed mauve purple shade. He raises the ashplant.*) Only the chimney's broken. Here is all he . . .

BELLA: (*Shrinks back and screams*) Jesus! Don't!

BLOOM: (*Warding off a blow*) To show you how he hit the paper. There's not a sixpenceworth of damage done. Ten shillings!

FLORRY: (*With a glass of water, enters*) Where is he?

BELLA: Do you want me to call the police?

BLOOM: O, I know. Bulldog on the premises. But he's a Trinity student. Patrons of your establishment. Gentlemen that pay the rent. (*He makes a masonic sign*) Know what I mean? Nephew of the vice-chancellor. You don't want a scandal.

BELLA: (*Angrily*) Trinity! Coming down here ragging after the boat races and paying nothing. Are you my commander here? Where is he? I'll charge him. Disgrace him, I will. (*She shouts*) Zoe! Zoe!

BLOOM: (*Urgently*) And if it were your own son in Oxford! (*Warningly*) I know.

BELLA: (*Almost speechless*) Who are you incog?

ZOE: (*In the doorway*) There's a row on.

BLOOM: What? Where? (*He throws a shilling on the table and shouts*) That's for the chimney. Where? I need mountain air.

(*He hurries out through the hall. The whores point. Florry follows, spilling water from her tilted tumbler. On the doorstep all the whores clustered talk volubly, pointing to the right where the fog has cleared off. From the left arrives a jingling hackney car. It slows to in front of the house. Bloom at the halldoor perceives Corny Kelleher who is about to dismount from the car with two silent lechers. He averts his face. Bella from within the hall urges on her whores. They blow ickylickysticky yumyum kisses. Corny Kelleher replies with a ghostly lewd smile. The silent lechers turn to pay the jarvey. Zoe and Kitty still point right. Bloom, parting them swiftly, draws his caliph's hood and poncho and hurries down the steps with sideways face.*)

The last chapter of Ulysses *is taken up by Molly Bloom's internal monologue, her stream-of-consciousness memories.*

It is gone two o'clock in the morning. Leopold has lurched home and is sleeping beside her in the uncomfortable, creaking bed she is always meaning to get rid of. As a child Molly was brought up in Gibraltar. She is 32 years old now, musical, full-bodied with healthy sexual appetites.

Lying in bed, half asleep and restless, disjointed fragments of her life flit across her mind; her life as a pretty girl in the 1890s, her daughter Milly, her husband, men she made love with; the love-making itself, mostly coarse and unpleasing but a necessity of life and occasionally deeply exciting:

yes I think he made them a bit firmer sucking them like that so long he made me thirsty titties he calls them I had to laugh yes this one anyhow stiff the nipple gets for the least thing Ill get him to keep that up and Ill take those eggs beaten up with marsala fatten them out for him what are all those veins and things curious the way its made 2 the same in case of twins theyre supposed to represent beauty placed up there like those statues in the museum one of them pretending to hide it with her hand are they so beautiful of course compared with what a man looks like with his two bags full and his other thing hanging down out of him or sticking up at you like a hatrack no wonder they hide it with a cabbageleaf the woman is beauty of course thats admitted when he said I could pose for a picture naked to some rich fellow in Holles street when he lost the job in Helys and I was selling the clothes and strumming in the coffee palace would I be like that bath of the nymph with my hair down yes only shes younger or Im a little like that dirty bitch in that Spanish photo he has the nymphs used they go about like that I asked him that disgusting Cameron highlander behind the meat market or that other wretch with the red head behind the tree where the statue of the fish used to be when I was passing pretending he was pissing standing out for me to see it with his babyclothes up to one side the Queens own they were a nice lot its well the Surreys relieved them theyre always trying to show it to you every time nearly I passed outside the mens greenhouse near the Harcourt street station just to try some fellow or other trying to catch my eye as if it was 1 of the 7 wonders of the world O and the stink of those rotten places the night coming home with Poldy after the Comerfords party oranges and lemonade to make you feel nice and watery I went into 1 of them it was so biting cold I couldnt keep it when was that 93 the canal was frozen yes it was a few months after a pity a couple of the Camerons werent there to see me squatting in the mens place meadero I tried to draw a picture of it before I tore it up like a sausage or something I wonder theyre not afraid going about getting a kick or a bang or something there and that word met something with hoses in it and he came out with some jawbreakers about the incarnation he never can explain a thing simply the way a body can under-stand then he goes and burns the bottom out of the pan all for his Kidney this one not so much theres the mark of his teeth still where he tried to bite the nipple I had to scream out arent they fearful trying to hurt you I had a great breast of milk with Milly enough for two what was the reason of that he said I could have got a pound a week as a wet nurse all swelled out the morning that delicate looking student that stopped in No 28 with the Citrons Penrose nearly caught me washing through the window only for I snapped up the towel to my face that was his studenting hurt me they used to weaning her till he got doctor Brady to give me the Belladonna prescription I had to

get him to suck them they were so hard he said it was sweeter and thicker
than cows then he wanted to milk me into the tea well hes beyond everything
I declare somebody ought to put him in the budget if I only could remember
the one half of the things and write a book out of it the works of Master
Poldy yes and its so much smoother the skin much an hour he was at them
Im sure by the clock like some kind of big infant I had at me they want
everything in their mouth all the pleasure those men get out of a woman I
can feel his mouth O Lord I must stretch myself I wished he was here or
somebody to let myself go with and come again like that I feel all fire inside
me or if I could dream it when he made me spend the 2nd time tickling me
behind with his finger I was coming for about 5 minutes with my legs round
him I had to hug him after O Lord I wanted to shout out all sorts of things
fuck or shit or anything at all only not to look ugly or those lines from the
strain who knows the way hed take it you want to feel your way with a man
theyre not all like him thank God some of them want you to be so nice about
it I noticed the contrast he does it and doesnt talk I gave my eyes that look
with my hair a bit loose from the tumbling and my tongue between my lips
up to him the savage brute Thursday Friday one Saturday two Sunday three
O Lord I cant wait till Monday

> ◆ Robert MacAlmon, in his memoirs of Paris in the twenties, records that
> Nora Joyce, who loved her husband but did not really understand his
> writings, confessed that she had sneaked a look at his Molly Bloom soli-
> loquy. 'Sure,' was her cheerful reaction, 'and hasn't he the dirty mind!'

*As sleep still eludes Molly Bloom, her memory turns to a happy occasion: that
moment years ago, on a rocky point above Dublin Bay, when she at long last
contrived to persuade Leopold to propose to her:*

the sun shines for you he said the day we were lying among the rhododendrons on Howth head in the grey tweed suit and his straw hat the day
I got him to propose to me yes first I gave him the bit of seedcake out of my
mouth and it was leapyear like now yes 16 years ago my God after that long
kiss I near lost my breath yes he said I was a flower of the mountain yes so
we are flowers all a womans body yes that was one true thing he said in his
life and the sun shines for you today yes that was why I liked him because I
saw he understood or felt what a woman is and I knew I could always get
round him and I gave him all the pleasure I could leading him on till he
asked me to say yes and I wouldnt answer first only looked out over the sea
and the sky I was thinking of so many things he didnt know of Mulvey and
Mr Stanhope and Hester and father and old captain Groves and the sailors
playing all birds fly and I say stoop and washing up dishes they called it on
the pier and the sentry in front of the governors house with the thing round
his white helmet poor devil half roasted and the Spanish girls laughing in
their shawls and their tall combs and the auctions in the morning the Greeks
and the jews and the Arabs and the devil knows who else from all the ends

of Europe and Duke street and the fowl market all clucking outside Larby Sharons and the poor donkeys slipping half asleep in the shade on the steps and the big wheels of the carts of the bulls and the old castle thousands of years old yes and those handsome Moors all in white and turbans like kings asking you to sit down in their little bit of a shop and Ronda with the old windows the posadas glancing eyes a lattice hid for her lover to kiss the iron and the wineshops half open at night and the castanets and the night we missed the boat at Algeciras the watchman going about serene with his lamp and O that awful deepdown torrent O and the sea the sea crimson sometimes like fire and the glorious sunsets and the figtrees in the Alameda gardens yes and all the queer little streets and the pink and blue and yellow house and the rosegardens and the jessamine and geraniums and cactuses and Gibraltar as a girl where I was a flower of the mountain yes when I put the rose in my hair like the Andalusian girls used or shall I wear a red yes and how he kissed me under the Moorish wall and I thought well as well him as another and then I asked him with my eyes to ask again yes and then he asked me would I say yes to say yes my mountain flower and first I put my arms around him yes and drew him down to me so he could feel my breasts all perfume yes and his heart was going like mad and yes I said yes I will Yes.

James Joyce (1882–1941), *Ulysses* (1922).

NANCY MITFORD, *high-spirited, elegant, funny, daughter of the second Lord Redesdale, was an old friend of Evelyn Waugh's first wife Evelyn (who was known to their friends as she-Evelyn and Evelyn Waugh as he-Evelyn to diminish confusion).*

When she-Evelyn and he-Evelyn were first married they rented a tiny house in Canonbury Square, Islington, and as he-Evelyn was frequently away in hotel rooms writing Vile Bodies, *she-Evelyn invited her friend Nancy Mitford to live with them and keep her company. Nancy Mitford jumped at this as she was 24 and anxious to get away from her authoritarian parents and make a life of her own.*

Miss Mitford's company did not seem to be enough for she-Evelyn because a few months later she left he-Evelyn and bolted with an old boy-friend, but Nancy Mitford and he-Evelyn stayed in touch and remained close friends for life.

Nancy Mitford had five sisters and a brother. Their father did not believe in educating daughters, in fact he did not believe in educated women. The brother was destined for Eton but the 'Mitford girls', as they became known, had to make do with such instruction as they could get at home, first rather vaguely from their mother and then from a succession of governesses.

When one of Nancy Mitford's younger sisters, Jessica, grew up she moved to America, married, and became politically left-wing (as did Nancy Mitford; unlike

Unity Mitford who became a friend and admirer of Hitler, and Diana Mitford who married Sir Oswald Mosley, the British fascist leader).

Jessica Mitford became a successful writer of books exposing corruptions which she detected in the fabric of American life. One of her most successful was The American Way of Death, *a factual exposé of the mortician industry which Evelyn Waugh had satirized in* The Loved One.

Then in 1960 Jessica Mitford turned to autobiography and published fascinating details of the highly unconventional upbringing which the Mitford girls enjoyed:

Muv [the girls' pet name for their mother] had invented a method of teaching which obviated the necessity for examinations. We simply read the passage to be mastered, then closed the book and related whatever portion of the text we happened to retain. 'I always think a child only needs to remember the part that seems important to her,' she would explain vaguely. Sometimes it didn't work very well. 'Now, Little D., I've read you a whole chapter. Tell me what you remember of it.' 'I'm afraid I don't remember anything.' 'Come now, Little D., can't you remember a single word?' 'Very well then—THE.' Fatal sentence! For years after I could be reduced to tears by sisters and cousins teasing in chorus, 'Very well, then—THE.'

I graduated to the schoolroom when I was nine. Our schoolroom at Swin-brook, big and airy, with bay windows, a small coal fireplace and chintz-covered furniture, was on the second floor, next to the governess's bedroom. It was separated from the visitors' rooms and my parents' rooms by a green-baize door. Here we spent most of our time. We had lunch, and sometimes dinner, downstairs with the grown-ups except when there were visitors, in which case meals were sent up and we ate in the unenthralling company of the governess, regretfully wondering what delicious things they were having downstairs.

Unity—Bobo to the rest of the family, but Boud to me—was the only other schoolroom-age child; Debo was only six, still having lessons with Muv, and otherwise in the nursery under the jurisdiction of Nanny. Nancy and Pam were long since grown up, Tom had gone to live abroad for a bit, and Diana was in Paris, restlessly poised between schoolroom and first London season.

Boud was a huge, outsize child of twelve. She reminded me of the expression 'great girl' in Victorian children's books. 'Oh dear, poor Boud, she *is* rather enormous,' Muv complained when the semi-annual boxes of children's clothes arrived on approval from Daniel Neal's in London, to be tried on and invariably, in Boud's case, sent back for a larger size. Nancy gave her the blunt nickname of Hideous, but Boud wasn't really hideous. Her immense, baleful blue eyes, large, clumsy limbs, dead straight tow-coloured hair, some-times in neat pig-tails but more often flowing loose, gave her the appearance of a shaggy Viking or Little John. She was the bane of governesses, few of whom could stand up for long to her relentless misbehaviour, and as a result we never had the same one for any length of time. They came and left in bewildering succession, and each replacement brought with her a new slant on the sum total of human knowledge.

Miss Whitey taught us to repeat, 'A-squared-minus-B-squared-equals-A-squared-minus-2-AB-plus-B-squared,' but she did not stay long enough to explain why that should be. Boud found out that she had a deadly fear of snakes, and left Enid, her pet grass snake, neatly wrapped around the w.c. chain one morning. We breathlessly awaited the result, which was not long in coming. Miss Whitely locked herself in, there was shortly an ear-splitting shriek followed by a thud. The unconscious woman was ultimately released with the aid of crowbars, and Boud was duly scolded and told to keep Enid in her box thereafter.

Miss Whitey was succeeded by Miss Broadmoor, who taught us to say Mensa, Mensa, Mensam all the way through. Nancy, even in those early days preoccupied with U and Non-U usage, made up a poem illustrative of the main 'refainments' of Miss Broadmoor's speech: 'Any huff a loft, and oft, as ay lay on may ayderdown so soft (tossing from sade to sade with may nasty coff) ay ayther think of the loft, or of the w-h-h-h-h-eat in the troff of the loft.' We couldn't resist reciting it each morning as lesson time drew near.

Latin lessons came to an end after Miss Broadmoor left. Miss McMurray grew beans on bits of wet flannel and taught the names of different parts of these growing beans—Plumule, Radical, Embryo.

She was soon followed by Miss Bunting, whose main contribution to our education was to teach a little mild shop-lifting. Miss Bunting was a dear little round giggly woman, shaped like a Toby jug, with a carefree and unorthodox approach to life that we found most attractive. Boud towered over her, and sometimes scooped her up and put her, squealing, on the schoolroom piano.

We made occasional trips to Oxford. 'Like to try a little jiggery-pokery, children?' Miss Bunting suggested. There were two main methods: the shopping-bag method, in which an accomplice was needed, was used for the larger items. The accomplice undertook to distract the shop-lady while the lifter, or Jiggery-poker in Miss Bunting's idiom, stuffed her bag with books, underclothes or boxes of chocolates, depending on the wares of the particular store. The dropped-hanky method was suitable for lipsticks or small pieces of jewellery. Miss Bunting in her governessy beige coat and gloves, Boud and I in matching panama straw hats, would strut haughtily past the deferential sales-people to seek the safety of Fuller's Tea Room, where we would gleefully take stock of the day's haul over cups of steaming hot chocolate.

Jessica Mitford (b. 1917), Hons and Rebels (1960).

Nancy Mitford, *encouraged by Evelyn Waugh, began to write. To begin with she had articles accepted by* Vogue *and* Harper's *and between 1931 and 1941 she published four light novels, none of which attracted or deserved much in the way of sales or critical notice. But a year or two later everything changed sensationally for the better. She fell deeply in love with a Free French officer, Gaston Palewski, who later became a minister in de Gaulle's government, and she wrote a novel dedicated to him which was published in 1945. The book was wildly successful, made her fairly rich and quite famous almost overnight, and eventually sold over a million copies. She moved to Paris and after writing some more delightful novels became a successful and respected biographer.*

The novel was The Pursuit of Love, *a title suggested by Evelyn Waugh. For its story Nancy Mitford turned to memories of her own childhood and much of the book is a lightly fictionalized version of the true story told by her sister Jessica of life in the Mitford household and the upbringing and subsequent love-affairs of the Mitford girls.*

Nancy Mitford constantly acknowledged her debt to Evelyn Waugh. He was not working on a book of his own at the time and so was able to help her with hers (he could be most kind and generous to young writers). He made good her grammar which, when present at all, was hopeless, he suggested improvements, and he was responsible for at least one passage: in the book the Mitfords have become the Radletts, the narrator is a cousin of the Radletts and Nancy's eccentric father, Lord Redesdale, becomes Uncle Matthew.

According to Nancy Mitford, it was Waugh who drafted the splendid description of Uncle Matthew's grim country house, where the girls spent their childhood:

Alconleigh was a large, ugly, north-facing Georgian house, built with only one intention, that of sheltering, when the weather was too bad to be out of doors, a succession of bucolic squires, their wives, their enormous families, their dogs, their horses, their father's relict, and their unmarried sisters. There was no attempt at decoration, at softening the lines, no apology for a façade, it was all as grim and bare as a barracks, stuck up on the high hillside. Within, the keynote, the theme, was death. Not death of maidens, not death romantically accoutred with urns and weeping willows, cypresses and vale-dictory odes, but the death of warriors and of animals, stark, real. On the walls halberds and pikes and ancient muskets were arranged in crude patterns with the heads of beasts slaughtered in many lands, with the flags and uniforms of bygone Radletts. Glass-topped cases contained, not miniatures of ladies, but miniatures of the medals of their lords, badges, penholders made of tiger's teeth, the hoof of a favourite horse, telegrams announcing casualties in battle and commissions written out on parchment scrolls, all lying together in a timeless jumble.

Waugh's Men at Arms, *with its unforgettable portrait of the fire-eating Brigadier Ritchie-Hook, did not appear until seven years after* The Pursuit of Love *but it seems likely that either Waugh's Brigadier was modelled on aspects of Nancy*

Mitford's Uncle Matthew, or that Waugh helped her to create Uncle Matthew originally and rewrote him later as the Brigadier.

One clear point of resemblance is the bloodthirsty nature of both men. The Brigadier was 'a legendary wielder of the entrenching tool', noted for returning from a raid on enemy trenches bearing a brace of severed heads.

Uncle Matthew was an equally enthusiastic wielder of the tool, as the opening lines of the book reveal:

There is a photograph in existence of Aunt Sadie and her six children sitting round the tea-table at Alconleigh. The table is situated as it was, is now, and ever shall be, in the hall, in front of a huge open fire of logs. Over the chimney-piece, plainly visible in the photograph, hangs an entrenching tool with which, in 1915, Uncle Matthew had whacked to death eight Germans one by one as they crawled out of a dug-out. It is still covered with blood and hairs, an object of fascination to us as children.

Another resemblance is the way in which both warriors, ferocious most of the time, could be reduced to displays of almost girlish emotion when they were moved by something.

With Brigadier Ritchie-Hook it was the sight of a tatty calendar which had a design on it featuring gnomes, toadstools and pink bare babies ('That's a lovely thing. My word, it is lovely. Isn't it lovely?').

Uncle Matthew's emotional experience was brought on by one of his very rare visits to the theatre:

Uncle Matthew went with Aunt Sadie and Linda on one occasion to a Shakespeare play, *Romeo and Juliet*. It was not a success. He cried copiously, and went into a furious rage because it ended badly. 'All the fault of that damned padre,' he kept saying on the way home, still wiping his eyes. 'That fella, what's 'is name, Romeo, might have known a blasted papist would mess up the whole thing. Silly old fool of a nurse too, I bet she was an R.C., dismal old bitch.'

Uncle Matthew was an irascible old codger, the kind of half-barmy eccentric who had been the mainstay of a hundred and fifty years of old-fashioned English sentimental comedy. Yet Nancy Mitford, elegant and witty stylist in the modern, crisply satirical Waugh fashion, wrote easily and naturally about him and with palpable affection:

Linda, Louisa and I were packed into Louisa's bed, with Bob sitting on the end of it, chatting in whispers. These midnight talks were strictly forbidden, but it was safer, at Alconleigh, to disobey rules during the early part of the night than at any other time in the twenty-four hours. Uncle Matthew fell asleep practically at the dinner-table. He would then doze in his business-room before dragging himself, in a somnambulist trance, to bed, where he slept the profound sleep of one who has been out of doors all day until cockcrow the following morning, when he became very much awake. This was the time for his never-ending warfare with the housemaids over wood-ash. The rooms at Alconleigh were heated by wood fires, and Uncle Matthew maintained, rightly, that if these were to function properly, all the ash ought to be left in the fireplaces in a great hot smouldering heap. Every housemaid, however, for some reason (an early training with coal-fires probably) was bent on removing this ash altogether. When shakings, imprecations, and being pounced out at by Uncle Matthew at six a.m., had convinced them that this really was not feasible, they became absolutely determined to remove, by hook or by crook, just a little, a shovelful or so, every morning. I can only suppose they felt that like this they were asserting their personalities.

The result was guerrilla warfare at its most exciting. Housemaids are notoriously early risers, and can usually count upon three clear hours when a house belongs to them alone. But not at Alconleigh. Uncle Matthew was always, winter and summer alike, out of his bed by five a.m., and it was then his habit to wander about, looking like Great Agrippa in his dressing-gown, and drinking endless cups of tea out of a thermos flask, until about seven, when he would have his bath. Breakfast for my uncle, my aunt, family and guests alike, was sharp at eight, and unpunctuality was not tolerated. Uncle Matthew was no respecter of other people's early morning sleep, and, after five o'clock one could not count on any, for he raged round the house, clanking cups of tea, shouting at his dogs, roaring at the housemaids, cracking the stock whips which he had brought back from Canada on the lawn with a noise greater than gun-fire, and all to the accompaniment of Galli Curci on his gramophone, an abnormally loud one with an enormous horn, through which would be shrieked 'Una voce poco fa'—'The Mad Song' from *Lucia*—'Lo, hear the gen-tel lar-ha-hark'—and so on, played at top speed, thus rendering them even higher and more screeching than they ought to be.

Nothing reminds me of my childhood days at Alconleigh so much as those songs. Uncle Matthew played them incessantly for years, until the spell was broken when he went all the way to Liverpool to hear Galli Curci in person. The disillusionment caused by her appearance was so great that the records remained ever after silent, and were replaced by the deepest bass voices that money could buy.

> 'Fearful the death of the diver must be,
> Walking alone in the de-he-he-he-he-epths of the sea . . .'

or

> 'Drake is going West, lads . . .'

These were, on the whole, welcomed by the family, as rather less piercing at early dawn.

The story of The Pursuit of Love *moves away from Uncle Matthew and Alconleigh as the girls grow up and the second half of the book is mostly concerned with the bitter-sweet tragedy of Linda's unfortunate marriage, but the remarkable success of the book is most certainly due to Nancy's descriptions of the early days, particularly the childhood of the Hons (i.e. the Mitford girls, those most attractive little savages) and the Rebels, as the Hons called all those who were stuffy and un-Hon minded.*

The Hons met regularly to exchange riveting news and gossip and to discuss Life:

The Hons' meeting-place was a disused linen cupboard at the top of the house, small, dark, and intensely hot. As in so many country houses the central-heating apparatus at Alconleigh had been installed in the early days of the invention, at enormous expense, and was now thoroughly out of date. In spite of a boiler which would not have been too large for an Atlantic liner, in spite of the tons of coke which it consumed daily, the temperature of the living-rooms was hardly affected, and all the heat there was seemed to concentrate in the Hons' cupboard, which was always stifling. Here we would sit, huddled up on the slatted shelves, and talk for hours about life and death.

Last holidays our great obsession had been childbirth, on which entrancing subject we were informed remarkably late, having supposed for a long time that a mother's stomach swelled up for nine months and then burst open like a ripe pumpkin, shooting out the infant. When the real truth dawned upon us it seemed rather an anticlimax, until Linda produced, from some novel, and read out loud in ghoulish tones, the description of a woman in labour.

'Her breath comes in great gulps—sweat pours down her brow like water—screams as of a tortured animal rend the air—and can this face, twisted with agony, be that of my darling Rhona—can this torture-chamber really be our bedroom, this rack our marriage-bed? "Doctor, doctor," I cried, "do something"—I rushed out into the night'—and so on.

We were rather disturbed by this, realizing that too probably we in our turn would have to endure these fearful agonies. Aunt Sadie, who had only just finished having her seven children, when appealed to, was not very reassuring.

'Yes,' she said, vaguely. 'It is the worst pain in the world. But the funny thing is, you always forget in between what it's like. Each time, when it began, I felt like saying, "Oh, now I can remember, stop it, stop it." And, of course, by then it was nine months too late to stop it.'

At this point Linda began to cry, saying how dreadful it must be for cows, which brought the conversation to an end.

It was difficult to talk to Aunt Sadie about sex; something always seemed to prevent one; babies were the nearest we ever got to it. She and Aunt Emily, feeling at one moment that we ought to know more, and being, I suspect, too embarrassed to enlighten us themselves, gave us a modern textbook on the subject.

We got hold of some curious ideas.

'Jassy,' said Linda one day, scornfully, 'is obsessed, poor thing, with sex.'

'Obsessed with sex!' said Jassy, 'there's nobody so obsessed as you, Linda. Why if I so much as look at a picture you say I'm a pygmalionist.'

In the end we got far more information out of a book called *Ducks and Duck Breeding*.

'Ducks can only copulate,' said Linda, after studying this for a while, 'in running water. Good luck to them.'

This Christmas Eve we all packed into the Hons' meeting-place to hear what Linda had to say—Louisa, Jassy, Bob, Matt, and I.

'Talk about back-to-the-womb,' said Jassy.

'Poor Aunt Sadie,' I said. 'I shouldn't think she'd want you all back in hers.'

'You never know. Now rabbits eat their children—somebody ought to explain to them how it's only a complex.'

'How can one *explain* to *rabbits*? That's what is so worrying about animals, they simply don't understand when they're spoken to, poor angels. I'll tell you what about Sadie though, she'd like to be back in one herself, she's got a thing for boxes and that always shows. Who else—Fanny, what about you?'

'I don't think I would, but then I imagine the one I was in wasn't very comfortable at the time you know, and nobody else has ever been allowed to stay there.'

'Abortions?' said Linda with interest.

'Well, tremendous jumpings and hot baths anyway.'

'How *do* you know?'

'I once heard Aunt Emily and Aunt Sadie talking about it when I was very little, and afterwards I remembered. Aunt Sadie said: "How does she manage it?" and Aunt Emily said: "Skiing, or hunting, or just jumping off the kitchen table."'

'You are so lucky, having wicked parents.'

Nancy Mitford (1904–73), The Pursuit of Love (1945).

PARENTS *in Beryl Bainbridge's stories are not especially wicked but are usually ill-assorted, and are not very good at rearing children.*

Beryl Bainbridge, slender, dark-haired, tiny, began a career as an actress but started to write a novel whilst waiting for her baby to arrive and became a writer instead. She grew up in wartime Liverpool, a world as different from Nancy Mitford's as a chip butty from a cucumber sandwich, but in their work there are parallels. Nancy Mitford's The Pursuit of Love *was a enormous success, critically and commercially: Beryl Bainbridge's novels are best-sellers and have so far won her the Whitbread Award, the Guardian Fiction Award, and two nominations for the Booker Prize.*

Nancy Mitford wrote about a young girl in a bleak and uncomfortable but rich home and the amusing antics of her eccentric father, who was at the same time also remote, frightening, and obsessed with hunting and shooting. In the following short story Beryl Bainbridge writes of being a young girl in drab, wartime, suburban Liverpool, of a father who is a dreamer, a failure, and a bit peculiar (only the rich are called 'eccentric'), of an ineffectual mother, and of a boring old grandfather obsessed with the game of cricket.

Beryl Bainbridge's wry, dry, watchful, black humour is concerned with domesticity and family relationships which go wrong, with cosiness into which a twinge of violence unexpectedly intrudes. This story tells of a small family incident, the sort of sudden little dramatic happening which a young girl might well remember for life:

THE LONGSTOP

Words and cricket seem to go together. Whenever I watch the game, by myself, on television, I think it's not true you can't get blood from a stone.

I only ever played the game once myself, in the park with some evacuees from Bootle. I was allowed to join in because I held a biscuit tin filled with shortbread that my mother had baked. They said I could have a turn if I gave them a biscuit afterwards. I didn't make any runs because I never hit the ball, and when I kept my promise and began to open the tin the evacuees knocked me over and took every bit of shortbread. They threw the tin over the wall into the gentlemen's lavatory. I had to tell my mother a six-foot-high naughty man with a Hitler moustache had chased me; she would have slapped me for playing with evacuees.

Mr Baines, who was my maternal grandfather, was a lover of cricket. Mr Jones, my father, didn't care for the game. He cared even less for my grandfather. In his humble estimation Mr Baines was a mean old bugger, a fifth columnist, and, following his self-confessed denouncing of a neighbour in Norris Green for failing to draw his curtains against the black-out, a Gauleiter into the bargain. He was also a lounge lizard, a term never satisfactorily explained, though it was true that my grandfather fell asleep between meals.

Apart from words, my father was keen on sailing ships. He subscribed to a monthly magazine on the subject. If he was to be believed, he had, when no more than a child, sailed as a cabin boy to America. In middle age, his occupation a commercial traveller, he prowled the deserted shore beyond the railway line, peering of an evening through the barbed wire entanglements at the oil tankers and the black destroyers that crawled along the bleak edge of the Irish Sea; it was a gloomy mystery to him where that fearless lad before the mast had gone.

Every week Mr Baines came for Sunday dinner. There had been a moment at the outbreak of war when he had contemplated coming to live with us, but after three days he returned home. He said he preferred to take his chances with the Luftwaffe. His conversation during the meal was always about cricket, and mostly to do with a man called Briggs. Briggs, he said, had just missed greatness by a lack of seriousness. If only Briggs had taken batting more seriously he would have been, make no bones about it, the best all-round cricketer in England since W. G. Grace. Briggs, he informed us, took bowling and fielding in deadly earnest, but as a batsman he was a disaster; he seemed far more anxious to amuse the crowd than to improve his average.

Nobody listened to my grandfather, certainly not my father who was often heard to remark quite loudly that, had he been in control, he wouldn't give the old skinflint the time of day, let alone Sunday dinner, world without end.

However, one particular Sunday in the summer of 1944, Mr Baines, without warning, excelled himself when describing a cricketer called Ranjitsinghi.

'Just to set eyes on him,' said Mr Baines, 'was a picture in motion. The way his shirt ballooned—'

'A black chappie,' my father exclaimed, taken aback at my grandfather speaking civilly of a foreigner.

'An Indian prince,' said Mr Baines. He was equally taken aback at being addressed in the middle of his monologue. He was used to conversing uninterrupted throughout the devouring of the black-market roast pork.

'They're two a penny,' my father said.

'More potatoes?' asked my mother, worriedly.

'Even when it wasn't windy,' continued Mr Baines, 'his shirt ballooned. Whether half a gale was blowing on the Hove ground or there wasn't enough breeze to shift the flag at Lord's, the fellow's shirt flapped like the mainsail of six-tonner on the Solent.'

'Blithering rubbish,' said my father. He stabbed at a sprout as though it was alive.

My mother told Mr Baines that they played cricket in the park every Sunday afternoon. Not a proper team, just old men and young lads. Not what he was used to, of course. 'But,' she said, eyeing my father contemptuously, 'it will do us good to get out into the pure air.'

She didn't mean my father to come. We were never a family who went anywhere together. My father's opinion, had he voiced it, would have been that the family who stood together fell out together. Often we would attempt an outing, but between the closing of the back door and the opening of the front gate, misunderstandings occurred and plans were abruptly abandoned. She was astonished when, having washed up and taken off her pinny, she found my father in the hall putting on his trilby hat. She didn't like it, you could tell. Her mouth went all funny and the lipstick ran down at one corner. Shoulder to shoulder, more or less, we set off for the park.

I wanted to nip over the garden fence and through the blackberry bushes into Brow's Lane, but my mother said my grandfather wasn't about to nip anywhere, not at his age. We trotted him down the road past the roundabout and the Council offices. The brass band was practising in the hut behind the fire station. When he heard the music, Mr Baines began to walk with his arms held stiffly at his sides, only the band kept stopping and starting and the tune came in bits, and after a while he gave up playing at soldiers and shuffled instead. My father looked at the ground all the time; there was a grey splodge on the brim of his hat where a pigeon had done its business.

The park was quite grand, even though it had lost its ornamental gates at the entrance. My mother said they'd been removed to make into tanks. My father swore they were mouldering away in a brick field down by the Docks, along with his mother's copper kettle and a hundred thousand front railings. The park had a pavilion, a sort of hunting lodge with mullioned windows and a thatched roof. People were worried about incendiary bombs. The park keeper kept his grass roller inside and buckets of water. In front of the pavilion was a sunken bowling green, and beyond that a miniature clock-golf course. We used to ride our bikes up and down the bumps. Beyond the pavilion, within a roped enclosure, was a German Messerschmidt. It had been there for two years. It hadn't crash-landed anywhere near our village; it was on loan. The park keeper was always telling the Council to tell someone to come back for it. At first we had all run round it and shuddered, but after a few weeks we hardly noticed it any more. It just perched there, propped on blocks, one wing tipped up to the sky, the cockpit half burned away, its melted hood gleaming beetle-black in the sunshine.

When he saw the aircraft, my father cried out, 'Good Lord, look at that!' He flung his arms out dramatically and demanded, 'Why wasn't I told?'

No one took any notice of him; he was always showing off. He stared up at the plane with an expression both fearful and excited, as though the monster was still flying through the air and he might yet be machine-gunned where he stood.

My mother and Mr Baines sat on wooden chairs pressed against the privet hedge. My mother was worried in case we were too near the wicket. She was for ever ducking and flinching, mistaking the white clouds that bowled across the sky for an oncoming ball. It wasn't an exciting game as far as I could tell but my grandfather sat on the edge of his chair and didn't fall asleep once. There was a man fielding who was almost as old as Mr Baines, and when the bowler was rubbing the ball up and down the front of his trousers preparing to run, the old man rested in a deck-chair on the pitch. The butcher's boy from the village shop was crouching down behind the wicket wearing a tin hat and smoking a cigarette.

'That fellow,' said Mr Baines, pointing at the elderly batsman in Home Guard uniform, 'is taking a risk. If he misses the ball he will be out leg before or he'll get his skull stove in.'

'Heavens,' cried my mother, cringing backwards on her chair.

'Briggs used to play that sort of stroke,' said Mr Baines. 'Of course, he knew what he was doing.'

My father came and sat down beside him. He said: 'I never knew it was there. I never knew.' He still looked excited. He'd taken his hat off and there was a mark all round his forehead.

'As soon as he saw what ball it was,' Mr Baines said, 'he'd stand straight in front of the wicket and wait until it looked as if it would go straight through his body—'

'I never knew,' repeated my father. 'I never even guessed.' He was very unobservant. He'd been morosely loping to and from the railway station night and morning for twenty years and never bothered to look through the trees.

'Be quiet,' said my mother. 'We're concentrating.'

'At the last moment,' Mr Baines said, 'Briggs would hook it. Glorious stroke. Poetry in motion.'

'If I could have served,' remarked my father, 'I would have chosen the Merchant Navy.'

'Mind you,' Mr Baines said, 'it had to be a fast ball.'

'Failing that, I think I'd have fancied the Air Force,' said my father.

There wasn't anything one could reply to that piece of poppy-cock. If my father had been healthy enough to join up, he wouldn't have been of any use. When Wilfred Pickles said on the wireless, 'And how old are you, luv? Ninety-seven!' my father had to blow his nose from emotion. If he happened to hear 'When the lights go on again all over the world' on Forces' Favourites, he had to go out into the scullery to take a grip on himself. According to my mother, Auntie Doris had turned him into a cissy. He was a terrible cry-baby. He cried one time when the cat went missing. My mother said that most of the time his carrying on like that was misplaced. Once we went all over Southport pressing shillings into the hands of what he called 'our gallant boys in blue'. They were soldiers from the new hospital down by the Promenade. My father told them he was proud of them, that they were the walking wounded; he had a field day with his handkerchief. Afterwards it turned out there was nothing wrong with them, nothing wounded, that is, it wasn't that sort of hospital. They were soldiers all right, my mother said, but they'd all caught a nasty disease from just being in the army, not from fighting or anything gallant like that, and it was certainly nothing to be proud of.

'I'm not criticising,' said Mr Baines, looking at the fielder resting in his deck-chair, 'but these fellows lack self-discipline. The true sportsman is a trained athlete. He dedicates himself to the game. Only way to succeed. Same with anything in all walks of life—cotton, fishing, banking, shipping—'

'Doesn't he ever get tired of his own voice?' said my father savagely.

I sat on the grass with my back propped against my mother's knees. I could feel her trembling from indignation. My grandfather began to clap, slapping the palms of his hands together above my head as the elderly batsman left the crease and began to trail towards the pavilion. Mr Baines was the only one applauding; there were few spectators and most of those had swivelled round the other way to look at the bowling green. The new batsman was younger and he had a gammy leg. When he heard Mr Baines clapping he glared at him, thinking he was being made fun of.

'One time,' said Mr Baines, 'Briggs got stale. The Lancashire committee suggested he should take a week's holiday. He went to a remote village in Wiltshire—'

'Don't think I don't know what the old beggar's getting at,' said my father. 'Talking about cotton like that. Did he think I wanted to come a cropper in cotton—'

'Word got round as it will,' Mr Baines said. 'Second day there a fellow came up to Briggs and asked him how much he'd take for playing in a local match. Ten pounds, said Briggs, thinking that would be prohibitive—'

The park was shimmering in sunshine. You couldn't see the boundary by the poplar trees; all the leaves were reflecting like bits of glass. The man with the gammy leg was out almost at once. I didn't know why, the bails were still standing. I couldn't follow the rules. A fat man came out in a little peaked cap. I could hear the dull clop of the ball against the bat and the click of the bowls on the green as they knocked against each other. Behind me the voices went on and on, another game in progress, more dangerous than either cricket or bowls, and the rules were always changing.

'Briggs's side lost the toss,' said Mr Baines, 'and he had to begin the bowling. His first ball was hit out of the ground for six—'

'If I'd had any appreciation all these years,' my father said, 'things might have been different. When I think how I tramp from door to door in all weathers while you and your blasted Dad put your feet up—'

'Finally he had two wickets for a hundred and fifty runs. The crowd was looking quite nasty,' Mr Baines said. 'But what finished them off was that when he went in to bat he was bowled second ball.'

'All I needed was a few bob at the right moment,' said my father. 'Just a few measley quid and the old skinflint wouldn't put his hand in his pocket—'

'Don't speak about him like that,' cried my mother. 'I won't have him called names.'

'Only a stalwart policeman and the train to London saved him from a jolly good hiding,' said Mr Baines. 'He never tried village cricket again.'

'If you'd been any proper sort of woman,' groaned my father, 'you'd have been a help-mate.'

'Be quiet,' my mother cried. 'Shut your mouth.'

'You've only been a bloody hindrance,' my father shouted. He jumped up and knocked over his chair. He walked away in the direction of the aeroplane, leaving his hat on the grass.

'What's up?' I asked. Though I knew. 'Is he off home, then?'

'Ssh,' said my mother. 'He's gone for a widdle.' Her voice was all choked.

'Don't upset yourself,' said Mr Baines. 'It's not worth it.'

'He sickens me,' my mother said. 'Sickens me. Whimpering over the least thing when inside he's like a piece of rock. He's hard. He's got no pity for man nor beast.'

'Don't waste your tears,' said Mr Baines. 'You can't get blood from a stone.'

At that moment the ball flew past the wicket and striking the ground rolled to my grandfather's feet. He leapt up and striding to the side of the pitch chucked the ball at the batsman. He didn't exactly bowl it; he sort of dipped one shoulder and flung the ball like a boy skimming a stone on water. The batsman, taken by surprise at such an accurate throw, swung his bat. The scarlet ball shot over Mr Baines' shoulder and went like a bullet from a gun after my father.

When we ran up to him he was stood there in the shadow of the Messerschmidt with his hand clutched to the side of his head. The ball hadn't hit him full on, merely grazed the side of his temple. But he was bleeding like a pig.

'That's a turn-up for the book,' said Mr Baines.

Beryl Bainbridge (b. 1934), reprinted: Mum and Mr Armitage (1985).

GRAHAM GREENE *is one of this century's greatest novelists and his novels deal much with good and evil, with moral and theological dilemmas, with good-intentions failing amidst seedy surroundings.*

But he has another side. He also writes thrillers and highly amusing stories and novels, and before the war he called these his 'entertainments' (he stopped using the word soon after the war when he decided that there was no real distinction between the 'entertainments' and the novels).

In a letter to a friend, he wrote that the three books which he was most pleased to have written were Brighton Rock, The Power and the Glory, *and* Travels with my Aunt. *Perhaps surprisingly for readers devoted to his more sombre works, the list shows that one and a half of his three favourites would have come into the category of 'entertainments' (the half being* Brighton Rock *which for some reason was called a novel in Britain and an 'entertainment' in America). Of the other two books,* The Power and the Glory *is undeniably a novel, and* Travels with my Aunt *is a witty comedy with touches of farce in which Graham Greene's inventive and mischievous humour is all.*

The aunt of Travels with my Aunt *is Aunt Augusta and the narrator is her nephew Henry. Henry, a retired bank accountant, is wrenched from his orderly and comfortable suburban villa to act as his aunt's protector as she sets out on one final wild and dubious mission.*

Aunt Augusta, splendidly grand, amoral, unrepentant, has had many, many, many lovers in her long, brilliantly-lived life and Henry finds it difficult to place them when she drops their names into the conversation.

For instance, there was a Mr Visconti.

On a train through Bulgaria, while Aunt Augusta is poring over a map of Istanbul, Henry seizes the moment to ask her for more details about this Mr Visconti who seems to have loomed so spectacularly in her past:

'He was a quite impossible man,' my aunt said, 'but I loved him and what he did with my money was the least of his faults. For example he was what they call a collaborator. During the German occupation he acted as adviser to the German authorities on questions of art, and he had to get out of Italy very quickly after the death of Mussolini. Goering had been making a big collection of pictures, but even he couldn't easily steal pictures from places like the Uffizi where the collection was properly registered, but Mr Visconti knew a lot about the unregistered—all sorts of treasures hidden away in *palazzos* almost as crumbling as your uncle Jo's. Of course his part got to be known, and there'd be quite a panic in a country place when Mr Visconti appeared taking lunch in the local *taverna*. The trouble was he wouldn't play even a crooked game straight or the Germans might have helped him to escape. He began to take money from this marquese and that not to tip off the Germans—this gave him liquid cash or sometimes a picture he fancied for himself, but it didn't make him friends and the Germans soon suspected what was going on. Poor old devil,' she added, 'he hadn't a friend he could trust. Mario was still at school with the Jesuits and I had gone back to England when the war began.'

'What happened to him in the end?'

'I thought for a long time he'd been liquidated by the partisans, for I never believed that story above the gondolier. I suspect he got someone to spread it for him. Mr Visconti, as I told you, was not a man for fighting with knives or fists. A man who fights never survives long, and Mr Visconti was great at survival. Why, the old sod,' she said with tender delight, 'he survives to this moment. He must be eighty-four if he's a day. He wrote to Mario and Mario wrote to me, and that's why you and I have taken the train to Istanbul. I couldn't explain all that in London, it was too complicated, and anyway I hardly knew you. Thank goodness for the gold brick, that's all I can say.'

'The gold brick?'

'Never mind. That's quite another thing.'

'You told me about a gold brick at London Airport, Aunt Augusta, surely . . . ?'

'Of course not. It's not that one. That was quite a little one. Don't interrupt. I'm telling you now about poor Mr Visconti. It seems he's fallen on very lean times.'

'Where is he? In Istanbul?'

'It's better you shouldn't know, for there are people still after him. Oh dear, he certainly escaped the hard way. Mr Visconti was a good Catholic, but he was very very anti-clerical, and yet in the end it was the priesthood which saved him. He went to a clerical store in Rome, when the Allies were coming close, and he paid a fortune to be fitted out like a monsignor even to the purple socks. He said that a friend of his had lost all his clothes in a bombing raid and they pretended to believe him. Then he went with a suitcase to the lavatory in the Excelsior Hotel, where we had given all those cocktail parties to the cardinals, and changed. He kept away from the reception-desk, but he was unwise enough to look in at the bar—the barman, he knew, was very old and short-sighted. Well, you know, in those days a lot of girls used to come to the bar to pick up German officers. One of these girls—I suppose it was the approach of the Allied troops that did it—was having a *crise de conscience.* She wouldn't go to her friend's bedroom, she regretted her lost purity, she would never sin again. The officer plied her with more and more cocktails, but with every drink she became more religious. Then she spied Mr Visconti, who was having a quick whisky in a shady corner. "Father," she cried to him, "hear my confession." You can imagine the tension in the bar, the noise outside as the evacuation got under way, the crying children, people drinking up what there was in the bar, the Allied planes overhead . . .'

'How did you hear the story, Aunt Augusta?'

'Mr Visconti told Mario the essentials when he got to Milan, and I can imagine the rest. Especially I can picture poor Mr Visconti in his purple socks. "My child," he said, "this is no fit place for a confession."

'"Never mind the place. What does the place matter? We are all about to die, and I am in mortal sin. Please, please, Monsignor." (She had noticed his socks by this time). What worried Mr Visconti most was the attention she was provoking.

'"My child," he told her, "in this state of emergency a simple act of contrition is enough," but oh no, she wasn't going to be fobbed off with something cheap like that—"Bargain sale owing to closing down of premises." She came and knelt at his knees. "Your Grace," she exclaimed. She was used to giving officers a superior rank—it nearly always pleased a captain to be called a major.

'"I am not a bishop," Mr Visconti said. "I am only a humble monsignor." Mario questioned his father closely about this episode, and I have really invented nothing. If anyone had invented a detail it is Mario. You have to remember that he writes verse plays.

'"Father," the girl implored, taking the hint, "help me."

'"The secrecy of the confessional," Mr Visconti pleaded back—they were now, you see, pleading to each other, and she pawed Mr Visconti's knee, while he pawed the top of her head in an ecclesiastical way. Perhaps it was the pawings which made the German officer interrupt with impatience.

'"For God's sake," he said, "if she wants to confess, Monsignor, let her. Here's the key of my room, just down the passage, past the lavatory."

'So off went Mr Visconti with the hysterical girl—he remembered just in time to put down his whisky. He had no choice, though he hadn't been to confession himself for thirty years and he had never learnt the priest's part. Luckily there was an air-conditioner in the room breathing heavily, and that obscured his whispers, and the girl was too much concerned with her role to pay much attention to his. She began right away; Mr Visconti had hardly time to sit on the bed, pushing aside a steel helmet and a bottle of schnapps, before she was getting down to details. He had wanted the whole thing finished as quickly as possible, but he told Mario that he couldn't help becoming a little interested now she had got started and wanting to know a bit more. After all he was a novice—though not in the ecclesiastical sense.

'"How many times, my child?" That was a phrase he remembered very well from his adolescence.

'"How can you ask that, Father? I've been at it all the time ever since the occupation. After all they were our allies, Father."

'"Yes, yes, my child." I can just see him enjoying the chance he had of learning a thing or two, even though his life was in danger. Mr Visconti was a very lecherous man. He said, "Always the same thing, my child?"

'She regarded him with astonishment. "Of course not, Father. Who on earth do you think I am?"

'He looked at her kneeling in front of him and I am sure he longed to pinch her. Mr Visconti was always a great pincher. "Anything unnatural, my child?"

'"What do you mean unnatural, Father?"

'Mr Visconti explained.

'"Surely that's not unnatural, Father?"

'Then they had quite a discussion about what was natural and what wasn't, with Mr Visconti almost forgetting his danger in the excitement, until someone knocked on the door and Mr Visconti, vaguely sketching a cross in a lop-sided way, muttered what sounded through the noise of the air-conditioner like an absolution. The German officer came in in the middle of it and said, "Hurry up, Monsignor. I've got a more important customer for you."

'It was the General's wife who had come down to the bar for a last dry Martini before escaping north and heard what was going on. She drained her Martini in one gulp and commanded the officer to arrange her confession. So there was Mr Visconti caught again. There was an awful row now in the via Veneto as the tanks drove out of Rome. The General's wife had positively to shout at Mr Visconti. She had a rather masculine voice and Mr Visconti said it was like being on the parade ground. He nearly clicked his feet together in his purple socks when she bellowed at him, "Adultery. Three times."

'"Are you married, my daughter?"

'"Of course I'm married. What on earth do you suppose? I'm Frau General"—I've forgotten what ugly Teutonic name she had.

'"Does your husband know of this?"'

'"Of course he doesn't know. He's not a priest."'

'"Then you have been guilty of lies too?"'

'"Yes, yes, naturally, I suppose so, you must hurry, Father. Our car's being loaded. We are leaving for Florence in a few minutes."'

'"Haven't you anything else to tell me?"'

'"Nothing of importance."'

'"You haven't missed Mass?"'

'"Oh, occasionally, Father. This is war-time."'

'"Meat on Fridays?"'

'"You forget. It is permitted now, Father. Those are Allied planes overhead. We have to leave immediately."'

'"God cannot be hurried, my child. Have you indulged in impure thoughts?"'

'"Father, put down yes to anything you like, but give me absolution. I have to be off."'

'"I cannot feel that you've properly examined your conscience."'

'"Unless you give me absolution at once, I shall have you arrested. For sabotage."'

'Mr Visconti said, "It would be better if you gave me a seat in your car. We could finish your confession tonight."'

'"There isn't room in the car, Father. The driver, my husband, myself, my dog—there simply isn't space for another passenger."'

'"A dog takes up no room. It can sit on your knee."'

'"This is an Irish wolfhound, Father."'

'"Then you must leave it behind," Mr Visconti said firmly, and at that moment a car back-fired and the Frau General took it for an explosion.

'"I need Wolf for my protection, Father. War is very dangerous for women."'

'"You will be under the protection of our Holy Mother Church," Mr Visconti said, "as well as your husband's."'

'"I cannot leave Wolf behind. He is all I have in the world to love."'

'"I would have assumed that with three adulteries—and a husband . . ."'

'"They mean nothing to me."'

'"Then I suggest," Mr Visconti said, "that we leave the General behind." And so it came about. The General was dressing down the hall porter because of a mislaid spectacle-case when the Frau General seated herself beside the driver and Mr Visconti sat beside Wolf at the back. "Drive off," the General's wife said.

'The driver hesitated, but he was more afraid of the wife than the husband. The General came out into the street and shouted to them as they drove off— a tank had stopped to give precedence to the staff car. Nobody paid any attention to the General's shouts except Wolf. He clambered all over Mr Visconti, thrusting his evil-smelling parts against Mr Visconti's face, knocking off Mr Visconti's clerical hat, barking furiously to get out. The Frau General may have loved Wolf, but it was the general whom Wolf loved. Probably the General concerned himself with his food and his exercise. Blindly Mr Visconti fumbled for the handle of the window. Before the window was properly open Wolf jumped right in the path of the following tank. It flattened him. Mr Visconti looking back thought that he resembled one of those biscuits they make for children in the shape of animals.

'So Mr Visconti was rid of both dog and General and was able to ride in reasonable comfort to Florence. Mental comfort was another matter and the General's wife was hysterical with grief. I think Curran would have dealt with the situation a great deal better than Mr Visconti. At Brighton Curran would offer the last sacrament in the form of a ritual bone, which the poor beast of course could not possibly chew, to a dying dog. A lot of dogs were killed by cars on Brighton front, and the police were quite annoyed by owners who refused to have the bodies shifted until Curran had been summoned to give the corpse absolution. But Mr Visconti, as I have told you, was not a religious man, and the consolations he offered, I can well imagine, were insufficient and unconvincing. Perhaps he spoke of punishment for the Frau General's sins (for Mr Visconti had a sadistic streak), and of the purgatory which we suffer on earth. Poor Mr Visconti, he must have had a hard time of it all the way to Florence.'

'What happened to the General?'

'He was captured by the Allies, I believe, but I'm not sure whether or not he was hanged at Nuremberg.'

'Mr Visconti must have a great deal on his conscience.'

'Mr Visconti hasn't got a conscience,' my aunt said with pleasure.

Graham Greene (b. 1904), Travels with my Aunt (1969).

Even when Graham Greene became accepted as an important and serious novelist he never became solemn.

Once, on learning that Cyril Connolly was throwing a drinks party for a group of friends, he rang Connolly up in an assumed voice in the middle of the party announcing that he was the chimney-sweep and that he had to make an early start in the morning, and he persuaded Connolly to cover the entire flat with dust sheets.

In 1965, under the nom-de-plume 'Malcolm Collins', he entered a literary competition in the New Statesman *magazine for the best parody of a Graham Greene biography of his brother Hugh, then Director-General of the BBC. Graham Greene's parody of his own writing style won him an honourable mention (the winner was his brother Hugh).*

In the 1950s, in a book review entitled 'Portrait of a Lady', he proved conclusively from interior evidence that the author, Beverley Nichols, was a woman.

Perhaps his most notable jeu d'esprit happened in the 1930s when he was film critic for the brilliant magazine Night and Day *(theatre critic—Elizabeth Bowen, book critic—Evelyn Waugh). In a review of the film* Wee Willie Winkie, *starring the new screen sensation, Shirley Temple, aged 9, Graham Greene suggested that Twentieth-Century Fox could be prosecuted for procuring Miss Temple for immoral purposes as the moppet's clothing and performance were clearly designed to pander to paedophiles.*

Twentieth-Century Fox, to whom Miss Temple represented an enormous investment, sued the magazine. After a trial resounding with fine British legal nincompoopery, they won. Graham Greene moved back to the Spectator.

His short stories demonstrate the range of his prose humour. In the following example, which is quite different in style from the frolics of Travels with my Aunt, *a schoolboy, and later the grown man, has to face a small, embarrassing situation; a social predicament so odd yet so uncomfortably real that only a brilliant novelist, perhaps only Graham Greene, could have thought of it:*

A SHOCKING ACCIDENT

Jerome was called into his housemaster's room in the break between the second and the third class on a Thursday morning. He had no fear of trouble, for he was a warden—the name that the proprietor and headmaster of a rather expensive preparatory school had chosen to give to approved, reliable boys in the lower forms (from a warden one became a guardian and finally before leaving, it was hoped for Marlborough or Rugby, a crusader). The housemaster, Mr Wordsworth, sat behind his desk with an appearance of perplexity and apprehension. Jerome had the odd impression when he entered that he was a cause of fear.

'Sit down, Jerome,' Mr Wordsworth said. 'All going well with the trigonometry?'

'Yes, sir.'

'I've had a telephone call, Jerome. From your aunt. I'm afraid I have bad news for you.'

'Yes, sir?'

'Your father has had an accident.'

'Oh.'

Mr Wordsworth looked at him with some surprise. 'A serious accident.'

'Yes, sir?'

Jerome worshipped his father: the verb is exact. As man re-creates God, so Jerome re-created his father—from a restless widowed author into a mysterious adventurer who travelled in far places—Nice, Beirut, Majorca, even the Canaries. The time had arrived about his eighth birthday when Jerome believed that his father either 'ran guns' or was a member of the British Secret Service. Now it occurred to him that his father might have been wounded in 'a hail of machine-gun bullets'.

Mr Wordsworth played with the ruler on his desk. He seemed at a loss how to continue. He said, 'You know your father was in Naples?'

'Yes, sir.'

'Your aunt heard from the hospital today.'

'Oh.'

Mr Wordsworth said with desperation, 'It was a street accident.'

'Yes, sir?' It seemed quite likely to Jerome that they would call it a street accident. The police of course had fired first; his father would not take human life except as a last resort.

'I'm afraid your father was very seriously hurt indeed.'

'Oh.'

'In fact, Jerome, he died yesterday. Quite without pain.'

'Did they shoot him through the heart?'

'Nobody shot him, Jerome. A pig fell on him.' An inexplicable convulsion took place in the nerves of Mr Wordsworth's face; it really looked for a moment as though he were going to laugh. He closed his eyes, composed his features and said rapidly as though it were necessary to expel the story as quickly as possible, 'Your father was walking along a street in Naples when a pig fell on him. A shocking accident. Apparently in the poorer quarters of Naples they keep pigs on their balconies. This one was on the fifth floor. It had grown too fat. The balcony broke. The pig fell on your father.'

Mr Wordsworth left his desk rapidly and went to the window, turning his back on Jerome. He shook a little with emotion.

Jerome said, 'What happened to the pig?'

This was not callousness on the part of Jerome, as it was interpreted by Mr Wordsworth to his colleagues (he even discussed with them whether, perhaps, Jerome was yet fitted to be a warden). Jerome was only attempting to visualize the strange scene to get the details right. Nor was Jerome a boy who cried; he was a boy who brooded, and it never occurred to him at his preparatory school that the circumstances of his father's death were comic— they were still part of the mystery of life. It was later, in his first term at his public school, when he told the story to his best friend, that he began to realize how it affected others. Naturally after that disclosure he was known rather unreasonably, as Pig.

Unfortunately his aunt had no sense of humour. There was an enlarged snapshot of his father on the piano; a large sad man in an unsuitable dark suit posed in Capri with an umbrella (to guard him against sunstroke), the Faraglione rocks forming the background. By the age of sixteen Jerome was well aware that the portrait looked more like the author of *Sunshine and Shade* and *Rambles in the Balearics* than an agent of the Secret Service. All the same he loved the memory of his father: he still possessed an album filled with picture-postcards (the stamps had been soaked off long ago for his other collection), and it pained him when his aunt embarked with strangers on the story of his father's death.

'A shocking accident,' she would begin, and the stranger would compose his or her features into the correct shape for interest and commiseration. Both reactions, of course, were false, but it was terrible for Jerome to see how suddenly, midway in her rambling discourse, the interest would become genuine. 'I can't think how such things can be allowed in a civilized country,' his aunt would say. 'I suppose one has to regard Italy as civilized. One is prepared for all kinds of things abroad, of course, and my brother was a great traveller. He always carried a water-filter with him. It was far less expensive, you know, than buying all those bottles of mineral water. My brother always said that his filter paid for his dinner wine. You can see from that what a careful man he was, but who could possibly have expected when he was walking along the via Dottore Manuele Panucci on his way to the Hydrographic Museum that a pig would fall on him?' That was the moment when the interest became genuine.

Jerome's father had not been a very distinguished writer, but the time always seems to come, after an author's death, when somebody thinks it worth his while to write a letter to the *Times Literary Supplement* announcing the preparation of a biography and asking to see any letters or documents or receive any anecdotes from friends of the dead man. Most of the biographies, of course, never appear—one wonders whether the whole thing may not be an obscure form of blackmail and whether many a potential writer of a biography or thesis finds the means in this way to finish his education at Kansas or Nottingham. Jerome, however, as a chartered accountant, lived far from the literary world. He did not realize how small the menace really was, or that the danger period for someone of his father's obscurity had long passed. Sometimes he rehearsed the method of recounting his father's death so as to reduce the comic element to its smallest dimensions—it would be of no use to refuse information, for in that case the biographer would undoubtedly visit his aunt who was living to a great old age with no sign of flagging.

It seemed to Jerome that there were two possible methods—the first led gently up to the accident, so that by the time it was described the listener was so well prepared that the death came really as an anti-climax. The chief danger of laughter in such a story was always surprise. When he rehearsed this method Jerome began boringly enough.

'You know Naples and those high tenement buildings? Somebody once told me that the Neopolitan always feels at home in New York just as the man from Turin feels at home in London because the river runs in much the same way in both cities. Where was I? Oh, yes. Naples, of course. You'd be surprised in the poorer quarters what things they keep on the balconies of those sky-scraping tenements—not washing, you know, or bedding, but things like livestock, chickens or even pigs. Of course the pigs get no exercise whatever and fatten all the quicker.' He could imagine how his hearer's eyes would have glazed by this time. 'I've no idea, have you, how heavy a pig can be, but these old buildings are all badly in need of repair. A balcony on the fifth floor gave way under one of those pigs. It struck the third floor balcony on its way down and sort of ricochetted into the street. My father was on the way to the Hydrographic Museum when the pig hit him. Coming from that height and that angle it broke his neck.' This was really a masterly attempt to make an intrinsically interesting subject boring.

The other method Jerome rehearsed had the virtue of brevity.

'My father was killed by a pig.'

'Really? In India?'

'No, in Italy.'

'How interesting. I never realized there was pig-sticking in Italy. Was your father keen on polo?'

In course of time, neither too early nor too late, rather as though, in his capacity as a chartered accountant, Jerome had studied the statistics and taken the average, he became engaged to be married: to a pleasant fresh-faced girl of twenty-five whose father was a doctor in Pinner. Her name was Sally, her favourite author was still Hugh Walpole, and she had adored babies ever since she had been given a doll at the age of five which moved its eyes and made water. Their relationship was contented rather than exciting, as became the love-affair of a chartered accountant; it would never have done if it had interfered with the figures.

One thought worried Jerome, however. Now that within a year he might himself become a father, his love for the dead man increased; he realized what affection had gone into the picture-postcards. He felt a longing to protect his memory, and uncertain whether this quiet love of his would survive if Sally were so insensitive as to laugh when she heard the story of his father's death. Inevitably she would hear it when Jerome brought her to dinner with his aunt. Several times he tried to tell her himself, as she was naturally anxious to know all she could that concerned him.

'You were very small when your father died?'

'Just nine.'

'Poor little boy,' she said.

'I was at school. They broke the news to me.'

'Did you take it very hard?'

'I can't remember.'

'You never told me how it happened.'

'It was very sudden. A street accident.'

'You'll never drive fast, will you, Jemmy?' (She had begun to call him 'Jemmy'.) It was too late then to try the second method—the one he thought of as the pig-sticking one.

They were going to marry quietly in a registry-office and have their honeymoon at Torquay. He avoided taking her to see his aunt until a week before the wedding, but then the night came, and he could not have told himself whether his apprehension was more for his father's memory or the security of his own love.

The moment came all too soon. 'Is that Jemmy's father?' Sally asked, picking up the portrait of the man with the umbrella.

'Yes, dear. How did you guess?'

'He has Jemmy's eyes and brow, hasn't he?'

'Has Jerome lent you his books?'

'No.'

'I will give you a set for your wedding. He wrote so tenderly about his travels. My own favourite is *Nooks and Crannies*. He would have had a great future. It made that shocking accident all the worse.'

'Yes?'

Jerome longed to leave the room and not see that loved face crinkle with irresistible amusement.

'I had so many letters from his readers after the pig fell on him.' She had never been so abrupt before.

And then the miracle happened. Sally did not laugh. Sally sat with open eyes of horror while his aunt told her the story, and at the end, 'How horrible,' Sally said. 'It makes you think, doesn't it? Happening like that. Out of a clear sky.'

Jerome's heart sang with joy. It was as though she had appeased his fear for ever. In the taxi going home he kissed her with more passion that he had ever shown and she returned it. There were babies in her pale blue pupils, babies that rolled their eyes and made water.

'A week today,' Jerome said, and she squeezed his hand. 'Penny for your thoughts, my darling.'

'I was wondering,' Sally said, 'what happened to the poor pig?'

'They almost certainly had it for dinner,' Jerome said happily and kissed the dear child again.

Collected Stories (1972).

B RITISH *artists and authors, unlike their counterparts on the Continent, have never been much good at joining things and having Movements.*

With the brilliant exception of the Pre-Raphaelite Brethren, which was a very colourful affair indeed, like a schoolboys' secret society with its private jargon full of oddly jolly, hearty phrases, a club magazine, and a secret symbol on its members' paintings, most British artists and writers battled away on their own. They tended not to know each other all that well. But when several of them understandably reacted simultaneously and in a radical way to what was going on around them, a Movement was wished upon them by journalists.

The Angry Young Men, a press catch-phrase of the 1950s and early 1960s, was just such a non-existent literary movement (the phrase 'Angry Young Man' originated as the title of a much-talked-about autobiography published in 1951 by a young man named Leslie Paul). Few of the writers dubbed Angry Young Men knew each other well enough to be friends let alone comrades fighting some kind of ideological battle: Colin Wilson was a lone figure who went off to the West Country

*to write complicated books about occultism and crime ; John Wain became Professor
of Poetry at Oxford ; John Osborne—perhaps the only young man who was deeply
and bitterly angry, was an actor/playwright who expressed himself with great
power in plays, notably* Look Back in Anger; *and then there was the poet and
novelist Kingsley Amis, born the year in which* Ulysses *was published,* 1922.

*Kingsley Amis was dubbed by the press an Angry Young Man with the pub-
lication in* 1954 *of his novel* Lucky Jim, *which has proved over the years to be
one of the most deservedly popular comic novels of the century, inviting a comparison beween Amis and Evelyn Waugh as to which is the funnier serious novelist.*

In fact Amis, when writing about Jim Dixon the hero of Lucky Jim, *was not
being an Angry Young Man at all. The novel was intended to be a love story and to
be funny and that is what it chiefly is, although with such a gifted novelist as its
author the book also has other qualities. In the story, Jim strikes out not to
denounce angrily the values of post-war Britain but to win his girl, and to alleviate
the immediate boredoms of his life in a provincial university which include a
neurotic and wildly possessive non-girlfriend, his boss the dreadful Professor Welch,
the Professor's awful wife and pretentious children and their arty social life of little
classical music recitals (Amis has always been a jazz man).*

*Jim fights back against his enemies in his own way, coolly, using his wits
to avoid humiliations and to engineer small victories, and sustaining himself in
black moments by pulling one of a large repertoire of carefully created funny
faces.*

At the end of Lucky Jim, *Jim wins his girl and gives up teaching in favour of
working as a minder-cum-Public Relations officer in London. Hardly the gesture of
an Angry Young Man despising Britain's post-war ethics.*

Lucky Jim *is an ironic title to begin with: Jim is steadily unlucky throughout
most of the novel. Indeed, in the very first week of his academic career he is very
unlucky in managing to infuriate not one but several important senior colleagues :*

How had he made his bad impression? The most likely thing, he always
thought, was his having inflicted a superficial wound on the Professor of
English in his first week. This man, a youngish ex-Fellow of a Cambridge
college, had been standing on the front steps when Dixon, coming round the
corner from the library, had kicked violently at a small round stone lying on
the macadam. Before reaching the top of its trajectory it had struck the other
just below the kneecap at a distance of fifteen yards or more. Averting his
head, Dixon had watched in terrified amazement; it had been useless to run,
as the nearest cover was far beyond reach. At the moment of impact he'd
turned and begun to walk down the drive, but knew well enough that he
was the only visible entity capable of stone-propulsion. He looked back once
and saw the Professor of English huddled up on one leg and looking at him.
As always on such occasions, he'd wanted to apologise but had found, when
it came to it, that he was too frightened to. He'd found the same when, two
days later, he'd been passing behind the Registrar's chair at the first Faculty

meeting, had stumbled and had knocked the chair aside just as the other man was sitting down. A warning shout from the Registrar's Clerk had avoided complete disaster, but he could still remember the look on the face of that figure, stiffened in the shape of a letter S.

Kingsley Amis (b. 1922), *Lucky Jim* (1954).

Like Evelyn Waugh (who is one of the three novelists Amis most admires, the others being Anthony Powell and P. G. Wodehouse) and his Decline and Fall, *Amis's* Lucky Jim *was instantly and hugely successful: it was reprinted twenty times in its first four years of life.*

And like Waugh, Amis went on from his first fine flowering to other and deeper things. He showed an unusual versatility in subject-matter and each of his books differed in approach from its predecessor. After Jim's pursuit of love there was the reality of a modern marriage in That Uncertain Feeling (1955) *followed by* I Like it Here (1958), *a xenophobic outburst against the regrettable un-Englishness of foreigners told by Bowen, a young lecturer in English Literature, who had uprooted himself and family and gone off to live in Portugal.*

I Like it Here *is graced with a memorable passage which shows Amis's splendid gift for reproducing foreign pronunciations exactly with the use of commonplace English words.*

Bowen and his family are on board a ship taking them away from England. Bowen is slumped in a chair in the saloon, brooding. He suddenly remembers the exasperation of trying to discuss English Literature with foreign students who could understand but could not convincingly speak, English:

His mind drifted back to the time when he had been too hard up to resist an invitation to Birmingham, where some foreign persons needed to be addressed on CONTEMPORARY BRITISH NOVELISTS (vi): *Graham Greene*. There was a brief interlude in an underground canteen with fluorescent-strip lighting and lino; the coffee was the prescriptive licquorice with a lacing of varnish. Surrounded by blue-eyed, tanned young men in open-necked shirts, slim-waisted girls in white blouses and no make-up, and a selection of middle-aged bit players from French films, he felt several times like apologising for the inroads which both decor and victuals must be making upon these sensitive continental psyches. But they all chattered away gaily, even a little loudly, throwing down the horrible draught with abandon and stubbing out their cigarettes on the barbaric wooden tables in a spirit of careless ease. Two of them had addressed him in English, and he had answered them, for he saw it as his duty to help foreign guests practise being in Great Britain. The only bad moment came on the way upstairs, when he caught sight of a figure in priest's garb and 'Christ, a Jesuit' was his panicked thought. But a snatch of Dublin drollery, audible an instant later, calmed him.

The lecture was all right. After it there was talk of the views, the attitudes, the obsessions, the values of Grim-Grin. One question seemed to relate to the face of Grim-Grin, and he was at a loss to frame an answer until they all assured him that the fellow was on about the faith of Grim-Grin. Bowen gave them the treatment on that. Then a woman with a lot of beads said:

'We have been hearing of your Grim-Grin and his *Power and the Glory*.'

He agreed that this was the fact.

'But we have been surprised that we have not been hearing of your Edge-Crown.'

'Oh, really?' He searched his brain frantically. Grim-Grin he had been ready for, together with Ifflen-Voff, Zumzit-Mum and Shem-Shoice. This was new. 'Could you amplify that a little?' He ran through the possible variants— Adj-, Ash-, Each-, Age-,. . . Some foreigner? But no, it had been *his* Edge-Crown.

'Sickies of sickingdom,' the woman explained irritably.

'Yes . . . of course . . . Well . . .' He began nodding his head with little hope of ever having reason to stop.

After a brief explanatory uproar he was enabled to wonder aloud what had led his questioner to detect a resemblance between *The Power and the Glory* and *The Keys of the Kingdom*, by A. J. Cronin. 'I think I've done enough talking for a bit,' he added, smiling hard and turning his face to and fro for everyone to see, in the hope of suggesting that he was not to be taken altogether seriously. 'Perhaps one of you would like to have a shot at that.'

One of them at once did, saying in a baritone growl: 'There is a priest in both.'

I Like it Here (1957).

A steady output of novels and miscellaneous works flowed, each one a departure from the last. In 1960 Take a Girl Like You *told the story of a nice Northern girl trying to hang on to her virginity in a London society which was discouraging such unfashionable attitudes. There were volumes of belles-lettres, some books of poetry, a James Bond novel written under the pseudonym Robert Markham, a novel about the extremely rich, a period detective story. Amis also wrote extensively about wines and spirits; he was drinks correspondent for the magazine* Playboy *for some years as well as writing on booze generally for sedater journals.*

His ghost story The Green Man *(1969), was set in an old (and haunted) inn whose proprietor was the story's narrator. The opening lines, beginning with the inn's entry in the* Good Food Guide, *not only provide us with a pastiche of this kind of amateur prose (the exclamation mark in the third line is perfect) but also reveal what the author, a professional wine-writer, thinks about Britain's most popular imported tipple, white Burgundy:*

FAREHAM. Herts   THE GREEN MAN
$\frac{1}{2}$ mile off A595.   Mill End 0043

No sooner has one got over one's surprise at finding a genuine coaching inn less than 40 miles from London—and 8 from the M1—than one is marvelling at the quality of the equally genuine English fare (the occasional disaster apart!). There has been an inn on this site since the Middle Ages, from which parts of the present building date; after some 190 years of service as a dwelling its original function and something of its original appearance, were restored in 1961. Mr Allington will tell its story to the interested (there is, or was, at least one ghost) and be your candid guide through the longish menu. Try the eel soup (6/-), pheasant pie (15/6), saddle of mutton and caper sauce (17/6), treacle roll (5/6). Wine list short, good (except for white Burgundies), a little expensive. Worthington E, Bass, Whitbread Tankard on draught. Friendly, efficient service. No children's prices.

Cl. Su L. Must book L; F, Sa & Su D. Meals 12.30–3; 7–10.30. Alc main dishes 12/6 to 25/-. Seats 40. Car park. No dogs. B & B from 42/6. Class A

App. Bernard Levin; Lord Norwich; John Dankworth; Harry Harrison; Wynford Vaughan-Thomas; Denis Brogan; Brian W. Aldiss; and many others.

The point about white Burgundies is that I hate them myself. I take whatever my wine supplier will let me have at a good price (which I would never dream of doing with any other drinkable). I enjoyed seeing those glasses of Chablis or Pouilly Fuisse, so closely resembling a blend of cold chalk soup and alum cordial with an additive or two to bring it to the colour of children's pee, being peered and sniffed at, rolled round the shrinking tongue and forced down somehow by parties of young technology dons from Cambridge or junior television producers and their girls. Minor, harmless compensations of this sort are all too rare in an innkeeper's day. The Green Man (1969).

Although Lucky Jim *was hardly the work of an Angry Young Man, Kingley Amis changed as the years rolled on to become quite a Furious Middle-aged Man. As a student he had enrolled briefly in the Communist party, the only party he had ever joined, but this left-wing radicalism evaporated quite early to reveal a staunch and patriotic conservative, prepared to defend aggressively those parts of the English way of doing things which he believed to be under threat and which he considered to be worth retaining.*

An indication of the maturing Amis was his distaste for most foreigners and foreign ways expressed so strongly in I Like it Here. *At the time this was an unmodish attitude and it worried the critics who would probably have thought the book funnier had Amis been a little less Tory about it all, a little more woolly liberal. But Amis, unrepentant, struck again with two novels,* Jake's Thing *(1978), and* Stanley and the Women *(1984), which, in an era of fashionable feminism, argued that many women, just by being the kind of women they were, were responsible for inflicting the woe and it was upon the men closest to them that they instinctively inflicted it.*

Jake of Jake's Thing *is a middle-aged lecturer at an Oxford college who has lost his sexual drive, his libido. His doctor, unaware that it is Jake's deep disillusion with the women around him that has stopped him desiring any of them in bed, sends Jake to an exquisitely embarrassing communal sex-therapy clinic in South London.*

One of the first pieces of homework he is then given is to buy a batch of soft-porn magazines and find out whether the pictures excite him.

He sneaks off to a newsagent, buys three girlie magazines, and hurries home with them. There he has to negotiate himself past the cleaning woman. He suspects that her ability to get in his way and to infuriate him with her mindlessness is part of the anti-Jake conspiracy brought to bear upon him by his wife Brenda, her friends, and his own lady academic colleagues, and that she might well be one of the minor causes of his impotence:

Jake wielded his latchkey and opened the front door slowly, cautiously. As soon as he had created an aperture wide enough for it to do so, a human head came into view at about the level of his knee and no more than a few inches from it. The eyes caught his and showed astonishment. He wanted to kick the head, which ascended and receded as part of a move from a crouching to a standing posture. It belonged to Mrs Sharp, the woman who came in three mornings a week to clean the house. He had told her about three-quarters of an hour earlier that he was going out for about three-quarters of an hour, so it was no more than natural that after about forty minutes she should have settled down (as he now saw) to polish the brass frame round the mat immediately inside the front door, nor that astonishment should have visited her to find him of all people entering the house and by such a route. It was sensing enough of this that must have led him to open the door in the way he had . . .

A round-shouldered woman of about forty with prominent but otherwise rather good teeth and a trick of murmuring indistinguishably in tones of self-reproach or mild alarm, Mrs Sharp was always in the way. His way at least. On the stairs, on the thresholds of rooms, in the narrow bit of passage from between the foot of the stairs and the dining-room door to the kitchen door (especially there), dead in front of whichever part of whichever shelf held the book he wanted—always, always. She monitored his shits, managing to be on reconnaissance patrol past the lavatory door or standing patrol in sight of it whenever he went in and out; he couldn't have said why he minded this as he did. Keeping at him in this way meant so much to her that she took 10p an hour less than the going rate and so, in these thin times, rendered herself virtually unsackable . . .

On his entry she had flattened herself against the wall to allow him, and any twenty-stone friends he might have brought with him, to pass. He got out of range of her, so that if she fell over at this point she wouldn't be able to knock the magazines out of his hand in the process, and said weightily,

'I'm going up to my study now, Mrs Sharp.'

'Yes, Mr Richardson.' (Already a most unusual exchange: it was her habit never to speak except while she was being spoken to.)

'I've got some important work to do.'

'Yes, Mr Richardson.'

'I don't want to be disturbed for the next hour.'

'No, Mr Richardson.'. . .

He settled down comfortably in his handsome brass-studded red-leather armchair, a present from Brenda on his fiftieth birthday, and opened *Kensington* . . .

Guiltily he flipped over a page and came upon a small photograph and a large photograph, both a bit misty on purpose, of a very pretty girl who at the same time looked like President Carter, in the sense that her face looked like his, and who had almost no clothes on without giving much away. Over the next page, three more photographs, arty angles, unlikely poses. Over the next page, well this is it folks. Wham. And (there being two such) bam. And thank you most awfully mam.

Jake is no stranger to girlie magazines; he had been a keen enjoyer of their pleasures as a young man but that had been a good many years ago and in the interim the magazines had become somewhat explicit. Whereas in Jake's youth he had gawped at a girl with her upper clothing disarranged to reveal a, to him, rare glimpse of 'them', he is now horrified to find himself staring much lower down at a sharply focused, full-colour close-up of 'it'.

Amis's description of 'it' as seen through Jake's eyes is a line of comic genius:

In itself it had an exotic appearance, like the inside of a giraffe's ear or a tropical fruit not much prized even by the locals.

Jake's reaction to 'it' is to decide that the girl in the photograph is not a lady because although her antics are well within the scope of a lady, allowing herself to be thus photographed isn't, and because of this he finds the photograph curiously off-putting, even slightly offensive.

But the doctor ordered him to persevere for fifteen minutes and this he does:

After a while, this way or that he was getting interested. Then the dead silence was broken by a tremendous rattling of the lock on the door.

That fairly hurtled him back not far off fifty years. He went into a kind of throe and made wild, self-defensive motions. 'What is it?' he asked. He had to ask most of it twice or more.

No answer. Further rattling, but the door itself did seem to be holding for the moment.

'What do you want, Mrs Sharp?' This was louder and steadier. 'I told you I didn't want to be—'

'—thought your knob looked as though it could do with a polish.' No, no, of *course* she didn't say that, couldn't have done; she must have been talking about th' door-knob or y' door-knob, but it had sort of come through to him different.

Jake's Thing (1978).

In later books Amis deals sympathetically with what he sees as the wearisome, frequently blackly funny business of growing old. This he treated somewhat wryly and sadly in Ending Up *(1974), and he returned to the theme again in* The Old

Devils (1986), *a more amusing novel about four old couples in Wales and their affectionate, wary, interleaved relationships.*

This novel at last won for Amis Britain's most prestigious literary award, the Booker Prize.

In The Old Devils *each chapter is devoted to one character's point of view. This suits one of Amis's techniques which is to go into the minutiae of everyday living, describing it as meticulously as Laurence Sterne described Corporal Trim reading the sermon in* Tristram Shandy. *Each of the men in* The Old Devils *is pictured in detail going through his tedious routine of getting up in the morning.*

It is a bad time for Charlie, old, heavy, unhealthy, a steady drinker, who is not at his best at the moment of waking up:

He was not at all fine, nowhere near.

As usual at this time, his morning self cursed his overnight self in having purposely left the Scotch in the drinks cabinet downstairs. Without that sort of help it was quite out of the question that he should ever get up. A mug of tea and a plastic flask containing more tea stood on the bedside table. He would in no sense be committing himself to getting up if it so turned out that he drank some. With this clear all round he got on his elbow and drank some, drank indeed the whole mug's worth in one because it was half cold, and dropped flat again. Before very long the liquid had carved a new and more direct route to his bladder. He rolled over and fixed his eye on the stout timber which framed the quilted bed-head, counted a hundred, then, with a convulsive overarm bowling movement, gripped it, counted another hundred and hauled with all his strength, thus pulling himself half upright.

In this position, still clutching the frame, he paused again, said 'With many a weary sigh, and many a groan, up a high hill he heaves a huge round stone,' and plunged a foot to the floor.   The Old Devils (1986).

Peter, uneasily married to Muriel who has all the money, is almost as fat as Charlie and just as keen a boozer. When his stomach ballooned and stiffness became a problem with age he worked out for himself a set of getting-up procedures which are strenuous but work rather well:

The section that really took it out of him was the actual donning of clothes, refined as this had been over the years, and its heaviest item was the opener, putting his socks on. At one time this had come after instead of before putting his underpants on, but he had noticed that that way round he kept tearing them with his toenails.

Those toenails had in themselves become a disproportion in his life. They tore the pants because they were sharp and jagged, and they had got like that because they had grown too long and broken off, and he had let them grow because these days cutting them was no joke at all. He could not do it in the house because there was no means of trapping the fragments and Muriel was bound to come across a couple, especially with her bare feet, and that was obviously to be avoided. After experimenting with a camp-stool in the garage and falling off it a good deal he had settled on a garden seat under the rather fine flowering cherry. This restricted him to the warmer months, the wearing of an overcoat being of course ruled out by the degree of bending involved. But at least he could let the parings fly free, and fly they bloody well did, especially the ones that came crunching off his big toes, which were massive enough and moved fast enough to have brought down a sparrow on the wing, though so far this had not occurred.

The socks went on in the bathroom with the aid of a particular low table, height being critical. Heel on table, sock completely on as far as heel, toes on table, sock round heel and up. Quite recently he had at last found the kind of socks he wanted, short with no elastic round the top. They did his swollen ankles good, not by making them swell less but by not constricting them, and so leaving them looking less repulsive and frightening when he undressed at night. Pants on in the bedroom, heel and toe like the socks but at floor level, spot of talc round the scrotum, then trousers two mornings out of every three or so. On the third or so morning he would find chocolate, cream, jam or some combination of these from his bedtime snack smeared over the pair in use, and would have to return to the bathroom, specifically to its mirror for guidance in fixing the braces on the front of the fresh trousers, an area which needless to say had been well out of view these many years.

There was nothing non-standard about the remainder of his dressing routine except perhaps for the use of the long shoe-horn, a rare and much prized facility he had once mislaid for a whole miserable week, filling the gap as best he might with a silver-plated Georgian serving-spoon from Muriel's kitchen, where it had naturally had to be returned after each application. He had worn the same pair of featureless slipper-types for years now, hoping to die or become bed-ridden before they fell to pieces and forced him to go to one of these do-the-whole-thing-yourself shoe-shops which he understood were all they had these days.

The part of the course that involved the bathroom hand-basin was less demanding only than the first. The foam went on to his face in two ticks, the sweeps of his razor were bold and swift and he hardly did more with his toothbrush than spread paste over his gums. But even so some bending and stretching and arm-raising was unavoidable, enough to see to it that by the time he was as ready to face the world as he would ever be he was breathing fairly hard and pouring with sweat, especially from his scalp.　　Ibid.

Amis's work is a succession of simply told stories of a remarkably consistent standard which illuminate the way people behave and speak and pretend, and mock those things which anger him, cant of all sorts, stupidity, artistic pretension. And the stories make funny those small but awful disasters which every day wait the other side of the door for most of us.

The best of Kingsley Amis's sadly funny disasters is to be found in Lucky Jim. *Most humorous writers have knocked out a good comic scene where their hero gets unspeakably drunk—there is a good one later on in* Lucky Jim *but Kingsley Amis has written the definitive piece about the morning-after. Once read, the full 'I-could-so-easily-have-done-that' horror of it stays in the mind.*

Jim Dixon is spending a reluctant weekend as a guest in the house of his loathed Head of Department, Professor Welch, and has arranged that if the whole experience is too dire he will telephone his friend Bill Atkinson who will immediately ring Jim back with a story of a family crisis.

Jim has been given a bedroom which has a door through to the communal bathroom.

The previous evening, intensively disliking the concert of chamber music being played by Professor Welch and friends, Jim had slunk off to a pub and got beastly drunk.

It is now the following morning:

Dixon was alive again. Consciousness was upon him before he could get out of the way; not for him the slow, gracious wandering from the halls of sleep, but a forcible, summary ejection. He lay sprawled, too wicked to move, spewed up like a broken spider-crab on the tarry shingle of the morning. The light did him harm, but not as much as looking at things did; he resolved, having done it once, never to move his eyeballs again. A dusty thudding in his head made the scene before him beat like a pulse. His mouth had been used as a latrine by some small creature of the night, and then as its mausoleum. During the night, too, he had been on a cross-country run and then been expertly beaten up by secret police. He felt bad.

He reached out for and put on his glasses. At once he saw that there was something wrong with the bedclothes immediately before his face. Endangering his chance of survival, he sat up a little, and what met his bursting eyes roused to a frenzy the timpanist in his head. A large, irregular area of the turned-back part of the sheet was missing; a smaller but still considerable area of the turned-back part of the blanket was missing: an area about the size of the palm of his hand in the main part of the top blanket was missing. Through the three holes, which appropriately enough had black borders, he could see a dark brown mark on the second blanket. He ran a finger round a bit of the hole in the sheet, and when he looked at his finger it bore a dark-grey stain. That meant ash; ash meant burning; burning must mean cigarettes. Had this cigarette burnt itself out on the blanket? If not, where was it now? Nowhere on the bed; nor in it. He leaned over the side, gritting his teeth; a sunken brown channel, ending in a fragment of discoloured paper, lay across a light patch in the pattern of a valuable-looking rug. This made him feel very unhappy, a feeling sensibly increased when he looked at the bedside table. This was marked by two black, charred grooves, greyish and shiny in parts, lying at right angles and stopping well short of the ashtray, which held a single used match. On the table were two used matches; the remainder lay with the empty cigarette packet on the floor. The bakelite mug was nowhere to be seen.

Had he done all this himself? Or had a wayfarer, a burglar, camped out in his room? Or was he the victim of some Horla fond of tobacco? He thought that on the whole he must have done it himself, and wished he hadn't. Surely this would mean the loss of his job, especially if he failed to go to Mrs Welch and confess what he'd done, and he knew already that he wouldn't be able to do that. There was no excuse which didn't consist of the inexcusable: an incendiary was no more pardonable when revealed as a drunkard as well— so much of a drunkard, moreover, that obligations to hosts and fellow-guests and the counter-attraction of a chamber-concert were as nothing compared with the lure of the drink. The only hope was that Welch wouldn't notice what his wife would presumably tell him about the burning of the bedclothes. But Welch had been known to notice things, the attack on his pupil's book in that essay, for example. But that had really been an attack on Welch himself; he couldn't much care what happened to sheets and blankets which he wasn't actually using at the time. Dixon remembered thinking on an earlier occasion that to yaw drunkenly round the Common Room in Welch's presence screaming obscenities, punching out the window-panes, fouling the periodicals, would escape Welch's notice altogether, provided his own person remained inviolate. The memory in turn reminded him of a sentence in a book of Alfred Beesley's he'd once glanced at: 'A stimulus cannot be received by the mind unless it serves some need of the organism.' He began laughing, an action he soon modified to a wince.

He got out of bed and went into the bathroom. After a minute or two he returned, eating toothpaste and carrying a safety-razor blade. He started cutting carefully round the edges of the burnt areas of the bedclothes with the blade. He didn't know why he did this, but the operation did seem to improve the look of things: the cause of the disaster wasn't so immediately apparent. When all the edges were smooth and regular, he knelt down slowly, as if he'd all at once become a very old man, and shaved the appropriate parts of the rug. The debris from these modifications he stuffed into his jacket pocket, thinking that he'd have a bath and then go downstairs and phone Bill Atkinson and ask him to come through with his message about the senior Dixons a good deal earlier than had been arranged. He sat on the bed for a moment to recover from his vertiginous exertions with the rug, then, before he could rise, somebody, soon identifiable as male, came into the bathroom next door. He heard the clinking of a plug-chain, then the swishing of tap-water. Welch, or his son, or Johns was about to take a bath. Which one it was was soon settled by the upsurge of a deep, untrained voice into song. The piece was recognisable to Dixon as some skein of untiring facetiousness by filthy Mozart. Bertrand was surely unlikely to sing anything at all, and Johns made no secret of his indifference to anything earlier than Richard

Strauss. Very slowly, like a forest giant under the axe, Dixon heeled over sideways and came to rest with his hot face on the pillow.

This, of course, would give him time to collect his thoughts, and that, of course, was just what he didn't want to do with his thoughts; the longer he could keep them apart from one another, especially the ones about Margaret, the better. For the first time he couldn't avoid imagining what she'd say to him, if indeed she said anything, when he next saw her. He pushed his tongue down in front of his lower teeth, screwed up his nose as tightly as he could, and made gibbering motions with his mouth. How long would it be before he could persuade her first to open, then to empty, her locker of reproaches, as preliminary to the huge struggle of getting her to listen to his apologies? Desperately he tried to listen to Welch's song, to marvel at its matchless predictability, its austere, unswerving devotion to tedium; but it didn't work . . . He sat up and by degrees worked his feet to the floor.

There was an alternative to the Atkinson plan; the simpler, nicer one of clearing out at once without a word to anybody. That wouldn't really do, though, unless he cleared out as far as London. What was going on in London now? He began to take off his pyjamas, deciding to omit his bath. Those wide streets and squares would be deserted at this time, except for a few lonely, hurrying figures; he could revisualise it all from remembering a week-end leave during the war. He sighed; he might as well be thinking of Monte Carlo or Chinese Turkestan; then, jigging on the rug with one foot out of, the other still in, his pyjamas, thought of nothing but the pain that slopped through his head like water into a sand-castle. He clung to the mantelpiece, nearly displacing the squatting Oriental, crumpling like a shot film-gunman. Had Chinese Turkestan its Margarets and Welches?

Some minutes later he was in the bathroom. Welch had left grime round the bath and steam on the mirror. After a little thought, Dixon stretched out a finger and wrote 'Ned Welch is a Soppy Fool with a Fase like A Pigs Bum' in the steam; then he rubbed the glass with a towel and looked at himself. He didn't look too bad, really; anyway, better than he felt. His hair, however, despite energetic brushing helped out by the use of a water-soaked nail-brush, was already springing away from his scalp. He considered using soap as a pomatum, but decided against it, having in the past several times converted the short hairs at the sides and back of his head into the semblance of duck-plumage by this expedient. His glasses seemed more goggle-like than usual. As always, though, he looked healthy and, he hoped, honest and kindly. He'd have to be content with that.

He was all ready to slink down to the phone when, returning to the bedroom, he again surveyed the mutilated bedclothes. They looked in some way unsatisfactory; he couldn't have said how. He went and locked the outer bathroom door, picked up the razor-blade, and began again on the circumferences of the holes. This time he made jagged cuts into the material, little inlets from the great missing areas. Some pieces he almost severed.

Finally he held the blade at right angles and ran it quickly round the holes, roughening them up. He stood back from his work and decided the effect was perceptibly better. The disaster now seemed much less obviously the work of man and might, for a few seconds, be put down to some fulminant dry-rot or the ravages of a colony of moths. He turned the rug round so that the shaven burn, without being actually hidden by a nearby chair, was none the less not far from it. He was considering taking the bedside table downstairs and later throwing it out of the bus on his journey back when a familiar voice came into aural range singing in a way that suggested head-wagging jollity. It grew in volume, like the apprehension of something harmful or awful, until the locked bathroom door began to be shaken and its handle rattled. The singing stopped, but the rattling went on, was joined by kicking, even momentarily replaced by the thudding of what must be a shoulder. Welch hadn't thought in advance that the bathroom might bear signs of occupancy by another when he wanted to get back into it himself (why, in any case, did he want to get back into it?), nor did he soon realise it now. After trying several manœuvres to replace his first vain rattling of the handle, he turned his attention to a vain rattling of the handle. There was a final orgasm of shakings, knockings, thuddings and rattlings, then footsteps retreated and a door closed.

With tears of rage in his eyes, Dixon left the bedroom, first unintentionally treading on and shattering the bakelite mug.

Lucky Jim (1957).

THE 1960s saw an extraordinary change in the youthful social climate of most Western countries, signalled by a seemingly spontaneous protest movement which erupted among students and young people everywhere.

One of the young's dissatisfactions was with what they considered to be the outdated and hypocritical Victorian and Edwardian ethical and moral standards of their elders. No doubt with the proliferation of nuclear weapons well in mind, the young then threw themselves into a number of peace-seeking philosophies like the Flower-Power movement of San Francisco. They sought guidance as to how they could combat materialism by sitting at the feet of deeply-bearded (and frequently very rich) Eastern gurus. They believed for a time that hallucinatory drugs were a good thing in releasing the mind from conventional thought and encouraging creative imagery but one of the outcomes of this was, sadly, a number a deaths and an army of walking wounded.

Popular music became for the first time in its history the music of young people. Some of its heroes like the Beatles and Elvis Presley had staying power but from the sixties on the majority of groups and solo singers, the lucky ones at least, tended to have rocket-like careers; Top of the Pops within a few weeks, millionaires within months, and forgotten within a couple of years.

When the dust of all this hubbub and change settled, what emerged was called the Permissive Society.

In humour this new permissiveness took the form of an acceptance of sketches and pieces on subjects which had been previously suppressed for being in utterly bad taste, or for involving unacceptable language, or for simply not being thought fit for comedy.

In Swinging London, the permissiveness was partly created and certainly consolidated by the succesful debut, in May 1961, of the immensely influential revue Beyond the Fringe, *written and played by four young men just down from university who, with intelligence, freshness, and wit, set about mocking hitherto unmocked targets like films about wartime heroism, Church of England sermons, the dialogue in Shakespeare's histories, and the smell of armpits.*

In October 1961, one of the revue's co-writers and performers, Peter Cook, with a friend Nicholas Luard, opened a 'fringe' nightclub in Soho called The Establishment, *an English version of the continental* boîte, *which featured a cabaret of rich and rude political comment and gave England a chance to make up its mind whether the American comedian Lenny Bruce was an iconoclast with a shocking but highly moral point of view, or a filthy maniac.*

On 24 November 1962, Ned Sherrin of BBC Television began producing a series of weekly late-night shows entitled That Was The Week That Was (*known as* TW3), *which provided the somewhat startled nation with a taste of this new, topical, near slanderous, cheerfully malicious entertainment.*

The whole phenomenon was dubbed by newspapers the Satire Boom, to the irritation of most of the writers and performers in it. To them it was great fun suddenly to be allowed to be more irreverent and personal, and a very great deal dirtier, but this was not being satirical in its honourable literary sense. Party-political squibs, mentions of Princess Margaret, impersonations of Prime Minister Harold Macmillan being vague, and frequent use of words like bum and tit were not really the same thing as Swift's A Modest Proposal.

A frequent criticism levelled by the older generations was that it was 'under-graduate humour' but at the time this was tantamount to high praise. The point of the Swinging Sixties culture was that it was a celebration of youth (which for the first time had enormous spending power). Many of the striking and original sketches in Beyond the Fringe *were written and performed when the cast were under-graduates at Oxford and Cambridge. When Peter Cook opened* The Establishment *club he was 24.*

The most interesting event as far as humorous prose was concerned was the founding of the 'satirical' magazine, Private Eye, *first issue published (and mostly given away) 25 October 1961. Typical of the time, the founders were not only just down from university where they had helped run an undergraduate magazine but had been to the same public school, Shrewsbury, where they had all worked on the school magazine, the* Salopian.

They were William Rushton, a very able cartoonist with an effortless flow of humour; Christopher Booker, intellectual, Christian; Paul Foot, intelligent campaigning journalist of the Left; and Richard Ingrams, who just wanted to mock everybody and edit Private Eye.

Just as Punch *was founded as the English equivalent of the Parisian satirical magazine* Charivari, *and* The Establishment *club was modelled on continental political nightclub/cabarets, so* Private Eye *was based upon the French magazine of political scandals and exposés,* Le Canard Enchaîné.

Its opening years were fraught with problems. The editors kept changing places and money frequently ran out but Peter Cook took over a majority shareholding and became both proprietor and amiable supplier of free ideas (such as the the magazine's front cover of a news photograph with 'balloon' captions, the pop group 'The Turds', and the compulsive letter-writer, Sir Herbert Gussett ('My dear wife, whose name for the moment escapes me . . .').

Eventually Richard Ingrams became editor and Private Eye's *circulation rose to be greater than that of* Punch, *the* Listener, *the* Spectator, *and the* New Statesman *put together.*

The first successfully sustained humorous prose series in the magazine came from a suggestion from Peter Cook that a parody of the comfortable, middle-class, radio soap-opera 'Mrs Dale's Diary' might be fruitful if based upon Mrs Wilson, wife of the incoming Prime Minister, Harold Wilson. The idea was taken up by Richard Ingrams and John Wells. Wells, humorist and comic actor, had been at Oxford with Ingrams and the others. The Diary ran in Private Eye *for the duration of Harold Wilson's term in No. 10 Downing Street and was adapted into a stage farce which, continually up-dated with topical material, was a long-running success.*

Mrs Wilson was known to be a comfortable, middle-class lady herself, kindly, and given to writing (and what is more, getting published) thoughtful, homely verses:

We had a gorgeous card from Her Majesty and the Duke who have been very kind to Harold, and I was so moved by their lovely greeting that I jotted down the following humble lines of royal tribute.

'A Merry Xmas to you, your Majesty
And to the sailor Prince
Here's hoping the Yuletide will be zesty
With many pies of mince.

Though storm-clouds loom and famine stalks
Throughout the gloom-struck world
Let us hope you will be able to take the Corgis for many walks
Beneath the British flag unfurled.'

'Mrs Wilson's Diary', *Private Eye* (18 Dec. 1964).

The character which Ingrams and Wells wished upon the luckless Mrs Wilson for purposes of the Diary was that of a dutiful suburban wife, incurious, whose small domestic world was brightened by her fondness for consumer goods as advertised on TV and for Nimmo the cat.

It is midsummer and the Wilsons have settled in at No. 10 Downing Street. The political position is that Mr Wilson has just returned from the USA and is congratulating himself on having made a good impression on President Lyndon B. Johnson:

MRS WILSON'S DIARY

The hot weather seems to have had a strange effect on Harold. The other morning I was just pegging out his tropical drip-dry 'brute' breefidrawers on the line when an enormous furniture van drew up outside the garden gate. A rather fat man got out, wearing a cloth cap, followed by a smaller man with a rather distressing cough. 'Good morning ducks' he remarked in a familiar tone, 'hot as a Turkish wrestler's watchstrap, eh? Just the weather to take your clothes off and live. Ho ho.' And with this he peeled off his rather damp shirt, revealing a plump torso with the words 'I love Fanny' written across his chest in blue pencil. With this he let the back of the lorry down with a loud bang, and assisted by his small companion, began lifting out an enormous wooden crate, with pieces of straw sticking out through the cracks.

'Are you sure you have the right house?' I enquired, attempting to examine the label. 'H. Wisson Esq. re No. 10 Downing Street, that's right, isn't it?' remarked the smaller gentleman, 'One Garden Figure in Portland Marble, This Side Up Use No Hooks. I bloody well hope so, I am not lumbering this load of rubbish back in the van.' 'Deary me' I cried, still holding a pinny full of clothes pegs, 'I must run inside and phone Harold. I am sure he is not expecting it.' I finally discovered that he was having lunch with Lord Thomson of Fleet in a private suite at the top of the GPO Tower. 'Gladys' he remarked as he came to the telephone, 'I am extremely busy. What the devil do you want?' I explained that even as I spoke the two men were removing the garden gate prior to carrying in the huge box. 'Ah yes' Harold remarked, 'that will be my statue. I asked Wheeler to do it at the Royal Academy Dinner. Kindly ask the men to put it up in our bedroom. I think where the wardrobe stands would be a nice place for it.' At this stage he rang off. Alas, easier said than done.

All went well until the two gentlemen tried to turn the corner of the stairs. The smaller of the two, whose name appeared to be Mr Cock, had unfortunately become wedged against the wall, and was making several uncalled-for remarks, interspersed with fits of coughing. At this juncture, naughty Nimmo came prancing playfully down the stairs, getting under the feet of the fat gentleman, who fell backwards with an oath. Fortunately just then there came the clank of a cistern, and Inspector Trimfittering emerged from the bathroom on the landing. 'What goes on?' he cried, in a jovial manner, 'experiencing a spot of bother, are we?' I explained the situation as best I could from the foot of the stairs, and with the help of the Inspector the enormous packing case was eventually dragged into our little bedroom, though not without some damage to the pale blue paint on the bannisters.

'Well there we are then Madam' remarked Mr Cock, holding out his hand in a curious manner as if wondering whether it was going to rain, 'thirsty work that.'

'Thank you' I remarked, shaking his hand and smiling at his heavily built companion, whereupon they both looked rather disgruntled and retreated down the stairs muttering in an impolite fashion.

'Now then' said the Inspector, and seized up the brass poker from the firedogs and shovel set we were given as a wedding present by Manny Shinwell, and applied it to the wooden crate. Alas, it immediately bent in two, and he was compelled to go downstairs and borrow a jemmy from Jim Callaghan's tool-box. Imagine my surprise, on dismantling the crate and pulling out the straw packing, to discover a huge male bottom, exquisitely carved in white marble. 'Who can it be?' I cried, standing back in some alarm. 'Leave this to me Madam!' replied the Inspector, 'I think it might be more seemly if you left the room.'

I stood outside the door for some moments listening to the Inspector's grunts of exertion and finally heard him remark 'There!—you can come in now Madam.' I could hardly believe my eyes. 'President Johnson!!' I cried, 'but why is he wearing Harold's bathrobe?' 'In the absence of a figleaf, Madam, I took the liberty. I feared you might be caused unnecessary alarm.' I must say the likeness is quite excellent, Mr Johnson standing with his fist clenched, and the motto written on the plinth 'All the Way with LBJ' When Harold returned he seemed delighted. He made light of the damage to the staircase and the straw over the bedroom carpet, and insisted on the bathrobe being removed. I myself was slightly displeased at having to move the wardrobe out onto the landing, and I find some difficulty in getting round the statue to dress and make the bed.

I was just dozing on Thursday morning, thinking that I must get up, when Harold woke with a start, climbed over me and flung on his dressing gown, slamming the door behind him and running downstairs to the sitting room. I found him huddled in front of the television watching little white sparks run across the screen from right to left. 'Look Gladys' he cried 'the first ever pictures of the moon by television. This is a historic moment. I must ring up Lyndon at once.'

At this he snatched up the telephone and dialled a number. Soon I heard the President's voice on the line. 'Mr President' remarked Harold rather pompously, 'may I on behalf of Her Majesty the Queen congratulate you on a magnificent achievement. This must surely rank beside the exploits of Vasco da Gama and Christopher Columbus.'

'Enough of this bullshit' I heard Mr Johnson's voice exclaim on the booster, 'When are we going to get your boys in Vietnam? Hold your horses Lady Bird, I'll be right back. Do you realise it is one o'clock in the morning over here?' Then the voice became rather muffled, and the President remarked, 'It's Wilson, baby. I know, but he's so dumb he can't find his ass with both hands.' I thought this rather strange as the last time Harold had a donkey was in the Scilly Isles before the war. It was called Dobbin and we had to get rid of it when it started eating the daffodils. Finally however the President remarked 'Well Harold, there you go, and keep your pecker up.' Harold had listened to the entire conversation with an expression of distaste on his face, and there was now a loud click from the other end. I was just going to ask Harold what he had meant about the donkey when he snatched up the early edition of the *Daily Telegraph* and stamped off to his den, kicking Nimmo aside and slamming the door.

> Richard Ingrams and John Wells (b. 1937; b. 1936), *Private Eye* (10 June 1966).

When Harold Wilson was defeated at the polls, 'Mrs Wilson's Diary' had to come to an end. The new Prime Minister, Edward Heath, was a staunch campaigner for a united Europe and was much involved in negotiating terms for Britain's entry into the Common Market, which meant discussing farm produce prices, milk output, and so on.

Private Eye dubbed him 'Grocer' Heath and chose the 'Grocer' aspect of the Prime Minister as the basis of their next lampoon. They set up a series which pretended that Britain was a giant supermarket chain, Heathco. Its Managing Director was Edward Heath and in each edition of the magazine he wrote a stirring memo to his workforce, i.e. the British public.

In this series Ingrams had a different collaborator, the cartoonist, novelist, and musician, Barry Fantoni. Fantoni, like Peter Arno joining the New Yorker, *just walked in off the streets and started work. He has been one of the magazine's strengths in spite of being the only member of the team not to have been to public school and university. As he put it, he represented the urban working-class Jewish-Italian vote.*

The prose style of Heathco was a brilliant parody of the kind of businessman's English dictated in anger and at great speed by a not very literate Managing Director who signed what he had dictated without bothering to read it through first.

The political inspiration for the piece was an irritating and fierce series of attacks on Mr Heath's policies made by his ex-Cabinet Minister, the Rt. Hon. Enoch Powell:

HEATHCO
A MESSAGE FROM THE MANAGING DIRECTOR

Hullo.

I have been asked recently whether I have anything to say with regard to the quite unprecedented remarks which have been made with increasing regularity about the way Heathco's is being run by one of my former board-room colleagues, namely Mr E. Powell.

Well quite frankly I simply haven't got the time to waste with this sort of childish nonsense.

Quite frankly I've got far better things to do with my time than to argue the toss with someone who to my mind doesn't know the first thing about how to run a business.

With the greatest respect to Mr Powell who I've no doubt is a highly intelligent person in his own right, when it comes to running a mammoth organisation like Heathco's is today you won't get very far with just book-learning—Latin and Greek and so forth with regard to this one.

But I say it again. If some people think I'm going to spend my mornings trying to answer some ridiculous points which Mr Powell has raised about the way Heathco's is going then they've got hold of completely the wrong end of the stick.

Don't get me wrong. I have no doubt at all that Mr Powell is a very capable man in many ways and has in the past contributed a great deal to the firm.

But ever since he left the board and I say this with all due regard to his many varied talents he has quite obviously completely gone off the rails.

But to get back to the point. I simply have got too much on my plate right now to be bothered with this quite honestly completely trivial matter of Mr Powell.

I would just like to say one thing to him. If he thinks he can run this business better than me then alright fair enough. Let him come forward at the next Annual General Meeting and put himself up to the board.

Quite frankly I'm sick to death of this constant carping and moaning from the sidelines. It drives me bloody well up the wall to have to listen day after day to what is to all intents and purposes Mr Powell's insults and accusations because quite frankly that's what they are quite frankly.

I will not stand for it any more. I've had it up to here with regard to this one. I've had just about as much as I can take of this non-stop bickering and backbiting.

The latest thing I hear is that 'I'm afraid of him'. Well of all the ridiculous ideas. Quite honestly if Mr Powell thinks that, he should have his head examined.

But I say it again. I just DO NOT intend to take the slightest fraction of notice with regard to anything that Mr Powell says, writes or whatever else he does. If he or anyone else thinks that as Managing Director of this company I can afford to spend my valuable time going into a totally minor matter such as this then all I can say is they don't know me and they don't know Heathco's.

APBDU

At the time of writing no firm decison has yet been taken viz a viz this one.

In the meantime it has come to my attention that some people are in the habit of using their beakers as ash trays and so forth.

It surely is obvious even to a child of two that PLASTIC IS HIGHLY FLAMMABLE.

What's more it catches fire very easily besides making a revolting smell. My office is right the other end from the canteen and yet at lunchtime and tea-breaks I have to close the window because of the disgusting black smoke pouring out of the canteen.

Kindly will those responsible in future use the temporary litter bins provided.

EDWARD HEATH

Man. Dir.

> Barry Fantoni and Richard Ingrams (b. 1940; b. 1937), *Private Eye* (27 July 1973).

The next incumbent of No. 10 Downing Street was the Rt. Hon. James Callaghan, Labour, and he proved not to have capability as a comic prose figure.

After him came the Rt. Hon. Margaret Thatcher, Conservative. Mrs Thatcher, too, proved an elusive subject to pin down in parody. But Mrs Thatcher was married and Mr Thatcher was another matter. Mr Thatcher was rich in those personal characteristics at which Private Eye *delighted to poke fun: he was a retired and rich businessman, late of Burmah Oil; he played golf; his closest friend was William Deedes, editor of the* Daily Telegraph, *a deeply Conservative newspaper. And so Ingrams and John Wells got together again and wrote* Dear Bill, *a series of letters purporting to be from Denis Thatcher, beleaguered in Downing Street, to a friend and drinking chum, Bill, at large in the real world of golf and large gin-and-tonics.* Dear Bill *proved to be* Private Eye's *most successful series and was a hit in the theatre where a dramatized version,* Anyone for Denis?, *starred the co-author John Wells looking uncannily like Denis Thatcher.*

The topical events touched upon in the following letter are: (a) Parliament has closed for the Summer recess and the Thatchers are off to Switzerland; (b) Lord Hailsham, the Lord Chancellor, has been voted a large rise in salary; (c) President Reagan (Hopalong) has had his nose examined for possible skin cancer; (d) More disturbances in South Africa with a drop in value of krugerrands (NB, the 'Fat Friend in the Waistcoat' living next door at No. 11 Downing Street is the Chancellor of the Exchequer, the Rt. Hon. Nigel Lawson, who always wears a waistcoat and is unslim); (e) BBC documentary makers at Lime Grove Studios are prevented from going ahead with a film about the IRA; (f) more bombs go off in Northern Ireland:

> *10 Downing Street*
> *Whitehall*

Dear Bill,

Just a quick line before we hang the Swissair tags on our Duty Free and jet off to Gnomeland.

As you will have seen in the *Daily Telegraph*, the term at Halitosis Hall ended with the usual high spirits and vandalism, all because somebody in Whitehall had the bright idea of jacking Hailsham's pay up to seventy-five grand a year—not a large emolument in this day and age—but considering all he does is doze on the Woolsack sneezing and scratching his ass from time to time it was hardly to be wondered at that there should be some angry murmurs from the Proles. You can't rely on our lot either nowadays, even in support of a fair day's pay for a fair day's work. The Wets predictably hollered a lot of SDP rubbish, got pissed and trailed off through the wrong lobby.

The Boss blew her top over this, and actually threatened to resign, in my view never a good card to play. Witness the melancholy tale of poor old Wino Henderson at Burmah, who as you may recall was reprimanded after some malfeasance at the Christmas Party, stormed into the Boardroom to say he'd never been so insulted, his private life was his own affair, and was tendering his resignation forthwith. Blow me, when he got back on Monday morning expecting the red carpet and the Entertainments Officer Ferney-Whittingstall on his knees pleading for forgiveness, they'd walled his office up and turned it into the Ladies' Wash Room. Luckily for the Boss, her ploy seems to have succeeded and Hailsham's pay rise has gone through, although the old boy has announced he's going to give it all to Oxfam. Rum world, eh?

Hopalong seems to be falling to bits, which I suppose was only to be expected. The latest scare was when he noticed his nose had turned a funny colour and insisted on taking a bit of it to the doctor's to have it looked at under a magnifying glass. You or I could have told him that a shiny red nose is perfectly normal in anyone over the age of forty, and nothing whatever to worry about, but these Americans are all obsessed about their health and rush off to the medic on the slightest pretext. That is why Dr O'Gooley, whose own nose actually glows in the dark, so often talks about toddling over there and upping his salary by six or eight noughts.

I hope you managed to sell your Krugerrands in time. I got a tip from the Portuguese woman who cleans at Number 11 that our Fat Friend in the Waistcoat had been on the blower to the Cape and that things sounded pretty grisly, and Furniss very decently unloaded mine in about ten minutes to some unsuspecting mug from Kuwait. A p.c. from Mrs Van der Kafferbesher asking for food parcels told a pretty poignant tale. Apparently Brer Coon has finally put his foot down and is refusing to buy any more Water Biscuits and Mature Cheddar from the local Safeways, with the result that Mrs Van der K's friends in trade are having to put the shutters up. The Boss I think has remained pretty sound on S.A. insisting on business as usual, confidence in an expanding market, and the best way to bring Mr Botha to see reason is to do nothing at all. Meanwhile Botha, ignoring the wishes of miscellaneous busybodies all round the world, very wisely decided to wield the big stick and arrest the clergy, in my opinion the true niggers in the woodpile, with Moscow chipping in pretty heavily whenever the collecting plate goes round. Mrs Van der K told me the last time I was down there that this Bishop Tutu man who is always being garlanded with Swedish peace prizes is actually a close friend of Mr Gorblimov and is always going off for free holidays on the Black Sea. None of that has been in the paper, obviously, but Mrs Van der K has her ear pretty close to the ground, and it made me wonder whether

Runcie isn't up to some nonsense of that kind too. (You saw he sent some minor sky-pilot out to one of their funerals.)

For once I thought Britain acted in a statesmanlike way in bringing the Pinkoes of Lime Grove to heel over this IRA Party Political they were planning. Not that it would have made a blind bit of difference as all the viewers are plastered by that hour of the night. But it was high time that somebody made it clear that there is a limit to the sort of bare-faced cheek Margaret had to listen to day after day on the wireless and the TV from assorted shirt-lifters and Trotskyites masquerading as entertainment. Incidentally after all this guff from M. about oxygen and violence which she got from McGregor during a somewhat rambling lunch when the talk turned to putting out fires on oil rigs—entre nous, the old geezer is now very over-ripe for the Farm—where was I? Anyway Hurd, our mastermind in Belfast, announced last week that the IRA were running out of steam, and within seconds you could hardly hear him speak for the noise of Best U.S. TNT blowing comestibles into the street all over the Province. I suppose that sort of prat learns his lesson eventually.

When you receive your annual p.c. of the Matterhorn you may find the message a little cryptic as all the post is opened by Dr Bosendorfer, the in-house shrink. For 'weather conditions' read M., for 'gentians in short supply this year' read the inevitable drought, and 'having a lovely time' draw your own conclusions. My best to Mrs Flack and all the gang under the thatched bar on the beach. You lucky buggers.

Yrs by a thread,
DENIS

Richard Ingrams and John Wells, *Private Eye* (9 Aug. 1985).

The humorous prose content of Private Eye, *and the magazine's circulation, profited in 1970 by the arrival as a regular contributor of the literary journalist, political columnist, and novelist, Auberon Waugh.*

Auberon Waugh's 'Diary' in Private Eye, *which ran until 1985, began as a parody of Alan Brien's highly personal, literary diary in the* Sunday Times *but, as so often happens, the parody element was soon dropped and the column developed its own style. And it was an extraordinary style. Auberon Waugh proved to be as eccentric and virtuoso an antagonist as his father, Evelyn Waugh, and the column bristled with nonsense, cheerful and unrepentant prejudices and sometimes quite vicious insults.*

The Diary, startling though it was, was more than an exercise in over-the-topmanship. The venom was in keeping with the magazine's house-style of cheeking its betters, and Auberon Waugh's point of view, an hilarious inversion of every woolly liberal attitude, was in line with the provocative nature of the 'satire boom' as well as being original and funny. Waugh took it upon himself to present the mandarin's-eye-view, to champion the over-dog.

In the following selection, from the last collection of his Private Eye *Diary pieces to be published in book form, Auberon Waugh expresses himself clearly on poor people who take caravan holidays, tea at Buckingham Palace, the importance of massage parlours, some thoughts on nuns' urine, a press reception given by Miss Olga Deterding, the Rt. Hon. Maureen Colquhoun, MP and her struggles as a lesbian, Miss Glenda Jackson's (highly) personal appearance, and a possible solution to the problem of old age pensioners:*

June 11, 1976

THE ROADS of West Somerset are jammed as never before with caravans from Birmingham and the West Midlands. Their horrible occupants only come down here to search for a place where they can go to the lavatory free. Then they return to Birmingham, boasting in their hideous flat voices how much money they have saved.

I don't suppose many of the brutes can read, but anybody who wants a good book for the holidays is recommended to try a new publication from the Church Information Office: *The Churchyard Handbook* (CIO, £2.40).

It laments the passing of that ancient literary form, the epitaph, suggesting that many of the tombstones put up nowadays dedicated to 'Mum' or 'Dad' or 'Ginger' would be more suitable for a dog cemetery than for the resting place of Christians.

The trouble is that people can afford tombstones nowadays who have no business to be remembered at all. Few of these repulsive creatures in caravans are Christians, I imagine, but I would happily spend the rest of my days composing epitaphs for them in exchange for a suitable fee:

> He had a shit on Gwennap Head,
> It cost him nothing. Now he's dead.
>
> He left a turd on Porlock Hill.
> As he lies here, it lies there still.

February 12, 1977

TO BUCKINGHAM PALACE for my weekly tea with the lady whose identity I do not propose to reveal. We laugh a lot about Marcia's theory [Marcia Falkender, later Baroness Falkender, personal assistant to the Prime Minister, Harold Wilson] that she was never invited to the Palace because the Queen knew she was of Royal blood!

It is a little known fact that the Queen has a marvellous sense of humour, especially if one tickles her feet with an ostrich feather.

February 28, 1977

THE *EVENING STANDARD* reveals that there are 13 officials in Westminster Council with the duty of inspecting massage and sauna parlours in what is becoming the Massage Capital of the World.

This is a job I might well apply for when *Private Eye* is closed down.

Massage Inspectors have the power to enter any premises where they have reason to believe that massage may be occurring, or may have recently occurred, or be about to occur.

It is important to keep standards high in this vital field. Massage and escort agencies between them now account for 27.4 per cent of all foreign earnings from tourism, according to figures released by the Central Statistics Office.

The scandal is that no government assistance is available. All state subsidy in this field has been grabbed by the resident homosexual community for its own personal pleasures.

These are English diversions, and while I am not necessarily urging an end to all buggers' subsidies, I feel it is time we started to think of our foreign guests, not to mention the resident heterosexual minority.

GOOD NEWS for the religious revival. The clotted blood of St Januarius, the fourth-century martyr and patron saint of Naples, has liquified again.

Even more remarkable is a discovery by doctors at King's College, Denmark Hill, London. In a project financed by the World Health Organisation, they have found that an extract from the urine of Italian nuns, called Pergonal, allows infertile women to have babies without the risk of multiple birth.

For my part, I never doubted the miraculous property of nuns' urine. Where the nun is Portuguese, her urine may be used in place of anti-freeze in your motor car. Make friends with a German nun, and she will show you unusual ways of polishing silver.

RATHER TO my surprise, as I have never met the lady, I find myself invited to a party given by Miss Olga Deterding, the elderly Dutch philanthropist, in her Piccadilly penthouse.

It is a strange scene. All the men, as one would expect, are homosexual, and all the women extremely ugly, but Miss Deterding (who is very into journalists) has supplemented them with some tailor's dummies. She also has some model sheep under which she has picturesquely scattered handfuls of raisins.

I am not at home in this *milieu*. Miss Deterding herself, with her white hair *en brosse*, sits with a walking-stick looking rather like the Maharishi's grandmother and exuding a faint aura of saintliness.

But she does not look at all well, and I wonder whether she may not have picked up a spot of leprosy from her noble work with Albert Schweitzer in Gabon many years ago. When we shake hands I find several of her fingers left behind. The most alarming thing is that she does not appear to notice.

> ✒ Mr Waugh's reluctance to be impressed by the extremely rich Dutch oil heiress did not falter. When Miss Deterding died he wrote: 'The last time I saw her she reminded me of Rider Haggard's Ayesha after one trip too many through the Fire of Eternal Life—hairless, shrivelled and black as a tinker's nutting bag.'

September 16, 1978

WOMAN'S OWN carries a poignant interview with 'Ms' Maureen Colquhoun, 49-year-old Lesbian MP for Northampton North. She announces that she intends to fight on, but I wonder whom she intends to fight.

It is wrong to attack Lesbians, but if they attack first one is permitted to fight back. I always advise people on these occasions to stand at a distance and throw lumps of coal at them. Another way of retaliating is to spray them with scent, but probably nothing annoys a Lesbian so much as to be patted on the bum.

September 21, 1981

LAST NIGHT, unable to sleep for worrying about badgers, I watched Glenda Jackson in Ken Russell's *The Music Lovers*. Hideous women, dreadful film. One can't really blame Tchaikowsky for preferring boys. Anybody might become a homosexualist who had once seen Glenda Jackson naked.

Since she has been kind enough to show it to us, I must remark that she has a most unusual configuration in her pubic hair. It seems to grow in a narrow tuft, like the hairstyle of the Last of the Mohicans. I wonder if Ms Jackson has any Red Indian blood. If so, it might explain why there are no more Mohicans.

December 10, 1982

MORE HORROR stories about the treatment of old people. A gang of thieves in St Albans has been giving them drugged tea and then robbing them while they slept. Or so it is claimed.

The reason why old people are at risk nowadays is that they are so rich. When their pension was only a few shillings a week, everybody left them alone. Now they are to be seen hobbling away from the Post Office every Monday morning carrying great fistfuls of £5 and £10 notes, even my fingers begin to twitch.

Something must obviously be done about this epidemic of granny bashing, and the first thing is for the Government to stop giving them so much money.

> Auberon Waugh (b. 1939), *Private Eye*, reprinted: *The Diaries of Auberon Waugh: a turbulent decade 1976–1985* (1985).

═══════════

THERE was a startlingly rapid growth of sexual explicitness in literature published after 1960, a burst of some twenty-five years of frank and fearless descriptions of sexual fun and games which lasted until the arrival of AIDS took the edge off the fun.

1960 was the year when Penguin Books were taken to court under the Obscene Publications Act for publishing Lady Chatterley's Lover *but won the right to publish.*

Descriptions of the sexual act became more frequent and detailed until by the 1980s best-seller lists were dominated by so-called block-busters, brick-thick paperback romantic novels mostly written by women who would perhaps be better described as professional best-seller manufacturers than authors, and their immensely successful 'novels' inevitably contained a quota of hair-raisingly explicit, physiologically imaginative couplings.

The surprising thing was that the Obscene Publications Act, meant to suppress soft as well as hard pornography, was still in force. But public opinion was in favour of permissiveness and juries were reluctant to convict. The imposing of censorship by legal action was unpopular, uncertain of success and, if pursued frequently, wasteful of public funds, so the authorities became increasingly cautious about bringing cases to court.

As far as authors were concerned the legal walls were still in position around them but the ramparts were no longer manned and could now be safely climbed or walked around.

Bad things came out of pornography when it became socially acceptable. As Kingsley Amis warned at the time, and has carried on warning, sexual explicitness encourages sloppy writing and has contributed towards the degeneration of literature by making rubbish saleable; the block-buster romances would never have got anywhere near the best-seller lists without their dirty bits. 'Breasts and buttocks are child's play,' Kingsley Amis wrote, 'but those important moments and days and whole relationships, which are deeply sexual but in which nobody even looks like touching anybody, can be quite difficult to write about. It is simply easier work retailing a series of bedroom tussles than trying to emulate Hardy, Tolstoy, or Richardson.'

But good things emerged from permissiveness, too. For an essentially serious novelist like Philip Roth who makes his points through humour, freedom from censorship means that he is able to write comically about human problems which were unmentionable before 1960.

Much of Roth's work is concerned with the Jewish dilemma, the dreams of genteel middle-class status amidst a sordid reality in an American-Jewish society where refinement and vulgarity are clearly marked areas but inseparable. His writing style is also paradoxical; even during the wildest and bawdiest comedy passages his prose is precise and controlled.

In Portnoy's Complaint, *the great taboo-breaker published in 1969, Alexander Portnoy is a 33-year-old New York lawyer, Jewish, with an unsatisfactory sex-life. He lies on a couch throughout the book, telling the story of his frustrations to a silent psychoanalyst, Dr Spielvogel. In the following extract from the most famous and stunning chapter, Portnoy tells Dr Spielvogel how he tried hard to be a dutiful son but growing up in a loving Jewish household just made him want to rebel against his parents' kind of suffocating Jewishness and this rebellious feeling made*

*him feel ungrateful, alone, and guilty. Which led to another and deeper problem,
which left him feeling even guiltier.*

He became a compulsive masturbator:

WHACKING OFF

Then came adolescence—half my waking life spent locked behind the bathroom door, firing my wad down the toilet bowl, or into the soiled clothes in
the laundry hamper, or *splat*, up against the medicine-chest mirror, before
which I stood in my dropped drawers so I could see how it looked coming
out. Or else I was doubled over my flying fist, eyes pressed close but mouth
wide open, to take that sticky sauce of buttermilk and Clorax on my own
tongue and teeth—though not infrequently, in my blindness and ecstasy, I
got it all in the pompadour, like a blast of Wildroot Cream Oil. Through a
wad of matted handkerchiefs and crumpled Kleenex and stained pyjamas, I
moved my raw and swollen penis, perpetually in dread that my loath-
someness would be discovered by someone stealing upon me just as I was in
the frenzy of dropping my load. Nevertheless, I was wholly incapable of
keeping my paws from my dong once it started climbing up my belly. In the
middle of a class I would raise a hand to be excused, rush down the corridor
to the lavatory, and with ten or fifteen savage strokes, beat off standing up
into a urinal. At the Saturday afternoon movie I would leave my friends to
go off to the candy machine—and wind up in a distant balcony seat, squirting
my seed into the empty wrapper from a Mounds bar. On an outing of our
family association, I once cored an apple, saw to my astonishment (and with
the aid of my obsession) what it looked like, and ran off into the woods to fall
upon the orifice of the fruit, pretending that the cool and mealy hole was
actually between the legs of that mythical being who always called me Big
Boy when she pleaded for what no girl in all recorded history had ever had.
'Oh shove it in me, Big Boy,' cried the cored apple that I banged silly on that
picnic. 'Big Boy, Big Boy, oh give me all you've got,' begged the empty milk
bottle that I kept hidden in our storage bin in the basement, to drive wild
after school with my vaselined upright. 'Come, Big Boy, come,' screamed the
maddened piece of liver that, in my insanity, I bought one afternoon at a
butcher shop and, believe it or not, violated behind a billboard on the way to
a bar mitzvah lesson.

It was at the end of my freshman year of high school—and freshman year
of masturbating—that I discovered on the underside of my penis, just where
the shaft meets the head, a little discolored dot that has since been diagnosed
as a freckle. Cancer. I had given myself *cancer*. All that pulling and tugging
at my own flesh, all that friction, had given me an incurable disease. And
not yet fourteen! In bed at night the tears rolled from my eyes. 'No!' I
sobbed. 'I don't want to die! Please—no!' But then, because I would very
shortly be a corpse anyway, I went ahead as usual and jerked off into my
sock. I had taken to carrying the dirty socks into bed with me at night

so as to be able to use one as a receptacle upon retiring, and the other upon wakening . . .

> *Sophie Ginsky the boys call 'Red',*
> *She'll go far with her big brown eyes and her clever head.*

And that was my mother! . . .

'He eats French fries,' she says, and sinks into a chair to Weep Her Heart Out once and for all. 'He goes after school with Melvin Weiner and stuffs himself with French-fried potatoes. Jack, you tell him, I'm only his mother. Tell him what the end is going to be. Alex,' she says passionately, looking to where I am edging out of the room, '*tateleh*, it begins with diarrhoea, but do you know how it ends? With a sensitive stomach like yours, do you know how it finally ends? *Wearing a plastic bag to do your business in!*'

Who in the history of the world has been least able to deal with a woman's tears? My father. I am second. He says to me, 'You heard your mother. Don't eat French fries with Melvin Weiner after school.'

'Or ever,' she pleads.

'Or ever,' my father says.

'Or hamburgers out,' she pleads.

'Or hamburgers out,' he says.

'*Hamburgers*,' she says bitterly, just as she might say *Hitler*, 'where they can put anything in the world in that they want—and *he* eats them. Jack, make him promise, before he gives himself a terrible *tsura*, and it's too late.'

'I *promise*!' I scream. 'I *promise*!' and race from the kitchen—to where? Where else.

I tear off my pants, furiously I grab that battered battering ram to freedom, my adolescent cock, even as my mother begins to call from the other side of the bathroom door. 'Now this time don't flush. Do you hear me, Alex? I have to see what's in that bowl!'

Doctor, do you understand what I was up against? My wang was all I really had that I could call my own . . .

The hysteria and the superstition! The watch-its and the be-carefuls! You mustn't do this, you can't do that—hold it! don't, you're breaking an important law! *What* law? *Whose* law? They might as well have had plates in their lips and painted themselves blue for all the sense they made! Oh, and the *milchiks* and *flaishiks* besides, all those *meshuggeneh* rules and regulations on top of their own private craziness! It's a family joke that when I was a tiny child I turned from the window out of which I was watching a snowstorm, and hopefully asked, 'Momma, do we believe in winter?' Do you get what I'm *saying*? I was raised by Hottentots and Zulus! I couldn't even contemplate drinking a glass of milk with my salami sandwich without giving serious offence to God Almighty. Imagine then what my conscience gave me for all that jerking off! The guilt, the fears—the terror bred into my bones! . . . Who filled these parents of mine with such a fearful sense of life? . . .

Doctor Spielvogel, this is my life, my only life, and I'm living it in the middle of a Jewish joke! I am the son in the Jewish joke—*only it ain't no joke*!

Philip Roth (b. 1933), *Portnoy's Complaint* (1969).

———————

THE *comic novelist Tom Sharpe*—Indecent Exposure, Porterhouse Blue, Blott on the Landscape, *and all the other best-sellers, a dozen published between 1971 and 1985—is a true child of the permissive society in that it is difficult to visualize his books even being considered for publication let alone becoming best-sellers before the 1960s had happened.*

Tom Sharpe's line is what might be termed intelligent, full-frontal farce. He mixes savagely funny sexual comedy with violence. Fires, explosions, minor but painfully embarrassing injuries and sudden deaths abound. He has developed a repertoire of characters which he uses in various permutations so in his novels you can be fairly certain to meet one or more of the following: a very fat or very thin nymphomaniac, a murderously brutal soldier or police officer, a lesbian, a cabinet minister or bishop with some unfortunate personal problem, a sexually unsatisfied wife, and a mild, intelligent, liberal-minded hero who is busily lusting after a full-breasted neighbour or the au pair girl.

As an example of the strong language which Tom Sharpe has been one of the first 'permissive era' humorists to make an essential part of his comic style, here is a typical Sharpe scene, a confrontation between the reasonable hero and some of the unsympathetic people with whom he has to work, illiterate pupils, right-wing and obstructionist members of the Education Committee, hostile and unco-operative left-wing colleagues.

Henry Wilt is Head of the Department of Liberal Studies at a technical college which exists mainly for the technical training of apprentice gasfitters, cooks, bakers, and bricklayers. Somebody in Wilt's department has borrowed the department's ciné-camera and with the help of some of the apprentices has made a most unusual little film:

He didn't much want what he found on his desk on Monday morning. It was a note from the Vice-Principal asking Wilt to come and see him at, rather sinisterly, 'your earliest, repeat earliest, convenience'.

'Bugger my convenience,' muttered Wilt. 'Why can't he say "immediately" and be done with it?'

With the thought that something was amiss and that he might as well get the bad news over and done with as quickly as possible, he went down two floors and along the corridor to the Vice-Principal's office.

'Ah Henry, I'm sorry to bother you like this,' said the Vice-Principal, 'but I'm afraid we've had some rather disturbing news about your department.'

'Disturbing?' said Wilt suspiciously.

'Distinctly disturbing. In fact all hell has been let loose up at County Hall.'

'What are they poking their noses into this time? If they think they can send any more advisers like the last one we had who wanted to know why we didn't have combined classes of bricklayers and nursery nurses so that there was sexual equality you can tell them from me . . .'

The Vice-Principal held up a protesting hand. 'That has nothing to do with what they want this time. It's what they don't want. And, quite frankly, if you had listened to their advice about multi-sexed classes this wouldn't have happened.'

'I know what would have,' said Wilt. 'We'd have been landed with a lot of pregnant nannies and—'

'If you would just listen a moment. Never mind nursery nurses. What do you know about buggering crocodiles?'

'What do I know about . . . did I hear you right?'

The Vice-Principal nodded. 'I'm afraid so.'

'Well if you want a frank answer I shouldn't have thought it was possible. And if you're suggesting . . .'

'What I am telling you, Henry, is that someone in your department has been doing it. They've even made a film of it.'

'Film of it?' said Wilt, still grappling with the appalling zoological implications of even approaching a crocodile, let alone buggering the brute.

'With some apprentice class,' continued the Vice-Principal, 'and the Education Committee have heard about it and want to know why.'

'I can't say I blame them,' said Wilt, 'I mean you'd have to be a suicidal candidate for Krafft-Ebing to proposition a fucking crocodile and while I know I've got some demented sods as part-timers I'd have noticed if any of them had been eaten. Where the hell did he get the crocodile from?'

'No use asking me,' said the Vice-Principal. 'All I know is that the Committee insists on seeing the film before passing judgement.'

'Well they can pass what judgements they like,' said Wilt, 'just so long as they leave me out of it. I accept no responsibility for any filming that's done in my department and if some maniac chooses to screw a crocodile, that's his business, not mine. I never wanted all those TV cameras and cines they foisted onto us. They cost a fortune to run and some damned fool is always breaking the things.'

'Whoever made this film should have been broken first if you ask me,' said the Vice-Principal. 'Anyway, the Committee want to see you in Room 80 at six and I'd advise you to find out what the hell has been going on before they start asking you questions.'

Wilt went wearily back to his office desperately trying to think which of the lecturers in his department was a reptile-lover, a follower of *nouvelle vague* brutalism in films and clean off his rocker. Pasco was undoubtedly insane, the result, in Wilt's opinion, of fourteen years continuous effort to get gasfitters to appreciate the linguistic subtleties of *Finnegans Wake*, but although he had twice spent a year's medical sabbatical in the local mental hospital he was relatively amiable and too hamfisted to use a cine-camera, and as for crocodiles . . . Wilt gave up and went along to the Audio-Visual Aid room to consult the register.

'I'm looking for some blithering idiot who's made a film about crocodiles,' he told Mr Dobble, the A.V.A. caretaker. Mr Dobble snorted.

'You're a bit late. The Principal's got that film and he's carrying on something horrible. Mind you, I don't blame him. I said to Mr Macaulay when it came back from processing, "Blooming pornography and they pass that through the labs. Well I'm not letting that film out of here until it's been vetted." That's what I said and I meant it.'

'Vetted being the operative word,' said Wilt caustically. 'And I don't suppose it occurred to you to let me see it first before it went to the Principal?'

'Well, you don't have no control over the buggers in your department, do you Mr Wilt?'

'And which particular bugger made this film?'

'I'm not one for naming names but I will say this, Mr Bilger knows more about it than meets the eye.'

'Bilger? That bastard. I knew he was punch-drunk politically but what the hell's he want to make a film like this for?'

'No names, no packdrill,' said Mr Dobble, 'I don't want any trouble.'

'I do,' said Wilt and went out in pursuit of Bill Bilger. He found him in the staff-room drinking coffee and deep in dialectics with his acolyte, Joe Stoley, from the History Department. Bilger was arguing that a truly proletarian consciousness could only be achieved by destabilizing the fucking linguistic infrastructure of a fucking fascist state fucking hegemony.

'That's fucking Marcuse,' said Stoley rather hesitantly following Bilger into the semantic sewer of destabilization.

'And this is Wilt,' said Wilt. 'If you've got a moment to spare from discussing the millennium I'd like a word with you.'

'I'm buggered if I'm taking anyone else's class,' said Bilger adopting a sound trade-union stance. 'It's not my stand-in period you know.'

'I'm not asking you to do any extra work. I am simply asking you to have a private word with me. I realize this is infringing your inalienable right as a free individual in a fascist state to pursue happiness by stating your opinions but I'm afraid duty calls.'

'Not my bloody duty, mate,' said Bilger.

'No. Mine,' said Wilt. 'I'll be in my office in five minutes.'

'More than I will,' Wilt heard Bilger say as he headed towards the door but Wilt knew better. The man might swagger and pose to impress Stoley but Wilt still had the sanction of altering the timetable so that Bilger started the week at nine on Monday morning with Printers Three and ended it at eight on Friday evening with part-time Cooks Four. It was about the only sanction he possessed, but it was remarkably effective. While he waited he considered tactics and the composition of the Education Committee. Mrs Chaterway was bound to be there defending to the last her progressive opinion that teenage muggers were warm human beings who only needed a few sympathetic words to stop them from beating old ladies over the head. On her right there was Councillor Blighte-Smythe who would, given half a chance, have brought back hanging for poaching and probably the cat o'nine tails for the unemployed. In between these two extremes there were the Principal who hated anything or anyone who upset his leisurely schedule, the Chief Education Officer, who hated the Principal and finally Mr Squidley, a local builder, for whom Liberal Studies was an anathema and a bloody waste of time when the little blighters ought to have been putting in a good day's work carrying hods of bricks up blooming ladders. All in all the prospect of coping with the Education Committee was a grim one. He would have to handle them tactfully.

But first there was Bilger. He arrived after ten minutes and entered without knocking. 'Well?' he asked sitting down and staring at Wilt angrily.

'I thought we had better have this chat in private,' said Wilt. 'I just wanted to enquire about the film you made with a crocodile. I must say it sounds most enterprising. If only all Liberal Studies lecturers would use the facilities provided by the local authority to such effect . . .' He left the sentence with a tag end of unspoken approval. Bilger's hostility softened.

'The only way the working classes are going to understand how they're being manipulated by the media is to get them to make films themselves. That's all I do.'

'Quite so,' said Wilt, 'and by getting them to film someone buggering a crocodile helps them to develop a proletarian consciousness transcending the false values they've been inculcated with by a capitalist hierarchy?'

'Right, mate,' said Bilger enthusiastically. 'Those fucking things are symbols of exploitation.'

'The bourgeoisie biting its conscience off, so to speak.'

'You've said it,' said Bilger, snapping at the bait.

Wilt looked at him in bewilderment. 'And what classes have you done this . . . er . . . field work with?'

'Fitters and Turners Two. We got this croc thing in Nott Road and . . .'

'In Nott Road?' said Wilt, trying to square his knowledge of the street with docile and presumably homosexual crocodiles.

'Well, it's street theatre as well,' said Bilger, warming to his task. 'Half the people who live there need liberating too.'

'I daresay they do, but I wouldn't have thought encouraging them to screw crocodiles was exactly a liberating experience. I suppose as an example of the class struggle . . .'

'Here,' said Bilger, 'I thought you said you'd seen the film?'

'Not exactly. But news of its controversial content has reached me. Someone said it was almost sub-Buñuel.'

'Really? Well, what we did is we got this toy crocodile, you know, the ones kiddies put pennies in and they get the privilege of a ride on them . . .'

'A toy crocodile? You mean you didn't actually use a real live one?'

'Of course we bloody didn't. I mean who'd be loony enough to rivet a real fucking crocodile? He might have been bitten.'

'Might?' said Wilt. 'I'd have said the odds on any self-respecting crocodile . . . Anyway, do go on.'

'So one of the lads gets on this plastic toy thing and we film him doing it.'

'Doing it? Let's get this quite straight. Don't you mean buggering it?'

'Sort of,' said Bilger. 'He didn't have his prick out or anything like that. There was nowhere he could have put it. No, all he did was simulate buggering the thing. That way he was symbolically screwing the whole reformist welfare statism of the capitalist system.'

'In the shape of a rocking crocodile?' said Wilt. He leant back in his chair and wondered yet again how it was that a supposedly intelligent man like Bilger, who had after all been to university and was a graduate, could still believe the world would be a better place once all the middle classes had been put up against a wall and shot. Nobody ever seemed to learn anything from the past. Well, Mr Bloody Bilger was going to learn something from the present. Wilt put his elbows on the desk.

'Let's get the record clear once and for all,' he said. 'You definitely consider it part of your duties as a Liberal Studies lecturer to teach apprentices Marxist-Leninist-Maoist-crocodile-buggerism and any other -Ism you care to mention?'

Bilger's hostility returned. 'It's a free country and I've a right to express my own personal opinions. You can't stop me.'

Wilt smiled at these splendid contradictions. 'Am I trying to?' he asked innocently. 'In fact you may not believe this, but I am willing to provide you with a platform on which to state them fully and clearly.'

'That'll be the day,' said Bilger.

'It is, Comrade Bilger, believe me it is. The Education Committee is meeting at six. The Chief Education Officer, the Principal, Councillor Blighte-Smythe—'

'That militaristic shit. What's he know about education? Just because they gave him the M.C. in the war he thinks he can go about trampling on the faces of the working classes.'

'Which, considering he has a wooden leg, doesn't say much for your opinion of the proletariat, does it?' said Wilt warming to his task. 'First you praise the working class for their intelligence and solidarity, then you reckon they are so dumb they can't tell their own interests from a soap advert on TV and have to be forcibly politicized, and now you tell me that a man who lost his leg can trample all over them. The way you talk they sound like morons.'

'I didn't say that,' said Bilger.

'No, but that seems to be your attitude and if you want to express yourself on the subject more lucidly you may do so to the Committee at six. I am sure they will be most interested.'

'I'm not going before any fucking Committee. I know my rights and—'

'This is a free country, as you keep telling me. Another splendid contradiction, and considering the country allows you to go around getting teenage apprentices to simulate fucking toy crocodiles I'd say a free fucking society just about sums it up. I just wish sometimes we were living in Russia.'

'They'd know what to do with blokes like you, Wilt,' said Bilger. 'You're just a deviationist reformist swine.'

'Deviationist, coming from you, is great,' shouted Wilt, 'and with their draconian laws anyone who went about filming Russian fitters buggering crocodiles would end up smartly in the Lubianka and wouldn't come out until they had put a bullet in the back of his mindless head. Either that or they would lock you up in some nuthouse and you'd probably be the only inmate who wasn't sane.'

'Right, Wilt,' Bilger shouted back, leaping from his chair, 'that does it. You may be Head of Department but if you think you can insult lecturers I know what I'm going to do. Lodge a complaint with the union.' He headed for the door.

'That's right,' yelled Wilt, 'run for your collective mummy and while you're about it tell the secretary you called me a deviationist swine. They'll appreciate the term.'

But Bilger was already out of the office and Wilt was left with the problem of finding some plausible excuse to offer the Committee. Not that he would have minded getting rid of Bilger but the idiot had a wife and three children and certainly couldn't expect help from his father, Rear-Admiral Bilger.

Tom Sharpe (b. 1928), *The Wilt Alternative* (1979).

━━━━━━━

A NOTHER *novelist whose comedy made good use of 'permissiveness' is Martin Amis whose first novel* The Rachel Papers *was published in 1973 (it won the Somerset Maugham Award), two years after Tom Sharpe's first,* Riotous Assembly. *The explicit language Amis uses in his novels is, where called for, perhaps even riper than that used by Tom Sharpe but Amis uses it for a different purpose. Much of Sharpe's comicality consists of the dropping-of-trousers of conventional farce updated into the dropping-of-everything, with jokiness promoted into dirty-jokiness; it is a kind of comedy which is continually probing and testing where the perimeters of contemporary taste have got to because, generally speaking, the more acceptably dirty this kind of farce is the more commercially successful it is likely to be.*

Amis is an essentially literary man. In fact, a literary young man; he was only 24 when The Rachel Papers *was published. His novels tend to be about young people who are highly intelligent and express themselves with humour; the permissiveness inherited from the 1960s enabled Amis to put into these characters' dialogue the previously disallowed ideas, words, and sexual allusions which in life they would have used all the time.*

Also, when there is a scene as in Dead Babies, *with a hideously fat, terminally vulgar family, such as the Whiteheads, Amis is able to record faithfully their appalling dialogue:*

The Whiteheads have several claims to being the fattest family alive. At the time of writing you could go along to Parky St. Wimbledon, any Sunday, one o'clock in the afternoon—and you'd see them, taking their seats in the Morris for the weekly Whitehead jaunt to Brighton.

'Get your huge fat arse out of the way'—'Whose horrible great leg is this?' —'Is this bit your bum, Keith, or Aggie's?'—'I don't care whose guts these are, they've got to be moved'—'That's not Dad's arm, you stupid great bitch, it's my leg!'

'It's no good,' says Whitehead Sr eventually, slapping his trotters on the steering-wheel. 'The Morris can't be expected to cope with this. You can take it in turns staying behind from now on.'

And indeed, as each toothpaste Whitehead squeezes into the Morris, the chassis drops two inches on its flattened tyres, and when Frank himself gets in behind the wheel, the whole car seems to sink imploringly to its knees.

'Flora, close that sodding door,' Frank tells his wife.

'I can't, Frank. Some of my leg is still out there.'

A crowd has gathered on the pavement. Neighbours lean with folded arms on half-washed cars. Curtains part along the terraced street.

'Oh, God,' says Whitehead Sr, 'they're all watching now. Keith! Give your mother a hand with her leg.'

Keith squats forward and fights his mother's thigh up into the car, while Frank leans sideways and tugs at the far door-strap with one hand and a fistful of Mrs Whitehead's top with the other. Aggie, Keith's sister, sits crying with shame in the back seat; she sees her family conflate into one pulsing balloon of flesh.

'Come on—nearly home.'

'No!' shrieks Flora. 'There's still a bit of arm hanging out!'

'Got it,' pants Keith.

The door closes noiselessly and to ironic cheers from the crowd the four grumpy pigs chug out into the street.

'Get your arse off the gear-lever, woman,' Frank demands as they pull up at the lights, 'How'm I expected to drive with arse all over the gear-lever? Keith! Move over, can't you, you fat little sod. You're weighing down the right rear wheel. I can feel her listing to the right.'

'Ah shut up, you fat old turd. How can I move with Aggie all over the place back here? It's you who's weighing it down, you great fat old fool.'

'I happen to have reduced considerably of late. And there's no cause for you to be so heavy—your'e only four foot and a fart.'

'Ah shut up. You fat old bugger. You fat old cunt.'

'Keith,' said his mother, 'don't talk to your father like that.'

'Ah, shut up. You fat old bitch. You fat old slag.'

'Keith,' said Aggie.

'Ah shut up.'

'This can't go on,' says Mrs Whitehead as the car wobbles down through the motorway heat-haze. 'Starvation diet, all of us, all next week. You too, Keith. All next week. Starvation diet. This can't go on.'

One hour later they sit in silence round a sea-front coffee-shop table, paw-like hands dipping occasionally into a dome of cream, jam and custard slices. Warm sugary tea runs down their chins.

Martin Amis (b. 1949), Dead Babies (1975).

In his novels Martin Amis uses complex plot constructions; he sometimes includes himself in the story and sometimes he speaks as author directly to the reader, all symptoms of a Modernist style which his father, Kingsley Amis, cannot bring himself to admire even in his son ('I say give the reader something to enjoy in every sentence but he goes further, so that after a while I'm dying for an ordinary sentence that just says something like "They finished their drinks and left." ').

In The Rachel Papers *the hero is Charles Highway who is 19 years old, as was Martin Amis when he worked on the book. Highway is precociously intelligent, literary, and introspective, as is Martin Amis.*

Charles Highway is waiting to go up to university and meanwhile is spending much of his spare time examining his body for signs of decay, worrying about his appearance, and sleeping around with girls without much pleasure. But Charles has one driving ambition: he is determined to sleep with an Older Woman before he reaches his twentieth birthday. The honour of being this Older Woman has fallen to Rachel who is just a year older than Charles.

Charles has managed to get to know Rachel slightly and as he pursues her he begins to fall in love with her; or at least as much in love as a 19-year-old's self-obsession and hypochondria will allow him to fall.

And at last his single-mindedness is rewarded. One evening he is alone in a room with Rachel and what happens then is set out by Martin Amis in the kind of assemblage of minute detail which Laurence Sterne used to describe Corporal Trim reading aloud and Kingley Amis used to decrlbe his Old Devils getting up in the morning.

Both Charles and Rachel are a little drunk.

They kiss:

As regards structure, comedy has come a long way since Shakespeare, who in his festive conclusions could pair off any old shit and any old fudge-brained slag (see Claudio and Hero in *Much Ado*) and get away with it. But the final kiss no longer symbolizes anything and well-oiled nuptials have ceased to be a plausible image of desire. That kiss is now the beginning of the comic action, not the end that promises another beginning from which the audience is prepared to exclude itself. All right? We have got into the habit of going further and further beyond the happy-ever-more promise: relations in decay, aftermaths, but with everyone being told a thing or two about themselves, busy learning from their mistakes.

So, in the following phase, with the obstructive elements out of the way (DeForest, Gloria) and the consummation in sight, the comic action would have been due to end, happily. But who is going to believe that any more?

Ready?

Now, as an opener, I decided to try something *rather* ambitious. I rose, poured out drinks, held her eye as we sipped, took her glass away. You really need to be six foot for this, but I gave it a go anyway: knelt on the floor in front of her, reached out and cupped her cheeks, urged her face towards mine . . . No good, not tall enough, she has to buckle inelegantly, breasts on thighs. Rise to a crouch, start work on ears, neck, only occasionally skimming lips across hers. Then, when leg begins to give way, I do not churlishly flatten her on to the sofa nor shoo her downstairs: I pressure her to the floor, half beside half on top of me. (It was bare boards so it must have seemed pretty spontaneous.) Reaching to steady her my hand has grasped her hip; not sober enough to be over-tactical, I let it stay there.

Hardly seemed worth bothering with her breasts. In one movement her skirt is above her waist, my right leg is between her legs, and my hand floats on her downy stomach. 'Doing' one of her ears I bulged my eyes at the floor.

Phase two.

Move my hand over her bronze tights, tracing her hip-bone, circling beneath the overhang of her buttock, shimmer flat-palmed down the back of her legs, U-turning over the knee, meander up her thighs, now dipping between them for a breathless moment, now skirting cheekily round the side. It hovers for a full quarter of a minute, then lands, soft but firm, on her cunt. Rachel gasped accordingly—but the master's hand was gone, without waiting for a decisive response, to scout the periphery of her tights. And her stomach was so flat and her hip-bones so prominent that I had no problem working my hand down the slack. By way of a diversionary measure (as if she wouldn't notice) I stepped up the tempo of my kisses, harrying the corners of her mouth with reptile tongue. It must be so sexy. How can she bear it?

Meanwhile the hand is creeping on all fours. At the edge of her panties it has a rest, thinks about it, then takes the low road. The whole of me is along with those fingers, spread wide to salute each pore and to absorb the full sweep of her stomach. Mouth toils away absently, on automatic. I nudge her with my right knee and give a startled wheeze as she parts her legs wide. Still, the hand moves down, a hair's breadth, a hair's breadth.

On arrival it paused to make an interim policy decision. Was now the time for the menace? Had the time come to orchestrate the Lawrentiana? What I really wanted more than anything—yes, what I really wanted more than anything else in the world was a cup of tea and a think. Covertly I looked at Rachel's face: it included clenched eyelids, parted lips, smallish forehead wistfully contoured; but there was no abandonment to be read there.

Nor to be read here. I begin to find all this rather alarming. It makes me feel confused, frightened, sad. Because we have come to the heart of the matter, haven't we? This is the outside looking in, the mind moving away from the body, the fear of madness, the squirrel cage. How nice to be able to say: 'We made love, and slept.' Only it wasn't like that; it didn't happen that way. The evidence is before me. (If any respectable doctor got hold of these papers he would have no choice but to cut my head off and send it to a forensic laboratory—and I wouldn't blame him.) I know what it's supposed to be like, I've read my Lawrence. I know also what I felt and thought; I know what that evening was: an aggregate of pleasureless detail, nothing more; an insane, gruelling, blow-by-blow obstacle course. And yet that's what I'm here for tonight. I must be true to myself. Oh God, I thought this was going to be fun. It isn't. I'm sweating here. I'm afraid.

Back on the breakfast-room floor, my fingertips awaited instructions. They had me know that I was dealing with mons hair of the equilateral-triangle variety, the pubic G-string variety, the best, not that of the grizzled scalplock, the tapered sideburn, the balding fist of stubble, fuzz and curls. So impelled— who knows—by a twinge of genuine curiosity, a mere presence now, the hand went *over* the mound; straining against the pull of her tights and pants, and, once in position, began its slow descent.

This is what I thought. Since Henry Miller's *Tropic* books, of course, it has become difficult to talk sensibly on the question of girl's cunts. (An analogy: young poets like myself are forever taunted by subjects which it is no longer possible to write about in this ironic age: evening skies, good looks, dew, anything at all to do with love, the difference between cosmic reality and how you sometimes feel when you wake up.) I remember I overheard in an Oxford pub one undergraduate—a German, I believe—telling another undergraduate that Swedish girls were okay, he supposed, but 'their conts are too big'. In the same place on a different occasion I talked sex with a pin-cocked Geordie who dedicated himself to the proposition that Oxford girls weren't nearly as good as Geordie girls, the reason being that their cunts were too small. Narcissistic rubbish. Size doesn't matter—unless, that is, you have troubles unknown to the present reviewer.

Which isn't to say that cunts are homogeneous. Now Rachel's was the most pleasing I had ever come across. Not, for her, the wet Brillo-pad, nor the paper-bagful of kedgeree, nor the greasy waistcoat pocket, the gashed vole's stomach, the clump of veins, glands, tubes. No. It was infinitely moist but not wet, exquisitely shaped and yet quite amorphous, all black ink and velvet recessed into pubic hair that resembled my own as a Persian carpet resembles a mat rug. And it was warmer than me; it was, actually, hot.

Meanwhile my fingers paddled there, enclosing it with the flat of my hand, entering with one, two fingers, one, two inches, flicking the clitoris. Rachel was quaking and warbling away: however, it seemed right out of context when I pressed my mouth against her ear and (well I never) my sharp erection against her thigh, and said, with a nicely gauged crack in my voice:

'How do you undo this dress?'

Her movements ceased at once. Her eyes opened. 'I'm not on the pill.'

Martin Amis (b. 1949), The Rachel Papers (1973).

TEN *years after* The Rachel Papers *came out another novel was published,* The Secret Diary of Adrian Mole, Aged 13¾ *which purported to record the daily diary of a schoolboy, Adrian Mole, whose problems turned out to be strikingly similar to those of Charles Highway of* The Rachel Papers.

Both boys were self-confessed intellectuals, both kept reminding us that they were poets, and both thought that they might well turn out to be geniuses. Both had too little money and too many facial eruptions and both had fervent sexual ambitions involving older woman.

The Secret Diary of Adrian Mole, Aged 13¾ *began life as a monologue written as an exercise for a theatre workshop by the playwright-in-residence, Sue Townsend. Sue Townsend was persuaded to work up the material into a radio play for the BBC, after which she made it into a book.*

The Secret Diary *and its sequel,* The Growing Pains of Adrian Mole, *published in 1984, became the publishing sensation of the early 1980s: over five million hardback and paperback copies were sold in the first five years. Then came a stage musical, a television series . . .*

The Growing Pains *carried on where* The Diary *left off. Adrian Mole is still writing his poetry and keeping his head above life's treacherous waters: his parents are both having affairs and his mother is pregnant by her lover, O-Level exams are looming, he has gone off religion in spite of his Granny, and the Falklands war has broken out.*

But Adrian is now 15 and sex is working in his veins like yeast. He is passionately in love with a girl in his class, Pandora, who is three months older than he is and posher. Adrian has made little headway physically in the relationship because Pandora is prudish.

The big difference between the two fictional boys (the small difference being that Charles was at a public school and Adrian is at a comprehensive school) is in their ages, exemplified by the extent of their sexual ambitions: Charles (19) wanted to seduce Rachel and make her his mistress.

Adrian Mole (15) was desperate for a glimpse of one of Pandora's nipples:

Sunday April 4th

I feel guilty about mentioning a personal anguish at this time of national crisis but ever since last night when a model aeroplane bacame stuck fast to my nose with glue, I have suffered torment. My nose has swollen up so much that I am frantic with worry that it might burst and take my brain with it.

I rang the Casualty Department and, after a lot of laughing, the nurse who removed the plane came on the line. She said that I was 'probably allergic to the glue' and that the swelling would go down in a few days. She added 'Perhaps it will teach you not to sniff glue again.' I tried to explain but she put the phone down.

Pandora has been round but I declined to see her. She would go straight off me if she saw my repulsive nose.

Monday April 5th

Just my luck! It is the first day of the school holidays and I can't go out because of my gigantic swollen nose. Even my mother is a bit worried about it now. She wanted to prick it with a sterilized needle, but I wouldn't let her. She can't sew an accurate patch on a pair of jeans with a needle, let alone do delicate medical procedures with one. I've begged her to take me to a private nose specialist, but she has refused. She says she needs the money for her 'Well Woman' test. She is having her primary and secondary organs checked. Yuk!

The dog is in love with a cocker spaniel called Mitzi. The dog stands no chance, though: (*a*) it isn't a pedigree, and (*b*) it doesn't keep itself looking smart like most dogs. I tried to explain these things to the dog, but it just looked sad and mournful and went back to lying outside Mitzi's gate. Being in love is no joke. I have the same problem with Pandora that the dog has with Mitzi. We are both in a lower class than our loved ones.

Tuesday April 6th

The nation has been told that Britain and Argentina are not at war, we are at conflict.

I am reading *Scoop* by a woman called Evelyn Waugh.

Wednesday April 7th

Wrote and sent Pandora a love letter and a poem. The letter said:

Pandora my love,
Due to an unfortunate physical disability I am unable to see you in person, but every fibre of my being cries out for your immediate physical proximity. Be patient, my love, soon we will laugh again.

Yours with undying love,
Adrian

P.S. What are your views on the Argentinian conflict, with particular reference to Lord Carrington's resignation?

The Discontented Tuna
I am a Tuna fish,
Swimming in the sea of discontent.
Oh, when, when,
Will I find the spawning ground?

I hope Pandora sees through my poem and realizes the symbolism of 'spawning ground'. I am sick of being the only virgin in our class. Everybody but me is sexually experienced. Barry Kent boasts about how many housewives he makes love to on his father's milkround. He says they are the reason why he is always late for school.

Thursday April 8th

Nose has gone down a bit.
My mother came home from her 'Well Woman' check in a bad mood.
I allowed Pandora to visit me in my darkened bedroom. We had a brilliant kissing session. Pandora was wearing her mother's Janet Reger full-length silk slip under her dress and she allowed me to touch the lace on the hem. I was more interested in the lace near the shoulder straps but Pandora said, 'No darling, we must wait until we've got our "O" levels.'
I pointed out to Pandora that all this sexual frustration is playing havoc with my skin. But she said, 'If you really love me you will wait.'
I said, 'If you really love me you *wouldn't* wait.'
She went then; she had to replace the Janet Reger slip before her mother got back from work.
I have got thirty-eight spots: twenty-eight on my face and the rest on my shoulders.

Tuesday April 13th

After *Crossroads* had finished I asked my father why he had married my mother. Talk about opening the floodgates! Fifteen years of bitterness and resentment spilled out. He said, 'Never make the mistake I made, Adrian. Don't let a woman's body blind you to her character and habits.'
He explained that he met my mother when miniskirts were in fashion. He

said that in those days my mother had superb legs and thighs. He said, 'You must realize that most women looked bloody awful in miniskirts, so your mother had a certain rarity value.'

I was shocked at his sexist attitude and told him I was in love with Pandora because of her brain and compassion for lesser mortals. My father gave a nasty laugh and said, 'Oh yeah! And if Pandora was as ugly as sin you wouldn't have noticed her bloody IQ and bleeding heart in the first place.'

He ended our first man-to-man talk by saying, 'Look, kiddo, don't even think about getting married until you've spent a few months sharing a bedroom with a bird. If she leaves her knickers on the floor for more than three days running forget it!'

Saturday April 17th

Still in bed with toothache.

My parents are showing me no sympathy, they keep saying, 'You should have gone to the dentist's.'

I have phoned Pandora. She is coming round tomorrow. She asked me if I needed anything; I said a Mars bar would be nice. She said (rather irritably I thought), 'Heavens above, Adrian, aren't your teeth rotten enough?'

The dog has been howling outside Mitzi's gate all day. It is also off its Pedigree Chum and Winalot.

Sunday April 18th
LOW SUNDAY

Pandora has just left my bedroom. I am just about devastated with frustration. I can't go on like this. I have written to Aunt Clara, the Agony Aunt.

Dear Aunt Clara,

I am a fifteen-year-old schoolboy. My grandma tells me I am attractive and many people have commented on how mature I am for my years. I am the only child of a bad marriage (except for the dog). My problem is this: I am deeply in love with an older girl (by three months). She is in a class above me (I don't mean in school: we are in the same class in school. I mean that she is a social class above me) but she claims that this doesn't matter to our relationship. We have been very happy until recently when I have started to become obsessed by sex. I have fallen to self-manipulation quite a lot lately, and it is OK for a bit but it soon wears off. I know that a proper bout of lovemaking would do me good. It would improve my skin and help my mind to concentrate on my 'O' level studies.

I have tried all sorts of erotic things but my girl-friend refuses to go the whole hog. She says we are not ready.

I am quite aware of the awesome things about bringing an unwanted baby into the world and I would wear a protective dildo.

Yours in desperation,
Poet of the Midlands

Tuesday April 27th

Got a letter from Aunt Clara! I read it on the way to school.

Dear Poet of the Midlands,

Well, well, well, you are in a lather aren't you, lovey! Look, you're fifteen, your body's in a whirl, your hormones are in a maelstrom. Your emotions are up and down like a yo-yo.

And of course you want sex. Every lad of your age does. But, my dear, there are people who crave penthouse apartments and exotic holidays. We can't have what we want all the time.

You sound as if you've got a nice, sensible lassie; enjoy each other's company. Take up a hobby, keep physically and mentally alert and learn to control your breathing.

Sex is only a small part of life, my dear lad. Enjoy your precious teenage years.

Sincerely
Aunt Clara

Enjoy my precious teenage years! They are nothing but trouble and misery. I can't wait until I am fully mature and can make urban conversation with intellectuals.

Sunday May 9th

I have just realised that I have never seen a dead body or a real female nipple. This is what comes of living in a cul-de-sac.

Monday May 10th

I asked Pandora to show me one of her nipples and she refused. I tried to explain that it was in the interests of widening my life experience, but she buttoned her cardigan up to the neck and went home.

Wednesday May 12th

I received the following letter from Pandora this morning:

Adrian,

I am writing to terminate our relationship. Our love was once a spiritual thing. We were united in our appreciation of art and literature, but Adrian you have changed. You have become morbidly fixated with my body. Your request to look at my left nipple last night finally convinced me that we must part.

Do not contact me,
Pandora Braithwaite

P.S. If I were you I would seek professional psychiatric help for your hypochondria and your sex mania. Anthony Hopkins, who played the maniac in *Psycho* was in analysis for ten years, so there is no need to be ashamed.

Thursday May 13th

Yesterday before I opened *that* letter I was a normal type of intellectual teenager. Today I know what it is to suffer. I am now an adult. I am no longer young. In fact I have noticed wrinkles forming on my forehead. I wouldn't be surprised if my hair doesn't turn white overnight.

I am in total anguish!

I love her!

I love her!

I love her!

Oh God!

Oh Pandora!

2 a.m. I have used a whole Andrex toilet roll to mop up my tears. I haven't cried so much since the wind blew my candy floss away at Cleethorpes.

3 a.m. I slept fitfully, then got out of bed to watch the dawn break. The world is no longer exciting and colourful. It is grey and full of heartbreak. I thought of doing myself in, but it's not really fair on the people you leave behind. It would upset my mother to come into the room and find my corpse. I shan't bother doing my 'O' levels. I'll be an intellectual road sweeper. I will surprise litter louts by quoting Kafka as they pass me by.

Sue Townsend concludes the drama of Adrian's burning but unwelcome curiosity about his girl-friend's bosom with a masterly touch:

Friday May 14th

Why oh why did I ask Pandora to show me *her* nipple? Anybody's nipple would have done. Nigel says that Sharon Botts will show *everything* for 50p and a pound of grapes.

Sue Townsend, The Growing Pains of Adrian Mole (1984).

———

O NE *of the most prolific of the post-1960, permissive-wave authors is Leslie Thomas, who became a happy orphan at Dr Barnado's when his parents died, joined a newspaper at the age of 16, wrote his first book at the age of 33, followed it with* The Virgin Soldiers *which was a best-seller and a popular film, and thereafter became a full-time author with another twenty or so successful novels and travel-books to his credit. Nearly all Leslie Thomas's novels are cheerfully humorous and many of them are joyfully explicit in their descriptions of couplings: there are probably more, and more varied, sexual docking-manœuvres in Leslie Thomas's books than in most other light fiction of the period. Typical reviews from distinguished literary reviewers ran:*

> 'Leslie Thomas is at it again.' *Daily Telegraph.*
> 'Funnier than Balzac and some would say filthier.' *Sunday Times.*

But what makes Leslie Thomas's fictional sex different is that it is kindly. Unlike Tom Sharpe's funny but cruel farce, or Martin Amis's sharp descriptions of inadequacy, or Sue Townsend's picture of engaging ignorance, Leslie Thomas writes of affectionate sex. He actually likes women. And his descriptions of the sexual act are depictions of moments of sudden, deep, usually fugitive pleasure; he describes love-making rather than 'having sex', and he celebrates it.

At the beginning of Arthur McCann and all his Women *the hero Arthur was 15; he was the same age as Adrian Mole but was shorter, weedier and very much luckier in his first love affair. Little Arthur lived in Newport, South Wales, and in the early months of the war a platoon of RAF airmen and airwomen with a huge silver barrage balloon were stationed in the local park.*

One night, when owing to circumstances entirely beyond his control he was being made love to by a large aircraftswoman named Rosie, the barrage balloon Rosie was supposed to be guarding caught fire. Because of this, little Arthur was persuaded by his ne'er-do-well and slightly barmy father that he was to be shot by the police for sabotage. Arthur ran away, stowed away on board a ship in the harbour, and his adventures began.

Many years later Arthur describes the bitter-sweet beginning of that first and never-to-be-surpassed affair:

In my fifteenth year I became very frightened because I believed that Mr Winston Churchill, our popular prime minister, had personally sanctioned my execution and was dispatching a firing squad to carry out the deed . . . In any case it was my father who told me they were coming to execute me and if a boy cannot believe his father, who is there to believe?

'Sabotaging one of His Majesty's balloons!' he howled, after the police had been around to tell him what had happened. 'Leaving this town wide open to German air attack. Hitler must be pleased with you.' The next day he told me that Mr Churchill had written a nice letter to him at the docks (so my mother would not know) and had regretfully said that I had to be done away with. He said I ought to stay in my room and pray as much as possible and that I should on no account tell anybody that I was to be executed because it would only give the family a bad name. This, coming on top of the discovery that I was wearing my sister's knickers at school was almost more than my sanity could stand.

The saddest thought was that it was my own junior patriotism and my first clash with uncharted sex and love that brought on the tragedy.

The barrage balloon, which arrived in Newport Park just after the war began, floated for days like a happy, watchful elephant, silver above our dusty street . . . The young airmen in the unit looked after their silver bundle, blowing it up like children, letting it down, flying it, mooring it, generally tending its wants.

One day I saw some of the airmen, and the airwomen who were conveniently billeted alongside them, swimming in the black River Ebbw, shouting and laughing in the water under the coal-rooted trees. I was sitting openly on the bank, watching them, when one of the larky men pulled down the front of a young airwoman's bathing costume. In a blinding moment I saw the forbidden puddings, exposed, huge, luscious. (My father had said that if a boy under eighteen saw a naked woman he would turn to stone, and although I didn't believe him, I thought just then that this was happening.)

The airwoman had huge ripe things. Memory may have inflated them over the years, but I don't think I have, even now, ever seen bigger. She shrieked a laugh and in an impromptu movement grabbed two handfuls of muddy Ebbw coal-dust from the bank and slapped them to her exposed front. It was my first erotic experience. Thinking about it that night (and many nights after) I wondered that she had not simply pulled up the front of her swimming costume again. Then I knew nothing about the strange perversity of women . . .

But patriotic I was. Wearing my scout uniform and with my stout scout pole in a military position I would stand, unrequested, for hours guarding our local doctor's car. People stared at me from buses and bikes, but I put on a stern face indicating that I alone knew the national importance of my duty. But one evening I heard the doctor's wife shout clearly from the house: 'Glynn! There's that mentally defective boy standing by your car again.'

This discouraged me somewhat from the self-imposed duty and I therefore transferred my decent enthusiasm to the park and barrage-balloon unit, and every evening I would run, walk and eventually stagger on innumerable journeys to the fish and chip shop on behalf of the balloon men and women. To do this I had to run the gauntlet of an army smoke-screen platoon which used to park its trucks along the main road with the duty of belching oily clouds over the town and the docks, thus further confusing the German bombers, already bemused by the barrage balloons.

It was, as can be imagined, a nasty, greasy job, manning the smoke screen trucks and I suppose they had selected a certain rough type of person to do it. Which is why I had to run the gauntlet with the fish and chips, for the smoke screen men would grab at my scout's shorts, pinch me and pull at my lanyard, and try to steal the airmen's supper . . . sometimes I got through with little hurt or annoyance and my cargo intact, but at others I was near to tears, clutching the almost empty wrapping of the *South Wales Argus* and, like as not, half a piece of hot cod fillet stuffed with boorish malevolence down my young trousers . . .

The barrage balloon crew were occasionally grateful, sometimes less so especially when their supper had been drastically mauled by the smoke men. I was thanked and rebuked in almost equal portions. For my trouble, they gave me a few pence which I put away, intending to make a major contribution to Newport's Buy-a-Bomber Week Fund.

Unfortunately my scout's shirt, woggle and neckerchief had become so foul with grease that I reluctantly had to put replacements before a new parachute for a pilot. Otherwise, I was warned, I would be drummed out of the scouts.

On the first evening I wore my new shirt I had a terrible ten minutes . . . they caught me, my parcels were ravaged, and when I arrived in the park the remaining fish and chips were mashed into what could easily be taken for a thick soup. One of the balloon men was particularly annoyed and berated me. It was then that Rose came in.

She had been in the park for about a year, a large and pretty girl, with a pink face and stormy black hair. She typed in the orderly office every day and when she saw me she would call out cheerily and wave. Her smart blue uniform was very swollen at the top and I tried not to look at it too much, or think about it at night. She probably had a large bottom and fat knees too, but I don't remember. To me she was a formidable, friendly and desirable balloon girl. She pushed aside the complaining airman, picked up one of his few remaining unmashed chips, dropping it casually into her mouth in the same movement, and then guarded me out of the hut.

'Your shirt, lad,' she sighed when we were outside in the evening sun. 'What a terrible muck.' She had a Yorkshire voice, almost unknown to my ears.

'The chips get squashed against it,' I explained with more sorrow than I felt, for her large calico hand was on my shoulder and part of it touched my neck. 'It's a new one, as well. I've even got a mess on my woggle.'

'Which is your woggle?' she asked quietly.

'This is,' I said, pointing to the leather band holding my scout neckerchief at my throat. She touched it and I felt the back of her fingers against my enlarging Adam's apple.

'How come they always get so mushed up?' she said. She took me by the hand and we reached the door of a hut . . .

'You didn't tell me how the chips always get mushed up,' Rosie repeated. She had sat me on the rough blanket of her bed and she was kneeling in front of me, rubbing something into the grease of my shirt. Her breasts were hanging forward heavily against my knees giving me agonies of happiness and fear.

'It's the smoke screen men,' I explained, wanting her to stay like that for ever. To my annoyance she backed away from my knees.

'What's it to do with them?' she asked.

'I have to run past them and they try to grab the chips from me,' I said resignedly. 'They do it all the time.'

She stared at me with speechless concern. Then, I thanked God, she leaned forward again, those great tender tits against my boy's bony knees, and began working again . . .

On the next fish and chip run I crept in my usual fearing Indian fashion to the edge of the smoke screen vehicles to be greeted with a shout of 'Hello Little Arthur!' It was the sentry. 'Come on, son. Nothing to be afraid of.' Nor was there. For the smoke screen men had suddenly become benevolent escorts, seeing me safely on my way, asking me, if I had time, to go for fish and chips for them and sending their love to Rosie. For the first time I came through without a scratch or a bruise or a single crushed chip. I don't know what Rosie did to them. Nor will I know.

I only know what she did to me.

My association with Aircraftswoman Rose Kirby is, I imagine, somewhere documented, written up, and filed in the archives that tell the detailed story of Britain's fight against Nazism from 1939 to 1945. It probably makes plum reading for any clerk who knows where it can be located. For me it is among the sweetest memories I have. I can even remember her number. 842912.

In that golden wartime summer nothing happened between us for a long time. I used to go down to the park and carry out my fish and chip run as before, but now with no danger from the smoke screen men. She always behaved like a big rosy friend, smiling at me with her round and pretty face and touching me with her expansive chest; sometimes gently making fun at me. In the empty evenings, when nobody seemed to be about, and the vapour trails of the day's planes had faded from the sky, we would sit comfortably in the lee of the tethered balloon. She was reading *Gone With The Wind* and she was a slow reader. It took her half of July, all of August and into September. I would be reading *Wulf the Saxon* by Henty, or Baden Powell's *Scouting for Boys*, for I was anxious to get several proficiency badges that summer.

We would read passages to each other, quite long pieces sometimes. I found it difficult to get unduly enthusiastic about the blighted love of Scarlett and Rhet, and I don't think that she always followed what I was saying about following a spoor or lighting a fire without matches, although she used to help me to memorise the nature signs I had to learn for my woodcraft badge.

Very few people used to see us or bother us. When the balloon was not flying the others in the unit would go into their huts or disappear into the park or visit the picture house in town. She had a full-blown, melodious laugh, like a sweetly played tuba. When she came to the description of a battle in her book she would put her wide plain hand on my thin arm to arrest my reading and in an almost comically flat Yorkshire voice she would relate the passage, supposing that, as a boy, I must be interested in battles and blood. I would wait patiently while she retold the slaughter and then I would enlist her aid in rehearsing the woodcraft signs; the signs which signified the presence of water or a mad dog, or the two stones which told the tracker that the quarry had gone home to tea.

'That looks like a cottage loaf,' she said, when I showed her how the stones were placed, the smaller sitting on top of the other. 'Gone home, is it? I think that's really neat, Arthur, that is. Really neat. Much better than writing it down.'

'Well,' I said logically, 'in the forest you wouldn't be likely to have pencil and paper and even if you did the message would probably get blown away.'

I looked up at her and saw she was regarding me with a potent, serious smile.

'Will you help me with some of the others?' I asked carefully. Something nervous began wriggling inside my chest. I hesitantly glanced at her again to make sure I was not mistaken, and my throat clogged with the sudden and powerful excitement.

'Come here Arthur, lad,' she said quietly, moving up closer to the balloon.

'I *am* here, Rose.' The sentence stumbled out like a man staggering from a fire.

'I mean here,' she urged, half laughing. 'Here. By me. A bit nearer.'

I shuffled towards her childishly, on my bottom, and sat there, stark with anticipation. Quickly I turned to look at her again and I saw that her peachy face was shiny with perspiration. Her lips seemed enormous and fruity and her eyes shone like lights.

'Move around to me a bit, love,' she muttered seriously. 'Round facing me.'

I felt my limbs do as she required. Then, abruptly, her head lolled forward as though with tiredness and, astounded, I felt the lovely, full, flow of her heavy hair against my face and my neck. My boy's face went into it, my nose burrowing into its luxury. Instinctively I rubbed myself against her face and I could feel it wet through the strands of her hair although I did not know whether it was tears or sweat. She made short little sobbing noises and I asked her helplessly: 'What's wrong? What's the matter, Rose?'

A moment later I knew for sure what was the matter. Her fingers were picking at the buttons of my shorts. I felt the cool evening air whistle through the front and her beautifully soft, big, comfortable airwoman's hands dip inside. I would have had a choking fit but I fought it back in case I spoiled it all. My breath came popping out in plaintive gasps, I could feel my face burning, and my legs shuddered.

Her head was still against me, the hair still smothering me, so I could not see, only feel, what she was about. She had all my personal bits cupped in her wide-winged hands now and had taken them out, as though they were quite separate parts from the rest of my body. She did it with gentleness and concern, like Old Moses, the poacher who used to take rabbits from their burrows on the banks of the Ebbw, with the rabbit hardly moving or protesting at all.

(He was a very interesting man, Old Moses, which, needless to say wasn't his real name but a nickname made up by the children of the district. But he had a marvellous way with animals and I had thought of trying to contact him with regard to the habits of the badger, which I was studying in connection with my woodcraft badge. A family of badgers had made a home a bit further up the river and Old Moses knew all about their habits and their mating and all that sort of thing.)

Well, anyway, she was holding me like that down there, like Old Moses, kneeling against me still so that I couldn't see, only feel, what was going on. I felt ashamed that my thing was so stiff, like a little signpost, but it was something I found I honestly could not prevent even when I became even mildly excited. There it was, the bloody nuisance, stuck up, impudent, disgraceful. I could feel it and, worse, I knew she could see it.

'I'm sorry, Rose,' I apologised. 'I'm very sorry.'

Then she did begin to cry. Her head was jogged with sobs and her large tears kept plopping on my bare knees.

'I'm wicked,' she sobbed. 'Wicked.'

I was just about to tell her she wasn't wicked when she did something to me, well, to mine, which indisputably was. I do not intend to enlarge on it here, since it still remains, despite all that has happened since, as the supreme shock of my life. At that age I did not even know that such things *could* be done. But she lowered her head and she did it right there and then. I fainted.

*　　*　　*

Rose parcelled away my private parts and pounded off for some smelling salts. When she returned on huge and anxious tiptoe I was sitting against the flank of the balloon desperately memorising my woodcraft knowledge, repeating the signs aloud to myself as a barrier against what I was convinced was rapidly approaching insanity. It could *not* have happened, I told myself. I was just going crazy. My mind was going to curds as the scoutmaster said it would if you did certain things which I could not resist doing.

But when Rose came back like a sweet-smelling cloud I knew that it was unbelievable reality. Neither of us mentioned it, but I could see by her overflowing expression that it had been and would be again. I said I ought to be going back home or my mother would start looking for me in the dark.

'You *will* come back, won't you, little Arthur?' she said with sincere anxiety, waving the smelling salts in front of my face. Then she smiled and said one word, one thrilling, adult, fantastic word—'Lover'. As she said it my eyes began to spiral in my head and I thought I was going off into another faint. I grabbed the smelling salts and took a deep sniff. 'I'll come back, lover,' I gurgled through the invisible stranglehold around my throat. 'Tonight.'

I ran home like a beserk redskin, seething with jubilant boiling emotions. They escaped like steam jets from every joint and hole and seam of my body . . .

Although that night I was creeping out on a grown-up assignation, I was still barely more than a child. As I went timidly through the darkness of the house and out into the street I felt like Wee Willie Winkie. It was two o'clock, an opaque summer night, close and still, with cats arched in the street and a policeman propped asleep beneath a lintel at the bottom of our road. I took fright when I saw a face in a shop window and then realized it was the mirrored moon. For the occasion I had put on my best suit, brown shoes, white shirt, tie, and my Odeon Saturday Morning Club badge.

I went like a shadow through shadows, gently avoiding the sniffing Home Guard sentry outside the off-licence, reaching the park, and letting myself in through a gap in the hedge. The balloon was like a fat woman asleep, rolling a little in the touch of night breeze. The excitement I had seething through my body left no room for any fear. I knew where she slept, the hut and the very bed. It occurred to me that the door might be locked, but it wasn't.

There was a short squeak as I turned the little brass door knob but the door swung without sound and I stepped in. It was close and scented in there. Suddenly I realized with a thrill of strange masculine power that I was in a room full of sleeping women. I could sense their breasts moving in the dark; I could see a white female face pinned beneath a column of moonlight coming in at a window.

Rose was snoring, a little lilt of a snore, lying on her front with her lovely big face buried in her pillows, her blankets kicked down the bed, a sheet half covering the moonlit breadth of her sweating back. I stood small by her bed, fighting down a sudden and urgent feeling that I ought to run, that every-thing was imagined. But I had her scent in my nose now and that made me stay. I knew that it was true, that her hair had been in my face, that she had done that extraordinary thing she did. It was true, and I knew it would be all right.

At first I thought I would rouse her with a kiss, and I hovered over her, lips pursed, trying to select a spot on which to put it, her cheek, her forehead, her shoulder, bare but for the single bridging strap of her nightdress, or the very middle of her fine large back. But my courage was only a lad's and I pulled away at the final instant. Instead I extended a worried finger and tapped her almost formally on the arm. She mumbled and stirred and did not wake. I put the finger into the nightdress strap and gave it a brief tug, letting the palm of my hand drop on to the shoulder. The sensation of her flesh went through me like a shock. I thought I was going to be taken short. I closed my hand over the warm skin I loved so much and felt her move and half wake. 'Fuck off,' she whispered.

I was transfixed. I pulled my hand away in some sort of terror. My whole body seemed to have dried up with those awful discouraging words. She stirred again and murmured: 'Fuck off, Danny, will you.'

Danny! I thought the top of my head was going to fly off. Danny? Who was Danny? Who the hell was he to be told to fuck off? Jealousy and wrath flooded my interior, already well occupied with apprehension. I stood up and regarded her with indignation and tears. She opened one eye, quickly fol-lowed by the other: 'It's you,' she breathed in immediately happy surprise. 'Little Arthur.'

'It's not Danny,' I muttered sullenly.

'Hush,' she warned sweetly. She propped herself up on one elbow to look around me at the others in the room. They still slept, but the action brought her half way from the sheet. The moon brushed her neck and flooded the indolent mounds inside the front of her nightdress. She saw my transfixion, reached for my hand and blatantly laid it against her skin. My sweat began to cascade inside my best suit. That lovely, swollen, soft, piece of Rose. And I was touching it.

She levered her feet from the bed. It was a long silk nightdress and big and statuesque as she was she reminded me of the picture of Britannia which we had on the wall at school. Or Boadicea, whichever it was. She took my hand, and glancing round the room again, made for the door. We went out into the soft night of the park and trod gleefully across the dewy grass to the somnolent barrage balloon.

We hardly bothered to look towards the sentry post. She pulled me down into the silver folds of the balloon and hugged me to her.

'You've got a collar and tie and long trousers on,' she whispered.

'It's my best suit,' I said. 'I thought I'd look nice if I was coming to see you.'

'Let's take it off,' she giggled. 'You'll get it all screwed up sitting down here.'

She helped me out of my clothes, just like my mother used to do when I was a few years younger, making the same little clucks as she did so, then folding the clothes up in a careful pile at our side. I had taken off everything except my underpants and I told her shyly I wanted to retain them, at least for a while. Underneath that wretched uncontrollable spike was up to its tricks again. Why wouldn't the bloody thing behave? I could see her looking at the tent it made in my underpants and felt myself blush.

'I don't know what to do,' I said because she was just kneeling and watching me.

'Come and have a rest down here,' she replied, turning and stretching herself out along the loose folds of the balloon. She was flat, laid out in her nightie, like Mrs Hughes was when she died and everybody in the street was allowed to go and have a look at her. Up to then Mrs Hughes was the only woman I had seen lying in a nightie and she couldn't compare with Rose, not for a moment. Not only was she dead, she was a lot older.

I stood, for a moment, hesitating, not sure what to do, how to launch myself, just as once I had stood at the top of the slide in the park playground, childishly frozen before the first descent. Rose's confident fingers encouraged me. She crooked one from each hand mischievously towards me and then reached out and held me behind my trembling knee with her strong but exquisite hand.

I went to her, buckling at the knees, then going head first as I would into the Newport municipal swimming baths. She gave a short grunt as I landed on her and I muttered an apology. I had no time or room or words for anything else.

For in a moment I was involved in a situation so exotic, so erotic, so incredible, that though I have known many women since, and varied positions and techniques, I have never again captured the pure joy of that first sensation. For me, ever since, it has been my sexual lost chord. All childhood vanished in a moment, my fears and barriers, my unawareness, my doubts, my joyless loneliness. I wallowed in her. That is the only word, *wallowed*. It was like swimming on a warm and wavy ocean. It was all I could do not to throw my arms into an exultant freestyle stroke. Her arms were hugging me with great, lovely enjoyment and, somewhat to my astonishment, she had my ear in her mouth. I've never had very attractive ears; they project and at school the others say they can see the light through them. But that's what Rose was doing. She *liked* my ears.

She began to groan and mumble while she was still doing this with my ear and I had to pull my head away from her and my ear out of her mouth before I could comprehend what she was saying, for the total effect was to render me half deaf and her half dumb. It was only my name: 'Arthur, Little Arthur.' Her forearms went around my sweating head and then I was all but smothered in her voluminous breasts. My face kept slipping all over the place for we were both very wet, up and down the slopes, into the middle and up and over again.

She steadied me strongly and more or less forced my mouth to the middle of her left breast until I had my lips around it, something I had not done since babyhood. I was conscious, despite all this, of my sharp knees sticking into the broad parts of her thighs, my hips tucked inside hers and my naked belly on the hot silk of the nightdress. Several times I thought I was going to fall off, but she held me tight.

All this. But we had done nothing yet. That was coming. Rose, when roused, became excessively violent, as I learned from the beginning. Her hand swooped down and came away with my tattered underpants which, well washed and old as they were (underwear, like other clothes, was in short supply in wartime), more or less disintegrated at her powerful grab. I heard them rend and made some forlorn movement to save them, but they shattered before I got my hand even in their vicinity.

I don't know exactly how the next few minutes felt for her and much worse, I cannot now remember exactly how they felt for me. The years have worked on the edge of the memory and all I know now is that I *loved* it, by God how I did; loved it much more than anything I can ever remember either before or after. I was still scrabbling all over the place in my unaccustomed eagerness and once I actually did tumble off. She pulled me on again with eager tenderness and then, using those splendid hands, guided my body until it was going to and fro in some regular movement, like a steam iron.

Trying to recall it now is, of course, very difficult but I remember that I loved it and I loved her because although she was so powerful she was very kind to me. She even stopped for a few moments in her grown-up passion to let me get my breath back. I had a good idea, from my own experiments, conducted despite the scoutmaster's curdled brain warnings, what happened at the climax. But when it actually occurred I realized that I had only been a boy riding a rocking horse.

We lay quietly against the balloon afterwards, letting the night air cool our bodies. My bum began to get cold and I wished she had not ripped my pants like that. I began to worry about my pants, because my mother knew exactly how many pairs I had and one missing would soon be noticed.

'Rose,' I whispered.

'Yes, love?'

'I don't suppose there's any chance of you sewing my underpants together again is there?'

She was still lying beneath me and she began to laugh a breathless little laugh, turning her face away from me as though she realized I would not understand. She let her hand search about and she found my pants. She held the tatters up and even with my poor knowledge of sewing I knew that nothing could ever be done to renovate them.

'I'll buy you some more,' she said, smacking my cold buttocks.

Leslie Thomas (b. 1931), Arthur McCann and all his Women (1972).

———

B Y an odd coincidence, which probably has no significance apart from giving hope to the compiler of this book that Fate may have decided to smile upon it and wish it well, the first piece of humour included was printed by William Caxton in the year 1477, and the last entry comes from P. G. Wodehouse whose last novel was published in 1977.

A span of exactly five hundred years.

Caxton and Wodehouse, as long as one does not push the thing too far, make a suitable bracket in which to enclose five centuries of humorous prose, if only because the humour of both men was unmistakably English; affable, observant, gentle, aiming to amuse.

The difference between them was that Caxton was England's only printer, there were as yet no publishers or booksellers to distribute his wares, and, as there were hardly any readers either, his circulation and fame was restricted at the time to some of the clergy and a handful of educated nobles and professional men.

P. G. Wodehouse, five hundred years later, had countless legions of readers including Her Majesty Queen Elizabeth, the Queen Mother, a committed Wodehouse reader for many years (legend has it that when asked once whether there was something which she would really like to have instead of the usual formal presentation gift, the Queen Mother replied, 'May I have the complete works of P. G. Wodehouse?' An excellent idea by any standards: complete sets are extremely rare).

Other distinguished self-confessed devotees included a former Prime Minister, the Rt. Hon. Herbert Asquith; the poet and classical scholar A. E. Housman; Hilaire Belloc (in the middle 1930s he broadcast a rather embarrassingly fulsome tribute to the modest Wodehouse with such phrases as 'the best writer of our time—the best living writer of English—the head of my profession'); Arnold Bennett; Rudyard Kipling; the novelist and playwright Ian Hay; four generations of Waughs including Evelyn Waugh and his son Auberon ('Wodehouse has been more read than any other English novelist by his fellow novelists'); Malcolm Muggeridge; Kingsley Amis; Bernard Levin (in The Times *he likened the impact of the line 'in my heliotrope pyjamas with the old gold stripe' to one of the great speeches in* Macbeth); *and so on.*

Perhaps an even more remarkable example of the diversity of Wodehouse's appeal occurs towards the end of Evelyn Waugh's biography of the eminent Catholic theologian and translator of the Bible, Father Ronald Knox, when Waugh noted: 'For the remaining years of his life, Ronnie Knox applied himself to devotional reading and the works of P. G. Wodehouse.'

But Wodehouse's stories were not meant to be either caviare to the general or incense to the priest but beans-on-toast to the troops, a bit of pleasure and fun for amusement only. He was a completely professional writer whose only intent was to make as many people as possible laugh. In this he was phenomenally successful.

Pelham Grenville Wodehouse, known as 'Plum', had his first piece of prose published during the reign of Queen Victoria, in 1900, while he was still a schoolboy at Dulwich College. When he died in 1975, aged 93, still working (he had written almost every day of his life through five reigns), he had published ninety-six books and hundreds of short stories. His books and stories have been translated into fifteen languages and most of them are still in print in paperback. His total sales run into many tens of millions, and there are Wodehouse appreciation societies and clubs in various spots around the world—Denmark's Wodehouse Society meets in Copenhagen in the 'Drones Club' and in Amsterdam there is a bar for Wodehousians called 'Mr Mulliner's Wijn Lokaal'.

Wodehouse also either wrote or collaborated in sixteen stage-plays, supplied all or part of the lyrics for twenty-eight musical comedies, and for eighteen of these he worked on the libretto (which is more libretti than Gilbert of Gilbert and Sullivan produced). For a time he contributed regularly to Punch, *wrote humorous verse for many magazines, and worked on six major film scripts in Hollywood.*

For somebody so unashamedly, irredeemably English, Wodehouse's work has always been extraordinarily popular in the USA, but his reputation is high there for another reason. In 1928, trying to meet the limitations of writing musical comedies for a tiny New York theatre, the Princess, *Wodehouse, in company with the composer Jerome Kern and the librettist Guy Bolton, managed to transform the nature of the American musical.*

Before the Princess *shows, most musical comedy was a gaudy version of Viennese Operetta, with simplified music for New Yorkers with tin ears, settings in Munich beer-gardens, Sahara sand-dunes, or Alpine chalets, and much spectacle.*

*The three new young writers had to work on a much smaller scale so they devised
a form which was not an operetta at all but a play with music, with more plot and
with the songs integrated into the action. Furthermore, the lyrics and the plots
were about contemporary Americans and the songs used everyday vernacular
American speech. They were highly successful shows, and important for their
influence. They broke up the old ground of musicals enabling Rodgers and Hammerstein to come along and plant the seeds of the new.*

*Nobody remembers many of those Wodehouse/Kern songs because they were of
their time, but one haunting romantic song has lasted. Written in 1917 it turned
up again in 1927 in* Show Boat *because Kern needed a show-stopper and it didn't
matter what the song was about because the scene was an audition. The lyric was
typically Wodehousian: a love song about a man who is so ordinary that his girl
is baffled trying to explain what she sees in him:* (Just My) Bill.

*In the late 1940s Peter Quennell wrote: 'Though not one non-literary reader in
a thousand will lift his eyes from the page to consider Wodehouse as an artist, a
fellow hack cannot fail to admire the extraordinary skill with which, judged by
professional literary standards, he goes about his business. Every sentence has a
job to do and—in spite of the air of lunatic irresponsibility which hangs around a
Wodehouse novel—does it neatly and efficiently.'*

*Fellow-hacks did not fail to admire; to writers almost everywhere Wodehouse
was The Master. In an interview with Wodehouse's biographer, Frances Donaldson,
Evelyn Waugh gave just one of many reasons why: 'One has to regard a man as a
Master who can produce on average three uniquely brilliant and entirely original
similes to every page.'*

*Here are some of these: they might be termed 'plums' except that they all come
from Richard Usborne's collection of over two thousand which he calls* Wodehouse
Nuggets:

The unpleasant, acrid smell of burnt poetry.

> P. G. Wodehouse (1881–1975), *Young Men in Spats* (1936). Reprinted:
> *Wodehouse Nuggets*, ed. Richard Usborne (1983).
>
> ☛ This was Evelyn Waugh's favourite Wodehouse line.

The drowsy stillness of the summer afternoon was shattered by what sounded
to his strained senses like G. K. Chesterton falling on a sheet of tin.

> *Mr Mulliner Speaking* (1929).

I became aware of somebody coughing softly at my side, like a respectful
sheep trying to catch the attention of its shepherd.

> *Thank You, Jeeves* (1934).

Into the face of the young man who sat on the terrace of the Hotel Magnifique
at Cannes there had crept a look of furtive shame, the shifty, hangdog look
which announces that an Englishman is about to talk French.

> *The Luck of the Bodkins* (1935).

'Alf Tod,' said Ukridge, 'has about as much chance of winning the heavy-weight championship, as a one-armed blind man in a dark room trying to shove a pound of melted butter into a wild-cat's left ear with a red-hot needle.'

Ukridge (1924).

His whole aspect was that of a man who has been unexpectedly struck by lightning.

Eggs, Beans and Crumpets (1940).

Wodehouse and his three brothers were brought up in England by a variety of aunts because their father and mother were usually in Hong Kong where Mr Wodehouse was a magistrate. His family was of upper-middle-class stock, comfortably off rather than well off, with close aristocratic connections (Wodehouse would certainly have met many butlers; there were a lot of them about in the nineties—even Mr Pooter could afford a maid). His most enjoyable days were those he spent at school.

Wodehouse was a great success at Dulwich. He was bright, he edited the school magazine, was in the Classical Sixth, and wrote Latin and Greek as fluently as he wrote English; he had a fine voice and sang in the choir, and he was a school prefect. And he wrote. He found that there was nothing he liked to do better, for as long as possible, at any time of the day, and whilst still at school he sold his first story. When the time came to leave Dulwich his father fixed him up with a lowly job at the Hong Kong and Shanghai Bank and off he went to the City, still writing at every free minute.

After two years in the bank his free-lance earnings exceeded his bank salary and he resigned, publishing his first novel about schoolboys, for schoolboys, The Pothunters. *He began writing for* Punch *and was taken on to help write a funny newspaper column in* The World, *and he went to America for the first time, really to see some famous boxers who all seemed to be American then as now, but also to try and sell a few stories.*

In 1907 he thought of an entirely new character, more sophisticated and grown-up than any before, and introduced him in Mike, *a two-part schoolboy serial he was writing. It turned out to be the turning-point in Wodehouse's writing career.*

According to Wodehouse, the character, Rupert Psmith (pronounced Smith), was closely based upon a real person, Rupert D'Oyly Carte, a schoolfriend of one of Wodehouse's cousins at Eton. The rich and unconventional Rupert had embraced communism and called everybody at Eton 'comrade', was always immaculately dressed, sported a monocle and when asked by a housemaster how he was, replied, 'Sir, I grow thinnah and thinnah'.

The entry of Psmith marked the point where Wodehouse stopped writing exciting school stories and moved up into the world of humorous adult fiction.

Psmith's first appearance in print came about when Mike, the decent, cricket-playing eponymous hero of Mike, *is forced by his father, through exam failures, to move to a non-sporting, lesser public school, Sedleigh. Thoroughly dispirited on arrival, he is mooching about when he comes upon an odd-looking figure:*

A very long, thin youth, with a solemn face and immaculate clothes, was leaning against the mantelpiece. As Mike entered, he fumbled in his top left waistcoat pocket, produced an eyeglass attached to a chord, and fixed it in his right eye. With the help of this aid to vision he inspected Mike in silence for a while, then having flicked a speck of invisible dust from the left sleeve of his coat, he spoke. 'Hello,' he said.

He spoke in a tired voice.

'Hello,' said Mike.

'Take a seat,' said the immaculate one. 'If you don't mind dirtying your bags, that's to say. Personally I don't see any prospect of ever sitting down in this place. It looks to me as if they meant to use these chairs as mustard-and-cress beds. A Nursery Garden in the Home. That sort of idea. My name,' he added pensively. 'is Smith. What's yours?'

'Jackson,' said Mike.

'Are you the Bully, the Pride of the School, or the Boy who is led Astray and takes to Drink in Chapter Sixteen?'

'The last, for choice,' said Mike, 'but I've only just arrived, so I don't know.'

'The boy—what will he become? Are you new here too, then?'

'Yes. Why, are you new?'

'Do I look as if I belonged here? Sit down on yonder settee, and I will tell you the painful story of my life. By the way, before I start there's just one thing. If ever you have occasion to write to me, would you mind sticking a P at the beginning of my name? P-s-m-i-t-h. See? There are too many Smiths, and I don't care for Smythe. My father's content to worry along in the old-fashioned way, but I've decided to strike out a fresh line. I shall found a new dynasty. The resolve came to me unexpectedly this morning. I jotted it down on the back of an envelope. In conversation you may address me as Rupert (though I hope you won't), or simply Smith, the P not being sounded. Cf. the name Zbysco, in which the Z is given a similar miss-in-baulk. See?'

Mike said he saw. Psmith thanked him with a certain stately old-world courtesy.

'Let us start at the beginning,' he resumed. 'My infancy. When I was but a babe, my eldest sister was bribed with a shilling an hour by my nurse to keep an eye on me, and see that I did not raise Cain. At the end of the day she struck for one-and-six, and got it. At an early age, I was sent to Eton, everybody predicting a bright career for me. But,' said Psmith, fixing an owl-like gaze on Mike through the eyeglass, 'it was not to be.'

> *Mike* (1909), first published as a serial 'The Lost Lambs', in *The Captain* (1907).

A year before Wodehouse invented Psmith he had written his first funny adult novel, based upon what happened to a man William Townend knew who tried to start a chicken farm. *Wodehouse's novel,* Love Among the Chickens, *introduced Stanley Featherstonehaugh (pronounced Fanshaw) Ukridge (pronounced Yew-kridge), an ill-starred, eccentric opportunist based upon a mixture of Townend's acquaintance and a rather odd friend of Wodehouse. The book sold well but Wode-house (pronouncd Woodhouse) did not follow it up at the time, perhaps because Psmith had become more interesting to write about.*

The Ukridge stories were of failure, amusing failure but, nevertheless, failure: Ukridge was always short of the ready and the stories were set in cheap Soho restaurants and tatty (but highly respectable) lodgings. Psmith was rich; his was a different world from Ukridge's. Psmith moved in the elegant ambience of Mayfair and clubland. It was Psmith who opened up to Wodehouse the possibilities of writing about the idle but attractive and amusing rich.

Years later, in the 1920s, Wodehouse revived Ukridge, unmarried him, changed him a bit, and wrote a series of short stories about his ingenious, desperate schemes to get rich quick. The brilliant ingenuity of the plots, the character of Ukridge himself, bulky, crafty, totally untrustworthy, never without his yellow mackintosh and spectacles held together with ginger-beer wire, the picture drawn of bright young sparks in Edwardian London yet to make their way in the world and in the meantime without a bean, the kindly narrator 'Corky' Corcoran (Wodehouse himself), all combine to show that by the 1920s Wodehouse had mastered the humorous short-story form:

UKRIDGE'S ACCIDENT SYNDICATE

'Half a minute, laddie,' said Ukridge. And gripping my arm, he brought me to a halt on the outskirts of the little crowd which had collected about the church door.

It was a crowd such as may be seen any morning during the London mating-season outside any of the churches which nestle in the quiet squares between Hyde Park and the King's Road, Chelsea.

It consisted of five women of cook-like aspect, four nurse-maids, half-a-dozen men of the non-producing class who had torn themselves away for the moment from their normal task of propping up the wall of the Bunch of Grapes public house on the corner, a costermonger with a barrow of veget-ables, divers small boys, eleven dogs, and two or three purposeful-looking young men with cameras slung over their shoulders. It was plain that a wedding was in progress—and, arguing from the presence of the camera-men and the line of smart motor-cars along the kerb, a fairly fashionable wedding. What was not plain—to me—was why Ukridge, sternest of bachelors, had desired to add himself to the spectators.

'What,' I enquired, 'is the thought behind this? Why are we interrupting our walk to attend the obsequies of some perfect stranger?'

Ukridge did not reply for a moment. He seemed plunged in thought. Then he uttered a hollow mirthless laugh—a dreadful sound like the last gargle of a dying moose.

'Perfect stranger, my number eleven foot!' he responded, in his coarse way. 'Do you know who it is who is getting hitched up in there?'

'Who?'

'Teddy Weeks.'

'Teddy Weeks? Teddy Weeks? Good Lord!' I exclaimed. 'Not really?'

And five years rolled away.

It was at Barolini's Italian restaurant in Beak Street that Ukridge evolved his great scheme. Barolini's was a favourite resort of our little group of earnest strugglers in the days when the philanthropic restaurateurs of Soho used to supply four courses and coffee for a shilling and sixpence; and there were present that night, besides Ukridge and myself, the following men-about-town: Teddy Weeks, the actor, fresh from a six-weeks' tour of the Number Three 'Only a Shop-Girl' Company; Victor Beamish, the artist, the man who drew that picture of the O-So-Eesi Piano-Player in the advertisement pages of the *Piccadilly Magazine*; Bertram Fox, author of *Ashes of Remorse*, and other unproduced motion-picture scenarios; and Robert Dunhill, who, being employed at a salary of eighty pounds per annum by the New Asiatic Bank, represented the sober, hard-headed commercial element. As usual, Teddy Weeks had collared the conversation, and was telling us once again how good he was and how hardly treated by a malignant fate.

There is no need to describe Teddy Weeks. Under another and more euphonious name he has long since made his personal appearance dreadfully familiar to all who read the illustrated weekly papers. He was then, as now, a sickeningly handsome young man, possessing precisely the same melting eyes, mobile mouth, and corrugated hair so esteemed by the theatre-going public today. And yet, at this period of his career he was wasting himself on minor touring companies of the kind which open in Barrow-in-Furness and jump to Bootle for the second half of the week. He attributed this, as Ukridge was so apt to attribute his own difficulties, to lack of capital.

'I have everything,' he said, querulously, emphasising his remarks with a coffee-spoon. 'Looks, talent, personality, a beautiful speaking-voice—everything. All I need is a chance. And I can't get that because I have no clothes fit to wear. These managers are all the same, they never look below the surface, they never bother to find out if a man has genius. All they go by are his clothes. If I could afford to buy a couple of suits from a Cork Street tailor, if I could have my boots made to order by Mykoff instead of getting them ready-made and second-hand at Moses Brothers, if I could once contrive to own a decent hat, a really good pair of spats, and a gold cigarette-case, all at the same time, I could walk into any manager's office and sign up for a West-end production tomorrow.'

It was at this point that Freddie Lunt came in. Freddie, like Robert Dunhill, was a financial magnate in the making and an assiduous frequenter of Barolini's; and it suddenly occurred to us that a considerable time had passed since we had last seen him in the place. We enquired the reason for this aloofness.

'I've been in bed,' said Freddie, 'for over a fortnight.'

The statement incurred Ukridge's stern disapproval. That great man made it a practice of never rising before noon, and on one occasion, when a carelessly-thrown match had burned a hole in his only pair of trousers, had gone so far as to remain between the sheets for twenty-four hours; but sloth on so majestic a scale as this shocked him.

'Lazy young devil,' he commented severely. 'Letting the golden hours of youth slip by like that when you ought to have been bustling about and making a name for yourself.'

Freddie protested himself wronged by the accusation.

'I had an accident,' he explained. 'Fell off my bicycle and sprained an ankle.'

'Tough luck,' was our verdict.

'Oh, I don't know,' said Freddie. 'It wasn't bad fun getting a rest. And of course there was the fiver.'

'What fiver?'

'I got a fiver from the *Weekly Cyclist* for getting my ankle sprained.'

'You—*what?*' cried Ukridge, profoundly stirred—as ever—by a tale of easy money. 'Do you mean to tell me that some dashed paper paid you five quid simply because you sprained your ankle? Pull yourself together, old horse. Things like that don't happen.'

'It's quite true.'

'Can you show me the fiver?'

'No; because if I did you would try to borrow it.'

Ukridge ignored this slur in dignified silence.

'Would they pay a fiver to anyone who sprained his ankle?' he asked, sticking to the main point.

'Yes. If he was a subscriber.'

'I knew there was a catch in it,' said Ukridge, moodily.

'Lots of weekly papers are starting this wheeze,' proceeded Freddie. 'You pay a year's subscription and that entitles you to accident insurance.'

We were interested. This was in the days before every daily in London was competing madly against its rivals in the matter of insurance and offering princely bribes to the citizens to make a fortune by breaking their necks. Nowadays papers are paying as high as two thousand pounds for a genuine corpse and five pounds a week for a mere dislocated spine; but at that time the idea was new and it had an attractive appeal.

'How many of these rags are doing this?' asked Ukridge. You could tell from the gleam in his eyes that that great brain was whirring like a dynamo. 'As many as ten?'

'Yes, I should think so. Quite ten.'

'Then a fellow who subscribed to them all and then sprained his ankle would get fifty quid?' said Ukridge, reasoning acutely.

'More if the injury was more serious,' said Freddie, the expert. 'They have a regular tariff. So much for a broken arm, so much for a broken leg, and so forth.'

Ukridge's collar leaped off its stud and his pince-nez wobbled drunkenly as he turned to us.

'How much money can you blokes raise?' he demanded.

'What do you want it for?' asked Robert Dunhill, with a banker's caution.

'My dear old horse, can't you see? Why, my gosh, I've got the idea of the century. Upon my Sam, this is the giltest-edged scheme that was ever hatched. We'll get together enough money and take out a year's subscription for every one of these dashed papers.'

'What's the good of that?' said Dunhill, coldly unenthusiastic.

They train bank clerks to stifle emotion, so that they will be able to refuse overdrafts when they become managers. 'The odds are that none of us will have an accident, and then the money would be chucked away.'

'Good heavens, ass,' snorted Ukridge, 'you don't suppose I'm suggesting that we should leave it to chance, do you? Listen! Here's the scheme. We take out subscriptions for all these papers, then we draw lots, and the fellow who gets the fatal card or whatever it is goes out and breaks his leg and draws the loot, and we split it up between us and live on it in luxury. It ought to run into hundreds of pounds.'

A long silence followed. Then Dunhill spoke again. His was a solid rather than a nimble mind.

'Suppose he couldn't break his leg?'

'My gosh!' cried Ukridge, exasperated. 'Here we are in the twentieth century, with every resource of modern civilisation at our disposal, with opportunities of getting our legs broken opening about us on every side—and you ask a silly question like that! Of course he could break his leg. Any ass can break a leg. It's a little hard! We're all infernally broke—personally, unless Freddie can lend me a bit of that fiver until Saturday, I'm going to have a difficult job pulling through. We all need money like the dickens, and yet, when I point out this marvellous scheme for collecting a bit, instead of fawning on me for my ready intelligence you sit and make objections. It isn't the right spirit. It isn't the spirit that wins.'

'If you're as hard up as that,' objected Dunhill, 'how are you going to put in your share of the pool?'

A pained, almost a stunned, look came into Ukridge's eyes. He gazed at Dunhill through his lop-sided pince-nez as one who speculates as to whether his hearing has deceived him.

'Me?' he cried. 'Me? I like that! Upon my Sam, that's rich! Why, damme, if there's any justice in the world, if there's a spark of decency and good-feeling in your bally bosoms, I should think you would let me in free for suggesting the idea. It's a little hard! I supply the brains and you want me to cough up cash as well. My gosh, I didn't expect this. This hurts me, by George! If anybody had told me that an old pal would—'

'Oh, all right,' said Robert Dunhill. 'All right, all right, all right. But I'll tell you one thing. If you draw the lot it'll be the happiest day of my life.'

'I shan't,' said Ukridge. 'Something tells me I shan't.'

Nor did he. When, in a solemn silence broken only by the sound of a distant waiter quarrelling with the cook down a speaking-tube, we had completed the drawing, the man of destiny was Teddy Weeks.

I suppose that even in the springtime of Youth, when broken limbs seem a lighter matter than they become later in life, it can never be an unmixedly agreeable thing to go out into the public highways and try to make an accident happen to one. In such circumstances the reflection that you are thereby benefitting your friends brings but slight balm. To Teddy Weeks it appeared to bring no balm at all. That he was experiencing a slight dis-inclination to sacrifice himself for the public good became more and more evident as the days went by and found him still intact. Ukridge, when he called upon me to discuss the matter, was visibly perturbed. He sank into a chair beside the table at which I was beginning my modest morning meal and, having drunk half my coffee, sighed deeply.

'Upon my Sam,' he moaned, 'it's a little disheartening. I strain my brain to think up schemes for getting us all a bit of money just at the moment when we are all needing it most, and when I hit upon what is probably the simplest and yet ripest notion of our time, this blighter Weeks goes and lets me down by shirking his plain duty. It's just my luck that a fellow like that should have drawn the lot. And the worst of it is, laddie, that, now we've started with him, we've got to keep on. We can't possibly raise enough money to pay yearly subscriptions for anybody else. It's Weeks or nobody.'

'I suppose we must give him time.'

'That's what he says,' grunted Ukridge, morosely, helping himself to toast. 'He says he doesn't know how to start about it. To listen to him, you'd think that going and having a trifling accident was the sort of delicate and intricate job that required years of study and special preparation. Why, a child of six could do it on his head at five minutes' notice. The man's so infernally particular. You make helpful suggestions, and instead of accepting them in a broad, reasonable spirit of co-operation he comes back at you every time with some frivolous objection. He's so dashed fastidious. When we were out last night, we came upon a couple of navvies scrapping. Good, hefty fellows, either of them capable of putting him in hospital for a month. I told him to jump in and start separating them, and he said no; it was a private dispute which was none of his business, and he didn't feel justified in interfering. Finicky, I call it. I tell you, laddie, this blighter is a broken reed. He has got cold feet. We did wrong to let him into the drawing at all. We might have known that a fellow like that would never give results. No conscience. No sense of *esprit de corps*. No notion of putting himself out to the most trifling extent for the benefit of the community. Haven't you any more marmalade, laddie?'

'I have not.'

'Then I'll be going,' said Ukridge, moodily. 'I suppose,' he added, pausing at the door, 'you couldn't lend me five bob?'

'How did you guess?'

'Then I'll tell you what,' said Ukridge, ever fair and reasonable; 'you can stand me dinner tonight.' He seemed cheered up for the moment by this happy compromise, but gloom descended on him again. His face clouded. 'When I think of all the money that's locked up in that poor, faint-hearted fish, just waiting to be released, I could sob. Sob, laddie, like a little child. I never liked that man—he has a bad eye and waves his hair. Never trust a man who waves his hair, old horse.'

Ukridge's pessimism was not confined to himself. By the end of a fortnight, nothing having happened to Teddy Weeks worse than a slight cold which he shook off in a couple of days, the general consensus of opinion among his apprehensive colleagues in the Syndicate was that the situation had become desperate. There were no signs whatever of any return on the vast capital which we had laid out, and meanwhile meals had to be bought, landladies paid, and a reasonable amount of tobacco acquired. It was a melancholy task in these circumstances to read one's paper of a morning.

All over the inhabited globe, so the well-informed sheet gave one to understand, every kind of accident was happening every day to practically everybody in existence except Teddy Weeks. Farmers in Minnesota were getting mixed up with reaping machines, peasants in India were being bisected by crocodiles; iron girders from skyscrapers were falling hourly on the heads of citizens in every town from Philadelphia to San Francisco; and the only people who were not down with ptomaine poisoning were those who had walked over cliffs, driven motors into walls, tripped over manholes, or assumed on too slight evidence that the gun was not loaded. In a crippled world, it seemed, Teddy Weeks walked alone, whole and glowing with health. It was one of those grim, ironical, hopeless, grey, despairful situations which the Russian novelists love to write about, and I could not find it in me to blame Ukridge for taking direct action in this crisis. My only regret was that bad luck caused such an excellent plan to miscarry.

My first intimation that he had been trying to hurry matters on came when he and I were walking along the King's Road one evening, and he drew me into Markham Square, a dismal backwater where he had once had rooms.

'What's the idea?' I asked, for I disliked the place.

'Teddy Weeks lives here,' said Ukridge. 'In my old rooms.' I could not see that this lent any fascination to the place. Every second and in every way I was feeling sorrier and sorrier that I had been foolish enough to put money which I could ill spare into a venture which had all the earmarks of a wash-out, and my sentiments towards Teddy Weeks were cold and hostile.

'I want to enquire after him.'

'Enquire after him? Why?'

'Well, the fact is, laddie, I have an idea that he has been bitten by a dog.'

'What makes you think that?'

'Oh, I don't know,' said Ukridge, dreamily. 'I've just got the idea. You know how one gets ideas.'

The mere contemplation of this beautiful event was so inspiring that for a while it held me silent. In each of the ten journals in which we had invested dog-bites were specifically recommended as things which every subscriber ought to have. They came about half-way up the list of lucrative accidents, inferior to a broken rib or fractured fibula, but better value than an ingrowing toe-nail. I was gloating happily over the picture conjured up by Ukridge's words when an exclamation broke me back with a start to the realities of life. A revolting sight met my eyes. Down the street came ambling the familiar figure of Teddy Weeks, and one glance at his elegant person was enough to tell us that our hopes had been built on sand. Not even a toy Pomeranian had chewed this man.

'Hallo, you fellows!' said Teddy Weeks.

'Hello!' we responded, dully.

'Can't stop,' said Teddy Weeks. 'I've got to fetch a doctor.'

'A doctor?'

'Yes. Poor Victor Beamish. He's been bitten by a dog.'

Ukridge and I exchanged weary glances. It seemed as if Fate was going out of its way to have sport with us. What was the good of a dog biting Victor Beamish? What was the good of a hundred dogs biting Victor Beamish? A dog-bitten Victor Beamish had no market value at all.

'You know that fierce brute that belongs to my landlady,' said Teddy Weeks. 'The one that always dashes out into the area and barks at people who come to the front door.' I remembered. A large mongrel with wild eyes and flashing fangs, badly in need of a haircut. I had encountered it once in the street, when visiting Ukridge, and only the presence of the latter, who knew it well and to whom all dogs were as brothers, had saved me from the doom of Victor Beamish. 'Somehow or other he had got into my bedroom this evening. He was waiting there when I came home. I had brought Beamish back with me, and the animal pinned him by the leg the moment I opened the door.'

'Why didn't he pin you?' asked Ukridge, aggrieved.

'What I can't make out,' said Teddy Weeks, 'is how on earth the brute came to be in my room. Somebody must have put him there. The whole thing is very mysterious.'

'Why didn't he pin you?' demanded Ukridge again.

'Oh, I managed to climb on to the top of the wardrobe while he was biting

Beamish,' said Teddy Weeks. 'And then the landlady came and took him away. But I can't stop here talking. I must go and get that doctor.'

We gazed after him in silence as he tripped down the street. We noted the careful manner in which he paused at the corner to eye the traffic before crossing the road, the wary way in which he drew back to allow a truck to rattle past.

'You heard that?' said Ukridge, tensely. 'He climbed on to the top of the wardrobe!'

'Yes.'

'And you saw the way he dodged that excellent truck?'

'Yes.'

'Something's got to be done,' said Ukridge, firmly. 'The man has got to be awakened to a sense of his responsibilities.'

Next day a deputation waited on Teddy Weeks.

Ukridge was our spokesman, and he came to the point with admirable directness.

'How about it?' asked Ukridge.

'How about what?' replied Teddy Weeks, nervously, avoiding his accusing eye.

'When do we get action?'

'Oh, you mean that accident business?'

'Yes.'

'I've been thinking about that,' said Teddy Weeks.

Ukridge drew the macintosh which he wore indoors and out of doors and in all weathers more closely around him. There was in the action something suggestive of a member of the Roman Senate about to denounce an enemy of the state. In just such a manner must Cicero have swished his toga as he took a deep breath preparatory to assailing Claudius. He toyed for a moment with the ginger-beer wire which held his pince-nez in place, and endeavoured without success to button his collar at the back. In moments of emotion Ukridge's collar always took on a sort of temperamental jumpiness which no stud could restrain.

'And about time you *were* thinking about it,' he boomed.

We shifted appreciatively in our seats, all except Victor Beamish, who had declined a chair and was standing by the mantelpiece. 'Upon my Sam, it's about time you were thinking about it. Do you realise that we've invested an enormous sum of money in you on the understanding that we could rely on you to do your duty and get immediate results? Are we to be forced to the conclusion that you are so yellow and few in the pod as to want to evade your honourable obligations? We thought better of you, Weeks. Upon my Sam, we thought better of you. We took you for a two-fisted, enterprising, big-souled, one hundred-per-cent he-man who would stand by his friends to the finish.'

'Yes, but—'

'Any bloke with a sense of loyalty and an appreciation of what it meant to the rest of us would have rushed out and found some means of fulfilling his duty long ago. You don't even grasp the opportunities that come your way. Only yesterday I saw you draw back when a single step into the road would have had a truck bumping into you.'

'Well, it's not so easy to let a truck bump into you.'

'Nonsense. It only requires a little ordinary resolution. Use your imagination, man. Try to think that a child has fallen down in the street—a little golden-haired child,' said Ukridge, deeply affected. 'And a dashed great cab or something comes rolling up. The kid's mother is standing on the pavement, helpless, her hands clasped in agony. "Dammit," she cries, "will no one save my darling?" "Yes, by George," you shout, "*I* will." And out you jump and the thing's over in half a second. I don't know what you're making such a fuss about.'

'Yes, but—' said Teddy Weeks.

'I'm told, what's more, it isn't a bit painful. A sort of dull shock, that's all.'

'Who told you that?'

'I forget. Someone.'

'Well, you can tell him from me that he's an ass,' said Teddy Weeks, with asperity.

'All right. If you object to being run over by a truck there are lots of other ways. But, upon my Sam, it's pretty hopeless suggesting them. Yesterday, when I went to all the trouble to put a dog in your room, a dog which would have done all the work for you—all you had to do was stand still and let him use his own judgement—what happened? You climbed on to—'

Victor Beamish interrupted, speaking in a voice husky with emotion.

'Was it you who put that damned dog in the room?'

'Eh?' said Ukridge. 'Why, yes. But we can have a good talk about all that later on,' he proceeded, hastily. 'The point at the moment is how the dickens we're going to persuade this poor worm to collect our insurance money for us. Why, damme, I would have thought you would have—'

'All I can say—' began Victor Beamish, heatedly.

'Yes, yes,' said Ukridge; 'some other time. Must stick to business now, laddie. I was saying,' he resumed, 'that I should have thought you would have been as keen as mustard to put the job through for your own sake. You're always beefing that you haven't any clothes to impress managers with. Think of all you can buy with your share of the swag once you have summoned up a little ordinary determination and seen the thing through. Think of the suits, the boots, the hats, the spats. You're always talking about your dashed career, and how all you need to land you in a West-end production is good clothes. Well, here's your chance to get them.'

His eloquence was not wasted. A wistful look came into Teddy Weeks's eye, such a look as might have come into the eye of Moses on the summit of

Pisgah. You could see that the man was mentally walking along Cork Street, weighing the merits of one famous tailor against another.

'I'll tell you what I'll do,' he said, suddenly. 'It's no use asking me to put this thing through in cold blood. I simply can't do it. I haven't the nerve. But if you fellows will give me a dinner tonight with lots of champagne I think it will key me up to it.'

A heavy silence fell upon the room. Champagne! The word was like a knell.

'How on earth are we going to afford champagne?' said Victor Beamish.

'Well, there it is,' said Teddy Weeks. 'Take it or leave it.'

'Gentlemen,' said Ukridge, 'it would seem that the company requires more capital. How about it, old horses? Let's get together in a frank, business-like cards-on-the-table spirit, and see what can be done. I can raise ten bob.'

'What!' cried the entire assembled company, amazed. 'How?'

'I'll pawn a banjo.'

'You haven't got a banjo.'

'No, but George Tupper has, and I know where he keeps it.'

Started in this spirited way, the subscriptions came pouring in. I contributed a cigarette-case, Bertram Fox thought his landlady would let him owe for another week, Robert Dunhill had an uncle in Kensington who, he fancied, if tactfully approached, would be good for a quid, and Victor Beamish said that if the advertisement-manager for the O-So-Eesi Piano-Player was churlish enough to refuse an advance of five shillings against future work he misjudged him sadly. Within a few minutes, in short, the Lightning Drive had produced the impressive total of two pounds six shillings, and we asked Teddy Weeks if he thought he could get adequately keyed up within the limits of that sum.

'I'll try,' said Teddy Weeks.

So, not unmindful of the fact that that excellent hostelry supplied champagne at eight shillings the quart bottle, we fixed the meeting for seven o'clock at Barolini's.

Considered as a social affair, Teddy Weeks's keying-up dinner was not a success. Almost from the start I think we all found it trying. It was not so much the fact that he was drinking deeply of Barolini's eight-shilling champagne while we, from lack of funds, were compelled to confine ourselves to meaner beverages; what really marred the pleasantness of the function was the extraordinary effect the stuff had on Teddy. What was actually in the champagne supplied to Barolini and purveyed by him to the public, such as were reckless enough to drink it, at eight shillings the bottle remains a secret between its maker and his Maker; but three glasses of it were enough to transform Teddy Weeks from a mild and rather oily young man into a truculent swashbuckler.

He quarrelled with us all. With the soup he was tilting at Victor Beamish's theories of Art; the fish found him ridiculing Bertram Fox's views on the

future of the motion-picture; and by the time the leg of chicken with dan-
delion salad arrived—or, as some held, string salad—opinions varied on this
point—the hell-brew had so wrought on him that he had begun to lecture to
Ukridge on his mis-spent life and was urging him in accents audible across
the street to go out and get a job and thus acquire sufficient self-respect to
enable him to look himself in the face in a mirror without wincing. Not,
added Teddy Weeks with what we all thought uncalled-for offensiveness,
that any amount of self-respect was likely to do that. Having said which, he
called, imperiously, for another eight bobs's-worth.

We gazed at one another wanly. However excellent the end towards all
this was tending, there was no denying that it was hard to bear. But policy
kept us silent. We recognised that this was Teddy's evening and that he must
be humoured. Victor Beamish said meekly that Teddy had cleared up a lot of
points which had been troubling him for a long time. Bertram Fox agreed
that there was much in what Teddy has said about the future of the close-up.
And even Ukridge, though his haughty soul was seared to its foundations by
the latter's personal remarks, promised to take his homily to heart and act
upon it at the earliest possible moment.

'You'd better!' said Teddy Weeks, belligerently biting off the end of one of
Barolini's best cigars. 'And there's another thing—don't let me hear of your
coming and sneaking people's socks again.'

'Very well, laddie,' said Ukridge, humbly.

'If there's one person in the world that I despise,' said Teddy, bending a
red-eyed gaze on the offender, 'it's a snock-seeker—a seek-snocker—a—well,
you know what I mean.'

We hastened to reassure him that we knew what he meant and he relapsed
into a lengthy stupor, from which he emerged three-quarters of an hour later
to announce that he didn't know what we intended to do, but that he was
going. We said that we were going, too, and we paid the bill and did so.

Teddy Weeks's indignation on discovering us round him upon the pavement outside the restaurant was intense, and he expressed it freely. Among
other things, he said—which was not true—that he had a reputation to keep
up in Soho.

'It's all right, Teddy, old horse,' said Ukridge, soothingly. 'We just thought
you would like to have all your old pals round you when you did it.'

'Did it? Did what?'

'Why, had an accident.'

Teddy Weeks glared at him truculently. Then his mood seemed to change
abruptly, and he burst into a loud and hearty laugh.

'Well, of all the silly ideas!' he cried, amusedly. 'I'm not going to have an
accident. You don't suppose I ever seriously intended to have an accident,
do you? It was just my fun.' Then, with a sudden change of mood, he seemed
to become a victim to an acute unhappiness. He stroked Ukridge's arm
affectionately, and a tear rolled down his cheek. 'Just my fun,' he repeated.

'You don't mind my fun, do you?' he asked, pleadingly. 'You like my fun, don't you? All my fun. Never meant to have an accident at all. Just wanted dinner.' The gay humour of it all overcame his sorrow once more. 'Funniest thing ever heard,' he said cordially. 'Didn't want accident. Wanted dinner. Dinner daxident, danner dixident,' he added, driving home his point. 'Well, good night all,' he said cheerily. And, stepping off the kerb on to a banana-skin, was instantly knocked ten feet by a passing lorry.

'Two ribs and an arm,' said the doctor five minutes later, superintending the removal proceedings. 'Gently with that stretcher.'

It was two weeks before we were informed by the authorities of Charing Cross Hospital that the patient was in a position to receive visitors. A whip-round secured the price of a basket of fruit, and Ukridge and I were deputed by the shareholders to deliver it with their compliments and kind enquiries.

'Hallo!' we said, in a hushed, bedside manner when finally admitted to his presence.

'Sit down, gentlemen,' replied the invalid.

I must confess even in that first moment to having experienced a slight feeling of surprise. It was not like Teddy Weeks to call us gentlemen. Ukridge, however, seemed to know nothing amiss.

'Well, well, well,' he said, buoyantly. 'And how are you, laddie? We've brought you a few fragments of fruit.'

'I am getting along capitally,' replied Teddy Weeks, still in that odd precise way which had made his opening words strike me as curious. 'And I should like to say that in my opinion England has reason to be proud of the alertness and enterprise of her great journals. The excellence of their reading-matter, the ingenuity of their various competitions, and, above all, the go-ahead spirit which has resulted in this accident insurance scheme are beyond praise. Have you got that down?' he enquired.

Ukridge and I looked at each other. We had been told that Teddy was practically normal again, but this sounded like delirium.

'Have we got that down, old horse?' asked Ukridge, gently.

Teddy Weeks looked surprsied.

'Aren't you reporters?'

'How do you mean, reporters?'

'I thought you had come from one of these weekly papers that have been paying me insurance money, to interview me,' said Teddy Weeks.

Ukridge and I exchanged another glance. An uneasy glance this time. I think that already a grim foreboding had begun to cast its shadow over us.

'Surely you remember me, Teddy, old horse?' said Ukridge, anxiously.

Teddy Weeks knitted his brow, concentrating painfully.

'Why, of course,' he said at last. 'You're Ukridge, aren't you?'

'That's right. Ukridge.'

'Of course. Ukridge.'

'Yes. Ukridge. Funny your forgetting me.'

'Yes,' said Teddy Weeks. 'It's the effect of the shock I got when that thing bowled me over. I must have been struck on the head, I suppose. It has had the effect of rendering my memory rather uncertain. The doctors here are very interested. They say it is a most unusual case. I can remember some things perfectly, but in some way my memory is a complete blank.'

'Oh, but I say, old horse,' quavered Ukridge. 'I suppose you haven't forgotten about that insurance, have you?'

'Oh, no, I remember that.'

Ukridge breathed a relieved sigh.

'I was a subscriber to a number of weekly papers,' went on Teddy Weeks. 'They are paying me insurance money now.'

'Yes, yes, old horse,' cried Ukridge. 'But what I mean is you remember the Syndicate, don't you?'

Teddy Weeks raised his eyebrows.

'Syndicate? What syndicate?'

'Why, when we all got together and put up the money for the subscriptions to those papers and drew lots to choose which of us would go out and have an accident and collect the money. And you drew it, don't you remember?'

Utter astonishment, and a shocked astonishment at that, spread itself over Teddy Weeks's countenance. The man seemed outraged.

'I certainly remember nothing of the kind,' he said, severely. 'I cannot imagine myself for a moment consenting to become a partner to what from your own account would appear to have been a criminal conspiracy to obtain money under false pretences from a number of weekly papers.'

'But, laddie—'

'However,' said Teddy Weeks, 'if there is any truth in this story, no doubt you have documentary evidence to support it.'

Ukridge looked at me. I looked at Ukridge. There was a long silence.

'Shift-ho, old horse?' said Ukridge, sadly. 'No use staying on here.'

'No,' I replied with equal gloom. 'May as well go.'

'Glad to have seen you,' said Teddy Weeks, 'and thanks for the fruit.'

The next time I saw the man he was coming out of a manager's office in the Haymarket. He had on a new Homburg hat of a delicate pearl grey, spats to match, and a new blue flannel suit, beautifully cut, with an invisible red twill. He was looking jubilant and, as I passed him, he drew from his pocket a gold cigarette-case.

It was shortly after that, if you remember, that he made a big hit as the juvenile lead in that piece at the Apollo and started on his sensational career as a *matinée* idol.

Inside the church the organ had swelled into the familiar music of the Wedding March. A verger came out and opened the doors. The five cooks ceased their reminiscences of other and smarter weddings at which they had participated. The camera-men unshipped their cameras. The costermonger moved his barrow of vegetables a pace forward. A dishevelled and unshaven man at my side uttered a disapproving growl.

'Idle rich!' said the dishevelled man.

Out of the church came a beauteous being, leading attached to his arm another being, somewhat less beauteous.

There was no denying the spectacular effect of Teddy Weeks. He was handsomer than ever. His sleek hair, gorgeously waved, shone in the sun, his eyes were large and bright; his lissome frame, garbed in faultless morning-coat and trousers, was that of an Apollo. But his bride gave the impression that Teddy had married money. They paused in the doorway, and the camera-men became active and fussy.

'Have you got a shilling, laddie?' said Ukridge in a low, level voice.

'Why do you want a shilling?'

'Old horse,' said Ukridge, tensely, 'it is of the utmost vital importance that I have a shilling here and now.'

I passed it over. Ukridge turned to the dishevelled man, and I perceived that he held in his hand a large rich tomato of juicy and over-ripe appearance.

'Would you like to earn a bob?' Ukridge said.

'Would I!' replied the dishevelled man.

Ukridge sank his voice to a hoarse whisper.

The camera-men had finished their preparations. Teddy Weeks, his head thrown back in that gallant way which has endeared him to so many female fans, was exhibiting his celebrated teeth. The cooks, in undertones, were making adverse comments on the appearance of the bride.

'Now, please,' said one of the camera-men.

Over the heads of the crowd, well and truly aimed, whizzed a large, juicy tomato. It burst like a shell full between Teddy Weeks's expressive eyes, obliterating them in scarlet ruin. It spattered Teddy Weeks's collar, it dripped on Teddy Weeks's morning-coat. And the dishevelled man turned sharply and raced off down the street.

Ukridge grasped my arm. There was a look of deep contentment in his eyes.

'Shift-ho?' said Ukridge.

Arm-in-arm, we strolled off in the pleasant June sunshine.   *Ukridge* (1924).

Wodehouse began to prosper. In 1909 he went to New York again, the beginning of a shuttle service he kept up for many years between England and the USA, a cheap and simple boat trip in those days.

In 1914 he was in New York—bad eyesight ruled out military service—and he met and a month later married a young widow, Ethel Rowley, who brought with her a 9-year-old daughter Leonora. Leonora provided to be the delight of Wodehouse's life. She began as his stepdaughter but he immediately adopted her to make the relationship closer.

He took up golf—with his sturdy, athletic figure, candid blue eyes and amiable grin he must have been the only man in the world who looked good in plus-fours— and his prose was enriched with a new wave of golf similes:

'Over my dead body!'
'That would be a mashie-niblick shot,' said Sidney McMurdo.

Nothing Serious (1950).

'After all, golf is only a game,' said Millicent.
Women say these things without thinking. It does not mean that there is any kink in their character. They simply don't realise what they're saying.

The Clicking of Cuthbert (1922).

The least thing upsets him on the links. He misses short putts because of the uproar of the butterflies in the adjoining meadows.

The Clicking of Cuthbert (1922).

Walter clasped her to his bosom, using the interlocking grip.

A Few Quick Ones (1959).

After Wodehouse's marriage his personal life was organized which gave him even more time to write, always providing that he could duck out of his wife's parties and social occasions which he frequently managed to do. And it all went very well indeed over the next few years.

In 1915 he wrote a short story, 'Extricating Young Gussie', about a new character, a 'chinless wonder', a well-off young man-about-town whom he called Bertie Wooster. Bertie had a manservant whom Wodehouse named Jeeves. The character of Bertie Wooster then was simply that of a stage 'dude' as performed by his friend George Grossmith, plus the characteristics of a couple of Wodehouse's more irresponsible friends. Jeeves was an extension of a manservant he had already invented called Jevons and was named after a county cricketer. He only had a few lines in the original story.

It was not until ten years later, when he began to plan a new series of Jeeves and Bertie stories, that Wodehouse realized the capabilities of the characters.

Psmith overcame his adversaries because he was rich and ruthless which wasn't really Wodehouse's style, and Ukridge's schemes always failed, so both were a little limited as perpetual subjects round whom to build short stories and series. In Bertie Wodehouse had a comical narrator, which meant that with hard work the author could, potentially at any rate, make every line of the story funny and not just the action and dialogue. And in making Jeeves a brainy, omnipotent gentleman's gentleman, he had a useful and highly original character. The relationship between the two of them gave Wodehouse a new and seemingly inexhaustible well of humour:

'What ho, Jeeves,' I cried, entering the room where he waded knee-deep in suitcases and shirts and winter-suitings, like a sea-beast among rocks. 'Packing?'

'Yes, sir,' replied the honest fellow, for there are no secrets between us.

Very Good, Jeeves (1930).

Jeeves had described Gussie as disgruntled, and it was plain at a glance that the passage of time had done nothing to gruntle him.

The Mating Season (1949).

Jeeves entered—or perhaps one should say shimmered—into the room . . . tall and dark and impressive. He might have been one of the better class ambassadors or the youngish High Priest of some refined and dignified religion.

Ring For Jeeves (1953).

'Yes, sir,' said Jeeves in a low, cold voice, as if he had been bitten in the leg by a personal friend.

Carry On, Jeeves (1925).

Jeeves lugged my purple socks out of the drawer as if he were a vegetarian fishing a caterpillar out of his salad.

My Man Jeeves (1919).

'Very good,' I said coldly. 'In that case, tinkerty-tonk.'
And I meant it to sting.

Right Ho, Jeeves (1934).

The period between the wars was Wodehouse's most successful and rewarding. He became one of America's highest-paid authors and pleasantly rich, though he had no interest in spending money. He and Ethel moved continually between rented and bought houses in England, France, and the USA, but increasingly in the USA where the work was. In 1934 they left England for good and only returned on visits.

In the twenties Wodehouse, like a puppeteer assembling a repertory company, steadily added to his permanent cast of characters until he had a considerable number to call upon when required: there were the stalwarts of the Drones Club (fifty-three members are named in stories), servants (as well as Jeeves, sixty-three butlers come into various books), aunts and uncles, girl-friends, the clergy (usually nervous but worthy curates and daunting bishops), members of the nobility, and assorted extras given the names of what they habitually ate or drank, for example, Eggs, Beans, Crumpets, Brandy-and-Sodas, and Small Ports. Many members of Wodehouse's repertory company were related or knew each other so they continually popped up in each other's stories, which gave much of Wodehouse's output an agreeable coherence ; the reader felt among friends.

Among his stock of minor characters perhaps the most memorable, certainly the most productive of splendid similes, were Bertie Wooster's awesome aunts:

Aunt is calling Aunt like mastodons bellowing across primeval swamps.

The Inimitable Jeeves (1923).

For some moments there was nothing to be heard but the sloshing sound of an aunt restoring her tissues.

Ibid.

There came from without the hoof-beats of a galloping relative, and Aunt Dahlia whizzed in.

Ibid.

It is bad to be trapped in a den of slavering aunts, lashing their tails and glaring at you out of their red eyes.

The Mating Season (1949).

Aunt Agatha's demeanour now was rather like that of one who, picking daisies on the railway, has just caught the down express in the small of the back.

The Inimitable Jeeves (1923).

The sort of house you take a look at and say to yourself, 'Somebody's aunt lives there.'

Carry on, Jeeves (1925).

A great many of the stories were based upon Bertie and his friends getting themselves entangled with unsuitable girls, from whom they had to be disentangled by Jeeves.

These unsuitable girls were deemed to be so for various personal reasons:

Honoria, one of those robust, dynamic girls with the muscles of a welterweight and a laugh like a squadron of cavalry charging over a tin bridge.

Ibid.

She looked like something that might have occurred to Ibsen in one of his less frivolous moments.

Summer Lightning (1929).

Madeleine Bassett laughed the tinkling, silvery laugh which was one of the things that had got her so disliked by the better element.

The Code of the Woosters (1938).

She looked like a vicar's daughter who plays hockey and ticks off the villagers when they want to marry their deceased wives' sisters.

Laughing Gas (1936).

Veronica was radiant. Not even in the photograph taken after the Pageant in Aid of Distressed Public School Men and showing her as the Spirit of the Playing Fields of Eton had she exhibited a more bone-headed loveliness.

Full Moon (1947).

Happy, carefree marriages were rare in the World of Wodehouse. Most of the aristocrats were married and some of the Drones took the plunge but the relationships were usually wary on both sides, at best a respite in the struggle for advantage in the balance of power, or, in the case of most of the impoverished Drones, a pause in their attempts to get their hands on their wives' money.

The girls seemed to know all this and their attitude, even when they dearly loved their young man, was summed up by one adored:

'I am going to forgive him the day after tomorrow,' she said. 'Not earlier, because we must have discipline.'

The Mating Season (1949).

Babies and children were not generally treated in Wodehouse's stories as sweet bundles of joy. If they put in an appearance at all it was not in order to be cooed over but to be part of the plot. Wodehouse's characters did not, on the whole, regard the very young as nature's little benisons:

Jane regarded him with quiet intentness.

'Does mother's little chickabiddy want his nose pushed sideways?' she said. 'Very well, then.'

Nothing Serious (1950).

Introduced to his child in the nursing home, he recoiled with a startled 'Oi!' and as the days went by the feeling that he had run up against something red-hot in no way diminished. The only thing that prevented a father's love from faltering was the fact that there was in his possession a photograph of himself at the same early age, in which he, too, looked like a homicidal fried egg.

Eggs, Beans and Crumpets (1940).

'Frederick won't be staying long, will he?' Lord Emsworth asked, with a father's pathetic eagerness.

Full Moon (1947).

Wodehouse was writing at full stretch in the early twenties. His short stories were much in demand and finding plots for great quantities of stories was becoming a problem. In 1922 he had begun to write golfing stories using the clubhouse as the locale and the Oldest Member as narrator. He was also well into more Jeeves and Bertie Wooster short stories, five volumes of which were in the shops. But he needed another approach.

The answer came in 1927 with his creation of Mr Mulliner. Mr Mulliner sat in his customary chair in the bar-parlour of the Anglers' Rest and monopolized the conversation by telling—as the name of the pub might indicate—rather tall stories. He spoke with dignity, usually about something dramatic or poignant or romantic which had occurred to one of his peculiar nephews.

Each story commenced formally, with a little of the Anglers' Rest's stimulating general conversation:

The man in the corner took a sip of stout-and-mild, and proceeded to point the moral of the story which he had just told us.

'Yes, gentlemen,' he said, 'Shakespeare was right. There's a divinity that shapes our ends, rough-hew them how we will.'

We nodded. He had been speaking of a favourite dog of his which, entered by some error in a local cat show, had taken first prize in the class for short-haired tortoiseshells; and we all thought the quotation apt and apposite.

'There is, indeed,' said Mr Mulliner. 'A rather similar thing happened to my nephew Lancelot.'

'You mean to say your nephew took a prize at a cat show?'

'No, no,' said Mr Mulliner hastily. 'Certainly not. I have never deviated from the truth in my life and I hope I never shall. No Mulliner has ever taken a prize at a cat show. No Mulliner, indeed, to the best of my knowledge, has even been entered for such a competition. What I meant was that the fact that we never know what the future holds in store for us was well exemplified in the case of my nephew Lancelot, just as it was in the case of this gentleman's dog which suddenly found itself transformed for all practical purposes into a short-tailed tortoiseshell cat. It is rather a curious story, and provides a good illustration of the adage that you never can tell and that it is always darkest before the dawn.'

At the time at which my story opens (said Mr Mulliner) Lancelot, then twenty-four years of age and recently come down from Oxford, was spending a few days with old Jeremiah Briggs, the founder and proprietor of the famous Briggs' Breakfast Pickles, on the latter's yacht at Cowes . . .

'Came the Dawn', reprinted: *Mulliner Omnibus* (1927).

Wodehouse knew about The Oxford Book of Humorous Prose *in its early days of research and obligingly contributed his own theory of humour; he wrote, refreshingly, 'I think I can recognize humour when I see it but that's as far as I am prepared to go.' But when asked which items from his enormous output he would most like to see included he named two pieces. His first choice was surprising but author's favourites often are. It was a brief Mr Mulliner short story, 'From a Detective's Note Book', written for* Punch, *in which one of Mr Mulliner's odd nephews proves that Sherlock Holmes was Dr Moriarty in disguise.*

The other choice was rather different and would probably be the first choice of most Wodehouse devotees, arguably Wodehouse comedy at its best and almost certainly the most memorably funny scene to be found in any of the Jeeves and Bertie Wooster stories—Gussie Fink-Nottle presenting the prizes at the Grammar School, Market Snodsbury, from Right Ho, Jeeves.

*The plot has the classic Jeeves/Bertie construction: Bertie has returned from the French Riviera with an outré item of clothing, a white dinner-jacket with brass buttons ('these mess jackets had been all the rage—*tout ce qu'il y a de chic—on the Côte d'Azur'). *Jeeves does not approve ('I fear that you inadvertently left Cannes in the possession of a coat belonging to some other gentleman, sir . . . surely you are not proposing to wear it in England, sir?'). The young master insists. The plot then gets under way and fizzes along at great speed. Gussie Fink-Nottle, an old school friend of Bertie's, described to Jeeves as having a face like a fish ('possibly a certain suggestion of the piscine, sir'), only interest in life—newts, has fallen in love with the dread Madeleine Bassett, a girl of elfin charm ('She holds the view that the stars are God's daisy chain, that rabbits are gnomes in attendance on the Fairy Queen, and that every time a fairy blows its wee nose a baby is born, which, as we know, is not the case'). Gussie has consulted Jeeves as how best to conquer his nervousness and propose to the Bassett.*

Sub-plots then multiply. Everybody converges on Bertie's Aunt Dahlia Travers and her husband Tom in rural Market Snodsbury. Bertie undergoes indignities,

*lovers are parted, but Jeeves manipulates events and the story ends happily with
an exhausted Bertie, in bed, being served by Jeeves with a restorative omelette and
half a bot., and a last victory ('In the matter of your mess jacket, sir . . . I am
sorry to say, sir, that while I was ironing it this afternoon I was careless enough
to leave the hot instrument on it. I very much fear it will be impossible for you to
wear it again, sir.'. . .'Right ho, Jeeves.' 'Very good, sir.').*

*Wodehouse always liked to place a strong comic set-piece towards the end of his
novels and in this one he arranged for Gussie Fink-Nottle to give the prizes away
at the local grammar school. The shy Gussie is terrified, not only from lack of
self-confidence but also because a general who once gave the prizes away at Gussie's
prep-school split his trousers on the platform. Bertie (who won the Scripture prize
at his prep-school) gives Gussie a good line about the race being not always to the
swift and a joke about adenoids. Jeeves obliges with the line about education being
a matter of drawing out rather than putting in and a joke about two Irishmen
called Pat and Mike walking along Broadway.*

*Gussie is now in such a nervous state that Jeeves and Bertie decide the only hope
is to fortify him by lacing his orange juice with lashings of gin. They overdo the
gin.*

Gussie is a teetotaller.

It is a very hot afternoon:

The Grammar School at Market Snodsbury had, I understood, been built
somewhere in the year 1416, and, as with so many of these ancient foundations, there still seemed to brood over its Great Hall, where the afternoon's
festivities were to take place, not a little of the fug of the centuries. It was the
hottest day of the summer, and although somebody had opened a tentative
window or two, the atmosphere remained distinctive and individual.

In this hall the youth of Market Snodsbury had been eating its daily lunch
for a matter of five hundred years, and the flavour lingered. The air was sort
of heavy and languorous, if you know what I mean, with the scent of Young
England and boiled beef and carrots.

Aunt Dahlia, who was sitting with a bevy of the local nibs in the second
row, sighted me as I entered and waved to me to join her, but I was too
smart for that. I wedged myself in among the standees at the back, leaning
up against a chap who, from the aroma, might have been a corn chandler
or something of that order. The essence of strategy on these occasions is to
be as near the door as possible.

The hall was gaily decorated with flags and coloured paper, and the eye
was further refreshed by the spectacle of a mixed drove of boys, parents and
what not, the former running to a good deal of shiny faces and Eton collars,
the latter stressing the black-satin note rather when female, and looking as
if their coats were too tight, if male. And presently there was some applause—
sporadic, Jeeves has since told me it was—and I saw Gussie being steered by
a bearded bloke to a seat in the middle of the platform.

And I confess that as I beheld him and felt that there but for the grace of God went Bertram Wooster, a shudder ran through the frame. It all reminded me so vividly of the time I had addressed that girls' school.

Of course, looking at it dispassionately, you may say that for horror and peril there is no comparison between an almost human audience like the one before me and a mob of small girls with pigtails down their backs, and this, I concede, is true. Nevertheless, the spectacle was enough to make me feel like a fellow watching a pal going over Niagara Falls in a barrel, and the thought of what I had escaped caused everything for a moment to go black and swim before my eyes.

When I was able to see clearly once more, I perceived that Gussie was now seated. He had his hands on his knees, with his elbows out at right angles, like a nigger minstrel of the old school about to ask Mr Bones why a chicken crosses the road, and he was staring before him with a smile so fixed and pebble-beached that I should have thought that anybody could have guessed that there sat one in whom the old familiar juice was splashing up against the back of the front teeth.

In fact, I saw Aunt Dahlia, who, having assisted at so many hunting dinners in her time, is second to none as a judge of the symptoms, give a start and gaze long and earnestly. And she was just saying something to Uncle Tom on her left when the bearded bloke stepped to the footlights and started making a speech. From the fact that he spoke as if he had a hot potato in his mouth without getting the raspberry from the lads in the ringside seats, I deduced that he must be the headmaster.

With his arrival in the spotlight, a sort of perspiring resignation seemed to settle on the audience. Personally, I snuggled up against the chandler and let my attention wander. The speech was on the doings of the school during the past term, and this part of a prize-giving is always apt rather to fail to grip the visiting stranger. I mean, you know how it is. You're told that J. B. Brewster has won an Exhibition for Classics at Cat's, Cambridge, and you feel that it's one of those stories where you can't see how funny it is unless you really know the fellow. And the same applies to G. Bullett being awarded the Lady Jane Wix Scholarship at the Birmingham College of Veterinary Science.

In fact, I and the corn chandler, who was looking a bit fagged, I thought, as if he had had a hard morning chandling the corn, were beginning to doze lightly when things suddenly brisked up, bringing Gussie into the picture for the first time.

'Today,' said the bearded bloke, 'we are all happy to welcome as the guest of the afternoon Mr Fitz-Wattle—'

At the beginning of the address, Gussie had subsided into a sort of daydream, with his mouth hanging open. About half-way through, faint signs of life had begun to show. And for the last few minutes he had been trying to cross one leg over the other and failing and having another shot and failing again. But only now did he exhibit any real animation. He sat up with a jerk.

'Fink-Nottle,' he said, opening his eyes.

'Fink-Nottle.'

'Fink-Nottle.'

'I should say Fink-Nottle.'

'Of course you should, you silly ass,' said Gussie, genially. 'All right, get on with it.'

And closing his eyes, he began trying to cross his legs again.

I could see that this little spot of friction had rattled the bearded bloke a bit. He stood for a moment fumbling at the fungus with a hesitating hand. But they make these headmasters of tough stuff. The weakness passed. He came back nicely and carried on.

'We are all happy, I say, to welcome as the guest of the afternoon Mr Fink-Nottle, who has kindly consented to award the prizes. This task, as you know, is one that should have devolved upon that well-beloved and vigorous member of our board of governors, the Revd William Plomer, and we are all, I am sure, very sorry that illness at the last moment should have prevented him from being here today. But, if I may borrow a familiar metaphor from the—if I may employ a homely metaphor familiar to you all—what we lose on the swings we gain on the roundabouts.'

He paused, and beamed rather freely, to show that this was comedy. I could have told the man it was no use. The corn chandler leaned against me and muttered 'Whoddidesay?' but that was all.

It's always a nasty jar to wait for the laugh and find that the gag hasn't got across. The bearded bloke was visibly discomposed. At that, however, I think he would have got by, had he not, at this juncture, unfortunately stirred Gussie up again.

'In other words, though deprived of Mr Plomer, we have with us this afternoon Mr Fink-Nottle. I am sure that Mr Fink-Nottle's name is one that needs no introduction to you. It is, I venture, a name that is familiar to us all.'

'Not to you,' said Gussie.

And the next moment I saw what Jeeves had meant when he had described him as laughing heartily. 'Heartily' was absolutely the *mot juste*. It sounded like a gas explosion.

'You didn't seem to know it so dashed well, what, what?' said Gussie. And, reminded apparently by the word 'what' of the word 'Wattle,' he repeated the latter some sixteen times with a single inflexion.

'Wattle. Wattle, Wattle,' he concluded. 'Right-ho. Push on.'

But the bearded bloke had shot his bolt. He stood there, licked at last; and, watching closely, I could spot what he was thinking as clearly as if he had confided it to my personal ear. He wanted to sit down and call it a day, I mean, but the thought that gave him pause was that, if he did, he must then either uncork Gussie or take the Fink-Nottle speech as read—and get straight on to the actual prize-giving.

It was a dashed tricky thing, of course, to have to decide on the spur of the moment. I was reading in the paper the other day about those birds who are trying to split the atom, the nub being that they haven't the foggiest idea what will happen if they do. It may be all right. On the other hand, it may not be all right. And pretty silly a chap would feel, no doubt, if having split the atom, he suddenly found the house going up in smoke and himself torn limb from limb.

So with the bearded bloke. Whether he was abreast of the inside facts in Gussie's case, I don't know, but it was obvious to him by this time that he had run into something pretty hot. Trial gallops had shown that Gussie had his own way of doing things. Those interruptions had been enough to prove to the perspicacious that here, seated on the platform at the big binge of the season, was one who, if pushed forward to make a speech, might let himself go in a rather epoch-making manner.

On the other hand, chain him up and put a green-baize cloth over him, and where were you? The proceeding would be over about half an hour too soon.

It was, as I say, a difficult problem to have to solve, and, left to himself, I don't know what conclusion he would have come to. Personally I think he would have played it safe. As it happened, however, the thing was taken out of his hands, for at this moment, Gussie, having stretched his arms and yawned a bit, switched on that pebble-beached smile again and tacked down to the edge of the platform.

'Speech,' he said affably.

He then stood with his thumbs in the armholes of his waistcoat, waiting for the applause to die down.

It was some time before this happened, for he had got a very fine hand indeed. I suppose it wasn't often that the boys of Market Snodsbury Grammar School came across a man public-spirited enough to call their headmaster a silly ass, and they showed their appreciation in no uncertain manner. Gussie may have been one over the eight, but as far as the majority of those present were concerned he was sitting on top of the world.

'Boys,' said Gussie, 'I mean ladies and gentlemen and boys, I will not detain you long, but I propose on this occasion to feel compelled to say a few auspicious words. Ladies—boys and gentlemen—we have all listened with interest to the remarks of our friend here who forgot to shave this morning— I don't know his name , but then he didn't know mine—Fitz-Wattle, I mean, absolutely absurd—which squares things up a bit—and we are all sorry that the Reverend What-ever-he-was-called should be dying of adenoids, but after all, here today, gone tomorrow, and all flesh is as grass, and what not, but that wasn't what I wanted to say. What I wanted to say was this—and I say it confidently—without fear of contradiction—I say, in short, I am happy to be here on this auspicious occasion and I take much pleasure in kindly awarding the prizes, consisting of the handsome books you see laid out on that table. As Shakespeare says, there are sermons in books, stones in the running brooks, or, rather, the other way about, and there you have it in a nutshell.'

It went well, and I wasn't surprised. I couldn't quite follow some of it, but anybody could see that it was real ripe stuff, and I was amazed that even the course of treatment he had been taking could have rendered so normally tongue-tied a dumb brick as Gussie capable of it.

It just shows, what any member of Parliament will tell you, that if you want real oratory, the preliminary noggin is essential. Unless you are pie-eyed you cannot hope to grip.

'Gentlemen,' said Gussie, 'I mean ladies and gentlemen and, of course, boys, what a wonderful world this is. A beautiful world, full of happiness on every side. Let me tell you a little story. Two Irishmen, Pat and Mike, were walking along Broadway, and one said to the other, "Begorrah, the race is not always to the swift," and the other replied, "Faith and begob, education is a drawing out not a putting in."'

I must say it seemed to me the rottenest story I had ever heard, and I was surprised that Jeeves should have considered it worth shoving into a speech. However, when I taxed him with this later, he said that Gussie had altered the plot a good deal, and I dare say that accounts for it.

At any rate, this was the *conte* as Gussie told it, and when I say that it got a very fair laugh, you will understand what a popular favourite he had become with the multitude. There might be a bearded bloke or so on the platform and a small section in the second row who were wishing the speaker would conclude his remarks and resume his seat, but the audience as a whole was for him solidly.

There was applause, and a voice cried: 'Hear, hear!'

'Yes,' said Gussie, 'it is a beautiful world. The sky is blue, the birds are singing, there is optimism everywhere. And why not, boys and ladies and gentlemen? I'm happy, you're happy, we're all happy, even the meanest Irishman that walks along Broadway. Though, as I say, there were two of them—Pat and Mike, one drawing out, the other putting in. I should like you boys, taking the time from me, to give three cheers for this beautiful world. All together now.'

Presently the dust settled down and the plaster stopped falling from the ceiling, and he went on.

'People who say it isn't a beautiful world don't know what they're talking about. Driving here in the car today to award the kind prizes, I was reluctantly compelled to tick off my host on this very point. Old Tom Travers. You will see him sitting there in the second row next to the very large lady in beige.'

He pointed helpfully, and the hundred or so Market Snodburyians who craned their necks in the direction indicated were able to observe Uncle Tom blushing prettily.

'I ticked him off properly, the poor fish. He expressed the opinion that the world was in a deplorable state. I said, "Don't talk rot, old Tom Travers." "I am not accustomed to talk rot," he said. "Then for a beginner," I said, "you do it dashed well." And I think you will admit, boys and ladies and gentlemen, that that was telling him.'

The audience seemed to agree with him. The point went big. The voice that had said 'Hear, hear,' said 'Hear, hear' again, and my corn chandler hammered the floor vigorously with a large-size walking stick.

'Well, boys,' resumed Gussie, having shot his cuffs and smirked horribly, 'this is the end of the summer term, and many of you, no doubt, are leaving the school. And I don't blame you, because there's a froust in here you could cut with a knife. You are going out into the great world. Soon many of you will be walking along Broadway. And what I want to impress upon you is that, however much you may suffer from adenoids, you must all use every effort to prevent yourselves becoming pessimists and talking rot like old Tom Travers. There in the second row. The fellow with a face rather like a walnut.'

He paused to allow those who wished to do so to refresh themselves with another look at Uncle Tom, and I found myself musing in some perplexity. Long association with the members of the Drones has put me pretty well in touch with the various ways in which an overdose of the blushful Hippocrene can take the individual, but I had never seen anyone react quite as Gussie was doing.

There was a sort of snap about his work which I had never witnessed before, even in Barmy Fotheringay-Phipps on New Year's Eve.

Jeeves, when I discussed the matter with him later, said it was something to do with inhibitions, if I caught the word correctly, and the suppression of, I think he said, the ego. What he meant, I gathered, was that, owing to the fact that Gussie had just completed a five-year stretch of blameless seclusion among the newts, all the goofiness which ought to have been spread out thin over those five years came to the surface on this occasion in a lump—or, if you prefer to put it that way, like a tidal wave.

There may be something in this. Jeeves generally knows.

Anyway, be that as it may, I was dashed glad I had had the shrewdness to keep out of that second row. It might be unworthy of the prestige of a Wooster to squash in among the proletariat in the standing-room-only section, but at least, I felt, I was out of the danger zone. So thoroughly had Gussie got it up his nose by now that it seemed to me that had he sighted me he might have become personal about even an old school friend.

'If there's one thing I can't stand,' proceeded Gussie, 'it's a pessimist. Be optimists, boys. You all know the difference between an optimist and a pessimist. An optimist is a man who—well, take the case of two Irishmen walking along Broadway. One is an optimist and one a pessimist, just as one's name is Pat and the other's Mike . . . Why, hello, Bertie; I didn't know you were here.'

Too late, I endeavoured to go to earth behind the chandler, only to discover that there was no chandler there. Some appointment suddenly remembered—possibly a promise to his wife that he would be home to tea—had caused him to ooze away while my attention was elsewhere, leaving me right out in the open.

Between me and Gussie, who was now pointing in an offensive manner, there was nothing but a sea of interested faces looking up at me.

'Now there,' boomed Gussie, 'is an instance of what I mean. Boys and ladies and gentlemen, take a good look at that object standing up there at the back—morning coat, trousers as worn, quiet grey tie, and carnation in buttonhole—you can't miss him. Bertie Wooster, that is, and as foul a pessimist as ever bit a tiger. I tell you I despise that man. And why do I despise him? Because, boys and ladies and gentlemen, he is a pessimist. His attitude is defeatist. When I told him I was going to address you this afternoon, he tried to dissuade me. And do you know why he tried to dissuade me? Because he said my trousers would split up the back.'

The cheers that greeted this were the loudest yet. Anything about splitting trousers went straight to the simple hearts of the young scholars of Market Snodsbury Grammar School. Two in the row in front of me turned purple, and a small lad with freckles seated beside them asked me for my autograph.

'Let me tell you a story about Bertie Wooster.'

A Wooster can stand a good deal, but he cannot stand having his name bandied in a public place. Picking my feet up softly, I was in the very process of executing a quiet sneak for the door, when I perceived that the bearded bloke had at last decided to apply the closure.

Why he hadn't done so before is beyond me. Spellbound, I take it. And, of course, when a chap is going like a breeze with the public, as Gussie had been, it's not so dashed easy to chip in. However, the prospect of hearing another of Gussie's anecdotes seemed to have done the trick. Rising rather as I had risen from my bench at the beginning of that painful scene with Tuppy in the twilight, he made a leap for the table, snatched up a book and came bearing down on the speaker.

He touched Gussie on the arm, and Gussie, turning sharply and seeing a large bloke with a beard apparently about to bean him with a book, sprang back in an attitude of self-defence.

'Perhaps, as time is getting on, Mr Fink-Nottle, we had better—'

'Oh, ah,' said Gussie, getting the trend. He relaxed. 'The prizes, eh? Of course, yes. Rightho. Yes, might as well be shoving along with it. What's this one?'

'Spelling and Dictation—P. K. Purvis,' announced the bearded bloke.

'Spelling and Dictation—P. K. Purvis,' echoed Gussie, as if he were calling coals. 'Forward, P. K. Purvis.'

Now that the whistle had been blown on his speech, it seemed to me that there was no longer any need for the strategic retreat which I had been planning. I had no wish to tear myself away unless I had to. I mean, I had told Jeeves that this binge would be fraught with interest, and it was fraught with interest. There was a fascination about Gussie's methods which gripped and made one reluctant to pass the thing up provided personal innuendoes were steered clear of. I decided, accordingly, to remain, and presently there was a musical squeaking and P. K. Purvis climbed the platform.

The spelling-and-dictation champ was about three foot six in his squeaking shoes, with a pink face and sandy hair. Gussie patted his hair. He seemed to have taken an immediate fancy to the lad.

'You P. K. Purvis?'

'Sir, yes, sir.'

'It's a beautiful world, P. K. Purvis.'

'Sir, yes, sir.'

'Ah, you've noticed, have you? Good. Married, by any chance?'

'Sir, no, sir.'

'Get married, P. K. Purvis,' said Gussie earnestly. 'It's the only life . . . Well, here's your book. Looks rather bilge to me, from a glance at the title page, but, such as it is, here you are.'

P. K. Purvis squeaked off amidst sporadic applause, but one could not fail to note that the sporadic was followed by a rather strained silence. It was evident that Gussie was striking something of a new note in Market Snodsbury scholastic circles. Looks were exchanged between parent and parent. The bearded bloke had the air of one who has drained the bitter cup. As for Aunt Dahlia, her demeanour now told only too clearly that her last doubts had been resolved and her verdict was in. I saw her whisper to the Bassett, who sat on her right, and the Bassett nodded silently and looked like a fairy about to shed a tear and add another star to the Milky Way.

Gussie, after the departure of P. K. Purvis, had fallen into a sort of daydream and was standing with his mouth open and his hands in his pockets. Becoming abruptly aware that a fat kid in knickerbockers was at his elbow, he started violently.

'Hello!' he said, visibly shaken. 'Who are you?'

'This,' said the bearded bloke, 'is R. V. Smethurst.'

'What's he doing here?' asked Gussie suspiciously.

'You are presenting him with the drawing prize, Mr Fink-Nottle.'

This apparently struck Gussie as a reasonable explanation. His face cleared.

'That's right too,' he said . . . 'Well, here it is, cocky. You off?' he said as the kid prepared to withdraw.

'Sir, yes, sir.'

'Wait, R. V. Smethurst. No so fast. Before you go, there is a question I wish to ask you.'

But the bearded bloke's aim now seemed to be to rush the ceremonies a bit. He hustled R. V. Smethurst off stage rather like a chucker-out in a pub regretfully ejecting an old and respected customer, and started paging G. G. Simmons. A moment later the latter was up and coming, and conceive my emotion when it was announced that the subject on which he had clicked was Scripture knowledge. One of us, I mean to say.

G. G. Simmons was an unpleasant, perky-looking stripling, mostly front teeth and spectacles, but I gave him a big hand. We Scripture-knowledge sharks stick together.

Gussie, I was sorry to see, didn't like him. There was in his manner, as he regarded G. G. Simmons, none of the chumminess which had marked it during his interview with P. K. Purvis or, in a somewhat lesser degree, with R. V. Smethurst. He was cold and distant.

'Well, G. G. Simmons.'

'Sir, yes, sir.'

'What do you mean—sir, yes, sir? Dashed silly thing to say. So you've won the Scripture-knowledge prize, have you?'

'Sir, yes, sir.'

'Yes,' said Gussie. 'You look just the sort of little tick who would. And yet,' he said, pausing and eyeing the child keenly, 'how are we to know that this has all been open and above board? Let me test you, G. G. Simmons. Who was What's-his-name—the chap who begat Thingummy? Can you answer me that, Simmons?'

'Sir, no, sir.'

Gussie turned to the bearded bloke.

'Fishy,' he said. 'Very fishy. This boy seems to be entirely lacking in Scripture knowledge.'

The bearded bloke passed a hand across his forehead.

'I can assure you, Mr Fink-Nottle, that every care was taken to ensure a correct marking and that Simmons out-distanced his competitors by a wide margin.'

'Well, if you say so,' said Gussie doubtfully. 'All right, G. G. Simmons, take your prize.'

'Sir, thank you, sir.'

'But let me tell you that there's nothing to stick on side about in winning a prize for Scripture knowledge. Bertie Wooster—'

I don't know when I've had a nastier shock. I had been going on the assumption that, now that they had stopped him making his speech, Gussie's fangs had been drawn, as you might say. To duck my head down and resume my edging towards the door was with me the work of a moment.

'Bertie Wooster won the Scripture-knowledge prize at a kids' school we were at together, and you know what he's like. But, of course, Bertie frankly cheated. He succeeded in scrounging that Scripture-knowledge trophy over the heads of better men by means of some of the rawest and most brazen swindling methods ever witnessed even at a school where such things were common. If that man's pockets, as he entered the examination-room, were not stuffed to bursting point with lists of the kings of Judah—'

I heard no more. A moment later I was out in God's air, fumbling with a fevered foot at the self-starter of the old car.

The engine raced. The clutch slid into position. I tooted and drove off.

My ganglions were still vibrating as I ran the car into the stables of Brinkley Court, and it was a much-shaken Bertram who tottered up to his room to change into something loose. Having donned flannels, I lay down on the bed for a bit, and I suppose I must have dozed off, for the next thing I remember is finding Jeeves at my side.

I sat up.

'My tea, Jeeves?'

'No, sir. It is nearly dinner-time.'

The mists cleared away.

'I must have been asleep.'

'Yes, sir.'

'Nature taking its toll of the exhausted frame.'

'Yes, sir.'

'And enough to make it.'

'Yes, sir.'. . .

There was a pause.

'Well, Jeeves, it was certainly one of those afternoons, what?'

'Yes, sir.'

'I cannot recall one more packed with incident. And I left before the finish.'

'Yes, sir. I observed your departure.'

'You couldn't blame me for withdrawing.'

'No, sir. Mr Fink-Nottle had undoubtedly become embarrassingly personal.'

'Was there much of it after I went?'

'No, sir. The proceedings terminated very shortly. Mr Fink-Nottle's remarks with reference to Master G. G. Simmons brought about an early closure.'

'But he had finished his remarks about G. G. Simmons.'

'Only temporarily, sir. He resumed them immediately after your departure. If you recollect, sir, he had already proclaimed himself suspicious of Master Simmons's bona fides, and he now proceeded to deliver a violent verbal attack upon the young gentleman, asserting that it was impossible for him to have won the Scripture-knowledge prize without systematic cheating on an impressive scale. He went so far as to suggest that Master Simmons was well known to the police.'

'Golly, Jeeves!'

'Yes, sir. The words did create a considerable sensation. The reaction of those present to this accusation I should describe as mixed. The young students appeared pleased and applauded vigorously, but Master Simmons's mother rose from her seat and addressed Mr Fink-Nottle in terms of strong protest.'

'Did Gussie seem taken back? Did he recede from his position?'

'No, sir. He said that he could see it all now, and hinted at a guilty liaison between Master Simmons's mother and the headmaster, accusing the latter of having cooked the marks, as his expression was, in order to gain favour with the former.'

'You don't mean that?'

'Yes, sir.'

'Egad, Jeeves! And then—'

'And then they sang the national anthem, sir.'

'Surely not?'

'Yes, sir.'

'At a moment like that?'

'Yes, sir.'

'Well, you were there and you know, of course, but I should have thought the last thing Gussie and this woman would have done in the circs. would have been to start singing duets.'

'You misunderstand me, sir. It was the entire company who sang. The headmaster turned to the organist and said something to him in a low voice. Upon which the latter began to play the national anthem, and the proceedings terminated.'

Right Ho, Jeeves (1934).

In 1939 Wodehouse was honoured by Oxford University with the degree of Hon. D.Litt., Oxon. He came to Oxford for the graduation ceremony and it turned out to be the last time he saw England.

When the war broke out Wodehouse and Ethel ill-advisedly decided to stay in their house in Le Touquet. When the German forces overran France, Wodehouse was arrested as an enemy alien and taken away to a camp. A few months before he was due to be freed—all detainees were released when they reached the age of 60— Wodehouse made an extremely silly and grave error of judgement. In order to reassure his American friends that he was all right—America was not at war with Germany—he wrote and recorded five talks, to be broadcast on American radio, giving a funny account of his life in internment.

Wodehouse was pleased with the recordings. It was a chance to make the public laugh again, he mocked the Germans, and he managed to represent the looking-on-the-bright-side, no-whining spirit of his hut-mates. The broadcasts went well in America where it seems the War Department used them in its Intelligence School at Camp Ritchie as models of subtle anti-Nazi propaganda.

It all went disastrously wrong in Britain. Somebody in Goebbels's Ministry realized that a propaganda coup had dropped into their hands and broadcast the recordings to Britain. A storm broke over Wodehouse's head.

The journalist Cassandra (William Connor), on Government instructions, wrote a vicious and inaccurate attack on Wodehouse in the Daily Mirror *and broadcast another similar diatribe on the BBC. This too was such a squalid personal attack that the BBC governors refused to transmit it but were ordered to do so by the Government. No official action could be taken because upon investigation it emerged that Wodehouse had, in fact, done nothing legally wrong. Writers sprang to his defence. Major Malcolm Muggeridge officially reported on the whole affair, interviewed everybody concerned, and exonerated Wodehouse from guilt.*

But a cloud still hovered over the name of Wodehouse. The general public, also politicians, lawyers, academics, and others too important and busy to read widely, tended to react rather vaguely to the name of Wodehouse with some remark like: 'Oh, yes—wasn't he a traitor or something?' or, 'Writer bloke who did a Lord Haw-Haw, wasn't he?,' or, 'Wasn't he a Nazi?'

The notion of the gentle, kind, shy, argument-hating, leave-me-alone-to-get-on-with-my-work recluse being a closet Nazi does not make any kind of sense.

Wodehouse's appalling error of judgement was due to just the factors which would have got him drummed out of the Nazi Party on the Tuesday after he had joined: apart, possibly, from how his current plot was shaping and the state of the musical theatre, there was nothing at all he felt strongly about but the public-school cricket results. He was a kind of holy innocent; his crime was being unable to hate anybody, not even the enemy.

And not even Cassandra, even after the columnist had attacked him so viciously and unfairly. An enterprising editor got the two of them together in New York over lunch expecting fireworks but Wodehouse immediately took to Cassandra. When Wodehouse heard that Evelyn Waugh was going to speak on the BBC about the affair he wrote a letter asking Waugh not to be nasty about Cassandra who seemed to him rather a nice chap. It seems that during the lunch Wodehouse discovered that Cassandra loved cats. Some Nazi.

So, what with the mood of the British Government, plus the early tragic death of Leonora, Wodehouse and Ethel made their home in America after the war and never returned to Britain. At the age of 74 Wodehouse became an American citizen and held dual nationality.

The Wodehouses moved to Remsenburg, on the tip of Long Island. Ethel collected up any stray dog or cat lucky enough to have wandered in for food and bought another basket to house it. Wodehouse wrote, and worried whether he could get the last page funnier, and went for walks with the dogs.

In January 1975 the British Government, in an extremely rare moment when a burst of common-sense came together with the awareness of literary genius in its bailiwick, honoured Wodehouse at last with a knighthood.

Sir Pelham Wodehouse, KBE, aged 93, was too frail to make the journey to London to be dubbed. Indeed, the next month he was taken to hospital with a complicated skin and circulatory problem. Typically, he took with him the book he was then working on, Sunset at Blandings, *so that being ill would not mean he would have to stop writing. A few days later, on 14 February 1975, he got out of bed to cross the room and died.*

The first excerpt in this book was chosen for two reasons and there are two reasons for picking the last, the short story Lord Emsworth and the Girl Friend.

First, it lays a claim to being the most autobiographical of Wodehouse's stories.

There are conflicting schools of thought as to how much of the Wodehouse world is fantasy and how much is autobiographical. The fantasy theory is held by J. B. Priestley, George Orwell, and others but has been knocked on the head recently by the diligent researches of Lt.-Col. Murphy who has discovered that almost every place and person in the works can be traced back to Wodehouse's past. Wodehouse himself, never a theorist or an intellectual about these matters ('Isn't it extra-ordinary how these fellows always want to dissect and analyse. I should have thought that anyone who wrote himself would realize that a writer just sits down and writes'), cheerily explained that there was nothing Freudian about his choice of subject-matter—he wrote about Bertie and Lord Emsworth because he was in America at the time and as he was no good at writing American stories he wrote the sort of stuff which Americans found funny about the British, i.e. barmy old Earls and silly asses (until very recently, not-very-good American films indicated that a character was British by having him say things like 'Pip-pip, old fruit').

And Wodehouse made Aunts beasts not in order to wreak revenge for childhood misery at the hands of aunts but because his stories needed female villains and, as he pointed out, in comedy you cannot have villainous mothers.

The truth probably lies half-way in that many of his characters and places came out of his memory and were then transformed by his imagination.

What is evident is that in to the character of Lord Emsworth, Wodehouse put much of himself: the agony of having to get dressed up and waste valuable time being social; the disinclination to argue with anybody (he once tried to arrange with Guy Bolton that should one of them be talked about insultingly, the other would not argue but agree and, if possible, add details); the dislike of facing the human race, singly or in bulk, at any time; the sublime unworldliness, as demonstrated by Lord Emsworth talking to the steward of his club:

'Tell me Adams, have I eaten my cheese?'

'Not yet, your Lordship. I was about to send the waiter for it.'

'Never mind. Tell him to bring the bill instead. I remember that I have an appointment. I must not be late.'

'Shall I take the fork, your Lordship?'

'The fork?'

'Your Lordship has inadvertently put a fork in your coat-pocket.'

Lord Emsworth felt in the pocket indicated, and, with the air of an inexpert conjuror whose trick has succeeded contrary to his expectations, produced a silver-plated fork.

Something Fresh (1915).

Lord Emsworth's whole life was organized for him by an extremely domineering woman, his sister Lady Constance, and so was Wodehouse's, in his case by Ethel.

Ethel was no ogre like Constance, but nevertheless she ran everything to do with the Wodehouse home, took charge of all the money, negotiated the Hollywood deals, bought and sold their houses. Both Wodehouse and Lord Emsworth badly needed looking after.

And there is Lord Emsworth's girl friend in the story. Wodehouse's step-daughter Leonora was a long way from being like his Lordship's cockney friend externally but the deep pleasure which the cockney girl brings to Lord Emsworth might well be a little tribute from Wodehouse to Leonora for the pleasure which she had always brought him. It is the one story in which Wodehouse allows himself to mix a touch of sentiment with the humour.

The second reason for ending with this story is the best possible reason, the quality of it.

Rudyard Kipling told the novelist Ian Hay that it was one of the most perfect short stories he had ever read:

LORD EMSWORTH AND THE GIRL FRIEND

The day was so warm, so fair, so magically a thing of sunshine and blue skies and bird-song that anyone acquainted with Clarence, ninth Earl of Emsworth, and aware of his liking for fine weather, would have pictured him going about the place on this summer morning with a beaming smile and an uplifted heart. Instead of which, humped over the breakfast table, he was directing at a blameless kippered herring a look of such intense bitterness that the fish seemed to sizzle beneath it. For it was August Bank Holiday, and Blandings Castle on August Bank Holiday became, in his Lordship's opinion, a miniature Inferno.

This was the day when his park and grounds broke out into a noisome rash of swings, roundabouts, marquees, toy balloons and paper bags; when a tidal wave of the peasantry and its squealing young engulfed those haunts of immemorial peace. On August Bank Holiday he was not allowed to potter pleasantly about his gardens in an old coat: forces beyond his control shoved him into a stiff collar and a top hat and told him to go out and be genial. And in the cool of the quiet evenfall they put him on a platform and made him make a speech. To a man with a day like that in front of him fine weather was a mockery.

His sister, Lady Constance Keeble, looked brightly at him over the coffee-pot.

'What a lovely morning!' she said.

Lord Emsworth's gloom deepened. He chafed at being called upon—by this woman of all others—to behave as if everything was for the jolliest in the jolliest of all possible worlds. But for his sister Constance and her hawk-like vigilance, he might, he thought, have been able at least to dodge the top hat.

'Have you got your speech ready?'

'Yes.'

'Well, mind you learn it by heart this time and don't stammer and dodder as you did last year.'

Lord Emsworth pushed plate and kipper away. He had lost his desire for food.

'And don't forget you have to go to the village this morning to judge the cottage gardens.'

'All right, all right, all right,' said his lordship testily. 'I've not forgotten.'

'I think I will come to the village with you. There are a number of those Fresh Air London children staying there now, and I must warn them to behave properly when they come to the Fête this afternoon. You know what London children are. McAllister says he found one of them in the gardens the other day, picking his flowers.'

At any other time the news of this outrage would have affected Lord Emsworth profoundly. But now, so intense was his self-pity, he did not even shudder. He drank coffee with the air of a man who regretted that it was not hemlock.

'By the way, McAllister was speaking to me again last night about that gravel path through the yew alley. He seems very keen on it.'

'Glug!' said Lord Emsworth—which, as any philologist will tell you, is the sound which peers of the realm make when stricken to the soul while drinking coffee.

Concerning Glasgow, that great commercial and manufacturing city in the county of Lanarkshire in Scotland, much has been written. So lyrically does the *Encyclopaedia Britannica* deal with the place that it covers twenty-seven pages before it can tear itself away and go on to Glass, Glastonbury, Glatz and Glauber. The only aspect of it, however, which immediately concerns the present historian is the fact that the citizens it breeds are apt to be grim, dour, persevering, tenacious men; men with red whiskers who know what they want and mean to get it. Such a one was Angus McAllister, head-gardener at Blandings Castle.

For years Angus McAllister had set before himself as his earthly goal the construction of a gravel path through the Castle's famous yew alley. For years he had been bringing the project to the notice of his employer, though in anyone less whiskered the latter's unconcealed loathing would have caused embarrassment. And now, it seemed, he was at it again.

'Gravel path!' Lord Emsworth stiffened through the whole length of his stringy body. Nature, he had always maintained, intended a yew alley to be carpeted with a mossy growth. And, whatever Nature felt about it, he personally was dashed if was going to have men with Clydeside accents and faces like dissipated potatoes coming along and mutilating that lovely expanse of green velvet. 'Gravel path, indeed! Why not asphalt? Why not a few hoardings with advertisements of liver pills and a filling-station? That's what the man would really like.'

Lord Emsworth felt bitter, and when he felt bitter he could be terribly sarcastic.

'Well, I think it's a good idea,' said his sister. 'One could go there in wet weather then. Damp moss is ruinous to shoes.'

Lord Emsworth rose. He could bear no more of this. He left the table, the room and the house and, reaching the yew alley some minutes later, was revolted to find it infested by Angus McAllister in person. The head-gardener was standing gazing at the moss like a high priest of some ancient religion about to stick the gaff into the human sacrifice.

'Morning, McAllister,' said Lord Emsworth coldly.

'Good morrrrning, your lorrudsheep.'

There was a pause. Angus McAllister, extending a foot that looked like a violin-case, pressed it on the moss. The meaning of the gesture was plain. It expressed contempt, dislike, a generously anti-moss spirit: and Lord Emsworth, wincing, surveyed the man unpleasantly through his pince-nez. Though not often given to theological speculation, he was wondering why Providence, if obliged to make head-gardeners, had found it necessary to make them so Scotch. In the case of Angus McAllister, why, going a step farther, have made him a human being at all? All the ingredients of a first-class mule simply thrown away. He felt that he might have liked McAllister if he had been a mule.

'I was speaking to her leddyship yesterday.'

'Oh?'

'About the gravel path I was speaking to her leddyship.'

'Oh?'

'Her leddyship likes the notion fine.'

'Indeed!'

Lord Emsworth's face had turned a lively pink, and he was about to release the blistering words which were forming themselves in his mind when suddenly he caught the head-gardener's eye and paused. Angus McAllister was looking at him in a peculiar manner, and he knew what that look meant. Just one crack, his eye was saying—in Scotch, of course—just one crack out of you and I tender my resignation. And with a sickening shock it came home to Lord Emsworth how completely he was in this man's clutches.

He shuffled miserably. Yes, he was helpless. Except for that kink about gravel paths, Angus McAllister was a head-gardener in a thousand, and he needed him. He could not do without him. That, unfortunately had been proved by experiment. Once before, at a time when they were grooming for the Agricultural Show that pumpkin which had subsequently romped home so gallant a winner, he had dared to flout McAllister. And McAllister had resigned, and he had been forced to plead—yes, plead—with him to come back. An employer cannot hope to do this sort of thing and still rule with an iron hand. Filled with the coward rage that dares to burn but does not dare to blaze, Lord Emsworth coughed a cough which was undisguisedly a bronchial white flag.

'I'll—er—I'll think it over, McAllister.'

'Mphm.'

'I have to go to the village now. I will see you later.'

'Mphm.'

'Meanwhile, I will—er—think it over.'

'Mphm.'

The task of judging the floral displays in the cottage gardens of the little village of Blandings Parva was one to which Lord Emsworth had looked forward with pleasurable anticipation. It was the sort of job he liked. But now, even though he had managed to give his sister Constance the slip and was free from her threatened society, he approached the task with a downcast spirit. It is always unpleasant for a proud man to realize that he is no longer captain of his soul; that he is to all intents and purposes ground beneath the number twelve heel of a Glaswegian head-gardener, and, brooding on this, he judged the cottage gardens with a distrait eye. It was only when he came to the last on his list that anything like animation crept into his demeanour.

This, he perceived, peering over its rickety fence, was not at all a bad little garden. It demanded closer inspection. He unlatched the gate and pottered in. And a dog, dozing behind a water-butt, opened one eye and looked at him. It was one of those hairy, nondescript dogs, and its gaze was cold, wary and suspicious, like that of a stockbroker who thinks someone is going to play the confidence trick on him.

Lord Emsworth did not notice the animal. He had pottered to a bed of wallflowers and now, stooping, he took a sniff at them.

As sniffs go, it was an innocent sniff, but the dog for some reason appeared to read into it criminality of a high order. All the indignant householder in him woke in a flash. The next moment the world had become full of hideous noises, and Lord Emsworth's preoccupation was swept away in a passionate desire to save his ankles from harm.

As these chronicles of Blandings Castle have already shown, he was not at his best with strange dogs. Beyond saying 'Go away, sir!' and leaping to and fro with an agility surprising in one of his years, he had accomplished little in the direction of a reasoned plan of defence when the cottage door opened and a girl came out.

'Hey!' cried the girl.

And on the instant, at the mere sound of her voice, the mongrel, suspending hostilities, bounded at the new-comer and writhed on its back at her feet with all four legs in the air. The spectacle reminded Lord Emsworth irresistibly of his own behaviour when in the presence of Angus McAllister.

He blinked at his preserver. She was a small girl, of uncertain age—possibly twelve or thirteen, though a combination of London fogs and early cares had given her face a sort of wizened motherliness which in some odd way caused his lordship from the first to look on her as belonging to his own generation. She was the type of girl you see in back streets carrying a baby nearly as large as herself and still retaining enough energy to lead one little brother by the hand and shout recriminations at another in the distance. Her cheeks shone from recent soaping, and she was dressed in a velveteen frock which was obviously the pick of her wardrobe. Her hair, in defiance of the prevailing mode, she wore drawn tightly back in a short pigtail.

'Er—thank you,' said Lord Emsworth.

'Thank you, sir,' said the girl.

For what she was thanking him, his lordship was not able to gather. Later, as their acquaintance ripened, he was to discover that this strange gratitude was a habit with his new friend. She thanked everybody for everything. At the moment, the mannerism surprised him. He continued to blink at her through his pince-nez.

Lack of practice had rendered Lord Emsworth a little rusty in the art of making conversation to members of the other sex. He sought in his mind for topics.

'Fine day.'

'Yes, sir. Thank you, sir.'

'Are you'—Lord Emsworth furtively consulted his list—'are you the daughter of—ah—Ebenezer Sprockett?' he asked, thinking, as he had often thought before, what ghastly names some of his tenantry possessed.

'No, sir, I'm from London, sir.'

'Ah? London, eh? Pretty warm it must be there.' He paused. Then, remembering a formula of his youth: 'Er—been out much this Season?'

'No, sir.'

'Everybody out of town now, I suppose? What part of London?'

'Drury Lane, sir.'

'What's your name? Eh, what?'

'Gladys, sir. Thank you, sir. This is Ern.'

A small boy had wandered out of the cottage, a rather hard-boiled specimen with freckles, bearing surprisingly in his hand a large and beautiful bunch of flowers. Lord Emsworth bowed courteously and with the addition of this third party to the *tête-à-tête*, felt more at his ease.

'How do you do?' he said. 'What pretty flowers.'

With her brother's advent Gladys, also, had lost diffidence and gained conversational aplomb.

'A treat, ain't they?' she agreed eagerly. 'I got 'em for 'im up at the big 'ahse. Coo! The old josser the plice belongs to didn't arf chase me. 'E found me picking 'em and he sharted somefin at me and came runnin' after me, but I copped 'im on the shin wiv a stone and 'e stopped to rub it and I come away.'

Lord Emsworth might have corrected her impression that Blandings Castle and its gardens belonged to Angus McAllister, but his mind was so filled with admiration and gratitude that he refrained from doing so. He looked at the girl almost reverently. Not content with controlling savage dogs with a mere word, this super-woman actually threw stones at Angus McAllister—a thing which he had never been able to nerve himself to do in an association which had lasted nine years—and, what was more, copped him on the shin with them. What nonsense, Lord Emsworth felt, the papers talked about the Modern Girl. If this was a specimen, the Modern Girl was the highest point the sex had yet reached.

'Ern,' said Gladys, changing the subject, 'is wearin' 'air-oil todiy.'

Lord Emsworth had already observed this and had, indeed, been moving to windward as she spoke.

'For the Feet,' explained Gladys.

'For the feet?' It seemed unusual.

'For the Feet in the pork this afternoon.'

'Oh, you are going to the Fête?'

'Yes, sir, thank you, sir.'

For the first time, Lord Emsworth found himself regarding that grisly social event with something approaching favour.

'We must look out for one another there,' he said cordially. 'You will remember me again? I shall be wearing'—he gulped—'a top hat.'

'Ern's going to wear a stror penamaw that's been give 'im.'

Lord Emsworth regarded the lucky young devil with frank envy. He rather fancied he knew that panama. It had been his constant companion for some six years and then had been torn from him by his sister Constance and handed over to the vicar's wife for her rummage-sale.

He sighed.

'Well, good-bye.'

'Good-bye, sir, thank you, sir.'

Lord Emsworth walked pensively out of the garden and, turning into the little street, encountered Lady Constance.

'Oh, there you are, Clarence.'

'Yes,' said Lord Emsworth, for such was the case.

'Have you finished judging the gardens?'

'Yes.'

'I am just going into this end cottage here. The vicar tells me there is a little girl from London staying there. I want to warn her to behave this afternoon. I have spoken to the others.'

Lord Emsworth drew himself up. His pince-nez were slightly askew, but despite this his gaze was commanding and impressive.

'Well, mind what you say,' he said authoritatively. 'None of your district-visiting stuff, Constance.'

'What do you mean?'

'You know what I mean. I have the greatest respect for the young lady to whom you refer. She behaved on a certain recent occasion—on two recent occasions—with notable gallantry and resource, and I won't have her bally-ragged. Understand that!'

*

The technical title of the orgy which broke out annually on the first Monday in August in the park of Blandings Castle was the Blandings Parva School Treat, and it seemed to Lord Emsworth, wanly watching the proceedings from under the shadow of his top hat, that if this was the sort of thing schools looked on as pleasure he and they were mentally poles apart. A function like the Blandings Parva School Treat blurred his conception of Man as Nature's Final Word.

The decent sheep and cattle to whom this park normally belonged had been hustled away into regions unknown, leaving the smooth expanse of turf to children whose vivacity scared Lord Emsworth and adults who appeared to him to have cast aside all dignity and every other noble quality which goes to make a one hundred per cent British citizen. Look at Mrs Rossiter over there, for instance, the wife of Jno. Rossiter, Provisions, Groceries and Home-made Jams. On any other day of the year, when you met her, Mrs Rossiter was a nice, quiet, docile woman who gave at the knees respectfully as you passed. Today, flushed in the face and with her bonnet on one side, she seemed to have gone completely native. She was wandering to and fro drinking lemonade from a bottle and employing her mouth, when not so occupied, in making a devastating noise with what he believed was termed a squeaker.

The injustice of the thing stung Lord Emsworth. This park was his own private park. What right had people to come and blow squeakers in it? How would Mrs Rossiter like it if one afternoon he suddenly invaded her neat little garden in the High Street and rushed about over her lawn, blowing a squeaker?

And it was always on these occasions so infernally hot. July might have ended in a flurry of snow, but directly the first Monday in August arrived and he had to put on a stiff collar, out came the sun, blazing with tropic fury.

Of course, admitted Lord Emsworth, for he was a fair-minded man, this cut both ways. The hotter the day, the more quickly his collar lost its starch and ceased to spike him like a javelin. This afternoon, for instance, it had resolved itself almost immediately into something which felt like a wet compress. Severe as were his sufferings, he was compelled to recognise that he was much ahead of the game.

A masterful figure loomed at his side.

'Clarence!'

Lord Emsworth's mental and spiritual state was now such that not even the advent of his sister Constance could add noticeably to his discomfort.

'Clarence, you look a perfect sight.'

'I know I do. Who wouldn't in a rig-out like this? Why in the name of goodness you always insist . . .'

'Please don't be childish, Clarence. I cannot understand the fuss you make about dressing for once in your life like a reasonable English gentleman and not like a tramp.'

'It's this top hat. It's exciting the children.'

'What on earth do you mean, exciting the children?'

'Well, all I can tell you is that just now, as I was passing the place where they're playing football—Football! In weather like this!—a small boy called out something derogatory and threw a portion of coco-nut at it.'

'If you will identify the child,' said Lady Constance warmly, 'I will have him severely punished.'

'How the dickens,' said his lordship with equal warmth, 'can I identify the child? They all look alike to me. And if I did identify him, I would shake him by the hand. A boy who throws coco-nuts at top hats is fundamentally sound in his views. And stiff collars . . .'

'Stiff! That's what I came to speak to you about. Are you aware that your collar looks like a rag? Go in and change it at once.'

'But, my dear Constance . . .'

'At once, Clarence. I simply cannot understand a man having so little pride in his appearance. But all your life you have been like that. I remember when we were children . . .'

Lord Emsworth's past was not of such a purity that he was prepared to stand and listen to it being lectured on by a sister with a good memory.

'Oh, all right, all right, all right,' he said, 'I'll change it, I'll change it.'

'Well, hurry. They are just starting tea.'

Lord Emsworth quivered.

'Have I got to go into that tea-tent?'

'Of course you have. Don't be so ridiculous. I do wish you would realize your position. As master of Blandings Castle . . .'

A bitter, mirthless laugh from the poor peon thus ludicrously described drowned the rest of the sentence.

It always seemed to Lord Emsworth, in analysing these entertainments, that the August Bank Holiday Saturnalia reached a peak of repulsiveness when tea was served in the big marquee. Tea over, the agony abated, to become acute once more at the moment when he stepped to the edge of the platform and cleared his throat and tried to recollect what the deuce he had planned to say to the goggling audience beneath him. After that, it subsided again and passed until the following August.

Conditions during the tea hour, the marquee having stood all day under a blazing sun, were generally such that Shadrach, Meshach and Abednego, had they been there, could have learned something new about burning, fiery furnaces. Lord Emsworth, delayed by the revision of his toilet, made his entry when the meal was half over and was pleased to find that his second collar almost instantaneously began to relax its iron grip. That, however, was the only gleam of happiness which was to be vouchsafed him. Once in the tent, it took his experienced eye but a moment to discern that the present feast was eclipsing in frightfulness all its predecessors.

Young Blandings Parva, in its normal form, tended rather to the stolidly bovine than the riotous. In all villages, of course, there must of necessity be a tough egg—in the case of Blandings Parva the names of Willie Drake and Thomas (Rat-Face) Blenkiron spring to the mind—but it was seldom that the local infants offered anything beyond the power of a curate to control. What was giving the present gathering its striking resemblance to a reunion of *sans-culottes* at the height of the French Revolution was the admixture of the Fresh Air London visitors.

About the London child, reared among the tin cans and cabbage stalks of Drury Lane and Clare Market, there is a breezy insouciance which his country cousin lacks. Years of back-chat with annoyed parents and relatives have cured him of any tendency he may have had towards shyness, with the result that when he requires anything he grabs for it, and when he is amused by any slight peculiarity in the personal appearance of members of the governing classes he finds no difficulty in converting his thoughts into speech. Already, up and down the long tables, the curate's unfortunate squint was coming in for hearty comment, and the front teeth of one of the school-teachers ran it a close second for popularity. Lord Emsworth was not, as a rule, a man of swift inspirations, but it occurred to him at this juncture that it would be a prudent move to take off his top hat before his little guests observed it and appreciated its humorous possibilities.

The action was not, however, necessary. Even as he raised his hand a rock cake, singing through the air like a shell, took it off him.

Lord Emsworth had had sufficient. Even Constance, unreasonable women though she was, could hardly expect him to stay and beam genially under conditions like this. All civilized laws had obviously gone by the board and Anarchy reigned in the marquee. The curate was doing his best to form a provisional government consisting of himself and the two school-teachers, but there was only one man who could have coped adequately with the situation and that was King Herod, who—regrettably—was not among those present. Feeling like some aristocrat of the old *régime* sneaking away from the tumbril, Lord Emsworth edged to the exit and withdrew.

Outside the marquee the world was quieter, but only comparatively so. What Lord Emsworth craved was solitude, and in all the broad park there seemed to be but one spot where it was to be had. This was a red-tiled shed, standing beside a small pond, used at happier times as a lounge or retiring-room for cattle. Hurrying thither, his lordship had begun to revel in the cool, cow-scented dimness of its interior when from one of the dark corners, causing him to start and bite his tongue, there came the sound of a subdued sniff.

He turned. This was persecution. With the whole park to mess about in, why should an infernal child invade this one sanctuary of his? He spoke with angry sharpness. He came of a line of warrior ancestors and his fighting blood was up.

'Who's that?'

'Me, sir, thank you, sir.'

Only one person of Lord Emsworth's acquaintance was capable of ex-pressing gratitude for having been barked at in such a tone. His wrath died away and remorse took its place. He felt like a man who in error had kicked a favourite dog.

'God bless my soul!' he exclaimed. 'What in the world are you doing in a cow-shed?'

'Please, sir, I was put.'

'Put? How do you mean, put? Why?'

'For pinching things, sir.'

'Eh? What? Pinching things? Most extraordinary. What did you—er—pinch?'

'Two buns, two jem-sengwiches, two apples and a slicer cake.'

The girl had come out of her corner and was standing correctly at attention. Force of habit had caused her to intone the list of the purloined articles in the sing-song voice with which she was wont to recite the multiplication-table at school, but Lord Emsworth could see that she was deeply moved. Tear-stains glistened on her face, and no Emsworth had ever been able to watch unstirred a woman's tears. The ninth Earl was visibly affected.

'Blow your nose,' he said, hospitably extending his handkerchief.

'Yes, sir, thank you, sir.'

'What did you say you had pinched? Two buns . . .'

'. . . Two jem-sengwiches, two apples and a slicer cake.'

'Did you eat them?'

'No, sir. They wasn't for me. They was for Ern.'

'Ern? Oh, ah, yes. Yes, to be sure. For Ern, eh?'

'Yes, sir.'

'But why the dooce couldn't Ern have—er—pinched them for himself? Strong, able-bodied young feller, I mean.'

Lord Emsworth, a member of the old school, did not like this disposition on the part of the modern young man to shirk the dirty work and let the woman pay.

'Ern wasn't allowed to come to the treat, sir.'

'What! Not allowed? Who said he mustn't?'

'The lidy, sir.'

'What lidy?'

'The one that come in just after you'd gorn this morning.'

A fierce snort escaped Lord Emsworth. Constance! What the devil did Constance mean by taking it upon herself to revise his list of guests without so much as a . . . Constance, eh? He snorted again. One of these days Constance would go too far.

'Monstrous!' he cried.

'Yes, sir.'

'High-handed tyranny, by Gad. Did she give any reason?'

'The lidy didn't like Ern biting 'er in the leg, sir.'

'Ern bit her in the leg?'

'Yes, sir. Pliying 'e was a dorg. And the lidy was cross and Ern wasn't allowed to come to the treat, and I told 'im I'd bring 'im back something nice.'

Lord Emsworth breathed heavily. He had not supposed that in these degenerate days a family like this existed. The sister copped Angus McAllister on the shin with stones, the brother bit Constance in the leg . . . It was like listening to some grand old saga of the exploits of heroes and demigods.

'I thought if I didn't 'ave nothing myself it would make it all right.'

'Nothing?' Lord Emsworth started. 'Do you mean to tell me you have not had tea?'

'No, sir, thank you, sir. I thought if I didn't 'ave none, then it would be all right Ern 'aving what I would 'ave 'ad if I'd 'ave 'ad.'

His lordship's head, never strong, swam a little. Then it resumed its equilibrium. He caught her drift.

'God bless my soul!' said Lord Emsworth. 'I never heard anything so monstrous and appalling in my life. Come with me immediately.'

'The lidy said I was to stop 'ere, sir.'

Lord Emsworth gave vent to his loudest snort of the afternoon.

'Confound the lidy!'

'Yes, sir, thank you, sir.'

Five minutes later Beach, the butler, enjoying a siesta in the housekeeper's room, was roused from his slumbers by the unexpected ringing of a bell. Answering its summons, he found his employer in the library, and with him a surprising young person in a velveteen frock, at the sight of whom his eyebrows quivered and, but for his iron self-control, would have risen.

'Beach!'

'Your lordship?'

'This young lady would like some tea.'

'Very good, your lordship.'

'Buns, you know. And apples, and jem—I mean jam-sandwiches, and cake, and that sort of thing.'

'Very good, your lordship.'

'And she has a brother, Beach.'

'Indeed, your lordship?'

'She will want to take some stuff away for him.' Lord Emsworth turned to his guest. 'Ernest would like a little chicken, perhaps?'

'Coo!'

'I beg your pardon?'

'Yes, sir, thank you, sir.'

'And a slice or two of ham?'

'Yes, sir, thank you, sir.'

'And—he has no gouty tendency?'

'No, sir, thank you, sir.'

'Capital! Then a bottle of that new lot of port, Beach. It's some stuff they've sent me down to try,' explained his lordship. 'Nothing special, you understand,' he added apologetically, 'but quite drinkable. I should like your brother's opinion of it. See that all that is put in a parcel, Beach, and leave it on the table in the hall. We will pick it up as we go out.'

A welcome coolness had crept into the evening air by the time Lord Emsworth and his guest came out of the great door of the castle. Gladys, holding her host's hand and clutching the parcel, sighed contentedly. She had done herself well at the tea-table. Life seemed to have nothing more to offer.

Lord Emsworth did not share this view. His spacious mood had not yet exhausted itself.

'Now is there anything else you can think of that Ernest would like?' he asked. 'If so do not hesitate to mention it. Beach, can you think of anything?'

The butler, hovering respectfully, was unable to do so.

'No, your lordship. I ventured to add—on my own responsibility, your lordship—some hard-boiled eggs and a pot of jam to the parcel.'

'Excellent! You are sure there is nothing else?'

A wistful look came into Gladys's eyes.

'Could he 'ave some flarze?'

'Certainly,' said Lord Emsworth. 'Certainly, certainly, certainly. By all means. Just what I was about to suggest my—er—what *is* flarze?'

Beach, the linguist, interpreted.

'I think the young lady means flowers, your lordship.'

'Yes, sir, thank you, sir. Flarze.'

'Oh?' said Lord Emsworth. 'Oh? Flarze?' he said slowly. 'Oh, ah, yes. I see. H'm!'

He removed his pince-nez, wiped them thoughtfully and gazed with wrinkling forehead at the gardens which stretched gaily out before him. Flarze! It would be idle to deny that those gardens contained flarze in full measure. They were bright with Achillea, Bignonia Radicans, Campanula, Digitalis, Euphorbia, Funkia, Gypsophila, Helianthus, Iris, Liatris, Monarda, Phlox Drummondi, Salvia, Thalictrum, Vinca and Yucca. But the devil of it was that Angus McAllister would have a fit if they were picked. Across the threshold of this Eden the ginger whiskers of Angus McAllister lay like a flaming sword.

As a general rule, the procedure for getting flowers out of McAllister was as follows. You waited till he was in one of his rare moods of complaisance, then you led the conversation gently round to the subject of interior decoration, and then, choosing your moment, you asked if he could possibly spare a few to be put in vases. The last thing you thought of doing was to charge in and start helping yourself.

'I—er . . .' said Lord Emsworth.

He stopped. In a sudden blinding flash of clear vision he had seen himself for what he was—the spineless, unspeakably unworthy descendant of ancestors who, though they may have had their faults, had certainly known how to handle employees. It was 'How, now, varlet!' and 'Marry come up, thou malapert knave!' in the days of previous Earls of Emsworth. Of course, they had possessed certain advantages which he lacked. It undoubtedly helped a man in his dealings with the domestic staff to have, as they had had, the rights of the high, the middle and the low justice—which meant, broadly, that if you got annoyed with your head-gardener, you could immediately divide him into four head-gardeners with a battle-axe and no questions asked—but even so, he realized that they were better men than he was and that, if he allowed craven fear of Angus McAllister to stand in the way of this delightful girl and her charming brother getting all the flowers they required, he was not worthy to be the last of their line.

Lord Emsworth wrestled with his tremors.

'Certainly, certainly, certainly,' he said, though not without a qualm. 'Take as many as you want.'

And so it came about that McAllister, crouched in his potting-shed like some dangerous beast in its den, beheld a sight which first froze his blood and then sent it boiling through his veins. Flitting to and fro through his sacred gardens, picking his sacred flowers, was a small girl in a velveteen frock. And—which brought apoplexy a step closer—it was the same small girl who two days before had copped him on the shin with a stone. The stillness of the summer evening was shattered by a roar that sounded like boilers exploding, and Angus McAllister came out of the potting-shed at forty-five miles an hour.

Gladys did not linger. She was a London child, trained from infancy to bear herself gallantly in the presence of alarms and excursions, but this excursion had been so sudden that it momentarily broke her nerve. With a horrified yelp she scuttled to where Lord Emsworth stood and, hiding behind him, clutched the tails of his morning-coat.

'Oo-er!' said Gladys.

Lord Emsworth was not feeling so frightfully good himself. We have pictured him a few moments back drawing inspiration from the nobility of his ancestors and saying, in effect, 'That for McAllister!', but truth now compels us to admit that this hardy attitude was largely due to the fact that he believed the head-gardener to be a safe quarter of a mile away among the swings and roundabouts of the Fête. The spectacle of the man charging vengefully down on him with gleaming eyes and bristling whiskers made him feel like a nervous English infantryman at the Battle of Bannockburn. His knees shook and the soul within him quivered.

And then something happened, and the whole aspect of the situation changed.

It was, in itself, quite a trivial thing, but it had an astoundingly stimulating effect on Lord Emsworth's morale. What happened was that Gladys, seeking further protection, slipped at this moment a small, hot hand into his.

It was a mute vote of confidence, and Lord Emsworth intended to be worthy of it.

'He's coming,' whispered his lordship's Inferiority Complex agitatedly.

'What of it?' replied Lord Emsworth stoutly.

'Tick him off,' breathed his lordship's ancestors in his other ear.

'Leave it to me,' replied Lord Emsworth.

He drew himself up and adjusted his pince-nez. He felt filled with a cool masterfulness. If the man tendered his resignation, let him tender his damn resignation.

'Well, McAllister?' said Lord Emsworth coldly.

He removed his top hat and brushed it against his sleeve.

'What is the matter, McAllister?'

He replaced his top hat.

'You appear agitated, McAllister.'

He jerked his head militantly. The hat fell off. He let it lie. Freed from its loathsome weight he felt more masterful than ever. It had just needed that to bring him to the top of his form.

'This young lady,' said Lord Emsworth, 'has my full permission to pick all the flowers she wants, McAllister. If you do not see eye to eye with me in this matter, McAllister, say so and we will discuss what you are going to do about it, McAllister. These gardens, McAllister, belong to me, and if you do not— er—appreciate the fact you will, no doubt, be able to find another employer—ah—more in tune with your views. I value your services highly, McAllister, but I will not be dictated to in my own garden, McAllister. Er— dash it,' added his lordship, spoiling the whole effect.

A long moment followed in which Nature stood still, breathless. The Achillea stood still. So did the Bignonia Radicans, the Digitalis, the Euphorbia, the Funkia, the Gypsophila, the Helianthus, the Iris, the Liatris, the Monarda, the Phlox Drummondi, the Salvia, the Thalictrum, the Vinca and the Yucca. From far off in the direction of the park there sounded the happy howls of children who were probably breaking things, but even these seemed hushed. The evening breeze had died away.

Angus McAllister stood glowering. His attitude was that of one sorely perplexed. So might the early bird have looked if the worm ear-marked for its breakfast had suddenly turned and snapped at it. It had never occurred to him that his employer would voluntarily suggest that he sought another position, and now that he had suggested it, Angus McAllister disliked the idea very much. Blandings Castle was in his bones. Elsewhere, he would feel an exile. He fingered his whiskers, but they gave him no comfort.

He made his decision. Better to cease to be a Napoleon than be a Napoleon in exile.

'Mphm,' said Angus McAllister.

'Oh, and by the way, McAllister,' said Lord Emsworth, 'that matter of the gravel path through the yew alley. I've been thinking it over, and I won't have it. Not on any account. Mutilate my beautiful moss with a beastly gravel path? Make an eyesore of the loveliest spot in one of the finest and oldest gardens in the United Kingdom? Certainly not. Most decidedly not. Try to remember, McAllister, as you work in the gardens of Blandings Castle, that you are not back in Glasgow, laying out recreation grounds. That is all, McAllister. Er—dash it—that is all.'

'Mphm,' said Angus McAllister.

He turned. He walked away. Nature resumed its breathing. The breeze began to blow again. And all over the gardens birds who had stopped on their high note carried on according to plan.

Lord Emsworth took out his handkerchief and dabbed with it at his forehead. He was shaken, but a novel sense of being a man among men thrilled him. It might seem bravado but he almost wished—yes, dash it, he almost wished—that his sister Constance would come along and start something while he felt like this.

He had his wish.

'Clarence!'

Yes, there she was, hurrying towards him up the garden path. She, like McAllister, seemed agitated. Something was on her mind.

'Clarence!'

'Don't keep saying "Clarence" as if you were a dashed parrot,' said Lord Emsworth haughtily. 'What the dickens is the matter, Constance?'

'Matter? Do you know what the time is? Do you know that everybody is waiting down there for you to make your speech?'

Lord Emsworth met her eye sternly.

'I do not,' he said. 'And I don't care. I'm not going to make any dashed speech. If you want a speech, let the vicar make it. Or make it yourself. Speech! I never heard such dashed nonsense in my life.' He turned to Gladys. 'Now, my dear,' he said, 'if you will just give me time to get out of these infernal clothes and this ghastly collar and put on something human, we'll go down to the village and have a chat with Ern.'

'Lord Emsworth and the Girl Friend', *Blandings Castle and Elsewhere* (1935).

Acknowledgements

THE editor and publisher are grateful for permission to include the following copyright material in this volume:

George Ade, from *Fables in Slang* (1899). Reprinted by permission of Dover Publications, Inc.

James Agate, excerpts from *Ego*, *Ego 4*, *Ego 5*, and *Ego 9* (published by Victor Gollancz Ltd.). Reprinted by permission of the Peters Fraser & Dunlop Group Ltd.

Kingsley Amis, from *Jake's Thing*, copyright © Kingsley Amis 1978, All rights reserved. Reprinted by permission of Century Hutchinson Ltd. and Viking Penguin, a division of Penguin Books USA, Inc.: from *The Old Devils*, copyright © 1986 by Kingsley Amis. Reprinted by permission of Century Hutchinson Ltd. and Summit Books, a division of Simon & Schuster, Inc.; from *I Like It Here*, copyright © 1958 by Kingsley Amis, and excerpt from 'The Red-Haired Woman' in *The Green Man*, copyright © 1969 by Kingsley Amis. Reprinted by permission of Harcourt Brace Jovanovich, Inc.; from *Lucky Jim*, copyright 1953 by Kingsley Amis. Reprinted by permission of Doubleday, a division of Bantam Doubleday Dell Publishing Group, Inc.

Martin Amis, from *Dead Babies* and from *The Rachel Papers*. Reprinted by permission of the Peters Fraser & Dunlop Group Ltd., and Jonathan Cape Ltd. on behalf of the author.

Elizabeth von Arnim, *see* Elizabeth, Countess Russell.

Daisy Ashford, from *The Young Visiters*. Reprinted by permission of Chatto & Windus on behalf of the Executors of the Daisy Ashford Estate.

from *The Australian* and *Australian Worker*, quoted by Bill Wannan. Reprinted by permission of Curtis Brown (Aust.) Pty Ltd., Sydney.

Beryl Bainbridge, from *Mum and Mr Armitage* (1985). Reprinted by permission of Gerald Duckworth.

Maurice Baring, from *Dead Letters*. Reprinted by permission of A. P. Watt Ltd. on behalf of the Trustees of the Maurice Baring Will Trust.

Max Beerbohm, 'A Clergyman' from *And Even Now* (1920). Reprinted by permission of Mrs Eva Reichmann.

Ludwig Bemelmans, from *Hotel Splendide* (Hamish Hamilton Ltd.). Reprinted by permission of Laurence Pollinger Ltd.

Robert Benchley, from *The Early Worm*, copyright 1926 by Robert Benchley, copyright renewed 1954 by Gertrude Benchley: from *The Treasurer's Report and Other Aspects of Community Singing*, copyright 1930 by Robert Benchley, renewed 1958 by Gertrude Benchley; from *The Benchley Round Up*, edited by Nathaniel Benchley, copyright 1954 by Nathaniel Benchley, copyright renewed 1982 by Nathaniel Benchley. Reprinted by permission of Harper & Row, Publishers, Inc.

E. F. Benson, from *Lucia's Progress*, copyright 1927 by Doubleday, Doran & Company, Inc. Reprinted by permission of Harper & Row, Publishers, Inc., and William Heinemann Ltd.: from *Paying Guests* (1929), reprinted by permission of The Hogarth Press on behalf of the Executors of the Estate of the Revd K. S. P. McDowell.

Humphrey Berkeley, from *The Life and Death of Rochester Snaith: A Youthful Frivolity* (Davis-Poynter, 1974). Reprinted by permission of Grafton Books, a division of William Collins & Sons.

Basil Boothroyd, reproduced by permission of *Punch*.

Caryl Brahms and S. J. Simon, from *No Bed for Bacon*, copyright Caryl Brahms and S. J. Simon 1941. Reprinted by permission of Chatto & Windus on behalf of the authors, and Curtis Brown, London.

Art Buchwald, from *I Chose Caviar* (1957). Reprinted by permission of Boccador Enterprises.

Patrick Campbell, from *Lilliput*. Reprinted by permission of Irene Josephy on behalf of Lady Glenavy.

Gavin Casey, from *It's Harder for Girls*, © Gavin William Casey 1964. Reprinted by permission of Angus & Robertson Publishers/Collins.

Henry Cecil, from *Brothers in Law* (1955), copyright The Estate of Henry Cecil 1955. Reproduced by permission of Curtis Brown Ltd., London.

G. K. Chesterton, from *Tremendous Trifles*.

Sir William Connor ('Cassandra'), extracts from his column in the *Daily Mirror*.

Alan Coren, from *The Sanity Inspector* (Robson Books, 1974) and from *Golfing for Cats* (Robson Books, 1975). Reprinted by permission of Robson Books Ltd., Publishers.

Richmal Crompton, from *Just William*. Reprinted by permission of Richmal C. Ashbee and Macmillan, London and Basingstoke.

Barry Crump, from *No Reference Intended* (1960). Reprinted by permission of Barry Crump Associates.

Paul Dehn, from *For Love and Money* (1956). Reprinted by permission of James Bernard, Executor.

E. M. Delafield, from *As Others Hear Us* and *The Provincial Lady in Wartime*. Reprinted by permission of the Peters Fraser & Dunlop Group Ltd.

Mary Dunn, from *Lady Addle Remembers*. Reprinted by permission of Methuen & Co.

Lord Dunsany, from *Fifty-one Tales*, copyright the Estate of Lord Dunsany. Reprinted by permission of Curtis Brown Ltd., on behalf of John Child Villiers and Valentine Lamb as literary executors of Lord Dunsany.

Lawrence Durrell, from *Esprit de Corps: sketches from Diplomatic Life* (1957). Reprinted by permission of Faber & Faber Ltd.

Elizabeth, Countess Russell, from *The Caravaners*. Reprinted by permission of Ann E. Hardham and Virago Press on behalf of William Ritchie.

Barry Fantoni and Richard Ingrams, 'Heathco', *Private Eye* (27 July 1973). Reprinted by permission.

Corey Ford, from *In the Worst Possible Taste* (1932), copyright 1932 by Corey Ford, copyright renewed 1960 by Corey Ford. Reprinted by permission of Harold Ober Associates, Inc.

Michael Frayn, 'A Hand of Cards', originally published in the *Observer* and reissued in *The Original Michael Frayn* (The Salamander Press 1983), copyright © The Observer Ltd. 1967. Reprinted by permission of Elaine Greene Ltd.

Stella Gibbons, from *Cold Comfort Farm*. Reprinted by permission of David Higham Associates Ltd.

Wolcott Gibbs, from *A Bed of Neuroses*.

Myles na Gopaleen (Brian O'Nolan), from his 'Cruiskeen Lawn' column in *The Irish Times*, 1939–66. Reprinted by permission of the copyright holder, Mrs Evelyn O'Nolan.

Richard Gordon, from *Doctor in the House* (1952). Reprinted by permission of Michael Joseph Ltd.

A. K. Grant, from *An Inquiry into the Construction and Classification of The New Zealand Short Story* (1977). Reprinted by permission of the author.

Graham Greene, from *Travels with My Aunt*, © 1969 by Graham Greene; from *Collected Stories*, © 1957, © 1985 by Graham Greene. Reprinted by permission of Laurence Pollinger Ltd. and Viking Penguin.

Nathaniel Gubbins, from his column 'Sitting on the Fence'. Reprinted by permission of Sunday Express Newspapers.

Joseph Heller, from *Catch-22* (Cape/Simon & Schuster, 1961), copyright © 1955, 1961 by Joseph Heller. Reprinted by permission of A. M. Heath and Simon & Schuster, Inc.

A. P. Herbert, 'The Negotiable Cow' from *Misleading Cases in the Common Law*. Reprinted by permission of A. P. Watt Ltd. on behalf of Crystal Hale and Jocelyn Herbert.

Diana Holman-Hunt, from *My Grandmothers and I* (1960). Reprinted by permission of Hamish Hamilton Ltd., Publisher.

Richard Ingrams and John Wells, from 'Mrs Wilson's Diary', *Private Eye* (18 Dec. 1964, 10 June 1966); from 'Dear Bill', *Private Eye* (9 Aug. 1985). Reprinted by permission.

W. W. Jacobs, from *Sea Whispers*. Reprinted by permission of The Society of Authors as the literary representative of the Estate of W. W. Jacobs.

Paul Jennings, from *Golden Oddlies*. Reprinted by permission of the author and Methuen London.

James Joyce, from *Ulysses*, copyright 1914, 1918 by Margaret Caroline Anderson and renewed 1942, 1945 by Nora Joseph Joyce. Reprinted by permission of The Bodley Head on behalf of the Executors of the Estate of James Joyce, Random House, Inc., and The Society of Authors as the literary representative of the Estate of James Joyce.

P. J. Kavanagh, from *The Spectator*, 27 Apr. 1985. Reprinted by permission.

Garrison Keillor, from *Lake Wobegon Days*, copyright © Garrison Keillor, 1985. All rights reserved. Reprinted by permission of Viking Penguin, a division of Penguin Books USA, Inc. and Faber & Faber Ltd.

Ring Lardner, 'I. Gaspiri', from *What Of It?* by Ring Lardner, copyright 1925 by Charles Scribner's Sons, copyright renewed 1953 by Ellis A. Lardner: from 'On Conversation', from *First and Last* by Ring Lardner, copyright 1934 by Ellis A. Lardner, copyright renewed © 1962 by Ring Lardner, Jr. Both used by permission of Charles Scribner's Sons, an imprint of Macmillan Publishing Company.

Stephen Leacock, from *Literary Lapses* (1910) and from *Nonsense Novels* (1911).

Fran Lebowitz, from *Metropolitan Life*, copyright © 1974, 1975, 1976, 1977, 1978 by Fran Lebowitz. Reprinted by permission of the publisher, E. P. Dutton, a division of Penguin Books USA, Inc., and Janklow & Nesbit Associates, for the author.

Anita Loos, selections are reprinted from *Gentlemen Prefer Blondes* by permission of Liveright Publishing Corporation. Copyright 1925 by Anita Loos. Copyright 1925 by the International Magazine Co., Inc. Copyright renewed 1953 by Anita Loos Emerson. Copyright © 1963 by Anita Loos.

Lennie Lower, from *Here's Luck*, © Mrs P. M. Pearl, 1947. Reprinted by permission of Angus & Robertson Publishers/Collins.

A. G. Macdonell, from *England, Their England*. Reprinted by permission of Macmillan, London and Basingstoke.

Richard Mallett, 'Do Something' from *Punch*.

Katherine Mansfield, 'The Modern Soul', copyright 1926 by Alfred A. Knopf, Inc.

and renewed 1954 by John Middleton Murry. Reprinted from *The Short Stories of Katherine Mansfield*, by permission of Alfred A. Knopf, Inc.

Arthur Marshall, from *Girls Will Be Girls* (1974) and from *Smile Please: Further Musings from Myrtlebank* (1982). Reprinted by permission of Hamish Hamilton Ltd.

Groucho Marx, from *The Groucho Letters*, copyright © 1967 by Groucho Marx. Reprinted by permission of Simon & Schuster, Inc.

H. L. Mencken, from *A Book of Burlesques*, copyright 1916 by Alfred A. Knopf, Inc., and renewed 1944 by H. L. Mencken; from *A Mencken Chrestomathy*, copyright 1924 by Alfred A. Knopf, Inc., and renewed 1952 by H. L. Mencken; from *Prejudices: A Selection*, copyright © 1958 by Alfred A. Knopf, Inc. All reprinted by permission of Alfred A. Knopf, Inc.

George Mikes, from *How To Be An Alien* (Wingate, 1946). Reprinted by permission of Andre Deutsch Ltd.

Jessica Mitford, from *Hons and Rebels* (Gollancz, 1960). Reprinted by permission of Rogers Coleridge & White Ltd.

Nancy Mitford, from *The Pursuit of Love* (Hamish Hamilton Ltd.). Reprinted by permission of the Peters Fraser & Dunlop Group Ltd.

J. B. Morton ('Beachcomber'), extracts from his column 'By the Way' in the *Daily Express*, 1924–75, reprinted from *Beachcomber: The Works of J. B. Morton* (ed. Richard Ingrams, 1974). Reprinted by permission of the Peters Fraser & Dunlop Group Ltd.

Eric Nicol, from his column in *The Vancouver Province*, © Eric Nicol. Reprinted by permission of the author.

Frank O'Connor, 'First Confession', copyright 1951 by Frank O'Connor, from *The Stories of Frank O'Connor* (Hamish Hamilton Ltd.), published in the USA in *Collected Stories*. Reprinted by permission of the Peters Fraser & Dunlop Group Ltd. and Alfred A. Knopf, Inc.

Dorothy Parker, 'You Were Perfectly Fine' from *The Collected Dorothy Parker*. Published in the United States in *The Portable Dorothy Parker*, copyright 1929, renewed © 1957 by Dorothy Parker, All Rights Reserved. Reprinted by permission of Gerald Duckworth, and Viking Penguin, a division of Penguin Books USA, Inc.

C. Northcote Parkinson, from *Parkinson's Law: The Pursuit of Progress*, copyright © 1957 by C. Northcote Parkinson, copyright © renewed 1985 by C. Northcote Parkinson. Reprinted by permission of John Murray (Publishers) Ltd., and Houghton Mifflin Company.

A. B. Paterson, 'Bill & Jim Nearly Got Taken Down' from *Singer of the Bush*, © Retusa Pty. Ltd. Reprinted by permission of Angus & Robertson Publishers/Collins.

S. J. Perelman, from *Contact*; 'How Sharper than a Serpent's Tooth' from *Keep It Crisp* (1946); 'Kitchen Bouquet' and 'Somewhere a Roscoe' from *Crazy Like a Fox*; 'Cloudland Revisited . . .', 'Strictly from Hunger' both from *Strictly from Hunger* (1937). Reprinted by permission of the Peters Fraser & Dunlop Group Ltd.

Stephen Potter, from *Gamesmanship* (Hart-Davis, 1947). Reprinted by permission of Grafton Books, a division of William Collins & Sons.

V. S. Pritchett, 'Oedipus Complex' from *Collected Stories* (Chatto & Windus, 1956). Reprinted by permission of the Peters Fraser & Dunlop Group Ltd. and Chatto & Windus on the author's behalf.

Frank Richards, from *Backing Up Billy Bunter*, copyright © 1955 by Frank Richards. Reprinted by permission of Tessa Sayle Agency.

Leo Rosten, from *The Education of H*y*m*a*n K*a*p*l*a*n* (1937). Reprinted by permission of Constable Publishers and the author.

Philip Roth, from *Portnoy's Complaint*, copyright © 1967, 1968, 1969 by Philip

Roth. Reprinted by permission of Jonathan Cape Ltd., on behalf of the author and of Random House, Inc.

Damon Runyon, from *Guys and Dolls*, copyright 1929, 1930, 1931 by Damon Runyon. All rights reserved.

Charles (Chick) Sale, from *The Specialist* (1930).

Walter Sellar and Julian Yeatman, from *1066 And All That*. Reprinted by permission of Methuen London.

Tom Sharpe, from *The Wilt Alternative*. Reprinted by permission of Martin Secker & Warburg Ltd.

Bernard Shaw, extracts from *The Star* and from *The Saturday Review*. Reprinted by permission of The Society of Authors on behalf of the Bernard Shaw Estate.

Max Shulman, from *Barefoot Boy With Cheek*, copyright 1943 by Max Shulman. Reprinted by permission of Doubleday, a division of Bantam, Doubleday, Dell Publishing Group, Inc.

Logan Pearsall Smith, from *Afterthoughts* (1931). Reprinted by permission of Constable Publishers.

Edith Somerville and Martin Ross, from *Further Experiences of an Irish R.M.* Reprinted by permission of John Farquharson Ltd.

Jan Struther, 'Christmas Shopping', from *Mrs Miniver*, copyright 1939 by Jan Struther and renewed 1967 by J. A. Maxtone Graham. Reprinted by permission of Virago Press and Harcourt Brace Jovanovich, Inc.

Frank Sullivan, excerpt from 'The Cliche Expert Testifies on the Tabloids' and 'The Night the Old Nostalgia Burned Down', copyright 1946, 1948 by Frank Sullivan. First appeared in the *New Yorker*. Used by permission of Little Brown and Company.

Angela Thirkell, from *The Brandons* (1939), copyright 1939 by Angela Thirkell and renewed 1966 by Graham McInnes and Lance Thirkell. Reprinted by permission of Hamish Hamilton Ltd. and Alfred A. Knopf, Inc.

Leslie Thomas, from *Arthur McCann and All His Women* (Michael Joseph, 1972: Pan Books, 1974). Reprinted by permission of Desmond Elliott, and Michael Joseph Ltd.

James Thurber, 'Nine Needles', copyright 1937 James Thurber, copyright © 1965 Helen Thurber and Rosemary A. Thurber from *Let Your Mind Alone* (published in the UK in *Vintage Thurber*, Vol. 1); 'The Night the Bed Fell', copyright 1933, © 1961 James Thurber from *My Life and Hard Times*; 'The Shrike and the Chipmunks' and 'The Unicorn in the Garden', copyright 1940 James Thurber, copyright © 1968 Helen Thurber, from *Fables In Our Time*, all published by Harper & Row (all published in the UK in *Vintage Thurber*, Vol. 2); 'The Secret Life of Walter Mitty', copyright 1942 James Thurber, copyright © 1970 Helen Thurber and Rosemary A. Thurber from *My World—And Welcome To It*, published by Harcourt Brace Jovanovich (published in the UK in *Vintage Thurber*, Vol. 1). All reprinted by permission of Lucy Kroll Agency on behalf of the copyright holder, and by permission of Hamish Hamilton Ltd. as UK Publisher.

James Thurber and E. B. White, from *Is Sex Necessary?*, copyright 1929 by Harper & Row, Publishers, Inc. Copyright renewed 1957 by James Thurber and E. B. White. Reprinted by permission of Hamish Hamilton Ltd., and Harper & Row, Publishers, Inc.

Sue Townsend, from *The Growing Pains of Adrian Mole*. Reprinted by permission of Methuen London.

Kenneth Tynan, extract from Kenneth Tynan's review of a stage adaptation of William Faulkner's novel, *Requiem for a Nun*, from the *Observer*, © K. Tynan 1957. Used with permission.

Peter de Vries, from *The New Yorker*, reprinted in *Without A Stitch in Time* (1950). Reprinted by permission of Watkins/Loomis Agency, Inc.

Ira Wallach, from *Hopalong-Freud Rides Again* (1952).

Keith Waterhouse, from *Fanny Peculiar* (Michael Joseph). Reprinted by permission of David Higham Associates Ltd.

Auberon Waugh, 'Diary', from *Private Eye*. Reprinted by permission.

Evelyn Waugh, from *Men at Arms*, copyright 1952, © renewed 1979 by Evelyn Waugh; from *Put Out More Flags*, copyright 1942, © renewed 1977 by Evelyn Waugh; from *Scoop*, copyright 1937, 1938, © renewed 1965, 1966 by Evelyn Waugh; from *Black Mischief*, copyright 1932, © renewed 1960 by Evelyn Waugh; from *Decline and Fall*, copyright 1928, © renewed 1956 by Evelyn Waugh; all reprinted by permission of Little, Brown and Company and the Peters Fraser & Dunlop Group Ltd.

H. G. Wells, 'The Truth About Pyecraft' from *The Complete Short Stories of H. G. Wells* and excerpt from *Kipps*. Reprinted by permission of A. P. Watt Ltd., on behalf of The Literary Executors of the Estate of H. G. Wells.

Michael Wharton ('Peter Simple'), 'The Way of the World', from the *Daily Telegraph*. Reprinted by permission of Ewan MacNaughton Associates.

E. B. White, 'Isadora's Brother' from 'The Talk of the Town Feature' in *The New Yorker*, 7 Dec. 1929; 'Farewell My Lovely', from *Essays of E. B. White* (Harper & Row); copyright 1936, © 1964 The New Yorker Magazine, Inc. Originally published in *The New Yorker* in 1936 over the pseudonym 'Lee Strout White'. Richard L. Strout had submitted a manuscript on the Ford, and White, with his collaboration, rewrote it. Used by permission.

P. G. Wodehouse, from *Mike* (1909); from *Ukridge* (1924); 'Came the Dawn' from the *Mulliner Omnibus* (1927); from *Right Ho Jeeves* (1934); from *Something Fresh* (1915); 'Lord Emsworth and the Girlfriend' from *Blandings Castle and Elsewhere* (1935) and brief quotes from other works by P. G. Wodehouse. Reprinted by permission of A. P. Watt Ltd. on behalf of The Trustees of the Wodehouse Trust No. 3 and Century Hutchinson.

Tom Wolfe, from *In Our Times*, copyright © 1961, 1963, 1964, 1965, 1968, 1971, 1972, 1975, 1976, 1977, 1978, 1979, 1980 by Tom Wolfe. Reprinted by permission of Farrar, Straus & Giroux, Inc.

Alexander Woollcott, from *While Rome Burns*. Copyright 1934 by Alexander Woollcott. Copyright renewed © 1962 by Joseph P. Hennessey, Executor of the Estate of Alexander Woollcott. All rights reserved. Reprinted by permission of Viking Penguin, a division of Penguin Books USA, Inc.

Dornford Yates, from *Berry and Co.* Reprinted by permission of A. P. Watt Ltd. on behalf of Robin Humphries and D. C. Humphries, CMG.

There are instances where we have been unable to trace or contact the copyright holder before our printing deadline. We apologize for this apparent negligence. If notified the publisher will be pleased to rectify any errors or omissions at the earliest opportunity.

Index of Authors

AND OTHER NAMES

This index excludes fictional characters. Authors who are quoted from are printed in roman type; other references are printed in italics.